The Study of Society

Contributors

Phillip Whitten Publisher

Lance Bennett
University of California, Irvine

Beverly Cigler
Pennsylvania State University

Donald A. Clelland
University of Tennessee

Adam Curle
Harvard University

Robert A. Dentler
Boston University

Lois Dicker
W. M. Krogman Center for Research

Marvin Dicker
Glassboro State College

Christopher Bates Doob
Southern Connecticut State College

Herbert Gintis
Harvard University

David E. Hunter
Southern Connecticut State College

Mark Hutter
Temple University

Dennis Krebs
Harvard University

Judith Lorber
Brooklyn College

Robert C. Mitchell
Swarthmore College

Donald Pearsall
Zomeworks Corp.

Jack Nusan Porter
State University of New York, Cortland

Ian Robertson
Cambridge University, England

Neil Shister
Yale University

Steven Spitzer
University of Pennsylvania

Michael Totten
University of California, Irvine

David Tresemer
Harvard University

Peter M. Wickman
State University of New York, Potsdam

Interviewees

Stanislav Andreski *University of Reading, England*
Robert F. Bales *Harvard University*
Peter M. Blau *Columbia University*
Robert Blauner *University of California, Berkeley*
Kenneth E. Boulding *University of Colorado*
John Burton *University of London, England*
Kenneth B. Clark *City University of New York*
Lewis A. Coser *State University of New York, Stony Brook*
Thomas J. Cottle *Massachusetts Institute of Technology*
Harvey Cox *Harvard University*
Paul R. Ehrlich *Stanford University*
Amitai Etzioni *Columbia University*
Dana L. Farnsworth *Harvard University*
Eliot Freidson *New York University*
Johan Galtung *University of Oslo, Norway*
Herbert J. Gans *Columbia University*
Nathan Glazer *Harvard University*
Chad Gordon *Rice University*
Germaine Greer *University of Warwick, England*
Michael Harrington *New School for Social Research*
Irving Louis Horowitz *Rutgers University*
Alex Inkeles *Stanford University*
Christopher Jencks *Harvard University*
Suzanne Keller *Princeton University*
John H. Knowles *Rockefeller Foundation*
Lawrence Kohlberg *Harvard University*
Charles R. Lawrence *Brooklyn College*
Seymour Martin Lipset *Harvard University*
David Matza *University of California, Berkeley*
Zhores A. Medvedev *Biologist and Author*
David Pilbeam *Yale University*
Edward H. Spicer *University of Arizona*
Gresham Sykes *University of Houston*
Robert Townsend *Business Executive and Author*
Kurt H. Wolff *Brandeis University*

Reviewers

Robert F. Bales *Harvard University*
Mary Jo Bane *Center for the Study of Public Policy*
Wendell Bell *Yale University*
Elise Boulding *University of Colorado*
Donald A. Clelland *University of Tennessee*
Rose Laub Coser *State University of New York, Stony Brook*
Bruce K. Eckland *University of North Carolina*
Richard Flacks *University of California, Santa Barbara*
Arthur W. Frank III *Yale University*
Chad Gordon *Rice University*
Leroy C. Gould *Yale University*
David M. Heer *University of Southern California*
John C. Henretta *Harvard University*
Thomas Hood *University of Tennessee*
Irving Louis Horowitz *Rutgers University*
David E. Hunter *Southern Connecticut State College*
Suzanne Keller *Princeton University*
Dennis Krebs *Harvard University*
Sheldon L. Messinger *University of California, Berkeley*
Stephen Mick *Yale University*
Robert C. Mitchell *Swarthmore College*
Wilbert E. Moore *University of Denver*
Peter Paulhe *California State University, Dominguez Hills*
Richard Quinney *University of North Carolina*
Ian Robertson *Cambridge University, England*
David Tresemer *Harvard University*
Joseph D. Yenerall *State University of New York, Potsdam*

the
dushkin
publishing
group, inc.
guilford, connecticut

The
Study
Of
Society

Library of Congress Catalog Card Number:
73–87071

Manufactured in the United States of
America

First Printing

Contents

vi

About the Contributors

Lance Bennett
Lance Bennett contributed two units to *The Study of Society*—Unit 10, "Personality and Society," and Unit 26, "Social Change." He will receive his Ph.D. from Yale University in 1974 and is currently lecturing at the University of California, Irvine. His interdisciplinary background includes training in political sociology, political psychology, cognitive psychology, and personality psychology.

Beverly Cigler
Beverly Cigler, co-contributor of Unit 17, "Urban Society," teaches at Pennsylvania State University. Her interests lie in urban studies and public policy analysis, with emphasis on environmental, welfare, and housing policies. She will receive her Ph.D. from Pennsylvania State University in 1974 and is the author of *The Urban Political System* (1973).

Donald A. Clelland
Donald A. Clelland, co-contributor of Unit 9, "Social Stratification," received his Ph.D. from Michigan State University in 1970 and is currently an associate professor of sociology at the University of Tennessee. He is the author of several articles concerning social stratification, and his current research focuses on community power-structure, status politics, and civil religion.

Adam Curle
Adam Curle, co-contributor of Unit 27, "Social Conflict and Peace," left his position as senior professor of education and development at Harvard University in 1973 to become the first holder of the chair of peace studies at the University of Bradford, England. He received his doctorate in anthropology from Oxford University in 1952 and, after doing field work in the Arctic and the Middle East, taught psychology and education at Oxford and Exeter. During the next 18 years he lived in some 20 Third World countries, where he worked on problems of development and conflict. His most recent books are *Making Peace* (1971) and *Mystics and Militants* (1972). *Education for Liberation* is forthcoming.

Robert A. Dentler
Robert A. Dentler, contributor of Unit 18, "The Sociology of Education," is Dean of Boston University School of Education and was Director of the Center for Urban Education until 1972. He received his Ph.D. from the University of Chicago in 1960 and is the author of more than 70 articles. Recent books by him include *Major American Social Problems* (1967), *American Community Problems* (1968), and *The Urban R's: Race Relations as the Problem in Urban Education* (with others, 1967).

Lois Dicker
Lois Dicker, co-contributor with Marvin Dicker of Unit 3, "Biology and Society," received her Ph.D. in human biology and physical anthropology from the University of Wisconsin in 1969. She is presently Research Investigator at the W. M. Krogman Center for Research in Child Growth and Development in Philadelphia and is coauthoring a book on the biological basis of human society.

Marvin Dicker
Marvin Dicker, the co-contributor of Unit 3, is associate professor of sociology at Glassboro State College. He received his Ph.D. in sociology and social psychology in 1968 from the University of Wisconsin and has done research in the areas of the biological origins of human society, sex roles, religion, and the distribution and nature of intellectualism within society.

Christopher Bates Doob
Christopher Bates Doob, the contributor of Unit 20, "Sociology of Politics," received his Ph.D. in sociology from Cornell University. He now teaches at Southern Connecticut State College and is the author of several articles on politics, education, poverty, and work.

Herbert Gintis
Herbert Gintis, contributor of Unit 21, "Sociology of Economics," received his Ph.D. in economics from Harvard University in 1969 and is currently assistant professor of economics there. A member of the Union of Radical Political Economists, he has published articles in most of the leading economics journals and is working on a book on education and the American class structure.

David E. Hunter
David E. Hunter played a major role in the creation of *The Study of Society*. The contributor of Unit 4, "Culture," he also served as graphics conceptualizer for the entire book; in that position he was responsible for generating the academic input for all the figures, tables, models, and photographs used in the book. In addition, he conducted the interview with Edward H. Spicer. He received his Ph.D. in cultural anthropology from Yale University in 1970 and is currently assistant professor of anthropology at Southern Connecticut State College. He has engaged in field work on Swiss peasants, and his research interests include revolution and peasant society, cognitive processes, and cross-cultural psychological universals.

Mark Hutter
Mark Hutter, contributor of Unit 7, "Marriage, Kinship, and the Family," received his Ph.D. in sociology from the University of Minnesota in 1969 and is currently assistant professor of sociology at Temple University. His major research areas are industrial-urban family life styles and adult socialization processes, and he is writing a cross-cultural analysis of social change and the family.

Dennis Krebs
Dennis Krebs, contributor of Unit 12, "Social Interaction," and an academic adviser for the book, earned a Ph.D. in social psychology from Harvard University in 1970. Currently assistant professor of psychology and director of undergraduate studies in psychology and social relations at Harvard, he has published articles on the effect of physical attractiveness on person perception and social interaction, altruism, and empathy and is currently writing a book on theories of socialization and moral development.

Judith Lorber

Judith Lorber, contributor of Unit 19, "Sociology of Medicine," received her Ph.D. from New York University and is currently assistant professor of sociology at Brooklyn College. Coeditor with Elliot Freidson of *Medical Men and Their Work,* she has written on various aspects of the sick role and the nature of sex roles.

Robert Cameron Mitchell

Robert Cameron Mitchell, co-contributor of Unit 27, "Social Conflict and Peace," and an academic adviser for the book, is assistant professor of sociology at Swarthmore College, where he has taught since 1968. He received his Ph.D. from Northwestern University, spent three years in Nigeria studying religion and social change, and recently coauthored *Black Africa: A Comparative Book* (1972).

Donald Pearsall

Donald Pearsall, contributor of Unit 6, "Population and Demography," studied at Yale University, has done solar-energy research for Zomeworks Corporation, and recently completed editing a book on life-support technology.

Jack Nusan Porter

Jack Nusan Porter, co-contributor of Unit 15, "Race and Ethnic Relations," was born in the Ukraine and educated in the United States, receiving his Ph.D. in sociology from Northwestern University in 1971. The coeditor with Peter Dreier of *Jewish Radicals: A Selected Anthology* (1973), he has taught at Northwestern University, DePaul University, and State University of New York, Cortland, and his articles have appeared in several academic and popular journals.

Ian Robertson

Ian Robertson played the major academic role in the creation of *The Study of Society.* He contributed Unit 2, "The Sociology of Knowledge," Unit 5, "Socialization and Moral Development," Unit 8, "Religion," Unit 13, "Sex Roles," Unit 16, "Formal and Complex Organizations," Unit 24, "Drugs and Drug Subcultures," and Unit 25, "Youth Culture." He was co-contributor of Unit 9, "Social Stratification," and Unit 15, "Race and Ethnic Relations," and served as an academic adviser for the book. He also conducted the interview with Germaine Greer. Dr. Robertson, who teaches in Cambridge, England, received a doctorate from Harvard University and has taught and lectured in England, the United States, and Africa. He has published numerous articles on both sides of the Atlantic on various sociological and political topics. A native of the Republic of South Africa, he was banned by order of the Prime Minister for his opposition to that country's racial policies; he is currently co-editing a book on southern Africa with Phillip Whitten.

Neil Shister

Neil Shister, co-contributor of Unit 17, "Urban Society," is completing his doctorate at Yale University. He spent two years in West Africa with the Peace Corps and has worked as a professional journalist. He recently accepted a teaching position at Hampshire College in Massachusetts.

Steven Spitzer

Steven Spitzer, who contributed Unit 23, "Criminology," received his Ph.D. in 1971 from Indiana University and is presently assistant professor of sociology at the University of Pennsylvania. The author of several scholarly articles on police behavior and labeling theory, he is planning a series of studies relating bail and capital punishment to economic change.

Michael Totten

Michael Totten, contributor of Unit 14, "Death, Dying, and Society," left Yale Divinity School to become a graduate student at the University of California, Irvine, where he is a doctoral candidate in the School of Social Sciences.

David Tresemer

David Tresemer, contributor of Unit 11, "Small Groups," received his Ph.D. in the Department of Social Relations at Harvard University. He has written a number of articles in the field of small groups, and his current research concerns sex roles. He conducted the interview with Robert F. Bales.

Phillip Whitten

Phillip Whitten served as publisher and academic editor for *The Study of Society.* As such, he had overall responsibility for the creation of the book. He contributed Unit 1, "The Science of Social Behavior," and was co-contributor of Unit 17, "Urban Society." In addition, he interviewed Thomas J. Cottle, Harvey Cox, Irving Louis Horowitz, Christopher Jencks, Lawrence Kohlberg, and Robert Townsend. Mr. Whitten, who is publisher of the Dushkin Publishing Group, has masters degrees from San Jose State University and Harvard University, where he is currently completing his doctorate. He has written numerous articles and currently is coediting a book on southern Africa with Ian Robertson. He has also produced two educational films, one of which, *Learning,* won the 1972 Merit Award of the American Psychological Association for "best educational film of the year." His areas of interest and research are moral development, dynamics of social change in east and southern Africa, educational vouchers, and peace.

Peter M. Wickman

Peter M. Wickman, contributor of Unit 22, "Deviance," received his Ph.D. from Michigan State University in 1969 and has done postdoctoral work in sociology at the New School for Social Research and Emory University. Professor of sociology at the State University of New York, Potsdam, he has written a number of scholarly articles, primarily in the area of deviance and corrections.

Preface

The Study of Society offers systematic coverage of the basic principles, concepts, and terminology of *sociological inquiry.* Equally important, it conveys, through its consistent and predictable organization, the processes of such inquiry. Customarily, each individual chapter of a sociology textbook is organized along its own lines, presumably reflecting the author's particular approach to the subject matter. This method, no doubt, makes writing a textbook easier, but does not necessarily create a book from which it is easy to learn. Studies of the learning process have clearly shown that we learn better if materials are presented in a predictably structured manner rather than in a loose, unpredictable way. As an academic discipline, sociology brings its unique, habitual perspectives and approaches to bear on the phenomena it investigates. This underlying structure of the discipline is reflected in the organizational scheme of this textbook, its *Generic Structure,* which is explained in detail in Unit 1.

A number of other features combine to help make *The Study of Society* unique. To mention some of them:

———The overall organization of the text is such that the thought of Marx, Weber, Durkheim, Parsons, Merton, and other key sociologists recurs as touchstones for analysis. Issues of vital continuing significance, such as alienation, bureaucratization, and urbanization, are given consideration in several different contexts. Thus the book serves as an introduction to classical and contemporary subjects and techniques of sociological research and analysis.

———The book is specifically organized to be a *learning vehicle* for the student: The opening page of each unit is a pre-experience of what is to come and a review for study after reading; key or technical terms are italicized to draw the student's attention to them; to immerse him or her in the scholarly experience of the field, generally the title, author, and date of first publication of books and articles quoted or significantly referred to are provided within the flow of the text itself; a selected bibliography is also provided at the end of the book, containing standard or most accessible editions of works significant to each unit.

———The interviews with leading sociologists and people in related disciplines at the end of each unit function both as dialogue and essay. Dialogue inasmuch as they are relatively informal give-and-take with a variety of interviewers, sometimes taking issue with other interviewees or even with the unit or discipline itself. Essay inasmuch as they consist, because they are with outstanding scholars or experts, of coherently developed thoughts extending and amplifying the unit. The selection of interviewees—from Australia, Britain, Norway, the Soviet Union and all parts of the United States—provides an international perspective on the topics at hand as well as a variety of backgrounds and outlooks.

———Finally, an extensive and balanced program of artwork—introductory graphics, figures, tables, models, paintings, drawings, photographs—has been developed with great care both to illustrate and comment upon the text. Captions also have an active function in the book. In addition to identifying an item of artwork, they often challenge the student with issues for further thought.

The Study of Society is the core of an entire *system* of instructional materials for the introductory course in sociology. The accompanying *Encyclopedia of Sociology,* with over 2,000 entries and more than 1,300 articles, provides detailed analyses of many topics that go beyond the scope of the usual introductory text. *Teaching and Testing From The Study of Society,* an instructor's resource book, includes for each unit of the text: an overview of the unit; a series of behavioral objectives for the student; case studies or applications of the topics dealt with in the unit; a list of entries in the *Encyclopedia of Sociology;* suggested student projects; 20 objective questions for examinations; four questions suitable for classroom discussion or essay examinations; an extensive bibliography of research materials; and a list of related articles in the Annual Editions *Readings in Sociology '73/'74* and *Readings in Social Problems '73/'74.* The Annual Editions *Readings in Sociology* and *Readings in Social Problems* are collections of articles from the public and popular press, updated each year. Finally, *Working With The Study of Society,* a student workbook, can accompany the text. Designed to help students review the important points of *The Study of Society,* the workbook includes for each unit of the text: an introduction outlining the unit; a list of terms, concepts, and names to be mastered; a fill-in review of the unit; questions for study; and a self-test review.

Phillip Whitten Publisher

The Study of Society

This unit aims to introduce the reader to sociology. It does so by addressing the following questions:

1. What is sociology?

2. How did the discipline of sociology develop?

3. In what ways does sociology relate to other disciplines?

4. How does the sociologist go about his work?

5. Can sociology be objective?

6. Should the sociologist be neutral regarding social issues?

At the end of this introductory unit there is a brief account of how the sociological endeavor is related to the Generic Structure of **The Study of Society.**
This account explains how and why the book is structured to maximize student interest and enhance learning skills.

Unit 1
The Science of Social Behavior

WHAT IS SOCIOLOGY?

Sociology is the scientific study of human society. The poet John Donne observed centuries ago that "no man is an island, entire of itself." There are of course many other social animals, but it is the nature of man's association with his fellows that sets him apart from the animal world. Man's forms of association are *cultural* and are *learned*. He learns to interact in various ways with other human beings and constructs enduring *social norms*—patterns of relationships, groups, institutions, societies. Society is more than a mere aggregate of individuals. The existence of society precedes the existence of any of its members, and it continues long after they are gone. We constitute society, but we are born into it and become human through it. We remain individuals yet necessarily participate in and are shaped by the *mass of interdependent relationships* that constitute social reality. Man is in society, but society is in man.

The sociological perspective focuses on these social relationships—how they arise, why they persist, what effects they have, how they maintain social order or contribute to social change. The sociologist applies theory to society—sometimes broad and imaginative and highly abstract, sometimes narrowly focused on a single phenomenon—but his perspective is a disciplined one. It aims at precision and objectivity through rigorous methods of scientific inquiry and analysis of evidence. The sociological perspective, like any other perspective, focuses on some elements in the world and relegates others to the background. But, unlike many other perspectives, it is a perspective of which the practitioner is aware: most individuals rarely appreciate that their own view of things is but one of an infinite number of possibilities, that their "self-evident facts" may be someone else's "patent nonsense." C. Wright Mills in *The Sociological Imagination* (1959) argued that the sociological perspective has had immense consequences for our understanding and awareness of ourselves:

> It is by means of the sociological perspective that men now hope to grasp what is going on in the world and to understand what is happening in themselves as minute points of the intersection of biography and history within society. In large part, contemporary man's self-conscious view of himself as at least an outsider, if not a permanent stranger, rests upon an absorbed realization of social relativity and of the transformative power of history. The sociological imagination is the most fruitful form of this self-consciousness.

Similarly, the contemporary sociologist Peter Berger has suggested that sociology is a special form of consciousness that induces skepticism about the "common sense" and "official" explanations of human society and human action. The sociologist's perspective, in Berger's view, lends a capacity for seeing through the facades, the accepted explanations, the conventional wisdoms. It makes us see in a new light what we once took for granted—the social world into which we were born and in which we have lived all our lives. In *Invitation to Sociology* (1963) Berger describes the sociologist as:

3

Karl Marx (1818–1883). Marx's social theory and analysis of society in terms of inherent, ongoing conflicts remains today, more than 90 years after his death, a major perspective of the social sciences.

a person intensively, endlessly, shamelessly interested in the doings of men. His natural habitat is all the human gathering places of the world, wherever men come together. . . . His consuming interest remains in the world of men, their institutions, their history, their passions. And since he is interested in men, nothing that men do can be altogether tedious for him. . . . Nobility and degradation, power and obscurity, intelligence and folly—these are equally *interesting* to him, however unequal they may be in his personal values or tastes. Thus his questions will lead him to all levels of society, the best and the least known places, the most respected and the most despised.

HOW DID THE DISCIPLINE DEVELOP?

Robert K. Merton has described sociology as a very new science of a very old subject. The ancient subject is human society, but the new science emerged about a century and a quarter ago, when it was conceived and named by a Frenchman, Auguste Comte (1798–1857). Modeling his new discipline on the natural sciences, Comte developed an elaborate *social physics*. He believed that all the existing sciences could be ranked in a hierarchy and that sociology, the queen of the sciences, was the crowning glory of man's intellectual achievement.

The system of social physics won few adherents, but firmer foundations for a science of society were laid by three intellectual giants, the Germans Karl Marx (1818–1883) and Max Weber (1864–1920) and the Frenchman Emile Durkheim (1858–1917). Their work defined many of the issues that are still relevant and prominent in social science today, and they produced richly imaginative theories and methods of analysis that still illuminate the sociological enterprise. They remain our intellectual contemporaries, and their names figure again and again in the pages of this book.

Marx, Durkheim, and Weber faced a world in which massive and apparently unpredictable social change had become a continuing and permanent feature of human existence. Industrialization was threatening or destroying traditional social factors—the church, the small community, the peasantry. Human society was being radically transformed before their eyes. Did the transformation signal a collapse into chaos and disorder or evolution to some new social form? The social world could no longer be comprehended in terms of traditional understandings and the experience of the past. The sociological enterprise today cannot be fully understood without an awareness of the concerns, influence, and continuing relevance of the classical thinkers of the nineteenth century.

During the twentieth century the main development of sociology has taken place in the United States. Earlier thinkers lacked the statistical techniques and other research methods to make precise observations of human action and institutions, and there was little systematic empirical investigation that might verify, modify, or invalidate theoretical speculation. Much of the impetus for the development of these techniques came through the close involvement

4

Max Weber (1864–1920). Weber's analyses of religion, economy, bureaucracy, class, status, power, authority, and law in capitalist society made him one of the greatest influences on modern sociology.

of sociologists with the reform movement in the early part of the century. Indeed, in the public mind the word "sociologist" almost inevitably implied "reformer." The close link between sociological research and social reform was based on the belief that a better world could be built through understanding of the principles of society. The accumulation of these scientifically verified principles would provide a rational and unanswerable basis for tackling problems ranging from the plight of migratory workers to the endemic poverty of the poorest fifth of the nation.

During the years between the world wars and afterwards this early zeal for reform gradually gave way to a concentration on the development of sociology as a science. Sociologists tended to withdraw from active involvement in social issues and to focus instead on developing the quantitative techniques and methodological procedures that they considered essential for a truly scientific discipline. It is only since the turbulent decade of the 1960s that a significant number of American sociologists have once more argued that a purely academic pursuit of sociology is an unjustifiable luxury and that sociologists must actively apply their tools and understanding to the creation of a better society. Most sociologists, however, still believe that sociology can render its most effective service through a stance of neutrality and objectivity, providing the undisputed facts on which others can base policy decisions.

IN WHAT WAYS DOES SOCIOLOGY RELATE TO OTHER DISCIPLINES?

Sociology is one of the *behavioral* or *social sciences.* The social sciences are commonly distinguished from the *natural sciences* (such as astronomy, physics, or oceanography), which deal with the natural world, and from the *humanities* (such as literature, art, or philosophy), which are concerned with humanity in a "nonscientific" way. As the most recent group of disciplines to emerge, the social sciences have tended to draw their subject matter from the humanities but their methods from the natural sciences. Even today the social sciences do not have a monopoly on the study of man: the natural sciences often contribute to our understanding (we can learn, say, from biology, ethology, or genetics), and the humanities provide a profound insight into many areas of human conduct. The sociologist's inquiries often venture into other disciplinary areas, because he focuses on man in so many of his interactions.

Within the social sciences there are several other disciplines besides sociology: political science, history, psychology, economics, and anthropology. The divisions between these disciplines are arbitrary and in a constant state of flux. Often practitioners from several of these disciplines will work together to develop an interdisciplinary approach to a particular problem, and the findings from one discipline are often useful data in another.

Political science deals with abstract theories of government (political philosophy) and with the actual practice of politics (decision making and the functioning of political institutions). One area of overlap between sociology and political science is *political soci-*

ology, which studies questions of political behavior in society —analyzing, for example, the social composition of revolutionary movements. Political science and sociology often draw on the same body of theory: Karl Marx, for example, is as much a political philosopher as a social theorist.

History was formerly considered one of the humanities; today it is usually regarded as a social science. This shift is partly the result of the introduction of the sociological perspective to historical investigation. Historians no longer simply chronicle battles and other significant events; they seek to discover underlying social forces involved in the events they describe and interpret. *Historical sociology* is an emergent and influential discipline. The task of the historian is very similar to that of the sociologist, except that the historian is dealing with a finite amount of past data and cannot utilize many of the techniques available to the sociologist.

Psychology deals with human mental processes. It studies both the *cognitive* aspect of the mind (how we think about the world around us) and the *affective* aspect (how we feel about our experiences). Psychology usually focuses on the individual; but one important area of overlap with sociology is *social psychology,* which studies the individual as a member of the group, focusing on the effect that socialization and group processes have on the individual in society.

Economics is primarily the study of the production, distribution, and consumption of goods, services, and wealth in society. It is a highly developed theoretical and empirical discipline, focusing on such subjects as the relationship between demand and supply or the requirements for long-range economic planning. A significant interface with sociology is *economic sociology.* Economic factors can pervasively influence society, and social factors can profoundly affect the development and functioning of the economic system. The sociologist and the economist can aid each other in their understanding of their respective fields.

Anthropology is the study of human culture. *Physical anthropology* uses techniques developed by biology and archaeology to study man's current physical development, as deduced from ancient bones and artifacts and to discover the geographic distribution of morphological and genetic traits. *Cultural or social anthropology* focuses on the cultures of peoples all over the world, particularly in small-scale, preliterate societies. As the supply of primitive men diminishes, however, anthropologists are concentrating increasingly on the culture of other groups all over the world. The anthropological perspective is important to the sociologists, particularly for its implication of the need to avoid ethnocentrism— the tendency to think only in terms of the values of one's own culture and to use these values as a standard for judging other cultures.

HOW DOES THE SOCIOLOGIST GO ABOUT HIS WORK?

Ever since Comte founded the discipline in the nineteenth century, sociologists have regarded their activity as a scientific one. Science is distinguished not only by the nature of its content, but

6

also by a method and by its spirit of inquiry. A science is a body of organized knowledge that has been accumulated systematically and that posits a series of logically connected propositions about the recurrent behavior and relationships of certain phenomena.

The *scientific method* involves systematic analysis of reality in such a way as to attain an understanding of truth—to seek, discover, understand, and explain recurrent relationships in the real world. The scientific spirit aims at objectivity. It takes nothing for granted; everything is uncertain until proven. Preconceived notions and biases are excluded from the search for truth as far as possible, and the results are made available to the scientific community, which can then evaluate, replicate, or modify them.

The sociologist uses methods similar to those of the natural scientist. He attempts to measure and quantify behavior by objective techniques, he analyzes and verifies data and findings, he controls the conditions surrounding his experiments, and he usually attempts to retain an orientation of neutrality toward his work.

Sociology, like other sciences, comprises two distinct but necessarily related elements, *theory* and *research*. Theory gives meaning to facts that might otherwise simply be units of information providing no particular enlightenment to anyone. Research makes theory more than a useless set of abstractions. The two are thus complementary: research is meaningless and irrelevant without theory, and theory without research is simply speculation unrelated to the world.

The most important elements in a theory are concepts. A *concept* is a unit of meaning, a symbol that supplies a label for a particular segment of reality. Some basic concepts in sociology, for example, are *personality, group, culture, interaction, society*. These concepts can be combined into theories, which are statements of the probable or predicted relationship between concepts.

There are several levels of theoretical generalization—low-level *empirical generalizations,* usually based on a few observations; *middle-range theories* that interrelate two or more of these empirical generalizations; and *grand theory,* into which all concepts, generalizations, and middle-range theories can be fitted. The attempts at grand theory by the classical social theorists have been a rich and provocative source of inspiration. to modern sociologists but do not lend themselves as readily to empirical investigation as middle-range theories, which are less abstract and more easily related to ongoing investigations.

A theory that remains to be validated or invalidated is called a *hypothesis;* it states a probable relationship between two concepts whose properties vary—that is, between two variables (for example, economic status and drug usage). The researcher first defines a problem from some area that he wishes to investigate. Then he frames a hypothesis, a suggested theory that lends itself to systematic investigation and verification—for example, "Middle-class youth are more likely to use illicit drugs than working-class youth." The variables must then be *operationally defined* so that it is clearly specified what is included in the definition and what is not. Operational definitions are usually achieved by establishing some *index*—for example, "middle class" may be defined with reference to a specific range of parental income, "youth" may refer to individuals between particular ages, and "illicit drugs" may be defined to refer only to some drugs and not to others. A *research design* is then chosen. How can the subject best be studied? How can the influence of other variables—like differential exposure to drugs—be discounted? How can we be sure that the subjects are telling the truth? How can we know that the sample is representative?

Research designs commonly use one of three methods. In the *experimental* method only one condition is varied at a time. Every effort is made to keep the others constant, so that cause-and-effect relationships can be disentangled. Frequently an attempt is made to compare *experimental subjects* and *control subjects*. The former are exposed to the experimental conditions, but the latter, who otherwise resemble the experimental subjects, are not. The two groups can then be examined at the conclusion of the experiment to see if significant changes have taken place in the experimental group that have not taken place in the control group. This procedure discounts the possibility that any changes in the experimental group happened independently of the experimental conditions.

In the *sample survey* method a representative group of people is chosen from a particular "population"—of, say, the nation, the city, the state police, or the local college. A statistician can construct his sample in such a way that conclusions valid for the whole population can be drawn from a small sample with very little error. The sample subjects may be asked to complete a questionnaire or take part in an interview. This method lends itself well to the analysis of a series of variables, *multivariate analysis*. Particularly if the information is fed into a computer, it is possible to extract valid generalizations about the correlations between many different variables for the whole of the population from which the representative sample was drawn. The method is also useful for following changes in variables, such as attitudes or income, over a period of time; the questionnaires or interviews can be repeated periodically.

The *case study* method involves intensive examination of a particular social group over a long period of time. Careful records are taken of significant events, and these are subsequently analyzed in the light of the original hypothesis. Case studies tend not to prove anything definitively—a small number of studies is an inadequate basis for establishing generalizations—but they often provide rich insights and serve as a source of fresh hypotheses and research.

CAN SOCIOLOGY BE OBJECTIVE?

Sociology, as a science, attempts to apply the scientific method to the objective study of man. But this endeavor creates thorny problems, for man is himself a product of the social world. His relationship to that world is thus different from his relationship with the natural world. Is the same degree of objectivity possible in studying both?

Many social scientists have denied that objectivity is possi-

8

THREE APPROACHES TO RESEARCH

Features	1 Experiment	2 Surveys	3 Participant Observation
Location of research	In a laboratory	In a real community or communities (large, extended)	In a real community (small)
Selection criteria for communities, persons, groups, etc.	Careful design of experiment includes specification of subject group parameters	Random selection from the wider society	Depends on availability of community, nature of study
Cost factor	Highly dependent on nature of equipment used	Depends on size of sample and whether mailed questionnaire or formal interviewing is used	Relatively inexpensive
Number of subjects	Usually very few	Usually quite large, depends on size of society, nature of problem	Relatively few
Nature of problem usually investigated	Hypothesis and variables to be investigated clearly articulated in advance and controlled for in the lab	Hypothesis and variables to be investigated clearly articulated in advance, but not under researcher's control	Subjecting general theory to case study validation; often unpredictable, growing out of study situation itself
Usual researcher/subject interaction	Mostly formal, face-to-face	When face-to-face inevitably formal; often indirect (e.g., via mail)	Mostly informal, face-to-face
Ways in which variables are controlled	Comparing data from the experiment vis-a-vis the control groups	Through statistical manipulation and analysis	Through testing against case materials, revision of research or theory
Extent to which independent variable(s) can be manipulated by researcher	Totally	Not at all	Slightly
Extent to which the results can be generalized to the wider society	Depends on whether groups have been selected with this in mind	Usually can, because random selection techniques are normally employed	Depends on nature of problem
Possibility of using this approach to determine distribution of a population variable (e.g., age)	No	Yes – because of sampling technique	Yes – to the extent that the community is an adequate example of the wider society
Are the results of the research at all influenced by the act of research?	Yes	Yes	Yes

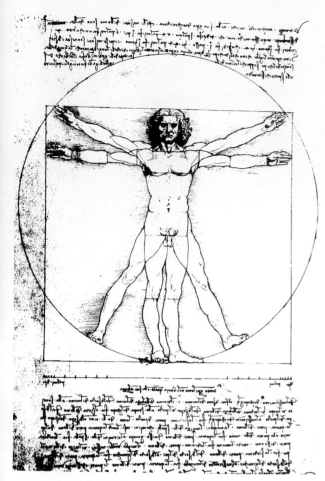

Leonardo Da Vinci's *The Proportions of Man.* No matter how systematically we investigate human nature, the neo-idealist maintains, we are inevitably a part of the process we are investigating, and our research is a part of its results. Thus human nature will always remain an elusive object for study.

ble in their field. The *neo-idealist* school, associated particularly with Max Weber, has argued that the division between the natural and the social sciences is so great that the methodology from the former cannot be applied to the latter. Man is a conscious being, with wishes, intentions, emotions, and reason. His consciousness places him in quite a different category from, say, an asteroid or a molecule. We can observe such natural phenomena from the "outside." We cannot empathize with a star or a molecule; we need not and cannot attribute intent or reasons to them; and only an analysis in terms of mechanical, cause-and-effect relationships is possible or appropriate. But we must deal with the social world "from the inside." We are part of what we study; we can empathize with other people and place ourselves in their position; in this case we must recognize that an analysis in terms of cause-and-effect relationships is inadequate. Full explanation must take account of values, emotions, and intentions—and these are subjective, not objective. Weber asserted, and many social scientists still agree, that objective measurements are not enough: sociologists must use *Verstehen* ("understanding") in their investigations. A full explanation of social phenomena will necessarily include a comprehension of their subjective meanings in the minds of others—a problem that the natural scientist never has to face.

An opposing tradition is that of *positivism,* which asserts that the methods of natural science can be applied to the study of man, even though the task may be difficult. Positivism exerted a tremendous influence in American sociology in the 1930s, when there was frequent effort to achieve great methodological rigor in the social sciences through the use of quantification, statistics, a supposedly highly precise technical jargon, and arrays of tabulations and graphs. The positivist assumption is that the natural and social sciences have basic similarities that can be analyzed by use of sane, logical, scientific method. The difficulties, it is alleged, lie in the inadequacy of our tools rather than in the applicability of these techniques. Some social sciences, such as economics, have already developed highly sophisticated tools, and the same should ultimately be true of sociology. At that point, it is argued, objective knowledge will be achievable in the social as well as the natural world.

Much contemporary opinion rejects the possibility of complete objectivity in either the natural or the social sciences. Instead, objectivity in social science is thought to consist of being sufficiently disciplined to reduce or eliminate distortions that might be produced by one's own feelings and attitudes to one's subject matter. But the desire to be objective, however sincerely held, does not necessarily lead to objectivity; the sociologist may be biased without realizing it. Furthermore, the very decision to investigate one problem rather than another is largely a matter of personal judgment, as is the construction of a hypothesis, the determination of a research design, the evaluation of data, the decision to regard some material as irrelevant and some as relevant, and the final pronouncement that one's original question has been adequately answered. The aim, however, is a dispassionate analysis of reality. The individual sociologist hopes that by submitting his findings to the critical and equally dispassionate view of the scientific community, he will avoid gross distortions of reality.

SHOULD THE SOCIOLOGIST BE NEUTRAL?

If the problem of objectivity is a difficult one, the problem of neutrality is even more troublesome. Sociology differs from the humanities in that it attempts, among other things, to apply the method of the natural sciences to the objective study of social life. Many sociologists accordingly insist that it is not their function as sociologists to take stands on social issues, however strongly they may feel about them and however much they may act on these feelings in their role as citizens. Instead, the sociologist's duty is to develop reliable knowledge about society; his own moral or political convictions should not color his work. The issues raised by such neutrality are complex and topical, for they deal with the role of science in human society and the social responsibilities of the scientific community.

Although the sociological enterprise in the early part of this century was focused on a partisan concern for change in American society, since World War I the tendency has been toward a conscious ethical neutrality. This neutral stance was much criticized in the 1950s by C. Wright Mills and in the 1960s by such sociologists as Irving L. Horowitz. Today there are indications of a renewed trend toward deep involvement in social problems and overt commitment to their solution. Many younger sociologists feel that their profession has a moral obligation to take an active leadership in the struggle against social injustice and inequality. They argue that it is impossible, in contemporary society, for sociology to be ''value-free''; to pretend otherwise is simply a delusion. The sociologist has access to knowledge and techniques that place him in an advantageous position to propose and work for more equitable solutions to social problems. The stance of neutrality is false and demeaning, and because it recommends no clear alternatives, it by implication supports the status quo. These critical views have unquestionably become more popular in recent years, and several sociologists are more radical in their attitudes than students or faculty members from almost any other subject area.

Other sociologists—certainly a majority—continue to argue for a value-free position. It would be quite wrong to view all of these sociologists as necessarily conservative; many of them are political radicals. They define their task separately from their politics, however, and insist that the discipline of sociology is not the appropriate place for identification with and involvement in social causes. They argue that preconceptions and biases can prejudice the findings of sociologists or even influence them not to investigate certain ''taboo'' areas if they suspect the findings might not be congenial to their beliefs. According to this view, the good sociologist guards against the corruption of his work and the truth by subjective opinions; if he abandons his position of neutrality, how is the discipline to be developed as an objective science? Why should the public and the policy makers pay attention to sociologists who are using their discipline not to provide a factual basis for decisions, but to influence policy so that it accords with their personal tastes? If the sociologist is tempted to suppress evidence because it does not suit him, the development of the discipline will be stunted, and the sociologist will not be trusted. There is ample scope for the sociologist to pursue his objectives, it is argued, in his role as citizen; the roles of concerned citizen and scientific sociologist must be distinguished and kept separate. The issue is one that each student and practitioner of sociology must decide for himself.

THE TWO-BOOK SYSTEM

Each unit of *The Study of Society* is prefaced by a unit-opening page that includes a Schematic Outline, a list of Supporting Units, and a list of Encyclopedia Entries. The Encyclopedia Entries are to be found in *Encyclopedia of Sociology,* which was developed to accompany this text as part of a **two-book system.** The list of Encyclopedia Entries for this unit follows:

anthropology, cultural
case study
Comte, Auguste (1798–1857)
concept
Durkheim, Emile (1858–1917)
ethnocentrism
experiment
generalization
grand theory
hypothesis
learning theory
Marx, Karl (1818–1883)
Merton, Robert K. (b. 1910)
methodology
middle-range theory
Mills, C. Wright (1916–1962)

multivariate statistical analysis
neo-idealism
political sociology
positivism
radical sociology
self-fulfilling prophecy
social change
social organization
social structure
social theory
sociology
sociometry
statistics
survey
variable
Weber, Max (1864–1920)

THE GENERIC STRUCTURE OF THIS BOOK

Research on learning processes, as Jerome Bruner points out in *The Process of Education* (1960), has taught us at least one significant fact—that learning depends largely on *structure,* a formal pattern into which the student can "lock" the various items in the content of that which is to be learned. Every discipline has its own structure, but this structure may not be immediately apparent to the beginner. Yet in any discipline there are recurrent themes, issues, and problems located within a framework that is unique to the particular discipline in question. *The Study of Society* is the first sociology textbook to apply a consistent and reliable structure—a *Generic Structure*—to the teaching and learning process. You will soon become familiar with this structure, and you will find that it greatly facilitates your understanding and hence your learning of the sociological content of this book and, perhaps more importantly, of the processes of sociological inquiry.

The Generic Structure is simply a basic format or skeleton that is repeated in every unit of this book. It is made up of four main "chunks"—**A, B, C, D**—with recurrent "elements" in several of the chunks. Every unit, for example, starts with a graphic introduction; every unit then defines the unit topic; every unit asks three basic questions; and every unit concludes with a final interview or interviews with some expert or experts in the field being discussed. The reasons for this Generic Structure are:

1. The book is easier to understand because of its predictable organization. Unlike other texts, *The Study of Society* does not present a haphazard jumble of facts, theories, research, and comparisons. The student knows exactly where to go for any item in any unit, and the items are consistently related to one another in each unit.
2. Students know what to expect as they read through each unit. They always know where they are in the text and what to expect next, so that learning expectancies are developed right from the start.
3. The structure permits the student the unique opportunity to read a particular series of chunks comparatively right across all units in the text, picking out only those items he or she wishes to focus on at the time—for example, classical theories.
4. The Generic Structure that forms the skeleton of each unit repeats the characteristic concerns of sociology. Hence the student is reinforced not only in his learning of content but also in his understanding of the "generic" qualities of the discipline itself.

The Generic Structure comprises the chunks and elements depicted in the following two pages.

A

Introductory Graphics

This chunk is a pictorial pre-experience of the subject matter of the unit. It illustrates the process or concepts involved in the unit topic.

Detail of introductory graphics from Unit 6 illustrating Demography—The Study of Populations.

B

Definition and Context

1 Definition
This element always provides a brief introduction to the topic and an *italicized* definition of the subject matter under consideration. There is also a brief explanation and definition of any other terms or concepts essential for an early understanding of the particular unit.

2 World Context
This element locates the topic in human experience and history, providing a perspective that extends beyond our time and country. Special attention is given to examples that differ significantly from American social institutions and practices.

3 American Context
This element lays the groundwork for the subsequent discussion in the unit. It introduces the student to specific facts and practices connected with the unit topic, showing, with examples, the nature, history, and scope of the topic in American society.

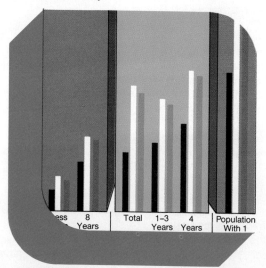

Detail of chart from Unit 18 relating level of educational attainment with income levels for both black and white people.

C

Questions and Evidence

This chunk is the core of each unit. Any textbook or textbook chapter in sociology necessarily only samples the field—usually haphazardly. But in *The Study of Society* three particular types of questions are consistently chosen. First is a *"burning issue" question,* a problem that is of real importance today and that reveals the contemporary relevance and fascination of sociology. Second is a *"classical" question,* a theoretical issue that is of wide scope and contemporary import, although it may have been asked for a century or more. Third is the *"research" question,* one that is more narrowly focused upon a specific sociological problem that has been recently investigated.

1 Questions
In this element the three questions are stated in everyday language.

2 Evidence
In this element each of the three questions is examined in turn. The examination always proceeds through four distinct stages: Context, Theory, Research, Evaluation.

i Context This element establishes a context for the question, explains why sociologists are interested in it, and restates the question in terms a sociologist might use.

ii Theory This element states the theory or model (or theories or models) that addresses the question at issue. When appropriate, equilibrium theories or models are contrasted with conflict theories or models.

iii Research This element introduces the most important study or studies relating to the question. For the "burning issue" question the research is usually a general summary or theoretical speculation inspired by the original theoretical model. For the "classical" question the research is usually a historical survey of the major pieces of research over an extended period of time. For the "research" question it is usually a finely focused single experiment, with a stress on methodology.

iv Evaluation This element evaluates the original theories in the light of subsequent research and summarizes our present understanding of the problems raised by the question in each particular case.

3 Overview
This element is a brief summary of the sociological endeavor discussed in the unit. Its aim is to provide some final sharp insights into the topic, bringing the area together for the reader.

D

Looking Ahead

This chunk consists of one or more interviews with prominent sociologists or personalities closely acquainted with the problems raised by the unit topic. Each interviewee answers questions and speculates on where the discipline in that particular area is headed, sometimes taking issue with the approach of the unit or with other interviewees.

Professor Charles R. Lawrence discussing black families in interview in Unit 7.

Detail of model from Unit 11 providing a set of categories for the observance of small groups in interaction based on Bales' interaction process analysis.

LOOKING AHEAD

1 Interview: Seymour Martin Lipset

Seymour Martin Lipset, professor of government and sociology at Harvard University, is one of America's most distinguished social scientists. His major publications include *Union Democracy* (with Coleman and Trow), *Political Man, The First New Nation, Revolution and Counterrevolution, The Politics of Unreason* (with Raab), and *Rebellion in the University*. His areas of current research are comparative stratification and mobility and the sociology of the intellectual life.

DPG *What are the main problems in sociology today?*

LIPSET If you mean problems of the discipline, then I'd say it's the fact that the discipline is highly disparate in its conception of what it's all about. One probably gets more heterogeneity among sociologists' judgments as to what is good sociology and how it should be done than in any other academic field I can think of. What we have as a field isn't a field. I think that probably there is less consensus in sociology today—about where it is and where it's going—than there was a decade ago.

DPG *Do you see sociology as getting close to being a science or approaching that goal?*

LIPSET No. If one means by science a field of inquiry that somehow is modeled on an image of certain natural sciences—an integrated body of theories that can be formulated as a very explicit model that is presented in mathematical and statistical terms—I don't think that is possible. I rather think that sociology is currently inclined to be more like medicine, meaning that it brings to bear on specific problem areas the approaches, knowledge, and hypotheses coming from a variety of areas. Sociology is inherently much more complex than the natural sciences. In the natural sciences one can limit the variables and the relationships; to do this would be much too artificial in sociology, although economics is basically such a discipline, based on a very limited set of variables and assumptions.

DPG *It seems you wouldn't even want to approach the natural sciences.*

LIPSET It is not a matter of preference but of what is possible. Some people feel unhappy unless they have a theory that explains everything. I have more tolerance for ambiguity.

DPG *If you don't see sociology as approaching a science, then in what directions do you think sociology should be moving or is moving?*

LIPSET It is moving largely in reaction to diverse external and internal pressures. Where it ought to be going, I'm increasingly less certain myself. It has as its job the effort to explain human behavior, overlapping with social psychology. Obviously our goal should be to try to explain as much as possible with as few variables and as few assumptions as possible. In principle I feel this is where we should be going. But we're not making that much progress.

DPG *Do you see that there could be a homogeneity, that people could be working toward that one goal?*

LIPSET Goals are never attainable really, and I think that people can have very different perspectives but still agree that optimally one should be able to formulate propositions about behavior that are testable, so that people of different views and approaches come up with the same results. One can then disagree as to how much—how many such findings, how many such relationships, how many such propositions—can actually be secured, and how important they will be.

The different findings that can be formulated in very rigorous terms tend to be less interesting facts. The larger the problem, the bigger the area you're working on, the less rigorous the approach and the less certain the findings. So you can, in effect, sacrifice scope of importance for rigor. Now the people who stress rigor will say, "OK, you can go in for your scope, and then that isn't scientific. It's just a question of popular success. Such work is literary." They would say that most macroscopic research is not really "scientific" scholarship.

DPG *Do you find that you vacillate between "macroscopic" and "microscopic" approaches?*

LIPSET No. Most of my work has dealt with what I call macroscopic problems, but I try to bring to bear on them as rigorous

methods as one can use. But to say I think this is like coming out for virtue against sin. Everyone will say that no matter what the problem he is dealing with, he tries to be as rigorous as possible. Most sociologists will

definitely accept that as the objective. The only question is how rigorously we can deal with different problems.

I don't want to undervalue the very useful work being done by people who do attempt to construct rigorous models of behavior. Formulating mathematical models enables the analyst to see all the relevant cases. One of the troubles with formulating propositions or theories purely in words is that you don't see the empty boxes—you only see what you want to see—whereas when you specify a formal model, it points up all the possible relationships. Therefore such work is both intellectually important and useful.

DPG *Could you say something about value-free research?*

LIPSET It's a very curious phenomenon that a lot of people, particularly radicals, keep attacking a simple-minded target they call value-free research or value-free scholarship. But the people they claim espouse it never have espoused it. Almost no major sociologist has ever believed social research is, or could be, "value-free" in any meaningful sense of the term.

DPG *What are you doing right now?*

LIPSET A variety of things. I've been working for some time on a book on "The Politics of Academe," based in part on the data from a big survey collected by the Carnegie Commission, which inquired into the political opinions of faculty. I'm mainly interested at the moment in the sociology of the intellectual life.

2 Interview: Stanislav Andreski

Stanislav Andreski is head of the department of sociology at the University of Reading in England. He has studied in Poland and England and has taught in South Africa, England, Chile, Nigeria, and the United States. His writings include *Military Organization and Society, Parasitism and Subversion, The Uses of Comparative Sociology,* and the controversial *Social Sciences as Sorcery.* Forthcoming books will deal with the prospects of revolution in the United States and "mental pollution."

DPG *Your book,* Social Sciences as Sorcery, *seems to have upset some people.*

ANDRESKI This is inevitable. I imply that 80 percent of the writing these days is not only worthless; it is pernicious. If people just used their common sense they would know more than if they studied, say, Talcott Parsons.

A lot of things can be solved by the use of jargon—for example, the effort of thinking or the danger of saying something that someone else may not like. You don't have to be clever, and you're always on the side of whoever has the money or power. This is true whether you are in Britain or Russia or the United States; in fact, anywhere. Actually I have coined the expression "promiscuous cryptoconformism," which means that you are on the side of the powers that be in whatever context you are.

The psychologist B. F. Skinner, is one of the people, for example, who pretend to know more than they do. I wouldn't say he's dishonest in the sense that he intentionally misleads people. Some social scientists pretend that they have an exact social science, but he hasn't got it at all. He can predict next to nothing that matters about human behavior.

DPG *Do you think the social sciences can predict anything?*

ANDRESKI Of course, prediction is a very complicated matter. But I think we can predict mostly negative things; we can eliminate certain possibilities. But then we can never know. I think one of the biggest obstacles is that because of your prediction certain possibilities are not tried out, whereas if they had been tried out they might have been found impossible.

DPG *Do you think that it is a function of the social sciences to attempt to predict social developments?*

ANDRESKI If you can predict nothing, then you are useless. For example, if you call in a plumber or a doctor, you expect him to be able to give some advice about the problem that led you to call him in the first place. The basis of that advice is some kind of prediction, and there is always some kind of theory involved. But the point is that social scientists shouldn't pretend to have the ability to predict when in fact they don't.

DPG *It would seem that the social sciences failed to predict the rise of the civil rights movement in America, or the development of the youth culture, or even the women's liberation movement.*

ANDRESKI I wouldn't hold that against anybody except those who claim to have an exact science of society. If you say that you can't claim to make any predictions about a complicated and difficult social matter of the kind that astronomers can make about the movement of the stars, at least you've admitted that you can't. You just try to make the best of the overwhelmingly difficult task at hand.

DPG *Apart from the question of prediction, do you think that sociology has any useful function?*

ANDRESKI How are you going to deal with this civilization, how are you going to solve anything unless you understand it better? The social sciences serve as a useful analytical tool. This depends on how it's done. The kind of jargon one finds in sociology and political science is in fact no use; it is rubbish that clutters up people's minds and makes them less able to understand.

DPG *Can you give some examples or illustrations of this?*

ANDRESKI Yes. The pretension that you have a very exact quantifiable science, despite the fact that you haven't quantified the most crucial variable because you don't really know how to quantify it. In order to maintain your claim that you have an exact science, you just conceal these other factors. There are all kinds of examples that can be given. For instance, the siting of a new airport: you can quantify the cost of the land, the cost of building, and so on, but you can't quantify the effect on people—the effect of the noise on their lives and on their nerves. So you rule these out, and the whole thing is useless. Take also this ques-

tion of the war in Vietnam: you can't quantify the reluctance of the American soldier to fight or the determination of a Vietcong soldier to fight; you can't quantify corruption and its effect on morale. There are any number of examples where pretending that you have an exact science has led to disastrous consequences, and I would say this is the result of unconscious dishonesty and delusion. Scientists don't like to think of themselves as crooks; no one does.

DPG *What would you think would be the ideal sociology?*

ANDRESKI I think it's always easier to find fault than to give a recipe, but my answer is, essentially, that one shouldn't make false claims. This use of language to confuse is a disease that originated in Germany and was then transplanted to America and is now being taken over by the Europeans.

DPG *Do you think that sociologists' research should be related to current human problems and needs?*

ANDRESKI I think that often even the most abstract and theoretical things are relevant. I don't think people should try to

relate their work only to the "burning issues" of the day, because you never actually know what will contribute to the solution. For example, you can study the myths of the American Indians and something may occur to you, an insight into some aspects of the human mind or some relationship, that may eventually help either you or somebody else. I would say let freedom prevail as long as one's work is done seriously and honestly without false pretenses. What has happened in the social sciences isn't that they are not relevant, but almost that they are deliberately irrelevant. One of the motives behind this addiction to jargon or pseudoquantification is that the addicts don't want to say anything relevant because it is dangerous.

DPG *Why dangerous?*

ANDRESKI Because then you take sides.

DPG *Can social science be objective?*

ANDRESKI Yes, if by objectivity you mean the desire and the determination to be impartial, not to twist evidence, to recognize the truth whether you like it or not. If this idea is rejected, then you might as well close the shop. You would have just propaganda. So I think objectivity is a necessary ideal to strive for. It is the justification of our existence as scholars.

On the other hand, I think it is dishonest to maintain that one can achieve this 100 percent. You must strive for this ideal, but you must recognize that no human being is infallible. Let us not pretend we are gods; we are all subject to human error. Even your most careful and intelligent scholar is human and liable to commit logical inconsistencies.

DPG *Would you say that honesty in the social sciences requires research to be harnessed to a value—that research should contribute to making the world a better place?*

ANDRESKI The only ideal that I think is indispensable is the conviction that you might be doing good by adding to the sum total of human knowledge and understanding. If you believe that understanding is an important achievement then I don't think you have to be committed to a definite social reform—although, as a matter of fact, I think that everybody has some kind of idea of what he would like society to be.

DPG *Would you say that all research in the social sciences is morally permissible? Suppose that a social scientist was to find, for example, that certain groups of people were genetically inferior?*

ANDRESKI It all depends on your belief in the value of knowledge and truth. If you believe that it is always better to know the truth, then I think the conclusion is inescapable that if the research uncovers an important problem it should be investigated. If it were true that the genetic potential of blacks for learning were lower than that of another race, then you could say that in terms of humanitarian ideals one should formulate policies that take this into account. However, a more difficult question is how you diffuse this type of information. I think it should be written up in scholarly journals, but whether a great fuss should be made about it on television and in other mass media is an entirely different matter. I think it should be insulated from distortion by the mass media.

DPG *Looking ahead to the future, what would you say are the most important areas that the social sciences might be most usefully turning their attention to?*

ANDRESKI I would not like to legislate this. I think one of the gravest faults of the social sciences is that too many people are trying to force others to pursue studies that perhaps they wouldn't have done otherwise. Knowledge is better served when people are allowed to explore whatever they feel to be important. I think the concentration of power through the control of money is a great danger to the free choice of research areas in the social sciences.

DPG *Could you make any predictions as to important social problems we may face in the future?*

ANDRESKI If you want a prediction from me about an important issue, I would venture this: if the present antisocialization and cretinization of the public mind by the mass media continues, then civilization as we know it now must end. If the mass media, prompted by commercial considerations, are allowed to debase the public mind, then democracy will collapse, because if they extirpate all the civic virtues, democracy will not function.

Culture

Part 1

and Society

Unit 2
Sociology of Knowledge

SCHEMATIC OUTLINE

A Introductory Graphics: Human Knowledge and Social Context

B Definition and Context

1 Definition
The sociology of knowledge studies the processes by which knowledge, very broadly defined, arises in a particular culture, why it takes the form it does, how it is sustained by the culture, and the effects it has on social action.

2 World Context
Although knowledge has become increasingly similar in the advanced industrial nations, their belief systems differ. The difference between the belief systems of modern states and those of traditional societies is even more significant.

3 American Context
The amount of knowledge available to Americans is unsurpassed in human history. Many of their beliefs are subject to close criticism and debate, but others remain unquestioned.

C Questions and Evidence

1 Questions
Sociologists ask: (1) How does progress in knowledge take place? (2) How are particular ideas related to a particular society? and (3) What is the relationship between knowledge, thought, and language?

2 Evidence
a The "Burning Issue" Question
In recent decades attention has been given to the relationship between social processes and scientific innovation. Robert K. Merton postulated four socially determined values accepted by the scientific community—universalism, communalism, disinterestedness, and organized skepticism—whereas Thomas Kuhn stressed disciplinary paradigms, which tend to resist change. Case studies tend to confirm Kuhn's viewpoint.
b The "Classical" Question
Karl Marx's analysis of the economic substratum and the cultural superstructure of society raised the question of whether it is possible to attain completely objective knowledge. Max Weber and Karl Mannheim also provided important discussions of the question. Today most social scientists recognize that complete objectivity is an unattainable goal.
c The "Research" Question
Two linguists, Edward Sapir and Benjamin Whorf, challenged the assumption that thought can be accurately translated from one language to another. However, recent studies by Basil Bernstein and others have shown that the linguistic relativity hypothesis cannot be accepted, at least in its extreme form.

3 Overview
The sociology of knowledge is particularly significant because of the importance of knowledge to social unity and action. The differential distribution of specialized knowledge has profound implications for democracy.

D Looking Ahead

1 Interview: Kurt H. Wolff
2 Interview: Zhores A. Medvedev

SUPPORTING UNITS

ENCYCLOPEDIA ENTRIES

Kuhn
Merton
Whorf

1. **Knowing.** To know things is to put them into categories. These categories as an aggregate constitute our cognitive system. Meaningful social change necessitates the creation of breaks in the cycle.

2. **Action.** Our actions are structured in terms of the cognitive systems we use to categorize our experiences — which creates our social settings.

3. **Learning.** The cognitive systems we learn are a part of the social reality we are born into.

B   DEFINITION AND CONTEXT

1   Definition

In the Middle Ages most men knew that the world was flat and that the sun moved around the earth; in modern times, most men know that the earth is round and that it revolves around the sun. The devout Christian knows that Christ was the only-begotten Son of God; the devout Moslem knows that Christ was nothing of the kind, but that Mohammed was the great prophet of Allah. Millions of people in the world know that the nuclear power of the United States could extinguish all human life; millions of different people in other parts of the world do not even know that the United States exists.

We do not understand the world simply by perceiving an objective reality apparent to all men. On the contrary, our perceptions and interpretations are colored and even determined by the society in which we happen to live. The truth of one people or era is the falsehood of another. Even such elementary concepts as those of time, space, and causation, which philosophers such as Immanuel Kant have held to be innate in the human mind, are in fact culturally variable.

The sociology of knowledge studies the process by which knowledge arises in a particular culture, why knowledge takes the form it does, how knowledge is sustained by the culture, and the effects that knowledge has on social action within the culture.

"Knowledge" in this sense is broadly conceived and comprises many different elements—ranging through philosophical beliefs, religion, and science to the system of inarticulate, common-sense ideas that ordinary people have about the society and universe in which they live.

2   World Context

Knowledge is socially constructed. Each society has unique features, and so each society will possess a unique system of knowledge. The development of global communications and the tendency toward an increasing identity of life styles and social mores among the advanced industrial nations have meant that, for these societies at least, knowledge has become increasingly similar. Scientific knowledge, in particular, tends to become the common property of all these societies.

Even so, there are striking differences in the *belief systems* of modern industrial societies. In the liberal democracies of the West knowledge often includes different perspectives and beliefs: the individual can, in theory at least, pick and choose among a broad range of viewpoints. In the totalitarian state, however, knowledge is deliberately tailored to suit the programs and policies of the regime; and a variety of social institutions—especially the mass media and the schools—are utilized as agencies of social control and ideological reinforcement to a greater extent than is the case in liberal democracies. It is worth bearing in mind that the free play of ideas in the liberal-democratic model is, in both historical terms and in the reality of the contemporary world, very much a rarity.

(Left top) Wooden double-face mask from Baule tribe, Ivory Coast; (left bottom) Vikonov's *Going for Their Daily Work,* poster, Soviet Union; (above) Francis Bacon's *Painting,* oil and tempera on canvas, Britain, 1946. The works produced by a society's artists reflect its basic orientations. Primitive art is produced in isolated, relatively tradition-oriented societies, and basic themes, forms, and materials are utilized generation after generation. "Socialist realism" allows for greater individual diversity among artists but is limited to a set of rather predictable conventions tied into the political and economic analyses of socialist societies such as the Soviet Union and China. The intensely competitive atmosphere of the art world of industrialized Western countries, with individual artists and "schools" of artists seeking to establish themselves as the "most" *avant garde,* shows many of the characteristics of the capitalist economic system—a great deal of individual innovation, but little in the way of commitment to fixed ethical and esthetic standards, values, and principles.

The greatest contrast of belief systems occurs between the modern industrial state and the traditional society. In the static tribal society knowledge scarcely increases at all from one generation to another. Such societies lack any relativistic viewpoints, and the consequent absence of competing belief systems tends not only to encourage social stasis, but also to ensure a high degree of social unity through the total integration of all members of the community into a single unquestioned belief system. The prime repository for knowledge therefore tends to be the older members of the community rather than the young, and it is they who hand down the traditional lore that constitutes the body of knowledge in the community. In traditional tribal societies religion is rarely differentiated from other aspects of life. Eating, hunting, and other activities are suffused with religious significance to such an extent that the members of such communities are usually incapable of conceiving of religion as a separate category. The distinctions "modern" men make between the natural and the supernatural realms may not exist—ghosts and spirits who are just as "real" as ordinary men may populate the world. We discuss religion in detail in Unit 8.

Even such seemingly basic notions as those of causality, time, and space may be conceived quite differently in traditional societies from the way they are in modern societies. The linguist Benjamin Whorf argued that language shapes our knowledge of the universe: the vocabulary, categories, and syntactical relations that characterize the language we speak necessarily characterize the nature of all our thought because we are obliged to think in the very terms our language provides. Whorf drew attention to the world view of the Hopi Indians, who, he claimed, divided up the spatiotemporal universe quite differently from ourselves, though in a manner equally coherent and meaningful to them. Their view of the universe was so encoded in the Hopi language (which lacks a future tense and other syntactic forms pertaining to notions of time) that our own notions would be virtually untranslatable to the Hopi, while theirs would, correspondingly, seem almost incomprehensible to us:

> The metaphysics underlying our own language, thinking and modern culture . . . imposes on the universe two grand cosmic forms, *space* and *time;* static three-dimensional infinite space, and kinetic one-dimensional uniformly and perpetually flowing time—two utterly separate and unconnected aspects of reality. . . .
>
> The Hopi metaphysics also has its cosmic forms comparable to these in scale and scope. . . . It imposes upon the universe two grand cosmic forms, which as a first approximation in terminology we may call *manifested* or *manifesting* . . . or again, *objective* and *subjective.* The objective or manifested comprises all that is or has been accessible to the senses. . . . The subjective or manifesting comprises all that we call future [and] it includes equally . . . all that we call mental. ("An American Indian Model of the Universe," c.1936)

Trofim Lysenko, Soviet biologist. Lysenko (b. 1898) felt he had proved that acquired physical characteristics could be genetically inherited. Although this belief was contrary to the principles of the established science of genetics throughout the world, Lysenko was able to obtain the backing of the Soviet Union's political power structure. Joseph Stalin named him head of the Soviet Agricultural Academy, and "Lysenkoism," by decree of the Central Committee of the Communist Party, became Soviet doctrine until it was replaced in the 1960s and orthodox genetics accepted. Here Lysenko *(left)* is shown with some Soviet agricultural technicians and professors.

Such a division of the universe, which neglects to recognize, let alone emphasize, the notions of time and space that seem so self-evident to us, at first may appear to be the product of "primitive" thinking, to be "wrong." But we should remember that our own cosmological concepts are ultimately just as hypothetical—indeed often as "mystical"—as those of the Hopi. Both are simply socially constructed interpretations of reality.

3   American Context

Because of the complexity and technological sophistication of the United States, combined with its collection of diverse and competing belief systems, the sheer quantity and variety of knowledge available to the average American are unsurpassed in human history. Information is endlessly generated from diffuse agencies and institutions; it can be instantly spread throughout society by means of the most elaborate communications network in the world—the United States has more TV sets per capita; produces more books, periodicals, and newspapers; and has more radio stations than any other country. Indeed, the dissemination of knowledge has become a major function both of the administrative bureaucracy and of corporate commercial enterprise.

One characteristic feature of industrial societies is particularly emphasized in the United States. This characteristic is the development of differentiated institutions for the specialized pursuit and transmission of knowledge—schools, universities, research institutes, and the like. More than half of American youth go on to some form of higher education—compared with, for example, less than 10 percent of British youth. Throughout most of history most men have relied for their knowledge on the common-sense understandings developed in the course of their daily lives and thus have felt relatively self-sufficient in the basic areas that affect their exist-

The compartmentalization of knowledge in industrial society. As human endeavors are split into more and more roles in an increasingly compartmentalized society, so too knowledge becomes increasingly fragmented and major ideas become less accessible to any given individual.

ence. But Americans today turn increasingly to the experts. Areas that were once the domain of common sense or of religion have been eroded by the advance of specialized forms of knowledge, and so rapid is the accumulation of knowledge within each discipline that the locus for this knowledge is now the educated young. The old, consequently, no longer enjoy status as respected purveyors and retainers of knowledge, and are instead more and more likely to suffer from *"future shock"* in their efforts to comprehend a world that changes faster than their capacity to adjust to it.

American beliefs are subject to a relatively high degree of critical examination and debate by the members of the society. But there are many aspects of knowledge that Americans still do not really question—the belief that nothing can travel faster than the speed of light, the view that education is good for people, the acceptance of money as a necessary element in the national economy, the conviction that certain sexual behaviors are undesirable and taboo. Yet all of these beliefs might be challenged by or be seen as irrelevant in other societies: just as they may one day be challenged by or seem irrelevant in American society itself.

C   QUESTIONS AND EVIDENCE

1   Questions

Three sets of questions typify the concerns of the sociologist who studies knowledge: (1) How does progress in knowledge, especially in the natural and social sciences, take place? Does scientific knowledge increase cumulatively through random experimentation, or do social factors exercise a decisive influence? (2) What is the relationship between ideas and the society in which they are found—how do ideas arise? To what extent can ideas "act back" on society? (3) What is the relationship between knowledge, thought, and language? Does the language a person speaks really influence the way he perceives and understands the world?

2   Evidence

a   The "Burning Issue" Question
i   Context   It is only in the last few decades that the process of scientific innovation has been considered an appropriate subject for sociological study. This new interest is linked with the widespread critical scrutiny of the entire scientific enterprise. The earlier tendency was to have a naïve faith in science as some lofty endeavor immune to attack, especially from sociologists. Today, however, it is recognized that scientific knowledge is of fundamental importance in shaping both the form and the direction of modern society—and many citizens are beginning to question whether that form and direction are even desirable. Sociologists ask: *How do social processes affect scientific innovation?*
ii   Theory   The foundations for a sociology of scientific innovation were laid down by Robert K. Merton in several of the essays in *Social Theory and Social Structure* (first ed., 1949). Merton's *function-*

Scientific research—a chart for would-be explorers. This illustration is an attempt to convey the inevitable difference between what is held to be the ideal in research and what in fact actually occurs. Scientists are, after all, human; and petty jealousy, competitiveness, selective distortion, denial of the obvious, bureaucratic blockages, and other human foibles plague the scientific pursuit of knowledge just as they do other realms of human endeavor.

alist approach postulated a set of scientific values that are implicitly accepted by the research community. Scientific innovation, in Merton's view, will take place as long as four major imperatives—universalism, communalism, disinterestedness, and organized skepticism—are followed. *Universalism* refers to an objectivity that views considerations of race, religion, national origin, and the like as being unconnected with truth; no scientific career should be curtailed and no scientific view rejected on grounds connected with these considerations. *Communalism* refers to the need for scientific discoveries to be made available to the whole community—although priorities can be assigned by individuals, there can be no private intellectual property. *Disinterestedness* refers to the requirement that scientists not improperly allow personal motives or commitments to distort their findings or to influence their evaluation of the work of their colleagues. *Organized skepticism* refers to the suspension of judgment until all the relevant facts are at hand, after which the facts are to be analyzed in terms of established empirical and logical criteria—and there can be no "sacred areas" to which such scrutiny cannot apply.

An alternative theoretical view is put forward by Thomas Kuhn, who feels that the Mertonian approach, though adequate to account for scientific advance over time, cannot explain *radical scientific innovation*. Any scientist, Kuhn points out, works within a matrix of existing beliefs, both theoretical and procedural, that is specific to his particular branch of established knowledge. Kuhn calls such a set of concepts a *paradigm*. These disciplinary paradigms determine what is to count as a problem, a solution, a discovery, an appropriate research method, and so on. In consequence, Kuhn says, "Preconception and resistance seem to be the rule rather than the exception in mature scientific development. . . . Scientific education inculcates a deep commitment to a particular way of viewing the world and of practicing science in it." *(The Structure of Scientific Revolutions,* 1962)

The paradigm, says Kuhn, characterizes some of the best science: nature is too vast to respond to random investigations, and the paradigm defines the problems available and the means of attacking them. In preparadigmatic situations—such as investigations of electricity before Franklin—little progress is made; only after a fruitful paradigm emerges can a science leap ahead. Research guided by a paradigm produces a rapid accumulation of knowledge by directing the attention of a defined community to the systematic and detailed consideration of a specified and circumscribed field. Such research will continually generate new *problems and anomalies* that can be assimilated to the existing paradigm only through its modification or reconstruction. Because there is such a heavy investment in the paradigm or basic theory, many alterations will be permitted in the theory in order to account for newly discovered phenomena that seem to contradict or invalidate it. Such alterations are part of the effort to retain a theory that has previously proven so useful and compelling. Eventually, however, anomalies may emerge that are so numerous or so significant that the theory becomes a patchwork incapable of containing them. This situation arose, for example, in Newtonian physics before Einstein. In such a crisis scientists are obliged to cast around for a new paradigm that will more economically account for the full range of phenomena. Several contending paradigms may co-exist initially, but the one that yields the best empirical results will eventually gain the allegiance of the relevant scientific community.

Yet there will always be immense resistance to change. Not all scientists will switch allegiance. The reasons are many: some are too stricken with intellectual inertia; others are too timid to venture from the reassuring certainties of a lifetime to new worlds of which they know little; others are perennially skeptical and reject the new paradigm; others have a considerable stake in the maintenance of their research projects and funds; others may feel that they will be incompetent in research under the new paradigm; others find the old paradigm still useful for their purposes, though it may have failed elsewhere in the discipline; and others (whose number should never be underestimated) remain ignorant that any changes have occurred at all.

iii Research Research on the question of scientific innovation has taken place largely within the framework supplied by the work of Merton and Kuhn. Typically, research takes the form of case studies, in which the sequence of events in a given attempt at innovation is analyzed to see to what extent it conforms to the theories outlined above.

Michael Mulkay, for example, has studied a number of cases of scientific innovation, and he finds that scientists do not conform to the Mertonian norms—although they would like to think that they do. Mulkay's research, which he described in *The Social Process of Innovation* (1972), suggests that Merton's account is more valuable as an ideal set of standards against which actual practice can be measured than as a descriptive analysis of an actually existing situation. Mulkay's study of the scientific reception accorded to Dr. Immanuel Velikovsky and his work *Worlds in Collision* (1950) revealed that a marked deviation from the Mertonian norms can take place when a radical challenge is made to existing assumptions. (Velikovsky challenged assumptions in the fields of astronomy, geology, and historical biology, rejecting much established methodology in the process.) The response of the scientific community was emotional. Velikovsky's book was attacked before it had gone to press; his personal scientific status was called into question; he had difficulty publishing his views or replies to his critics in the professional journals; a movement arose to apply sanctions to his publisher; and little attempt was made to show the truth or falsehood of his theories experimentally. All the Mertonian norms, in fact, were violated. The real norms operating were those of contemporary theory and methodology.

W. O. Hagstrom has conducted similar investigations of scientific innovation, and he places great emphasis on the importance of social recognition to the scientist. Although the researcher is supposedly concerned only with the pursuit of truth, his outrage if he is beaten to the punch in his findings by someone else and therefore cannot take credit for the discovery suggests that a desire for public approval, appreciation, and status is also operating. On the basis of his analyses, Hagstrom argues, in *The Scientific Community* (1965), that the organization of science can be seen as an exchange of information for social recognition. Research publications are "contributions" (frequently financed by the contributor himself) that are offered in a ritual of "gift-giving." Acceptance of the gift, as in other social institutions, implies recognition of the status of the donor and the existence of reciprocal rights. Recognition is not important just because it provides massage of the ego or material rewards and professional ranking, however. It is important because the recognized scientist is in a better position to further the interests of his discipline—funds will flow freely in his direction and his findings will be more widely publicized. The desire for recognition, Hagstrom finds, will influence the scientist in his selection of problems and methods. Research that deviates too far from accepted channels will not be published in professional journals, and an awareness of what constitutes acceptable science will constantly pressure the practitioner towards conformity with established norms. Hagstrom's studies show how sanctions may be applied to "doctrinal deviants": there will be attempts to enforce conformity in appointments, in publications, and in the course of instruction offered to students.

Nevertheless, Hagstrom does find that in rare cases the desire for recognition can lead, not to conformity, but to a venturesome attack on new areas of ignorance, in the attempt to locate problems that other researchers are less likely to solve. Case studies show that, as a new area opens up and gains recognition as "hot," there will be a great influx of scientists eager to stake a claim in this more fertile ground. The "phage group" represents a striking example of this phenomenon—in this particular case a number of scientists deserted nuclear physics because they felt they could apply their talents more profitably in the new fields of microbiology and biophysics. Such crossovers into fields without established paradigms, where there is likely to be a minimum of resistance to new ideas, seems to be a significant source of scientific advance.

iv Evaluation Research findings tend to support the Kuhnian rather than the Mertonian model. In times of normal scientific activity, Mertonian norms may be applied, but when radical innovation threatens the existing theoretical and methodological paradigms, the scientific community often mounts a swift and hostile counterattack.

There have been too many examples of this reaction to innovatory science for us to doubt this tendency: Galileo was forced to retract his advocacy of the Copernican view that the sun rather than the earth was the center of the universe. Freud was pilloried and abused when he advanced his notion of infant sexuality. The examples are not only historical: witness the current derogatory reaction to the assertion by such ethologists as Konrad Lorenz that men may retain some residual instincts, notably those of territoriality and aggression. There is no necessary or inherent implausibility in this thesis—if the research and conclusions were restricted to chimpanzees, no scientist would raise any objection. But the findings are unacceptable from the start to many people of a humanist or liberal frame of mind, because the construction of an ideal society becomes more difficult if we grant that man is innately aggressive and selfish. Some scientists tend to reject Lorenz's thesis because it violates their social preconceptions rather than because of the questionable reasoning and research Lorenz advances to support his view. The problem for the scientific community, of course, is how to distinguish between a radical innovation worthy of consideration and a crackpot or malicious theory that merits being rejected out of hand. In sorting out the geniuses from the charlatans amid a continual profusion of new theories, scientists are primarily (and sometimes wrongly) guided by expedient and conventional notions of what constitutes acceptable knowledge and the appropriate procedures for obtaining it.

Kuhn's theory is more promising than Merton's, and it clearly has implications beyond the field of scientific research—how often in our daily lives do we find ourselves thinking in terms of paradigms, fitting facts into preconceived intellectual frameworks in order to make sense of them? It is debatable, however, whether all scientific advance can be contained within Kuhn's model—most of his examples are either from nuclear physics or from disciplines devoid of paradigms but moving into a paradigmatic state, and Kuhn never convincingly demonstrates that the theory can be applied equally well to other disciplines. The progress of science is probably much more messy than Kuhn allows. Many disciplines operate under conditions in which the ideas that compete with and complement one another are too vague and untidy to be assigned so elegant a title as paradigm. Even when overarching assumptions exist, they may be by no means as systematic or as universally accepted as Kuhn implies.

Another inadequacy of Kuhn's theory is that it cannot account for all innovation, some of which occurs in the normal course of scientific investigation without any prior crisis condition. Several other mechanisms exist to induce scientists both to seek and to accept new ideas. One of the most obvious and neglected is what the sociologist and economist Thorstein Veblen termed ''idle curiosity'' —the creative desire to discover something new. Another mechanism comes into play when, for whatever reason, the *mental set* of the experimenter is changed. For example, innovation frequently stems from the experience of individuals who fill two or more roles (such as experimenter and practitioner) so that they are constantly obliged to view the same problem from different angles. The desire for social recognition will also impel scientists to seek out new problem areas for their research initiatives. Finally, pressures from the wider society, which are often translated into an outpouring of public funds to support projects in a particular area, will also stimulate scientific innovation. After the launching of the first Soviet sputnik for example, American concern at the United States lag in the space race led to a massive concentration of resources on scientific research in the physical sciences. In the 1970s, public concern over the environment is becoming translated into new research opportunities in ecology and pollution control, and major innovation is to be expected in these fields.

b   The "Classical" Question

i Context   What is the relationship between ideas and the society in which they are found? To what extent can ideas ''act back'' on society? If all ideas are subject to some limitation because of the social context in which they originate, can we ever suppose any view is objective? The question is an important one, both for sociologists and for many contemporary students who are concerned with social action, with assessing what influence ideas can have on social structure, and with the problem of objectivity (in advancing some cause or course of action as the "right" one). Sociologists ask: *What is the relationship between knowledge and the social location of its producers?*

ii Theory The theoretical foundations for a sociology of knowledge were laid by Karl Marx, and most subsequent theoretical work tends to consist of amplifications, modifications, or refutations of his ideas. Marx held that the products of human society can be roughly divided into two strata—an economic or material substratum and a cultural or ideological superstructure. The content of the latter is dependent on the economic relations pertaining in the former. *Cultural products* such as ideas, law, political philosophy, religion, or art are therefore conditioned by the economic substructure of society, and these products merely reflect the position of their producers in the class structure of society. The *dominant ideas* at any time will necessarily be the ideas of the *ruling class*, whether these ideas find expression in legal statutes, in religious doctrines, in political structures, or in other social institutions. Ideas should be seen as weapons in the class struggle. Marx termed idea systems *ideology*; the prime function of the dominant ideology is to make the rule of the dominant class seem legitimate.

To Marx any such ideology clearly distorts social reality because it is constructed by the dominant class to maintain its privileged position. Its use for this purpose may often be unconscious. Social phenomena—such as the notion of the divine right of kings—may therefore appear to both kings and peasants to be as much a part of an external order of things as natural phenomena themselves are. This tendency for man to lose the awareness of his own authorship of and potential control over his cultural products is termed *alienation*. To Marx, the alienated man is the man whose own products confront him as something oppressive, so that he feels separated from the world that he himself has created. Frequently the dominant ideology will be accepted by members of the oppressed class as well (for example, the "Uncle Toms" in the black community). Marx termed this phenomenon *false consciousness*—that is, a consciousness that does not accord with the *objective situation* of those who experience it. Although the dominant ideology represents the interest of the ruling class, other ideologies can exist. These ideologies also tend to reflect the material interests of their producers, but the ideas can never become dominant unless there is an appropriate change in the class structure (as when feudal notions were superseded by classical liberalism, the ideological justification for laissez-faire capitalism).

Marx argued that economic relationships are the decisive factors in shaping people's conceptions of the world and that this fact constitutes a serious distorting barrier to the discovery of truth. He did not insist that ideas were totally dependent on the economic or material substratum; he conceded that certain idea systems (such as mathematics) could exist largely unaffected by changes in the

Sputnik I. This small sphere of shiny metal was the first satellite launched by human beings successfully to achieve a stable orbit around our planet. Its launching by the Soviet Union in 1957 propelled the United States into a nationwide mobilization of academic resources in order to redirect research and application efforts toward the eventual goal of placing a man on the moon before 1970. That goal was achieved in 1969.

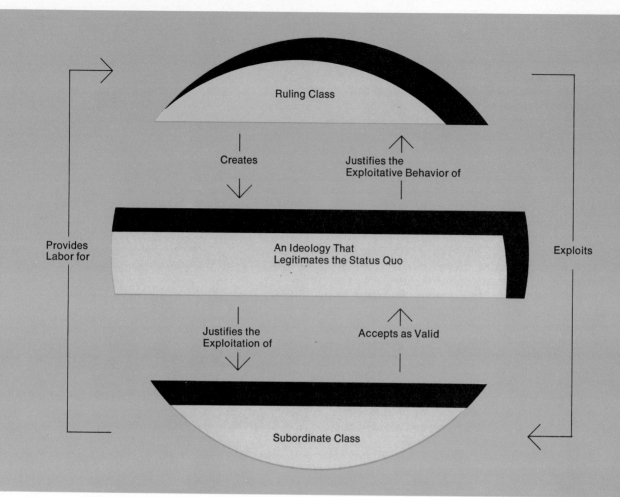

Model 1. Marx's Theory of the Relationship Between a Society and Its Ideology. The contradictions and inherent conflict in the relationship between the ruling and subordinate classes inevitably result in social change, and social change produces new ideologies.

social location of their producers—although the use to which such ideas were put might be a different matter. But other idea systems—such as sociology—were entirely dependent on the class structure of the society in which they arose. According to Marx, all sociologies are necessarily distorted in this way, with one exception: his own. Capitalist (or bourgeois or liberal) social science merely legitimates the existing social structure; the Marxist analysis alone is correct because it discerns the objective laws of historical development. Unit 4 discusses the Marxist view further with reference to culture.

iii Research (Survey)   Unless one accepts the Marxist stance, which relativizes all perspectives but regards Marxism itself as an objective foundation for all inquiry and scientific endeavor, how is one to handle the problem of objectivity? If all knowledge (including Marxism) is necessarily subject to the ideological biases and societal limitations of those who produce it, then is it ever possible to attain *completely objective knowledge?*

This problem has vexed most social scientists who do not accept the Marxist framework. Max Weber recognized that his own assumptions were affected by the underlying values of his society and that his interpretations were necessarily colored and limited as a consequence, even when he was trying his utmost to be objective. Even the notion of objectivity is, after all, the product of a particular social context; concepts of what constitutes objectivity and of the appropriate methods for arriving at objectivity are historically and culturally variable. Weber recognized that reality is infinite; the very decision to choose some part of it for sociological investigation is itself a judgment of value. Thereafter the methods chosen for the research, the assumptions on which the research proceeds, the basis for the interpretation of the data, and the final decision to pronounce one's own understanding as adequate can all involve personal bias, and must all take place within the confines of the unique historical and cultural context in which the researcher is embedded. Weber's conclusion was that although the scientist was welcome to his personal opinions, he should always make clear in his work what his assumptions were and should attempt as far as possible to exclude all conscious bias from his research. Complete objectivity, however, was an impossibility.

Another German sociologist, Karl Mannheim, in *Ideology and Utopia* (1929) picked up the threads of Marx's argument. However, he reserved the term *ideology* for essentially conservative doctrines—those that sought to justify some present situation or go back to some past situation. To these ideologies he contrasted *utopias,* or revolutionary ideologies, which were grounded in some messianic vision of an alternative social organization in the future. Mannheim also distinguished between a *particular* and a *total* ideology. The former is an idea or set of ideas that serves some specific function or purpose; that is, a given social group may interpret some event in terms of a particular ideology. A total ideology, on the other hand, refers to a more general system of beliefs and values that suffuses the entire culture—the taken-for-granted assumptions implicitly shared by the whole community.

Mannheim also accepted Weber's reasoning on the problem of objectivity, but believed he saw one way out. He claimed that the relatively "free-floating" intellectual tended to be only loosely attached to the social structure and therefore would have an unusually detached perspective, enabling him to enjoy the maximum opportunity for attaining the truth. Mannheim did not claim that the intellectual was free of commitments, passions, material interests, or ideological biases. He did feel, however, that this free-floating characteristic enabled the intellectual to obtain a richer, more varied understanding of reality by seeing several perspectives at the same time. And the intellectual would have the awareness—denied to most men—of the *relativity* of his own knowledge.

iv Evaluation   The Marxist view of the relationship between knowledge and the social location of its producers remains influential; in particular, Marx's theory of the justificatory nature of ideologies has been provocative and useful in aiding sociological understanding. In the Communist-governed countries of the world, such as the Soviet Union and China, sociology takes place almost entirely within the framework of the Marxist analysis. In effect, their sociology is simply the application of Marxist theory to social phenomena. In the West and elsewhere, however, the Marxist interpretation has been treated with considerable reservation. If the Marxist perspective is applied to

Marxism itself, then Marxism must be seen as the product of a particular time and place—mid-nineteenth century capitalist Europe—and thus denied its panhistorical significance. Even in the West, however, there are social scientists and philosophers who are profoundly influenced by Marxist notions of objectivity. Herbert Marcuse, for example, has argued that the views of the political right are self-evidently wrong and evil, although those of the political left are self-evidently right and good; and he argues that the political left would be accordingly justified in suppressing the political right.

Other social scientists still believe in the possibility of objectivity, provided that the social sciences operate on the model supplied by the natural sciences. Much of the jargon and pseudoscientific verbiage that clutters the vocabulary of contemporary social sciences—especially sociology—stems from the very attempt to develop a supposedly neutral ''scientific'' terminology (that is, one more conducive to quantification and verification) in imitation of the allegedly more objective natural sciences, particularly physics. Physicists themselves, however, admit the impossibility of complete objectivity in their own field; the act of investigating any natural phenomenon has been shown to distort it to some degree, and therefore its nature when undistorted by scientific observation cannot be known with certainty (that is, what it is ''really'' like when undisturbed by our efforts to find out what it is ''really'' like).

Some social scientists deny that objectivity is ever possible, or that it is even a desirable goal. They argue that the investigator may as well assert his commitments and work in accordance with them, leaving others to evaluate his findings in the light of their own interpretations of his procedures and conclusions.

In American social science at least, the Weberian position has triumphed. It is recognized that absolute objectivity is probably impossible to attain. However, as long as the researcher sticks to acceptable standards of methodology and exposes his work to the criticism and evaluation of the research community, there will be some safeguard against serious distortions of reality. But it must be remembered that the pre-Copernican geocentric view of the universe met all the standards of objectivity, methodology, and public evaluation of the time—yet it was objectively wrong, and Copernicus and Galileo were right. Future generations may look back on our own standards of impartiality and methodology with the same kind of amusement that we apply to the pre-Copernicans.

c   The "Research" Question

i   Context   Does the language we speak really influence the way we perceive and understand the world? The relationship between language, thought, and knowledge has stimulated a good deal of theoretical speculation and research effort; the problem has been tackled collaboratively by investigators from such different fields as sociology, psychology, education, philosophy, and the relatively new field of linguistics. There are thousands of languages in the world, and for thousands of years it has been assumed that ideas are freely translated from one language to another. In the United Nations a diplomatic subtlety spoken in Chinese is immediately translated into English, Russian, French, and Spanish on the assumption that accurate translation is possible. Sociologists, however, have raised the question of whether such translatability can really be achieved —or whether different languages "code" the world in different ways, giving quite different interpretations of objective reality. Sociologists ask: *To what extent does the language spoken in a particular society affect the cognitive perceptions and subsequent social actions of individuals within that society?*

ii   Theory   The long-standing belief in the translatability of thought from one language to another was challenged in this century by two linguists, Edward Sapir and his student, Benjamin Whorf. Einstein's theory of relativity had revolutionized the physical sciences, and Sapir and Whorf attempted to apply a new principle, *linguistic relativity,* to human society. Their argument was initially a very *determinist* one. Sapir declared:

> The worlds in which different societies live are distinct worlds, not merely the same world with different labels attached. We see and hear and otherwise experience very largely as we do because the language habits of our community predispose certain choices of interpretation. (*Language*, 1921)

And Whorf argued:

> We cut nature up, organize it into concepts, and ascribe significances as we do, largely because . . . the patterns of our language . . . are absolutely obligatory. ("Science and Linguistics,") 1940)

This argument implies that speakers of a language will be virtually incapable of perceiving the world except through the "colored glasses" supplied by the forms and categories of their language—so that if a language has no future tense (like Hopi) or several words for snow in different forms (like Eskimo) the visuali-

(Facing page) The planet Earth as photographed from the Apollo 17 spacecraft in 1972 during the final lunar landing mission in the Apollo program. The visibly spectacular results achieved through the use of technology reinforce our civilization's commitment to the technological and positivist definition of the nature of things.

Mark Spitz, winner of seven gold medals in swimming at the 1972 Olympics. Why do we measure the 200-yard freestyle? Why not the 240-yard freestyle? Clearly, the numerical categories our language recognizes structure our behavior in athletics. We seek the round numbers—a four-minute mile is the great barrier, not the 3.58. The distances and times are arbitrary; they simply conform to our linguistic habits.

zation of the world is bound to be restricted or extended accordingly. In their later work Sapir and Whorf tended to adopt a less determinist approach, but they still insisted that language structurally influenced thought. Whorf's evidence came largely from his studies of the Hopi Indians, whose world view (as noted earlier) does not recognize the fundamental categories of time and space so essential to our own conceptual framework, and whose language lacks the forms associated in our language with temporal and spatial distinctions.

More recent supporters of the linguistic-relativity hypothesis have shown that there are major relevant differences of several kinds between languages. First, some words may be missing in one language that are present in another—Aztec, for example, has only one word for snow, frost, ice, and cold. Second, an overall category may be missing—a tribe may have no word for "tree," only words for particular types of tree. Third, there may be major syntactic differences—one language may have grammatical and syntactic forms not found in another. Finally, different languages impose different categories on the physical world. The color spectrum, for example, is broken up in different ways by different communities—the Bassa-speakers of Liberia recognize only two colors, *hui* and *ziza*, roughly corresponding to the cold and warm colors of the spectrum, respectively.

The British sociologist Basil Bernstein, noting the tendency in all industrial societies for working-class children to do less well in school than middle-class children, has hypothesized that different linguistic codes have a causal significance in this respect. Bernstein argues that educational success is largely dependent on linguistic skill. Through language the child can organize his ideas and experiences; he is enabled to develop a wider perspective, to think in terms of possibilities and options, to manipulate or reorganize a problem mentally when attempting to solve it. In general, the more success depends on abstract thinking and the use of symbolism, the greater the influence of language is likely to be—thinking is never more precise than the language it uses. Bernstein believes that working-class and middle-class people are characterized by two quite distinct modes of speech. These speech modes are a consequence of the differing social relationships and values dominant in each class, and they are also a major factor in the perpetuation and reinforcement of these differences. Bernstein's theme is that the two modes may be characterized as *restricted code* and *elaborated code*—both of which are available to the middle-class child, but only one of which is available to the working-class child. The restricted code has a high degree of lexical and syntactic predictability; although speech may have vigor and color, it tends toward simple constructions accompanied by repetitiveness, limited use of adjectives and adverbs, and short or grammatically incorrect sentences. The elaborated code, on the other hand, is a much more flexible instrument. Its lexical and syntactic manifestations are not highly predictable and will vary considerably from individual to individual. The elaborated code has accurate grammar and syntax and a full range of subordinate clauses. It employs a wide range of parts of speech and uses more refined distinctions and greater abstraction. Meaning is made explicit through the precise use of sen-

Upper-class child and lower-class child. Not all students of linguistics share Basil Bernstein's view concerning the code differential between upper-class and lower-class children. In *Speaking and Language* (1971) Paul Goodman wrote: "It is plausible that the upper group would find the lower speech simpler and something like their own careless speech. But though the lower speakers hear the others' words, they do not really hear the distinctions, the concessions, the subordinations, and the abstractions; they quickly dismiss it as all bullshit. And the upper speakers are fatally put off by the bluntness and violence, much of which is ritual insult precisely to calm things down; they take the stereotypes too literally; they think that because the language is childish, the reasoning is—but it's not. When the atmosphere heats up, communication breaks down badly."

tence structure and a wide vocabulary.

Bernstein argues that working-class children who have access only to the restricted code will have great difficulty in mastering processes of generalization, classification, and conceptualization. Their thinking will be channeled by their early linguistic environment to such an extent that exposure to the elaborated code in the school will have little impact:

> The type of learning . . . initiated and sustained through a restricted code is radically different from learning induced through an elaborated code. . . . The orientation towards these codes, elaborated and restricted, may be independent of the psychology of the child, independent of his native ability. . . . The code orients the child progressively towards a pattern of relationships which constitute for the child his psychological reality and this reality is reinforced every time he speaks. ("A Socio-Linguistic Approach to Social Learning," 1965)

iii Research (Methodology) Several experiments have been conducted to test aspects of the linguistic relativity hypothesis. One of the best known is a study by J. B. Carroll and J. B. Casagrande, who investigated the relationship between linguistic structure and behavior among Navaho children ("The Function of Language Classifications in Behaviour," 1958). Some of the children in the sample spoke only English; others spoke only Navaho. The Navaho language has a particularly distinctive feature: verbs of handling (referring to processes such as picking up, dropping, holding in the hand, and so on) require special forms depending on the shape of the object that is being handled. There are some 11 different forms—for example, one for round objects, one for long, flexible objects, one for round but thin objects—and the young Navaho has to master these distinctions in order to speak his language accurately and grammatically.

Carroll and Casagrande established that the young Navahos did in fact speak their language grammatically. They then compared Navaho-speaking and English-speaking Navaho children, matched for age, on a sorting task in which they had to use shape, form, or material as a basis for classifying objects. Their finding was that the Navaho-speaking children were superior at the task; they tended to sort objects on the basis of form at a much younger age than the English-speaking Navahos. But Carroll and Casagrande also showed that although language can apparently influence behavior in this way, it is not the only factor capable of producing precocious sorting behavior. English-speaking children in Boston were also found to be able to sort material on the basis of form at a younger age than English-speaking Navahos—presumably because their more extensive experience with toys prepared them for the task.

Bernstein's hypothesis about the effects of language on scholastic performance has also been explored through empirical research. Studies have shown that scores on vocabulary tests in the early years of childhood correlate very highly with social class. From the age of seven onward social-class differences become very apparent in the complexity of sentence structure, as evidenced through sampling of the speech patterns of children from different economic backgrounds. It has also been found that deaf children tend to suffer retardation more than blind children, and differences in IQ relating to social class are less among deaf children than among hearing children, suggesting that these differences are associated with language differences. Bernstein himself has compared the performance of working-class and middle-class pupils on tests of both verbal and nonverbal intelligence. He found that even those working-class boys who scored highly on the nonverbal test tended to score lower on the verbal test—a difference amounting in some cases to over 20 IQ points. The scores of middle-class boys did not show this pattern. Instead, middle-class pupils tended to be equally skilled at both verbal and nonverbal problems. Bernstein concluded that the verbal difficulties of the working-class pupils were acting to depress their academic performance.

On the other hand, work by Denis Lawton (*Social Class, Language and Education,* 1968) has shown that if placed in a situation that demands an elaborated code response (such as discussing an abstract ethical question like capital punishment), working-class children are capable, although with some difficulty, of providing that response. Other experiments have shown that working-class mothers, who normally use restricted code, are capable of employing an elaborated code when talking to a middle-class interviewer. The different speech modes may, therefore, be a matter of habit and stimulus rather than necessity and may be capable of adaptation if the situation demands it.

iv Evaluation It seems that the linguistic relativity hypothesis cannot be accepted in its extreme form. If concepts cannot be accurately translated across languages, then Whorf should not be able to explain the Hopi universe to us. The more successfully he is able to describe that universe, the more he undermines his own argument. The fact that a language lacks certain forms does not mean that its speakers are incapable of conceiving the concepts to which those forms relate. The Arabs have hundreds of words for "camel"; we have only one. Yet it would be possible for an Arab to explain to us the precise distinctions that his language makes between various categories of camel, and it would be possible for us to perceive and express those distinctions, even if we were required to use many words for the purpose. Similarly, we are capable of thinking of "fruit and nuts" as a single category of seed-bearing pods, even though, unlike the Chinese, we have no one single word for that particular concept. In its more moderate form, however, the linguistic-relativity hypothesis is accepted by sociologists: that is, the resources of the language we speak may predispose us to make certain categorizations and interpretations of reality.

Bernstein's theory has aroused a good deal of speculation and has won guarded support from many sociologists. His theory is based on certain assumptions about the influence of language and thought that although persuasive are by no means proven. The relationship between language and thought may be far more complex than Bernstein suggests, and it may be that thought is much more independent of language than Bernstein's theory allows. His theory also appears to be too determinist; Bernstein offers no convincing reason why early linguistic experience should necessarily have so permanently limiting an effect on children reared in a restricted-code environment. The frequent failure of working-class children to achieve educational success is at least as likely to be the product of social influences (the effects of overcrowded and impoverished background, negative reactions of middle-class teachers, lack of incentives, and so on). There is no reason why this failure should be attributed solely to the limiting effects of the linguistic factor alone. And Bernstein's delineation of the two codes seems altogether too tidy—the truth is surely that the codes Bernstein outlines are merely the polar models on a more fluid and blended linguistic continuum. Much of Bernstein's determinism may stem from a failure to appreciate this fact. Nevertheless, Bernstein's theory does show how language can reinforce the working-class child in the values of his culture and how the child may fail to respond to much of the teacher's speech, particularly when the teacher is making fine distinctions or using unfamiliar syntactic constructions. Although we cannot be as sure that linguistic factors are as influential as Bernstein suggests, his theory yields a number of provocative and persuasive perspectives on the relationship between linguistic and intellectual abilities.

3 Overview

The sociology of knowledge is one of the most fascinating and vital aspects of sociology, because of the importance of knowledge and belief for social cohesion and social action. Men's beliefs about their past, their present, and their future are inseparably linked to the shape and nature of their society.

As theorists such as Marx, Mannheim, Bernstein, and Whorf have pointed out, knowledge is differentially distributed, both among different societies and among different elements within particular societies. In the modern world this differential distribution is increasingly significant, because knowledge—particularly scientific knowledge—is becoming an organizing principle of hierarchy both in international affairs and in the structure of specific societies. The contemporary social theorist Jürgen Habermas believes, for example, that the United States has become a postcapitalist society in which knowledge, not capital, is the basis of production and the basis of social stratification. In his view expertise rather than wealth is the prerequisite for admission to the ruling elite of the modern state—an elite that includes corporate management, the controllers of the media, bureaucratic personnel, and the military hierarchy as well as the political rulers.

In the ancient Greek city-state each individual could, in principle, assimilate all the knowledge necessary to make rational decisions about the issues facing the community. In modern America the mass of information in specific fields such as, say, economics or the Apollo space program seems to be beyond the capacity of any but the most skilled experts to comprehend, and even legislators and presidents are obliged to take in trust the information and recommendations of specialists upon which crucial public policies, programs, and priorities are based. The implications for democracy—real control by people over their lives—are profound.

D LOOKING AHEAD

1 Interview: Kurt H. Wolff

Kurt H. Wolff studied in Germany and Italy, where he received his doctorate, and is now professor of sociology at Brandeis University. He was a student of Karl Mannheim, and the sociology of knowledge has long been one of his major interests. He was chairman of the Research Committee on the Sociology of Knowledge of the International Sociological Association and is president of the International Society for the Sociology of Knowledge. He has contributed many articles to professional journals and symposia and is an author, editor, and translator of books.

DPG *It is sometimes claimed that the sociology of knowledge is a rather nihilistic discipline because it ends up relativizing everything, including itself. What is the real point of the discipline?*

WOLFF Karl Mannheim and some other sociologists of knowledge claimed that truth is relative to social position. Of course, on the face of it this is a statement that relativizes itself, because it, too, is relative to the position of the speaker. Theoretically speaking, it is a denial of the possibility of an objective or universal truth. The question is: How can absolutes be established despite the relativity of any one particular truth? The first thing to do is to examine what relativity means in a sense that is pertinent not only to the sociology of knowledge but to other social sciences as well, most particularly cultural anthropology.

Cultural relativism or any other relativism has two quite distinct meanings, one of which I entirely affirm, the other of which I think is utterly untenable. One meaning is the injunction to the social scientist to do his best in understanding what he wishes to understand in *its* own terms rather than in his. This methodological injunction presupposes the possibility of understanding, of course, which means that it is a stricture on relativism. If there were nothing common between the student and his subject, no such understanding could be expected.

But the other meaning of relativism says that there is no such thing as universal validity—of truth, of knowledge, of attitudes, of moral judgments or whatever—there is only relative validity. And that view allows for no common features that would account for the possibility of truth being more lasting than a moment or more widely valid than for a given person. Now I think this is certainly untenable because it makes it impossible to account for all kinds of activities that we in fact engage in and take for granted, such as the study of cultural anthropology or the study of history.

DPG *Are we getting nearer to an understanding of the concept of objectivity today?*

WOLFF I think with the development of technology, the world has become so small that we are forced constantly to recognize other kinds of peoples, other kinds of institutions, other kinds of convictions, some of which may strike us as incredible or even repulsive. The "global village," as Marshall McLuhan puts it, is itself an unintended but very powerful impetus to move, to work toward a grasp of that which all men share. Think only of one invention, television, that brings totally unknown worlds to people that may not be able to read, so that they confront the questions: What is man? What is human nature?

But, of course, technology also involves the developments in weapons. An increasing number of people are aware of the possibility of being annihilated by nuclear bombs, and I think that this awareness also brings about a change—the realization that all people have something in common and a search for what that is and how it can be formulated.

DPG *Is science becoming the new ideology?*

WOLFF Again it depends on what one means by science. If you mean by science the mastery and domination of nature in a systematic fashion, then I'm afraid it has a very strong ideological component. But I think that the very developments I have just mentioned may well raise questions about the propriety of that notion. An increasing number of voices plead for *cooperation* with nature. This position does not mean to advocate something antiscientific or unscientific, but rather a revision of our theory and practice of science.

I don't see how scientific inquiry itself can ever become an ideology—if, that is, by scientific inquiry you mean an inquiry as unbiased, as thorough, as undisturbed by extraneous considerations as possible. It seems to me that's the only way you can get at the truth of anything. The truth the scientist seeks is not truth in any absolute sense; it is rather what I would call hypothetical truth—that is, truth within the limits of whatever hypothesis he is working with. It is stipulative truth or theoretical truth or, in other senses, relative truth. It is truth that goes only so far—as far as that particular piece of research. You can also call it pragmatic truth.

Most people agree, I think, that science takes all kinds of things for granted about which a person may have doubts, about which he wants to know something. The scientist tells him that he is not here to supply answers. In much of science, including social science, people engage in research without quite knowing why—because it's an opportunity for a grant, it looks good on the bibliography, or it satisfies a request of a professor or a foundation. But they don't raise the question of the ultimate end of that research. In fact, they comfort themselves with the attitude of ''Why should I?'' They're not philosophers.

DPG *In order to pursue science with an end in view, one would have to satisfy oneself about the question: What is the good life? And that is a major philosophical undertaking.*
WOLFF Yes. And it is not considered to be a scientific question. In fact, some peo-

ple say it's not even a philosophic question, but a question of one's fate or one's existence, or perhaps a religious question.

DPG *It almost seems that if one were to pursue science with an end in view, one would have to answer the philosophical question before the scientific one.*
WOLFF Yes. I think that in normal times this question isn't pressing because the ends are supplied by the ordinary cultural traditions. You ''know'' you go to church, you ''know'' the family is good, you ''know'' what the virtues are, and so forth. You're not pushed to answer end questions. And you can pursue your science because in some fashion or another it will serve them, it will be compatible with them. But that's not our time at all.

DPG *What about times of radical innovation?*
WOLFF Then such questions as those I've just mentioned come up. And then we have no tradition to fall back on, because if we had it, the question wouldn't come up. The tradition would supply the answer.

There are all kinds of responses to this kind of a situation. My own answer is that the scientist has to ask himself as best he can, exactly what, at his most honest, he can believe to be the case. That is, he must suspend—or, using a phenomenological term, ''bracket''—whatever traditional answers he may be able to review. Here to suspend means neither to reject nor to accept. The scientist must try to find out what, on the basis of the most serious and moving and important experiences he has ever had in his life, he can believe.

DPG *Then it comes back to the philosophical?*
WOLFF Yes, of course. Now this effort I've just sketched I call surrender. It may be surrender to whatever particular question the occasion gives rise to. What can I answer when asked about good or evil, or why I live, or who I am—or whatever a similar question may be? There may be less profound issues than these examples, but the pursuit of the answer must be as uncon-

ditional as the person can make it. And then he comes up with an answer that is, at that time, true for him. He knows he has done the best he can to get at the truth. That is, he has considered—just as a scientist does —whatever negative cases may have come to his mind, he has worked as hard as he can in his imagination, and he stands there and says, ''God help me, Amen, that is the best I can do now,'' without fooling himself into being convinced that tomorrow it may not change because he may have, again as a scientist, come across new evidence that forces him to change. To take such a stand, of course, presupposes a considerable amount of ego strength or maturity. It entails a throwing away of whatever traditional crutches there are, and that is a very uncomfortable feeling. You think you'll fall, and in fact you may fall.

DPG *How does the process end?*
WOLFF It ends, I think, with a redefinition of science. A relation of trust and honesty, it seems to me, should be the prerequisite of our social science.

DPG *What are the implications for our society of the pace at which new knowledge is accumulating? Can generational conflict be explained in these terms?*
WOLFF I think that among the matters that the young people object to certainly is knowledge for its own sake. They ask what this scientism is good for. The danger of that attitude is, of course, that it is terribly close to anti-intellectualism—that is, to an unwillingness to learn, to read, to think, to analyze, all of which seem so ''remote from life.'' On the other hand, I think the enmity to factual knowledge for its own sake is entirely proper. Nobody can possibly have all the information anyway because there's such an explosion of it. So in the field of education, for instance, there is a very justified objection to a perpetuation of knowledge and types of knowledge that at one time were perhaps properly held to be important or germane to the time and that no longer are.

Now, I said ''factual knowledge'' because it seems to me, on the other hand, that much thought that is laid down in what some people call the great books is not passé. And this should be among the traditions that ought to be known in order to be suspended in that situation I sketched a moment ago. Such knowledge cannot be suspended if it is not available of course. It should be made accessible. But it may not be possible to make it accessible to many people by suggesting that the writing that contains it be read. Because for many young people—and no doubt older people too—reading is no longer a habit, or no longer something to enjoy. Consequently, some other means of education must be devised. I have no objection to mediating the problems by means of films or by other means that would move students to get interested in what, after all, are or seem very theoretical matters. Technically, I have great hopes in microfilm and the microfiche. I'm always intrigued by the idea that I can carry a 10,000-volume microfiche library in my briefcase. And such institutions as abstracting services are, I think, extremely important because it is simply impossible to keep up with anything.

DPG   *What about the problems of selection? We have so much to choose from. How does one get the basic equipment with which to choose what one would like to do, what one would prefer to do, what would be best to do?*
WOLFF   I think the criterion is, as usual in science, the problem. What is the problem? That tells you what's relevant and what's not relevant. And any device such as those I've just mentioned—for example, abstracting, microfilming—that facilitates surveying the mass of things that might possibly be candidates for relevance is to be welcomed. I don't see anything new in that except the technical side.

2 Interview:

Zhores A. Medvedev

Zhores A. Medvedev is the former head of the department of molecular biology at the Institute of Medical Radiology at Obninsk in the Soviet Union. Dr. Medvedev was also affiliated with the Laboratory of Proteins and Amino Acids of the Research Institute of Physiology and Biochemistry of Farm Animals, Borovsk, Kaluga Region, USSR. He is the author of *Protein Biosynthesis* (Oliver and Boyd Ltd., 1966), *The Rise and Fall of T. D. Lysenko* (Columbia University Press, 1969), *Molecular-Genetic Mechanisms of Development* (Plenum Press, 1970), *Medvedev Papers* (Macmillan, 1971) and *Ten Years After "One Day in the Life of Ivan Denisovich"* (Macmillan, 1973). Medvedev is also the author, with his brother Roy, of *A Question of Madness* (Macmillan, 1971). He is currently researching molecular and genetic aspects of development and aging.

DPG   *What effect does government restriction on the free exchange of scientific information and on scientific ideas and meetings among scientists have on the progress of scientific research?*
MEDVEDEV   It all depends on the kind of restriction. I can roughly indicate several kinds. The first is connected with the different kinds of social systems in the so-called East and West and the so-called Cold War. This situation makes it necessary for any government to restrict the flow of scientific information (so-called classified research), and any government places restrictions on certain information in certain areas. If we consider the tremendous resources that governments commit to experiments that are in fact repetitions of costly research already done in other countries—the endeavors to send rockets to the moon, for example, cost more than all research done in the field of biology—and if one thinks in terms of the benefit of mankind, one realizes that restricting scientific information eats up tremendous resources.

Also, the cost to one country of developing a scientific product may be twice the cost to another country developing the same product independently. For example, the Soviet version of the nuclear accelerator may cost half that of the American version. But if scientific information was shared, then all countries could benefit from the cheaper methods of producing the accelerator. Therefore, I think it's important that we calculate how much natural and human resources are wasted in this way, without any significant scientific achievement.

DPG   *What about the disadvantageous effects of restricting meetings among scientists across international boundaries?*
MEDVEDEV   Meetings between scientists are important when scientists are united in respect to a single problem. Small meetings are infinitely more useful than large ones. Free meetings between scientists can be very useful for research. I must point out, however, that at large scientific conventions, where a single scientist cannot be expected to have a knowledge of or involvement in the whole field, personal contacts very often seem to supersede the importance of scientific contacts. For me, for example, as an expert in a definite field, it is more important to go to one laboratory or another to discuss my problems with persons and scientists whom I know and whose research I know. This is more useful to me than attending a symposium of a more general nature, where I may find a lot of papers and contributions that are very important but not very interesting for my own research. Therefore, I consider it very important for governments to give permission for scientists to make contact with other scientists based on their judgment of what would be helpful to their research.

We also have another type of restriction—that on technical and scientific research that has a commercial value. This type of restriction is usual in any country and is defended by certain international conventions in respect of inventors' rights, patents, and so on. These restrictions are common, and I suppose we can't really construe them as restrictions on the free exchange of scientific information of a political nature.

Also, I think generally that there is no restriction on the free exchange of published scientific information. However, restrictions in respect of travel are different at present. These cannot be explained by the attempt of any government, including my own government, to restrict the exchange of scientific information; these restrictions have some political background. They are connected with ideological differences and primarily concern research in the political, social, and economic sciences. They have been introduced because of the differences between social systems.

DPG *Do you think these restrictions in the area of the social sciences have had a negative effect on the state of social science in the Soviet Union?*
MEDVEDEV Yes, I certainly do. I think that the Soviet social sciences are in an especially difficult situation. As a biologist, I can

read any scientific information in my field and be informed about any discoveries or any special aspect of research that affects my work. Social scientists and philosophers, however, are restricted from receiving free information in their fields from the United States, Western Europe, and so on. For example, Russian sociologists are not free to receive information about living standards in other countries. They can't even receive information concerning their own country or investigate situations in different parts of the USSR in connection with their own social research.

DPG *Precisely what damage does this do?*
MEDVEDEV I think it makes a lot of things in the USSR unpredictable. Because we find that a lot of social processes that could be predicted are not. If social scientists found it possible to have and discuss information freely, a lot of negative social consequences could be avoided in, for example,

the field of agriculture or in connection with the problem of pollution.

In the specific instance of Lake Baikal, the economic planners, because of national economic objectives, had planned to build a large paper mill on the lake. The lake is an extremely beautiful one, world unique, is used by many people for recreational purposes, and has valuable fish resources. There was a lot of protest about the location of the mill from scientists and from other people. Unfortunately, planning for the mill did not include the input of social scientists about the effect on the area. The chief interest of the planners was the economic goal of producing more paper, so the damage was done. This situation reflects the importance of the contribution of the social sciences to development plans.

So, as I say, I think it is important that it is made possible for social scientists to have access to the data for their research and also that their findings should be taken into account for overall planning goals.

Unit 3
Biology and Society

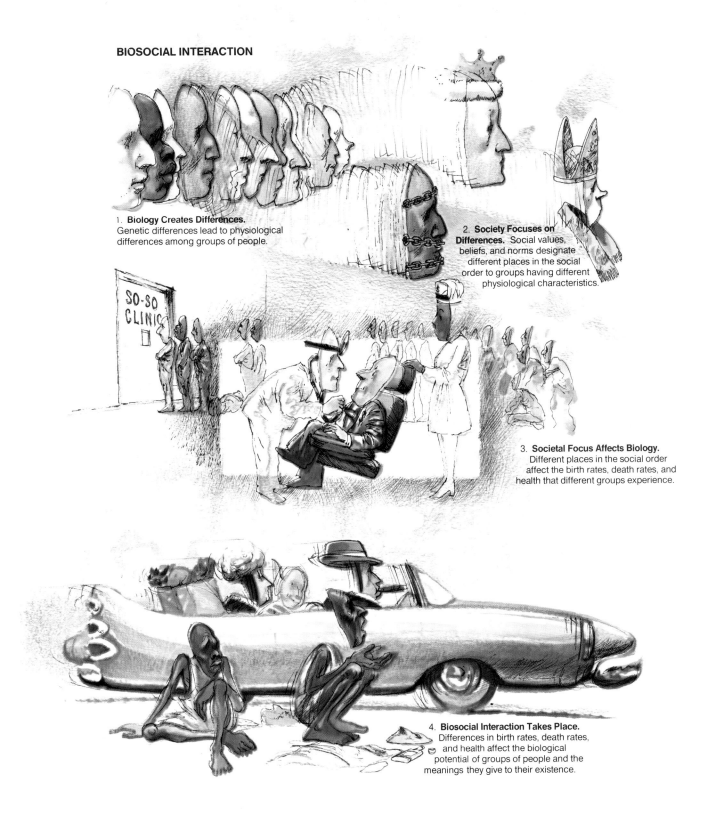

BIOSOCIAL INTERACTION

1. **Biology Creates Differences.**
Genetic differences lead to physiological
differences among groups of people.

2. **Society Focuses on Differences.** Social values,
beliefs, and norms designate
different places in the social
order to groups having different
physiological characteristics.

3. **Societal Focus Affects Biology.**
Different places in the social order
affect the birth rates, death rates, and
health that different groups experience.

4. **Biosocial Interaction Takes Place.**
Differences in birth rates, death rates,
and health affect the biological
potential of groups of people and the
meanings they give to their existence.

SO-SO CLINIC

B DEFINITION AND CONTEXT

1 Definition

Throughout history man has struggled to overcome his biological limitations, to extend his powers beyond the boundaries of purely inherited capabilities, to view his nature as fundamentally *discontinuous* with the rest of the animal kingdom. In the very beginning, according to the Bible, "God created man in his *own* image. . . .

(to) have dominion over the fish of the sea, and over the fowl of the air, and over every living thing that moveth upon the earth." The history of civilization is in part the record of man's efforts to aspire to, and to justify, the quasi-divine attributes he has imputed to the human condition. Definitions of what qualities constitute the unique difference between *homo sapiens* and the rest of the biological universe have preoccupied philosophers and artists for thousands of years.

These definitions have tended to isolate three qualities as essential determinants of human behavior—*reason, culture,* and *free will.* By no means do these three human variables figure equally in the different formulations that have been proposed. Nor are the definitions applied with impartial generosity to people everywhere: it seems that some folk (one's own kind) are more human than others (called "barbarians" or "savages"). How else, for example, can we explain the fact that those who emigrated from the Old World to the New in search of equal opportunity for all could systematically exterminate almost the entire population of native Americans as if they were an alien species?

In the nineteenth century Charles Darwin's theory of biological evolution (particularly the notions that all mammals, including man, share a common ancestry, and that all organic species have evolved according to a principle of selection called "survival of the fittest") drastically challenged man's conception of himself as a godlike creature whose domain had little in common with every other "living thing that moveth upon the earth." This new perspective furthered the *ethnocentric* convictions of certain groups who felt that they were themselves the "fittest" members of society. Herbert Spencer, the major proponent of *Social Darwinism,* could

Belle, an adult female chimpanzee, acts as dentist. A striking example of learned role-differentiation among chimpanzees was observed at the Delta Regional Primate Center in Covington, Louisiana, in 1973. Belle used the occasion of social grooming to attempt to examine the teeth of other chimpanzees. When one allowed her to do so, she examined the individual teeth carefully, cleaned them with the aid of stripped twigs and other instruments, and even extracted a loosened "baby tooth."

thus point to the unequal distribution of power, privilege, prestige, wealth, and opportunity among the various echelons in any society, and develop a convenient rationale for the defense of privilege and the maintenance of the existing social hierarchy.

Two far-reaching implications of the "biological approach" to human behavior quickly became manifest. If human traits are genetically determined, then certain genetic strains may be deemed "preferable" to others. (The Nazi destruction of over 6 million Jews was based on the presumption of their genetic "inferiority.") Fur-

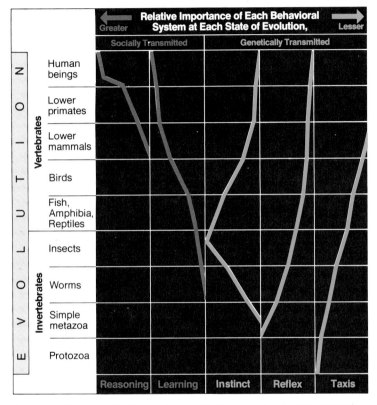

Figure 1. Biologically Programmed Versus Socially Learned Behavior. The lines indicate the relative importance of each behavioral system at each stage of evolution. *Reasoning* is the ability to make abstract connections and perceive relationships between two or more experiences. *Learning* is the ability to make direct associations between two or more experiences. *Instinct* is genetically encoded and transmitted patterned behavior-response to predetermined stimuli. *Reflex* is genetically encoded and transmitted behavior response to predetermined stimuli. *Taxis* is genetically encoded and transmitted simple movement reaction to predetermined stimuli. Note that human beings and other primates mostly learn and reason rather than inherit genetically programmed behavior patterns.

thermore, if human traits are thought to be genetically determined, human corruption, avarice, and mendacity can be regarded as inevitable expressions of biological destiny; hence social reformers ought to abandon attempts to forge a nobler or more just society.

Obviously, these implications were unacceptable to most social theorists—especially because they tended to justify the least attractive aspects of human society (inequality, depravity, aggression, even genocide)—and they focused their study on the role of environment in molding the individual and the behavior of entire populations. This approach, in turn, eventually gave rise to a debate as to which constellation of factors should be regarded as most decisive—heredity versus environment, or "nature" versus "nurture." Today, however, the question is no longer either/or; it has shifted, instead, to a concern with both the separate and joint contributions of heredity and environment to the production of observed behavioral phenomena.

Indian women receiving instruction in the use of contraceptive devices. Even in societies where poverty is chronic and widespread, as in India today, social and cultural pressures to have children may well override considerations of economic cost.

The sociology of biology seeks to determine how the principles and findings of biology can be applied to the study of human behavior, social structures, and institutions. This effort encompasses a wide range of investigations. Some studies are directed toward an understanding of the extent to which behavioral differences between social classes and between races may in fact be genetically determined. Others concentrate primarily on describing the dynamics of biosocial interaction or using observations based on nonhuman primate groups (such as apes) to form new perspectives on human behavior. Still others anticipate the integration of genetic and sociological principles: in the next several decades biology will cross over the threshold of genetic mastery, and social scientists will be expected to provide the guidelines and policies that will influence the future course of human evolution itself.

2   World Context

Examples of biosocial interaction can be found in all human societies regardless of their level of technology. One clear-cut case concerns the prevalence of the disease kuru among the Fore people in the eastern highlands of New Guinea. The disease was once thought to be hereditary in nature but is now believed to be caused by a virus via the ingestion of uncooked flesh. Because kuru, usually fatal, occurs from four to 20 years after ingestion, it did not appear to be in any way connected to the event or environmental factor that was later discovered to have produced each instance of it: namely, the Fore custom of eating dead kinsmen—including those who had died of kuru—as a sign of respect. The disease occurred much more frequently among females than males and was therefore thought by interested observers to be a genetically dominant trait in females and recessive in males; actually the distribution pattern of the disease was due to the fact that custom barred adult males from participating in the feast of flesh that was saved for, and savored by, women and young children. When these social customs were stopped by government intervention in 1950, the incidence of kuru decreased, and there was a drastic change in the death and disease expectations of females in the Fore society.

Biosocial interactions in general are far more complex, subtle, and entangled than this simple illustration. Most studies have sought to discover which characteristics can be modified by diverse environments. Moreover, because diverse environments tend, over time, to promote certain hereditary traits at the expense of others, these studies have attempted to learn the ways in which various distinct populations differ from each other. Such populations are not necessarily geographically distinct groups, but rather are made up of individuals who are statistically distinct from those in other groups with respect to some *gene frequencies.* Thus social classes can be viewed in the same terms as "races" that exist side by side in the same country where intermarriage is the exception rather than the rule (for example, the United States and the Republic of South Africa).

It has been demonstrated, for example, that there is a striking positive correlation between the IQ of parents and their offspring with social class. This correlation gave rise to the fear that because those in the lower classes tend to have larger families than those in the higher social strata (due to environmental factors), the biological future of the world's population could be characterized as a "galloping plunge toward intellectual bankruptcy." But the prediction of deteriorating intelligence has not been fulfilled. In fact, studies by R. B. Cattell, the man who gloomily predicted the declining quality of each successive generation, have shown that intelligence, like height and health, is actually increasing. As J. McVicker Hunt explains, "If intelligence tests measure fixed intellectual capacity or innate potential, and if the majority of each new generation comes from parents in the lowest third in tested intelligence, something very, very strange is happening." ("Black Genes—White Environment," 1969) The implication, of course, is that intelligence tests are *not* qualitatively all that different from achievement tests, and that as environment and diet become more enriched, one's intellectual mastery over that environment improves as well. Marvin Bressler, in his 1968 paper "Sociology, Biology, and Ideology," suggests a different possibility: "This seeming anomaly may be resolved by noting that 'although the least intelligent groups produce more children within marriage, they are the least likely to marry.'"

Studies that attempt to deal with "genotype-environment interactions" among human subjects are hampered and immeasurably complicated by the difficulty of separating genetic from environmental factors. (*Genotype* refers to the fundamental constitution of an organism as determined by heredity.) However, a noted experiment with rats by Roderick Cooper and John Zubek ("Effects of Enriched and Restricted Early Environments on the Learning Ability of Bright and Dull Rats," 1958) yielded a number of interesting observations that were relatively free of ambiguities. Of two groups of rats raised in a laboratory, one strain was bred to be "clever" at finding the way through a maze, the other bred to be "dull." Under normal conditions the bright rats did indeed find their way through the maze with fewer trials and errors than their less able counterparts; in a more restricted environment, however, both strains gave equally poor performances, and in a more stimulating environment both kinds of rats did equally well. This experiment shows how greatly problem-solving activities (intelligence) are influenced by aspects of the environment: the more interesting, variegated, and challenging the environment, the more agile and able the response.

3 American Context

Modern medicine has extended the human life span and increased population tremendously through reducing infant mortality rates and deaths from childbirth. Technology has also improved contraception methods, and it is believed that the introduction of the birth control pill has substantially reduced birth rates in the United States. However, technology alone has rarely caused major changes in population structure: sociocultural changes influencing attitudes toward family life, female role, ideal family size, use of contraceptives, and morality of abortion are major factors determin-

Women's liberation movement abortion counseling session. A basic theme of the women's liberation movement is that a woman has ultimate jurisdiction over her own body and, accordingly, has the right to decide whether or not she wishes to become or remain pregnant. As the ideas of the women's movement are accepted more and more by the wider society, they may significantly affect the birth rate.

ing the extent to which the available technology can be effective. Differing attitudes on these issues within the various *subcultures* of American society contribute to different rates of fertility based on religious, class, racial, or ethnic factors.

The types of diseases that afflict man have also come under the control of modern society. Those that were once the scourge of the human species (plague, tuberculosis, polio, and the like) have been all but eliminated in the United States today as a result of deliberate scientific efforts. However, a different crop of afflictions has emerged and somehow seems specifically intertwined with the striving, dollar-oriented, American life. Illnesses of stress—heart disease, mental illnesses, and alcoholism—although present in other societies, are particularly prevalent in the present-day United States. Of course, increased longevity itself will increase diseases of old age, including heart disease. Our affluent society has also fostered obesity to such an extent that diet fads and weight-reducing salons are a booming business. Although it is culturally undesirable to be overweight, the mass media bombard us daily with the glories of carbohydrates, vending machines offer them profusely, and our pocketbooks can afford second helpings.

In these and many other ways, the fast-paced life of affluent America has given rise to a new range of physical conditions that have, in turn, distinctly affected the state of American social life. For example, although the average life span of both sexes in the United States today has been greatly extended, the life expectancy for females is greater than for males. This difference can lead to profound social effects when the female role changes from wife to widow. Because many more people are living to be 70 years or older, our population of senior citizens is rapidly increasing; this shift is bound to create special social problems, including the care of increasing numbers of people prone to illness and no longer able to take part in the work force.

Perhaps the most urgent social problem facing Americans today is racial conflict. Unequal life opportunities are accorded to members of different groups distinguished by ranges of skin color, variations of physiognomy, and cultures appreciably unlike that of the white Protestant majority. The limited access these minorities have to the rewards at the top of the social hierarchy are often justified on "biological" grounds. White Americans are divided between those who think blacks have been kept down by social prejudice and those who think blacks have remained in their low socioeconomic status because of their "innately" lower capabilities.

It is important to realize that there is no undisputed biological definition of race. Physical anthropologists use racial categories to attempt to classify certain biological variations observed in human populations, but they are somewhat arbitrary devices. Depending on the biological criteria used, the human species has been divided into as few as three or as many as 100 different races. Thus there is no such thing as a "pure" race, and there is considerable overlap in the biological traits found in any two populations classified as different races.

From a sociological perspective, racial distinctions are symbolic labels usually connoting positive qualities for *in-group* members and negative qualities for *out-group* members. These distinc-

Age Group	1971
All ages	207,049,000
Under 5 years old	17,289,000
5 to 9 years old	19,318,000
10 to 14 years old	20,902,000
15 to 19 years old	19,688,000
20 to 24 years old	18,163,000
25 to 34 years old	15,820,000
35 to 44 years old	22,961,000
45 to 54 years old	23,459,000
55 to 64 years old	18,884,000
65 years and older	20,567,000

Table 1. United States Population by Age Group in 1971.
(Source: Bureau of the Census)

tions are not necessarily related to any objectively measured biological traits of the groups in question. In the social world racial labels tend to be either/or distinctions. One is or is not a member of a particular race; consequently, one has or does not have *all* the positive or negative qualities associated with membership.

Problems arise when the social use of racial categories is believed to signify genetically homogeneous populations. When dealing with such a specific issue as the difference between the IQs of black and white children, it must be kept in mind that "black" and "white" refer to social distinctions rather than to genetically pure populations. In so far as these terms indentify biologically distinguishable groups, they do so only in the sense of statistical aggregates.

C   QUESTIONS AND EVIDENCE

1   Questions

Three problems are of interest to both biologists and sociologists: (1) Is a lack of success of American black children in academic achievement the result of inherently lower IQ or of conditions in their environment? (2) What is the biological basis of human society? (3) Are human violence and war due to man's intrinsically aggressive nature?

2   Evidence

a   The "Burning Issue" Question
i Context It is an axiom of sociology that if conditions allow it, a subordinate group will attempt to improve its position in society relative to that of the dominant group, and the dominant group will tend to resist this change. It is within this context of changing group relationships and group conflict that the scientific question of the relative importance of genetic and environmental factors in determining measured intelligence (IQ) has become a major social and political issue. The charge has been made by some whites that blacks have a subordinate position within American society because they are intellectually less capable than whites. Blacks have answered that their subordinate position is the result of the environmental factors of systematic discrimination and long-term social and economic deprivation directly attributable to their original status as slaves. The basic question is: *Is the lower performance of black children on IQ and related tests the result of genetic or environmental factors?*
ii Theory The idea that hereditary factors are more important than environmental factors in explaining IQ differences between American blacks and whites became a controversial issue again recently when an eminent psychologist, Arthur R. Jensen—in the lengthy article "How Much Can We Boost IQ and Scholastic Achievement?" published in the *Harvard Educational Review* in 1969—charged that the attempts to overcome the environmental gap between blacks and whites by compensatory education programs (special education for young blacks) had failed. Blacks were still unable to demonstrate

Project Head Start in operation. Once one assumes biological causation for the social problems of ethnic minorities, efforts such as the Project Head Start program of compensatory education become meaningless exercises. Because such biological explanations undermine serious attempts to deal with society's ills on the social level, one should be extremely cautious before accepting these explanations.

educational achievements comparable to those of whites. The reason for this situation, according to Jensen, was that blacks, considered as a racial group, had been shown to have lower IQs than whites, by an average difference of about 15 points. Admitting that environmental influences—especially prenatal influences—can affect IQ, Jensen nevertheless stressed that racial variation in intelligence cannot be accounted for by environmental differences alone. Therefore, he argued, it must be primarily due to genetic differences.

The publication of Jensen's article immediately ignited a major controversy. Many sociologists, psychologists, and educators challenged his position, arguing that environmental factors can indeed account for the 15-point average IQ differences observed between American blacks and whites. Their critique centers around three points.

First, compensatory education has not failed; it has yet to be given a proper trial. Environmental conditions affect individuals in a cumulative manner over a long period, whereas compensatory education has only been available for a few years. Consequently, it cannot be adequately evaluated at the present time.

Second, his critics argue that Jensen ignored the complexity of American social reality. For example, being black in contemporary America opens one to all kinds of negative social experiences irrespective of one's economic or educational achievements. This reality of discriminatory society makes it impossible simply to compare the IQs of blacks and whites with similar socioeconomic status. Because of the discriminatory situation, the environmental conditions surrounding blacks and whites are never the same and cannot be equated.

Finally, the critics argue that many studies have been conducted that provide evidence that the IQ differentials can be explained by reference to environmental factors. Of course, Jensen did not deny that qualitative differences in environment do exist, nor that they have an effect on intelligence and achievement scores.

iii Research   Because humans cannot be manipulated over generations in a laboratory situation, studies of the inheritance of human intelligence (as in the study of most human traits) must rely on indirect methods. The most common techniques are extrapolations from animal studies, investigations of human pedigrees, studies of adopted children, and twin studies. Research in all these areas supports the notion that IQ is predominantly an inherited trait.

First, experiments have suggested that animals (particularly rats) can be bred for certain aspects of intelligence, notably the ability to solve maze problems. (But even these findings are ambiguous: the rat that learns a maze fastest may be less cautious, not more intelligent, than the rat that takes longer.) Second, when human family pedigrees are studied, related individuals have been found to exhibit IQ test scores that are more similar than those of unrelated persons. These family pedigrees follow the pattern expected for an inherited multigene trait. Third, adopted children show IQ test scores that correlate more closely with those of their natural mothers than those of their adopted mothers. Finally, twin studies have enabled researchers, to some extent, to separate genetic from environmental effects. Assuming that identical twins have the same genetic endowment, all differences in observed IQ must be due to environmental differences. Identical twins reared apart show closer average IQ scores than fraternal twins reared together. But fraternal twins, unlike identical twins, are genetically different. Therefore, the environment affects total IQ much less than heredity. On the basis of twin studies, it has been estimated through a complex mathematical formulation that approximately 80 percent of the variability in IQ test scores among white populations is due to genetic factors.

Those arguing for the importance of environmental factors in the observed IQ differences between whites and blacks have generally accepted the fact that genetic factors do affect test scores. They contend that they are not dealing with the total nature of IQ, but only with the marginal differences between blacks and whites. There is ample research, they claim, to support the importance of environmental factors in producing this marginal difference. For example, among the studies that correlate positive changes in IQ scores with beneficial changes in environment are reports on successful compensatory education programs, investigations showing that Southern blacks increased their IQ by migrating to the North, and surveys of draftees from different environmental backgrounds, which show that black draftees from the North have higher IQs than white draftees from the South.

Furthermore, the testing situation (an environmental factor) can affect the distribution of IQ scores. Blacks score significantly higher in IQ tests when the tester is black than when he is white and when the tester takes pains to show that he is friendly and supportive rather than judgmental. A number of studies also indicate that scholastic performance is related to environmental factors in the homes of students. These factors included the presence of educational materials in the home, the parents' interest in and responsiveness to the child's learning, and the security the child feels in the home environment.

Identical twin studies have indicated that a difference in IQ test scores as large as 15 points (the average difference between whites and blacks) can occur among identical twins raised in different environments. But, as C. O. Carter points out in *Human Heredity* (1965):

> twins raised apart differ on the average by about seven points in I.Q. Two people chosen at random from the general population differ by about seventeen points. Only four of the 122 pairs of twins differed by as much as seventeen points. Ordinary siblings raised in the same household differ by twelve points. . . . And finally, fraternal twins raised in the same home differ by an average of eleven points, which was equaled or exceeded by only twenty-three of the 122 pairs [of identical twins].

Finally, studies have shown the importance of prenatal health of the mother and early infant care in the development of intelligence: for example, children with low birth weight were found to have lower IQs than children of higher birth weights. The fact that a multigenic

An IQ test in progress. Many social variables play a role in determining IQ scores. One significant variable is the conditions under which the test is administered. Black children do significantly better when the test they are given is administered by a black tester.

trait such as height can be drastically influenced by poor nutrition in no way invalidates the fact that heredity accounts for most of the variation seen in height. The same can be said for intelligence. Heredity may account for most of the variation in intelligence, but the environment can exert a decisive influence.

iv Evaluation There is no doubt that IQ is predominantly inherited. And, of course, there is no a priori reason why there should be no IQ differences between American blacks and whites; similar differences can be found in other traits, such as limb-trunk ratio. But the observed differences in average IQ between blacks and whites in America are more readily explained by reference to the environments within which American blacks and whites live out their lives. Differences in those environments have been conclusively shown to affect the distribution of many traits, including IQ. Until those differences cease to exist there will be no conclusive way to demonstrate how much—if *any*—of the average difference between white and black intelligence-test scores can be attributed to genetic factors alone.

Perhaps the most interesting aspect of this controversy is that the argument has tended to be political rather than scientific. Some people believe they can use Jensen's argument to attack the integration of schools, the busing of children, the equalization of educational opportunity, and the need for special help to disadvantaged minority groups. Other people use contrary evidence to support all of the same positions. The policy direction any society will follow on questions concerning intergroup conflict often depends more on the relative power of the groups involved than on the findings of social science.

Those who disagree with Jensen for political reasons have tended to dismiss his argument on two grounds: racial strains are so mixed in America that it makes no sense to speak of such a fundamental difference between the IQ of the white population and that of the black; and the environments for the two populations are so different that it is impossible to sift out purely hereditary factors. Even in the highly doubtful eventuality that it is proved that the two populations do exhibit genetically unequal average levels of intelligence, should the idea of a socially just climate for everyone—regardless of skin color—suffer a decisive setback? Not at all, for such evidence could not impose any rational restrictions on the struggle for racial justice.

b The "Classical" Question

i Context Sociology studies the human group and its social processes. But as *social groupings* have been found throughout the animal world, an ongoing problem of sociology has been to determine what constitutes a specifically *human grouping*. Human societies have a biological base somewhat similar to that found for other animals; at the same time, they represent properties that, in evolutionary terms, are still emergent. Sociologists ask: *To what extent is the nature of human society determined by the innate characteristics of individuals as biological organisms?*

ii Theory Societies, from those of insects through those of vertebrates, appear to exhibit certain common properties. Foremost among these characteristics are social bonding and social organization. *Social bonding* refers to the fact that the individuals within the society (whether they be insects, monkeys, or men) are involved in a network of interaction that constitutes a relatively permanent association. *Social organization* refers to the fact that this association is constituted so that the members of the society support each other in achieving both common and individual objectives.

In *Human Society* (1949) Kingsley Davis postulated that all societies must meet certain conditions in order to survive. First, there must be a population—that is, some means of providing for the reproduction of new members, nourishment, and protection against injury. Second, a division of labor must be developed that enables the members of the population to function as an interdependent social unit achieving common goals (such as the needs just mentioned). For example, among primates the males usually provide protection whereas females tend to be involved with the nurturance of the young. Third, the social bond must be maintained by encouraging contact between the members of the society, mutual toleration of insiders, and avoidance of or resistance to outsiders. Finally, the system of interaction that maintains the first three conditions must be continued beyond the lifetime of any given individual or set of members. Otherwise, the society would die out with the

Carpenter ants in nest. Ant society is a biosocial system. The insects are not taught what to do and how to do it. They are born with complex, genetically encoded, behavioral-response patterns that predetermined stimuli elicit.

passing of a single generation.

Nonhuman societies may be said to exhibit biosocial systems of organization. By *biosocial systems* we mean that the social patterns of these groups are relatively fixed by heredity. Among biosocial systems major innovations depend upon changes in the *gene pool*, because individuals within the group are *genetically programmed* to respond in specific ways to specific stimuli.

By contrast, human societies are usually thought of as exhibiting a sociocultural system of social organization. A *sociocultural system* is one in which the social patterns are regulated by cultural elaboration rather than by genetic programming. *Cultural elaboration* refers to the symbolic network of values, norms, and beliefs that govern much of man's behavior. In sociocultural systems innovation is no longer exclusively dependent on changes in the gene pool,

but may involve cultural experimentation and contact between cultures not previously exposed to each other. As a consequence, although mankind is a single biological species, its social patterns vary immensely from place to place and from time to time.

iii Research (Survey) (Adolf Portmann (*Animals as Social Beings,* 1961) and others have shown that social groupings that have the properties of a society are found throughout the animal kingdom. Thus the question of what elements in human society are found only among human beings is one of continuing interest.) Researchers have come up with different answers, depending on their field of study, their methodology, and their theoretical outlook.

(The contemporary school of thought that has perhaps been most insistent in denying any basic differences between human social development and that of lower animal forms is the tradition associated with *reinforcement theory* in psychology. This *behaviorist* tradition, which includes such names as Pavlov, Watson, and Thorndike and culminates in the work of B. F. Skinner, suggests that man differs from other animals only in the complexity of his behavior rather than in any of its basic mechanisms.) On the basis of a series of impressive experiments conducted on rats and pigeons, but only occasionally on humans, these behaviorist psychologists have developed a theory of learning based on the concept of the positive or negative reinforcement or extinction of a response. According to the theory, if an act is followed by some pleasur-

Nonverbal greeting behavior among New Zealand Maoris *(top)* and Japanese Zen Buddhist priests. Not only do humans learn that greeting behavior itself is appropriate, but they also learn exactly what specific forms of behavior constitute greeting behavior in their particular culture. Changes in group greeting behavior involve socially learning new actions, not genetically acquiring new patterns.

able sensation it will tend to be repeated; if followed by a negative sensation it will tend to be extinguished. This simple formulation is seen as the basic mechanism underlying all social behavior. Implicit in this theory is the idea that the learning processes of rats and men do not differ in any scientifically important way.

(By contrast, some sociologists have developed the extreme opposite position. These theorists argue that the animal nature of man is irrelevant to an explanation of anything that happens in human social activity. They believe that sociability is uniquely human and that it alone is a sufficient explanation for the nature of human society.) In this view, everything about human society is specifically human, not simply a more complex form of phenomena found in lower animal societies.

Whereas reinforcement theorists tend to ignore the uniquely human elements in human societies, their opponents tend to ignore the impressive body of zoological and ethological research concerning animal societies. *All* societies do in fact have common properties. The major research question has been to discover what is shared and what is unique.

Research by Jane van Lawick-Goodall, Alison Jolly, and others on primate societies in their natural habitats has indicated that sociability is not uniquely human, but a general primate characteristic. Primates tend to live together in relatively peaceful, highly sociable communities. A number of other attributes thought to be unique features of human culture, such as intergenerational learning, tool using, and cooperation, have also been found to be general in primate groups.

Another group of studies has shown that the evolutionary history of social organisms has been one of constantly increasing individuation. *Individuation* refers to the emergence of the individual as a distinct entity within the group. In the social insects, such as bees and ants, the individual is completely subordinated to morphologically defined castes, but among social vertebrates the individual

has become distinctive enough to be related to other members of the group through personal recognition. This process of individuation has been carried further in the primates than in any other social vertebrate. And within the primates the evolutionary higher forms—gorillas, chimpanzees, and, finally, man—all exhibit progressively greater individuation.

Other research findings have suggested that the cooperative tendencies found among primates were probably reinforced as a result of the unique ecological niche in which early man developed. Man is the only primate to develop a hunting way of life, and social

Chimpanzees, mankind's closest living relatives. Detailed chemical analysis of blood and urine has confirmed morphological and evolutionary evidence that the chimpanzee is phylogenetically closer to mankind than is any other animal. Like human beings, chimps have a relatively long infant-dependency on their mothers; are extremely gregarious; often touch, groom, and even caress each other; show great positive emotion when encountering certain individuals from whom they have been separated for a long time; learn most of their habits in social groups; and frequently use specially prepared "tools" for particular tasks.

(Pages 60–61) East Africa, 2.5 million years ago. Possibly as early as 40, but certainly by 10 million years ago, our ancestors had split off from other primates in their evolutionary development. By around 2.5 million years ago, a crucial stage of human evolution known as the *Australopithecine* stage had evolved in east and south Africa. These ancestors were completely bipedal, had brains slightly larger than and apparently organized differently from those of modern apes and eventually invented the production of stone tools, which irrevocably changed the course of human evolution as our ancestors came to depend on an artifically created technology to solve problems of subsistence and defense.

There were at least two main branches of *Australopithecus:* the gracile line and the robust line. There is a great deal of disagreement regarding how these two lines fit into the evolutionary scheme of things, but gradually more and more specialists are accepting the version that argues that the robust line (shown here foraging for berries and roots) was herbivorous—that is, did not hunt or eat meat (in the usual course of events). As the environment gradually became drier, these creatures (who also failed to invent stone tools) gradually became unable to maintain themselves and became extinct. The gracile line apparently went through two stages: first came *Australopithecus africanus,* shown here with some freshly killed game. They apparently had not yet invented stone tools, but they continued to evolve into a larger form known as *Australopithecus habilis,* which did have stone tools and even hunted large game, such as the ancestral elephant. It is possible that this advanced form of *Australopithecus* hunted the less culturally advanced *robustus*—possibly causing his extinction around 1 million years ago. On the other hand, *robustus* might well have become extinct simply because he did not adapt to the changing climate.

The advanced form of *Australopithecus* eventually evolved into the first humans (called *Homo erectus*) around 1 million years ago. Those theorists who ascribe to humans an innate aggressiveness or predatory bloodthirstiness point to the events described here and argue that the fact that the line of *Australopithecus* that evolved into humans was the line that chose a toolmaking and hunting way of life suggests that *Australopithecus habilis* was indeed a murderous sort (killing off placid and pleasant *robustus*) and that we have inherited his vicious temperament. However, there is no concrete evidence to support this view—*robustus* may well have died off due to inability to adapt to changing environmental conditions. Furthermore, recent studies of animals in the wild suggest that contrary to popular ideas, many other animals kill members of their own species and that humans are thus less exceptional in this regard than has been previously assumed.

The student is thus well advised to take any argument that stresses biologically inherited mental characteristics due to the evolutionary history of the human species with a grain of salt. There is far from general agreement on the details of human evolution, and such speculations may distract us from those very real causes of social problems that lie in the nature of our contemporary social, political, and economic systems.

hunting emphasizes cooperation, food sharing, and an increased division of labor. It has been suggested that out of this biosocial matrix human society developed in two distinctive but complementary directions. First man developed self-awareness as a unique thinking, feeling, responding individual. Next man developed *culture* as a mechanism for maintaining group social processes for a highly individuated animal. The biological and psychological changes that accompanied these developments allowed for the higher development of intelligence, the invention and elaboration of language, and an increased ability to learn—all of which in turn reinforced the development of self-awareness and culture.

iv Evaluation   It is clear at this point that human society is an evolutionarily emergent type of social organization. Man as a strongly individuated animal with highly developed reasoning capabilities exists within a sociocultural system where social interaction is controlled by symbols, values, norms, and beliefs rather than by genetic programming.

c The "Research" Question

i Context   Violence at all levels of society has always been a major social problem. Aggression seems a part of everyday life, and warfare is almost a part of normal human experience. If we are not actually at war, we are in the process of preparing for possible war or recovering from a past one. Indeed, the threat of a nuclear war is a constant reminder that violence is a problem of worldwide consequence.

The sociologist is concerned with the major issue of whether violent behavior in our society can be controlled by social means, and if so, whether these means can be implemented in a democratic society. Is human violence solely an outcome of social situations, or is there an inherent aggressive element in man, which must be taken into account? If combinations of factors are necessary to produce violent behavior, what are they?

Although aggression has sometimes been defined as an all-inclusive process involving the entire spectrum of assertive behaviors (covert as well as overt), this unit will deal with aggression only as it is manifested in violent activities. Violence will be defined as the actual inflicting of physical damage on persons or property. The question is: *Is man innately aggressive?*

ii Theory   Theories concerning the origin of aggressive behavior can be divided into two main groups: those that consider aggression as part of the innate biological nature of man and those that consider it as the outcome of certain environmental situations.

The biological-instinctual theory of aggression states that human aggression is an *innate* biological instinct developed through natural selection and essentially *adaptive* in nature. Adaptive behavior is behavior that assists the survival of the species. From an evolutionary point of view, aggressive behavior in man may be understood as adaptive in its capacity to assist in the survival of early man. It enabled him to defend the young, to hunt for food, to maintain stability within the group (by establishing a *dominance order*), and to space the population. The strongest individuals survived fights between rivals. Environmental conditions have changed drastically since the time of early man, however, and aggressive behavior

Prize fight between Sugar Ray Robinson and Kid Gavilan. The behavior portrayed here is accepted behavior in American society, even though it is clearly violent in nature and leads to individuals getting hurt and sometimes even killed. In what context is violent behavior accepted in American society? Who is apt to participate? What are the consequences likely to be?

may be no longer adaptive in today's complex society. (Perhaps the most aggressive individuals tend to be killed off as a result of wars or of criminal or antisocial activities.) Today cooperative behavior may be most adaptive. Yet man appears to have inherited a behavior pattern derived from an earlier stage of human development.

In the 1960s a discovery was made that had a number of fascinating implications, many of which are still unfolding. Chromosome studies in Sweden showed that a large number of "difficult" patients in mental hospitals had an extra Y (male sex-determining) chromosome. Follow-up studies in maximum-security prisons and hospitals for the criminally insane in Scotland revealed the same surprising prevalence of this abnormality. In the United States findings in case after case indicated that the double-Y syndrome was operating in many unusually aggressive criminals. (Richard Speck, who stabbed eight nurses to death in Chicago in 1966, was one prominent example.) The discovery of what has come to be known as *XYY individuals*—tall, below average in intelligence, with a tendency toward acne and a record of antisocial behavior (including unusual sexual inclinations)—has served to reinforce the biological theory of aggression.

Environmental theories subdivide roughly into three types: frustration-aggression theories, learning theories, and theories of societal processes.

Frustration-aggression theories state that aggressive (and often violent) behavior is the result of interference with ongoing purposeful activity. Classical exponents of this theory often cite such examples as a boy whose mother prevents him from getting an ice cream cone after he has heard the ice cream vendor's bell and the boy is on his way to buy it. Previous experiences of frustration, available alternatives to violence, the nature of the frustration, and the individual's maturity all influence the type and intensity of the aggressive response in such circumstances. This theory suggests that

63

the reduction of violence requires a reduction of existing frustrations and/or the redirection of aggressive responses into nonviolent channels.

Learning theories state that violence and aggression can be learned just as other forms of behavior are learned and can be carried out without the stimulus of any frustration. From childhood onward people learn their expected behaviors from their culture and subcultures (for example, little boys learn how to fight). In most societies there is culturally accepted violent behavior, and some forms of it are actually admired. Some examples from our culture are football players, who are expected to "kill" the opposition, and sportsmen, who are expected to be expert marksmen in contests against unarmed (and unsuspecting) prey. These theories conclude that social violence is the result of learning experiences and that changes in the nature of those experiences will change the level of violence in society.

Theories of societal processes state that aggression and violence are the result of the breakdown or ineffectuality of *social bonding mechanisms*. If people do not feel integrated into a single cooperating community, if they feel themselves in competition with others for scarce resources, if they do not share structures of authority and values, or if they do not recognize the legitimacy of institutions, they will organize themselves into conflict-oriented groups and, essentially, make war on each other. The solution here is to improve social bonding mechanisms. In regard to possibilities of international harmony, however, social bonding would have to be effective on a worldwide scale to overcome the spirit of nationalism that now encourages groups of individuals who are socially bonded to each other (nations) to fight other socially bonded individuals.

iii Research (Methodology) Ethologists such as Konrad Lorenz and Niko Tinbergen have established through a series of experiments and field observations that many animals have an innate instinct for aggression. By *innate instinct* they mean that the same stimulus always elicits an aggressive response; for example, a male stickleback fish always attacks an object that looks like a rival male exhibiting courtship display. These researchers have postulated that man may also have an innate instinct for aggression that can be similarly triggered.

An instinct for possessing and defending *group territory* has been postulated to explain aggressive behavior in man. Many animal groups, including some species of fish, birds, and mammals, defend territory, and among primate groups there is a great diversity in territorial behavior. The gibbons are perhaps the most territorial (they preserve group spacing mainly by means of loud calls), although the chimpanzees do not defend a territory at all. Field experiments have shown that different environments will elicit different territorial behavior among monkeys. Thus territorial behavior in primates depends on both biology and environmental conditions.

The biological basis of aggression is also supported by research on the brain, which demonstrates that electrical stimulation will elicit threat and escape behavior in cats and monkeys, by studies of the effect of the male hormone, testosterone (aggressive behavior increases in testosterone-injected female monkeys), and by comparing castrated with noncastrated males.

The case for the innate aggressive nature of man, then, lies in the fact that man has evolved as a primate-carnivore and may not yet have lost certain aspects of his biological heritage. Field and laboratory studies point to aggression as a general characteristic of animal life, and man, as an animal, shows this characteristic.

Many social scientists consider that man is not innately aggressive, as claimed by the animal behaviorists. Their arguments focus mainly on three main areas: human cultures that exhibit little aggression; animals that exhibit little aggression and no territorial behavior; and the impact of learning, experience, and environmental situations in producing aggressive behavior.

There are some human societies that can be considered nonaggressive. War does not take place in them, and they do not place a premium upon aggressive behavior. These include the Arapesh of New Guinea, the Lepchas of Sikkim, the Pygmies of the Ituri forest in Africa, and the Shoshone of the western United States. These societies have no ideal of a brave, aggressive, virile hero.

Field research on free-living animals has also raised questions about an innate instinct for aggressiveness. In particular, primates in their natural habitat do not exhibit much aggression. There is, however, variation by species. For example, macaques and baboons are among the more aggressive primates, whereas gorillas are among the least. Despite this variation, in all nonhuman primate groups, physical combat is kept to a minimum by the use of ritualized gestures of threat and submission and the acceptance by all the members of the troop of the established dominance hierarchy. Furthermore, there are many animal societies (including those of the gorilla, orangutan, chimpanzee, California ground squirrel, elephant, and red fox) that do not defend territories. Thus it may not be valid to postulate that man has an innate territorial instinct that accounts for his aggressiveness.

There is considerable evidence that learning and experience can influence the production of aggressive behavior. For example, monkeys reared in isolation exhibit an increase in aggressive behavior not seen in monkeys reared with a mother. Also a study of "normal" nursery school children exposed to aggressive TV programs showed that they exhibited more aggressive behavior than children not viewing the programs. The view that the environmental situation does have an effect on aggressive behavior is also supported by research by John Hurrell Crook. In "The Nature and Function of Territorial Aggression" (1968) he reports that the more aggressive children are more likely to come from homes where there are neither rules nor punishments for bad behavior, and less aggressive children are more likely to come from homes where bad behavior is controlled in a nonpunitive manner. Studies reporting that some animals become increasingly more aggressive with an increase in population density also support the environmentalists' position.

Finally, there is much research supporting the frustration-aggression hypothesis. Most specialists in international relations consider war to be the consequence of societal processes rather than the aggressive nature of man.

iv Evaluation   Human behavior is rarely explained by simple answers, and human violence is no exception. Violence and particularly war result, in all likelihood, from combinations of factors, including the biological nature of man. To say this is not to beg the issue, but to assert that here we have a good example of a biosocial interrelationship.

Margaret Mead titled an article "Warfare Is Only an Invention—Not a Biological Necessity" (1968). This is true, but the intellectual level that man has reached through his biological development enables him to create novel kinds of war and to understand the advantages that can come to him by pursuing warfare.

Any policy-making decisions aimed at solving the problem of human violence and war must take into account the possibility of biological drives toward violence, the psychological conditions that tend to foster violence, and the particular nature of societal processes that lead to aggression and war.

3   Overview

The study of biosociology is an exciting subdiscipline within the general sociological study of group processes and social interaction. This focus appears to have emerged as the result of two increasingly insistent trends. Biologically trained investigators have questioned the sociological solutions to such important issues as IQ and learning, the basis of human society, and the nature of human aggression. And the recent innovative research on nonhuman primate societies in their natural habitats has forced theorists to reexamine their thinking concerning the nature of human enterprise. Biologists are beginning to see the importance of sociological thinking for understanding nonhuman societies, and sociologists are beginning to appreciate the importance of biological findings in building a comprehensive life science that would define the nature and limits of human variability. This critical research has made it apparent that for certain problems neither a totally biological nor a totally sociological perspective is sufficient. It is now obvious that more can be understood through the study of biosocial interrelationships. Thus a vital new interdisciplinary area has been born.

Preparation for war: Jale warriors, New Guinea Highlands. In the Highlands of New Guinea, before the coming of Europeans, chronic warfare between neighboring groups was commonplace. However, unlike warfare waged by Europeans, the object was not to capture the enemy's territory, nor even to decimate his ranks. Warfare was a prestige system. Groups gained prestige-ascendancy over each other by killing members of the other groups. Such killings, of course, touched off counter-killings with a never-ending cycle of raids and agreed-upon battles assuming a very important, ongoing role in the organization of these people's lives.

D   LOOKING AHEAD

1   Interview:
David Pilbeam

David Pilbeam is associate professor and associate curator in the department of anthropology of Yale University. He is the author of *The Ascent of Man* and is currently researching primate and human morphological and behavioral evolution and the application of quantitative methods to paleoanthropology.

DPG   *Do you see the interaction of biology and society as a meaningful analytical framework for studying human problems?*
PILBEAM   I think it will be eventually, when we understand more about the interactions of the brain and the social contexts in producing behavior. One way of getting at this problem of how much of behavior is biological and how much of it isn't is to look at animals whose behavior is simpler than humans' but is related to humans'. Many anthropologists have turned to primates, using them as simple models where, theoretically at any rate, it is possible to separate behavior into genetically determined and socially learned components. But nobody has as yet satisfactorily unraveled the behavior of any species of primate.

There are a number of different research groups working on that problem. We are just beginning to do it at Yale by working with macaque monkeys. We are going to adopt a variety of approaches, observing these monkeys in a habitat that resembles as closely as possible their natural habitat and at the same time doing physiological experiments on them, implanting their brains with electrodes. It is now possible to stimulate by remote control animals who actually are interacting with each other in social groups. Once we have an established social group functioning properly, with all the animals relaxed and reasonably contented with each other, knowing each other very well (hopefully a group of animals that are related to each other because that's normally the structure of the primate social grouping)—we'll begin to interfere in various ways with their behavior, both directly by stimulations of various kinds and also by manipulating their environment, changing their food supply, influencing population density, and things like that.

DPG   *Do you see the possibility of manipulating the genetic make-up of human beings in such a way as to eliminate certain traits such as aggression? Already neurophysiologists have found in other animals many centers in the brain that when stimulated produce instant aggression.*
PILBEAM   It is hardly surprising. We can probably do this kind of manipulation with many kinds of behavior. Quite what it means, I don't know. Clearly this topic is very complicated. Whether or not we should consider doing away with aggression is another question altogether. If we do that, I suspect that we will interfere with many other kinds of behaviors, since the brain is a highly integrated organ. It is highly interactive, organized, and is therefore much more than the sum of its parts.

DPG   *Some say that human violence is primarily the outcome of innate human aggression. Others say it is caused primarily by environmental or cultural factors. What do you say?*
PILBEAM   My feeling tends toward the latter view rather than the former, but I think that the question as phrased—and it's a question that's frequently posed—implies a rigid dichotomy between what is called "nature" and what is called "nurture." I think most behaviorists would argue that almost all behavior has both learned and innate components. Most human behaviors tend toward the environmental end of the continuum. Even aggression is, like most human behavior, not very well understood. It seems fairly clear that there are certain social circumstances and social contexts in which humans are clearly not aggressive. At times aggression is easy to learn, like a seventh sense, and at other times it is hard

to suppress. Any premium placed on reinforcing affectional behavior will tend to reduce human aggressiveness. But nevertheless, I don't think there is any way we will completely eliminate aggression, or want to eliminate it.

DPG   *What do you mean? Do you see aggression as a desirable characteristic?*
PILBEAM   Well, if you look at other animals, you see some situations where it's necessary for them to be aggressive—for protection. In certain situations there has been an increase in population density and therefore competition for scarce resources. The animals that are most aggressive will survive. There are a number of circumstances in which a peaceful animal will drive off other animals.

DPG   *Do you think that approaches for solving the problem of individual aggression would be appropriate for solving the problems of war? And do you see war as something that is possible to eliminate?*
PILBEAM   Looking at historical data concerning human warfare, it would appear that it would be very difficult to get rid of war. I find it sometimes a little puzzling to really understand the relationship between individual aggression and war. War is a political decision generally made by not more than a handful of people relative to the population of the country that will be involved in the war. People get involved in wars who are not very aggressive in their everyday life, who are not warlike. It is quite possible now—it wasn't so possible 200 years ago—to be completely emotionally detached and unaggressive in warfare, to be involved very distantly with sophisticated equipment. Therefore, I think it possible to consider warfare as something that is peculiarly human—different from the fighting that you see in other animals. Animals don't go in for that sort of thing.

In fact, it is quite likely that warfare is a relatively recent invention. It is an activity that can take place only after human beings have settled down, once they have ceased to be hunters. Hunters don't have wars.

They have better things to do with their time. Their populations are so low that you couldn't get an army together. And even if you got an army together, they couldn't maintain it because a hunter is doing his own food gathering. He is either hunting or gathering—he doesn't store his food. If he does store it, he stores enough quantities to support only a handful of people. So there is no way of putting together an army, and there is no reason why you'd want to do it. There is no political structure or kind of land tenure system on a grand scale that you'd want to protect. So you invent things like stratified divisions of society, which come after hunting/gathering gives way to agricultural society. Now the idea of chieftain is developed. We reach a settled way of life where there is harvesting and domestication, where some people are beginning to specialize. You have to have a high enough population density so that you can have a separate class of people who will be the chiefs or the priests in order to have warfare. This now becomes an aspect of political dealing between people.

It is true that it helps to have soldiers who are individually aggressive. But not necessarily, because we might have people who are recklessly aggressive. So one thing that leads to war—certainly as well as, if not instead of, aggression—is the ability to plan. This ability is something that is not characteristic of aggressive behavior. I think that the major mistake made is in treating warfare and war as an aspect of aggressive behavior. I don't think that it is. I think that wars are essentially political problems, not problems of aggression.

DPG   *That point brings up questions about the definition of aggression. To be aggressive, do you have to show outward signs of rage, or can it be manifested in other ways? When a political leader coldly makes a decision to declare war, having full knowledge that it will be the cause of many deaths, what do you call the motivation behind this decision? Is it aggression, and if not, what is it?*
PILBEAM   Just look back at recent wars. To what extent were they related to the fact that the presidents or prime ministers of the countries were aggressive human beings or were being aggressive at the time? I would suspect that they really weren't. They proba-

bly made the decisions to go to war at a time when they were not especially angry. One would have to be very precise in defining the term "aggression." It's a word that physiologically speaking presents all kinds of problems—especially in terms of human aggression.

DPG *How much do we know about the way in which biological determinants shape human interaction?*
PILBEAM I would give a short answer to that. Not very much. Far less than most people think.

DPG *So you are saying that manifested behavior has both biological and environmental roots, but that it is the environmental that determines how the biological components will come out?*
PILBEAM That is what is going on. It is almost like stating a truism. What we want to know is: what determines what kind of learning takes place?, when is a behavior learned?, is it unlearnable? Psychologists, of course, are trying to do work along these lines. But one of the dimensions they often leave out is the cultural one—the extent to which the experiments that they do on Western people may not in fact be relevant to humans as a whole. But there is some interesting work being done. Some of it concerns the early effects aggressive models shown on television have on children. And this research has shown that there is probably a differential response between young males and young females. But at the moment it appears that there's not very much that man has not learned.

DPG *Some say that human society is only quantitatively different from other primate societies; others contend that it is also qualitatively different. What do you think about all of this?*
PILBEAM Again I'm not knocking the question—even though human beings have got the same basic primate central nervous system as the chimpanzee, there is no doubt that humans are qualitatively different. No one will confuse the behavior of a chimpanzee with the behavior of a human being.

There is a very great difference between a man and a chimp in a way that there isn't between a chimp and a cat, even though those two animals are different.

What is it that contributes to human behavior being qualitatively different? Well, I think language is one of the great contributors. Also the fact that one of the main results of having language is the existence of our cultural atmosphere. Although other primates learn a lot of their behavior, human learned behavior is a particular kind—it is cultured. We don't have time to go into what is specifically peculiar and different about our culture as opposed to other kinds of behavior, but there are a number of quantitative differences between human learned behavior and learned behavior of other animals that have accumulated to the extent that they result in a qualitative difference. We've taken a sort of quantum jump, which is made possible, I think, primarily because of language.

Unit 4
Culture

1 Definition
Culture is the knowledge that is necessary to function as a member of a particular social group. The objects used and produced by the group and the psychological characteristics of its members are the products of that culture.

2 World Context
Every human group has its own culture. Hence different cultures define reality differently, and there can be no transcendent reality that all people experience in the same way.

3 American Context
American society may have not an integrated culture, but a mosaic of diverse cultures held together by the economic, political, educational, and legal systems.

1 Questions
Sociologists study both specific cultures—(1) Can the so-called primitive cultures survive in the modern world?—and broader theoretical matters—(2) How does culture interact with other systems in a society? (3) Do all adult human beings share the same thought processes?

2 Evidence
a The "Burning Issue" Question
All cultures must adapt in order to survive. And the societies committed to a technological and industrial culture are now expanding at the expense of less developed, isolated, traditional groups. Yet those groups certainly provide their members with a satisfying way of life. The important issue is how to use cultural change to create a humane world for all the diverse people who inhabit it.
b The "Classical" Question
Culture interacts dynamically with the social, political, and economic systems and even the natural environment of a particular group. Talcott Parsons and Neil Smelser developed the equilibrium model to describe the stable, self-adjusting nature of these interactions. The Marxian conflict model, on the other hand, stresses the strains and contradictions in every society.
c The "Research" Question
Recent studies by Claude Lévi-Strauss and other structuralists have shown that all adults do use the same mental processes, regardless of the cultural sources of the things they think about.

3 Overview
Each culture must be understood on its own terms. But the differences among them must not obscure the fact that all human beings share certain fundamental characteristics.

INTERACTION OF CULTURE WITH OTHER SYSTEMS

1. **A Cultural Value.** American suburbanites believe in the primacy of the individual.

2. **The Economic System.** Each suburban family has its own house, cars, swing set, and television.

3. **The Social System.** Each suburban household tries to keep its problems a secret from the surrounding households.

4. **The Political System.** Collective solutions to problems are viewed with suspicion.

5. **The Biological System.** The emphasis on individual success and the competition for ownership of material goods can have harmful effects on the body of the individual.

A LOW SALT DIET SHOULD KEEP YOUR BLOOD PRESSURE DOWN, AND BLAND FOODS WILL...

B DEFINITION AND CONTEXT

1 Definition

Sir Edward Burnett Tylor (1832–1917), considered by many to be the father of modern cultural anthropology.

Although Sir Edward Burnett Tylor wrote *Primitive Culture* in 1871, many of the thoughts developed in it continue to exercise a strong influence on contemporary studies of culture. Tylor defined culture as ''that complex whole which includes knowledge, belief, art, morals, law, custom, and any other capabilities and habits acquired by man as a member of society.'' All modern definitions of culture relate back to the central themes suggested by Tylor: Culture is learned and taught in the context of groups; it is not inherited genetically, but rather passed on from generation to generation through social communication between adults and children; it is indeed a complex whole and every aspect of our life as human beings is influenced (if not determined) by it.

In search of rigorous theoretical formulation many social scientists have followed Ward Goodenough's definition (in ''Cultural Anthropology and Linguistics,'' 1957). *Culture is ''whatever it is one has to know or believe in order to operate in a manner acceptable to [a society's] members, and to do so in any role that they accept for any one of themselves.'' Thus culture is knowledge—knowledge learned and taught in groups.* This knowledge includes the definitions, relations, and categories of reality through which group members are taught to perceive the universe, and it also includes the values, goals, norms, ethical prescriptions and proscriptions that govern the behavior of group members toward each other and toward outsiders. Art, architecture, and all the other diverse material objects used and produced by a given group are seen not as culture itself, but rather as *products of culture.*

Other products of culture are the patterned psychological characteristics shared by group members. Manifestations and objects of anxiety, defense mechanisms, and even forms of mental illness are culturally patterned. For example, an Irish schizophrenic exhibits very different symptoms from an Italian schizophrenic. Keeping the distinction between culture and the products of culture clear is extremely important. If everything that human beings do, think, and make as members of human groups were included within the definition of culture, it would be difficult systematically to examine such a grab-bag whole. When we limit the concept of culture to include only the knowledge that it is necessary to have in order to function as a member of a given group, we can study this body of knowledge as a system by itself and then see the nature of its interactions with other systems operating in the life of the group—subsistence activities, art, political organization, psychological make-up, and so on.

2 World Context

From the definition it is obvious that every human group has its culture. It would be impossible for an aggregate of individuals to be a group if they did not share a body of knowledge regarding what is appropriate behavior among themselves, toward outsiders, and even how group members should interact with their natural environ-

Just a cow? For Americans a cow is to milk or to eat. In India it is a sacred animal and must not be killed. But the cow, despite its sacred status, does nevertheless serve some economic functions: its dung provides fertilizer for peasants who cannot afford to purchase commercial fertilizers, and dried dung is burned as a cheap source of fuel.

American tourists at the Pantheon in Rome. We see concrete remains of the roots of European civilization. What are our American roots?

ment. Any American who has traveled outside the United States has observed that it is very difficult to know what is "correct behavior" in other lands. We are familiar with our own culture but find it hard to know how to meet the expectations of other cultures —or even to know what those expectations are.

One reason it is so difficult to know what expectations people from other cultures have is that different cultures may define any given situation differently. For an American killing a cow is simply a way to get meat; for a Hindu in India it is a sacrilege. Part of our knowledge of how one should behave depends on our definition of what is going on. Thus we must keep in mind that not only do people from different cultures *do* things differently, they also *see* things differently.

This train of thought leads us to a rather remarkable conclusion. Because different cultures define reality differently, there can be no transcendent reality that all people experience in the same manner. Small wonder, then, that it is often so difficult for people from different cultures to get along with or even to understand each other. They are operating with different comprehensions of reality itself.

One understandable result of this state of affairs is that each group tends to believe that its definition of reality is right and any other definition of reality is wrong. Thus people tend to judge and evaluate the behavior of others in terms of the culture of their own group. This attitude is known as *ethnocentrism.* It manifests itself in the form of racial prejudice, nationalistic fanaticism, religious intolerance, and various other social phenomena that keep the peoples of the world from respecting and enjoying one another.

Anthropologists, the social scientists who specialize in the study of different cultures, have consistently fought against ethnocentric thinking, arguing instead for *cultural relativism.* A cultural relativist is willing to try to see another culture on its own terms. He attempts to reserve judgment regarding the behavior of people from different cultures until he understands the cultural definitions and prescriptions in terms of which these people are acting. Anthropologists believe that until the vast majority of the world's people embrace the concept of cultural relativism, significant movement in the direction of world unity is impossible.

3   American Context

The United States is one of the youngest countries in Western civilization. We trace our history back a scant 350 years or so. Furthermore, our population is the result of a rapid series of "waves" of immigrants who displaced the original inhabitants and attempted to create viable niches for themselves. Some came against their will; the captured Africans who were imported as slaves certainly had no vested interest in coming here. Others were more happy to arrive; various contingents from the European countries migrated here with a hope for a better life. But even the people who came voluntarily did so in pain. Most were refugees from conditions in their home countries that made life there intolerable. Some fled from famine, others from political or religious persecution. The United States is thus unique: this country was populated more rapidly, more recently, and by a more diverse aggregate of disaffiliated and troubled ethnic groups than any other country in the history of Western civilization.

With its short history and its tremendously pluralistic composition, can the United States be said to have a national culture that transcends and integrates the cultures of all the ethnic groups of which it is constituted? What—aside from historical accident and legal citizenship—makes Southwestern Chicanos, Appalachian mountain people, inner-city blacks, Little Italy Italians, Chinatown Asians, Midwestern farmers, all tribes of American Indians, and the highest layer of Boston high society all "Americans"? Many students of American society call these various groups *subcultures* of the wider American society. But are they subcultures *united* into a larger whole, or are they discrete cultural and social entities with minimal cultural relationship to each other?

Some authors argue that although diversity is indisputably the cornerstone of American society, the "common experiences" of our short history—the westward expansion and the frontier experience, the escape from previously intolerable conditions to the land of opportunity (Africans excluded, of course), an economic system giving more people more material things than any other

(Facing page) Prejudice: ethnocentrism brought to its extreme. The power of ideas is not to be underestimated. People kill and die in defense of their world views.

Americans all. What makes all these people American? Do they share a world view? An identical language? A set of goals? A value system?

country in history (with the exception of the "unfortunate" fifth of the population that suffers from chronic poverty generation after generation), and even our great success in war (somehow Korea and Vietnam always escape notice when this point is made)—all these experiences are said to contribute to a unique American experience and provide the components for a unique American culture. It is further argued that the awesome power of the public schools and mass media to mold American minds continues this homogenizing process and that a distinctive American culture is becoming increasingly more evident.

Even the critics of American society seem to believe in the existence of an overarching American culture. Both Charles Reich in his naïvely optimistic book *The Greening of America* (1970) and Philip Slater in his more pessimistic *The Pursuit of Loneliness* (1970) see an American culture. In fact, they believe this American culture is thrown into bold relief by the glare of the newly emerging *counterculture* of the young. Whereas Reich believes the counterculture rejects the cultural assumptions of the older generations, Slater argues that it merely emphasizes strong themes that have lain dormant in the old culture and reverses some of the old culture's priorities. According to Slater it is incorrect to say, for instance, that young people are rejecting technology: motorcycles, expensive stereo equipment, and diverse synthetic drugs are hardly attainable without a sophisticated technology. For that matter, even the slogan "Do your own thing" is firmly rooted in what is considered to be the traditional American culture's emphasis on individualism and independence.

But when we get beyond the picture of America as portrayed by the media, when we can see behind the glass facades of our cities of skyscrapers, when we remember the people living in rural mountain areas, in desolate Southwestern canyons, on vast plains, in crumbling slums, in tin-roofed dormitory huts, if we contemplate the diverse churches, synagogues, tents, football stadi-

ums, and open fields in which people are praying (and if we remember how many don't pray), where shall we search for the common theme, the shared definition of reality that would signify the presence of an integrated culture?

It is even difficult to argue for the presence of an integrated counterculture. What, beyond disaffection with American society, unites hippies, Yippies, Black Panthers, new left radicals, drug freaks, drop-outs in rural communes, Jesus freaks, women's liberationists, motorcycle gangs, ostentatiously bored college students, and the radical chic?

In what sense are Indians "American"—or, for that matter, what unites them besides a shared historical experience of defeat and humiliation? Are there not a large number of Indian tribes and even nations? A dominant and ruthless society has imposed a superficial homogeneity on the American Indian groups; does this situation mean that the Indians experience this commonality? Analysis suggests that the belief in an *integrated American culture* is a myth—a myth held by the advantaged, dominant groups in the country in whose interest it is to perpetuate this view of things. Perhaps America is not composed so much of subcultures as it is a *mosaic of diverse cultures* held together by the *interlocking mechanisms* of the economic, political, educational, and legal systems of the nation.

C   QUESTIONS AND EVIDENCE

1   Questions

Sociologists who focus on the study of culture are interested in the characteristics of specific cultures as well as in broader theoretical concerns. Among the questions they ask are these: (1) Can the so-called primitive cultures survive in the modern technological world? (2) How does culture interact with other systems in a society? (3) Do all adult human beings share the same thought processes—no matter which culture they were raised in? The first question relates to a specific type of culture; the latter two relate to the abstract, theoretical meaning of the term "culture."

2   Evidence

a   The "Burning Issue" Question

i   Context   There can be no doubt that peoples with a great cultural capacity for producing and contolling energy—that is, industrial, technologically sophisticated cultures—are expanding across the world at the expense of peoples whose cultures are much less technologically developed. There are still people in the world today who literally are living in the Stone Age, people whose tools are made of wood and stone and who sustain themselves by hunting and gathering vegetable materials or who may engage in horticulture (using hoes, not plows) with a relatively low yield. As the industrial peoples of the world expand, these technologically less developed peoples are either being killed off, pushed to ever more remote and inhospitable areas, or absorbed in the expanding industrial society—but at the lowest socioeconomic levels.

(Even within the technologically advanced societies a selection process is going on. Industrialized countries are experiencing a "flight from the countryside.")Small farmers and peasants are leaving their family holdings and migrating to the cities, looking for the greater material benefits offered by work in manufacturing and service industries. Those who remain in the country are turning to such activities as creating tourist facilities (hotels, ski areas, resort towns, and so on) to raise their standard of living. (The traditional way of life of these rural people is breaking up and their cultures are vanishing. Sociologists ask: *Is the survival potential of a given society directly correlated with its technological mode and orientation?*)

ii   Theory (Before it is possible to discuss the relative *adaptive capabilities* of particular cultures, it is necessary to understand the role played by culture in the life of human beings.

Basically, a culture tells people what needs they have and how to go about meeting them.)If they live in the Arctic their culture tells them how to build shelters with the most available material —snow. If they live in the heat of the tropics their culture tells them how to build sleeping devices that allow the air to circulate around their bodies—hammocks. Culture tells people what they should eat and how to go about getting it. It tells people how they should go about gratifying their sexual needs, how to deal with anxiety, and what to do about disease.

(Culture is a device, then, that enables human beings to interact with their particular environment(s). A human being without a culture could not survive; he could not talk, find food, build a shel-

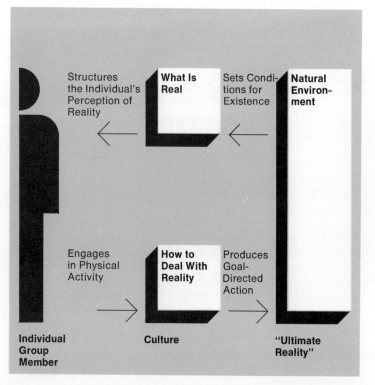

Model 1. Culture. Culture tells us what is real, what to do, and how to do it.

ter, or defend himself from predators, because human beings have to learn how to do all these things—they do not inherit these behavior patterns through their genes.

A device that enables an organism to survive must be flexible enough to change as the environment changes. A device that adapts people to living only on lake shores is useless if the lakes are drying up. It is nonadaptive to know only how to hunt if game is disappearing. Nor is it wise to have a technology based on massive consumption of coal and oil if there is only a finite amount of these natural resources.

The only certainty in the universe is change. The natural environment is changing. The social environment is changing. The introduction of a new medicine controls a given breed of bacteria, but some new strains evolve that are immune; thus a new medicine must again be introduced. No culture can survive *as it is.* Although at any given moment some cultures will appear to be more successful in meeting people's needs than are other cultures, if their success results from a too rigid specialization in either *technology, social organization,* or *cultural patterns,* these cultures will not adapt easily to new circumstances. Overspecialization is bad for long-term evolutionary prospects. This dictum holds both on the biological and on the cultural levels.

The story of human evolution is also the story of cultural evolution and adaptation. It is not easy to evaluate the "worthwhileness" of inventions and cultural changes. In the Near East, one of the places where agriculture was invented, the surplus food produced in this manner eventually allowed people to congregate in cities and supported newly emerging classes of individuals who produced no food, but rather provided services in the areas of religion, art, architecture, trade, government, and warfare. There was a tremendous surge of human creativity as whole groups of persons were freed from the necessity of having to hunt or gather their own food. Even the absolute number of people increased tremendously. However, at the same time, the division of society into classes of food producers and nonproductive consumers became rigid, dividing human beings for the first time into *self-perpetuating classes* of rich and chronically poor; power to make decisions drastically affecting the lives of masses of people became concentrated into the hands of a few; even the human relationship to nature changed from that of friendly cooperation to one of *exploitation.* Was the newly agricultural and urban Near East more "fit"—in terms of potential for survival—than the Near East of hunters and gatherers of wild grasses? There is no easy answer to this question.

iii Research Although it is difficult to assess the long-term evolutionary significance or usefulness of the survival of one culture at the expense of another, it is very clear that this process is taking place. In the modern world the technologically advanced societies are expanding into ever more remote areas. As this expansion occurs, the small indigenous groups, with their relatively less sophisticated technology, are being disrupted, displaced, and often destroyed.

Currently the government of Brazil is pressing forward with its construction of a highway linking the Atlantic shore with the distant

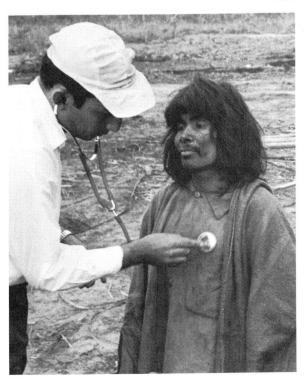

An Indian in the Mato Grosso region of Brazil is examined by a physician. Elsewhere in Brazil, surveyors, prospectors, plantation-builders, and skin-hunters are ready to kill Indians who oppose them.

A Tasaday family. The Tasaday life-style is characteristically one of great interpersonal warmth.

interior and providing for the easy expansion of the culture of technology into the depths of the Amazon jungle. This expansion is seen as a great step forward, a triumph of modern civilization. What effect has it had on the indigenous Amazon Indian tribes?

Some groups, such as the Kreen Akrore, are fleeing ever deeper into the jungle and are attempting to ensure their survival by simply killing every person they meet who is not a member of their group. Others are being placed on reservations. Some are attempting to tie their subsistence activities into the expanding market economy of the dominant society. It is clear, however, that the traditional way of life is undergoing radical disruption.

But this disruption is not all the damage. A shocked world has read newspaper accounts of the Brazilian air force napalming and strafing Indian villages in an attempt to wipe out large segments of the indigenous population. Reportedly, this policy was followed so that plantation companies could move in and make use of the land. Although many view such actions as atrocities, they are offensive because of their blatancy, not because most people question the underlying assumption that primitive societies are no longer viable and thus are doomed to extinction anyway.

Recently in the mountain jungles of the Philippines a Stone Age group was discovered whose members had never even seen a white person. This group, called the Tasaday, became a focus of tremendous anthropological interest because they were thought to be relatively uncontaminated by industrial society and thus offered a unique opportunity to study a truly Stone Age culture. A large research team of cultural anthropologists, biologists, zoologists, filmmakers, and linguists were helicoptered in to study them. Reports indicate that they are a very happy people who spend a great deal

Evonne Goolagong, an Australian Aborigine who became Wimbledon Women's Singles Champion in 1971. An individual star lives an exhilarating life of success, but most Aborigines suffer chronic poverty and racial discrimination.

of their time hugging each other and uttering terms of mutual endearment. Apparently they do not even have a word to express the concept of hostility.

The government of the Philippines has set aside the surrounding country as a reservation so that the Tasaday may continue their way of life for the time being. Had this action not been taken, it is probable that they would have been killed off by the lumber companies that are expanding into the area and are engaged in bloody skirmishes with each other for the rights to the land.

International attention may be focused for a brief time on isolated groups of primitive peoples encountering the expanding industrial world. But the attention is brief. And in many parts of the world the same process goes on with scant attention paid. In Australia (as in the United States) the aboriginal population has been pushed into the most unlivable areas. Those who have attempted to integrate themselves into the dominant white society have found their way blocked by job, housing, and educational discrimination that keeps them at the bottom socioeconomic stratum of Australian society. Although a few Aborigines do achieve wealth and fame, as in the case of international tennis star Evonne Goolagong, for the group as a whole their participation in the white-dominated racist society is a life of chronic poverty and a great deal of misery.

Even within the countries of Europe the traditional peasant communities are losing the younger generations to the seductions of city life and higher standards of living. Although governments subsidize agriculture, the subsidies generally favor the large farms, which can operate more efficiently than the small, isolated farmsteads. In all probability, much of Europe's peasant population will no longer exist within 50 years. Farmsteads will have been consolidated into mechanized farms, and the steep hillsides now being tilled will be abandoned or used solely for pasture.

iv   Evaluation It is undeniable that the picture of human society has always changed and is continuing to do so. It is clear that at this time the societies committed to a technological and industrial culture are expanding and extending their interests at the expense of less technologically developed, isolated, small, traditionally oriented groups.

Does that mean that these vanishing groups are less ''fit''? They are certainly fit enough to provide their members with a satisfying way of life. Their technology is sufficiently developed to enable them to make a living on their own terms in the natural environments in which they live. Despite various technological accomplishments, modern Western society can hardly claim to have created a way of life that allows all citizens equal access to goods and services or to power, that enables us to experience ourselves in a relaxed, untense, unharried, emotionally integrated way. We have made no more progress along these lines (and perhaps less) than the societies we are actively destroying. Shall we limit the meaning of ''fitness'' to the capacity to destroy or absorb other, less technologically advanced groups? Does this trait in itself suggest significant evolutionary potential?

In a controversial book called *Evolution and Culture* (1960) Marshall Sahlins and Elman Service suggest that the greatest evolutionary potential does not reside in the United States or other so-called *developed countries* but rather in the currently less developed *Third World nations* of Asia, Africa, and Latin America. Their ''law of evolutionary potential'' states that ''specific evolutionary progress is inversely related to general evolutionary potential.'' It is thus advisable not to accept uncritically the complacent assumption of America's evolutionary cultural ''fitness.''

To the extent that America's economic system must constantly expand in order to survive, it depends for its existence on the presence of less developed economies. As these develop, the survival potential of our current economic system is diminished. To the extent that American society insists on continuously expanding its use of limited natural resources, its life style must be ultimately unviable. To the extent that we continue to rely on technological innovation as the source of solutions for the vast social and economic problems (such as chronic poverty and runaway environmental pollution) rather than examine our values and create new priorities, to that extent we shall not be able to meet the long-term challenges to our society's survival.

Evidence of America's waning ability to cope with fundamental problems is to be found in her large cities, where decaying housing, chronically improverished populations, inadequately functioning schools, spiraling crime rates (especially of violent crime), epidemics of drug addiction, widespread corruption of public officials, and an erosion of confidence in the police force as an agent of social stability and control all combine to make urban life less and less tolerable for those who have the financial means to leave. (We discuss the urban crisis in Unit 17.)

By contrast, although the Third World nations certainly face

Australian Aborigine in a changing world. What should be the priorities in social and cultural change?

tremendous problems generated by the process of developing new social, political, and economic forms, they are not yet overly committed to one or another direction of development, and the problems inherent in industrial society are not yet so severe in these countries that they cannot be dealt with in the course of their development. It is impossible to know for sure whether the developing Third World nations will be able to ameliorate (through careful planning) many of the problems that plague us. But at least they have the opportunity to do so in a situation of flux—whereas we are cramped and constrained by the vast economic and political bureaucratic structure that we labored so hard to create.

But in the final analysis, perhaps the issue of which cultures are more "fit" is less important than the question of how human beings can go about creating societies in which it is possible for all members to live with a sense of their own worth, with meaningful possibilities to contribute to the ongoing functioning of the society, and with a satisfying sense of responsibility for the welfare of the society. The important issue is how to control inevitable change in human society and use it to create a humane world—for all the diverse peoples who inhabit it.

b The "Classical" Question

i Context Culture is knowledge systematically taught and learned in human groups. This knowledge is of tremendous significance for human beings, because it provides all the information about the universe and techniques for dealing with the surrounding environment that an individual possesses. Although it takes a long time for an individual to learn his culture (*adulthood* is essentially recognized in all cultures and means that the individual has mastered enough of the culture to be able to function adequately) the very fact that behavioral patterns are learned rather than genetically inherited enables human beings to be almost infinitely flexible. Human beings occupy more ecological niches than does any other species of animal, because human knowledge can be modified to meet new situations on the spot, whereas it takes many generations of natural selection for genetically coded behavior patterns to change. Sociologists ask: *How does culture as an adaptive system interact with other systems relevant to the human experience?*

ii Theory There are two ways of approaching this question. One can take the point of view that four basic sets of phenomena—human culture, biology, the mind, and the natural environment—are interacting in a remarkably successful manner. After all, no matter where human groups live, they have cultures that tell them how to survive and bodies constructed to function well in that environment (such as the barrel chest of the Indians living high up in the Andes), and they apparently conceive of themselves as reasonably satisfied with their life styles. This concept is called the *equilibrium model* because it stresses the self-adjusting interaction of those four systems in the direction of stability. Social change is therefore seen as episodic—a temporary state of affairs operating within a generally stable context.

The equilibrium model has been refined to its highest degree by the American sociologists Talcott Parsons and Neil Smelser. Parsons' model of society, described in his book *Societies: Evo-*

lutionary and Comparative Perspectives (1966), consists of four *action systems* through which human beings relate to "ultimate reality" on the one hand, and the "physical-organic environment" on the other. These action systems are the *cultural system,* which functions to maintain patterns; the *social system,* which functions to integrate action; the *personality system,* which directs goal attainment; and the *behavioral organism,* which adapts to the natural environment. The conditions that set the boundaries of possible human behavior come ultimately from the *physical-organic environment* and influence these four systems sequentially—that is, through the behavioral organism, then the personality system, the social system, and finally the cultural system. The information necessary to control the specific actions individuals undertake originates in *ultimate reality* and operates *hierarchies of control mechanisms* in the reverse order—through the cultural system downwards through the social and personality systems, and finally expressed in the behavioral organism (which is any given individual).

How does the equilibrium model approach the question of social change? Basically, it traces the original causation of change to individuals' dissatisfaction with the ways in which resources are allocated and/or with the behavior expected of them in the performance of their roles. These individuals further perceive that the society has available facilities to remove the sources of their deprivation. Feeling anxious, tense, frustrated, and finally angry, such individuals threaten to coalesce into an oppositional social movement. This situation causes the various agents of social control to step into the picture and to channel the upwelling dissatisfaction by creating structural changes in the social system. These *structural changes* consist of the *differentiation of social roles* and the *integration* of these newly designed roles into the functioning social order. *Social change,* then, is seen basically as a result of the actions taken by a society's managers, who are acting to remove the source(s) of social dissatisfaction that have produced a temporary disequilibrium. By thus ameliorating these dissatisfactions through modifications in the social structure they restore the society to a state of equilibrium (and, not coincidentally, keep themselves in positions of control).

It is possible to view society from another perspective, however. Instead of focusing on the homeostatic equilibrium of a society interrupted by temporary spasms of social change, it is possible to see society as in fact being in a constant state of change due to dynamic forces that are built into it and that operate continuously in a dialectic manner. This is the *conflict model,* which sees social stability as the temporary state of affairs reached when the inexorable processes of social change are interrupted by the coercive power of a ruling elite, or through concessions made by the social elements that are in opposition to each other. We will discuss the equilibrium and conflict models further in Units 26 and 27.

The writings of Karl Marx provide perhaps the best example of the conflict model. Marx was primarily interested in the relationship between culture, which he thought of as an *overarching ideational superstructure,* and the subsistence activities and economic relations of a society, which form its *material basis.* The culture and

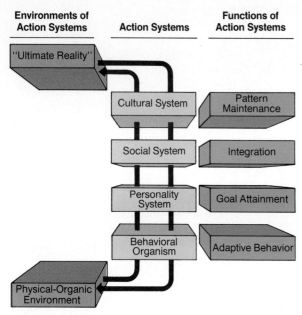

Environments of Action Systems   **Action Systems**   **Functions of Action Systems**

"Ultimate Reality"

Cultural System — Pattern Maintenance

Social System — Integration

Personality System — Goal Attainment

Behavioral Organism — Adaptive Behavior

Physical-Organic Environment

Model 2. Talcott Parsons' Equilibrium Model of Society. The upward flow indicates the hierarchy of conditioning factors; the downward flow indicates the hierarchy of controlling factors. (Source: Adapted from Parsons, *Societies*)

all other systems, such as the political system, educational system, and so on, are supported on this material base; consequently, changes in the material base produce cultural change and not vice versa. Naturally it takes some time for changes in the economic basis of a society to be reflected in the overarching cultural superstructure, and this *cultural lag* is an inevitable and constant source of *strain and contradiction* in every society.

Marx describes the logical priority of the material condition over human consciousness (culture) eloquently in his ''Preface to *A Contribution to the Critique of Political Economy*'' (1859):

> In the social production which men carry on they enter into definite relations that are indispensable and independent of their will; these relations of production correspond to a definite state of development of their material powers of production. The sum total of these relations of production constitutes the economic structure of society—the real foundation, on which rise legal and political superstructures and to which correspond definite forms of social consciousness. The mode of production in material life determines the general character of the social, political and spiritual processes in life. It is not the consciousness of men that determines their existence, but, on the contrary, their social existence determines their consciousness.

The causal origin of social change as viewed by conflict theorists rests, ultimately, in changes in the ''relations of production'' that obtain at any given time. Ralf Dahrendorf, author of *Class and Class Conflict in Industrial Society* (1957) and *Essays in the Theory of Sociology* (1968), is one of the better-known modern sociologists who has elaborated on Marx's original formulations. He sees society as inevitably involving the dialectical opposition of two groups with conflicting interests: *power* seeks to maintain the social structure that gives it control over scarce (or limited) resources (for example control over the means of production); *resistance to power* arises in response to the unequal distribution of resources and seeks to change the social structure that deprives it of positions of authority, the value system that legitimates the social structure, and, finally, the economic system that underlies the organization of the society.

iii   Research (Survey)   In order to examine the relative merits of the equilibrium model and the conflict model, let us look at some features of social and cultural evolution in general, and then focus on one community in particular.

Until about 12,000 years ago, all human groups made a living through hunting game and foraging for vegetable foods. Even today there are still bands of hunters and gatherers in remote areas of the world who have not adopted any other more sophisticated form of subsistence activities. Although there are, of course, tremendous cultural differences between these groups, they do have enough features in common to suggest a causal relationship between their culture and social organization and the level of their economic development.

Hunters and gatherers do not usually produce surpluses.

Spanish explorer Ferdinand De Soto committing atrocities against the Florida Indians. (Engraving by De Bry, c.1598)

They gather what they can eat and no more. Though the kinds of groups they live in vary a great deal, they tend to be very egalitarian. Naturally in all areas there are some people who can do things better than others and consequently play a leadership role in that area; but full-time leaders with power to enforce their decisions are not prevalent. Leadership is exercised through persuasion and appeal to group values and prestige rather than force. The *division of labor* is generally structured along age and sex lines, with men usually doing the work of hunting larger game, while women hunt smaller game, such as rodents, and also do most of the gathering of vegetable food. Children generally help the women in their food-gathering activities.

The *exchange systems* of hunters and gatherers are characterized by an emphasis on gifts and reciprocity rather than on trade. Gifts are often given along kinship lines and are usually food items rather than decorative or luxury goods. There is no attempt to try to get more in value from another person when he reciprocates a gift, as is the case in trading relationships, where each person tries to maximize his gain.

Once human groups acquire the technological capacity to produce *food surpluses* (usually through some form of domestication of plants and/or animals), the nature of their social groups changes remarkably. Individuals or groups of individuals inevitably acquire rights to the surpluses and to their redistribution. This situation gives them the direct economic power that underlies the emergence of centralized political authority and power. No longer is government by persuasion—decisions are made by those who have the centralized economic and political power, and these decisions are enforced through economic as well as other sanctions.

The division of labor becomes much more complex once surpluses are available to support groups of people who do not need to produce food themselves. Full-time specialists emerge in such areas as religion, medicine, warfare, and trade. These specialists are also able to gather a certain degree of power into their hands. Thus these societies are no longer egalitarian, but rather structured in terms of hierarchies of power to make and enforce decisions that affect the lives of others. Exchange is in the form of trade, and *markets* provide loci for economic networks far beyond the lines of *kinship relationships*.

This general scheme of the evolution of culture and social organization in response to the change of the economic systems of human societies has been observed in all areas of the world. Elman Service made a systematic study of these phenomena in *Primitive Social Organization* (1962).

In order to gain a deeper insight into the dynamics of the relationships between culture and other systems, let us examine one particular community of peasants living in the Alpine foothills of central Switzerland. These farmsteads are strung out along a high ridge that runs approximately east to west. Thus the farm land lies both on the northern and southern slopes of the ridge. The snow adheres sooner and melts later on the northern side than on the southern. About 50 years ago, before mechanized equipment was used in the area, the households on the northern slopes would go to help those on the southern slopes with their sowing and harvesting (because the ground was ready and the crops ripen sooner on the southern slope than on the northern); then the help would be reciprocated. Regular reciprocal labor relations existed between households on the "sun-side" (south) and "shade-side" (north) of the ridge. The entire community conceived itself thus divided into sun-side households and shade-side households. This bifurcation of the community not only structured work relationships between homesteads, but also patterned who drank with whom in the local tavern (there were different tables informally agreed upon to be appropriate for sun-siders and shade-siders to drink at), who fought with whom in school (usually sun-siders against shade-siders), and a whole variety of social interactions.

The division of this community into the two groups was clearly rooted in the ecological situation and the patterns of labor exchange that developed from it. With the introduction of power mowers and tractor equipment, labor exchange became unnecessary and in fact has diminished to very minimal levels at the present time. Whatever labor exchange still exists between households is no longer structured by the sun-side/shade-side bifurcation. However, patterned drinking in the tavern persists and so does *stereotyping*. In terms of the local culture, sun-siders and shade-siders are thought of as being somehow different, with the latter often described by sun-siders as more moody and less spontaneous than the sun-siders.

Interestingly, this division of the community has perpetuated itself even in the area of economic development. Recently a group of 11 men got together to build a local ski lift. Although it was built on the shade-side of the ridge, only two members of the founding group were shade-siders, and then only because the lift was built on their land.

Thus the picture is clear. Originally there was an ecological reason for bifurcating the community in terms of the patterns of reciprocal work relations. The structure of the economic system was expressed on the level of social organization and in terms of the local culture. However, the introduction of technological innovation eliminated the economic basis of the social and cultural community split more than 15 years ago. Nevertheless, these social and cultural patterns have persisted and continue to influence the course of events in the community. We have here, then, a good example of (1) the interaction of the economic basis of a society and its culture and (2) the cultural lag in reflecting a basic change in the economic organization.

iv Evaluation We have seen the value of defining the term "culture" as the shared system of knowledge, expectations, and beliefs that influence the behavior of any given group of human beings, and we have also seen that culture bears a dynamic relationship to other systems such as the social system (patterned social interaction), political system (patterns of power relationships), economic system (relations of productive behavior), and even the natural environment. If we are to understand the functionings of human society, all these relationships must be examined and their dynamic characteristics understood.

It is beyond dispute that there is a certain element of *pattern maintenance,* a resistance to change, in human societies. Were this

Peasant farmsteads in central Switzerland. Along these steep slopes peasant families labor to extract an existence by meticulously tilling every square foot of land.

not the case, groupings of people would fragment before they could even generate a self-identity—or they would be changing so fast that the concept of a *group identity* would have no meaning. However, despite these mechanisms for group stability, it is also undeniable that groups are in constant change. How can we account for the omnipresence of change without resorting to a sort of simplistic environmental reductionism in which we trace all change in groups to changes in the environment (a position once held by many scholars but now abandoned as being useless for explaining most social phenomena)?

We can account for change in a systematic and useful way if we analyze human group phenomena in terms of the built-in cultural lags, strains, stresses, and even contradictions that seem to characterize all known societies. The culture, social system, political system, economic system, and environment are never in complete harmony either with one another or even in complete equilibrium within themselves. Change manifests itself unequally in the different systems, and it is not always sufficiently explained in terms of role differentiation resulting from decisions made by society's managers. Thus it appears that the conflict model has a greater explanatory power than the equilibrium model (although in the last decade several theorists, notably Pierre L. van den Berghe, Robert Cole, and Gerhard Lenski, have attempted to integrate both models into one general theory).

Alvin Gouldner and Richard Peterson provide further support for this position in *Notes on Technology and the Moral Order* (1962). Using complicated statistical techniques, they analyze data on 71 primitive and preindustrial societies in order to ascertain which factors, if any, have a direct causative effect on the moral orders (culture) of human societies. After analyzing 11 social factors (including sexual dominance, kinship, and norm-giving factors), they conclude that "technology is the single most influential factor, in that it predicts more of the variance in all of the other factors than does any other single factor." Thus this research reinforces the position taken by Marxian conflict theorists that the economic system plays the primary causative role in structuring the nature of social life in any given society.

c The "Research" Question

i Context How do we experience the world? How do we organize our experiences and deal with them conceptually? Students of these questions agree that all human beings perceive the world through sets of categories that they carry in their minds and into which all perceived objects are sorted. These categories are called *cognitive categories,* and we can manipulate our experiences of phenomena conceptually only after we identify the perceived objects in terms of membership in one or more of these categories.

All our experience is sorted in terms of cognitive categories. For example, we know that the category "sandwich" is a subcategory of "something to eat" and that "BLT" and "tuna on a hard roll with lettuce and tomato" are subcategories of "sandwich." We know that "mashed potatoes," although beyond doubt "something to eat," do not belong to the category "sandwich." We also know that the item "cousin" belongs to a different category altogether.

"The Thinker." What do *you* think he's thinking?

Now it has been amply demonstrated through cross-cultural studies that these categories—or ways of sorting and grouping together diverse phenomena and experiences—are *culturally determined*. They are learned and taught in group contexts and serve to define the nature of reality for all group members. It follows, then, that different cultures can (and usually do) have different sets of cognitive categories. Although, for example, nineteenth-century Eskimos no doubt had a category "something to eat," the items they identified as belonging to that category included many items that we would not include (maggots and raw seal blubber, for example, which we would categorize as "inedible") and did not include many items that we feel belong (such as sandwiches). Thus "something to eat" literally means something different to us than it did to those Eskimos. This difference in meaning is not at all trivial, because it affects us so deeply that we might get sick when we contemplate eating maggots and raw seal blubber. Sociologists ask: *To what extent are the mechanisms of thought structurally equivalent across cultural boundaries?*

ii **Theory** There is no way a social scientist studying a foreign group of people can predict either what kinds of cognitive categories they will have or what items will be classified as being members of the diverse categories they do have. One of the devices anthropologists use to investigate this topic is the concept of the folk taxonomy.

Although the theory in this area has been elaborated into great complexity, in essence it may be stated as follows. All cultures have cognitive categories into which all culturally meaningful experiences (of all things—objects, feelings, and so on) are sorted. These categories are not isolated, but rather are systematically related to at least some other categories. Often this relationship is *hierarchical;* that is, some categories are seen to be subcategories of other, more inclusive categories. Thus, to recall the discussion of "something to eat," a "BLT" is a category that has several subcategories

Model 3. Two Alternate Ways of Schematizing Identical Taxonomies. The vertical single-headed arrows indicate the dimension of hierarchical inclusion (only goes in one direction); the horizontal double-headed arrows indicate the dimension of contrast (goes in both directions); Levels I, II, III, IV are levels of contrast. Level I: *A* contrasts with *non-A*. Level II: *B* contrasts with *C*. Level III: *B, D,* and *E* contrast with each other. Level IV: *B, F, G,* and *E* contrast with each other. Along the dimension of hierarchical inclusion: *B* is a kind of *A* but not a kind of *C; C* is a kind of *A* but not a kind of *B;* therefore, *B* and *C* are both included in *A,* though each is separate from the other; similarly, *F* and *G* are included in (kinds of) *D* but not in *B* or *E;* also, *F, G, D,* and *E* are included in *C* and *A* but not in *B;* finally, although *F* is included in *D* and *D* in *C* and *C* in *A,* one cannot say the reverse (that *A* is included in *C,* and so on).

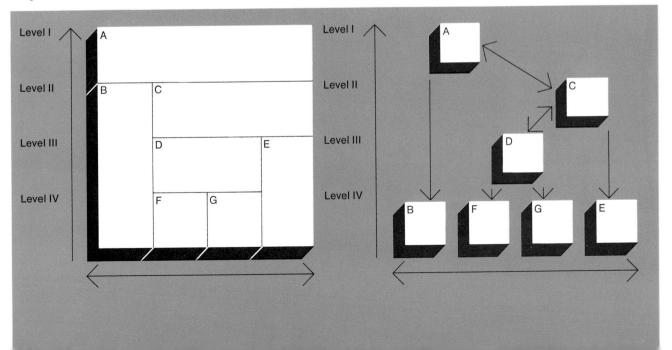

Model 4. A Partial Folk Taxonomy of "Something to Eat." The vertical single-headed arrow indicates the dimension of hierarchical inclusion; the horizontal double-headed arrow indicates the dimension of contrast. Try extending the taxonomy yourself. Where would "stew" fit? How about "salami grinder"? "Roast turkey"?

(for example, ''toasted,'' ''on plain bread,''); it is also itself a sub-category of ''sandwich,'' which includes other subcategories on the same level as ''BLT'' (such as ''tuna fish,'' ''grilled cheese,'' and so on); furthermore, ''sandwich'' is itself a subcategory of ''something to eat'' and contrasts at its level with such other categories as ''steak dinner'' and ''pizza.''

What we have been doing, essentially, is to begin construct-ing a *taxonomy,* which is a set of categories that are related to each other hierarchically. (''BLT'' is included in ''sandwich,'' ''sandwich'' is included in ''something to eat,'' but the reverse is not true.) *Folk taxonomies* are the particular taxonomies that cultures use to relate their cognitive categories (as opposed, say, to scientific taxonomies of such things as the animal kingdom, the plants, and so on). The taxonomy we have been working on is the folk taxonomy of Ameri-can English categories of ''something to eat.'' Although our analysis of this folk taxonomy is by no means complete, it is obvious that it is quite complicated and involves at least four (and probably several more) *levels of contrast.*

At the lowest level of contrast we find such things as ''toasted'' versus ''on plain bread.'' The next higher level includes ''BLT,'' ''tuna fish,'' and all other varieties of ''sandwich.'' (No doubt the various kinds of ''pizza'' would be placed at this level of con-trast. Try it out yourself.) Immediately above this level is the level that includes ''sandwich,'' ''pizza,'' and so forth. All these are sub-sumed under the highest level we have so far identified—that is, ''something to eat,'' which itself contrasts (probably) with ''inedible.'' At every horizontal level of the taxonomy the categories of the tax-onomy (or *taxa,* as they are properly called) are thus seen to con-trast with one another: hence the term ''levels of contrast.'' As we move vertically up the taxonomy, however, instead of the rela-tionship of contrast we are dealing with the relationship of inclu-sion.

Cognitive categories have other types of relationships to one another. One such relationship is the *part-whole relationship,* which is often confused with the *relationship of inclusion* of the taxonomy proper. This relationship may be illustrated by our classification of parts of our anatomy. A ''finger'' is certainly part of a ''hand'' (but is not included as a subcategory of ''hand''—''left hand'' and ''right hand'' are subcategories of ''hand''). A ''hand'' is part of a ''limb'' (but is not a subcategory of ''limb'' as are ''arm'' and ''leg''). Part-whole relationships are very easily confused with the relationships of inclusion. In fact, the systems of classification of the cultures of the world usually include both—and the scientist who investigates such· folk systems (or even tries to investigate his own system of classifi-cation) must be careful to ascertain which relationship (part-whole or inclusion) is actually being employed by an informant in constructing a particular hierarchy. Most people seldom analyze their own folk hierarchies in a systematic manner, and often one classificatory system is in reality a mixture of both kinds of hierarchical relation-ships.

iii   Research (Methodology)   Once it has been established that there is a tremendous difference in the cognitive categories recog-nized by different cultures and that these categories are arranged in highly differing taxonomies and other patterns of relationship, it seems very reasonable to ponder the question: Do all adult people of the world use the same thought processes?

For a long time anthropologists and psychologists firmly believed that the answer was no: the so-called primitive peoples thought at a prerational level analogous to the ways children were believed to think. Such people as Lucien Lévy-Bruhl believed, for example, that primitives could not engage in detached logico-deductive thought, but rather interacted with the world in a manner in which thoughts and feelings were hopelessly intermixed.

In the last 15 years, this point of view has come under severe attack as an example of ethnocentric thinking. Perhaps the most famous and brilliant statement on behalf of the complexity and logico-deductive nature of "primitive" thinking is *The Savage Mind,* published in 1962 by the French anthropologist Claude Lévi-Strauss. Lévi-Strauss examined the systems of classification of many technologically less developed societies and demonstrated the logical bases for systems of classification that to previous students had appeared "mystical" and nonrational. "The savage mind is logical in the same sense and the same fashion as ours . . . its thought proceeds through understanding, not affectivity, with the aid of distinctions and oppositions, not by confusion."

In other words, Lévi-Strauss has demonstrated that no matter what categories are employed by a particular culture, thinking ultimately involves making distinctions and defining contrasts between categories—and all peoples of the world do this. He further argues that all contrasts between categories can be broken down to their most simple levels of contrast, and that at this level the contrast will be *dyadic* (that is, reduced to only one either/or possibility).

For example, let us look at a familiar object of our culture: the traffic light. Although at first glance the red (for stop), yellow (for caution), and green (for go) may appear to be a *triadic* (three-way) relationship, it can be broken down and shown to be the product of two two-way (dyadic) relationships. That is, there are two dimensions of contrast each with two poles (or possibilities). One dimension is *caution* (yellow) versus *no caution* (red means *stop*—thus no caution is necessary; green means *go*—also without the necessity of caution); the other dimension is *stop* (red) versus *go* (green).

In his insistence that it is the underlying structural relationships between categories that are the crucial aspect of human thought (rather than the categories themselves), Lévi-Strauss has been joined by an ever-increasing number of scholars in different disciplines: Jean Piaget in psychology, Roman Jakobson and Noam Chomsky in linguistics, Roland Barthes in literary criticism, and so forth. This point of view is called *structuralism* and is one of the vital and invigorating movements in the scholarly world today.

Recent painstaking research by cultural anthropologists such as Oswald Werner (for example, that reported in his "Ethnoscience 1972") has further strengthened the position of those who claim that thought processes are panhuman in their nature. This research has focused on eliciting the folk classificatory systems of diverse cultures and then asking the informants questions based on the logical principles of Western thought—that is, based on the syllogism. In

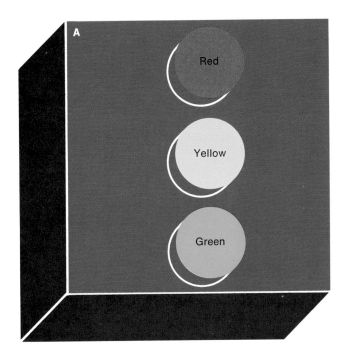

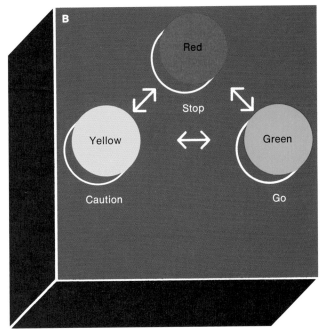

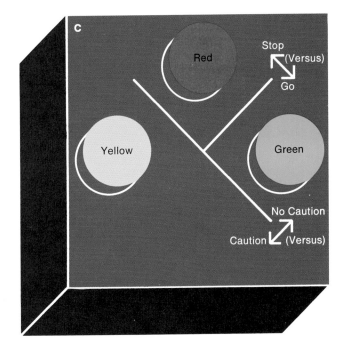

Model 5. Surface Contents and Underlying Structural Relationships.
The traffic signal *(A)* apparently involves a triadic relationship *(B)* among
the three colors and their associated meanings. However, the apparent
triad *(B)* can be analyzed as resulting from the intersection of two dyadic or bi-
polar dimensions *(C): (1) caution* versus *no caution* and (2) *stop* versus *go.*

other words, informants were asked to confirm or disconfirm conclusions that followed from their own categories if one used the Western mode of logical deduction. So far researchers have reported 100 percent agreement between the conclusions that would be drawn on the basis of Western logical thought when applied to these folk classifications and the conclusions drawn by the informants themselves. This fact further substantiates the point of view that no matter what categories one happens to be using, all adult people—regardless of their culture—use the same logical rules for examining the relationships between their categories.

iv Evaluation Recent investigations have demonstrated that all adults do think with the same mental processes no matter which culture they have been brought up in. They do not necessarily think about the same things; but the processes involved in making distinctions in terms of oppositions or arranging cognitive categories in terms of taxonomies of hierarchical inclusion and part-whole relationships are the thought processes all human beings make use of, regardless of the cultural source of the items being thought about.

3 Overview

This unit has shown that the concept of culture can be used to analyze human social groups both in relation to other groups and also to the natural environment. Culture is a system of knowledge that interrelates with other systems like the economic system and the political system.

There are many different human groups in this world, each with its own culture. Each group passes its culture on to the next generation and so ensures the survival of the group beyond the lifetime of any individual member. Culture thus exhibits a constancy —a stability—over time. But, like any other system, culture is also in a constant state of flux. As an adaptive mechanism it must continually meet new situations and modify accordingly. And it is not simply handed down from parents to children. As Margaret Mead argues in her study of contemporary American society, *Culture and Commitment* (1970), a society's young people may well be their parents' teachers—especially in societies undergoing rapid social change, because the young people are adapting more quickly to the changes than their elders. Culture is thus both tenacious in perpetuating traditional patterns and flexible in meeting new conditions for human survival. Cultures that are too specialized lose this flexibility and thus have less evolutionary potential than more generalized cultures.

Although there are a very great number of cultures and although each culture provides for its adherents a unique perspective on the nature of the universe (that is, a unique world view), underneath the level of the different cultural contents all adult human minds share the same fundamental structures and operate using the same processes. All human beings are the result of the evolution of the species. There is a panhuman, shared, "collective body." Although every human body is different, there is a basic, underlying structure that characterizes all human bodies (and differentiates human bodies from the bodies of other animals). So too with the mind. Every culture provides different inputs of contents, every individual has a unique set of life experiences; but the dynamic processes of the mind are panhuman, shared, collective.

The concept of cultural relativism is of critical importance in understanding the behavior of people from different cultural backgrounds, and the remarkable mosaic of cultures constitutes the world's richest resource. But these abundant and important differences must not obscure the fact that all human beings share with each other fundamental human characteristics, such as a long gestation period in their mother's womb, a long period of infantile dependency, the acquisition of a vast amount of knowledge and ability as they learn to speak and gradually assimilate their culture, the ability logically to order and correlate whatever ideas their culture provides, an ability to reflect back upon themselves (to search their souls), and the omnipresent (but often avoided) awareness of their inevitable death.

What are the various ways in different cultures that old people define themselves as useful?

1 Interview:
Edward H. Spicer

Edward H. Spicer, president of the American Anthropological Association, is professor of anthropology at the University of Arizona in Tucson. He is author of *Human Problems in Technological Change, Cycles of Conquest,* and *Plural Society in the Southwest.* His research focuses on questions of ethnic identity and acculturation in the American Southwest, Mexico, Spain, and Ireland.

DPG   *What do you consider to be the social responsibility of the scientist who does research on the ways people live?*
SPICER   There are a whole series of such responsibilities, but I think responsibility to the people studied takes priority over all the others.

DPG   *Does that imply that the people studied should have a say in the decisions made about the materials and the use to which they are put?*
SPICER   The use of the material—the final product of a piece of research—can hardly be restricted in any way. If you take the position that it should be restricted, then you always come back to the question of who determines the restrictions. I do think that the people studied should have the opportunity to participate in the planning of the research if they care to. That doesn't mean participation in the formulation of the particular scientific objectives, but in the way in which those objectives are pursued. I think here it's important to have some kind of reciprocal interaction between the investigator and the people being studied.

DPG   *Do you think that such interaction is usually the case in social research?*
SPICER   More and more research by anthropologists is being carried on in this way—with some kind of reciprocity in planning. In the past, however, many anthropologists made no attempt to introduce this

element into the research process. All kinds of captive subjects, like Indians on the reservations, have been turning against anthropology, largely because there was a violation of basic ethical principles in the past. Probably one of the classic examples is that of the Pueblo Indians in New Mexico. There was a great deal of cloak-and-dagger anthropological study until recently. The Pueblos built up defenses against anthropologists—excluded them. But I think this hostility is moderating now. Anthropologists recognize the rights of the Pueblos.

DPG   *There's a lot being written nowadays on the value system—or lack of it—of the wider American society. Could you comment on what you see as the constellation of values operating in American society today and what developments are possible in the future?*
SPICER   I see several different value systems in terms of which people's lives are focused in the United States. The Navaho value system is an example. Then there's what I call the old-fashioned modernization culture—industrialization and the acceptance of a whole series of values in connection with it. There's also the value system that could, in a superficial sense, be labeled the counterculture.

DPG   *Do you believe that the counterculture is a systematic oppositional force?*
SPICER   It may be systematic in the sense one might use the term in systems analysis, but it's not systematic in the sense that it's organized with a high degree of social solidarity and cultural integration. It has periods of cohesiveness, and then it seems to disintegrate into several parts. The industrial, technological value focus, on the other hand, seems to have a different kind of base that carries it along, although it's also subject to periodic disintegration in terms of its social organization—like that experienced in the Depression, for instance.

DPG   *Do you share the apparently widespread concern about the liberalization of moral standards in American society—a sort of hedonistic input that probably did not characterize our society in the 1950s?*
SPICER   I think that that kind of thing is an accompaniment to the breakdown of local communities, to the weakening of small-

scale social ties. It's a product of the strong tendencies for individualization in our society. In themselves, tendencies like the spread of pornography don't seem to me to be a very big threat. They're symptoms of something much deeper—a general loss of interest on the part of the individual tied up with the whole industrialization complex. The work value, a major value orientation, had changed. Work is dehumanizing today; it's not interesting. It's been broken down into simple units and then reorganized purely on the basis of the efficiency of production. Things are put together on a shoddy basis without regard to either the satisfaction of the worker or the lasting satisfaction of the user.

DPG   *In many of the more traditional, smaller societies these problems probably haven't emerged yet. Do you have any thoughts of the inevitability and meaning of the disappearance of traditional societies?*
SPICER   I take issue first with calling such societies traditional. I think we now have a well-established, traditional, industrial society in the United States. We have technological traditions, for example, and they really ought to be put in the same category as the customs of everyone in the world. But cultures have been disappearing all through the human experience. We can't assume that any culture that exists today has existed for longer than a few centuries at most. The disappearance or the change of any culture is inevitable—the real questions are how they will change and who will have a say in directing that change.

DPG   *One generally thinks of "modernization" when one speaks of change in traditional societies. Do you think modernization should be pushed in all areas of the world?*
SPICER   If you mean what I call "traditional modernization"—straight industrialization—the answer is a simple no. Neither would I advocate pushing the kind of modernization that includes reactions against the traditional type—antipollution activities, save-the-environment campaigns and so on. I don't think any modern cultural or technological development should be imposed from above or outside. That means

that a highway through the Brazilian wilderness should not be built unless the hitherto isolated groups that it will impinge upon have an opportunity to participate in the planning process.

DPG   *Even if that would conceivably slow down the building of the road for 50 years?*
SPICER   I think 50 years is no time at all when you consider that these small isolated groups can be destroyed as societies. That kind of destruction involves ignoring a certain people's values.

DPG   *Are you really arguing then that you have an overriding ethical notion that people should have the power to make decisions that affect their lives?*
SPICER   That's right. And I think this concept takes precedence over the values that derive from technological advance.

DPG   *Do you think your ethical concerns are being actualized or overridden in the process of social change?*
SPICER   Both processes are going on. Look at Title IX of the Equal Opportunity Act, the one that called for the "maximum, feasible participation of the poor" in the antipoverty programs. The principle was revolutionary at the time. Its application has been variable—some local governments have adapted or modified it; some have circumvented it. But it's had tremendous influence. On the Navaho reservation, its impact is almost incalculable. The extension of participation to the local community proceeded in a way that hadn't been approached since the Bureau of Indian Affairs programs started. The principle of participation has been followed in other areas too—the community-development programs sponsored by the United Nations and various national governments in Latin America and elsewhere.

DPG   *So you see the principle in operation, but you also believe that social change falls short of the ideal in many cases.*
SPICER   Definitely. In many cases social change is brought about by a change in specific material conditions—building a dam, for example. The decision is often made only at the top level. Local people are simply expected to adapt to the new conditions. It doesn't have to be this way, though. In Mexico, for example, the nation-state has made local participation a basic consideration in its efforts to bring people into the technological age. I'm talking about the *ejido* system of land holding, which was introduced during the Mexican Revolution as a reaction to the big landlord system of the nineteenth century. The *ejido* system is based on collective ownership of pieces of land and the collective management of agricultural production. The whole country is committed to the system—no politician who wanted to abolish it could get elected.

DPG   *The traditional anthropologist has focused on the more isolated societies. This situation is changing, as you know. Urban anthropology is now respectable. Do you have any thoughts about priorities for social-science research in the next decade?*
SPICER   I think there should be several focuses in anthropology, including the older tendency to concentrate on what were regarded as simpler, rather remote societies. I'll mention one that I think has been neglected: the nature of systems of ethnic relations in modern nations. This work is urgently needed to provide perspective to managers of modern nations in dealing with the issues of political versus ethnic advantage and the importance of ethnic systems of relations for any kind of development and planning. I'm thinking here about practical problems that are sensationalized—for example, the situation in Ireland. Of course, the peasant societies and the transitional societies should be studied. But not because they're about to disappear. All social systems are about to disappear—including our own.

Unit 5

Socialization and Moral Development

Socialization is the process by which an individual, usually during childhood, learns and adopts the behavior patterns and norms appropriate for his social environment. Moral development is one of socialization's most crucial aspects.

Although all societies socialize their children, the process differs in form and content from one culture to another.

In the United States socialization by the family is complemented by contacts with peer groups, schools, and the mass media. The process does not prepare individuals successfully for adolescence or old age.

Three questions deal with various aspects of the socialization process: (1) How important is social interaction for the development of the individual? (2) What part does emotional and psychosexual development play in the process? (3) How do people acquire their beliefs about right and wrong?

Early in this century Charles Horton Cooley and George Herbert Mead argued that man is the product of his social interactions and developed the concepts of the *looking-glass self* and the *generalized other* to describe socialization. More recent studies have confirmed their views.

Sigmund Freud's description of psychosexual development profoundly influenced later thinking about personality formation. Erik Erikson extended Freud's ideas, stressing identity confusion. These psychological analyses have shown that even the most private and individual aspects of human life can have meaning only in their social context.

The psychologist Jean Piaget conducted empirical investigations that showed that moral development is both a cognitive and a social process. Lawrence Kohlberg suggested a more subtle set of moral stages. This research shows the importance of social interaction in the acquisition of morality.

Socialization is a complex process that accounts for the continuity of human society over generations and also allows for individual personality differences.

THE PROCESS OF SOCIALIZATION

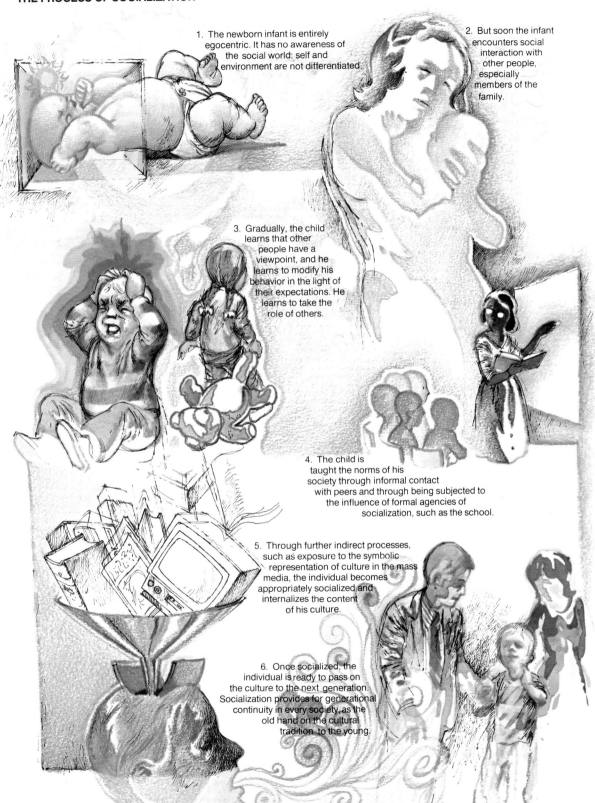

1. The newborn infant is entirely egocentric. It has no awareness of the social world: self and environment are not differentiated.

2. But soon the infant encounters social interaction with other people, especially members of the family.

3. Gradually, the child learns that other people have a viewpoint, and he learns to modify his behavior in the light of their expectations. He learns to take the role of others.

4. The child is taught the norms of his society through informal contact with peers and through being subjected to the influence of formal agencies of socialization, such as the school.

5. Through further indirect processes, such as exposure to the symbolic representation of culture in the mass media, the individual becomes appropriately socialized and internalizes the content of his culture.

6. Once socialized, the individual is ready to pass on the culture to the next generation. Socialization provides for generational continuity in every society, as the old hand on the cultural tradition to the young.

B   DEFINITION AND CONTEXT

1   Definition

Man is a social animal. Yet the human infant enters the world not as a social being, but simply as a biological organism. Only through a long process can he cease to be merely animal and become fully human—that is, a person with values, attitudes, goals, patterns of behavior, a notion of who and what he is. Basic *biological givens* underlie the *personalities* that later emerge, but heredity supplies only the needs, potential capabilities, and limitations of the human organism. Even the basic drives of hunger and sex are general and undirected: they need reshaping through *cultural definitions* into socially approved channels.

Socialization is the process by which an individual learns and adopts the behavior patterns and norms appropriate for his social environment. Sometimes the term is applied to the process by which a newcomer is acculturated to a group, as when a person learns to be a teacher, a soldier or a convict. But usually socialization refers to the process by which children internalize the norms of their society, develop individual personalities, and learn to behave appropriately—to identify objects, to attach meanings to events, to use language, to tie shoelaces or harpoon whales, to respect taboos, rights, and wrongs. Indeed, the moral development of the individual is one of the most crucial elements in socialization, for social living is based on general internalization of shared moral imperatives governing behavior.

Two characteristics make human beings uniquely receptive to the socialization process. The first is the fact that in the early years of life humans have a much longer period of helplessness and dependence on the adult than any other animal does. The second is that language gives them the capacity to create and use an infinite system of symbols. The complexity of human culture is largely based on this capacity for *linguistic symbolism*, and most socialization takes place through the medium of language.

2   World Context

All societies socialize their children. Yet the *cultural content* of each society—its language, its roles, its skills, its traditions, its norms—is different. Hence the form and content of socialization are different in every society, although the underlying focus is the same. The *norms* of each society vary in content. In the United States, for example, it is considered highly improper for people to expose their bodies, and public nudity is associated with feelings of guilt and shame. In many other societies partial or full nudity is the norm, and feelings of guilt are inconceivable in such a context. In the United States it is considered quite acceptable to lick an ice cream cone in public, but in parts of Africa the extrusion of the tongue involved is highly offensive to decent people. The sociologist, then, often finds it convenient to analyze socialization in terms of the society in which it takes place: to be socialized for one society does not necessarily mean that one is appropriately socialized for another.

Three generations of an American Indian family. In many technologically less developed societies the elderly were a valuable resource. In them reposed the detailed knowledge of tribal lore, values, and cosmology, which they passed on to the young in a loving and mutually gratifying manner.

Another difference between societies lies in the varying *personality types* that children are implicitly urged to copy. In some parts of the world an aggressive, assertive temperament is considered highly appropriate and is rewarded; in other societies a pacific, gentle personality is the ideal. It follows that in some societies the aggressive individual will be considered maladjusted, whereas in other societies he will be the product of successful socialization.

A third difference lies in the *agencies of socialization* that operate in each society. In most societies *the family* is the initial and the most important of these agencies. Although its structure varies considerably across cultures, the family is invariably the primary group to which the responsibility for the care of the young is assigned. And the family does not tend merely to the physical needs of the infant; it assumes the task of teaching moral rules and social skills as well. In small-scale traditional societies the only other significant agency of socialization is the clan or tribe itself. There is little *generational discontinuity* in such societies; knowledge reposes in the older generation, which has a powerful and honored place in the community, and socialization consists broadly of the handing on of the cultural tradition from one generation to the next.

When traditional societies encounter change, however—as is happening today in those parts of the less developed world where urbanization and industrialization are taking place—members of the younger generation find themselves poorly socialized for their new roles. Much of their earlier experience is irrelevant or dysfunctional, and new agencies of socialization—particularly the schools—assume greater importance. In the complex societies of the modern world there are multiple agencies of socialization and a variety of *subcultures* into which the individual can become socialized. In such societies, where the individual is confronted with a range of models, goals, choices, and changing situations, socialization is a complex and always partially incomplete process.

3 American Context

The United States is an extremely complex society: there are many regional, ethnic, religious, and age-based subcultures, and the society as a whole is in a state of continual flux associated with technological change. One consequence of these features of American life is the number of agencies of socialization that operate to create a mosaic of cultural forms.

The *peer group* complements the family in the socialization of the individual. Initially the peer group socializes the child into the world of young children and adolescents, and into the particular values that these age groups hold. In these early contacts with peers the individual learns to modify his behavior so that he is accepted by others, and he learns to acknowledge the impersonal authority of the group as well as the personal authority of parents. But the individual continues to learn from peer groups for as long as he lives, for in American society each individual will fill many roles in his or her life—as pupil, Boy Scout, student, lumberjack, secretary, housewife, salesman, retired person.

A further important agency of socialization in America is the *school*. The heterogeneous complexity and technological sophistication of the United States make a long period of formal education necessary so that the young can be taught those elements of the culture whose acquisition cannot be left to chance: for example, how to read and write—or, at higher levels, how to be a doctor or engineer. American schools are formal bureaucratic structures designed to produce individuals who emerge with socially approved additions and modifications to their knowledge and behavior. The schools are oriented to middle-class values, and the teachers themselves are largely drawn from the middle class. Thus the norms of the school are often at variance with those the non-middle-class child has learned from his family and his peer group, and the school may counteract or conflict with earlier trends in the socialization of the individual. This effect of decreasing individual differences and reinforcing responses and goals felt to be consistent

Two children's bedrooms. Children from chronically impoverished families are at a competitive disadvantage in the mass, bureaucratized school systems of this country, which are oriented toward the white, middle-class population.

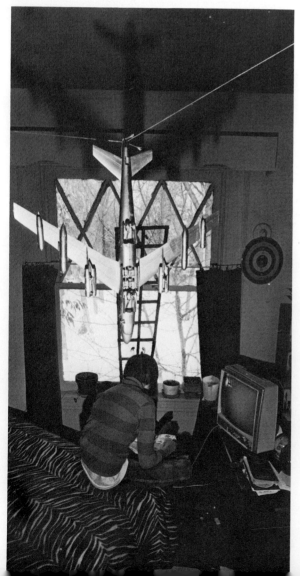

with middle-class norms is achieved not only through the formal curriculum, but also, and perhaps more importantly, through the child's *incidental learning* of attitudes toward authority, of conceptions of right and wrong.

Other important agencies for socialization in America are the *mass media.* Americans own more television and radio sets per capita than any other nation on earth. In many American homes the TV is turned on throughout the waking hours of the family, and viewing takes up approximately one-sixth of the waking hours of the average American between the ages of 3 and 16. Furthermore, newspapers, magazines, comics, and movies reach everyone. From these diverse sources, with their advertisements, stories, details of the lives of heroes, rock singers, and actors, the individual learns the elements of the popular culture.

Socialization in America is markedly unsuccessful in two areas. Americans are ill-prepared for *adolescence,* which is often a time of turmoil and confusion. A total ban on sex is imposed in childhood, but later in life this internalized prohibition must be unlearned. It is not surprising that the process is often marked by feelings of doubt and guilt. Similarly, the young are taught formal rather than actual rules of conduct. When adolescents observe how far short the real society falls from the ideal notions with which they were imbued, they often react with cynicism, confusion, or anger.

American socialization also fails to prepare the individual adequately for *old age.* The current premium placed on youth and the lack of a clearly defined and honorable status for the old (an increasingly significant number of whom live more than one-fourth of their lives beyond the age of 65) make the acceptance of one's role as one of the aged difficult. The discontinuity between the cultures of young and old in the United States aggravates this problem. In traditional societies the experience and wisdom of the old make them valuable members of the community; but in the United States today a person socialized as much as half a century ago is unlikely to have much to offer that is not regarded as hopelessly outdated by the young.

A large variety of *total institutions* exist in the contemporary United States—such as the armed forces, prisons, orphanages, sanitaria, and asylums and hospitals for the mentally ill. In these institutions a systematic if unintended *resocialization* takes place. In *Asylums* (1961) Erving Goffman has described the process as involving isolation from the outside world, spending all day in the company of the same people, shedding all possessions and identity, breaking with past existence, and losing freedom of action.

C QUESTIONS AND EVIDENCE

1 Questions

Three sets of questions deal with various aspects of the socialization process. (1) How important is social interaction for the development of the individual? How is this influence brought to bear? (2) How does emotional and psychosexual development take

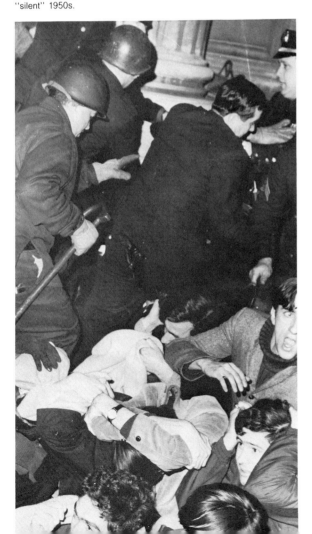

Police break up student sit-in at Columbia University in 1968. Social scientists failed to predict the student unrest of the 1960s, nor have they fully explained it after the fact. Subsequently, social scientists in the late 1960s predicted more of the then-current unrest for the 1970s—and were, on the whole, quite mistaken. The 1970s are unfolding with a great flourish of student inactivity reminiscent of the ''silent'' 1950s.

Entering the military. The armed forces are total institutions with resocializing rituals of transition for moving the recruit from his civilian identity as an individual to his new identity as a "nameless," replaceable cog in the military machine.

place? What part does society play in this process? (3) How do people acquire beliefs about right and wrong? What is the basis for their judgments?

2 Evidence

a The "Burning Issue" Question

i Context A decade ago a favorite topic in high school debates and college freshman examinations was the "nature-nurture" argument: Which is more important, environment or heredity? The question has since been recognized as pointless. It is now appreciated that both elements are significant, but that neither can be seen as the main or sole factor affecting the socialization of the individual. Instead, attention is now focused on how individual and society interact to produce the results that they do. How amenable to cultural modeling is man? Is he passively shaped by his society? Does he participate in the process in some way? What role do his fellow men play? The basic question is: *In what ways do society and individuals interact in the process of socialization?*

ii Theory The view that man creates society was firmly implanted by early political philosophers. In *Leviathan* (1651) Thomas Hobbes spelled out his theory of the *social contract.* Early man, said Hobbes, had lived in an age of aggressive, selfish individualism; the result was that life was "solitary, poor, nasty, brutish, and short." Because this state of constant conflict could not endure, men contracted by mutual consent to form a society and to submit to its authority for their own good. John Locke somewhat later put forward a similar contract theory, although he placed less stress on man's innately brutish nature. He saw society and government as being constructed by rational men for their convenience and emphasized the natural dignity of man and his right to rebel against central authority that grew too tyrannical.

In the early twentieth century the sociological perspective presented an alternative to this view. Charles Horton Cooley and George Herbert Mead argued that society creates man—that man is a social product, the result of interaction between the human organism and the society into which it is born. In *Human Nature and the Social Order* (1902) Cooley formulated the concept of the *looking-glass self* to describe this process. We all imagine ourselves as we appear to the minds of others. Each of us examines this concept of another's judgment and modifies his own behavior accordingly. Thus other people define us; we learn our identity from them and modify that identity under the influence of the sentiments and judgments we impute to them. Socialization, argued Cooley, depends on this socially learned capacity to be an object to oneself, as in a mirror image. Cooley believed that the individual and society arise in the same process: "A separate individual is an abstraction unknown to experience, and so likewise is society when regarded as something apart from individuals." Human society is simply a series of interactions among individuals, and the individual personality is the product of these *social interactions.*

Cooley's views were carried a great deal further by George Herbert Mead, who founded the school of social psychology now known as *symbolic interactionism.* Although Mead loathed literary composition and never wrote a book, his students at the University of Chicago realized the importance of his ideas and published their own transcripts of his lectures (*Mind, Self, and Society*, 1934). Mead particularly stressed the role of language in learning and socialization: language gives the child a *mind*, the capacity to think and to engage in symbolic interaction with others. The child, by taking on the *roles* of others (initially through imitating the parents), gradually learns to think and feel the way other people do. At first the child will adopt the viewpoint only of particular others—specific relatives or friends or *significant others*. But eventually the child will adopt the view of *the generalized other*—that is, will develop a less specific notion of the expectations and attitudes of others in his society. The individual internalizes social attitudes—the attitudes not only of his parents, but of his society as a whole. Mead distinguished between the *I*—the spontaneous, natural, self-interested self—and the *me*—the socialized self imbued with the norms of the community and aware of the individual's obligation to society as a whole.

iii Research Investigations in this area face an obvious methodological problem. It would be unethical to deprive "test-case" children of the advantages of a warm and encouraging early environment simply to see what effect, if any, this deprivation has on personality and development. Evidence is accordingly much more circumstantial and derives from three main sources: case studies of so-called feral (wild) children; investigations of children who have been raised in total institutions, such as orphanages; and studies of other animals, particularly primates.

Illustration of Mead's concepts of the "I" and the "me."

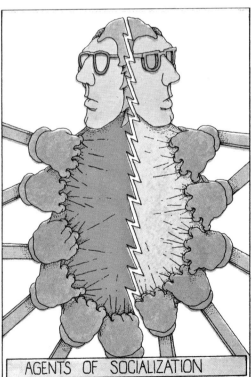

AGENTS OF SOCIALIZATION

The label ''feral'' is used because of dubiously authenticated reports of children brought up by wild animals (''wolf boys'' and ''ape boys''), but attention is focused today on children who are for some reason *social isolates*. As a result of abandonment or parental neglect, they have sustained only a minimum of human contact. Kingsley Davis studied two such children in *Human Society* (1949). One of them was an illegitimate girl raised by a deaf-mute mother and kept in a dark room until the age of six and a half years; she was incapable of human speech, reacted to strangers with hostility and fear, and could only grunt and crawl around on all fours. A second child of similar age was not only unable to speak, but could not even make any move for herself and seemed completely apathetic and emotionless. Neither had any mind as we know it, and both seemed scarcely human. Initially, the two girls were considered feeble-minded, but after two years of careful attention, they made considerable progress in socialization, learning to speak and to relate to others in a relatively normal fashion.

Evidence from institutions for young children also strongly suggests that when sustained human affection is not provided for the young, the process of socialization is considerably impeded. René Spitz, in an article on ''Hospitalism'' (1945), found that institutionalized children deprived of social stimulation and maternal affec-

Statue of Romulus and Remus, mythical founders of the city of Rome, being suckled by a wolf. Classical mythology contains many instances of children reared by wolves and other animals after they have been cast into the wilds. These children, combining as they do the best of both the animal and the human, usually go on to achieve great feats in the legends. In reality, however, children raised without frequent human interaction are severely damaged, and if their deprivation has been great enough, they may not even learn to speak when they are taken out of the ''feral'' situation.

tion suffered severe emotional and physical disabilities, even though the standard of facilities in the institution was good. The lack of cuddling and interaction seemed crucial, and it was precisely this attention that the nurses did not have the time to provide. The children, suggested Spitz, were subject to a very high mortality rate and those that survived were emotionally and intellectually deprived and socially inadequate.

Numerous studies have tended to confirm Spitz's findings. William Goldfarb's "Psychological Privation in Infancy and Subsequent Adjustment" (1945), which traced the later development of children from institutions, indicated that even when the children are adopted into more stimulating foster homes, they continue to be more retarded mentally, more aggressive, more dependent, more distractible, and more hyperactive than a control group; they also appear emotionally cold and capable of only superficial human relationships. Researchers have attributed these and similar social inadequacies in large measure to the lack of a secure social relationship in infancy.

Harry F. Harlow has conducted extensive research on rhesus monkeys, rearing these subjects away from their mothers and their peers. His article "Social Deprivation in Monkeys" (1962) showed that such animals are socially inadequate, display bizarre mannerisms reminiscent of human psychotics, are unable to mate, and if artificially inseminated prove to be unloving and even abusive mothers. Animal studies must always be treated with caution: monkeys are not people, and the results are not necessarily applicable to other primate species. But Harlow's findings are consistent with other evidence on the effects that lack of social interaction has on the development of personality and the socialization of the individual.

iv   Evaluation   Human socialization is a complex process that is not fully understood. Yet the evidence is overwhelming that, without social interaction, the existence of a human being in any sense in which we understand that term is impossible. Not only do we learn the specific content of our culture from our social environment; we also learn to become ourselves.

The collective product of man's activity is *culture,* which includes the language and symbols with which man shapes his social relations. In fully successful socialization there is a symmetry between the objective world of society and the subjective world of the individual. In fact, this symmetry is never fully achieved, particularly in a complex society like the United States. For although all persons are socialized, each person is different. The child is always somewhat resistant to the effects of the social environment, and every person remains to some extent unpredictable. None of us is totally molded by social convention, though all of us owe our essential humanity to socialization.

b   The "Classical" Question

i   Context   Our emotional and psychosexual development largely defines the kind of individuals we become. But what role does the social environment play in the development of our *affective relations* with others? If early experience is of prime importance, such traits as hostility, rejection, optimism, initiative, ambition, or withdrawal

Monkey love for a mother-surrogate. Higher primates have an innate need for interaction. These photos show macaque and rhesus monkeys at the University of Wisconsin Regional Primate Research Center clinging to warm terry-cloth "mother surrogates." The monkey at the top right is reaching for milk on a bare-wire surrogate.

may have their foundations in infancy. This area is one where social scientists from several disciplines have a contribution to make; sociologists will call on the perspectives of the psychologist—the social psychologist in particular—to answer the question: *What is the role of social experience in the psychosexual and affective development of the human individual?*

ii   Theory   Any consideration of human psychosexual and emotional development must start from the work of the psychologist Sigmund Freud. His ideas have profoundly influenced not only subsequent psychoanalytic theory, but also many of the "common sense" notions about people that abound in our own culture today.

Freud's theory of personality development was based on a conflict between the self and society. Especially in *Civilization and its Discontents* (1930), he described the continual tension between the demands of society for compliance with its codes of right and wrong and the individual's instincts for self-indulgence and independence. The manner in which the individual handles this con-

Life-Cycle Stage	Approximate Ages	Most Significant Others	Major Dilemmas
Infancy	0–12 Months	Mother	Affective Gratification/ Sensorimotor Experiencing
Early Childhood	1–2 Years	Mother, Father	Compliance/ Self-control
Oedipal Period	3–5 Years	Father, Mother, Siblings, Playmates	Expressivity/ Instrumentality
Later Childhood	6–11 Years	Parents, Same Sex Peers, Teachers	Peer Relation-ships/ Evaluated Abilities
Early Adolescence	12–15 Years	Parents, Same Sex Peers, Opposite Sex Peers, Teachers	Acceptance/ Achievement
Later Adolescence	16–20 Years	Same Sex Peers, Opposite Sex Peers, Parents, Teachers, Loved One, Wife or Husband	Intimacy/ Autonomy
Young Adulthood	21–29 Years	Loved One, Husband, or Wife, Children, Employers, Friends	Connection/Self-Determination
Early Maturity	30–44 Years	Wife or Husband, Children, Superiors, Colleagues, Friends, Parents	Stability/ Accomplishment
Full Maturity	45 to Retirement Age	Wife or Husband, Children, Colleagues, Friends, Younger Associates	Dignity/Control
Old Age	Retirement Age to Death	Remaining Family, Long-term Friends, Neighbours	Meaningful Integration/ Autonomy

Table 1. Stage-Developmental Model of the Ideal-Typical Life Cycle in Contemporary, Urban, Middle-Class United States, With Approximate Ages, the Most Significant Other Persons, and the Major Dilemmas of Value-Theme Differentiation and Integration. (Source: Gordon, "Role and Value Development Across the Life Cycle")

flict largely determines the contours of personality and behavior.

Most human motivation, Freud argued, lies hidden in the subconscious forces that largely determine our thoughts and actions, our values and fears. He divided the self into three categories, each characterized by a special role or function it performs for the individual: the id, the ego, and the superego. The *id* is the reservoir of infantile pleasure-seeking drives and instincts—the deep unconscious desires that demand instant satisfaction. The *superego* is a form of conscience for the individual; it comprises the internalized authority of society (especially as represented by the parents) and works through shame and pride to mold the individual to social ideals. The *ego* is the conscious part of the self; it attempts to mediate rationally between the chaotic and childish impulses of the id and the highly self-critical and repressive responses of the superego, and thus it brings about a continuous bargain between the individual's need for a certain amount of self-gratification and his need to exist day by day in the real world with a minimum amount of friction between himself and the social order. Self and society are often in oppostition, with socialization imposing great sacrifices on man's urges, particularly those for sexual satisfaction and aggressive outlets. But the balance achieved within the three components of the personality, on the one hand, and between the tripartite self and the environment, on the other, is the basis for personality development.

Freud's account of personality formation centered on the early years: most subsequent personality disturbances, he felt, were based on early childhood *repressions,* often of forbidden sexual wishes. Freud believed that psychosexual development began in early infancy and progressed through a series of stages in which the center of sensual interest shifted from one part of the body to another; many personality characteristics were formed during this period, which continues until early adolescence. In the first year, Freud believed, the infant is at the *oral stage:* the action of the mouth gives a great deal of sensual satisfaction. In the second and third years of life is the *anal stage,* in which pleasure is derived from the rectal and anal area and the retention and expulsion of feces. From ages 3 to 4, during the *phallic stage,* the prime sensual pleasure is derived from manipulation of the sexual organs. During this stage arises the *Oedipus complex,* which occurs in the fourth and fifth years of life. The young boy develops sexual desires for his mother and views his father as a rival. He senses his father's hostility (sometimes through the fear that the father will castrate him) and resolves his tension by identifying with the father and repressing both his sexuality and the memory of his childhood sexuality. Freud made little attempt to apply this stage to girls, although he did experiment with a parallel theory (the "Electra complex").

From ages 6 to 11 a *latency stage* continues the sexual repression that occurred in the previous stage. Finally, from about 11 onwards is the *genital stage;* this stage marks the beginning of the period of normal adult genital sexuality. If the social environment is inappropriate or not supportive, however, an individual may *fixate* at a particular stage; or he may find the stresses of a later stage too great, and may *regress,* much later in life, to an earlier stage.

iii Research (Survey)   Perhaps the most influential of the recent theoretical accounts of psychosexual development is that of Erik Erikson, a psychologist who works in the Freudian tradition. Erikson's ideas constitute important innovations in psychoanalytic theory, but he does not reject or ignore the major contribution made by Freud. His work does stress, however, the particular problems of both adolescents and adults in contemporary society. Furthermore, Erikson emphasizes the social experience of the adolescent and the adult as being vitally important in the continuing development of personality throughout life. In this respect he modifies Freud's greater emphasis on the importance of childhood experience in later personality development and behavior.

Erikson's early experience as a Freudian analyst led him to doubt the adequacy of his theoretical tools. Many of his subjects seemed to have a problem of *identity* that was related more to the sense of self and the cultural environment than to sexual drives. They had apparently lost the sense of who and what they were, and what their goals in life should be. The main problem, Erikson determined, was "identity confusion," not sexual neurosis.

Erikson presented his conclusions in *Childhood and Society* (1950). In that book he argues that, in addition to the *psychosexual stages* of development outlined by Freud, there is a series of *psychosocial stages,* in each of which the individual has to establish new orientations both to the self and to the world. Personality development, Erikson feels, continues throughout the *life cycle,* through a series of stages each of which has both a positive and a negative component. Each component is a *polar ideal:* all people are somewhere in between, with elements of both poles.

Erikson identifies eight stages in the life cycle. In each of these a new dimension of social interaction becomes possible. The stages are as follows:

1. *Trust Versus Mistrust:* This stage extends through the first year of life and involves trust at one extreme and mistrust at the other. The infant whose needs are met in a warm, consistent manner will view the world as a secure, dependable environment. The infant whose care is inconsistent and rejecting will come to mistrust his environment.
2. *Autonomy Versus Doubt:* In this stage, covering ages two to three, the child attempts to develop a sense of personal autonomy—over impulses, self, and environment. If he is encouraged and succeeds in his efforts, his autonomy is confirmed; if he is treated in an overprotective or highly critical way by his parents, he is handicapped in his efforts to achieve autonomy and experiences feelings of doubt and shame instead.
3. *Initiative Versus Guilt:* This stage extends from the ages of four to five, when the child is capable of initiating motor and social action on his own. If this initiative is reinforced, the child experiences feelings of competence; if he is made to feel that his explorations or questions are bad or stupid, he may develop a sense of guilt over his own capacities.
4. *Industry Versus Inferiority:* This stage runs from ages six to 11. The child is highly active and industrious at this time, constantly constructing ideas, objects, and situations. If these products are

rewarded, the sense of industry is enhanced; if they are discouraged and regarded as a nuisance by the parents or the school, the child may develop a sense of inferiority. From this stage onwards social institutions, as well as the family, come to influence the development of the individual.

5. *Identity Versus Role Confusion:* From roughly ages 12 to 18, the individual develops many new ways of thinking about and looking at the world; in particular, he can conceive of ideal situations and contrast them with the realities that confront him. If the adolescent has a sense of trust, autonomy, initiative, and industry, then he is likely to arrive at a meaningful self-concept and ego identity. But the young person who enters adolescence with feelings of mistrust, doubt, guilt, and inferiority is open to the risk of role confusion. The attainment of a sense of personal identity depends largely on the social milieu. Young people in the turbulent social climate of America, for example, will experience more difficulty in forming identities than their counterparts in more stable or static societies.

6. *Intimacy Versus Isolation:* This period covers young adulthood. Intimacy is the capacity to share with another person without the fear of losing the self in the process. Inability to form this bond may imply isolation for the individual—a feeling of being alone in the world without anyone with whom to share one's feelings and existence.

7. *Generativity Versus Self-Absorption:* This stage covers middle age. Generativity is a concern for others than the self—for the social world, for the future of one's children. Those who fail to achieve a sense of generativity may relapse into a self-absorbed state, in which their prime concern is their own needs and cares.

8. *Integrity Versus Despair:* This stage covers the last years of the life cycle. A feeling of integrity arises in the individual who can look back with satisfaction on his life's achievements; despair is the fate of those who regret their many mistakes and failings and can think only of what might have been.

iv Evaluation Freud's work is one of the most significant theoretical contributions to social science: its implications have been profound and have deeply influenced the way we think about ourselves and others. Yet his system has been widely criticized as fanciful in some respects and culture-bound in others. Ideas that seemed to fit the facts in his environment, late nineteenth-century Vienna, may not be as fruitful when applied elsewhere. In fact, many of Freud's theories have been modified by anthropological research, such as Bronislaw Malinowski's *Sex and Repression in Savage Society* (1927). Malinowski studied the society of the Trobriand Islanders, where the maternal uncle has the major share in the socializing and disciplining of the child. The child still lives with the parents, however, and they enjoy a monogamous sexual relationship that is often conducted with the full awareness of the child—and often in his sight. Malinowski found that a good deal of hostility was often expressed toward the uncle by the children, but seldom any toward the father. It may be, then, that any hostility to the father in our culture derives from his role as disciplinarian, rather than from sexual jealousy.

Freud may have placed too much emphasis on biological drives rather than social factors in the determination of personality, although he did give importance to the child's early social experiences. He was probably correct, however, in his assertion that many human motives are subconscious and do not necessarily harmonize with the requirements of society. Freud's notions of the id, ego, and superego represent ways of looking at personality rather than actual entities in the mind, of course, and they have proved a fruitful conceptual tool in the past. It may be, however, that new forms of analysis will be developed that will be of even greater value.

One such attempt is that of Erik Erikson. Yet his theories are also not to be taken as a literal description of all human development; they are merely a particular conceptual perspective on the problem of the human life cycle in society, a perspective whose value is to be judged in terms of its usefulness as a tool in analysis. For sociologists the particular importance of work by psychologists such as Freud and Erikson is this: that even the most private and individual aspects of human life can have meaning only in terms of the *social context* in which they originate and by which they are modified and sustained.

c   The "Research" Question

i   Context   All theories of socialization attempt to explain how the child grows—or fails to grow—into an adult who is willing to cooperate with others and make the personal sacrifices necessary for social living. But how is this orientation toward moral behavior acquired? Do people behave in a moral fashion because their society punishes those who deviate from the norms? Do they believe in or internalize the rules of acceptable social behavior, or do they evolve their own ethical principles?

Early research shed little light on this problem. In a famous experiment described in "Studies in Deceit" (1928) Hugh Hartshorne and M. A. May examined the behavior of children in a situation where there was an opportunity to cheat. Their findings were a moralist's nightmare: nearly everyone cheated. There was little correlation between cheating in one situation and another. Children's verbal responses bore no relation to their actual behavior. There was no relationship between cheating and teaching of religious values. Cheating was not a character trait; it was a situational phenomenon. Values of honesty, Hartshorne and May concluded, are relative to each class or group; there is no absolute morality, because the content of notions of right and wrong are determined by cultural values.

Other theorists, however, did not accept that the analysis of moral behavior had met a dead end, and the issue has been studied by social scientists for the past half century. The question is: *What role does social interaction play in the acquisition of moral attitudes?*

ii   Theory   A novel approach to the problem of moral behavior was developed by the Swiss philosopher and cognitive psychologist Jean Piaget. Viewing moral development as part of the general process of intellectual development, he chose to concentrate not on the behavior of his subjects, but on their reasoning. This approach proved highly fruitful and revolutionized the study of moral development.

Piaget's brilliant monograph *The Moral Judgment of the Child* (1932) recounts a series of empirical experiments he conducted with children, out of which his theories emerged. For example, when children playing with marbles were asked the origin of the rules they were following, the younger children, ages 5 to 7, saw the rules as sacred and inviolable; rules had a semimystical authority and were derived from the older children, or even from God. Later, however, the child realized that the rules were socially constructed, that they could be changed if other participants agreed, but that their purpose was to make the game possible. At first, Piaget believes, the child sees rules as absolute, external products imposed on him; later they are accepted as the product of mutual agreement.

In another experiment Piaget presented children with hypothetical situations to assess their judgments of right and wrong actions. He found that the young child can discriminate between an unintentional and a deliberate act but takes no account of this distinction in assigning blame; instead, the sheer amount of damage is crucial. Thus the person who deliberately breaks one cup is less culpable than the person who accidentally breaks six. Lies, too, are judged to be ''bad'' to the degree that they depart from the truth; no account is taken of the motives of the person who tells the untruth. Only when he grows older does the child give precedence to the intentions of others by taking their point of view and appreciating their reasoning.

When Piaget examined the child's notions of punishment and justice, he found that young children have an expiatory notion of punishment: the greater the punishment, the better. Obedience is equated with virtue, and punishment is seen as right simply because of its source—usually, the unquestioned power of the parent. The older child, however, takes a different view. Punishment is seen as a means not only to balance a misdeed, but also to deter the offender and to protect the group from a recurrence of the offense. Older children may also accept that there is no need for punishment if the offender is reformed without its application. Punishment is no longer seen as justified in itself purely because those in authority have the power to inflict it.

Piaget theorized that the morality of the young child is a *morality of constraint,* whereas that of the older person is a *morality of cooperation.* The young child has an *egocentric viewpoint:* he is unable to appreciate even that others have a point of view and has difficulty differentiating his own thinking from the events he is thinking about. His parents receive a unilateral respect; every command is an obligatory moral rule whose authority derives from its source. Whereas the young child does not see the relativity and fallibility of his own viewpoint, and fails to recognize himself as the source of the judgment that a particular authority is absolute, the older child has an awareness of other points of view and a sense that rules grow from human relationships. The morality of cooperation emerges through social contact and particularly the clash of wills with peers.

Although this child's behavior is clearly ''inappropriate'' in terms of the role-expectations that society has for the *teacher-pupil dyad* in general, it is not necessarily inappropriate in terms of the interaction between the two as individual *persons.* It is possible that this particular adult has been sufficiently unfair to this particular child to warrant this response.

Moral development, then, is both a *cognitive* and a *social* process. The child gradually develops the capacity to think, to reason; simultaneously he learns, as a result of his social interaction, to see the viewpoints of others. The two stages of moral reasoning are not entirely distinct, according to Piaget. The young child will display only the morality of constraint, but older children and even adults will often retain some elements of this earlier morality, even though most of their moral reasoning may be conducted under the morality of cooperation.

iii Research (Methodology) Piaget's approach to moral development has been carefully elaborated by the American psychologist Lawrence Kohlberg, whose research has suggested a more subtle gradation of stages of moral development. Kohlberg presented children with hypothetical moral dilemmas and then probed the reasoning they gave in their response. A typical hypothetical situation is that of a man whose wife is dying of cancer; only one drug can save her, but the man cannot afford it. Having no other means of obtaining it, the man steals the drug. Was he right or wrong?

An exhaustive analysis of the responses of his subjects to such questions, summarized in his article "Stage and Sequence: The Cognitive-Developmental Approach to Socialization" (1969), led Kohlberg to the view that human moral development proceeds through three fundamentally different levels of moral development—a *preconventional, conventional,* and *postconventional* morality. Within each of these levels Kohlberg delineates two stages. In all, then, there are six stages through which the individual may pass. Everyone moves through them in a fixed order, starting with stage 1. It is impossible to skip a stage because each succeeding stage involves a "higher" or more adequate form of reasoning that logically subsumes its predecessor. Each stage builds upon, and eventually transforms, the one below it. The stages form a hierarchy of increasingly adequate forms of moral judgment. Most children perceive morality in preconventional terms, and most adults in conventional terms. Very few people ever reach the highest, postconventional stages of moral development. The stages are defined as follows:

I. *Preconventional Level*

At this level the child is responsive to cultural rules and labels of good and bad, right or wrong, but interprets these labels in terms of either the physical or the hedonistic consequences of action (punishment, reward, exchange of favors), or in terms of the physical power of those who enunciate the rules and labels. The level is divided into two stages.

Stage 1: The punishment and obedience orientation. The physical consequences of action determine its goodness or badness regardless of the human meaning or value of these consequences. Avoidance of punishment and unquestioning deference to power are valued in their own right, not in terms of respect for an underlying moral order supported by punishment and authority (the latter being stage 4).

Stage 2: The instrumental-relativist orientation. Right action consists of that which instrumentally satisfies one's own needs and occasionally the needs of others. Human relations are viewed in terms like those of the marketplace. Elements of fairness, of reciprocity, and of equal sharing are present, but they are always interpreted in a physical or pragmatic way. Reciprocity is a matter of ''You scratch my back, and I'll scratch yours,'' not of loyalty, gratitude, or justice.

II.   *Conventional Level*

At this level maintaining the expectations of the individual's family, group, or nation is perceived as valuable in its own right, regardless of immediate and obvious consequences. The attitude is one not only of conformity to personal expectations and social order, but of loyalty to it. The order is actively maintained, supported, and justified, and is identified with the persons or group involved in it. At this level there are also two stages: 3 and 4.

Stage 3:   The interpersonal concordance or ''good boy—

Real children becoming real adults. The process of development from childhood to adulthood is still poorly understood. Various theories and models are crutches for our limited knowledge.

nice girl'' orientation. Good behavior is that which pleases or helps others and is approved by them. There is much conformity to stereotypical images of what is majority or ''natural'' behavior. Behavior is frequently judged by intention: ''He means well'' becomes important for the first time. One earns approval by being ''nice.''

Stage 4:   The ''law and order'' orientation. There is respect for authority, fixed rules, and the maintenance of the social order. Right behavior consists of doing one's duty and maintaining the given social order for its own sake.

III.   *Postconventional, Autonomous, or Principled Level*

At this level there is a clear effort to define moral values and principles that have validity and application apart from the authority of the groups or persons holding these principles, and apart from the individual's own identification with these groups. This level again has two stages: 5 and 6.

Stage 5: *The social-contract legalistic orientation, generally with utilitarian overtones.* Right action tends to be defined in terms of general individual rights and of standards that have been critically examined and agreed upon by the whole society. There is a clear awareness of the relativism of personal values and opinions and a corresponding emphasis upon procedural rules for reaching consensus. Aside from what is constitutionally and democratically agreed upon, the right is a matter of personal "values" and "opinion." The result is an emphasis upon the "legal point of view," but stressing the possibility of changing law in terms of rational considerations of social utility (rather than freezing it in terms of stage 4, "law and order"). Outside the legal realm, free agreement and contract is the binding element of obligation. This orientation is the "official" morality of the United States government and constitution.

Stage 6: *The universal ethical principle orientation.* Right is defined by the decision of conscience in accord with self-chosen ethical principles appealing to logical comprehensiveness, universality, and consistency. These principles are abstract and ethical (the Golden Rule, the categorical imperative); they are not concrete moral rules like the Ten Commandments. At heart these are universal principles of justice, of the reciprocity and equality of human rights, and of respect for the dignity of human beings as individual persons.

Kohlberg and his associates have conducted research in several other cultures and have determined that children elsewhere follow the same sequence in the development of their moral reasoning. And other experiments have shown that it is possible to accelerate the rate at which moral development takes place—by consistently presenting the child with moral reasoning conducted at a stage above that employed by the child at the time. Real difficulty in raising the stage of people's moral reasoning is only encountered at the postconventional level, which involves abstract reasoning too sophisticated for many.

iv Evaluation Kohlberg's work displays a firmer empirical anchorage and greater theoretical refinement than that of Piaget, and his theories are attracting increasing attention. Further research is needed on the validity of his stages. It has been suggested, for example, that the sequence of stages need not be invariant; some individuals who have achieved a postconventional morality may regress to an earlier, hedonistic, stage-2 morality; others may be overwhelmed by the responsibilities of moral autonomy and may seek refuge in an earlier, "do your own thing" code. Moreover, Kohlberg's stages are merely a test of reasoning; they do not necessarily predict how a given individual will behave in the real world.

The fact that Kohlberg's stages are defined on the basis of how people think about morality indicates that a fundamental prerequisite of moral development is cognitive development. In general, the more adequate a person's ability to think, the more adequate his ability to think about morality. But although cognitive development is a necessary condition for moral development, it is not sufficient. A second determinant of moral development is the capacity to take the view of others, to transcend one's egocentricity.

For the sociologist, the value of the work of Piaget and Kohlberg in the field of moral development lies in this stress on social interaction as the basis for the acquisition of moral attitudes. The individual is first constrained by his society, especially as represented through his parents. Later he internalizes the rules and norms of his society and attempts to conduct his life in accordance with them. Later still the individual may be able to transcend these conventions and explore a morality based on ethical principles. And those principles must necessarily be founded on a respect for his fellow man.

3 Overview

Socialization is a complex process of learning whereby man is transformed from a mere biological organism to a human being, capable of functioning as an individual in society. Socialization involves the learning of the knowledge, norms, and morals of society as well as the achievement of individual personality and identity. At birth the young child is egocentric. Development is essentially a progressive trend away from this egocentricity. The individual learns to see things from the point of view of others—at first particular others, then "generalized others." As the child acquires an increasingly sophisticated ability to take on various roles, he gains an increasingly adequate perspective on the social and moral world. Socialization and the development of morality consist of a series of advances in the child's understanding of himself, his relationship with others, and the rules and principles that most meaningfully govern these relationships.

The process of socialization accounts for the continuity of human societies over successive generations—not only the observable practices, but also the linguistically encoded symbolic elements of the cultural tradition are, in principle, available to each member of the community. But socialization is never fully successful: all individuals reveal temperamental differences from the time of birth, and every individual learns from situations in his own unique way. The result is an infinite variety of personality configurations among the mass of interacting individuals who make up society.

D LOOKING AHEAD

1 Interview: Lawrence Kohlberg

Lawrence Kohlberg is professor at the Harvard University Graduate School of Education. He has worked as a psychologist with the U.S. Veterans Administration and was Russell Sage Resident at Boston Children's Hospital. He has taught at Yale and the University of Chicago and was a Fellow of the Institute of Advanced Study in the Behavioral Sciences. His major publications in the field of child psychology include *The Development of Modern Moral Thinking and Choice in the Years 10–16* and "Stage and Sequence." His areas of current research involve moral development and the new social studies and moral development and correctional institutions.

DPG *How important is moral development as an aspect of socialization?*
KOHLBERG Until roughly 100 years ago, social thinkers assumed that socialization and moral development were the same thing. That is, they believed that the fundamental problem for social psychology and sociology was the explanation of how the individual came to be a moral being. The whole concept of socialization really arose as a response to the development of a more relativistic view of moral behavior or moral judgment. So that essentially what one means by socialization is the learning of conformity to the rules and norms of one's culture, a problem with which all societies are confronted. It's apparent that the universal and most important features of socialization are the things that we call moral development. Moral philososphers have tried to abstract from the arbitrary rules and conventions that vary from society to society some universally human aspects of being social, and these aspects are called being moral.

There are really three ways in which moral development is the central issue or problem area in the field of socialization. First, it refers to the *universal* features of socialization, not to the learning of particular arbitrary cultural rules that vary from one group to another, but to the universal features of regulating one's own behavior in terms of the consideration of the other human beings in one's society in general. Second, what's considered moral is the *central* kinds of rules and principles and decisions that guide an individual. In general when we talk about something being a moral issue, we mean that it is of central significance to the individual and to society. In that sense, moral considerations take primacy over other considerations in the broader field of social behavior and socialization. Third, of course, a concept of moral development is used as a criterion of desirable or undesirable forms of socialization. In other words, a Nazi storm trooper was successfully socialized, perhaps more successfully socialized than, say, Martin Luther King, because the Nazi had conformed to and internalized the norms of his group. But when one tries to evaluate the outcomes of socialization in terms of some kind of criterion of better or worse, one's forced to return to some notion of moral principles.

DPG *Socialization in a small-scale, static society does not pose quite the same problems as socialization in a mass society in flux. What are the implications?*
KOHLBERG The problems of socialization in a mass society in flux fundamentally revolve around the lack of a kind of social consensus on values. In this kind of society there are continuing changes in values, and there's an awareness of conflicting values between various subgroups in one's society and between one's own society and other societies. This awareness of conflict and change in values leads to a higher awareness of the relativity of moral values and a kind of questioning of the particular values of one's own parents, one's own social group, and authoritative institutions. This lack of a consensus society is a challenge to moral development, in the sense that the awareness of value change and value conflict seems to be a fairly necessary condition for movement to a postconventional or principled moral orientation. It's only through the awareness of the relativity of

the values of one's own group and one's own society that one can move on to the formulation of more universal, self-chosen principles. On the negative side, lack of consensus means that movement into the conventional stages of morality can become more difficult for certain groups. Adolescents, particularly those who are deprived or disadvantaged, can see a lack of social consensus as representing the fact that everybody's out for himself, that there are no genuine socially shared moral values and so on. This situation can leave an individual at what we call a preconventional, instrumental, egoistic orientation. This relativism leads adolescents to question all the traditional authoritative institutions, particularly the school and the family. It requires that the institutions that deal with young people no longer base their norms and their reasoning about adherence to norms on authority and conventional reasoning, but engage in a philosophic dialogue with the young. Educational institutions have to demonstrate to adolescents that their own objectives are not arbitrary and relative but have some universal basis. That represents a whole new approach to education.

DPG *What are the areas in moral development that are likely to gain research attention in the future?*
KOHLBERG Although it's not new, the most vital movement is the one I've been involved in—reevaluating socialization in terms of stages and structures of development. This movement includes Erikson's and Loevinger's stage approaches to ego development, for example. This developmental-structural approach is distinguished from the social-learning approach, which sees socialization merely as the learning—through various mechanisms like reward, punishment, modeling, and so on—of fixed behavior patterns and culture patterns. And it's different from the psychoanalytic approach, which views socialization essentially as the taming of basic instinctual drives. Elaborating this new developmental-structural approach means relating cognitive and moral development systematically to broader notions of ego development like Erikson's. It means more systematic work on the relationship of judg-

ment to action. It means a better account of the conditions that lead to movement from stage to stage. This kind of work has to go on in an educational and action context. The only way to find out how people move is to try to get them to move, and the only way to understand the relations of judgment and action is to try to change judgment and see how that influences action or to try to change action. For this reason we've gone into intervention projects in prisons and schools.

DPG   *The child growing up in America to-day is confronted with what are apparently two cultures—that of his parents and the counterculture of his peers. Is this a histori-cally unusual situation?*
KOHLBERG   I think that there has always been the same conflict between the peer culture and the adult culture, but the gap today is deeper and it revolves around the issue of relativism. In the past the peer culture of the adolescents, although it con-

flicted with the adult culture with regard to the superficials of behavior, didn't question the fundamental authority of the adult cul-ture. Adolescents simply accepted that the adults were too strict and too demanding and that adolescents needed to have a good time and had their own norms. There was always a fundamental acceptance, however, that when you grew up you did move into the adult culture and accepted those norms as authoritative. Today that's being questioned.

DPG   *Do we yet have an adequate theory of psychosexual development?*
KOHLBERG   No, we don't. Again, it's an issue of integrating the kind of cognitive-developmental theory that I've worked on, and Piaget has worked on, with Freudian in-sights and theory and Eriksonian insights and theory. I think that we can dispense with the notion of libido, that is, a fixed childhood sexual instinct. From a more gen-eral view of the child's cognitive develop-ment and self-development, it is possible to understand why it is that sex and issues of sex identity are so important to the young

child. I think that without an instinct theory, which is the most questionable part of psy-choanalysis, most of the fundamental in-sights of psychoanalysis hold in this area, although they need to be theoretically refor-mulated.

DPG   *How can parents and schools social-ize their youngsters in such a way as to promote the development of their sense of justice?*
KOHLBERG   Generally, we have to pro-vide kids with a sense of participation—op-portunities to role-take and responsibility and power in the groups and institutions to which they belong, including the family, the school, and so on. Second, we have to see that these groups and institutions are "just" institutions. The best way, obviously, to pro-mote a sense of justice is to see that in the social world in which the child lives, injus-tice is not the rule but the exception.

Unit 6
Population and Demography

Demography studies the size, distribution, and composition of human populations by analyzing statistical data on births, deaths, and migrations. Because of the complex interactions between population and society, such analysis is crucial to the understanding of whole social systems.

2 World Context
The human population crept steadily upward for centuries but doubled between 1650 and 1850. At the beginning of the twentieth century, however, the rate of population growth unexpectedly declined in several industrial nations. But population pressures continue to be overwhelming in the world's developing nations.

3 American Context
The high birth rate and massive influxes of immigration that characterized the United States through most of its history were encouraged because they made rapid national growth possible. Only recently has population growth become a matter of concern.

C Questions and Evidence

1 Questions
Sociologists interested in demography consider a wide range of questions, including: (1) Can the world's overpopulation problem be resolved? (2) What are the consequences of the influx of people into metropolitan areas? (3) Who will the American people be?

2 Evidence
a The "Burning Issue" Question
Research by Kingsley Davis, Bernard Berelson, and others has shown that measures for controlling the world's population—family planning and abortion—have not been effective enough so far. Parents must be motivated to have smaller families, but the necessary changes are often too radical to be accepted by governmental leaders, religious organizations, and other groups.
b The "Classical" Question
Studies by Ferdinand Toennies, Emile Durkheim, the "Chicago school," and Kingsley Davis defined the characteristics of rural, urban, and surburban life. But such differences are lessening as the trend toward widespread urbanization continues in the United States.
c The "Research" Question
Mathematical estimates of population may be inaccurate in the long run. Accurate predictions about social status and the quality of life for the population are even more difficult to make.

3 Overview
The problems of population and energy use are two aspects of the urgent dilemma facing the world today.

Population density and the percentage representation of age groups, racial groups, ethnic groups, and social classes in a given population are the result of the complex interaction of many factors.

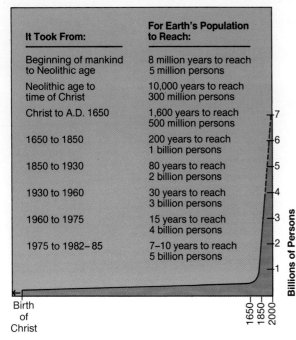

It Took From:	For Earth's Population to Reach:
Beginning of mankind to Neolithic age	8 million years to reach 5 million persons
Neolithic age to time of Christ	10,000 years to reach 300 million persons
Christ to A.D. 1650	1,600 years to reach 500 million persons
1650 to 1850	200 years to reach 1 billion persons
1850 to 1930	80 years to reach 2 billion persons
1930 to 1960	30 years to reach 3 billion persons
1960 to 1975	15 years to reach 4 billion persons
1975 to 1982–85	7–10 years to reach 5 billion persons

Figure 1. World Population Growth. Until about 1650 the world's population grew very slowly, but improvements in technology, medicine, public health, and the standard of living have since then sent the growth rate skyrocketing. (Source: Ehrlich and Ehrlich, *Population, Resources, Environment*)

B   DEFINITION AND CONTEXT

1   Definition

The study of human population is known as demography. Demographic studies focus on a population's size, its distribution, and its composition by analyzing statistical data on its birth, deaths, and migrations. Demography does not fall entirely within the realm of sociology: it is an independent field that draws on many other disciplines, including anthropology, biology, economics, mathematics, medicine, and political science. Yet demography and sociology are inseparably linked, for the sphere of each exerts a powerful determining influence on the other.

The three primary variables governing population are the *birth rate,* the *death rate,* and the *rate of migration.* What controls these variables? Obviously biology plays a critical role in determining birth and death rates, and a variety of other biological, political, and economic factors—wars, famines, plagues, depressions—are active from time to time. But it is largely social factors that account for the more systematic differences from one population to another. Is there strong pressure to marry? What is the proper age for marriage? Is a large family or a small family more desirable? Should a newly married couple live near the family or move away to seek new lives of their own? Are men taught to court danger, whereas women learn to avoid it? To what measures will people resort to postpone death?

In turn, the nature of a population has much to do with a people's social behavior, organizations, and institutions. How does social life in Washington, D.C., with its large population of professional women and female office workers, differ from that in Alaska, where men far outnumber women? How will overcrowding of schools affect children's learning of social values? How does the trend toward urbanization change the nature and function of the groups people choose to join? Because of these complex, two-way interactions between population and society, the study of basic demographic principles is crucial to the understanding of whole social systems.

2   World Context

Since the species *homo sapiens* first appeared, the human population level has crept slowly upward. Only the most gradual increases were possible at first, because the high birth rate was matched by an almost identical death rate. Serious setbacks surely occurred before the dawn of history—disease, famine, periods of adverse climate, and other natural disasters—but because people lived in small, scattered bands, these setbacks hardly slowed the population's steady growth. Other events brought about dramatic increases in the level of population: the "invention" of culture and the beginning of agriculture with division of labor and specialization gave mankind a degree of control over the food supply. But in spite of these sudden leaps, the population's growth rate remained slow. The history of ancient China reveals that famine was practically an annual event, while in Europe the bubonic plague wiped out a quarter of the population during the fourteenth century. The world's population had reached only an estimated 500 million by A.D. 1650.

But the period around 1650 proved to be a turning point. In Europe it marked the beginning of an era of peace and the establishment of new political and economic systems. Strong monarchies replaced decentralized feudal hierarchies, and mercantile capitalism was on the rise. In addition, great advances were made in agriculture. These factors combined in drives for national supremacy that centered around national prosperity; improvements in living conditions were extended to all social classes. The death rate began to decline, populations grew more rapidly, and the passage of time brought better sanitation and radical innovations in medicine. Events in Asia followed a similar pattern, though less pronounced and not as well documented. The nature of African civilization at the time was such that no account of its population trends was preserved.

In 1798 an English clergyman named Thomas Malthus, who is now popularly considered the father of population studies, expressed his controversial views in *An Essay on the Principle of Population*. He contended that population increased according to a geometric progression (1, 2, 4, 8, 16, 32, 64, 128, and so on), although production of food could at best grow by arithmetic progression (1, 2, 3, 4, 5, 6, 7, 8, and so on). Because population could not continue to increase indefinitely, it must fall subject to controls. Initially Malthus emphasized the "*positive checks*" of starvation, disease, and war—a death rate solution to the population problem. In his later writings Malthus noted in addition the importance of "*preventive checks*" on fertility—late marriage, "moral restraint," and the like.

In spite of Malthus' predictions the Industrial Revolution sent the population skyrocketing. The world population had taken about 16 centuries to double by 1650, but by 1850 it had doubled again. The next doubling took about 80 years. Malthus' predictions were also overturned by the bounties of three continents new to Europeans—Australia and the Americas—which further fueled the European population explosion by providing food, vast amounts of raw materials, and abundant terrain into which the population could migrate. Malthus could not have foreseen the full impact of these new reasons for optimism, and his theories passed into obscurity—temporarily.

Around the beginning of the twentieth century something unexpected began to happen: the rate of population growth decreased in industrial nations. Until this time changes in human numbers had been almost exclusively a story of death-rate fluctuations, but since the middle of the seventeenth century the death rate had been falling steadily. Now the birth rates of industrial nations were falling as well. Instead of finding children an economic advantage, parents were finding large families an economic burden. Because of the changing nature of labor and because of child labor laws, children could no longer add to a family's income; they only provided more mouths to feed and required additional funds to finance an increasingly important education. Throughout Europe a pattern was becoming apparent. The death rate fell with industri-

American Indians interacting with newly arrived Europeans. What at any given time looks like a successfully thriving population may be doomed to near extinction through unforeseen causes, such as sickness, starvation, natural disasters, or another population's avaricious acts.

alization, causing a sharp increase in population; then, after some years' lag, the birth rate also fell, bringing the rate of population growth back down to nearly the same level as before industrialization. This important phenomenon became known as the *demographic transition.*

Around the time of World War II the industrial nations began exporting to developing nations the technology that had made possible their low death rates. Sri Lanka (formerly known as Ceylon) is often cited as an example. In 1945 its annual death rate stood at 22 per 1,000. The introduction of DDT brought malaria under control and reduced the incidence of a variety of other insect-borne diseases. Sri Lanka's death rate dropped startlingly and by 1954 reached 10 per 1,000. Similar stories were repeated throughout Asia, Africa, and Latin America: death-rate reduction affected primarily children and young adults, and this situation meant more babies. The impact of this humanitarian effort to cut death rates has been and will certainly continue to be overwhelming in the world's developing nations—where many populations are doubling every 30 or 35 years.

3   American Context

When English colonists landed at Jamestown in 1607, the native American population is estimated to have been about 1 million. It was a stable population with a high birth rate and a high death rate, but the colonies soon introduced the Indians to "negative population growth." As colonies sprouted all along the eastern seaboard, entire tribes were wiped out. The Wampanoags, who made possible the first Thanksgiving, vanished along with the Chesapeakes, Potomacs, and many others. Only their names are preserved in the names of our states, rivers, cities, lakes, and other places as reminders of the areas they once inhabited. By 1860 the Indian population was estimated at only 340,000; just 30 years later it had been reduced by one-third.

The English colonies flourished at the expense of the Indians. New land was constantly being cleared as the population expanded. Most settlers lived in rural areas, where large families meant more hands to work the land, and ships loaded with new colonists arrived often. In 1790 the first census of the United States placed the population at 3,929,214, including 757,000 black slaves (19.3 percent of the population). Ten years later the population had grown by 35.1 percent, to 5,308,483. In 1800 the crude birth rate (number of births per 1,000 population, including both sexes and all ages) was 55.0, more than three times the present rate (15.6 in 1972). For comparison, the 1972 birth rate was 37 in Asia, 38 in Latin America, and 47 in Africa. Although the incredibly high birth rate was offset by a very high death rate, every United States census until 1870 showed a population increase well above 30 percent over the previous decade's census. Even in the developing world today only a few West African nations can equal this rate of growth; the United States *doubling time* in 1870 was only slightly longer than 20 years.

This rapid growth alarmed no one. In fact, almost everyone believed it was highly beneficial, because the multiplying population

Burying the dead after the P of Wounded Knee, S.D. -1890

Americans of European descent interacting with American Indians: trench burial of dead Indians following Battle of Wounded Knee, South Dakota. In 1890 a band of Sioux, fearful of punishment from government authorities for practicing their "Ghost Dance" religion (which mingled Christian and traditional Indian elements), attempted to move from one reservation to another. Surrounded by the U.S. Cavalry, the Indians were disarming peacefully when a gun went off accidentally. The troops opened fire on the Indians with Hotchkiss machine guns. About 300 Indian men, women, and children were killed and buried in a common grave. This massacre was the last "battle" of the Indian wars. Its site is now a highway intersection.

made rapid national growth possible, and for this reason the United States encouraged *immigration*. This country is unique for the role immigration has played in its history. Because it was commonly viewed as a new and uncrowded land of freedom and opportunity for all, the United States attracted millions of people from all parts of the Old World. By the early twentieth century, nearly 40 percent of the population was either foreign-born or first-generation American; in New York City, the most important center of immigration, this number reached 80 percent, and percentages in other Northern and Midwestern cities were also much higher than the national average.

The massive influx began in the 1840s, when the number of immigrants more than tripled that of the previous decade; the annual rate during that decade stood at 8.4 immigrants for every 1,000 residents, including the previous year's arrivals. This was more than double the previous decade's rate, and the rate continued to increase until the Civil War and its aftermath temporarily slowed the influx.

During the period just after 1840, the vast majority of immigrants arrived from northern Europe, especially England, Ireland,

Germany, and Scandinavia. But when heavy immigration resumed in the late 1870s and continued on a larger and larger scale into the twentieth century, most of the immigrants came from southern and eastern Europe. They were more visible to the rest of the population than were earlier immigrants, partly because of ethnic differences and partly because they tended to be poor rural folk who lacked the education and "sophistication" of their predecessors. Often they were resented, ridiculed, and discriminated against. (Irish Catholics had earlier also undergone severe discrimination.) In the face of this cold welcome, many immigrants chose to return to their native lands.

World War I effectively halted immigration from Europe. Shortly after the war, Congress enacted a *quota system* that drastically limited all immigration but gave northern Europeans a relative advantage.

Immigrants arriving at Ellis Island, New York City. Many of American society's characteristics are traceable to the fact that the United States absorbed more immigrants from more diverse social backgrounds in less time than any other country in modern history. In 1907 alone, 1,285,349 immigrants arrived in the United States.

C   QUESTIONS AND EVIDENCE

1   Questions

Sociologists interested in demography consider a wide range of questions, including: (1) Can the world's overpopulation problem be resolved before it is too late? (2) What are the consequences of the influx of people into metropolitan areas? (3) Who will the American people be?

2   Evidence

a   The "Burning Issue" Question

i   Context   The accuracy of the term *population explosion* becomes all too clear in light of a figure supplied by the World Health Organization: 3.7 human beings are born every second. This fact means 13,260 new people every hour; 318,240 every day; 2,227,680 every week. (According to the Population Reference Bureau, Inc., of Washington, D.C., daily births have currently increased to 342,000.) The number of babies born every year equals the combined populations of Austria, Belgium, Denmark, Finland, Great Britain, Ireland, The Netherlands, Norway, Sweden, and Switzerland.

But those countries, along with the other industrial nations of the world, are not the ones most directly involved in the population explosion. Less than a third of the world's population lives in the industrial nations; over two-thirds inhabit the so-called underdeveloped or developing countries of the Third World—Asia, Africa, Latin America. Perhaps a better term might be the "hungry" countries, for the standard of living in most of them is barely above the subsistence level. In addition to having most of the world's population and most of the world's poverty and hunger, these countries have the world's highest population growth rates, which sap the most determined efforts to raise the standard of living. For example, if, through herculean effort on their own part and massive assistance on the part of industrial nations, these countries manage to raise their agricultural output by 50 percent in the next generation, each person will have less to eat than he or she does at present—*if* population growth continues at the current rate.

It can be said with assurance that population growth *will* decrease in the future, but it remains to be seen whether that decrease will be caused by falling birth rates or by rising death rates or by some combination of these two trends. The "death-rate solution" is clearly unacceptable to most people, for in the last 100 years the world has cheered dramatic reductions in the death rate. In order to prevent the death rate from rising by the dictates of nature, the solution must be achieved by lowering the birth rate. Sociologists ask: *Can social planning reduce the birth rate in time to avert a sharp rise in the death rate?*

ii   Theory   Of the theories concerned with lowering the birth rate, *family planning* is by far the most popular and widely practiced. Its guiding principle is that parents should be able to determine and achieve the number of children they want, spaced at the intervals they deem best. Proponents of family planning operate on the as-

Peruvian peasant family working in the fields. Unlike households in mass, urbanized society, the peasant household continues to function as the basic economic as well as social unit of its society. Children are crucial as sources of labor for peasant households. It will therefore be very difficult to convince such families to change their value system (which promotes having many children) toward having fewer children for long-term demographic considerations when short-term economic needs must be met.

sumption that parents—especially parents in poor and crowded areas where the birth rate is high—would have smaller families if only they had the means to prevent conception. Thus the task of family planning is twofold: it must make simple and effective contraceptives widely available at little or no cost, and it must spread knowledge of the availability of the contraceptives, instruction in their use, and encouragement to actually use them. But the family planning movement faces enormous obstacles. In areas where the need is greatest, transportation and communication facilities are often poorly developed, much of the population is illiterate, and trained personnel are in short supply. The scale of the problem is tremendous, but not beyond solution. The family planning movement has been active in the industrial countries for more than half a century; in the Third World (where the real population problem began around the time of World War II) serious family planning efforts only began about 1965. Often political leaders were slow to recognize rapid population growth as a problem or opposed birth control for political or religious reasons. Even now many governments give family planning only token support, but only a few nations remain without programs.

The most natural thing in the world? Ideas, like anything else, have a natural history, and nonadaptive ideas must fall by the wayside. For instance, we take it for granted that all adult couples are "naturally entitled" to have children—unless the family is on welfare. The time has come to face the question: *Why?* Why shouldn't the wider society play a role in deciding the reproductive future of its members? Rather than evoking merely visceral responses, this question needs serious consideration, with a dispassionate listing of the pros and cons.

Because of the dominance of family planning, few other schemes for reducing the birth rate have been tried on a large scale. The exception is an indirect attempt to lower birth rates in Third World countries through industrialization (or *modernization*) of agrarian societies. Many hope this industrialization will lead to a demographic transition like that experienced by the Western countries about the turn of the century. For over a generation Third World governments have been encouraging development, and industrial countries have been supplying technical and financial aid in an effort to provide an economic solution to population pressure as well as to improve the standard of living.

Another theory holds that the birth rate remains high because parents are not motivated to have small families and that this motivation can best be achieved through socioeconomic pressure. A few Third World nations have tried mild forms of pressure, such as propaganda extolling the advantages of a small family. (The propaganda can be made subtle and pervasive—for example, commercial advertisements that depict families may never show more than two children.) But governments have shied away from stronger—and politically more risky—forms of pressure, such as changing the tax laws to reduce or eliminate deductions for more than one or two children, or allocating public housing without regard to family size. Obviously these measures could not be used in many countries, because a great many families are too poor to be taxed at all or because there is no public housing to allocate. But a variety of other methods have been proposed. The difficulty lies not in finding a feasible technique for applying pressure, but in the vehement and almost universal opposition to coercive methods of population control. Distasteful as the coercive methods may be, some scholars contend that they may become necessary and gain popularity as the crisis worsens. Such proposals as implantation of sterilant capsules, compulsory abortion or sterilization, or strong penalties for bearing an unlicensed child sound like a science-fiction nightmare, but a time may come when they will be more attractive than the miseries of a grossly overpopulated planet.

The task of reducing the world's population growth is made especially difficult because of the youth of the world's present population. In most Third World nations the proportion of the population 15 years old or younger hovers near 50 percent; in the United States this figure is under 30 percent, and in Europe, even less. As this tremendous proportion of children matures to childbearing age, their sheer numbers will ensure rapid population growth for many years to come, even if no couple bears more than two children. This phenomenon can be observed in the United States today, even though the United States population has now reached the *zero population growth* level of two children per family; if this current fertility rate were to continue indefinitely into the future, the population would continue to grow well into the twenty-first century because of the "baby boom" of the late 1940s and 1950s. (Those babies will be bearing babies.) In the Third World the situation is already far worse, and the baby boom continues at full speed.

iii Research   India, whose population is second only to China's, is among the nations most sorely beset with the population crisis.

Although its campaign to reduce births began in the early 1950s, little progress was made until the program was reorganized in 1965. Its family planning program has been extensively studied since then, and the research findings present little cause for optimism.

In 1965 the Indian government's goal was to reduce the country's birth rate from 40 to 25 per 1,000 population "as soon as possible." According to a 1973 estimate, it has only been reduced to 38 per 1,000 and the original goal has been put off to 1980. Charles Loomis' survey ("In Praise of Conflict and its Resolution," 1967) of 364 villages found that 59.7 percent of the men had heard of family planning, and 31.5 percent expressed an interest in it; of the women, 45.6 percent had heard of it, and 28.9 percent expressed an interest. But only 4.5 percent of the men and 3.2 percent of the women had actually tried a method of family planning. Part of the problem lies in the difficulty of making contraceptive devices available, but the trouble goes far beyond that. As Kingsley Davis points out in his 1967 article "Population Policy," "Among 5,196 women coming to rural Punjabi family planning centers, 38 percent were over 35 years old, 67 percent over 30. These women had married early, nearly a third of them before the age of 15; some 14 percent had eight or more *living* children when they reached the clinic, 51 percent had six or more." Furthermore, studies indicate that after two years less than 50 percent of the women who are fitted with intrauterine contraceptive devices (IUCDs) still have them in place. (There are rumors that some women remove them and return for another fitting to collect the small incentive payment again.) Sterilization, especially vasectomy for males, appeared promising for a time, but (in "Husband-Wife Communication and Motivational Aspects of Population Control in an Indian Village," 1969) Shirley and Thomas Poffenberger cite a 1968 study of farmers in eight villages indicating that, although 86 percent knew of vasectomy, only 9 percent had had the operation. (Two percent of the wives had been fitted with IUCDs). In an article in *The New York Times* Joseph Lelyveld reported that the sterilization program, which had roused so much hope, was losing ground; the number of vasectomies performed was declining.

Discouraging though the research findings are, many people believe that the problems result primarily from family planning's current state of development. They contend that once all the bugs are eliminated, the program can achieve population control. But Davis expresses quite a different opinion:

> Logically, it does not make sense to use *family* planning to provide *national* population control or planning. The planning in family planning is that of each separate couple. The only control they exercise is control over the size of *their* families. . . . There is no reason to expect that the millions of decisions about family size made by couples in their own interest will automatically control population for the benefit of society. On the contrary, there are good reasons to think they will not do so.

Family planning intends to give people what they want, and in most nonindustrial countries people want a lot of children. *Family Plan-*

Teaching about birth control to villagers in India. Many governments, such as that of India, have given high priority to massive family planning programs in order to deal with a population explosion that wipes out economic gains.

ning and Population Programs (1965), Bernard Berelson's survey of research by W. Parker Mauldin and others, compares the actual family size with "ideal" family size (as determined by population councils and government agencies) in several countries. This and other studies show that as long as attitudes remain unchanged, family planning can provide only a token growth rate reduction. Clearly, any true solution must go beyond eliminating unwanted births and concentrate on reducing the number of children wanted.

In the West substantial reduction in the birth rate was an unintended but proven side effect of industrialization. Many concerned observers were encouraged when the first non-Western nation underwent a demographic transition in record time: between 1947 and 1957 Japan cut its birth rate in half and thereby drastically reduced its population growth rate. Perhaps this occurrence marked the beginning of a trend in the Third World. But Japan can hardly be considered a typical Third World nation: even in 1947 it had well-developed systems of communication and transportation and a high literacy rate, and by 1957 it was well on its way to becoming the industrial giant it is today. The people of Japan, not the government, took the initiative against population growth, and credit must be given to the large Japanese corporations for their role in providing information and services to their workers. Perhaps most significant is the fact that in Japan (as well as in Eastern Europe) legalized abortions played a crucial role in bringing the birth rate under control; in many countries abortion remains illegal and is opposed by government and religious leaders. (Japan, however, is now considering measures for population increase.)

For most of the developing countries, chances of industrialization along American, Soviet, European, or Japanese lines are very slight indeed. For one thing, the necessary resources are nonrenewable and are being rapidly used up by those nations that are already industrialized. For another, the financial resources required for capital accumulation cannot be spared by Third World nations and are far beyond the means of current "foreign aid" programs of industrial nations. Progress toward industrialization of underdeveloped countries has barely kept ahead of the expanding needs caused by rapid population growth. Again, youth is an important factor; slightly more than half of the population is old enough to work (although older children do provide some assistance in agriculture), but that part of the population must provide food, shelter, clothing, and energy—and the government must finance education—for almost an equal number of nonworking children. To make matters worse, many women are kept out of the labor force by frequent childbearing and the necessity of caring for young children. Thus a reduction in the ideal family size in developing countries cannot be expected to result from industrialization and the demographic transition. Because socioeconomic pressures have been tried only in mild forms, they have scarcely affected social and cultural values favoring large families. Effects of these pressures are difficult to isolate from the effects of other ongoing programs, and virtually no research has been focused upon them.

iv Evaluation   Theories and research cannot directly address the question: Can social planning reduce the birth rate in time? At best they can suggest more effective or rapid ways of cutting back births. Unfortunately, most of the suggestions are at odds with current policies.

Family planning receives the lion's share of the funding and attention, and other more effective approaches are thereby short-changed. For example, the experiences of Eastern Europe and Japan have proved the effectiveness of *abortion.* Although not ultimately the most desired method of population control, abortion has been especially useful in the early stages of campaigns to reduce the birth rate. A woman faces less danger from the procedure than from childbirth, and up to the twelfth week of pregnancy abortion can be performed safely by specially trained paramedical personnel without need for hospitalization of the woman. Yet abortion is outlawed by the majority of nations, although illegal abortions are quite common and popularly accepted throughout the world (even though these are usually more dangerous than childbirth). Abortion is legal and prevalent in the Communist-governed countries (in Hungary, abortions even exceed births), and the rest of the world seems to be progressing toward legalization. Sripati Chandrasekhar, the leading Indian demographer, has recommended legal abortions in India, and the United States Supreme Court overturned most American anti-abortion laws in January of 1973.

But abortion, along with efforts to devise and distribute improved mechanisms of contraception, still does not deal with the basic issue: How can the number of children that parents desire be reduced? The answer frequently involves changes too radical to be accepted by governmental leaders, religious organizations, or groups within the society. As Kingsley Davis notes, "Changes basic enough to effect motivation for having children would be changes in the structure of the family, the position of women, and in sexual mores." It has been shown that parents who marry late do have fewer children than those who marry at earlier ages, but what factors favor late marriage? Sociological research has documented the validity of existing facts, but it has done little to suggest how new trends or changes might be encouraged. Even if the discipline of sociology had the answers, it would probably have little effect on leaders of developing nations or religious or ethnic minority groups who refuse to accept zero population growth as a goal or who see an increase in numbers as a solution to their political problems.

b The "Classical" Question

i Context Until recently cities held only a tiny fraction of the world's population; the vast majority of people lived in rural areas. Today the urban-industrial society dominates the world and is considered the most "advanced" form of civilization. The United States exemplifies this type of society and the proportion of its population living in *metropolitan areas* (essentially defined by the Bureau of the Census as cities of 50,000 or more and their closely related areas) was 68.6 percent in 1970. Sociologists ask: *What is the sociological and demographic effect of the trend toward concentration of the population in urban areas?*

Women's liberation movement pro-abortion rights demonstration. Many of the goals of the women's liberation movement are in keeping with the social necessity to deal with demographic and other pressures. It is quite likely that the wider society will continue its incorporation of many of the changes for which the women's movement is now working.

ii   Theory   Earlier we mentioned one type of *migration*—immigration—that once accounted for much of American cities' growth. Today another type of migration—*internal migration*—is taking place at a tremendous pace. Scarcely half the people in the country live in the same house they lived in five years ago. People are constantly moving from farm to town, from town to city, from city to suburb, from suburb to countryside, from one metropolitan area to another. All this moving about gives rise to two related phenomena. *Urbanization* is a result of a large concentration of people in a limited area: *urbanism* is the effect of a densely settled area on the people who inhabit it. Our primary concern in this unit is with the effects of the urban environment on its inhabitants in industrial nations, especially the United States. But a brief discussion of the theory of urbanization here will help explain the nature of its consequences in terms of human life. Unit 17 is devoted to a full discussion of urban society.

The development of the cities became possible when agriculture advanced to the point where more food could be produced than the people directly involved in its production needed and when the means for transporting food to the nonfarmers become available. People were then able to go to the cities and earn their daily bread without having to grow the grain for it. But they also *wanted* to go to the cities. The urban centers offered attractions that were not available in the villages or on the farms.

Urbanization in the developing countries has been a more recent phenomenon, and it has accelerated for a very different reason. Instead of being pulled to the city by its attractions, rural people have been pushed there by lack of available land to farm. For both developed and developing countries, however, the theory of urbanization implies that migration, rather than the natural increase of the urban population, was the main factor in the growth of cities.

Urban areas in industrial nations are seldom defined strictly in terms of particular political boundaries. Most cities have suburbs, and many have grown to merge with neighboring urban areas (as in New York or Los Angeles). In this country a few suburbs were in existence by the time of the Civil War, but in the last three decades the popularity of the private automobile has probably done more to change the nature of metropolitan areas than any other factor in American history. Millions of people living in the suburbs think nothing of commuting two hours to and from work. Families need no longer live near schools, shopping districts, and friends, because they are all only minutes away by car. People can now move out to escape the crowds, the noise, the dirt associated with city life.

The flight to the suburbs has been and is still led by people with higher incomes. The well-kept townhouses they leave behind often become apartments or rooming houses, the ''better'' shops follow their high-income customers, and industries often relocate outside the city limits to take advantage of lower land prices without losing transportation advantages. Thus the central city is left to poor people and racial and ethnic minorities. The rush to the suburbs leads to ''deterioration'' of the central city and sparks the drive for urban renewal: low-income housing is replaced by civic centers, sports arenas, and new superhighways to make it easier for suburb-

Abandoned automobile and city slum. The automobile was a key factor in the development of the suburbs and contributes—through congestion, pollution, and housing demolition for highways—to the urban crisis. The automobile, which was supposed to be a liberating force, has in fact become a nemesis in many ways. It uses tremendous amounts of gasoline and oil (thus draining natural resources), causes over 50,000 deaths per year in the United States alone, and maims millions. It has its interests protected by corporate lobbies that promote highway construction instead of the development of efficient mass transit systems that the cities desperately need.

anites to get in and back out of the city even faster than they could before.

These trends of urbanization describe gross historical facts, sheer numbers of people moving from one place to another, shifts in areas of residence. What of the difference in people's lives? Popular theory holds life in rural areas to be personal and friendly; everybody knows everybody else by first name; family and friends (the primary group) are very important; strangers are treated hospitably (but people can be wary of them); old ways are clung to; and there is little tolerance for new or strange ideas. The pace of life is slow, and everyone is something of a jack-of-all-trades.

City life is viewed as the polar opposite, depersonalized and anonymous. Many people do not know their next-door neighbor's name. Friends are few, and the vast sea of strangers is ignored. The *primary group* is replaced by the city's many cultural opportunities and by *secondary groups*—buddies at work, the bridge club, the bowling team. A stranger who makes contact is viewed as a threat, but there is great tolerance for diverse types of people, ways of life, and different ideas and beliefs. Life moves quickly, and in order to succeed financially, a person must specialize in a particular trade or service.

Suburban life is a compromise. It is an attempt to return to the friendly informality of rural life, to revive the primary group in the neighborhood, to regain independence through owning land, being a gardener or a do-it-yourselfer. There is less tolerance of difference than in the city and more homogeneity than in the country; "keeping up with the Joneses" is the order of the day, and woe be unto the woman whose clothes are not whiter than white or the man who does not mow his lawn every weekend. Popular mythology demands a bored wife and a husband with an ulcer. Occupational specialization remains the key to success.

What about demographic differences? Do rural people have more children so there will be more hands to help with chores? Do the competition and fast pace of life in the city lead to a higher death rate? Who has greater mobility? Where is the marriage rate highest? Where do single people live?

iii   Research (Survey) In 1887 in *Gemeinschaft und Gesellschaft* Ferdinand Toennies advanced the concept of *Gemeinschaft*—the close communal relationship that often characterizes life on the farm or in small villages—and *Gesellschaft*—the organized impersonal relationship found in society at large. He applied the term *burgerliche Gesellschaft* (bourgeois society) to the commercial activity of cities and towns, in which competition was universal and, in Adam Smith's words, "Every man . . . becomes in some measure a merchant." Although Toennies' concept of *Gemeinschaft* and *Gesellschaft* was not developed specifically to explain relationships based on environment, it served as a foundation for later theories and research that were.

Emile Durkheim, in *The Division of Labor in Society* (1893), spoke of the necessity of increasing the "physical and moral density" of the population to achieve *economy of scale*. A specific distribution of the population, Durkheim said, is necessary before division of labor is possible. This possibility of specialization makes cities more efficient, but only up to a point: cities reach a size where

diminishing returns negate economy of scale. This fact is demonstrated by a rise in per capita public service costs as a city's population rises past a certain point.

Urban sociology flourished in the 1920s and early 1930s, led by the "Chicago school" of sociologists including Robert Park, Ernest Burgess, R. D. McKenzie, and Louis Wirth. Their work and its impact was extensive, and it largely defined the direction of urban sociology since them. (For example, Burgess' theory of the city's growth as occurring in *concentric zones* is still the most widely used model.) Because of limitations of techniques of data collection and analysis, many of their theoretical formulations were not proven until years later. During the same period, Pitirim Sorokin and Carle C. Zimmerman were producing their monumental *A Systematic Source Book in Rural Sociology* (1930–1932), which set the standard for rural-urban comparisons in all fields of sociology. In the 1920s Sorokin and Zimmerman predicted an eventual unification of rural and urban ways (with urban influence predominating), which they called "rurbanization."

Kingsley Davis' *Human Society* (1949) contains an excellent discussion of urban society, including eight principal characteristics of urbanism: *social heterogeneity, secondary control, social mobility, secondary association, social tolerance, voluntary association, individuation,* and *spatial segregation.* Rural life, Davis maintains, embodies the opposite of these principles. He emphasizes the importance of the suburban trend and predicts the spread of urban attitudes to rural areas, resulting in the spread of urbanism throughout the entire country. This view differs slightly from Sorokin's and Zimmerman's concept, mainly in its emphasis on the specifically *suburban* aspects of the development.

For the time being, however, differences between rural and urban ways of life do still exist. Davis' characteristics outline the major sociological differences. Modern methods of data collection and computer analysis make possible a detailed enumeration of urban-rural demographic variations, and Ralph Thomlinson has provided a concise account of the differences.

> The sex ratio (number of men per 100 women) is higher in rural areas. . . . In urban areas there are more foreign-born persons, and the educational attainment is much greater. The ages below 20 are better represented in rural areas, whereas all other age groups are slightly better represented in urban places. There are more working women in cities. Urban incomes are higher.
>
> The urban family tends to have fewer members, smaller quarters, greater mobility, more scattered activities, and less stability than its rural counterpart. City dwellers marry later, produce fewer children, and divorce more frequently. A higher proportion of the rural people are single, and a larger percentage of urban residents are widowed or divorced. There are more housing accommodations and recreational facilities for unmarried people in cities.
>
> The death rate is higher in cities, but not so high as the birth rate. Cities survive through a combination of

Luca Carlevaris' *The Dock With the Ducal Palace at Venice* (c. 1715). In the later Middle Ages and in the Renaissance in Europe, cities were often vibrant and efficient in meeting their citizens' needs and economically and politically successful. But today cities are an increasing liability for mass society, using more than their per capita share of natural resources and exhibiting concentrations of poverty, crime, corruption, deteriorated housing, and pollution. What is the future of cities in mass society?

natural increase and an excess of in- over out-migrants. Rural areas survive through a high natural increase despite a net outward migration. Thus cities are partially ''biologically'' parasite on rural areas. (*Population Dynamics,* 1965)

iv   Evaluation (The United States population is now about three-quarters urban, and the trend toward urbanization continues.) The President's Commission on Population Growth and the American Future estimates that by the year 2000, 60 percent of the population will live in metropolitan areas of *1 million* or more. The latest census shows that many central cities actually declined in population or grew only slightly in the last decade, but the suburban rings that surround them registered a tremendous gain. (We are becoming a nation of suburbanites.) To realize that the suburban life style is the ideal, if not already the dominant form, one has only to watch an hour's worth of television commercials. The rural-urban-suburban differences suggested by the theories discussed earlier still persist, but there is less and less difference every year.

(Meanwhile the plight of the cities grows increasingly grave.) Kingsley Davis in *Human Society* worries that most officials view urban growth as something to be planned *for* rather than something to be *planned.* Can urbanization go on indefinitely? Can sociological and demographic studies be put to intelligent practical use? Will central cities die of ''suburbanitis''? Can urban renewal save them? Time alone will tell.

c   The "Research" Question

i   Context (In December 1972 the United States Bureau of the Census announced that women between 18 and 24 years old in 1972 ''would complete their childbearing with an average of about 2.1 births per woman''—if they had the number of births that this age group of women said they expected to have and if the past relation between birth expectations of this age group and their actual fertility were repeated.) This birth rate would lead to a reduction of about one child per family since 1960. As a result, the Bureau of the Census made a major downward revision in its projections of the future population. (The drop in the *fertility rate* will change not only the population's *size,* but also its *composition,* and it will have a profound influence on the nature of such social groups as families, the aged, and racial and ethnic minorities. It may alter the status of women and children, and it will surely affect the economy, government, education, the use of resources, and the environment. All the factors involved in this demographic change—a small reduction in the fertility rate—will interact to produce significant changes in the American population. Sociologists ask: *Can demographic data and sociological research predict the future composition of the United States population?*)

ii   Theory (As indicated earlier, the new low United States fertility rate does not mean that zero population growth has actually been achieved; for although fertility has reached *replacement level,* that is only one of the conditions for zero growth. But many observers maintain that if the fertility rate does not rise again, the population will stop expanding by the year 2000 or shortly thereafter and that

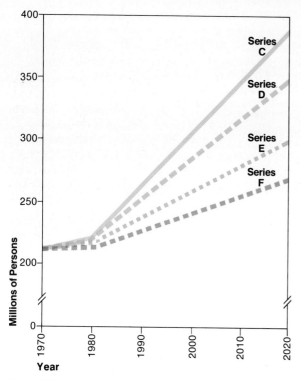

Figure 2. Four Different Series of Projections of the Population of the United States, 1970–2020. Each projection series has a different "fertility assumption" (average number of births per woman). Series *C* assumes 2.8; Series *D* assumes 2.5; Series *E* assumes 2.1; Series *F* assumes 1.8 (Source: Bureau of the Census)

slight demographic changes will have greater impact in a stationary population than in a growing population. That is, the one-child decrease in American family size over the last 15 years will have a greater effect on age composition, the family, the economy, and so on, than would a one-child decrease in a country where families average four or five children. This hypothesis heightens the significance of the current low fertility rate in the United States.

The youthfulness of the United States is a popular legend. The evidence usually cited is a *median age* that is in the twenties and going down. The United States does place tremendous emphasis on youthfulness, and the population is younger than most European populations, but it should be noted that in 1800 the median age in this country was 16 years, and in most developing countries today it does not exceed 20 years. The median age in the United States rose steadily from its first measurement until 1950, when the tremendous number of babies born during the boom of the subsequent two decades lowered the age slightly. The current trend will have the opposite effect. In a stationary population the number of people 50 years old is very nearly as great as the number of five-year-olds. The predicted low birth rate will mean a much higher proportion of elderly people and hence a much greater emphasis on them and their problems and needs.

By definition, a lower fertility rate results in fewer children per family. Fewer children mean fewer mouths to feed, so the same family income can provide better meals, more toys, books, vacations, and clothing, and more comfortable housing. Mothers will have increased opportunity to pursue careers or interests outside the family, because they will no longer have such extensive demands on their time inside the home. Thus lowered fertility could indirectly contribute to raising the status of women in the working world, changing sex roles, and alleviating poverty. In families with two breadwinners, for example, the husband will not need to gear his earnings to a five-day work week, and the labor force in general will be able to enjoy increased spending power and fewer hours at work. However, a few theorists fear that this greater proportion of the population in the labor force could lead to increased unemployment. In addition, several prominent economists have pointed out that a lower fertility rate will increase the average age of the labor force, which in turn will cause the level of productivity to suffer because it is the younger persons—those who have just completed their education—who have the higher technical training, and their proportion of the population will be much smaller.

Economic changes will also have a strong influence on the quality of the environment and the availability of resources, but theorists are divided on what the influence will be. Some believe that the lower projections of future population will mean fewer people to pollute the environment and deplete natural resources and smaller demands on industries for goods whose manufacture pollutes and depletes. But others believe that the increase in affluence and leisure time will more than make up the difference, putting increased pressure on society to produce more goods, more cars, more highways.

There is a widespread belief that the older a population is, the greater are its resistance to change and its political conserva-

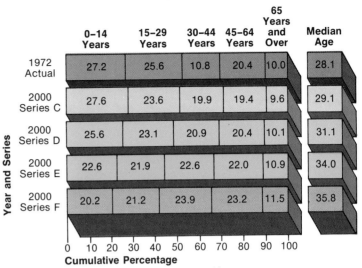

Year and Series	0–14 Years	15–29 Years	30–44 Years	45–64 Years	65 Years and Over	Median Age
1972 Actual	27.2	25.6	10.8	20.4	10.0	28.1
2000 Series C	27.6	23.6	19.9	19.4	9.6	29.1
2000 Series D	25.6	23.1	20.9	20.4	10.1	31.1
2000 Series E	22.6	21.9	22.6	22.0	10.9	34.0
2000 Series F	20.2	21.2	23.9	23.2	11.5	35.8

0 10 20 30 40 50 60 70 80 90 100
Cumulative Percentage

Figure 3. Actual Percentage Distribution of United States Population by Age in 1972, With Four Different Series of Projections of Distribution in 2000. See Figure 2 for fertility assumption of each series. (Source: Bureau of the Census)

tism. France is cited as a case in point, but opponents of this theory usually counter by citing Sweden, which is known both for its population control and its strikingly liberal politics. There seems to be no solid theoretical ground for predicting political trends on the basis of population change, but there is almost unanimous agreement that a smaller population is easier and cheaper to govern. To some extent its government tends to be more democratic and representative.

The low fertility rate cited by the Bureau of the Census is an average, of course. Some groups in the society have higher rates, others lower rates. Higher education is one factor that can be correlated with low fertility; to a certain extent income and social class also work the same way. Again, no one is certain whether low fertility is the cause or the result, but the correlation is well known, and it has prompted some citizens to theorize with alarm that the process of evolution has been reversed to favor multiplication of the "less fit." Presumably these alarmists are also (or perhaps primarily) worried about the high fertility rate among many racial, ethnic, and religious minorities. Will the current low fertility rate significantly change the racial, ethnic, and religious composition of the United States? One way to approach this question is to compare changes in *differential* fertility or birth rates among the various groups.

iii Research (Methodology) Central to all aspects of the question of who the American people will be is an examination of the methods used by the Bureau of the Census to estimate future populations. The Bureau uses a *cohort component method* to arrive at separate *projections of fertility, mortality, and migration* that spell out the mathematical consequences of certain beginning assumptions. The basis of the fertility projections is the *completed cohort fertility rate*—the total number of children born to a group of 1,000 women by the completion of their childbearing years. Past *expectations* of a cohort of women differ from their actual *performance*, and this statistical difference can be applied to the current expectations of a younger cohort of women to predict what their performance will be. Timing of births is also computed, both because women who begin childbearing later tend to have fewer children and because the timing influences the population in a given future year and governs the year at which these children will themselves reach childbearing age. Despite the thoroughness with which fertility projections are computed, researchers cannot be certain that women currently too young to have children (or women yet unborn) will have the same fertility expectations as women today, and this factor and other less important factors make fertility the most uncertain of the three components of population change. For this reason, four different *fertility assumptions* are used. For each assumption, the number of children born each year is projected and added to the total.

Mortality rates are also carefully plotted. Researchers assume no major medical breakthrough that would significantly decrease mortality rates for people over 10 years old, but they do take into account the continuing decline in infant and childhood mortality. They also use separate mortality rates for men and women. For each subsequent year the number of people who survive is plotted from standard tables for each age group (at one-year intervals). Using this method, researchers can project, for example, the number of people born during 1965 who will die between 1990 and 1991. The number of immigrants is projected to be a constant 400,000 per year; this figure is added to the population for every future year, observing the age and sex distribution of immigrants who arrived during fiscal 1972.

Through careful analysis of detail, Census Bureau researchers can project the future *age composition* of the population with considerable accuracy. If the current fertility rate holds true for the future, the median age will be 5.9 years greater in the year 2000 than in 1972. The number of people 65 years old and over will increase by 37.7 percent, compared with a 26.6 percent increase for the entire population. If the fertility rate continues to decrease from the current level, the median age and the proportion of people aged

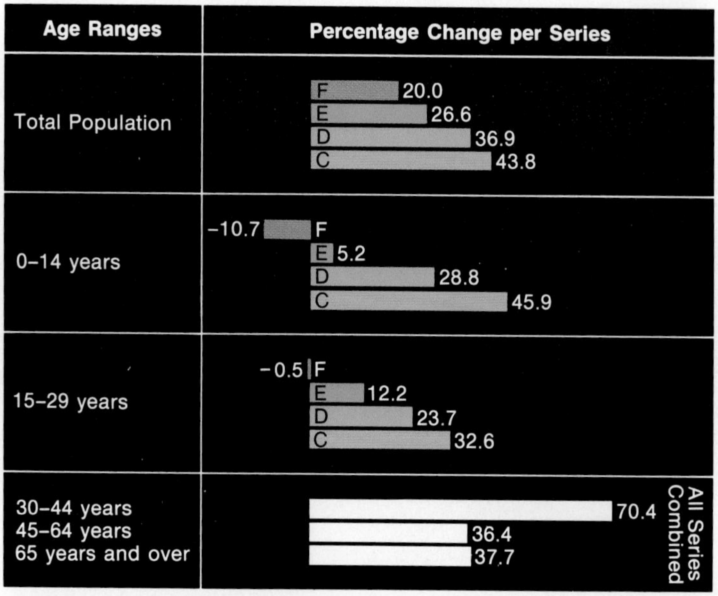

Age Ranges	Percentage Change per Series		
Total Population	F 20.0	E 26.6	D 36.9 / C 43.8
0–14 years	−10.7 F	E 5.2	D 28.8 / C 45.9
15–29 years	−0.5 F	E 12.2	D 23.7 / C 32.6
30–44 years 45–64 years 65 years and over	70.4 36.4 37.7		All Series Combined

Figure 4. Four Different Series of Projections of Percentage Change in Distribution of United States Population by Age from 1972 to 2000. See Figure 2 for fertility assumption of each series. (Source: Bureau of the Census)

65 and over will be still higher. Regardless of the fertility rate, *life expectancy* will increase slightly, for women from 75.1 years in 1971 to 75.8 years in 2000, and for men from 67.4 years to 69.6 years. But if concern for old people and their problems depends on any demographic factor (as opposed to social and political factors), it is their proportion in the population, which depends on the fertility rate. This proportion will increase as long as the fertility rate remains below approximately 2.5 children per family.

The United States has always stood out among industrial nations for the low age at first marriage. In the last decade the average age at first marriage began to rise, partly because of the effects of the *"sexual revolution."* The fact that late marriage favors lower fertility will reinforce the current population trends. Although many people have predicted the disintegration of the family because of the tremendous recent rise in the divorce rate, some researchers predict that late marriage will have the effect of increasing the family's strength.

In 1972 the Presidential Commission on Population Growth and the American Future compared the effects on the economy of a two-child-per-family population projection and a three-child projection and concluded:

1. Major economic changes are on the horizon regardless of future changes in population growth rates.
2. The nation has nothing to fear from a gradual approach to population stabilization.
3. From an economic point of view, a reduction in the rate of population growth would bring important benefits, especially if the United States develops policies to take advantage of opportunities for social and economic improvement that slower population growth would provide.

The commission predicts that, regardless of the magnitude of population growth, the average family income will exceed $21,000 by the year 2000 (a sharp rise from the $12,000 figure for 1972) and that consumption will more than double. Per capita income will be about 15 percent higher with a two-child-per-family growth rate, but the gross national product will be lower than it would with a three-child growth rate. In the 1970s the number of people entering the labor force will be far greater than in the 1960s, straining the ability of the economy to provide jobs for all. If the two-child growth rate prevails, this problem will be eased during the 1980s and 1990s, because the number of new entrants will not increase significantly during those decades. As for poverty, the commission states, "We have found that the general improvement in average income associated with slower population growth would assist in reducing poverty, but would not eliminate it."

The commission also evaluated the future of resources and the environment. In some areas slow population growth could significantly reduce *ecological damage.* The use of pesticides and artificial fertilizers would have to be increased greatly to feed the population that would result from the three-child growth rate. In 50 years the deficit of clean water would be twice as great with a three-child growth rate as with a two-child growth rate. But it will be primarily the economy rather than the population growth rate that determines the rates of depletion of nonrenewable resources, energy production and consumption, and pollution. Slow population growth will reduce the damage to some extent, but the better economic life we will all enjoy will continue to devastate the Earth's *life-support systems*. In short, population growth is not the central problem; "The real risk lies in the fact that increasing numbers press us to adopt new techniques before we know what we are doing."

Although there is no convincing research on the future political climate of the United States, the commission contends that slow population growth will minimize the problems of government, both by keeping down demands for government services and by increasing per capita financial resources to fund government programs. Nevertheless, the problems faced by government should not be minimized; the heaviest burden will fall on governments in metropolitan areas, which are already in grave difficulty.

Throughout the history of the United States most racial, ethnic, and religious minorities have had higher fertility rates than the Northern European, Protestant majority. (But Jews have a lower fertility rate than the WASP majority.) But racial, ethnic, and religious fertility differences are marred by the comparison of minority and majority. An examination of birth rates in most industrial nations found the rate among Catholics to be higher than the Protestant rate when Catholics were the minority, but lower than the Protestant rate when Catholics were the majority. Minorities are frequently denied educational, occupational, and economic opportunities; a low fertility rate is usually found among people who rank high in these areas. Birth rates for minority groups are decreasing along with the birth rate for the entire population. (The lowest fertility rate in the United States is found among black women with college degrees.) It is difficult to say whether the rate of decrease for minority birth rates differs from that of the rest of the population—different methods of computation yield conflicting results—but on the basis of current demographic data, no major change in present trends is apparent.

iv Evaluation In predicting the future, research often lapses into speculation. The estimates of the future size of the United States population are prepared scientifically, with great attention to methodology, but the Bureau of the Census cautions that its projections may be inaccurate. Of course short-term projections are more accurate than long-term ones, and the bureau's projections for the people already alive should prove nearly exact. Thus we can have a reasonable estimate of the number of people over age 65 in the year 2000, but can we say with certainty anything about what their *social status* will be? Because status, even more than statistical projections, depends heavily on variables related to the unfathomable political, social, and economic events of years to come, we can say only that because the elderly will probably make up a more significant segment of the society in future decades if Americans have two children instead of three, the intense emphasis our society currently places on youth will be replaced by greater concern for the needs, interests, attributes and values of those on the far side of 30.

If it continues to expand, the Anaconda Corporation's open pit mine will eventually take the city of Butte, Montana.

But this fact does not fully address the original question: Who will the American people be? The mixture of research and speculation presented here may be able to predict accurately the nature of one aspect of American society, but suppose all the most optimistic estimates are correct. In that event the American population will be older and richer, have more leisure time, enjoy redefined sex roles, and the like. Even when all these changes are added up, we still are not able to predict how happy the American people will be, how harmoniously the various components of the population will interact —with each other and with the environment.

3 Overview

The sudden and drastic reduction of death rates in nonindustrial nations may well lead to a far more dangerous situation than the spread of nuclear weapons. The control of disease and the distribution of medicines (especially in relation to the impressive reduction of malaria in Asia) has diminished one of what Malthus called "positive" checks on population—death—and the result is that those countries *least* able to support more life are now experiencing a doubling of their already swollen numbers every 25 years. Starvation and deprivation are therefore increasing in these Third World nations as well, and eventually they will serve as further "positive" checks on population growth; meanwhile, they render the *quality of life* there increasingly impoverished and harsh.

"Consider what it would mean for a country like the Philippines or Honduras to double its population in some 20 years," write demographers Paul and Anne Ehrlich:

> There would be nearly twice as many families in 20 years; today's children would be adults and have their own children. In order to maintain present living standards, such a country must, in two decades, duplicate every amenity for the support of human beings. Where there is one home today there must be two (or their equivalent). Where there is one schoolroom there must be two. Where there is one hospital, garage, judge, doctor, or mechanic, there must be two. Agricultural production must be doubled. Imports and exports must be doubled. The capacity of roads, water systems, electric generating plants, and so on must be doubled. It is problematical whether the United States could accomplish a doubling of its facilities in 20 years, and yet the United States has abundant capital, the world's finest industrial base, rich natural resources, excellent communications, and a population virtually 100 percent literate. The Philippines, Honduras, and other UDCs [underdeveloped countries] have none of these things. They are not even going to be able to maintain their present low standards of living. (*Population, Resources, Environment,* 1970)

It has been demonstrated that family planning is not in itself an adequate way of curbing the birth rate. But affluent nations cannot simply allow unchecked nature once again to eliminate excess

Seventeenth-century engraving by Stradanus Galle of windmills and water wheels in operation. Nonpolluting energy-producing devices used in the past may become sources of hope for the future.

(Facing page) In search of the future American.

population in developing or "hungry" nations; they cannot withhold vaccines or pesticides so that disease will restore *population balance*. More constructive approaches to reducing the birth rate include legal, safe, and easily accessible abortions and incentives to make families want to have fewer children through preferential housing, employment, and favorable tax rates. (In India many couples feel the need to keep producing more children in hopes that some will be sons and flourish long enough to provide for their parents' old age.) *Standards of living* must be improved so that the correlation between education and the desire to have fewer offspring will become effective on an international scale that includes the Third World.

In the United States, where the fertility rate is declining, average income is expected to go up, as is the average age of the population. These beneficial circumstances will involve some further adjustments, among them the fact that there may be no really convincing argument for continued national economic growth at the continued expense of the *biosphere,* the part of the world in which life can exist. Because the United States, with only 6 percent of the world's population, consumes an astounding 35 percent of the world's energy, the responsibility for developing new, clean, and inexpensive sources of power clearly falls on its shoulders, and it must similarly enforce measures to reduce domestic drain on the current supply. The problems of population and of energy resources and distribution are two aspects of the most complex and urgent dilemma facing the world today. The way we resolve it will determine the health of both the natural and the human environment as our children and grandchildren enter the year 2001.

D   LOOKING AHEAD

1   Interview:
Paul R. Ehrlich

Paul R. Ehrlich is professor of biology at Stanford University. He has done field and laboratory research on a wide array of problems ranging from studies of the ecological and evolutionary interactions of plants and herbivores to experimental studies of the effect of crowding on human beings. He collaborates with his wife Anne in work on the dynamics and genetics of insect populations and, especially, in policy research relative to problems of human ecology. His books include *Population, Resources, and Environment* (with Anne Ehrlich) and the controversial *The Population Bomb*. Other interviews in *The Study of Society* were conducted by The Dushkin Publishing Group. The interview with Prof. Ehrlich, however, is extracted from *Playboy* magazine. (Extracted from "PLAYBOY" Interview: Dr. Paul Ehrlich," PLAYBOY Magazine, August 1970; Copyright ©1970 by Playboy.)

PLAYBOY   *Why do you say the death of the world is imminent?*

EHRLICH   Because the human population of the planet is about five times too large, and we're managing to support all these people—at today's level of misery—only by spending our capital, burning our fossil fuels, dispersing our mineral resources and turning our fresh water into salt water. We have not only overpopulated but overstretched our environment. We are poisoning the ecological systems of the earth —systems upon which we are ultimately dependent for all of our food, for all of our oxygen and for all of our waste disposal. These very complex ecosystems are made up of many different kinds of organisms; we're killing off those organisms and simplifying the systems. The stability of ecosystems is dependent on their complexity; if they become simple, they become unstable.

Suppose, by analogy, that our lives depended on the functioning of a very complex computer. If transistors were being removed from that computer at random, we would have reason to be concerned. In the same way, every time we turn over more land to one-crop farming, every time we eliminate a species, as we are doing with the California condor, the peregrine falcon and the brown pelican, we reduce the complexity of the systems upon which our very existence depends.

In a balanced ecological system, the effects of sudden fluctuations in the population of one species are canceled out by the actions of other species. Should one natural predator of a pest fall prey to a new disease, the complexity of the system ensures that other predators will keep the pest population in check while the diseased species builds new immunities. What man does is counter to this natural process and, in the long run, to his own best interests. When we use synthetic pesticides to increase crop yields, we reduce the population of the pests' natural enemies, because most of these chemicals are toxic to both the pests and their predators. Once we eliminate the natural controls, we have to use even more pesticides. The insects build up immunities and become resistant to the pesticides, while their predators may very well be wiped out. So by spraying miracle crops, we simplify the system to the point where we have not only miracle crops but miracle pests, and the only way we can keep on is to use more chemicals that slowly poison *us*.

If we do something to an ecological system in one place, the whole system is affected. We must learn to look at the whole world and the people in it as a single interlocked system. It's impossible to do something somewhere that has no effect anywhere else. There are a number of ecological rules it would be wise for people to remember. One of them is that there is no such thing as a free lunch. Another is that when we change something into something else, the new thing is usually more dangerous than what we had originally. We can't affect one part without affecting another. People must learn those laws of dependencies and interrelationships. One of the greatest defects of our Government is its failure to educate people about the interconnections among population, pollution, environmental deterioration, war and resource depletion. . . .

PLAYBOY *Isn't the public becoming aware of these problems and aren't we beginning to move toward remedies?*

EHRLICH We're hearing a lot of talk now, but that's one of the problems. Politicians are talking about ecology and most of them don't have the vaguest idea of what it's all about. Even many of those involved in ecology don't really have the facts. But the main hang-up at the moment isn't just that people are doing a tremendous amount of talking without much knowledge; it's that no *action* has been taken—no action whatsoever—on either the population or the environmental front. The things the Administration is talking about doing to help the environment—emission standards for automobiles and so forth—are like giving aspirin to a cancer victim.

PLAYBOY *But hasn't all the rhetoric begun to spur research into possible technological remedies that may make ecological disaster much less likely?*

EHRLICH Man's technology hasn't eliminated all of the natural controls on his population, but it has artificially expanded, at least temporarily, the carrying capacity of the planet. Let me give you an analogy. Suppose we put gelatin nutrient, banana and a pair of fruit flies into a bottle. The fruit flies breed, their offspring breed and the population builds up. Eventually, the population becomes so large that the excreta of the flies fouls the medium and the food supply diminishes to a critical level. The fly population dies off or dies back to a lower level. By increasing the size of the bottle or putting more food into it, we haven't removed any natural controls; we have only temporarily increased the carrying capacity of the environment. Eventually, the flies will again overshoot the carrying capacity of the bottle and die. Man's technology has temporarily expanded the carrying capacity of the earth, but increasing that capacity without population control only guarantees that a larger number of people will die in misery than would have died if we hadn't increased the carrying capacity.

You have to understand the sheer numbers of the problem and the rate of acceleration of population growth. It took about 10,000 years for world population to grow from 5,000,000 to 500,000,000 in 1650 A.D., so population was doubling approximately

every 1000 or 1500 years. World population reached one billion in 1850; the doubling time had been reduced to 200 years. Two billion was reached by 1930; that's a doubling in 80 years. We've almost completed the next doubling, only 40 years later. We're adding 70,000,000 people to the world every year. This means that we have a new United States—in population and all that implies in terms of environmental stresses—*every three years*. Let me put it another way. In all of the wars fought by the United States, we have suffered around 600,000 combat deaths. World population makes up that amount in about half a week. If current growth could continue, in 900 years there would be about 100 people per square yard of the earth's surface. Needless to say, population growth will come to a screeching and disastrous halt long before then.

PLAYBOY *What is the maximum population the world could support without environmental damage?*

EHRLICH It's difficult to determine the ideal population. There probably is no such static figure, but many scientists think the population of the United States should eventually be reduced to well under 50,000,000 and that of the world to an absolute maximum of 500,000,000.

PLAYBOY *Could family planning cut the birth rate and reduce population to this optimum level?*

EHRLICH In general, around the world, the problem isn't unwanted babies but *wanted* babies. This doesn't mean we shouldn't have an all-out campaign to reduce the number of unwanted births, even if they aren't that important, on the whole. Some people estimate that in the United States, a third of the babies are unwanted and that if we can eliminate these births, we will go a long way toward solving our population problem. Perhaps, but it's very difficult to determine how many children people want. They say one thing and perform differently. Certainly, it's important that no woman be compelled to have a child she doesn't want; but as far as the world demographic situation is concerned, we have to change people's attitudes on how many children they *do* want. Despite the fact that family planning has existed in many countries for a long time and in the United States for well over 60 years, we still have rapid population growth. We've tried family planning and we know it doesn't work. That doesn't mean family planning isn't valuable, but more is needed to persuade people not to have too many children.

PLAYBOY *How many is too many?*

EHRLICH Any more than two is too many. With a limit of two children per family, the average will move down to somewhere around 1.3 or 1.4, and that's what we need to bring rapid population growth in the United States to a halt before the end of this century.

PLAYBOY *Do you think Government regulations will be necessary to achieve this?*

EHRLICH The first thing we should try is a Government propaganda campaign in which the President says, "Starting now, no patriotic American family should have more than two children." And we should start a TV campaign of spot commercials to keep reinforcing the idea that it's better for all concerned—especially the parents—to have families of two children or, if you want more, to adopt them; that it's stupid and irresponsible to have large families. We should also eliminate the notion that there is something strange or barren about a childless couple.

PLAYBOY   *What if simple reason doesn't work and people continue to reproduce at an excessive rate?*

EHRLICH   If we're going to attack this problem, the Government has to act intelligently, starting with the least coercive measures to remove the pressure, the conditioning, to reproduce. If propaganda doesn't work, the Government could give *incentives* not to reproduce. If those fail, it could resort to disincentives—such as changes in the tax structure. The thing is that eventually, if we don't manage population control with voluntary means, the Government will have to step in and employ sanctions of some sort. Laws control the number of wives you can have now and, if necessary, they'll control the number of children you can have, too.

PLAYBOY   *Wouldn't people resist Government interference with what most consider an inviolable individual freedom?*

EHRLICH   People aren't sufficiently aware that their freedoms are rapidly disappearing *because* there are more and more people. As population grows, we find that there are more and more restrictive laws on where we can drive, whether we can own a gun, whether we can fly an airplane, where we can throw our garbage, whether we can burn leaves. And as conditions become more crowded, even stricter and more comprehensive Government controls and regulations will be implemented. . . .

PLAYBOY   *Aren't some nations, such as Japan, with fewer resources and greater population densities than ours, attempting to increase population?*

EHRLICH   Japan's recent move to increase the birth rate may go down in history as one of the most idiotic moves ever made by a government, although there are many contenders for that honor. Japan already has to import around half of her food and she has to take from the sea roughly one and a half times the protein she is able to grow on land. She's involved in a race with other countries to get the last protein out of the sea. She is soon going to have very grave feeding problems and, with her present population-doubling rate of about 70 years, she will eventually have to turn aggressively toward the mainland. But even

without military aggression, highly developed nations such as Japan, Russia and the United States are far more serious ecological threats than the underdeveloped nations in Asia or Latin America.

PLAYBOY   *Even though the populations of countries such as India are growing much faster than those of the highly developed nations?*

EHRLICH   Absolutely. The average white, middle-class baby born in the United States has a future of consumption and pollution ahead of him that cannot be matched by *50* of his counterparts in Calcutta, who will probably not have enough food to survive as long as it will take the American kid to reach his peak consumption years. To keep that American baby in the style this country has decided is necessary, a large quantity of the natural resources of underdeveloped nations will have to be mined and made available to American industry. Most of the time, this exploitation doesn't require legions of occupying troops. We have the technology to extract the resources and use them; the underdeveloped nations don't. So we go in and build our plants or set up our mines, which employ a number of the natives who lived in absolute poverty before industry came along. In return for beefing up the local economy, we get the minerals, some of which may filter back into the economy of the nation that owned them. But as resources become scarcer, the populations of the developed countries grow larger and the governments of the poorer nations turn more nationalistic, competitions and frictions will develop that may very well lead us to war. The earth is running out of some very critical natural resources; the demand isn't easing, it's increasing; and in many cases, no substitutes are readily available. . . .

PLAYBOY   *Haven't there been radical advances in agriculture that will make it possible to meet the nutritional needs of our expanding population?*

EHRLICH   That's the famous "green revolution." The best way to evaluate the wildly optimistic claims of its proponents is to refer to *Time* magazine, November eighth, 1948, which reported that the agriculturalists expected in 12 years—by 1960—to be able to feed everybody in the world without any problem. Although some people thought there would be two and a quarter billion people by 1960, *Time* said other experts believed this was an overestimate. Well, in 1960 there were *three* billion people and the agricultural experts weren't feeding half of them. My reply to the prophets of agricultural utopia is: When you can adequately feed the 3.6 billion people we have now—including the 10,000,000 to 20,000,000 who are dying of starvation each year—come back and tell us how you'll feed the seven billion we'll have by the year 2000. Until you can do that, why don't you just shut up and get back to work? . . .

PLAYBOY   *Can the complexity of the ecological problem be made clear to people through advertising? Wouldn't such a program be likely to suggest simplistic answers that might be counterproductive in the long run?*

EHRLICH   There is a great danger of rampant know-nothingism from all sides in this area. The problems are so complex that you can be fairly sure that no single simplistic solution is right. But people *have* learned the word ecology, and now they're going to have to start learning what ecology is all about and how it relates not only to their welfare but to their survival. The essentials of the science of ecology won't be hard for this well-educated society to learn; the hard part will be learning to live differently than we do now—to conserve rather than to consume, to abstain rather than to indulge, to share rather than to hoard, to realize that the welfare of others is indistinguishable from our own.

PLAYBOY   *Can people be persuaded to modify their high standards of living in order to save the environment?*
EHRLICH   The usual concept of a standard of living is really absurd. How do you measure a standard of living? By the number of four-slot toasters per capita? Or by the quality of education, recreational facilities, cultural events and physical health? But

whether or not we decide to make sacrifices, the population-environment problem in the United States is going to cause a decline in any genuinely human standard of living. As I think everyone knows, we're falling farther and farther behind in the effort to keep our air and water clean, to provide adequate schooling for our children and to supply good transportation and decent housing for our citizens. Even without a major disaster, our lives seem doomed to become nastier, shorter and more brutish as a result of our unceasing pursuit of a "high standard of living," which is simply not a rational measure of what's desirable in life. I think people will begin to see that and move toward ecological sanity. . . .

PLAYBOY   *What happens, though, if public interest fades and the problems remain?*
EHRLICH   Well, most likely, we as a race will fade away, too. For good. I sometimes start my speeches by saying the environmental crisis began on January second, 8000 B.C. The levity escapes my audiences, more often than not, but the message is there. As soon as man began to farm the land, he began to significantly alter the ecology of the planet. Everything he has done since has made the situation worse. For most of man's life on the earth, however, his disruptions were small enough in scale to be handled by the biosphere—that thin layer of earth, air and water which supports and binds together all forms of life on earth. But with the Industrial Revolution, man tipped the scales; it became possible for him to overload the biosphere and destroy it piecemeal. He's been doing it, rather stubbornly, ever since.

When man mastered his own tools and intelligence enough to escape the earth and view it from space, however, he learned that what he has been given is not infinite. Those striking pictures of earth taken from the moon may be the greatest reward of the entire space program—an effort that certainly isn't ecologically sound in any other way. All anyone who doesn't believe in the severity of the crisis has to do to convince himself is look at those pictures of space-

ship earth suspended in the black void. That's it—all we have, one little orb.

That orb and most of the other heavenly bodies are much older than man. Many of the creatures of the earth have seniority over us. They made it this far by remaining compatible with their environment, by adapting and adjusting to the natural circumstances of their existence. There are many species that have vanished because they could not adapt. It's not at all inconceivable that man will follow these creatures into extinction. If he continues to reproduce at the present soaring rate, continues to tamper with the biosphere, continues to toy around with apocalyptic weapons, he will probably share the fate of the dinosaur. If he learns to adapt to the finitude of the planet, to the changed character of his existence, he may survive. If not, nothing like him is likely to evolve ever again. The world will be inherited by a creature more adaptable and tenacious than he.

PLAYBOY   *Is there such a creature?*
EHRLICH   Yes. The cockroach.

Unit 7

Marriage, Kinship, and the Family

SCHEMATIC OUTLINE

A Introductory Graphics: Marriage and Social Organization

B Definition and Context

1 Definition

Marriage is an institutionally sanctioned union between a man and a woman that assumes some permanence and conformity to societal norms. "The family" refers to the marriage partners plus their children, and "kinship" refers to the larger network of affinal and consanguineal relatives.

2 World Context

Monogamy is the prevalent form of marriage in most societies, but the conjugal family varies widely in its relationship with extended kinship organizations.

3 American Context

In recent years Americans have challenged many conventional assumptions about marriage and the family. Robin Williams has described the characteristic American kinship system, and Evelyn Duvall has identified the stages of the family life cycle.

C Questions and Evidence

1 Questions

Three questions are of significance to the general population as well as to sociologists: (1) Do poor people tend to have less substantial or stable relationships than those of the more affluent classes in the United States? (2) Why are the patterns of marriage and family attitudes changing throughout the world? (3) How has the shift in population from rural to urban areas changed family and kinship patterns?

2 Evidence

a The "Burning Issue" Question

The highly publicized "Moynihan Report," a political statement of the "culture of poverty" position developed by Oscar Lewis and others, has been challenged on methodological and empirical grounds. Herbert Gans and other advocates of the situational approach to poverty focus on the behavioral consequences of economic and political deprivation.

b The "Classical" Question

William Goode argued that the worldwide tendency toward the conjugal family has multiple causes but is significantly related to changes in ideologies and values connected with industrialization. His viewpoint has been extended and modified by several researchers.

c The "Research" Question

Recent studies have shown that the modified extended family is more prevalent and more functional in the city than is the isolated conjugal family. The research by John Mogey, Evelyn Bott, and Lee Rainwater is particularly stimulating.

3 Overview

Shifts in family patterns reflect changes in the social fabric and should be thoroughly studied.

D Looking Ahead

1 Interview: Charles R. Lawrence

SUPPORTING UNITS

ENCYCLOPEDIA ENTRIES

aging
arranged marriage
bigamy
common-law marriage
courtship
dating behavior
day care
divorce
endogamy
exogamy
family
group marriage
incest taboo
marital roles
marriage
marriage counseling
matriarchal family
mixed marriage
monogamy
patriarchal family
polygamy
trial marriage
widowhood

MARRIAGE AND SOCIAL ORGANIZATION

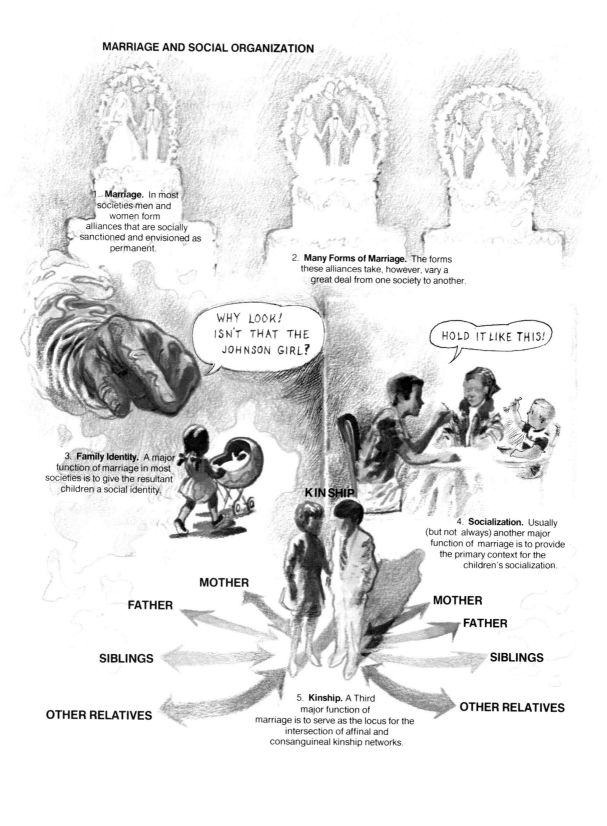

1. **Marriage.** In most societies men and women form alliances that are socially sanctioned and envisioned as permanent.

2. **Many Forms of Marriage.** The forms these alliances take, however, vary a great deal from one society to another.

WHY LOOK! ISN'T THAT THE JOHNSON GIRL?

HOLD IT LIKE THIS!

3. **Family Identity.** A major function of marriage in most societies is to give the resultant children a social identity.

KINSHIP

4. **Socialization.** Usually (but not always) another major function of marriage is to provide the primary context for the children's socialization.

MOTHER

FATHER

MOTHER

FATHER

SIBLINGS

SIBLINGS

OTHER RELATIVES

OTHER RELATIVES

5. **Kinship.** A Third major function of marriage is to serve as the locus for the intersection of affinal and consanguineal kinship networks.

B DEFINITION AND CONTEXT

1 Definition

The family is the most important group to which most individuals belong. It provides a framework for intimate and enduring interaction among its members and acts as a mediator between them and the larger society from birth until death. It is the primary socializing agent as well as a continuous force in shaping the course of the individual's life.

Because the family is such a pervasive and socially valued institution, it is vital that we understand its various functions in relation to the rapid technological and cultural changes occurring in the modern world and in contemporary American society. This unit will deal with variations in marriage, family, and kinship systems and with the factors that influence stability and change in them.

First it is necessary to define some key terms. *Marriage is an institutionally sanctioned union between a man and a woman that assumes some permanence and conformity to societal norms.* Such unions may be legally or socially sanctioned (common-law marriage being an example of the latter). *"The family" refers to the marriage partners plus their children and connotes a set of statuses and roles acquired through marriage and procreation. Kinship refers to the network of relatives associated either through marriage (affinal kin) or by common blood (consanguineal kin).*

2 World Context

Debates on the universality of the family frequently center on semantic arguments about varying definitions and conceptualizations. A more useful line of investigation focuses on the significance of the family for individuals, kinship groups, and the social structure as a whole.

The basic family group is the *nuclear family*, which consists of husband, wife, and children. It is also referred to as the *conjugal family*, emphasizing the importance of the marriage bond. The number of people in the marriage bond varies: one man and one woman *(monogamy)*, one man and several women *(polygyny)*, one woman and several men *(polyandry)*, and several men and women *(group marriage)*. In George P. Murdock's *World Ethnographic Sample* (1957), an analysis of a carefully selected sample of 565 of the world's societies, only about 20 percent of the societies are designated as strictly monogamous; roughly 75 percent could be classified as favoring polygyny; less than 1 percent sanction polyandry; and virtually no society practices group marriage. But monogamy is the prevalent form of marriage in almost all societies; in all *polygamous* (polygynous *or* polyandrous) societies the privilege of having multiple spouses is restricted to a small minority, usually members of the higher social strata.

In *The Family in Cross-Cultural Perspective* (1963) William Stephens states that polygyny serves as a status distinction, a mark of prestige, because of the economic and political advantages of having several wives. (That is, when women have economic or political value, there is a greater demand for polygyny

Monogamy

Nuclear or Conjugal Family

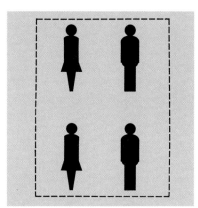

Spouses and Their Children

Vertical Extended Family

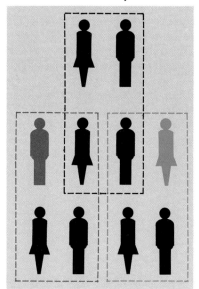

A three- (or more) generation family formed by the linking of three (or more) conjugal families. The offspring of the highest generation are the connecting links. This situation is a monogamous one, even though several conjugal families are linked.

Model 1. Forms of Family and Other Kinship-Based Organizations.

Polygamy

Polygyny: The Marriage of One Man to Several Women

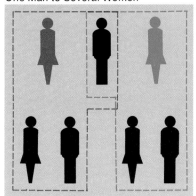

The man is the connecting link between the diverse conjugal families he forms with each spouse.

Polyandry: The Marriage of One Woman to Several Men

The woman is the connecting link between the diverse conjugal families she forms with each spouse.

Key

"X" "Y" = Marriage of "X" and "Y."

"A" "B" = "A" and "B" are siblings.

"X"
|
"A" = "A" is the child of "X."

☐ = Delineation of a single conjugal family.

than monogamy.) Conversely, polyandry, which is relatively rare, tends to prevail where there is a limited amount of land, conditions are hard, and wives are not economic assets. In polyandrous marital systems there is a *patriarchal* (male-dominant) organization in which one male agrees to share his wife with other men in exchange for their work services. Group marriage has not been a permanent characteristic of societal family patterns; it occasionally occurs during periods of societal turmoil and transition or in such short-term experiments as the Oneida Community in New York State from the 1840s to the 1880s.

Although the conjugal family group is a recognizable unit in most societies, there is a great variation in its autonomy. It is less autonomous if it is part of an *extended family system,* which is composed of two or more conjugal families related by blood. Unlike conjugal families, which emphasize the importance of the marital relationship, extended families place greater value on the consanguineal relationship. Upon marriage—which is usually arranged by the married couple's extended kinship families—the couple traditionally resides in the parental home of one spouse or the other. The residential pattern is called *patrilocal,* when they live in the husband's family's home, or *matrilocal,* when they reside in the wife's family's home. In either case the couple's relationship is subservient to the larger kinship organization. The extended family emphasizes continuity; the individual nuclear family emphasizes autonomy.

Extended kinship structures frequently are organized in *consanguineal lineages* or *clans,* which have served as the major structural units in most societies in the world. Inheritance, authority, and economic and status patterns in these societies are determined through kinship lineages; they also control marital and sexual partnerships. Many of the functions of these kinship groups are changing in response to technological and cultural innovations in the contemporary world. However, they still serve as the underlying principles for the organization and regulation of interpersonal and structural relationships.

In "The Family" (1956), Claude Lévi-Strauss, one of the world's most eminent anthropologists, has analyzed the marriage, family, and kinship groups that link man to woman, family to family, and kinship groups to the wider social organization all as a chain of exchanges. The division of labor between husband and wife serves to increase their dependency on one another, whereas the marriage of man to woman serves to develop links between kinship groups. Lévi-Strauss sees the continued accumulation of reciprocal obligations as the basis of the social structure of a given society. If this is the case, changes in the family structure can eventually have far-reaching societal results.

3 American Context

In recent years, as part of their intensive analysis of many of their fundamental ideas about the quality of life, Americans have challenged the conventional assumptions about the necessity of maintaining kinship relations, the desirability of the nuclear family, the inherent nature of male-female sex-role differences, the function of

The Louds of Santa Barbara, California, were chosen as a "typical" American family for a 1972 television documentary series. During the course of the series, William Loud was shown to be having extramarital liaisons, long-standing difficulties in the marriage led Patricia Loud to seek a divorce, and Lance, the eldest son, openly became a homosexual in New York. Many generalizations are made about the seemingly successful, white, middle-class family, but there are surprisingly little "hard" data on it. Social scientists have studied other types of family life more intensively than they have this.

the marital relationship (especially as it pertains to sexual fidelity or monogamy), and the importance of parenthood. Skepticism about these traditional relationships is manifest in the activities of the women's liberation movement, in the new sense of freedom from old social norms reflected by some segments of the youth culture, and in the reexamination of previously "sacred" attitudes against trial marriages, out-of-wedlock pregnancies, and abortions. The mass media have devoted much attention to the future of the family, and divorce statistics are constantly cited as evidence of conventional matrimony's declining validity in today's society. A prevalent attitude declares that the family is a dying institution, and much concern is expressed about the implications for mankind, its offspring, and the health of the social order.

Contemporary American marriage, family, and kinship systems vary to some extent according to social class, ethnicity, race, religion, geographical region, and urban-rural residence. Nevertheless, an overall kinship structure and its normative or cultural system can be identified. In *American Society* (1970), for example, Robin Williams emphasizes 10 characteristics of the American kinship system. The first four regulate family lineage and organization structure and the first three are legally as well as socially enforced.

First, the incest taboo forbids marriages with certain relatives: an individual cannot marry his parent, sibling, grandparent, uncle, aunt, niece, or nephew in any of the 50 states, and 29 states prohibit the marriage of first cousins. *Second,* polygamous marriage is prohibited; marriage must be monogamous. *Third,* a person is not required to marry individuals who are related to him or her paternally or maternally. *Fourth,* the descent system tends to be *bilineal* (or *multilineal*); that is, no special preference is given to the lineage of either the mother or the father (except that the children take on the father's last name). Thus neither lineage can maintain or exert structural dominance over the conjugal family.

The *fifth* important characteristic is the emphasis on the conjugal family as opposed to the extended kin group. Societies that have highly developed *unilineal* systems (preference to lineage of either mother or father) deemphasize the marital relationship; in those societies the spouse is viewed as a "symbolic" outsider. Urban, middle-class couples typify American society's emphasis on the conjugal family.

The *sixth* and *seventh* characteristics focus on the importance of the husband-wife-child relationship. Conjugal families tend to set up their own households (*neolocal* residences) and to act as the effective consumption and social unit. Except in extraordinary crisis situations, extended kin are expected not to interfere with the autonomy and privacy of the conjugal family. Furthermore, the conjugal family is not now a producing economic unit, as it was in the era of the small farm and shop. With the growth of American industry and the birth of the giant corporation, the family has been transformed primarily into a consuming unit.

Multilineality and the emphasis on the conjugal family results in the *eighth* characteristic, the lessened importance of family tradition and family continuity. But a notable exception appears in the upper-upper class of inherited wealth, where there is great concern with family tradition and lineage.

The *ninth* characteristic is the relative independence of the mate selection from kinship control. The *tenth,* which is linked to this free marriage choice, is the widespread geographical dispersion of adult children from the parental household. This characteristic appears especially when the children are striving for or have achieved upward social mobility.

The delineation of these major structural elements of the dominant kinship system in America provides a model that can serve as the comparative base for an analysis of various social class and substructural variations as well as for an understanding of emerging marital and familial patterns.

Sociologists of the family have schematically presented the development of the typical American family relationship through the concept of the *family life cycle.* In *Family Development* (1969) Evelyn Duvall views that cycle as consisting of eight stages. The *first stage,* which lasts two years, involves young married couples without children. The *second stage,* childbearing families, lasts from the birth of the first child until he or she is two and one-half years old. *Stage three,* families with preschool children, covers the three-and-one-half year period just before the oldest child enters school. The *fourth* (families with school children) and *fifth* (families with teenagers) stages both last seven years. *Stage six,* families as launching centers, covers the approximately eight-year period until the youngest child leaves home. During the *seventh* and *eighth stages* the married couple is once again without children living within the household. Duvall estimates that this period is approximately half of the family life cycle.

Duvall emphasizes that throughout its life cycle, the family, both as a whole and through its individual members, performs certain "developmental" tasks that are essential to its survival, growth, and continuity. These include the socialization of its members, physical maintenance (providing food, clothing, and so on, for the family), and the maintenance of motivation and morale (that is, rewarding members for achievements and satisfying individual needs for acceptance). Questions concerning socialization were discussed in Unit 5.

This *ideal type* of the American marriage, family, and kinship system largely ignores the variations that can be attributed to social class, ethnicity, regionalism, and the like. Such variations, and their implications for the social order, can best be presented by contrasting them with the "normal" family system.

C   QUESTIONS AND EVIDENCE

1   Questions

Three questions about marriage, kinship, and family systems are of significance to the general population as well as to sociologists: (1) Do poor people tend to have less substantial or stable family relationships than those of the more affluent classes in the United States? Is the model of the American family really just a middle-class ideal? (2) Why are the patterns of marriage and family attitudes undergoing significant changes around the world? Why is there a trend toward the nuclear family unit and away from the mutual interdependence of relatives in family compounds? (3) How has the shift in population from rural to urban areas changed family and kinship patterns?

2 Evidence

a The "Burning Issue" Question

i Context After the 1954 Supreme Court school desegregation decision, and especially following the assassination of President Kennedy in 1963, a number of civil rights acts were passed by Congress. Yet such events as the riots in the black community of Watts still occurred. White Americans could not understand why such a problem would arise in 1965, when the range of opportunities open to blacks had ostensibly been improving steadily. Weren't things better than ever before?

This quest for a simple solution was partially satisfied by accounts of an unpublished and officially confidential report that claimed to pinpoint the causes of discontent within black ghettos. Entitled *The Negro Family: The Case for National Action,* this document was prepared by the Office of Policy Planning and Research of the United States Department of Labor under the supervision of the Assistant Secretary of Labor, Daniel P. Moynihan. The report was eventually made public and is popularly referred to as the "Moynihan Report." It opened with the following statements:

> At the heart of the deterioration of the fabric of Negro society is the deterioration of the Negro family.
>
> It is the fundamental source of the weakness of the Negro community at the present time.

This explanation of ghetto riots—the "tangle of pathology" occurring within the black community, particularly within the black family—was widely publicized in the national media. But it raised a number of questions. Do poor people tend to have less substantial or stable family relationships than those of the more affluent classes in the United States? Is the model of the American family really just a middle-class ideal? In the face of the controversy the Moynihan Report provoked, sociologists asked: *Do poverty families perpetuate poverty conditions?*

ii Theory To make sense of the sociological discussions of poverty and its relationship to lower class families, the two major positions must be delineated. The first focuses on cultural factors, the second on situational factors.

The *cultural position* argues that social conditions under poverty may have long-range effects on individuals' and families' behavior and values. More importantly, these conditions may lead to the development of self-perpetuating cultural patterns. For example, Oscar Lewis, in *La Vida* (1965) and other case studies, hypothesizes the development in class-stratified, highly individuated capitalist societies of a *culture of poverty*—a virtually autonomous subculture existing among the poor that is self-perpetuating and self-defeating. As an adaptation and reaction to societal conditions, the culture of poverty "represents an effort to cope with feelings of hopelessness and despair that arise from the realization by members of the marginal communities in these societies of the improbability of their achieving success in terms of the prevailing values and goals." This hopelessness and despair, this sense of resignation and fatalism, involves an inability to put off the satisfaction of immediate desires in order to plan for the future, which in turn results in an endlessly reinforcing cycle: low educational motivation leads to inadequate job preparation, which perpetuates poverty, unemployment, and despair.

Black Muslim family. If we take the point of view of the "culture of poverty" analysts, we would see the Black Muslims as attacking the problem of ghetto decay at the most productive level—working to cement the solidarity of black ghetto families.

Based on his own research in Mexico, Puerto Rico, and New York, Lewis describes certain characteristics of poverty families that he believes hold true under every capitalist system:

> On the family level the major traits of the culture of poverty are the absence of childhood as a specially prolonged and protected stage in the life cycle, early initiation into sex, free unions or consensual marriages, a relatively high incidence of abandonment of wives and children, a trend toward female- or mother-centered families and consequently a much greater knowledge of maternal relatives, a strong predisposition to authoritarianism, lack of privacy, verbal emphasis upon family solidarity, which is only rarely achieved because of sibling rivalry, and competition for limited goods and maternal affection.

The *situational approach* postulates that although the behavior of the poverty family does not follow the middle-class pattern, the values or culture of that group is basically the same as those of the middle class. Herbert J. Gans and others view the poor as an economically and politically deprived group whose values and behavior are specific adaptations to poverty conditions, just as the behavior and attitudes of the affluent are adaptations to their social situation. In *Tally's Corner* (1967), for example, Elliot Liebow argues that although each generation may provide *role models* for each succeeding one, the similarities between generations "do not result from 'cultural transmission' but from the fact that the son goes out and independently experiences the same failures, in the same areas, and for much the same reasons as his father."

Perhaps the lower classes do not reject the dominant values of society, but instead stretch them to fit their circumstances where they cannot fulfill them. Based on his observations of West Indian family life, Hyman Rodman developed this concept:

> By the value stretch I mean that the lower-class person, without abandoning the general values of the society, develops an alternative set of values. . . . The result is that the members of the lower class, in many areas, have a wider range of values than others within the society. They share the general values of the society with members of other classes, but in addition they have stretched these values, or developed alternative values, which help them to adjust to their deprived circumstances. ("The Lower Class Value Stretch," 1963)

These two theoretical positions affect the way sociologists design their research projects and interpret their data. More importantly, they have profoundly different or contrasting implications for social policy. The Moynihan Report is, of course, a case in point.

iii Research Although the Moynihan Report dealt with discrimination, unemployment, and poverty as basic causes of the difficulties of black lower-class family systems, its primary emphasis was on the deterioration of the Negro family and on the high incidence of broken families, illegitimate births, high delinquency and crime rates, and welfare dependency. It was based on data from census and governmental reports.

As Lee Rainwater and William Yancey emphasize in their masterful compilation of the popular and scholarly reactions to the report (*The Moynihan Report and the Politics of Controversy,* 1967), the document was neither an article prepared for a professional journal nor a simple governmental position paper; rather, it was a mixture that presented certain social science statistics while arguing a general policy position. It advocated a national effort to strengthen the black family to a position of "equality" with other American families. Without recommending any detailed policies, Moynihan argued that:

> The policy of the United States is to bring the Negro American to full and equal sharing in the responsibilities and rewards of citizenship. To this end, the programs of the Federal government bearing on this objective shall be designed to have the effect, directly or indirectly, of enhancing the stability and resources of the Negro American family.

The much-maligned black matriarchal family: "tangle of pathology" or realistic adaptation to conditions of chronic poverty that negatively sanction the presence of a man through curtailing welfare assistance? When this photo was carried in the famous Edward Steichen exhibit "The Family of Man," it was captioned "She is a tree of life to them."

Essentially, the report supported the "culture of poverty" position, stressing the social deprivations that blocked the Negro family from taking advantage of the opportunities of America, especially since the passing of civil rights legislation for equality of opportunity. Although antidiscrimination action had resulted in the removing of some barriers to liberty, the problem of inequality still existed. The freedom of blacks to compete with whites was not at issue, but the question of whether they have the equal resources to do so. The report demonstrated that the socioeconomic system played a role in the "deterioration of the Negro community" but emphasized the dysfunctional characteristics of the black *matriarchal* (female-headed) family structure and the resultant "tangle of pathology."

This argument was criticized on both methodological and theoretical grounds. Rainwater and Yancey state some of the methodological criticisms of the report:

1. The data were oversimplified. Moynihan failed to include figures that tended to contradict his hypothesis, and the data that were used did not lead to such semantically loaded conclusions as "rapid deterioration" and "alarming rate of illegitimacy."

2. The thesis did not consider the effects of the economic position and the differences between social classes. Analysis of these variables would wipe out the differences between black family life and the "norm."

3. The report downplayed the great range and variability in the black family and family behavior—including the great diversity of low-income families—and tended to focus on a narrow sampling of urban families on welfare. As Hylan Lewis pointed out, "When [this variability is] overlooked for any reason, there is danger that the depreciated, and probably more dramatic and threatening, characteristics of a small segment of the population may be imputed to an entire population." Other research has also shown that many families in the black inner-city ghettos have demonstrated an impressive capacity to adapt to the social, cultural, and economic deprivations foisted on them by the larger society and have developed strong familial relationships.

4. Data gathered by Rainwater contradict the notion that the matriarchal family is dysfunctional. He finds that there is an adaptive (that is, functional and appropriate) urban matricentric family.

The *situationalist* conterargument was exemplified in Elliot Liebow's study of lower-class black males in Washington, D.C. Liebow found no evidence indicating deviation from white middle-class norms or that family-role deviancy is perpetuated between generations. Thus he concluded that there is a clear relationship between socioeconomic discrimination and family instability; the former causes the latter, but the relationship does not operate in the reverse direction.

iv Evaluation The cultural emphasis on a special category of "poverty families" implies that the poor are poor through their own lack of ability and initiative and should thus be held responsible for implementing the necessary reforms. Such concepts as lower-class culture, cultural deprivation, social disorganization, family deprivation, and tangle of pathology have contributed to distorted views of the poor. Hyman Rodman believes they reflect middle-class judgments and argues that terms such as "pathological" should be applied to the total society rather than to lower-class behavior. He says that "promiscuous" sexual relationships, "illegitimate" children, and "unmarried" mothers should not be seen as problems peculiar to the lower class, but, in fact, as solutions to problems that lower-class persons face in the social, economic, and perhaps legal and political spheres of life.

Most social scientists agree that the Moynihan Report was more of a polemic than a scientifically valid argument. Herbert Gans' "The Negro Family" (1967)—which Rainwater and Yancey acknowledge to be the only thorough analysis of the report's social science base and political implications—describes the report as a call for a rash of "pseudopsychiatric programs" and a wave of social work and psychiatric solutions intended to change the Negro female-headed family to a middle-class model. Gans argues that knowledge about the black lower-class family is still relatively weak and notes that there is much greater certainty about the importance of economic deprivation in causing social problems. "It would thus be tragic if the findings were used to justify demands for Negro self-improvement or the development of a middle-class family structure before further programs to bring about real equality are set up."

b   The "Classical" Question

i   Context   In the ninetenth century the *Social Darwinists* attempted to apply the theory of biological evolution in such a way as to determine the origin and development of the family as well as other social institutions. Usually the family was depicted as advancing through states of primeval promiscuity, group marriage, polygamy, and finally to the apex of civilization—Victorian monogamy. Although Herbert Spencer, J. J. Bachofen, Henry Sumner Maine, and Lewis Henry Morgan gathered their data through historical literature and cross-cultural evidence of "primitive" peoples, they failed to develop a valid model of unilinear evolutionary family forms. The historical evidence was more fiction than fact, and the reports by missionaries and travelers were impressionistic and distorted. More importantly, these thinkers' basic assumption of unilinear evolution was wrong. The idea of the "primitiveness" of non-Western civilization was erroneous; such cultures are not relics of the Stone Age, but rather autonomous civilizations with distinctive evolutionary histories.

Even after Social Darwinist thought had been discredited, however, sociologists were still concerned with the relationship between social change and the family. During recent decades they have noted that marriage and family attitudes are undergoing significant changes around the world. There is a trend toward the nuclear family unit and away from the interdependence of relatives in family compounds. Confronting these changes, they ask: *What are the basic causes for the world revolution in marriage, family, and kinship patterns?*

ii   Theory William Goode's comprehensive analysis of changing family patterns during the last 50 years, *World Revolution and Family Patterns* (1963), notes a worldwide trend toward some type of conjugal family emphasizing the married couple and its children, with fewer kinship ties with distant relatives. Goode's conclusions are based on a massive historical analysis of comparative research data from Western countries, Arab countries, sub-Saharan Africa, India, China, and Japan.

Goode takes issue with the Marxist idea that the degree of family change is *primarily* a function of industrialization and technology. (It should be noted that Marx's co-writer Friedrich Engels in 1884 in *The Origin of the Family, Private Property and the State* had modified the Social Darwinist unilinear evolutionary theory so that monogamy was no longer viewed as the apex of civilization, but was instead regarded as a result of the subjugation of woman; therefore it represented the victory of private property over economic collectivism.) Goode argues that changes in family patterns are probably more closely related to changes in ideologies and values than to industrialization and technology themselves. He suggests that the hypothesis that the conjugal family emerges only *after* a society is exposed to industrialization ignores the theory that the conjugal family "fits" the modern industrial system and is particularly suited for helping to advance it. (For example, the independence of the conjugal family from extended kinship ties permits it to move where the jobs are, and the increased emotional component of the conjugal family relationship compensates for the increased pressures from the industrial order and the absence of kin relations.)

Goode believes that the ideology of economic progress and technological development as well as the ideology of the conjugal family both arose in non-Western societies before industrialization and worldwide changes in family patterns. An emphasis on industrial growth and social change placed tradition and custom on a lower level of importance; the worth of the individual was considered more important than his lineage, and personal welfare more important than family continuity. A third ideology, egalitarianism between the sexes, emphasizes the uniqueness of each individual within the family and gives lesser importance to sex status and seniority. This ideology reduces the sex and age inequalities of members within families and also undermines the traditional subordination of the young to the old.

All three of these ideologies aim directly or indirectly at terminating the dominance of extended family systems over the conjugal family units—and in particular over the young and over women. Furthermore, all three minimize the traditions of societies and assert the equality of the individual as against class, caste, or narrow sex-role definitions.

iii   Research (Survey) In *The Family* (1964) Goode compared the Chinese and Japanese family systems during the late nineteenth and early twentieth centuries to illustrate the importance of family patterns in assisting or hindering industrial change. In Japan patterns of inheritance, attitudes toward nepotism, narrow patterns of social mobility within the merchant class, and a feudal loyalty of individuals to their extended families and of the extended families to the state imperial system, all assured the rapid industrialization of the society. In China the patterns of inheritance—equal particulate inheritance in contrast to the Japanese system of the eldest inheriting all—prevented the accumulation of family capital, and the Chinese attitudes toward nepotism handicapped social mobility. Unlike the Japanese, the Chinese accorded a low social rank to merchants. Hence, when they became wealthy, individuals attempted to achieve prestige and power by becoming members of the gentry. That attempt prevented the steady accumulation of financial and technical expertise. Finally, although an individual owed loyalty to both the state (personified by the emperor) and his family, in the case of conflict between the two his first loyalty was to the family. Goode concluded that these different family systems played an important part in the industrial achievement of Japan and the lack of achievement in China.

Goode's argument that there is a worldwide trend to some type of conjugal family system has been questioned by several researchers. Sydney Greenfield, in "Industrialization and the Family in Sociological Theory" (1961), combined secondary analysis of historical and contemporary sources with his own research on the society of Barbados. He concluded that "there is no necessary and sufficient causal relationship, whether expressed in terms of necessary functional interdependence or consequence, between the small nuclear family and urbanization and industrialization." He found that the small conjugal family type was predominant even without the presence of urbanization and industrialization.

In "Industrialization and the American Family" (1966), Frank F. Furstenberg, Jr., conducts a historical analysis of accounts of foreign travelers who visited the United States between 1800 and 1850. He focuses on courtship and mate selection, the conjugal relationship, parent-child relations, and the position of women in society. He finds striking similarities between that period and the present day; free mate selection and the romantic love complex existed prior to American industrialization. He concludes that many family strains and tensions presumably caused by industrialization may in fact have assisted the development of the industrial society.

Robert F. Winch and Rae Lesser Blumberg, in "Societal Complexity and Familial Organization (1963), report on research testing the correlation between the type of *subsistence pattern* and type of *familial system*. Using data from Murdock's *World Ethnographic Sample,* their report indicates that nuclear families exist in hunting and gathering societies (which have the least complex level of subsistence) as well as in industrial societies. The extended family is found mainly in societies with a middle range of technological development—agricultural societies with a stable food supply and low geographical mobility, in which the family serves as the economic unit and owns the land. Thus a curved relationship between societal complexity and family complexity seems to exist.

This report questions the notion that there is a worldwide trend toward the conjugal family system. In an analysis of samples drawn from the United States, three familial types are found to exist in contemporary America—an "isolated" nuclear family, the nuclear family embedded in a network of extended kin, and the mother-child family. These family types vary by *ethnicity;* white Protestants characterize the first type, the extended family is predominant among Italians and Jews, and blacks in poor urban centers have a higher than average number of mother-child families.

iv   Evaluation   William Goode's great contribution to the sociology of the family has been his emphasis on the *multiple causes* of social phenomena. In particular, he emphasizes the importance of avoiding theories that suggest that all change and all relations stem from some single factor, such as technology or industrialization. His assertion that there is a worldwide trend to some form of conjugal family system, which should be viewed as a combined product of technology, family patterns, and ideology, is not without critics. There is still a great deal of work to be done in accurately assessing the full significance of the relationship between a society's technology and its family system.

Arlene and Jerome Skolnick see a further limitation on the reported research. In their introduction to *Family in Transition* (1971) they contend that most studies, like Goode's, "assume that industrialism is the last stop in technical history." Instead, they believe that a deeper understanding of the family can be accomplished by studying the nuclear family as a social problem—that is, by viewing its problems as arising out of its very nature and structure. They also feel that the sociological study of the family can be strengthened by extending the line of inquiry to a new stage of economic development—postindustrial or postmodern society. These suggestions have provocative implications for the family and for social policy.

c   The "Research" Question

i   Context   Since the turn of the century America has undergone a rapid transformation from a predominantly rural society to a society dominated by large urban centers. Between 1900 and 1930, for example, Chicago increased its population by over 2 million. Extensive migration of Americans from rural areas and the last great wave of European immigration accounted for this tremendous jump in urban population. Sociologists have been concerned with determining what impact the city has had on the family and kinship relationships and they ask: *What are the major characteristics of urban family life?*

ii   Theory   The classical tradition in sociology, as exemplified by such theorists as Emile Durkheim, Georg Simmel, and Ferdinand Toennies, has stressed that the urban family is relatively uninvolved with external social networks of friends, neighbors, and, especially, kin. The American sociologists Louis Wirth and Talcott Parsons have supported this view. Wirth contends that the family as a unit of social life is emancipated from the larger kinship group characteristic of the countryside and that the individual members pursue their own diverging interests in their vocational, educational, religious, recreational, and political life. According to Parsons, in "The Kinship System of the Contemporary United States" (1943), the nuclear family lives separately from its extended kin, including parents, and is economically independent from them. Theoretically, such a relatively "isolated" family is ideally suited to the demands of occupational and geographical mobility that are inherent in industrial urban society.

iii   Research (Methodology)   It was not until the end of World War II that sociologists began to test the standard hypothesis about the isolated nuclear family empirically. Contrary to their expectations, they found that viable relations do exist among relatives and, in fact, constitute a family's most important social contact. Most importantly, these researchers argued that the isolated nuclear family is not the most functional type for the modern industrial city. The work of Marvin Sussman and Eugene Litwak is the most interesting in this regard.

In "The Use of Extended Family Groups in the Achievement of Social Goals" (1960) and other papers, Litwak argues that the middle-class urban family structure consists of a series of kin-related nuclear families joined together on an egalitarian basis for mutual aid. He calls this the *"modified" extended family system,* and he believes that it is more functional in the city than is the isolated nuclear family. Considerable mutual aid is assumed to exist between family members in times of need, and thus the family does not face the world as an isolated unit.

The modified extended family is joined together by *affectional* as opposed to *obligatory* ties. This system does not require that conjugal units live in the same geographical area; in fact, extended kin relations in other cities provide services for the newly moved family, such as aid in finding new homes and jobs. In contrast, the classical extended family usually has a single authoritarian head, demands conjugal family subordination, and tends to prevent and discourage occupational and geographical mobility. As Goode has also pointed out, this type of system tends to be dysfunctional for an industrial urban society. The modified extended system is also more functional than the isolated nuclear system because when the conjugal family is completely divorced from extended kinship ties, its members cannot get assistance from the extended family in times of need and are unable to use kin to help them achieve occupational mobility.

The research that provided the basis for the idea of the modified extended family system was based primarily on middle-class populations. Data have also begun to be accumulated on urban working-class families. Drawing on some of this material, John Mogey, in "Family and Community in Urban-Industrial Societies" (1964), develops a theoretical framework distinguishing between "open" and "closed" communities. A *closed community* is characterized as one where scenes of intense interfamilial cooperation exist —especially within extended kinship groups that are cohesive and homogeneous in cultural values and closed against nonmembers. *Open communities* are those where members have selective attachments to a variety of associations or secondary groups. Families who live in these communities interact with individuals and extended family relations in other areas as well as in their own. The closed community is characteristic of the working class, whereas the open community resembles the middle-class modified extended family.

Mogey describes the impact of the closed community on *marital roles*. Husbands and wives each perform a separate set of household tasks, and in times of emergency aid for either is provided by other husbands and wives—usually kin and, to a lesser extent, neighborhood friends. The separation of tasks—husbands are involved with the work sphere and wives with the home—is so strict that even leisure-time activities are segregated. Within this type of family the mother-daughter relationship tends to be as strong as the husband-wife relationship (if not stronger). This situation is particularly true when the husband has moved his residence at the time of marriage to a place close to the home of his wife's mother.

Mogey hypothesizes that the conjugal family and the modified extended family system are not prevalent in the closed community. Those patterns require an open community structure, with secondary group relationships as well as primary ones. The greater geographical mobility of such families also leads to the sharing of tasks and activities and to a greater emotional attachment between husband and wife.

Researchers have started exploring the interrelationships of husbands and wives and their extended kin, friends, and neighbors in urban communities. In *Family and Social Network* (1968), a book that promises to generate extensive future study, Elizabeth Bott reports the results of the thousands of hours she and her associates spent intensively interviewing 20 London couples. Their interviews focused on the conjugal role relationship between husband and wife and on their respective involvements with friends, relatives, and kin. Bott suggests that when husbands and wives who are members of close-knit social networks (friends, relatives, and kin who all know and interact with each other) marry and continue to maintain such close-knit relationships, their conjugal-role organization is based on a clear differentiation of tasks, with few shared interests or activities. If either partner needs assistance, he or she can call upon other members of the social network. Bott also observes that the network's continuing support lessens the expressive demands each spouse needs to make of the other. Conjugal-role organization will be different when few of the partner's friends and relatives know each other. Because such loose social networks exert less social control over the couple and provide less mutual assistance, husbands and wives must gain emotional satisfaction from each other. Hence they maintain a joint relationship with a minimum division of labor. These couples are characterized by the sharing of common interests and leisure activities. A third group of conjugal families and social networks tends to fall between these two extremes.

The families described by Bott as participating in close-knit social networks are similar to the families associated by Mogey with the closed community. Moreover, the families linked by Bott to loose social networks are similar to those associated with Mogey's open community in their tendency to be more self-enclosed. After early reports of Bott's research, Lee Rainwater tested her hypothesis on a sample of 168 couples who were categorized into Bott's three types of conjugal role relationships. The couples were asked first to tell something about their family life and about the important things that happened during their marriage. Then they were asked how decisions were made in the family, about the main duties of husband and wife, and about the interests and activities of each. Finally, each respondent was asked to evaluate how his or her spouse felt about him or her. From all of this material a judgment was made as to which of the three types of relationship the couple most closely approximated. The results, reported by Rainwater in *Family Design* (1965), indicated that marital relationships show sharp class differences. The upper-middle class and lower-lower class patterns are particularly distinct: the former overwhelmingly emphasize sharing and joint participation in married life, whereas the latter almost equally strongly emphasize separateness and isolation of the marital partners from each other. The lower-middle and upper-lower class group falls into the intermediate pattern.

iv   Evaluation   The vast amount of research on the viability of kinship and family relations in the city has disproved the isolated nuclear family hypothesis. By and large, the modified extended family system seems to be quite prevalent. But surprisingly little study has been carried out on the social networks and conjugal roles of middle-class urban families, and relatively little work has focused on the study of social networks and conjugal roles for the geographically nonmobile working class. Herbert J. Gans' study of Italian-Americans in Boston (*The Urban Villagers,* 1962) supports the finding that there is marked sexual segregation both inside and outside the geographically and socially nonmobile working-class conjugal family. Gans also found that the Italian-American working class male shows little involvement between generations. He does not interact with his father or father's peers; his intimate kin network is composed of brothers and cousins. This finding suggests that comparisons between different ethnic groups of the working class ought to be investigated further.

3   Overview

Studies of the cross-cultural variations of the family systems have called attention to the fact that kinship systems, especially in preindustrial societies, are the dominant social structure linking families with the societal organization. As William Goode's analysis of the "world revolution in family patterns" has indicated, ideological and value changes (seen as partially independent of industrialization) have had decided impact on family action. More significantly, technology, family patterns, and ideology are now viewed as independent but converging forces that ultimately change the very fabric of the social order.

The examination of urban family life styles, interrelationship of marital roles, and involvement of couples with external social networks within the context of the modern industrial city has drawn further attention to the dynamics that characterize the interaction between the family and the social order. Finally, analyses of poverty families in industrial urban society demonstrate the fundamental dynamism of sociological thought and its central relevance to the formation of public policy.

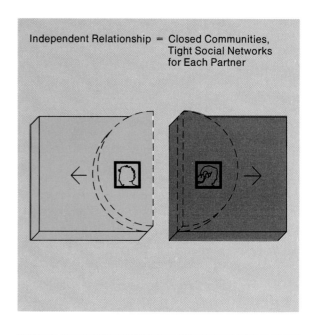

Independent Relationship = Closed Communities, Tight Social Networks for Each Partner

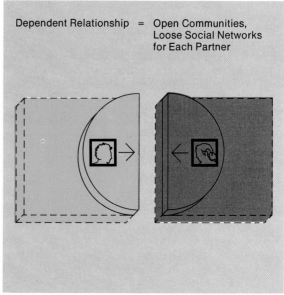

Dependent Relationship = Open Communities, Loose Social Networks for Each Partner

Model 2. Marriage Relationship as a Dependent Variable Connected With the Nature of the Community to Which Each Partner Relates.

D   LOOKING AHEAD

1   Interview:
Charles R. Lawrence

Charles R. Lawrence is professor of sociology at Brooklyn College of the City University of New York. He edited *Man, Culture, and Society* and is author of "Color, Class, and Culture: A Minority View" and other articles. His interests focus on social change, the family, race, and culture.

DPG   *Does the impact of modernization tend to produce a trend away from the traditional family and kinship systems and toward the conjugal, or nuclear, family?*
LAWRENCE   To a large extent that contention is true. The conjugal family seems to be a more mobile family. It doesn't have the burdens that the extended family places on vertical mobility as well as on horizontal mobility. Of course, the extended family persists in very many groups. Several studies indicate, for example, that Jews maintain numerous relationships among cousins and siblings (particularly brothers and sisters). So do some Roman Catholic groups and Negroes, particularly lower-class Negroes. In addition, models of the extended family persist to a considerable extent, even when the extended family itself is no longer present. Very often they persist in terms of continued interdependence of the conjugal units rather than in residence patterns.

DPG   *Is the persistence of the extended family a reflection of a minimum level of modernization?*
LAWRENCE   Not necessarily. For example, one study has shown that Jewish people tend to move to cities where they have relatives. This tendency may grow out of the long history of persecution, of insecurity, of living in a world of strangers for centuries. Blacks also move into city neighborhoods where they have relatives or distant kinsmen. Living in more modern and more technologically organized societies does diminish the importance of the extended family system in relation to the conjugal family, the nuclear family, but the tenacity of the extended family in many groups is still impressive.

DPG   *Is there a predominant family system within the black community?*
LAWRENCE   There are class-related family forms. Strangely enough, despite all the sociological gossip to the contrary, the predominant family form among most blacks is a quasi-paternalistic, quasi-patriarchal family. As E. Franklin Frazier pointed out, beginning back in slavery, the most exploited groups (namely the field hands) had to depend on the female line, particularly the grandmother, to hold the family together. The grandmother continues to be very important, particularly in lower-class black families. On the other hand, whenever possible, in working-class black families the father takes a very dominant role. And black families of the upper middle class (professionals, successful business people, and so on) are very egalitarian, which is true of American families of this class in general, I think.

DPG   *So there are income and class variations. What about regional variations among black families?*
LAWRENCE   The difference is urban and rural rather than Southern and Northern. In some of the old Southern cities, there were the old black families who had social status because of their descent. Very often they were descended from freedmen rather than from slaves. But this phenomenon is fading, and achievement has become the predominant yardstick, even though there are still certain recognizable "old families." By and large, however, the measure of social status among blacks in the Southern cities is achievement. The more you get into the urban environment, the more achievement, rather than family relationships, becomes the important measure. Of course, family relationships also have something to do with achievement.

DPG   *Is this pattern unique to the black community or does it apply to other minority groups and ethnic groups as well?*
LAWRENCE   It certainly applies to other national minority groups—to Jews of European background, to Italian-Americans, to Polish-Americans, even to the Chinese, who we always thought were the most familistic of all the ethnic groups. Generally, at least in the United States, as people move up the economic ladder, their families begin to resemble the prevailing pattern. Strong cultural patterns and ties give a more distinct flavor to the family than otherwise. The black family, of course, has experienced a strong discontinuity in the cultural pattern because of the nature of slavery in America.

Although currently young black scholars and ideologues are trying to show that the black family in the United States is really a transplanted African family, the facts, as I understand them, are that very few residuals of African culture persisted here, except in isolated areas such as the Sea Islands of South Carolina. The very nature of slave trading in the United States militated against the perpetuation of tribal or ethnic customs. In West Africa, where most of the slaves

that came to the United States orginated, though families had a kind of matrifocality in the sense that each woman had primary responsibility to her own family, it was always patriarchal, even where it was matrilineal. So the American experience, the slave experience, particularly for field hands, where the man had neither responsibility for the children nor the privilege of having anything to do with them, shattered the pre-existing cultural pattern. I tend to agree with Frazier's thesis that the Negro family in the United States is an example of the evolution of a family in a strange culture in which there are very few if any guidelines from the old culture.

DPG *Is the black community a political and cultural entity? Do you think that the future family or kinship system of black America will be distinct and different from that of mainstream America?*
LAWRENCE I don't think so. I think that the growing black consciousness will probably lead to attempts to maintain the distinct flavor of black families in general. On the other hand, black families of a given socioeconomic status and educational background are more likely to resemble non-black families of similar social status than they are to resemble economically dissimilar black families.

DPG *What are the patterns in the so-called underclass of the black community?*
LAWRENCE Despite the relatively high

proportion of families headed by females, role models are always near—the surrogate fathers, temporary stepfathers, grandfathers, uncles. I think that the absence of fathers interferes with the socialization of children, but, particularly in the black underclass, models of adaptations exist, although they're inadequate from the middle-class point of view. However, the fact that such role models exist makes the situation less bleak than, say, Daniel P. Moynihan would have us believe.

DPG *Would you say that other nonwhite American minority groups experience the same family dislocation as the blacks?*
LAWRENCE By and large, when people are uprooted from rural backgrounds, or, as in the case of the Chicanos, uprooted from peasant backgrounds, and brought into cities, the traditional forms of the family are changed. The one big difference between the American Indians and the Chicanos on the one hand, and blacks on the other, is that the underclass blacks did have an opportunity in the rural areas to stabilize what we think of generally as the standard American family. What Moynihan calls the disintegration of the black family is very visible in the urban environment, but actually this phenomenon has been happening in the rural areas for decades, even centuries. Much of what we think of as pathology in the urban environment was produced in rural areas, particularly as people were displaced from traditional sharecropping agriculture, let us say, in the Deep South. They're displaced without urban skills, without urban working patterns, and without any kind of program for helping them in the transition.

DPG *Is this true of the Third World developing countries?*
LAWRENCE To a degree. But we do assume (although it may not be true) that the people migrating to the cities in Third World countries are coming from at least functional social organizations in the rural areas. It would be hard to make a case that there was an idyllic family existence for blacks in the American rural South.

DPG *Would you say the communal experiments of the last decade present a potential and viable alternative kinship form for the future?*

LAWRENCE I doubt that they will become a distinct alternative, although a few of the forms developed by the various communal movements in the United States will persist. I do think, however, that the experiences of the communes will leave their impact on future relationships, probably providing stimulus for other kinds of cooperative interfamily activities.

DPG *Does contemporary American society tend to act against the nuclear family?*
LAWRENCE Certainly, among intellectuals, there's a great deal of questioning of the nuclear family, but these same intellectuals keep right on forming nuclear families, with or without benefit of clergy. And even in the face of the high divorce rate the marriage rate doesn't go down. The romantic ideal, as screwy as it is, persists even among the most blasé people. I think that the present questioning of the nuclear family will have some lasting effects, but mainly with regard to modifications of the roles within the nuclear family rather than to a rejection of the nuclear family. You must note that even in tribal societies where the extended family is very important there are still recognizable nuclear units.

DPG *What trends are identifiable now that can suggest the future of the family in the 1970s and 1980s?*
LAWRENCE Immediately I think of the trend in family size. Despite contrary experience in the past, I think smaller families will be a lasting trend because of the greater availability of information about fertility control and the growing consciousness of a need for a more independent or more autonomous existence for women. I would hope that we will develop more adequate institutional forms to supplement the family—family centers, prenatal care, family counseling, child care for working parents, preschools for children of all social backgrounds. These would not be substitutes for the family but would enable the family to do its job better. In fact, developing these kinds of supportive institutions may even be necessary if the family is to survive. But in view of the political situation, with such things as President Nixon's veto of the child development bill, I think provision of such facilities is problematic.

Unit 8
Religion

RELIGION AND SOCIETY

1. Individual human beings . . .

2. . . . group together to form society.

3. Society gives birth to religion.

4. Religion in turn influences society . . .

5. . . . . and thus affects individual human beings.

Human beings in society create various social products — including religious ideas. The shared
ideas of a society pattern the social actions of its members. Individuals participating in social actions,
including religious activities, experience a sense of belonging and well-being.

B DEFINITION AND CONTEXT

1 Definition

Religion appears in all human societies. In some it is the dominant social feature, enveloping the consciousness of the inhabitants; in others it is a secondary, minority activity. Religion can be a powerful source of social conflict, or it can be the basis of social unity. It takes so many forms, in fact, that there is no agreement among sociologists as to exactly what constitutes a religious phenomenon.

There are many plausible ways to define religion. Some sociologists would include superstition in any definition because it expresses belief in supernatural influence on human affairs. Other sociologists would include Confucianism in a definition of religion as a coherent system of ethical principles—even though its doctrines specifically refrain from any speculation about the supernatural. Still other sociologists insist that certain surrogate relations must be included in the definition.

One such *surrogate* or *functional equivalent* of religion is communism, which has been compared to the traditional church in many respects (although Christian critics have argued that it is the opposite of religion). Communism has its founding prophet—Karl Marx. It has its unquestioned sacred texts—Marx's writings. It has its saints and shrines—such as Lenin's preserved body in Moscow's Red Square. Communism has a missionary zeal—the desire to convert the world to acceptance of its doctrines. It has its unchallenged dogmas—such as a belief in the dialectical progression of history. It has its vision of a better life in the future—the communist utopia. It places an ethical injunction on all men—"From each according to his ability, to each according to his needs."

Each definition of religion must allow scope for some disagreement. For the purposes of this unit, a relatively restricted definition will prove a useful analytic tool and will accord with the intuitive understanding of religious phenomena that most people in our society have. *Religion is a communally held system of beliefs and practices that are directed toward some transcendent, supernatural reality.*

Sociological analysis does not deal with religious beliefs as such. A theologian may wish to prove or disprove the view that souls transmigrate from men to animals, that Jesus rose from the dead after three days, that totem poles have magical properties, that Jupiter hurls thunderbolts at those who offend him, or that the universe was created by a scarab beetle, but this is not the concern of the sociologist. It is no part of his function to make pronouncements, in his professional capacity, about the truth or falsehood of a particular belief. Instead, the sociologist of religion studies the ways in which society influences religion—its origins, its practices, its doctrines, and he also examines the way in which religion influences society and human behavior.

2 World Context

All societies have a system of beliefs and practices that may be termed religious—but not necessarily in the sense familiar to

Some sociologists feel that social movements such as communism can be considered functional equivalents of religion. In the People's Republic of China, for example, attitudes toward Communist Party Chairman Mao Tse-tung have sometimes verged on cult-like adulation. Here a worker in the ceramics center of Fushan puts the finishing touches on a bust of Mao, which is the most-produced item at this factory.

(Facing page) Ceremonial object used by the Uli people of New Ireland, an island near New Guinea. These flamboyantly carved and decorated wooden objects were used for the *Malagan,* a ritual dedicated to clan ancestors.

Americans. It is important that we should not project assumptions about our own religion onto the belief systems of other societies.

Religion, then, takes many forms. It includes the drug-induced communal ecstasy of the peyote cult and the mystical experience of the visionary hermit, the formal services of the conventional modern church and the messianic movements that prophesy the imminent arrival of God's kingdom on earth. In tribal society religion embraces the consciousness of the entire community, and almost all activity—hunting, preparing food, initiation rites, sickness, death—is suffused with religious significance. In undeveloped and developing societies religion remains largely undifferentiated from other social institutions. It is difficult for us today to conceive how in medieval Europe, for example, the church permeated society to the extent that there was no distinct religious sphere—religion pervaded and informed every aspect of experience, so that social organization and religion were almost identical.

But religion has been pushed to the sidelines in many modern societies. In the Communist-governed countries it is often suppressed, and in Western Europe religious practice has dropped steadily throughout this century. For example, only about 10 percent of the population of Great Britain attends a weekly church service, and only about 25 percent attend as often as once a year. Yet most marriages and nearly all funerals remain religious functions in Western Europe.

The most appealing religions have usually been those that promise some kind of *salvation*. This concept represents the attempt to answer the moral problems man constantly faces. Max Weber pointed out in his studies of religion in *Economy and Society* (1922) that human intelligence in every society sooner or later comes to terms with the fact that, inexplicably, the good often goes unrewarded and the evil often triumphs. Man appears frail and alone in a hostile or indifferent universe. The religions that most frequently win converts are those that offer a solution to this problem of injustice and misery in the world, usually by claiming that in some metaphysical realm redress is assured and a higher moral order revealed.

Weber regarded the *prophet* as the agent through whom new religious ideas emerged. In instances of *exemplary prophecy* the prophet makes the route to salvation clear by his own life and example but does not put forward any claim to a divine mission or impose an obligation on others to follow him. The guru of India is an example of the exemplary prophet. In *ethical prophecy* the prophet advances a divine mission, a set of ethical imperatives, and sees compliance with them as a moral duty, to be enforced if necessary with the sword. The Christian crusader is an example of the ethical prophet.

Weber argued that three religions gave the most satisfying systematic answers to the problem of evil and misfortune. The first was Hinduism with its doctrine of karma—the transmigration of souls through a cycle of compensating existences. The second was Zoroastrian dualism, which sees the whole universe as an arena in which spiritual forces of good and evil are locked in endless combat so that human misery is merely the product of a temporary victory for the forces of evil. The third was ascetic Protes-

The Sun Dance. Among various Great Plains Indians, such as the Al-
berta Blackfoot tribe depicted in this 1892 photograph, individual
men underwent public rituals of torture and vision quest known as
the Sun Dance. The volunteer dancer would have his chest pierced
by thongs attached to a pole. He would walk in an ecstatic trance
around the pole until he fainted, or his muscles and skin ripped free.
A successful dance was believed to bring supernatural benefits to
the tribe by revitalizing the earth.

Total Christian		**924,274,000**
Roman Catholic	580,470,000	
Protestant	218,120,000	
Eastern Orthodox	125,684,000	
Moslem		**493,012,000**
Hindu		**436,745,000**
Confucian		**371,587,000**
Buddhist		**176,920,000**
Shinto		**69,662,000**
Taoist		**54,324,000**
Jewish		**13,537,000**
Zoroastrian		**138,000**

**Table 1. Estimated Membership of the Principal World Reli-
gions.** The Christian religion has almost twice as many adherents as
the next largest, Islam, the Moslem religion. The Roman Catholic
church is the largest single Christian body in the world. (Source: *Bri-
tannica Book of the Year, 1969*)

tantism, which views God as absolutely mysterious; the intentions and motives of the Almighty cannot be judged by human standards, and man's only duty is to bow to God's unfathomable will.

3 American Context

In the 1830s Alexis de Tocqueville wrote in *Democracy in America* that "there is no country in the world where . . . religion retains a greater influence over the souls of men than in America." At first sight Tocqueville's comment would still seem to be true. About 98 percent of Americans questioned in a 1968 Gallup Poll on religious beliefs in 11 countries claimed to believe in God, and church participation and attendance have remained fairly constant throughout the century (although they have declined slightly since their peak in the 1950s). This situation is in sharp contrast to that in all other industrial nations, where church attendance has steadily and rapidly dropped; less than 80 percent of the people in five Western European countries claim belief in an ultimate deity.

Most Americans are Protestants. Indeed, high social status is closely correlated with Protestantism because the Protestants were the first to arrive in numbers and gain control of power and wealth. (Some sociologists also maintain that certain elements of the "Protestant ethic" strongly support the competitive spirit of capitalism.) But the United States is noted for embracing a great many religious beliefs and affiliations. This appeal of such a variety of religions in the midst of the most sophisticated industrial society in the world may be difficult to understand unless one explores the way in which religion represents a major institutional aspect of American society.

In fact, many sociologists have questioned whether Americans really are religious—and whether the variety of religious beliefs is really significant. Will Herberg, author of *Protestant, Catholic, Jew* (1955), commented that the United States paradoxically is "at once the most secular and the most religious of nations." High church membership levels do not necessarily indicate strong religious impulses in individuals or in the society as a whole. One must ask, for example, whether weekly attendance at church services necessarily implies intense religious convictions—or whether church going is serving as a social outing rather than an act of faith. (There are also "C and E" Christians, who attend church only at Christmas and Easter.) Do church members see themselves as having made a pervasive commitment whose implications determine their lives—or are their religious beliefs mere lip service, restricted to an isolated fragment of their experience? And to what extent are the churches still "religious" bodies? Or have they become narrow, bureaucratic institutions that have lost contact with their original ethical impulses because of their need to survive in an unsympathetic and materialistic society?

Many researchers have concluded that the variety and intensity of religious life in the United States are more apparent than real. Herberg has argued that, a few sects apart, all churches in the United States in fact worship "the American way of life," which includes the notion of being "religious" and finding in religion a justification for American values of individualism, efficiency, and

	1950	1960	1970
Protestant	51,080,000	63,669,000	71,713,000
Roman Catholic	28,635,000	42,105,000	48,215,000
Jewish	5,000,000	5,367,000	5,870,000
Old Catholic, Polish National Catholic, Armenian Churches	250,000	590,000	848,000
Buddhist	73,000	20,000	100,000
All Others	142,000		449,000
Total Number of Church Members	86,830,000	114,449,000	131,046,000
Church Members As Percentage Of Total Population	57%	64%	63%
Average Number Of Members Per Local Church	304	359	399

Table 2. Church Membership in the United States. Americans belong to a great variety of churches, but there are far more Protestants in the United States than adherents of all other religions put together. (Source: *Yearbook of American Churches, 1971*)

self-improvement. The following prayer, delivered by the Reverend J. Lawrence Yenches, D.D., at the Florida League of Cities Banquet in December 1972 and reported in *The New York Times*, provides a striking example of this phenomenon.

> Almighty God, we thank Thee for a free land where private property is a sacred reality. For millions it is not. Among us, Lord, are millions who own no home, no land, and no business. Owning nothing, they demand everything from a paternal government. Dear Lord, we fear they are potential victims for the panacea of Socialism. . . .
>
> Help us, our Father, to remember that all we have— our schools, businesses, homes, banks, farms, mines, and buildings—are here because somebody worked for them and worked hard. . . .
>
> Bless all among us who work, produce, save, and invest, creating real wealth for our well-being.
>
> Help us to rely less on government and more on ourselves. Gird us to fight anything that destroys incentive, kills initiative, penalizes superior ability, and subsidizes laziness.
>
> Remind us strongly, O God, that without good business with a good profit, we can have no non-profit churches, schools, foundations, hospitals, tax-paid politicians, or a government giving away so-called free benefits or welfare subsidies.
>
> Preside at our meal: O Lord, sanctify our conversation, and may the glow of Thy Presence shine on all our faces. In the Master's Name, Amen.

Research by Rodney Stark and Charles Glock and their associates at the University of California at Berkeley in the 1960s revealed that more people see the church as a basis for security in this life or the next than as a cause or a challenge. Churchgoers tend to be more prejudiced and bigoted than nonchurchgoers. Significantly, only 8 percent of Protestant ministers felt that their congregations would approve if they gave a sermon on a controversial political or social topic.

But the fact that the American dream has permeated religion is only part of the explanation for the unique persistence of organized religion in America.

Certain historical factors are involved in this development. The United States lacks a feudal past; there has never been a politically-established church on the national level, and so irreligion has never emerged, as it did in Europe, as a protest against the status quo. Furthermore, immigrant groups have used the church as a means of maintaining ethnic community unity. And it may be that in a vast, rapidly changing society, the churches provide unique opportunities for membership in a community offering warm personal relationships. By accommodating itself to the predominant culture, religion in the United States has become internally secularized; the religious content has been drained from the churches without radically altering the form of religious institutions. In Europe, on the other hand, a less compromising church has simply become increasingly less important.

The Children of God. Millenarian and charismatic movements still arise in the midst of modern industrial society. Here young members of the Children of God, a controversial Jesus cult based in New York, march in monks' robes while calling for repentance and a return to Bible belief.

Attention has focused recently on the rise of the ''Jesus freak'' movement—often seen as a response to the ultimate meaninglessness of life in an arid, mechanized society. The movement has a particular appeal for young people who have been detached, through their exposure to countercultural or ''hippie'' values, from the norms of mainstream America. As sociologists Robert L. Adams and Robert J. Fox point out in ''Mainlining Jesus: The New Trip'' (1972):

> The Jesus trip seems tailor-made for adolescents. Not only does commitment to Jesus preserve childhood morality with its absolutist definitions of right and wrong, but it also provides an ideology based on personal, internal, and for the most part, unexplainable experience rather than on critical, rational or realistic analysis.

Adams and Fox note that there are several similarities between the drug and ''Jesus freak'' experiences. Both are anti-establishment in their attempts to create alternatives to the middle-class life style. Both are concerned with subjective experience, as opposed to the objective, scientific, rational style of the dominant culture. And the religious experience is in tune with previously experienced drug ''highs.'' There are, however, several significant differences between the two movements. The ''Jesus freaks'' are attracted to severely authoritarian leaders and social structures, in sharp contrast to the ''hang-loose'' ethic of the ''hip'' culture. After extensive interviewing, Adams and Fox found a shift to a conservative position by 76 percent of their subjects and warned: ''The Jesus culture bears watching in the future because . . . it is a victim area of right wing politics, and we foresee its steadily increasing exploitation by reactionary political forces.''

Young people searching for new religious certainties have often turned to cults rather than to an organized church. Enthusiasm and ecstasy have never been much prized in the major white American churches—in fact, great intensity is an object of reproach, and undue transcendence is liable to be seen less as a communion with God than as a matter for the psychiatrist. Young people often see the conventional church as a bureaucratic, disenchanted, and hypocritical institution, drained of its original ethical content and supporting the existing social order. Even within the church there are many dedicated religious activists who criticize its formality, coldness, anonymity, material concerns, and political timidity but who work for reforms in the hope that organized religion can once more supply a basis for political activism and social concern.

C   QUESTIONS AND EVIDENCE

1   Questions

Typical of the varied questions the sociologist of religion asks are: (1) Is the modern world really becoming less religious? If so, why? (2) What function, if any, does religion have in society? Is it merely a harmless myth, or does it serve a useful social purpose? (3) Can

''The Jesus Music Festival'' held in Dallas, Texas, in 1972. Both the ''Jesus freak'' movement and ''straight'' evangelical Christianity are currently gaining adherents among American youth. Both movements tend to emphasize simple and emotional forms of religion. This evangelical festival also attracted some ''Jesus freaks.''

Bengali Moslems praying for the independence of Bangladesh during 1971 war with Pakistan. Political, economic, and ethnic differences led to a bloody conflict between the two regions of Pakistan despite the fact that both shared the same religion, Islam. As a result of the conflict, the region of East Pakistan (East Bengal) became the new nation of Bangladesh.

religion influence people's social actions on a large scale? For example, can whole societies and economies take the shape they do because of the influence of religion?

2   Evidence

a   The "Burning Issue" Question

i   Context   Many people believe that religion is becoming less and less important in modern societies—that the area that religion once occupied in the social structure and in the minds of men is steadily shrinking to insignificance. If this view is true, it signals a profound change in the belief systems of industrial societies. To account for such a change, sociologists ask: *To what extent, and for what reasons, is the modern world becoming secularized?*

ii   Theory   Max Weber believed that the irrational, magically oriented religion of simple traditional societies was occasionally disrupted by the rise of a prophet—an individual of enormous personal power—*charisma*—who proclaimed a new and decisive break with the old order. Such prophecies supplied the decisive historical source of doctrines that brought about radical changes in traditional religious belief systems. The successful prophets—such as Moses, Zoroaster, Jesus, Mohammed, Buddha—*rationalized* religious belief, converting a confused set of ideas, magical notions, and superstitions into a more coherent system. Once the leader and his successors are gone, however, such rationally based religions tend to release the minds of men from the grip of superstition and to become increasingly routine and schematic. Losing their original vision, they increasingly focus on preserving themselves as institutions of the secularized society they had unintentionally helped to create. The prime example of this process, Weber felt, was Protestantism. Its worldly asceticism had so "de-enchanted" the universe that it paved the way for capitalism—and capitalism in turn made possible a modern world in which religion no longer seems appropriate.

Modern theorists tend to see the decline of Western religion in terms that rely heavily on Weber's insights. They acknowledge that the churches have been obliged to make continual accommodations to a changing and hostile society. Indeed, the pendulum has swung so far in the direction of secularism that those who remain committed to traditional religion are becoming a minority. As Peter Berger has said in *A Rumor of Angels* (1969), "The theologian more and more resembles a witchdoctor stranded among logical positivists." In consequence, Berger argues, the genuinely religious content in American churches has been profoundly eroded—in extreme cases to the point where nothing is left but the hollowest rhetoric. The fundamental choice for those who remain actively religious, he continues, is to remain in their minority status or surrender their beliefs.

It is only in a community of considerable strength that a particular religious doctrine can be maintained, for members can provide each other with "continuing therapy against creeping doubt." Berger points out in *The Sacred Canopy* (1967) that such communities no longer exist and argues that the church must either retreat into virtual *sectarianism*—refusing to compromise with the spirit of the age and losing members rapidly in consequence—or venture into the new world and make whatever compromises are necessary. The churches generally prefer the latter course, and the results are likely to be a contamination of the traditional distinctive features of the church, which is the weaker partner in the bargaining process with the world. Even modifications that are intended only to be tactical may in the end result in genuinely substantive changes, such as "God is dead" theology.

Attempts to make the church and its teaching more "relevant" to the contemporary world often take the form of political activism on the part of the clergy. But it is possible that such activity, regardless of its other merits, merely antagonizes many lay members of the church without winning new supporters. A political program based on religious principles is unlikely to offer any particular attractions over a secular program. Paradoxically, Berger concludes, many attempts to "dechurchify" the church, to modernize and reorganize its rituals and trappings, may ultimately diminish the appeal of traditional religion by stripping it of the mystery that may be its most attractive feature in an arid age.

iii Research   In the modern world, *secularization* has been found to take several forms that are empirically related but conceptually quite distinct.

First there is secularization in the sense of the *institutional differentiation* of the church from other areas of society—especially from the state, but also from economic, legal, educational, and other institutions. In this sense secularization is an uncomplicated matter. Historical evidence reveals a long-term process, extending from the Middle Ages, of institutional separation of the church from the social structure as a whole. The church was once identified with political authority and could exert that authority to further its influence but can no longer make such claims.

In modern societies there is little religious control over most social institutions. The rise of industrialism allowed new classes first to influence and eventually to replace the older order based on the identity of church and state. This diversification of society redistributed the functions of the church. Some of these functions have been assigned to new institutions. (The Social Security Administration, for example, has taken over many tasks earlier considered appropriate only for the church, and the state now has dominant control of primary and secondary education.) Many other institutions have separated themselves from religious influence (the universities being a notable case in point).

This tendency toward secularization has not been universal, even in modern industrial states. In Italy and Spain, for example, the church still retains a virtual monopoly of belief and is closely intertwined with the apparatus of government. (In Spain earlier trends toward secularization were halted and reversed after the civil war ended in 1939, although the circumstances there are exceptional.) In the United States the Catholic church has had considerable success in establishing and maintaining its own educational system in parallel with the public schools. And in many countries there may be a strong link between the church and, if not the state, at least one political party: the Republic of South Africa and Ireland provide striking examples of this phenomenon.

Protesting priest. Attempts of the clergy to achieve greater contemporary relevance for the church can lead to clashes with established political authorities. For example, Episcopalian priest Father Malcolm Boyd, author of *Are You Running With Me, Jesus?*, was arrested for celebrating an antiwar mass on the concourse of the Pentagon in 1970.

(A second form of secularization is the *diminished religiosity* of the organized church and its participants. Sociologists studying secularization in this sense have focused on the increasing ''worldliness'' of the church itself and the declining allegiance to the church and its doctrines on the part of the population at large. They have found that faced with the pressures of a changing world, the churches often focus more on preserving their own social standing and rational functions than on implementing their religious obligations.) There seems little doubt that much of the religious content, doctrine, and ritual of the major churches—particularly the Protestant ones—is being abandoned.

(The other sense in which the concept of secularization is applied to the churches relates to a *declining popular participation* in their affairs. This view implies an identity between church and religion (that is, that those who no longer attend church have lost their religious faith) and has been encouraged by the churches. As Thomas Luckmann points out in *The Invisible Religion* (1967), secularization in this sense is a process of ''religious pathology,'' a sickness that can be measured by the diminishing membership of the churches. Because there is no ''counterchurch,'' the conclusion is that society is becoming irreligious.

(Sociologists strongly question whether church and religion can be equated in this way, but there seems little doubt that the church as an institution is becoming more and more marginal to the lives of those who live in industrial societies.) Although nearly every American claims to believe in God, only about 40 percent actually attend church. Lessening attendance among the nation's younger adults has accounted for most of the decline of church participation since 1958, when 49 percent attended church in a typical week. A mere 5 percent of the people in Finland regularly go to church, but as many as 83 percent still maintain that they have religious faith.

Clearly this trend is difficult to measure. What behavior, for example, indicates religious activity—identification with the church, participation in church activities, or purely personal devotion? What criteria are to be used to measure membership when some churches view membership as a birthright and others demand a positive act of commitment in adulthood? What criteria establish participation when some churches—such as the Roman Catholic— make far more stringent demands on their members than others? If a person is religious in one respect—say attendance at worship—does it automatically follow that he is religious in another— say in the moral principles by which he guides his daily actions?

According to a 1967 Gallup Poll, a majority of people in the United States believe that religion is losing its influence on American life, as opposed to less than 15 percent of the people who shared that sentiment in 1957. When a 1968 Poll asked, ''Do you believe that life today is getting better or worse in terms of morals?'' 78 percent responded that it was getting worse. Studies also show that the decline of popular participation in the church is statistically related to the progress of industrialization and urbanization: rural areas are more church-oriented than towns, women are more church-oriented than men, and the old are more church-oriented than the young; that is, the degree of involvement in modern indus-

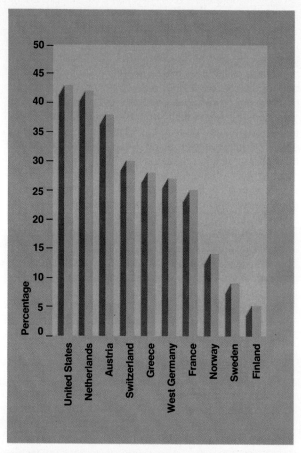

Figure 1. Percentage of Adult Population That Attends Church Each Week in Various Countries. The United States leads other industrial countries in church attendance. (Source: Gallup Poll, *New York Times*, Dec. 22, 1968)

trial activities seems to correlate negatively with church-oriented religious participation.

A final sense in which the term "secularization" is used refers to the question of whether there is in modern society any lessening of belief in some *transcendent, supernatural reality* itself. Is such belief fading along with the institutions that proclaimed it? To those who identify church and religion, secularization in this sense is clearly taking place; but to those who do not accept the equation, the issue is much more problematic. Some writers, such as Peter Berger, have tried to find a new religion in such secular realms as play, hope, order, and humor, but other sociologists point out that these elements have coexisted with traditional religion since prehistory and are in no sense a substitute for traditional religion. Other writers have tried to find a new religion in such mass movements as communism, fascism, and the American counterculture.

There is evidence, however, that individuals continue to express an unorganized but massive belief in some transcendent reality. Berger reports that 80 percent of American students feel the need for a religious faith, and Gallup Polls indicate that 98 percent of Americans believe in God and that 75 percent believe in life after death. David Martin, in *A Sociology of English Religion* (1967), presents the discovery that even in irreligious Britain half the population believes in both life after death and a God. One in 10 believes in reincarnation, one in six in hell, one in six in ghosts, and one atheist in 10 even believes in immortality. The widespread faith in luck, fortune telling, astrology, and even magically protective objects suggests that despite our technological sophistication, there has been no withering of the capacity for belief.

iv Evaluation Secularization is a major sociological feature of the modern world. The institutional differentiation of the church from the rest of society and its declining membership and influence are not in doubt. In popular mythology these developments are often attributed to a battle between religion and science—a contest from which science emerges victorious because of its superior ability to decipher the universe. But secularization cannot be reduced to such an automatic process. Urbanization and industrialization have led to widespread changes in the social structure, creating a complex society with various specialized institutions. Those institutions encourage and distribute different world views, and individuals come to experience the church and religion as merely one isolated component of their daily lives. Religious values become less and less relevant to political, economic, and other activities; thus what were once total life commitments become at best part-time norms.

The attempts to find a new religion in mass movements such as communism, fascism, or youth culture have not been convincing. There is a superficial resemblance between these movements and institutionalized religion, but the similarity does not extend far enough. None of these movements claims to mediate an ultimate, transcendent, or sacred reality. Their concerns are essentially with the mundane, and they cannot be considered religious phenomena in any meaningful sense.

A much more promising area for research would be the popular attitudes to ghosts, spirits, charms, life after death, "imma-

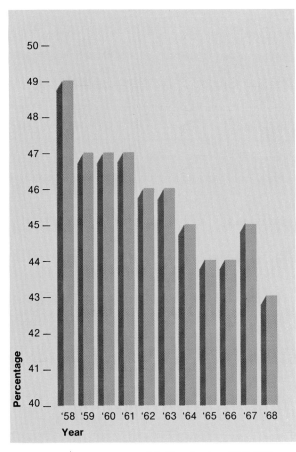

Figure 2. Percentage Trend in U.S. Churchgoing, 1958–1968.
Adult church attendance has declined steadily (except for 1967) from its peak of 49 percent in 1958 to 43 percent in 1968. Sociologists are investigating whether or not the decline in church attendance among adults means a decline in the impact of religion on American lives. (Source: Gallup Poll, *New York Times*, Dec. 22, 1968)

nent justice," and the power of drugs to "unlock the universe," and so on. It is likely that such research would reveal a surprisingly rich, if disorganized, collection of beliefs and superstitions that could only be characterized as religious. The capacity for a belief in some "other" reality may die far harder than traditional faiths.

b   The "Classical" Question

i   Context   Does religion have any particular value in society? If not, why is it found in all societies, and why does it still persist to some extent in the modern industrial world? Sociologists who examine this question often take a *functionalist* approach—that is, they examine the phenomenon of religion in relation to the wider social structure in order to determine what purpose it serves in the ongoing life of the society concerned. In this case they ask: *What is the social function of religion?*

ii   Theory   In his "Introduction to *The Critique of Hegel's Philosophy of Right*" (1844), Karl Marx summarized his attitude to religion: It was a mere illusion, and an oppressive one.

> Religion is the sigh of the oppressed creature, the sentiment of a heartless world, and the soul of soulless conditions. It is the opium of the people. The abolition of religion, and the illusory happiness of men, is a demand for their real happiness.

Marx was the first major sociologist to give his attention to religion. Most other sociologists of the nineteenth century regarded it as unworthy of study. Religion was seen as an irrational hangover from an ignorant and superstitious past, of no real significance to modern man. But Marx believed that his attack on religion was fundamental to his entire sociology; "The criticism of religion," he wrote, "is the premise of all criticism."

As we saw in Unit 2, Marx believed that men in life together create social products of two kinds—*material products* (such as houses and clothes) and *ideological products* (such as law or religion). In a simple society men recognize these products as their own and realize that they can refashion them at will. But as *class divisions* begin to develop, men lose their sense of independence and domination, and *alienation* sets in. Man comes to feel himself a stranger in the world he himself has created. As he loses his sense of control over his own constructs and well-being, he projects his powers onto certain objects and into abstractions. This projection is most striking in the case of religion.

Marx recognized that in a simple, undifferentiated society people would create mythic explanations for the universe, but he explained that this situation was the consequence of their ignorance of natural processes. Later, he argued, religion expanded and took on quite a different function. The dominant religious ideas at any time served to legitimate the interests of the dominant class in society—and because men had lost the awareness that religion was a social creation, the oppressed orders accepted these dominant religious ideas as absolute. The notion of the divine right of kings, for example, was promoted by the church—and believed in by the masses. Protestantism, with its stress on individual effort rather than communal solidarity, became the dominant religion of

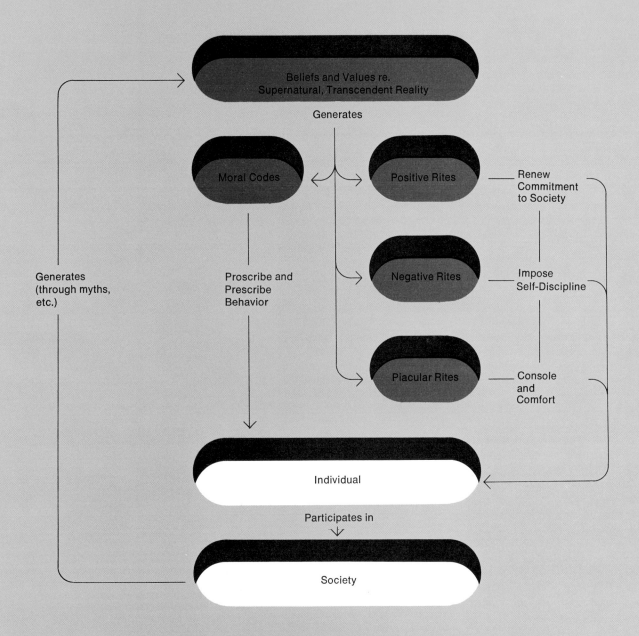

Model 1. Durkheim's View of the Relationship Between Religion and Society. The orange boxes taken together represent a society's religion.

the go-getting entrepreneurs of early laissez-faire capitalism—and the religiously promoted notions of the value of thrift and the virtues of hard work were also accepted by the masses.

This analysis of the social function of religion has been criticized. But Marx's basic concept—that religion is a communally created ideological product that serves some function in society—has become fundamental to sociological research since his time.

iii Research (Survey) Emile Durkheim in *The Elementary Forms of Religious Life* (1915) developed a functionalist but non-Marxist approach to religion. Durkheim's theory was not based on any exhaustive study of religious phenomena. Instead, he sought to discover the origins of religion by analyzing the religious beliefs of what he supposed to be the most primitive society he could find—on the assumption that subsequent changes in form were simply elaborations and disguises of some lasting essence. Like other evolutionists of his time, Durkheim believed that societies could be graded from the simple to the complex, and he saw religion as a variable that could be traced along such a continuum.

The religion Durkheim selected for analysis was the *totemism* of Australia. The totem is a stylized representation of some environmental commonplace, usually an animal or a plant (such as mice or clovers), that serves as a symbol of a *clan*. Although it is a material object, the totem is believed to possess sacred properties—a curious fact because the totemic objects themselves do not seem capable of inspiring the powerful feelings associated with them. The totem, then, is both a symbol of the clan and a sacred representation. Exploring the dual function of various totems, Durkheim developed his famous idea that sacred things are, in reality, the symbols of the society that practices the religion: ''Divinity is merely society transformed and symbolically conceived.'' The mechanism by which religion arises, he suggested, is the periodic clan gathering. On important social occasions the entire group comes together in a fervent and excited atmosphere, and this awesome feeling is attributed to supernatural forces.

Durkheim saw religion and its associated rituals as performing a function essential to the integration of society; they restrain deviants and ensure a high degree of adherence to existing rules and values. He classified religious rites into three types. *Positive rites* involve a renewal of commitment to the values of society; such rites bring people together, reaffirm their solidarity, and confirm the social values of the group. Next, *negative rites* maintain taboos and prohibitions; these rites impose on the individual the self-discipline that is essential for a social life based on general acceptance of controls and restraints. Third, *piacular rites* comfort and console, tide the community over in times of disaster, and ensure the piety of the individual. All these rites give the individual an opportunity for social communion. Members of the community are kept aware of their social heritage, tradition is maintained, values are embedded and transmitted, faith is renewed, and society strengthened. Religious forces are, therefore, ''human forces, moral forces.''

Every society, Durkheim insisted, needs a religion—or at least a common system of belief. But in contemporary society, which is moving from a simple to a complex form, ''the old gods

Three generations of an American Jewish family celebrate a Passover Seder. Such positive rites are one way that religion serves to confirm the solidarity and values of a group. This Jewish ceremony involves a ritual meal and prayers to commemorate the exodus of the Hebrews from Egypt thousands of years ago.

are growing old or are already dead, and others are not yet born." Traditional religion does not meet the requirements of the scientific spirit and hence is no longer acceptable to the industrial world.

Later studies have suggested that religion has other functions. For example, J. Milton Yinger in *Religion in the Struggle for Power* (1946) points out that during certain periods in history fissures begin to appear in a social structure because of new pressures from within and from without. The old foundation of values no longer appears structurally sound, and character deviations become more widespread and pronounced. In the midst of this chaos various individuals search for more meaningful conceptual frameworks —and from these the most acceptable solutions will take hold. It was through such a process, Yinger argues, that the Protestant Reformation arose. The growth of cities, trade, and travel introduced a "wobble" into the previously stable medieval system. Peasants who emigrated to the urban centers and warriors and merchants who returned from other countries faced new opportunities and ideas, which in turn gave rise to new needs and inclinations that could not be expressed through behavior patterns suited to a more provincial and homogeneous agrarian society. As large numbers of people sought to relieve their stress and to reestablish personal balance through values and motives more in harmony with their new circumstances, the growing religious reform movements offered new versions of traditional religious beliefs. Thus religion acted as an "agent of modernization, . . . helping to carry people over into a new world by furnishing ultimate definitions and procedures relevant to that world."

iv   Evaluation   Marx's analysis of the social function of religion has not been generally accepted in Western sociology. Religion may serve to legitimate a ruling class, but many sociologists feel that the Marxist viewpoint overlooks religion's independent status as a social fact apart from its relation to class structure. It fails to take into account the other functions that religion performs.

Both Durkheim and Marx emphasize the dependency of religious thought on variations in the social structure. But Marx sees religion as a product of man's alienation from himself, while Durkheim sees a system of common belief or values as essential to social cohesion. Durkheim's views have exerted a deep influence on his successors, although his analysis of Australian totemism—based as it is on a discredited evolutionary view of religion—is no longer acceptable on methodological grounds.

What Durkheim does neglect are the potentially *dysfunctional,* divisive aspects of religion. Religion does not necessarily play the invigorating role posited by Durkheim. Religious beliefs and institutions can resist change and may stultify a culture to such a degree that it no longer thrives in its environment. The papal opposition to birth control, for example, may become highly dysfunctional for those already overpopulated countries where religious dogma continues to prevent contraception. Durkheim's thesis rests on the assumption that all members of the collectivity share the same system of belief; but there is certainly plenty of sad historical and contemporary evidence of the disruptive influence of religion where this presupposition does not hold true.

c The "Research" Question

i Context Sociologists have long been fascinated with the way in which belief systems can alter the course of history and influence both the character and the development of nations. Because the secular belief systems of societies are usually poorly delineated, the dominant ideas of a culture are largely studied in relation to their religions. Some sociologists maintain that religion merely reflects the more fundamental relationships that underlie the social and economic order, but others argue that religion has a definite effect on the society from which it originates. Sociologists ask: *Can religion operate as an independent social fact causing or influencing social action?*

ii Theory Karl Marx's determinist view of the relationship between belief systems and human society maintained that religion, law, political philosophy, and the like are projections of class relationships. In his view these institutions had no function other than to represent the interests and legitimate the rule of the exploiting class. Other sociologists, although they admit that all belief systems must have a social base, maintain—as did Durkheim—that ideas are not mere reflections of an underlying social reality. They can be social facts in their own right and can act as causative influences on other social phenomena.

The main statement of this latter view came from Max Weber. Weber in fact greatly admired Marx's materialist method—but only as an approach that happened to prove particularly fruitful. He saw this method, like all such intellectual constructs, as providing an *ideal type* against which an actual situation could be compared, and he resisted all attempts to insist on its absolute truth. Referring to the early settlers arriving on the Atlantic seaboard of North America, who promptly attempted to establish a capitalist economy in the midst of the utmost material deprivation, he states: "To speak of a reflection of material conditions in the ideal superstructure would be patent nonsense." Weber did not wish to turn Marx's view upside down—that is, to claim that ideas influence society rather than vice versa—but he was determined to show that, in some cases at least, belief systems could have a profound and independent effect on social action and economic development. His attempt to prove this view resulted in the *Protestant ethic thesis*—one of the most provocative, ambitious, and best-known hypotheses in sociology.

iii Research (Methodology) Marx based his sociology of religion on an intuitive understanding of the phenomenon, supplemented with some sketchy historical data. Durkheim analyzed all religion through the study of a single religious form, Australian totemism. But

Amd en amfi de quant
tes uertus et de quantes
biens il a este auctcur
a ceuly de sa lignice. et
combien plain de grant aigre il est
moit nous lauons delaine on li

The great cathedrals of Europe, which took hundreds of years and thousands of workers to construct, are apt symbols of the dominant role of religion in medieval society.

duuuut dur Quuud falouno
fil: auuoues iciue enfuut eut
us le iopuuue te fon pue. et fu
us ou fiege iopul. ront le puple
nuchueut fuueur. conuue on
le fuue a uu iop au conuueure

Max Weber, a man of prodigious learning, undertook an exhaustive study of most of the major world religions. The central focus of his analyses was the influence of men's religious ideas on their social action, especially in the field of economic behavior.

Starting from the contemporary and historical fact that there is a strong correlation between membership in an entrepreneurial class and adherence to the Protestant faith, Weber in *The Protestant Ethic and the Spirit of Capitalism* (1904–1905) set out to demonstrate a significant relationship between the doctrines of ascetic Protestantism—particularly of the Calvinist variety—and the rise of modern capitalism. He argued that the modern capitalism of the West differed radically from the capitalistic enterprises of other periods and societies—such as the simple greediness of merchants or mere seizures by pirates. The whole modern operation is routinized, systematized, and rationalized in terms of the supreme goal of capital accumulation. Furthermore, capitalism provides a strong ethical orientation to commercial activity—making money is not perceived as something disreputable but becomes a legitimate and inherently worthwhile enterprise, to such an extent that it is even considered a duty. Finally, there is an ascetic refusal to employ the accumulated wealth for immediate personal enjoyment; instead profits are to be saved or reinvested for the sole purpose of creating still more capital.

Weber's argument is that a certain interpretation of Protestantism created some of the motivations that led to the development of modern capitalism. Although he did not insist that it was the prime cause, he did regard it as a major influence. The relevant religious element was derived from the psychological consequences of the doctrines of ascetic Protestantism. That belief system sees the individual as being in stark confrontation with his Maker. That confrontation is unmediated—in contrast to the view of the Catholic church—by priestly intervention. The omnipotent Maker has predestined each individual to salvation or damnation from the beginning of eternity, and no man can by his conduct alter the divine decree. Nevertheless, it is the duty of each man to work for the greater glory of God. Although Protestantism does not instruct the faithful to discover indications of religious salvation in worldly success, the doctrine of predestination forces each anxious believer to seek some sign of his "election," some clue to his ultimate destiny, in his daily endeavors. Each individual embarks on regular, dedicated work in obedience to God, but any material success he achieves seems an indication of God's favor. Thus, argues Weber, the pioneers of modern capitalism could find a positive ethical and religious value in their work; it served as a means by which they could selflessly serve God and allay their own anxieties.

Weber's studies of other world religions revealed their relative inappropriateness as ideological supports for the development of capitalism. Catholicism supports monasticism and encourages the individual to be satisfied with his lot in life and to seek his rewards in heaven rather than on earth. Buddhism is also monastic and supports otherworldly asceticism, strongly deprecating all actions designed to win worldly goals. Taoism demands that the believer limit all self-seeking acquisitiveness, preferably by withdrawing from activities that offer worldly temptation. Hinduism stresses the in-

185

dividual's obligations in a static caste system, though even these duties are not the most important aspect of life; the mundane world is an illusion in any case, and a transcendent reality is available to those who seek it through meditation. Confucianism emphasizes a paternalistic social structure in which individual enterprise is subdued; the highest values are not imagination, innovation, or personal achievement, but benevolence and faith in an unchanging society. Weber saw Islam as being primarily a religion of warriors, oriented to values of conquest and plunder; the warrior is fatalistic rather than disciplined, and asceticism is inappropriate. Judaism, because it is a relatively rationalized religion and because of its minority status, does from time to time play a significant part in economic advance, but like Islam, it lacks ascetic values; therefore its capitalism has tended to be of the political or adventurist type common in the medieval period. In each of these complex social situations, argues Weber, the religious element may have played a role in retarding modern capitalist development.

Many recent lines of sociological investigation have focused on the ability of different religions to develop new frameworks of living and the extent to which these frameworks not only influence the growth and orientation of nations but also encourage or inhibit the achievement levels of individuals as well. Gerhard Lenski in *The Religious Factor* (1961) found that among Protestants in the United States children of devout working-class or farm parents grow up to have a higher economic achievement level than children of less devout families; the relationship among Catholics is the reverse. Furthermore, on a comparative basis, 51 percent of the Protestants sampled acquired middle-class status, as opposed to 39 percent of the Catholics. Nevertheless, other national studies have indicated that younger Catholics from lower-income brackets now have the highest achievement scores on tests measuring motivation—perhaps because of the desire to overcome their unequal status. This finding about motivation may also be correlated to some degree with a factor singled out in another study: that the recent drop in church attendance is greater among young Catholics than among their Protestant peers.

iv Evaluation   The Protestant ethic thesis continues to arouse much controversy. Some writers have argued that although a connection does exist between Protestantism and the development of capitalism, Weber misconceived the nature of the connection. Robert Bellah in "Reflections on the Protestant Ethic Analogy in Asia" (1963) argues that it was the very fact of the eruption of the Reformation that made possible the rise of capitalism: the old European order was being shaken to its foundations, and it was natural that those who were taking the lead in religious innovation should be found exploring new economic forms as well. Others have suggested that the crucial factor was the marginal status of Calvinists, who after the Catholic Counter-Reformation were often exiles and outcasts denied participation in other areas of national life. It has also been argued that the influential characteristic of ascetic Protestantism was not the "salvation panic" mechanism described by Weber but rather the Calvinist stress upon individualism, activism, and responsibility.

186

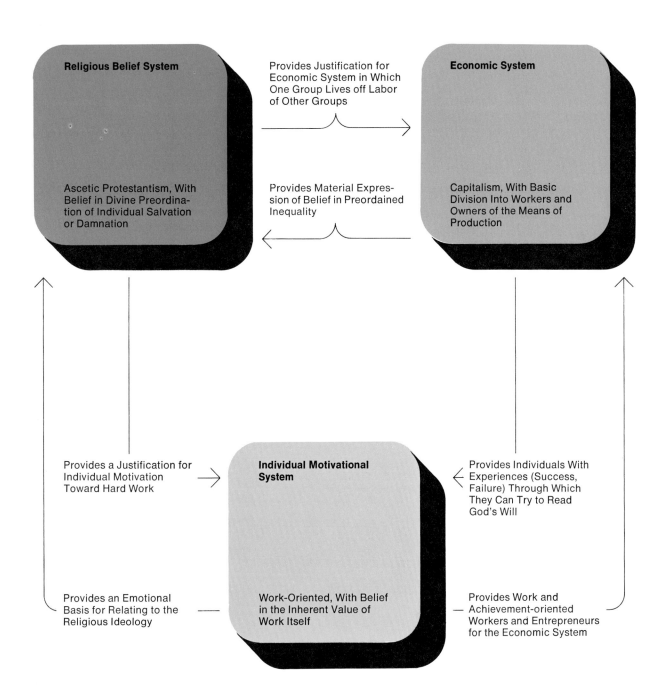

Model 2. Weber's Protestant Ethic Thesis. Each box provides some material that allows the system indicated by another box to function.

(Guy Swanson in *Religion and Regime* (1967) maintains that political factors were of prime importance to modern capitalism. A high degree of political centralization was characteristic of Catholic areas, whereas the low degree of centralization found in Protestant areas allowed more independent innovation.) The interrelationship here is complex, because these political features were themselves largely the product of religious attitudes. But Swanson argues that political decentralization involving a more flexible social structure was more open to innovation and hence more conducive to capitalist development.)

(Most sociologists, however, feel that the interrelationship of such diverse factors as the breakdown of the feudal system, the effects of the Reformation, and the growth of towns and of political authorities is so complex that no one can satisfactorily demonstrate the extent (if any) to which the Protestant ethic played a significant role in the development of modern capitalism.) In a sense, it seems that Weber bit off more than he could chew: the problems of isolating the relevant variables in a study of such scope are so great that even his exhaustive surveys leave his thesis as a continuingly provocative but unproven hypothesis. But his insistence that belief systems can function independently of the social structure in which they arise is so persuasive that it is now generally accepted by sociologists.)

(As to the influence of the Protestant ethic on individual economic achievement, sociologists have observed that the distinction between the two dominant religious groups in the United States is becoming more and more marginal) and that the issue involves many complex considerations and perspectives that are sometimes hidden by the methods of investigation. J. Milton Yinger reminds us that ''in some measure Catholics have been 'Protestantized' and Protestants have been influenced by Catholics . . . and both have been Americanized,'' and he defers to Weber's view that ''the pursuit of wealth is now quite secularized in the West.''

3   Overview

The fact that religion is not central to the consciousness of modern man should not obscure its global importance. For most people in most of history, religion has encompassed knowledge and permeated the social structure. Classical social theorists, such as Marx, Durkheim, and Weber, were deeply concerned with religious phenomena, and for good reason. The subject still captures the attention of sociologists today.

In particular, the study of the sociology of traditional religions has made sociologists aware of the implications of the various functional equivalents of religion that are to be found in the industrialized world—communism, fascism, hippie cults, and the like. Drawing on the study of religion, they are able to approach such phenomena with an enriched perspective.

But it is not only surrogate religion that captures the attention of the modern sociologist. The *messianic* and *millenarian movements* that arise in the midst of the rationalized technological society—such as the ''Jesus freaks''—are a sociological phenome-

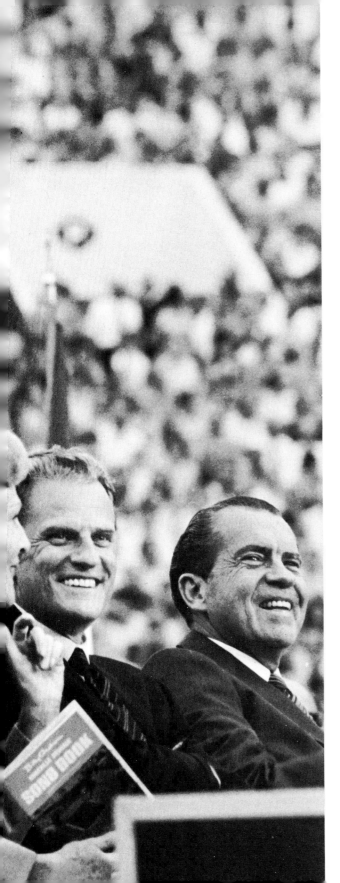

non of the first importance. Although the hold of the traditional church may be slipping, and although the contents of its doctrines may be steadily eroded, the capacity of millions of men and women in the modern world for a belief in some mysterious realm of ultimate and surpassing significance for humanity remains surprisingly strong. The sociologist of religion need not be confined to distant lands or historical records; fresh material for the discipline is at hand in his own society.

President and Mrs. Nixon appear with Rev. Billy Graham at a Crusade for Christ in Tennessee. In the United States public religiosity is used as a positive sanction for certain social values.

D   LOOKING AHEAD

1   Interview: Harvey Cox

Harvey G. Cox, Jr., is Victor S. Thomas Professor of Divinity in the Divinity School of Harvard University. Dr. Cox is an ordained Baptist minister who has held positions with Oberlin College, the American Baptist Home Mission Society, Andover Newton Theological School, the Gossner Mission in East Berlin, the World Council of Churches, the Blue Hill Christian Center, the Boston Industrial Mission, the Pontifical University of Lima, Peru, and *Christianity and Crisis* magazine. He is the author of *God's Revolution and Man's Responsibility*, *The Secular City*, *On Not Leaving It to the Snake*, *The Feast of Fools*, and *The Seduction of the Spirit*.

DPG   *What is the role of traditional religion in the modern industrial world, and why does it persist?*
COX   Well, religion does a lot of different things for people. There was a time when

religion was too easily explained as a kind of residue of superstition, as giving answers that other things couldn't. But it also gives people a kind of sense of where they fit in the whole of life and history. It legitimates occasions for what are now called "alternative states of consciousness." In some ways I think that people in an industrial society need even more such occasions because the others are taken away from them. And one very important thing that religion seems to do for people is provide a sense of community.

I'm especially interested, for example, in the growth of Pentecostalism in Latin America. Wherever there is rapid social change, urbanization, uprooting of villages, Pentecostalism grows. Pentecostalism provides a small, intimate, warm, emotionally valid kind of community for people. So I think all the predictions about religion's disappearing in industrial society seem not to have come true, and I wouldn't be surprised to see industrial society begin to fade before religion does.

DPG   *Is an analogy to the Pentecostalism of Latin America the kind of religious communes that have grown up in recent years here?*
COX   Yes. Here the communes are serving the same kinds of needs—the needs that people express all the time for belonging with people, for sharing a sense of intimacy,

for feeling that somebody cares about them. And they express these not just in conventional words, but in the things they do together—the kind of songs, the rituals or liturgies that people seem to have. Every successful commune has that kind of symbolic dimension to its life. If they don't, they seem to fall apart.

DPG   *What about the "Jesus freaks" and similar movements? How do you account for their appearance in a society as secular and rational as ours?*
COX   Well, there are two things about the "Jesus freaks." One is that they're "freaks," and one is that they're interested in Jesus. So let's take those two points separately. They have taken over the word "freak," you see, which was coined by the counterculture. "Freaks" say: we don't fit; we don't believe in this society; we're differ-

ent from you; we have different values; we have different hopes; we have a different way of life. So I think it's a conscious dissent from certain aspects of the majority culture. But in this case, it is rooted and legitimated, not by Oriental religion, as some of the early countercultural religion was, but by a reappropriation of a very simple, uncomplicated, institutionally unelaborate form of Christianity, based on a particular understanding of Jesus that is quite emotional, very direct, very feeling-oriented, not political, at least in any conventional sense, and not concerned about institutional structures. I'm personally a little worried about certain aspects of the Jesus movement, just because so much of it seems to be based on very strong charismatic leadership and authoritarian patterns. But I don't dismiss it out of hand as simply a kind of neofascism or something like that. In a way it's a reinjection of a certain kind of emotional vitality into conventional Christianity, which doesn't have a whole lot of that left.

DPG   *How is it that part of the new-left political movement evolved into the drug culture, some of which evolved into the Jesus movement?*
COX   Well, you know there always were in the new left in the United States, as opposed to the left in other countries, two characteristic features. It was not as anticlerical or antireligious as the European left movements are. And there were always religious people, including religious professionals, involved in it, all along the line. And it was anti-ideological. I mean you couldn't have a consistent discussion about ideology. Even then it was always very much based on feeling. There was no "program" either.

You see, that's structurally very similar to an old and persistently recurring brand of American religion, namely American pietism. Pietism holds that religion is based on feeling. The pietist says: don't talk to me about theology; I don't care about your theology; I want to know if your heart is right with God; or if you feel the movement of the Spirit; or if you've been saved. And that goes back to the Great Awakening in the eighteenth century, all the way back to Jonathan Edwards. It's one of the strongest traditions—I think a greatly overlooked one. When people talk about American Protestant history, for example, it's always identified with Puritanism. But pietism has been the major expression of American Protestantism.

What we have now that reminds me of it more than anything else are encounter centers. When I first went to Esalen Institute, I thought that it was more like the old camp meetings that my great grandparents went to than anything else. You go there, and you have a great experience, and you talk about your feelings, and you have some kind of reconciliation with divine forces and with each other. And you go away and see everything new, and you love everybody, and so on. I think there's a direct continuity there, so I'm not surprised to see what we call the new left fading gradually into a religious movement. And, in fact, into a religious movement without much theology and without much structure. And when you have a nontheological and institutionally amorphous movement, charismatic figures are bound to arise. That's the only authority you have left.

There are, in fact, two different types of religious movements that are emerging. One is the evangelical, theologically conservative, more-or-less authoritarian kind of Jesus movement. Pentecostalism, Mormonism, and the Nazarenes are all growing. On the other side, you have the Sufi communes and the Zen movements, and the love communes, with the Jesus people too. My real interest is whether there's going to be a movement toward some kind of a merger. I think I can see in a couple of churches the beginnings of a really new type that combines certain aspects of the evangelical-pentecostal with the new kind of countercultural religion. When that happens, there's going to be a very potent movement.

DPG *You have predicted that the Protestant ethic would return by the late 1970s. That seems to be another strain from the one you were just talking about.*
COX Yes. Let's take the Puritans as an example. What they were interested in and what shape their religious devotions took may, in fact, provide some models in the next five or 10 years along the following lines. One would be simplicity. They were very much against ostentation, conspicuous consumption, elaborate things. They were really interested in how one lived simply, as were the Quakers, Mennonites, Amish, and all those people. Simplicity is a very old Christian value. The other thing about the Puritans is they were suspicious of hierarchical authority. They wanted to assume

responsibility at the congregational level for their own religious life. In fact, the whole idea of the separatists who came over here was that they didn't want to wait for the religious authorities to reform the church. It had to be done congregation by congregation. It was decentralization.

But the most important thing that interests me about the Puritans—and I realize that it's not really terribly popular to talk about the Protestant ethic and all that—is that, after the decade of the 1960s where tripping was the idea—exploring the limits, pushing the very edges of experience, tasting everything, trying it all—I can see now a movement toward what I would call "centering," that is, making choices, doing this instead of that, finding some kind of focus for one's life. The need to find a spiritual and an autobiographical focus is very strong in the Puritan ethic.

So I can see where, if you discount now the kind of acquisitive, competitive side of the Protestant ethic that was allied with a certain form of capitalism, the religious substance of it still has something that may become interesting and attractive to people in the decade to come. Maybe this fact is one of the reasons why these conservative groups are growing. They're disciplined. Everybody who belongs to them tithes. It isn't a kind of a trippy thing. It's more structured, more disciplined. But the discipline is a self-discipline, especially in Puritanism.

DPG *To what extent is the Protestant ethic responsible for stunting the uninhibited, expressive, Dionysian side of human beings?*
COX I think it is to some extent responsible for stunting the Dionysian elements. Everybody needs periodic episodes of Dionysian expression. In fact, I wrote a whole book about it, *The Feast of Fools*, trying to understand what holidays are all about. What are feasts? I think in the human person there is a built-in need for episodic escapes from the structure of order and expectation and symmetry. If you don't have such episodes, then the need becomes very destructive. The Puritans had a decree in the early days of New England about not celebrating Christmas. They had Thanksgiving, but they were very suspicious of holidays because the whole life had to be focused on service to God and the building

of the holy commonwealth, and they were very suspicious of anything that was not productive, anything that wasn't instrumental.

DPG   *But in our society today Christmas seems to have become subordinated to business again. Is there anything that serves officially that feast function?*
COX   Very little. In fact, the holidays have now become ways in which you rest up so you can come back and be even more competitive and more efficient. The idea that a holiday is in itself a viable and valuable human activity that doesn't have to be justified on the basis of productivity is a difficult one for us. That's why I said in *The Feast of Fools* that there's a relationship between ''play'' and ''pray.'' You see, prayer is also not productive, and we're just as critical of people who go to monasteries because we say that they're not contributing anything. The point I was making was the similarity between, on the one hand, prayer, meditation, comtemplation, the monastic life, and all of the things that seem so strange and weird to a lot of people in the modern world, and, on the other hand, play and festivity, which are also proscribed. I think there's a close relationship in that all these activities are nonproductive. They don't produce anything beyond themselves. They're not instrumental. A society that is suspicious of play and festivity is also suspicious of contemplation. I think that the Protestant ethic, insofar as it has informed our culture, has been hard on both play and prayer. Prayer gets to be used as a means to an end. It's a way of achieving something or getting something. And play is perverted in the same way. It's made into a way of shoring up your energies or having a change of pace so that later you can compete or accumulate better.

It seems to me that one of the basic affirmations of all religions is that there is something more important about one's relationship to reality than changing it, manipulating it, accumulating it, competing with it. This affirmation is the act of awe, the attitude of worship, which is simply affirming, saying yes. In the Jewish tradition, it's the Sabbath. The old idea of the Sabbath was that you did *nothing* on the Sabbath. The Sabbath itself is the symbol of the highest relationship of man to God and man to the world, simply enjoying it, simply being with it.

DPG   *Does the proscription of play in our society account, at least in part, for the popularity of a place like Disneyland?*
COX   I think you have to understand Disneyland as more basic than a playground. It's a pilgrimage site. It's where we go in America to make sure that the lost image of a small town and the intimate community, where everything was in scale, where we didn't feel overwhelmed, is still there somehow. It functions, for many people, I think, in a religious way, in the broad sense of religious. That is, it nourishes an archetypal vision that they feel is disturbed

or distorted in the world that they generally live in. But what this does for me is to suggest that a narrow definition of religion as what happens in churches or people's relationship to the supernatural simply misses a wide range of religious phenomena—activities, attitudes, gestures—that the culture is absolutely inundated with. If you watch television for one night, there are heroes and saviors and demons, and there are sacraments that can save you from your sin and can redeem you. You see, what we do is define religion in a very narrow way so that we don't have to bother with it, although we're really evangelized daily by all

of these powerful symbols. What I'm trying to do in my own teaching here is to help my students see that theological analysis and evaluation have to be turned toward so-called secular phenomena.

I suppose the first thing that I ever became notorious for was the theological analysis of *Playboy* magazine, which I paired with an analysis of Miss America. I couldn't help seeing the striking similarity between aspects of the Miss America festivity—the ritual and the crowning and the taboos around her person and the showering with gifts—and the old fertility cults. Why does that happen? I'm convinced that the religious dimensions of human life are far more persistent than most people have ever believed. They're really there. And the most secular, rational man or woman who claims that he's really free of all that stuff, falls asleep, and, instantly upon falling asleep and dreaming, is back into a mythical realm. There are monsters, and there are ordeals, and there are mystical flights, and there's ritual violence, and there's all the stuff that religion is made of. So it's pretty close to the surface and it comes up everywhere. Disneyland is only one example of it.

DPG   *What's the future of the organized church and religion in America?*
COX   They're two different questions, I think, because we don't have *an* organized church in America. We have over 225 recognized religious denominations as tabu-

lated by the Bureau of the Census. And we have God knows how many other un-tabulated religious organizations, movements, cults, and what have you. And despite all of the predictions, I see no evidence whatever of a decline in religious vitality, religious organization, religious belonging, religious adherency, or anything. There is a difference in where it's happening and how it's being organized. The major denominations, the Episcopal, Congregational, Methodist, and Roman Catholic even, seem to be experiencing a decline in membership, in rates of growth, building, and all the rest. Not a spectacular one, but nevertheless an ascertainable decline—say from 1950 to 1960 to 1970. At the same time, we seem to see a growth of sectarian, cultic, nontraditional, unconventional types of religious movements. So there just isn't any evidence at all that religion is disappearing or withering away. I think it's proliferating, but I think that the pattern of large, bureaucratically organized, national denominations is fated for extinction. I think they're declining, and within 10, 20, 30, 40 years, depending on how long it takes, they will no longer be the center of focus, if they are now, of religion in the narrow sense in America. I might also point out, by the way, that a very similar tendency is at work everywhere I know in the world.

DPG   *Where in an industrial society like ours do we go for theology in an age in which fantasy has been said to be the salvation for intellect?*

COX   Theology is not to be equated with religion any more than musicology is to be equated with music. Theology is something different. Yes, the basic myths that people have lived by are still there. They are there in our ethnic and standard religious tradition. They're there in our dreams, in our unconscious. They come out all the time in small-group interaction. They're there in our music. Who would have predicted the enormous new interest in Jesus in every second or third musical that comes out or in all the movies? To find a myth today, we just have to look around. They're simply there. A lot of people are tuned out, so they can't appreciate or live mythologically or perceive the mythical and religious quality of life around them. But that's their fault. It's there,

and I think we have mistrained people in public schools and in other kinds of education to such a narrowly cognitive and instrumental way of thinking that they miss all this.

DPG   *Can any secular idea ever replace religion?*

COX   I doubt it. If by "secular" you mean a way of perceiving reality that leaves no place for mystery, for transcendence, for the terror of the unknown, for the ecstatic, for the noncognitive. I think that when man becomes totally secular—if that ever happens—then something of what we now think of as essentially human will have been lost. When that dimension is lost, then we're really getting into *1984* or *Brave New World,* or something. Partly as a prediction and partly as a hope, I would say that I see no possibility of a really postreligious society.

One of the things we should watch for in the coming period is a kind of a battle of the gods. If you watched President Nixon's Inauguration in 1973, it was a religious event. On the one hand, there is a civic religion in America that is built around the flag and a kind of mythologized history of our country. Then on the other hand there are the major religious traditions and the charismatic movements. I think we're becoming more aware now of the clash. These phenomena are not easily assimilable to each other, and we're going to see more sharply defined friction, which I think some people like the Berrigans have begun to show us. There are certain demands that the Catholic heritage, for example, puts on people that are going to be in conflict with the American civic religion. And vice versa. So I look forward to more conflict between religious perspectives in the period to come.

Unit 9
Social Stratification

1 Definition
Social stratification is a system of inequality based on hierarchical orderings of groups according to their members' share in such rewards as wealth, power, and status. The principal forms that stratification takes are estate, caste, and class.

2 World Context
For most of human history social stratification has been unquestioned. The most striking inequalities in the world today are international.

3 American Context
Americans tend to consider themselves a relatively classless people, though wealth, status, and power are unequally distributed in the United States.

1 Questions
Contemporary sociologists raise three significant questions about stratification: (1) Can Marx's prediction that class tensions would ultimately lead to the destruction of the capitalist system still be applied? (2) Is stratification an inevitable and necessary feature of human society? (3) Can the class structure of modern societies be analyzed solely by reference to the economic positions of individuals?

2 Evidence
a The "Burning Issue" Question
The notion of class struggle was central to Marx's thought. Numerous social theorists have challenged his economic determinism, pointing out that the workers in capitalist societies have not developed a militant class consciousness. The current consensus is that his predictions were only partially correct.
b The "Classical" Question
Functional theories regard social stratification as necessary and unavoidable. These theories have been strongly criticized both theoretically and on empirical grounds.
c The "Research" Question
Marx's economic definition of class was expanded and modified by Max Weber's multidimensional analysis of stratification. Empirical research by W. Lloyd Warner, Floyd Hunter, and others have shown that prestige, wealth, and power may vary independently of one another.

3 Overview
Social stratification is a complex phenomenon whose origin and function are not yet fully understood. Clearer comprehension of it may emerge from interdisciplinary studies and may lead to modification of hierarchical systems.

SOCIAL INEQUALITY AND ECONOMIC PROCESSES

1. In small-scale hunting and gathering communities, there is no surplus production and relationships are too intimate to allow the formation of rigid strata.

2. More advanced agrarian economies allow the production of surplus wealth and the development of inequality. Stratification in these societies tends to be static and to have a hereditary basis.

3. In most contemporary societies class is based on income and related criteria, such as access to status and power. Class lines are not inflexible, and there may be some individual mobility between classes.

NO

YES

4. Greater equality of access for all people to the power to influence decisions regarding production and to the goods and services actually produced is necessary to lessen the exploitation inherent in economically class-structured society.

Although there is little inequality in small-scale societies, inherited inequalities emerge in more complex agrarian societies, and modern industrial societies tend to be stratified on the basis of economic class. The elimination of economic classes would necessitate the restructuring of the productive processes.

B   DEFINITION AND CONTEXT

1   Definition

Over 2,000 years ago Aristotle commented that populations tend to be divided into three groups—the very rich, the very poor, and those in between. He observed a prominent and almost universal feature of human societies that is as evident today as it was in his time: Society is divided into classes or strata arranged in hierarchies of property, influence, and prestige. For centuries the phenomenon of stratification has attracted the attention of social theorists, philosophers, and activists. It remains one of the most crucial issues in sociology today.

Social stratification is a system of social inequality based on hierarchical orderings of groups according to their members' share in socially valued rewards. The nature of these rewards varies from society to society, but generally they consist of *wealth, power,* and *status.* Members of each stratum are normally accorded deference by those below, are treated as equals by members of the same stratum, and are deferential to members of the stratum above.

The principal forms that stratification takes are estate, caste, and class. *Estate* describes each group with a feudal system in an agrarian society: in medieval Europe, for example, there were three estates—the nobility, the clergy, and the serfs. *Caste* applies to a rigid system, such as that prevailing for centuries in India, in which an individual is inevitably destined to spend his entire life in the stratum into which he was born. *Class* refers to groups whose stratification is primarily economically based. Legal sanctions are the basis of estate systems, and religious criteria underlie caste systems. But an individual's class is normally determined by the economic position of the head of his family.

Of the three systems, class stratification offers the greatest possibility of *social mobility;* that is, an individual born into a particular class may, through his own efforts or through external circumstances, move up or down in the social hierarchy. In a caste or estate system there is almost no individual mobility. If an individual's position in a stratification system is based on characteristics over which he has no control, such as race, age, sex, or birth, his status is said to be *ascriptive;* if the individual's position depends on other modifiable variables, such as high income or marriage into a higher stratum, his status is said to be *achieved.* If the stratification system is sharply defined and offers no way for an individual to rise to a higher position, it is said to be *closed;* if the boundaries between the strata are more blurred and an individual may legitimately hope for a change in his position, the system is said to be *open.* Open systems emphasize achievement rather than ascription and offer considerable mobility as compared to hereditary systems. The class system that characterizes modern industrial societies is relatively open and mobile, and such variable, economically based criteria as occupation, education, and life style are usually the determinants of class.

For the lower strata inequality often implies poverty. *Absolute poverty* refers to extreme inadequacy in the essentials of life—food, clothing, and shelter. *Relative poverty* refers to the compara-

G. R. Boulanger's *Slaves of Ancient Rome* (1882). The various forms of slavery that have existed in many parts of the world at various times constitute a clear-cut example of social stratification rooted in a society's economic structure. However, wherever one group makes a living off the labor of another group of persons, the society is both economically and socially stratified.

tive poverty of the lower strata in relation to the affluence of the higher strata. Absolute poverty combined with inequality represents a vital issue in politics and social policy. If absolute poverty overlaps with issues of race, language, or religion the potential for *social conflict* may be particularly explosive.

2   World Context

For most of recorded human history the inequality of man has been unquestioned. It was viewed as a part of the natural order and was approved not only by law and custom, but also by religion; for example, the notion of the divine right of kings legitimated the feudal system. The revolutions of the eighteenth century and early nineteenth century fought against the notion that stratification was part of an unchanging and unchangeable order. Yet the revolutionary changes ultimately instituted a new form of inequality, based this time not so much on birth or wealth alone as on a new form of production (industrial capitalism). These new social inequalities have been attacked in turn, particularly by those who, under Marxist inspiration, conceive of a *classless society.* These ideas are a key element in contemporary sociology: the notion that stratification systems can be modified by human intervention is accepted in all modern societies.

The most striking inequalities in the world today are international. Two-thirds of the world's population shares only one-third of the world's income, and only a quarter of mankind lives in those industralized states that enjoy relatively high incomes and standards of well-being. About half the population of the world spends less than $100 per year on goods and services, but the average citizen of the United States spends more than thirty times that amount. The United States alone accounts for one-third of the world's gross national product. The gap between the very rich and the poor is particularly wide in the developing nations. There is usually no middle class of any size in them; and there are wide variations in the degree of *social distance* between strata and in the degree of *class consciousness* within any one stratum. Moreover, the basis for stratification is culturally variable: a man may be in the top rank because of his skill in war, the wealth of his parents, or his membership in a priestly order.

The outstanding example of an ascriptive caste system is that of India, where neither wealth nor success can remove a person from the stratum of his birth. In theory there are four major castes in India: the Brahmans—the priests and teachers of lore; the Kshatriyas—the warriors and princes; the Vaisyas—the peasants and merchants; and the Sudras—a caste of manual laborers who exist to serve the other castes. All those who are below the Sudras and thus beyond the Hindu spiritual community are *outcastes* and *untouchables;* in fact, there are some 3,000 castes and subcastes in India. Although the influence of the caste system has waned rapidly in the urban areas, it still dominates social relations in small villages and the countryside. There are complicated rules about the cooking and serving of food by different castes, and great concern is expressed about the ritual avoidance of pollution from contact with untouchables—or even with their passing shadows. For most

Nikita S. Khrushchev, First Secretary of the Communist Party and Premier of the Soviet Union in the 1950s and early 1960s, with President John F. Kennedy at the Vienna conference in 1961. Many of the Soviet Union's leaders since the Bolshevik Revolution in 1917 have come from peasant families. Sometimes their class background colors their behavior in international settings, upsetting more ''refined'' diplomats. Khrushchev, for example, was famous for his earthy language and gestures and is the only world leader ever to have pounded on a United Nations desk with his shoe in order to make a point.

Mohandas K. Gandhi (1869–1948). Besides leading the Indian people in a decades-long struggle for liberation from British subjection, Gandhi, a high-caste Hindu, also challenged his own traditional heritage and actively campaigned for inclusion of the ''untouchables'' into modern Indian society. Under his influence laws discriminating against the untouchables both socially and economically have been eliminated, but informally their outcaste status remains operative in most of the Indian countryside and, to some extent, in urban society as well.

Indians the formal abolition of castes in 1949 has had little impact on the system.

Industrialization brings with it pervasive changes in the stratification of societies. The demand for skills opens up new opportunities and breaks down ascriptive barriers. The *peasantry* becomes a *proletariat,* and education becomes a key to advancement. Most modern industrialized societies are relatively mobile, and an individual can rise rapidly in the stratification system through achievement—normally through the acquisition of wealth. Great Britain is one of the few societies that retains an elaborate and distinct system of snobbery based on *class origins* rather than *current wealth:* an individual's class is recognizable by one signifier immediately identifiable to other Britons—his accent. The prevalence of this acute sensitivity to class origins is probably related to the fact that Britain, almost alone of the European feudal societies, did not undergo a revolutionary overthrow of its aristocracy. Even as late as the end of World War II, some 1 percent of the British population still owned half the private property in the country.

The socialist societies of Eastern Europe claim to have abolished private property and to be working toward the construction of a new, classless society. The fact remains, however, that in the Soviet Union and other East European countries the top incomes are many times higher than the lowest, and the bureaucratic hierarchy has in its hands a concentration of economic and political power unparalleled in the West. There is, however, very high social mobility in the USSR, with no element of heredity in the apportionment of social rewards. No *leisure class* exists on inherited wealth, and only a relatively small ''new class'' lives on the labor of others. Instead, the *dominant elite* is stratified as the upper echelon of an open, *bureaucratic hierarchy.* In the People's Republic of China there is considerable *egalitarianism* at the local level, but this egalitarianism is counterbalanced by a continuing deference to the decisions of central authority.

3   American Context

Americans tend to consider themselves a relatively classless people: theirs is the land of opportunity, the home of the free. Equality is a core value in American culture, expressed in the early history of the country, in the Declaration of Independence, and in the Constitution. The United States has no history of feudal ranking or of a dominant aristocratic order; the nation was influenced in its ideology by the upheavals in Europe against precisely such hierarchies. Ownership of property was relatively widely diffused, and it was not until large-scale industrialization in the 1880s and 1890s that considerable inequalities of wealth developed among the whites. Between the 1890s and the 1930s the United States had a singularly bloody history in the area of labor-management relations, but no major nationally organized socialist movement developed. Today the United States remains, along with Canada and the Republic of South Africa, one of the few highly industrialized countries in the world in which neither the government nor the leading opposition party is a socialist one.

Inequality is a significant feature of contemporary American society; the good things in life are scarce and are unequally distributed. Furthermore, this distribution is not always on the basis of achieved status: we need only consider the advantages in life accruing to one who is white, male, and Protestant to see that much of the American stratification has an ascriptive foundation. Several studies, notably *Social Mobility and Industrial Societies* (1959) by Seymour Martin Lipset and Reinhard Bendix, have shown that the rate of social mobility in the United States is not significantly higher than that of a number of other industrial societies. Nevertheless, the belief in the ideology of egalitarianism still persists in America today, although it tends to be modified from an insistence on the equality of men to a belief in the right of all men to equal opportunity.

The traditional concept of the United States as a highly mobile society, the land of equal opportunity, has probably acted to diminish the development of *class consciousness* among workers. Rapid *social change* and *geographic mobility* have prevented the establishment of stable classes. Moreover, the presence of the black American has meant that the white worker need never feel himself to be at the lowest level of the social hierarchy. As T. B. Bottomore points out in *Classes in Modern Society* (1965):

> The negroes have formed a distinctive American proletariat, with the lowest incomes, the most menial and subservient tasks, and the lowest social prestige (in part because of their slave origins) of any group in American society. The existence of this large, relatively homogeneous, easily identifiable, and exploited group has meant that every white American, even the lowest-paid laborer, possesses a certain social prestige which raises him, at least in his own view, above the level of a proletarian.

In the United States today more than 40 percent of the national income goes to the richest one-fifth of the people; the poorest fifth receives about 5 percent—much the same portion, in fact,

The American working class. Much to the frustration of Marxist theorists and organizers, the American working class does not yet perceive itself as a unified social entity created by its position in the socioeconomic system. Rather, differences of racial and ethnic origin are emphasized, as are rather arbitrary distinctions between ''white-collar'' and ''blue-collar'' workers. This situation results in an inability of the working class to fight collectively for its interests. Even labor unions find it difficult to cooperate with one another.

as the lowest fifth received in 1935. The contrast is even greater when we consider total wealth rather than just income. Some 10 percent of the people in America own over 60 percent of the wealth and are able to continue to do so through tax loopholes and other untaxed personal benefits (such as expense accounts or corporation yachts). In recent years there have been cases of individuals with annual incomes of millions of dollars who have, quite legally, paid little or nothing in income taxes, and the same is true of some of America's largest and most profitable corporations. The general affluence of the United States has not filtered down to the 20 percent of the population at the bottom of the hierarchy. The highest incidence of poverty occurs among nonwhites, the aged, residents of certain regions such as Appalachia, families with no breadwinner or large numbers of children, and unskilled workers. Often these categories overlap: a quarter of the poor families in America are headed by females, a quarter are headed by nonwhites, and 40 percent of the poor nonwhite families have a female head.

If wealth and status are unequally distributed among Americans, what about power? The traditional view has been that the United States is a *pluralistic society* in which various groups counterbalance one another. In this setting power is considered to be diffused through a series of "veto groups." However, C. Wright Mills argued in *The Power Elite* (1956) that the United States is actually dominated by an interlocking directorate of several thousand men placed in the most important corporations, foundations, universities, government bureaucracies, mass media institutions, and private associations. The members of this group have not seized power intentionally; rather they happen to occupy influential positions in institutions that have grown progressively stronger during this century. They occupy the command posts in the major institutional hierarchies that control society today. They tend to know one another and are linked together in various formal and informal ways. Particularly in times of national crisis, they have to be rapidly coordinated. Mills contended that conflict between interest groups does not occur at this level. Instead, such conflict arises at the middle levels of power and takes the form of bargaining over issues of lesser importance. At the bottom of the hierarchy are the members of *mass society*, which exerts little influence on the course of decision taking; indeed this group is usually unaware that decisions are being taken at all.

Disillusionment with the course of the Vietnam war increased the popularity of Mills' analysis among college students and perhaps among the public at large. A number of sociologists are attempting to verify the *power elite thesis* empirically. The most notable is G. William Domhoff (author of the books *Who Rules America?*; *The Higher Circles*; *Fat Cats and Democrats*), who has accumulated a body of data that supports the thesis that the power elite governs in the interests of the upper class and is particularly effective in the area of foreign policy. But Domhoff's radical argument has not been as widely accepted among sociologists as the *interest-group pluralist model*, which is reaffirmed in the work of Arnold Rose (*The Power Structure*, 1967).

C QUESTIONS AND EVIDENCE

1 Questions

Contemporary sociologists raise three significant questions about stratification: (1) Can Marx's prediction that class tensions in industrial societies would tend ultimately to the revolutionary destruction of the capitalist system still be applied to modern capitalist societies? (2) Is social stratification, which appears in all but a few small-scale tribal societies, an inevitable and necessary feature of human society? (3) Can the class structure of modern societies be analyzed solely by reference to the economic position of individuals—or must other criteria be used as well?

2 Evidence

a The "Burning Issue" Question

i Context In 1848, a year of revolutionary ferment in Europe, Karl Marx and Friedrich Engels published the *Communist Manifesto*. In it, they proclaimed class conflict to be a dominant feature of human history and the vehicle for the creation of the perfect social order—the classless or communist society. The communist ideal has since won the allegiance of hundreds of millions of people. Wars and revolutions have been fought under Marxist inspiration, and the industrialized countries of the world are today grouped into opposing blocs on the basis of their acceptance or rejection of Marxist theory. Marx predicted that class divisions would lead to the doom of the capitalist system: Have his predictions been supported by the trend of events? The basic question is: *Can the Marxist theory of class struggle be validly applied to contemporary capitalist societies?*

ii Theory The third volume of Marx's *Capital* (1867, 1885, and 1894) breaks off at precisely the point at which he intended to give a systematic account of his theory of class. But the notion of class and class struggle is central to all his work; throughout his writings he affirms the economic basis of class distinctions and the significance of class as the basis for all social organization. We have discussed Marx's theory with reference to knowledge, culture, and religion in earlier units.

Marx was an *economic determinist*. He believed that the mode of production of a particular society is fundamental to the whole social order. All other social institutions—law, the dominant ideology, religion, government—derive their form and content from the economic foundations of society, and the upper stratum in society uses these institutions to justify and maintain its privileged position. The government of the capitalist state, says Marx, is but "the executive committee of the bourgeoisie." The struggle between the classes is the primary means of social change throughout history, and the endpoint of this process is the classless society.

In the *Communist Manifesto* Marx and Engels declared:

> The history of all hitherto existing societies is the history of class struggle. . . . Freedman and slave, patrician and plebeian, lord and serf, guildmaster and journeyman, in a

Classes in America. Despite popular mythology to the contrary, there is in actuality little interclass mobility for individuals in the United States. Of course, as long as people continue to believe in the myths (backed up by the occasional true-life "Horatio Alger" story of "from rags to riches by pluck and luck") there will be little public pressure to change the American system of social stratification.

word, oppressor and oppressed, stood in constant opposition to one another, carried on an uninterrupted, now hidden, now open fight, a fight that each time ended, either in a revolutionary reconstruction of society at large, or the common ruin of the contending classes.

According to this view, all except the most primitive human societies are divided into mutually antagonistic classes. These classes originated with the first historical expansion of productive capabilities beyond the level required for mere subsistence; the resulting division of labor and accumulation of surplus wealth made possible the emergence of private ownership of economic resources and products.

Human society, Marx believed, moves through a series of stages according to the *mode of production* predominant in each stage. He delineated five distinct stages: *primitive communism, slavery, feudalism, capitalism,* and *socialism.* Each system is more productive than the one before it, but each contains within it an inherent tension. The dynamic force of history is *class struggle:* each new stage is based on the *exploitation* of one group by another, and although each stage opens up new productive possibilities, the exploited will eventually revolt and initiate the next higher stage. Thus it was, for example, that the rising *bourgeoisie* (merchants, moneylenders, manufacturers) overthrew feudalism and the aristocracy of birth and instituted instead the capitalist system of production. In the same way, Marx predicted, the exploited working class, the *proletariat,* will eventually overthrow the exploiting capitalist class, this time introducing a socialist society in which the means of production will be publicly owned.

Initially a *dictatorship of the proletariat* will supervise the so-

(Below left) W. A. ("Tony") Boyle, charged by critics with corruption, collaboration with mine owners, and involvement in the murder of union reform leader Joseph Yablonski was ousted from the presidency of the United Mine Workers in 1972 by a rank-and-file movement. (Below right) George Meany, president of the American Federation of Labor-Congress of Industrial Organizations, applauds President Nixon before a speech to an AFL-CIO convention. In a number of ways "big unionism" has adopted the ills of "big business"; some union presidents, for example, receive salaries and retirement benefits of more than $100,000 a year, while rank-and-file workers continue to struggle to make ends meet.

cial order, preventing the attempts by reactionaries to reimpose the capitalist system. Finally the stage of socialism will give way to the *communist society*—a classless, democratic social order in which the alienation of man will be a phenomenon of the past, in which each individual will contribute according to his abilities and receive according to his needs.)

Marx contended that the trends in capitalist societies would lead to the sharpest class conflict in history:

> Our epoch, the epoch of the bourgeoisie, possesses, however, this distinctive feature: it has simplified the class antagonisms. Society as a whole is now splitting up into two great hostile camps, into great classes directly facing each other—bourgeois and proletarian.

(The *middle classes* between the bourgeoisie and the proletariat would tend to disappear, most of their members being absorbed into the proletariat. The capitalists would grow fewer and fewer in number as they eliminated one another by fierce competition.) Declining living standards would be the fate of the workers, and the economic system as a whole would become more and more unstable. Labor unions would contribute to the rising class consciousness of the workers, who would inevitably rise up to reconstruct the entire social order. In a capitalist society the proletarians and capitalists are locked in inevitable, unceasing struggle. Their interests are irreconcilable, but history, according to Marx, is on the side of the proletariat.

iii *Research* (Numerous social theorists have challenged the applicability of the Marxist concept of class struggle to modern capitalist societies. An early and representative critic was Selig Perlman, whose *A History of Trade Unionism in the United States* (1923) argued that Marx had failed to foresee changes in capitalism and had underestimated the adaptability of the capitalist system. The labor unions, for example, had not become more militant; on the contrary, they had won concessions for the workers and were far more interested in reform than revolution. The working conditions of the proletariat had considerably improved since Marx's time, and most of its members did not see themselves as inevitably locked into the working class.) The desire for and possibility of upward mobility operated against the development of a distinctive class consciousness. The result, argued Perlman, was that the workers were developing an increasing stake in the preservation of the status quo, rather than an urge to overthrow the system.

(Other writers, pointing to the lack of a militant class consciousness among the workers, have suggested that a process of *embourgeoisement* is making the workers and the middle class share similar attitudes and consumption patterns.)They argue that Marx neglected those important relationships that cut across class divisions and counteract the development of strong class consciousness. Workers are members of national groups, of churches, of communities, of ethnic groups; they may have high or low prestige jobs within their class; and a number of laborers frequently earn more than some white-collar members of the middle class.

Moreover, critics of Marxism claim that there is no evidence that the rich in capitalistic countries are growing richer, that the middle class is disappearing, or that the poor are becoming poorer. The high productivity of the industrial societies of the West has created an affluence that has made most of the working class substantially better off, both relatively and absolutely, than was the case when Marx wrote. The middle class is expanding and the traditional working class is shrinking because of changes in the occupational structure; that is, the number of white-collar and professional occupations is increasing, and there is a contraction in the proportion of blue-collar, manual jobs. Individual capitalists and monopolies have given way to large corporations with thousands of stockholders. The lines between the classes are, if anything, more blurred than when Marx wrote.

Historically, socialist revolutions have not occurred in highly industrialized capitalist societies at all, as Marx predicted they would. Instead, they have arisen exclusively in backward, illiterate, agrarian societies, such as Russia, China, and Cuba at the time of their revolutions. The experience of the socialist societies of the Soviet bloc has also increased skepticism about Marx's predictions. Although there is little private property in these countries, indications are that a hierarchy of Communist party officials and bureaucrats enjoys significantly greater power, income, and prestige than the masses. Milovan Djilas, a former vice-president of Yugoslavia who was imprisoned for his criticisms of the "new class," has written of how this stratum emerged in the socialist societies of Eastern Europe:

> The party secretary and the chief of the secret police in some places not only became the highest authorities but obtained the best housing, automobiles, and similar evidences of privilege. Those beneath them were eligible for comparable privileges depending on their position in the hierarchy. . . . The essential aspect of contemporary communism is the new class of owners and exploiters. (*The New Class*, 1957)

iv   Evaluation   The current consensus of opinion among Western sociologists is that Marx was only partly correct in his predictions. He wrote at a period of sharp antagonism and conflict between capital and labor, and he projected the trends he saw into the future. What he did not anticipate was that the distribution of national income might change in favor of the working class; that the middle class would expand in response to the emergence of new occupations requiring technicians, managers, scientists, and administrative personnel; that the capitalist economy would become more regulated and less subject to severe fluctuations and crises; that welfare states would emerge; and that the class consciousness of the workers would diminish as they gained a stake in the society Marx thought they would overthrow. It is not possible to regard the workers in the United States and most of the industrialized countries of Western Europe as bitterly alienated from their society and ready to support radical moves for the overthrow of the social order.

In fact, when Democratic candidate George McGovern suggested during the 1972 presidential campaign that too much of

America's wealth was controlled by an elite of families and that he would favor a government-imposed ceiling of $500,000 on all individual inheritances, the loudest cry of outrage was raised not by the aristocracy of wealth, against whom this proposal was directed, but by the workers themselves. Most workers will never be able to amass an estate of even 1 percent of that figure, but they evidently cherish the vision that *anyone* can become a millionaire. In anticipation of their own (purely hypothetical) vast fortunes, they oppose any regulation that would steal it away from their rightful heirs. This situation shows the degree to which many workers in America identify with the aspirations and outlook of the capitalist class rather than those of the "downtrodden proletariat."

Marxist sociologists have tried to account for the gap between Marx's predictions and empirical reality primarily through a reinterpretation of Marxist theory in the light of changed circumstances. The most powerful argument is based on V. I. Lenin's theory of *imperialism,* put forward in *Imperialism, the Highest Stage of Capitalism* (1916) and other works. In this view, the greater equality and diminished class conflict that now prevail in Western capitalist societies have been achieved only at the expense of the rest of the world. In this view the proletariat of the United States, for example, is considered to be external—residing in Africa, Asia, and Latin America—and the tensions between the classes are believed to have been transferred to the international scene. The wealthy, industrialized countries of the world are engaged in an economic conflict with the exploited and oppressed peoples of the less developed Third World. By using imperialism, the Western capitalists have postponed—but not avoided—the day of ultimate reckoning.

The theory of imperialism does provide a useful focus on the relationship between the rich and poor nations of the world, although it is not clear that the economic and political relationship between the Third World and the capitalist societies of the West is significantly different from the relationship between the Third World and the socialist societies of Eastern Europe.

It must also be pointed out that if Marx's theory of class revolution is viewed as a multistage process ranging from simple class identification to recognition of common interests in economic and working conditions to protest activity to revolutionary action, it can be seen that even in the United States, Marx's analysis is partially applicable. For more than two decades national public opinion polls and studies have shown no lessening in the solid majority of blue-collar workers who designate themselves as "working class" rather than "middle class." Polls have also consistently demonstrated the liberal orientations of blue-collar workers on many economic issues. Recent years have shown a marked rise in common interest in the problem of repressive working conditions, especially among young workers.

Despite the impact of the mass media, there is considerable evidence that the working class is not simply imitating middle-class life styles. Despite President Nixon's success in obtaining the blue-collar vote in 1972, the continued identification of the majority of workers with the Democratic party reflects the resilience of class-based party affiliation. American workers also continue to be more willing to strike for their economic interests than the workers in most industrial countries. The fact that American workers are far removed from *revolutionary* class consciousness should not blind us to the many ways that more rudimentary forms of economic group identity shape their attitudes and actions.

b   The "Classical" Question

i   Context   Social stratification is a feature of all but the smallest and most simple societies, and even in those communities it is often possible to detect the elements of differentials in power, prestige, and possession of property. Stratification is universal in communities of any size. But does this mean it is inevitable? Would it be universal if it did not perform some essential role in human society?

The tradition that sees social inequality as inevitable has a long ancestry in religious thought and in political philosophy. It is only since the French Revolution and the subsequent spread of egalitarian and Marxist thought that the possibility of an unstratified society has gained wide acceptance. The hope that mankind can be reorganized into unstratified communities based on cooperation has been the basis of wars and revolutions and a source of artistic and literary inspiration. Sociologists continue to ask: *Is social stratification an inevitable and necessary structural feature of human society?*

ii   Theory   The earliest modern argument for the inevitability of human inequality was presented by the *Social Darwinist* theorists of the last century. Once Charles Darwin had shown how evolution to higher forms in the natural world depended on the survival of the fittest, some social theorists attempted to apply this notion to the human world. Classes or races were considered to be dominant or inferior because they were biologically better or less well adapted to the conditions of life. The survival of the species depended on seeing to it that the fittest element in each society had the best chances in life.

This theory was based on a false analogy with the natural world and, in any case, failed to take account of the lack of equality of opportunity in the nineteenth century, which made talk of the "survival of the fittest" almost nonsensical. A more plausible theory was that of Gaetano Mosca, whose *The Ruling Class* (1896) concentrated on political inequalities. Mosca contended that a complex society necessitated some form of political organization, which would necessarily be hierarchical in the interests of efficiency: there could be no organization without leaders. Political power, Mosca argued, would then tend to be exploited in order to obtain other advantages.

The principal modern statement of the case for viewing stratification as inevitable, however, is a *functionalist* one and is largely derived from the social theories of Talcott Parsons. Functionalism views each element in social structure as contributing to the ongoing survival of the society; from this perspective, stratification—like any other feature of human society—performs some integral function in the maintenance of the system.

A functional theory of stratification was proposed by Kingsley

Davis and Wilbert E. Moore; their article "Some Principles of Stratification" (1945) argued that because stratification is universal, it must perform a vital, necessary, and inevitable function in the social structure. Davis and Moore contended that inequality is an inherent necessity in the operation of human societies. Their objective was not to justify such a situation, but merely to explain it. Some positions in society, they argued, require either scarce talents or prolonged training; the job of surgeon or military commander cannot be filled by just anyone. All societies must employ some method for distributing these jobs among appropriate members of the population. Because these jobs often impose great responsibility, stress, and sacrifice on the individuals who fill them, the positions have to carry remuneration in terms of those rewards that are most highly valued in the society concerned—prestige, power, or wealth. Thus in a society that rates warriors more highly than physicians, the warrior will be more highly rewarded; in a society that rates physicians more highly than film stars, the physicians will be more highly rewarded. Only in this way can people be motivated to train for and accept the responsibilities of those important social positions for which suitable candidates are in short supply. In this view social inequality is necessary, unavoidable, and functional.

iii Research (Survey) An influential analysis of social class is Gerhard Lenski's *Power and Privilege* (1966), which draws on the insights of Davis and Moore but considerably modifies their theory. Lenski asserts that people, though they are social beings, generally find it more rewarding to fulfill their own wishes, desires, and ambitions than those of others. This tendency may be regrettable, and it may even be modifiable, but it is a dominant feature of human behavior. Most of the things that human beings desire are in short supply: power, wealth, privilege, and prestige are never infinite, and the demand for them always exceeds the supply. Inevitably, then, there will be some degree of conflict over the distribution of these rewards in all human societies, and because the rewards are scarce and individuals are unequally adapted for the competitive struggle, some inequality will be the inevitable consequence. Such inequities are not necessarily functional, however. Although they may initially serve a functional purpose, forms of stratification will tend to persist as *social norms* long after they have ceased to be useful. This situation too is inevitable: no social system can ever attain perfection, and there will always be some degree of error, inefficiency, and dysfunction within any given system.

Lenski examines various types of human society and suggests that stratification can only be avoided in a simple, primitive, hunting and gathering community, where there is no *surplus production* and where the population is very small and intimate. In agricultural communities the potential for surplus wealth, and hence for social stratification, is far greater; indeed, the historical tendency has been for advanced agricultural societies to be highly stratified—as was the case in medieval feudalism. With the arrival of the industrial society the tendency to gross inequality is arrested and gradually reversed. The complex division of labor and the demand for an increasing variety of scarce skills provide numerous opportunities for

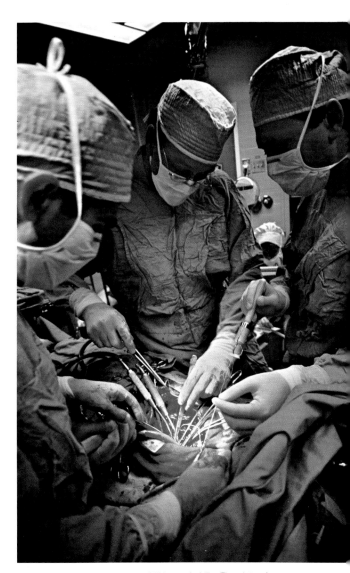

A specialist with special responsibilities and skills. Theorists who argue that inequality of standards of living is a necessity deriving from the inherent inequality of job-demands neglect to examine the possibility that challenging, responsibility-laden work may have its own emotional rewards for the individuals who perform it. These theorists confuse the necessity of role-segregation in modern society with the question of alleviating social, political, and economic inequality.

relatively high status and income. Moreover, industrialization tends to be accompanied by democratization; such measures as the provision of welfare and the institution of the progressive income tax tend to limit severe social inequalities.

Lenski's theory also allows for other influences on the stratification system, which may be independent of the economic level of the society in question. Individual leaders or bureaucratic elites may bring about profound changes in social stratification—examples might be Castro in Cuba, Mao Tse-tung in China, or the bureaucratic hierarchies in the countries of Eastern Europe. External or internal threat will tend to encourage a concentration of power in society, because this concentration is the most effective means of combatting such threats; these concentrations of power may lead to parallel concentrations of wealth and privilege. *Ideology* may also exert an independent influence on the form and direction of stratification, even though there is continuous interaction between ideology and social structure.

iv   Evaluation   Functional theories of the origins of and necessity for social stratification have been strongly criticized. The assumption of the structural inevitability of inequality is one that sociologists have been reluctant to accept on several grounds. Some have challenged the view that man is inherently self-interested. Such motivations, they argue, are learned rather than innate, and it should be possible to construct a human society in which a concern for one's fellows would be a distinguishing feature of human relationships. This view is strongly held and cannot be disproved, but no large-scale human society based on altruism has yet been created.

Another objection is based on empirical investigations, which have revealed that inequalities of wealth depend more on unequal distribution through *inheritance* than on the differentials in *income* that might reward those with singular talents. Most people, despite the potential for upward or downward mobility, stay in their class of origin. Stratification operates in general not to promote the talented or demote the functionally dispensable, but to ensure that most individuals remain in the social stratum into which they were born. This situation is most true of purely ascriptive stratification systems, such as those based on caste or color. To the degree that the assignment of roles is based on ascriptive criteria, and to the degree that the stratification system is a closed one, the functionalist argument seems quite invalid, for stratification *prevents* society from making the most effective use of its available talents.

The essential problem is that inequality tends to increase and diffuse with the passage of time until its ultimate form bears no relation to its origins, functional or otherwise. Individuals who are dominant by reason of birth rather than merit are able to exploit others, to increase their power and wealth, and to pass these privileges on to the next generation. Although some degree of stratification may serve a functional purpose in society, the likelihood is that most societies are much more stratified than any functional necessity would require. Finally, stratification does not necessarily contribute to systemic maintenance: often it can lead to flux, dissension, and conflict, even to the destruction of the social order.

The "jet set." What functional utility—beyond the consumption of goods and services—does the "jet set" serve to justify its receiving so many social rewards?

c The "Research" Question

i Context (Karl Marx regarded a class as a group of people who shared a common relationship to the means of production—as exploiters or exploited. The fundamental criterion for the determination of class, then, was economic.) Although most sociologists have focused their studies on questions of prestige and life style, even today many of them assign an individual to a particular class on the basis of economic criteria—usually the occupation or income of the head of his or her family. But does this criterion provide an adequate basis for the analysis of class phenomena? In what class is the impoverished aristocrat or the penniless dethroned king? What are we to make of the hippie who drops out of his upper class home and begs on the street? In what class is the wealthy member of a despised minority group?

Problematic cases such as these should make us aware of other, more subtle elements than just economic ones in the stratification of modern industrial societies. Hence sociologists ask: (*Can stratification in modern industrial societies be analyzed in terms of characteristics that vary independently of economic position?*)

ii Theory (Like Marx, Max Weber saw class as based on relationship to the means of production. In a famous essay on class, status, and party in *Economy and Society* (1922) he proposed a multidimensional framework for the analysis of social stratification. According to Weber, " 'classes,' 'status groups,' and 'parties' are phenomena of the distribution of power within a community." The field of stratification, then, encompasses the study of the unequal distribution of *power* in the economic order, the social order, and the legal order. Power is defined as the capacity of an individual or group to realize its will, even against the opposition of others. Power resources (means of control) vary in each of the three orders. The economic order is stratified in terms of *classes*—categories of people who share similar life chances because they share a similar "market situation." The social order is stratified in terms of *status groups*—categories of people who share similar styles of life and, consequently, similar degrees of social honor. The legal order is stratified in terms of political groups oriented toward influencing communal action: these political groups, which Weber designated as *parties,* can be more accurately designated as *interest groups* or political factions.)

(These stratification orders are partially independent, and the degree of communal identity felt by persons sharing in any of these dimensional quasi-hierarchies varies from situation to situation.) Just as there is no necessary conjunction between economic elites and status elites, there is no necessary conjunction of either of these with "political power" elites. At any level of the various quasi-hierarchies there may exist a variety of groups that are always, potentially at least, in conflict with each other. Interest groups in the "political power" hierarchy may represent a wide array of combinations of economic and status interests.

(Many social theorists have been particularly influenced by Weber's analysis. With the blurring of class lines and the tendency for some blue-collar workers to earn more than white-collar salaried employees, gradations of status rather than income may be assum-

ing more significance.) Status groups interposed among the economic classes in society form a continuum of positions defined by a
variety of noneconomic criteria. The relationship between a lower
and higher status group may not be one of conflict, as Marx held
would be the case with classes, but rather one of competition, or
sometimes emulation. Claims to social status are based not so
much on earnings as upon *life style*—the nature of one's occupation, the use of one's leisure, the pattern of one's consumption and
recreation, the social standing of one's friends.)

iii Research (Methodology)   Although American sociologists
tended to accept Weber's multidimensional analysis of stratification,
they were slow to conduct empirical studies of social class in the
United States. One of the earliest investigations was carried out by
William Lloyd Warner in the 1930s; his work stimulated a spate of
similar studies that have consistently supported his general conclusions. Warner and a group of social anthropologists undertook a
systematic study of the New England town of Newburyport (disguised under the name of "Yankee City" in their reports). The results were presented in *The Social Life of a Modern Community*
(1941) and other books. The studies were initially based on subjective judgments by some members of the community about the status
of other members. The experimenters undertook lengthy, open-
ended interviews with members of the community, attempting to
establish how many levels the interviewees perceived in the social hierarchy and on what basis these levels were assigned.
The life styles of various groups were closely observed and recorded by the researchers. For more objective measurements,
Warner constructed an index of status characteristics based on
four indicators—occupation, source of income, type of house, and
area of residence. Two other indicators, amount of education and
amount of income, were also used initially, but they correlated so
well with the other characteristics that they were dropped as unnecessary.)

Presidential adviser Henry A. Kissinger and friend. Kissinger is an
example of the blurring of lines regarding class, power, and prestige. He is of middle-class background and not particularly wealthy
but has a great deal of power through his access to President Nixon's confidence, and he certainly enjoys very high social prestige.

It soon became apparent that this small community (17,000 at the time) was anything but a homogeneous mass. Instead, the town was divided into a number of distinct groups, with lines being drawn largely in terms of prestige—which itself was closely linked to income. Warner and his associates were able to distinguish six social classes: *upper-upper, lower-upper, upper-middle, lower-middle, upper-lower, and lower-lower.* Some 3 percent of the population were members of the upper classes, 38 percent were in the middle classes, and the remainder constituted the lower classes.

Not all sociologists supported Warner's general conclusions; C. Wright Mills, for example, immediately criticized Warner's lack of recognition of Weber's multidimensional approach and his acceptance of "social class"—a concept that parallels Weber's "status group"—as the complete description of stratification. There have been scores of studies touching upon power in American communities—notably *Middletown, A Study in American Culture* (1929) and *Middletown in Transition* (1937) by Robert S. and Helen M. Lynd, and *Elmtown's Youth,* by A. B. Hollingshead (1949)—but these did not treat community power as a separate stratification variable. That approach was initiated by Floyd Hunter in his study of "Regional City" (*Community Power Structure,* 1953).

Hunter introduced a reputational technique for analyzing power that closely paralleled Warner's subjective method for analyzing status. Most of the men in the small group who were the reputed power-wielders in Regional City were not officeholders but big businessmen. The conclusion could be drawn that economic class was the main source of power in the local community, and a number of studies following Hunter's methods supported this conclusion.

As in the case of Mills' power elite thesis at the national level, "pluralists" were quick to respond to Hunter's conclusions about local power. Using a different research technique, the close analysis of the participants in three major community issues, Robert Dahl claimed that the power-wielders in New Haven basically were *not* the same people as the economic or social prestige elites (*Who Governs?,* 1960).

Over the past two decades the dispute between "pluralists" and "elitists" has raged as many new studies were completed. Although this dispute may never be completely resolved, we can conclude that community power is stratified in the sense that a small number of persons necessarily must make decisions on community issues; that the vast majority of citizens have little power, are uninvolved and apathetic; that wealthy businessmen are a particularly powerful group in most communities; and that other classes, status groups, and interest groups exert power on a wide variety of issues.

In 1947 and again in 1963 two national studies were conducted to determine the degree of prestige attached to particular occupations by the public at large. The 1963 findings were very much the same as the results of the poll conducted 16 years previously, and parallel studies in over 20 other countries have revealed a similar ranking of occupations on the basis of prestige evaluations. As the listing (from Robert W. Hodge, Paul M. Seigel, and Peter H. Rossi, "Occupational Prestige in the United States, 1925–

Occupation	Score	Occupation	Score
U.S. Supreme Court Justice	94	Welfare worker for a city government	74
Physician	93	Newspaper columnist	73
Nuclear Physicist	92	Policeman	72
Scientist	92	Reporter on a daily newspaper	71
Government scientist	91	Bookkeeper	70
State governor	91	Radio announcer	70
Cabinet member in the federal government	90	Insurance agent	69
College professor	90	Tenant farmer—one who owns livestock and machinery and manages the farm	69
U.S. Representative in Congress	90	Local official of a labor union	67
Chemist	89	Manager of small store in a city	67
Diplomat in the U.S. Foreign Service	89	Mail carrier	66
Lawyer	89	Railroad conductor	66
Architect	88	Traveling salesman for a wholesale concern	66
County judge	88	Plumber	65
Dentist	88	Barber	63
Mayor of a large city	87	Machine operator in a factory	63
Member of the board of directors of a large corporation	87	Owner-operator of a lunch stand	63
Minister	87	Playground director	63
Psychologist	87	Corporal in the regular army	62
Airline pilot	86	Garage mechanic	62
Civil engineer	86	Truck driver	59
Head of a department in a state government	86	Fisherman who owns his own boat	58
Priest	86	Clerk in a store	56
Banker	85	Milk route man	56
Biologist	85	Streetcar motorman	56
Sociologist	83	Lumberjack	55
Captain in the regular army	82	Restaurant cook	55
Accountant for a large business	81	Singer in a nightclub	54
Public schoolteacher	81	Filling station attendant	51
Building contractor	80	Coal miner	50
Owner of a factory that employs about 100 people	80	Dock worker	50
		Night watchman	50
Artist who paints pictures that are exhibited in galleries	78	Railroad section hand	50
Author of novels	78	Restaurant waiter	49
Economist	78	Taxi driver	49
Musician in a symphony orchestra	78	Bartender	48
Official of an international labor union	77	Farmhand	48
County agricultural agent	76	Janitor	48
Electrician	76	Clothes presser in a laundry	45
Railroad engineer	76	Soda fountain clerk	44
Owner-operator of a printing shop	75	Sharecropper—one who owns no livestock or equipment and does not manage farm	42
Trained machinist	75	Garbage collector	39
Farm owner and operator	74	Street sweeper	36
Undertaker	74	Shoe shiner	34

Table 1. Occupational Prestige Ratings in the United States, 1963. The 90 occupations are ranked from most prestigious (U.S. Supreme Court Justice) to least prestigious (shoe shiner). (Source: Hodge, Seigel, Rossi)

1963'') shows, there is some relationship between prestige, power, and income, but this relationship is not inevitable or uniform.

iv Evaluation Weber's analysis of stratification is sometimes more helpful to the social scientist than an analysis that concentrates exclusively on earnings and wealth. However, a purely economic analysis of class is adequate for much sociological investigation, because class, status, and power are usually tightly correlated: numerous studies have shown that class is the greatest single influence on an individual's life style (and hence status) and on his position in the political structure of society (and hence power). When we meet an individual for the first time, one of the earliest questions we ask is "What do you do?" The reason is that the answer will enable us to predict, with reasonable assurance, a great deal of information about him—his education, his income, his attitudes, his life style, his influence, his social status.

Studies of both subjective and objective rankings in the United States have shown that prestige, wealth, and power may vary independently of one another. The survey of prestige rankings, for example, shows that a physician enjoys more prestige than a congressman, who wields more power, and that a minister has more prestige than an accountant for a large business firm, who has far greater income. Studies have also shown how power need not be a function of the ownership of the means of production or even of high income: the merely middle-level bureaucrat in the large-scale formal and complex organizations of government and business can often take decisions that profoundly affect the lives of many other citizens.

A comprehensive theory of stratification must take into account the existence of overlapping economic, prestige, and power strata—all of them subject to the further influence of *cross-cutting affiliations* of age, region, sex, ethnicity, or religion.

3   Overview

Social stratification is an ancient and dominant feature of human existence. It is a potentially explosive topic: although social stratification is inherently conservative in its effect on the individual and society, the rigidity of stratification may give rise to resentments that provoke radical efforts to overthrow the status quo. Social stability will depend on whether the members of the lower strata are

A blue-collar family. Liberal on some issues, conservative on others, the lower-class family struggles to make ends meet and staunchly backs the status quo—to which it feels its sole (though admittedly remote) possibility of climbing the ladder of socioeconomic success is securely tied.

prepared to tolerate a continuing inequality in society, or whether they are willing, by force if necessary, to seek a change in the social order. Inequalities of some kind have been the source of popular uprisings throughout history.

Social stratification is a complex phenomenon whose origins and function are not yet fully understood. A clearer comprehension may well emerge in the future from interdisciplinary studies by sociologists, anthropologists, political scientists, and psychologists, all of whom have an interest in the processes and effects of stratification. The issues raised by class divisions and the inequality of mankind are not only sociological, but also moral. It is important that we realize that these hierarchical systems form part of the social order, not the natural order. Stratification is a social construct that is subject both to historical changes and, in principle, to social modification.

His/her future may seem limitless, but in a highly stratified society such as ours it is actually highly predetermined.

D   LOOKING AHEAD

1   Interview:
Michael Harrington

Michael Harrington has been associate editor of *The Catholic Worker;* organizational secretary and member of the board of directors of the Workers Defense League; consultant to the Fund for the Republic; editor of *New America;* organizer of the marches on the Democratic and Republican national

conventions in 1960; chairman of the board of the League for Industrial Democracy; member of the national executive committee of the Socialist Party from 1960 to 1972; national chairman of the International Union of Socialist Youth; delegate to the Congress of the Socialist International; member of the board of directors of the American Civil Liberties Union and the A. Philip Randolph Institute. He is author of *The Other America, The Retail Clerks, The Accidental Century, Toward a Democratic Left,* and *Socialism. The Other America* has been credited with influencing President Kennedy to initiate the War on Poverty.

DPG   *Are the poor becoming "invisible" again?*
HARRINGTON   I think that the black poor and perhaps the Spanish-speaking poor, the Chicanos and the Puerto Ricans, are still visible because they're organized and militant. But even after the rediscovery of poverty in the 1960s, invisibility still persisted somewhat with the white poor. People assumed that most poor people were black. Now that President Nixon has turned his back on so many programs, the white poor may well become invisible again.

DPG   *Was the "war on poverty" a failure?*
HARRINGTON   I think it was a fundamental failure with some significant successes. Today, years after President Lyndon Johnson announced an unconditional war on poverty in 1964, the government's figures still show that about 12 or 13 percent of the people are poor. I'd say that a more accurate computation would be between 15 and 20 percent. The broad contours of poverty are the same; that is, poverty is most severe among the aging, the minorities, people in certain regions such as Ap-

palachia. So the structure of poverty was not destroyed by the government's efforts. On the other hand there were some gains. Perhaps the most notable single gain was the decline in unemployment under Kennedy and Johnson. Primarily as a result of the drop in unemployment during the 1960s, a significant number of people, those that lived in families where the head of the family was in the labor market, were able to escape from poverty. Nixon has annulled that gain, of course. Second, although the community-action programs of the war on poverty did not in any way live up to some of the romantic expectations people had for them, they did make a difference. They helped the insurgencies led by Martin Luther King, by Cesar Chavez, and by other leaders. Third, I think there were gains in providing legal services for the poor, although the poor are still largely deprived before the bar of justice in the United States. But the fact that some gains were made is evidenced by Nixon's attempts to get the legal services program under his control.

DPG   *What are the basic reasons for the existence of poverty in an affluent country like America?*
HARRINGTON   I think there are a number of reasons. First of all, an extremely rapidly changing technology is transforming the class structure and the economic geography of the country. Through technological change many of the semiskilled jobs that traditionally were the point of exit from poverty for the earlier immigrant groups have been destroyed. Therefore, the late arrivals—the black poor coming from the rural South, the Puerto Ricans, the Chicanos— come to the cities at a time when the labor market is not at all as propitious for an unskilled and not well-educated worker as it was a generation or so ago. Rapidly changing technology affects the white poor too, of course. One of the greatest concentrations of white poor people is in Appalachia. The decline of the main industry of the area, coal mining, has cost the people there hundreds of thousands of jobs and has been a prime cause of some very bitter poverty. A second reason for poverty is the fact that there are strong institutional forces that profit from poverty and therefore resist efforts to abolish it.

DPG *Can you illustrate that point?*

HARRINGTON Southern congressmen resisted Nixon's Family Assistance Plan. Now in the South the Nixon plan would have done more for the white poor than the black poor, for the simple reason that there are more white poor in the South than black poor. So the reason for resistance wasn't solely racism, although naturally if you can keep blacks impoverished, you can control them more easily. Southern congressmen resisted the Nixon program because they represent a class of people who have a vested interest in a cheap labor market in the South. Similarly, the growers in California have an interest in maintaining a pool of migrant workers who will do stoop labor in blazing heat at the appropriate season for very little money.

DPG *Are there any corporate interests that have an institutional interest in poverty-level wages?*

HARRINGTON Leaving aside agriculture, which is a very big business in the United States, the really giant corporations that are dependent on very sophisticated and advanced technology are not particularly guilty of that. Indeed the evidence is that, say in dealing with problems of racial discrimination, big corporations are perhaps more amenable to doing something than smaller businesses. Furthermore, I think poverty in America is against the sophisticated and long-run interest of business. Any shrewd capitalist would be in favor of abolishing poverty because that action would create a much larger market than now exists.

DPG *Will the emergence of a postindustrial society bring about a new class structure?*

HARRINGTON I think a new class structure is already emerging. In America there is a contraction of semiskilled jobs a little above the bottom, a stagnation of unskilled jobs at the very bottom, a certain narrowing of skilled industrial jobs, and a considerable increase in the number of professional and technical workers. This situation is going to make it more difficult for the people at the bottom to get out of poverty. On the other hand, in the middle and the upper-middle reaches of American society there is now a vast college-educated professional and technical population, which has already been the source of political support for the

Kennedy, McCarthy, and McGovern movements, and the antiwar movement. This group might play a significant political role in abolishing poverty in the future.

DPG *Has the working class forever lost its revolutionary and even reformist momentum?*

HARRINGTON It's not clear the working class ever had revolutionary momentum in the United States. The American labor movement is unique because it was formed

out of the coming together of diverse and often antagonistic immigrant groups. The American working class had a heterogeneity that no other working class had in its formative period. The result was that the national, ethnic, and religious differences among American workers inhibited the development of a consciousness of class and of a class politics. The revolutionary tradition among American workers was confined to somewhat isolated groups and to minority groups. I'm thinking of the Industrial Workers of the World, the Western Federation of Miners, and so on. These revolutionary workers tended to be migrant workers, loggers, metal miners, even migrant agricul-

tural workers. They did not create any kind of lasting movements for themselves. Second, in terms of reform the American labor movement today—the AFL-CIO, the Teamsters, the United Auto Workers—are the most effective organized body pushing for reforms, such as full-employment policies, government spending for education, housing, medicine, and the like. So I think that the American labor movement has continued its reformist impulse, although less dramatically than in the 1930s.

DPG *Are ethnic and life-style identifications eclipsing social identification based on economic similarities?*

HARRINGTON That's a difficult question. What often appear to us to be ethnic conflicts are often as much class conflicts as they are ethnic. For example, if impoverished blacks start spreading into a Polish-American working-class community, the resulting antagonisms appear as a race conflict or an ethnic conflict. Yet it's also a class conflict over scarce resources, housing and education. The economic root is basic, and the ethnic differences are important but not decisive.

DPG   *What about the life-style identifications—things like upper middle-class or rich kids running around in bib overalls and jeans and boots?*

HARRINGTON   The degree to which the life-style changes are jumping class barriers is striking. In 1969 Malcolm Denise, who was a vice-president of the Ford Motor Company, analyzed why the young workers in the shop were so militant against speed-up, hostile to authority, and so on. He commented that the young workers have been affected by the life-style revolution, by a sort of libertarian revolution, by the anti-authority revolution. I think that's true. Profound class differences remain, but I suspect that the style differences may be getting blurred.

DPG   *In your writings you refer to "class structure" and "corporate interest," but you seem to avoid reference to "ruling class" or even "power elite." Why is that?*

HARRINGTON   I think that C. Wright Mills' work on the power elite was enormously suggestive and represented a tremendously important antidote to the consensus theories of the 1950s. But the basic proposition about this elite has not been proven. In a sense I criticize Mills from a more orthodox

Marxist point of view. The term "elite" implies a kind of selection and a merit principle. It divorces the question of power at least somewhat from social class based on wealth, income, and either ownership or domination of the means of production. I regard class categories, with all the problems in this new structure of society that we're evolving into, as the most revealing. Therefore, I would tend to think in terms of "ruling class" rather than "power elite." But most of the people who use the term "ruling class" in America are suggesting a kind of unitary class, which is an oversimplified analysis. Therefore, as a kind of rhetorical strategy, I may try to stay away from the term.

DPG   *How can the emergence of a new, bureaucratic, antidemocratic ruling class be avoided under socialism?*

HARRINGTON   There is no formula for that. It's obvious that the great danger of a

socialist society is that the governmental institutions required for planning and for implementing the decisions of the society may acquire an independent and excessive and antidemocratic power that then can become the basis of a ruling class. Socialists have realized that for a long time. The danger of a bureaucratic ruling class, however, is a danger that confronts all social systems of the late twentieth century. You can only combat it if you have some kind of vibrant democratic movement of the people. If you've got that, then the actual tactics you'd use to control it are easy enough. For example, the Paris Commune of 1871 proposed that all governmental figures would be paid the same wage as working people. There are all kinds of things you can do. For example, in every bureaucratic institution, be it public or private, there should be an independent review board that would allow people who have suffered from bureaucratic decisions to appeal those decisions outside the bureaucracy. The United Auto Workers has this kind of board, and it should be universalized. But if you don't have a population that is committed to a vibrant democracy, none of these fine schemes will work.

DPG   *What makes you think that the corporate elite would not be able to prevent the gradual emergence of the sort of democratic socialism you advocate?*

HARRINGTON   I lean rather heavily on one of the greatest conservative thinkers of this century, Joseph Schumpeter, in believing that the corporate elite is becoming demoralized. The corporate elite has actually very little loyalty to capitalism or to private property. Therefore if you had a socialist political movement, if you had a socialist majority, I think the attitude of the corporate elite would be "Well, we'll go along with it because we're going to make out under this majority the way we made out under the previous majority." By the way, at least in the first stage, they'd be right. The class structure would not change overnight. So I think that the evolution of capitalist society, the separation of ownership and control, the bureaucratization, the socialization of corporate property has made it at least possible to envision a lack of great resistance on the part of the corporate elite.

DPG   *Some feel that the key to positions of power today doesn't seem to be money or family or class background any more, but knowledge. Are expertise and knowledge the keys to power positions in our society?*

HARRINGTON   Right. Galbraith has made this kind of argument in *The New Industrial State*. I think that this argument recognizes Marx's perception that as capitalism developed it would become increasingly dependent upon science and the application of science to production. For Marx that whole development was one more argument in favor of socialism because it meant that the individualistic and entrepreneurial element in growth and production was declining and the rational, scientific, and therefore social element was growing. Marx was right in saying that science in a modern society is fundamentally dependent on the effort of the entire society. He therefore argued that the fruits of science should belong to the entire society.

DPG   *Do you think that the United States can be developing toward a classless society?*

HARRINGTON   The United States right now is developing in an ambivalent way. I think it has profound tendencies toward a corporate, collectivist kind of society in which the state intervenes in the economy on behalf of the corporations and the rich. I think that is what is the significance of Nixon's conversion to Keynesianism, his wage-price controls, his activist government intervention. On the other hand, I think there is still the possibility of organizing a movement in America to democratize these collective structures. And therefore I think that the real debate is not between state intervention and free enterprise. It's between corporate collectivism and democratic collectivism.

Human

Part 1
Relations

Unit 10
Personality and Society

SCHEMATIC OUTLINE

A Introductory Graphics: The Individual in Society

B Definition and Context

1 Definition
Personality is the set of needs and dispositions that manifest themselves in behavior that contributes to a person's identity. Although personality is generally postulated of individuals, it is possible, with care, to make some sociological generalizations about the relationships between the dynamics of personality operating within the individual and the dynamics related to an entire group of people who share a similar framework of living.

2 World Context
Members of certain groups within every society differ from members of other groups in the same society, and citizens of one nation differ from those of another.

3 American Context
The concepts of individual identity and competition are highly valued by the dominant culture in the United States. Hence its members often find it difficult to understand the behavior of other groups, even within American society.

C Questions and Evidence

1 Questions
Among the questions about personality and society are: (1) Is it personal needs or social factors that account for the widespread use of drugs in America today? (2) Do we need to understand individual personality in order to understand social behavior in groups? (3) Can we really talk about the "personality" of a society or nation?

2 Evidence
a The "Burning Issue" Question
General research suggests that the use of marijuana is best understood in terms of social factors, whereas the use of stronger drugs is best understood in terms of personal factors. But longer-term studies, especially of the personalities of drug users, are necessary.
b The "Classical" Question
Early sociologists, such as Emile Durkheim, C. H. Cooley, and G. H. Mead, advocated the idea that the individual self was socially determined. Later theorists, including Robert K. Merton and Talcott Parsons, have modified this position by integrating personality perspectives into general sociological theory.
c The "Research" Question
Recent theoreticians have developed the concept of the modal personality of a group. The application of this methodology to specific groups is difficult, although there have been significant studies of the sociopolitical "personality" of the Soviet Union. Further refinements may open another valuable area for sociological research.

3 Overview
Even the most traditional sociologist cannot avoid the question: Where does society end and the person begin?

D Looking Ahead

1 Interview: Alex Inkeles

SUPPORTING UNITS

ENCYCLOPEDIA ENTRIES

THE INDIVIDUAL IN SOCIETY

1. **Social Demands.** People adapt to social life by learning the demands and expectations attached to various roles and behaviors.

2. **Socially Motivated Behavior.** Social demands, expectations, and constraints often produce compliant behavior. Such behavior may establish group solidarity and identity but does not express the differences between individuals.

3. **Personal Needs.** Although most people accept common rules of conduct, each person's unique life experiences give him or her a unique perspective on every social event. People develop distinctive ways of expressing themselves and satisfy the particular personal needs they have acquired when they engage in social behavior.

4. **Personality Styles.** Personality styles are the behaviors that express or "act out" individuals' needs and dispositions. They characterize a person's behavior across different situations and roles and cannot be explained as direct responses to external circumstances and social demands.

5. **Social Expression.** The self-expressive styles and social needs of the individual adapt to the demands of situations and roles. This adaptation results in socially acceptable behavior that reflects the nature of the individual.

6. **Social Continuity.** The personality component of behavior is a common dimension running through the different roles that a person plays. This component provides continuity to an individual's identity and action. External social influences on behavior produce shared ways of understanding and relating to others. These shared ways lend continuity to collective action and social organization.

Three public figures: John F. Kennedy, Lyndon B. Johnson, Lady Bird Johnson. Although John F. Kennedy and Lyndon B. Johnson each successively occupied the same social position—the highest public office in the United States—their individual personalities caused them to interpret their duties differently and to enact the obligatory role behavior with different styles and emphases. The same was true of Mrs. Kennedy, Mrs. Johnson, and other "First Ladies."

B   DEFINITION AND CONTEXT

1   Definition

Social behavior is formed and influenced by both social and individual factors. The *social factors* include the norms, conventions, and expectations that a society or group has about what constitutes appropriate behavior in a given situation and the sanctions and pressures that are applied to one who deviates from these standards. The fundamental *individual factor* is *personality,* which enters into behavior to the extent that social prescriptions are flexible or ambiguous, sanctions are weak or insignificant, and the individual's needs and dispositions are strong. The person in whose behavior the social factors appear to predominate is often dismissed as a "conformist" or praised as a "solid citizen," whereas the person whose behavior exhibits a high degree of individuality may be condemned as "headstrong" or admired for having the courage to "do his own thing."

The judgment "He has a wonderful personality" has been ascribed to such markedly contrasting showmen as Sammy Davis, Jr., and Dick Van Dyke. One factor common to both entertainers is the recognizably distinctive and characteristic manner in which each reacts to a wide variety of circumstances, and it is this strongly individual component in their behavior that allows them to be categorized together as "personalities."

Despite its complex and elusive connotations, *personality may be functionally defined as the set of individual needs and dispositions that manifest themselves in behavior that contributes to a person's identity, that cannot be entirely explained by constraints in the external social situation, and that possess some definite structure and organization in terms of pattern, intensity, and frequency of occurrence.* The statement "He sees red whenever a student questions his authority" conveys something definite about a particular professor's personality not only because it points to a recurring pattern that has been observed in the past and that may be predicted of the future, but also because it describes an idiosyncratic reaction in these situations that differs from behavior others might expect or prefer. The statement "He became angry when the students ransacked his office" is *not* descriptive of the personality involved because this particular reaction took place on a single occasion and is one we would expect anyone to have on the basis of the external provocation alone.

Personality is generally posited of an individual rather than a group: it is one of the ways people are distinguished from each other in similar situations, and it provides a continuous thread of *identity* through the different roles an individual plays in the course of his daily social existence. Although no two people share exactly the same personality, it is, however, possible, with care, to make some generalizations about the relationships between the dynamics of personality operating within the individual *(psychology)* and the dynamics of personality related to an entire group of people who share a similar framework of living *(sociology).* We can try to determine, for example, the degree to which a group of people—such as ghetto delinquents, blue-collar workers, "Horatio Alger" business executives, Jewish voters, young voters, or even the American people viewed collectively as a national entity—share certain dispositions and behavior patterns. We can attempt, by applying our knowledge of personality to the group as a whole, to understand and anticipate social attitudes and problems associated with the group. Sociologists are careful, though, to emphasize the difficulties involved in making accurate *aggregate personality assessments.*

Our understanding and grasp of social situations will be aided by determining the degree to which various expressions of personality and *social constraints* are operating in the social environment. For example, do those who have defected from Castro's Cuba share certain personality traits not prevalent among the majority of Cubans who have remained in their homeland? What social changes were instituted by Castro's regime that made it impossible for people of a certain disposition or orientation to adjust to the new system? Another example, this time closer to home: what personality expressions and social constraints have caused a sizable number of America's teenagers from reasonably affluent backgrounds to become such vigorous and habitual shoplifters that many businessmen regard shoplifting as the major threat facing retailers today?

The constant interplay between the dynamics of the individual and the dynamics of a social group or situation is a fundamental aspect of all social phenomena, but insights into these two distinct but overlapping realms have not always taken place at the same time. Sigmund Freud published his landmark theories of personality structure and development at the turn of the century, and for several decades his conclusions about the psychology of the individual were projected onto the general nature of civilization as well. His theories, along with important revisions by such psychologists as Erik Erikson and Harry Stack Sullivan, inspired anthropologists Margaret Mead and Ruth Benedict in the 1930s and 1940s to investigate ways in which different cultures influenced the character development of their young through their traditions of childrearing. Much of the personality structure Freud had thought of as reflecting *universal* patterns of behavior, social pressures, and taboos was eventually reinterpreted as being *relative* to a particular culture at a particular time. By the 1950s sociologists had begun to look at the pervasive influence of complex social environments on character development and social adaptation. Today's sociologist is likely to examine his subject from three points of view: (1) how social needs arise, (2) how these needs are accommodated or frustrated by the group or the society, (3) and what the consequences of this accommodation or frustration for the individual, the group, and the society are.

2   World Context

Because social factors affect the basic nature of a person's behavior, and the behavior of individuals in turn affects the nature of their society, it may be reasonable to suppose that members of certain groups within a society differ from members of other groups in the same society and that citizens of one nation or culture differ from citizens in another—and indeed our experience demonstrates this supposition to be true. Nevertheless, such differences are often misinterpreted and negatively judged. Throughout the course of history visitors to other societies have found themselves in seemingly familiar situations in which the members of the host culture behave quite differently from "the folks back home," and from these experiences stereotypes have developed about *national characters*. The British are said to be reserved, the Chinese inscrutable, the Scots thrifty, the Germans austere. Efforts to explain these postulated character differences have produced theories that are often as misguided as the stereotypes themselves. The Greek philosopher Hippocrates attributed differences in national "humors" to the influence of climate on the lives of a population. The ancient Romans at one time believed that character traits of a people depended on mythical lines of descent from the greater or lesser gods. Psychologists of the Nazi regime claimed that differences among social groups could be traced to lines of descent from various ancient tribes. Ethnic slurs and jokes capitalize on the notion of national, religious, and racial "personalities" and tend to reinforce their negative connotations.

3   American Context

Qualities connected with individualism and competitiveness are highly valued in the United States and considered as personality attributes. The Puritans and pioneers left a legacy in which individual initiative, hard work, and self-determination are regarded as basic aspects of the American national character. The frontier spirit of "rugged individualism" is succinctly summed up by an old maxim that pioneers used to quote to explain the "new breed" of people who had negotiated the journey west: "The weak never started, the slow never got there." The subsequent growth of more easily accessible routes to the still largely unclaimed tracts of land west of the Mississippi and the dramatically expanding economy that characterized the nation's development through the nineteenth and the beginning of the twentieth century further compounded the notion of the United States as the land of opportunity where the self-made, self-willed, quick-witted individual could go from humble origins to an envied position at the top. In a 1971 Labor Day speech President Richard Nixon declared that "America's competitive spirit, the work ethic of this people, is alive and well. . . . The dignity of work, the value of achievement, the morality of self-reliance, none of these is going out of style."

Because of the emphasis on this view of the national character, noncompetitive behavior by certain minorities is viewed by many Americans as evidence of "laziness." Sociologists, however, emphasize that things generally considered personality traits may really be necessary response patterns to a particular environment —in other words, environmental attributes rather than personality attributes. Corroboration of the persistence of the competitive spirit has recently been provided by a number of experiments by Linden Nelson and Spencer Kagan in which Anglo-American, second-generation Mexican-American, and rural Mexican children participated—with sharply contrasting results.

What do these people have in common? In what ways are they different? How do we learn our stereotyped images of members of different groups? To what extent are these images entirely fictitious? To what extent can they be verified through close observation of these group-members' behavior?

The experiments involved a number of board games in which the children could (1) compete for prizes by trying to win at each turn, (2) cooperate for prizes by alternately sacrificing a turn, or (3) forfeit their own chance for reward in order to prevent their competitors from receiving a reward. The games were devised so that cooperation would prove the most effective prize-getting strategy. Of the three groups, the Anglo-American pairs won the least number of prizes because they chose to compete in a majority of the trials—despite the fact that it was irrational and self-defeating to do so within the context of the experiments. When presented with the opportunity, Anglo-American children also exhibited an acutely rivalrous attitude toward each other's possessions, taking prizes away from their peers on 78 percent of the trials—even when they could not keep the toys for themselves. Rural Mexican children proved the least competitive. Although they cooperated to win prizes that had eluded their Anglo-American counterparts, they failed to defend their possessions with opposing moves on all but 14 percent of the trials (in contrast to the Anglo-Americans, who made countermoves on 72 percent of all responses).

Thus a child from rural Mexico who was suddenly transplanted into an urban environment in the United States would be at a considerable disadvantage within the new social framework, and the reasons for his *culture shock* would go beyond the barriers of language and custom to the fundamentally different social values and constraints operating within the two societies. Often we fail to understand both the dimension and the sources of other people's problems and incorrectly infer that the element of their behavior that we find conspicuous or different from ours is due to personality factors rather than to social constraints of which we may be unaware; that is, Anglo-Americans may infer that the Mexican child is lazy or indifferent to his plight.

The United States is made up of so many racial and ethnic groups and socioeconomic stratifications that it is frequently difficult for members of one group to understand the behavior of another group or to fully grasp the pressures, constraints, and problems that contribute to the differences in observed behavior. Second-generation and third-generation white Americans, whose immigrant forebears "pulled themselves up by their bootstraps," may be derisive about the fact that many seventh-generation black Americans have not been able to secure adequate employment, education, or housing. The mistaken assumption is that both groups have been operating within a similar social context and that therefore "innate character differences" must be playing a crucial role. However, sociologists, psychologists, historians, and black artists, writers, and spokesmen have demonstrated how complex and unique has been the social experience of black Americans.

We often call in experts to explain the problems of a group or the interaction of groups within society, and each expert has his particular personal orientation as well as the orientation of the specific discipline in which he has earned his credentials. The economist, the psychologist, the political scientist each emphasize certain dynamics and downgrade the importance of others. (There is even a well-known nutritionist who claims that wars are the result of vitamin deficiencies.) Sociologists have their biases too: one soci-

Newark, New Jersey. It is easy to see symptoms; identifying the nature of the problem(s) is much more difficult.

Motorcycle gang. Although individuals such as these may be said to be poorly adjusted to the wider society, they are nevertheless members of an integrated social group with norms, values, cognitive systems, and behavioral patterns to which they are themselves all well adjusted. Clearly, we must look at social factors as well as psychological factors in order to understand such "deviant subcultures."

ologist's analysis of a situation may be put purely in terms of variables related to the structure and process of groups, whereas another's may lean toward more psychologically subtle and individual variables pertaining to members of the group. The tendency of most sociologists, however, is to focus almost exclusively on social context and to "underattribute" behavior to personal characteristics of *social actors*—much as the average layman "overattributes" the causes of behavior to personal characteristics rather than to situational influences and constraints.

The fragmentary, incoherent, and unsatisfactory pronouncements that various experts offer as explanations for many of today's critical social problems have underscored the need for a more balanced and rounded interdisciplinary approach in the social sciences. One such trend in this direction has been the gradual integration of perspectives on personality (psychology) into traditional sociological theory. The sociologist should be sensitive not only to both the social and psychological causes of problem behavior, but also to the ways in which both groups of factors *interact*.

C   QUESTIONS AND EVIDENCE

1   Questions

Among the questions explored by sociologists concerned with the relationship between personality and society are these: (1) Is it personal needs or social factors that account for the widespread use of drugs in America today? (2) Do we need to consider the personality of the individual in order to understand social behavior in groups? (3) Can we really talk about the "personality" of a society or a nation?

2   Evidence

a   The "Burning Issue" Question

i   Context   The large-scale use of such "nonaddictive" and "mind-expanding" drugs as marijuana, mescaline, and LSD is a relatively new phenomenon in this society, and we deal with it in detail in Unit 24. When social practice affects large numbers of people, sociologists seek to identify its roots, its practitioners, its nature, and its social implications. Is drug use simply a new way of expressing traditional social patterns? (People who now use drugs might have swallowed goldfish in the 1930s.) Does the drug subculture reflect a major change in society? Is drug use restricted to certain groups of people? What causes people to use drugs? All of these questions are interrelated and seem to crystallize around the last one, which sociologists rephrase as: *What are the critical social variables and personality factors related to the use of the so-called mind-expanding drugs?*

ii   Theory   An explanation of drug use that emphasizes *social factors* might begin with an assumption about the group of people involved with the behavior, which is often referred to as the "drug subculture." When a sociologist speaks of a *subculture* he is referring to the product of frequent and extended contact among individuals who recognize that they share certain meaningful social

"Coke" spoon: new status symbol for the young and rich. "Snorting" cocaine (which gives feelings of great power) has become an "in" drug trip for the "jet set" and young elite. The spoon from which the cocaine is sniffed is worn as a group symbol.

attitudes and values that differ from those of the *dominant culture.*
In this particular instance members of the subculture may share
such problems as poor relationships with parents or with people in
positions of authority and an inability to accept the "materialism" of
the larger society. Repeated contact among similarly inclined people aids the evolution of *behavior patterns* that act as a buffer
against the sources of their commonly recognized problems and
also demonstrate mutual solidarity. Acceptance by other members
of the subculture becomes dependent upon conformity to these
newly established *norms* and *styles* of the group, and this conformity offers the member a secure environment in which to act out the
differences that seem to separate him from the larger society. Drug
use provides a highly visible way for people to identify themselves
as members of a special group, and it is associated with a specific
range of interests and personal styles and idioms that serve as further *lines of access* among members. For example, such questions
as "Where's your head at?" "What are you into?" "What's your
sign?" "What's your trip?" may signal that both the speaker and
the person to whom he's speaking are oriented in the direction of
"self-exploration"—a value heavily stressed in the drug subculture.

An explanation of drug use based on *personality factors*
would begin with a different set of assumptions—assumptions that
have to do with the nature of the individual user. People who use
drugs may have intense personal needs that have been frustrated
in past social contexts, or they may be disposed to behave in ways
that make their social adaptation to the "straight" world difficult or
personally unacceptable, although the personal and/or social life
related to drug use satisfies these previously frustrated needs. The
situation may mean simply that an individual with high *affiliation
needs* may find that other drug users respond to him in ways that
are more accepting, attentive, friendly, intimate, or "meaningful"
than the ways that others have responded to him in the past. However, this acceptance may be based on the fact such an individual
only loses his usual self-consciousness and shyness when he is
"high," and he might then feel he is relating to others more naturally than he normally does. The basic assumption remains that
people use drugs because personal needs and dispositions are
better satisfied through the physiological or psychological effects
and/or the social response styles associated with drug experience
or drug environments.

Note that the explanation in terms of personality does not
assume that similarities must exist in the social histories, circumstances, or problems of drug users. Although this explanation does
not deny that such common characteristics may exist (or be
created), it attributes the basic motivation for drug use to personality factors, and places more emphasis on the possible psycho-
physiological effects of drugs than the explanation based on social
factors does. Neither of these theories discounts the possibility
that people use drugs simply because they find the experience
pleasurable. Both explanations do imply, however, that the pleasurable experience is interwoven with other social or psychological processes.

iii Research   The reader has probably considered each of these
explanations in light of his own observations about drug use. Per-

haps the use of marijuana seems somehow different from the use of drugs such as LSD. Is this difference significant? Does it reflect on the ability of either of the theories to explain the phenomenon? The answer to both questions is "yes." General findings from research suggest that the social-factors theory best explains marijuana use, although the "personal factors" theory best explains the use of stronger drugs.

A 1971 study by James Preston and Patricia Fry reveals some support for the subculture-pressure explanation of marijuana use. Their survey of students in five Houston, Texas, high schools disclosed that 95 percent of the marijuana users had friends who were also users. In contrast, only 32 percent of nonusers had friends who were users. This division is a rather startling one for a community as small as a high school. Also in keeping with the subculture-pressure explanation was the finding that marijuana use was most regular among students from schools where clear norms existed supporting the use of marijuana. In "Multiple Drug Use Among Marijuana Smokers" (1969) Erich Goode has added support to these findings. Goode found that people who smoke marijuana tend to maintain long-term relations with other smokers, and that those who smoke together express agreement on a wide range of social values. He concludes that marijuana smoking reaffirms social bonds and secures social integration. Furthermore, the "common social problems" hypothesis of the social-factors explanation was also supported by Nechama Tec's "Family and Differential Involvement with Marijuana" (1970), a study of the family backgrounds of 1,700 teenagers. Tec found that regular users of marijuana felt that they received little recognition from their families and that the users tended to see their families as cold and rigidly controlling.

The investigating team of C. P. McAree, R. A. Steffenhagen, and L. S. Zheutlin recognized the important possibility that differences might exist among people who use different types of drugs. In "Personality Factors and College Drug Users" (1969) they broke their sample of University of Vermont student drug users into three groups. The first group used marijuana only; the second used marijuana and amphetamines; and the third used all types of drugs, including psychedelics. To serve as a comparison base, they also formed a control group composed of students who did not use drugs. Their questionnaire included the Minnesota Multiphasic Personality Inventory, an omnibus personality measure that taps many dimensions or phases of personality. They came up with the interesting finding that the "marijuana only" group did not differ significantly from the nonuser group in terms of personality variables. However, the group that used psychedelic drugs differed significantly from both the "marijuana only" and the control group: those who used psychedelic drugs were less able to cope with pressure, more likely to reject social mores and standards, and more inclined to withdraw from contact with others. Similar findings were reported in the research of Reginald Smart and Dianne Fejer, who compared LSD users with nonusers.

iv Evaluation The study by C. P. McAree and his colleagues is an important one. It calls attention to the fact that those who restrict their drug use to marijuana are not different in personality terms from the general population, although they do differ in respect to some social dimensions. Adding the finding that personality differences do characterize users of psychedelic drugs, we begin to see drug use in this perspective: the social-factors theory best explains the use of marijuana, and the personality theory best explains the use of stronger, hallucinogenic drugs. The combination of the two theoretical perspectives can give us a clearer picture of drug use across the entire spectrum than either theory taken by itself could do.

The comparison and empirical testing of these two theories have shown us how inappropriate it is to make blanket generalizations about drug use or drug users. Because the nature of marijuana issue is in fact quite different from the nature of the LSD issue, we should be hesitant to make statements like "People who smoke marijuana will end up using LSD." It appears that the reasons people use LSD are quite distinct from the reasons people use marijuana. Without considering both personality and social theories related to drug use, we might not have illuminated this important distinction.

Empirical studies in this area have certain limitations. The samples in these studies differ in terms of geographic region, age, institutional setting, and social composition. More studies that tap representative national samples are needed in order to establish a standardized comparison base. Personality studies face certain unique problems; for example, membership in a drug subculture or the use of the drugs themselves may produce personality changes in users. If such changes do occur, it is difficult to distinguish between those personality dispositions that existed prior to drug use and those that are simply responses to the phenomenon itself. Longer-term studies are thus needed to measure the personality attributes of persons both before and after their exposure to drugs. Despite such limitations, however, the general strength and recurrence of findings like those cited earlier help to establish that drug use does not form merely one dynamic continuum.

b The "Classical" Question

i Context In early sociological thinking people were seen exclusively as role players, position holders, status representatives, or group members, and sociologists understood people by referring to the groups to which they belonged as if their attributes were all socially determined. This *social determinist* position has been the center of a lengthy debate between sociologists and psychologists, because it often appears unable adequately to account for the dynamic qualities of society and social life. One of the characteristic questions in this debate has been: *Does personality theory have a place in the sociological study of society, and, if so, how can conceptions of personality be made compatible with existing sociological perspectives?*

ii Theory Many nineteenth-century schools of philosophical thought saw man as a rational, autonomous being motivated by principles of self-interest. Early sociologists rejected this position because it failed to explain much of the uniformity and cooperation in social relations as well as the tendency of people to carry *group solidarity* through many different situations. It appeared to the early

High! I'm Abbie Fly me to Miami

Ten Days to Change the Wor July 10-14   August 20-

Abbie Hoffman, "non-leader" of the Youth International Party (Yippies). Abbie Hoffman's anarchistic political movement emphasized the absurd side of contemporary life and identified itself strongly with the use and legalization of marijuana. Here Hoffman parodies airline advertisements and urges youth to demonstrate at the 1972 Democratic and Republican presidential nominating conventions in Miami.

232

sociologists that clear standards for behavior existed in society outside of the person; where these standards were lacking or ambiguous, people lost their sense of belonging as well as the sense of their own identity. People were conceived of as extensions of the groups to which they belonged, and these groups transmitted the demands, rules, moralities, and conscience that shaped the identities and behaviors of their members.

A personality perspective criticizes this "oversocialized" conception of people by suggesting that behavior is situationally determined only to the extent that a situation is inflexible or emotionally neutral. To the extent that norms are ambiguous or contradictory, that goals are unclear, or that emotions are aroused in social relations, personal dispositions and needs will enter into the behavioral equation. The implication of this argument is that sociological analysis will profit by looking at the degrees of flexibility and emotion-arousing potential in forms of social organization. The combination of these dimensions of personality analysis and standard sociological variables offers the possibility of resolving the dichotomy between "automatic sociological man" and "atomic psychological man."

Let's consider an example of this merger between personality and sociological variables. As we saw in Unit 5, the *role* is the key person-related variable in traditional sociology, and its description invokes the elements of *structure, conception,* and *behavior.* These mean that a role is determined by: (1) externally given demands associated with a social position, (2) a person's perception of, and orientation to, the part that he will play in the situation, and (3) the resulting behaviors that have an impact on the social situation. In this narrow view people appear to be social automatons,

A marriage. No mechanistic theory can account for the enormous variation in the ways in which individuals enact what is considered to be "proper" behavior.

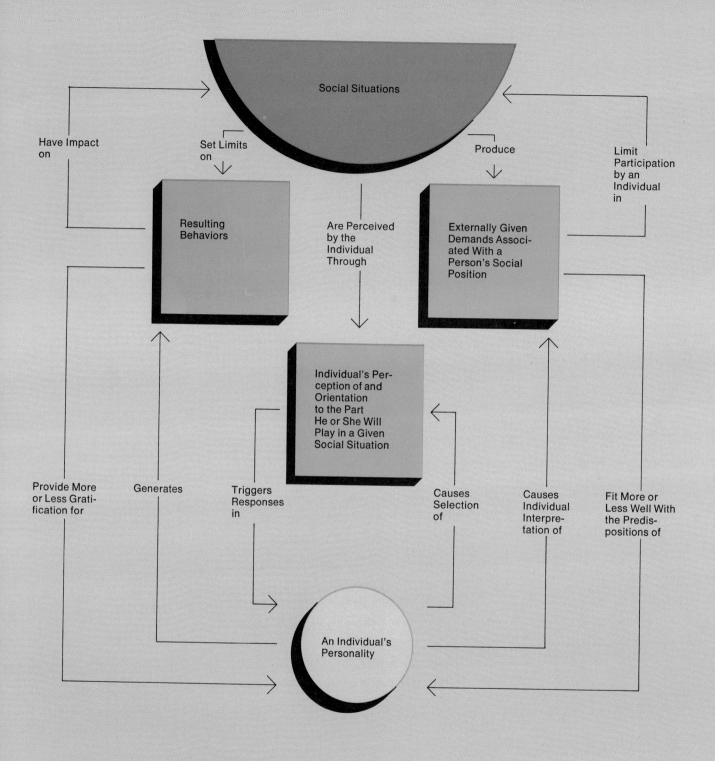

Model 1. Schematization of How Social Roles Mediate Between the Individual and Social Situations. The boxes indicate the three elements of a social role.

receiving an input, accepting its implications, and acting accordingly.)

The addition of a personality factor to role theory allows personal needs and dispositions to mediate between the three phases of a role—for instance, with respect to the selective interpretation and incorporation of various external demands made on an individual with regard to the role he or she plays. A woman from HOME (Happiness of Motherhood Eternal) has clearly emphasized and selected different aspects of the social role assigned to women than has one from WITCH (Woman's International Terrorist Conspiracy from Hell). Individual dispositions obviously are a factor. From this position, as formulated by Daniel Levinson in "Role, Personality, and Social Structure in the Organizational Setting" (1970), role conception may be seen as an "ego achievement," "a reflection of the person's capacity to resolve conflicting demands, to utilize existing opportunities and create new ones to find some balance between stability and change, conformity and autonomy, the ideal and the feasible, in a complex environment."

iii Research (Survey) The social determinist position concerning personality finds its roots in the thought of the brilliant Emile Durkheim, who, in opposition to much nineteenth-century thinking, saw the individual as a being of purely social orientation, the product of the social community and its moral traditions.)

While collective *representations* and *consciousness* were the focus of Durkheim's radical thought in this area, Sigmund Freud was proposing revolutionary theories concerning the psychology of the individual. Freud saw the person as being in a state of conflict between his self-centered biological drives and impulses and the self-denying demands of the real world. According to Freud, the self, or the *ego,* developed as a result of each person's unique resolution of this conflict.)

Despite the fact that early personality theorists, such as Freud, Alfred Adler, Harry Stack Sullivan, and Erik Erikson, were also interested in social processes and theories, early sociologists did not return the compliment: the sociological conception of the self was a social self. About 1900 Charles Horton Cooley proposed the conception of the *looking-glass self,* and 30 years later George Herbert Mead formulated the concept of the *generalized other.* In both cases the basic principle was that other people acquire their "selfness" through observing the responses of others to them and through processes of identification with groups.

Some sociologists, however, began to see the importance of personality for the understanding of social life. Robert K. Merton reasoned that social frameworks emphasize certain goals and reward certain means or *instrumentalities* for achieving them. The nature of personal adaptation in a social setting depends on whether the person is frustrated or encouraged, disposed or not disposed, to behave in proper instrumental fashion in the pursuit of socially valued goals. It wasn't until the 1950s, however, that sociologist Talcott Parsons and some of his colleagues in the Harvard Department of Social Relations began work on an interdisciplinary "theory of social action." Following theories of personality and society down from their heritage of Freud and Durkheim, Parsons proposed an integration of personality perspectives into general sociological theory by viewing the dynamics of *conformity-aliena-tion* as those in which person and society meet. The *need disposi-tions* of the individual were believed to result in conforming or alienating behaviors, depending on whether *patterns of social rela-tionships* satisfied or frustrated these basic needs. The emphasis in this theory is obviously social and involves the basic assumption that patterns of social experience are generally shared and result in a high degree of "fit" between basic personal needs and social rewards. Nevertheless, this theory has been a significant step in liberating sociology from the "oversocialized" conception of man.

iv Evaluation Early sociology had a somewhat intransigent ap-proach against adopting theories of personality. Durkheim reacted strongly against the practice of "psychologizing" in sociology be-cause, as he stated in *Suicide* (1897): "On the pretext of giving the science a more solid foundation by establishing it upon the psycho-logical constitutions of the individual, it is thus robbed of the only object proper to it. It is not realized that there can be no sociology unless societies exist and that societies cannot exist if there are only individuals." As a result of this foundation, a firm conceptual dichotomy between the individual and the society became charac-teristic of sociological thought.

The gradual change in this position illustrates the interplay between the cluster of abstractions that we call a science and the reality that it studies. The pressure from other disciplines like psy-chology and social psychology in combination with the need of new tools of social analysis gradually stimulated the change in sociological thinking. The adoption of personality perspectives —even though somewhat limited as yet—has strengthened socio-logical abilities to deal with problems like the nature of social adap-tation, the process of social change, and the effects of change on members of society. There is much work that still needs to be done on sociological conceptions of personality, but the initial steps of theory building are under way and empirical applications are not far behind. The next section explores some of these.

c   The "Research" Question

i Context In recent years sociologists have searched for some middle ground in order to talk about the elements of "groupness" in people and the elements of "peopleness" in groups. Some breakthroughs concerning this problem have come in the area of national-character research. This research began primarily when cultural anthropologists used psychoanalytic theories to analyze re-lationships and cultural habits in simple, homogeneous, tribal socie-ties. With the tensions produced by World War II and its aftermath, attention turned to the problem of understanding national character in more complex and modern societies. The methods of cultural anthropology were not as well suited to the investigation of hetero-geneous societies as were the methods of sociology. The task for the sociologist was to combine his techniques for the analysis of patterns of social organization with compatible personality theories in order to answer questions like: *How do personality factors relate to and influence patterns of adaptation in a given society?*

ii Theory Early anthropological studies of national character re-lied on Freudian theories of human development. These theories di-

(Facing page) The image of self. Our self-image is a composite of many factors. On the level of social interaction we constantly monitor others' behavior toward us and try to figure out what *we* think *they* think of us. Sometimes we are unhappy with the image we think they have of us, sometimes we are glad. And sometimes it doesn't make much of a difference to us. But through speculating about what others think of us, we constantly confront our own images of ourselves. Parts of the image we like, parts we do not like, and parts leave us indifferent. (*Hand With Reflecting Globe*, 1970, print by M. C. Escher.)

Cross-cultural variety in child care. Different societies have different patterned customs for raising their children. Such patterning of behavior toward children results in culturally related emotional and behavior patterns in these individuals when they become adults. The process of growing up is, however, a very complicated one. So far researchers have not been able to delineate specific emotional or behavior patterns as being directly caused by specific patterns of child care.

rected the researcher's attention to the ways in which the social environment of childhood systematically rewarded, frustrated, and redirected basic human drives or impulses. The researcher could construct hypotheses from these *behavior-shaping patterns* and make predictions about *dominant cultural practices* in adult society. For example, particular feeding and weaning practices involving the infant might be traced forward to such styles of adult conduct as selfishness, generosity, trustfulness, or withdrawal, to name a few.

When anthropologists applied these theories to modern societies, they were often criticized by other social scientists. The critics agreed that early childhood shaping of need dispositions had an effect on adult personality, but in a complex society there were many other intervening influences on personality between childhood and adulthood, and there were also countless classes, strata, and significant subculture groupings. Each of these societal divisions, it was argued, would provide certain unique experiences, demands, and rewards for its members. Thus it might be useful to look for a distribution of personality types in a society. The concept of *modal personality* was born. This term refers to the statistical concept of *mode*, which means the most frequent observation in a population. Many populations may be *multimodal* in the sense that more than one cluster of traits will appear with great frequency. Modal personality is a group concept. The determination of the dominant personality type in a group does not tell us what a particular individual will be like. Rather, we have a measure of group potentialities.

The sociological perspective on group personality begins with the basic premise that behavior dispositions, basic values, and social motives are shaped by certain dominant forces or pressures in the *social environment*, and thus that members of social groups —even groups as large as a society—will share in these basic experiences and frameworks for living. *Response dispositions* to these shared phenomena will be shaped by common sanctions in the social environment.

Social structures that have inconsistent or contradictory *sanctioning mechanisms* (rewards and punishments) or patterns of sanctions in a state of flux may frustrate the needs of the individual in some recognizable manner. They may thus result in a different behavior pattern from that intended. The effectiveness of a system of sanctions and the *adaptive potential* of the individual depend on the extent to which individuals are disposed to respond in expected ways to social sanctions.

Through "mapping" the dominant patterns of personality and social organization or structure in a society, it is possible to look at new changes in social organization and see how they were promoted because of underlying changes in personal dispositions. Similarly, the roots of particular social-psychological disorders, such as alienation, frustration, and maladaptive behavior patterns, may be traced to particular changes in social structure. In these ways patterns of social organization are seen to influence, and to be influenced by, the personality modes of a population at a given time. Personality and society are *functionally interdependent.*

iii   Research (Methodology)   Applying this theory to specific research questions is no simple matter. The first problem involves finding a methodology suitable for determining personality characteristics of large numbers of people in a foreign setting. Then the researcher must correctly identify the key behavior patterns that are linked to the personality dispositions of the population.

One of the classic studies on national character was conducted by Alex Inkeles, Eugenia Haufmann, and Helen Beir (reported in 1961 in their "Modal Personality and Adjustment to the Soviet Socio-Political System"). Its object was to explore the relationship between personality modes and adjustment to the Soviet sociopolitical order. Sampling the population of Russia was impossible for both political and economic reasons, but the Russian Research Center at Harvard was able to locate 3,000 persons who had defected from Russia during or after World War II, and thus the researchers had a sample of persons who did *not* adjust to the system. The question was why.

Of the 3,000 subjects who completed a general questionnaire, over 300 also gave a detailed life-history interview. From this group 51 people were selected as generally representative of the sample and were studied with a great variety of clinical tools and evaluative tests to yield specific personality profiles, inventories of cognitive styles, and general personality traits.

Analysis of these data revealed that the sample displayed certain dominant personality modes—for example, strong need for affiliation, a need for dependence on external support, conflicts involving trust versus mistrust in personal relations, high self-esteem, and high emotional volatility. The researchers attributed the failure

of these individuals to adapt to the Soviet system to certain government practices and rapid social changes that placed severe strains
on these particular dispositions.) Such practices and changes included political surveillance, distance between the regime's elite
and the masses, and the replacement of informal traditional communities with bureaucratic collective structures that deemphasized
the small group structure of society.

An interesting complement to the Inkeles study is a recent
one conducted and published in Russia itself on this relationship
between Soviet sociopolitical practices and the personality modes
of the Russian people. The Russian sociologist Georgii Smirnov reports in ''On the Concept of the Socialist Type of Man'' (1971) that
underlying the social arrangements and political demands of Russia
since the revolution is a developing personality type characterized
by such dispositions as ''collectivist orientation,'' ''comradely cooperation,'' ''internationalism,'' and a sense of ''public identity''
through public ownership of work products. Nevertheless, one
must always be careful in assuming that a given personality type is
fundamentally linked to a social practice: the adaptation may be
more apparent than real, and it may merely represent the fact that
certain opportunities exist for certain forms of behavior to prove
more profitable than others at a particular point in time.

iv Evaluation   As our initial definition of personality indicated,
personal dispositions manifest themselves in behavior that cannot
be entirely attributed to environmental factors alone. When the researcher is distant from the complex social patterns of a society, it
is often difficult to identify the network of constraints that are at
work in the social environment and influencing behavior patterns.
Moreover, as Reinhard Bendix points out in ''Complaint Behavior

and Individual Personality'' (1952), national-character research must be careful not to confuse the response with the stimulus and attribute socially constrained behaviors to personality traits. Because the core instruments of national character research are personality inventories, scales, and tests that were largely developed and validated by American psychologists on American populations, the challenge of establishing a universally valid theory and methodology is formidable. Indeed, *cultural bias* is an obstacle of such magnitude that many social scientists doubt that it can be overcome. If, however, the continuing efforts to perfect these theories and techniques succeed, the results will provide another valuable area in which the sociologist can pursue his concern with the nature of groups without losing sight of the individuals involved.

3   Overview

A respected sociologist has noted that the only place where personality theories regularly occur in sociology is in the introductory textbook. At more advanced levels they are mainly ignored in sociological theory and in practice. Nevertheless, one central question about personality and society does not allow itself to be easily bypassed even by the most unconvinced (traditional) sociologist: Where does society end and the person begin? If you think about this question with reference to yourself and your daily life, you may be able to appreciate how complex and elusive it is. How much of your behavior can be traced to some sort of social pressure, group influence, or loyally followed rule of conduct? How much of your behavior can be traced to unique personal qualities that operate independently of these social constraints? If there is a unique aspect to your behavior, is it genetically determined or do you existentially create it? The implications of the question have fascinated philosophers and novelists as well as psychologists and sociologists in their exploration of the human condition, and our views on the issue also greatly influence our concept of moral responsibility and criminal guilt.

A family meal. The patterned interaction within families is a factor that varies along societal lines. This variation not only produces patterns of behavior that are accepted by a given society as being ''correct'' but also produces patterned psychopathology. Thus, for instance, Irishmen who have been brought up in families dominated by mothers who habitually treat their sons as ''forever boys and burdens'' tend, when they become schizophrenic, to become withdrawn, latently homosexual, compliant toward authority, and chronically alcoholic. Italians brought up by dominating fathers tend, on the other hand, when they become schizophrenic, to be loud and aggressively expressive, defiant of authority-figures, overtly homosexual, and not at all inclined toward alcoholism. (Drawing by Ben Shahn.)

Japanese child with grandmother. The problem of rapid social change in industrial and industrializing societies complicates the study of national character. It is difficult to assess, for example, the degree to which this child growing up in contemporary Japan will share ''Japanese'' traits with her grandmother more or less than she will share ''Western'' traits with Americans or West Europeans. And it is even more difficult to predict the cultural configurations in which the little girl will herself participate.

D LOOKING AHEAD

1 Interview: Alex Inkeles

Alex Inkeles is Margaret Jacks Professor of Sociology and Education at Stanford University. His research interests have centered on studies of Soviet society and on socio-cultural aspects of economic development. His major publications include *Public Opinion in Soviet Russia*, *How the Soviet System Works* (with Kluckhohn and Bauer), *The Soviet Citizen* (with Bauer), and *Social Change in Soviet Russia*.

DPG *What are the problems involved in evaluating whether personal dispositions are suited or unsuited to a system of social organization?*
INKELES This kind of research takes us beyond the question of national character. As a matter of fact, what it gets one into is a concern for transnational character—that is to say, for qualities of the individual that, independent of national and cultural differences, may be related to a particular kind of social structure. The two forms in which we are most interested to begin with are the forms that distinguish, broadly speaking, between the less-developed countries and the more-developed countries. Then there are further questions about the differences between the path that's described broadly as socialism and the path that's described broadly as capitalism.

Now some of the most interesting research on this field is concerned with attempting to ascertain whether or not there is a particular kind of personality that both develops in and suits an individual more effectively to participate as a citizen and a producer of the modern, industrial, large-scale, bureaucratic, complex, urbanized society. What I have concentrated on is trying to determine whether there is a meaningful psychological syndrome that we can speak of as being the "modern man." I think we've identified a syndrome of that kind. That syndrome is evident, that kind of person emerges, in all of the underdeveloped countries that we have studied, and, as the theory would indicate, that kind of person is found much more in the modern sector of the underdeveloped countries; that is, they

are found much more among the people who have had formal schooling, those who participate in industry, those who work in large-scale bureaucratic organizations, those who participate in certain types of economic cooperatives in the countryside, those who are urban. They are decidedly more prevalent among the people who are much exposed to the media of mass communication and who participate in voluntary organizations.

DPG *What this fact implies is that the modern world demands certain personality traits from everybody, whether he's born in Ghana or the United States.*
INKELES Exactly. And we are able to demonstrate quite unambiguously with our measures on the Omm scale, the overall measure of modernity, that the qualities that define a person as "modern" are the same in all six countries that we have studied, and they cover quite a range of culture and level of economic development. Two were in South America, and two were in Asia.

DPG *Does this finding set aside for the time being the things like temperament?*
INKELES As a matter of fact, we have no reason to minimize the continued existence of things like temperament, but they are independent of, or marginal to, this measure of individual modernity. Obviously, no man can be all things, but one of the things that we find to be quite important and of great concern to the people we talked to in developing countries is the fact that they lose some of the highly valued attributes that they think of as unique or special in their culture in the course of the process of modernization. Our results suggest that the fear of that loss is probably greatly exaggerated because most of the qualities that in the past have been used to identify people in terms of some unique national characteristic of the temperamental kind don't really seem to be much affected by the modernization process.

The qualities that do change are things that, by and large, most people are not at all unhappy to give up—like, for example, the sense of passivity. A passive attitude seems to be built into some religious systems, like Islam, but if you look carefully at any great world religion you will find that, in fact, there is a basis for a wide variety of personal types that are perfectly consistent with the theology that's developed by the religion. In any event, things like passivity are things that are given up in the process of modernization, but variations in temperament don't necessarily have to change one

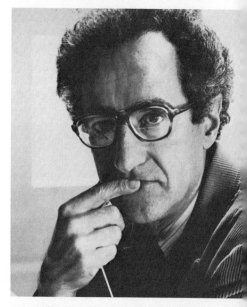

way or the other. A Japanese is still identifiable as a Japanese before and after the process of Japanese industrialization and modernization, but some other qualities, like the openness to new experience, the readiness to try new ways of doing things, the importance of a substantial amount of personal choice in making intimate daily life decisions—those are the qualitites that seem to transcend national boundaries and develop more or less equally in all of the developing countries, depending on the amount of influence you have coming from the institutional side. One important feature of this theory stresses that these changes don't come about spontaneously. They come about in good part as the response to the introduction into the system of modern institutions—of things like the factory, large-scale bureaucratic organizations, and modern schools.

DPG *It would also seem that there are certain personality types in a developing country who are tied to traditional passive social roles and wouldn't be adventurous enough to go into a factory, say, and reject all their early upbringing. If they'd grown up in the United States, though, they would never have had to cope with that problem because the society is oriented toward the "modern man" culture already.*

INKELES I think we have evidence for the second part of your statement. The more generally developed the country, the more individuals get a bonus, above and beyond the actual extent of their exposure to modernizing institutions, that seems to come from the environment in general. In a sense their culture has become a modern culture; so in absorbing their own culture spontaneously, they absorb some of the dispositions that go with modernity. We don't find a great deal of evidence to support the idea that the individuals who get more exposed to modern institutions in the developing countries, especially if you consider industry as the chief means of this exposure, are particularly selected in advance on the basis of their psychological predispositions. We find that the biggest factor in causing people to leave the countryside and move to urban industrial pursuits is actual need.

The people who have the least land and the least opportunity in the countryside are the individuals most likely to migrate; yet they are not psychologically the most adventuresome. That makes the situation all the more interesting. If only the more energetic people were the ones who got recruited from the countryside, the fact that you found them in the modern sector wouldn't indicate that the modern sector had done much to change them. It would be rather a problem of differential recruitment. But we find the evidence does not support the differential recruitment theory very strongly. On the contrary, recruitment seems pretty much a neutral factor, and that strengthens the argument that changes are brought about after people come in contact with modern institutions. This fact leads to another part of our emphasis. The earlier

emphasis on national character, personality, and social structure tended almost exclusively to focus on the early years of life and development. We find very substantial evidence of great changes that occur in the later years of development, after age 16. In explaining the attitudes and values and behavior of the modern man, we find that approximately half of the variance is accounted for by early socialization factors, and half is accounted for by late socialization experiences—things that happen after the age of 16.

DPG *What are the implications of this fact?*

INKELES One of the implications is that, to a degree that we have not experienced since the Middle Ages in Europe, the whole world is increasingly going to have in it people who have a personality that's more like the personalities of people from other cultures and countries than was true in the past. We feel one of the implications is that it increases the opportunity for cross-national or cross-cultural understanding.

DPG *Will the national or societal leaders be those people who are most "modernized"?*

INKELES Well, they may be, but the outstanding feature of leaders is that they are responsive to local cultural traditions and values. However, some other types—for example, scientists, some kinds of businessmen, some sorts of teachers, industrial workers—may find a lot more in common with individuals from other cultures. Indeed, they may find that in some ways they feel more of a sense of affinity with someone who is from a different culture but like them in their orientation towards modern living than they feel with someone from their own culture but from a different segment of the socioeconomic hierarchy. That is one of the things that we find quite striking.

The other thing that we find very interesting is that, oddly enough, this model of "modern man" in some ways seems to be most eroded in the most advanced countries. In the most advanced countries, you get a phenomenon that we are referring to increasingly as "postindustrial" or "postmodern" man, and that is a feature that we don't understand very well yet. It is presumably connected with the notion of alternative life styles so popular in the United States

and some parts of Britain and France, and there is a lot of argument about whether or not these tendencies really are a reaction against the institutions of the modern world by people who themselves have basically a modern character or whether the people who most manifest that tendency actually were raised in social climates or environments that had begun to disembody some of the features of the modern orientation. For example, the people who seem to reject the modern model for themselves often went to schools in which time and scheduling, which are very much a part of this

larger syndrome, were deemphasized and in which, instead of basing knowledge on empirical procedures in science, people were urged much more to look inside themselves. Their orientation becomes a more mystical, archaic, bucolic one and not so much a modern, industrial orientation.

Unit 11
Small Groups

SCHEMATIC OUTLINE

A   Introductory Graphics: The Small Group—Stages of Development

B   Definition and Context

1   Definition
Sociologists define a small group as any collection of *interrelating* human beings. Most research concentrates on deliberately formed groups that have an intentional psychological focus.

2   World Context
Studies by Gustave LeBon, Sigmund Freud, and others examined such groups as the French revolutionaries, the army, and the church. The group setting of personality change has been of particular interest.

3   American Context
Research by Kurt Lewin, Carl Rogers, and Jacob Moreno after World War II stimulated the study of group processes. Recently there has been great popular interest in various kinds of intentional psychological groups as a way of achieving personal and organizational change.

C   Questions and Evidence

1   Questions
Among the questions about small groups are: (1) Under what conditions are they harmful to individual members? (2) How do they evolve in style and concerns? (3) How are roles divided within them?

2   Evidence
a   The "Burning Issue" Question
Some theorists see casualties of small groups as victims of the harmful release of man's innate aggression; others regard such aggression as an intrinsic part of the social system rather than of human nature and argue that social constraints should be stripped away. Empirical research supports both viewpoints, and more, and firmer, investigations are needed.
b   The "Classical" Question
Theoretical studies, mainly derived from Freud, offer only sketchy predictions about the evolution of small groups. But the empirical models of group development may be too specific. More inclusive research is needed.
c   The "Research" Question
Sociologists have long been interested in possible patterns of role allocation and performance. The classic description of the instrumental-expressive dichotomy was given by Talcott Parsons and Robert F. Bales. Bales has developed the method of interaction process analysis, but his empirical research has generated more data than can be dealt with readily in existing theories.

3   Overview
Small groups have been an exciting testing ground for ideas about all sizes of social systems. Most experimental investigations concentrate on quite small groups; inclusive studies sacrifice a certain amount of rigor. But no unified theory has yet emerged from either the selective or comprehensive approach.

D   Looking Ahead

1   Interview: Robert F. Bales

SUPPORTING UNITS

ENCYCLOPEDIA ENTRIES

cohesion
conformity
consciousness-raising groups
counterdependence
encounter group
feedback
formal and complex organizations
group dynamics
group process
participant observation
psychology, humanistic
small groups
sociometry
study group
therapy group
training group
transactional analysis

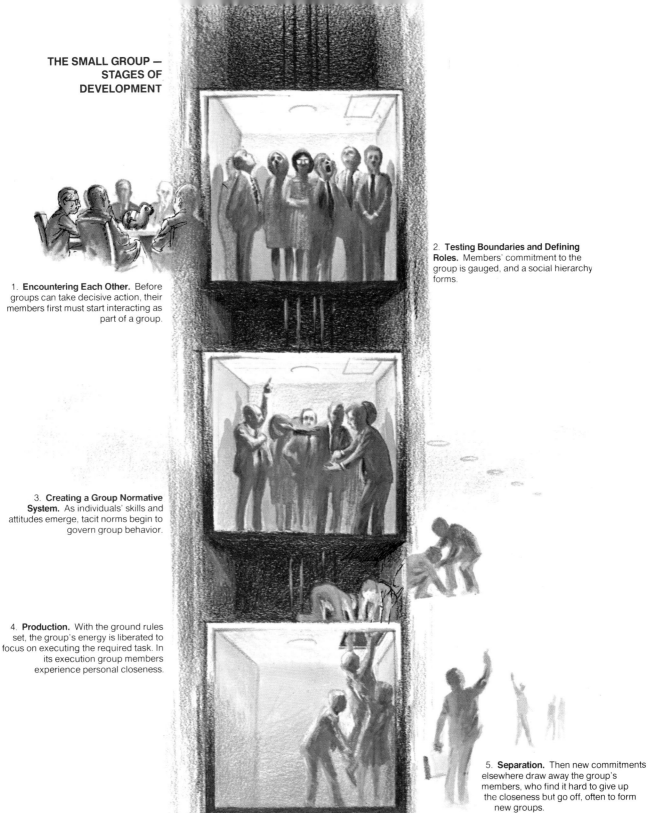

**THE SMALL GROUP —
STAGES OF
DEVELOPMENT**

1. **Encountering Each Other.** Before groups can take decisive action, their members first must start interacting as part of a group.

2. **Testing Boundaries and Defining Roles.** Members' commitment to the group is gauged, and a social hierarchy forms.

3. **Creating a Group Normative System.** As individuals' skills and attitudes emerge, tacit norms begin to govern group behavior.

4. **Production.** With the ground rules set, the group's energy is liberated to focus on executing the required task. In its execution group members experience personal closeness.

5. **Separation.** Then new commitments elsewhere draw away the group's members, who find it hard to give up the closeness but go off, often to form new groups.

Getting away from it all. But not getting away from small groups. In almost every situation in society some kind of small group is operating to structure the dynamics of interaction—even if, as in the case of these trailer-campers, the group is not deliberately formed and is of limited duration.

B   DEFINITION AND CONTEXT

1   Definition

Only fairly recently has the study of small groups attracted any attention, for the most part because social scientists could not see how so many diverse kinds of groups—including, for example, a mountain rescue team, occupants of a college dormitory, a baseball team, a rural commune, President Nixon's cabinet, a professional repertory company, and the travelers in a bus from New York to Miami—had anything in common. This problem is still one of the greatest difficulties of the field, although current theory spans all the different manifestations of small groups. Most research has concentrated on small groups that can be easily observed and that last for more than a short time (unlike, for example, the small group in an airport men's room at any one time). However, principles of small-group interaction derived from the kinds of groups that are studied in the laboratory are felt to apply to all sorts of naturally occurring small groups. For this reason sociologists use this definition: *A small group is any collection of interrelating human beings.*

This definition has certain limitations. By far the most important is the size of the group. Clearly the minimum size can be no smaller than two, and many studies in this field have been done with groups of three people. The maximum size allowable is determined by a number of factors, all pertaining to various interpretations of the term "interrelating." Some theorists emphasize that each member of a small group must have some knowledge of and communication with each other member—a "face-to-face" luncheon group would fit this criterion. Some merely emphasize that the members must have the same goal in mind—this requirement could permit study of a large peace demonstration or march. Because large crowds are known to have special characteristics of their own and because most of the research in this field has been done with groups no larger than about 30 people and averaging about 10 meeting at the same place at the same time, we will emphasize in this unit the *ongoing interaction* in what we call a small group. Thus, although the group of travelers in a large jet would be too large, the pilot and his crew in the same jet would qualify. Theodore Mills estimates in *The Sociology of Small Groups* (1967) that the average person is in five ongoing small groups.

Other factors are important in distinguishing between kinds of small groups. The *salience* of a group—how important it is to a person and how much it affects him—is a crucial variable related to size. On the average, the smaller the size of the group, the more salient it can become for the members, partly because of the abundant opportunities for face-to-face interaction that reinforces the sense of belonging shared by all members of the group. If an individual is constantly checking to see how members of a certain group behave, that group may be a *reference group* or *peer group* for him.

Among the small salient groups, those that have been most extensively researched have certain distinguishing features. First, these groups have a *psychological focus.* The primary emphasis of members is on each individual's feelings, thoughts, beliefs, and values. In contrast to other groups—such as a board of directors' meeting or a theater group—these groups focus on the very personal psychological interactions among members. Second, the psychological focus is *intentional,* rather than, say, a by-product of the camaraderie developed in the course of touring the college circuit as members of a basketball team. Finally, these groups are *deliberately formed;* they are not created by the accidents of circumstance, but are consciously organized for a particular purpose.

It is important to distinguish between these particular factors, which may occur in different combinations and degree, because much research on small group processes is concentrated exclusively on deliberately formed groups that have an intentional psychological focus. However, many of the observations resulting from this research are felt to extend to other kinds of groups. For example, a group of survivors in a life boat is not a deliberately formed group, and at first it is intentionally nonpsychological in focus. As the days pass and resources become scarce, however, the group develops a nonintentional psychological focus, which must soon become intentional so that the members can confront their own fears and combat them.

2 World Context

Recent work in anthropology has shown that man's primate relatives roaming the vast African grasslands have highly developed forms of social organization. A roving band of baboons, for example, can have about one or two dozen members. When they move or feed, they form a large circle; the females and children are in the center, the adolescents just outside, the dominant males come next, especially in the forward and rear positions, and on the perimeter are the young males, not yet strong enough to win closer access to the females, who protect the group (unless the threat is so serious that one of the dominant males must step in). This pattern is a *group space* very similar to the kind that will be described later in our discussion of group roles.

The modern family had its roots in these early small groups. It is only very recently, as we saw in Unit 7, that the *nuclear family* (a father, a mother, and their children) has become isolated from others in separate living units. Throughout human history—from nomadic tribes to primitive hunting and gathering groups to societies using agriculture and domestication of animals—the predominant form has been the *extended family,* which includes in the same household as the nuclear family others related through *kinship.* The extended family was the focus of survival efforts and of interpersonal contact. Perhaps it is the contraction of the extended family unit, which led to the loss of its opportunities for intense interrelationships with many others, that has increased interest in other groups (especially deliberately formed groups with an intentional psychological focus).

Gustave LeBon was the first modern social scientist to study group phenomena in and of themselves. In a book entitled *The Psychology of Crowds*, published in 1895, he began to describe

An informal small group. What interaction do you think is taking place here?

the characteristics of the angry Paris mobs of the French Revolution. Sigmund Freud in *Group Psychology and the Analysis of the Ego*, first published in 1922, discussed LeBon's work at length and included an examination of other groups, such as the army and the church. Indeed, Freud's analysis became the foundation of modern-day organizational analysis. But his ideas were applicable to small groups too (where they were much easier to observe in practice). Freud felt, for example, that members of a group substitute the *group leader* for their *ego ideal* and identify themselves with one another through this common attachment. This idea might explain the well-known power of groups to change a member's opinions and modify his behavior. Throughout history, from Sufi religious groups to Outward Bound mountain survival groups, the group setting has been used as a powerful agent of personality change.

3   American Context

Most of the effort in developing models of small groups began only after World War II. Kurt Lewin, who founded the Research Center for Group Dynamics at the Massachusetts Institute of Technology, did much to encourage this work. Lewin's initial interest was trying to understand how to change people's attitudes, including toward one's self. He found that group discussions and group decision making, in which the leader functioned as a *facilitator* or moderator rather than as a director, were powerful tools for motivating attitude change. During World War II rationing days, for example, Lewin found that group discussions were an effective way to convince people to eat such unpopular foods as turnips, beef hearts, and kidneys.

In a classic study with Ronald Lippitt and R. K. White ("Patterns of Aggressive Behavior in Experimentally Created 'Social Climates,' " 1939), Lewin also experimented with different group "climates." Groups of 10-year-old boys were observed in hobby activities under conditions of autocratic, democratic, and laissez-faire adult leadership. The *autocratic leader* directed all the group activities in an impersonal but controlling way. The *democratic leader* allowed the group to determine matters of policy, suggesting alternatives when appropriate. The *laissez-faire leader* was essentially a nonparticipant, and the group was given complete freedom. Hostility, aggression, and scapegoating were many times as great in the autocratic as the democratic groups, while the quality of production was better in the democratic groups. This early study did much to advance interest in analyzing processes in small groups.

Another development in the use and study of small groups occurred at about the same time at the University of Chicago. After World War II Carl Rogers was asked by the Veterans Administration to create some kind of training program to prepare educated men to work effectively with returning GIs as personal counselors. The staff felt that ordinary classroom training would be insufficient for this task, so they experimented with an intentional psychological group experience in which trainees met for several hours each day to learn more about themselves and how they related to others. This attempt to tie together experiential and cognitive learning in a process that had therapeutic value for the individual was so successful that Rogers and the staff continued to use the procedure in workshops from that time on.

Another early worker in this field was Jacob Moreno, who formulated the *sociometric method* for understanding the nature of networks in groups. In its simplest form, members of a group answer the question "Name the two people in the group you like best." The resulting *sociogram* reveals who the best-liked people in the group might be—perhaps they are also central—and the least-liked people are also visible. Thus a picture of the group as a whole is possible. Moreno also did much work on the use of *role-playing techniques* (*psychodrama*) in small groups.

Model 1. Sociogram. The letters represent respondents; the arrows represent direction of choice. This model illustrates several patterns often found in sociograms: (1) two different subgroups within the larger group, (2) cliques of people who choose each other (for example, *DEG*), (3) popular people *(B)*, and (4) isolates *(C)*.

More striking than the growing study of groups is the promotion of many kinds of intentional psychological groups as a way of producing personal and organizational change. This concept is reaching the proportions of a fad in contemporary American society. Psychologist Sigmund Koch has said that "today the group movement has become the most visible manifestation of psychology on the American scene." Various models of groups have been applied in numerous settings. In 1947, shortly after Lewin's death, his students started the National Training Laboratories in Bethel, Maine, where they devised the *T-group* or *training group model* of group process. The T-group has been the model most used by businesses and organizations to develop communication, trust, and caring within, say, an executive staff or a group of black and white employees. A number of popular new models of psychotherapy that also utilize group interaction have emerged: a *transactional analysis group* emphasizes the analysis of important state-

·ments made by members of the group; an *encounter group* or *sensitivity group* emphasizes the direct experience by each person of each other person facilitated by various exercises and games; the *Synanon group* uses a strong attack on the defenses of the participant in an attempt to expose the "true self") and so on.

Why has this fantastic growth in the use of small groups taken place at this time in the United States? Perhaps specific factors in American society are causing people to seek a new way of relating to others. There has been an increase, especially in certain urban situations, in the fragmentation of social relationships in response to the greater complexity of society and the competing demands of many social commitments, extending far outside of the nuclear family and de-emphasizing its importance. Most social contacts in this situation are transitory and thus not characterized by the gratifying intensity of a close, long-term relationship with another person.

This fact might explain the tremendous interest in joining groups or making ones that already exist more satisfactory through the application of techniques developed from research. (Intentional pyschological groups often emphasize feeling and emotion rather than reason, and they provide a situation in which the individual can try to look inward (or to reach out to others) instead of constantly striving to achieve and produce.) Many individuals turn to psychological groups to find the sense of security, camaraderie, and love that they miss in daily life, and the ideal within such groups is that each member is accepted for who he is. (At the extremes some of the new groups have identified with the much-advertised "youth-love culture," and participants are not supposed to think, but only to feel.) They are encouraged to express their sexual and aggressive energies freely, to love or hate without self-censorship. Overall, the impact of recent concentration on the possibilities of experiences in groups to bring about personal changes has come from increased awareness of the research in this field and an acceptance of both feeling *and* thinking, or as Freud once said, "love and work."

The psychologist Carl Rogers proclaims that "the encounter group is the most important social invention of this century." But can the fragmentation of social relations in modern life really be healed by intense experiences in small groups? Or is this American emphasis on groups an indication of the desperate dependence of *other-directed man* (David Riesman's term in *The Lonely Crowd* for the person who is no longer concerned primarily with his own views but is guided solely by others) and a surrender to the tyranny of the mass?) Of course, a general answer cannot yet be given, but it is important to remember that these issues have been at the roots of the research in this field.

C   QUESTIONS AND EVIDENCE

1   Questions

Among the questions sociologists working on small groups ask are these: (1) Under what conditions are small groups harmful or de-

Sensitivity groups emphasize getting to know oneself and others through close personal interaction, often of a nonverbal nature.

structive to their members? (2) How do small groups evolve in their style and central concerns over time? (3) What is the regular division of roles within small groups? Are they the same from group to group?

2 Evidence

a The "Burning Issue" Question

i Context Concern for how people are affected by the groups they are in is nothing new, but recently the issue has begun to receive more urgent attention. The burgeoning of intentional psychological groups has left a small percentage of group participants with more acute pyschological problems than when they joined the group. A number of them have suffered such adverse reactions to the group experience that they have been consigned to mental institutions. Data from National Training Laboratories show 25 serious psychiatric incidents among 11,000 participants in 22 consecutive summer programs and 8 incidents among 3,000 participants during 13 years of programs specifically designed for industry. Commentators have noted that less responsible group-training centers have even less enviable records. Sociologists have become increasingly concerned with this and related negative group phenomena, and they ask: *How can the dynamics of interaction in small groups exert pressures that exceed the personal capacities of its members?*

ii Theory It must be pointed out that there is no absolute set of standards as to what constitutes "benefit" or "harm" to the human psyche. Personality theorists, who have been hard put to define what is good, bad, or normal about personality in a static sense, have found even greater difficulty in defining values, variables, and processes with regard to *personality change.* Vague and conflicting ideas about how personalities should develop and how such growth should be measured have plagued this field, but a generally accepted definition of personal growth is given by Jack and Lorraine Gibb in "Emergence Therapy" (1968):

> Growth is a movement toward greater acceptance of self and others. The trusting person comes to accept more parts of himself. . . . Growth is a movement toward intimacy and away from social distance . . . . a movement toward feelings of freedom, power, and interdependence.

Because most groups are concerned with developing positive goals such as personal growth, negative effects tend to be brushed aside or ignored. In "A Study of Encounter Group Casualties" (1971) Irvin Yalom and Morton Lieberman define a *group casualty* as a member who increasingly develops feelings of anxiety or depression, suicidal thoughts, acts of aggression, and so on, as a consequence of the group experience. Though Yalom's and Lieberman's emphasis was on intentional psychological groups, these disheartening symptoms can occur in individuals as a result of participating in many different sorts of groups—for example, the excessive alcohol intake, intestinal pains, or lethargy some people experience after weekly staff meetings where they work. Though such meetings might not pretend to be therapeutic,

their psychological effects can be evaluated with the same criteria. As for the tools of measurement, group effectiveness is often assessed by self-evaluations of the participants in a small group or by outside observations of changes in their behavior. For example, Betty Meador had trained judges rate randomly chosen film clips of actual group sessions. She found that the raters affirmed significant increases over time in group members' abilities to express feelings more spontaneously and to relate more openly to others. Assessments of negative effects have, on the other hand, all been limited to lengthy clinical interviews conducted after the group experience was over.

The question as to how a group can have the opposite of the intended beneficial effect on one or more of its members has not been dealt with directly in sociological theory. Sociologists understand casualties as victims of aggressive energies converging within a social system. Thus the question is linked to one of the classical concerns of sociology—the dynamics of the expression of aggression in a social system. There are two major popular views of these dynamics, and each has different implications for understanding how and why different kinds of groups can be harmful to their members.

The first view is one furthered by LeBon and Freud. They see man as a savage animal. Civilization binds him down and makes him appear respectable. Were it not for these ties, he would burst out and murder his fellows. It is thus the tenuous *social contract* of the group, which guarantees survival through cooperative use of resources, that demands the *repression* of these aggressive energies. (The social contract concept received classic formulation in political theory in the thought of Hobbes and Locke, mentioned in Unit 5.)

When the group contract breaks down or when an individual finds himself an anonymous member of a large crowd or mob, these restrictions are lifted, and aggressive energies flow in every direction. Sometimes these repressed energies build up tremendous pressure, as in a pressure cooker, and some outlet must be found. Because the person does not want to direct these aggressive energies toward himself, he finds someone who is different from himself—a member of the opposite sex, a person whose skin is a different color, and so on. Casualties in small groups are understood as the unfortunate victims of this aggressive energy. A good example of this view is found in William Golding's novel *Lord of the Flies* (1955), in which an airplane full of English schoolboys crashes on a tropical island, and all the adults are killed. Slowly at first, but then with increasing acceleration, the boys revert to a primitive existence where minorities in the group are savagely destroyed.

The other major view, which is much more popular among encounter group leaders than the first, sees man as dependent on his immediate surroundings for clues as to how he should behave. This theory regards man as *socius*, "as an undifferentiated and diffused region in a social space inhabited concurrently by all other men thus diffused" (Sigmund Koch, "The Image of Man Implicit in Encounter Groups," 1971). Thus, if there is aggression or strain resulting in casualties, it is because there are positive group sanctions for it or because it is an intrinsic part of the system. The comparable fictional example here is Thomas Hughes' famous novel *Tom Brown's School Days* (1857), also about English schoolboys, which describes a situation of bullying and punishment that although it definitely leads to group casualties, is part of the tradition of the school. Encounter group leaders feel that such *social constraints* on the individual must be stripped off, allowing the inner man—whom they believe to be naturally good—to emerge.

iii   Research   In their 1971 investigation of casualties in intentional psychological groups, Irvin Yalom and Morton Lieberman recruited 209 unscreened Stanford University undergraduates and assigned them to 18 groups led by well-recommended group leaders representing a variety of approaches. Yalom and Lieberman dubbed the types of leaders as "aggressive stimulators" (charismatic), "love leaders" (supportive), "social engineers" (steering the groups), "laissez-faire," "cool-aggressive," "high structure" (emphasizing group games), and two who used taped instructions for the encounters. Of the 170 students who stayed with their groups until the end, 17 (or 9.6 percent) were rated as casualties. Leader style rather than ideological approach seemed to be the most important determinant of harmful effects. What Yalom and Lieberman call "aggressive stimulators"—the charismatic, challenging, impatient, and authoritarian group leaders—ran the five groups that produced nearly half of the casualties. High-risk subjects turned out to be those who needed and expected most from the group experience but "lacked the self-esteem and interpersonal skills to operate effectively in the group." Although it is hard to draw firm conclusions from the very small numbers of cases, Yalom and Lieberman suggest that persons without sufficient strength to undergo a difficult experience would be likely to suffer especially in groups where aggression is aroused.

Relevant to this question is a series of studies by Chris Argyris at Harvard's Graduate School of Education, described in his article "The Incompleteness of Social-Psychological Theory" (1969). Argyris studied 163 different meetings in 10 different business organizations (from a top management planning discussion group in a manufacturing firm to a meeting of a university executive development program), which resulted in 45,802 units of behavior coded in terms of his own system for scoring verbal interaction. Argyris compared these findings with 3,610 units of observed behavior in 13 T-groups. The observed *modes of interactions* in the business groups he termed "Pattern A," in the T-groups "Pattern B." Pattern A was characterized by norms of conformity, antagonism, and individuality; individuals were very rarely observed expressing feelings, being open to feelings, showing concern or trust, or helping others own up to, be open toward, or experiment with ideas or feelings. Pattern B was most often characterized by high levels of expressed concern and trust, taking responsibility for ideas and feelings, and helping others do the same, both as intellective and feeling expressions. Argyris argues strongly that Pattern A leads to defensiveness, closed-mindedness, readiness to ignore others in favor of a task, tendencies to make

Two views of aggression: aggression as innate and aggression as caused by reaction to a social situation.

silent assumptions about others without testing them out, and the like. These are all very harmful consequences. He does not document the contention that interacting in Pattern A leads to negative effects outside the group with actual cases because such documentation would require a long-term study. Furthermore, Pattern A interaction is widely accepted as normal for business groups. (See Theodore Whyte's *The Organization Man,* 1956.)

The Stanford psychologist Philip Zimbardo has been conducting a series of experiments on the effects of *deindividuation* on expression of aggression. Very briefly, his general finding has been that under the cover of anonymity (for example, when subjects don an oversize lab coat and hood with eye slits as they enter the experimental laboratory), subjects will deliver painful electric shocks of greater intensity and duration to victims in a rigged learning situation than when the subjects are clearly identified. He has also found that general hostility levels are lower in groups where everyone has a name tag than in groups where each wears a hood over his or her head. Again the results are only suggestive of how individuals might react in naturally occurring anonymous groups. (It was known in advance that none of the "victims" would actually suffer.)

Carol Wolman and Hal Frank at the University of Pennsylvania studied six groups varying in size from nine to 13 members, each including just one woman: three T-groups of degree candidates in business administration and three work groups of psychiatric residents. Wolman and Frank concluded that the lone woman in professional peer groups—a situation that is occurring with greater frequency as sex-role standards change and more women move into the professions—"runs a higher risk than the other members of becoming a casualty of the group and . . . her presence is likely to undermine the productivity, satisfaction, and sense of accomplishment of her male peers." The researchers led or observed each of these groups and noted that the men felt that their traditional male aggressive joking relationship (a subtler version of locker room boasting and sparring) had been violated by the intruding woman.

> They fear that she will act weak and demand that they take care of her, violating the norm of independence and toughness. They fear that she will compete successfully with them, violating the norm that women are seen as objects, and threatening their masculinity. And they fear that she will stir up sexual rivalry among them, disrupting their friendships and violating the norm that sexual feelings are taboo. ("The Solo Woman in a Professional Peer Group," 1972)

The woman was labeled a deviate in the group or was isolated and ignored in a process that took many weeks and of which no one was clearly aware. Most of the women became depressed, and some dropped out as a result.

iv Evaluation It is extremely hard to compare these various studies. Together they do not support one of the theoretical models more than the other, but seem to give tentative support to both. Whether behavior in a group that leads to a casualty is a result of

The Ku Klux Klan, a totalitarian organization dedicated to keeping black and Jewish persons outside of the mainstream of white (Southern) American life. Although most people believe that KKK members wear hoods so that they cannot be identified for legal purposes (which is no doubt true), a deeper reason may be the fact that personal anonymity apparently allows individuals to release less-controlled aggressive behavior.

the particular *normative constraints* of that group or of the surrounding society or whether such behavior results from the loosening of certain social conventions, a loosening that exposes an *underlying human savagery,* cannot be known from the research available today. The Yalom and Lieberman study suggests that aggression is aroused by strong leaders and results in lasting damage to those whose defenses are too weak to cope with their own and others' aggressive impulses. The Argyris study, on the other hand, suggests that it is the social situation—defined by either an organizationally-oriented group or a growth-oriented group—that leads to either the undesirable characteristics of Pattern A or the positive outcomes of Pattern B. Yet in the Wolman and Frank research, how much of the harmful strain directed at the lone woman member is a result of innate masculine aggressive energy? How much is it the result of conformity to pervasive culturally defined sex-role stereotypes that demand that the man be assertive and dominating and the woman passive and accepting? In the deindividuation research, how much of the potentially destructive aggression is due to the unlocking of deeply hostile impulses and how much to the feeling that when wearing a Ku Klux Klan mask, one should act like a Ku Kluxer? Perhaps we can conclude that generally both dynamics are operating. Strictly defined social roles offer acceptable outlets for the expression of basic energies. When norms are undermined, controls over aggressive energies are lost and victims have no protection.

This search is also plagued by a more fundamental disagreement about the image of man and what he *should* be. The investigators have no firm definitions of "help" and "harm" and no clear idea of how much each can or should be regulated in group situations. Some group leaders and researchers, for example, say, "None should suffer," but others say, "That's life—some people benefit from intense group interaction, some don't." The result is an unprecedented experimentation with group experiences, ranging from trying to create peak emotional experiences for drug addicts to the forceful breaking down of defenses through nude group dancing. Until more research is done on the potential effects of group settings, we undertake each new experiment with an element of risk.

b The "Classical" Question

i Context There are a great many common-sense notions about what happens in a small group over time. Many people hold the beliefs that groups get stronger the longer the members are together, that communications get subtler as more *nonverbal behavior* develops, that *factions* arise over issues of leadership and power, and so on.

But do we know enough about how collections of interrelating human beings change as they spend more and more time together to be able to support such beliefs? Are there consistent patterns in all sorts of small groups? Why do committees take so much longer than individuals to get things done? Sociologists have now begun to take a closer look at the way small groups develop, and they ask: *What interpersonal factors influence the structure and course of behavior in small groups over time?*

ii Theory Again Freud's thinking is central to notions about the ways in which groups change over time. In particular, two of Freud's positions have been elaborated by later theorists to form two major hypotheses about the nature of change in groups. The first of these hypotheses is the *centrality of the leader.* Freud's famous metaphor of the "primal horde," though originally developed in *Totem and Taboo* (1912), was also used in *Group Psychology and the Analysis of the Ego* to explain the central importance of authority and power in groups ranging from marital dyads to entire societies. The metaphor describes the time when man the hominid was just becoming *homo sapiens*, the time of the birth of consciousness. The father of the group was autocratic and cruel, reserving all the females for himself and preventing the younger sons from having sexual partners. Out of jealously and hatred,

> these many individuals eventually banded themselves together, killed [the father], and cut him in pieces. . . . They then formed the totemistic community of brothers all with equal rights and united by the totem prohibitions which were to preserve and to expiate the memory of the murder. *(Group Psychology and the Analysis of the Ego)*

So even after death, the father lives on as the central power in the group.

Philip Slater, in his book *Microcosm: Structural, Pyschological and Religious Evolution in Groups* (1966), discusses the centrality of the group leader to everything that goes on in a group, proposing that the "revolt" against the leader—whether a literal casting out or a symbolic uprising—is the most important crisis the group must confront and a turning point in the group's evolution. "In the last analysis independence cannot be conferred; it can only be seized." Along with Freud, however, Slater points out that this independence is marked by a deep identification with the deposed leader.

The second major hypothesis deriving from Freud's work sees group process as *antidevelopmental.* If development in a group setting means the eventual emergence of interpersonal honesty and caring and the appearance of cooperative work on mutually defined problems, then most groups cleverly prevent their own development. They go as far as needs be to construct a system of relationships whereby further development is made impossible—risk is minimized and change slows to a standstill. Freud, summarizing LeBon, put it this way: "Groups have never thirsted after truth. They demand illusions, and cannot do without them. They constantly give what is unreal precedence over what is real."

In *Experiences in Groups and Other Papers* (1959) W. R. Bion described some of the stances a group can take to prevent development based on an understanding of the fundamental personality needs of the individual members. He called these stances *"basic assumptions."* The entire group can make them at any time without recognizing it, and they are often taken in succession. In the dependent group (which Bion called *baD*, or "basic assumption of dependency"), "the group has met together to obtain security from one individual on whom they depend" in an attempt to gain

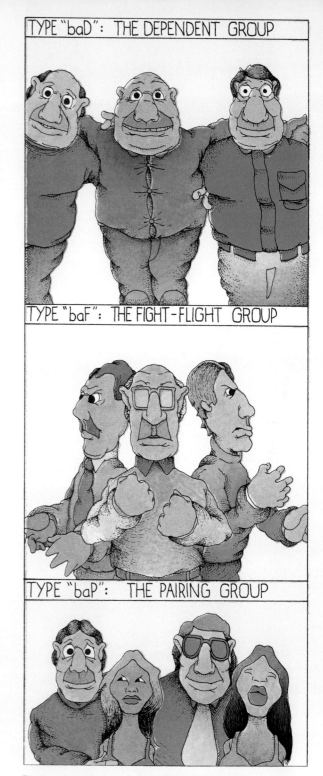

Bion's analysis of group dynamics that inhibit growth. Bion's theory, which derives from Freud's work and sees group process as antidevelopmental, describes the stances a group can take to inhibit the growth of group members.

nourishment and support. In the fight-flight group *(baF)*, the main aim is the preservation of the group and the combatting of the ever-present threat to the group's survival. In the pairing group (*baP*), all relationships are seen as sexual, because the assumption is that the group has met to find a mate of some sort. Over time and with the increased awareness of the unspoken group assumptions, the group can (the process is facilitated by a trained leader) become a work group (*W*). Instead of being held together by dependency, anxiety, or sex, the members are in a sophisticated and reality-based cooperative endeavor for their mutual benefit. Bion's theory, then, talks very generally about stages through which a group must evolve to achieve maturity.

iii Research (Survey) Although studies of this question have been based on such theories, they are very much concerned with exactly in what order different phenomena, such as the basic assumptions and the revolt against the leader, occur. Though Bion never said that the basic assumptions occur in a fixed progression from group to group, such investigators as W. G. Bennis and H. A. Shepard have tried to find a general invariant pattern of development toward the work group. Thus the research efforts extend beyond the limits of the theories.

It has been difficult to define the divisions of time in a group, but in "Phases in Group Problem Solving" (1951), Robert F. Bales and F. L. Strodtbeck give a definition of *time spans* that can apply to all sorts of small groups. Bales and Strodtbeck define time spans as "qualitatively different subperiods within a total continuous period of interaction in which a group proceeds from initiation to completion of a problem involving group decision." The judgment of when a time period starts, when it ends, and what the characteristics are of the atmosphere and quality of interaction between start and finish, however, are all subject to the decision of the researcher. Some employ best guesses, some expert opinion, and some exceedingly complex systems of scoring members' statements and analyzing the resulting data.

A number of the most important studies of group development are presented in Table I. They are placed side by side in order to compare the different conceptions of the important changes in small groups. Although these studies have been conducted with various types of salient groups over the last 25 years, it is surprising how much the different models of time spans agree with each other. By putting them all together, perhaps you can get a better idea of how small groups have been observed to change over time. The least vague scheme, that offered by T. M. Mills, is presented first. R. D. Mann's system is based on the idea that everything that takes place in a group is centered around the relations between members and the leader. He has devised a scoring system to pick up the most subtle *cues* revealing the orientation of a member to the group leader. In the W. G. Bennis and H. A. Shepard model leader-member issues dominate the first part of the group time. The members rebel against their dependence and come to a resolution about the leader by identifying with his aims.

It appears that groups will move steadily toward resolution, toward intimacy and work group (which is equivalent to Mills'

Still from film *Mutiny on the Bounty* (1935): Clark Gable as Fletcher Christian confronts Charles Laughton as Captain Bligh. First mate Christian led a mutiny against the hard-driving Bligh on the *H.M.S. Bounty* in 1789. This dramatic historical incident was later depicted in popular books and films and is a good example of small group dynamics. Problems of the hierarchy of power, personal loyalties and antagonisms, and the role of a newly emergent (in this case, mutinous) leader are issues that affect almost all human groups at some time or other.

Mills (1964): Non-Directive Learning Groups	Mann (1967): Self-Analytic Groups	Bennis and Shepard (1965): Self-Study Graduate Seminars in Group Dynamics	Bales and Strodtbeck (1951): Problem-Solving Groups	Yalom (1970): Psychotherapy Groups
Phases and Issues	Stages	Phases and Subphases	Phases	Stages
1. Encounter Individual objectivity versus involvement	1. Appraisal	1. Dependence: Authority and power a. Dependence-Submission: Flight from anxiety b. Counterdependence: Fight; Rebellion c. Resolution: Catharsis and group solidarity; Pairing	1. Orientation: Relevant material made available by individuals	1. First meeting: Invariably a success
2. Testing boundaries and modeling roles Preoccupation with group versus with processes external to group	2. Confrontation with leader and other members			2. Initial stage: Orientation; Concern for who is "in" or "out"
3. Negotiating an indigenous normative system Coping with relationships between leader and peers and with group task	3. Reevaluation of leader and of group situation; Group image changed	2. Interdependence: Love and intimacy a. Enchantment: Flight to cohesive and relaxed relations b. Disenchantment: Fight; Anxiety; Distrust; Disparagement of the group c. Consensual validation: Resolution; Pairing; Understanding of group and persons in reality; Acceptance of individual and group needs; Work-group	2. Evaluation: Differences in values and interests resolved; Task better defined	3. Second stage: Conflict; Rebellion; Concern for who is "top" or "bottom"
4. Production Expression of affection; Solidification	4. Internalization: Identification with the leader and the stated task of the group; Work		3. Control: Regulation of members in pursuit of the task	4. Third stage: Concern with how "near" or "far" one is from others
5. Separation Preparation for termination	5. Separation: Sadness and final expression of stifled feelings; Frustration at inability to accomplish expected progress			5. Development of cohesiveness and cooperation

Table 1. Different Models for Group Development. References are to the authors of major recent studies of the topic, the year of publication of the studies, the type of group observed, and the label of the units of group evolution. Time moves downward from initiation of each group to its termination. The studies are: Mills, *The Sociology of Small Groups;* Mann, *Interpersonal Styles and Group Development;* Bennis and Shepard, "A Theory of Group Development"; Bales and Strodtbeck, "Phases in Group Problem Solving"; Yalom, *The Study and Practice of Group Psychotherapy.*

fourth phase). But it is not as simple as that, because (1) the models of time spans presented in the table outline the development of successful groups, not of those that become rigidified in a basic assumption that prevents development; and (2) the process described is fraught with conflict—finding a balance between the personal needs of each member and the needs of the group as a whole involves great strains for all. (Bennis and Shepard construe it as a Hegelian dialectic—thesis, antithesis, synthesis.) It is clear that groups cannot skip the earlier (perhaps more comfortable, but unproductive) stages in group evolution. The capacity for production has its price.

iv   Evaluation   It is immediately clear that the theories of group development offer only a few sketchy predictions about how central issues will take shape in the evolution of a small group. (And there *are* central issues—many groups have been observed to focus on these issues for the entire time they are together.) But the models of group development used are perhaps too specific. More inclusive research is needed to define the general processes in groups and determine when they occur.

In evaluating this and future research, the basic problem of the validity of a model or a measuring tool should always be kept in mind. The most striking aspect of research in this field is its reliance on *content-analysis techniques* for understanding various group phenomena. In using these techniques, the researcher must create what he considers to be meaningful categories of behavior to be assessed in a number of groups. The phenomena thus observed from group to group will be somewhat similar, yet there is enough looseness of terminology and of measurement methods to make crisp comparisons between any two of those models almost impossible. Some research tools provide better understanding of the *latent intention* beneath *manifest behavior,* and, of course, there are many different approaches to the material. We need greater efforts at integrating these apparently diverging schemas.

c   The "Research" Question

i   Context   The morning that any family leaves for a vacation trip, there is a flurry of activity. Everyone is doing something different —someone is hitching up the trailer, someone is writing notes to the mailman and the milkman, someone is late packing his or her suitcase and is throwing clothes together, and so on. These different kinds of activities may represent a division of labor in the family unit that is characteristic in many situations with which this family is confronted. The behavior that makes up any of these routine jobs can be called a "role."

Sociologists have long been interested in finding possible patterns of *role allocation* (assignments to separate jobs) and *role performance* (the actual behaviors performed by individuals in the group) in closed social systems like the family. Of major interest are how the necessary jobs are divided among those within a group (Does one person cook, another clear the dinner table, and another wash the dishes?); how this division is understood by the other members of the group (for example, is it understood that the mother is the one who listens to everyone's problems?); and how stable or consistent these constellations are over time (Are these divisions of jobs always changing, or do they hardly change at all?). In other words, what *place* and what responsibilities does each person have in the group? Sociologists ask: *Does every group have a unique solution to the problem of finding appropriate roles for group members, or are there generalizations that can be made about what sort of roles can be found in any group?*

ii Theory Large or small, certain things must be done to keep an organization of human energy operating. These things are done most efficiently by dividing up the jobs and assigning each individual a specialty at which he can become highly expert. In this sense a *role* is a standardized form of behavior related to the performance of a necessary social function. In a small tribe or community there is the medicine man or physician, there is the expert weapons maker or blacksmith, the shaman or pastor, and so on. If the town doctor dies, someone else must be found to fill his place or, more correctly, to fulfill his social function. Each doctor has a somewhat different personality, but the abstract idea of healer is common to them all.

More recently the emphasis has been placed on how the personalities of group members affect the way that roles are performed and how individual needs are met by certain divisions of roles. For example, the classical example of the different functions that go to make up a social system defined the parts in terms of their tasks and thus ignored completely the important contribution of the people who maintain the cohesive interrelationships between all those parts—such as, in the examples used above, the women.

This fundamental distinction between orientation toward a *task* versus orientation toward *social and emotional (cohesive) issues* was first made by Talcott Parsons and Robert F. Bales in *Family, Socialization, and Interaction Process* (1955). This classic work is best known for presenting a basic pattern in the family— the *instrumental husband* and the *expressive wife*. The husband and father characteristically deals with the outside world in terms of tasks to be performed in order to support the family; the wife and mother has her place in the home where she facilitates the expression and fulfillment of emotional needs. By analyzing the family this way, Parsons and Bales unintentionally rigidified our view of what comprised sex-role stereotypes. (See Unit 13.) Actually their ideas about these divisions were not derived originally from observations of the family but from observations of small groups, where the filling of these functions was not rigidly determined by sex-role identification. Certainly many instances bear their findings out: business groups are notorious for ignoring social-emotional interaction in an attempt to concentrate on the task, and there are numerous women's groups noted for their inability (and lack of desire) to "get anything done," while they spend all their time interacting at a social-emotional level. But our *stereotypes* about these distinctions are stronger than the actual behavior in naturally occurring groups. What is certain is that a successful group must have developed both of these internal orientations (the instrumental and the expressive) to a high degree.

The concept of the *instrumental-expressive dichotomy* was derived not from the deductive analysis of the needs of a social system characteristic of earlier theoretical work, but through infer-

Group activity. Identify the patterned role-behaviors in this scene of group activity and decide *why* each individual has taken such activity upon himself or herself.

ences made from the observations of interaction patterns in small groups (inductive method). Bales' first attempts along these lines grew out of many hours observing meetings of the local chapters of Alcoholics Anonymous. From these experiences he constructed the method of *interaction process analysis,* a set of categories for scoring group interactions. Raters can observe an ongoing group from behind a one-way mirror and encode every statement made by each member into specific categories. Members of any group have different average *profiles* from each other, one way of defining their different roles in the group.

The idea that groups might have different specialists for the instrumental and expressive functions came directly from the research of Parsons and Bales. Thus there is a task (or instrumental) leader in a group who might seem the most dominant; he talks more and puts most pressure toward working on the job at hand. There is also a social-emotional (or expressive) leader, who probably doesn't talk as much but directs many of his or her statements toward the feelings of the group and its members and toward interpersonal problems and their resolution. There may be other leaders who fulfill valuable functions for the group and become foci for certain aspects of group interaction. There may be other *role specialists* in the group—persons who are highly defined, that is, their behavior is consistent and clear, and they fulfill some of the needs of the group. An example is the *scapegoat,* a person who elicits and submits to an inordinate amount of aggressive hostile energy from the other members. His existence allows these destructive energies to be channeled off in one direction, thus relieving a threat to the solidarity of the group as a whole. And the person who becomes the scapegoat might need to feel rejected or guilty for some reason fundamental to his own personality. In this case, as in others, the group leader or the group itself must be careful to check what it is doing; otherwise, overly severe or destructive experiences may result, as the earlier discussion of group casualties indicates.

iii Research (Methodology)   Researchers in this field are confronted with tremendous difficulties. Seldom are roles clearly defined in a group. One of the reasons is the sheer complexity of interpersonal relationships. A group of three has three different possible dyadic relationships, a group of 10 has 45. The formula is $n (n - 1)/2$. Yet there are special interrelationships involving triads and the like that increase the number of potential forms of interaction within the group fantastically. Another factor that increases the number of possible forms is variation in the *level of interaction—* many communications are carried on at subtle, latent, nonmanifest levels of interaction, and some are fully clear and conscious. People may relate to each other at a number of different levels with each statement or gesture they make. Taking these extra factors into account is a challenge to any research.

In his recent book *Personality and Interpersonal Behavior* (1970) Robert F. Bales reports a major program of research spanning a number of years. The main study involved several small groups whose members filled out numerous ratings of each other, while judges behind a one-way mirror observed the behavior and filled out other sets of ratings. Bales distinguished hundreds of variables taken from studies of personality, psychopathology, and group behavior.

The method for evaluating all these data was *factor analysis,* an elegant means for obtaining important independent dimensions, or clusters of correlated variables, from observed behavior. Bales found three major independent dimensions from his data. These can be visualized together as a cube called the *group space:*

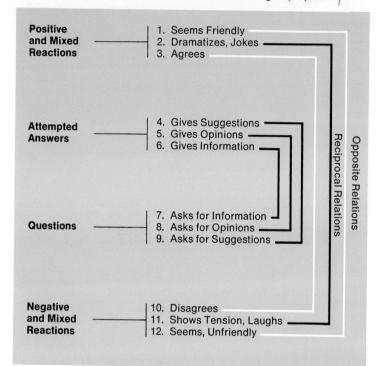

Positive and Mixed Reactions	1. Seems Friendly 2. Dramatizes, Jokes 3. Agrees
Attempted Answers	4. Gives Suggestions 5. Gives Opinions 6. Gives Information
Questions	7. Asks for Information 8. Asks for Opinions 9. Asks for Suggestions
Negative and Mixed Reactions	10. Disagrees 11. Shows Tension, Laughs 12. Seems, Unfriendly

Opposite Relations
Reciprocal Relations

Model 2. A Set of Categories for the Observance of Small Groups in Interaction. The black lines indicate reciprocal relations; the white lines indicate opposite relations. The categories are those of Bales' interaction process analysis. The "acts" or simple statements can be stored for each member in the group and a "profile" obtained to describe the extent and nature of each member's participation in the group. (Source: Adapted from Bales, *Personality and Interpersonal Behavior*)

Scapegoating? The concept of scapegoat comes from an ancient custom described in the Book of Leviticus in the Old Testament:
"And Aaron shall lay both his hands upon the head of the live goat, and confess over him all the iniquities of the children of Israel, and all their transgressions in all their sins, putting them upon the head of the goat, and shall send him away by the hand of a fit man into the wilderness."

1. *U-D or Upward-Downward: Dominance.* Dominant group members (*U*) may have spoken more than others, be seen as particularly influential in the group, or have been the first to emerge in group discussions or events. Submissive group members (*D*) may have been less involved in discussions.

2. *P-N or Positive-Negative: Affective Style or Likeability.* Supportive and relatively uncritical group members (*P*) may have expressed liking for other members; they seem warm and friendly. Critical group members (*N*) may have been more likely to confront others and less likely to accept without question what others say; they seem unfriendly to others.

3. *F-B or Forward-Backward: Task Orientation.* Task-oriented and instrumental group members (*F*) may support decisions or goals of the group members and activity toward those goals; they tend to give mostly opinion or analysis. Expressive group members (*B*) may express disagreement with the decisions and tasks decided upon by the group or may favor goals unlike those favored by the group leader or other group members; they do not analyze but, rather, express feelings.

Thus there are 27 different places in the group space formed by combinations of these factors: *U, U* plus *F* or *UF, U* plus

N plus F or UNF, and so on, including the center of the space, which is called "average."

To find out where one group member thinks the place of another is in the group space, he answers 52 questions about that person. Two examples are: "Does he seem able to give a lot of affection?" (*Yes* indicates the person rated is *P; No* indicates he is *N*); "Does he seem to be very acceptant of authority?" (*Yes* indicates the person rated is *DF*; *No* indicates *UB*). By adding up the indications from all these questions, one can derive a summary of where he feels another should be in the group space. By averaging all the ratings of a single person by the other group members, one can find a rough consensus for where that person is in that group. When we do this averaging for all members, we have a completed group space.

An example of the ratings from an actual group appears in Model 3. It is important to study this model closely to get an idea of what this group constellation might look like in three dimensions. Each person has a place in the group space, and he is related or is not related to others by *coalition relationships* (indicated by the lines in Model 3), which were determined by finding how close the individuals were to each other in the group space. The idea behind coalitions is that people who are similar in the group will have similar places in the group space; they will also have similar interests and will pursue these interests in the same way. The most dominant member of a coalition (in the case diagrammed in Model 3, Arthur heads up a large subgroup within the group) will be relied on for direction in pursuing these interests. Analysis of coalitions helps us to see how resources are shared to determine the outcome of group decisions and events. In Model 3 there is one major coalition and two minor ones. The Phil-Rick-Steve triad is very important because it is so tightly knit and because it controls the most dominant (*U*) sector of the group. Yet this triad is Type *UPB*: "Toward Emotional Supportiveness and Warmth." The triad uses its power to give and arouse affection in the rest of the group. The major coalition nearly monopolizes the *DPF* part of the group space, described by Bales as

Type DPF: Toward Salvation Through Love.
The member located in the downward-positive-forward part of the group space by his fellow members seems friendly and submissive, and at the same time, task- and value-oriented. He is ready to follow and obey, ready to confess wrongs and conform. He is respectful, loving, gentle, idealistic, and altruistic. In the realization of his own values he seems to be trying to move toward salvation of some kind, religious or social, or perhaps interpersonal, through the giving and receiving of love. "There are no human problems that love cannot solve."

Also interesting are the few *isolates* in the group space—David (the group leader), Gayle, Rufus, and Anne. From her place in the space, Anne would be described as Type *DNG*: "Toward Failure and Withdrawal." She is passively alienated, unfriendly, cynical, and discouraged. Indeed, she was the scapegoat for this group, a role that she sets for herself by her behavior. Bales has used the

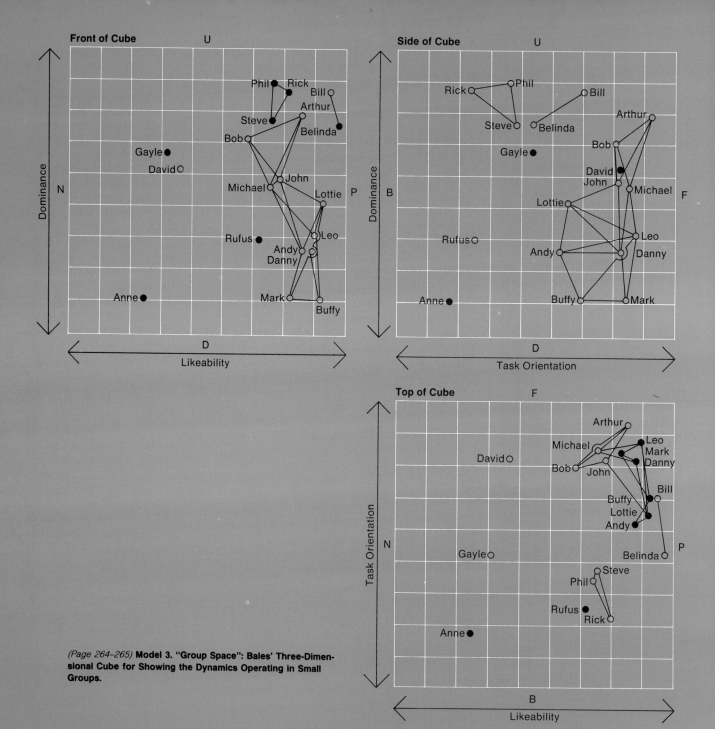

(Page 264–265) **Model 3. "Group Space": Bales' Three-Dimensional Cube for Showing the Dynamics Operating in Small Groups.**

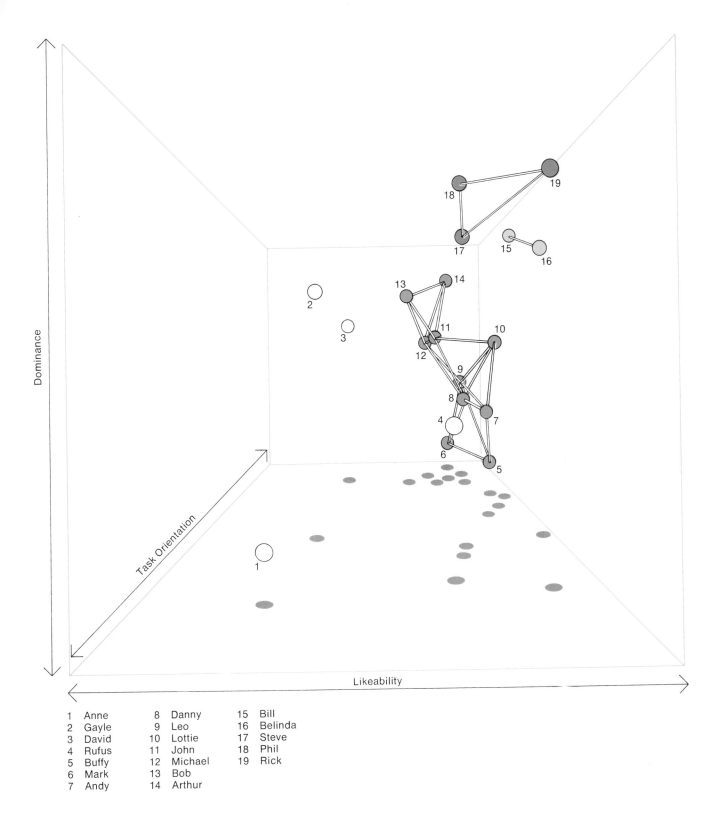

1	Anne	8	Danny	15	Bill
2	Gayle	9	Leo	16	Belinda
3	David	10	Lottie	17	Steve
4	Rufus	11	John	18	Phil
5	Buffy	12	Michael	19	Rick
6	Mark	13	Bob		
7	Andy	14	Arthur		

Dominance

Task Orientation

Likeability

(Page 264–265) **Model 3. "Group Space": Bales' Three-Dimensional Cube for Showing the Dynamics Operating in Small Groups.** The model depicts the "group space" for an actual intentional psychological group of 19 members—five females and 14 males, with David the leader. The "group space" is depicted two-dimensionally from three viewpoints (front, side, top) on page 264 and three-dimensionally on page 265. Each group participant is rated by observers and group members along three social dimensions: dominance, likeability, and task orientation. As a result of these ratings, each person can be shown to occupy a unique position in terms of the three-dimensional space defined by the intersection of these dimensions. This space, then, is essentially a cube, and each person occupies a unique position in the cube. Each person is represented in the model by a ball or circle suspended in space. In the front view the ball indicates "located backward," the circle "located forward." In the side view the ball indicates "located negative," the circle "located positive." In the top view the ball indicates "located downward," the circle "located upward." It is further possible to measure quantitatively the interactions between individuals. These interactions are seen to be patterned—that is, certain individuals interact more frequently with each other than they do with other individuals. Those persons who consistently interact with each other more frequently than they do with other group members are shown in the figure by connecting them together with "sticks." Individuals so connected may be said to belong to "subgroups" of the larger group. An inspection of the figure will show that there are two phenomena indicated: (1) clusters of individuals who occupy closely adjoining space (and therefore are operating in a very similar manner in the group), and (2) clusters of individuals connected by "sticks" (and who thus form subgroups defined in terms of the frequency of their interaction with each other). There are three such subgroups or "coalitions"—one having two members, one having three members, and one having 10 members. There are also four individuals (Anne, Gayle, David, and Rufus) who are "loners" or "isolates" within the group; that is, they are not members of any subgroup. One of these persons is the group leader. Not surprisingly, another of these persons turned out to be the group scapegoat. (Source: Adapted from Bales, *Personality and Interpersonal Behavior*)

group space in the analysis of different kinds of groups and found the same general group space profile for each.

iv Evaluation Clearly this research has gone far beyond the theory of roles within groups presented earlier. The research has generated more data than the theory can deal with readily—precise mathematical measurement of each member's place in the group space and coalitions within the group. This new wealth of data is partly due to the approach. Bales carefully rejected all the previous a priori conceptions of what roles there *ought* to be in a group system and decided to extract the key factors through empirical observation. Of course, the data were based on the judgments of group members and observers who might have had their own biased preconceptions, but the large number of variables serves to counteract this somewhat. The technique of factor analysis is an exceptionally good one for organizing large amounts of data. However, it has two major problems. First, if the whole evaluation process were run through again, changes in a number of correlations might change the position of the factors considerably, or even totally, thus requiring a new conception of the group space. Second, in the end it is the researcher who labels his own factors, thus adding an element of unavoidable nonobjective interpretation.

The Bales instrumentation represents a third generation in *psychometrics*. The first generation used questionnaires that had what is called high "face validity": to find out if someone is dominant, one simply asks the person and his or her friends, "Is this person dominant?" This obvious approach was often found to be unreliable. (The answer will change from time to time, and various friends will give various answers.) The second generation was an empirical approach that used carefully tested items for assessment of the unknown variable but was lacking in face validity. For example, two important items on the Terman-Miles scale for rating masculinity-femininity are relative liking for artichokes and preference for George Washington versus Abraham Lincoln. Such standards may not make sense, but they seem to work. The third generation brings *face validity, internal reliability,* and *replicability* together so that the measures make sense and work well—clearly an important step in this whole area.

By purposefully rejecting *role labels* (such as scapegoat, idol, seducer, joker, hatchet man) in favor of profiles of actually observed interactive behavior, Bales destroys common illusions about group roles and exposes the great difficulty of thoroughly understanding what roles there are in groups, how they are assigned, and how they are similar from group to group.

3 Overview

The theory and research presented in this unit do not represent the majority of work in this field. Most studies take place in experimental laboratories, involve groups that meet only once or only a few times, and compare group sizes of two and three to perhaps as many as seven or eight. Furthermore, they use complex instructions for analyzing communications patterns in different sorts of groups and such group phenomena as *brainstorming* (the production of more alternative solutions to a problem in the group setting than when individuals work on it alone), the *risky shift* (the incorporation in group decisions of more risk than any of the individual members would be willing to take by themselves), or *conformity to group pressure* (agreeing with the wrong answer to a problem when it is a group norm).

The studies chosen for discussion in this unit were intended to be more inclusive. The sizes of groups employed vary more and are larger than those usually studied in the laboratory. Most are *naturally occurring groups* even if they are deliberately formed and have an intentional psychological focus. The theories employed are far more comprehensive, touching upon the essential ideas in the field of sociology. Small groups have been an exciting testing ground for ideas about all sizes of social systems—how roles are allocated within groups, how they develop over time, and what characterizes destructive situations.

The price paid for the greater relevance and magnitude of such theory and research is the loss of a certain amount of rigor in experimental control. The main instruments of these field studies have been interpretive observations, clinical interviews, content analysis of statements, and factor analysis, and all these depend a great deal on the researcher's professional judgment. From a methodological point of view, these methods are far less reliable than such techniques as blips on a counter or self-ratings on a scale from 1 to 9 supplied by the subject, but it is hard to know which approach will in the long run lead to more understanding of small groups.

A unified theory of small groups has not yet emerged. In some cases, notably Bales' recent work, the abundant data now available have outstripped existing theories and have opened up exciting possibilities for further investigation and insight. We need now to develop a comprehensive theory sufficient to explain our wealth of actual observations of the behavior characteristic of interactions in small groups.

D   LOOKING AHEAD

1   Interview:
Robert F. Bales

Robert F. Bales, professor of social relations and psychology at Harvard University, is well-known for his studies of small groups. His books include *Interaction Process Analysis*, *Working Papers in Theory of Action* (with Parsons and Shils), *Family, Socialization, and Interaction Process* (with Parsons), and *Personality and Interpersonal Behavior*. He is now dealing with the training of observers in the study of natural social interaction.

DPG   *Would you briefly describe your early work with Alcoholics Anonymous groups and what the study of small groups was like then?*

BALES   There was no field called the study of small groups at that time. There was no recognition that there might be a huge field of study that cut across practically all of social life. It was not really recognized that therapy groups had any resemblance to task groups in industry, that groups formed for educational purposes, such as classroom groups, were anything like therapy groups, and so on.

When I first heard of Alcoholics Anonymous, I was much impressed with their apparent therapeutic success. I got acquainted with the members of the local group. They kindly invited me to their meetings, and I attended for some period and talked with members after the meetings. Then at a certain point, like a dutiful sociological researcher, I brought a pad of paper and started taking notes on the behavior in the groups. This made the members a little nervous, and I had to discontinue, but I had found my problem—how to describe social interaction. I have been working on observation methods ever since.

I became convinced that whatever it was Alcoholics Anonymous was able to do was done in interaction between the ''sponsor,'' as he was called, and the alcoholic, that somehow you should be able to see more and understand better what was happening in the concrete interaction of individuals with each other. So I guess from

the first my interest in groups has centered around an interest in social interaction. I have never been very well satisfied with a treatment of group behavior or characteristics that glossed over differences between individuals or that didn't deal with phenomena at the interaction level. My motivation in studying groups and studying social interaction all this time has been a concern for arriving at an understanding of what concepts ordinarily used in sociology and psychology mean when transferred to the interaction level. Many of our concepts in sociology and psychology are not explicitly reduced to the interaction level but are anchored at a level of generalization and abstraction somewhat above interaction. They cause a certain amount of discomfort in me simply because of their lack of semantic clarity.

DPG   *How do you think that such efforts have led towards a theory of small groups? Do you think that there really is a theory of small groups?*

BALES   Yes. I think that there are a number of different theories operating at different semantic levels. For example, in group therapy we know that a lot of therapists work from essentially a psychoanalytic point of view that really has its clearest application to the dynamic structure of the individual personality and to the relationship of the individual to the therapist. This point of view isn't particularly well fitted to the study of group phenomena in all respects. There have been many crude sorts of extensions of concepts—such as group ego, group superego, and so on—that have a clearer application at the individual level than to group characteristics, such as the division of labor that one finds among persons in a group.

Another theory, the field theory of Kurt Lewin, doesn't really deal very well, I feel, with internal dynamics of the individual personality but helps to understand what you might call the patterns of circular influence that are set up when you get a great many different behavorial elements interacting with each other—as among individuals within a small group. These kinds of circular patterns that I'm talking about are often called "group dynamics." A group dynamic effect is a kind of pattern effect that occurs when a number of people find themselves in a certain constellation that begins to move toward some outcome, such as finding a scapegoat and attacking him. But there may not be much interplay between a field of force conception, such as you find in Lewin, and a dynamic conception of personality, such as you find in psychoanalytic theory, unless you are able to relate the two semantically to each other.

DPG   *It seems that your own work with the "group space" concept has actually done that to an extent by elucidating how the entire group is made up of separate parts and where each individual fits and why.*
BALES   I believe that the "group space" concept is one that enables us to span over all of the well-known bodies of theory that potentially deal with social interaction. I've mentioned two, but there are others.

There's a new brand of group theory that goes with operant conditioning and reinforcement theory from experimental psychology. There's another brand of group theory that proceeds from sociometry, the measurement of interpersonal liking. There's another brand that proceeds from the study of leadership and has a kind of practical slant. There's another brand that is modeled after economics and considers the interchanges between individuals as if they were economic transactions. There are still other brands that are modeled after processes that go on in individual cognition. All of these bodies of theory are very difficult to relate to each other, but they do all come to a focus in the natural interactions of persons in small groups. I have an interest in theory, and I have an interest in integrating these major bodies of theory with each other. So my choice of the small group as a focus of interest is motivated in a very important way by these general theoretical interests and the possibility of making the reconciliation or tracing the relationships in detail.

DPG   *What do you think the important new work will be in groups? Maybe you could say something about what you're currently involved in.*
BALES   I'm currently involved in developing the concept that we just talked about, the idea of a "group space" and in the training of observers who are able to deal with natural social interaction. That's what I needed when I first began to study Alcoholics Anonymous. One may have a good theory, but if he's going to do much with it in the practical world, he must depend upon observation. So the observation must be something that is practical to do. I've been busy with changing and embedding my earlier method, called "interaction process analysis" in a larger way of looking at things, the theory of "group space." I'm trying to work out a way of looking at things that will be useful to practical leaders, administrators, educators, and therapists; that will enable them to improve their observation of what is going on, their understanding of it, their ability to infer from it, their ability to make decisions on what they should do next to improve their effectiveness. This really involves not only improvements in the pragmatic abilities of leaders, but it also makes necessary a better theoretical understanding upon their part as they observe.

I have a strong feeling that the important advances we're going to make in the next five or 10 years in this field will be in the synthesis of what we know in these various languages that I've mentioned earlier— the language of sociology, the language of psychoanalysis, the language of learning theory, the language of personality trait theory and so on—in being able to put these all together in practical working situations. This synthesis will mean that many kinds of groups that have not been very much studied will be studied carefully and compared with each other. There's a social movement now in the use of groups for almost every conceivable purpose—not only for therapeutic purposes, as was the case earlier, but for all kinds of hoped-for growth in human potential, for the formation of utopian communities, and for the solution of large social problems. These groups have now been added to the many traditional types of small groups we all know.

I think the many varieties of groups that we see today will quite soon be much more carefully compared with each other. This comparative study of groups may well be the matrix from which the applied social psychology of small groups will come to be effectively developed.

There now are very active movements, for example, in the field of family therapy. It has begun to develop theory from its own empirical base, and it is very relevant for group therapy, for instance. But it's hardly been put together with group therapy as yet. It's very relevant for leadership in the classroom, but it hasn't been put together with that yet.

These various fields of application seem very different from each other, and they belong in all kinds of different academic fields and in different social institutions. It's only a rather abstract point of view taken by social psychology that puts them all in the same perspective. But we need to make generalizations that apply to some extent to all small groups and to develop methods of observation that can be used in all and to develop ideas of leadership, individual development, learning, therapy, education, and so on, that also can be applied in very different concrete ways.

Unit 12

Social Interaction

1 Definition
Social interaction is the reciprocal influence that people have on one another's behavior, thoughts, and emotions through symbolic and nonsymbolic modes of expression.

2 World Context
All animals interact, and human interaction involves both biologically innate and socially acquired factors.

3 American Context
Americans have ways of interacting that are associated with their particular society and its characteristic roles. Different conventions also distinguish various subcultures within the United States.

1 Questions
Three questions about social interaction are of great interest to contemporary sociologists: (1) What do we communicate about ourselves and our feelings toward others through body language? (2) What is the function of role playing in social interaction? (3) What factors basically determine who interacts with whom and direct the course of the interaction?

2 Evidence
a The "Burning Issue" Question
Body language has been the subject of serious research by such social scientists as Roy L. Birdwhistell, Albert E. Scheflen, and Edward T. Hall. Their work suggests that the verbal and nonverbal channels of expression can reinforce or work against each other and that humans do display a sense of territoriality. But their findings have not yet been integrated into a fully developed sociological theory.
b The "Classical" Question
G. H. Mead and, more recently, Erving Goffman examined the relationships between role playing and the projection of individual identity in social interactions. Recent research has tended to confirm Goffman's dramaturgical perspective, which focuses on the complexities of social occasions themselves rather than on the psychological disposition of individual participants.
c The "Research" Question
George Homans and other social scientists have argued that the basic determinant of interaction is social exchange motivated by self-interest. This theory has been restated in mathematical terms and supported by both sociological case studies and psychological experiments.

3 Overview
Social interactions involve biologically inherited expressions as well as role playing and are based on behavior exchange.

THE PERSON IN SOCIAL INTERACTION

1. **Ego: The Person Whose Behavior in a Social Situation Is the Object Under Investigation.** Each person brings his or her own bundle of self-definitions into any social situation.

2. **Alter: The Individual(s) Ego Encounters in Social Situations.** Ego makes a choice of which "self" to present to alter.

I THINK SHE'LL BE FUN TO DATE

I THINK HE'D LIKE TO DATE ME SO, IF I ENCOURAGE HIM, I WON'T BE GOING OUT ON A LIMB.

3. **Ego's Initial Dilemma.** Ego's choice depends on what ego thinks alter's expectations are.

4. **Ego's Decision.** The choice also depends on the extent to which ego wishes to meet the expectations he or she believes alter to have.

Nonverbal interaction. Until recently social scientists have focused on spoken interaction for the most part. However, simple nonverbal gestures often convey complex, emotionally powerful statements. Here a grief-stricken American infantryman, whose friend has been killed in combat, is comforted by another soldier, while a corpsman counts out casualty tags.

B DEFINITION AND CONTEXT

1 Definition

Everyone has a general idea of what social interaction involves. People interact when they influence one another. They communicate through speech, through expressive gestures, through nonverbal sounds, through various types of behavior ("Actions speak louder than words"). Furthermore, there is a full range of influence that people exert upon each other in nonsymbolic forms. These include direct exchanges of goods and services, bodily expressions of pleasure and pain, and other modes of physical behavior.

Sociologists traditionally have emphasized the symbolic aspect of social interaction. In the words of Max Weber:

> Action is social insofar as by virtue of the subjective meaning attached to it by the acting individual (or individuals) it takes account of the behavior of others and is thereby oriented in its course. (*Economy and Society,* 1922)

More recently, Herbert Blumer has discussed social interaction:

> The term "symbolic interaction" refers of course to the peculiar and distinctive character of interaction as it takes place between human beings. The peculiarity consists in the fact that human beings interpret or "define" each other's actions instead of merely reacting to each other's actions. Their "response" is not made directly to the actions of one another, but instead is based on the meaning which they attach to such actions. Thus human interaction is mediated by the use of symbols, by interpretation, or by ascertaining the meaning of one another's actions. This mediation is equivalent to inserting a process of interpretation between stimulus and response in the case of human behavior. (*Symbolic Interactionism,* 1969)

These definitions emphasize the uniquely human aspect of social interaction. Unlike animals lower on the phylogenetic scale humans interpret the behavior of others and react to it in terms of what is believed to be its meaning. Yet not all human interaction involves such cognitive processes: Unit 3 pointed out that man shares many characteristics of lower animals, and, like them, he reacts emotionally to others in a way that is relatively direct and often independent of his interpretation of a situation. People communicate with and influence others in ways that are unintentional, unconscious, nonsymbolic, and nonverbal. Therefore, a complete definition of social interaction must include both its symbolic and nonsymbolic aspects. *Social interaction is defined as the reciprocal influence that two or more people have on one another's behavior, thoughts, and emotions through symbolic and nonsymbolic modes of expression.*

2 World Context

All animals interact. It is commonly assumed that the interaction of animals low on the phylogenetic scale is *instinctual* and *reflexive* and, as such, irrelevant to the understanding of human social interaction. Recently, however, such *ethologists* as Konrad Lorenz and Niko Tinbergen have argued that although humans interact in ways that are unique—that is, through interpretations of each other's behavior—their interaction is closer to that of other animals than they think. This observation is especially apparent in regard to *dominance, sexual behavior* and *territorial behavior.* For example, male monkeys often can be seen threatening each other and, by all indications, preparing to fight. Yet they rarely engage in outright battle, and these encounters usually end when one monkey "presents" himself to another in the female sexual position. This ritualistic mock battle serves to establish dominance. Similar bluffing behavior, with its characteristic posture, facial expression, and appropriate verbalizations, can be observed in children's playgrounds, athletic contests, neighborhood bars, and other human settings. There is even evidence that humans equate submissiveness with female sexuality, at least on an unconscious level: such derogatory terms as "get shafted" and "screw you" are employed aggressively, and sex is often equated with dominance and subordination in the fantasy life of patients in psychotherapy.

Many other parallels could be given. Robert Ardrey's speculations in *The Territorial Imperative* (1966) are now common knowledge: humans, like animals, Ardrey claims, are genetically programmed to define and defend a space or region from encroachment by other members of the species.

One implication of this view of human social interaction as partly a product of man's evolutionary heritage is that forms of *biologically determined* behavior should be common to all members of the species. In other words, dominance, sexuality, and territoriality

Tense-mouth facial gesture. This facial gesture apparently has similar meanings when exhibited by chimpanzees and humans. In both cases it involves making confident threats and is usually displayed by dominant males.

should exert a major influence on social interaction in all societies of the world. And, of course, they do: people everywhere have "pecking orders," engage in sexual intercourse and have courtship rituals, and express a sense of territory.

These aspects of interaction are associated with basic biological responses. Interactions involving man's higher processes—his ability to reason, employ symbols, and transmit information from one generation to another—tend to vary in form and content across cultures. But neither set of responses exists in isolation from the other. What and how we think helps determine what and how we feel, and vice versa. The relationship between what is *innate* (and true of people regardless of their culture) and acquired through tradition (and thus *culturally relative*) is nicely demonstrated by research on facial expressions.

Whether or not facial expressions of emotion are innate in the human species has been a topic of debate since Charles Darwin (who thought they were). After several years of research Paul Ekman and Wallace Friesen concluded ("Constants across Cultures in the Face and Emotion," 1971) that emotions such as happiness, sadness, anger, fear, surprise, and disgust are associated with distinct patterns of facial muscle contractions. These facial expressions are similar in all humans and are not culturally determined; people from New Guinea, Borneo, Brazil, and Japan could identify pictures of people from other cultures experiencing specific emotions associated with particular stories. But the way people deal with the emotions and the gestures they use to symbolize them are specific to particular cultures. Researchers have shown that some gestures do vary widely in meaning. In the United States, for example, hissing is a sign of disapproval, but in Japan it is a way of showing deference to superiors, and among Basutos a way of applauding. It would be difficult to imagine a gesture of greater disdain in America than urinating on another person but for some tribes in Africa it is a way of transferring medical and healing powers.

Although every culture is unique in many respects, all human communities share certain essential characteristics. Comparisons of various societies tend to take the similarities for granted and emphasize the differences. Indeed, the variations in language, tradition, climate, resources, level of technology, or metaphysical beliefs often create problems when members of one culture observe the customs and behavior of members of another. Nevertheless, the human condition is such that people around the globe possess similar inherent emotional dispositions that affect both the nature and the range of interactions possible between people.

All humans undergo a basic series of stages in physical and mental development. Jean Piaget has shown, as we saw in Unit 5, that the human mind develops through an orderly sequence of stages, and Noam Chomsky and other linguists have suggested that there are universals in language. As Eric Lenneberg explains in "A Biological Perspective of Language" (1964):

Although language families are so different from one another that we cannot find any historical connection between them, every language without exception is based

Faces. What emotions do you "read" on these faces?

Tooth display in humans and monkeys. The "forced" or "frozen" smile seen at cocktail parties may be traced back to its original manifestation in infrahuman primates as a mildly aggressive gesture of tooth display. At such gatherings people are generally less than fully at ease—and the best defense is a good offense.

on the same universal principle of *semantics, syntax, phonology*. All languages have words for relations, objects, feelings and qualities. . . .

People everywhere interact in similar ways because their statements are structured similarly. This is not to say, of course, that Americans and people from other lands share the same daily contexts of living or that differences in the way they interact are not important.

Anthropologist Benjamin Whorf suggested that the structure of thought is reflected in the structure of language, and that cross-cultural linguistic differences indicate differences in the way people think about and perceive the world. (See Unit 2.) In this view, language is not merely part of a culture: it is the basic set of tools that defines that culture. Language can reflect social status. For example, a Japanese writer cannot use a direct quotation without referring to the social rank of the persons he is referring to; verb endings always indicate the relative superiority of the person talking. In other languages, such as English, this is not the case.

But all people—regardless of the special categories and feelings that can be expressed in their particular language—propagate the species, join together for the common good, divide up workloads, protect themselves from outside threats, maintain internal order, and so on. To achieve these goals, all societies develop *divisions of labor* and associated *roles.* Specific groups take care of the children, supervise workers, obtain food, guard the safety of the family or the larger community, and teach the young. All of these roles are associated with basically similar forms of social interaction: mothers mother, bosses boss, teachers teach, and policemen police.

All mothers do not mother in the same way, however. Different *behavioral expectations* are associated with various roles from culture to culture. In the African country of Dahomey, for instance, an unmarried woman who has become rich and wishes to acquire an heir may act as a "husband," "marry" another woman, give sexual rights to a favored male, and officially be considered "father" to the resulting children. Thus it is difficult to refer to the roles of other societies in the terms that describe the roles in Western cultures. *Ethnocentrism* must always be avoided in such discussions.

3   American Context

Americans have ways of interacting that are associated with their particular society and its characteristic roles, and, like most people, they tend to assume that their way is right. In what has been called the "Ugly American" phenomenon, diplomats often defeat their purpose by unintentionally alienating the people they are sent to help: they mean well, but because they fail to learn the customs of the countries to which they have been assigned, they are unable to communicate with the people there.

Learning the language of another culture means more than translating words. It means learning how to think and feel the way the people of the culture do. It also means observing the custom-

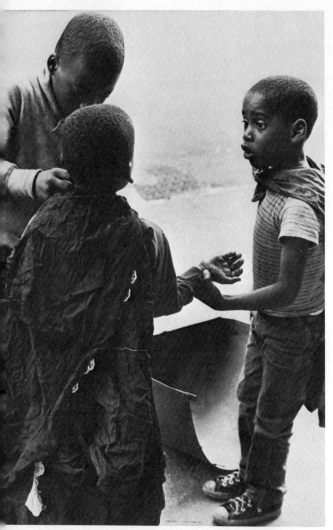

Body language speaks at least as loud as words. Like many aspects of black culture having to do with personal interaction, handslapping as an expression of joyous participation in another person's experience is spreading into the dominant white culture. This tendency is particularly noticeable among athletes.

ary rules about *interpersonal space*. The same American who is viewed as aloof by a Latin American can be seen as pushy by a European, simply because he has stood too far away from the first and too close to the second.

Similar variations characterize subgroups within the United States. There is no such thing as a "typical American": social classes observe different conventions of behavior from each other, as do various ethnic and regional groups. Groups of people who share a common subculture have certain customary modes of social interaction, even different conventions of body language. "Hippies," jazz musicians, young radicals, homosexuals and other counterculture groups each have their own language. So do broader categories, such as women, mothers, teenagers, teachers, and doctors.

In its general sense, *role* refers to relatively standard patterns of interaction. The concept is associated not only with an individual's formal position in a social organization (he can be a son, a husband, an accountant, vice president of the club, and so on), but also with his informal positions in social interactions (he might act as a "clown," a hard worker, a follower, and so on), and with his relationship to more abstract societal values (as a patriot, a rebel, an honest man, and so on). Some roles, such as those associated with age, sex, race and ethnicity, are determined by circumstances of birth in conjunction with characteristics imputed to those circumstances by a given culture. Others (husband, musician, "ladies' man") are aspired to by the individual. *Role labels* can denote categories as broad as American, laborer, Jew, or woman or categories as specific as "people who get colds easily."

Most people occupy many roles at the same time. For example, a Jewish-American laborer may also be a woman who gets colds easily. Not infrequently, however, some of each person's roles conflict with each other. A female Jewish-American laborer who gets colds easily would probably have a high rate of absenteeism on the job. Or a teacher who is a ladies' man on the job might find his tenure terminated.

Many roles in society are, so to speak, deliberately designed to conflict. A policeman and a thief, for example, are expected to behave antagonistically to each other; their roles prescribe it. Other roles are more ambiguous in relation to each other—a judge and a defendant, for example, or an insurance investigator and the survivor of an auto accident. Some roles are supposed to be mutually enhancing—pupils who want to learn, teachers who want to teach —but become mutually destructive instead, because the pupils are also black and poor, and the teachers are white and middle-class. Interaction among people is a highly complex process not only because of the multiplicity of roles in society, but also because of the multiplicity of roles each individual himself or herself occupies.

C QUESTIONS AND EVIDENCE

1 Questions

Three questions about social interaction are of great interest to

contemporary sociologists: (1) What do we communicate about
ourselves and our feelings toward others through body language?
(2) What is the function of role playing in social interaction? (3)
What factors basically determine who interacts with whom and direct the course of the interaction?

2   Evidence

a   The "Burning Issue" Question

i   Context   "Body language" is a hot topic in the pop culture.
People are becoming aware of the degree to which various physical gestures, postures, positions, and facial expressions communicate feelings and attitudes to others and help to create an overall
impression of the individual (who may be unaware of what he is indicating). Nonverbal exercises are a part of every aspiring actor's
training, sensitivity groups touch each other in an effort to overcome the barriers of words, and nonverbal parties are even in
vogue.

But body language is more than a fad. It is also the subject
of serious study by such social scientists as Roy L. Birdwhistell, Albert E. Scheflen, and Edward T. Hall. These men have founded the
sciences of *kinesics* ("body language" in general) and *proxemics*
(the way we handle space). They and other researchers ask: *What
are the dynamics of non-verbal communication?*

ii   Theory   A unified theory of body language does not yet exist.
Most research in the field has been confined to the descriptive
level—the how of nonverbal communication rather than the why.
Roy Birdwhistell has attempted to develop a written language to
characterize gestures: for example, the symbols

refer to an expression in which the left eye is winked, with a squint
at the corner, the nose is depressed, and the mouth is drawn
down into a pout.

Albert Scheflen divides body language into points, positions,
and presentations. *Points* are the smallest units of movement—for
example, nodding the head, blinking the eye, and waving the hand.
Positions are sequences of points, postural changes that involve at
least half the body. A *presentation* is the sum of the positions a
person employs in an encounter.

As a psychiatrist, Scheflen has been concerned with the information revealed by patients about themselves through their bodies. He has found that certain positions are associated with particular emotions in particular patients; an accurate reading of the
association between position and emotion can supply cues to
sources of psychological difficulty.

Another approach to body language is presented by the anthropologist Edward T. Hall, who founded the science of proxemics. The study of personal space is based on the assumption that:

spatial changes give a tone to a communication, accent it and at times even over-ride the spoken word. The flow and shift of distance between people when they interact with each other is part and parcel of the communication process. (*The Silent Language*, 1959)

Hall identifies four *zones of interpersonal interactions*, each one involving more distance between the subject and any other individual than the zone that precedes it: (1) intimate distance, (2) personal distance, (3) social distance, and (4) public distance. The first zone is characterized by close proximity. The second is the most common zone of informal social interaction: it allows some intimacy but within definite limits. The third zone is the distance employed by people in instrumental relationships, the space at which we talk business; status differences are especially apparent in this zone. Finally, public distance is the zone of relative impersonality: public speakers generally stand toward the end of this area. Hall defined his zones on the basis of observation of average Americans. He acknowledged, of course, that different individuals have different customary zones. As a matter of fact, it was differences in the way people from different cultures handle space that alerted him to its significance in interpersonal interaction.

Information of this sort is classificatory. Birdwhistell, Scheflen, and Hall have offered ways of breaking down and analyzing posture and interpersonal space. But to the extent that there is a theory underlying such discussions of body language, it is the one associated with ethology, which in turn relies strongly on the theory of evolution. Ethology suggests that people inherit tendencies to employ various postures and zones of interaction that, ultimately, have developed over generations through natural selection. Such an approach can hardly be considered sociological. In his book *Body Language and the Social Order* (1972), however, Scheflen suggests that the social environment consists of *contexts*—places, groups, and people that exert particular behavioral demands. Although individuals have a large repertoire of possible performances, the situations in which they find themselves reduce the range of acceptable behaviors considerably. One might say each of us is programmed from birth by our social structure and culture to behave in a limited number of predictable ways, and we perpetuate these established forms of action and interaction by teaching them to our own children. Thus the primary function of body language—like other forms of behavior—is to maintain and regulate the structure of all the social *transactions* that make up society. Interactions of this sort maintain dominance and affiliative relationships, territorial claims, and the flow of communication.

iii Research   The nonverbal language described by Birdwhistell is the result of his analysis of thousands of films of human interaction. Scheflen has also devoted a great deal of attention to films —in his case, of psychiatric sessions—and warns against overinterpretation. He argues that movements have meaning only in context. It is impossible to identify a *particular position*—crossing the legs, for example—and equate it with a *psychological disposition*, such as sexual frigidity. Nevertheless, the meaning of some

Bodies. What emotions do the various postures express?

gestures is amazingly transparent. Scheflen himself has cited numerous incidents where the psychiatrist interprets messages from a patient's body that are different from those the patient verbalizes. Such evidence is largely anecdotal, however.

One study tested the anecdotal evidence experimentally. Paul Ekman and Wallace Friesen shot films of a large number of interviews of patients in a psychiatric hospital, and selected a small number of incidents where patients attempted to deceive themselves or their psychiatrist—for example, by acting happy and contented when they were really distressed. They then showed different silent films of these patients to three groups of observers. The first group saw only the faces of the patients; the second group saw their bodies from the neck down; the third group saw both faces and bodies. The observers were asked to describe their impressions of each patient.

In "Non-Verbal Behavior in Psychotherapy Research" (1968) Ekman and Friesen reported that the latter two groups were able to identify accurately the emotional state of patients who were attempting to act differently from the way they felt. Observers who saw only the faces were unable to describe the patients' real emotional states, and observers who saw the bodies only were more accurate than observers who saw both faces and bodies. The researchers concluded that people who attempt to deceive pay more attention to controlling facial *cues* than cues associated with their bodies. Therefore, their bodies are more apt to give them away.

There is also a growing body of experimental evidence in support of the concept of human territoriality. In *Interpersonal Space* (1969) Robert Sommer described a series of experiments conducted by Nancy Russo. In one aspect of the experiments, when Russo sat next to people who were studying in a library and then moved increasingly closer to them, she found that the students fidgeted, moved away, or ultimately got up to leave. Only one of 80 students verbally requested her to move. In most cases a social interaction had transpired without a word being spoken.

It has also been shown that interpersonal zones are open to *ethnic modification.* O. M. Watson and T. D. Graves observed Arabs and Americans interacting in a laboratory and found that Arabs looked more directly at one another, sat close together, touched more, and talked more loudly than Americans ("Quantitative Research in Proxemic Behavior," 1966). In another study, "Body Buffer Zone in Violent Prisoners" (1970), Augustus F. Kinzel asked prisoners in a federal penitentiary to stand in the center of an empty room while a research assistant approached them slowly. Each of them was asked to say "Stop" when he became uncomfortable. Kinzel found that each man had a *zone of comfort*—Kinzel termed this his "body buffer zone"—and that there was a great difference between the zones of violent and nonviolent criminals: the former became uncomfortable much sooner than the latter. Kinzel concluded that this greater discomfort may be due to overcrowding in the ghettos and the failure of police to understand the significance of body zones. The existence of such zones may also suggest one reason why a high incidence of aggression is associated with crowded living conditions.

(In humans territoriality is associated with status as well as dominance.) Status reveals itself in many ways. Some are obvious—people of high status are usually seated at the head of the table, above other guests—but others are not. One interesting study focused on behavior in a business situation. Sound films with two actors playing the roles of executive and visitor showed one man knocking at the office door of another who was sitting at his desk, then entering the office, and finally approaching the other. The spectators could easily assess the relative status of each man. When the visitor stopped just inside the door, he was thought to have low status; when he walked half way up to the desk, he was seen as having more status; and when he walked directly up to the desk, he was assigned the highest status of all.

iv Evaluation (Careful research suggests that verbal and nonverbal channels of expression can reinforce each other or can work at cross purposes, with the nonverbal channel displaying a reality that the verbal channel is attempting to deny.) In general, humans have more control over what they say than how they feel. Often they do not want to admit (or perhaps even recognize) how they feel. In sociologist Erving Goffman's terms, people learn more about others by the messages they "give off" than the messages they "give." (Lie detector tests work on this principle.) Subjects are asked questions while their physical responses are measured, on the assumption that if they are lying they will react with heightened physiological activity to a question that would ordinarily not be associated with an emotional response.

Recent studies also support the general claim that humans have a sense of territory. Such evidence provides some confirmation for the ethological perspective, but the fact that there are individual differences in reactions to invasions of territory suggests that culture also has an effect.) Ethology has important implications for the study of society. Territoriality is associated with dominance and aggression: wars are fought for land; the goal of the average American is to possess property, to have a house of his own; juvenile gangs in large cities stake out "turfs" and protect them in much the same way as primate animals; executives define their status by the size of their office. Until recently such findings were not joined together in any integrated sociological theory. But Scheflen has begun to develop a framework that includes interpersonal acts as small as winks, arm movements, and nods and sociological phenomena as large as institutional change.

b The "Classical" Question

i Context Children often attempt to act like grownups. They play "house" and make-believe they are mommies and daddies; they play school and make-believe they are teachers; and they play doctor and nurse. Their ability to project themselves into the character of someone else almost makes them "become" the people they imitate. With age such make-believe declines, but humans never lose their tendency to act (although they are not always ready to admit it). Each of us "comes on" to others as we would like to have them see us. What we say has the dual purpose of communicating information and of establishing ourselves as a particular kind of person—"good guy," man of the world, glamour girl,

People in public interaction. What images of themselves do you think these persons are trying to project? What "personality traits" do you ascribe to them?

intellectual, socialite, Jewish mother, or Catholic martyr. In short, we behave like actors; we play roles.

Many sociologists have noted the parallel between social interaction and theatrical performance. In the process of *socialization* children learn to play appropriate roles. Parents and other socializing agents are the directors. The role playing of children is a rehearsal. The situations they invent, and which later confront them in reality, involve props and a supporting cast. The observers are the audience. Because the parallel is so compelling, sociologists ask: *What are the functions of role playing in social interaction?*

ii Theory George Herbert Mead, one of the founders of a school in sociology called *symbolic interactionism* (also discussed in Unit 5), held that the form of human social interaction is determined by the shared system of symbols that exist in societies. People communicate by exchanging symbolic *gestures* (acts that elicit the same response from the actor and his audience), especially those contained in language. Mead was particularly concerned with the relationship between social interaction and development of the *self*. He argued that the only way people can know themselves is by "taking the role of another" and viewing their behavior from the other's vantage point. (*Mind, Self and Society,* 1934) People are able to know themselves only when they can act toward themselves in the way that other people act toward them.

In stressing symbols, Mead focused on the aspects of interaction that are uniquely human. Because humans can take the role of others, they are able to "put on acts." In the words of Robert Park, a distinguished colleague of Mead,

> One thing that distinguished man from the lower animals is the fact that he has a conception of himself, and once he has defined his role he strives to live up to it. He not only acts, but he dresses the part, assumes quite spontaneously all the manners and attitudes that he conceives as proper to it. Often enough it happens that he is not fitted to the role which he chooses to play. In any case, it is an effort for any of us to maintain the attitudes which we assume; all the more difficult when the world refuses to take us at our own estimates of ourselves. Being actors, we are consciously or unconsciously seeking recognition, and failure to win it is, at the very least, a depressing, often a heartbreaking, experience. This is one of the reasons why we all eventually conform to the accepted models and conceive ourselves in some one or other of the conventional patterns. ("Human Nature and Collective Behavior," 1927)

The contemporary sociologist who has most clearly employed the metaphor of the theater in his analysis of social interaction is Erving Goffman. As he explained in *The Presentation of Self in Everyday Life* (1959):

> The perspective employed . . . is that of the theatrical performance; the principles derived are dramaturgical ones. I shall consider the way in which the individual in

Self and others. By drawing and cutting out life-size figures of themselves, children in an experimental kindergarten can learn to distinguish self from others. They can consider their own paper self-images in relation to the images of their peers.

ordinary work situations presents himself and his activity to others, the ways in which he guides and controls the impressions they form of him, and the kinds of things he may and may not do while sustaining his performance before them.

Goffman suggests that although social interaction involves the communication of factual information, it also serves to convey information about the *projected identity* of the individuals who are interacting—their evaluation of one another and their definition of the situation. The form of social interaction is governed by an informal but powerful system that prescribes particular *performances* on particular *occasions,* and Goffman's analysis of social interaction focuses on those occasions rather than on the individual. He is concerned with identifying ritualistic regularities: as he put it in *Interaction Ritual* (1967), "Not, then, men and their moments. Rather moments and their men."

iii Research (Survey) Goffman's main contribution has been his organization of his ideas around a *dramaturgical perspective.* His research methodology is thus one of observation. Goffman argues by example, and although his analyses are often ingenious and intuitively powerful, they are vulnerable to defeat by counterexample. Nevertheless, specific research studies have tested a number of his ideas and in general supported them.

It is quite obvious that if you ask a person to make a favorable impression, he will exaggerate his attractive qualities. And, indeed, in their article "Some Determinants of Reactions to Being Approved or Disapproved as a Person" (1962), E. E. Jones, K. J. Gergen and K. E. Davis confirmed that the people who were instructed to make a good impression exaggerated their favorable qualities much more than people who were instructed to act "naturally." It also seems clear that people will exaggerate less about themselves when their "act" can be checked than when it cannot. K. J. Gergen and Barbara Wishnov found that people who anticipated further interaction with a partner were more honest about themselves than those who did not ("Others' Self-Evaluation and Interaction Anticipation as Determinants of Self-Presentation," 1965). And researchers also established that when a person's falsely favorable act was received with approval, the actor adjusted his *self-concept* and was ready to believe the best about himself.

These findings support a central assumption of symbolic interaction theory—that what people think of themselves depends on the reflected appraisals of others. Frank Miyamoto and Sanford Dornbusch tested this idea further. They asked each member of ten groups to (1) rate themselves on intelligence, self-confidence, physical attractiveness, and likableness, (2) rate all other members on the traits, and (3) attempt to predict the ratings of others. If Mead is correct, there should be (1) a high correspondence between self-ratings and ratings of others and (2) a higher correspondence between the perceived (predicted) ratings of others and self-ratings. In "A Test of Interactionists' Hypotheses of Self-Conception" (1956), Miyamoto and Dornbusch reported that such was in fact the case.

There are undoubtedly many senses in which man is an actor. But is he more? In separating the self, actor, or individual be-hind the mask from the roles he plays, role theory implies he is. Research by C. W. Backman and P. W. Secord ("The Self and Role Selection," 1968) clarified the relationship between the roles a person plays and his identity. They hypothesized that role categories determine people's behavior and thereby help shape their self-concepts; this relationship they called a *fashioning effect*. They also, however, hypothesized that the reverse can occur: peo-ple choose roles that allow them to behave in a manner consistent with their self-concept *(role selection)* or adapt roles to their style of interaction *(role portrayal)*. Three experiments provided evidence for all three processes. College students preferred occupations and marital roles most consistent with their personality characteristics and self-concepts (role selection). Once they had selected roles, however, their self-concepts became more in accord with the im-ages associated with the roles they had selected (fashioning ef-fect). And once they had chosen a particular role (such as wife), subjects chose the *style* (such as companion or partner or wife-mother) that was most consistent with other aspects of their self-concept (role portrayal).

iv Evaluation The dramaturgical perspective supplies a valid characterization of social interaction. Man is, at least in part, an ac-tor because the process of socialization involves conforming to the roles of a society. And "all the world's a stage" inasmuch as each society contains roles that are independent of the people who oc-cupy them.

Almost all sociological theories accept the concept of role and view social interaction as role performance. But theorists em-ploy the concept of role in different ways. Such grand theorists as Talcott Parsons and Robert K. Merton view a role as a set of ex-pectations associated with a particular status or position in the so-cial structure. Social behavior is mainly conforming to the expecta-tion of particular roles. Other theorists suggest that this view is too mechanistic. For example, in *Identities and Interactions* (1966) George McCall and J. L. Simmons argue that:

> To the role theorist [like Parsons and Merton], the ar-chetypical role is that seen in ritual or classic drama, in which every line and every gesture of each actor is rigidly specified in the sacred script. In our view, the archetypical role is more nearly that seen in improvised theater—which performs extemporaneously within broad outlines of the sketches and of the characters assumed.

The dramaturgical perspective has also been criticized for portraying human beings as manipulative or "phony." But this criti-cism may result from an incorrect interpretation of the perspective. S. L. Messinger, Harold Sampson, and R. D. Towne interviewed mental patients and discovered that they forced themselves to act "normal," even though they knew they felt otherwise, in order to speed up their release from the institution. The patients were able to recognize the times when they were "on"—when they were act-ing—and could distinguish such moments from those when they were "natural." They viewed being "on" as an interruption of their

Karateka. There are two sets of questions we must ask to under-stand the behavior of this karateka fully. The first set involves psy-chological issues relating to her as an individual: what personality traits, fears, goals, and so on led her to engage in karate role-behavior? The second set concerns her enactment of the role-behavior as it is culturally defined. How does *she* (as a unique individual) enact the expected behavior? In what ways is her inter-pretation of the role-behavior unique? In what ways does it conform to what is culturally prescribed?

Multiple statuses are involved at one time but one pair predominates in structuring this interaction—the ceremony in 1969 in which Queen Elizabeth II invested her son Prince Charles as Prince of Wales. The ceremony is a survival of the feudal system under which England was once governed. Following the investiture, Charles' first act was to offer his allegiance to the Queen—his mother.

normal perspective. The researchers concluded that:

> In viewing "life as a theater" the dramaturgic analyst does not present us with a model of the actor's consciousness; *he is not suggesting that this is the way his subjects understand the world.* Instead, the dramaturgic analyst involves the theatrical model as a device, a tool, to permit *him* to focus attention on the consequences of the actor's activities for others' perceptions of the actor.
>
> In other words people need not self-consciously put on acts or play roles, in order to qualify as actors. ("Life as Theater," 1970)

The dramaturgical perspective also has been criticized for viewing man as a chameleon who changes his appearance to meet each new encounter. But psychologist K. J. Gergen has argued that the assumption that people have one basic underlying self-conception or identity is incorrect. The many masks that people wear reflect their many identities, and, contrary to popular belief, it is neither normal, nor psychologically healthy to have one firm unified identity. As Gergen put it in "Multiple Identity" (1972), "Perhaps our true concern should be aroused when we become too comfortable with ourselves, too fixed in a specific identity."

c The "Research" Question

i Context Whenever people gather together—at a cocktail party, a business convention, or a political rally, in the office, or at someone's home—some of them pair off while others remain isolated. Some cluster into groups, and others wander from person to person. Some individuals seem to dominate and attract everyone's attention; others remain inconspicuous or even totally withdrawn. As he or she leaves, one person may comment, "Now you know why I dreaded coming here in the first place"; another will proclaim, "Now you know why I have such wonderful feelings about this group."

What causes some human relationships to work and others to fail? What determines the direction of a conversation? Why do some people seem to have advantages over others in social situations? Why are some people difficult to talk to while others "make you feel as if you've known them for years"? Sociologists seek to throw light on these questions when they ask: *What are the key variables in human interactions?*

ii Theory The most basic determinant in one's choice of a "partner" in social interaction is *self-interest.* Although many theories do not explicitly identify self-interest as the guiding force of social interaction, most theories assume that human beings are motivated to maximize pleasure and minimize pain.

George Homans, in *Social Behavior: Its Elementary Forms* (1961), argues that the oldest theory of social behavior is one of social exchange: people interact in order to exchange material and nonmaterial goods that are of value to them. He further maintains that each alternative presented to an individual involved in an interaction contains a reward and a cost. The goal of social interaction is to maximize one's profit—be it in material goods, such as

Kitchen as ''stage.'' The dramaturgical approach to analyzing human interaction stresses the view that all interactions may be seen as taking place on identifiable ''stage settings.'' Part of understanding the interaction of the social actors (even mother and child) involves discovering the demands made upon them by the nature of the setting itself (even an untidy kitchen).

money, or nonmaterial goods such as approval, self-respect, or prestige. In Homans' formulation: profit = reward − cost.

Interaction may seem straightforward when viewed from the point of view of one person, but the process involves at least two people. And both of them are similarly motivated. What is rewarding to one may be costly to another. Therefore, social interaction involves a compromise: each gives that which is least costly to him (and most rewarding to the other) in order to receive that which is most rewarding to him (and, usually, least costly to the other). To complicate matters, people often enter interactions with unequal expectations of profit. Those who make great investments, such as in their own education, status, beauty, and expertise, have a right to expect more profit, Homans argues.

In *The Social Psychology of Groups* (1959) J. W. Thibaut and H. H. Kelley supplied a detailed model for analyzing the behavioral outcomes of social interaction. Their unit of analysis is pairs of outcomes—one for each interactant, each accompanied by a cost and gain—which can be schematized into a matrix (Figure 1). Thibaut and Kelley argue that because each interactant is motivated to maximize the reward value of his outcome, social interaction is a compromise. Both people adjust their responses until they arrive at the combination that has the largest reward value for both. Or they may jump back and forth between two sets of ''cells'' associated with respective rewards.

Although some social interactions end with one encounter, most do not. As they make each move, people worry about the next response of their partner in the interaction. The Thibaut-Kelley model is most applicable to such extended sequences. The interactants try out various combinations of outcomes until they find the one that is the most mutually rewarding.

iii   Research (Methodology)   Interactions of this sort have been studied in both sociological and psychological terms. Sociological research has generally relied on case studies of naturally occurring relationships; these are interpreted according to the principles of *behavior exchange*. Psychological research generally involves experiments in which one or more variables are manipulated, so that their effect on particular outcomes can be measured.

One of the best examples of sociological research in this area appears in Peter Blau's *The Dynamics of Bureaucracy* (1955). Blau studied 16 agents in a federal law-enforcement agency who were engaged in the highly technical work of investigating particular firms and preparing reports on the legality of their activities. Although agents are supposed to prepare reports by themselves, they often consult with one another. Blau observed and analyzed their social interaction as follows:

A consultation can be considered an exchange of values: both participants gain something, and both have to pay a price. The questioning agent is enabled to perform better than he could otherwise have done, without exposing his difficulties to his supervisor. By asking for advice, he implicitly pays his respect to the superior proficiency of his colleague. This acknowledgement of inferiority is the cost of receiving assistance. The consultant gains prestige, in return for which he is willing to devote some time to the consultation and permit it to disrupt his own work. The following remark of an agent illustrates this: "I like giving advice. It's flattering, I suppose, if you feel that others come to you for advice."

Given an equal loss of prestige, it would be in an agent's interest to seek advice from his most competent colleague. But if all agents did this, the most competent agent would have no time for his own work. Therefore, he could either refuse to give aid or increase the cost of requesting aid by exaggerating the incompetence. Blau's observations indicated that agents tended to interact with agents with whom they could negotiate an equal exchange—that is, with colleagues similar to them in competence. In this way they could reciprocate both advice and prestige.

Experimental research on social interaction has attempted to reduce the complexity of real life in order to investigate minimal social situations, stripped of everything except the reward-cost exchange. In 1956 J. B. Sidowski and his colleagues isolated two people and wired shock electrodes to them. The researchers then asked them to press one of two buttons. The purpose of the exercise was to gain as many "points" as possible. The buttons were arranged such that if both people pressed the right-hand button, person A received a shock and person B a "point." If both pressed the left-hand button, person B received a shock and person A "a point." If person A pressed the left-hand button and person B the right-hand button, both received a shock. Both received a "point" if A pushed the right-hand button and B the left-hand button.

This arrangement was designed to supply a rough test of the idea that social interaction involves an exchange between two people that results in maximum benefit. In "Reward and Punishment in a Minimal Social Situation" (1957) the researchers reported that, as predicted, after about five minutes both subjects made the choices that resulted in their greatest mutual benefit. Later experiments were similarly designed, but brought the subjects together and required them to adopt some type of *interactional strategy*—cooperation, individual initiative, or comparative responses. There have been hundreds of experiments in this tradition, which has come to be called *game theory*. Probably the most popular are those that stem from the "prisoners' dilemma," described by R. D. Luce and Howard Raiffa in *Games and Decisions* (1957):

Two suspects are taken into custody and separated. The District Attorney is certain that they are guilty of a specific crime, but he does not have adequate evidence to convict them at a trial. He points out to each prisoner that he has two alternatives: to confess to the crime the police are sure they have done, or not to confess. If they both do not confess, then the District Attorney states he will book them on some very minor trumped-up charge such as petty larceny and illegal possession of a weapon, and they would both receive minor punishments; if they both confess they will be prosecuted, but he will recommend less than the most severe sentence; but if one confesses and the other does not, then the confessor will receive lenient treatment

(Top left) **Figure 1. Thibaut and Kelley's Matrix of Act Combinations, Indicating Goodness of Outcome Values for Selected Pairs of Responses.** Thibaut and Kelley developed this kind of a matrix for the study of social interaction. The actions available to the first person in this hypothetical interaction are indicated in each vertical column by the designated value for the person of each action. Each of these actions is accompanied by a response available to the second person, also with a designated value; these accompanying responses are contained in each horizontal row. The resulting square cells are act combinations, each associated with a net "reward"—a positive or negative number—for each interactant. Because each interactant is motivated to maximize the reward value to him of an outcome, social interaction is a compromise in which both people adjust their behavior (travel through the columns and rows) until they come to the act combination that has the largest reward value for both—or jump back and forth between two sets of cells associated with selective rewards. (Source: Adapted from Jones and Gerard, *Foundations of Social Psychology;* from Thibaut and Kelley, *Social Psychology of Groups*)

(Top right) **Figure 2. Minimal Social Situation Containing Only Reward-Cost Exchange.** This figure illustrates the situation in the experiment by Sidowski, Wycoff, and Tabony in which two people (*A* and *B*) each had two alternatives: to press either the right-hand button or the left-hand button. Being granted a point (indicated by "+") was a positive outcome; being given an electric shock was a negative outcome (indicated by "–"). The subjects of the experiment soon learned that there was only one combination of presses in which both would receive positive outcomes. This combination is indicated in the upper-left quadrant of the figure. This happy outcome could be achieved only by cooperation. Once they learned it, all subjects kept repeating this combination.

(Bottom left) **Figure 3. Concrete Form of the Prisoners' Dilemma.** This figure depicts the dilemma by means of specific terms of imprisonment placed in a matrix. (Source: Adapted from Jones and Gerard, *Foundations of Social Psychology*)

(Bottom right) **Figure 4. Abstract Form of the Prisoners' Dilemma.** This figure depicts the dilemma by means of numerical units (based on one unit equaling three months of imprisonment) placed in a matrix. (Source: Adapted from Jones and Gerard, *Foundations of Social Psychology*)

	A's Response Repertory					
B's Response Repertory	a_1	a_2	a_3	a_4	$\cdots$	a_n
b_1	6 / 2	1 / 0	−1 / −2	−4 / 0	$\cdots$	
b_2	4 / 4	2 / 5	0 / 0	3 / −5	$\cdots$	
b_3	0 / 0	−4 / −4	0 / 0	1 / −1	$\cdots$	
b_4	0 / 0	−1 / 0	1 / −3	0 / 0	$\cdots$	
$\vdots$	$\vdots$	$\vdots$	$\vdots$	$\vdots$	$\vdots$	$\vdots$
b_n						

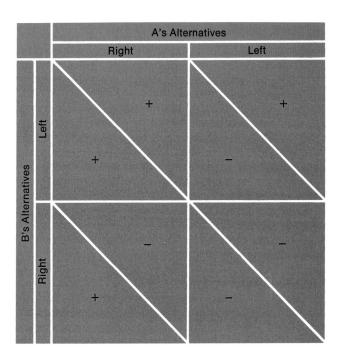

	Prisoner A's Alternatives	
Prisoner B's Alternatives	Not Confess	Confess
Not Confess	(1) One year each	(2) ⌐ Ten years for B / Three months for A
Confess	(3) ⌐ Three months for B / Ten years for A	(4) Eight years each

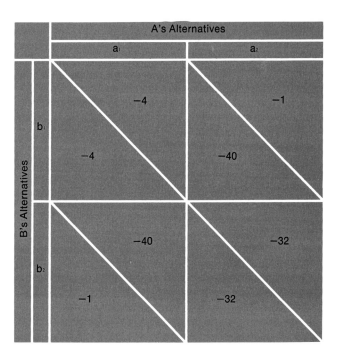

for turning state's evidence, whereas the latter will get
"the book" slapped at him.

The cooperative choice for both subjects is not to confess, the
competitive choice is to confess.

In "The Effect of Motivational Orientation upon Trust and
Suspicion" (1960) Morton Deutsch reported that the average subject in such a dilemma behaved quite competitively when he was
able to respond *after* his partner, making an average of only 21
percent cooperative responses. However, when subjects were allowed to change their responses until they were satisfied (in view
of the responses of their partner), they became much more cooperative, 77 percent making cooperative responses. In general, researchers have found that subjects are quite willing to exploit a
clearly cooperative partner and that cooperation is greatest in situations when partners appear to change from competitive to cooperative responses.

iv Evaluation The advantage of observing interactions in their
natural settings is that they reveal behavior that is meaningful to the
people who initiate it. It is the product of a complex convergence
of forces and is relevant to the participants' lives. But the disadvantage of the case study method is that it is usually difficult to determine which of the many possible variants actually caused the
behavior under examination.

These experimental methods supply a way of testing competing hypotheses, but at the cost of creating situations removed
from the real world. People do not walk around with electrodes on
their thumbs, pressing buttons to make "points." But this criticism
is only partially valid. For example, the argument that it makes a
difference whether we know that another person has hurt us or not
does not invalidate Sidowski's results, but suggests yet another experiment to test this particular variable. Researchers have in fact
carried out such experiments. One of the main problems with testing behavior exchange theory is in the quantification of reward and
punishment, pleasure and pain. There is something quite arbitrary
and artificial about this process. First, can pleasures really be
placed on a continuous scale, or are they qualitatively different?
Second, how can we know ahead of time what the appropriate values are?

The first question is manageable: one can tell which of two
alternatives is most rewarding by watching which a person actually
chooses. But the second is not. There is no way to determine how
desirable an alternative is, and therefore, every response can be
explained only after it has been made. If the researcher believes
that people always make the most rewarding response, then, by
definition, every response they make is the most rewarding available. But there is no way to test the underlying assumption.

The subjects in one experiment were given a chance to
make cooperative choices that also resulted in greatest gain to
themselves. Even though it cost them money *not* to make cooperative choices, they made the cooperative choice only half of the
time. These results seem to contradict the principle of behavior exchange, but the researchers argued that they did not (J. S. Minas,
Alvin Scodel, David Marlowe, and Harve Rawson, "Some Descrip-

tive Aspects of Two-Person Non-Zero-Sum Games,'' 1960). They suggested that the subjects were rewarded by *exploiting* their partners: although it cost them money, their partners lost even more.)

Does a competitive social and economic framework, such as that which characterizes American society, ''teach'' us to avoid cooperative activity as if it was opposed to maximum self-interest —even when the evidence is clearly shown to be otherwise? Or is competition the more basic human impulse and cooperation a form of behavior that has to be learned? As we also saw in Unit 10, these are among the many questions about the principle of behavior exchange that sociologists are still seeking to answer today.

3   Overview

The biological component of social interaction is reflected in dominance, sexuality, and body language. Such interactions also involve the performances and presentation of self in everyday life and are based on the overriding principle of behavior exchange. No theory yet integrates all these components, but some of their relationships seem apparent. Body language is an element of the actor's role, and the principle of behavior exchange determines the roles that are selected and the style with which they are portrayed; it also guides the interaction between the available roles of two or more actors.

In discussing face-to-face interaction, Erving Goffman identifies body language as the central subject matter: ''The ultimate behavioral materials are the glances, gestures, positionings, and verbal statements that people continuously feed into the situation, whether intended or not.'' Scheflen suggests that body language actually regulates face-to-face interactions:

> Two acquaintances may approach each other on the street with uncertainty about whether they should exchange greetings in passing or stop and chat. Or people may assemble in the living room of a friend with a different understanding of the nature of the gathering. . . . In such cases the situation needs further definition. . . . This may be done by verbal instructions or negotiations. In any case, it will be done or attempted with kinesic cues and signals. (*Body Language and the Social Order*)

Goffman and Scheflen are concerned with the *how* of social interaction—the techniques employed to convey impressions, play roles, and create performances. Behavior exchange theorists comment on the *why*—the directions that social interactions take according to anticipated rewards or punishment.)

There are several questions in this area that require further clarification. What is the nature of gain to a social actor? What are the common-sense rules of rational behavior? How do these roles differ from actual decision-making roles? How are they reconciled (or how do they conflict) in the social order? Are particular interactions determined by individual selves through a negotiative process? Or is interaction predetermined by immediate perceptions of characteristics of the other (such as social class) that define the situation according to normative rules?

D   LOOKING AHEAD

1   Interview: Chad Gordon

Chad Gordon is chairman of the department of sociology at Rice University. His interests focus on symbolic interaction, including investigations into self-conceptions and socialization at various periods in the life cycle, particularly adolescence and retirement. His writings have also dealt with methodology and with power, influence, and decision-making structures. He is the author of *Looking Ahead* and is working on Volume 2 of *The Self in Social Interaction.*

DPG   *What do you think about the current interest in "body language"?*

GORDON   Body language is really a special topic within communication. Let's go directly to the idea of interaction, because I have some corrections to the points made in your unit. It essentially defines interaction as communication and makes them equal. But, as Erving Goffman has pointed out in his book *Relations in Public,* they really aren't equal. Communication is one very important part of interaction, but interaction is broader than communication.

Interchange of clearly social meanings is certainly the bulk of what sociologists deal with in interaction, but there are many forms of interaction beyond communication. Interaction includes *all* of the ways in which people directly affect each other through any kind of exchange, whether of information, of material objects, or physical contacts. On conscious levels first, there are strictly material exchanges, involving all kinds of goods and services. They certainly have social meanings that can be studied, but they are important in their own right even without the elaborate or subtle forms of status and deference and other "moral" meanings that sociologists like to analyze. In a sense, therefore, evaluation, status, power, and attraction meanings get overlaid on routine everyday activities.

It is also possible to have all kinds of bodily situations strike one below or beyond cognitive levels. These interactions are at a level broader than strictly cognitive communication involving social topics, and they are important in interaction even though

they might be excluded from the study of human communication because it's thought that they don't involve symbolic processes. The definition of communication at a very symbolic and highly socialized, highly cultural level tends to stress and overstress that which is uniquely human—involving the frontal lobes and high capacity for symbolization—and to miss those things that are operating at the level of physical signs that may not even be "noticed" at conscious levels.

DPG   *Do you think that that is a built-in limitation on the whole discipline?*

GORDON   That's correct. The most recent things about body language—the whole run of popularizations that tell you about the crossing of the legs, the posture of the body and so forth—these tend to be "automatic" in their interpretations. That is, if legs are crossed in a certain way, that implies tightness; if they're not crossed, then that implies that the woman is accepting one sexually, or something of the sort. Those are much too simplistic. The key feature of human interaction is that all expressions, all gestures, all signs and symbols are inherently ambiguous in and of themselves. Their meaning is constructed over time from a large number of cues and their sequence, so that no given signal can stand for the whole elaborate message. It takes much more than just single gestures. They're built up into patterns, and they're phased over time. Each is part of the interpretive context for the rest and is in turn interpreted in relation to the rest. Thus we have the symbolic meanings of many actions, plus the forms of the nonsymbolic and direct interactions at the level of energy transmission. Stroking and touching and fondling and all kinds of things of that sort have interpretations that are quite social, but they're also far more basic and physiological: an electrochemical interaction is going on that isn't really "communication" directly. A whole new kind of research, brain wave research—in a cliché phrase, "biofeedback"—involves recognition by the person of when his waves are operating in a certain pattern, and the feelings that he gets when they operate with certain rhythms, and his capacity to control them, whether or not he understands at a cognitive level how he does it. As this kind of research progresses, people will want to do it in great quantities. But they will also put symbolic work around that, such as

thinking of all kinds of symbolic and social situations to go along with this pleasure stimulation, because they'll find it more satisfying to have both levels going.

DPG   *Both the communication and the basic response?*

GORDON   That's right.

DPG   *Do you think that people interact socially as a matter of rewards and punishment—that that is all that's going on—or is there something more to it?*

GORDON   There definitely is something more to it. We have to go back to the biochemical level, because interaction with one's environment starts long before social interaction. That is, one is interacting with an environment from the moment of conception. The fetus responds to the physiological stimuli of oxygen, nutriment, motion, and so on. At the time of birth, and from then on, there are very basic biological stimulation phenomena that don't involve any form of "interpretation." The infant will respond very differently to those stimulations that "feel good" as compared to those that "feel bad," long before it acquires abstract labels for these concepts. Now what happens very quickly through social interaction is that gestures—facial gestures in particular, but also stiffnesses of body position as opposed to gentle, caressing, tactile stimulation take on important self-referential meanings for the child. That is, he's being taught that he is worthy and wonderful and lovable, or that he is unwanted and unpleasant and a repugnant object in the world, deserving of only minimal physical care. Symbols are added onto the basic biological levels of rewards and punishments that are very undifferentiated. Approval is distinguished from respect, for example, and from acceptance and from sexual response, all of which are different forms of symbolic rewards. Different forms of physical rewards are also distinguished. For example, being rocked and cuddled and hugged is all of a piece at first, but later you have different forms of strokes that are thought of as the strokes between comrades as opposed to sexual partners, and so on. We begin to use nonverbal communication through different senses—that is, sight, sound, smell, touch,

seen, let alone touched, and sexuality is a repugnant form of carnal sin necessary only to reproduce the species—such attempts to repress sexuality will work against the basic biological drives for tactile stimulation and for genital pleasure and for mating activities. These repressions produce additional problems when they lead to the kinds of delusional religions that are attempts to provide huge symbolic rationales for this form of denial: you have to invent gods and devils and give them horrendous powers to be able to sustain any such repression of sensual interaction. When you have very elaborate, prolonged, and intense use of the bodily forms of interaction (I'm thinking particularly of sensuality, but also of very high-level chemical or electrical stimulations), sustained symbolic and social interaction with other persons may be severely disrupted. Just in the economy of time, bodily pleasures may be felt as so pleasurable that they may supersede human communication. Thus there is a possibility for conflict, although it's a personal value judgment whether supernatural religious or highly sensate pleasures are good things or not.

DPG   *What about further research?*
GORDON   I think that new forms of technology, particularly videotape, are going to allow strong breakthroughs in this research because of the capacity for a new form of self-awareness. Persons are allowed to see "instant replays" of their own verbal and nonverbal interaction styles, and this gives them part of the perspective of the other and of third parties. In addition the study of social situations themselves (more broadly than just the communications between persons) deserves far more sociological attention and research.

Finally, another topic is the expanded temporal dimension to interaction over the entire life cycle of individuals. Certain forms of body language are thought to be appropriate or taught to be appropriate to various persons of various ages. These are not at all well understood yet. All kinds of interaction and communication are possible all across the life cycle, far beyond what our culture has defined as appropriate or desirable. We tend to think that these stage-

specific interaction forms are biologically determined. For example, we socialize people to believe that they can expect sex drives to decline rapidly after age 40, but that is not physiologically valid. Stage-specific interaction forms are culturally defined, they are culturally bent and shaped and given their meanings. This situation is particularly true regarding forms of interaction that are expressive (ends in themselves) versus instrumental interaction (directed as means toward later goals). We often assign expressivity to children and adolescence, and then blindly equate dull instrumentality to "adulthood." A much better way would be to blend the expressive and the instrumental into what we usually call something like creativity, at all stages of the life cycle and in every conceivable realm of human existence.

balance, and such—and even within one modality, touch, different parts of the body are to be touched at different points of time by different persons in different acts. So we get great differentiation of the receptors for pleasure and pain and of the symbolic meanings of the pleasures and pains. The definitions of what people find worthy of reward and what rewards you receive are in principle quite cultural. They're not biological at all. The biological potentiality for a huge range of kinds of rewards and kinds of pains exists, but the cultures select from them certain performances to be rewarded and then determine when they're to be rewarded and how they're to be rewarded.

DPG   *Is there a danger of real conflict arising between the basic biological responses and cultural responses?*
GORDON   In cultures that try to deny sensuality as being something like devil's snares and delusions to trap the unwary soul into hell, where the body is not to be

Unit 13
Sex Roles

SCHEMATIC OUTLINE

A Introductory Graphics: Sex-Role Differentiation

B Definition and Context

1 Definition
A sex role is a pattern of behavior expected of males or females in a particular society. Such patterns involve functional roles, personality attributes, and sexual behavior.

2 World Context
Gender is used throughout the world as a basis not only for assigning activities, but also for ascribing and transmitting rights, duties, property, and social status. Despite great progress toward equality in the industrialized world, the status of women is still universally lower than that of men.

3 American Context
The traditional American sex roles are altering rapidly in response to the pressures of industrialization and the changing social structure.

C Questions and Evidence

1 Questions
Drawing on material from a wide range of sources and disciplines, sociologists ask: (1) Is there such a thing as natural sexual behavior? (2) How do sex-typed differences in personality arise? (3) How do sex roles develop?

2 Evidence
a The "Burning Issue" Question
Many social scientists, including Sigmund Freud, Alfred C. Kinsey, and Margaret Mead, have challenged the dominant Western sexual mores. Cross-cultural studies have found only one universal restriction—the incest taboo. Otherwise, the attitudes toward premarital liaisons, marriage, nudity, erotic stimulation, and homosexuality vary widely. This evidence strongly suggests that human sexuality is highly malleable and that human beings can be socialized into a variety of marital institutions and sex roles.
b The "Classical" Question
Studies of personality variables have found sex-linked differences very early in life. Some of these may have a genetic basis, but they are relatively minor. Most of the observed gender differences arise from the interaction of genetic and social factors.
c The "Research" Question
Most research supports the idea—advocated by Lawrence Kohlberg and other cognitive-development psychologists—that sex roles are learned as part of active self-definition rather than through social conditioning of a passive individual. This learning process involves complex interactions between innate cognitive capacities and social experiences.

3 Overview
Although research in this area has sometimes been hampered by taboos, much has been learned about the social basis of sex roles.

D Looking Ahead

1 Interview: Germaine Greer

SUPPORTING UNITS

- **3** Biology and Society
- **4** Culture
- **5** Socialization and Moral Development
- **6** Population and Demography
- **7** Marriage, Kinship, and the Family
- **22** Deviance
- **26** Social Change

ENCYCLOPEDIA ENTRIES

adultery
bisexuality
chaperonage
Civil Rights Acts
double standard
Equal Rights Amendment
ethnocentrism
gay liberation movement
heterosexuality
hippies
homosexuality
incest taboo
Kinsey, Alfred C. (1894–1956)
Kohlberg, Lawrence (b. 1927)
Mead, Margaret (b. 1901)
monogamy
polygamy
sex differences
sex roles
sexual morality
sexual variance
status
transvestism
unisex
woman suffrage
women's liberation movement

SEX-ROLE DIFFERENTIATION

1. **Sex-Role Differentiation.** A child's sex has social as well as biological meanings, and its identity as male or female is reinforced from birth onward.

2. **Sex-Role Socialization.** Boys and girls are socialized differently.

BOYS WILL BE BOYS

SUCH A LITTLE LADY

3. **Sex-Role Self-Definition.** They accept their roles and develop different kinds of interests and personalities.

4. **Transmission of Sex-Role Stereotypes.** All aspects of social life reinforce the individual's gender identity and sex roles.

5. **Ongoing Sex-Role Behavior.** During the course of one's life, the behavior appropriate to one's sex-role becomes second nature. Why does the man drive the car? Why does the woman suggest directions? What look like "natural" traits are the result of sex-role conditioning.

B DEFINITION AND CONTEXT

1 Definition

The first question asked by the parents after the birth of a child is the same around the world: "Is it a boy or a girl?" And the answer has profound implications for the rest of the infant's life. In every society men and women are acknowledged to be different—different not only in their physical characteristics, but also in their social behaviors as well.

The tendency to make significant systematic differentiations based on sex is universal in human society. But the specific forms these differentiations take—such as in matters relating to dress or hair length—are culturally and historically variable. In societies around the world women can be found wearing trousers and men wearing skirts as often as the reverse arrangement. The contemporary Western male is supposedly less interested in personal adornment than the female, but not so long ago in Europe it was the male who took the predominant interest in silks, satins, stockings, wigs, and perfumes. Long hair on Western males has been the rule rather than the exception throughout history; the current short-hair fashion of the middle-aged, which some regard as a cosmic imperative, actually dates from World War I, when troops in the trenches shaved their heads to rid themselves of crawling lice.

What Americans think of as distinctively masculine or feminine may be completely reversed in other societies. In fact, it would be impossible to find even an approximate definition of what men and women are like that would be acceptable to the human race as a whole. Masculinity and femininity are not characteristics with which we are born; in every culture boys and girls are socialized differently and internalize different expectations of the sex roles they are to fill.

A *sex role* is a pattern of behavior expected of males and females in a particular culture. Sex roles involve several related elements. First, there is the *functional role* that members of a particular sex play in their society: men customarily perform some tasks, women other. Second, there is the constellation of *personality attributes* that are considered appropriate for each role in a given society. Third, there is the actual *sexual behavior* that is considered role-appropriate in each culture.

There are important biological differences between the sexes. But when the sociologist studies sex differences he is generally considering not so much differences in biological characteristics as differences in culturally created roles—roles that can be reinforced or modified, perhaps even reversed or eliminated.

2 World Context

In all societies the physiological differences between men and women are elaborated into notions of *masculine* and *feminine*. The content of these notions varies, but in every culture distinctions of sex are associated with differences in social status and behavior.

One striking difference is in the functional role of each sex

Abraham Bosse's *The Dictatorial Husband* (1633). In many societies around the world it was—and is—considered appropriate for a man to beat his wife if she fails to please him.

Working woman in the Soviet Union. In the Soviet Union it is recognized that traditional notions regarding what is properly "male" and "female" work are inhibiting to many talented individuals and are a source of social waste. In the interest of creating a more productive society, traditional definitions of work are being altered.

in society. There is usually a clearly defined division of labor between the sexes. Inevitably, the fact that women bear and suckle
children tends to bind them to the home, so that in most societies
child care, food preparation, and light agriculture are women's
work. Men, on the other hand, are physically more powerful and
are not immobilized by periodic childbearing, so that tasks such as
hunting, fighting, heavy agriculture, and care of wandering livestock, are their concern. These institutionalized role differences in
the familial division of labor are especially evident in subsistence
economies and small-scale societies.

In 1937 G. P. Murdock in "Comparative Data on the Division
of Labor by Sex" presented the frequencies with which 224 societies operate a sex-based division of labor in activities relating to
food production and collection. He noted that the differences are
quite sharp for most activities except dairy work, soil preparation,
fowl tending, and the building of shelters. Generally, however, the
male activities are those that involve vigorous physical activity or
travel; the female activities are those that are physically less stren-
uous and require less mobility.

Activity	Number of Societies in Which Activity is Performed by:				
	Men Always	Men Usually	Either Sex Equally	Women Usually	Women Always
Metalworking	78	0	0	0	0
Weapon making	121	1	0	0	0
Boat building	91	4	4	0	1
Making musical instruments	45	2	0	0	1
Work in wood and bark	113	9	5	1	1
Work in stone	68	3	2	0	1
Work in bone, horn, shell	67	4	3	0	2
Making ceremonial objects	37	1	13	0	1
House building	86	32	25	3	14
Net making	44	6	4	2	11
Making ornaments	24	3	40	6	18
Making leather products	29	3	9	3	32
Hide preparation	31	2	4	4	49
Making nontextile fabrics	14	0	9	2	32
Making thread and cordage	23	2	11	10	73
Basket making	25	3	10	6	82
Hat making	16	2	6	4	61
Weaving	19	2	2	6	67
Pottery making	13	2	6	8	77
Making and repairing clothing	12	3	8	9	95

There are also sex-role differences in manufacturing activities in the same societies. Physical differences do not explain the
division of labor in this case. Weapon-making, for example, is a
predominantly "male" activity, but it does not necessarily require
more strength than making clothes, a "female" activity. The explanation here seems to lie in the anticipated use of the object: only
men use weapons, and so men also make them.

Table 1. Subsistence Activities and Division of Labor by Sex.
Data for the table were obtained from 224 societies. (Source:
Adapted from Murdock, "Comparative Data on the Division of Labor
by Sex")

Activity	Number of Societies in Which Activity is Performed by:				
	Men Always	Men Usually	Either Sex Equally	Women Usually	Women Always
Pursuit of sea mammals	34	1	0	0	0
Hunting	166	13	0	0	0
Trapping small animals	128	13	4	1	2
Herding	38	8	4	0	5
Fishing	98	34	19	3	4
Clearing land for agriculture	73	22	17	5	13
Dairy operations	17	4	3	1	13
Preparing and planting soil	31	23	33	20	37
Erecting and dismantling shelter	14	2	5	6	22
Tending fowl and small animals	21	4	8	1	39
Tending and Harvesting crops	10	15	35	39	44
Gathering shellfish	9	4	8	7	35
Making and tending fires	18	6	25	22	62
Bearing burdens	12	6	35	20	57
Preparing drinks and narcotics	20	1	13	8	57
Gathering fruits, berries, nuts	12	3	15	13	63
Gathering fuel	22	1	10	19	89
Preservation of meat and fish	8	2	10	14	74
Gathering herbs, roots, seeds	8	1	11	7	74
Cooking	5	1	9	28	158
Carrying water	7	0	5	7	119
Grinding grain	2	4	5	13	114

Table 2. The Manufacture of Objects and the Division of Labor by Sex. (Source: Adapted from Murdock, ''Comparative Data on the Division of Labor by Sex'')

Gender is used throughout the world not only as a basis for assigning activities, but also for *ascribing* and *transmitting* rights, duties, property, and social status. Most societies organize their institutions around males rather than females. In his 1957 ''World Ethnographic Sample'' of 565 societies, Murdock found that about three-quarters of the societies favored transmission of kinship status *patrilineally* (through the father) rather than *matrilineally* (through the mother). Some 376 of the 565 societies were found to be predominantly *patrilocal* (married sons and their wives residing with or near the parents of the husband), and only 84 were predominantly *matrilocal* (married daughters and their husbands living with or near the parents of the wife.) With regard to forms of multiple marriage, of the 431 societies that permit *polygamous marriage,* only four permit the wife to have more than one husband. Unit 7 is entirely devoted to a discussion of marriage, family, and kinship systems.

As far as personal relations are concerned, the husband almost always claims superior status to his wife. She is usually expected to be submissive and obedient, and in many parts of the world the husband is allowed to beat his wife if she fails to satisfy these requirements. A 1963 study of authority and deference between husband and wife in 36 societies (William N. Stephens, *The Family in Cross-Cultural Perspective*) found that the husbands exercised considerable authority over the wife in 21 of the societies; in six the husbands were slightly dominant; in five there was an equal sharing of authority; and in only four did women appear to have more authority than the males. In the latter four cases, however, the authority of the female did not extend beyond the family; in the wider society male dominance was undisputed.

In some 61 percent of the 139 societies for which information is available, a mated woman is forbidden to engage in extramarital sexual relationships. The male is similarly restricted in a number of societies, but these prohibitions are rarely taken as seriously as they are for women. Most societies believe that the man should take the initiative in sexual advance, and many believe that the man should take a more active role in the sex act itself.

(Despite great progress toward equality during the last century, the status of women is universally lower than that of men. In a classical study of women in European politics (*Political Role of Women*, 1955), Maurice Duverger found that females were substantially less likely than males to vote and that they rarely exceeded more than 5 percent of the membership of European legislatures. Even when they took their places in public life, their concerns remained typical of those conventionally assigned to their sex—education, children, women's rights. Men concentrate instead on "manly" issues—economics, foreign affairs, defense, crime. (Even in the Communist-governed countries, which insist on a formal equality between the sexes, this phenomenon persists:) in China, the Soviet Union, Cuba, and elsewhere, key political leadership is placed almost exclusively in male politicians, just as it is in the West.

(The Communist-governed countries have succeeded, however, in changing *job patterns* to a considerable extent. In the Soviet Union four out of five women between the ages of 20 and 55 hold full-time jobs.) About three-quarters of the physicians are women—compared with only 16 percent in Britain and 8 percent in the United States. Nearly half the instructors in Soviet universities are women, compared with 9 percent in the United States. (In the main academic fields, the American figure is 2 percent.) A third of Soviet engineers and scientists are women, compared with the United States figures of less than 2 percent and 1 percent respectively. (A few countries of Western Europe have also made considerable progress in eliminating sex-related job patterns:) in Denmark nearly half the lawyers are women; in West Germany, about a third—compared with 4 percent in the United States. (But even in those countries where considerable vocational emancipation of women has been a matter of urgent public policy, women hardly ever are promoted to leadership levels within their chosen professions;) in the Soviet Union, for example, where the field of medicine is dominated by women, women are still excluded from such high, prestigious positions as professorships of medicine and hospital directorships. Furthermore, changes in domestic relationships apparently have lagged far behind whatever gains have been made in changing job patterns: in the USSR women still keep their traditional separate role in the home—maintaining the household, preparing food, caring for children, washing the clothes.

3   American Context

The *women's liberation movement* has made the question of sex

Stele of Hammurabi (c. 1800 B.C.). Hammurabi, king of ancient Babylon, was the author of a code of laws in which, among other things, the civil rights of women were specified. Among the rights listed were that of a woman to own property apart from her husband's and to keep a separate "bank account." This code is engraved in cuneiform script on the shaft of the stele beneath the rendering shown here of Hammurabi before Shamash, the Sun God.

One source of input into gender identity is the omnipresent television. One estimate holds that by the time a child graduates from high school, he or she will have spent more than 11,000 hours in the classroom but more than 22,000 hours in front of the television set.

roles one of the most controversial topics in American society. The movement is ideologically linked to other searches for emancipation by more "historically visible" underdogs—the poor and the black—and feminists have claimed that the existing relationship between the sexes is exploitative and degrading. The movement has aimed not merely to achieve equality, but also to redefine the nature of the male and female roles in America. The notion that the existing roles are part of some natural order is strongly challenged: criticism is leveled not only at the submissive status of women, but also at the identification of men as the aggressive, dominant rulers in society. How valid are the claims of the feminists?

In international terms the American woman is in a fairly privileged position. She is not likely to be beaten by her husband for disobedience, and the division of labor between male and female is unusually flexible. Yet in the United States the status of women remains demonstrably lower than that of men. One social scientist, William J. Goode, argues that the sexual division of labor in the family "comes perilously close to the racial or caste restrictions in some modern societies. That is, the low-ranking race, caste, or sex is not only defined as not being able to do certain types of prestigious work, but it is also considered a violation of propriety if they do." (*The Family,* 1964)

The personality attributes associated with each sex are strongly contrasted. In particular, the American male is stereotyped as a model of go-getting aggressiveness that has no parallel in any other modern society—and very few parallels in preliterate tribes. He is expected to be undemonstrative, unemotional, competent, assertive, and dominant. The word "aggressive" can be used to describe a man in a complimentary sense in America; in any other modern society the term has a strongly pejorative connotation. The exaggerated masculinity of the stereotyped American male is, in fact, something of an international joke.

But, paradoxically, in America this masculinity is treated as a very fragile characteristic, easily undermined. Parents continually monitor and reinforce behavior of a little boy to ensure that he grows up to be a "real man." The little girl who occasionally acts in a boyish way is understandable: she aspires to a superior though unattainable status. But the little boy who fails to meet the requirements of aggressiveness, fighting, initiative, sturdiness, and ambition is likely to be called a sissy. Continued failure to live up to these requirements is a cause for great concern by parents and may even be seen as requiring medical or psychiatric action to make the child "normal." It is no accident that the current fashion for long hair on males (originally imported from London) has been branded "effeminate," and it is no accident that even the supposedly liberated younger American males still refrain from the sartorial extravagance of their counterparts in London and Paris. Most young American males reject laced sleeves, velvet jackets, and floral embroidery.

The American woman, on the other hand, is expected to be excitable, affectionate, intuitive, and sensitive. She is supposed to get her man not by brazen invitation but by subtle wiles, and her understanding of his little faults and favorite foods should enable her to manipulate him throughout his life. She is meant to be passive, ignorant of sport, politics, and economics, and happiest when absorbed in the cares of the home or chatting with the neighbors. In her relations with the children she (unlike the husband) is supposed to be expressive, emotional, tender. Goode suggests that the division of labor in the family and the associated sex-role stereotypes have led to a family that has a weak, ineffectual mother and a cold, unyielding father—and the family that does not approximate these characteristics does a poor job of socializing its young to meet the expectations of the wider society.

Yet these traditional roles are altering, probably faster than most people realize. As in other mature industrial societies, American women are moving toward positions of equality with men. When modernization takes place, the father-dominated family pattern of the past is inevitably shattered, its authority broken by pressures of industrialization and a rapidly changing social structure. The father has been increasingly robbed of his economic importance by having a wife and children who work; gradually, he is becoming just another member of the family, rather than its sole support and hence its head.

During the twentieth century equal rights for women have gradually become institutionalized in America. The process has included the extension of the right to vote, increasingly equal opportunities in education, the end of chaperonage, a slight decline in discrimination in employment, and erosion of the double standard of morality that regarded the premarital activities of the male indulgently but considered his partner a loose woman. Sex has come to be seen not simply as a prerogative of the male, but as an equal relationship—a change reflected in the shift of blame for poor sexual compatibility from the woman to the man. (Women are reportedly now less concerned about frigidity, men more concerned about potency). There is still considerable *specialization of domestic roles*—mother washes the clothes, father mows the lawn—but there is a *convergence of roles* as well—both may shop at the supermarket, both will be expected to contribute equally to the marriage relationship.

In the United States, as in all industrial countries, legislation restricts the hours a woman may work, the weights she may lift, and the jobs she may take. Such laws limit the prospect for equal pay for the sexes; women, in effect, have become victims of laws passed by men for women's protection. The 1963 Equal Pay Act overrides protective legislation only when men and women are engaged in similar work, and the courts have held that the 1964 Civil Rights Act does not overturn restrictions concerning women that result from protective labor legislation.

Changes in employment practices are proceeding slowly. At the end of the 1960s 28 percent of American men earned more than $10,000 per year, but only 2.9 percent of women did. Of the 3.5 million families in America headed by women, nearly 2 million live below the poverty line. At present the median pay for women is less than 60 percent that of men. Women comprise some 51 percent of the population but represent only 40 percent of the labor force. (Yet compared to past figures, this figure is a high percentage.) Nine out of 10 married women now work at some time during their marriage, and almost a third of mothers with children un-

The movement for women's rights had its origins in the era of revolutions in the eighteenth century and continued through the fight for women's suffrage. *(Above)* A meeting in Berlin of the International Council of Women in 1904. *(Below)* A poster advertising a rally against women's suffrage. *(Below)* Suffragettes marching on the United States Capitol.

Figure 1. Women's Income in the United States as a Percentage of Men's Income. The incredible shrinking woman? (Source: Koontz, ''Myth and Reality in the Employment of Women'')

der 18 are currently at work. (The normal pattern is for women to work before their marriage, to stop while they bear and rear children, and then to return to work. If the division of labor that so profoundly influences our *sex-role stereotypes* in America is primarily due to the necessity for women to spend part of their lives at home in close physical proximity to the children, there is a certain irony in the fact that the average American women spends only 3 percent of her total life span in the reproductive functions of pregnancy and lactation.) This period is a very small segment of a lifetime on which to base such generalizations as ''A woman's place is in the home.'' (The continuing preeminence of the male in American culture is maintained above all else by the continuing male control of the *family economy*.) Ultimately, the male is still responsible: his status is inseparably linked with his role as bread-winner and with the degree of financial success he has achieved. There is something ''wrong'' with the man who hasn't got a job—and there is something ''dominant'' about the man who has. There is something ''wrong'' with the woman who wants a career—and there is something ''domineering'' about the woman who succeeds.

C   QUESTIONS AND EVIDENCE

1   Questions

Sociologists who study the nature and development of sex roles in society draw on material from a wide range of sources and often cooperate with anthropologists, social psychologists, and developmental psychologists. Among the main questions sociologists ask are these: (1) Is there such a thing as natural sexual behavior—or can human beings be conditioned by their social environment to adopt roles involving the practice and acceptance of a specified range and type of sexual behaviors? (2) What, if any, are the innate differences between men and women? How do sex-typed differences in personality arise? (3) How do sex roles develop—by what process does the boy or girl come to know that he or she is a boy or girl, and to behave in accordance with that knowledge?

2   Evidence

a   The "Burning Issue" Question

i   Context   "You can't tell if it's a boy or a girl"—the comment is common enough these days, for the trend toward unisex fashions has wiped out many superficial distinctions between the sexes. And there are other more significant indications that a convergence of sex roles may be occurring. Thanks to the women's liberation movement, girls are becoming more confident, more assertive, more actively involved in nondomestic issues and areas of interest. Thanks to the percolation of "hippie" values through the middle-class youth, boys are apt to appear more gentle, more emotional, more caring. But the assault on our traditional notions of what constitutes proper sexual roles and behavior goes still deeper. Such "sexual minority groups" as the homosexuals in the gay liberation movement have refused to be defined as "abnormal" and offered "treatment" any longer, asserting instead that the existing, rigidly defined sex roles are repressive. Do our current *norms* of sexual conduct conform to some genuinely natural and proper *biological imperative,* or is human sexuality much more malleable and adaptable? Sociologists ask: *To what extent is human sexual behavior modifiable through the socialization process in a particular culture?*

ii   Theory   Western sexual mores have been profoundly influenced by a particular interpretation of Judaeo-Christian morality that views one, and only one, form of sexual activity as legitimate: *genital heterosexual monogamy.* Deviations from this pattern have been considered sinful, depraved, and/or illegal. Sexual behavior that was forbidden by the church gradually became a criminal matter in England only in the late fifteenth and early sixteenth centuries, but this criminal code was imported to the United States by the early settlers. The Puritans of the Massachusetts Bay Colony made adultery a capital offense, and fornicators were fined, flogged, or forced to marry. In 1642 Connecticut instituted the death penalty for adultery, homosexuality, and bestiality.

Traces of this morality are still to be found on the statute books of virtually every state in the union. Many of these laws are falling into disuse, but prosecutions for so-called deviant or immoral acts between consenting adults are by no means rare in America in the 1970s. Adultery is illegal in 41 states, cohabitation outside of marriage in 26. Fornication is illegal in 23 states and is punishable by a prison sentence of up to five years in Michigan. Oral intercourse is illegal in 41 states: in six states offenders can receive up to 20 years in prison. Anal intercourse is illegal in 45

Occupations	Percentage Women in 1950	Percentage Women in 1970
Nurses	97.6	97.3
Secretaries, typists	94.6	94.6
Telephone operators	95.8	94.5
Bank tellers	44.6	86.2
Retail clerks	48.9	56.5
Editors, reporters	32.1	40.6
Postmasters	44.9	31.8
Bakers	11.6	30.0
Buyers	24.6	29.8
College teachers	22.4	28.6
Bus drivers	2.9	28.0
Accountants	14.9	26.2
Bartenders	6.4	21.1
Doctors	6.7	9.3
Lawyers, judges	4.1	4.9
Architects	3.8	3.6
Clergy	4.4	2.9
Electricians	0.6	1.9
Engineers	1.3	1.6
Auto mechanics	0.6	1.4

Table 3. Percentage of Women in Selected Occupations, 1950 and 1970. A few occupations (for example, bus drivers and bank tellers) have shown dramatic increases in the percentage of women in the field. However, most professions and trades employed virtually the same percentage of women in 1970 as they had twenty years before. (Source: Adapted from *Newsweek,* 2/12/73)

1925

Sigmund Freud (1856–1939). Although his work in psychology contributed to the liberalization of moral standards regarding sexual behavior, Freud is currently seen as an oppressive figure by the women's liberation movement because of his insistence on the "natural superiority" of the vaginal orgasm over the clitoral orgasm.

states: in nine conviction carries a sentence of up to 20 years.

Many social scientists have challenged the dominant view of what is natural (by extension, normal or moral) behavior. Sigmund Freud, for example, was profoundly convinced that the human species was fundamentally *bisexual*. He also believed that the dominant morality was based on an unhealthy tension between private instincts and social repression. The result was that the illusions of chastity and restraint that were presented to children became the cause of a great many subsequent neuroses and psychoses, often with physical manifestations such as frigidity and impotence.

A similar view was taken by Alfred C. Kinsey, who published his massive works *Sexual Behavior in the Human Male* in 1948 and *Sexual Behavior in the Human Female* in 1953. His studies, the first major empirical research on the topic, shocked American society with their revelations of the amount of variation and extent of deviations from the accepted norms. Kinsey discovered a great deal more "forbidden" activity than had ever been suspected, and concluded in the first book:

> The world is not divided into sheep and goats. . . . It is a fundamental of taxonomy that nature does not deal with discrete categories. Only the human mind invents categories and tries to force facts into separated pigeon holes. The living world is a continuum in each and every one of its aspects. The sooner we learn this concerning human sexual behavior the sooner we will reach a sound understanding of the realities of sex.

Margaret Mead and other anthropologists have drawn similar conclusions from their field studies of other societies. Such cross-cultural research reveals much about the malleability or the rigidity of human sexual behavior, though such evidence must be evaluated in terms of cultural relativity. Each culture has its own validity, and the yardsticks of one cannot be used to measure the mores of another. For the social scientist it is a basic principle that all human beings are fundamentally similar, that their cultures have an intrinsic validity, and that all societies have something to learn from knowledge of one another. *Ethnocentrism* must be put aside.

iii Research Anthropologists have found only one constant in human sexual behavior—the *incest taboo.* No society allows people to mate at random. There is an almost universal taboo against sexual relations between parent and child, and between brother and sister. (The exceptions were the royal households of Hawaii, ancient Egypt, and Inca Peru and commoners in ancient Egypt and Persia.) Most societies have taboos against sexual relationships between other kin, but the definitions of who constitutes kin and who does not, or which kin fall within the taboo and which do not, are highly variable.

Beyond the incest taboo, the evidence from ethnographic studies is that a permissive attitude is much more common than a restrictive one. Murdock's 1949 cross-cultural study of 250 societies found only 54 societies that forbid or disapprove of premarital liaisons between nonrelatives, and many of these societies institutionalize sex relations between specified relatives, such as cross-cousins, for unmated persons. In another major cross-cultural study, *Patterns of Sexual Behavior* (1951), Clellan S. Ford and Frank A. Beach found that formal restriction to a single mate characterizes less than 16 percent of the 185 groups on which information could be obtained. Of these 29 societies, fewer than 10 wholly disapproved both premarital and extramarital liaisons. In many societies the idea of *virgin marriage* is absurd; these cultures not only permit sexual experimentation by unmarried young people, they institutionalize it as a socially approved and useful arrangement. Many societies also make provision for acceptable outlets for the widowed. In our society, in contrast, unmarried or widowed persons are theoretically obliged to remain celibate.

Americans tend to assume that marriage is based on love, but love and marriage are not necessarily linked in some invariant relationship. To many societies—especially in the Middle East and East Asia—the *arranged marriage* is the norm, and if love is present in these marriages it is as a consequence rather than a cause of the betrothal. A number of societies provide men with opportunities to find sexual satisfaction outside marriage through institutionalized relationships with a designated group of female relatives ("sexual hospitality"), through socially endorsed or tolerated arrangements involving prostitutes, concubines, or mistresses, or even through the formal recognition of periods of debauchery (such as the ancient Roman Saturnalia). In general, these outlets are available only to the male, reflecting the social location of power in these societies.

Many other aspects of sexuality are culturally variable. The practice of concealing the woman's genital region with some form of clothing is far more common than the covering of the male organs. A number of societies require the female but not the male to cover the pubic region. Several societies allow both sexes to go nude, but no society requires the male to be covered and allows the female to go uncovered. The position adopted for sexual intercourse is also a product of human culture rather than biological factors. The position normally adopted in the United States as natural is for the partners to lie down, face-to-face, with the male on top. Kinsey found that about 70 percent of American married couples had never experimented with any other position. In global terms, however, this position is something of an oddity. (It is often called the "missionary position," because several cultures were introduced to it by Christian missionaries.) Among several thousand portrayals of human intercourse left in the art of ancient civilizations, there is hardly a single example of the conventional American position. Yet some states have declared alternative positions to be unnatural, with criminal penalities for those practicing them.

Notions of what stimuli are to be considered erotic are also culturally variable. American men are much attracted by the female breasts, but many people—particularly in parts of Africa and the South Pacific—do not regard the female breast as a sexual feature at all. The female buttocks, however, frequently assume a sexual connotation far more intense than that experienced by the American male. Armpit and (thanks to recent advertising campaigns) vaginal odor are considered somewhat offensive by many Americans and some Europeans; but in most societies these odors are considered

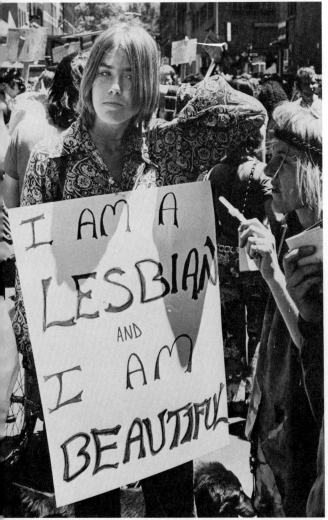

highly stimulating. Kissing is considered an erotic experience in most cultures, but there are several societies—such as the Thonga and Siriono of Micronesia—in which kissing is not practiced and is viewed with ridicule or with considerable distaste. Oral stimulation of the genitalia is relatively rare in other societies, but fairly common in the United States. (According to Kinsey's study of married couples, oral stimulation of the female genitalia is practiced by 45.3 percent of the well-educated and about 4.1 percent of the grade school husbands; oral stimulation of the male genitalia is practiced by the wives of 75.3 percent of the well-educated husbands and 57.1 percent of the grade school husbands.) The frequency of the sex act also varies across cultures. The common frequency in America is two or three times a week, but in most societies for which information is available every normal adult engages in sexual intercourse every day. The Aranda of Australia aim at intercourse from three to five times nightly, sleeping between each act. Some peoples, such as the Trobriand Islanders, do not require privacy for their sexual activity and will unself-consciously have intercourse in front of their children or other members of the community.

Attitudes toward homosexual behavior also vary widely. Ford and Beach found that in 28 of the 77 societies for which information was available homosexuality was rare, absent, or disapproved of. In all these societies there was strong social pressure against this behavior, ranging from ridicule to threat of death. In 49 of the societies (64 percent), however, homosexuality was considered normal and socially acceptable—sometimes for certain members of the community, sometimes for all of them (although never, of course, as sole outlet). Homosexual activity may be institutionalized in various forms. Sometimes it is reserved for religious rites, as in South American tribes and in Asian shamanism. In the contemporary Middle East bisexuality on the part of the male is very much the norm, especially in those traditional societies in which women are kept veiled and guarded. In America homosexuality is sometimes associated with effeminacy; historically, however, it has been commonly linked in other countries with an aggressive masculinity, as in the case of the warrior Spartans or the Japanese samurai. Homosexual relations between an older man and a boy are considered particularly reprehensible in the United States, but in ancient Athens this love was elevated to a noble ideal, exalted by Plato and institutionalized in art, literature, and custom. The Karaki bachelors in New Guinea universally practice sodomy, and in the course of his puberty rites each boy is initiated into anal intercourse by older males. The boy then plays a passive role for a year after his initiation, after which he spends the remainder of his bachelorhood sodomizing the newly initiated. One institutionalized form of male sexual inversion is *berdache,* practiced by the Plains Indians of the United States and found also in Siberia. The institution covers every biological and social variation from homosexual to hermaphrodite to transvestite; the berdaches were often considered to have magical powers and were given special status in most tribes. Homosexuality is much more common in the United States than is generally realized; indeed, it is thought to be significantly more common here than in any other industrial society. Kinsey found that some 37 percent of American males had experienced homosexual activity to the point of orgasm, and he estimated that about 30 percent of the males in in the United States have at some time or other been brought to orgasm as a result of oral stimulation by a member of their own sex.

iv   Evaluation (The evidence from cultures around the world strongly suggests that human sexuality is highly malleable and that human beings can be successfully socialized into a variety of marital institutions and sex roles—each of which has its advantages and perhaps disadvantages in the particular society concerned.)

(The cultural norms of American society, however—virgin marriage, genital sexuality, exclusive heterosexuality—seem to have only a superficial relation to the statistical norms.) Kinsey found that 92 percent of the male population had masturbated to orgasm and that 22 percent of all males had attempted intercourse by the age of 12. In a recent study Robert Sorensen reported that 44 percent of all males between the ages of 13–15 have had intercourse experience, and 36 percent of these had their first episode by the age of 12 or under. By the age of 19, 52 percent of all male and female adolescents in the United States have had sexual intercourse. About half the married men had had intercourse with someone other than their wives during the course of their marriage. One child in 10 is illegitimate. More than two-thirds of the men and nearly half of the women experience premarital sex. Between 40 and 50 percent of all farm boys have sexual contact with animals; in some Western areas, Kinsey secured incidence figures as high as 65 percent, and he found that about 27 percent of rural males of college level have had animal experience to the point of orgasm. As Kinsey drily observed, ''Practically every mammal that has ever been kept on a farm enters the record.'' The striking feature about these deviations from the conventional morality is not so much their range, nature, and frequency as the fact that they can exist in the face of such a strict socializing process. The comparative failure of this social pressure points to a much more flexible and explorative base to human sexuality than our conventional notions allow.

b   The "Classical" Question

i   Context (Until the last century almost no one questioned the assumption that the sexes inherited differences in temperament as well as physical differences.)But the pressures of egalitarian and feminist movements, coupled with the findings of modern psychology, have led to a reexamination of the old assumptions. (*Radical feminists* in particular have claimed that nonphysiological differences between men and women are either nonexistent or else insignificant, and they posit instead an *androgynous society* in which the treatment accorded to and expected from males and females would be identical. Sociologists ask: To what extent *are cultural factors responsible for any fundamental behavioral differences between men and women?*)

ii   Theory (Almost every culture has favored men over women in the allocation of prestige and status. Some theorists have concluded that this superiority is based on a differential genetic endowment. The idea that there are *genetic predispositions* derives from three types of evidence: cultural universals such as male dominance; sex-typed behavioral differences in other ground-dwell-

(Facing page) Demonstrations of the gay liberation movement in New York City. Both male and female homosexuals are organizing into serious political groups for the purpose of changing laws that discriminate against them and also to change public opinion regarding the issue of homosexuality.

ing primates; and behavioral differences in new-borns that seem to occur long before they are capable of perceiving and imitating the different characteristics of their parents.)

(Other theorists, particularly anthropologists, have stressed the importance of cultural factors in determining behavioral differences between the sexes. These theorists minimize or deny the effect of genetic differences, and instead stress *socialization patterns,*) such as were discussed in Unit 5. Ashley Montagu, an anthropologist and sociologist who has argued for many years for a reevaluation of existing sex roles, believes:

> What we have always taken as biologically determined, namely masculinity and femininity, are in fact genders which are virtually wholly culturally determined. We now know, beyond dispute, that whatever the sex of the child may be, its gender role is what it learns. ("The Pill, Sexual Revolution and the Schools," 1968)

(Anthropologist Margaret Mead has also stressed the role of the cultural environment in determining the content of gender roles. Her theory was based on her extensive field work with three primitive tribes in New Guinea, which she described in *Sex and Temperament in Three Primitive Societies* (1935). Mead found that both men and women in the Mundugumor tribe were typically aggressive and even violent—traits that Americans associate only with men. In the Arapesh tribe she found that both men and women were passive and gentle—traits that Americans associate only with women. And in the Tchambuli tribe she found that sex roles for men and women were highly differentiated—but the roles were "reversed," with the men being passive and subordinate and the women dominant and aggressive.)

No later researchers have found specific evidence as convincing as Mead's, but radical feminists have pushed this theoretical approach even further. Kate Millet, author of *Sexual Politics* (1970), for example, maintains that: "The sexes are inherently in everything alike, save reproductive systems, secondary sexual characteristics, orgasmic capacity, and genetic and morphological structure."

iii Research (Survey) (Studies of *personality variables* in young children have revealed *sex-linked differences* very early in life. Even in the cradle, male infants are more active:) they cry more, sleep less, demand more. Female infants react more strongly to the removal of a blanket and are more sensitive to sound, touch, cold, and pain. They also smile more and are more passive and content.) At 12 weeks girls will look longer at pictures of faces than at geometric figures; boys have no preference at first but eventually show a preference for figures. (The argument that these differences are innate is a strong one; as Jerome Kagan points out, the earlier a difference appears, the more likely it is to be caused by biological rather than environmental factors (*Personality Development,* 1969). Other primates also display behavioral differences between the sexes from a relatively early age:) young male rhesus monkeys, for example, are more aggressive, less interested in newborn monkeys, and less interested in grooming themselves or others than are their female counterparts.

Male aggressiveness occurs early—even before the child is able to perceive the difference between the sexes or to begin to imitate one rather than the other. But, whether or not there are inborn differences in temperament, no characteristic belongs exclusively to one sex. Some traits are more sex-specific than others from the earliest years on, but no matter what trait is under consideration, some females will exhibit or exceed the "male" norm, and some males will exhibit or exceed the "female" norm.

By the age of four, twice as many girls as boys cry when frightened in a strange laboratory. Girls learn to talk and to read earlier. They also demonstrate greater dependence and docility; boys begin to show greater autonomy and activity. IQ testing reveals intellectual differences between the sexes from an early age. Boys are better at subtests involving spatial ability, mechanical tasks, some forms of arithmetic and quantitative reasoning, and analytic ability; girls are better at subtests involving fine motor skills, verbal ability, memory, numerical computation, and some forms of symbolic manipulation. (Interestingly, Eleanor Maccoby in "Sex Differences in Intellectual Functioning," a 1966 article, reports that differences in mathematical skills appear first in high school, *not* in elementary school.) On nearly all IQ tests used today the effects of these differences are deliberately eliminated by excluding test items that give sex-specific results.

Some of the most important research on sex differences has been conducted by John Money, Joan Hampson, and John Hampson (reported in their "Imprinting and the Establishment of Gender Role," 1967). These researchers studied clinical evidence from case histories of *pseudohermaphrodites* whose gender had been mistaken at birth. (Errors arise particularly in conditions of congenital adrenal hyperglasia in which the internal organs may be female but the external organs appear to be male, especially in infancy.) The development of normal adult behavior in these cases apparently depends on the timing of the individual's reassignment to the proper sex. After the age of three or four it is exceedingly difficult to reverse roles: a boy who is initially raised as a girl will have adopted the gender role of a girl. The researchers concluded that gender role is quite independent of chromosomal, gonadal, or hormonal sex and that all humans are *psychosexually neuter* at birth.

In "A Critical Evaluation of the Ontogeny of Human Sexual Behavior" (1965), Milton Diamond examined clinical evidence on a variety of behavioral, endocrinal, anatomical, and genetic factors, and concluded that humans *are* predisposed to a particular gender orientation as a result of prenatal genetic and hormonal differences—but that this predisposition is potentially very modifiable. Frank A. Beach considers the issue unresolved; he believes that there are sex-linked differences in the functional characteristics of the brain at birth but accepts the importance of experience in subsequent development of gender-linked personality differences.

iv Evaluation Although it is extremely difficult to disentangle the social from the biological in the study of sex-linked personality differences, the evidence of different behavior patterns for males and females from birth strongly suggests that at least some of the variation has a genetic basis. It is true, however, that infants are treated differently from the time of birth, depending on their sex. Parental responses may vary in subtle ways, but the infant will inevitably respond and develop differentiated behaviors. As the child grows older, the problem becomes still more complex, for personality differences may be mediated by the sex-role identification that the child is making. A little girl will tend to select and develop those attributes that are socially endorsed as acceptable for her own gender role.

(Accordingly, several explanations can be offered for sex-linked differences among young children. The fact that girls learn to speak and to count sooner than boys, for example, can be attributed to the fact that the developmental process is different for boys and girls. The more rapid maturing of girls may imply a temporary lead in *cognitive functioning* as well as in *physical development*. But differences in adult behavior—as exemplified in the relatively low incidence of women in such fields as literature or art—are more properly seen as the products of environment rather than biology.) The creativity of women may be blocked and blunted by the discrimination, obstacles, and even ridicule that confront the woman who does not conform to established stereotypes.

(Few social scientists today would ask whether the observed differences between the sexes are the product of innate or social factors; rather, they ask how and in what proportion the two variables interact. It has also become clear that although innate differences may exist statistically, the differences that have been discovered in the early years are relatively minor and do not in any way imply a deficiency or superiority in either sex.) Most of the personality differences associated with the categories of male and female are culturally variable, and it may be that these differences can be overcome, leaving no real distinctions except in behavior associated with childbearing. Indeed, human development may be viewed historically as the victory of the social over the biological: as the struggle for sheer physical survival has become decreasingly important, sex-role differentiation has similarly assumed decreasing significance—especially with regard to the range of occupational opportunities. Nevertheless, whether a unisex society would be desirable or satisfactory to its members is highly questionable: no significant proportion of our own or any other society has advocated such experimentation. The likelihood remains that the facts of anatomy, gender, and parturition will continue to influence social structure. But societal history is by no means over, and as the findings of modern social-science research continue to demonstrate the potential flexibility of sex roles, men and women will be provided with an increasing sense of control over this area of their lives.

c   The "Research" Question

i   Context   The human infant is confronted by a social world whose inhabitants are divided into two distinct groups on the basis of their more conspicuous *primary sexual characteristics*. Each of these two groups exhibits, in every society, different roles—roles that may involve differentials in temperament, sexual behavior, clothing, economic function, familial authority, and social status. The ubiquity of sex-role stereotypes is impressive—and equally impressive is the capacity of the human infant to acquire, by the age

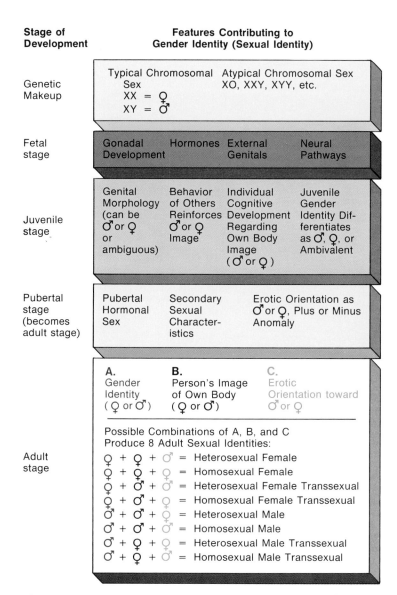

Stage of Development	Features Contributing to Gender Identity (Sexual Identity)			
Genetic Makeup	Typical Chromosomal Sex XX = ♀ XY = ♂	Atypical Chromosomal Sex XO, XXY, XYY, etc.		
Fetal stage	Gonadal Development	Hormones	External Genitals	Neural Pathways
Juvenile stage	Genital Morphology (can be ♂ or ♀ or ambiguous)	Behavior of Others Reinforces ♂ or ♀ Image	Individual Cognitive Development Regarding Own Body Image (♂ or ♀)	Juvenile Gender Identity Differentiates as ♂, ♀, or Ambivalent
Pubertal stage (becomes adult stage)	Pubertal Hormonal Sex	Secondary Sexual Characteristics	Erotic Orientation as ♂ or ♀, Plus or Minus Anomaly	

For the adult stage:

A. Gender Identity (♀ or ♂) **B.** Person's Image of Own Body (♀ or ♂) **C.** Erotic Orientation toward ♂ or ♀

Possible Combinations of A, B, and C Produce 8 Adult Sexual Identities:

♀ + ♀ + ♂ = Heterosexual Female
♀ + ♀ + ♀ = Homosexual Female
♀ + ♂ + ♂ = Heterosexual Female Transsexual
♀ + ♂ + ♀ = Homosexual Female Transsexual
♂ + ♂ + ♀ = Heterosexual Male
♂ + ♂ + ♂ = Homosexual Male
♂ + ♀ + ♀ = Heterosexual Male Transsexual
♂ + ♀ + ♂ = Homosexual Male Transsexual

Table 4. Developmental Schema for Human Gender and Sexual Identity. (Source: Adapted from Money, "Nativism Versus Culturalism")

of two or three, clear sex differences and to grow up to conform to the appropriate sexual stereotypes. Sociologists ask: *By what process do children come to acquire sex-typed behavior patterns?*

ii Theory Two basic models have been provided by social scientists to account for the acquisition of sex roles by young children. These models derive from each of the two main traditions in developmental psychology—the *social-learning* (or *behaviorist*) model and the *cognitive-developmental* model.

Social-learning theory posits an acquisition of behavioral patterns as a result of *reinforcement and rewards.* First the individual distinguishes between various sex-typed behavior patterns, then he generalizes from these particular patterns to new situations, and finally he comes to perform the appropriate sex-typed behavior. This process is made possible by the fact that the child, through explorative imitation and observational learning, will offer

various behaviors that will be either approved (positively reinforced) or disapproved (negatively reinforced) by members of the
surrounding society, particularly the parents. Accordingly, the little
boy who plays with dolls will be discouraged; the little girl will receive social approval for similar activity. Girls will be taught to sew,
to do housework; boys to enjoy rough games, to be aggressive.

An alternative account is given by Lawrence Kohlberg, who
works in the cognitive-developmental tradition established by the
Swiss philosopher and psychologist Jean Piaget. (See Unit 5.)
Kohlberg stresses the active self-definition of the individual rather
than his passive conditioning by society, and he sees sex-typing as
a specific instance of general cognitive development. The child, he
argues, selectively organizes his world: he selects his perceptions,
comes to understand his environment, and categorizes himself as
belonging to a particular gender. In this view sex-typing is seen not
as the result of identification and conditioning, but as the product of
the child's self-definition, which is only then followed by identification. According to Kohlberg, social-learning theory holds that the
child considers: ''I want rewards; I am rewarded for doing boy
things, therefore I want to be a boy.'' But from the cognitive-
developmental viewpoint, the child says: ''I am a boy, therefore I
want to do boy things; therefore the opportunity to do boy things is
rewarding to me.''

Kohlberg treats the formation of concepts of *gender identity*
as a particular example for overall *conceptual development*. He believes that children have a strong preference for whatever they perceive to be like themselves: once they have sensed that they are
members of a gender category, they will show a preferential identification with other members of that category. Furthermore, these
categories are not merely cognitive classes. The stereotypes of the
surrounding culture assume a quasi-moral character to the child,
and deviance from them is seen as ''wrong.''

The difference between the two approaches, then, lies in the
role played by the individual. Social-learning theory acknowledges
the existence of some internal mediating process, but does not
grant it causal influence. Antecedent events—stimuli and reinforced
responses—rather than some intropsychic cognitive acts, are used
to account for learned behavior. Cognitive-developmental theory,
on the other hand, posits some active, internal mediating state of
the organism, some inner ''person'' who selects the stimuli he or
she will respond to and the nature of the response and who actively constructs his or her own understanding of the world.

iii Research (Methodology) Considerable research effort has
been devoted to establishing just how children do adopt appropriate sex roles. Herbert Barry, Margaret K. Bacon, and Irvin Child, in
''A Cross-Cultural Survey of Some Sex Differences in Socialization'' (1957), which covered 110 cultures, found that there was a
strong pressure in most for girls to be obedient and boys to be
self-reliant. There is little question that in American culture very
clear expectations are presented to the child by the parents. But
does this adequately account for the process by which the child
comes to accept that he or she is a boy or a girl? Research evidence shows that the child does go through sequential intellectual
growth, as Kohlberg postulates.

The child's concepts of anatomy are found to be very different from the adult's. In *The First Five Years of Life* (1940), Arnold Gesell and his colleagues assert that at age two-and-a-half most children do not know if they are a boy or a girl, but by three years of age most of them do. But this labeling seems to involve simply a name rather than an intellectual category; full gender identity demands a level of intellectual conceptualization that the maturing child has not yet reached. In fact, research shows that young children remain unclear about the genital basis for assigning gender until after the time at which they have accepted their own sex role. In "The Discrimination of Sex Differences by Young Children" (1955) Allan Katcher shows that although almost all children are able by the age of four to assign the correct sex to themselves and to dolls, the basis of assignment typically involves such variables as clothing, hair length, and general size. In doll-play situations and figure assembly tests that involve matching the segment containing the genitals with other parts of the body, the majority of children show themselves to be confused and ignorant of genital differences. Up until the age of five, many children are unaware that there are genital differences at all. Up to the age of six or even nine, children may continue to have a number of erroneous beliefs—that both sexes have the same organs, but that girls' are smaller; that girls' organs had been or would be bigger; that girls' organs had been cut off; or that the opposite sex's organs were somehow "wrong," "funny." Even up to the age of six, children may believe that the boy-girl dichotomy is not permanent or invariant—that one may still, by changing clothes or hair, change gender. In spite of this confusion about the genital differences, however, children have clear and definite concepts of sex-role stereotypes and show clear preferences in behavior from the age of four or five.

iv Evaluation On the whole, the evidence from research supports the cognitive-developmental rather than the social-learning viewpoint—though it would be wrong to force the two perspectives into complete opposition to one another. Many social scientists, particularly those with a more humanistic viewpoint, reject the behaviorist model because it seems to ignore the role of the *self* in structuring the environment. Social-learning theory is criticized for its lack of a developmental perspective: it sees the child's initial viewpoint as stemming essentially from a lack of experience and conditioning. In contrast, the cognitive-developmental view assumes that children are quite unlike adults and that the differences are not merely in the child's ignorance but in the very structure of the child's thought. Moving from one stage to the next is a matter of specific intellectual activity on the part of the child, which is based on a complex interaction between innate cognitive capacities and experience of the social world. The child must define himself or herself—thereafter he does not really need reinforcement. Unless the child has accepted that he or she is and always will be a boy or a girl, there is no basis for the consistent adoption of the appropriate sex roles. After he or she has adopted a sex role, it would be virtually impossible to arrange suitable "stimuli" and "reinforcements" to reverse behavior patterns.

Sex roles develop, then, through a complex process. There

is undoubtedly some reinforcement of specific responses and interests by the parents. There is imitative behavior by the children. There is some innate biological predisposition to act in one way rather than another. There are cues and pressure from the surrounding society. And perhaps most important, there is a self-imposed gender identity.

3   Overview

Social scientists studying sexual behavior have often been hampered by the lingering taboo that attaches to discussion and research on sexual matters in American society. Many ethnographic studies of other societies avoid mention of sexual mores, and there is still a puritanical reaction to both laboratory research and field studies on sexual behavior in our own society. The situation has changed somewhat since the publication of the Kinsey Report in 1948 (when *The New York Times* refused to carry advertisements for the book), but for a subject of such psychological and sociological significance, human sexual behavior remains remarkably neglected. The work of Virginia Masters and William H. Johnson reported in *Human Sexual Response* in 1966 was the first laboratory investigation of many physiological aspects of sexuality.

Research has suggested, however, that much of the emotional reaction to the discussion or reevaluation of sex behavior is associated with attitudes that do not reflect actual experience but are pegged instead to outdated conventions more honored in the breach than the observance. Although the present younger generation is often criticized for its allegedly promiscuous behavior, the major change toward a permissive society occurred in the first two decades of this century. In the pre-1900 generation, 73.4 percent of the women had no premarital sex experience; in the generation born between 1900 and 1909, only 48.7 percent had no premarital sex experience, and this figure remained fairly constant at least up to the 1950s. Yet a Gallup Poll in 1970 showed that nearly 70 percent of adults (aged 29 and over) believed that premarital sex is "wrong." College students today may not behave markedly differently from their parents, but their expressed beliefs are more in harmony with their actual conduct: another 1970 Gallup Poll showed that three students in four, of both sexes, did not believe it was important that the person they marry be a virgin.

On the question of sex roles themselves, social scientists have learned a good deal from other cultures. Other societies, however, do not necessarily offer models for American society, because their conventions would be alien or artificial within the framework of our own. At the same time, we have learned that sex roles are extremely malleable. The arrangements that societies make in the content of their sex roles are highly variable, and this realization gives us a greater appreciation of the freedom that we have to modify society along lines more conducive to equal rights and equal opportunities for all—regardless of gender. It is important, whatever our objectives, that we see the sociocultural world as more of a human artifact than a biologically determined structure.

Drs. William H. Johnson and Virginia Masters, researchers into human sexuality. The contribution made by Masters and Johnson to understanding human sexuality can hardly be overestimated. In laboratory conditions they systematically measured human physiological responses during diverse sexual acts ranging from fantasizing through masturbation and coitus. They rebutted Freudian theories regarding the "superiority" of the vaginal over the clitoral orgasm in women and carefully documented the physiological stages of orgasm in both men and women. As a result of their work, rapid progress is being made in the area of sexual counseling and therapy for individuals who are experiencing difficulties in fulfilling themselves and their partners sexually. After years as colleagues in research, the two scientists married each other.

D   LOOKING AHEAD

1   Interview:
Germaine Greer

Germaine Greer holds degrees from the Universities of Melbourne and Sydney in Australia and Cambridge University in England. She now lectures at the University of Warwick in England. Her book *The Female Eunuch* attracted international attention, and she is recognized as a leading figure in the women's liberation movement.

DPG   *Sociologists and anthropologists have been challenging the old assumption that most sex differences in behavior are biological in origin. Is their message getting across?*

GREER   It depends what you think the message is. The mistake in the past has been to assume that we could be certain about what we knew about biology (like supposing we knew that one cell was a different shape from another). The logical collapse occurred when people assumed the difference had an effect on behavior. They assumed what they had to prove—say, the relationship between the fact that sex hormones enter the brain and the way the brain functions. The most interesting thing to the political theorist is that you can describe most of the attributes that women traditionally are given in our society as aspects of the pathology of oppression. They are characteristics that they share with oppressed classes in general. For example, because they are not adequately educated, women rely on something like native wit, which is then dignified with the name "intuition." In the working classes, it's called "common sense," or something like that. Even with certain physical characteristics, you have to consider that centuries of oppression will probably give rise to inherited acquired characteristics. This fact seems to me to be the basis of most evolutionary theory. What we don't know is, given the psyche, which is a very delicate thing, how quickly characteristics can be said to be inherited. But of course each girl child starts off with a clean slate which has had an injection of male acquired characteristics. There probably isn't anything to a theory that women are a class which has been bred to be useless for anything else but oppression. We are not a class in that sense. We are not self-contained, we constantly have to consort with the oppressor, and thereby we take on some of his pathology too.

It seems likely that there are going to be all kinds of massive changes in the study of biology. The present state of understanding about DNA, the substance that functions in the transfer of genetic characteristics, seems inadequate and wrong, and the assumptions drawn from it look hopelessly overblown. We're back where we started from—we really don't know the causes of human behavior. We can only trace certain patterns of causation.

DPG   *Is it clear to you that many of the characteristics of women and men in our society that are taken to be genetically endowed are in fact culturally determined?*

GREER John Money's work has probably proved this. You can't find an unconditioned subject on which to base an experiment—they don't exist. But you can find someone who has been conditioned wrongly, according to biological givens, and then try to discover if this fact has led to any collapse in the formation of a female psyche, say, in someone who has actually got male hormones and male genetic structure generally. Money's investigations indicate that men who have been wrongly identified as women from birth have grown up to be quite secure—as secure as anybody can be in his or her sex role. I'm often accused of arguing in paradoxes and contradictions, but they are inherent in my subject. The paradox is that there *are* probably ineradicable differences between men and women. But they are hopelessly exaggerated. And the difference in social treatment isn't based on the basic difference. It's based on the polarized difference—all men are treated as if they were muscular, strong, and hairy, and all women are treated as if they are small and fragile and helpless—although the actual number of people at either of the sexually identified extremes is quite small. I hope that there are lots of differences and that we vary the possible male and female roles as much as possible, so that instead of having unisex we have multisex. At the moment we seem to have no sex at all!

DPG *Would you see the unisex society as a possibility even if it were desirable?*
GREER I detest the idea of any uniformity imposed on people. It terrifies me even in cases where it looks like the only way to bring about any form of justice. There really ought to be plurality in everything, including sex, for a society to be at all vibrant.

DPG *When you talk about the multisex society, do you see some current forms of deviance as representing the vanguard of broad social change in the future?*
GREER Oh, I think so. But the important thing is for people to realize that dividing people off into segments of sexual behavior, and committing them to uniformity within

that segment—like "so-and-so s gay," or "so-and-so's straight"—has a self-perpetuating effect. For example, I believe that the apparent enormous increase in male homosexuality in urban centers has come about because of the extreme austerity of the male sexual role as accepted by a mercantile community. Lots of men who had a perfectly nonaligned desire for sensory excitements that were not included in the range of things that a solid citizen could permit himself became homosexual just out of anxiety. Men who really did feel that they should have pretty clothes and should be able to wear rushing things next to their skin found themselves committed to deviance because it just wasn't allowed. I have a feeling that what we will see in the future is a greater polymorphousness in ordinary sexual relations and not very much concentration on just what genital apparatus the recipient has got. And people won't feel that if they have sex with one man they've got to do it only with men for the rest of their lives, or that if they have sex with one woman they've got to do it with just women for the rest of their lives. But it doesn't show much sign of happening yet, because the sudden increase in women's vociferousness seems to have given rise to a degree of male anxiety and impotence, especially in the United States.

DPG *How do you account for the particularly aggressive stereotype of the American male?*

GREER   I think it's because of the myth of being frontiersmen. It's the same in Australia. In both countries it hasn't been true for generations. But these images die very hard, and they are constantly built up by things like Marlboro cigarette ads, so the puniest man imagines that inside him is John Wayne struggling to get out. But the American male isn't all that different. British construction workers are just as chauvinistic and just as anxious about their phallic endowment and performance as any American. In England, it's partly a working-class cultural tradition. The work ethos is strong in both countries—that mad single-mindedness that makes sex a kind of achievement and therefore a repository of intense anxiety.

DPG *What about men's lib? Do you think men have a role as demanding and demeaning as women, and that their opposition to changes in their role might be even more deeply entrenched than that of many women to the early women's liberation campaigns?*

GREER   I don't think you could argue that it was more deeply entrenched. The situation is probably roughly symmetrical. But men would have to undertake their liberation for themselves, and there'd be no reason for them to do that if they found themselves deriving satisfaction from breasts and bottoms and women who never asked any questions or never demonstrated any interest in anything. Women could help, mainly by insisting on what is due to them. Men's liberation is probably occurring in a subtle way. I wonder what the outcome of the

situation is going to be, because sometimes the anxieties come with redoubled force when they appear to have been laid aside. For example, there's the deliberate effeminacy—that's what my father would call it anyway—of pop stars in the last few years. They refuse to abandon a posture of potency, of *male* potency, and nevertheless they don't just dress themselves in an attractive or showbiz kind of way, they actually dress themselves like the whores of Alexandria, with malachite around their eyes, and their hair dyed and filled with silver paste. And they're getting into the politics of blandishment. But it could be a self-mocking procedure, a way of shortcircuiting the real change. It has a sort of exaggerated media expression which reality can't live up to. I don't know quite what's happening to men. A lot of the men I know have become really extraordinarily passive, as passive as women ever were.

DPG *Can the changes you envisage take place within the context of our existing society?*

GREER   It's not just a question of sexual behavior, it's a question of the whole concept of work and productivity. Women or men for that matter won't be liberated under anything like the present regime, the present structure of wealth or the distribution of power. When you have a very narrow concept in a community of what work is, and what activity is deserving of reward, and what production is, and you have a whole class which because of its power to reproduce is excluded from participating in the rewarded and power-bearing work structure, then you obviously have a class that's built for oppression. If you increase the differentials, if you constantly reward for a particular kind of service to the community, you then develop an oppressed class who are reproducing in order to support this structure of work-elitists. I don't believe you will ever dignify women's work until it is

given dignity by the economic structure, until having children is considered to be a valuable, productive activity and is rewarded as such. Women do something that machines cannot do. Many workers do something that machines can do and are highly paid for doing it. I do not condemn the role of motherhood at all. But the role of motherhood is hopelessly disadvantaged at present, and the children are paying the price.

You see, if women demand the right to work in the restricted sense, namely the right to go and toil at a factory in return for independence in the form of wages, it's perfectly understandable, but hopelessly ahistorical—it's out of date already. It's very ironic that just when the pressures of unemployment are beginning to grind the lowest-paid workers, just when the poor are going through their worst agony, women have suddenly started to put pressure on the employment structures at a critical point. They're coming in with greater advantages, better education, more ambition, and so on. All of a sudden the pressures of middle-class women have been acknowledged, and it's not by bloody accident. It's in the employer's interest to acknowledge it. The battle has already been set up between the poor and blacks and the women, and the women do not have a political strategy which will circumvent it.

DPG *Do you think violence will be involved in the change to a different society?*
GREER   I don't know. It's taken us a long time to work out that there's no value in dying for things at all, that the world purges it-

self of its best blood regularly, and that's one of the reasons why things don't change. I don't think we can purge our society by popular action like China did in its cultural revolution. Fighting in the streets would only give everybody the opportunity they want to kick the hell out of us. It seems obvious that the Black Panthers are a totally controlled and manipulated organization in the United States. Everybody gets excited about them supposedly firing rifles from the rooftops, but it gives the police carte blanche for the most horrifying repressive measures ever afterwards. I think Americans have learned the technique of encouragement and indulgence and then exposure and ruthless repression. But like all oppressed groups, women are politically naïve, so they'll probably go through that phase. I fight media battles all the time because I happen to think they are sometimes more conclusive than, say, getting myself arrested for pitching a rock through Revlon's showcase window. I'd love to do it but I can't indulge myself to that extent. It's actually the Australian libertarian anarchist position that I've held since I was about 19. When everyone was saying "Legalize marijuana," for example, I was one of the first people to say "Legalize marijuana—hell!" At least you can smoke a joint without thinking you're subsidizing a damn Polaris submarine or something. As soon as you legalize marijuana it's going to be exploited, and it'll just be expensive and bad-quality dope, and it will be enriching the same bunch we've always enriched. Let it stay illegal.

DPG *Antifeminists always point to the fact that very few women have become great artists or musicans in support of their view that women are somehow different or even inferior. What's your answer?*

GREER   The same answer as you give to why oppressed groups everywhere haven't performed the arts of the oppressor. It's a bit like saying that the black women who worked on the plantations were inferior to the white women because they didn't embroider very well. You bet they didn't embroider very well; their hands had been coarsened by the kind of toil that they had been doing. There are two separate questions. One is what the absolute value of those great works of art is. They have very great value to a group of people, an elite who have been taught to desire them. They've been taught that if you can't have an orgasm when you hear Beethoven, then you've got a deficient sensibility. The next question is whether or not the arts of an oppressed group are themselves important. The Whitney Museum in New York had an exhibition of patchwork quilts, which are the collective work of women, supervised by one woman who made the pattern. And somebody realized what should have been obvious, that what they were looking at was nonfigurative art of quite a high degree of sophistication. It was sewn—but what's the special magic about painting on two-dimensional surfaces? If the artists have no ego, they're not going to compete; they're not going to want to compete; they're not going to want to write a symphony. They're going to do other things, and it's a question of our aesthetic sensibility to what unregarded and disregarded people do. What's so hot about the damn Mona Lisa anyway?

Unit 14
Death, Dying, and Society

SCHEMATIC OUTLINE

A Introductory Graphics: Death—Past and Present

B Definition and Context

1 Definition
The sociology of death is an inquiry into the impact of man's dying upon his relationship to himself, to other human beings, and to the social structure as a whole.

2 World Context
Although death is a universal fact, different societies behave differently when confronted with it. There are various modes of counteracting it, depending upon the degree of threat it poses to the social framework.

3 American Context
American society has tended to deny the reality of death, to emphasize youthfulness and progress, and to institutionalize dying. Only recently have social scientists begun to take an interest in the terminally ill.

C Questions and Evidence

1 Questions
Among the questions about death that intrigue sociologists are: (1) What are the most urgent aspects of the "dying in dignity" controversy? (2) How do attitudes toward death and the process of dying affect attitudes toward life? (3) How has the hospital responded to its role as a "dying center," and what is its attitude toward the terminally ill patient?

2 Evidence
a The "Burning Issue" Question
Study of the last stage of life has been neglected by the social sciences and is not yet well understood. Elisabeth Kubler-Ross' *Death and Dying* shows that the stages of dying demand a tremendous amount of fortitude, courage, and exertion rather than passive submission to one's fate. A focus on the psychosocial aspects of death is now emerging.
b The "Classical" Question
Sigmund Freud viewed death as a psychological reality as well as a bodily event. His theories sparked interest in a previously forbidden area, and his model of psychological man has been revised and amplified by sociologists, psychologists (such as G. Stanley Hall and Erik Erikson), philosophers, and anthropologists.
c The "Research" Question
Barney Glaser and Anselm Strauss have carried out important research on social interactions between dying patients and hospital personnel. They suggest that information about his condition should not be withheld from the patient and recommend changes in medical training and planning.

3 Overview
Accelerated technological advances and social and institutional changes have left the issue of death relatively obscure and ambiguous.

D Looking Ahead

1 Interview: Robert Blauner

SUPPORTING UNITS

3 Biology and Society
6 Population and Demography
7 Marriage, Kinship, and the Family
8 Religion
10 Personality and Society
11 Small Groups
12 Social Interaction

ENCYCLOPEDIA ENTRIES

aging
alienation
Census, United States
death
death rate
family
generation gap
Golden Age Clubs
kinship systems
life expectancy
Medicare
middle years
old-age insurance
population
rites of passage
social insurance
social structure
thanatology
widowhood
zero population growth

DEATH — PAST AND PRESENT

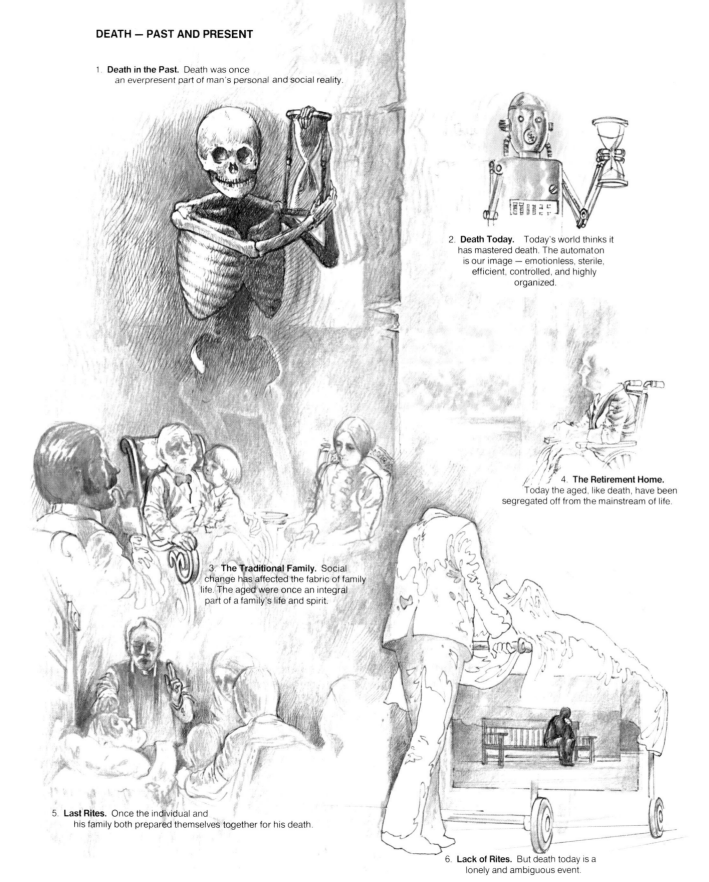

1. **Death in the Past.** Death was once an everpresent part of man's personal and social reality.

2. **Death Today.** Today's world thinks it has mastered death. The automaton is our image — emotionless, sterile, efficient, controlled, and highly organized.

3. **The Traditional Family.** Social change has affected the fabric of family life. The aged were once an integral part of a family's life and spirit.

4. **The Retirement Home.** Today the aged, like death, have been segregated off from the mainstream of life.

5. **Last Rites.** Once the individual and his family both prepared themselves together for his death.

6. **Lack of Rites.** But death today is a lonely and ambiguous event.

Sisyphus, figure from Greek mythology who had to push a boulder to the top of a mountain. As he approached the top, however, the boulder inevitably slipped from his grasp and rolled back down to the plains below. "Judging whether life is or is not worth living amounts to answering the fundamental question of philosophy"—Albert Camus, *The Myth of Sisyphus* (1940). (Copper engraving after M. Picart.)

B   DEFINITION AND CONTEXT

1   Definition

The fundamental nature of death and the significance it imparts to life have always been dominant concerns of religious and philosophical inquiry. As Plato said, "The true philosopher is ever pursuing death and dying." Death has been personified in many guises: the seducer, the gay deceiver, the Conqueror Worm. Today, however, it has been stripped to a considerable degree of its awesome and macabre connotations. The advances brought about by science and technology and the consequent vast improvement in public health have resulted in a substantial improvement of living conditions and have thereby considerably diminished the extent of death's domain. (See Unit 3.) In his *Psychology of Death* (1972) psychologist Robert Kastenbaum, a prominent figure in death research, says, "In a sense . . . death is becoming obsolete. It is an event that befalls only those people who have already become obsolete, therefore Death himself has been mustered out of his employment."

Its images have undoubtedly shifted, yet the act and fact of death still play an integral role in the drama of life. So little attention has been given to the subject in either professional or lay journals that some social scientists have termed American culture "death-denying." Death is part of reality. They ask what the social outcome will be if children live insulated and isolated from it. Dying is an institutional phenomenon; what attitudes are projected by those who occupy *death professional* roles—physician, nurse, funeral director, clergyman? How has the terminally ill patient's perception of reality been altered? There are a host of important questions in this area.

The sociology of death is an inquiry into the impact of man's dying upon his relationship to himself, to other human beings, and to the social structure as a whole. Its aim is a better understanding of how death and dying affect the everyday world in terms of the way people cognitively and emotionally perceive it and, most importantly, in terms of how people behave. How does our conception of death influence our construction of reality, and how does our social reality reflect our orientation toward death?

2   World Context

Although death is a universal fact of life, different societies behave differently when confronted by it. In the less-developed, preindustrial nations death is a commonly accepted occurrence. To take one example, the monsoons that seasonally descend upon the Indian subcontinent result in a devastating mortality rate. Poor public health measures are reflected by a high rate of epidemics, and famine brought about by the destruction of key crops further contributes to the prevalence of death. Because mortality as a fact tends to disrupt social structures on a day-to-day basis, *death systems* have been devised to counteract its impact.

In most preindustrial countries there are well-established *kinship networks,* and because each individual belongs to an exten-

X-Men. Although the mass media focus to a great degree on violent behavior, few of the figures one is meant to identify with ever actually dies. The media avoid the idea of one's personal death and treat death as an abstract concept, if and when they deal with it at all.

sive family, the loss of one member is compensated for by the continuing presence of the others. Fertility conditions ensure a high birth rate to offset the staggering death rate. Most important, religious myths and rituals provide concrete guidelines and roles for the bereaved individuals and the social group as a whole in the face of death. These ritual prescriptions range from cosmological explanations of what happens to the person after death down to the most pragmatic issues—for example, distribution of the deceased's land and provision of a new husband or wife for the remaining spouse.

Sociologist Robert Blauner in "Death and the Social Structure" (1966), one of the few studies of the subject, notes a number of ways societies attempt to meet the threat of death. A major method is to reduce the importance of those who die. Thus

Primitive societies, hard hit by infant and child mortality, characteristically do not recognize infants and children as people; until a certain age they are considered as still belonging to the spirit world from which they came, and therefore their death is often not accorded ritual recognition—no funeral is held.

Anthropologist Arnold van Gennep's classic study, *Rites of Passage* (1908), provided detailed examples of societies in which children are sometimes not accorded living status until their marriage.

But what happens when a person who is clearly engaged in a vitally important function of the society dies? That person's "unfinished business" must in some way be completed, and Blauner perceptively suggests:

(Facing page) A group of Txukahamal Amazon Indians in their jungle camp. South American Indians such as these do not define infants as human until they have survived a few months. If the mother is still suckling a previous child, the newborn may be strangled to death or left to die in the jungle. Because the infant is not defined as human, such action is not seen as murder. There is an underlying biological basis for this behavior; these Indians live on a low-protein, high-starch diet, and if the mother tries to nourish more than one infant from her milk, both are likely to contract kwashiorkor, a fatal protein-deficiency disease.

the almost universal belief in ghosts in preindustrial societies can be understood . . . not simply as a function of naïve, magical and other "unsophisticated" world views. Ghosts are reifications of this unfinished business, and belief in their existence may permit continuation of relationships broken off before their natural terminus.

Death, Blauner demonstrates, is a variable of social structures. Accordingly, it is counteracted in different modes, depending upon the degree of threat it poses to the existing social framework. The more sophisticated the technological status of the society, the less important is the function of any specific individual, and, therefore, the less entrenched are the rituals and social prescriptions surrounding death.

George A. Hillery, Jr., and some associates compared mortality rates from 41 countries and found that preindustrial countries show high birth and death rates, "transitional" countries exhibit low death rates but still maintain high birth rates, and a "mature" or fully industrialized country displays both low birth and death rates ("Causes of Death in the Demographic Transition," 1968). Parents are encouraged to choose when and how many children to have. The resulting reduction in family size brings about an important change in *primary groups:* parents place more emphasis and bestow greater attention upon their fewer offspring. Reduced family size also means that the children of a family are grown and gone sooner than in past generations, when the span of children's ages was so much greater.

3 American Context

It has been suggested that American culture is the first in the history of mankind to be relatively "death-free." The average life span of an American today is twice that of his ancestors: in 1900 the infant mortality rate in America was 162 deaths per 1,000 persons; by 1961 the equivalent figure had dropped by over 80 percent, to 23 deaths per 1,000. The major *communicable diseases*—influenza and pneumonia, tuberculosis, gastritis, duodenitis, and enteritis, and the infectious illnesses of childhood—have declined as major causes of death, giving way to the *degenerative diseases*—heart ailments, malignant neoplasms, arteriosclerosis, and strokes—usually associated with the *geriatric* patient. American parents now live more than one-third of their lives after their children have left home. But the American family has been modified by other factors as well. As corporate modes of employment replaced employment on the small farm and in the small local business, social and geographical mobility became increasingly viable ways to obtain better occupations. The close family and kinship system fragmented into more isolated nuclear families, and primary groups became less dependent upon kinship structure than upon interactions at work. *Socialization* tended to become divided between parental control and institutional instruction, and *rites of passage* evolved away from family or clan initiations to be replaced by attaining various rungs in the "corporate ladder." We have discussed many of these developments in earlier units.

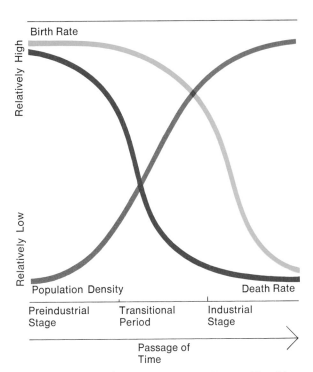

Figure 1. The Interaction of Birth and Death Rates as They Affect Population Density When Less-Developed Societies Modernize. The preindustrial stage has a stable population at low density, but high birth and death rates. In the transitional period there is a rapid population increase because the death rate is decreased by developments in the field of health more rapidly than there is a decrease in birth rates. In the industrial stage there is a stable population at high density with lower birth and death rates.

(Facing page) The faces of old age. When you look at the faces of elderly people, what are the thoughts, feelings, and associations that come into your mind? Is the dominant tone positive or negative?

(Pages 324–325) Often extraordinary measures are taken to keep hospital patients alive for just a few extra days. Gradually the medical profession is coming to grips with the moral question: When does a patient have the right to insist that he or she wants to die in peace—and possibly even at home, away from the medical environment?

The *nuclear family's* central concern with children also had far-reaching consequences. No longer afraid that their children would die before they reached one year of age, parents could wholeheartedly respond to each child's birth and individual dispositions. Applause greeted each new arrival, and cultural defiance of death was transformed into a denial of its reality. Society endorsed, developed, and (some would say) demanded a youth orientation. Advertising and merchandising created the image of the agile and attractive perpetual postadolescent bent essentially on consuming products ranging from maternity clothes to pseudo-racing cars. The "pop-top disposable" approach colors much of American life: some estimates claim that over $5 billion is spent each year on cosmetics, wigs, exercise equipment, and various youth-enhancing gadgets, although only one-twelfth of that figure is provided for the care of the elderly.

The roots of this situation go much deeper than the past 75 years. The characteristic American focus has always been on the bounty of the future: today's invention or discovery is but one more step toward the ultimate destination. The belief that "nothing stands in the way of progress" has been a credo of American life.

America's campaign to wipe out death has effectively institutionalized it: less than one-third of all deaths occur outside of hospitals or other appropriate institutional settings, and only 5 percent of all deaths occur violently. As degenerative diseases account for more and more deaths, aging and dying tend to become synonymous, and in a society bent on forgetting death the elderly have been cordoned off from the mainstream of American life. The devaluation of the elderly parallels the premium placed on vitality, vigor, mobility, freshness, and, most importantly, aggressive activity. A set of clear dichotomies—between young and old, productive and useless, mobile and immobile, important and unimportant, living and dying—has pervaded our social structure. Yet it has only been in the past two decades that serious questions have been posed and research generated about death and dying, the aged and aging. Death is still largely considered a morbid and tedious subject to pursue. Why, then, the sudden interest in recent years?

One reason is that there has been a downgrading of the American worship of progress. People have begun to notice that industrial advance has had substantial environmental costs, and for many "low status" individuals and groups progress has been slight. The public spotlight turned on such obvious shortcomings eventually led to interest in problems related to aging and death.

Other reasons for increased interest have been suggested: nuclear bombs pose a threat to our very existence, and at least two commentators, Hans J. Morgenthau and Robert Jay Lifton, have argued that our relationships to ourselves, others, death, immortality, and life in general have been radically altered since the attack on Hiroshima. Robert Kastenbaum suggests that as psychiatrists, psychologists, and other social scientists have experienced the aging and dying of their spouses, friends, and peers, they have begun to reflect on and discuss the reality of death. There is increasing concern about the hospital and the geriatric institution, and a controversy is underway over the *terminally ill* patient's relationship to his doctor, his hospital environment, and the changes

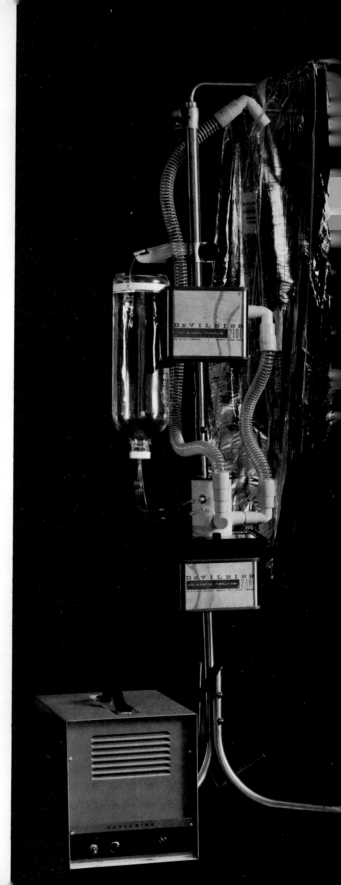

that occur in his perception and construction of reality. The rites that used to allow a dignified and optimally painless passing have been damaged by the impersonal institutionalization of present-day medical procedures.

C QUESTIONS AND EVIDENCE

1 Questions

Among the questions about death that intrigue sociologists are: (1) What are the most urgent aspects of the "dying in dignity" controversy? (2) How do attitudes toward death and the process of dying affect attitudes toward life? (3) How has the hospital responded to its role as a "dying center," and what is its attitude toward the patient? Should this attitude be changed?

2 Evidence

a The "Burning Issue" Question

i Context Although we are increasingly insulated from the actual fact of death, the mass media do provide a few stylized or abstracted images of it. These range from the news reports on war, famine, and starvation in various parts of the world to children's cartoons, daytime serials, and movies full of scenes of dying and mayhem. We are rarely allowed to empathize with the dying or the murdered: most such scenes are emotionally neutral and dramatically matter-of-fact. Presentations of this sort have intensified the already distant relationship Americans have with death.

It was most unusual when one television series, *The Bold Ones,* in 1972 offered a dramatic protrayal of the dilemmas facing a terminally ill patient. In an era when physicians are characterized in the media as young, dynamic "Ben Caseys" constantly involved in life-saving heroics or as older sage-like "Marcus Welbys" who endlessly dispense patience and advice (mostly to their younger colleagues), *The Bold Ones* presented a clear portrayal of a woman facing the possibility of remaining alive only through the use of several "life-prolonging" machines. Simply "keeping the patient alive" was her doctor's central concern—at whatever cost to her, her family, and other patients who might benefit more from the medical equipment and professional time required for her treatment. As the dying woman radically examined what meaning the temporary prolongation of life could have for her in such circumstances, the doctor faced a conflict in the Hippocratic oath: what to do when saving the patient's life not only failed to ease her suffering but caused her greater anguish. Sociologists must also confront complex situations of this sort, and they ask: *What are the personal and social factors relevant to the "dying in dignity" issue?*
ii Theory Although this incident of *The Bold Ones* was an anomaly for television viewers, it presented scenes that hospital personnel, doctors, and clergymen would not find uncommon. Whether or not a patient should be informed that he is dying has been an important issue not only to concerned professionals, but also to the patient's family as well. The meaning of *euthanasia* has become a

topic of heated dispute as complex machines increase the possibility of artificially prolonging a threatened life, thus challenging the very definition of a ''natural'' life span.

The problem of how to allow patients death with dignity is even more immediate. Although the hospital provides the patient with ''improved'' (meaning ''relatively painless'') conditions in which to die and offers the benefits of up-to-date medical facilities and specialized knowledge, the resulting environment has created pressing psychological problems for all involved. The patient is deprived of *sustaining or distracting interaction* with his friends, neighbors, and business associates and instead must depend on *routinized interaction* with a staff of relatively impersonal professionals. On the other hand, nurses are exposed to death as part of their daily routine; physicians are confronted by situations they have not been trained to handle; and clergymen are denied the traditional modes of ritual in communicating with the institutionalized patient. In *The Coming Crisis of Western Sociology* (1970) Alvin Gouldner says, ''Indeed if there is any modern organization more callous than the army to the dignity of the person, it is the modern hospital.'' This callousness affects not only the dying patient, but also all the other individuals around him. Although death and dying have become efficiently organized, the training of hospital staff and death professionals has been overly confined to the operational level, leaving large areas of emotional interaction totally untouched and unexplored.

Alienation in institutional settings has been a central concern of sociology, yet almost no research has been done on the moment of approaching death, which activates an enormous crisis for the individuals involved. The fear of the unknown overcomes the dying patient and is compounded by fears of loneliness and loss of family, friends, body, self-control—in short, loss of *identity*. An individual maintains his sense of *self* through his contact with others and the affirmation he receives from his family and his own body. In the dying process the patient is confronted with the task of continuing the integrity of the self in the face of disintegrating and annihilating forces.

Psychologist Erik Erikson's theory of psychosocial development (discussed in Unit 5) suggests a direction sociologists might

Grandparents. When old persons are given meaningful positions in society, they have a reasonable chance to experience themselves as valuable, worthwhile persons—especially when they are allowed to have meaningful relationships with children.

In the second stage of the dying trajectory the dying person starts to come to grips with the feelings that are brought to the surface as he or she faces the inevitability of death. The intensity of anger, initially directed outward, is eventually turned inward by the dying person on his or her own self. Deep depression follows.

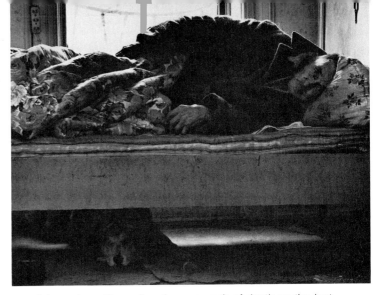

possibly explore. Regarding the approach of death as the last stage of man's *developmental life cycle,* Erikson characterizes it as optimally a time of

> acceptance of one's own and only life cycle and of the people who have become significant to it as something that had to be and that, by necessity, permitted of no sub-stitutions. . . . It is a sense of comradeship with men and women of distant times and of different pursuits, that have created orders and objects and sayings conveying human dignity and love. ("Identity and the Life Cycle," 1959)

Despair, on the other hand, is the result of the erosion of self-esteem—the inability to retain a positive belief in who one is and has been. The last stage of life, Erikson suggests, should be a vital step in the rounding out of one's entire existence. In the *bureaucratic setting* of today's hospital, however, the patient is given little psychosocial assistance, and the hospital staff is equally unprepared to meet, or even to perceive, such needs.

iii Research Elisabeth Kübler-Ross, one of the first physicians to conduct a seminar on death and dying, has done considerable study of the situation and status of the dying patient. In her interaction with terminal patients she has detected five stages the patient moves through from the time he is told he is dying until he actually dies.

Stage one is *initial denial,* usually expressed in disbelief—"No, not me, it can't be me." Kübler-Ross reports the case of one woman who refused to accept her diagnosis, convinced that her X-rays were "mixed up"; she then asked for reassurance that her pathology report could not have been processed so quickly and that therefore it must belong to someone else with the same name. When her hopes for reassurance were denied, she demanded to leave the hospital and went to a number of other doctors, although she kept in contact with her original doctor in order to have help available at all times.

From denial and isolation, the patient moves into the sec-ond stage: *anger.* The illusion ("It can't be me") gives way to fact ("Oh, yes, it is me, it was not a mistake"). A logical part of this

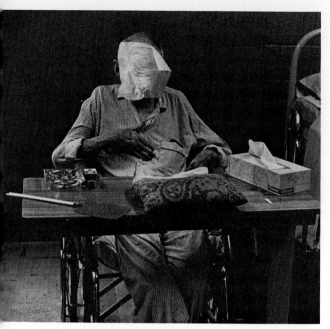

Elderly patient in a state mental hospital with face covered. The psychologist Carl Jung wrote extensively about old age. He held that part of preparing for one's death is a retreat from outer-directed behavior toward the "real world" and an intensification of the inner-directed energy with which the individual tries to come to grips with his or her "inner world." As this turning inward intensifies, the individual starts to think more and more in terms of archaic, mythological symbols and themes and thus may seem "crazy" to friends and family members. Instead of allowing this process to play itself out, we often commit such people to insane asylums.

stage involves the question, "Why me?" Much of the anger is projected outwardly onto the patient's family and doctor and the hospital staff.

Anger gives way to stage three: *bargaining*. The patient will agree to go quietly if God permits him to live just long enough to participate in or witness some important event: a son's wedding or a daughter's graduation. The patient promises "good behavior" in the hopes for an extended "deadline."

When the patient can no longer deny his illness, bargaining is overcome by stage four: *depression*. The heaviness of his fate engulfs the dying patient, and this situation may be compounded by anxiety over financial burdens, status loss in one's role as breadwinner or homemaker, as well as by the thought of impending loss of family and self.

"If a patient has time enough," writes Kübler-Ross, "and has been given some help in working through the previously described stages, he will reach a stage during which he is neither depressed nor angry about his 'fate'." This is the fifth and final one: *acceptance*.

Kübler-Ross' *Death and Dying* (1969) thus describes important aspects of the problem that are daily encountered in our institutionally designated *"dying centers."* It may seem that acceptance of death is like a surrender or resignation and means that the patient has "given up fighting." Yet, as Kübler-Ross has shown, the stages of dying demand a tremendous amount of fortitude, courage, and exertion: these indicate the very opposite of passive submission to one's fate.

iv Evaluation   The last stage of life is not yet well understood. Studies that have focused on patient-physician relationships seem to agree on the emotional inadequacy of medical training and medical care. "The care of the dying," writes Cicely Saunders in "The Last Stages of Life" (1965), "demands all that we can do to enable patients to *live* until they die. It includes the care of the family, the mind, and the spirit as well as the care of the body." According to Richard Kalish, the critical questions that continually present themselves in working with terminal patients are: "What is the major goal of the physician? Is it to keep the patient legally alive? To preserve a minimal level of alertness? How important a goal is the smooth running of the hospital? The anxiety of the other patients?" ("The Practicing Physician and Death Research," 1969)

A focus on the psychosocial aspects of death is emerging. One of the most obvious characteristics of the relationship between the patient and physician is its one-sided dependence. The physician "knows" what to do; the dying patient must absolve himself of any part in the business. Recent articles and research, however, point to a potentially significant change: the insights of the aging and dying can instruct us about the last stages of life. In *Death and Dying* Kübler-Ross provides a good illustration:

Early in my work with dying patients I observed the desperate need of the hospital staff to deny the existence of terminally ill patients in their ward. In another hospital I once spent hours looking for a patient capable to be inter-

Albrecht Dürer's engraving *The Knight, Death, and the Devil* (early sixteenth century) and still from Ingmar Bergman's film *The Seventh Seal* (1956). During the medieval period in Europe, death was a very real part of people's lives.

viewed, only to be told that there was no one fatally ill and able to talk. On my walk through the ward I saw an old man reading a paper with the headline "Old soldiers never die." He looked at me with anger and disgust, telling me that I must be one of those physicians who can only care for a patient as long as he is well but when it comes to dying, then we shy away from them. This was my man! I told him about my seminar on death and dying and my wish to interview someone in front of the students in order to teach them not to shy away from those patients. He happily agreed to come, and gave us one of the most unforgettable interviews I have ever attended.

b   The "Classical" Question

i   Context   Historically, death has conditioned people's responses to cultural situations. Religious systems have often involved concepts that offer man a way to overcome mortality—either by positing a life that goes on after death (the personality remains more or less intact despite incorporeality) or by interpreting death as a transition into other cycles of "being," which may involve physical existence in a radically different form (one may "come back" as a cat or a flower). In return for this anticipated reward of extended life—or, indeed, in order to earn it—religions also offer paradigms of behavior and action that members of the community are supposed to emulate. In this way, man's need to cope with the fact of death and to discover its meaning for each individual can clearly be seen to influence his daily social interaction and values.

With the development of modern technology and the consequent removal of death from center stage, the emphasis on death and a hoped-for afterlife has given way to an emphasis on life itself. Death has almost been robbed of any significance whatsoever. Because 95 percent of deaths today are considered "natural," people no longer need to huddle together to ward them off; social prescriptions, group cohesiveness, and kinship bonds have been replaced by the relationships of "psychological man"—separate, individual, the possessor of a unique personality. Nevertheless, sociologists feel that death as the ultimate phenomenon continues to pervade our social structure, even if only subliminally, and influences the development of personality. They ask: *What personal and social behaviors are associated with death, and how does modern society influence their expression? What is the relationship between death-related behavior and broader patterns of human interaction and social structure?*

ii   Theory   Sigmund Freud, the founder of psychoanalysis, provided social theorists with a dynamic structure of personality and social development. Although it did not consist of a single systematic message, it was supported by a network of interwoven intellectual and ethical implications. Freud envisaged and formulated the model of "psychological man," which he saw emerging as a contrast to the Marxist "economic man" of the nineteenth century.

Freud saw three stages in man's history: (1) the primitive stage, where taboos created a cohesive but repressive system; (2) the religious stage, where theology replaced taboos; and (3) modern culture, where old repressions are being loosened but not yet superseded. According to Freud, the modern period—a period of transition where morality is ebbing and *normative authority* is lacking—had given rise to an extraordinary increase in *neuroses,* because of the decline of traditional belief and group ritual and their replacement by self-absorption and individual preoccupation.

Freud examined the common incidents of everyday life and saw that they exhibited a split—a *cultural lag* between thought and action, ideology and technology, and the changing social context and traditional modes of behavior. His analysis of man and the basic processes of civilization was a kind of rigorous excavation and dissection of "civilized morality," and he concluded that much of our socially accepted behavior is actually a "sublimated" and disguised form of more aggressive and primitive drives that can still be glimpsed in their original composition and force in the "unconscious" and "subconscious" dimensions of man's psyche. If these drives and longings (Freud called them *wishes*) become too severely frustrated or blocked, the individual is compelled to behave in either an *antisocial* or a *self-destructive mode.* The person who turns his *aggression* inward too consistently and intensely may seek release from his tensions in death (or the idea of death), a response that may make him fear even more strongly the very termination he desires. Because the "civilizing" process to some degree always involves the inhibition of aggression and the inculcation of guilt, civilization is fundamentally "neurotic" (self-thwarting) in direct proportion to how repressive it is and how unreassuring are the answers it offers to problems shared by its members. Because death (or self-destruction) retains a hidden grip on our emotions, it is an area that must be brought to light and accepted on its own terms. To fail in this respect is to invite the tyranny of death rather than its demise.

iii Research (Survey)   Although sexuality was a predominant concern of Freud, it was not the only one. As sociologist Phillip Rieff points out in *The Mind of the Moralist* (1961), "Freud's one small hope, reason, is closely and properly linked to his mixed vision, half longing and half repugnance, of the force of death." Death and fate recur as significantly as sexuality in Freud's writings, and he attacked society's denial of death as strongly as he condemned sexual suppression. Writing in 1925 about the evolving status of physicians, he pointed out that "the contemporary generation of doctors has been brought up to respect only anatomical, physical and chemical factors. . . . They were not prepared for taking psychical ones into account and therefore met them with indifference and antipathy." Freud criticized medical training methods, which focused on the eradication of the illness-causing alien element and stressed disease as the exclusive concern of the physician—who was expected to counteract the pathos of his encounter with his patient by simulating certain bedside mannerisms, affectations, and an aloof demeanor.

Freud sought to understand death as more than a bodily event; he treated it as a psychological reality that he termed the *death instinct.* He felt that "a more studied appreciation of death could reinstruct us in the serious consequences of living." Writing in 1915, just after the outbreak of World War I, he talked about "our relation to death":

(Left) Sigmund Freud (1856–1939). Freud's interest in what he came to call *thanatos,* or the death instinct, foreshadowed a tragic development in his own life. He fell victim to cancer of the face, and as it became obvious that more and more of his face would have to be removed surgically, he asked a friend to kill him painlessly. The friend (who kept the secret until a posthumous publication of his diaries revealed it), proved his friendship by meeting Freud's request.

(Below) A funeral. Even in the ritual of interment, our society avoids facing the issue of death's finality. The casket is lowered into the grave, and the grave is covered over with a "lid" of artificial flowers before the funeral party arrives at the graveside. The casket is thus out of sight for the graveside ceremony, and the family and friends are expected to leave the graveside before the workmen begin to fill in the open grave with dirt.

If one listened to us, we were, of course, ready to declare that death is the necessary end of all life, that every one of us owed nature his own death and must be prepared to pay this debt—in short, that death is natural, undeniable and unavoidable. In reality, however, we used to behave as if it were different. We have shown the unmistakable tendency to push death aside, to eliminate it. ("Thoughts for the Times on War and Death")

Today people still show the same tendency to "keep a deadly silence about death."

iv Evaluation Though Freud's theory of psychoanalysis and the "psychological man" did not provide a specific system of action, they did create an imposing model that sociologists, psychologists, philosophers, and anthropologists have revised and amplified. Through the impetus of Freud, G. Stanley Hall, one of the earliest American researchers into death attitudes, published his "Thanatophobia and Immortality" (1915) and *Senescence* (1922). Erik Erikson modified Freud's stages of psychosexuality by emphasizing the social context in personality development. Erikson has been a major advocate of the view that parents should face up to the facts of death in order that their children may more fully face life.

Whether one views Freud positively or critically, the fact remains that he was the spark that generated interest in many forbidden areas. Sexuality became and continues to be a subject of intense study. Death, however, has received considerably less attention. As late as 1959 psychologist Herman Feifel could write:

> In the presence of death, Western culture, by and large, has tended to run, hide, and seek refuge in group norms and actuarial statistics. The individual face of death has become blurred by embarrassed incuriosity and institutionalization. The shadows have begun to dwarf the substance. Concern about death has been relegated to the tabooed territory heretofore occupied by diseases like tuberculosis and cancer and the topic of sex. ("Introduction to *The Meaning of Death")*

There are no longer any entrenched, well-defined supportive roles in our culture that help one to cope with dying or death. Pluralism, secularization, and social complexity have left death's status particularly ambiguous. Most recent studies revolve around condemnations or indictments of the death professionals, especially the physician for his impersonal mode of behavior and the funeral director for his businesslike attitude and financial interests. The fact that these two professions have drawn so much unfavorable criticism may very well reflect the much more burdensome task that they now face in a secularized society. Two questions must be answered in future studies: (1) How should the roles of death professionals best be redefined? (2) How should society as a whole reevaluate and reorient its approach to dying and death?

c The "Research" Question
i Context The most acceptable death, argues Talcott Parsons in

"Death in American Society" (1963), is that which comes at the end of a full life in which the individual can be said to come somewhere near having maximized the opportunities given him by his capacities and his situation." He terms this acceptance the *ideal-type orientation to death*. As the majority of studies show, however, a dying patient's situation is far from congenial, it is often a horror. He usually does not remain in the bosom of his family to contemplate his past accomplishments and friendships quietly, but instead is thrust into a frightening and unfamiliar institutional setting. Science by its very nature is aggressive, active, and forward-directed, but the orientation that Parsons speaks of is one of retrospection and necessarily subjective perspectives. The question sociologists ask is: *What institutional changes might facilitate the dying patient's positive acceptance of his situation?*

ii Theory The work of sociologists Barney Glaser and Anselm Strauss represents a rare bright spot in theoretical research on dying patients. With the support of the National Institutes of Health, Glaser and Strauss spent several years researching social interaction and organization of dying patients and hospital personnel in six San Francisco hospitals. Their intensive research, described in *Awareness of Dying* (1965), *Time for Dying* (1968), and several journal articles, has resulted in a theory of *awareness context* and the development of a *dying trajectory* model.

The dying trajectory consists of two important aspects: duration and shape. Duration covers the time span from the patient's admittance to the hospital until the moment of death. Shape expresses the progress or course of the patient's physical deterioration—steadily downward, erratic, slow change followed by a sudden sharp drop, and so on. These two main variables, *when* and *how,* provide a graph of the dying trajectory for the hospital staff and enable the nurses and doctors to determine their mode of operation and organization for each particular patient (and also serve as guidelines for their personal behavior in their constant interaction with dying persons). The mode of operation may involve routine measures for a steady trajectory or emergency measures mobilized when a predicted course suddenly plunges into a critical situation.

Glaser and Strauss find that several *critical junctures* ordinarily arise and are assimilated through the hospital network. First, the patient is defined as dying. Second, preparations are made for death by the hospital staff, the patient's family, and, if he is aware of it, the patient himself. Third, a point is reached where there is "nothing more to do" before death. Fourth, there is the culmination of the trajectory, which may take weeks, days, or several hours, and ends in three final stages: the "last hours," the death watch, and the death itself.

The movement is closely charted, and if the expected trajectory occurs on schedule, it provides a means of preparation for all participants. The nurses are prepared for a death watch if they know when the end is to come. On the other hand, an unexpected turn of events—that is, the appearance of an unanticipated critical juncture—leaves all participants ill-prepared. For example, a critically ill patient who has been given last rites and is surrounded by his relatives may abruptly change, but only temporarily, for the better. Often the relatives have to depart and again wait to be called. Sometimes such reversals occur several times before the patient finally dies, creating severe strain on both family and hospital.

Such unexpected occurrences or changes in a dying patient's "passage" affect not only organizational procedures but also what Glaser and Strauss term the ward's "sentimental mood." For instance, in an intensive-care ward, where death is frequent and speedy, the mood is relatively unaffected by the occurrence of one more expected death; the mood becomes dissembling, however, if the patient lingers on and on. (Another mood disruption is that caused by a spouse's inability to accept the death.)

One of the central problems of the dying trajectory is the interaction between the patient and death professionals. Glaser and Strauss term it the *awareness context:* the "total combination of what each interactant in a situation knows about the identity of the other and his own identity in the eyes of the other." Awareness contexts can be divided into four types: an *open* awareness context exists when each interactant (that is, the patient and a nurse, doctor, or family member) is aware of the other's true identity as well as his own identity in the eyes of the other. In a *closed* awareness context one interactant is not aware of the other's identity or the other's view of his identity. A *suspicion* awareness context is a modification of the closed one: one interactant suspects the true identity of the other or the other's view of his own identity, or both. The *pretense* awareness context is a modification of the open one: both interactants are aware of each other's identity, but pretend not to be. In their work with dying patients, Glaser and Strauss were able to construct a paradigm out of six more or less consecutive components of the awareness context: (1) a description of the type of awareness context, (2) the structural conditions, (3) the consequent interactions, (4) the changes of interaction that result in transformations of context, (5) the tactics of various interactants in attempting to maintain or change the context of awareness, and (6) some consequences that emerge out of the change in awareness contexts.

iii   Research (Methodology)   According to Glaser and Strauss' schema, the patient is usually in a closed awareness context at first. The hospital staff is aware of the impending death; the patient is not. Four structural conditions help maintain the closed awareness: (1) most patients are medically incompetent to interpret their own symptoms; (2) the hospital is impeccably well-organized for hiding the medical diagnoses from the terminal patient (charts are conveniently kept out of reach, and the medical staff is trained to act collusively when they are around the patient); (3) the physicians are provided with a professional rationale for withholding the information ("Why deny him all hope by telling him he is dying?"); (4) the patient is in a relatively helpless position, finding few allies even in his family or other patients.

The third, fourth, and fifth steps involve maintaining the closed awareness context, or attempting to move the context to a partial or full open awareness context. If it is decided that the passage of the dying patient should take place in a closed context, then the nurses, physician, and family, if they are knowledgeable, will employ a number of "situation as normal" interaction tactics.

The patient will be positively reinforced by his doctor that certain symptoms are not very serious; for example, an attempt may be made to focus the patient's attention on a minor medical ailment. Nurses may engage in "faith-oriented" talk of the future—for example, telling the patient, "You'll probably be going home soon after your operation." As death nears, however, the nurses may decrease the time they spend with the patient or find that they must leave the room to keep from an emotional outburst. The doctor may directly assure him that he will live, "lying with a clear purpose." One patient who was suffering from an advanced case of cancer and had been given a week to live was told by his physician that he was suffering from diabetes. The illusion was successfully carried through: the patient was provided with insulin, along with instructions in its use, and then sent home.

An ever-present danger in such *"collusive games"* is the possibility of disclosure. Although a closed awareness context gives greater control to the hospital staff in working with the terminal patient, it also demands rigorous attention to interpersonal *cues*. A patient may become suspicious when nurses suddenly spend less time around him or begin to minimize their talk with him. "Some treatments to sustain life," report Glaser and Strauss, "do not make sense to a patient who does not know he is dying. He may refuse a medicine, a machine, an awkward position or a diet, thus shortening his life." Unless the patient dies fairly quickly or goes into a state of coma, he may soon suspect or detect the real situation. (The patient may overhear a conversation, or the night shift may not be alerted about the collusive game and unwittingly disclose the truth.) "Eventually he may also understand that the hospital is organized not to give him all the information about his condition but rather to withhold most information."

If the patient becomes aware of the fact that others are withholding the information from him, he may bring about a changed context of awareness in one of the three remaining ways. He can continue at the level of suspicion, sounding out those around him for further evidence that his condition is indeed different, which can result in maintaining a "pretense," or he can openly confront the other interactants, peeling away the illusions that they have constructed.

Glaser and Strauss's results lend support to the other studies with dying patients that suggest maximizing the open awareness context. Withholding information from the dying person prevents him from talking to close kin about his impending fate. He cannot act toward himself or others as if he were dying. "The kinsmen and hospital personnel are saved from certain stressful scenes," write the authors, "that accompany open awareness about death, but they are also blocked from participating in various satisfying rituals of passage to death." Nurses take on an exceptionally heavy burden—much greater than that of the physician, who only occasionally interacts with the patient.

iv Evaluation   Glaser and Strauss have derived a set of recommendations from their studies. The first focuses on medical training: "Training for giving terminal care should be amplified and deepened in schools of medicine and nursing." This recommendation would require an experimental approach to training, carefully

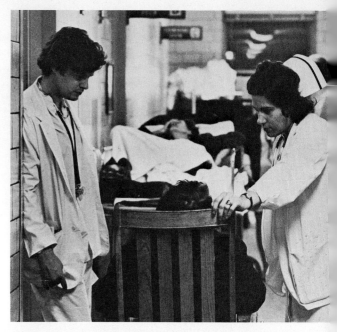

(Above) The human environment of the terminally ill. Hospital staff, clergy, friends, and family try to "keep it from" the patient and rationalize their behavior as an act of kindness. Perhaps the only person they are being kind to is themselves, because they are protecting themselves from having to confront the patient in a direct, sincere, and deep-felt manner. Avoidance is easier on them but may be harder on the patient who, among other burdens, must play along with the game that he sees through.

(Facing page) Where the elderly have social value. Away from industrial, highly technological society, old people often have meaningful positions. They are repositories of tradition and folklore. They keep alive connections with the past, providing the younger generations with spiritual and emotional roots in their ancestors' culture. The top photo shows an elderly couple in the rural United States and the bottom photo shows a 100-year-old man and his year-old grandson in Abkhasia, a region of the Soviet Union that has an extraordinarily high percentage of active very elderly persons. This photo may serve to illustrate an important concept formulated by psychologist Erik Erikson, who insists that only when we have learned to accept death will we be able to teach our children to embrace life.

bringing together social, psychological, and organizational aspects into a coherent program. Problems in this area, Glaser and Strauss say, will probably arise in the faculty's own personal anxieties and attitudes toward dying and death. Second, they suggest that "explicit planning and review should be given to the psychological, social, and organizational aspects of terminal care. The greatest reform in this area is the need for hospital institutions to provide more detailed actions and modes of behavior for their personnel in working with terminal patients." Third, "there should be explicit planning for phases of the dying trajectory that occur before and after residence at the hospital." To fill the needs of terminal patients who find themselves in and out of hospitals, better coordination between institutional settings and the outside world is necessary. Finally, they suggest that "medical and nursing personnel should encourage public discussion of issues that transcend professional responsibilities for terminal care."

Two critical problems that need greater public discussion are the "senseless prolonging" of life and the withholding of addicting drugs until "near the end." The controversy over life prolongation, as noted earlier, goes to the core of the American credo and becomes more heated as medical technology advances. Only a radical review of our philosophies of living and dying, as well as our social priorities, will make possible any genuinely significant institutional changes.

3   Overview

Death is the oldest conceivable human social issue, yet accelerated technological advance and social and institutional changes have left this issue relatively obscure or ambiguous. The most obvious ambiguity stems from the recent allocation of the process of dealing with death to the institution. The terminal patient, bereft of his friends, associates, and environment, must adapt to the new situation by constructing a new social reality. The nurses, encountering death as a daily reality, must also build up certain defenses, fabricate necessary cues and mannerisms, and in the majority of cases deny the reality of the situation. Physicians prefer to treat patients as if they were expected to live, which may reflect a conscious or unconscious desire to maintain a dominant relationship with the patient. Doctors show contradictory attitudes: they uphold a professional ethic of secrecy in relation to their patients, but express a desire to be informed if they themselves should be in a similar situation.

Just as important, however, is the growing concern for the aging and the aged. A revision of our cultural attitudes on death must also deal with our cultural biases against the aging. Again, our priorities need to be given clearer shape and form. Must geriatric and terminal patients assume second-class citizenship as if they were irrelevant to the primary interests and values of most Americans? Have they no important contributions to make to American life? On a larger scale, what lies ahead as people progressively seek to master death and extend the years of life? What qualities will make those added years worth living? The way we define the role of death in our social structure may well determine our own role in life.

D   LOOKING AHEAD

1   Interview:
Robert Blauner

Robert Blauner is associate professor of sociology at the University of California at Berkeley. His major publications include *Alienation and Freedom: The Factory Worker and His Industry* and *Racial Oppression in America*. His article "Death and Social Structure" has been influential in the field of the sociology of death. He is currently doing research on race and class in American society.

DPG   *We live in a society that seems to measure many aspects of our lives according to a yardstick of economic usefulness. Does this explain why our society treats dying people with so little consideration?*
BLAUNER   Yes. You could speak of a social death that afflicts some people long before their biological death. In the United States, old people, often even middle-aged people, are treated as superfluous or obsolescent in an economic and social sense.

DPG   *That's probably one result of the glorification of youth in American society.*
BLAUNER   Yes, but it's also related to the American inclination not to think about death. Such a "denial of death" may even have intensified in the past decade. The trend toward discarding and segregating aged people, toward finding them socially irrelevant is partially the result of their connection with death. But it also reminds me of our attitude toward America's involvement with mass death overseas, the bombing in Vietnam, for example.

DPG   *So you'd maintain that Americans feel detached from death? It's not terribly real to them?*
BLAUNER   It's all relative. Most people have experiences with death in the course of their lives, obviously. But our culture does tend to emphasize a certain detachment, and a sanitization of unpleasant things like death. Over the past 10 years, however, there has been a countertrend, although I don't think it has upset the dominant theme of society. There's been a general rejection of the larger society among some young people, and part of the reason is that they see American culture as "plastic." The American consciousness tends to exclude or to trivialize human experience of great depth, particularly tragic realities.

DPG   *Can you be more explicit about the ways you think the youth culture approaches the question of death?*
BLAUNER   I can give you my impressions. Many members of the youth culture have been attracted by what certain psychologists call "peak experiences"—intense states that are associated with the drug culture. Contemplating death is such an experience. Furthermore, some members of the youth or countercultural movements have looked for philosophical or religious guidance in Buddhism and other Eastern religions and philosophies. In these death is at the heart of things. It's much more central than in our culture.

DPG   *Would you say that a greater reverence for life leads to a greater reverence for death in its role in determining our lives, putting our lives in relief?*
BLAUNER   If you turned that statement around, I would agree with you. A concern for death and its meaning can definitely sharpen the sense of the preciousness and reality of life. But you have to strike a balance. In my studies of grief and mourning I found that people can be overwhelmed by

death and bereavement. Some never get out of that morass. In the two or three years that I made an intellectual specialization of death, I had both a certain intensification of experience and a depressing, morbid feeling. One of the reasons I shifted away from this field was that I felt that being primarily involved in philosophical and theoretical questions about death was a somewhat introverting personal experience.

DPG   *Do you foresee any cultural or philosophical shifts that might change the "plasticity" with which our culture approaches death?*
BLAUNER   I don't think it's going to be easy. All the long-term social trends are working against the giving of meaning and dignity to death. The most important of these are society's view of the aged, labor force pressures toward earlier retirements, and a shift in religion away from heavy theological consideration toward more superficial social purposes.

DPG   *But you did point out that the youth culture was taking another tack.*
BLAUNER   Yes. These pluralist trends are all to the good. There's also a new interest in what might be called "death education"; for example, setting up a situation in which a dying person could talk to young doctors or other hospital personnel. An emphasis on death education might be one positive countertrend, but I don't think it's going to make a radical change. Geoffrey Gorer has written an essay on the "pornography of death," which draws several parallels between the repression and denial of sex in the Victorian period and the repression and denial of death today. That parallel's interesting because just as sex education is needed to overcome residual Victorian attitudes—and it has gotten a great deal of emphasis—death education is also needed and it will probably come to the fore.

DPG   *What would be the purpose of this type of death education? What effect do you think it would have on the people exposed to it?*
BLAUNER   At least for some people, it might counteract the natural human tendency to either deny or trivialize the reality of death that is steadily reinforced by the culture and the media. It might counteract the tendency among people to put death and old people out of their minds. It might make people more aware, more frequently, of the finitude of their own lives. In that sense it could enrich their experience, their sensitivity, their values.

DPG   *If people's awareness of death were heightened in this way, how would it be reflected or expressed in social terms? Would there be changes in institutions or in attitudes toward death that would improve the quality of American life?*

BLAUNER   In social terms, increased awareness would hopefully reflect itself in attitudes toward old people. Perhaps it would raise the possibility of an appreciation of old people as part of the resources of the society. The aged obviously have the valuable experience of living over a long period. They are also facing the isolation and uncertainty that is likely to be the lot of many young and middle-aged people. Death itself is to some extent an abstract concept. It's real, but once you're experiencing it, you're no longer experiencing anything. The old, on the other hand, are real people and they may have serious problems of living. Yet they are really the cast-offs in this society.

DPG   *What directions do you think our approach toward death should take in the next 30 years or so?*
BLAUNER   Nobody likes death. You don't want to experience more of it than you need to. One desirable change might be increased acceptance of the old humanistic, internationalist idea that people should be able to feel diminished personally by the death of others, by the hurt of others. So that U.S. genocide in Vietnam, for example, would hurt people elsewhere so much that they might be forced into action. Furthermore, if people experienced it as a personal thing, it would be much less likely to happen in the first place.

DPG   *"No man is an island. . . ."*
BLAUNER   Something like that. The institutions or residences for the aged and the dying should provide more possibilities for communication and contact with younger people. There should be more contact between the generations, between the living and the dying. It's not easy because everyone wants to live his own family life.

DPG   *And people don't want to take responsibility for the community at large, relating to everyone, including the dying.*

Unit 15

Race and Ethnic Relations

RACIAL DISTINCTIONS AND CONFLICT

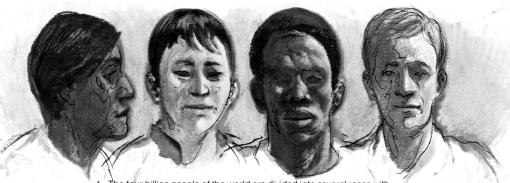

1. The four billion people of the world are divided into several races with numerous subdivisions. But all humans are part of a single species, and racial distinctions are significant only when people attribute meanings to them.

2. Sometimes racial distinctions form the basis for social inequalities, discrimination, and exploitation, with a dominant group developing myths about a subordinate group in order to justify their continued subjection.

3. If the subordinate group is unwilling to accept its inferior status and responds by separatism or militancy, the race relations problem becomes one of outright racial conflict. If the dominant racial groups insist on preserving their political, social, and economic advantages, racial conflict will be driven in the direction of massive, violent confrontation.

4. The modern world faces the challenge of reacting to racial conflict by creating a society in which dominant and subordinate racial categories are abolished. The dominant racial groups must come to see that it is in their own long-run self-interest for all racial groups to have equal access to the rights, duties, and benefits of modern society.

Human variation. More and more, biologists are finding it impossible to divide the human race systematically into clearcut distinct racial groups. It is becoming increasingly common for such biologists to refuse even to make use of the terms "race" or "subspecies." Rather, changes in gene frequencies over geographical areas are charted for each gene separately. This procedure helps assure that biologists will make no built-in assumptions regarding the genetic composition of a group of people as a whole.

B DEFINITION AND CONTEXT

1 Definition

There are almost 4 billion people in the world today. Biologists and physical anthropologists group most of them into three major racial constellations—the Negroid, the Caucasoid, and the Mongoloid. Sometimes other, smaller groups are recognized, such as the Australoid or the Khoisanoid, but there is no universal agreement on the precise subdivisions of mankind. Although the human species is believed to have emerged well over 200,000 years ago (starting with Neanderthaloids), the present division of the races can be traced back no more than 50,000 years at the outside. Thus the formation of the present-day races is a comparatively recent evolutionary phenomenon.

Biologists, confronted with the enormous range of peoples, have tried to bring conceptual order to the continuum. But there are no hard and fast dividing lines: many populations are almost impossible to classify because of their intermediate position between other groups. And even within established groups there are immense variations. The Negroid race, to give but one example, includes both the tallest and the shortest subdivisions of mankind. All humans share the same basic physical and genetic constitution, however, and all races can interbreed with one another.

The sociologist focuses on race as a social rather than a biological fact. He defines a *racial group* simply as any collection of people that, in its interactions with other groups, is believed to be and is treated as a distinct race. Relationships between the races derive their content and significance less from the physical characteristics of people than from the meanings men attach to various physical differences. Such differences become *categorical perceptions* and serve as a basis for *social distinctions,* including stigma and discrimination. Men oppose one racially defined category to another and posit the kind of social relationship that they believe should obtain between representatives of the groups on either side of the racial division. Sometimes distinctions of the same type are applied to *ethnic groups.* Such a group is not distinguished from others by physical characteristics; it is identifiable through cultural rather than physical criteria. Irish-Americans, for example, may be identified as members of an ethnic group on the basis of such factors as their last names.

Race or ethnic relations are social interactions that are based on or affected by the awareness of actual or imputed racial or ethnic differences between the peoples concerned. The problems and prejudices that characterize this acutely sensitive arena of human interaction make it one of the burning topics in the United States and in the world today—as the uprisings in American cities in the 1960s and the slaughter of millions of people in racial conflicts around the globe throughout this century attest.

2 World Context

As a result of wars, migrations, and changes in political boundaries, a great many modern societies are composed of a number of

Hutus awaiting their execution. A tragic example of the treatment of vanquished enemies occurred in the small central African country of Burundi in 1972. The ethnic makeup of the country consists of two tribes, the politically dominant Tutsis, who comprise 15 percent of the population, and the subordinate Hutus, who account for the remaining 85 percent. Great enmity has characterized the relations between the two tribal groups for as long as can be remembered. In 1972 the Hutus hoped to take advantage of some Tutsi infighting and launched a coup d'état. The coup was unsuccessful, and in the aftermath at least 80,000 Hutus were slaughtered, with special emphasis on the killing of all educated Hutus who might become future leaders. For reasons that are unclear, the Hutus apparently accepted their deaths with awesome apathy—some even showing up voluntarily for their own execution when told to do so. More massacres of Hutus took place in 1973.

different racial or ethnic groups. These various elements interact with one another in complex patterns that are not necessarily antagonistic; there are many multiracial or pluralistic societies in which the different groups live together in considerable harmony. Hawaii, for example, has a mixed population of "mainland American," Chinese, Japanese, and native Hawaiian stock; Switzerland has German, French and Italian components; The Netherlands has a substantial Indonesian population; and Tanzania has Arab, European, and Asian minorities.

Yet in many nations, racial antagonism and barriers are sharply defined, and the physical or cultural traits of one group are held in low esteem by the dominant segment of the population, usually the majority. This kind of broad inequality based on racial categories is particularly iniquitous: it designates some members of the society as inferior and denies them full participation in the society purely on the grounds of an accident of birth. The degree of disability suffered by such minority groups—Maoris in New Zealand, Aborigines in Australia, West Indians in Britain, Jews in the Soviet Union, indigenous tribes in Central America, or Asians in Uganda, for example—varies widely.

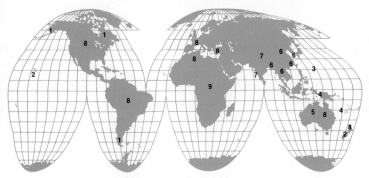

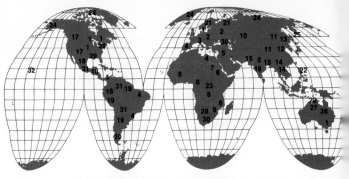

Type of Race: GEOGRAPHICAL—Collections of breeding populations, inhabiting geographically defined areas

Type of Race: LOCAL—Real breeding populations, significant evolutionary units

Races	Locations
1. Amerindian	Alaska to Labrador to tip of South America
2. Polynesian	Pacific Islands from Hawaii to Easter Island to New Zealand
3. Micronesian	Small Islands East of Japan
4. Melanesian	New Guinea, New Britain, and Solomon Islands
5. Australian	Australia
6. Asiatic	Main Continent of Asia, Japan, Taiwan, Philippines, Indonesia, Sumatra, Borneo, Java
7. Indian	Himalaya Mountains to Indian Ocean
8. European	Rapidly Expanding Since 1500, Extending from North Africa and Western Asia to New World, Europe, Australia, New Zealand, etc.
9. African	Sub-Saharan Africa

Figure 1. One Currently Accepted System of Racial Classification. (Source: Adapted from Garn, *Human Races*)

Races	Locations
1. Northwest European	Scandinavia, North Germany, Low Countries, British Isles, and Their Descendants Abroad.
2. Northeast European	Russia, Poland, Lithuania, Estonia, and Their Descendants Abroad
3. Alpine	Alps and Balkan Mountains
4. Mediterranean	North Africa, Levant, Turkey, Greece and Westward Through Spain, and Their Descendants Abroad
5. Iranian	Asiatic Turkey Through Iran and India
6. East African	East Africa to Sudan
7. Sudanese	North Sudan
8. Forest African	West Africa, Congo
9. Bantu	Southeast Africa
10. Turkic	Central Asia
11. Tibetan	Sikkim, Tibet, Central Mongolia
12. North Chinese	Northern China
13. Extreme Mongoloid	Siberia, Mongolia, to Kamchatka Peninsula
14. Southeast Asiatic	Expanding Group in Southeast Asia
15. Hindu	Indian Subcontinent
16. Dravidian	Southern India to Sri Lanka
17. North American Amerindian	Canada and United States
18. Central American Amerindian	Southwestern U.S. to Bolivia
19. South American Amerindian	Peru, Chile, Brazil, Etc.
20. Fuegian	Southern End of South America
21. Lapp	Tundra and Swamps of West Russia and Northern Scandinavia
22. Pacific "Negrito"	Australia to Philippines
23. African Pygmy	Congo Rain Forest
24. Eskimo	Circum-Polar Area
25. Ainu	Yezo Island of Northern Japan
26. Murrayian Australian	Central Australia
27. Carpenterian Australian	Northern Australia
28. Khoisan	Kalahari Desert (South Africa)
29. North American Black	Black population of U.S.A. (Forest African Plus European Mixture)
30. Cape Colored	South Africa (Bantu and Khoisan Plus European Mixture)
31. Ladino	Central and South America (Southern European Plus Amerindian Mixture)
32. Neo-Hawaiian	Hawaii (European Plus Polynesian, Chinese, Japanese, Filipino Mixture)

In *Race Relations in Sociological Theory* (1970) John Rex provided a typology of six groups that in particular situations may be dominated by a majority:

1. *Vanquished enemies,* such as the American Indians or the French in Canada
2. *Outright slaves,* notably the West African peoples enslaved during the early colonial period or the East Africans enslaved by the Arabs
3. *Poor immigrants*—for example, the Pakistanis in Britain or the Poles and Irish in the United States
4. *Political refugees,* such as the refugees from Castro's Cuba or Jewish fugitives from Naziism
5. *Indentured laborers,* such as the Indian and Chinese workers in several former British colonies in Africa
6. *Trading minorities*—for example, the Indian traders on the east coast of Africa

The extent to which the relationships between these groups and the dominant society become problematic depends largely on the attitudes adopted by the host country to the minority in its midst. Reactions may range from mild disapproval—as in the case of popular British response to mass immigration from her former colonies in the 1960s—to genocidal warfare—such as that occurring between the Arab and Negroid populations of several African countries in the 1970s.

Very occasionally the dominant group is a minority itself. The most striking example of this phenomenon in the modern world is the Republic of South Africa, where the white minority applies the strictest racial segregation in human history to the non-white majority. Although they are outnumbered by more than five to one in a multiracial society of blacks, mulattos, and Asians, white South Africans severely restrict these groups from voting and participation in the legislative process; they are virtually totally excluded. Every conceivable area of social life is segregated. Concern with racial "purity" has led to laws not simply against intermarriage, but against any sexual contact between races. Even to "conspire" to engage in interracial intercourse is a criminal offense under the "Immorality Act" and carries a sentence of a whipping and up to seven years imprisonment. Although the concern with *miscegenation* reaches an obsessive level in South Africa, it is common in lesser degree in many multiracial societies; racial mixing can in fact produce social confusion in the local norms governing differential racial status and interaction.

3   American Context

Race relations have always been a source of severe social tension in the United States. The status of diverse minority groups has been a persistent issue, that of the black American being the most serious enduring problem. The civil rights movement of the 1950s and the turmoil of the 1960s brought the issue to the forefront of contemporary concern, but antagonisms between ethnic and racial groups are nothing new in American experience. They have taken place since the earliest colonial settlement under a variety of condi-

Bantu gold miners in the Republic of South Africa. The economic system of the Republic of South Africa is based on the exploitation of the numerically greater Bantu population and imported black labor by the politically dominant white population (mainly of Dutch and British descent). Thus the social institution of *apartheid*—total racial segregation—has a very real economic basis.

tions: the conquests of native Americans by the original colonists, the enslavement and forced migration of black Africans, the waves of voluntary immigrants from Europe seeking a new life.

In 1607 there were about 800,000 native Americans. Disease and outright genocide reduced that number to 340,000 by 1860, and to 250,000 in 1890, according to the U.S. Bureau of the Census. Since then the native American population, much of it concentrated on 284 Indian reservations, has increased—to about 800,000.

Some 400,000 Africans had been brought to the United States by 1808, when the foreign slave trade was officially stopped. Their descendants are today the largest minority group in the nation, numbering some 25 million, or approximately 12 percent of the population. In several Northern urban centers they represent an absolute majority.

Fresh European migration began in earnest around 1820 and reached huge proportions in the 1840s when the Potato Famine brought large numbers of immigrants from Ireland, followed by others from the Catholic areas of northern Europe. Virulently anti-Catholic groups emerged among the local population, and Irish immigrants were killed and Catholic churches burned in riots during the 1830s, 1840s, and 1850s. A further wave of immigration between 1860 and 1890 brought more arrivals from the "Teutonic" and "Nordic" countries—Germany, Austria, and Scandinavia. Finally, between 1880 and 1914 millions of immigrants from the Mediterranean area and Eastern Europe—Italy, Greece, the Balkans, Poland, Russia, and other countries—arrived.

In each case, the new arrivals were resented by much of the established population. Legislation against further immigration was demanded, and antiblack, anti-Catholic, and anti-Jewish movements sprang up across the United States; the Ku Klux Klan was one of the largest and remains one of the most enduring examples. European minorities were often incorporated into American society not through the good will of the existing populace, but because political bosses found it expedient to work for their support.

Black Americans, native Americans, and the 5 million Mexican-Americans of the Southwest have not been so readily assimilated into American society, however. During the late 1960s and early 1970s their response to their situation has grown increasingly militant. A major change in strategy has been a rejection of the goal of integration and a denial of the moral authority of mainstream America. These minorities now assert the independence and validity of their own *subcultures*.

Has progress been made in the elimination of discrimination and racially prejudiced attitudes in America today? At least at the level of formal policy—through its executive, congressional, and legal apparatus—the nation has irreversibly committed itself to the equal treatment of all its citizens. *Segregation* has been outlawed, notably by the Supreme Court decision on school desegregation in 1954 and the Civil Rights Acts of 1964 and 1965. Yet there remains a good deal of institutionalized discrimination: blacks, Mexican-Americans, and native Americans are still systematically excluded from opportunities and treated unequally through such informal means as all-white residential areas or clubs and differential

Anti-Asian feeling in the United States. *(Right)* During the nineteenth century Asian laborers were brought in for such arduous tasks as building railroads. However, other lower-class economic and ethnic groups felt threatened by the newcomers, as this cartoon from the period shows, and there were numerous mob murders of Asians in Western cities and towns. *(Above)* During World War II persons of Japanese descent underwent extreme segregation by federal government action. More than 100,000 were removed from their homes and forced to live in relocation camps like this one in Manazar, California. In spite of the military's assessment that a sustained Japanese attack on or invasion of the West Coast was unlikely, it was the consensus of West Coast political leaders, the general public, and the mass media that a mass evacuation was necessary. Secretary of War Henry Stimson and President Franklin Roosevelt went with the tide, and General DeWitt, who supervised the evacuation, later summed up his feelings in a widely quoted and approved statement: "A Jap's a Jap. They are a dangerous element. . . . It makes no difference whether he is an American citizen; theoretically he is still a Japanese, and you can't change him." Total losses to the Japanese in property and bank accounts were estimated at $400 million, of which only $38 million was eventually repaid.

treatment from police and the legal system. The chronically higher rates of unemployment and lower average incomes found among these visible minority groups are symptoms of such discrimination.

Yet attitudes are unmistakably changing. The proportion of whites who accept crude notions of racial differences has consistently dropped during recent decades. In 1942 over half the whites surveyed in a national public opinion poll expressed a belief in innate differences in the learning potential of blacks and whites. By 1968, however, a CBS poll found that 14 percent of whites believe that "white babies have more natural intelligence than black babies"—although some 28 percent expressed no opinion on the subject. In 1942 only 30 percent of a national sample believed that all races should attend the same school, but in 1965 this view was held by 61 percent of the population, and by 1970 some 71 percent of Americans accepted the proposition.

The United States has always been characterized, to a greater extent than most societies, by a proclaimed belief in the doctrine of equality. Thirty years ago Gunnar Myrdal argued in *An American Dilemma* (1944) that the denials of these ideals in practice was placing great stress on American society and that the resulting tension was creating considerable pressure for change.

Both at the level of attitudes and at the level of practice, some of this change has come about. Nevertheless, the dominant white, Anglo-Saxon, Protestant group still discriminates, sometimes in subtle and sometimes in overt ways, against racial and ethnic minorities.

C QUESTIONS AND EVIDENCE

1 Questions

In studying race and ethnic relations, sociologists ask three questions: (1) What personality factors are involved in racial prejudice? (2) Do those racial myths that persist even when disproved by science serve some social function? (3) What are the possible patterns of antagonism or coexistence between racial and ethnic groups?

2 Evidence

a The "Burning Issue" Question

i Context Race relations is one of many fields in which the sociologist cooperates with social scientists from other disciplines, notably anthropology, political science, and psychology. American research on race relations has relied heavily on the contribution of social psychologists, whose emphasis on personal attitudes complements the sociologist's interest in systematic theory and social bases. The social psychologist analyzes attitudinal tendencies in individuals and groups and identifies other factors—age, personality, social background, income, or education—that correlate with or might contribute to the development of those tendencies. This information is of great value to the sociologist, both in his attempts to formulate theoretical perspectives and in his empirical research. He asks: *What personality factors correlate with racist attitudes?*

ii Theory Theoretical descriptions of the psychology of racial prejudice invariably refer to the concept of the *stereotype*. As the psychologist Gordon Allport explains in *The Nature of Prejudice* (1954), the *stereotype* is an exaggerated belief associated with a particular category of people. Stereotypes simplify the psychological processes of perception; they are based on a fixed mental image of some group or class and are applied to all members of that group without any attempt to test preconception against reality. By defining the characteristics of another group—its members may be perceived as lazy, inferior, smelly, childish, or less intelligent—the stereotype justifies a particular mode of conduct in relation to that group.

Two other concepts used by social psychologists are indirectly derived from Freudian theory. The first is *projection*—the tendency of the individual to attribute to others behavior or motives that are ingredients of his own personality but cannot be acknowledged as such. In this perspective the thousands of brutal lynchings for ''rape of a white woman'' that took place in the South can be interpreted as projections of the suppressed sexual desires of the whites onto black men, who were believed to have heightened sexual prowess; their punishment therefore had to be severe enough to expiate the whites' sense of their own guilt.

The second concept, *scapegoating,* refers to the tendency of an individual who is frustrated to respond with aggression. If it is impossible to direct aggression at the source of the frustration, the individual may channel the aggressive response at a third party incapable of offering resistance.) Thus the economically deprived white worker may vent his frustrations on minority groups whom he believes to be living largely on welfare, instead of striking out against his boss, the stockholders, or the government. (This tendency of each person to pick on the person one rung below him is known as the "pecking order" phenomenon.)

The most important contribution to the analysis of the relationship between racial prejudice and particular personality constellations is that of T. W. Adorno and his associates: their monumental analysis, *The Authoritarian Personality* (1950), has inspired a number of subsequent studies. According to Adorno, the authoritarian personality has a *hierarchical orientation* toward life; he shows submission to his superiors and expects deference from those he considers beneath him. His submissiveness to authority is linked to an admiration for power and an unquestioning respect for conventions. He is intolerant of ambiguity, judges others in terms of categorical alternatives, and condemns those who go against religious, sexual, or other *social norms*. He has a deep-rooted personal insecurity—the product of his own upbringing—and is particularly prone to racial prejudice.) He may also be a likely recruit for extremist movements.

In "Discrimination and the American Creed" (1948) sociologist Robert K. Merton pointed out that a distinction must be made between *prejudice* (a biased prejudgment) and *discrimination* (an act based on such prejudgments).) The relationship between prejudice and discrimination is not always a neat one. (Merton devised a paradigm that includes four "types" of persons and their characteristic responses:)

Type I: The unprejudiced nondiscriminator.) This "all-weather liberal" adheres to the formal values of American democracy and upholds the American ideals of freedom and equality in both belief and in practice. He is a vigorous champion of the underdog and takes his principles seriously.

Type II: The unprejudiced discriminator. This "fair-weather liberal" is not prejudiced but may occasionally discriminate when it is expedient for him to do so, because he may suffer loss of status or financial disadvantage if he does not.)

Type III: The prejudiced nondiscriminator. This "timid bigot" feels considerable hostility to other groups but recognizes that law and social pressure are against discrimination.) Therefore he reluctantly conforms to the American egalitarian ideal.

Type IV: The prejudiced discriminator.) This "all-round bigot" discriminates in both word and deed against other groups. He does not believe in the values of freedom and equality and consistently acts upon his prejudices.

Each of these cases is of course an "ideal type"; few people fit exactly into any particular category. But the typology does cover the range of possible variations.

iii Research (Studies of prejudiced personalities have focused on the failure of the individuals to check their stereotypes against reality. In a classic demonstration of this failure, reported by N. M. Jahoda ("X-ray of the Racist Mind," 1960), a questionnaire used

as part of a study of antagonism toward groups other than one's own referred to three entirely imaginary peoples. Listed among various actual ethnic and racial groups were the Danireans, the Piraneans, and the Wallorians. A large proportion of those who disliked blacks and Jews expressed a dislike of these three nonexistent peoples—and even advocated restrictive measures against them.

Allport's *The Nature of Prejudice* also showed that stereotypes often contain inherently contradictory elements—another indication of the failure of the prejudiced individual to confront reality. In a comprehensive scale to measure attitudes toward Jews, Allport deliberately inserted various propositions that were inherently contradictory. One of his subscales, for example, dealt simultaneously with "seclusiveness" and "intrusiveness," which are mutually contradictory traits. Yet the same people would often accept both propositions. Here are two such pairs:

—Much resentment against Jews stems from their tending to keep apart and exclude gentiles from Jewish social life.
—The Jews should not pry too much into Christian activities and organizations nor seek so much recognition and prestige from Christians.

And:

—Jews tend to remain a foreign element in American society, to preserve their old social standards and resist the American way of life.
—Jews go too far in hiding their Jewishness, especially such extremes as changing their names, straightening noses, and imitating Christian manners and customs.

Allport found a correlation of 0.74 in acceptance of these contradictory propositions; that is, roughly three-quarters of the same people who accuse Jews of being seclusive also accuse them of being intrusive. Similarly, people who dislike the Jews because they have all the money also dislike them because they are always begging; people who dislike them because they are capitalists and control business also dislike them because they are communistic; people who dislike the Jews because Jews think themselves better than others also dislike them because Jews have an inferiority complex.

These contradictions plainly show that people who dislike a particular group will accept any proposition or myth that feeds or justifies their prejudice. Genuine group characteristics are not at issue; rather there is a deep-seated prejudice that seeks its own justification. As Allport notes:

If one state of affairs exists we call on one proverb to "explain" it. If the opposite state prevails, we can call on the reverse proverb. And so it is with ethnic stereotypes. . . . The need for sequential and uniform logic does not trouble us.

Other studies have noted further double thinking. As Merton points out in "The Self-Fulfilling Prophecy" (1948), the fact that Abraham Lincoln worked far into the night shows that he was industrious, resolute, and persevering, but the fact that Jews and Japanese work equally hard is taken as an indication of their sweatshop mentality, their unfair competitive practices, and their undermining of American standards.

iv   Evaluation   Prejudice is a highly complex phenomenon, and one that is not easily measurable. Authoritarianism is a theoretical concept rather than an empirical fact, so interpretation of research in this area is often very difficult. But the early work of Allport and Adorno has stimulated a great many useful investigations of the personality characteristics of the prejudiced individual. Many of these expose the irrational and often contradictory nature of stereotyped images. The failure—even refusal—to check one's preconceptions against reality is a common characteristic of the prejudiced individual. He has something at stake in *not* finding out.

Valuable though the perspectives from social psychology are, sociologists consider that purely psychological explanations of social phenomena are inadequate. A fuller analysis must be more interdisciplinary, taking account of *social factors,* both in the immediate family setting and in the society beyond, that are conducive to the development of racial prejudice. There is evidence that homes whose atmosphere is harsh, suppressive, critical, intolerant, and authoritarian are likely to produce individuals who see power and authority, rather than trust and tolerance, as the dominant factor in human relationships; such individuals often use "them-versus-us" categorizations of the social world. If these personality tendencies are accepted, endorsed, or encouraged by broader social forces in the surrounding culture, the racially prejudiced personality and racist society may be the consequence.

b   The "Classical" Question

i   Context   Racism always involves attitudes that are based on myth. And such myths are often clung to in the face of all scientific evidence to the contrary. The prime example of racial myth is of course the Nazi view of the various races of man. In *Mein Kampf* (1925) Adolf Hitler declared:

> All the human culture, all the results of art, science and technology that we see before us today, are almost exclusively the creative product of the Aryan. . . . He is the Prometheus of mankind from whose singing brow the divine spark of genius has sprung at all times. . . . It is no accident that the first cultures arose in places where the Aryan, in his encounters with lower peoples, subjugated them, and bent them to his will.

Such theories led the world into World War II and the slaughter of millions of people.

Many other racial theories, less virulent and flamboyant than those of the Nazis, uphold discriminatory practices wherever they are found—and they are remarkably enduring. Beliefs in the superiority of this, that, or the other race have no scientific validity, yet people seem to perceive selectively, noting only those facts that seem to support their beliefs. To study the ongoing importance of these beliefs in multiracial societies, sociologists ask: *What is the social function of racial ideologies?*

ii Theory Racial myths generally arise in societies that accord some of their members different access to local resources on the basis of their racial or ethnic origin. The myths are used by the dominant group to justify its continued suppression or exploitation of the subordinate group. Any alternative theory that does not support existing social relationships is seen as a heretical attack on the natural order.

Marxist sociologists (following their general approach to social phenomena, which we have explored in other units) have tried to link racism with *class conflict:* the relationship between the dominant and the subordinate race, they argue, is in reality based on class and is only masked by an ideology of race. Theories and myths derived from various forms of *exploitation* are put forward by the *ruling class* to justify its position. One leading proponent of this view is O. C. Cox, who in *Caste, Class and Race* (1959) hypothesizes that:

> Racial exploitation and race prejudice developed among Europeans with the rise of capitalism and nationalism, and because of the worldwide ramifications of capitalism, all racial antagonisms can be traced to the policies and attitudes of the leading capitalist people, the white people of Europe and North America.

As Marx himself described these ramifications of capitalist exploitation in Volume I of *Capital* (1867):

> The discovery of gold and silver in America, the extirpation, enslavement and entombment in mines of the aboriginal population, the beginning of the conquest and looting of the East Indies, the turning of Africa into a warren for the commercial hunting of black skins, signalized the rosy dawn of the era of capitalist production. These idyllic proceedings are the chief momenta of primitive accumulation. On their heels treads the commercial war of the European nations, with the globe for a theatre.

This view of racism, however, has not found many supporters other than Marxists. Most sociologists find such analysis useful in some situations but too simplistic in others. Furthermore, there are a number of precapitalist societies where there is violent racial conflict, and certain racist societies have had little historical contact with Europeans.

Whether or not they accept the Marxist stance, all sociologists agree that racial ideologies are firmly rooted in the societies where they are found. As an integral part of the society's values, *racial myths* arise in and sustain a particular *social relationship.* They are integrated into the *belief system* of the society as a framework for ordering intergroup activities and to provide justifications for behavior that would otherwise appear completely irrational and immoral.

iii Research (Survey) In "Race and the Ideology of Race" (1962) Manning Nash provides an analysis of the functional importance of racial ideologies. Conscious political and social discrimina-

Jean León Gérôme's *The Christian Martyrs' Last Prayer* (1863–1883). Race and ethnic affiliation have not always been as major a dimension of social conflict as they are today. Among other things, religion has also been a focus of tremendous conflict throughout the history of civilization.

350

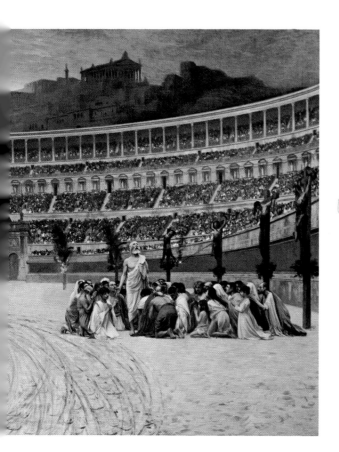

tion, he argues, requires and generates an ideology in terms of which race differences are employed to justify the discrimination:

> The ideology of race is a system of ideas which interprets and defines the meanings of racial differences, real or imagined, in terms of some system of cultural values. The ideology of race is always normative: it ranks differences as better or worse, superior or inferior, desirable or undesirable, and as modifiable or unmodifiable. Like all ideologies, the ideology of race implies a call to action; it embodies a political and social program; it is a demand that something be done.

No group of men, Nash continues, can systematically subordinate or deprive another group of men without appealing to a body of values that justifies the disprivilege and exploitation. Racial ideologies therefore legitimate the relationship between the two groups concerned. They also serve to quell dissension or doubt in the dominant group itself.

Nash believes that the conditions for the emergence of a racial ideology are (1) conflict between racial or ethnic groups, (2) the subordination or systematic deprivation of one group, (3) the unwillingness of the subordinate group to accept the disprivileges, (4) the structuring of the division of labor on racial or ethnic lines, and (5) the dissent of some of the dominant group to the prevailing facts of disprivilege. Under these circumstances, a racial ideology will provide a moral rationale for the systematic disprivilege of the subordinate group. If one believes, for example, that God designated as black those members of the human race who were fit only to be slaves, or that slaves are happier in slavery than in freedom, then the enslaving of others becomes morally more justifiable. In this way an ideology of race allows members of the dominant group to reconcile their activities with their values.

Furthermore, the ideology of race will discourage the subordinate group from making claims on society, particularly because some of them will come to believe the racial myths themselves. The ideology of race defends the existing order, especially the *division of labor,* as eternal, and it rallies the dominant group to a "just" cause—political action in defense of their position. In the face of these social functions, scientific evidence is of marginal importance. As Nash observes, "If one is promoting an ideology, it is better to have most of the facts on your side, but it does not really matter, as long as some of the facts can be absorbed or made consonant with the ideology."

iv   Evaluation It is often to the advantage of dominant groups to emphasize biological differences among ethnic or racial elements in a society, and to minimize or even deny the essential humanity of all men. Sometimes, indeed, racial differences will actually be invented to justify systematic disprivilege—as the Nazis invented imaginary differences between Jews and the so-called Aryan race.

At other times it may be to the advantage of the dominant group to alter its attitudes. For example, although Asians have always been classified as nonwhites in the Republic of South Africa and subjected to severe racial discrimination, in 1962 Japan com-

pleted a trade agreement with South Africa so favorable that South Africa modified its racial policies. Her Japanese residents (some 60 in all) are now officially classified as "honorary whites," whereas the Chinese and other Asians still remain "nonwhite."

(A racial ideology frequently becomes a central feature of the value system of a society in times of social crisis—when scapegoats are sought—or when a dominant group perceives itself to be threatened by a subordinate group. The group that feels insecure requires some ideology to justify its position and maintain the stability of the social and economic order. Gunnar Myrdal argued in the 1940s that the American value system was so explicit on the subject of equality and freedom that racial discrimination could not persist unless there was some intervening ideology that excluded black Americans from the applicability of the value system as a whole. This situation explained the racial ideology that stressed the supposed inferiority, laziness, and happiness-in-servitude of the black population.)

c The "Research" Question

i Context Between 1965 and 1967 racial disorders in the United States took 130 lives and injured more than 3,600 people. Some 29,000 arrests were made, and damage to property was estimated at over $700 million. These statistics reveal some of the costs of bad race relations, but other less tangible costs—hardened attitudes, stifled opportunities, unnecessary poverty, heightened antagonism between groups who could be working in harmony for their mutual benefit—are much greater.

The situation in the United States parallels in many respects the problems elsewhere in the world. Prejudice, misunderstanding, and vested interest often combine to poison human relationships, and the reduction or elimination of racial discrimination is an urgent and pressing need. Each society attempts its own solution, and each can learn from the successes or failures of the others.

In the United States, for example, there is much confusion about the ultimate nature of the society we want. Should our objective be the proverbial *"melting pot,"* in which each racial or ethnic group is an ingredient to be blended in a common nationhood? Or should the objective be a *pluralist society,* in which each group retains its distinctive characteristics while respecting the culture of the other groups and dealing with them on a basis of mutual equality?

The patterns other societies have adopted are therefore of great significance to the sociologist studying race relations. What attitudes have majorities historically adopted toward minorities, and what has been the reaction of those minorities? Which policies encourage racial harmony, and which aggravate strife? Sociologists ask: (What are the possible patterns of intergroup relations and what are the consequences of these patterns?)

ii Theory (Pierre van den Berghe's "The Dynamics of Racial Prejudice" (1958) suggests that the relationships between the dominant group and the subordinate group tend to polarize around two types of system, in both of which the ideology of the dominant group attributes different characteristics to the subordinate group.

The *paternalistic system* is usually found in an agricultural

The nineteenth-century American South has often been presented as an example of the paternalistic system of racial intergroup relationships.

(Facing page) Racial ideology follows political necessity. In order to be able to justify Germany's political alliances, Nazi theoreticians of Aryan supremacy proclaimed the "Aryanization" of the Japanese. The Mediterranean racial stock of the Italian fascists was a subject to be avoided. Thus the fighters for "racial purity" put political reality before ideological conviction. The top photo shows Japanese Foreign Minister Matsuoka with Italian Foreign Minister Ciano and German diplomat Von Mackensen. The bottom photo shows Hitler shaking hands with Mussolini.

society with a simple economy (such as the Old South). There is a wide gap in the living standards of the two groups, the division of labor is based on race, everyone knows his or her place, and there is no ideological conflict about the system. The dominant group has a paternalistic attitude and tends to consider the subordinate group as childish, immature, uninhibited, impulsive, happy-go-lucky, and generally inferior.

The *competitive system* develops in a more sophisticated and urbanized society (such as contemporary South Africa), where there is partial overlap in the standards of living. The economic status of the dominant group is continually threatened by the upward pressure and ambitions of the subordinate group, and there is severe conflict over ideology. In this case the dominant group develops an attitude of fear and hatred and tends to view the subordinate group as aggressive, insolent, oversexed, dangerous, and subhuman—traits that must be suppressed by sternly authoritarian measures.

John Rex's *Race Relations in Sociological Theory* (1970) examines patterns of racial dominance in the industrialized countries of the Western world, focusing on those former colonial powers in Europe whose relationship with immigrants from the now-independent colonies, Rex argues, parallels the pattern that existed in the colonies themselves. This analysis is relevant to the United States because of several "colonial" features in the blacks' migration to Northern cities from the traditionalist, agricultural South. Rex suggests that such minorities tend to be defined by the majority group as alien outsiders, despite their possession of formal citizenship, and that meaningful interaction is blocked by a complex system of *social and economic stratification.* The immigrants enter the stratification system near the bottom and tend to take "replacement jobs"—that is, functions that have not yet been eliminated by technical advance but are so arduous and unpleasant that they are not acceptable to members of the working class of the host society. In times of crisis the minority group becomes a target for blame and recrimination; it serves as a ready-made and virtually defenseless scapegoat.

iii Research (Methodology)   In *Racial and Cultural Minorities* (1965) G. E. Simpson and J. M. Yinger delineated six major strategies for a society confronted with a race relations problem. All of these have been tried in practice during recent history.

Assimilation may take place more or less by chance, or it may be the result of deliberate policy. It occurs when the dominant group has no strong and sustained objection to incorporating the subordinate group into its own culture. This pattern has been followed, though not necessarily as an act of policy and often with gross inconsistencies, in Brazil and the United States, both of which have to some extent been "melting pot" societies. There have been unassimilable elements, however—the blacks and native Americans in the United States and the Indians of the interior in Brazil. Portugal is following a policy of deliberate assimilation of the indigenous population in its African colonies, on the assumption that this strategy, rather than outright subjugation of the natives, is more likely to permit retention of the colonies in the long run. The indigenous population is resisting assimilation, however, so that

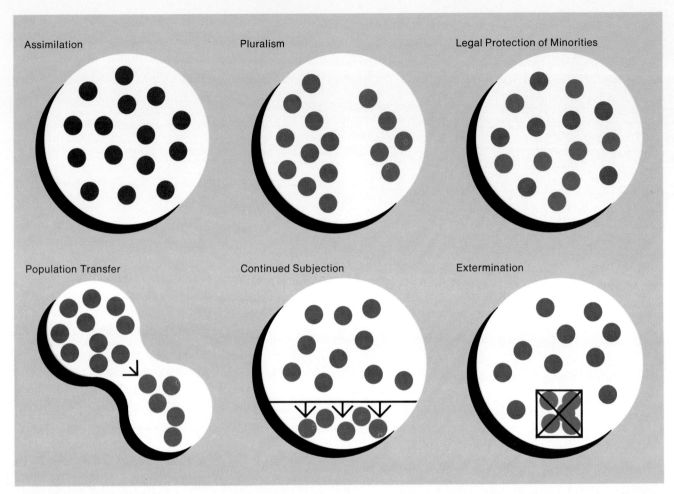

Assimilation Pluralism Legal Protection of Minorities

Population Transfer Continued Subjection Extermination

Model 1. Possible Relationships Between Subordinate Groups within a Society.

subjugation is also being employed, leaving Portuguese policy inconsistent and ineffectual.

Pluralism stems from a willingness of the dominant group to permit some degree of cultural variation within the context of overall national unity. The United States has always exhibited a considerable degree of pluralism, and pluralist values have been adopted by most multiracial societies that enjoy good race relations. The policy is most likely to be successful where the dominant group does not feel threatened by the minority elements within the society and where the minority culture is not so alien or antagonistic to the dominant culture that national unity and welfare are threatened.

Legal protection of minorities is appropriate where the dominant group is prepared to recognize the anxieties of the subordinate or minority group and to enact legislation protecting its interests. This strategy has been adopted by the United States through legislation aimed at preserving the civil liberties of minority groups, enforcing fair employment practices, and outlawing overt segregation. Another example is the British Race Relations Act, which outlawed discrimination in Britain when nonwhite immigrants from the

West Indies, India, and Pakistan complained of prejudice against them, particularly in employment and housing, during the 1960s.

Population transfer may be adopted on a voluntary basis by the subordinate group. A population will not leave its place of residence, however, unless discriminatory pressures have been intense (even if they have stopped short of outright expulsion). The emigration of Jews from Germany in the early years of the Nazi regime is an example of this "voluntary" migration. Several examples of forced population transfer have also occurred during this century—the deliberate expulsion of Jews from Germany later in the Nazi regime, the recent expulsion of Asians from Kenya and Uganda, the transfer of populations between India and Pakistan at the time of the dismemberment of the Indian subcontinent into predominately Moslem and Hindu states, and the expulsion of millions of blacks from urban centers in the Republic of South Africa over the past two decades.

Continued subjection of subordinate peoples is an increasingly rare policy in the modern world, although it was the basis of the colonialism of European powers in Africa and Asia until after World War II. Today several Central and South American countries apply it against the indigenous Indians. It is also the basis of continued rule by the white-minority regimes in South Africa, Rhodesia, and the remaining Portuguese colonies in Africa (Mozambique, Angola, and Guinea-Bissau).

Extermination of entire populations—*genocide*—has occasionally been practiced within the last two centuries. The Tasmanians of Australia were completely destroyed, the American Indians and the South African Hottentots and Bushmen were almost wiped out (the Bushmen were officially classified as "vermin," with a bounty on each one killed), and 6 million Jews were murdered by the Nazis as a part of Hitler's systematic attempt to eliminate the entire Jewish people.

iv   Evaluation   Any solution to the problem of race relations in the United States in the foreseeable future is likely to involve cultural pluralism combined with legal protection of the rights of minorities. The long-run tendency may be toward full assimilation of all groups, so that the "melting pot" will become a reality, but the society is currently tending to recognize the integrity and worth of the cultures of its various ethnic and racial minorities.

The law plays an important part in attitudinal change. Statutes do not necessarily reflect *social mores;* very often they create those mores. The public mood tends to alter after a law has been adopted. Laws provide a basis for the changing of group attitudes by defining and clarifying rights and obligations, and public attitudes tend to be modified as a result. People often are converted by an established legal principle, and the law has a certain educative function.

Harmonious race relations will depend not merely on legal measures, however, but also on changing attitudes. Although laws can prevent us from discriminating against our fellow men and women, they cannot guarantee that we will love our neighbor: a change in attitude requires education and personal knowledge about other groups. All the evidence suggests that racial attitudes

Anti-Asian feeling in Britain and Africa. The top photo shows a signboard put up by Air India in Delhi in 1970 that refers to the efforts of British Conservative politician Enoch Powell to have nonwhite immigrants to Britain sent back to their home countries. The signboard shows Powell as a travel agent offering an Indian free air passage from Britain to Delhi and a thousand pounds as *baksheesh* (tip). The airline used the signboard to boost its passenger traffic. The bottom photo shows persons of Indian descent leaving Uganda after President Idi Amin expelled most persons of Asian ancestry from that country in 1972.

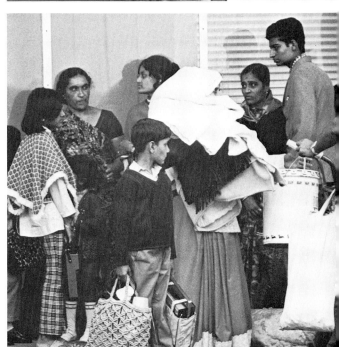

Challenge for the coming generations. Creating a society in which racial and ethnic identity will have no negative bearing on how and where human beings live and find fulfillment is a major task for the world as it moves into the twenty-first century. The bottom photo shows an interracial couple in Britain.

are learned early in life, but that they are modifiable by later events, such as personal experience of equality in the school or work situation. Overt discrimination can be fought in the legislatures and the courts, but the basic attack on prejudice must be made in the homes, the media, the churches, the schools, and the workplaces.

3 Overview

Race and ethnic relations present one of the major social problems of our time, both in the United States and in the rest of the world. The global gap between the affluence and power of the white nations of the Northern Hemisphere and the poverty and powerlessness of the nonwhite nations of the rest of the world is likely to be a breeding ground of tension for decades to come. The global problem is also found in microcosm within most industrialized countries.

Prejudice and discrimination can be eliminated if we understand their psychological and sociological bases. Prejudice is an element in the *norms* transmitted through *socialization* to new generations; it is associated with the *ethnocentric tendency* to rate one's own group as superior to others and to employ one's own standards as the yardstick for measuring other people's. To future generations it may seem barbaric that men could have hated, stigmatized, and even slaughtered one another on such grounds as the pigmentation of their skin. But the sociological perspective, by indicating how racial myths and attitudes are derived from underlying social factors, does suggest strategies for the improvement of race and ethnic relations. Changes in the structure of society and the economy may bring about changes in the ideology of race. Race relations can be meaningfully studied only in their historical and socioeconomic context, and racial prejudice and discrimination will not disappear until the socioeconomic conditions that sustain them no longer exist.

D   LOOKING AHEAD

1   Interview:
Kenneth B. Clark

Kenneth B. Clark is Distinguished University Professor of psychology at City College of the City University of New York and president of the Metropolitan Applied Research Center, Inc. He has held positions as officer or consultant with government and social agencies, foundations, and corporations and served as president of the American Psychological Association and the Society for the Psychological Study of Social Issues. He is author of *Desegregation, Prejudice and Your Child*, *Dark Ghetto*, and *A Relevant War on Poverty* (with Hopkins).

DPG   *Are race relations in the United States getting better?*
CLARK   They certainly aren't getting worse, although despair and pessimism have become somewhat fashionable. The focus has changed from a concentration on removal of the laws supporting exclusion from schools, public accommodations, and so forth, particularly in the South, to dealing with problems in the urban North—segregation in housing, de facto segregation in the schools. But these kinds of race problems are not easily dealt with in terms of the traditional methods of legislation, litigation, or even demonstrations. The paradox of the present complex pattern of race relations in America is that it reflects the successes of the past. The more flagrant forms of racial humiliation and cruelty that were characteristic of the South—the signs saying "white" and "colored" and the like—have been removed. Although this fact is unquestionably progress, the more insidious racism in the North does not lend itself to remedy by the traditional methods and techniques.

DPG   *What approaches and remedies could be used to cope with these problems in the North?*
CLARK   The first thing I would propose is the recognition of the need to think about new strategies. One of the things that seems pretty clear about the Northern form of racism is that, if the racial issue is permitted to be the dominant issue, it almost inevitably will result in polarization. The majority of whites will respond racially, and the backlash phenomenon will be reinforced. That would obviously not contribute to amelioration or remedy of the problems. Full employment and the quality and accountability

of education should be treated as issues that affect all citizens. The viability and vitality of the cities should be emphasized as a way of dealing with the elimination of ghettos.

DPG *The plight of the black American has had the limelight until recently. Can we expect more attention to problems of such minorities as the Chicanos and the Indians in the future?*

CLARK One of the most important consequences of the civil rights movement of the 1950s and 1960s is that it has helped the American public to understand that the problems of cruelty and injustice should be dealt with without regard to the particular victim. The blacks did dramatize the issue of injustice, and I think it's absolutely right and valuable for other dark-skinned minorities and such white minorities as the Appalachian whites to use similar techniques. I don't see this process as competitive at all.

DPG *To what factors would you ascribe the reluctance of the present administration and its "middle American" constituency to provide the funds necessary to achieve equality and economic justice in America?*

CLARK The Nixon administration seems to be demonstrating with disturbing frequency a rather anachronistic and constricted antipoor and antihuman view of social and economic problems. I think it won't be long before the self-destructiveness of this attitude will become apparent to the majority of Americans. They will begin to see that one cannot ignore the very real plight of the poor without risking social instability or jeopardizing the economic benefits that now exist for the middle class or the privileged. This kind of instability is inevitable unless the society opts for total repression, but I don't think the majority of the American people would accept that.

DPG *Is legislation adequate as a means of attacking problems of race relations? If not, how else might racism be eliminated in America?*

CLARK Federal and state legislation, court decisions, and executive policy positions are essential, but not sufficient. They are extremely important as a base upon which

one can seek to educate the American people as to the true ramifications of continuing racial inequities. One of the disturbing things about the Nixon administration is that the federal government no longer provides a baseline below which the attitudes and behavior of the American people cannot go. That has to be remedied. Even though it seems as if it has been conducive to political success to pander to the more primitive passions and prejudices of the people, I have to believe that in the long run it will be shown that such tactics benefit no one.

DPG *Do black power movements and other manifestations of ethnic feeling simply represent a passing phase, a practical necessity if the ethnic groups concerned are to make their way into American society, or has ethnic pride and feeling become a permanent and valued part of our way of life? Will the "melting pot" idea finally be discarded as a myth?*

CLARK The melting pot was never a literal reality in American history, but Americanization and assimilation have been and continue to be realities. It is a fact that America was a place where lower-class people from European countries migrated in order to avail themselves of the possibilities and op-

portunities that were clearly denied them at their point of origin. It's also a fact that, for European immigrants, America did fulfill its promises to a greater extent than many cynics believe. America has certainly never been classless, but social, economic, and educational mobility was more a reality here than in the countries from which the immigrants came.

DPG *There's been a development of separatism among American minorities. Do you think ethnic communities will begin to assert their ethnic identity and pride more and more?*

CLARK I think that various ethnic groups in America have done two things simultaneously. They have tried to maintain their ethnic unity, and at the same time they have provided individual members of their groups with the opportunity for melding or melting into the larger community. And it has never been either/or for white ethnic groups in the American social mobility process. Two generations ago, the Kennedys and the Fitzgeralds went into politics and emphasized their Irishness to the ultimate in their struggle against the Boston WASPs. After that base was established, Joe Kennedy concentrated on economic mobility and systematically diminished the Irish component of his identity. The Kennedy boys could afford to emphasize their Americanism.

DPG *Would you say that this pattern of working into the American system through emphasizing ethnic or group pride is likely to be successful for other minorities?*

CLARK The racial separatist groups and the ethnic pride groups are trying this approach now because they believe it worked successfully for European immigrant groups. And this approach may still have some validity. One of the problems I used to point out 20 or 30 years ago was that blacks at that time tended to buy the white perspective on blacks, which led to deep feelings of inferiority on their part. Black power ideology seems to be an attempt to deal directly with that point. I'm worried, however, by attempts to deal with problems only in terms of rhetoric or ideology. Other ethnic groups have reinforced their struggle for positive self-esteem and pride by establishing some

kind of realistic base—political organizations, economic organizations, perhaps even crime. Of course, it may be that words are the first step in finding some kind of valid, realistic base upon which blacks (or Chicanos or Indians) can obtain or exercise their power to get an equitable share in the spoils of the society.

DPG   *What would you say is the importance or the value of the role of the WASP in American society?*
CLARK   The value of the WASPs in America is that, whether they like it or not, they represent the standard against which all other groups measure themselves. The WASPs fulfill a role that is the opposite of the role of blacks, who represent the negative standard by which mobility of the other ethnic groups can be measured. About 25 years ago I pointed out that the rate of Americanization of ethnic groups can be measured in terms of the increase in their antiblack attitudes. In the past, the status of the blacks was held constant. They were not permitted the same access to mobility as European immigrants. The WASPs are the positive constant. Ethnic groups measure the degree of their assimilation in American society by the extent to which they are permitted participation in WASP clubs or WASP power or economic groups.

DPG   *Do you see antagonism between blacks and other ethnic groups as a forthcoming major problem?*
CLARK   I think it's always been a major problem. The only thing that's different is that now it can no longer be a quiet struggle, and, as a psychologist, I think that's progress. Quiet acceptance of inequities and injustices in the society is clearly much less healthy than a struggle against the inequities, no matter how painful the struggle. Interestingly, the dark-skinned groups are not so far challenging the basic democratic assumptions or machinery in any significant way, even though democracy has worked far less successfully for them than it has for white ethnics. In that sense the dark-skinned groups are not radicals, but conservatives.

DPG   *What impact have the claims of Arthur Jensen and William Shockley had on the state of scientific research or on race relations in America? Do you feel that research into the relationship between IQ and race should be taboo?*

CLARK   Obviously, as a scientist, I cannot possibly advocate that any area of inquiry should be immune from inquiry. The issue of genetic determination of psychological functions is a very legitimate scientific issue. Nevertheless, one does not passively accept what is sheer nonsense. And Jensen's statement that the academic achievement of dark-skinned minority youngsters, blacks, is genetically determined is nonsense for several quite obvious reasons. Genetics as a science is not by any means ready to make any association between genes and complex human psychological characteristics. Furthermore, intelligence is a complicated, confused phenomenon in concept. Jensen defines intelligence as whatever intelligence tests measure, which is a fascinating kind of nondefinition. To tie a nondefinition concept to something as specific and at the same time as ambiguous as genes is to me arrant, pseudoscientific nonsense. I have to be pushed to talk about Jensen and other people who talk about genetic inferiority as a psychological trait. It's like talking about witches, and we don't have time to talk about witches when we have so many real problems.

DPG   *What are the hot areas in the study of race relations? What do we need to know or do to solve our problems of race and ethnic relations?*
CLARK   Obviously, anybody who attempts to answer that question has to deal with it in terms of his own biases and limitations. I'm currently concentrating on the various aspects of power in this field. Power is a very fundamental issue, and we have to get a more precise understanding of the meaning of power in human interaction in order to understand a lot of things about human conflict. Bertrand Russell made a suggestion that the key phenomenon in the social sciences is power, just as the key phenomenon in the physical sciences is energy. Social scientists, it seems to me, have to be much more precise and systematic in their study and understanding of the origins, the determinants, and the dynamics of power in order to be more effective agents of social change. And that goes beyond race relations to involve all aspects of human interaction.

Institutions in

Part III

Mass Society

Unit 16

Formal and Complex Organizations

SCHEMATIC OUTLINE

A Introductory Graphics: Organizations and the Individual

B Definition and Context

1 Definition
A formal organization is a social unit that has explicit impersonal goals. The activities of its members are coordinated by means of a bureaucracy.

2 World Context
Complex organizations are rare on the international level. But within individual states, especially in Western and Eastern Europe, there is often a high degree of bureaucratization.

3 American Context
Large, formal, complex organizations pose a genuine dilemma for modern America. They often appear oppressive, but may be essential to social and economic well-being.

C Questions and Evidence

1 Questions
Three problems typify the interest of sociologists in formal organizations: (1) What are the political implications of the trend toward bureaucratization? (2) Is bureaucracy an inevitable concomitant of modern industrial society? (3) Do bureaucracies operate smoothly and efficiently to achieve the best results?

2 Evidence
a The "Burning Issue" Question
Early in this century Robert Michels argued that large organizations must necessarily give their officers a near monopoly of power. His "iron law of oligarchy" has been hotly debated, especially by those who argue that the socialist and capitalist systems are converging in bureaucratization. The appearance of a technocratic elite raises a fresh issue.
b The "Classical" Question
Karl Marx argued that bureaucracy could be eliminated only by the move from capitalism through socialism to the communist society. Max Weber, on the other hand, saw bureaucratization as part of the inevitable rationalization of industrial society. Emile Durkheim suggested the strengthening of secondary groups to intervene between the individual and the state. Ultimately, local charismatic upheavals may counteract bureaucratization.
c The "Research" Question
Most studies of bureaucratic operations have been based on Weber's concept of the ideal type, though some have concentrated on informal organization. The studies show that bureaucracies have many dysfunctions but are often an efficient and practical means of coordinating people to achieve a definite objective.

3 Overview
In response to a number of pressures most nations are currently seeking to reduce or modify bureaucratization.

D Looking Ahead

1 Interview: Peter M. Blau
2 Interview: Robert Townsend

SUPPORTING UNITS

5 Socialization and Moral Development
6 Population and Demography
8 Religion
9 Social Stratification
11 Small Groups
16 Formal and Complex Organizations
17 Urban Society

ENCYCLOPEDIA ENTRIES

Blau, Peter M. (b.1918)
bureaucracy
bureaupathology
capitalism
class
compliance theory
counterculture
division of labor
Durkheim, Emile (1858–1917)
feudalism
formal and complex organizations
Hawthorne studies
iron law of oligarchy
Marx, Karl (1818–1883)
Merton, Robert K. (b. 1910)
oligarchy
organization man
rationality
scientific management
socialism
technocracy
Weber, Max (1864–1920)

ORGANIZATIONS AND THE INDIVIDUAL

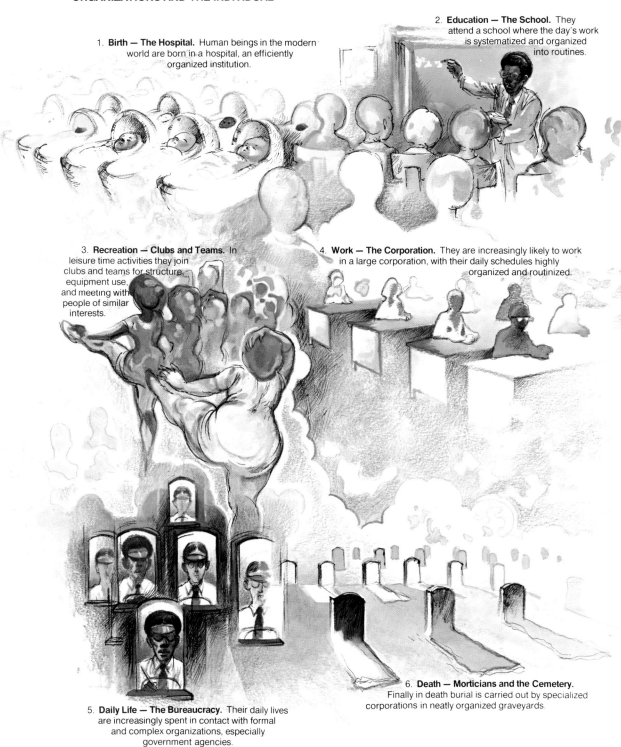

1. **Birth — The Hospital.** Human beings in the modern world are born in a hospital, an efficiently organized institution.

2. **Education — The School.** They attend a school where the day's work is systematized and organized into routines.

3. **Recreation — Clubs and Teams.** In leisure time activities they join clubs and teams for structure, equipment use, and meeting with people of similar interests.

4. **Work — The Corporation.** They are increasingly likely to work in a large corporation, with their daily schedules highly organized and routinized.

5. **Daily Life — The Bureaucracy.** Their daily lives are increasingly spent in contact with formal and complex organizations, especially government agencies.

6. **Death — Morticians and the Cemetery.** Finally in death burial is carried out by specialized corporations in neatly organized graveyards.

B   DEFINITION AND CONTEXT

1   Definition

Human life is social life: that is, human life involves participation in some forms of association. Often these associations are informal (such as friendships), transitory (such as a seminar group), and small (such as a family or kinship unit). But in the modern industrial state, the tendency is for the individual to spend more and more of his time in *formal, complex organizations.* Modern man spends most of his waking life participating in these institutions. And even when he is not an active participant, his behavior is still affected by the pervasive influence of the many formal organizations in his society. Schools, factories, offices, corporations, armies, government bureaucracies—all influence the kind of people we are and the kind of society we live in.

A *formal organization is a special-purpose social unit that has explicit, impersonal goals in terms of which the activities of its members are coordinated.* This coordination is achieved by the rational operation of a hierarchical authority structure known as a *bureaucracy;* bureaucratic procedures are followed by all formal, complex organizations. Although in common parlance the word "bureaucracy" has a pejorative connotation—one thinks of red tape, inefficiency, insufferable delays, bungled decisions, the conservatism of petty officials and their rigid adherence to the rule book—the sociologist uses it as a descriptive term in a neutral sense.

2   World Context

In international terms the formal, complex organization is a rather rare phenomenon. Most inhabitants of the earth live in preliterate or developing societies in which social and economic life is relatively undifferentiated, even if some central administrative apparatus is imposed on the society as a whole. This situation is particularly true of the tribal society, where lack of literacy alone would make the formation of a complex bureaucratic structure impossible, even if there were need for one. In these societies, as in many of the developing countries, there is relatively limited division of labor and a high interchangeability of individuals in different tasks: the farmer and the toolmaker may be the same person, and economic activity is based on the *extended family unit* and does not require complex coordination. Even where differentiated military, religious, and political leaderships have emerged through an incipient *division of labor and specialization,* their functions are still too limited and localized to require the development of formal organizations with a bureaucratic apparatus.

Formal organizations and bureaucracies began to appear with the development of the nation-state in the early civilizations of Mesopotamia and Egypt. Administrative organizations later reached a high level of bureaucratic sophistication in some preindustrial empires, such as the Roman, the Byzantine, the Chinese, and the Spanish. (The Roman army, whose disciplined ranks and hierarchical leadership contrasted so strongly and effectively with the relatively disorganized troops they were usually pitted against—thus

The architecture of some buildings is a literal representation of the formal organization of the company they house. In the penthouse is the office suite of the president. On the next floor down are the vice-presidential suites, below them the offices of the middle-managers, and on the lowest—and largest—floor at ground level is the secretarial pool.

making possible the conquest of the then-known world—is one of the earliest and most striking examples of a formal, complex organization.) It was only after the Industrial Revolution in England and the political revolution in France in 1789, however, that formal structures based on the bureaucratic administration of the entire economy and political system reached the level of refinement we know today. In fact, Napoleon Bonaparte, who was largely responsible for establishing state bureaucratic machinery, is reported to have done so in order to obtain complete organizational control over the various institutions of France and thereby assure that no group could compete with him for power.)

In the industrial countries of Western Europe there is often a very high degree of bureaucratization. It has been said, perhaps a little cynically, that French education is so tightly organized that the national minister of education can state, at any time of day, exactly what book every child at a particular grade level is using at that moment. In Britain railway workers have evolved an interesting and convenient method of going on strike, known as "working to rule." The rules that railwaymen are supposed to follow are so cumbersome and outdated that many of them are ignored in practice. If the workers do "work to rule" the result is a paralysis of the national rail network. But the men are not officially on strike or disobeying orders, and so they continue to draw full wages.

In the state-socialist societies of Eastern Europe, bureaucratization has also reached a very high level compared with the United States. In those societies areas that in the United States are left to chance or to private initiative are largely regulated instead by the administrative apparatus of the central government.)

3   American Context

The modern American has been called the "organization man." One of the most pervasive features of our lives is that we are dominated by large, formal, complex organizations that control finance, commerce, religion, telecommunications, education, entertainment, government, the military, law, philanthropy, research, medicine, and virtually every other institutional area of the national life. These administrative networks are so gigantic in scale that organizations such as the Pentagon, ITT, or General Motors have far larger budgets, far more personnel, and perhaps more power than whole national governments elsewhere in the world.

These organizations pose a genuine dilemma for modern America—as many of its youth are loudly pointing out. Theodore Roszak, in his *The Making of a Counter Culture* (1969), sees the American youth movement largely as a response to the increasing *rationalization* and *bureaucratization* of society—young people are not willing to become mere "cogs in a machine," to surrender control over the detail and direction of their lives to impersonal organizations. But although the organizations that influence or dominate our society may sometimes appear oppressive of all that is spontaneous, natural, and joyful in the life of man, they also seem to be a social invention without which no mass industrial society could exist. Census taking, voter registration, taxation and budgeting, health and welfare, long-range economic planning, military preparedness,

(Pages 366–367) Republican National Convention, 1972. The Republican presidential nominating convention in 1972 was an example of Michels' formulation regarding the powerlessness of the mass of low-level participants in formal organizations. President Richard Nixon had, in effect, "orchestrated" the entire event, even down to the "spontaneous" demonstrations on the part of the delegates on the floor, in order to give the impression of maximum unity behind his renomination.

the mass production and distribution of rock records and tapes—
how could all these take place without the use of formal structures
to develop policies and coordinate activities?

C   QUESTIONS AND EVIDENCE

1   Questions

Three questions typify the interests of sociologists who study formal
organizations and bureaucracies: (1) What are the political implications of the trend toward bureaucratization—are organizations denying people the democratic right to control their own lives and futures? (2) Is bureaucracy an inevitable concomitant of modern
industrial society—or is it possible for bureaucracies to be restricted, adapted, or even eliminated? (3) How do bureaucracies
really work—what are their characteristics? Do they conform to the
intentions of their designers in functioning smoothly and efficiently
to achieve the best results?

2   Evidence

a   The "Burning Issue" Question

i   Context ⟨Sociologists have been interested throughout this century in the problems that bureaucratization poses for democracy.
Two distinct but related problems have captured their attention.
First, does the existence of formal, complex organizations in the
political sphere—like the political party or the government department—limit or enhance the capacity of voters to exercise real influence on the course of events?⟩ (The same question can also be
asked, of course, about nonpolitical organizations—about the influence of the average church member in his church, of the average
stockholder in his corporation.) And ⟨second, are bureaucratization
and extension of the state apparatus creating a new ruling elite that
is independent of, and perhaps more influential than, formally
elected national leadership? Sociologists ask: *What are the implications of bureaucratization for democratic theory and practice?*⟩

ii   Theory ⟨The problem of the relationship between formal organizations and *oligarchy* (rule by the few at the top) was raised early
in this century by the German sociologist Robert Michels in his
classic work, *Political Parties* (1911). Michels had become deeply
disillusioned by the fact that the fledgling socialist parties of Europe
appeared to offer no more effective participation to their members
than the traditional conservative parties did. Despite a supposedly
more democratic structure, the new mass-based parties still appeared to be ruled from above with little attention to the opinions of
their mass membership. Michels sought the answer to this paradox
and found it inherent in the very nature of organizational structure:
"It is organization which gives birth to the domination of the
elected over the electors, of the mandatories over the mandators,
of the delegates over the delegators. Who says organization, says
oligarchy." This principle, which Michels held would operate in any
complex social organization, has come to be known as the "*iron
law of oligarchy.*"⟩

Why did Michels argue that large-scale organizations must necessarily give their officers a near monopoly of power? His belief was that because of the sheer problem of administration, organization necessitated bureaucracy. And bureaucracy, because of the need for a chain of command and responsibility, necessitated *hierarchic structure*—with oligarchic control. Hence the irresolvable dilemma of modern man: the functioning of the large-scale political and social units on which his very society depends must involve the allocation of effective power to the few who control these units. For several reasons, Michels argued, the mass membership has little opportunity to exercise influence. The leaders of an organization possess many resources to consolidate their position and further their own aims. Because of their position, they have superior knowledge. They have access to a mass of information that can be used to secure assent to their objectives, and they can manipulate this information because of their control over internal communications and over propaganda released for external consumption. The very fact that the officials have risen to positions of leadership implies that they are skilled in the arts of politics—they are far more adept than the rank and file at making speeches, organizing activities, writing articles, influencing discussions, manipulating people and meetings.

The position of the leadership is made even more secure by what Michels called "the incompetence of the masses." The influence of the mass membership, if it is to have any real effect, must be applied forcefully and continuously through full participation in organizational activities. But in fact relatively few rank-and-file members take a full and continuing part in the formulation and application of organizational policy. Unlike the full-time officials, the ordinary members have many other concerns, and the organization represents only one limited area of interest to them. The masses, too, have lower levels of education and of general sophistication, and they tend to regard their leaders (especially the more charismatic ones) with veneration and to take their proposals on trust.

So the leaders become a professionalized *power elite,* with many of their policies reflecting not so much the will and the material interests of the masses as the concerns of the officials. Sometimes these concerns may be purely self-interested; but sometimes the leaders may, for entirely idealistic reasons, pursue some objective that they believe to be in the interests of the organization or the wider society, even though most of the membership is apathetic or opposed to the objective. Even when such a cleavage of views becomes apparent, it is extremely difficult for the mass membership to take effective action. The leaders are strongly motivated to maintain their position, and they define criticism from within the organization as naïveté, disloyalty, or even treachery.

In Michels' view, the result of these oligarchic tendencies would be that, even after the socialist revolution, there would be "dictatorship in the hands of those leaders who have been sufficiently astute and sufficiently powerful to grasp the sceptre of domination. . . . The socialists might triumph, but not socialism, which would perish in the moment of its adherents' triumph."

iii Research The iron law of oligarchy has influenced social theory and research for half a century. Much of the debate has been

Hitler celebrates the anniversary of his first attempt to seize power in Germany. Did Hitler's power come from mass support or from his control over the German political machinery—or from both?

Meeting of communal revolutionary committees during China's Great Proletarian Cultural Revolution. The cultural revolution was initiated by Communist Party Chairman Mao Tse-tung in an attempt to allow all persons equal access to positions of responsibility and to prevent the state bureaucracy from creating a new basis for class privileges. Using the motto "Bombard the headquarters" Mao released forces of structure-breaking all across the country in an attempt to correct social ills through reorganizing an entire society.

focused on the theory that the socialist and capitalist countries of the modern world are *convergent*—that is, their governmental and economic institutions are becoming progressively more similar. The convergence argument hinges on the question of whether the technocratic bureaucracy that has arisen in the socialist countries has come to assume the status of a *dominant class* in its own right— paralleling the development in capitalist societies of a similar technocratic group that is gradually displacing the capitalism of the individual businessman and the aristocracy of birth. If such processes are taking place, then the state socialism of Eastern Europe may be in some respects very similar to the corporate capitalism of the West; it may be "state capitalism." The differences lie partly in the existence of a propertied *leisure class* in the West unknown in the East, partly in the greater stress on egalitarianism in the East in contrast to the emphasis on individual freedom and limited governmental intervention in the West.

Research in this general area has been greatly hampered by the absence of statistical material on the socialist-bloc countries as well as by the definitional problems involved in determining exactly what a "class" is. Some researchers have refused to accept the idea that the bureaucracy is becoming a class on the grounds that the term ought to be assigned only to a group that has an *exploitative relation to the means of production*. Other researchers, although they concede that the socialist bureaucracy is not exploitative, suggest that if class is defined in terms of the *control* that any group is able to exercise over the means of production, the bureaucracy in the socialist societies is in fact a distinct, coherent, and dominant class.

Many researchers have accepted the latter definition. Stanislaw Ossowski has shown that in countries such as the Soviet Union the rule of a single party unchecked by any organized opposition has permitted a highly authoritarian ordering of both rank and income. Similarly, the French sociologist Raymond Aron has drawn attention to the exceptional power held by the ruling group in the USSR—it holds power over both economic and political activities whereas in the capitalist societies divided elites compete for power. Most researchers have tended to accept the conclusion that the socialist countries are coming under the control of a technocratic bureaucracy that is as divorced from the rest of society as is the ruling elite in Western capitalist countries. In both types of society the elite consists increasingly of trained experts.

iv Evaluation Michels' view is a persuasive and disturbing one, but it must not be accepted uncritically. It is true that analyses of the internal life of many organizations, such as professional associations, corporations, churches, and student governments, have shown that something akin to the iron law of oligarchy operates. Trade unions are one prime example. Union after union in America has been revealed as being ruled by a "one-party" apparatus that is able to maintain itself in power indefinitely and to recruit its own successors. Some thinkers, such as V. I. Lenin, have even made a virtue of what Michels believed a scandal. Accepting the notion of the incompetence of the masses, Lenin advocated decision making by an elitist group of disciplined party *cadres* that would provide direction until the masses were competent to do it themselves.

Yet Michels sees only the restrictive side of bureaucracy and does not recognize the vital function that organizations may serve as a means through which groups can achieve desired (and otherwise unattainable) objectives. Furthermore, there are significant variations in the organizational structure of complex organizations such as political parties. The Democratic party of the United States, for example, is quite loosely structured, and its convention is easily dominated by a determined popular movement—as the McGovern forces showed in 1972. In contrast is the British Conservative party, where all decisions are taken by one man, the leader, who is elected for life without any formal mechanism for his removal. It is also true that the *policies* of an organization must not diverge too greatly from the *real interests* of its members—the results may range from loss of membership (in the case of a voluntary organization) to revolution (in the case of a state bureaucracy). Organizations, too, are not nearly so monolithic as the iron law holds. There may be two or more *competing elites* present within the structure, eager to step in if the dominant elite makes grave mistakes or loses the allegiance of the mass membership. Some writers, such as Joseph Schumpeter, have even applauded elitist organizations in politics, arguing that the citizens of modern democracies enjoy a high degree of freedom because the parties must so vigorously compete for their support.

Whether the socialist and capitalist models of social organization are converging must remain problematic until the relevant statistics and data are freely available in the socialist countries, but the hypothesis seems very plausible in the light of the evidence so far presented. This theory also raises the fresh issue of *technocracy*—the domination of all industrial societies by a technical elite. It may well be that the technocrat (the specialist within a sharply delimited area of knowledge or technical expertise) is replacing the bureaucrat as the elitist villain in the modern state. It is not clear whether this trend toward technocracy would assure more informed, coordinated, and forward-looking public policy or, instead, increasingly sacrifice liberal and humanistic values in favor of scientific priorities, computerized conformity, and even tighter regimentation and control.

b   The "Classical" Question

i   Context   The question of whether bureaucracy is an inevitable concomitant of modern industrial society has interested social theorists for some time and is now beginning to interest the average citizen as well. Witness the demands for local community control or the expressed desire of young people to seek a return to a simpler life style. And sociologists ask: *Is the trend toward bureaucratization an inevitable concomitant of the development of the modern industrial state?*

ii   Theory   Karl Marx was the first sociologist to tackle the problem of bureaucracy, which he discussed in reference to an allied phenomenon, the *state*. To Marx, the state—that is, a particular governmental form—is simply a projection of the class relationships existing in a given society, and its prime function is to safeguard the interests of the economically dominant group. Thus in the feudal society the monarchy will defend the landed aristocracy against

William D. ("Big Bill") Haywood (1869–1928), secretary-treasurer of the Western Federation of Miners, one of the founders and national secretary-treasurer of the Industrial Workers of the World, and member of the executive board of the Socialist party. In 1906 Haywood was tried for and acquitted of the assassination of the governor of Idaho. In 1917 he was jailed for opposing World War I. He escaped to the Soviet Union in 1921, died there, and was buried next to the Kremlin wall.

The American labor movement for a number of decades was a vigorous mass social movement with a high degree of decentralized decision making and tremendous commitment on the part of many members and leaders, such as Haywood. Currently, however, many unions are run by powerful oligarchies receiving lucrative salaries and retirement benefits. Pragmatic, conservative, political power-brokering has replaced ideological fervor as their operating tone.

the peasants; in the capitalist society the government is but "the executive committee of the bourgeoisie." It follows from this analysis that if class relationships are abolished, the main function of the state, and hence most of the trappings of the state, will be abolished also—an idea expressed by Marx's co-writer, Friedrich Engels, in the famous phrase that the state would "wither away." As a guide to the kind of political activity that would occur in the *classless communist society,* Marx pointed to the brief experience of the Paris Commune of 1871, with its short-term, recallable officials who merely executed the wishes of a citizenry that took a direct, continuing interest in policy matters.

This view of the ultimate stage of human society precludes even the possibility of a permanent, influential bureaucracy. Even specialization is to be abandoned. In the communist future, says Marx, a man may fish in the morning, hunt in the afternoon, and be a literary critic in the evening. Marx saw bureaucracy as an institutional embodiment of personal alienation; the apparent disinterestedness of the bureaucrats merely masked their exploitation of the whole community:

> The bureaucracy has in its possession the affairs of the state, the spiritual being of society; it belongs to it as its private property. . . . As far as the individual [bureaucrat] is concerned, the goals of the state become his private goals: a hunting for higher jobs and the making of a career. . . . The bureaucrat sees the world as a mere object to be managed by him. (*Critique of Hegel's Philosophy of Right,* 1843)

Marx, then, held out hope that bureaucracy could be eliminated, but only through the move from capitalism through socialism to the communist society. This view has been challenged by subsequent theorists, who have argued that the increasing *egalitarianism* in the modern industrial state will actually accelerate bureaucratization as the government apparatus assumes the privileges, functions, and powers that formerly characterized the dominion of one class over another. Furthermore, they contend, this steady accumulation of power by the state and by the civil officials and specialists whose status and livelihood depend on it may make the achievement of the communist society impossible in any case.

iii Research (Survey) The principal theoretical counterargument to the Marxist position was provided by Max Weber—a close friend of Robert Michels. If there is one concept that is fundamental to Weber's whole sociology it is that of *rationalization*. By rationalization Weber meant the process by which abstract, explicit, rationally calculable rules and procedures are substituted for sentiment, tradition, spontaneity, and rule of thumb in all spheres of activity. In architecture, for example, a haphazard arrangement of differing styles is obliterated by redevelopment—and a series of rectangular boxes is erected instead. In law, traditional judicial wisdom gives way to a uniform, codified system of statutes. In commerce, the small shopkeeper who gave his customers individualized attention is replaced by the supermarket. Religious explanation is succeeded by specialized science as the prime source of intellectual authority.

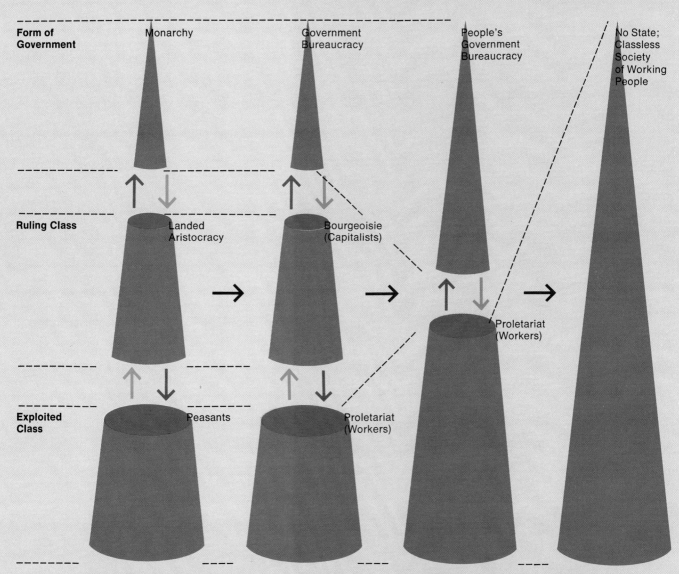

| Economic System | Feudalism | Capitalism | Socialism | Communism |

Form of Government — Monarchy — Government Bureaucracy — People's Government Bureaucracy — No State; Classless Society of Working People

Ruling Class — Landed Aristocracy — Bourgeoisie (Capitalists) — Proletariat (Workers)

Exploited Class — Peasants — Proletariat (Workers)

Model 1. Marxist View of the Evolution of Society From Feudalism to Communism. The upward-pointing red arrows indicate "creates"; the downward-pointing red arrows indicate "exploits"; the downward-pointing blue arrows indicate "protects the interests of"; the upward-pointing blue arrows indicate "provides labor for"; the horizontal black arrows indicate "change through time." The transition from capitalism to socialism is marked by the elimination of the bourgeoisie as the ruling class. The transition to communism from socialism is marked by the "withering away" of the state, that is, the political bureaucracy.

"Little boxes on a hillside." Housing developments, such as this collection of mobile homes near Los Angeles, consisting of slight variations of one or two basic styles of dwelling reflect the forces pushing our society toward the predictable, the matter-of-fact, the drab. To what extent do the prepackaged dwellings mirror the lives of the people living in them?

The trained technocrat is substituted for the cultivated man of letters. Machine technology makes the skilled craftsman obsolete.

Through this process of rationalization (which Weber saw as the distinguishing characteristic of industrial society), the quality of life was being rendered grey, drab, predictable, matter-of-fact. In an essay in *Economy and Society* (1922), Weber explained: "It means that . . . there are no mysterious incalculable forces that come into play, but that one can, in principle, master all things by calculation. . . . The world is disenchanted." Although Weber recognized this trend as inevitable, he lamented that "precisely the most ultimate and sublime values are retreating from public life" in the interests of achieving the goal of *maximum efficiency* as envisioned by "specialists without vision, sensualists without heart."

Why did Weber regard this dismal progression as inevitable? The growth of the bureaucratic state, he argued, proceeds in close connection with political *democratization,* because the demands made by democrats for political representation and for equality before the law require complex administrative and judicial provisions to prevent the exercise of unauthorized privilege. The formation of the socialist state would entail an even higher degree of bureaucratization, because it would place a still wider range of tasks in the hands of a centralized administration. Bureaucracy, too, is "escape-proof" wherever it has become entrenched. In ancient Egypt, Rome, and China, for example, once the officialdom gained control, it retained it until the end. Only when the social order as a whole collapses does the bureaucracy disappear.

Many sociologists have taken a similar view. Emile Durkheim, for example, was concerned at the possibility that, with the increasing expansion of state activity, a bureaucratic tyranny that might be completely out of touch with the individuals in the collectivity could emerge. As a solution he suggested the strengthening of *secondary groups*—such as workers' guilds—so that they could intervene between the individual and the state and maintain some balance of power. Durkheim's emphasis on the need for highly developed interest groups in a pluralist society contrasts markedly with Marx's insistence that it is only through the abolition of such pluralism that state power and bureaucracy can be contained.

iv Evaluation Most social theory on the question of whether bureaucratization is inevitable has been pessimistic. Weber put the issue clearly as he saw it: modern man was trapped in an "iron cage." For Weber the great question was not how the process of bureaucratization could be reversed, but, rather, "What can we set against this mechanization to preserve a certain section of humanity from this fragmentation of the soul, this complete ascendancy of the bureaucratic ideal of life?"

The Marxist answer—that the state will steadily shrink to insignificance—is based on the belief that politics can be reduced to economics, that if there is no conflict of class interest, political antagonisms will evaporate and the apparatus of the state will tend to disappear. But it is doubtful if a nonantagonistic society will arise simply as a result of the abolition of private property, for other group interests may remain, and decisions will have to be taken with which particular groups may not agree. Conflicts between peasant and worker, between those higher and those lower in the administrative apparatus, between those of one region or nationality and those of another—these are not necessarily based on class or economic interest. Even if the decisions in the communist society were taken by men of infinite wisdom, knowledge, and integrity, there is no guarantee that their decisions would be universally acceptable. The allocation of scarce resources must always involve some potential for political disagreement. The administrative functions of the state cannot disappear in any modern society. The very complexities of man's social organization requires some division of labor between rulers and ruled, manifested by some apparatus of social control. One can be a hunter in the morning, a fisherman in the afternoon, a literary critic at night—provided one's society is not too complex. But one cannot fly a Boeing 747 in the morning, design computers in the afternoon, and make long-range macroeconomic forecasts in the evening, nor can the hunter-fisherman-critic even hope to comprehend what experts and officials in such diverse fields are up to.

Durkheim's proposed solution seems more promising—but it runs counter to the general tendency toward complex organizations of greater and greater scale. Fragmentation of organizations at the local level, allowing communities and interest groups more control over their own destinies, is possible even in the modern industrial state, provided the resultant loss of efficiency (amounting perhaps to near chaos in some fields) is a price people are willing to pay.

Weber himself held out only one small hope—charismatic upheavals. The notion of *charisma* is another of Weber's seminal contributions to modern sociology. Charisma is a driving, creative force that surges ahead, destroying the established rules. It is a specifically irrational phenomenon, and attaches to both individuals and movements. Rationalized institutions are, in Weber's view, particularly liable to evoke charismatic reactions. This vulnerability results from what Weber termed "the paradox of unintended consequences": every rationalization will tend ultimately to create irrational outcomes that were never envisaged. Procedures that were originally a means to an end will tend to become ends in themselves. Rationalized organizations may solve certain problems, but they will create new ones as well. Thus it is that in the midst of the routinized, disenchanted modern church, a charismatic upsurge such as the "Jesus freak" movement (discussed in Unit 8) breaks forth; in the midst of union indifference and overwhelming power on the part of the nation's crop growers, a Cesar Chavez rises from obscurity and bypasses existing organizational structures to forge a vital change in the status of migrant workers; in the midst of corporate rigidity, a dynamic executive will suddenly sweep aside conventional ways of operating and institute far-reaching reforms. Similarly, the modern university may be routinized to the extent that it becomes virtually a factory for the efficient production of trained experts—but then, by the paradox of unintended consequences, the deeply alienated students burn some of the buildings down. Where rationalization and bureaucratization have progressed furthest, it seems, the likelihood of a reassertion of human spontaneity and independence seems greatest.

c The "Research" Question

i Context Because bureaucracies have become so important in the modern state, sociologists are anxious to find out how they really work. They attempt to define the major characteristics of the phenomenon of bureaucracy and to assess whether in fact bureaucracies operate as their designers intended. Basically they ask: *What are the structural and functional characteristics of bureaucracy?*

ii Theory Sociological research on bureaucracies has been conducted almost entirely in terms of the "ideal type" bureaucracy supplied by Weber. An *ideal type* in sociology is a configuration specifically delineated as an aid to the interpretation and explanation of social phenomena. It is constructed by the abstraction and combination of an indefinite number of elements that, although found in reality, are admittedly seldom if ever discovered in this exact configuration. The usefulness of a given ideal type can be determined only in relation to the light it sheds on concrete problems, and it must be modified and sharpened in the course of actually investigating such problems. In turn, the use of the ideal type alerts and guides the researcher to particular aspects of the problem and so increases the precision of his analysis. (This book evaluates the ideal types used in a number of areas of sociology.)

With reference to bureaucracy, Weber stated (*Economy and Society,* 1922):

> The fully-developed bureaucratic apparatus compares with other organizations exactly as does the machine with non-mechanical modes of production. Precision, speed, unambiguity, knowledge of the files, continuity, discretion, unity, strict subordination, reduction of friction and of material and personal costs—these are raised to the optimum point in the strictly bureaucratic organization.

According to Weber, the ideal type of such an organization will have the following main characteristics:

1. Organizational tasks are distributed among the various members of the organization as official duties. There is a clear-cut division of labor that makes possible a high degree of specialization.
2. Official positions are organized into a hierarchical authority structure. Usually this hierarchy takes a pyramidic shape, with each official both responsible for his subordinates' decisions and answerable to his immediate superior. The scope of each individual's authority is clearly defined.
3. A formal system of rules and regulations governs decisions and actions. The operations of the bureaucracy are based on the application of these general rules to specified cases.
4. There is a specialized administrative staff—managers, secretaries, record keepers and similar personnel—whose duty is to maintain the organization and the communications system within it.
5. Officials are expected to assume an impersonal orientation in their contacts with clients and with other officials. Clients are treated as "cases," and emotional detachment is required in dealing with other members of the organization. This requirement prevents the feelings of officials from distorting their ra-

(Page 373) Modern man in search of his soul. What are the long-term psychological implications of the current orientation toward technological solutions to human problems and the deemphasis of emotional considerations in the programming of social change?

Charismatic leaders. Social movements often constellate around individuals who have a magnetic power to attract people and impart excitement and vitality. Such figures always loom large in history—although the results of their actions may be either productive or destructive when seen in retrospect. Depicted here are *(clockwise from top left):* Fidel Castro, Franklin D. Roosevelt, Malcolm X, Adolf Hitler, David Ben-Gurion, Martin Luther King.

Perſonal=Ausweis

Eigenhändige Unterſchrift des Inhabers.

d biermit beſcheinigt, daß der Buchinbab
Lichtbild dargeſtellte Perſon und Mitgli

tional judgment.

6. Employment in the organization constitutes a career for the officials. They are typically full-time employees looking forward to a life-long career in the organization. Candidates are employed on the basis of their technical qualifications, and promotion is based on either merit or seniority or both.

iii   Research (Methodology)   This Weberian ideal type has provided the starting point for most research into bureaucracies. The methods most frequently used are case studies, in which particular bureaucracies are examined over a period of time, and interview and observation techniques to ascertain the subjective views and objective behavior of the bureaucrats themselves.

Far from being synonymous with filling out irrelevant forms in quintuplicate, Weber's ideal type of bureaucracy would be the most efficient and rational means known of organizing human resources to attain desired ends. Nevertheless, as Robert K. Merton points out in essays in *Social Theory and Social Structure* (1949, 1957, 1968), even structures that approach the ideal type display many inefficiencies, largely because officials tend to think in terms of unquestioned rules and procedures suited to standard situations. Regulations that make for general efficiency can produce inefficiency or even injustice in specific cases with unanticipated or exceptional features. In such cases the original programming becomes highly dysfunctional, because of the emergence of the phenomenon caustically described by economist and sociologist Thorstein Veblen as "trained incapacity." When unforeseen conditions arise, officials may be unable to act because of their acquired predisposition to do nothing that is not sanctioned by rules and precedent.

The hierarchical authority structure itself may also be dysfunctional in certain respects. Precisely because men find themselves in *segmental roles,* performing specialized duties in a situation over which they have little control, they are deprived of the opportunity to use their rational judgment. The result is considerable *alienation,* a feeling on the part of the official that he is not responsible for his own behavior at work, but rather that he is controlled by his job and separated from the product of his labor. Hierarchy may promote discipline and make possible the coordination of activity, but it discourages subordinates from accepting any real challenge or responsibility. In *Modern Organization* (1961) Victor Thompson has spoken of some of these dysfunctions as "bureaupathology"—all large hierarchical organizations, he found, will produce many tensions among their personnel. Thompson found anxieties and frustrations over promotions, failures, lack of recognition, and meaningless work routines. The end result was often an attempt to "play it safe"—by concentrating on report filing and record keeping, by passing the buck and ducking decisions—so that behavior became oriented to personal needs rather than organizational goals. And even within the organization, Robert MacIver found, the men at the top need not necessarily be the individuals with the superior talents, because the behavior of the incumbents is governed by their office rather than by their personal characteristics (*The Web of Government,* 1947). Some observers of large corporations consider that the man at the top is often one of the most dispensable figures in the entire hierarchy—most of the

Youth of the organized society. A major theme in the lives of many young people is a rejection of the values and priorities that underlie formal and complex organizations. The question of the future is whether such young people will create a positive alternative to the bureaucratized society or merely help to entrench it further by dropping out and leaving no viable opposition actively questioning it.

important, day-to-day decisions are taken not by the chief officers of the organization, but by middle-management personnel.

Other researchers, most notably Peter M. Blau, have pointed to the fact that the operation of an institution cannot be understood without reference to its informal structure. A procedural flow chart or a diagrammatic representation of organizational structure tells us only how the organization ought to operate in theory; in practice the personnel may behave rather differently. There is always an *informal organization* of cliques, friendship groups, and personal loyalties, all of which may cut across the official hierarchy, involving, say, the skilled "operator" who knows how to pull strings, the "old-timer" who recalls the precedents and mistakes of the past, and the "crown prince" who is marked out for promotion and is consequently more influential than others of the same rank. The implications of this interplay for the taking and execution of decisions can be considerable. We have discussed some of this interplay in Units 11 and 12.

Even at the lowest levels of the organization there can be a set of distinctive informal relationships. In their classic study of production workers (*Management and the Worker,* 1939), F. J. Roethlisberger and William J. Dickson found that output was regulated by *informal norms* rather than institutional requirements. Workers expected their fellows to be neither too fast nor too slow, and deviators were penalized by ridicule, loss of status, and ostracism. The workers had informally organized themselves to control output—with significant implications for the achievement of the goal of the organization, namely production.

iv   Evaluation   Weber's work on bureaucracy remains one of the outstanding theoretical contributions to sociology. His ideal type of bureaucratic structure has been the starting point of almost all subsequent investigation. As a result of this research, additional aspects of bureaucratic functioning that suggest some modifications of or additions to the Weberian model have come to light. More than 60 years ago the British classicist F. M. Cornford named three principles that characterize the bureaucratic tendency to support the status quo: the "principle of the wedge," the "principle of unripe time," and the "principle of the dangerous precedent." The first argues that you should not act justly now for fear of raising expectations that you may act still more justly in the future. The second argues that the time is not ripe, meaning simply that people should not do at the present moment what they think is right at that moment because the moment for which they think it right has not yet arrived. Finally, the dangerous precedent principle states that you should not do an admittedly right action now for fear that you should not have the courage to do right in some future case, which is essentially different but superficially resembles the present one. Every action which is not customary either is wrong, or, if it is right, is a dangerous precedent. From this principle it may be deduced that nothing should ever be done for the first time.

The dynamics pointed out by Cornford and the abundant objections already noted suggest that Weber overstresses the rationality and impersonality of bureaucracies—organizations have been found to vary significantly in the extent to which prescribed formal rules actually govern behavior. Officials do not interact merely in terms of the positions they occupy, and a preoccupation with the formal aspects of bureaucracy may direct attention away from the important unofficial patterns that develop. (These informal relationships can become a dynamic force; in fact, such relationships may even be essential for the continued operations of the bureaucracy.) It often happens that procedures that were originally instituted for specific purposes later create problems in unforeseen circumstances; at that point informal patterns typically arise to cope with these new problems efficiently.

The fact that organizations have been shown to operate with much less efficiency than the ideal type should not be interpreted as implying that some alternative form of social unit would necessarily be more efficient: bureaucracies, for all their demonstrated dysfunctions, have frequently proven to be an efficient and practical means of coordinating people to achieve some administrative objective. Ultimately, every bureaucracy must justify its existence by reference to standards of functional efficiency, even though in practice it may fall somewhat short of these standards.

3 Overview

Weber's warnings, over half a century old, have become ever more starkly confirmed. Organizations dominate our lives, and they are likely to do so to an increasing extent as we move into a technocratic age in which more and more decisions will have to be referred to trained experts. However, an awareness of the threat that rationalization of society poses to human freedom and spontaneity has at last developed in citizens of both capitalist and socialist industrial societies. Most socialist societies are now seeking to minimize the amount of government ownership and control and to maximize local and even individual initiatives, at least as much as is in harmony with promoting the welfare and egalitarian objectives that they have. In the United States and the countries of Western Europe the young have revolted against the rationalization and mechanization of life. It is likely that as members of the younger generation gradually come to participate in formal organizations—particularly when they visualize a career in such organizations—they will insist on a minimum level of informality and scope for initiative and innovation. Furthermore, the sociology of organizations has helped sensitize the general public to the dangers posed by bureaucratization and to the need continually to modify and adapt organizational behavior to human beings rather than human behavior to organizational requirements. Some industries have responded by implementing a number of experimental programs that alter traditional work patterns in the direction of greater flexibility and variety—employee-determined time schedules, shorter work weeks, self-organizing teams that tackle a broader spectrum of job functions, two-month and three-month vacations after a given interval of employment, paternity leaves for men, paired part-time patterns for women (one full-time job split into two complementary shifts) so that mothers with small children who wish to retain a primary role in raising their families can at the same time participate in the vocational mainstream of American life. Unit 21 is devoted to a discussion of the question of bureaucratic organization of work and some other issues relevant to this unit.

Bored people build bad cars. That's why we're doing away with the assembly line.

Working on an assembly line is monotonous. And boring. And after a while, some people begin not to care about their jobs anymore. So the quality of the product often suffers.

That's why, at Saab, we're replacing the assembly line with assembly teams. Groups

of just three or four people who are responsible for a particular assembly process from start to finish.

about who does what and when. And each team member can even do the entire assembly singlehandedly. The result: people are more involved. They care more. So there's less absenteeism, less turnover. And we have more experienced people on the job.

We're building our new 2-liter engines this way. And the doors to our Saab 99. And we're planning to use this same system to build other parts of our car as well.

It's a slower, more costly system, but we realize that the best machines and materials in the world don't mean a thing, if the person building the car doesn't care.

Assembly line at Pontiac Motor Division and Saab advertisement. Some forward-looking enterprises, such as Saab in Sweden, are willing to sacrifice some efficiency in the short run for long-term improvements in workers' commitment to the product they are making and to the company they work for. In some plants "work modules" and "assembly teams" are replacing assembly lines.

D LOOKING AHEAD

1 Interview:
Peter M. Blau

Peter M. Blau is professor of sociology at Columbia University. His research centers on formal organizations and bureaucracies, with special emphasis on the laws governing differentiation in organizations, social exchange, social mobility, and occupational structure. His books include *The Dynamics of Bureaucracy, Bureaucracy in Modern Society, Formal Organizations* (with Scott), *The American Organizational Structure* (with Duncan), and *The Structure of Organizations* (with Schoenherr). He is president of the American Sociological Association.

DPG Organizations are getting pretty big. Is there an optimal size?

BLAU The optimal size is probably different for different kinds of organizations. You also have to distinguish between what optimal size is for the organization itself—for the people who own a firm—and what is optimal for the workers in the firm and for the society at large. For example, it is in the interest of each company to have a lot of sales and to dominate the market, but in our system we believe that it is bad for society if one company or a few companies dominate the market.

DPG Some international corporations are huge. Would you say that such organizations are becoming dysfunctional because of their very size?

BLAU They certainly seem to be becoming dysfunctional for society's good, if not their own. I assume that in strictly economic terms the size of these international conglomerates is very advantageous—for the organizations concerned. That's why they have become so large. But if a person as much a part of the conservative American tradition as Dwight Eisenhower warns us against the military-industrial complex, then the size of organizations must represent a great danger. In a sense this situation applies not only to the large international organizations but to exclusively American organizations as well.

DPG Does this relate to the situation in international money markets—where private speculation by large organizations in hot money puts governments under pressure?

BLAU That's one of the things that I am very interested in. I think that organizations have become tremendously important in our power structure. More and more power is exercised in such complicated ways by organizations rather than individuals that we really don't have the proper tools for maintaining our democratic institutions. We need better ways of regulating organizations. The Constitution doesn't serve us here, because when it was adopted there were no such organizations.

DPG You say democracy demands better regulation of organizations. Are we being ruled by technocrats rather than elected rulers?

BLAU In one sense you can say we are being ruled by technocrats. For example, I imagine Nixon made the final decision to devalue the dollar, but he could not make this decision without having certain technical advice from high-powered economists, who probably made the most intelligent, rational decisions they could make. Large organizations are now very complex structures in which a lot of people combine and make their technical, professional decisions, which obviously influence the policy makers. The real problem is that we must continue to maintain our power and control over the organization. The Department of Defense in the last five years gives you an extreme example. The population drastically changed its attitude toward the war during that period, but we knew so little about what power the Department of Defense exercises and how it exercises its power that we could not control it. It's still true. Even though there's a cease-fire, the budget for the Department of Defense is apparently not going down.

DPG What about the problem of chief policy makers who have to rely on data and expertise presented by experts when they make decisions. Is it possible for technocrats to furnish the president, for example, with selective information in order to secure adoption of their own policy outlook? One example might be J. F. K. and the Bay of Pigs debacle.

BLAU I think we have to try to maintain the difficult distinction between the kind of decisions only experts can make and the

kind of decisions that involve basic values and therefore should be brought to the people. Perhaps something like our system of checks and balances should be built into high-level government agencies. Consider a decision like the devaluation of the dollar. Now obviously most people, including me, don't have the technical knowledge to make such decisions. On the other hand, there are clearly value implications to devaluation, and the decision makes a tremendous amount of difference for a lot of people. Ideally, there should be people on both sides of the fence trying to explain the pros and cons to the public. Of course, our elections are meant to do that. But we need better information to vote intelligently.

DPG *What is the shape of organizations to come? Have we learned anything from Parkinson's Law that "work expands to fill the amount of time available for it" and the Peter Principle that "each person rises to the rank just above his level of competence"?*
BLAU Parkinson's Law itself is very misleading. If you think about it, Parkinson seems to imply that bureaucracies maintain themselves for their own sakes. This is partly correct. Once an organization or any kind of institution is established, it tends to maintain itself even if its basic function has disappeared. But often people also interpret Parkinson's Law to mean that the larger the organization, the more bureaucratic it is. My own research indicates that in some respects large organizations are more bureaucratic than small ones; for example, they

have more rules. In other respects, however, they are less bureaucratic; for example, large organizations have proportionately smaller administrative machinery than small ones. Parkinson says, "Look—when the British Navy became much smaller after World War I, the number of admirals declined hardly at all." But if you think this fact through, it doesn't mean that large organizations have too much brass; on the contrary, it means that a smaller navy had too many admirals. In general, little organizations have disproportionately large administrative machineries, and the large ones are, in this respect, less bureaucratic. This implication is quite contrary to the bureaucratic stereotype. So is something else—namely that power in the large organizations tends to be more decentralized. I have written a book on universities and colleges that clearly shows that they are indeed becoming bureaucratic, but that the largest ones are in many ways least bureaucratic, particularly in respect to centralization of authority. The small college is much more likely to have a centralized authority structure than the large university.

DPG *Are large organizations becoming more cognizant of the human needs of the work force, or are workers as much as ever subjected to the impersonal requirements of automation and efficiency?*
BLAU There definitely has been somewhat more concern for the worker. At the beginning of the century scientific management

was the major focus. The stress was on rationalizing the work, making it more efficient, making workers work fast by teaching them how to run a machine. Then more and more the research showed that if people are very dissatisfied they will not work. At least in this respect, there was a change toward more concern with the dissatisfaction of workers. Sometimes the result of intensified concern for the workers was even contrary to their interest, because one of the things the graduate business schools sold business people on was that one of the ways to save money was to worry about the morale of the workers and not be too concerned about wages. Now there's been a reaction against that.

DPG *Do you have any proposals that might meet the threat of organizations that operate against the interests of the society in which they function?*
BLAU The first thing we have to recognize is that organizations do become independent entities and that the organization itself, not specific people, causes problems in a democracy. For example, an early Supreme Court decision developed the fiction that organizations are persons. So all the protections that are built into our Constitution in order to protect individual people have been used in order to extend the powers of the organization. Our problem now is to learn to make the distinction between people and organizations. We can pass laws to control organizations, and we do not need to protect the liberty of organizations as we protect that of individuals. We are willing to take the risk of allowing the public to see pornographic movies because we want freedom of speech for individuals. But organizations are different from individuals, and our laws have to treat them differently.

Another thing we have to change is our complete reliance on the profit principle, which is really competition among many organizations. I don't mean necessarily the nationalization of all industry that the socialists advocate. But monopolies should be nationalized, and sometimes you need a monopoly for an enterprise to function effectively. In order to have a good telephone company, you need an integrated system, and therefore we accept AT&T's monopoly. But should AT&T be run on the profit principle? Shouldn't it rather be run by and for the people? And the third point, which relates to the other two, is that Congress should take a much more active role in controlling the large organizations. We can hope for some independence in Congress, much more than in the big agencies such as the Department of Defense. A Congressman practically has to be dishonest to be under the control of a big business such as Lockheed. But that is not true for bureaucrats in the Department of Defense. The interests of the bureaucrats and the businessmen are so interlocking, they are really the same. It's not a question of honesty. The Department of Defense wants big appropriations in order to have big contracts for Lockheed and other defense contractors. In a sense, one of the good things that is happening now is that Congress is becoming worried about the increasing power of the present administration. We need constitutional protection against organizations, and Congress is really the only agent that can do that.

DPG   *Are there any other ways organizations can be controlled?*
BLAU   Other countries—Yugoslavia, for example—have done much more along the lines of worker participation in organizational management. And in foreign universities the faculty generally has considerable influence in running the institution.

DPG   *You mentioned worker participation in management in Yugoslavia. Why haven't there been more experiments of this kind in the United States?*
BLAU   First of all, I think the Yugoslav arrangement is successful to some extent, but the government has stated that it isn't as successful as it hoped, because management still has much more influence than the workers. That is probably inevitable. But the workers still have more influence than here. In a capitalist system with private industry, worker participation is troublesome. Democracy is always costly. If workers participate in decision making, it just makes trouble for management, particularly if workers participate in some of the big decisions—like the distribution of profits or how much goes for wages. It's interesting that some of the most socialist countries are opposed to allowing the workers to have a say in the big decisions because it interferes with centralized planning, which is a major socialist tenet. Some of the ideological battle between the Soviets and the Yugoslavs results from this controversy.

2   Interview: Robert Townsend

Robert Townsend is a businessman interested in research in nonbureaucratic forms of organization. He was an executive of American Express International, Inc. for many years and chief executive officer of Avis Corp. He is the author of the best-selling *Up the Organization.*

DPG   *Organizations are getting pretty big. Is there an optimal size for organizations?*
TOWNSEND   I think every organization has a different optimal size. It obviously takes a larger organization to build a Chevrolet than it does to handle the department of grounds and buildings at the University of Wisconsin. But I would think that the right direction for any organization lies in figuring out what the smallest possible size for it is and then in aiming actively at achieving that.

DPG   *Some of the international corporations are so huge that their organizations seem actually to be becoming dysfunctional. Is this so?*
TOWNSEND   Well, they're becoming dysfunctional the way any organization does when it gets too big. Secrecy becomes the method of control. The people who know what's going on lead the organization, and it makes them feel good to be in on something. The result is that there's an elite who knows and the rest of the people who don't. This kind of lack of communication is typical of big organizations and is one of the reasons they're so expensive and so inefficient. But they're large and powerful. They can influence governments, and, once they become international, they can move across borders and avoid laws. Just as tax avoidance—as opposed to tax evasion—is legal and reputable in capitalist countries, so law avoidance, I think, will probably become a wave of the future for these giant corporations.

DPG   *At what level do we find the technocrats who are making the most important decisions?*
TOWNSEND   A lot of people think that the top leaders in corporations are the most expendable. I think that's very true. So we may well be ruled by experts and technocrats and people who have specific talents that are needed at the moment rather than by the chief executive. The level of the technocrats who are taking the decisions is defi-

nitely near the top. Middle is nowhere: John Kenneth Galbraith's views notwithstanding, the middle management is not making important decisions.

DPG   *But don't they, in effect, make decisions by not doing things?*
TOWNSEND   Oh, sure. They can squat in the middle of the road to prevent anything from moving. But I don't call that ruling. It's preventing rule, if you will. The effect of middle management is mainly negative.

DPG   *What's the shape of organizations to come? Are working conditions in large organizations changing in recognition of the human needs of the workers, or is efficiency still equated with virtual automation of the worker?*
TOWNSEND   It's pretty clear to me what works and what doesn't work. Pyramids don't work. Hierarchy doesn't work. And it's a worldwide phenomenon, one that applies to the whole range or organizations. What does work is small partnership. That's the shape of organizations to come. A collection of partnerships, as small as possible, highly focused and motivated mainly by a desire to do the work well and to get paid for it.

DPG   *How do you measure whether small partnerships are more effective than pyramidal organizations?*
TOWNSEND   We have several measures. One is productivity. In small partnerships the

workers are given real power over matters that are very important to them, like the ways of organizing the work. They combine tasks like setup, machine operation, maintenance, and quality control into one job. Groups will be formed. These are the partnerships—where workers have a task to perform, have total power over how they organize it, and are paid on a group productivity basis rather than on an individual basis, so there's no competition within the group. When somebody comes up with an idea that can get the job done faster or better, all he has to do is convince his teammates to try it. If it works, it hits all of their pay envelopes. Because they have the right to try things, workers get more interested in their jobs. And as a result pay levels go up considerably. So a worker's take-home pay may be as much as 50 percent higher than, say, a machine operator in a conventionally organized plant. Productivity, however, also goes up substantially. Maybe it's more than twice as high as productivity in a conventional plant. Quality also goes up because workers will combine the job of quality inspector with the machine operator's job. And, because it's a function of productivity, there's no question about the motivation, so absenteeism and turnover go way down. As a result, although wages may be higher, there is such an increase in productivity that profits are substantially higher and costs are substantially lower than in a conventional plant.

DPG *Is this organizational structure that you're talking about similar to the kind that has been used in Yugoslavia for quite some time? And, if it's as successful as you say, why isn't it imitated by more American companies?*
TOWNSEND   Yes, it's related to the Yugoslav experiment. It's been going on for about 20 years in Yugoslavia, Germany, France, and, particularly, Scandinavia. It started in the United States recently. These developments are all related, but there's no textbook on it, so people are doing it their own way, and they're all growing like Topsy. But I think it can be concluded so far that the worst of the experiments are better than the conventional pyramid because they tend to get people to use more of their own intellectual and creative capacities than the pyramid does.

Why isn't it talked about more? Let's say you're Proctor and Gamble, which is one of the companies that's using this struc-

ture, and you've got a plant in Lima, Ohio, organized in this series of partnerships and turning out liquid detergent. How are you going to put this situation in your monthly magazine? Are you going to want to talk about the fact that in the Lima plant costs are substantially lower overall and that the company's profit margin is much higher than it is in the conventional plant? All you're going to do is create a revolution of rising expectations. It's pretty hard to convert a whole company at once. It has to be done plant by plant. And it has to be done slowly. The workers have to take charge, really, and they're not used to that. Some of them don't like it. Some of them are suspicious. They've got to talk it out and reason it out and work it out themselves. It's also pretty clear that in the United States the obstacles are union leadership and top management.

DPG *Are the progressive unions like the United Auto Workers likely to latch onto this idea, especially because of the boredom that so typifies the automobile assembly line?*
TOWNSEND   I don't think so, because the UAW, progressive as it is in some directions, happens to be tied to the world's most backward organization from a humanistic standpoint, General Motors. A perfect illustration is the Vega plant in Lordstown, Ohio, where GM put in every new mechanical and technological breakthrough possible and completely ignored the human element. The result was a disaster. The real breakthroughs are peripheral compared to the power of getting somebody to use 80 percent of his brain, creativity, imagination instead of the 20 percent that he's using now. But General Motors will be the last and the UAW will be the next to the last to see it.

DPG *Aren't you underestimating the necessary role of large organizations?*
TOWNSEND   You say in your unit that one of the most pervasive features of our lives is that we are dominated by large, complex, formal organizations. I agree with that. Then you say that organizations are a social invention without which no mass industrial society could exist. I claim that that is not true.

DPG *Was it ever true?*
TOWNSEND   I don't know. But I regard it as a disaster to leave this statement unchallenged. Saying voter registration couldn't be done without bureaucracy is hogwash. In

Australia 95 percent of the people vote. Everybody has an i.d. in the country. In order to vote, all people have to do is prove that they're citizens. They don't have to register by different state requirements. As for bureaucracy being the only efficient way to handle health and welfare—hogwash! The way we run it in this country—sure, you need a bureaucracy. But that's because the bureaucracy is there, and that's the way we've been attacking all our problems.

Suppose all you needed was proof of citizenship to be entitled to medical treatment. Why can't we have mobile units in every community, paid for out of local taxes, that can take care of 90 percent of the health problems for people? And have hospitals for only those 10 percent that require major surgery or sophisticated equipment that can't be moved. You know, there are other ways of operating.

DPG *Why is bureaucratic organization so pervasive throughout industrialized society then?*
TOWNSEND   I suspect it's because it's the easy way. There are a lot of people who feel secure in a job where the payoff is on the basis of seniority, where their tasks don't require them to use their minds or to strain their imaginations. I expect there are a lot of people who are very comfortable with bureaucracy. That's why I think that, if we're going to oppose it, if we're going to develop systems that will fight it, we're going to have to do it cautiously, and we're going to have to put a lot of effort into it. Otherwise, just by default, we will wind up being governed by bureaucratic organizations.

And too many sociologists are creatures of a bureaucratic way of thinking. My suggestion as a means of fighting that is this: I would make it a worldwide requirement for a doctorate that a candidate must have served two years in a bureaucracy in some capacity completely unrelated to his discipline, not as an expert or a technocrat. If he's a sociologist, he can't work in a bureaucracy as a case worker, we'll say. He'd have to work in a stockroom of Eastman Kodak or in a motor vehicle bureau. Bureaucracies are all the same. Once you've worked for two years,—not as an expert, but as a field hand in a bureaucracy—you can understand and cope with them all. I don't think we should be turning out intellectual leaders who are not aware of how bureaucracies really work.

Unit 17
Urban Society

SCHEMATIC OUTLINE

A Introductory Graphics: The City in History

B Definition and Context

1 Definition
Urban society is that form of social organization in which economic exchange and markets are vitally important, social roles are highly specialized, administrative and legal agencies rather than religious institutions provide political direction, the population is heterogeneous, and most interaction tends to be impersonal, functional, and transitory.

2 World Context
Cities have a long and complex history, but urban society as we know it is a creation of industrialization.

3 American Context
Massive urbanization has overflowed the central cities in the United States, creating metropolitan areas that also encompass the suburbs.

C Questions and Evidence

1 Questions
Sociologists raise three crucial questions about modern urban society: (1) Are American cities uninhabitable? (2) What is the nature of community? (3) How do living conditions in overcrowded urban areas influence the behavior of the people who live in them?

2 Evidence
a The "Burning Issue" Question
Louis Wirth's theory that the city produces relationships that leave it vulnerable to disorder has been borne out by research studies but has also been subject to serious criticism. Although it is difficult to offer a hopeful prognosis for the future of the American city, to conclude that it is dead or dying seems premature and overly pessimistic.
b The "Classical" Question
The ecological approach to the study of community, exemplified by the concentric zone, sector, and multiple-nuclei theories of the "Chicago School," concentrates on spatial organization. A second approach, based on Ferdinand Toennies' contrast of *Gemeinschaft* and *Gesellschaft,* analyzes shared institutions and values. Both theories have led to useful research, but the first is very limited and the second highly subjective. More empirical studies are needed.
c The "Research" Question
Ethological experiments have shown that overcrowded living conditions lead to disturbed behavior patterns, especially aggression, in animals. Their social applications are still very tentative, however. The direct effects of human population density have not yet been documented in a sophisticated way.

3 Overview
The modern city presents advantages as well as problems. But if it is to sustain itself, increased resources must be funneled into its housing, commercial, and transportation facilities.

D Looking Ahead

1 Interview: Nathan Glazer
2 Interview: Herbert J. Gans

SUPPORTING UNITS

3 Biology and Society
4 Culture
6 Population and Demography
7 Marriage, Kinship, and the Family
15 Race and Ethnic Relations
16 Formal and Complex Organizations
26 Social Change

ENCYCLOPEDIA ENTRIES

aging
alienation
anonymity
bureaucracy
central city
cities, growth of
city planning
class
community
concentric zone theory
crime
delinquency
deviance
divorce
dominance relationship
drug abuse and addiction
ghetto
greenbelt
leisure, sociology of
mass society
megalopolis
melting pot
metropolitan area
mobility
pollution
poverty
sector theory
segregation
suburb
territoriality
unemployment
urbanism
urban renewal
urban sociology
welfare programs
zone theory

THE CITY IN HISTORY

1. **Walled Cities.** Early cities were separated from the countryside by walls.

2. **Mass Society.** All the world is now a city via urbanization, mass transportation and mass media.

3. **Golden Age.** For the classical civilizations the city was the core, the intellectual center.

4. **The Age of Problems.** In our time the city has become a major locus of concentration of our "social pathology."

5. **The Future.** Will cities once again become the vital locus of our civilization, or will they crumble into irretrievable social blight?

B DEFINITION AND CONTEXT

1 Definition

"A walled towne," wrote Shakespeare in *As You Like It,* "is more worthier than a village." This emphatic declaration touches upon two characteristics that traditionally distinguish urban life—its unique physical context and the possibility for a more sophisticated and multifaceted way of life that it affords. The notion of a city has historically meant something more than merely a large, inhabited place. The ideal is a self-governing civil society, autonomous within itself and conferring on its members a freedom and richness of culture not possible elsewhere.

The ancient citadel, the kernel from which the modern city emerged, was surrounded by walls that marked off a special space for the transaction of very distinctive social phenomena. Gradually these innovative social practices and cultural forms spread beyond the expanding boundaries of the city to include more and more of what had originally been agricultural areas. The city as a social institution is so dominant now that it is almost impossible to locate an area, no matter how remote, completely untouched by its influence.

What, then, is an urban society? At the most basic operational level, it can be defined as a working-residential area of a certain population density. Although such a definition is unobjectionable, it ignores the various factors responsible for the distinctive characteristics of such societies. *Urban society is that form of social organization in which economic exchange and markets are vitally important, social roles are highly specialized, administrative and legal agencies rather than religious institutions provide political direction, the population is heterogeneous, and most interaction tends to be impersonal, functional, and transitory.*

The urban sociologist is concerned with identifying and ex-

Table 1. Some Qualitative Differences Between Simple and Urban Society. Many sociologists delineate these kinds of differences between the two types of societies.

Process	Simple Society	Urban Society
Nature of family	Extended kinship	Nuclear; "modified extended"
Socialization	Centralized; family	Decentralized; many institutions
Division of labor	Minimal; age and sex	Intricate and extensive
Social control	Informal	Legal; formal; hierarchical
Value structure	Homogeneous; little friction	Heterogeneous; conflict and disorganization
Orientation to change	Strong resistance; tradition; static	Future-oriented; conflict; pragmatic
Interaction patterns	Personal, integrated; persistent; primary group relations	Impersonal; functional; transitory; segmentalized; superficial; secondary
Social stratification	Minimal	Highly elaborated

amining the phenomena that are distinctive to the city and metropolitan life. The issues studied can be grouped into two general categories: *descriptive*—that is, involving analysis and description of demographic, institutional, and interpersonal relationships of the city—and *policy-oriented*—that is, involving consideration of what an urban society should ideally be like and proposing plans designed to implement that ideal. Units 6 and 26 also take up some of the issues involving urban society that are discussed in this unit.

2   World Context

The process of urbanization began with agriculture, the systematic cultivation of crops, which required more stable and permanent settlements than those necessary for hunting or gathering. Because the ''city'' population did not usually raise its own food and depended on an *agricultural surplus* to sustain itself, the rise of urban society was highly dependent on improved methods of farming. By 3000 B.C. distinctly urban settlements existed in the Indus River Valley, along the Persian Gulf, and on the banks of the Mediterranean. Their economic basis was largely agricultural, supplemented by trade.

Cities were generally centers of royal and priestly power. From the founding of Memphis in ancient Egypt to St. Petersburg in eighteenth-century Russia, the city took form as a ''control center,'' fusing secular with sacred authority, rather than simply as a marketing or manufacturing center. The first act of the king usually was the construction or rededication of a temple to serve as the home of the god that sanctified his claims to absolute authority. Within the citadel walls were the temple, palace, granary, and storehouses. Thus the ancient city was physically organized as a small-scale model of the universe. Its structure showed ''law and order'' prevailing over ''chaos,'' and its character was quasi-sacred.

The ''urban ideal'' assumed grandeur with the Greek city-

Acropolis in Athens and Juilliard School of Music in New York City. Classical architecture was designed in mass and scale to establish a positive relationship with human beings. Modern urban architecture, though often employing similar forms, is frequently dehumanizing or oppressive.

Area	1800 Millions	1800 Percentage of Total Population	1850 Millions	1850 Percentage of Total Population	1900 Millions	1900 Percentage of Total Population	1950 Millions	1950 Percentage of Total Population	1960 Millions	1960 Percentage of Total Population
World	15.6	1.7	27.5	2.3	88.6	5.5	313.7	13.1	601.5	20.1
Asia	9.8	1.6	12.2	1.7	19.4	2.1	105.6	7.5	207.4	12.6
Europe and USSR	5.4	2.9	13.2	4.9	48.0	11.9	118.2	19.9	186.0	29.1
Africa	0.3	0.3	0.2	0.2	1.4	1.1	10.2	5.2	30.1	11.0
America	0.1	0.4	1.8	3.0	18.6	12.8	74.6	22.6	170.3	41.4
Oceania	—	—	—	—	1.3	21.7	5.1	39.2	7.7	49.0

Table 2. Population in Large Cities, by Major Continental Regions, 1800–1960. In this table large cities are those of 100,000 population or over. (Source: U.N., *Report on the World Social Situation,* 1957; *United Nations Demographic Yearbook 1966*)

states, whose systems of law, moral order, and architecture created what Aristotle called "a common life for a noble end." Rome, whose contribution to urban society was the development of elaborate, highly efficient public administration, spread the city model throughout its conquered territories in western Europe.

The expansion of trade revitalized urbanization in the medieval period. Cities took a significantly new direction as merchants began to exercise the social dominance previously accorded royal courts. From the fourteenth through the sixteenth centuries the major advances in urban society occurred in the Italian commercial city-states.

Before 1800 little of the world was really urban. With the exception of Great Britain and The Netherlands, the proportion of a national population residing in cities nowhere exceeded 10 percent; there were only 45 cities with a population of over 100,000; and only 3 percent of the world's people lived in towns of more than 5,000. The vast growth of urban society resulted from the Industrial Revolution. Improvements in communication and transportation, advances in agricultural productivity, and the development of the factory system all led to the concentration of labor and services in relatively densely populated urban centers: as manpower needs for agriculture lessened and as increased labor could be absorbed into manufacturing and related industries, people flowed off the farms and into the cities. Between 1900 and 1950 the population living in cities of more than 100,000 rose by 250 percent. Urban society as we know it is a creation of industrialization.

On no continent now does less than 10 percent of the population live in "large" cities. About one-quarter of the world lives in urban communities of more than 20,000. Europe and North America are more than twice as urbanized as less-developed Africa, Asia, and Latin America, but the urban population in the Third World countries is growing at a rate more than twice as fast as that of Europe during its most rapid expansion. The growth of urban society in these less-developed regions does not parallel that of Europe and North America, however; its rate shows no consistent relationship with such economic indices as growth of manufacturing, capital accumulation, or increases in agricultural productivity. Even without significant change in the foundations of these societies, there has been a vast expansion of cities.

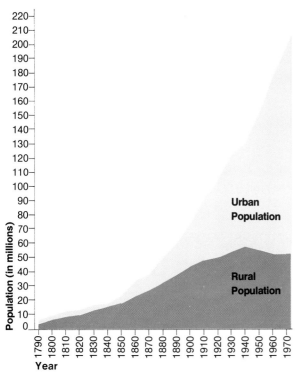

Figure 1. Rural and Urban Population of the United States, 1790–1970. (Source: Bureau of the Census)

3   American Context

Town life has been important in the United States since the organization of the country's first two important settlements, Plymouth, Massachusetts, and Jamestown, Virginia. From those rudimentary beginnings, cities have steadily grown, spreading from coast to coast and spilling over clearly defined boundaries. Yet, despite the clear evidence of an urban impulse, Americans retain a national ambivalence about and even hostility toward the city.

This country came of age with an idea of itself as a pastoral Eden in which independent yeomen could flourish. Such a vision contributed significantly to national ideology but could not easily accommodate an urban society of concrete buildings and social interdependence. Thomas Jefferson vividly expressed the tension between country and city when he wrote: "Those who labor the earth are the chosen people of God, if ever he had a chosen people [while] mobs of great cities add just so much to the support of pure government as sores do to the strength of the human body."

Nevertheless, the city's dominance has steadily increased. The rate of urbanization in the United States was one of the fastest in the world. In 1790 only one out of 30 Americans lived in settlements of 8,000 or more; on the eve of the Civil War, 70 years later, the ratio was one in six. Boston, New York, Philadelphia, Baltimore, Charleston, New Orleans—the first major cities—owed their growth to the fact that they were seaports favorably situated for carrying on trade with Europe and the West Indies. Then, as settlers began crossing the Appalachians, such raw western towns as Pittsburgh and Cincinnati arose to serve as distribution points between the coast and the west. Cleveland, Detroit, and Minneapolis-St. Paul prospered because of strategic locations on interior waterways. When the railroad allowed for a much fuller opening up of the frontier, cities such as Chicago, St. Louis, Denver, and Memphis boomed.

The era of the modern city began after the Civil War. By 1890 New York was nearly as big as Paris, and Chicago and Philadelphia were the sixth and seventh largest cities in the Western world. By the turn of the century the city had become a national institution rather than a regional curiosity. Railroads, financial combinations, and industrial power had transformed the nation into an urban society by 1920, when the Census Bureau noted for the first time that one out of every two people in the United States lived in an *urban area* (settlement of more than 2,500 persons).

Three factors are usually cited as encouraging America's urbanization: (1) the land was fertile enough to support a large non-agricultural population; (2) technology was highly developed, along with efficient use of capital; (3) the family structure, *nuclear* rather than *extended,* was well-suited for urban living. The urbanization of the country is still proceeding: the 1970 census classified 73.5 percent of all Americans as urban-based.

This massive urbanization has overflowed the cities, creating sprawling *metropolitan areas* that include separate politically incorporated units. Most observers believe that urban society in the United States has entered a "metropolitan phase" and is much less single-city-oriented than was the case before World War II. The

Bureau of the Census, responding to the shift outward into suburbs and satellite communities, now uses the concept of *standard metropolitan statistical area* (SMSA). This definition ignores usual political divisions of cities and towns in order to delineate the limits of regular daily influence of urban areas. In 1960 212 SMSAs (involving a core city of at least 50,000) were designated; 35 more were added by 1970. In 1970 68.6 percent of Americans lived in SMSAs.

Probably the most significant development affecting American urban society today is the growth of the suburbs and the relative decline of the central city within a metropolitan area. Between 1960 and 1970 the central cities increased their population by 4.7 percent, but metropolitan populations extending out from the boundaries of the city grew by over 25 percent. The *ethnic composition* of metropolitan areas is profoundly affected by this population shift. Although the population of central cities throughout the nation has been growing, the proportion of whites living in cities actually decreased by 0.2 percent in the 1960s. The white population of Chicago declined by over half a million, that of Detroit by 29.2 percent, and that of St. Louis by 31.6 percent. Four of the larger central cities—Washington, Atlanta, Newark, and Gary—were over half black by 1970, and many others are at least 40 percent black.

This suburban sprawl has been prompted by two main factors. Manufacturing and warehousing facilities have increasingly been moved outside central cities to more peripheral locations with lower labor and land costs. And the development of highway and mass transportation systems allows people to commute considerable distances between where they live and where they work. These influences mutually reinforce each other: new jobs create new residences, which in turn motivate more commercial establishments to relocate out of the city.

Some analysts view *suburbanization* as a reaction against urban society. The suburb may be an expression of people's desire to reestablish the more intimate personal contacts they feel are absent in the city. It seems more probable, however, that the suburb is a logical extension rather than an abrupt reversal of the urbanization process. The problem facing descriptive urban sociologists is to understand the nature of the connection between city and suburbs; policy-oriented students must find ways to integrate both into an optimally satisfying metropolitan community.

C   QUESTIONS AND EVIDENCE

1   Questions

Sociologists raise three crucial questions about modern urban society: (1) Are American cities uninhabitable? (2) What is the nature of community? (3) How do living conditions in overcrowded urban areas influence the behavior of the people who live in them?

2   Evidence

a   "The Burning Issue" Question

i Context   The city in America was once looked upon as a place

Although the problem of pollution seems to be most visible in cities, it is really a problem of industrial society as a whole. If rural and urban dwellers do not unite to finance the fight against pollution, the environment will become intolerable for both.

Commercial patterns are creating "strip" complexes that are the same from coast to coast. Do such strips constitute a kind of "visual pollution"—or even a "polluted vision"?

of excitement and personal opportunity. Nowadays it is regarded more and more as a symbol of dread. All kinds of people, from counterculture "hippies" to prosperous professionals, seem increasingly disenchanted with urban living. Novelist Norman Mailer has succinctly described the sense of being vulnerable to random violence and impending chaos:

> By afternoon the city is incarcerated. Haze covers the sky, a grim, formless glare blazes back from the horizon. . . . By the time work is done, New Yorkers push through the acrid lung-rotting air and work their way home avoiding each other's eyes in the subway. Later, near midnight, thinking of a walk to buy *The Times* they hesitate—the streets are not quite safe. We recognize one more time that the city is ill, that our own New York, the empire city, is not too far from death. ("Why Are We in New York," 1970)

Not all students of urban life share this sense of doom, however. For example, Raymond Vernon of the MIT-Harvard Urban Studies Center does not deny the problems of the city, but neither does he consider them beyond control. He feels that for most Americans the personal experience of urban living has been one of rather continuous improvement. In the midst of neighborhood dislocation and changes in social patterns, a long-term trend toward amelioration of conditions can be seen. (*The Myth and Reality of Our Urban Problems,* 1967)

The future of American cities thus depends to a large extent on answers that arise in response to certain key questions sociologists ask: *Do urban conditions produce life styles counter to American middle-class values? If so, are these conditions reversible?*

ii   Theory   The most influential theoretician of urban living in America was the sociologist Louis Wirth of the "Chicago School," which dominated urban sociology for several decades. In 1938 he published an essay considered a classic statement of urban sociology, "Urbanism as a Way of Life." This essay suggested that the city, by virtue of its population density and social organization, produces the kinds of personal relationships that leave it vulnerable to disorder. Wirth's analysis was essentially *ecological,* that is, it dealt with the pattern of interrelationships between organisms (human beings in this case) and their environment.

Emphasizing the decline of bonds of kinship and neighborly sentiment, Wirth argued that most urban relationships are held together by "utility." When life is overwhelmingly regarded as a means of achieving personal ends regulated by an economic nexus, social relationships become correspondingly impersonal, superficial, and even highly predatory. Anonymous, isolated, and alienated, urban man is a socially potent agent only as a member of some collective entity. His *identity* is derived from his *organizational status:* occupations figure preeminently in each individual's sense of self and self-esteem. Physical proximity and immediate expediency tend to define the possible range of social contacts, so that *psychic distance* arises in the urban context. People meet in *segmented roles,* often screened from each other by *hierarchical rank,* and relate to each other in one particular setting (on the work-shift, for example, or during the once-a-week trip to the laundromat, or at the same New Year's Eve party once a year). Wirth concluded by noting that frequent changes in the place of residence, place and character of employment, and income make it difficult to secure constant organizational identities and almost impossible to promote intimate and lasting relationships.

Thus Wirth saw *anomie*—a concept famously discussed by Emile Durkheim in *Suicide* (1897)—as the characteristic urban condition. He acknowledged that the work role and any collective groups to which the individual might belong worked against this sense of personal disintegration. But, in his view, the maintenance of an integrated identity, for both the individual and the community, was difficult. Accordingly, he concluded that many citizens would flee the city. Those left behind would feel little collective responsibility; property would cease to be sanctioned by anything beyond the power to protect it, and people would be prey to a jungle-like "survival of the fittest" ethic.

This theory of *ecological determinism* has been attacked by those who claim that urban living produces its own distinct cultural forms, which integrate the individual with his surroundings. Roles, choices, demands, and opportunities create social identity, and these are as available in the city as elsewhere. One need not assume that the urban environment is, because of some intrinsic and unavoidable flaw, *alienating,* and one can conceive of a properly planned city that would serve as a physical environment in which social feelings and communal identity could prosper. Land use could be managed, pollution could be reduced, people could be guaranteed a minimum standard of living, and authority could come from those being governed as well as from distant authorities.

iii Research   The demographic and class makeup of the central city has changed dramatically since World War II. Much of the current concern over the future of the city stems from a recognition of the extent of that change and a deep concern over what it heralds.

Both the "rich," defined as those prepared to pay $75 per room per month, and the "poor," who are unable to pay more than $15 per room per month, increasingly constitute the bulk of city population. With the post-World War II housing boom in one-family suburban residences, the middle class—falling between the two extremes of rich and poor—has steadily been leaving the city. This exodus has profoundly affected urban neighborhood structure. During the last decade of prosperity prior to World War II—the 1920s—a number of neat, middle-class residential areas were built within the city. But the children of the people who lived in these houses have, for the most part, not remained in the same area. Thus there has been an abrupt break in the ethnic continuity of *residence pattern;* older people of limited income remain, whereas their children, with real incomes close to double that of their parents, move away.

The expansion of income, which brought about increased consumption and heightened demands for land (even if only a suburban quarter-acre) appears to be the principal factor in this movement: urban residences cannot accommodate two cars or modern electrical appliances. Recent studies have failed to demon-

strate that a perception of growing violence or concern with crime affects white *mobility patterns* or explains the exodus to the suburbs. (It should be noted, however, that blacks, the segment of the population most affected by crime, are least able to relocate.) Perception of air pollution as a problem has likewise shown little correlation with actual residential movement.

Many researchers have tested the hypothesis that the social psychology of urban life significantly differs from that of other areas. Samuel Stouffer, in *Communism, Conformity and Civil Liberties,* (1955), reported that social tolerance was the highest in metropolitan areas and decreased in small towns and farms. However, a review of over 35 studies comparing rural and urban groups in the United States on a wide variety of personal attributes leads to the conclusion that such differences are not clearly defined.

There is evidence that certain forms of social "deviance" —delinquency and crime, mental illness, alcoholism, suicide—occur much more frequently in an urban than in a nonurban setting; burglary rates in the United States are generally three times as great in urban areas; robbery is six times as frequent; rape rates almost twice as great and significantly on the rise. Specific case studies suggest that crime increases with urbanization. Although most contemporary data show higher rates of mental disorders in urban areas, the evaluation of mental health is extremely difficult. Statistically, the chance that a rural person will become a chronic alcoholic is less than half as great as that of an urban dweller—but in relatively affluent suburbs today, housewives are increasingly afflicted with alcoholism. The suicide rate in American cities of more than 10,000 population is almost twice as great as the rate in less urban areas, and research throughout the world indicates that persons living in farms, villages, or small towns are much less likely to take their own lives.

However great the stresses and strains within the city may be, researchers have found evidence of ongoing social life and independent cultural constellations. Sociologist Herbert Gans has called these "urban villages." In "Urbanism and Suburbanism" (1951) and other writings, he has described "ethnic villages," where traditions brought to America from other countries maintain themselves and provide life with a coherent framework, and has also identified a "cosmopolite" culture—that of students, writers, intellectuals, entertainers, and professionals who create an autonomous *subculture* displaying stability and authenticity. Gans concludes that Wirth's description of urban life is appropriate for only certain areas of the central city, where people interact in segmental roles, but not in all areas at all times.

Most of the research conducted by urban planners has addressed specific questions of *land use* and *housing patterns*. The realization that cities are not "self-restorative" without external direction and assistance has been the key insight of these studies. The four vital aspects of city organization—industry, transportation, housing, and social services—tend to prosper or decline in unison. In order to be effective, urban planning must try to deal with these four components as a systematic whole. The evidence is considerable, Daniel P. Moynihan argues in "Toward a National Urban Policy" (1970), that many federal urban renewal programs have

(Facing page and above) The life and death of intimate neighborhoods. Even in our largest cities there are neighborhoods that still function as communities; businesses cater to unique cultural tastes, and patterns of social interaction have developed in terms of which individuals find fulfillment. Demolition for "urban renewal," corporate expansion, and highways has demolished many such neighborhoods in recent years, however.

treated only one of the four areas, thereby producing sharp imbalances in the "ecology" of urban areas and contributing to the further deterioration of the city. The highway expansion program, for example, destroyed existing housing and neighborhoods, which in turn led to increased demands for social services.

iv Evaluation It is difficult to offer a hopeful prognosis for the future of the American city. Yet to conclude that the city is dead or dying seems premature and more pessimistic than the facts at present fully support. The cities are in deep trouble: their economic well-being is steadily eroding, and the bulk of the middle class (whose presence is most essential in stabilizing urban patterns) has not found contemporary urban life congenial. But there are some encouraging signs. Children raised in the suburbs, says urbanologist Richard Sennett, express dissatisfaction with the blandness of life there and are returning to the city in growing numbers (*The Uses of Disorder,* 1970). And, as Moynihan, Gans, and others have argued, a national urban policy that includes supporting social and economic policies sustaining full employment and minimum income levels could significantly revitalize the city.

Although Wirth's theories have been borne out by much of the research on "deviance" and social disorganization in an urban setting, they have been subject to serious criticism. Social behavior has been shown to be much less one-dimensional and predetermined than Wirth claimed. The urban resident may conduct much of his social interaction in secondary relationships, but there also is a greater opportunity in the city to form primary relationships of one's own choosing. The city usually tolerates a broader range of groups and attitudes than do smaller communities, where there is greater pressure for conformity. It does appear that "pre-urban" social patterns require adaptation in the city, but this fact does not necessarily mean that the evolving group life is inferior—only different.

Self-conscious urban planning has suffered from the absence of a coherent, national urban policy. If much community planning policy has failed to achieve its objectives, this may be because the planners have been rooted in an outmoded concept of "the railroad city," which regards it as a "space market" for the efficient allocation of economic resources. But history has shown that the city has always been valued for its life-enhancing qualities as well as for its architectural landscape. Planners are beginning to appreciate that cities, in the first and last analysis, are for people. If they can successfully translate into a physical reality the ideal of an urban environment conducive to (in Shakespeare's phrase) "more worthier" human interaction and cultural exchange, cities in America need never become "uninhabitable."

b The "Classical" Question

i Context Sociologists traditionally have considered "society" to be synonymous with "community." Recently, however, they have begun to wonder whether contemporary mass society provides the kinds of relationships that have sustained and nurtured small, discrete communities. The efforts by the counterculture and women's liberation groups to develop new social patterns can be seen as examples of contemporary attempts to create living arrangements conducive to community.

"*Community*" is a word used so many times in so many ways that it often lacks clarity. In its most technical sense, it denotes the organization of social units and social behavior in a locality. Four major functions contributing to community have been identified: (1) economic production, consumption, and distribution; (2) socialization; (3) social control; (4) social participation and mutual support. Different sociologists have concentrated on different aspects of community, but their major theoretical statements may show how separate research studies can be integrated into a systematic definition of "community." The questions to be asked include: *Where does community begin? How is it organized in terms of social structure, interpersonal relationships, values, physical proximity? How does the individual become incorporated into it?*

ii   Theory The study of community has used two fundamental approaches. One concentrates on physical space; it pictures traditional society as a housing cluster surrounded by farms, and urban society as a trade center bordered by residential areas and then, perhaps, farm land. The second approach grew out of the idea that "community" refers less to physical proximity than to "people living together"; it analyzes the shared institutions and values that create common behavioral patterns—regardless of *where* the social actors reside. The two modes of study need not be contradictory and can complement each other. Indeed, the second approach developed as sociologists realized that modern, urban communities could not be adequately studied in terms of spatial organization alone.

Spatial theories of community figure prominently in rural sociology. On the basic assumption that by virtue of living in the same area people almost automatically share a set of attitudes and behavior, the neighborhood or settlement is seen as the critical social unit. The development of larger communities can then be understood as a process whereby individual, disparate neighborhoods or residence-unit groups are linked to each other over larger areas.

During the 1920s and 1930s Robert E. Park, Ernest W. Burgess, Roderick D. McKenzie, and their colleagues at the University of Chicago borrowed this concept of spatial relationship in their urban research. Assuming that detailed studies of Chicago would reveal general principles applicable elsewhere, they developed an ecological theory of community organization. They pictured the city as a ring of five *concentric zones*—(1) a central business district, (2) a zone "in transition," (3) a zone of "independent workingmen's homes," (4) a zone of "better residences," and (5) a zone of "commuters." In addition to the urban zones, they postulated "natural areas" occurring within or overlapping zones. Each of these natural areas displayed particular kinds of land use, social activity, and population makeup.

This model of dynamic community demonstrated the interplay between urban zones and natural areas. It postulated an interdependence between the *ecological process* of spatial organization and the *social functions* transpiring within a natural area. Although many contemporary students of community do not approach the problem in this way, they generally acknowledge the debt they owe

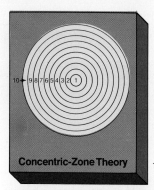

1 Central business district
2 Wholesale light manufacturing
3 Low-class residential
4 Medium-class residential
5 High-class residential
6 Heavy manufacturing
7 Outlying business district
8 Residential suburb
9 Industrial suburb
10 Commuters' zone

Concentric-Zone Theory

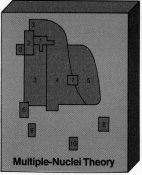

Multiple-Nuclei Theory

Sector Theory

Figure 2. Three Models of the Internal Structure of Cities. In the 1920s Robert Park, Ernest Burgess, and Roderick McKenzie developed the concentric-zone theory as a kind of ideal-type intended to apply to most cities. This theory delineated five zones. In the 1930s Homer Hoyt developed the sector theory and delineated five sectors. The arrangement of sectors was to vary from city to city. In the mid-1940s Chauncey Harris and Edward Ullman developed the multiple-nuclei theory. They delineated nine nuclei, with any particular arrangement of the nuclei being only one pattern among innumerable possible variations. The above figure shows the total number of categories (10) presented in the three theories and places all 10 categories simultaneously within each of the three different models for purposes of comparing where the placement of each might fall from model to model. It should be borne in mind that each model provides for the possibility of expansion, contraction, and overlap of categories. (Source: Adapted from Harris and Ullman, "The Nature of Cities")

Table 3. Family Income, Education Levels, and Poverty in New York City, 1960 and 1970. Although all groups in New York City are making gains in family income and educational level, the gap between whites and nonwhites continues to widen. (Source: Adapted from *New York Times*, 8/17/72)

the "Chicago School."

The second approach to community developed from the writings of German thinkers in the late nineteenth and early twentieth centuries, especially Ferdinand Toennies. These theories differentiated between human relationships bound by a community of affection, *Gemeinschaft,* and those bound by more mechanical, functional, utilitarian ties, *Gesellschaft.* True community emerged from the fraternal feelings of *Gemeinschaft; Gesellschaft* produced what these analysts called "group life"—organized behavior lacking sentiment or emotional warmth.

Various typological categories describing personality structure, cultural order, and social system have been heavily influenced by the original *Gemeinschaft/Gesellschaft* distinction. Especially noteworthy are Charles Horton Cooley's discussion of the primary versus the secondary group, Emile Durkheim's theory of mechanical and organic solidarity, David Riesman's inner-directed/outer-directed personality characters, and Talcott Parsons' attempt to develop a general theory of action based on certain pattern variables. All of these theories share the idea that community assumes importance to the extent that it shapes behavior, ideology, and social perception.

Although urban group life may be for many an unsatisfying emotional substitute for "small town" *Gemeinschaft,* it possesses many communal characteristics. Thus the problem of modern community may have less to do with how people organize themselves in space than with how they relate to each other as human beings.

iii   Research (Survey)   The "Chicago School" borrowed many of

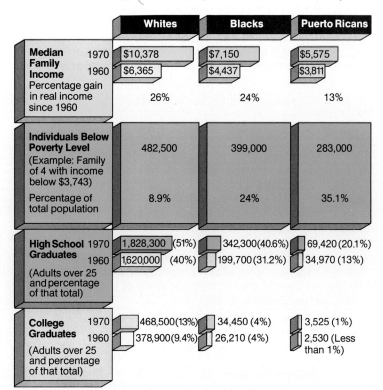

	Whites	Blacks	Puerto Ricans
Median Family Income 1970	$10,378	$7,150	$5,575
1960	$6,365	$4,437	$3,811
Percentage gain in real income since 1960	26%	24%	13%
Individuals Below Poverty Level (Example: Family of 4 with income below $3,743)	482,500	399,000	283,000
Percentage of total population	8.9%	24%	35.1%
High School Graduates 1970	1,828,300 (51%)	342,300 (40.6%)	69,420 (20.1%)
1960	1,620,000 (40%)	199,700 (31.2%)	34,970 (13%)
(Adults over 25 and percentage of that total)			
College Graduates 1970	468,500 (13%)	34,450 (4%)	3,525 (1%)
1960	378,900 (9.4%)	26,210 (4%)	2,530 (Less than 1%)
(Adults over 25 and percentage of that total)			

Demonstration in Forest Hills area of New York City against scatter-site housing in 1972. Scatter-site housing—public housing projects with large numbers of low-income residents deliberately placed in middle-class neighborhoods—may be a bad reform idea. It brings the problems of poverty into the middle-class neighborhoods, thus threatening the life style of the residents of the area. It also disperses the poor, weakening them politically so that they cannot organize themselves along community or neighborhood lines to fight the political and economic forces that oppress them.

the concepts it used in analyzing patterns of urban growth—such as competition, natural area, and symbiosis—from Darwinism and naturalism. Although some students disagreed with the theory of concentric zones, their alternatives tended to be variations on the common theme rather than radical departures. For example, Homer Hoyt's *sector theory* of urban growth, proposed in 1933, maintained that high-rent areas tend to be located on the fringes of particular sectors of the city rather than equally distributed within a concentric zone. His research demonstrated that industrial areas develop along river valleys, water courses, and railroad lines instead of forming a circle around the central business zone. Another model portrayed the city as organized around *multiple nuclei* instead of a single center, with each of the various centers or "nuclei" tending to specialize in a particular kind of activity—retailing, wholesaling, finance, government, recreation, or education.

The development of American urban areas after World War II has tended to confirm the multiple-nuclei theory. The expansion of population and the extension of the metropolitan area into the suburbs have made it largely impossible to consolidate all important functions into a single center. The modern metropolis is increasingly decentralized, with scattered pockets of concentrated shopping and professional areas performing the roles previously played by the central city.

Urban ecologists have also investigated ethnic and class segregation, showing that people of the same nationality, race, or social position tend to cluster, voluntarily or involuntarily, in the same residential area. However, ethnic neighborhoods in America, once the norm, have clearly begun to wane. Blocks and census tracts are increasingly "polyethnic" instead of being dominated by a single nationality group. Herbert Gans' study of Boston—*The Urban Villagers* (1962)—revealed an ethnic intermixing typical of that occurring throughout the country. Only 42 percent of the population in the "Italian" area was first-generation or second-generation Italian, the rest being Jewish, Polish, Slavic, and Irish. Nonetheless, Nathan Glazer and Daniel P. Moynihan, in *Beyond the Melting Pot* (1963), seriously questioned the extent to which ethnic identity is being amalgamated despite residential intermixing. They found ethnic differentiation highly articulated in New York City, and argued that Jews, Catholics, Anglo-Saxon Protestants, Negroes, and Puerto Ricans would continue to preserve their particular distinctiveness and choose to congregate among themselves, despite the continual housing shortage in the city that requires different groups to live next to each other in vast neighborhoods.

Although the residential segregation of white ethnic groups has been declining, neighborhoods still remain highly segregated on the basis of race. The most important fact concerning racial residential segregation in American cities is that it is generally increasing: over 80 percent of the black population in Chicago and over 70 percent of the black population in Detroit, St. Louis, Atlanta, and New York City lives in census tracts termed "predominantly Negro" (over 50 percent nonwhite). In most of the country's largest 100 cities there is very little racial intermixing within dwelling units. The makeup of public school population is another measure of racial segregation: seventy percent of all black pupils were enrolled in schools with 90–100 percent black student bodies; white students are equally segregated, with 80 percent of the white public school population attending schools between 90 and 100 percent white.

Much of the research analyzing the community in terms of patterns of shared institutions and values has taken the form of descriptive studies. The classic book in this field is *Middletown,* published in 1929 by Robert and Helen Lynd. The Lynds concluded that ''all things people do in this American city may be classed within six main-trunk activities: earning a living; making a home; training the young; using leisure; engaging in religious practices; and engaging in community activities.'' Later descriptive studies of daily living have assumed that community exists when people invoke common definitions and descriptions to explain recurring life situations and experience and derive behavior as a result of those definitions.

Talcott Parsons, whose work dominates much contemporary sociology, appraises community in terms of four coordinates: *goal attainment* of the individual social units; *adaptation* or manipulation of the environment in the pursuit of goal attainment; *integration* or the attachment of social units to each other; and *tension* or the malintegration of units that exist as independent but related systems. Research derived from Parsons' conception of social system analyzes such phenomena as status and power distribution, communication processes, and the kinds of linkages uniting individuals, institutions, and separate systems.

iv Evaluation The contributions made by the ''Chicago School'' to understanding the ecological structure and spatial organization of urban society were undeniably significant. But, as its critics have noted, this approach is limited and unable to analyze many of the main factors that characterize urban community. It still provides a useful topographical survey of the contours of a settlement pattern, but it fails to explain the nature of community.

On the other hand, studies derived from the *Gemeinschaft/ Gesellschaft* theory in contrast tend to be highly subjective. Descriptive insight is certainly not to be disregarded, but to study the community as a sociologist rather than as a novelist or a skilled journalist, one must have at his disposal a set of conceptual tools that are equally available to other students. These concepts, and the evidence they uncover, must lend themselves to some kind of objective validation. Although the theoretical propositions discussing community in terms of interpersonal relationships are highly suggestive, more empirical work is needed.

Professional sociologists, like other citizens participating in the life of our times, are increasingly realizing that community is vital to personal well-being. The quality of life depends not only on material prosperity and physical conditions, but also on the quality of our interpersonal relationships. Alienation and anomie result when people are unable to share meaningful experiences, either because of the absence of ''significant others'' or because there are limited opportunities for deeply personal transactions. (See Unit 5.) Discussions of the nature of community focus, in one way or another, on the nature of group life and the ways in which an individual shares in its dynamics.

The Savage Skulls, a Bronx street gang. Such groups flourished in the 1950s, declined in the 1960s, and are growing dramatically again in the 1970s. What theories help us to explain such developments?

High-rise, low-income housing projects such as this one replaced smaller multiple-family slum houses but did not get rid of slum conditions. Indeed, by increasing the population density and maintaining the level of poverty, slum problems such as high rates of crime, physical and mental illness, and suicide were intensified.

c The "Research" Question

i Context The idea of the role space plays in an urban setting has changed markedly since the beginning of the twentieth century. Before World War I open space was believed necessary largely for hygienic reasons, and parks within the city were accordingly known as "sanitary greens." Now, however, open areas are considered important in urban planning for more psychological or even physiological reasons. Open space in a city is conceived as an outlet where tensions generated by crowded living can be released. This new approach to the uses of space reflects the heightened attention being devoted to the problem of how people are affected by high-density living.

The United States Civil Rights Commission estimates that some blocks in Harlem are so densely populated that the entire American population could be housed in three New York boroughs if all blocks were comparably crowded. Although Harlem is, of course, extraordinary, in all cities the concentration of people is much greater than has been traditionally experienced in rural areas. The question of how environmental factors influence human behavior underlies much sociological research. What is the character of human behavior in an overcrowded environment? Do the higher rates of alcoholism, drug addiction, illegitimacy, delinquency, attempted suicide, and crime in the city reflect social disorganization prompted by difficulties in establishing and defending personal territory? Is violence caused by spatial intrusion? These are the kinds of research issues being examined by urban sociologists who ask: *What is the social-psychological impact of high-density urban living?*

ii Theory In approaching this relatively new area of inquiry, sociologists look to the natural sciences, as in Unit 3, for much of their theoretical orientation. Urban environmentalists, for example, are making use of work done by ethologists on animal behavior. It is much easier to study the relationship between behavioral adaptation and spatial requirements in animals than in human beings: time can be "compressed," so that several generations of animals can be examined within a short number of years; experimental situations can be manipulated in a way that would be intolerable with people; and investigations can be conducted in "natural environments," where the presence of an observer has slight impact on exhibited behavior.

Territoriality, a basic concept in ethology, has recently been popularized in the writings of Robert Ardrey and Konrad Lorenz. The concept is defined as the behavior through which an organism lays claim to an area and defends it against members of its own species. According to one of the world's most distinguished animal psychologists, Heini Hediger of Zurich, the function of territoriality is to ensure the propagation of the species by regulating *population density.* Only those animals that are strong enough to lay claim to a territory and maintain its integrity are able to establish a "safe home base" within which their progeny can be successfully reared. Territoriality has several dimensions. *Flight distance* is an inter-species spacing mechanism, the distance one animal will allow another animal to approach before it flees. The *critical distance* is the core area of an animal's territory; the animal will attack any in-

truder who enters this area. The normal spacing that noncontact animals maintain between themselves is known as *personal distance. Social distance* is the maximum distance across which social animals communicate: it is maintained by sight, hearing, or smell. Unit 12 was also concerned with some of these concepts.

Aggressive behavior appears to be related in some species more to territorial imperatives than to food supply, which was previously considered basic. Animals first communicate to an interloper that they construe his presence to be an intrusion. If this communication receives no response, the level of hostility escalates until it becomes overt, physical *aggression.*

Contemporary social students are exploring the possibility that man's spatial requirements are similar to those of animals. The common-sense notion that the individual begins and ends with his outermost sheath of skin seems increasingly mistaken and simpleminded. The types of exchanges that shape social behavior probably include some kinds of *spatial transactions.* Aspects of Western law reflect territoriality: trespassing, violating established boundaries, is a punishable act; English common law recognizes the sanctity of one's home and prohibits it from "unlawful" search and seizure; the distinction between "private" and "public" property is part of our social tradition.

Is a similar dividing line drawn in social interaction between "public" and "private"? Degrees of closeness or distance between people are often sensed rather than known; their perception may occur below the threshold of "reason." One can cognitively recognize the proximity of another by the loudness of the voice, the presence or absence of body smells, and feelings of warmth eradiating from skin. But it is possible that this sensation of closeness, of physical intimacy, also occurs in moments when the individual does not seek or is even repelled by it. The theoretical problem presented by urban density revolves around this question of "imposed nearness." When people live as close to each other as they do in high-density urban areas, what is the impact on natural spatial mechanisms that have previously operated to anchor social behavior?

iii Research (Methodology) The important ethological studies often cited by sociologists have been conducted on rats. A major experiment conducted in 1947 originated the term *behavioral sink* and is worth describing in some detail.

Colonies of rats were raised in pens and allowed freely to reproduce. In the natural state rat population per 10,000 square feet stabilizes at 150, but this experiment maintained 5,000 rats in a caged area. The researcher, John Calhoun, developed the concept of "sink" to describe that environmental state when gross behavioral distortions appeared and all forms of *social pathology* became accentuated. This condition arose when the population density was approximately double that which in natural circumstances produces maximum stress (that is, 400 rather than 200 rats).

In the natural, uncrowded state there is a short period of time during which the young, physically mature animals fight each other in order to establish territorial claims and a fairly stable social hierarchy. Under "sink" conditions territoriality became almost impossible. The maintenance of a fairly stable harem of females became equally impossible. Courting was totally disorganized, with some males refusing to approach a female, others mounting incessantly (which never happens in nature), and "pansexual" males indiscriminately mounting males and inappropriate females. The females, who normally do most of the work building the nest and attempt to keep litters separated, ceased to involve themselves with such domestic matters. The rearing of the young was completely neglected. The mortality rate of females and infants soared, and a great deal of "sadistic activity" was observed.

Other studies have demonstrated correlations between crowded conditions and glandular or physiological alteration. Improper glandular secretion suppresses pregnancy; animals raised in dense groups develop greatly enlarged adrenal glands, shrunken testes and reduced spermatozoa. Large portions of the population die even though food and water supplies remain adequate.

According to John Christian and David Davis ("Endocrines, Behavior, and Population," 1965), the biochemical changes stemming from overcrowding reflect the impossibility of regulating territorial claims under those conditions. Belligerent behavior constantly expressed cannot be resolved because of the absence of space. Increased levels of aggression, sexual activity, and accompanying stress overload the adrenals. An eventual population collapse results, caused by the lowered fertility rate, increased susceptibility to disease and mass mortality from shock.

Gerald Suttles, in *The Social Order of the Slum* (1968), reported considerable evidence of urban behavior that could be considered territorial. He studied the interaction among different ethnic groups in Chicago and found that each group laid out definite borders for its "area." Within these borders, which were effectively made known, organized social patterns prevailed. Suttles discovered that residents acquire a "cognitive map" of the differentiated regions and the behavior appropriate within them. Conflict was most likely to occur on the fringes of each "territory," where claims were tenuous and different groups competed for space.

Research stimulated by ethological findings has shown a tentative connection between crowding and indications of social breakdown. Population density was found to correlate positively with rates of juvenile delinquency, adult crime, suicide, mental hospital admissions, and infant mortality rates in 29 Honolulu census tracts. A Chicago study found that the greater the population per acre, the higher the rate of infant mortality, tuberculosis, and public assistance to persons under 18. Research conducted on attempted suicide indicates that the most important social correlate is overcrowding; the typical nonfatal gesture is made by a person harrassed beyond endurance by recurrent friction within a domestic group in cramped premises.

iv   Evaluation   Although the studies on the social effect of overcrowding are suggestive, their results are still preliminary. Density itself may not be the independent causal variable in the correlations; income or wealth or social class may be the root source of the observed behavioral patterns. Overcrowding, if only because of the stress it introduces into life, does appear to have biological

(Facing page) Two urban dwellings with high density of population. Although both these buildings house many persons in a relatively restricted space, the low-income project (on the right) has a high population density in each room, whereas the high-income building has a low population density per room. Thus these buildings offer qualitatively different life styles in a similar physical setting: the former is crowded (and deteriorates quickly as a consequence), noisy, dirty, and dangerous (because of high crime rates); the latter is spacious, well-maintained, and provides its residents with a restful, clean, and relatively undisturbed way of life.

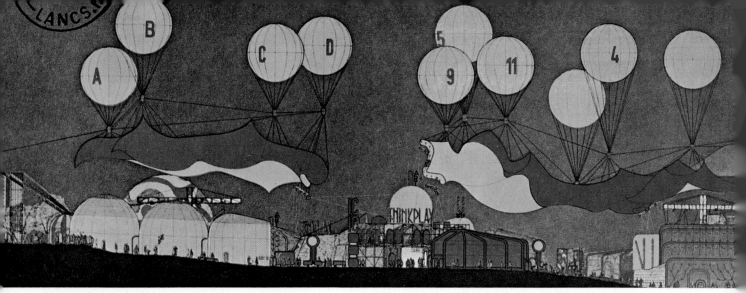

"Instant City." A group of English architects has devised plans for a portable resort city enclosed in a vast polythene-type wrapper held aloft by balloons. Like a giant traveling circus, the "Instant City" would transform, for example, a rain-drenched resort area into a holiday playground overnight as giant equipment mounted on trucks erected the city. In rain or shine the heated, neon-lit, "plug-in" city would operate like a mammoth fair, offering nightclub entertainment, cabaret and variety shows, computerized bingo, exotic restaurants, and luxurious electronic supermarkets and warehouses.

(Facing page) 3-D City. One problem of urban settlements is that they are two-dimensional; they and their suburbs spread over the countryside, destroying land and water. Architect Paolo Soleri suggests three-dimensional cities, such as "Hexahedron" shown here. "Hexahedron" could house 170,000 people, use up only 140 acres of land, have a height of three-fifths of a mile and a diameter of half a mile. No person would be more than 15 minutes away (by elevators and escalators) from any part of the city. Power supply, industrial production, and waste recycling would be in the earth beneath the building. The outside shell would carry utility networks. Between such cities the land now used for transportation, parking, junk yards, and suburban sprawl could be turned to agriculture and recreational use. Mass transit would link the city complexes to each other.

concomitants that heighten disruptive behavior, but the interaction of biological and social factors requires much more sophisticated documentation before definitive conclusions can be drawn.

The first efforts by social scientists to study density effects in controlled laboratory situations have yielded highly tentative results. It seems reasonable to argue that decreased space will adversely affect behavioral stability and encourage aggression, but this hypothesis remains to be demonstrated.

Planners and architects (responding intuitively to a condition in advance of empirical evidence) are reconsidering their utilization of space and designing urban environments and buildings more conducive to privacy and spatial isolation than was previously the case. If urban construction can be organized in a way that provides space for the individual to be alone when he or she so chooses, high-density living need not necessarily condemn society to a state of chaotic disorganization.

3 Overview

Urban living clearly poses major problems, but it also extends the promise of significant benefits. Although sociologists differ among themselves as to whether the advantages outweigh the disadvantages, all agree that the modern city is qualitatively different from the forms of communal organization that preceded it.

Twentieth-century urban man lives within complex physical and social environments that organize human behavior in separate systems. He often feels that his activity is disjointed, disconnected from a coherent "whole" that would unify the different aspects of life in a logically and emotionally satisfying way. Yet it is precisely this open-endedness that provides the city with its most vital quality. In the urban context the individual can define himself through personal experiences rather than through ritualized roles. Whereas in the Anglo-Saxon village a person's name might be drawn from his predominant role—Baker, Smith, Carpenter, Tailor, Mason, Johnson—in the city such one-dimensional identification would be inappropriate.

Increased resources must be funneled into the city if it is to sustain itself. Although the modern city was largely produced by nineteenth-century economic expansion, many of its economic functions are becoming obsolete with developments in communication and transportation. If the city is to thrive as a place where heterogeneous populations can intermix and enrich each other's social universe, the federal government must intervene and consciously direct resources for better housing, commercial facilities, and mass transportation toward the metropolis.

But the national commitment to cities has been tentative at best. Many political interest groups regard the city with distrust if not hostility. The Model Cities program, undertaken as part of Lyndon Johnson's Great Society to channel public funds and talent to the problem of revitalizing the central city, was insufficiently responsive to the real needs of minorities and often promised more than could be delivered. But its limited achievements marked a starting-point for future advances. The Nixon administration, however, is unwilling to carry on the program.

The city is a national resource that offers a society the values of diversity and cosmopolitan interaction. In such a heterogeneous country as the United States the city has served as an invaluable arena where different groups could come together. It will be a major tragedy if shortsighted politics deprives it of its health and leaves it abandoned to rot away.

D   LOOKING AHEAD

1   Interview:
Nathan Glazer

Nathan Glazer is professor of education and social structure at the Harvard University Graduate School of Education. He is co-author of *The Lonely Crowd* (with Riesman and Denney), *Faces in the Crowd* (with Riesman), *Beyond the Melting Pot* (with Moynihan), and author of *American Judaism, The Social Basis of American Communism,* and *Remembering the Answers.* His interests focus on the question of race and ethnic relations and social policy.

DPG   *What would you say are the main problems with urban sociology today?*
GLAZER   There are probably two main problems. One is determining sociology's position. Is it a science trying to develop theoretical principles or is it a discipline akin to sophisticated social history and record keeping? I feel that it would be very difficult to model sociology in the shape of a social science like economics. The second aspect —expanding sociology's links to history, journalism, census taking, and social analysis using whatever skills are necessary—is likely to be more productive. The works of Herbert Gans, *The Urban Villagers* and *The Levittowners,* are ideal examples of what sociology can do along these lines. But neither of those books contains authoritative advice concerning what should be done about their subjects—old immigrant communities or the development of new towns.

The second major problem is determining how sociology relates to current social problems and what advice it offers in dealing with them. Up to this point sociology's advice has been extremely crude and barely better than that of the informed layman. First of all, it doesn't take a large investment of time to master the theoretical orientations and the specific methodological techniques of sociology. Second, the kinds of problems on which sociologists are asked to give advice involve a number of inputs from many different orientations and fields in which a sociologist cannot give an authoritative position.

DPG   *Could you identify one or two areas in which a sociological orientation could be useful?*

GLAZER   One critical area is conflicts between races and ethnic groups (which is a problem in many countries besides the United States), the sources of those conflicts, the techniques or policies that moderate and ameliorate them. Another critical area is changes in the family, which is at the source of many other kinds of common social problems—juvenile delinquency or youth unemployment, for example. But sociology isn't likely to come up with a precise and positive program that's superior to others, although it does provide some tools for the development of programs. In a way, the best developed branch of sociology is demography, and even demography finds it hard to predict very far ahead. Demographers know that the people who will give birth to the next great baby boom are already born, but they don't know what their reproductive behavior will be. Demography is in this position. It's hardly likely that sociology is going to be better off.

DPG   *Does the city today have a distinct function that cannot be duplicated by other types of settlement or residence?*
GLAZER   This is a common view. But we now have the idea, based on developments in communication and technology, that the city, even as a relatively dense concentration, has no specific function. According to this argument, even those areas that are not very dense—suburbs, exurban areas, research parks, and so on—are actually "urban" in the sense that they are clearly based on an advanced industrial technology rather than a preindustrial technology. Nevertheless, we generally do think of the city as a dense center of residents and occupations, and in this sense it does have unique functions. It has been argued, for example, that a great deal of work involves person-to-person relationships. The magazines are still edited from New York; the books are still published from New York; the financial district is still in New York, despite the ridiculous taxes that the city imposes on it. Presumably these sorts of activities and many others involve a kind of personal interaction and immediacy of contact that is not satisfied by even the best communication devices.

DPG   *What advantages for society spring from the kind of interaction and close relationships that occur in the cities?*
GLAZER   For hundreds of years now society has been based on the notion that ex-

ploiting and developing the most advanced ideas, whether in culture or business or politics, results in a better society, a society that can manage the social problems of a huge population with a high standard of living. Presumably an urban social pattern makes exploitation of new ideas more possible.

DPG   *What do you see as the principal sickness of the cities?*
GLAZER   There are two basic sources. One problem concerns the reuse of old areas, which is really an economic problem. There is always a reason to settle newer areas. Land is cheap. You don't have to worry about past restrictions of land ownership when you build, and therefore residences, commercial development, industrial development, all tend to move out of the center. But the city has a politically drawn physical boundary, so its resources decline as people move out. Then you have a real crisis in terms of social services and urban upkeep and so on. This problem is independent of poverty. It's simply the inevitable tendency of a growing population to expand into new areas combined with the rigidity of the city's political boundaries. The second major problem relates to the fact

that agriculture has become highly mechanized and specialized. Rural migrants gravitate to the cities, where they believe they are most likely to find employment. Cities almost everywhere have the problem of adapting these newcomers, who have been raised and oriented to other styles of life, to an urban life style.

DPG   *How do you feel the sociopsychological aspects of city life—overcrowding, noise, pollution—affect the fabric of society?*

GLAZER   We may exaggerate that effect. It's interesting to point out that cities in developed countries like the United States get less and less crowded all the time. Manhattan had a population of 2.5 million in 1920. Now it's down to 1.5 million and probably dropping. That's true of the center of most cities. So in one sense, the problem of overcrowding in terms of those who are left is a less serious problem than it was. In another sense overcrowding becomes more serious because expectations as to space and privacy may be rising more rapidly than the drop in density. Very few Americans—something like 15 percent—live under circumstances of more than one person per room. So the crowding is perhaps more symbolic, a crowding of messages from the mass media, a crowding of demands by a complex society, particularly the huge number of bureaucratic messages. That kind of massive invasion by messages oppresses people considerably. However, people in suburbs on their lots of one-half to five acres are probably just as oppressed by television, newspapers, magazines, and bureaucracies, such as the Internal Revenue Service, as people living in more physically crowded circumstances. The social organization of society creates a problem of crowding for people, not so much the physical lack of space.

DPG   *Do you see any hope for the city in the future? Could you "dream a dream" in respect to the city?*

GLAZER   Clearly the city is reducing certain aspects of density. Some kinds of occasional encounter are being replaced by organized and formalized encounter. One drives to the theater instead of walking and talking to his neighbors on the way, for example. People have exchanged urban vitality for space, and on the whole they are satisfied with the bargain. Some individuals and some groups—young unmarrieds and older people whose children have left home and bohemians—are dissatisfied, of course.

In the future probably only a few cities like New York and San Francisco will be able to retain a kind of urban excitement and density that was once much more widespread in the United States. The rest may well be very spread out, with a lot of communications and a lot of planned activities substituting for the informal contacts. That's the choice people seem to prefer.

DPG   *You mentioned the economic decline of the center city and the concentration of poverty in the cities. Do you see any solution to this problem?*

GLAZER   I don't see any easy solution. We don't even know how to pour in money and solve the problem. One can rebuild the vandalized and burned-out houses, but if people find the neighborhood unsafe and unattractive, they'll keep on moving to the newer areas. I think the long-run solution to it is a kind of stability in the inner-city poor population. This stability might develop in two ways. First, the vicious cycle that has contributed to this decline may finally lead to some kind of counterreaction by those most subject to it. The epidemic of drug use may finally end, even if the social causes aren't eliminated, simply because it's just too painful, too degrading, too damaging. The cycle of crime may finally end, or at least stabilize, for the same reason, even if the social conditions aren't changed. There have been similar cycles of decay in the city in the past, and the trend toward social disorganization eventually wore itself out. The Irish and other immigrant groups in the nineteenth century ended the cycle without any particular social intervention. We don't know what happened. People may have decided that damaging themselves was less satisfying than taking advantage of whatever the society had to offer. Obviously society offers more now in some ways than it did in the nineteenth century.

The other possible route to stabilization lies in new forms of social intervention. After the experience of the 1960s, the most attractive forms are those that emphasize work, jobs with career potential and security and satisfaction. In a society in which 30 or 35 percent of the GNP moves through the government, the government has the responsibility to generate the necessary changes. Perhaps the government should guarantee such jobs in private industry, or take over some of the cost of such jobs, or even generate such jobs itself.

DPG   *Do you think that it's a political decision to focus this kind of attention on the poverty-stricken cities?*

GLAZER   It's a political decision, but it's also a problem of social design. You need an awful lot of experimentation, a lot of gambling. Social design involves consciousness and intervention. The problem has to be broken down. For example, you say: "The young blacks are not working because (1) either jobs are not available, or (2) they don't have the right attitudes, or (3) the right kinds of jobs aren't available, or (4) the jobs are available but they don't know about them." You try to find out what is true—the intervention has to be designed on this basis.

DPG   *What incentives could you offer others to come to the aid of the poor in the central city?*

GLAZER   First, the central city does not contain only blacks and Puerto Ricans and the poor. There are many whites in the central city, so the nation's white majority might have some incentives to help them. Second, there are many other kinds of interests in preserving the central city. Private investors obviously have an interest in protecting or improving their real estate values. Society has made a very heavy investment in the substructure of urban facilities and streets and schools and so on. Whether such interests are strong enough to lead to adequate intervention is an interesting question.

DPG   *Could you see any other ways in which one could approach a solution to improving the cities?*

GLAZER   In one sense I've addressed myself to the most urgent problems and in the least interesting way. The city is also a catalyst for other kinds of intervention—technical invention, aesthetic invention, the things that urban designers do that sometimes meet human needs and sometimes don't. All these things provide wonderfully intriguing possibilities to make cities better. But in this country we tend to think less about those things and more about dealing immediately with the social problems. Some people argue that if we dealt with the aesthetic and design features of the city and made them more attractive, they would have some impact on the social problems, perhaps by increasing sociability or even reducing crime, but I think basically the problems have to be dealt with at the level of national social policy.

2   Interview:
Herbert J. Gans

Herbert J. Gans is Ford Foundation Professor of Sociology at Columbia University and senior research associate at the Center for Policy Research. His books include *The Urban Villagers, The Levittowners, People and Plans,* and *More Equality.* He is now completing books on popular and high culture in the United States and on the ways in which the national news media cover American society. He is also doing further work on equality and its implications for American society and public policy.

DPG   *What do you see as the sickness of the cities?*
GANS   The sickness has two major sources. Suburbanization has reduced the economic functions and the economic importance of the central city; and at the same time, the city has been forced to become a haven for poor people who are unemployable or cannot find work. The good jobs, the affluent taxpayers, and the most vital part of the American economy are in the suburbs, but neither the suburbs, nor the corporations that dominate the economy, nor the federal government are willing to deal with the sickness of the city, and with the economic and other deprivations of the urban poor.

DPG   *What about the sociopsychological aspects of city life: crime, sexual and other deviance, overcrowding, and so on?*
GANS   There's surely more visible deviance in the city, but deviance is not necessarily equivalent to sickness, particularly when there are no patients or victims. One reason for New York City's attractiveness is its many different life-styles, some of which are called deviant by other people, but most of which do not hurt anyone. They are just different.

DPG   *What about crimes against one's neighbor? It does seem that there are more predator crimes in the overcrowded cities.*
GANS   Of course there is more crime in the city, but I don't think it's caused by overcrowding; the major cause is poverty. Rich or middle-class people do not mug each other; poor people who despair about getting a decent job may turn to crime both

to get money and to get even with society. Consequently, I suspect there's a good deal of crime in poor suburbs or poor small towns as well. However, if everyone knows everyone else, and people watch each other, as they do in smaller towns, the opportunity for crime is less, and in that sense, the city encourages crime somewhat more, both because of its size and the impersonality that is a consequence of size.

DPG   *You seem to believe poverty is the crucial urban social problem. Poverty has been seen as a deliberate product of our social system. Do you see any remedies?*
GANS   I think there are remedies. For example, a logical remedy would be a full-employment economy that has a high minimum wage and provides income grants for those who can't work. This is the best, and perhaps the only remedy for the urban sickness, but it is not a politically feasible remedy. The Nixon administration is eliminating even the minuscule antipoverty programs that were started during the 1960s, but then President Nixon was elected by the nonpoor and evidently feels no great political incentive to do anything about urban poverty, although the long-term consequences of his decisions, for example, a higher crime rate and increasing political unrest among the poor, may haunt him and his successor. Still, one cannot pin all the blame on President Nixon; many Americans still believe that poverty is the poor person's own fault, and as long as they do, politicians, whether Democratic or Republican, are not forced to take effective steps to eliminate urban poverty.

DPG   *Do you see any hope for the cities? If the political will to apply the necessary resources existed, could you "dream a dream" for the cities?*
GANS   No, I don't see any hope right now. I think those who can afford to get out of the cities will continue to get out, those who cannot will demand more police protection to insulate themselves from the poor, and the poor will continue to suffer. Consequently, it's hard and frustrating to dream. Moreover, even if poverty could be eliminated, and racial segregation likewise, the city as we have known it is still doomed, because, with the exception of New York and a number of regional capitals, the economic functions of the city cannot be re-

stored. Most people, including the poor, would prefer to live in low-density housing, particularly in the suburbs, and eventually, I suspect most cities will be redeveloped at lower densities. The high-density living associated with some American cities is a historical phenomenon; it came about because the cities were providing jobs and the people who held these jobs were too numerous and too poor to be housed at low-density levels. They didn't necessarily want to live in tenements but they had no choice, and now, when their descendants have a choice, they move to the suburbs.

DPG   *In what way do you think high-density living is shaping the lives of people in our society?*

GANS   Actually, very few people in this country live at high density; even in most cities, the typical house is a single-family house or a row house. Moreover, there have been a number of studies that attempted to relate high density to various kinds of pathology, and no one has ever been able to prove that density per se is pathological. Even dwelling-unit overcrowding seems to be less pathological than is often thought, although it is by no means desirable. For example, Robert Mitchell did a study in Hong Kong, where people live at inconceivably high levels of density and dwelling unit crowding by American standards, and the only problem he found was that if two families were forced to share one apartment, familial privacy boundaries were violated, and the families would fight. But one family, even if crowded into a small dwelling, seemed to be able to adapt; evidently standards of privacy are more flexible than we think, particularly among the poor—and they, after all, lived under crowded conditions even in the countryside.

DPG   *Do you really think that high-income people are unaffected by life under conditions such as those in New York City? Can even people with the advantages of wealth achieve serenity amid the concrete jungle and the hurtling cars? Doesn't this kind of environment inevitably diminish the quality of life for the individual?*

GANS   I think it depends upon exactly what conditions you are talking about. Rich New Yorkers live at high density on Park Avenue, but of course there's no dwelling unit crowding, and many have weekend and summer homes to which to retreat. Money brings a great deal of serenity, even in New York, although I don't think people live in Manhattan for serenity; those who have a choice live there for the excitement and variety that the big city provides. As for the poor and moderate-income people, they have no choice, and of course the lack of choice helps to diminish the quality of life for them. Still, I don't think serenity is determined by where you live as much as by other things, for example, one's occupation. People who work in industries that rise and fall with the fickleness of the consumer—the fashion industries, the mass media, and so on—rarely lead serene lives, even if they reside in a quiet suburb. Actually, if there has

been a decline in serenity for the urban rich and the middle classes, it stems from the fact that they are no longer protected from the unpleasantries of city life from which they were protected for so long. Air pollution affects them as much as the poor, and now the police can no longer prevent criminals from entering their neighborhoods.

DPG   *You seem to really play down the effects of city environment on the quality of life for the city dweller.*

GANS   Yes, I think the effects of the physical environment have been overrated. Moreover, however bad today's urban environment, it is much better than it was in the past. We tend to forget, for example, that nineteenth-century cities, with horse-drawn carts and carriages clattering on the streets, were noisier than contemporary ones, and more congested as well; and that they were in some ways more polluted too, at least in the sense that there was more garbage and feces on the streets. This fact doesn't justify present conditions, of course, particularly since standards for the quality of life have gone up so much faster than the reality. Nevertheless, the most important environments are economic and social; if people do not have enough money to live on, or work at demeaning jobs, or are segregated and discriminated against, they suffer a hundred times more than if they live in an inferior physical environment.

DPG   *Do you think that there's anything enriching about living in a city?*

GANS   I think enrichment is to a considerable extent in the eye of the beholder; if a place contributes something to the goals one is seeking, it is enriching, whether it is an exciting city or a dull rural area. When I studied one of the Levittowns, I asked people whether they felt their community was dull, but although the teenagers all said yes, the adults all said no, because they found what they were looking for in Levittown; friendly neighbors, friends, and a lot of social and civic organizations. Conversely, urban slums are hardly dull places to live in, but I can't imagine very many slum dwellers enjoy that particular kind of vitality, because it often means suffering for them. In the end one can only answer such a question for

oneself. I find New York very exciting despite all the inconveniences of living there and the fear of crime. I've lived in the country, but I find it boring. Other people may have entirely different reactions—in fact most people prefer just the opposite—and I don't think one reaction is "better" than another. The important thing is that people have the ability to choose where they want to live and then to implement their preference.

DPG   *Do you think that there's a community within the city based on the fact that one is part of the city culture?*

GANS   I don't think that there is one single city culture. There are hundreds and hundreds of cultures. The only place where you find one culture is in a primitive tribe where there's just one way of doing things. There are many cultures even in the most ordinary and seemingly homogeneous suburb. If you go to a public meeting in any suburb, you'll see the cultures clashing over school and other political issues.

DPG   *How do you feel about the decline of the city and its replacement by a suburban society that you seem to predict?*

GANS   I like the city, especially Manhattan, but I don't think my own preference should determine public policy. Some architects and planners want to preserve the city because they prefer it aesthetically to the suburbs, but again, I don't think they have a right to determine public policy on the basis of their feelings either. Most people seem to prefer suburbia—but with many urban conveniences nearby—and in a democracy, their preferences ought to be attended to. What's wrong with today's suburbia is that it excludes so many people on the basis of income and race. By my lights, a good society is one in which there is more equality of income and political power, and no discrimination on the basis of class, race, sex, and so on. Equality is far more important than density or urbanity. In fact, I've written a book making that point; it's called *More Equality,* published by Pantheon Books. I think greater economic and political equality is the most important urban—and national —issue of our time, and if America can become a more egalitarian society, it really doesn't matter whether most people live in cities or in suburbs, in apartments or in houses.

Unit 18

Sociology of Education

EDUCATION AND SOCIAL MOBILITY

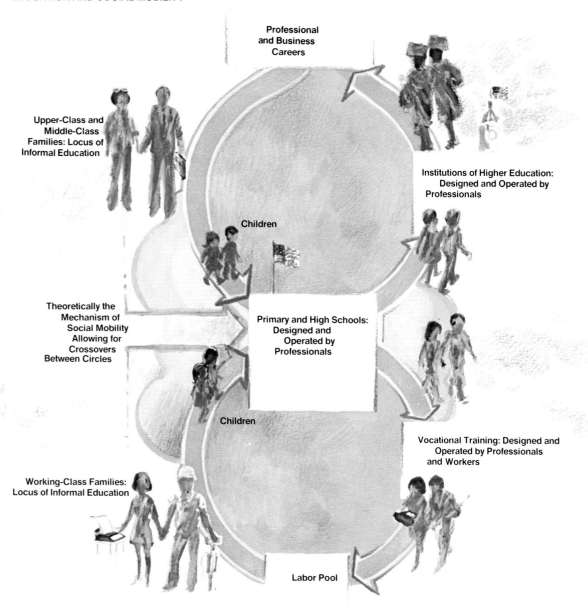

Professional
and Business
Careers

Upper-Class and
Middle-Class
Families: Locus of
Informal Education

Institutions of Higher Education:
Designed and Operated by
Professionals

Children

Theoretically the
Mechanism of
Social Mobility
Allowing for
Crossovers
Between Circles

Primary and High Schools:
Designed and
Operated by
Professionals

Children

Vocational Training: Designed and
Operated by Professionals
and Workers

Working-Class Families:
Locus of Informal Education

Labor Pool

The crucial question is to what extent this system approximates the ideal form of a figure-eight — and
what forces operate to keep the two circles relatively discrete with few crossovers.

Boys learning to be boys and girls learning to be girls. Even in our highly differentiated and institutionally specialized society, educational experiences are not confined to institutions of formal education. Values and knowledge are learned and taught informally in family and other reference group contexts and through the mass media.

B   DEFINITION AND CONTEXT

1   Definition

In all societies human beings become "human" by learning the *culture* that surrounds them—the great collection of beliefs and behavior patterns that people continuously observe and absorb from birth to death. In the process they also learn to teach this cultural system to others, along with new forms that include their own generation's emergent contributions to culture. Because man both builds and is bound by his culture, his survival and well-being rely heavily upon access to effective teaching-learning situations, and these develop within all human organizations. In highly complex industrial societies, many, but far from all, such situations for transmitting and binding culture become concentrated in special, separate organizations known as schools.

The sociology of education searches systematically for regular patterns in and empirical explanations of the relationships between society and its characteristic teaching-learning situations. Society can be interpreted as a *macrosystem* or a *microsystem*. The sociologist can study adolescent social life within a high school (a microsocial project) or the effect of a nation's overall social-class structure upon the individual or group's access to effective teaching-learning situations (macrosocial research).

The term *teaching-learning situation* is used to emphasize the fact that the sociology of education concerns itself with more than schooling. The Greek root for *school (scholè)* meant leisure reserved for learning or time set apart for learning. School then was a time, not a place. The modern school is a highly organized environment ostensibly designed for instruction in specific aspects of one's culture. But there are countless other situations of equal and often greater educational importance. Hence the sociology of schooling is only one subfield of the sociology of education.

2   World Context

Until a century ago the goals and methods of education had been thought of as the province of philosophers. The American sociologist Lester Ward (*Dynamic Sociology,* 1883) triggered interest in a new approach to education as a social institution through his writings on the special nature of genius and its influence upon society. Ward viewed education as an instrument of social improvement, with greater happiness for the educated individual as a valuable by-product.

In France Emile Durkheim, more conservative in this respect than Ward, emphasized the role of formal education as a conserver of culture. His pioneering concern was with the *social functions* of education rather than with its *personal functions;* he viewed education as an institution that essentially reflects rather than transforms the social structure (*Education and Sociology,* 1922). Today there is still uncertainty about whether schools can function as significant *agents of social change.* We know they cannot do so for very long without support from other parts of a society.

From 1900 to 1940 the sociology of education was an aca-

demic vehicle for stimulating positive *social engineering.* Its spokesmen were seldom systematic, and they were often quite moralistic in their approach to both teaching and learning. As a result, after only 35 years of objective research, sociologists today are often unprepared to meet the new demand for solid findings in the field.

Worldwide interest in the sociology of education has become intense. The leaders and aspiring peoples of many developing countries yearn for modernization, and they believe that acquisition of secular-industrial concepts and skills is basic to economic development and political independence. Although they are eager to design effective teaching-learning environments, they are also increasingly aware of the severe costs involved in traditional systems of public schooling. British, French, and American educational formulas are too expensive to be applied to Third World societies on a mass basis. Each such society must either choose to educate selected elites or must devise new types of instruction.

In democratic, authoritarian, and revolutionary societies alike, education is often viewed as a fundamental means of broad *social control.* Teaching-learning processes, both formal and informal, can be studied as instruments of conformity and compliance, and the uses to which education is put can be seen to influence the kind of society a nation will develop into in the future. The world is now aware of a connection between *social value choices* today and the individual adult of tomorrow.

3   American Context

The United States has developed a system of free, universal schooling. Because of their religious convictions, the New England Puritans placed a high value on education. From 1630 onward, in ways that were eventually paralleled throughout most of the thirteen colonies, New Englanders paid for lessons in both literacy and morality for their children. But these opportunities tended to be restricted to the church faithful and the socially ''deserving'' families. American historian Lawrence Cremin has shown that in the period from 1650 to 1700 the

> idea that schooling ought to be generally available for the advancement of piety, civility, and learning was accepted throughout the colonies. . . . Wherever it took root, schooling was viewed as a device for promoting uniformity. . . . And, like all other institutions of education, schools inevitably liberated at the same time that they socialized, and many a colonial youngster was doubtless freed from the social and intellectual constraints of a particular household, church, or neighborhood by attending a nearby school, which opened doors to new ideas, new occupations, and new life styles. (*American Education,* 1970)

The meaning of ''generally available'' varied from town to town, but usually meant ''generally available for mainstream whites.'' Only in a handful of communities did it include any Indians or blacks. Most schools also excluded the ''undeserving poor''—that is, children from families who were neither pious nor impoverished by specific misfortunes.

French and English ideals of equality and republicanism reinforced the ideal of the free common school in postrevolutionary America. In spite of the ravages of war, new and more inclusive schools at all levels were developed between 1780 and 1850. But secondary and higher schooling were seldom available to anyone below the middle class. Except at the college level, the burden of funding schools shifted progressively from subscribers and bene-factors to villages and townships. The pattern of excluding the Indi-ans, the blacks, and the impious poor persisted, however; and the common school was usually a very Protestant institution. Waves of anti-Catholicism, for example, drove immigrant Irish Catholics to es-tablish nonpublic schools wherever they settled. In short, until after the Civil War, the mass of the American population could expect only a rudimentary free education aimed at providing literacy fol-lowed by an apprenticeship in a trade. On the western frontier even these rudimentary phases of training were usually missing.

Each major war from the Revolution to World War II refor-mulated the central issue in American public education: Who shall be educated? State constitutions and local laws passed from 1850 to 1946 established a legal standard of equal educational oppor-tunity—some specified amount of education that was obligatory for all persons. Yet this norm was violated in practice in every region of the country. As schooling became more and more widely availa-ble, its orientation became more and more restricted to educating the sons and daughters of those whom we would today call the "establishment."

Between the Civil War and World War I, the period of most rapid growth of public education, educators and businessmen actu-ally agreed that schools should teach the *impossibility* of equality in the human condition. Public schools were expected to explain the rights of property and organized industry and the wrongfulness of labor unrest. Prior to the American Revolution schools had been or-ganized to reinforce religious and moral precepts. After the Civil War they were extended to reinforce business and industrial ethics. American schooling developed to include the public high school, but less than 20 percent of the nation's youth were enrolled in high schools in 1915, compared with more than 80 percent in 1973. The issue of *access*—of who should be formally educated—con-tinued to stimulate debate.

World War II framed the same issue for higher education. The GI Bill in 1946 brought the first large wave of less affluent stu-dents into colleges and universities. But not until 1965, with the passage of the Elementary and Secondary Education Act, was equal educational opportunity assigned federal priority and given fi-nancial support rather than merely being assisted by piecemeal grants.

As sociologist of education James S. Coleman has noted, the idea of *equal educational opportunity* has always had a special meaning in the United States. Since the American Revolution edu-cational equality has meant the provision of a free education up to a given level, common curriculum, attendance at the same school for students from diverse backgrounds but similar locality, and

(Page 409, top) Institutionalized education. As one type of social in-stitution among others, American society's educational institutions re-flect the structural patterns of other formal and complex organizations. The 50-minute lecture format, mass testing with rigidly structured questionnaires, and computerized grading are all expres-sions of the bureaucratic structure that has been adopted as the basic organizational form of mass, industrialized society. *(Page 409, bottom)* A classroom in the Highlands of New Guinea. The expan-sion of industrialized, mass society into remote corners of the world is forcing previously isolated peoples to adopt new forms of social organization and culture. A major mechanism through which the agents of the expanding industrial world seek to incorporate these groups is the institution of formal schooling. But no group of people can embrace the prospect of substantial social change with unal-loyed enthusiasm.

Two American schools: *(top)* Phillips Andover Academy, Massachusetts, and *(bottom)* public school in Brooklyn. The idea of equal educational opportunity has always had a special meaning in the United States. . . .

equal distribution of educational resources among the schools of a particular locality.

In practice the educational ideal has been applied discriminatively. The upper class went to private, separate schools. The very poor, especially the blacks, Indians, Mexican-Americans, Puerto Ricans, and the early contingents of Asian and Eastern and Southern European immigrants, got no schooling or some lesser amount that was both separate and inferior. By the end of the Great Depression of the 1930s, moreover, sociologists of education had shown that social classes within common schools were treated differentially, making inequality the rule rather than the patterned exception.

Despite these inequities, mass education has been so widespread in America that nearly everyone is an amateur sociologist of education. Almost all citizens have a minimum of five (usually eight) years of formal schooling, and most have at least several years of secondary education as well. Indeed, increasing numbers attend school for 16 to 20 years (an unprecedented span of time—the equivalent of one-half of an entire average lifetime in many of the developing nations). Every individual formulates his or her own opinions on the merits and effectiveness of such a mass institution—on its drawbacks; on curricula; on teachers; on methods of approach to subject matter; on what values (for example, promptness, docility, competition, neatness) should be rewarded in school and what values (for example, erratic attendance, autonomy, cooperation, sloppy appearance, or long hair) should be penalized; on what is learned in school versus what is learned at home, on the streets, or on TV.

Americans display a profound ambivalence toward schooling. Many believe that success and longevity in school help produce success in work, income, and other life opportunities, including self-realization. Yet from time to time these believers join the minority of skeptics who maintain that schooling makes little difference as a preparation for adult living and that the difference it does make often detracts from development of the personality, lessens the possibilities of creative innovation, and generally diminishes the individual.

Hence, in the American context, the sociologist is often pressed to provide social accounts of the public and individual consequences of formal education. Thus the sociology of education seeks to determine what differences school-based learning experiences make to the society, the economy, and the citizenry. How can these experiences be altered to achieve revised or expanded goals?

C   QUESTIONS AND EVIDENCE

1   Questions

Sociologists typically narrow such broad concerns down to smaller working hypotheses that can be tested by empirical evidence. Typical of the questions they ask are: (1) Does the busing of school children within or across public school districts increase the equality of learning opportunities and the level of individual academic achievement? (2) How does the class structure of a society, especially as reflected in particular local communities, shape its teaching-learning structure? (3) What social factors most affect academic achievement, and are some factors more amenable to control than others?

2   Evidence

a   The "Burning Issue" Question

i   Context   In its unanimous opinion in the 1954 case of *Brown v. Board of Education*, the United States Supreme Court asserted: "Education is perhaps the most important function of state and local government. . . . In these days it is doubtful that any child may reasonably be expected to succeed in life if he is denied the opportunity of education." The Brown decision defined public establishment of racially segregated schooling as a denial of equality of opportunity.

Today, 20 years and 10,000 community upheavals later, hundreds of school districts in the Deep South have been desegregated—yet seven out of 10 black students attend schools that are 90 percent or more black. Overt public opinion has shifted substantially. About three-fourths of the public states in polls that it agrees that "integrated education" is desirable. However, the same percentage also remains firmly opposed to certain specific methods aimed at actually bringing about integrated education. Opposition to *busing*, the mechanism for redistributing students among public schools by transporting a percentage of pupils from their neighborhood school to a more distant school that has a different racial composition, has become a political code word for opposition to school desegregation.

Busing was such an issue in 1972 that it affected the outcomes of the presidential primaries in Florida, Maryland, and Michigan, and the battle over it raged through heated debates over party platforms at the national nominating conventions. Richard Nixon and Spiro Agnew's campaigns against busing contributed to their victory in the election. The Republican candidates' stand not only reinforced the swing of all the Southern states to their ticket, but also helped deliver such key Northern states as Michigan, New York, New Jersey, and Illinois. Busing has become such an important issue and is so widely misunderstood that sociologists have been pressed to answer the question: *How does the busing of children influence academic achievement?*

ii   Theory   The broad idea of equality of educational opportunity rests upon several interrelated concepts. Sociologist James S. Coleman was commissioned by the United States Office of Education in 1965 to conduct a congressionally mandated survey of equality of educational opportunity in America, and published his findings in a famous report, *Equality of Educational Opportunity,* in 1966.

The Coleman Report defined five basic categories of relevant criteria. According to him, one type of inequality stems from *differences in community inputs* into the school, such as dollars per pupil, school plants, and quality of teaching staffs. A second type arises from the *racial composition* of the school: the Supreme Court's assumption is that inequality exists as long as schools within the same district have markedly different racial compositions. A third type includes such *intangible factors* as teacher and student morale, student interest in academic learning, and teachers' expectations of students. A fourth concerns *equality of results* from school, where community and student inputs are held constant but where levels of learning might differ significantly. A fifth concept defines equality as *equality of learning results* even where students begin with different advantages or disadvantages.

The first three concepts are part of three centuries of American educational history. By custom an American community is supposed to provide free, uniformly distributed resources for common or similar schooling of all the community's children and youth. Although this ideal has never been achieved, it underlies the criteria of equal inputs, student assignment to equally equipped schools and faculties, and provision of a learning environment within every school.

The fourth and fifth criteria, dealing with equality of results, are more recent in origin and less well understood. They grew out of the Supreme Court's Brown decision. According to Coleman, educational equality goes *beyond* the concept of simple protection against the violation of freedoms. He writes, "The responsibility to create achievement lies with the educational institution, not the child. The difference in achievement at grade 12 between the average Negro and the average white is, in effect, the degree of inequality of opportunity, and the reduction of that inequality is a responsibility of the school."

The issue of educational equality thus pivots around a basic value judgment that learning is more than, in the old phrase, a race that belongs to the swift. Equal opportunity means all students must receive whatever appropriate assistance is necessary in order to begin their learning from the same starting line; the differences in their *levels of learning*—not their rates and styles, which always vary greatly—should be equalized as a result of the effects of teaching within schools. The redistribution of students through busing is one method that can help to accomplish this goal, because it allows districts to fund and staff schools equally and to randomly distribute all students regardless of initial circumstances of ethnicity, family income, or literacy level. This deliberately random process assures access to the same starting line.

Busing for student redistribution does not address some of the newer aspects of the issue of educational equality, however. It cannot, for example, resolve the problem of individual differences. And most parents are not primarily interested in correcting *group injustices* but are instead concerned with obtaining the most advantageous *individual treatment and training* for their own child. When one United States Senator, who had publicly maintained a pro-busing position, was asked in a televised interview why he chose to avoid busing his son by sending him to a private school, he responded, "I don't think my children should be penalized for their father's political beliefs."

iii Research   Some social research has focused on the effects of desegregated schooling regardless of whether or not such schooling was achieved by means of busing. For example, on the basis of their survey of students in the first, third, sixth, ninth, and twelfth grades in more than 4,000 schools, Coleman and his associates reported in *Equality of Educational Opportunity* that what the child brings *with* him to school as strengths or weaknesses determined by his *social class* is the factor that best predicts his school achievement. This achievement is not influenced primarily by teachers or facilities or courses of studies, but by what other pupils bring with themselves.

In practical terms, Coleman found that as the proportion of white pupils increased in a school, achievement among blacks and Puerto Ricans increased. He attributed this change to the association between *white ethnicity* and *social class advantage;* white students have a greater sense of control over their environment and less belief in or resignation to luck or chance than black students. Coleman also found that although desegregated schools help the achievement of students from minority groups, they have no effect —negative or positive—on the academic achievement of the white students who attend them.

In 1967 social scientist Meyer Weinberg was commissioned by Phi Delta Kappa, the national education honorary fraternity, to review more than 1,000 studies of the nature and effects of segregation and desegregation upon student achievement. Weinberg found the great confusion of concepts, terms, and research designs made it difficult to reach conclusions. But he also reported (in *Desegregation Research*, 1968) that, on balance, segregated schooling is relatively more harmful educationally to nonwhites and desegregated schooling is relatively more beneficial to them.

In 1966 social scientists David Cohen, Thomas Pettigrew, and others were assigned to analyze the Coleman Report and to gather additional data on desegregation and education for the United States Commission on Civil Rights. Their report, *Racial Isolation in the Public Schools* (1967), reached the same conclusions as Coleman and Weinberg. However, it also showed that a desegregated school is not necessarily a good school and that the *level of interracial acceptance*—actual social desegregation of the student body rather than simply nominal desegregation of the school as an institution—determines how beneficial the educational experience is. In relatively integrated schools, where no racial tension is reported, black students showed higher verbal achievement, more definite college plans, and more positive social attitudes than black students in those desegregated schools where tensions were high. The report also demonstrated the important fact that racial "deisolation" is significant in its own right—that more than social class differences operate in schools to influence learning.

In a series of studies conducted from 1964 to 1968 (some collected in *The Urban Rs,* 1968) Robert Dentler and others found that sharp distinctions must be drawn between *types* of segregated and desegregated schools if their effects on student learning are to be understood. For example, a city school with a naturally mixed racial composition—it might be located in a neighborhood changing from all white to predominantly black, for example—is likely to be racially tense. It may be further handicapped by a curriculum aimed at a student body that departed five years earlier.

Another Northern city school may be mechanically desegregated; its attendance boundaries may have been redrawn or students may be bused in, but without plans and programs set up by the staff for hosting and teaching the newcomers. Still another school in the same city may be predominantly black yet relatively integrated socially, with a *social climate* that welcomes students from a variety of other ethnic backgrounds.

As part of this series of studies, sociologist Richard Boardman reviewed the literature on the effects of busing upon student achievement and then conducted a systematic analysis of these effects within a single pair of schools in one city. His findings led him to conclude that the effects of busing depend upon the conditions under which it is introduced, whether it is planned or not planned for educationally, and how it is carried out by administrators and teachers. According to Boardman's analysis, a poorly planned program of busing reduced the achievement levels of the children who were bused, the children who were left in the sending school, and the children in the receiving school.

Sociologist David Armor's study of student achievement at schools integrated through busing arrived at the most negative findings to date on the issue. His article "The Evidence on Busing" (1972) reviewed the data gathered on a number of different school programs and concluded that all had had remarkably similar and disappointing results. For example, in one carefully administered program the gap between blacks and whites in reading achievement actually increased after three years. Blacks were therefore jeopardized by an environment in which they were competing for grades with "students *three years ahead* of them in academic growth." Armor felt it important that the public be made aware "that black achievement is not being helped in any significant way by busing, and that therefore we have to raise the possibility of harmful psychological effects due to the achievement gap." ("Armor Answers Back About Busing," 1973) Armor's research design and data analysis have been repudiated many times by Pettigrew and other social scientists, however.

iv Evaluation During the turbulent 1960s, as racial and ethnic minorities grew impatient for rights long denied them, they became bitter and increasingly disenchanted with the liberal ideal of gradual desegregation of public institutions. Although most studies clearly demonstrated that academic achievement improved among nonwhites when they were carefully integrated with whites in schools that had specially devised programs, the resistance of the white community to actual desegregation was so strong that it led to racial tension that was too often counterproductive. As black political scientist Charles V. Hamilton pointed out in 1968:

It is absolutely crucial to understand that the society cannot continue to write reports accurately describing the failure of the educational institutions *vis-à-vis* black people without ultimately taking into account the impact those truths will have on black Americans. There comes a point when it is no longer possible to recognize institutional failure and then merely propose more stepped-up measures to overcome those failures—especially when the propos-

als come from the same kinds of people who administered for so long the present unacceptable and dysfunctional policies and systems. ("Race and Education: A
Search for Legitimacy")

With few exceptions, after 1968 Northern black educators and
community leaders turned to a concern with issues other than
school desegregation, and activity in pursuit of this ideal declined
sharply in local black and other minority communities. Emphasis
has shifted instead to voter registration, community self-determination, and self-help efforts on behalf of minority children and youth.

Nevertheless, increased educational opportunity through
such devices as *redistricting, racial balancing,* and *busing* has
been achieved in many schools throughout the Deep South and in
a handful of districts from California to New York and Massachusetts. In spite of stiffening white resistance, widening minority
disenchantment, and some doubts about whether integration does
in fact assure equal educational opportunity (or fundamentally re-
dresses social-class disadvantage), court actions today continue to
make the Brown decision the law of the land.

b The "Classical" Question

i Context Viewed in one way, racial inequality in education is
one type of *categorical discrimination.* It is overlapped by another
type: *social-class inequality.* Because sociologists of education are
concerned with studying the relation between teaching, learning,
and the society as a whole, they are interested in identifying those
pervasive aspects of social-class structure that affect the teaching-
learning process.

If the class structure is directly reflected in the society's educational institutions, for example, one may infer that education
serves to maintain the class structure. If a school markedly
changes the opportunities of its students—for example, if success
in school increases a student's chance to get a job with higher pay
than he or she would have obtained without schooling—one may
still infer that education reflects the overall class structure, although
it may change the social-class prospects of individual students by
providing *upward mobility.* In short, studies in this area reveal
something of value about basic interactive relations between society, the individual, and education. Sociologists ask: *How does social stratification, particularly at the local level, influence the educational process and determine educational goals?*

ii Theory In the middle of the nineteenth century sociologist
Lester Ward theorized that education worked upon the potentialities
of gifted individuals and channeled those abilities into the service
of social progress. As latent talents were identified and shaped by
educators into skills and scientific discoveries, for instance, society
was constantly improved, and individuals achieved happiness
through recognition of their contributions to social well-being. As
education became more generally available, and as teachers
learned to teach more effectively in response to rising popular demand, a wider range of genius and promise would be found
among the population. A reciprocal interaction could then take
place that would guarantee continued social progress.

Emile Durkheim, on the other hand, was preoccupied with the *disorganization* of Western societies. He believed that the well-being of individuals depended upon the maintenance of coherent societal institutions. Late in the nineteenth century, fearing a secularization of Western society and a disintegration of cultural values, Durkheim turned toward formal education as a source of structural "cement." He reasoned that the function of education was to transmit culture and hence to perpetuate it through succeeding generations.

In the midst of the Great Depression in America, William Lloyd Warner, Allison Davis, and August Hollingshead, along with many other sociologists, were studying community social structures. (We have considered some of their work in Unit 9.) They asked whether local schools provided avenues for movement up and out of poverty and from one social class to another. Their studies of the function of the school within the surrounding community did not support Lester Ward's vision. They reasoned that Durkheim's point of view was generally true, but that within American communities the school operated to transmit, not the ideals of liberty and equality for all, but the *dominant values of the upper-middle class*. Students who brought the values of competition, conformity, literacy, and expectations of conventional occupational success with them into school were rewarded. Students with other languages and values, especially those from the lower and working classes, were penalized with school failure or neglect.

Sociological analysis from 1940 to 1960 tended to confirm this view. It added new evidence that although schools function chiefly to reinforce the status quo, they sometimes put special strains on the socioeconomic structure. They occasionally enable groups to develop new statuses connected with their occupations and hence to avoid family-based social-class destinies. Usually schooling does little to modify, or even to strain, the class structure of the community, but it does contribute to expanding the frame of *social reference* of students from all social classes. The student *peer mix* and the shared experience of a common school *subculture* often extend the student's consciousness beyond the narrow setting of nuclear family, church, neighborhood, and workplace.

iii Research (Survey) In *Elmtown's Youth* (1949), his study of a Chicago suburb, August Hollingshead found that "Class V" students—those at the bottom of a local social hierarchy—were rated lower on all measures of achievement than were "Class I and Class II" students. Their test scores and course grades were lower, they received fewer prizes, and they were failed more often. For 20 years thereafter, sociologists confirmed a correlation between the socioeconomic status (SES) of the student and his or her school success. The correlation coefficient ran consistently, regardless of setting or age level, from 0.55 to 0.65. Because the correlation coefficient between measured intelligence (IQ) and SES is also between 0.55 and 0.65, it was obvious that a student's degree of conventional school success or failure could be fairly accurately predicted on the basis of his IQ and SES in about three out of five cases, without evidence about the school and its teaching.

C. Wayne Gordon (*The Social System of the High School*, 1957) and other sociologists demonstrated that a student's SES is

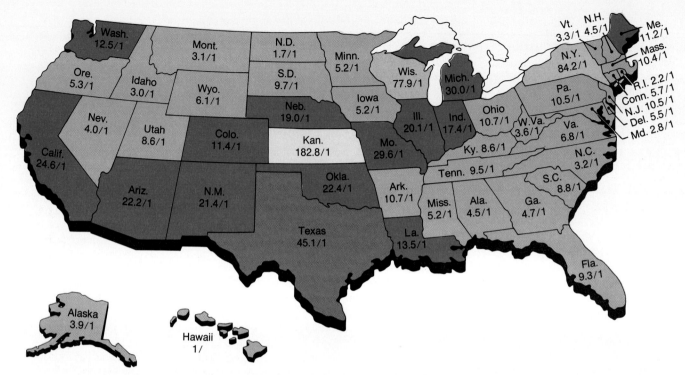

also a valid predictor of his degree of participation in extracurricular activities, election to student offices, and membership in peer group cliques. Patricia Sexton in 1961 showed that average family income within a census tract was strongly correlated with many different measures of school success or failure (*Education and Income*, 1961). Alan B. Wilson has shown that the achievement of entire student bodies varies according to their social-class composition; furthermore, a student's college and job aspirations are significantly correlated with the SES level of the student body of his or her school ("Residential Segregation of Social Classes and Aspirations of High School Boys," 1958).

These and similar studies also explored the social stratification of American communities. The degree of stratification and its rigidity and clarity varies from community to community, but it derives from a pyramid-shaped social hierarchy based upon differences in family income, occupational prestige, ethnicity, and educational attainment. Some theorists feel that socioeconomic status influences IQ as well (and that it is IQ that basically determines the other class-related factors). Furthermore, members of each stratum differ notably in some behaviors and attitudes from members of every other stratum.

The American public school is financed by all social strata, largely through collection of local property taxes. In actual fact, however, most American public schools are controlled by the upper-middle class. School-board members as well as teachers are drawn chiefly from the upper-middle and middle classes. Teachers from working-class families tend to have strong aspirations for upward mobility, which they achieve through educational attainment and the respectability that comes with their appointments to school positions.

Figure 1. The Gap Between Rich and Poor Schools: State-by-State Ratio of Assessed Property Valuation per Pupil in School District With the Largest Figure to That in District With the Smallest Figure, 1968–1969. Revenues from local taxes on property are used to support education in communities in all states except Hawaii, and nationally such revenue accounts for more than half of the $50 billion spent each year for public elementary and secondary education. The ratios shown in the figure indicate that the schools in the well-to-do communities receive a very significantly higher proportion of the total property tax revenue than do the schools in the poor communities. This situation perpetuates unequal educational facilities. (Source: *New York Times*, 3/1/73; from *Review of Existing State School Finance Programs*)

As guardians of the interests of the middle and upper-middle class, public schools discriminate against lower-class students and against lower-IQ students. Many children from poverty backgrounds and oppressed racial and ethnic groups are themselves alienated by the hostile, strange, or unsympathetic environment of their schools. Others are actively discouraged from continuing their studies; they are sometimes expelled for allegedly deviant conduct, if they do not drop out first from lack of reinforcement. In short, schools tend to have little positive effect upon learning for those who need it most and to function as a punitive force against already disadvantaged students.

iv   Evaluation   The sociology of education challenges the myth that formal education in America is a prime vehicle of social mobility. Some children of the poor and working classes are prepared for occupational "success" by virtue of school achievement. This type of mobility is found so frequently that there seems to be a kind of beneficient lottery stacked in favor of the students. Actually, however, the odds are stacked in favor of the "house": students are, in the mass, most likely to be measured, sorted, evaluated, and rewarded or penalized by teaching staffs in accordance with socioeconomic origins.

Social psychologist Bernard Mackler calculated more exact odds in one study (*The Little Black Schoolhouse*, 1969) of urban

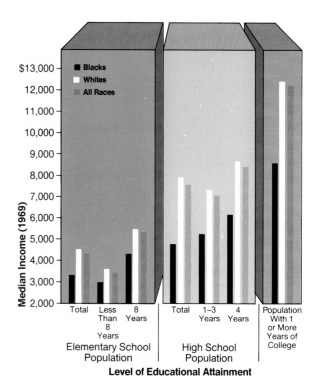

(Above) **Table 2. Median Income of Men 25–54 Years of Age, by Level of Educational Attainment.** Even to the extent that blacks do participate in the educational system, the wider society stacks the deck against them economically. The higher their level of educational attainment, the more blacks lose out economically in relation to whites. (Source: Bureau of the Census)

Race and sex	Number of Persons 25 Years Old or Older	Years of School Completed (Percentage Distribution)							Median School Years Completed
		Elementary School			High School		College		
		Less Than 5 Years	5–7 Years	8 Years	1–3 Years	4 Years	1–3 Years	4 Years	
Total, all races	110,627,000	5.0%	8.7%	13.0%	16.8%	34.4%	10.7%	11.4%	12.2
Male	52,357,000	5.6	8.9	13.4	15.8	30.6	11.1	14.6	12.2
Female	58,270,000	4.5	8.5	12.7	17.7	37.8	10.3	8.5	12.2
Total, white	99,211,000	4.1	7.8	13.3	16.2	35.5	11.1	12.0	12.2
Male	47,098,000	4.4	8.1	13.7	15.3	31.3	11.6	15.5	12.3
Female	52,113,000	3.8	7.5	12.9	17.0	39.2	10.7	8.9	12.2
Total, black	10,250,000	13.5	17.4	10.8	23.5	24.2	6.0	4.5	10.1
Male	4,675,000	16.7	17.4	10.5	21.6	23.3	5.8	4.7	9.9
Female	5,574,000	10.8	17.5	11.1	25.2	24.9	6.2	4.3	10.2

(Left) **Table 1. Levels of Education by Race and Sex (as of March 1971).** Blacks participate significantly less in the full range of the educational system than do whites. (Source: Bureau of the Census)

black and Puerto Rican students at the elementary level. He found that only about three children in every 100 with first-grade ability levels sufficient to do average or superior schoolwork were actually doing average or superior schoolwork by the end of the third grade. The Coleman Report found that teachers and school influences combined accounted for as little as 5 percent of the differences in the verbal achievement levels of Northern white students, contrasted with as much as 50 percent resulting from family SES.

Any vital public myth can withstand a substantial onslaught of sustained rational analysis before it is weakened. The myth that education opens a world of opportunity enables parents to send their children to school in the belief that the children will benefit from the experience, and encourages taxpayers to fund the public schools. Sociological analysis has contributed to the slight but steady erosion of this particular myth, but the myth is so central to the functioning of the society that it has withstood sociological wear and tear quite well. Student vandalism, unrest, and withdrawals from high school reached dangerously high levels during the 1960s, as did teacher militancy and organized dissent, yet opinion polls taken as late as 1969 showed that over 80 percent of the adult public still believed that public schools did a good to excellent job of preparing the young for adult life; 50 percent claimed they might be willing to spend more on public education. Few people know of a viable alternative to the way schooling is traditionally set up, and they resist the revised systems proposed by such articulate social critics as Ivan Illich, Edgar Friedenberg, and Paul Goodman, who have called for alternatives to compulsory schooling and a standardized curriculum. These alternatives would create less *bureaucratic* teaching-learning environments that would not be as likely merely to maintain the status quo.

The myth of the legitimacy and feasibility of schools today is maintained for two simple reasons. First, school experience at its most conventional does provide something like the three Rs for a considerable number of children. Even if only 40 to 50 percent of the students receive this benefit, this range and level of delivery of a public service seem impressive. The institution still seems more accessible, freer, safer, and sometimes more humane than others, even to families struggling against racial and ethnic oppression and urban poverty. Second, the importance attached to formal education by many social theorists and observers may have little correspondence with majority opinions. For all the hours it takes up and the demands it makes, school is still set apart from "life" in the lay imagination. And school is organized as a crude approximation—a benign micro-ordering—of adult conceptions of adult life as it "should" be conducted. Some observers have suggested that the real but unstated function of the school is that of a child-care center—a place that keeps the kids off the streets. Others have concluded that high school is mainly a way to postpone the entry of young people into the labor market.

Evaluations of the real results of schooling have just begun to reach a new level of sociological and educational sophistication. Stimulated by the landmark achievements of the Coleman Report, social scientist James W. Guthrie and a team of researchers recently reanalyzed 18 of the best studies of the effects of schooling upon student achievement (*Schools and Inequality*, 1971). They concluded that, contrary to many sociological interpretations, schooling has a positive effect upon student learning and that the extent of this effect is determined in part by *dollar inputs*. A school system that spends more per pupil on teacher salaries, facilities, and materials gets higher levels of student achievement as an outcome, even when IQ and SES factors are controlled. The weak but positive correlation between dollar inputs and student learning outcomes is statistically significant.

Christopher Jencks and associates at Harvard University

A learning experience.

reanalyzed every available study of the relation between educational quality and inequality and other socioeconomic factors, but they came to conclusions that are the direct opposite of Guthrie's. In *Inequality* (1972) they argued that quality of schooling has no measurable effect on anything—that the individual's capabilities, habits, expectations, and attitudes are largely a product of his *nonschool environment.* If social equality is a national goal, they concluded, it must be pursued through national social and economic policies, not primarily through emphasis upon equality by means of schools.

c The "Research" Question

i Context Teachers, students, and parents are eager to understand the way in which learning situations are influenced by diverse factors. They are also interested in altering the learning process so that it will yield greater results for a greater number of students involved in the educational system—regardless of initial advantage or disadvantage. Sociologists are thus pressed to provide instant formulas and cure-alls. They are often asked to explain, directly or by implication, how teaching-learning situations can be designed to achieve optimal results. Although many theorists have become reluctant to fill this role (for reasons indicated later in this unit), sociologists are interested in ascertaining: *What socioeconomic factors influence academic achievement, and what is the actual process that takes place in schools?*

ii Theory Willard Waller was the first American sociologist to develop a complete treatise on *The Sociology of Teaching.* Although Waller wrote 40 years ago, his ideas framed the sociological perspective on school-centered teaching and learning. In that perspective *status and role relations* between teacher and learner and between student peers are far more influential than the physical environment, the content of lessons, or the methods of instruction.

Herbert Hyman systematized sociological thinking about how social learning occurs in educational settings (*Applications of Methods of Evaluation,* 1962). Using studies begun during the Depression by Theodore Newcomb (and continued through the 1950s), Hyman theorized that learning can best be studied in terms of measurable, observable changes in behavior. These changes, he reasoned, were primarily the result of the learner's membership in and affiliations with a variety of *reference groups,* such as social class and religious, ethnic, and other relevant groups. The learner identifies psychologically with the members of these groups and looks to them for corroboration of his or her own attitudes and behavior. Viewed sociologically, learning in a school setting thus results from such affiliations rather than from the *didactics*—the content and method—of formal instruction.

In his sociological analysis *The Adolescent Society* (1971) James Coleman emphasized Hyman's perspective. Comparing the achievement and attitudes of high school students in 10 different high schools in terms of the social climates of interpersonal relations between student cliques and similar factors, Coleman concluded that the influence of didactic instruction was a minor factor.

A related but different factor was identified by psychologists Robert Rosenthal and Lenore Jacobson in *Pygmalion in the Class-*

room (1968), which studied school success in terms of a theory of *interpersonal expectation*. Rosenthal and Jacobson demonstrated that the grades students received and the scores they earned on achievement tests were powerfully affected by their teachers' expectations. A teacher who believed he or she was teaching "gifted" students, for example, taught and rewarded the students as if they were making outstanding progress. In turn, students did make significant learning gains. The power of positive thinking does indeed affect performance, and negative thinking similarly fulfills its own worst expectations.

iii Research (Methodology) The Coleman Report found that out of all the variables studied, student attitudes toward personal control over one's life, combined with their attitudes toward school learning, showed the greatest correlation with their actual level of achievement. Three statements were used to indicate attitudes toward control: "Good luck is more important than hard work for success"; "Every time I try to get ahead, something or somebody stops me"; and "People like me don't have much of a chance to be successful in life."

For example, in a Northeastern metropolitan area 5 percent of the white, 12 percent of the black, and 19 percent of the Puerto Rican students agreed with the statement that they did not have much of a chance to be successful. Students who disagreed with all three statements had significantly higher achievement levels. Both control and motivational attitudes are, of course, powerfully correlated with socioeconomic status (SES), but they also contribute their own effect. It is possible, however, to interpret Coleman's data differently, arguing that school success engenders feelings of self-confidence rather than vice versa.

R. M. Goff found that both girls and boys believe that lack of money and life opportunities are major interferences with their ambitions and goals in life. An effective school program can reverse these beliefs and encourage student self-esteem, of course, but such programs are rare. ("Some Educational Implications of the Influence of Rejection on Aspiration Levels of Minority Group Children," 1948)

Mildred Gebhard has demonstrated through research that success or even the hope of success nearly always increases both student interest and effort, and David Grant and James Cost have found that student expectation of a reward for attaining a goal is usually more powerful than the actual number of rewards received in completing a learning task. When teachers set learning goals that hold a high chance of success, students are likely to work harder.

Of course, the student group must accept the learning goal if expectations are to have this effect. In this respect Herbert Hyman's emphasis on *interpersonal relations* led to research on *social comparisons* and *student norms*. Irwin Katz found, for example, that black students scored higher on tests when they were told their scores would be compared with blacks, lower with whites ("Behavior and Productivity in Biracial Work Groups," 1958). Leon Festinger conducted an experiment that indicated that college sophomores—after taking a test—expected to do a little better on the next test if they were told their scores on the first test were be-

An example of the "Open Classroom." In the "Open Classroom" approach a number of demarcated "learning areas" with a profusion of materials are made available to the children. The children are free to wander from area to area, pursuing whatever interests them and using the teacher as a resource person. Apparently, however, the relaxed atmosphere contributes to the children's remarkably positive response to such classrooms as much as the architectural and learning-material innovations do.

low the college level, expected to do much better when told their scores were below high school level, and expected to do about the same when told their scores were equal to those of graduate students. He also showed that their actual test performance, not merely their aspirations, was affected by changing social comparisons of this kind ("Wish, Expectation, and Group Performance as Factors Influencing Level of Aspiration," 1942).

iv Evaluation These studies lend support to the importance of interpersonal attitudes as a mediating influence in the teaching-learning process. The content of teaching and the instructional methods used by the teacher are important, but much less so than the combined effects of teacher attitudes and student attitudes. The teacher's behavior does influence student learning, but less significantly than common sense would predict and more through the character of the interpersonal relationship than through the character of imparted knowledge and method. Unfortunately, sociologists of education have thus far made few contributions to our understanding of how *teacher effectiveness* may be increased, leaving this aspect of the process to educational researchers.

As Martin Deutsch has pointed out, "Most teachers would, I think, agree with me that we spend about 75 percent of our time disciplining the children and about 25 percent of our time teaching. Even the time spent in teaching is only about 10 percent effective because of having to stop several times during a lesson to speak to certain children." ("Minority Group and Class Status as Related to Social and Personality Factors in Scholastic Achievement," 1960) Although not much is yet known about what really constitutes teacher effectiveness, social scientists are certainly capable of designing a more efficient learning situation than the one Deutsch has outlined.

From 1957 to 1965 one creative sociologist, Omar Khayam Moore, designed a uniquely effective learning environment for preschool children. In his experiments hundreds of two-year or four-year-old children learned to typewrite, read, and take dictation. Moore's environment emphasized optimal freedom, self-motivation, and prompt positive reinforcements. (*Autotelic Response Environments and Exceptional Children,* 1963) Although his studies led to the development of new teaching machines, these were found to have little effectiveness when separated from Moore's special environment. His work suggests that within the next two decades behavioral scientists, working with parents and children, will begin to design teaching-learning environments unlike those we know today, with better results for the majority of students from diverse social backgrounds.

3 Overview

The American belief that education is a vital ingredient in determining a person's future economic achievement and that equal access to education will thereby ensure equal economic opportunities for all citizens has been the guiding spirit behind the movement in this country to extend quality schooling to minority youngsters and the children of the poor. The 1954 Brown decision gave added impetus to the notion that social and economic inequality could be corrected through improved formal education. Inequality of achievement in society was seen largely as a reflection of inadequate education received in relatively impoverished, understaffed, and underequipped ghetto schools. If black students attended the same schools as whites, the reasoning went, they would enter the competitive arena of American enterprise from the same starting line.

In practice, however, the resistance of whites to desegregation proved formidable, and the fact that blacks were physically present in formerly all-white schools did not mean that they were socially integrated into the student body. Racial isolation persisted as a counterproductive phenomenon, along with considerable interracial tensions and hostility in (and out of) school. Furthermore, when busing turned out to be the only mechanism that could actually provide "neighborhood" schools with a racially mixed composition of pupils, whites angrily resisted the transference of their children to formerly all-black or predominantly black schools.

The uproar caused by desegregation and by the increased attention paid to effective versus ineffective or inadequate education led to a number of studies that provided some unexpected insights into the nature of schooling and the nature of "success." James S. Coleman found that the *nonschool environment*—particularly with regard to social class—is the factor that best predicts a child's achievement at school. But the child's attitude is also influenced by the attitudes of those with whom he *interacts* in school, and for this reason Coleman felt that achievement among minority pupils would increase through association with *white ethnicity, ambition,* and *social-class advantage.* Christopher Jencks' study, on the other hand, asserted that *socioeconomic factors* were such pervasive determinants of all individuals' abilities that the quality of schooling was irrelevant; that is, it made little difference for the individual's eventual destiny.

In the past several years black communities have become less eager to send their children to predominantly white neighborhood schools and have turned instead to improvement of their own local school facilities and programs. Sociologists have begun to design alternative approaches to education because traditional methods obviously fail a large number of American students (and not only those who are socially disadvantaged).

Omar Khayam Moore's innovations are an example of this new disposition. Robert Hamblin, a sociologist at Washington University, has been hard at work since 1966 on the design of new learning environments; as he researches his designs, he installs and supervises their operation in real schools. Sociologists are also redesigning educational systems for less-developed countries. In the next 25 years the theories, methods, and accumulated knowledge of sociology will be applied directly and continuously toward creating and modifying teaching-learning environments in close collaboration with those most intimately involved—teachers, parents, and the students themselves.

D   LOOKING AHEAD

1   Interview:
Christopher Jencks

Christopher Jencks is lecturer in sociology at Harvard University and a fellow of the Cambridge Policy Studies Institute. He is co-author of *The Academic Revolution* (with David Riesman) and *Inequality* (with Bane, Gintis, et al). When the latter book appeared in 1972, it helped spark a national debate about the relationship of education to economic position in America.

DPG   *What is the major finding of your book* Inequality, *and why did it stir up so much controversy?*
JENCKS   I think the controversy was primarily attributable to the political context in which it was published. The Republicans were in power, and education budgets were being cut both nationally and locally. The book therefore became embroiled in the political controversies about whether or not education budgets should go up or down.

The most important finding of the book was that the use of schools as a device for reducing the economic gap between the rich and the poor didn't seem particularly likely to be effective. The level of economic inequality among people who have the same amount of schooling is almost as high as among people in general. The impact of changes in school quality on eventual earnings also appears to be very small. This finding has been used by people who want to cut school budgets as a way of saying, "Well, education doesn't make any difference." This statement is, of course, a gross exaggeration. But I think that explains a lot of the controversy.

DPG   *Didn't James Coleman some years ago find essentially the same thing as you did?*
JENCKS   Coleman found that qualitative differences between schools had very modest effects on the test scores of children in those schools. The findings that are reported in *Inequality* are quite consistent with Coleman's findings, but they take them a step further. First of all, we tried to look not only at some of the qualitative differences

between schools that you can measure in terms of expenditures, teacher credentials, class size, and things like that but also at unmeasured qualitative differences. That is, we just tried to rank schools from the most effective to the least effective, then see how big the differences in the achievement of specific children were between the schools.

Second, although a lot of people interpreted the Coleman Report as showing that schools didn't make any differences, that wasn't at all what his conclusions were. He concluded that one school has very much the same effect as another school. Although that's entirely consistent with our conclusions, we also argue that even variations in the amount of schooling people get don't explain very much of the economic inequality among adults. We're not denying that people who get graduate degrees make more money than people who drop out of high school. All we're doing is saying that those differences don't explain most of the overall level of economic inequality.

DPG   *What you found seems to deny the American mythology that education is the means up the economic ladder for poor people. Is that, in fact, what you're saying? Did school ever serve that function?*
JENCKS   I think what we're saying isn't really counter to the American mythology. If you get a college degree you'll make more money than if you drop out of high school. That's true. What we're saying is something a little bit different. We're saying that if you're interested not in the problem of getting yourself or your child a position at the top of the pecking order, but in the problem of eliminating poverty in society as a whole, then you'll find that changing the educational system isn't a particularly promising way of achieving your goal. Another way to put it is to say that if you stay in school longer than your neighbor, you'll make more money than he does; but if everybody stays in school longer than his or her parents, there will be as much poverty as before. So it's a difference in point of view. The American emphasis on education focuses on individuals getting an advantage over one another. In contrast, the problem

we addressed was: How can society as a whole lick the problem that large numbers of people are poor and seem to remain poor year after year after year despite all kinds of remedial efforts?

DPG   *Getting back to an earlier point, if schooling doesn't explain most of the variations between people's incomes, what does?*

JENCKS   We don't know very much about that question. We do know that IQ scores don't explain all that much. We also know that family background doesn't explain all that much. Both these things have some importance, but there's a tremendous amount of unexplained variation. If you think about that, it's not at all surprising. That is, if you think about two graduates of a leading university who have more or less the same scores on standardized tests and who both come from upper middle-class families, you won't automatically expect them to end up with similar incomes at the age of 50. One may be making a great deal of money—either in business or as a successful lawyer or as a surgeon or whatever—and the other may be teaching school or doing other things that will not be making him very much money. He will not be really poor, but there will be a tremendous dispersion of the incomes of those graduates. That comes as no surprise to anybody. I think it's fair to say that nobody ever expected the schools

really to make people equal, but if you don't expect them to do that, you can't really expect them to solve the problems of poverty either.

DPG   *Are there cheaper ways, both economically and in terms of human resources, of providing the instructive functions that schools provide?*

JENCKS   The research in our book *Inequality* suggests that if you're interested in simple, basic skills like reading, writing, and arithmetic, raising school expenditures doesn't help people acquire those skills. But the main argument for raising school expenditures over the past 50 years hasn't usually been that people would learn the three Rs better. If you look at a big, expensive, suburban high school, say, and ask what it is teaching that a small rural high school doesn't teach, the answer you would come back with is that it offers more different, advanced, and esoteric kinds of courses—foreign languages, calculus, and so on. Whether those things can be taught better at less cost, perhaps by television or programmed instruction, really isn't a question we tried to answer.

DPG   *Do you advocate reduced expenditures for schools or the disestablishing of schools?*

JENCKS   There are two excellent reasons for spending more on schools than we are now spending. The first is that children

spend some six hours a day in school, and schools ought to be pleasant places. Lots of schools are not now at all pleasant, particularly if you have large, crowded classes and terrific disciplinary problems. More money does seem to make it easier to make schools pleasant. You can keep paint from peeling off the walls; you can keep the plaster from falling on people's heads; you can have a playground so the kids don't have to play in the streets; you can have small enough classes so the teachers can actually pay some attention to the individual children. All these things are expensive.

The other reason for spending money is that if one of the purposes of schools is to pass on some notions about what Western civilization is about, what complicated abstract ideas are about, and so on, it helps to have some faculty members who know about these questions, to have books in the library so that people can read them, to have some classes that are specialized, and so forth. That doesn't mean that kids will come out with higher Scholastic Aptitude Test scores or know more arithmetic or whatever, but it probably means that they are more likely to have heard of ancient Greece and know something about it.

DPG *Why are you so concerned with the wide variation between incomes in the top fifth and the bottom fifth of the population?*

JENCKS There are two answers to that. One has to do with the problem of poverty and social disorganization and the attendant social disorders that go with it. The evidence is pretty powerful that people in the United States need a level of income that is roughly at least half the national average in order to participate in any meaningful way in the life of the society. When your income gets to be less than half the national average, you just can't afford to do the things that most members of the society do. People who find themselves in that circumstance tend to just drop out and be defeated. Their children tend to grow up in a very distorted and unhappy kind of environment. Getting the economic floor up is, it seems to me, a critical element in any strategy for dealing with all the problems of poverty and injustice that we spent so much time worrying about in the 1960s. That kind of strategy is much more likely to be effective than a social-services strategy of leaving people's incomes low and then trying to do things for them.

At the other end, there's the question of "What about the rich?" The problem there involves political power. The very rich have disproportionate influence on what happens in America. No one has found a way of making a man who has $200 million in capital assets politically equal to a man who has $200 in the bank. If you want a democratic society in which different people have somewhat proportionate influence, those huge concentrations of wealth pose a political problem. Everybody's income doesn't have to end up exactly the same. I certainly don't see that as a desirable objective. But I do think that the extremes of wealth and poverty that exist now aren't really compatible with a democratic society.

DPG *Are there any strategies for social change that will bring about less of a disparity between income levels?*

JENCKS It's relatively easy to think of mechanisms for doing this. There are various kinds of government actions that can raise the incomes of those at the bottom and reduce the concentration of wealth at the top. The Family Assistance Plan was an effort to raise the floor below which no family's income could fall, and a more adequate version of that could largely eliminate poverty in this country at a cost that would cer-

tainly be not more than two or three percent of the gross national product. It's not by any means prohibitively expensive. There are other kinds of strategies that basically have to do with regulating wages so that you don't have large numbers of families that have somebody working regularly but are unable to earn an adequate income.

DPG *You found a 5 percent difference in achievement between students in high and low quality schools and suggested that such a difference is relatively insignificant. Isn't a 5 percent gain worth considerable investment?*

JENCKS Actually what we referred to was five points—using points not as percentages but in the sense that they're used on an IQ test, where fifteen points is one standard deviation, or something like that. The economic benefits of that kind of gain don't seem to be huge. On the other hand, the main reason for learning to read, it seems to me, isn't to raise your future income. If you're going to try to evaluate the importance of a five point gain on a reading test, you really have to ask "important in what terms?" In economic terms it would be hard to justify spending huge sums to raise reading scores by five points, but in intellectual and social terms it might be quite easy to justify that. It depends on your priorities, and there's no easy way to say what is the cash value of having helped more people to enjoy reading books. It's clear, to me anyway, that a society where more people can read is a better society, but I don't know how to say how many dollars it's worth.

DPG *What do you think the next important step in research in education should be?*

JENCKS Probably the most important single area that's neglected and on which we have almost no information is outcomes of schooling other than test scores, going to college, and getting ahead in the world. Some schools have a whole range of other purposes. They're supposed to teach people to be good citizens. They're supposed to teach them to tell right from wrong. They're supposed to teach them to be patriotic, to drive automobiles safely, not to drink too much, to have a well-regulated sex life. You name it, schools are supposed to do it. We haven't got very much evidence about schools' effectiveness in most of these areas. It's perfectly possible that the difference between a good school and a bad school makes a lot of difference in terms of how bigoted or tolerant the graduates are, even though it doesn't seem to make a huge difference in their reading scores. So I would say that the major focus of additional inquiry would be to look at other areas of life besides just making a dollar or doing well on a reading test.

Unit 19
Sociology of Medicine

SCHEMATIC OUTLINE

A Introductory Graphics: Physicians and Patients—Decisions and Dependency

B Definition and Context

1 Definition
The sociology of medicine studies the social organization of modern medical institutions and the social roles of the people who work in those institutions and the clients who use them.

2 World Context
In every society the healer is elevated in status. Special knowledge and interpersonal skills characterize the primitive shaman as well as the modern professional physician.

3 American Context
Despite the ideal that personal feelings should not interfere with health care, American physicians and nurses tend to favor patients who are trusting and cooperative and who can report their symptoms unemotionally.

B Questions and Evidence

1 Questions
Contemporary sociologists explore three questions about medical institutions and the social effects of illness: (1) How can the quality and distribution of health services in America be improved? (2) What are the social dynamics, characteristics, and consequences of being ill or incapacitated? (3) What influence do different social factors have on the nature and distribution of mental illness?

2 Evidence
a The "Burning Issue" Question
In the present system of American health care, the further the patient gets from treatment by a familiar physician, the less control he or she has over the services received. Feelings of depersonalization and hopelessness become particularly acute when hospitalization is required. A thorough revision of the system is necessary to improve the personal quality of the care.
b The "Classical" Question
Theoretical and empirical studies have supported the ideas that illness is a social as well as a physiological concept and one that is particularly influenced by the definitions and approaches of medical professionals.
c The "Research" Question
Surveys using the disease, stress, and societal-reaction models of mental illness have shown that treatment varies according to the patients' social characteristics, that a vast number of cases are not treated, and that psychiatric labeling is inexact. Further long-range studies are needed.

3 Overview
Sociologists have shown that health and illness are social as well as biological or physiological phenomena. But their insights have not yet led to practical innovations in health care.

D Looking Ahead

1 Interview: Eliot Freidson

2 Interview: John H. Knowles

SUPPORTING UNITS

ENCYCLOPEDIA ENTRIES

PHYSICIANS AND PATIENTS — DECISIONS AND DEPENDENCY

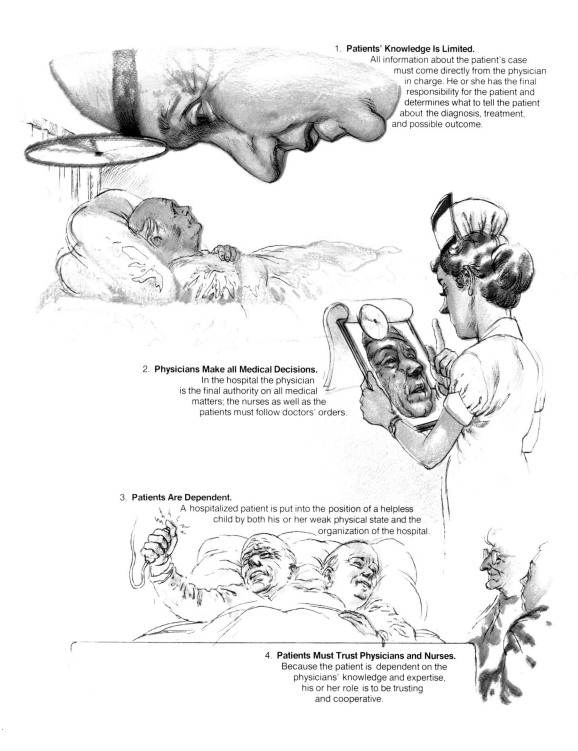

1. **Patients' Knowledge Is Limited.**
All information about the patient's case must come directly from the physician in charge. He or she has the final responsibility for the patient and determines what to tell the patient about the diagnosis, treatment, and possible outcome.

2. **Physicians Make all Medical Decisions.**
In the hospital the physician is the final authority on all medical matters; the nurses as well as the patients must follow doctors' orders.

3. **Patients Are Dependent.**
A hospitalized patient is put into the position of a helpless child by both his or her weak physical state and the organization of the hospital.

4. **Patients Must Trust Physicians and Nurses.**
Because the patient is dependent on the physicians' knowledge and expertise, his or her role is to be trusting and cooperative.

The family physician—nearly a thing of the past. The traditional family physician's role was multidimensional. Besides caring for the sick he played the role of "father confessor," counseled the family on the entire spectrum of human problems, and actively treated the family members' mental as well as physical health.

B   DEFINITION AND CONTEXT

1   Definition

The sociology of medicine studies the social organization of modern medical institutions, such as physicians' offices, out-patient clinics, hospitals, nursing homes, sanitoria, agencies for the handicapped, and departments of public health. Medical sociologists examine the social role of the men and women who work in these institutions and of the patients or clients who use them.

2   World Context

In every society the healer is set apart and elevated in status. In earlier times—and in many primitive societies today—the *shaman* was a priest and sorcerer as well as healer: he was said to be in contact with the gods and to have secret knowledge of magical spells and the curative properties of plants. Because many primitive peoples believed that illness was due to sorcery, witchcraft, or evil acts or thoughts, the healer had to be able to discover the source of illness through divination or elaborate rituals. Even without the aid of scientific medicine, the observant "doctor" probably had a working knowledge of the causes of various symptoms and what might remedy them. Also, his spells, rituals, and magical paraphernalia probably enhanced the sick person's belief in his curative powers and thus brought about many recoveries.

The physician's lore of ritual, observation, and pragmatic knowledge has always been passed on through some kind of apprenticeship system. Records show that the early Greek physicians (the most famous being Hippocrates and Galen) traveled from town to town with a band of disciples, who assisted them in their work. At the same time, the disciples learned the art of healing, the usefulness of first-hand observation, and the philosophical system the physician had developed to explain the causes of symptoms and their course. The Greek physicians' emphasis on careful naturalistic observation resulted in quite accurate descriptions of organs and biological processes, and they began the systematic classification of symptoms into specific diseases. However, the Hippocratic explanation of why diseases occurred was based on the notion of an imbalance of "humors" (blood, phlegm, black bile, and yellow bile).

During the Middle Ages and particularly later in the seventeenth and eighteenth centuries (when patients could be observed and autopsies done in charity hospitals), further discoveries about the workings of human bodies added to medical knowledge. But it was not until the techniques of scientific experimentation had been developed that the specific causes of symptoms could be determined and reliable means of treatment or prevention established.

The modern medical student learns anatomy, physiology, pathology, and the characteristic features of diseases through formal education. He also absorbs the lore and techniques of medical practice at the side of established physicians, accompanying them on "grand rounds" in hospitals, observing and trying his own hands in operating and delivery rooms, taking the histories of new patients,

 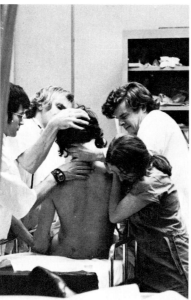  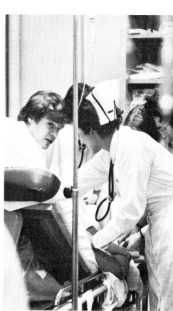

practicing the techniques of giving injections, and so on. Above all, as physicians have always done, he gains first-hand clinical experience with patients.

Emergency room. Both the perception of pain and the reaction to experienced pain vary across cultures. For example, persons of Mediterranean ethnic background tend to be quite expressive, giving dramatic reactions to pain and stress. Such reactions sometimes alienate professional staffs from northern European ethnic backgrounds, who may see such behavior as "excessive emotionality" or even as "childish self-indulgence."

3   American Context

In the United States, as in most countries where medical practice depends on scientific knowledge, the physician is the supreme expert in medical problems because only he has had extensive training. Patients have very little to say about their treatment, and non-physician health workers, such as nurses and laboratory technicians *(paraprofessionals),* must take orders from the doctors who supervise their work. Where care is poor, impersonal, or even harmful, the lay person has little recourse, for only other physicians have the expertise to judge their colleagues. In a *medical malpractice* suit, the standard by which a physician is judged is the standard of medical care in the community, as attested to by the other physicians in that community.

The protection of the patient rests on the ethical or *service orientation* of physicians, which is supposed to ensure that they will put the patient's interest before their own. The patient is also protected by the *professional expectations* that physicians will treat all patients alike, regardless of their social characteristics; that they will not let personal feelings influence care; and that they will concentrate on the task of treating each patient's physical or mental problems, without judging or evaluating his or her moral or social worth. The patient, in turn, is expected to seek professional help for physical or emotional incapacity and not resort to home remedies or to nonlicensed faith healers, herbalists, or quacks. Once in treatment with a licensed physician, the patient is expected to trust the doctor's judgment and to cooperate fully with the prescribed *regimen of treatment.*

Despite the ideal that physicians and nurses should not let

personal feelings interfere with the care of patients, they tend to favor patients who are trusting and cooperative and who report their symptoms unemotionally. They tend to disapprove of patients who take up more time than seems to be warranted, complaining a great deal, asking many questions, and refusing to cooperate with the treatment regimen. Doctors and nurses have a limited amount of time to devote to their patients and understandably tend to allocate more time to those they feel need more medical attention. Although laymen usually recognize that the sicker they are, the more attention they deserve, there is an inherent conflict of interest between the patient's view of each illness as an emergency and the physician's conventional view that it is a routine case.

Disapproval of "problem patients" is especially evident in hospitals and other institutions where patients must be cared for day and night. In general hospitals demanding, complaining, uncooperative patients may be given minimal care, sent home before they are entirely well, administered tranquilizers, or referred to psychiatrists. In mental hospitals uncooperative or aggressive patients may be given shock treatment, put in solitary confinement, or, as a last resort, given brain surgery.

In addition to the patient's behavior, criteria of social worth may influence treatment. Physicians in emergency rooms often make stronger efforts to save a well-dressed, middle-aged patient than an elderly derelict reeking of alcohol. In our society the young, particularly children, and adults with responsibilities are considered more deserving of medical attention than the very old and those whom medical workers consider immoral, such as alcoholics, drug addicts, promiscuous women, and people who have attempted suicide.

C QUESTIONS AND EVIDENCE

1 Questions

Contemporary sociologists explore three questions about medical institutions and the social effects of illness: (1) How can the quality and distribution of health services in America be improved? (2) What are the social dynamics, characteristics, and consequences of being ill or incapacitated? (3) What influence do different social factors have on the nature and distribution of mental illness?

2 Evidence

a The "Burning Issue" Question

i Context Availability of services, ease of access, and ability to pay are vital factors in the *delivery* of health care. But the best of care may not result in improved well-being, either in an individual or in a given population. If "health" means the absence of symptoms of illness, such a state is probably not a realistic possibility: one survey found that 90 percent of an apparently healthy sample nevertheless had some physical aberration or clinical disorder worthy of treatment. Immediate medical attention can control many acute infections, and infant *mortality rates* fall markedly with good prenatal and postnatal care. To raise the general health of a population, however, it may be equally necessary to improve housing, nutrition, and sanitation. In more affluent populations, where medical care is generally good and well utilized, people do not die of infections at an early age but succumb to cancer and heart disease and the debilitating effects of old age. (See Units 3, 6, and 14.)

With the understanding that lifelong perfect health for everyone is a utopian dream, then, the question is: Do Americans want more medical services, a better distribution of existing services, or higher-quality care?

At present medical care for ordinary illnesses and chronic conditions is stratified by income. The poor can receive care in municipal clinics. But they may have to wait for hours—or even days—to be scheduled for an appointment, and they may never see the same doctor twice in the course of being diagnosed and treated. Furthermore, in such clinics, and particularly in teaching hospitals, the more exotic illnesses are more valued by the staff than those that are more familiar. The fragmented and impersonal nature of services rendered fosters a certain degree of irresponsibility toward the patient's overall well-being. Poor people are most frequently treated not in such clinics, however, but in the *emergency room,* where service is geared toward immediate relief of only the most severe symptoms. Extensive diagnostic tests, patients' histories, and follow-up care are rarely pursued.

In contrast, the middle-class or upper-class patient is able to pay for visits to a private practitioner. In this case the physician knows or gets to know the patient individually and assumes responsibility for his or her overall health. If special care is needed, the private doctor not only recommends appropriate specialists but usually receives their reports on the patients and coordinates and oversees the various forms of treatment, medicines, and so on, that the patients receive. Private patients can initiate contact and make appointments with their doctors by phone, and they rarely have to wait more than an hour in a doctor's office on the day the appointment is scheduled. Middle-class and upper-class patients pay a fee for each visit to a private practitioner.

For more serious, life-threatening conditions that require hospitalization, a similarly stratified system exists. The *medically indigent* are usually placed in wards under the care of rotating interns, residents, and medical students. Patients whose hospital stay is covered by various insurance plans are under the care of their private doctor and occasionally a private-duty nurse; most often, their daily routines and treatment are managed by a resident and staff nurse. Upper-class patients, especially those with considerable social status, can command the services of the most prestigious physicians and round-the-clock private-duty nurses.

Nevertheless, few patients in America—rich, middle-class, or poor—receive fully coordinated care from cradle to grave. Complaints of lack of information and feelings of powerlessness abound. Therefore, sociologists ask: *How can the delivery of health care be improved, and how can it be made independent of income and other social factors?*

ii Theory Physicians are individually responsible for their patients and have complete authority over their treatment and over the con-

Income Level of Patient	Place of Treatment for Relatively Minor Illness	Major Illness Requiring Hospitalization	
		Ward-Type	Under Care of
Well-to-Do	Private Physician's Office	Single or Semi-Private Rooms	Private Physicians and Private-Duty Nurses (when needed)
Poor	Municipal Hospital Clinics	Mass, Dormitory-Style Rooms	Interns and Residents, Possibly Medical Students, Staff Nurses

Table 1. Medical Care and Income Levels.

ditions of their work. They are licensed by the state only after long years of training and certification by other doctors that they are fully competent to take such responsibility. Once licensed, however, the work of professionals is rarely observed or criticized, even by fellow professionals. Because of their total control over all aspects of their work and the training of new physicians, any change in the organization of medical care will be superficial unless physicians can be persuaded to alter their view that only they know what is best for their patients.

Various schemes have been proposed as solutions to this situation. These would increase consumer (that is, the patient and his family), citizen (that is, the community), and government participation and control over health services. They range from a system based on England's "socialized medicine"—in which the government assumes the cost of medical care for rich and poor alike—to government regulation of medical fees, government-imposed ceilings on physicians' earnings, more adequate health insurance for every citizen, and government prosecution of malpractice suits. Some recommend lay public representation on hospital boards, ombudsmen in hospitals to handle patients' complaints, regulation of hospital fees, standardization of services, and public review of what new or additional health facilities are needed and should be funded. It has even been suggested that all costs of training medical personnel should be borne by the public so that poor people can become doctors as easily as rich people and so that part of the medical community's justification for charging high fees ("Look how much money my family and I had to invest in my training") will be removed.

iii Research For very serious illnesses, the rich and the poor probably get the best medical care in America today—because both are likely to be treated in hospitals affiliated with medical schools, where the highest standards of medical practice are found. *Teaching hospitals,* which conduct research as well as train new physicians and care for patients, have the best equipment and laboratories and are staffed with medical personnel who are aware of the latest medical findings. Wealthy patients can afford the specialists affiliated with those hospitals, and the poor ward patients at those hospitals get the benefit of scientific medicine at its best. Although technologically outstanding, such care is likely to be impersonal, specialized, and oriented primarily toward clearly evident illnesses. The doctors who staff and are trained in the best teaching hospitals show little interest in routine sicknesses, in psychosomatic complaints, in the patient's personal stresses, or in continuity of care. The patient, unless he or she is a "V.I.P.," often feels like an object rather than a person.

Middle-class patients, the bulk of Americans, are usually treated by a family doctor who has their trust and confidence and who has known them for some time. They usually find their *primary-care physicians* (general practitioners, internists, pediatricians, obstetricians, gynecologists) through family members, friends, or co-workers who had used them and had been pleased with the care they got. Because of their dependence on good will and word-of-mouth referrals, primary-care physicians in private practice are said to have *client-dependent practices*. To avoid alienating their clientele, they are likely to take their patients' wishes and views into consideration, use methods of treatment that the patients prefer, and spend time talking to patients about personal problems.

Unfortunately, the general practitioner who has to devote time and effort to building up a private practice is likely to have outmoded medical knowledge and inadequate examination techniques a few years after he has left medical school. As a result, in order to receive specialized knowledge and treatment for a nonroutine or major illness, patients usually must be referred to surgeons, orthopedists, cardiologists, neurologists, and other specialists. Since such referrals are usually made by primary-care physicians, these *secondary-care physicians* are not dependent on the patients' good will, but on the good opinion of the referring physicians. Specialists' practices are thus said to be *colleague-dependent,* and the criteria by which they are judged are technical competence, up-to-date knowledge, and accuracy of diagnosis. On the other hand, such physicians, because they specialize in one branch of medicine, cannot give the patient the "whole-person" treatment a family physician can provide.

Thus, in the present system of medical practice, the further the patient gets from treatment by a familiar physician who is paid on a fee-for-service basis, the less control he or she has over the services received. The patient's feelings of depersonalization and powerlessness become particularly acute when hospitalization is required. Although only physicians can give patients information about their diagnosis, prognosis, and treatment, they are often rushed and do not like to deal with emotional reactions to bad news: hence patients often feel they do not know what is happening. Complaints about lack of information by patients in hospitals, particularly those who are better educated, are well documented. (We have discussed such complaints by *geriatric* and *terminally ill* patients in Unit 14.)

The introduction of medical insurance for everyone or totally free health services would probably not remove the difficulty of combining *personalized care* with *specialized treatment* or the unwillingness of most physicians to convey full information to hospitalized patients. A review of different kinds of national health systems in Britain, Europe, and the Soviet Union found that nowhere did the nationalization of health services challenge the physicians' power over all aspects of health and illness. Governments rarely question professional expertise based on long years of training.

iv Evaluation Although a system of national health insurance or

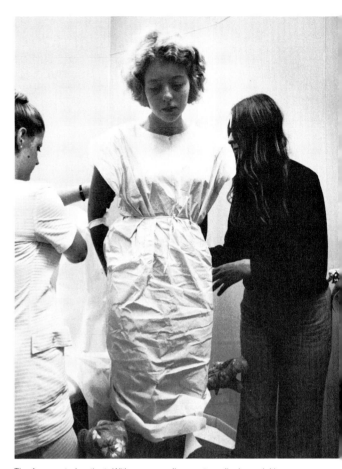

The fragmented patient. With so many divergent medical specialties now existing, seldom does one medical practitioner follow an individual patient through all stages of his or her diagnosis and treatment—even different body areas of the same patient are treated by different physicians. Although this specialization increases the efficiency and expertise brought to bear on each specific problem along the way, medical personnel may not see the larger picture, the comprehensive perspective that enabled the family physician of earlier times to treat the patient as a "whole person."

free medical services in America could make technically competent health care readily available to everyone, the kind of services received and the quality of care would probably not be altered. Indeed, when the individual patient no longer controls payment, he or she will have even less leverage. The dissatisfied patient can now threaten to take his or her medical business elsewhere.

A thorough reorganization of the current health-care system is necessary to improve the personal quality of care. Greater lay participation in the administration of medical care should be implemented, and medical ombudsmen might be assigned to represent the patients' interest. In addition, it has been suggested that medical care be reorganized to give hospitalized patients or members of their families more responsibility for their treatment. A more elaborate scheme of replanning has been outlined by Milton I. Roemer. In "Nationalized Medicine for America" (1971), he advocates the provision of personalized, continuous primary health care in localized health centers staffed by general practitioners, medical assistants, nurses, and social workers, with specialized services provided in a series of more centralized hospitals and teaching and research centers. Roemer argues for lay involvement at every level of care.

b   The "Classical" Question

i   Context   Everyone recognizes discomfort and pain and expects to suffer them in his or her lifetime. Yet no one considers illness a normal condition. Anything that incapacitates an individual, especially a fully functioning adult, disturbs the equilibrium of life, for both that individual and his or her associates. Because such a person cannot fulfill normal obligations, someone else must fill the gap. Because he or she must be cared for, time and energy must be taken from other tasks. A minor illness, such as a bad cold or the flu, can easily be handled by one's family, but incapacitation that lasts more than a few days creates a greater social upheaval and requires the adoption of a new social role. Illness is not only a *disvalued state* in itself, but also involves expectations on the part of others. Sociologists therefore ask: *To what extent does being seriously or chronically ill constitute a deviant social role?*

ii   Theory   Talcott Parsons' classic description of illness as a *deviant social role* in *The Social System* (1951) contrasts the condemnatory way society views criminals with the forgiving way it views the ill. (Units 22 and 23 deal with social attitudes toward deviance and crime.) Because the ill are not thought to be responsible for their condition, they are not punished as criminals are, but are excused from normal social obligations and treated with leniency. However, the privileged treatment is conditional on the ill person's seeking professional help. Cooperation with treatment by health professionals demonstrates that he or she is not simply lazy, self-indulgent, or attempting to avoid unpleasant tasks by claiming illness. Without a genuine effort to recover, the ill person can be accused of *hypochondria* or *malingering*—illegitimate "illnesses." This model of the sick role assumes that after a short period of time, any ill person will recognize the need for professional help and that consequent treatment will lead to a return to normal.

Several medical sociologists have refined Parsons' unitary conceptualization of the sick role. For example, David Mechanic in

Ward of a mental hospital. There is an interesting contradiction in our attitude toward ex-mental patients. On the one hand we tend to have great confidence in our society's specialists and the tools at their disposal. On the other hand we find it very difficult to accept ex-mental patients back into society. We apparently do not trust the "cure" for which we entrusted them to our specialists.

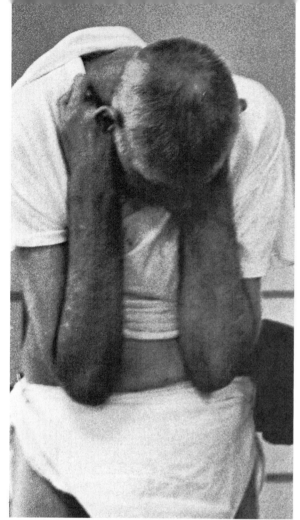

Medical Sociology (1968) argued that consultation with health professionals is as dependent on certain characteristics of ''illness behavior'' as it is on the extent of incapacity. According to Mechanic, before the sick role is adopted, the person with symptoms, usually in consultation with *significant others* (see Unit 5), has to define himself or herself as ill and not in some other condition. The individual must also decide whether or not the illness is routine, nonthreatening, and limited to itself, and, if not, whether to consult an internist, psychiatrist, or some other kind of healer. These lay diagnoses, prognoses, and prescriptions are shaped by the ill person's ethnic and religious group, cultural values, education, age, sex, and social situation. Eliot Freidson argued in *Profession of Medicine* (1970) that the views of the larger society also impose definitions on illness. These ''labels'' may block a return to complete normality once the sick role is adopted, even if health professionals consider the ill person cured. Certain conditions that are publically accepted as illnesses, such as drug addiction and mental illness, may be only partially legitimated because they are seen as shameful or stigmatizing, possibly for life.

Freidson also notes that the medical professional plays a significant role in illness processes. Professionals must validate the incapacitated person's claim to the exemptions and privileges of the sick status, but, according to Freidson, their monopoly over medical information, resources, and services means that they and they alone have the final say as to who is ''really'' sick and who is not. They determine what kind of sickness it is (physical or mental), what should be done about it (for example—drugs, surgery, psychotherapy, or physiotherapy, but not acupuncture or herbal medicine), and how patients in their care should act if they are to continue to receive treatment.

iii Research (Survey) Every stage of illness and health—from preventive care, to attention to symptoms, to seeking help, to being a

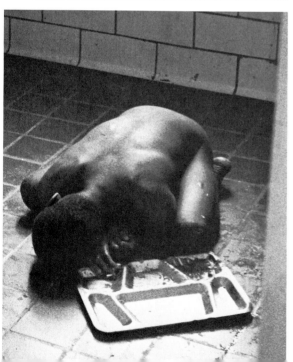

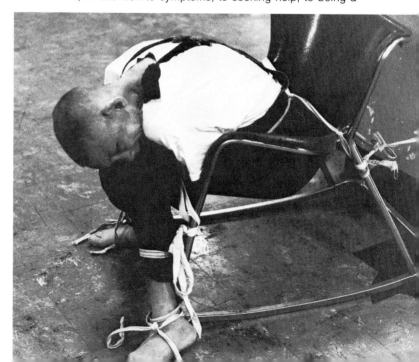

patient—has been shown to vary by sex, age, religious or ethnic group, education, and social class. In interviews with 137 people who had just experienced a severe illness, Edward A. Suchman found that men and younger people tended to minimize the impact of initial symptoms more than women and older people, but were also more likely to seek immediate care ("Stages of Illness and Medical Care," 1965). Comparing 144 Irish and Italian patients coming to an out-patient clinic for the first time, Irving K. Zola discovered that for the same disorder, Italian patients tended to complain more of pain and to describe more symptoms in more areas of the body than did Irish patients; the Irish also tended to postpone consulting the physician ("Culture and Symptoms," 1966).

Mark Zborowski, in a study of 146 men admitted to a veterans' hospital, found considerable cultural differences in reactions to severe pain. Italian patients tended to dramatize their pain with much moaning and groaning, but to relax when it was relieved. Jewish patients were also openly expressive about the eventual outcome of their illness. Patients of Anglo-Saxon descent tended to be stoical and objective about their illness (*People in Pain,* 1969). Rose Laub Coser's study of 51 hospitalized patients found that some of them expected solace and comfort from the doctor, did not question rules and regulations, and enjoyed being taken care of so much they wanted to stay in the hospital, whereas others expected only competence and efficiency from their physicians, were critical of hospital routines, and were eager to leave. The latter group of *instrumentally oriented* patients tended to be younger than the *primary care* patients ("A Home Away from Home," 1956).

Clearly, the sick role does not have universal dimensions, but varies considerably with the patients' social characteristics. The variations, however, take place within the limited set of possibilities allowed by current institutions and agencies for treatment. Erving Goffman's study of mental institutions, *Asylums* (1961), graphically described the extent to which medical workers impose restrictions and expectations on all patients. Goffman found that the staff systematically eradicates inmates' former varied social selves and substitutes an official model that is docile, submissive, easily managed, and homogeneous. Similarly, in *The Making of Blind Men* (1969) Robert A. Scott reported that the sightless who were clients of agencies for the blind, even though young and potentially employable, tended to be made dependent by the *sheltered-workshop philosophy* of *rehabilitation professionals*. The patient hospitalized for a physical illness, although conscious and able to take care of many needs, is never allowed responsibility for the treatment regimen, even though research has demonstrated that nurses make a shockingly high number of medication errors.

In sum, research on institutionalized or hospitalized patients supports Freidson's model of the sick role as one imposed by professionals. This role entails considerable refinement of Parsons' model of active cooperation between ill person and health professionals. Physicians and nurses tend to impose *norms of submissiveness and passivity* on patients, who are given no chance to question, choose, or modify what is done to them. Patients who might rebel against the doctors' authority are hampered by their lack of expertise, which is compounded by the slight amount of accurate information about their own cases doctors are willing to give them.

Finally, there is the problem of relinquishing the sick role and returning to normal. Derek L. Phillips asked 300 people if they would want as neighbors, club members, fellow workers, boarders, or in-laws individuals described as having had symptoms of mental illness. In "Rejection" (1963) he reported that those members of a group showing the same symptoms who were described as having consulted a psychiatrist or having been in a mental hospital were rejected to a significantly greater degree than those said to have sought help from a clergyman or general practitioner. For some illnesses, it seems, the deviant social role can never be dropped.

iv Evaluation The conception of illness as a deviant social role challenges the *medical model* of illness as purely biological or physiological entity and the treatment process as primarily scientific and rational. When "illness" is considered a *social product,* one can study the effects of the social characteristics of those harboring the symptoms or signs of abnormality, the cultural values of social groups, and the biases and expectations of those officially designated as managers of the social problems connected with physical and mental incapacity. A sociological perspective on illness and health permits the researcher to be more objective about patients and their treatment and less bound by the narrow beliefs of any time, place, or social group.

c The "Research" Question

i Context Numerous studies have shown that rates of treated mental illness and self-reported symptoms of emotional discomfort in those not being treated vary according to age, sex, ethnic group, religion, and social class. The findings to date are that the economically disadvantaged are hospitalized in state mental institutions to a markedly greater degree than their percentage in the total population; that women are more likely than men to be psychiatric outpatients; and that women, older people, Puerto Ricans, and Jews more frequently report symptoms of psychological difficulty in interviews, compared to men, middle-aged people, blacks, Irish, and Protestants. The attempt to explain the connection between rates of treated or reported mental illness and social factors has led to intensive questioning of the reliability and validity of the studies themselves.

The first problem of sociological research on mental illness is lack of agreement as to what a "case" should be. Who should be considered mentally ill—only mental-hospital patients, only those in some form of psychiatric treatment, or all those who report symptoms psychiatrists judge severe enough to be worthy of treatment? The selection of cases for study depends largely on the researcher's theoretical perspective on the nature of phenomenon under scrutiny. Sociologists are thus trying to determine: *How can the relationship between mental illness and such factors as poverty, age, sex, and ethnic group best be studied?*

ii Theory The most common view of mental illness is that it is a serious debility with a demonstrable pathology that will eventually cause such severe disturbance in the person's life that it will lead to hospitalization or intensive treatment. This model of mental illness as a true disease is essentially medical and is held by most psychiatrists. In sociology, its chief spokesman is Walter Gove ("Societal Reaction as an Explanation of Mental Illness," 1970). The logical cases for research are mental-hospital patients, out-patient clinic patients, and those in continuous long-term treatment with private psychiatrists. The goal of such research is to identify the social characteristics of those with the highest incidence of treated mental illness.

A second view of mental illness is that it is a reaction to stress, the result of problems in living or difficulty playing the game of life. Thomas Szasz (*The Myth of Mental Illness,* 1961) is the best-known proponent of this alternative to the *disease model.* Sociological researchers who use the *stress perspective* are interested in locating populations "at risk." In an attempt to determine which *social environments* are likely to produce high rates of *maladaptation,* they have surveyed random samples of untreated populations, seeking to determine the true prevalence of symptoms of mental illness.

A third theoretical viewpoint contends that at one time or another every individual exhibits symptoms of emotional distress or acts in bizarre or disapproved ways. Such "*residual deviance*" is usually ignored by one's family or friends or treated with leniency or permissiveness. If it continues, becomes too disruptive, or leads to trouble with official authorities, the *societal reaction* frequently locks the person into a mentally ill role. The role often becomes permanent because those who receive psychiatric treatment are stigmatized, especially if they are hospitalized, and also because those who are labeled mentally incompetent obtain such secondary gains as relief of responsibility and disability payments. The societal-reaction definition of mental illness proposed by Thomas Scheff (*Being Mentally Ill,* 1966) is the most radically sociological approach in any of the three models. This perspective calls for research not only on the person exhibiting the symptoms, but also on those who define him or her as mentally ill—family, friends, and *social-control agents,* such as policemen, teachers, and psychiatrists. The goal is to determine what *social characteristics* are most likely to lead to being defined as mentally ill.

iii Research (Methodology) In an attempt to discover how social class and mental illness are related in our society, August B. Hollingshead and Frederick C. Redlich took a "psychiatric census" of people residing in New Haven, Connecticut. Using the clinical records of 1,891 patients, they obtained data on paths to treatment, places of treatment, and type of treatment received by those of different social position in the community. (Social position was measured by place of residence, occupation, and years of schooling completed.) In *Social Class and Mental Illness* (1958) they reported that upper-class and middle-class patients were most likely to be referred to psychiatric treatment by family members, friends, or general practitioners, whereas lower-class patients were most likely to be referred by the courts, the police, or social agencies. The upper class was underrepresented in the patient population, whereas the percentage of patients who were of the lowest class was double the percentage of this class in the general population. Upper-class patients were likely to be diagnosed as *neurotic,* but 90 percent of the lowest-class patients were diagnosed as *psychotic.* As for treatment, upper-class and middle-class patients were treated in private hospitals or by private practitioners, whereas the only source of treatment

Breeding ground for mental illness? Research has shown that when other factors are held constant, crowded living conditions tend to produce greater frequencies of mental illness than more spacious environments do.

for lower-class patients was state mental hospitals or veterans' hospitals. In those institutions the few upper-class and middle-class patients were twice as likely as the lower-class patients to receive psychotherapy rather than physiological treatment.

Hollingshead and Redlich admitted their study's methodology suffered from reliance on "confused, discursive and contradictory" clinical records that made it extremely difficult to evaluate the findings. Although the documentation of the overrepresentation of those at the bottom of the social scale in the mental hospital population was useful, the study proved nothing about the relationship of social class to the causes of mental illness.

Another project, the "Midtown Study," attempted to explore the direct connection between social factors and mental illness symptoms in a field survey of a general population. A random sample of 1,660 residents of the East Side of Manhattan were interviewed in their homes. The respondents' reports of symptoms and interpersonal functioning were reviewed by psychiatrists, who determined that only 19 percent of this general population could be considered mentally well by their standards, while 24 percent exhibited impairment of a marked to severe degree. Only 5 percent of those considered impaired were currently in treatment, and 73 percent had never received any psychiatric treatment at all. As for social characteristics, the Midtown Study found that the percentage impaired rose as socioeconomic status declined; 47 percent of the lowest-status group were considered emotionally impaired. Older people were more likely to report severe psychological symptoms, as were single men, whereas Jewish respondents were most likely to report mild symptoms.

Leo Srole and his associates in the Midtown Study (*Mental Health in the Metropolis,* 1962) argued that low socioeconomic status, old age, and single status for males were clearly correlated with the symptoms of severe emotional disorders. Critics of such field surveys have challenged this interpretation, claiming that there is a built-in bias in interviews toward "socially desirable" responses. Thus those who feel the symptoms are shameful will deny having them, and those who admit to symptoms are likely to be members of groups who do not consider it shameful to have emotional problems or who do not know that the interviewer is probing for evidence of mental illness.

There have been no large-scale studies using the societal reaction perspective. In a small experiment conducted by David L. Rosenhan to test the situational effects of psychiatric diagnoses ("On Being Sane in Insane Places," 1973) eight sane people feigned symptoms of mental illness and were admitted to 12 mental hospitals in five different states. Once in the psychiatric ward, the pseudopatients dropped their pose of abnormality and acted as sane as the setting permitted. Although the lengths of hospitalization ranged from seven to 52 days, none of the hospital staff members (including psychiatrists) detected the hoax, and all the pseudopatients were discharged with diagnoses of schizophrenia "in remission." Later the medical staff at a prominent teaching and research hospital were told that one or more pseudopatients would attempt to gain admission to the psychiatric ward in the next three months; during that period 41 out of 193 actual patients were judged by the

(Page 442) Physician and patient interacting. In order to understand this interaction it is necessary to ask "What's in it?" for both participants. Both obviously feel that they have something to gain from being in this social situation—or they would not be in it. What do you think the patient has to gain? The physician?

staff to be pseudopatients.

These experiments cast some doubt on psychiatric labeling. They provide little or no evidence, however, about how the "true" symptoms of mental illness can be differentiated from pretended symptoms. Such distinctions apparently do exist, for several patients did unmask the pseudopatients. They evidently were able to recognize differences that the staff members could not.

iv Evaluation   Such field surveys provide some support for those who argue that there is a great reservoir of psychological symptoms, only a small portion of which receive treatment. Hollingshead and Redlich showed that the determination of who is seriously mentally ill, who is hospitalized, and who stays in state mental hospitals depends heavily on social characteristics, primarily social class. At this point a large-scale study of "mental illness careers" seems to be necessary, to examine in detail the components of processes that produce current rates of mental illness.

3   Overview

The sociological approach to health and illness shows that phenomena that seem purely biological or physiological are also, because they involve human beings in interaction, social creations. Surveys of populations at large found that the significance and meaning of physical and mental symptoms depend on *cultural values* and acceptable attitudes. As a result, far fewer people use medical services and become patients than those who show symptoms of illness. Those who do become patients tend to act in ways commensurate with their age, sex, ethnic group, religion, race, education, income, and social position. The views of health professionals on proper modes of treatment and on how patients should react further mold the social aspects of illness.

The attempt to determine the social nature of the *health-illness continuum* invokes important questions about the nature of conformity and deviance. The concept of abnormality for which the individual is *not* held responsible, but which he or she *is* expected to do something about, has added a new dimension to the sociology of deviance and social control.

When it comes to social policy, however, this perspective has only identified cultural variations in utilization of health services and cooperation with treatment. Few innovations—such as more responsibility for patients who want it—have actually been tried. The concepts and insights of medical sociology have often been coopted and shaped to the physicians' point of view, so that patients are seen as *management problems* rather than as participants in a *social interaction*. Physicians are human too, but policy makers (usually physicians themselves or those in their hire) still tend to organize medical services as if medical practitioners were always rational, efficient, and completely attuned to the patients' best interests. Administrators have not given serious consideration to the sociological perspective on medical institutions. That perspective sees doctors as workers who are trying to make their work lives as interesting and convenient as possible, patients as consumers who are trying to get the most for their money; and both as having frequently conflicting points of view.

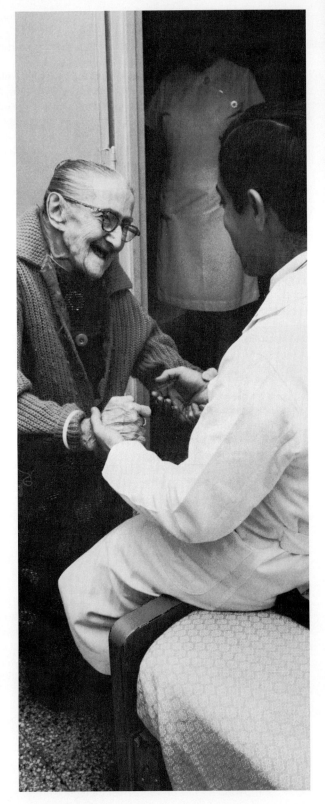

D   LOOKING AHEAD

1   Interview:
Eliot Freidson

Eliot Freidson is professor of sociology at New York University. He is the author of *Patients' View of Medical Practice, Profession of Medicine, Professional Dominance,* and *The Professions and Their Prospects.* He edited *Hospital in Modern Society* and (with Lorber) *Medical Men and Their Work.* He has been an adviser to the National Institutes of Health, the Social Security Administration, and the Social Rehabilitation Service of the Department of Health, Education, and Welfare. He is currently doing research on the social organization of labor.

DPG   *Both mentally and physically sick people find themselves in the hands of "the men in the white coats," the technocrats of medicine who dispense specialized knowledge in connection with the sick. What can be done to respect the human dignity of the individual in this situation?*

FREIDSON   For me the central thing in medicine is the central thing in all the so-called professions. It's the extent to which a professional has really special knowledge that nobody else has, knowledge that in effect really requires you, if you want a certain end accomplished, to put yourself in his hands. But the problem is that to apply that knowledge and that skill, a professional has to do other things about which he doesn't necessarily have any special knowledge. For example, the way you deal with a dying person can be treated both in strictly technical and medical terms and in social and moral terms. While the technical knowledge (concerning electrolytic balance or the state of the heart, for example) is solely in the hands of the doctor, that special knowledge doesn't really qualify a doctor to deal with the ethics and the social interaction involved.

DPG   *In your opinion, should the medical profession be concerned about ethical and social considerations?*

FREIDSON   They have to be. In order to apply their specialized knowledge, they have to assume some attitude toward the other person. They have to make decisions that don't solely refer to, let's say, the state of the heart or the lungs, and they have to apply some social or moral standards. Now

doctors claim that they see so many sick people that they become very wise, and, indeed, some certainly are as individuals. But their technical training does not equip them in any special way to be sophisticated and aware of the moral or social significance of their actions.

On the surface a very easy way of handling this question of significance would be simply to provide the patient with all the information and let him make his own decision. I am a member of the Privacy Committee of the American Civil Liberties Union, and we are working now on the privacy of the

medical record—whether a patient has a right to see his own record and to be informed of his diagnosis and prognosis, including the right to expect to be told he is dying. All kinds of stories have been collected about physicians withholding information, some shocking, some amusing. In one case a doctor told an employer that his butler was dying, but he didn't tell the butler or the other members of the butler's family. Now, patently, who you tell what has nothing whatsoever to do with the doctor's expertise in biology, biochemistry, physiology, or anything else connected with the body.

I personally feel the only way to cope with that issue is by some series of checks and balances, not by just overriding medicine's present autonomy. You can't just throw the expertise out the window and

make it a matter of voting. Furthermore, I also think the physician has some right to protect the way he works. Many medical decisions are made for the convenience of the doctor. For example, a lot of doctors don't want to tell patients that they are going to die, mostly because it creates what they call a "management problem." The doctor is going to have to take a lot of time and trouble. His own anxieties are going to be raised.

Now I can't blame them for wanting to make their work manageable. I want to. Every other worker does. But to make work manageable, doctors have to make work-

related moral and social decisions, and this process is somewhat selfish and doesn't necessarily refer to the patient's needs. It's for this reason that there should be a sort of checks-and-balances negotiative kind of relationship. This relationship is preferable to a situation in which the doctor runs everything for his convenience or one in which the patient makes the doctor simply somebody who cuts to order, like the medieval barbers who used to do the dissection on the table for the surgeon who was watching in the amphitheater. I don't think that medicine should be in the position of just having to do whatever the patient wants—there's not much point in training men so extensively for that.

DPG   *It sometimes seems that humane medical treatment is a privilege rather than a right in this country. The rich person, who can afford to pay for a private consultant, gets individual treatment. The poor person has to go to the clinic, where he is impersonally and perhaps impatiently funneled through the system. What kind of mechanism would you set up to see that a patient is treated as a human being with dignity who has a role to play in ordering his own life?*

FREIDSON   It's not a very imaginative suggestion, but I don't really see any lasting alternative to some kind of representative ombudsman. From what I've seen, most recent attempts to elicit patient participation and to mobilize poorly educated patients have tended either to fizzle out quickly or to damage what good medicine has to offer. I think there has to be some mediating agent

in a very weak position. The ordinary community hospital is totally run by the medical staff; the administration is essentially a custodian, doing housework, and that sort of thing. But they do logically constitute a kind of countervailing force.

An awful lot of people tend to feel that because it is impossible for a profession to regulate itself responsibly, physicians should be reduced to petty administrative functionaries, that their independence and their economic and, for that matter, intellectual power should be routinized by administrative accountability. I would like to feel that there is some chance that workers—and doctors are workers even though they're middle class and very well paid; they practice a skill and they produce goods and services and are not merely paper pushers—could conceivably regulate themselves, particularly if

own gain. I think it's led many people, and governments too, to try to develop programs of "accountability." The thrust of most of the young and therefore freshly thinking sociologists today is to destroy professional power. They don't talk about what they are going to put in its place, though, and that's what worries me. I would rather see if there are ways of developing an honest profession. Some of the techniques Communist China has tried might conceivably be useful. Such solutions ultimately require political power, of course. There's no other way.

DPG   *Patients today have to undergo institutionalized procedure, and doctors are also working within that context. Now it seems to be one thing when the patient is just physically ill but has by medical standards control of his mental faculties and therefore can*

who can be insulated from the medical workers enough so he will not simply be co-opted by them, but who will serve as a spokesman and, in a sense, a guide for all patients, poor or not. That sounds a little paternalistic, though. I do think every man ultimately should have the right of controlling what happens to him, but the problem arises when the knowledge he possesses can be used to do himself harm as well as good. You have to have some sophistication to be able to cope with medical knowledge in a way that will do justice to yourself.

DPG   *Do you think people trained in hospital administration could fill an ombudsman role within the present system?*

FREIDSON   Hospital administration is comparatively weak as an occupation except in the "avant garde hospitals"—big city hospitals, teaching hospitals, and the rest. In many other places hospital administrators tend to be nuns, clerks, nurses, and they are

their arms are twisted with some adequate checks and balances. In part because of the past irresponsibility of physicians, professors, and all the other professionals, however, the trend seems to be toward their becoming functionaries in a ghastly vast bureaucracy.

DPG   *I suppose a lot of physicians would prefer to stay with medicine and concentrate on that instead of being bogged down with a lot of paper work.*

FREIDSON   I didn't make myself clear. The problem is bigger than that. Although there are exceptions, members of prestigious professions are quite blindly selfish in a very immediate shortsighted sense. And they have developed a sort of absolute idea of their freedom—professional freedom, academic freedom, and so on. They deny, ignore, or excuse the deficiences of their work by asserting their freedom to pursue their

make some sort of judgments about the control of his body, and another when a person is mentally ill. Such a person's right to make decisions is removed from him even more than it is from a physically ill patient.

FRIEDSON   In many ways madness is the biggest problem of all, because you might call mad anybody who's unbearable to himself and/or to other people, and you can't find any legitimate cause for the situation except to say that he's crazy. Some people will slap a diagnostic category on it to make it respectable, and this procedure has quite properly been criticized. Now Thomas Szasz says mental illness is just a problem of living, not a disease, but he is basically fighting a semantic war. I'm not defending psychiatry, but unless they find that mental illness, or at least some portions of it, is in fact a sort of chemical, biochemical, genetic malfunction to be treated by conventional medical methods, I think that the problem will always remain. And some institutionalized solutions are necessary. I don't think eliminating it from the category of illness and from the jurisdiction of psychiatry is going to solve the problem. Simply eliminating medical jurisdiction and diagnosis without assuring a humane institutional alternative at the same time will probably eliminate the possibility of any care at all for the poor, and we'll be left with the sanitarium, the rest home, the drying-out place for rich alcoholics of the nineteenth century.

DPG   *What do you think is the major issue in the field of the sociology of medicine?*
FREIDSON   I've already referred to it in part. The issue is a general one—responsible self-regulation on the part of all workers, not just professionals. This issue could be put in Marxist terms, because Marx's whole orientation is that ultimately the worker should be able to control his own destiny. I don't simply put professionals beyond the pale because they are part of the overclass. I think they have a skill and they are committed to their skill, and that's a good thing. The problem is whether they can practice their profession in a way that doesn't sell the public, the client, and everybody else short. I think there are really only three alternatives. One is the current insistence on individual self-interest and freedom in a competitive free market. This insistence stems from the old laissez-faire ideal that permeates Western Europe, the United States, and Britain. It's the idea that if everyone pursued his own ends, everything would come out right. I don't think that concept works. When economic incentives are involved, it becomes even worse. That system is crumbling now. Another way is to organize things in some rationally planned way, with a set of administrators or managers, in theory responsible to the people.

DPG   *Like Plato's philosopher-kings?*
FREIDSON   Not so much philosopher-kings as administrator-kings. They're more likely today to be systems-analyst kings, men who rationalize, break everything down into small units, with every worker doing what the systems-analysts have determined to be an efficient unit of work without awareness of the philosophical conceptions involved. This is the bureaucratic, administrative solution. The Soviet Union and a number of planned economies in socialist societies have tried it, but I think it's bound to fail.

A third way is a kind of syndicalist system. Under such a system workers with some sense of solidarity based on sharing the same problems at work, with commitment to the value of their work, with intellectual and social involvement in their work that gives their life meaning, are somehow also made responsive to the good of the people. If it could be created, I think such an approach would be the most humanly satisfying system. It would require the elimination of barriers between patients and doctors in their interaction over the nontechnical aspects of the work.

For me, the central issue is responsible self-regulation and control. I have to stress again that the professional ideal is a very real and important one and shouldn't simply be thrown out of the window (which is what most people seem to have in mind), nor should it remain subordinate to the ideas of some kind of cost-benefit analysis or systems analysis, ideas predicated on treating people as things and human services as synonymous with automobiles or toasters. A society run on that logic is, to me, a nightmare.

2   Interview:
John H. Knowles

John H. Knowles received the M.D. degree from Washington University in St. Louis and also holds honorary doctorates from several universities. He is president of the Rockefeller Foundation in New York City. He is interested in research on the setting of priorities on medical, agricultural, social, and cultural problems and on economic development in the United States and abroad. He wrote *Respiratory Physiology and Its Clinical Application* and edited *Hospitals, Doctors and the Public Interest; The Teaching Hospital;* and *Views of Medical Education and Medical Care.* Dr. Knowles was general director of the Massachusetts General Hospital in Boston for ten years. In 1969, Dr. Knowles was nominated by President Nixon for the post of Assistant Secretary of Health, Education, and Welfare for Medical Affairs. Dr. Knowles' name was withdrawn by the president several months later because of pressure from an alliance of the American Medical Association and other conservative health delivery institutions.

DPG *Can the medical profession regulate itself? If not, how can more lay control be exerted over it?*

KNOWLES The sociologist will tell you that any professional group is never in the best ultimate position to judge itself. Harold Laski said that experts should always be on tap and never on top. You don't ask the general of the army whether or not to go to war, because he is hired to go to war. You put the statesman above the general. Second, journalists or the public at large frequently root out incompetent members of the various professions when their peers are unable to do so. That isn't to say that the expert pro-

available to them. There are other groups— like the million-dollar beef trusts of the athletic teams, or the very rich who are apt to indulge in medical faddism—who are not getting the quality of care that they should have. There is also a steadily increasing number of medically indigent people in the middle class who cannot afford the skyrocketing costs of care.

DPG *What would be the ideal system of health care in the United States?*

KNOWLES The ideal system would involve responsible producers and responsible consumers. I think 50 percent of the problem is

producers. The almost 1,000 different forms of health insurance that are offered by the private insurance companies should have some standardization; they should insist on quality controls and standards before payments are made. Legislation along these lines could raise the standards of a voluntary private sector.

DPG *Would you say there's a trend toward medical people becoming functionaries in a vast bureaucracy?*

KNOWLES Unfortunately, for the last half century in this country the people who teach medicine and the people who practice it

ducer shouldn't take part in evaluation of the quality of his work. But you've got to have the unbiased, neutral view of the consumer equally represented to make sure the standards and quality of work in any given profession are maintained. That's why, for example, you don't ordinarily put doctors on boards of trustees of hospitals. You have a lay board interpose itself between the expert's interest and the public interest.

DPG *Would you say that the system of health care in the United States today serves the needs of the people adequately?*

KNOWLES It serves large segments of the people, but in our so-called free-market economy certain elements have been left out. Some 25 to 40 million Americans who live in, or border on, poverty certainly do not have health services of acceptable quality

due to the producers and their inadequacies. For example, the average person today often demands X-rays and antibiotics when he has a cold. If a responsible doctor refuses to prescribe such treatment, the patient goes to another doctor who will. Then they all complain about rising costs. Furthermore, we've done an abysmal job in preventive medicine and health education, so that consumers are not as responsible for their own health as they should be.

DPG *Can you see any specific kind of checks-and-balances structure that would assure the layman's involvement in medicine?*

KNOWLES Actual legislation could do it. Blue Cross and Blue Shield have got to represent consumers as much as they do

have seen their role solely as superspecialized technocrats who can function in glorious isolation without any moral or ethical concern about the work they do. I think their inattention to these concerns is reflected by the proliferation of groups who are concerned with these issues of human dignity and social welfare. Some elements of organized medicine and the doctors themselves have now begun to rivet their attention on these concerns. I think that's healthy.

DPG *Sick people find themselves in the hands of the "men in white coats"—the technocrats of medicine who dispense specialized knowledge. What can be done to guarantee respect for the human dignity of the individual in this situation?*

KNOWLES Just knowing about social and humanistic concerns doesn't guarantee a more compassionate person, but the knowledge and perspective of those fields can certainly do a lot to leaven the view of the doctor. Today a premedical college education essentially excludes the liberal arts. Then in medical school the student is drawn into the vortex of superspecialization. Doctors end up as technical "idiot savants."

DPG *Is there any kind of institutional approach or structure that might enable doctors to devote more time to the personalities of their patients?*
KNOWLES There are numerous possibilities. For example, there might be a filtering

mechanism that allows paramedical people to do the routine work with the patient so that when the doctor finally sees the patient he can carry out his unique role of listening to the patient and giving him empathy and understanding, instead of quizzing him about the details of one symptom and then throwing him into the cold clutches of the machines for the next three weeks. Certainly there are a number of ways of automating the routine of medicine so that the doctor and the patient will once again have the satisfaction of the human element, the personal encounter, which is what both of them want.

DPG *Should patients have the right to die without life-prolonging treatment if they choose?*
KNOWLES I think under certain circumstances that the request to reject life-prolonging treatment should be respected. On the other hand, refusal to accept such treatment can be an ultimately selfish act. There are other people involved in the patient's death—children, wives, parents—and they should have some say. Under the duress of chronic illness many people do get discouraged, but when the sun comes up the next day and they have a little less pain, they change their minds. One has to be very careful that one doesn't become a lord high executioner in this process.

DPG *What about the case of the mental patient whose civil liberties have been severely restricted by commitment to a mental institution?*
KNOWLES Clearly, in extreme cases it is necessary to sequester and isolate patients who are either dangerous to the people around them or to themselves. However, there's a large grey area where the question must be asked whether the psychiatrist is representing the patient's interest or the family's selfish interests. Still, in acute situations, you have to rely on the psychiatrist. After that, I think you probably should have the judgment of two doctors.

DPG *How can the health care of the poor be improved?*
KNOWLES Services have to be made more accessible. That can be done either by busing the poor to where the services are or by taking the services on wheels to where they are. Improvement involves a massive health education. It involves more assiduous attempts to bring health education into the school system where the children will at least learn how to get into the system and how to use it, as well as the language of the system. Of course, the health of poor people ultimately depends on the availability of jobs, on decent housing, to say nothing of adequate nutrition. The health of the poor depends to a great degree on our ability to redistribute income and wealth.

DPG *How should scarce medical resources be allocated?*
KNOWLES We are making allocations right now. For example, we've paid a lot of atten-

tion to sickle-cell anemia, even though venereal disease and malignant hypertension are much more important public health problems for black people. I think the priorities are askew. We spend 25 percent of all our personal health expenditures on 10 percent of the population—the 20 million people over the age of 65, the majority of whom are over 70. By contrast, we allocate very little to infant and child care or to the problems of 30 million adolescents, many of whom need help desperately. I think it's in the long-range interests of the country to pay more attention to the beginning of the cycle than to its end. In order to do this effectively, we've got to regain our ability to make certain decisions about life and death and allocate resources to where the needs are most profound, as contrasted to where the votes and the money are.

DPG *What do you think is the major issue in the field of sociology of medicine today?*
KNOWLES One of the major issues is the fact that the medical profession, indeed all members of the health profession, are denied access to the body of knowledge that would assist their overall prospective of the social good. When we talk about the sociology of medicine, we're talking about attitudes and behavior of the consumers of health services, about the economic determinants of who gets these services, about the cultural anthropology of health services, and all those issues that determine how producers and consumers behave. If we had more knowledge of these things, we could structure a much more effective and efficient health service—and a better life for the vast majority of the people.

Unit 20
Sociology of Politics

SCHEMATIC OUTLINE

A Introductory Graphics: Political Periods and the Sociologist

B Definition and Context

1 Definition
The sociology of politics is concerned with the relationship between such basic sociological variables as class, caste, ethnicity, and race and how they intersect and interpenetrate the political variables of power, authority, sovereignty, and representation. The basic concept in this study is power.

2 World Context
The gradual development of Protestantism created an ideological climate that gave individual initiative and the urge for personal power and wealth religious justification.

3 American Context
To discover the social effects of American political ideals, sociologists must look behind and beneath the workings of formal political institutions.

C Questions and Evidence

1 Questions
Sociologists concerned with politics focus on three central questions: (1) Can revolution take place in this country? (2) How is one system of political leadership replaced by another? (3) Why do political organizations sometimes fail to achieve their goals?

2 Evidence
a The "Burning Issue" Question
Theodore Roszak has suggested that Karl Marx's theoretical description of the processes leading to the revolution of the working class must be modified to accord with conditions in contemporary America. Descriptive studies by William Ellis, Kenneth Keniston, and William Hinton indicate that collective goals—which are foreign to most Americans—are essential to successful revolution.
b The "Classical" Question
Karl Marx, Max Weber, and Vilfredo Pareto all developed theories about the processes of political replacement. Their views, based largely on historical documents, tend to be narrow in certain respects but complement one another significantly.
c The "Research" Question
Irving Janis' analysis of groupthink and Christopher Doob's concept of dynamic stagnation, both of which are based on descriptive case studies, provide some insights into the failures of political decision making. Further studies focusing both on group activities and on the wider context of the group members' lives are necessary.

3 Overview
Ideally, sociology should be both historical and biographical in order to portray the raw realities of power.

D Looking Ahead

1 Interview: Irving Louis Horowitz

SUPPORTING UNITS

9 Social Stratification
15 Race and Ethnic Relations
16 Formal and Complex Organizations
21 Sociology of Economics
25 Youth Culture
26 Social Change
27 Social Conflict and Peace

ENCYCLOPEDIA ENTRIES

anarchy
authoritarianism
bureaucracy
capitalism
charisma
class consciousness
communism
conservatism
democracy
dialectical materialism
Durkheim, Emile (1858–1917)
fascism
feudalism
imperialism
iron law of oligarchy
liberalism
Marx, Karl (1818–1883)
military-industrial complex
Mills, C. Wright (1916–1962)
monarchy
neocolonialism
pluralism
political sociology
power elite
progressivism
Protestant ethic
ruling class
socialism
state
totalitarianism
Weber, Max (1864–1920)

POLITICAL PERIODS AND THE SOCIOLOGIST

1. Until the 1960s sociologists tended to
   report "how" society was functioning.

2. In the dissent-ridden 1960s many
   sociologists became troubled along
   with their students as the students
   began to confront the society in a
   critical, activist manner.

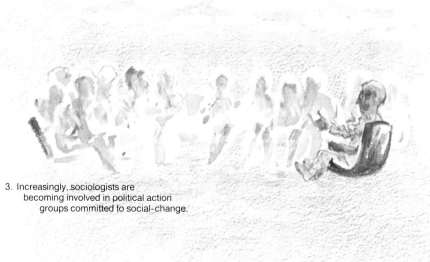

3. Increasingly, sociologists are
   becoming involved in political action
   groups committed to social-change.

"The Big Stick in the Caribbean" (*New York Herald* cartoon, 1905). President Theodore Roosevelt formulated his view of the policy he wished to maintain between the United States and Latin America as "Speak softly, but carry a big stick." Underlying this formulation is the concept of the initially disguised, but ultimately naked, use of power to obtain what United States policy-makers want in terms of international relations.

(Facing page, above) H. A. Ogden's *Signing of the Declaration of Independence, July 4, 1776.* This painting in a patriotic vein depicts various of the Founding Fathers of the United States. *(Below)* Boy coal miners, c. 1909. The social mobility that public schools were and are supposed to facilitate and teach as an accomplished fact is and was largely illusory. Chronic poverty continues to plague our country, the richest on earth. Only when we refuse to "see" the poor can we speak complacently of American accomplishments.

B   DEFINITION AND CONTEXT

1   Definition

As part of its effort to understand group process in general, a portion of sociology studies the processes of government. More specifically, the sociology of politics is concerned with, in the words of Irving Louis Horowitz, *"the relationship between the basic social variables of class, caste, ethnicity and race and how they intersect and interpenetrate the key political variables of power, authority, sovereignty and representation."* (*Foundations of Political Sociology*, 1972)

The political sociologist is especially interested in such questions as: Why has labor moved from the radical to the conservative side of the political spectrum? What is the relation between social class and political activism today? What is the relation between educational attainment and age and voting patterns? How do social systems influence political ideologies? What conditions are particularly favorable to guerrilla insurgency? To what extent does social science legitimate public policy, and to what extent does it foster policy changes? Why do certain disadvantaged minorities support the status quo? What is meant by "the ethnic vote"?

The basic concept of political sociology may not be fully recognized if only *formal systems* of government are studied. That basic concept is *power*—in the simplest relationship, the ability of one person or group to compel another to do what the first wants, whether or not the second wishes to obey.

Political *institutions* alone reveal relatively little about the workings of power. There are an increasing number of books and articles about how political leaders have reached important decisions, but to see power pulsating, one must look beyond such intellectual portrayals of institutions.

2   World Context

Preliterate societies are unified by and structured around specific religious experiences. Their religion, as Emile Durkheim pointed out (see Unit 8), reaches into all institutions of life, including the political. Their sacred sites, rituals, and festivals bring people, they feel, close in space and time to the eternal cycles of the universe. Feeling at one with powers transcending earthly existence, they do not perceive themselves as separate entities. On the whole, societies with such an outlook do not endorse the search for wealth and power, because that process necessarily involves a high degree of personal ambition, and they also have no economic surplus to facilitate the acquisition of power.

Although the drive to accumulate wealth and power certainly did not begin with the Judaeo-Christian tradition, it is likely that it was nurtured by the idea that God had designated the Jews to be his chosen people and led them on a chartered course through history. With Christianity the idea of irreversible progress became clearer. Gradually transcendent rituals receded, and individuals became free to follow their own ambitions.

As also discussed in Unit 8, Max Weber theorized that the religious beliefs of the Calvinists (which he called *the Protestant ethic)* supported the development of Western capitalism. For Calvinists God is an all-knowing, all-controlling deity, and his motives are inscrutable. Each individual's destiny is predetermined, and only an *elect* will be saved. But worldly success can be a sign of *salvation,* failure the proof of *damnation.* Success has no merit in itself, but simply serves as an indication of what is coming—and hard work and good deeds are the only way man can counteract his inherent sinfulness. These concepts combined at the time of the Protestant Reformation to create an ideological climate giving individual initiative and the urge for personal power and wealth religious justification.

3 American Context

Among the early Puritan settlers of America the Protestant ethic provided support for the so-called *free enterprise system.* The individual could exploit Indians, blacks, later immigrants, and even his Anglo-Saxon neighbors. Their own lack of worldly success showed that such people were predestined to be damned. As the Calvinist strongholds in New England began to break up, the explicit influence of religion receded; yet the idea of the value of capitalistic venturing became part of American culture.

But what about American political ideals? The Founding Fathers declared the following beliefs:

Fundamental dignity of the individual, with city, county, state, and country established only to serve him
Equality of individuals, with the pursuit of life, liberty, and property regarded as every individual's inalienable right
Freedom, with each person regarded as entitled to maximum opportunity to select his own life purposes

One school of thought holds that the Constitution was written to keep government off the backs of the people. Another believes the rich and powerful received special attention, that the Constitution was essentially written to keep government off *their* backs. Probably both arguments are correct. In the late eighteenth century this country must have seemed large, rich, and empty enough to permit little restriction upon anybody, rich or poor.

But the fact is that, no matter how noble the Constitution may have been in intention, the document has allowed the spirit of capitalism to go on little checked. From one root, the *primacy of the individual,* has emerged an emphasis upon unrestricted individual rights and, at the same time, the opportunity for the unrestrained pursuit of capitalistic ventures.

Support for American capitalistic democracy also came from unsolicited sources. Touring the eastern United States in the 1830s, the Frenchman Alexis de Tocqueville was impressed:

In America, the most democratic of nations, those complaints against property in general, which are so frequent in Europe, are never heard, because in America there are no paupers. As everyone has property of his own to defend, everyone recognizes the principles upon which he holds it.

The two volumes of Tocqueville's *Democracy in America* (1835, 1840) are filled with cogent insights and impressive predictions. But for him, as for many today, the poor were "invisible."

Many social scientists still claim that Americans have put their political ideals into practice literally. For example, distinguished political scientist Robert Dahl and economist Charles E. Lindblom describe the *pluralistic* tendencies of American government.

> Social pluralism develops a complex distribution of control. . . . Ordinary citizens control their immediate leaders and are controlled by them. These leaders in turn control other leaders and are controlled by them. Hence a society of reciprocal relationships exists to control government policy. (*Politics, Economics, and Welfare*, 1953)

In *Sociology* (1972) Peter and Brigitte Berger argue that political scientists have focused too exclusively on the abstract qualities of the political order and on the behavior of people in the formal activities of institutions, especially voting and participation in political parties. Sociologists, they feel, can examine power "behind and beneath" the formal political structure.

But not all sociologists do so. Talcott Parsons, the most influential American figure in the profession, intended the following as a criticism of C. Wright Mills, who *did* attempt to penetrate beneath the surfaces of political institutions:

> The essential point is that, to Mills, power is not a facility for the performance of function in and on behalf of the society as a system, but is interpreted exclusively as a facility for getting what one group, the holders of power, want by preventing another group, the "outs," from getting what it wants. ("The Distribution of Power in American Society," 1957)

In time, however, Mills has been vindicated. An increasing number of sociologists are wondering whether capitalist democracy can realize its ideals, or whether those ideals can emerge only in a radically different system.

C   QUESTIONS AND EVIDENCE

1   Questions

Sociologists concerned with politics focus on three central questions: (1) Can revolution take place in this country? (2) How is one system of political leadership replaced by another? (3) Why do political organizations sometimes fail to achieve their goals?

2   Evidence

a   The "Burning Issue" Question

i   Context   Since Shays' Rebellion in 1786, right after the establishment of the independent United States, part of our national heritage has been the frequent willingness of a few people to be stirred

Alexis de Tocqueville (1805–1859). Tocqueville was a French aristocrat sent to the United States to study its penal system. He traveled extensively in Jacksonian America and his two-volume *Democracy in America* (1835, 1840) is a classic study of American national character and society, especially the effects of political systems upon the larger social system. Other of his writings, particularly *The Old Regime and the French Revolution,* contributed to the development of early sociology. (Lithograph by Chasseriau)

V. I. Lenin (1870–1924), chief theoretician and organizer of the Bolshevik Revolution of 1917, addresses a crowd of workers. The Bolshevik Revolution overthrew the old ruling class in Russia and accomplished a sweeping redistribution of power and property; much bloodshed occurred in the process. (The famous photo above originally showed Leon Trotsky, like Lenin a revolutionary intellectual, standing to Lenin's left, but under Stalin, Lenin's successor, the photo was "doctored" and Trotsky cut out of it.)

to insurrection when what are supposed to be the rights of all citizens are violated by a few. But any *revolution* that involves more than superficial changes in life style, that actually achieves *massive redistribution of wealth and power,* will not simply happen. It may require violent overthrow of those in control, or perhaps a more gentle overturning, most likely through the electoral process. In any case, sociologists contemplate the possibility of social change as a fundamental overhaul of the existing social structure and culture and ask: *What are the societal conditions that lead to a radical redistribution of wealth and power among people in a society?*

ii   Theory   Karl Marx's revolutionary theory swept across the fields of philosophy, history, economics, political science, and sociology and developed the world's most influential theory of revolutionary change. Marx and Engels viewed revolution in the context of *dialectical materialism*. The term *dialectic* refers to a three-stage process of conflict and reconciliation—thesis, antithesis, synthesis—as history moves forward through successive stages toward its goal. In this interpretation there was a temporarily stable condition *(thesis)* when capitalist society finally emerged from the crumbling feudal order that had produced it. It should be emphasized that Marx viewed capitalism as a higher stage than feudalism. It was, in fact, a necessary step in the evolution toward a still more advanced economic and political order.

Within capitalism the ordinary person must sell his labor, the only thing he has of value, to the capitalist, whose basic concern is to turn money into more money. The worker must labor on the capitalist's farms and in his factories, and for his effort he receives wages. But his wages fall short of the value for which the commodities he produces are sold. The amount beyond his wages is *surplus value,* the profit of the capitalist.

The jobs of the workers, Marx held, would become increasingly specialized and unfulfilling and the *exploitation* by the capitalists more and more pronounced. The opposition of the workers to this exploitation would produce the *antithesis* to capitalism. What was once a stable order would be polarized by the conflict between the contradictory, irreconcilable interests of the owners of the *means of production* and the workers. Marx argued that the workers would eventually become aware of their common plight—would know themselves as a *class*—and then would rise up and overthrow the propertied class, the owners. A *synthesis,* the new order, would emerge when the working people owned all the means of production. Thus Marx predicted the arrival of socialism. This Marxist view is detailed further in Units 4, 9, 16, 21, and 26.

In *The Making of a Counter Culture* (1969) Theodore Roszak suggests that the Marxist model of revolution must be updated to reflect new forms of oppression. Americans now live in a *technocracy* and are expected to accept the following premises:

The vital needs of people are technical and can be solved by formal analysis.

The analysis of our needs is virtually 99 percent complete and whenever something goes wrong, it is only a temporary breakdown in effective systems.

The experts who understand people's needs are employed by government or big business.

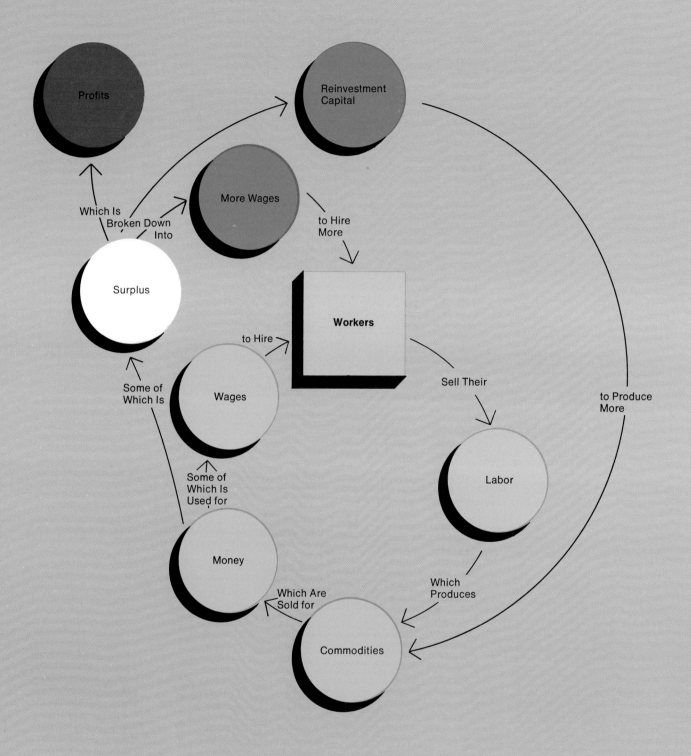

Model 1. Capitalism as a System. There are two fundamental features of capitalism: (1) workers always produce more in commodity worth than they are paid for in their wages; (2) because profits are removed from the flow, the system must constantly expand in order to continue to function.

These assumptions provide no allowance for people's feelings, no acknowledgment of the presence of immense problems in our present society, no opportunity for most people to participate in the decisions affecting their own lives. It is against these conditions, says Roszak, that many young people find themselves in the kind of rebellion we deal with in Unit 25. But *revolution,* actually overthrowing the social system, is of course quite another matter from *rebelling,* simply turning against or away from the values of society.

iii   Research   Let us look at three pieces of research dealing with characteristics of rebellion and revolution and compare these situations with the Marxist model. The first two pieces deal with the groups—blacks and student radicals—currently considered the most opposed to the American establishment. The third piece deals with social change in a foreign country, China.

William Ellis' *White Ethics and Black Power* (1969), a study of a black, antipoverty agency in Chicago, argues that the organization he discusses (the West Side Organization) was revolutionary because its members looked unblinkingly at the oppression of poor blacks in a racist society and asserted themselves in their every act by working to eradicate it. The staff provided jobs that removed people from welfare, but at the same time worked to help those still on it. While helping individuals, the leaders of the organization also became prominent figures in the local black power movements, serving on steering committees and participating in demonstrations. The West Side Organization leaders and their associates planned to offer themselves as replacements for the local politicians in the belief that in their new positions they would be able to meet the needs of their constituents even more effectively.

In *Young Radicals* (1968) Kenneth Keniston studied an upper-middle-class student group trying to mobilize protest against the Vietnam war. They debated whether they should work toward a *cultural revolution,* whose goal would be a full transformation of people's perspectives, priorities, and character, or be content with more modest, *political change,* working toward effective control over misguided governing structures. They could see conditions favoring both courses.

In *Hundred Day War* (1972) William Hinton describes a period of intense activity at Tsinghua University in China that was part of the "Great Proletarian Cultural Revolution," an enormous upheaval in the mid-1960s intended to wipe out entrenched individual ambitions and interests that were diluting the socialist intentions of the original Chinese revolution. Communist Party Chairman Mao Tse-Tung and other Chinese leaders allowed a "war" between student factions to continue for two years without interruption, until any hope that the students would reach peace among themselves had dissipated. The workers, over 30,000 of them, moved onto campus, shouting, "Use reason, not violence. Turn in your weapons. Form a big alliance." A few workers were killed and many wounded, but in two days they broke the fighting of two years.

Then began the problem of reconciliation. The workers explained that both factions were to be commended for seeking to follow the teachings of Chairman Mao, but each was also responsible for the violent division that had developed. They called for each group to weed out those who were "class enemies," who clearly

Great Proletarian Cultural Revolution in China. Youths at a Peking rally in 1966 wave copies of *Quotations From the Thoughts of Chairman Mao Tse-tung.* For several years in China all social factions were urged to wage ideological warfare in order to create a social dialectic that would result in a positive restructuring of the values and priorities of the society. The Cultural Revolution may have been the largest-scale social experiment in the history of the human species and involved great turmoil and loss of life. Its benefits will be ascertainable in coming years.

were pursuing their own interests and not those of the people. Slowly, painfully the members of each faction began to do this, and ultimately reconciliation was reached.

iv Evaluation Ellis' antipoverty workers and Keniston's students certainly opposed the political-economic leaders of the society. In neither case, however, were they simply workers exploited by capitalists. Ellis' informants faced the particular oppression of being *both* black and poor. Keniston's students were not workers at all, and their "revolution" can best be seen from Roszak's perspective, as an opposition to the technocratic order and what it represented, especially the Vietnam war.

Furthermore, neither the antipoverty workers nor the students received much support. In fact, Ellis' informants seem to be saying that revolution is simply "staying in one piece in Whitey's world." Blacks face unique problems that they feel set them in opposition to all whites, even if the latter are also oppressed. This position, of course, is inimical to the Marxist idea of a dialectical process in which all oppressed people will (or should) become aware of their common plight and band together.

But not only blacks see themselves as set apart from the wider society. One of the reasons Keniston's students felt that *they* could not develop a cultural revolution across class and ethnic lines was because their middle-class socialization and education had made them more aware of the potential benefits of such a change than most Americans are. They were *atypical* in a society where individual economic and social success within capitalism remains the cherished goal. In startling contrast the student factions at Tsinghua University shared an underlying sense of common purpose despite their violent differences. In fact, it was that common goal that ultimately annihilated the factionalism.

Collective goals are quite foreign to most Americans. Yet even in the current quiet following the social storms of the late 1960s, efforts to build *revolutionary coalitions* between different ethnic, class, and occupation groups are occurring in scattered locations across the United States. How large a force is needed to initiate an actual revolution is an issue that remains crucial but unresolved. It is clear, however, that a powerful movement for fundamental change can only begin with the sort of modest efforts presently underway.

b The "Classical" Question

i Context Classical sociologists of the nineteenth and early twentieth centuries read widely in modern and ancient history. It is hardly surprising that they were interested in historical questions, including those that concern rulers and the fate of rulers. Many modern political sociologists have realized that replacement is at the essence of power, their basic concept. They ask: *Is the replacement of political leaders a single-factor or multi-factor process, and precisely what sequence of events does it usually involve?*

ii Theory Max Weber developed important ideas about systems of political leadership and their replacement and their connection with moral and technological conditions. Writing with constant awareness of, almost in dialogue with, Marx, who preceded him by several decades, Weber discussed the right of those in authority to

(Facing page) Pentagon power. The expansion of the power of the military-industrial complex has profound implications for Americans at home as well as for the particular peoples against whom the United States government wages war.

command. He argued that whereas *power* concerns single or sporadic acts, *authority* is sustained, and he delineated three systems for legitimating authority—the *traditional,* the *charismatic,* and the *legal-rational.*

In a traditional system the legitimacy of those in authority is maintained by *precedent.* This system most frequently takes a form akin to that of a vast patriarchal family, and violation of its rules is felt to be almost a kind of religious evil. At the same time, the *patriarchal leader* has considerable leeway in his enforcement of the rules.

Weber developed the concept of *charisma* from Rudolph Sohm, a church historian and jurist. The term means "gift of grace" and refers to leaders who are followed because of some extraordinary personal qualities that have enormous appeal to others who are in distress. Such a charismatic leader comes from outside established structures, and in order to do justice to his mission, he must remain outside of them. He gains and holds support simply by the success of his acts. If he is a prophet, he prophesies; as a warrior, he wins battles; as the Son of God on earth, he walks on water —or at least is reported to do so. The charismatic leader knows no earthly laws. He establishes a movement that unquestionably is revolutionary.

But it is also a movement that is unstable. The authority of the system depends on the charismatic leader himself, and when he leaves, dies, or simply loses his touch, it is difficult for a replacement to retain the same personal loyalty that has been pledged to him. Hence the charisma becomes *routinized,* loses its excitement, its spark, and becomes boring, merely routine. (We have discussed *charisma* in connection with religion in Unit 8.) The system centered

Styles of leadership: *(top row, left to right)* Martin Luther King, John F. Kennedy, Indira Gandhi, Jomo Kenyatta; *(bottom row, left to right)* Mohandas K. Gandhi, Golda Meir, Robert F. Kennedy, George C. Wallace. How many of these famous twentieth-century leaders could be considered charismatic? Mohandas K. Gandhi, leader of the Indian independence movement, clearly was, but what about Indira Gandhi, present Prime Minister of India? How does Indira Gandhi compare with Golda Meir, Premier of Israel? How does John F. Kennedy compare with his brother, Robert F. Kennedy? How does American nonviolent civil rights leader Martin Luther King compare with Jomo Kenyatta, founder of the Mau Mau and current president of Kenya? How does King compare with segregationist leader George C. Wallace? How many twentieth-century leaders have suffered violent deaths at the hands of political enemies?

around the charismatic leader may be replaced by a traditional system, with the authority carried through the *blood line* of the charismatic leader's descendants.

On the other hand, if the office, not the person, becomes the source of authority, the legal-rational system appears. This system can also evolve out of traditionalism and, like charismatic movements, can bring about massive change. In all areas of life it substitutes *rational practice,* in which there is a logical relationship between means and ends in social activity, for traditional order.

Legal-rational systems are maintained by *bureaucracies.* Each bureaucracy has a fixed area of jurisdiction, levels of graded authority, a staff to maintain the written documents on which the office is based, rational expertise, and rules which govern the behavior of all. In a modern, complex society such as our own the amount of bureaucratic detail that penetrates into the lives of all of us is staggering. The nature and functions of bureaucracy were described in Unit 16.

The replacement of one *authority system* by another, Weber argues, is a complex process involving the intellectual, psychic, political, economic, and religious spheres. Given this complexity, power-seeking is an unpredictable, irrational process. No one can anticipate the effects of his actions in such an arena.

Vilfredo Pareto, an Italian contemporary of Weber, developed a theory involving the *circulation of two types of elites* and presented it in *The Mind and Society* (1916). One of his starting points was the concept of *residue*—a basic human drive that, unlike an instinct, has considerable flexibility in its social manifestation.

Pareto described six classes or complexes of residues, two of which provide the foundation for a political theory. The *residue of combination* produces an innovative and reflective but inactive approach to life, and the *residue of the persistence of aggregates* generates an active effort to maintain a conservative condition in society.

Pareto also described *derivations,* the speech reactions or ideologies used to veil the basic quality of these residues. Different derivations and actions often hide the same residue. For example, one man might openly express intolerance for any religious beliefs different from his own and another stridently condemn intolerance of any sort, yet the residue would be the same in each case—an effort to impose on others one's own beliefs and standards. Human behavior, according to Pareto, is generally illogical because most of the time individuals are subjected to residues that contradict each other.

Throughout history, however, certain individuals emerge who have primarily residues of combination; these are the *"foxes."* Others have mostly residues of persistence; these are the *"lions."* The foxes are manipulators, and when they predominate in a government, they engage in reforms. Eventually they will bring about their own downfall by softness, plasticity, and corruptibility. Their successors, the lions, emphasize duty, determination, willpower, and decisiveness. They are rigid and unbending, and eventually the scheming foxes appealing to the need for change will be able to overthrow them. Thus the cycle of replacement goes on and on indefinitely.

iii   Research (Survey)   Both Weber and Marx are more inclined to

Vilfredo Pareto (1848–1923). Pareto's analyses of income distribution led him to the belief that inequality was inherent in the nature of things. His theory of elites dealt with decay and division within a ruling class and conflicts among elites as the prelude to revolution. Social stability, in his theory, required the "circulation of elites," that is, access to the ruling class by talented newcomers and elimination of less-fit members of the elite. His works, such as the million-word *The Mind and Society* (1916), are often said to have influenced the development of Italian fascism.

see the source of power coming from outside the individual than is Pareto, who sees it emerging from within, from one's own residues (though Weber's charismatic form of authority is close to Pareto's view). Like Marx, Pareto deemphasizes values and ideology: he sees derivations as subordinate to residues, just as Marx argued that all institutions are shaped by economic conditions. But Weber —as was apparent in the discussion of the Protestant ethic—suggests that *ideology*—that is, values in general—can help determine *power arrangements.*

To both Pareto and Weber, at least in his charismatic authority system, the individual is the focus of power. Marx, on the other hand, unequivocally contends that power emerges out of the economic system—whether feudalism, capitalism, or socialism. Both Pareto and Weber consider power-seeking irrational and uncontrollable, a mighty force that descends upon society in varying forms and with unpredictable results. For Marx, however, power-seeking is fully rational, and on the part of the workers is a banding together of economically oppressed people for the distinct purpose of overthrowing the oppressors and establishing an equitable distribution of wealth. But Marx considers capitalism as ultimately irrational—it nurtures the conditions for revolution against itself and so contains the seeds of its own destruction—whereas Weber designates it as rational, with bureaucracy the epitome of that rationality.

iv Evaluation   More than simply presenting a theory, Marx presented a call to action, to revolution, and he mapped a way for its rational achievement. His was a narrow view, ready for action. Weber, on the other hand, was basically a scholar rather than activist, and although he was a liberal in his day, he was no supporter of socialism. He set out to look at power in all its sociological diversity, but, though critical of capitalism in some ways, he basically supported it. Here his view was quite narrow: it lacked the exhaustive, highly critical approach pursued by Marx, especially in the three volumes of *Capital* (1867, 1885, 1894).

Both Marx and Weber appear to favor whichever system they approach narrowly, seeing it as rational; those systems that they do not favor are analyzed much more thoroughly and deemed irrational. Marx's analysis of capitalism as a system is more penetrating and revealing than Weber's; but Weber's examination of power relations adds interesting dimensions to Marx's outlook. But both approaches are limited not only by personal bias, but also by the material used by the theorists—*historical material.*

c The "Research" Question

i Context   The sociologist examining an organization that fails in its fundamental purposes is like a doctor with a sick patient. He may see signs of visible disease, he can ask questions, but he knows he must do a thorough examination. He is studying the most intimate functioning, or malfunctioning, of the group, not just in terms of static goals but to determine the processes leading to those goals.

Such organizational or small-group research must consider the context of the whole society. After all, the individual who is attending a meeting of an organization has not discarded all his previous values, beliefs, and knowledge. Sociologists therefore ask:

What are social and psychological factors that influence the success political groups and organizations have in achieving their goals?

*ii   **Theory***   In *Victims of Groupthink* (1972) psychologist Irving Janis argues that the greater the cohesiveness (sense of shared values, interests, and activities) within a group, the more likely critical thinking is to dissipate. It will tend to be replaced by *groupthink* —that is, the amiable, conflict-free, and, above all, uncritical resolution of issues, often carried through with enormous expense to *out-groups.*

There is precedence for this proposition in small-group research (see Unit 11), but Janis' conclusion is based upon the analysis of several political-military events—the unsuccessful Bay of Pigs invasion in 1961, the abortive American effort to invade North Korea in 1950, the unpreparedness for invasion at Pearl Harbor in 1941, and the escalation of the Vietnam war. He argues that the process of groupthink emerges out of an unyielding belief in group invulnerability, morality, and unanimity; a stereotyping of the enemy; collective rationalization of basic assumptions; and group pressure and self-imposed pressure against deviant views.

Sociologist Christopher Doob observed a four-stage process in an anti-poverty agency and argues that it frequently occurs in political organizations, especially those seeking reforms:

1. There is a primary task directed toward a goal that is collective and perhaps revolutionary.
2. Although the staff members emphasize the priority of this task, they spend little time engaged in it, because firm pursuit would mean a head-to-head confrontation with powerful economic and political representatives, who would be adversely affected by such action.
3. There are two ways in which the staff can reduce or conceal this gap between word and deed. (a) Certain secondary, less volatile tasks can absorb staff time and, if these are performed adeptly, little time will remain for the primary goal. (b) Staff members sympathetic to the primary goal can claim that certain powerful people directly related to their organization are dangerous adversaries and are hampering its success. Probably such claims are no mere ruse; these individuals believe their own words of indictment.
4. The relationship with the strategic enemies is a precarious one. They must have high social status; otherwise they would not justify the attention. Furthermore, they must be people with whom the members of the organization have frequent contact and on whom they are dependent. The staff members must sustain public relations with them in order to survive as an organization, but must be disparaging of them in private if they wish to maintain the respect of their colleagues and their own respect.

Public outbursts may occasionally bridge the inconsistency between the prevailing public and private images, but these are infrequent. Usually the struggle is to stabilize the inconsistency. Doob terms this ongoing process to preserve an inconsistent position *dynamic stagnation.*

iii   Research (Methodology)   To examine the Bay of Pigs invasion, which he calls the "perfect failure" of groupthink, Janis uses material from the accounts of President John Kennedy's advisors and aides who were participants in the decision making, especially Arthur M. Schlesinger, Jr.'s *A Thousand Days* (1965), which contains extensive coverage of their meetings. As these sources report, on April 17, 1961, a brigade of about 1,400 Cuban exiles assisted by American armed forces and the Central Intelligence Agency invaded Cuba at the Bay of Pigs. All plans broke down, and by the third day some 1,200 members of the brigade, virtually all those who had not been killed, were captured. The venture was clearly badly planned. From the beginning, the President and his advisors miscalculated the strength of the Cuban air force, overestimated the collective morale of the invading forces, underestimated the strength of the Cuban army, and even failed to scan a map to discover that the escape route was a geographical impossibility.

Groupthink emerges from group cohesiveness that is, paradoxically, created and maintained by the leader. Any threats to its continuance are squashed. In this specific case Schlesinger wrote memos criticizing the prospective invasion. When he finally voiced weak criticism in a meeting, Attorney General Robert Kennedy, the President's brother, took him aside and explained that the decision had been made to go ahead and that only support for the President was expected. In the meetings run by President John Kennedy there was actually little or no opportunity for a discussion of the course of action that had been planned. Undersecretary of State Chester Bowles, who had opposed the whole program from the beginning, was fired soon after the fiasco.

Doob's theory is based on a 15-month examination of a federally funded antipoverty organization with a staff of 14 people, primarily poor, black, and female. The staff members, especially the leaders, said one task was most important—*community organizing.* The staff members would seek out common problems from among the local poor, unite them in neighborhood groups, and then explain how to engage in various protest actions demanding changes in the oppressive conditions of their lives. The essential purpose of such organizing was to enable poor people to remove the control of their destiny from the powerful and assume it themselves—that is, to attain power.

It was soon apparent, however, that although the leaders continued to discuss organizing, most of their time and energy was devoted to a series of much easier, short-term tasks. Those tasks received considerable recognition from local, often prominent, individuals and groups and did not create much controversy. The leaders realized that they could not organize effectively. If they did, they would be out on their ears.

Their solution, apparently an unconscious one, was to fixate upon the board of directors and other white, middle-class groups as strategic enemies. In the privacy of agency meetings, the leaders would explain that the board members had to be watched carefully, or they would disrupt the organization and make it impossible to carry on the work being done for the local poor. Such statements were made only in private. The leaders maintained cordial relations with their "strategic enemies" in public. And those strategic enemies did little to justify the attention they received: they were stodgy and uncooperative but not dangerous. Yet, as prominent local individuals overseeing the local antipoverty agency, they were sitting ducks for the label of oppressor. All in all, as long as the leaders continued the private attacks upon board members their militant *public image* and *self-image* was assured—even though they did not organize poor people.

iv   Evaluation   Both of these theories barely touch on the driving force of *personal ambition.* Above all, they tend to disregard the intimidating effect of the group leader. Janis certainly acknowledges the influence of the leadership role but does not give it the powerful position that his facts would suggest. He sees the Bay of Pigs decision as a perfect example of groupthink failure. But the researcher must also realize that the members of the organization he is scrutinizing do not exist only in the group context where he sees them.

3   Overview

In *The Sociological Imagination* (1959) C. Wright Mills said that sociology should be about history and biography, about the lives of real people set within the historical context of their society. The *historical context* gives breadth; the *biographical focus,* broader than the mere psychological, gives concreteness. To understand the raw realities of political power both of these dimensions must be considered. Unfortunately they are often lacking in the research done by political sociologists, research that in content or method or both emphasizes the unusual, the obscure, the esoteric rather than issues of significant concern to people.

Students with guns. Black students emerge from a building they occupied in a protest at Cornell University in 1969. The blacks felt that they needed the arms to protect themselves against white students and police. Considerable research was conducted to explain this event, and recommendations were made to improve the situation for the faculty and students. This social-science research was largely ignored by the Cornell board of trustees.

D   LOOKING AHEAD

1   Interview:
Irving Louis Horowitz

Irving Louis Horowitz is professor of sociology and political science at Rutgers University and chairman of the sociology department at Livingston College. He is also director of Studies in Comparative International Development at Rutgers. Professor Horowitz is author of a number of works in political sociology, including *Radicalism and the Revolt Against Reason, The War Game, Three Worlds of Development, Professing Sociology, The Knowledge Factory, The Struggle is the Message,* and *Foundations of Political Sociology.* He is editor-in-chief of *Society* magazine.

DPG   *What are your most prominent satisfactions and fears about the current American political scene?*
HOROWITZ   I have more prominent fears than satisfactions. This results from the fact that the United States is shifting from a political society as a mass activity to a policy-making society based upon elite activity. And this shift has been the critical factor and dynamic since the onset of the New Deal. The Nixon era is thus not the repudiation of New Dealism, but, at the organizational level, the fulfillment and the completion of the New Deal impulse toward a solution of problems through expertise rather than popular will. This situation leads to what has been called a genteel fascism, which has none of the overt manifestations of European degradation—no holocaust or concentration camps— but which has the essential elements of the fascistic system—decision making through gubernatorial fiat and the statist management of the bourgeoisie, the proletariat, and the marginal classes in society. These managerial concepts are accompanied by the rise of a technocracy within the federal administration. This kind of genteel fascism is prominent not only in the United States but in many other advanced industrial societies, whose commitments to democratic channels

have become eroded over time—such as Germany and France. Under different rubrics and different conditions, bureaucratic statism prevails even in the Soviet Union. What you really have, political and ideological labels aside, is a tremendous and widening gulf between masses and elites, servants of power and masters of power.

One other depressing aspect of the current situation is that the masses have reacted more like Ortega y Gasset's masses than like Karl Marx's classes. The masses have renounced responsibility, not simply because they are oppressed, but because they have a revulsion from responsibility and an oversimplified model of life in which their pressure brings significant relief to them. Political elites do not function in American life as simple conservative elites. They function as a repository of the total spectrum of sentiment and opinion—liberal and conservative. The danger is that the elites are fighting out within their own stratum what the masses should be fighting out in the citizen arena. As a result, elites are more likely to make mistakes than masses, on the simple premise that fewer people making decisions make more mistakes than when greater numbers of people participate. Even the articulate critical factions who are no longer content with labels and who are seriously attempting to participate in the universities and in government represent, in effect, a counterelite, a counterestablishment rather than an anti-

establishment. As such, such countercultural forces have the limits and the constraints of any elite groups, whatever may be their political or ideological characteristics.

DPG   *Did technocratic decision making contribute to the United States involvement in the war in Indochina with virtually no dissent among the people in the government?*
HOROWITZ   The plain irony is that the United States entered the Vietnam war and the United States exited from the Vietnam war in roughly the same manner—as a response to elite decision making rather than to mass pressure. Now I realize that there was a strong peace movement, but I also know that this social force reached its high point in 1968. When the war was actually brought to a halt in early 1973, the peace movement had all but dissolved in a miasma of internal confusion. As a result, I do not believe that it is accurate, numerically, historically, or analytically, to claim that the end of the war was any less elitist in character than the beginning of the war. The American public was able to accept with equanimity and calm the savage and routine bombing of Hanoi only a week or two before the winddown actually occurred. This constitutes considerable evidence for the absence of mass

participation as the key to the end of the Vietnam war. The character of the war from beginning to end, within the American policy context, was defined by elites and not by masses. (It is just not possible to think of Henry Kissinger as less elitist in character than Robert McNamara.) As a result, the American nation remains prone to other kinds of foreign adventures in the future; although perhaps not as blatant or as damaging as the Vietnam war.

DPG   *Do you feel, then, that massive protest movements are unable to produce meaningful changes in our society?*
HOROWITZ   Mass movements are necessary as a form of protest in the same way counterelite activity is a form of protest. Very often people raise the question of mass protest as if it were in contradistinction to elite forms of protest. In point of fact, the real issue is always what side of an issue we are drawn to. The question of street demonstrations, or the question of mass activity generally, is a tactical question—not a matter of principle, but a matter of moment. Once seen in this way, the sorts of protest activities engaged in by ordinary people can be dealt with empirically, rather than dogmatically.

DPG   *Social scientists were unable to predict the civil rights movement and the youth movement in the early 1960s. Do you feel that there will be major political protests in the near future?*
HOROWITZ   It is true that certain conservative wings, certain behaviorists and functionalists were completely unable to predict mass movements. The dominant wing of social science was unable to perceive *any* future. Their frame of reference is functional analysis and is thereby restricted to *that which is* rather than to *that which is coming* into existence. But some social scientists, including myself, did understand that there would be a period of mass movement and mass social change, and there are considerable writings to this effect. It is important to bear in mind that, like everyone else, some social scientists are right and some are wrong. Some had a historical vision, and some did not. It is not a matter of correct or incorrect predictions in this area, but rather of a generic inability to deal with prediction

as the essential task of explanation within the social sciences. There is a methodological problem involved relating to the nature of social science itself. Does social science have any responsibility to address itself to questions of prediction or explanation? This question goes to the heart of problems of the philosophies of social sciences and not simply to the question of ineptitude in this area of political sociology.

But you also asked what the future looks like. My feeling is that the 1970s will be a period of consolidation of the protest era. Not a defeat or a rout, but a consolidation. Retrenchment in terms of mass action is obviously taking place. This is self-evident to everyone. But students do have more options than they had in the past. Marginal groups are more widely accepted. Alternate life styles have insinuated themselves more thoroughly than at any time in the past. Sexual revolution, stylistic innovation, the drug culture, and so on, have taken place, and there is no going back at the social and cultural levels. However, it would be dangerous to consider all these gains as somehow nonpolitical or politically neutral in character. They represent a somewhat peculiarly American pattern of undulating currents of overtly cultural and covertly political phenomena that are called "social." America is a land that is highly sociological. People think, act, and dream in terms of family units, personal units, community organizations. Their notion of direct political behavior and political participation is still quite remote and consists largely of letting the "politicians" run the world. This situation has broken down to some extent with the ongoing politicization of all American cultural life and cultural forms. But cynicism about the political machinery has led to a generalized cynicism about the political process as such. And this only reinforces elitism.

DPG   *What do you feel is the role of the sociologist in contemporary political events?*
HOROWITZ   For most sociologists, participation in political events represents very little more than citizen participation. Now there is a relatively small group of social scientists whose inputs are both real and extensive at

national, state, and local levels. These people are consultants, who prepare reports and do research. They make a real contribution to policy making, because they are largely responsible for those inputs of exact information and knowledge that permit policy to be made. The main point to note about the Moynihans and the Kissingers and their less well-known colleagues is that they are *not* responsible for making policy, so much as they are for executing and evaluating policy. A great deal of confusion at this level results from the ideas of such outstanding scholars of an earlier generation as Harold Lasswell and Paul Lazarsfeld and Bernard Berelson, who assumed an autonomous policy-making role for social scientists that they actually did not have. The truth of the matter is that social scientists are, if anything, legitimizers. We legitimate certain political positions and postures. We have a notion of constituency. We have a notion of doing a service on behalf of a client. And we have a notion of truth as partisan, rather than as transcendental. Social scientists must never forget they are performing a service. They legitimate a policy. They rationalize a policy. They accelerate policy discussions among certain select constituencies. They poke logical holes in policies already made. But they do not *make* the policy. The belief that they do make policy was the Great Functionalist Fallacy. Thus, before we discuss participation, we should be both more aware and more modest as to what sorts of participations (as social scientists) are currently practiced.

DPG   *Do you think social-science findings can be misused by policy makers?*
HOROWITZ   There is no doubt that such fears are well-founded. A considerable part of my own work has been dedicated to showing just how such misuse has happened. On the other hand, all information has the potential of being used by different kinds of people. Different constituencies use social science findings for different ends. All social scientists face the problem of having the work that we do employed by people that we do not necessarily agree with. How-

ever, the central problem is not the misuse of information, but rather the simple *use* of information. Very little information generated by social scientists is actually used in a creative or an imaginative way by government apparatuses or policy-making agencies. Social scientists presume that the people "out there" are breathlessly waiting to take their information and convert it to immediately negotiable ends. In fact, it is extremely difficult to get constituencies to use any sort of exact information in their decision-making processes. Even when you are not concerned with the abuse of the material by the political powers that be, you have to worry about the frequent failure of imagination of the minority constituencies you do appeal to. It is extremely hard to get minority groups to sponsor exact research—or to get labor unions to sponsor precise social science analysis on their own practices. With considerable cause, they are often afraid that the information will be misused by people who have power. But much greater utilization of information by the organizational fabrics and frameworks that one designates as underprivileged, undernourished, under-rewarded would help correct the current imbalance in the uses of information. Informational cloture, trying to prevent access to data, is both counterproductive and leaves present power arrangements unchanged.

DPG *If you have one idea or concept about political sociology that you could be certain to lodge in the heads of students in introductory sociology, what would it be?*

HOROWITZ The paramount idea, for me at least, is that the twentieth century is the age of political sociology just as the nineteenth century was the age of political economy. In the twentieth century the essential pivot is the relationship between social class and political participation. I do not simply mean voting. Voting may prove one of the least significant acts of political participation, especially in the majority of cases where the multiparty system either has broken down (as in parts of Europe or Latin America) or where it never existed in the first place (as in parts of Asia and Africa). This relationship is as important in understanding the dynamics of the twentieth century as the relationship between occupational classes and the mar-

ket exchange system was in understanding the nineteenth century. The base of society is no longer the "free market." It is now increasingly the political marketplace—increasingly a matter of fiscal allocation and decreasingly a matter of economic production. As the societal base and superstructure have been transformed, the character of the relationship of society to politics and of society to the economic system also alters. That is the key to understanding the twentieth century: the domination of the political-military-bureaucratic apparatus of the economy, or at least the parity of all of these social sectors.

DPG *Would you say then Marx's analysis of society and how change might be brought about in society is essentially outdated?*

HOROWITZ No. Marx is not outdated. Classical political theory may be altered, augmented, amplified, but rarely is it outdated. This is for the obvious reason that people who raise basic issues in "normative

theory"—whether Plato, Aristotle, Vico, Hobbes, or Marx—deal with the interrelationship of empirical events to moral judgment; and, though events change, the moral judgments remain far more constant. Marx said early in his career, in opposition to the German idealist tradition, that he and his colleague Engels were embarked on a uniquely scientific socialist crusade in which they would move analysis from elites to masses, from idealism to naturalism, from mechanistic to dialectical modes of reasoning. And in the realm of political sociology, this emphasis meant a transformation of the weapon of criticism into a criticism of weapons.

Marx and Engels never ignored military and political factors. Their major work focused on state power and political power, on the forms in which social classes triumph and are defeated. It is true that Marx and Engels studied economic systems, but it is not true that they were economic determinists who always assumed that the economic factors had base relationships in connection with the other superstructural phenomena. By the time Marx prepared his *Critique of the Gotha Programme,* he and Engels were dealing in hard, straight-ahead political analysis and political programatics. The seizure of State power, rather than the change in productive modes became central in their definition of the social system. This aspect is what most captivated Lenin, specifically the idea of the dictatorship of the proletariat. The older Marx and Engels became, the more they came around to realizing that economic units were not the only critical factors, that political and military factors were at least as critical in determining the present condition and future aims of a society.

DPG *Is that one of the major points you make in your book* The Foundations of Political Sociology?

HOROWITZ That is the overriding theoretical point of the book, its alpha and omega. But from that theme developed a number of other points. For example, the world is broken down differently today from the way it was in the nineteenth century. The twentieth-century world is divided in terms of national systems no less than economic systems. It is also broken down in terms of policies and policy options rather than politics as an activity of the bourgeoisie. It is broken down in terms of military inputs in contrast to civilian sectors. Militarism has become a major study area of political sociology. The military factor is enormously important, because it is one of the essential ways in which bureaucratic change is made in the twentieth century.

All of these considerations axiomatically derive from the collapse of the notion of base and superstructure and a recognition that politics is not a superstructure or a reflex action of economic systems, but very real and fundamental in and by itself. Under the fascist state Hitler did not take orders from the bourgeoisie. He gave *them* orders. That was also true in the United States under the New Deal. It remains largely true throughout the technocratic welfare states of Western Europe. One can no longer seriously speak of the bourgeois class defining and determining the nature of political state outcomes. Rather, the State has come to have a reality and an autonomy all of its own. The bureaucratic base is employed by and owes its allegiance exclusively to the State. The military sector of the State is but the advanced power guard of the State. In this situation the idea of the State as simply the repository of bourgeois power or

proletarian power is simply a nineteenth-century anachronism. We live in a far more ferocious epoch precisely because the State is not responsible for its authority to any of the traditional classes; but acts with an autonomy and an independence that derives from having power, and not simply exercising power on behalf of others. The State is thus the center of gravity, and not the class. It is the source of law and of lawlessness, of peace and of war, of order and of change. Thus to speak of social change has led invariably to further talk of social revolution. In the popular imagination the State has come to play a central role—for better or for worse—and on this, the popular imagination has understood things rightly.

DPG *What are some of the major problems with contemporary sociology as a discipline?*
HOROWITZ One of the important problems relates to the boundaries of the sociological imagination. The question is: what does sociology study beyond the platitudes of interaction? In the past deviant behavior was one boundary and normative behavior the other. But there has been a decline in the knowledge of what constitutes normative behavior and deviant behavior; or better, a declining belief that such labeling categories have any meaning. The world has simply changed. The difference between marginal political behavior and deviant sociological behavior is quite slim. It is hard to know if a theft is criminal or political, especially if the money is turned over to a political movement in the classical tradition of anarchist "revolution of the deed." Further, it is hard to know whether the kind of symbolic rape that Eldridge Cleaver talks about in *Soul on Ice* is an intentional act of deviant behavior or a symbolic retribution for historical injustices. We are moving into a period of American life where the boundaries of both sociology and political science are shifting. One of the main problems for the social sciences is in defining its position in relation to the physical and biological sciences and worrying less where sociology leaves off and political science or psychology commences.

DPG *In which directions do you think sociology will move in the near future?*
HOROWITZ There are now many contradictory tendencies in the field. First, greater

attention is being paid to historical subject matter. Second, sociology will probably continue to devote critical attention to its own past performances. There will be more study of sociological methodology, the study of the sociology of sociology, more of what's been called reflexive approaches to sociology, critical approaches. Third, there may be more attempts to deal with the crucial question of ways to study large macro units with the same degree of efficacy as one studies small group units in the laboratory. Do large phenomena involve the same kind of parameters, the same sorts of measurements? Are there such phenomena as middle-range analysis or middle-range phenomena? These are some of the areas that have to be dealt with in the near future.

This pluralization of the field is healthy—following as it does a rigorous succession of monisms, from organicism to functionalism. It is also a reflection of the growing impact the political culture has had on the life of sociology as a profession: from the legitimacy of overseas research for government agencies to the worthwhileness of domestic research for minority and underprivileged groups. There are, of course, crudities and exaggerations in any such broad-scale reawakening or renaissance. Justice and history rarely form a perfect isomorphic coupling. Nonetheless, the big lessons have been learned: sociology is dedicated not just to social problems, but to political solutions. And beyond that, sociology exists to serve society, and not the other way around. Hence, we must better understand the nature of social structure and social change themselves if we are to come to a truer understanding of the life of sociology and sociologists.

Unit 21
Sociology of Economics

SCHEMATIC OUTLINE

A Introductory Graphics: Economic Life and Social Stratification

B Definition and Context

1 Definition
The sociology of economics studies the social relations of production and consumption and the influence of economic institutions on social organization and social change.

2 World Context
Modern economic development, which has affected most of the world in the past 200 years, has involved changes in the class structure of societies, the basic beliefs and values of individuals, and the nature of work.

3 American Context
Although the United States has the most successful economy in the world in terms of per capita consumption, many of its social problems—including economic inequality and discontent with work—are clearly related to its economic institutions.

C Questions and Evidence

1 Questions
Typical of the sociologist's questions about work are: (1) Does industrial efficiency necessarily require a large and relatively powerless labor class controlled by a small and relatively powerful elite? (2) Does a person's work have total impact on his or her life, or can it be separated from leisure, family, and culture? (3) How do education and socialization prepare young people for work positions?

2 Evidence
a The "Burning Issue" Question
Theoretical criticism and empirical research have shown that the traditional economic concept of the labor market is not realized in modern organizations. Efficient production as well as worker satisfaction tend to be subordinated to the need of the bureaucracy to retain its control.
b The "Classical" Question
Karl Marx, Max Weber, Robert K. Merton, and Talcott Parsons developed theories about the relationship between work and personality. Although all of these theories defy simple statistical verification, there is clear evidence of the impact of work on all aspects of the individual's life.
c The "Research" Question
A great deal of evidence indicates that the nature of work and the class structure that derives from the capitalistic hierarchy have a strong influence on family life and education. Those agencies of socialization, in turn, tend to limit rather than expand job opportunities for lower-class individuals.

3 Overview
Although the United States is in theory a democracy, its economic system tends to perpetuate inequalities of opportunity and income.

D Looking Ahead

1 Interview: Kenneth E. Boulding

SUPPORTING UNITS

ENCYCLOPEDIA ENTRIES

ECONOMIC STRUCTURE AND SOCIAL STRATIFICATION

1. **Production.**
In all societies a basic
minimum amount of
food must be
produced.

2. **Surplus.** When more than the
minimum amount of food is produced,
a surplus is available.

3. **Control.** Persons or groups acquire
the right to collect and redistribute
the surplus.

4. **Social Stratification.** Once they can
pass these privileges on to their heirs,
the society is stratified.

B   DEFINITION AND CONTEXT

1   Definition

Economics is the study of the production and consumption of goods and services. Economic theory attempts to answer many diverse questions that relate to social life. What particular goods and services are produced and in what quantities? How does production change to meet shifts in the demands of consumers? How is production allocated among such components as consumption and investment in factories and machines and among such social services as hospitals, roads, and schools? How is the distribution of income among individuals determined, and how can it be altered? Under what conditions does the market efficiently regulate economic activity, and when must political controls be employed? What determines the rate of inflation and unemployment? What are the sources of economic growth?

Such questions are the daily fare of economists, but they are only marginally related to sociology. Indeed, the vast majority of economists are quite unconcerned with matters outside the realm of prices, wages, and profit rates. Nevertheless, many have expressed interest in the ways in which economic activity and social behavior mutually affect each other. One can claim that it is no more possible to understand economic life without considering the social situations that surround it than it is to comprehend social activity without analyzing its economic characteristics and contexts. Hence there is an important place for sociology in economics, and for economics in sociology.

The sociology of economics studies the social relations of production and consumption and the influence of economic institutions on social organization and social change. Some sociologists are also interested in the mutual interactions between economy and social structure—or, indeed, in the ways social organization influences economic institutions. For example, they might study the different social factors in China and Japan that led to the development of strikingly dissimilar economic systems in both countries following World War II.

Automobile assembly line and a factory parking lot. The nature of the system of production has direct implications for the nature of socially organized behavior.

2 World Context

Brewing for hundreds of years on the European continent, the Industrial Revolution erupted vigorously in England in the late eighteenth century and spread quickly in the nineteenth century to France, Germany, the United States, Japan, and other nations. Today scarcely any area of the world is unaffected by modern economic development. Those nations in Asia, Africa, and Latin America that retain the vestiges of preindustrial society are labeled "underdeveloped" and the worth of their political regimes is judged by their success in emulating European and American patterns. Thus the main issues in the sociology of economics deal with the social causes and effects of *modernization*.

Experience has shown that the transition to an industrial society cannot proceed without two basic developments. First, the *class structure* of society must change. In preindustrial society the bulk of economic activity lies in agriculture and livestock production, and power, wealth, and prestige are based on ownership of land. In medieval Europe, for example, power lay with the class of feudal lords, in the pre-Civil War American South with the owners of slave plantations, and in present-day Latin America with the wealthy landowners. Although agriculture remains very important in industrial society, there is a strong tendency for power to shift from ownership of land to ownership of industrial and financial capital. The Industrial Revolution led to the demise of the French and English aristocracy and the American plantation class. Today American agriculture is dominated by the vast corporate conglomerates whose power derives from manufacturing, trade, and finance. In present-day underdeveloped countries the landowning classes vigorously resist widespread development as basically antagonistic to their status, and this attitude gives rise to political and social struggles of the first magnitude. Thus the swift development of the Chinese economy was based on the abolition of landlords' property rights and the rise of communal agriculture; on the other hand, in neighboring India, where caste-based land tenure still holds, modern economic development touches only a small segment of the population.

The second prerequisite of economic development is the change in *basic values and beliefs* of individuals. In preindustrial society, personal fulfillment is based on relations with nature, spiritual rewards, community activities, rituals, pride in work, and, when available, leisure. In capitalist society personal fulfillment is conceived in more *individualistic* terms—that is, as freedom, social position, prestige, wealth, power, and initiative. Controllers of production who care more for social niceties or spiritual rewards after death than for personal profit will show little drive toward capital accumulation and technical innovation. Workers who merely desire enough to live on will not be properly motivated by the lure of wages. Indeed, individualistic values are central to what Max Weber called *the Protestant ethic*—the belief that through hard work and individual striving each person can judge by the degree of his resultant economic success whether he is among God's elect. This ideological climate is uniquely conducive to the growth and flowering of capitalism. Units 8 and 20 discuss a number of issues connected with the Protestant ethic thesis.

Trading floor of the Tokyo Stock Exchange. The ownership of industrial and financial capital is a relatively new basis of group power in human society. It has replaced the ownership of land, which was the basis of social and political power in preindustrial society.

Traditional weaver in the Andes and textile factory workers in the United States. The traditional craftsman creates the entire artifact, possessing it in both an economic and affective sense. The modern factory worker on a production line creates or assembles only a part of the whole artifact and has no ownership rights in it. Thus he becomes alienated both emotionally and economically from the products of his or her labor.

The social implications of the transition to an industrial society are many and varied. Emulating the models of Western European and American capitalism or Eastern European and Soviet state-socialism involves—in addition to the obvious benefits of increased income, medical care, and education—several major *social costs:* the fragmentation of communities, the detachment of individuals from their natural environment, ecological disruption, the persistence of extensive social and economic inequality, and domination by impersonal and centralized political control. In addition, a basic transformation in the nature of work occurs. Whereas in preindustrial societies most individuals have direct control over their activities as farmers and craftsmen, in capitalist society workers lose this sphere of freedom. In exchange for a wage, they agree to vest disposition over their work activities in a capitalist or manager, who in turn determines the *organization of work.* This arrangement creates *hierarchy* and *bureaucracy.* Nevertheless, the factory worker frequently works far fewer hours, and far less arduously, than the rural peasant—and for more monetary compensation. Industrial workers also have a certain amount of choice both in regard to their particular trades or skills and the employers they work for. Thus there is an increased mobility and a wider range of opportunities that appear very enticing to those who are "down on the farm."

Increasingly being raised is the question of the *inevitability* of the pattern of social transformation that has heretofore accompanied modern economic development. The Chinese with their emphasis on balanced growth and suppression of social class privileges and the Yugoslavs with their emphasis on worker control of production are drawing more and more attention as countries consider whether it is possible to follow a course that reaps the benefits of modernization but avoids its costs.

3 American Context

In the years from 1890 to 1920 the outlines of modern America were set. The modern form of corporate enterprise became dominant, large-scale immigration ended, the structure of urban life crystallized, the West was closed, and the intervention of the govern-

ment in economic life came to seem legitimate. Americans, however, had little time to assess the shape of modern society. In 1929
the collapse of the stock market set off the Great Depression, recov-
ery from which came only with the results of full participation in
World War II. The return to normal conditions between 1945 and
1950 was broken by the Korean War, so that Americans could
hardly focus the future shape of their society before 1955. During
the next decade, the first predictions were for an unending and harmonious stretch of prosperity and social cohesion in the pursuit and
enjoyment of affluence. But by 1964 the civil rights movement was
in full swing, and not long after, disappointed blacks were rioting in
central cities. Radical protest and peace groups changed the tenor
of student life and, with a fair degree of tacit and active support
from their peers, sounded the call for a new society. The *counterculture* flowered, with its plea for personal liberation, communalism, re-

Bread line during the Great Depression. The series of crises of wars
and depression that have marked twentieth-century history have
made it difficult for America to pause and assess herself objectively.
As we do so now, some of our previous optimism seems misplaced.

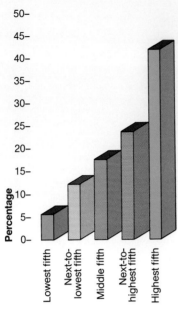

Figure 1. Percentage of Total Income Earned by Each Fifth of the Wage-Earning Population in the United States, 1970. The highest fifth of all wage-earners earned over 40 percent of the total wages earned. The lowest fifth earned only 5.5 percent. These figures have remained virtually constant for more than a quarter-century. (Source: Henle, "Exploring the Distribution of Income")

ligious experience, love, and a return to the earth. These developments, along with the movement for women's liberation and ecological integrity, have recently fallen into relative quiescence—a quiescence based not on solutions of the underlying problems, but on recognition by millions of individuals of the enormity of the changes required for such solutions.

Discontent with the quality of life remains widespread in America today. The United States has the most successful economy in the world—successful in the purely "economic" sense of per capita consumption. But its high rates of drug use, crime, neurosis, divorce, discontent, alcoholism, racism, poverty, and alienation are evidence of deep problems, if not unhappiness. And these social issues relate to economic institutions in a fairly direct way. Americans may believe that social well-being derives from the qualities of the social activities individuals enter into, the degree to which they may control the conditions of their lives, and the extent to which they are provided rewarding opportunities for individual development. But the major *social contexts* of such activity are *environment, community,* and *work,* and those contexts are themselves molded by *economic institutions* through the mechanisms that allocate land and labor to productive use.

The environment is shaped by the nature of industrial expansion, land speculation, and uneven spatial development based on the goals of profit maximization, and the drive toward ever greater volumes of marketable products. The development of communities is based on the sale, purchase, and use of community property according to the criteria of private gain. Most clearly of all, work is the product of economic forces that seek to minimize the costs of labor and thereby increase the margin of profit. The structure of jobs is certainly not controlled by workers themselves: whereas in 1850 most individuals were farmers and craftsmen who controlled their own labor, in 1950 over 80 percent of workers were wage and salaried employees, and by 1970 the figure had risen to 90 percent. Workers who are their own bosses now comprise only 8 percent of the work force, and many of these are only temporarily self-employed.

The discussion in this unit will be limited to the subject of work—not because other areas in the sociology of economics are less important, but in the interest of pursuing a single problem in some depth. Moreover, the nature of work does involve many of the social problems of America in the 1960s and 1970s.

First, *inequality* is largely an outcome of the economic process. Although extreme differences in inherited wealth do account for much income inequality, a great deal is also the product of wage and salary differentials among workers. This inequality is built into work organization. Most workers participate in corporate and government bureaucracies characterized by the hierarchical division of labor. Lines of authority pass from the managerial apex of a hierarchical pyramid through intermediate supervisory levels to the base of the pyramid composed of the mass of clerical and secretarial white-collar and semiskilled and unskilled blue-collar workers. Each descending level involves lower wages as well as more limited areas for independent initiative and control. Much income inequality is due to this organization of production.

Inequality is built into "job ladders" in such hierarchical enterprises. In the medieval guild authority was also organized hierarchically, with master craftsmen above skilled journeymen and journeymen above apprentices. But in the normal course of his lifetime the craftsman would pass from apprentice to journeyman to master. In the modern enterprise, however, a similar passage does not usually occur. Unskilled workers, maintenance personnel, clerical help, secretaries in the typing "pool," key-punch operators, and other low-level employees have limited opportunities for advancement. At more skilled levels blue-collar, white-collar, and managerial jobs are rarely held by the same individual "working his way up the corporate ladder." Even within each category vertical movement is limited, although to a lesser degree. The discontent of blacks, other minority groups, and women is due to the fact that they are by and large limited to the lower levels of jobs and to jobs with severely limited opportunities for advancement.

But the *quality* of work is also the subject of much discontent. Most of today's college graduates, for example, demand creative jobs that involve participation, personal control, and social relevance, but they are offered rigid, fragmented, limited positions in corporate or government bureaucracies. Although this job prospect doubtless accounts for the sympathy of college students for aspects of the radical and counterculture movements, discontent is prevalent among the majority of Americans as well. A special task force to the Secretary of Health, Education, and Welfare, in its report *Work in America* (1973), describes these sentiments as "blue-collar blues" and "white-collar woes." Although wages, physical working conditions, and job security have improved dramatically in the past

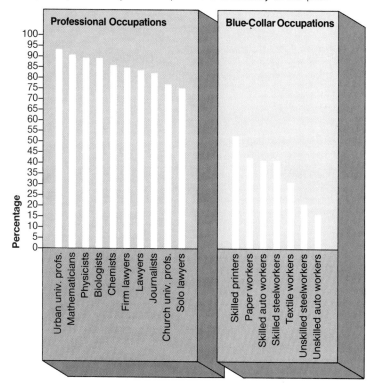

Figure 2. **Percentage of Workers in Various Occupational Groups Who Would Choose Similar Work Again.** Blue-collar workers express less job-satisfaction than professionals. (Source: Special Task Force, *Work in America*)

decade for most workers, absenteeism, high turnover, wildcat strikes, industrial sabotage, and willful laxity of job performance have increased equally dramatically. Only 43 percent of white-collar and 24 percent of blue-collar workers express satisfaction with their jobs. Good pay and working conditions are not enough: workers want creative and meaningful jobs. In the words of the report, "What the workers want most, as more than 100 studies in the past 20 years show, is to become masters of their immediate environments and to feel that their work and they themselves are important—the twin ingredients of self-esteem."

Moreover, the rising level of social consciousness in America in the past few years has brought about even more disenchantment. For instance, when the Project Talent, a 1960 survey of over 400,-000 high school students, was repeated for a representative sample of students in 1970, there was a marked shift from the students' valuing job security and opportunity for advancement to their valuing "freedom to make my own decisions" and "work that seems important to me." Similar results for college students were revealed in Daniel Yankelovich's surveys: in 1968 over half (56 percent) of all students indicated that they did not object to the prospect of being "bossed around" on the job, but by 1971 only one out of three (36 percent) saw themselves as willing to submit to such authority. (*The Changing Values on Campus*, 1972)

Similar problems face even those who are destined for the relatively rewarding professional positions. *Work in America* gives a dramatic, yet typical observation of a young Chicago lawyer:

> You can't wait to get out and get a job that will let you do something that's really important. . . . You think you're one of the elite. Then you go to a place like the Loop and there are all these lawyers, accountants, etc., and you realize that you're just a lawyer. No, not even a lawyer—an employee; you have to check in at nine and leave at five. I had lots of those jobs—summers—where you punch in and punch out. You think it's going to be different but it isn't. You're in the rut like everybody else.

C QUESTIONS AND EVIDENCE

1 Questions

The seemingly pervasive historical tendency toward alienation and inequality in work and the discontent it creates inspire several basic questions: (1) Does efficiency in mass production necessarily require a large and relatively powerless labor class controlled by a small and relatively powerful elite? Can worker-controlled production result in a more equitable distribution of income and increase worker satisfaction? (2) Does a person's work have a total impact on his or her life, or can work be separated from leisure, family, and culture? For instance, will the negative impact of work be reduced merely by shortening the work week and increasing the length of vacations as the nation becomes richer and more productive? (3) How do education and family socialization prepare young people for their later positions in the economic hierarchy?

2 Evidence

a The "Burning Issue" Question

i Context Economists argue that capitalists and managers of private enterprises (and nonprofit concerns, such as hospitals and governmental bureaus) organize work to minimize production costs. In this sense they are *technically efficient,* and their practices are inevitable if people want high incomes. Moreover, it is clear that the state-socialist countries, such as the Soviet Union, with divergent *social goals* and *power relations* from those of the capitalist countries, have chosen the same form of work organization.

In terms of the sociological perspective, this theory of conventional economists may not be valid. Radical social scientists in America and Europe, following the lead of Karl Marx, argue that the hierarchical division of labor serves a far different purpose: it maximizes the power of managers and capitalists to control the work process, and it reduces the power of workers by dividing them through fragmented tasks and through *vertical stratification* and *horizontal segmentation* on the basis of race, sex, ethnic origin, and social class. To examine the issue carefully, sociologists ask: *Is the hierarchical organization of authority in production a necessary concomitant of advanced technology and efficient production?*

ii Theory The traditional economic argument attempts to prove that when firms maximize profits, and when labor and all other *factors of production* are bought and sold on free markets where prices and wages are determined by supply and demand, then the structure of jobs will reflect workers' preferences, subject to the availability of natural resources and known technologies of production. This situation can be termed *workers' sovereignty,* because workers essentially choose their job structures within the limits imposed by nature and the level of scientific knowledge of production possibilities.

To understand the workings of this process, suppose that in one year workers are faced with a job structure characterized by alienating and routine jobs subject to hierarchical authority and that they decide they would prefer more satisfying and integrated work. They will express this preference by offering their services at a lower wage or salary to a capitalist who provides the kind of work they desire. Some enterprising capitalist will now realize that he can obtain cheaper labor than his competitors if he provides jobs structured in this particular manner, and he will look around for a *production technique* that is both compatible with the workers' desires and profitable to him. If he finds one, not only will the workers get the jobs they prefer, but his competitors will be forced to adopt the same production technique in order to hold their labor supply.

According to this theory, if jobs are unrewarding, it must be because of the nature of the technology or because workers prefer higher incomes to more desirable jobs. The desirability of jobs is reflected in the *supply price* of labor (the wage at which the worker is willing to accept the job). Indeed, each individual, in deciding his or her life's work makes some *trade-offs* between income and job desirability. The capitalist does have some *incentive* to make work attractive and thereby lower his labor costs.

That this theoretical aspect of the labor market is not actually operative to any significant extent should be clear from the fact that wages and salaries are generally higher for more desirable jobs, not lower. The labor force is stratified, so that only a restricted number of alternatives are open to a given individual. An assembly-line worker may aspire to become an electrician, a salesman, or a university professor, but the obstacles he would encounter along the way are so formidable that they effectively operate to prevent, or at least discourage, attempts at this kind of *upward mobility.* Realistically speaking, there are few real alternatives available to the workers in a given *occupational stratum.* And the capitalist system has a stake in preserving a large pool of inexpensive labor.

Radical theorists go far beyond this criticism, however, and argue that a *profit-maximizing* capitalist will never introduce a form of work organization that threatens to lessen secure control at the top of the hierarchy of production. Any loss of control is likely to lead to a *transfer of profits* from management to workers. For instance, if there is an efficient technology that allows workers autonomy, community, and solidarity in organizing their tasks, that affords a more equal distribution of an exercise of skills, that provides intrinsic work satisfaction, and that embodies group decision-making in the design of work—then a capitalist could secure labor more cheaply and obtain higher initial profits by using *worker control* under this technology. But such control, by shifting power from management to workers, would increase the solidarity and power of the latter in negotiating future wage agreements. In essence, workers might gain not only more desirable jobs, but higher pay as well. Thus the rational capitalist will not introduce this form of work organization, even if it is more efficient.

The traditional concept of worker sovereignty clearly will not hold. It assumes that the *labor-wage exchange,* whereby the worker accepts money in return for giving up the disposition of his work activities to the employer, symmetrically parallels other economic exchanges—say apples for pennies, or raw materials for cash credits. Most economic exchanges are legally binding contracts, however, enforced by a political power outside the jurisdictions of the parties engaged in exchange. The employer-employee exchange is different in that if workers fulfill only the legally enforceable aspects of the agreement (that is, come to work on time), little production will take place. The internal organization of production must therefore be designed to motivate individuals to produce, to limit the aspirations and *self-concepts* of workers to those compatible with the hierarchy of production, and to divide the workers against each other so as to reduce their aggregate power vis-à-vis management. In short, the integrity of the wage-labor contract is enforced not outside, but within the jurisdiction of those involved. It is on this distinction that the sociology of work focuses.

iii Research   The study of organizations in their modern form began with Max Weber's brilliant analysis of the place held by bureaucratic organization in the great civilizations of the past and in nineteenth-century Europe and America. As we saw in Unit 16, Weber argued that the merit of bureaucratic organization lay in its *rationality,* characterized by a power structure legitimated by rational values, run by trained experts, and based on the principle of hierarchy. ''The principle of hierarchical authority'' Weber says, ''is found in

Drafting pool. Although individuals may have quite a large choice regarding the particular firm for which they will work, the nature of their jobs, for example, janitoring or drafting, is pretty much the same from place to place. And, in a bureaucracy the personalities of the individuals occupying specified positions in the organization are assumed to be irrelevant. Tasks and procedures to be followed are specified for all employees, and they are expected to follow these prescriptions in a uniform manner. It is usually wrong to take too much as well as too little responsibility. But bureaucracies never run as efficiently as they are designed to. What goes wrong?

all bureaucratic structures." It involves a "firmly ordered system of super- and sub-ordination."

> Bureaucratization . . . very strongly furthers the development of "rational matter-of-factness." . . . Its specific nature, which is welcomed by capitalism, develops the more perfectly the more completely it succeeds in eliminating from official business love, hatred, and all purely personal, irrational, and emotional elements which escape calculation. (*Economy and Society,* 1922)

Finally, Weber emphasizes that the power of the bureaucratic form lies in its subjecting individuals to rigid *rules* and *behavior criteria,* allowing production to proceed independent from the particular desires of its members.

What Weber does not elucidate, however, is whether the "rationality" of the hierarchical division of labor is toward technical efficiency or secure and flexible controls on the part of its directors. The latter is certainly, on the face of it, more likely: on efficient standards, the organization will run at a higher level if its participants care about the results of their productive activities and derive satisfaction from the successes of cooperation. Yet the alienation and impersonality of bureaucratic organization explicitly avoid this identification of workers with their work and each other.

Empirical research indicates that bureaucratized and routinized tasks do not in fact flow from the nature of *technology* but from the needs of *centralized control.* As Victor H. Vroom notes in his masterful survey "Industrial Social Psychology" (1969), "decentralized structures have an advantage for tasks which are difficult, complex, or unusual, while centralized structures are more effective for those which are simple and routinized." That is, given that the corporate unit is based on centralized control, the most efficient technologies will be those involving routinized, dull, and repetitive tasks. In a decentralized environment the exact reverse would be true.

Moreover, workers do not like fragmented jobs. The experimental literature shows that job enlargement and decision-making control on the part of workers increases their satisfaction and lowers absenteeism and turnover. Nevertheless, managers have organized the usual bureaucratic division of tasks in such a way that actual worker performance is substantially independent of the worker's attitudes and satisfactions. This startling observation is one of the major results of 50 years of investigation by industrial psychologists.

In addition, although bureaucratic organization or production may ensure managerial control and corporate security against the ups-and-downs of workers' morale, it is by no means efficient in the wider sense. For even moderate worker participation in decisions and goal-setting increases *productivity:* the best results are obtained when people work out solutions individually and then evaluate and choose among them as a unified team.

For example, the MIT-generated Scanlon Plan of "participatory management" has been tried in some 10 plants in the United States. This arrangement gives workers unlimited power to organize and improve the work process and working conditions, guaranteeing them a share in the proceeds of cost reduction. In those plants

General Motors Vega plant at Lordstown, Ohio. Contrary to Weber's assumptions, dehumanized social hierarchies are not populated by superrational workers, but rather by workers who often are bored, alienated, routinized, inflexible, and—worst of all, in Weber's sense—inefficient. Unfortunately, instead of trying to figure out how to apply modern technology to situations of decentralized control, our society is, for the most part, moving in the opposite direction.

where it has been put into practice the average yearly increase in productivity has amounted to 23.1 percent; in one company 408 out of the 513 innovative ideas suggested by workers were successfully implemented because they led to real improvements in the productive process. Clearly a stable dialogue between workers, technicians, and planners would increase this fertile activity even more.

These results are confirmed by many other individual studies showing that when workers are given control over decisions and goal-setting, productivity rises dramatically. As Paul Blumberg concludes:

> There is scarcely a study in the entire literature which fails to demonstrate that satisfaction in work is enhanced or . . . productivity increases accrue from a genuine increase in workers' decision-making power. Findings of such consistency, I submit, are rare in social research. . . . the participative worker is an involved worker, for his job becomes an extension of himself and by his decisions he is creating his work, modifying and regulating it. (*Industrial Democracy*, 1968)

But such instances of even moderate worker control have been instituted only in marginal areas and in isolated firms fighting for survival. When the crisis is over, there is a tendency to return to "normal operating procedure." The threat that workers will escalate their demand for control is simply too great, and the takeover of the prerogatives of hierarchical authority is quickly quashed. Hence efficiency in the broader sense is subordinated to the needs of the bureaucracy to continue its control.

iv Evaluation   Clearly more research is needed in this area. Indeed, there will undoubtedly be further studies in coming years, as more and more workers begin to object to alienated labor. The bulk of the evidence certainly favors the view that the *hierarchical division of labor* basically serves the interests of control as opposed to technical efficiency. But the central question is the *extent* to which this is true.

In addition, all of modern technology has been developed with an eye toward its application to bureaucratic settings. It is scarcely any wonder, therefore, that science and creative work appear opposed to one another. The possibilities of using modern communications techniques, cybernation, computers, and the like in decentralized production remain to be explored. Nevertheless, it is clear that if corporate and governmental enterprises are organized according to the needs of secure control from the top, these technical possibilities never will be explored.

If such social research is to bear fruit, social scientists may have to give up their traditional Weberian views, detailed in Unit 16, about the *inevitability* of alienated labor and the efficiency of top-down control. They must at least entertain the possibility that workers, under proper conditions, have the capacity and will to direct their lives to the benefit of both themselves and society.

b   The "Classical" Question

i Context   Work organization obviously has strong impact on society through the immediate experiences of the worker during his or her hours of employment. Work occupies more than one-third of the average person's waking hours, but its effects do not necessarily end there. And the greater the "spill-over" from work to such social spheres as family, political participation, culture, and leisure, the more crucial the quality of work becomes.

In the popular mind work and other aspects of life are usually considered quite distinct. No matter how frustrating one's job, one can still expect to find solace in leisure time. When young people consider the not-so-pleasant prospect of their coming work lives, they often console themselves with visions of a fulfilling private social activity. Nor are they consistently disappointed. Nevertheless, the connection between work and leisure is closer than most people would like to admit and poses one of the classic questions in sociology: *To what extent does the quality of work determine the quality of life for the individual?*

ii Theory   According to Karl Marx, work guides and shapes the psychic development of the worker. "By acting on the external world and changing it," he argues in *Capital* (1867, 1885, 1894), the worker "at the same time changes his own nature . . . and develops his slumbering powers." Accordingly, in proportion as

Company team. Company-sponsored athletic teams are one mechanism through which large corporations are trying to "humanize" the company image and thus achieve greater worker loyalty. This is but one superficial example of the great influence that our work life exerts over our leisure activities—structuring times, recreational preferences, and recreational partners.

work is broad or narrow, stimulating or monotonous, it expands or stunts the individual's abilities. Only variety of work can develop the many sides of human ability and character. This principle, Marx and Engels insist, must guide the organization of labor in a communist society.

Marxist theorists go on to argue that because individuals develop their personalities and consciousness through the way they relate to productive activity, work is the basis for the formation of social classes. *Classes* consist of groups of individuals who hold similar positions in the division of labor. Insofar as the system is characterized by capitalists versus workers, farmers versus wage laborers, white-collar versus blue-collar workers, wage laborers (men) versus domestic workers (women), and insofar as each group is subject to different experiences in production, the groups develop distinct cultures, life styles, interests and ideologies. Thus, in this view, social stratification (which we discussed in Unit 9) is itself based on the experience of individuals in production.

Marx's famous emphasis on *materialism* is based squarely on the relation between work and social life. It asserts that forms of consciousness embodied in ethics, religion, science, and law are derived from people's experience in work and social life, rather than vice versa. (Various aspects of this view are also discussed in Units 2, 4, 8, 9, 16, 20 and 26.) Marx's argument that such "ideals" have a concrete economic basis is based on historical evidence that changes in the organization of production lead to changes in the experiences of individuals as well as changes in the class structure. From these changes spring new values and new forms of *consciousness*. For example, in the early stages of capitalism, when wages are low, workers are led to seek salvation through fundamentalist religions such as Methodism. In later stages of capitalism wages rise, and the worker will be properly disciplined only if he values income more than leisure—and more than desirable work conditions. Thus there is a shift toward *commodity fetishism;* that is, "salvation" is believed to derive from high-level consumption.

The relation between work and social life was also one of Max Weber's basic concerns. He acknowledged and approved of Marx's emphasis on the intimate tie between work and consciousness but disputed the argument that the direction of influence is always from work to consciousness, ideology, and values. His famous *The Protestant Ethic and the Spirit of Capitalism* (1904–1905) argued that the rise of capitalism in Western Europe was encouraged by the simultaneous flowering of Protestantism—with its asceticism, emphasis on work in this life as a sign of after-life salvation, and non-Catholic focus on individualism.

However brilliant Weber's demonstration of the close connection between capitalism and Protestant consciousness may be, modern research tends to indicate that Protestantism itself arose as an ideological response to the change in work patterns that occurred at the close of the Middle Ages. As urban trade centers began to develop, the simple agrarian life was challenged by the exodus of peasants away from the countryside and into the emerging cities. There the older religious perspectives failed to "fit" the new economic and social climate.

Weber also examined the relationship between bureaucratic

El Greco's *Purification of the Temple* (1574). Christ drove the money-changers out of the temple. If modern capitalists were to take their Christian doctrine literally, what would happen to their economic system? Whatever may have been the relationship between capitalism and religion in the past, is a waning of religious faith crucial for the further development of capitalism?

organization of production and individual personality, and this analysis has been extended by Robert K. Merton. According to this view, the individual working in a bureaucratic setting learns to be disciplined and subordinate and to react *cognitively* rather that *emotionally* to social situations. He must place independent value on the *outcomes* and *external rewards* of his activities rather than on the *processes* amd *intrinsic rewards* of the activities themselves.

This characterization of the "bureaucratic personality" was developed further in Talcott Parsons' *pattern-variable* schema. First, the bureaucratic personality is *affectively neutral* as opposed to *affective* in social relationships; that is, he tends to keep his feelings withdrawn or repressed. Second, he is *specific* rather than *diffuse* in his relations with others; he reacts to them not as total personalities, but only in terms of the specific and limited purposes that bring him in contact with others. Third, he is *universalistic* as opposed to *particularistic* in judging other individuals' behavior and worth; he values and judges others without reference to their particular relationship (wife, lover, son, fellow Presbyterian) to him and uses cognitive as opposed to emotional criteria in defining relationships. Fourth, he defines his relations to others in terms of their *performance* rather than their *qualities*—their *achievements* rather than their *ascriptive characteristics* (age, sex, caste, color). Finally, he betrays a *self-orientation* as opposed to a *collectivity-orientation* in choosing goals; he acts out of personal interest rather than interest in the groups of individuals with whom he is associated.

Parsons does not discuss the extent to which constant requirements to act according to bureaucratic standards (affective neutrality, specificity, universality, performance, and self-orientation) in work actually affect other areas of the worker's life.

Psychologist Kenneth Keniston's well-known study *The Uncommitted* (1965) argues that such spill-over not only does occur, especially among workers with some supervisory functions, but also causes severe distortions and tensions in the individual's private life and prevents him from relating to himself and to others as a full human being.

iii Research (Survey) These broad theories can be verified only through extensive historical and cross-cultural analysis. However, a number of observations can be made on the basis of far more limited and specific statistical studies.

First of all, doctors, medical researchers, and psychiatrists have noted a direct relation between work satisfaction and basic physical and mental health. In an impressive 15-year study of aging, Erdman Palmore ("Predicting Longevity," 1969) found that the most accurate predictor of longevity was job satisfaction. Satisfaction and general happiness on the job were more closely correlated with long life than a rating by an examining physician of physical functioning or measures of the use of tobacco or genetic inheritance. Moreover, Arthur Kornhauser's *Mental Health of the Industrial Worker* (1965) found that 40 percent of a sample of 407 auto workers had symptoms of mental instability and that the key correlation was between job satisfaction and mental health.

Although the political behavior of individuals would seem to be quite unrelated to work, there is in fact a good deal of evidence that the socioeconomic status of individuals—a measure of their income, occupational status, and level of education—is a basic determinant of degree of alienation from or participation in the political process. Those with higher status and income, who have relatively more opportunity to participate in decisions on the job, are more likely to participate in politics. Thus Sydney Verba and Norman Nie report in *Participation in America* (1972):

> The social status of an individual—his job, education, and income—determines to a large extent how much he participates. It does this through the intervening effects of a variety of ''civic attitudes'' conducive to participation: attitudes such as a sense of efficacy, of psychological involvement in politics, and a feeling of obligation to participate.

The close relationship between work experience and leisure activities has been noted repeatedly in research studies. William R. Torbert demonstrated the direct relationship between degree of control in work and the vitality of leisure activity in *Being for the Most Part Puppets* (1973). Torbert studied 209 men, using a job rating that reflected their degree of control over decision making, control over pace and quantity of work, and the routine versus creative character of their activities. He also measured the learning and exploration that characterized their free-time activities in terms of (1) degree of discrimination, (2) extent of contribution to self-improvement or community improvement, (3) amount of activity, and (4) level of commitment. Finally, his measure of job involvement reflected the subjective satisfactions of the worker, his feelings of challenge, variety, and interest on the job. Torbert found that there is a very strong relationship between job rating and job involvement, on the one hand, and leisure involvement, on the other. Indeed, the two measures of control and involvement on the job explain 81 percent of the variation in leisure involvement.

iv Evaluation Perhaps the most obvious fact of social life is the amazing diversity among human beings: even individuals with the same social class, age, sex, ethnic origin, work experience, and education manifest a seemingly unlimited variety of personal characteristics. Nevertheless, there are broad uniformities as well. No reputable sociologist has even offered a theory asserting that common work experiences have no effect, or even a small effect, on the total life spaces of individuals. Moreover, every body of evidence bearing on the issue shows the effect of work on the worker's social activities is great.

Because the classic theories in this area are historical and comparative in nature, they defy simple statistical verification. There is research supporting Marx's emphasis on work as formative of consciousness and personality, although the direct impact of work experience is only partially relevant here. Alex Inkeles' transnational studies of modern man as a modal personality type (see Unit 10) support the Parsonian and Weberian emphases on cognitive orientation, universality, and achievement orientation. That the class structure is a reflection of the social relations of production seems to be a historical truth, and studies such as Richard Schlatter's on the theory of property rights (*Private Property*, 1951) and Ronald Meek's on economic theory (*Economics and Ideology*, 1967) show that changes in the nature of economic life lead to changes in the conceptions of ethics, religion, and social theory.

Unfortunately, modern statistical researchers too often overlook the classical theories altogether or else interpret them far too narrowly to support fruitful studies. Clearly more work needs to be done in this area, not only to demonstrate the spill-over of work attitudes into leisure or political activities (which has already received some attention), but, more importantly, to demonstrate the degree to which alienated work patterns sap life of its vitality and integrity and thereby diminish our most important resource—human productivity.

c   The "Research" Question

i   Context   Another, less direct connection between work and individual development relates to the preparation of individuals for their occupations. The factory or office is itself a minisociety, with unique social relations, and preparing individuals to assume roles in the hierarchical order of such a setting is a role of the *socialization agencies.*

Socialization is one of the main functions of the family and the school. (See Units 5, 7, 18.) To the extent that an individual's performance in the economic system is predicated upon the fostering of particular paths of personal development by families and schools, those institutions themselves will come to reflect the social relations of economic production. The more total and embracing the socialization requirements for work, the closer must be the correspondence between the structure of work and the structure of families and schools. And the closer this correspondence, the more valid Marx's emphasis on the nature of work as the basic determinant of personality and individual consciousness. Hence sociologists ask: *How are the hierarchical features of capitalism perpetuated from generation to generation?*

ii   Theory   To deal with this question, we must have some idea of what the requirements of proper job performance are. We can then examine how the characteristics of family and schools in America conform to the need to fulfill those requirements.

One of the major theses in this area is the *technocratic perspective* (also discussed in Units 9 and 16). According to this view, the hierarchical division of labor arises from the need to motivate the most able individuals in society to undertake the extensive training necessary to perform the most difficult and important high-level occupational roles (doctor, engineer, professor, judge, physicist, financial analyst, and the like). Salaries and/or status are the enticements offered to those few individuals who are both able and willing to train for these positions. In 1945 Kingsley Davis and Wilbert E. Moore set forth their highly influential *functional theory of stratification,* which locates the ''determinants of differential reward'' in ''differential functional importance'' and ''differential scarcity of personnel.'' ''Social inequality,'' they conclude, ''is thus an unconsciously evolved device by which societies insure that the most important positions are conscientiously filled by the most qualified persons.'' (''Some Principles of Stratification'')

This technocratic justification of the hierarchical division of labor leads smoothly to a *meritocratic* view of the process of matching individuals to jobs: an efficient and impersonal bureaucracy assesses each person purely in terms of his or her expected contribution to production or the community well-being. The main determinants of the individual's expected job fitness are seen as those cognitive and psychomotor capacities relevant to a worker's technical ability to do the job.

The technocratic view of production and the meritocratic view of *job allocation* yield an important corollary—namely, that there is always a strong tendency in an efficient industrial order to ignore caste, class, sex, color, and ethnic origins in occupational placement. This tendency will be particularly strong in a capitalist economy, where competitive pressures constrain employers to hire on the basis of strict efficiency criteria.

In terms of this technocratic perspective, the basic function of family and schools in relation to the economy is to supply youth with the proper skills to hold jobs. The *family* is expected to provide the child with basic cognitive abilities (either genetically determined or socially nurtured) and a set of orientations toward learning, whereas the *school* actually develops the work-related cognitive skills relevant to economic success.

This view of schooling, economic success, and the requisites of job functioning supplies an elegant explanation of the historical rise of mass education. Because modern industry relies on increasingly complex and sophisticated operational technologies, the cognitive demands it makes require an increasing level of competence on the part of the labor force as a whole. Thus the expansion of educational opportunity becomes a requisite of modern economic growth. The technocratic perspective, which emphasizes the ability and willingness to apply skills as the focal requirement of economic success, has been dominant, indeed virtually undisputed, until recently. (See Unit 18.)

That view is now being challenged by a *social relations perspective,* which shifts the emphasis from cognitive factors to a number of other factors and characteristics that determine an individual's position in the economic hierarchy. In this view, families become more important and schools less important in influencing the future economic position of children. The family has relatively greater impact on behavior, character, personality, outlook, and attitudes, and the schools affect the future positions of students mainly by teaching *work habits* and by teaching *skills* only secondarily.

This theory argues that mass education had its beginning in cities and towns where the dominant industries required little skill —and far less cognitive ability—among the work force. Thus the growth of the modern educational system did not reflect the rising cognitive requirements of the economy. Rather, the birth and early development of universal education was sparked by the critical need of a burgeoning capitalist order for a stable work force and a citizenry reconciled, if not inured, to the wage labor system. Order, docility, discipline, sobriety, and humility—attributes required by the new social relations of production—were admitted by all concerned as the social benefits of schooling.

iii   Research (Methodology)   A growing body of historical research may be interpreted to bolster the social relations perspective. American schooling can be seen as a more or less conscious and coordinated attempt to generate a disciplined industrial labor force and to legitimate the rapid hierarchization of the division of labor in the

The work of cleaning up after work. The lessons taught in school of the necessity to defer to authority and behave docilely may be more useful to employers than most of the specific skills that a student is likely to learn. Also, racial, ethnic, and sexual discrimination often operates to close off certain jobs from particular groups in the population.

late nineteenth and early twentieth centuries.

The technocratic perspective is supported by statistics that show that individuals with higher IQ obtain better jobs, that better jobs require more cognitive skills, and that education, whose primary function is inducing cognitive skills, is therefore the major social determinant of economic success. Statistics also show that the members of families of higher social class have proportionally higher intelligence (in statistical terms) than the rest of the population in the classes below them. They pass their abilities on to their children, thus perpetuating the social stratification of IQ. This situation, it is claimed, explains how families affect the economic positions of their offspring, and the causes of *intergenerational status transmission* as well.

But the social relations perspective claims that these observations are not sufficient to account for why different people end up in different positions in the economic hierarchy. It also maintains that the main effect of families and schools is *not* cognitive.

Critics of the traditional view claim that the technocratic perspective argues that more education leads to higher income and occupational status *because* each year of education supplies an increment of skills and those skills are rewarded on the job market. According to the technocratic view, the longer the individual attends school, the more developed will be his cognitive abilities and thus his eligibility for high-status jobs. It is certainly true—as many studies have shown—that if one examines a large sample of individuals in terms of (1) the level of education they attained, (2) the level of cognitive skills they possess—say IQ scores, objective achievement tests, and the like—and (3) their incomes and occupational statuses as adults, one can observe a correlation between level of education and economic success. But suppose that one chooses to examine a subset of individuals in the sample, a subset *all of whom have the same level of cognitive skills*. Then, if the technocratic perspective is correct, there should no longer be any relation between level of education to economic success in this subgroup; that is, if two individuals have the same level of skills, differences in their education should have no effect on their economic position. Using a wide variety of statistical data, this proposition appears to be false. When cognitive skills are held constant, the correlation between education and economic success remains almost as strong as the observed gross correlation over a range of skill levels.

A similar experiment can be performed concerning families. If for a sample of individuals, one knows (1) the socioeconomic status of the families in which they were raised, (2) an objective measure of their cognitive abilities, and (3) their own adult economic position, one will note a strong correlation between socioeconomic background and economic success. But, again, if one chooses a subset of this sample with a particular level of cognitive skills, the relationship between family background and economic success remains virtually the same. Thus the technocratic theory is not valid: cognitive skills alone cannot be the prime determinant of economic success.

The social relations theory suggests the explanation of economic success lies in a *correspondence* between school and work—that the social relations of schooling are structured similarly to the social relations of production in several essential respects.

The school is a bureaucratic order with hierarchical authority, rule orientation, stratification by "ability" (tracking) as well as by age (grades), and a system of external incentives (marks, promise of promotion, and threat of failure) much like pay and status in the sphere of work. Therefore schools are quite likely to develop in students traits corresponding to those required on the job, and those traits will play a large part in teacher evaluations of students' performance. Thus it is less *what* is learned than the *way* it is learned that is most directly relevant to the future economic position of students.

Social relations theorists go on to suggest that this correspondence is not confined to schooling. There is strong evidence for a similar correspondence in the structure of family life. In his massive ten-year study sponsored by the National Institute for Mental Health (*Class and Conformity,* 1969), Melvin Kohn reports that

> middle class parents . . . are more likely to emphasize children's self-direction, and working class parents to emphasize their *conformity to external authority.* . . . The essential difference between the terms, as we use them, is that self-direction focuses on *internal* standards of direction for behavior; conformity focuses on *externally* imposed rules.

Thus parents of lower-status children value obedience, neatness, and honesty in their children, whereas higher-status parents emphasize curiosity, self-control, and happiness. Kohn concludes:

> In this exceptionally diverse society—deeply marked by racial and religious division, highly varied in economy, geography, and even degree of urbanization—social class stands out as more important for men's values than does any other line of demarcation, unaffected by all the rest of them, and apparently more important than all of them together.

To refine the relation between social class, values, and child-rearing, Kohn classifies his 1,400 test subjects according to the amount of "occupational self-direction" inherent in their jobs. He used as indices whether the worker was closely supervised; whether the worker dealt with things, data, or people; and whether the job was complex or repetitive. His analysis indicates that the "relationship of social class to parents' valuation of self-direction or conformity for children is largely attributable to class-correlated variation in men's exercise of self-direction work." And he concludes:

> Whether consciously or not, parents tend to impart to their children lessons derived from the conditions of life of their own social class—and thus help prepare their children for a similar class position. . . . Class differences in parental values and child rearing practices influence the development of the capacities that children will someday need. . . . The family, then, functions as a mechanism for perpetuating inequality.

To school: in Appalachia *(above)* and Greenwich Village *(page 490)*. The Coleman Report found that the situation at home that each child brings with him or her has greater predictive value in assessing the child's likely future than does the child's schooling. *Inequality,* by Jencks, Gintis, Bane and others, asserted that socioeconomic factors are such pervasive determinants of all individuals' abilities that the quality of schooling was irrelevant; that is, it made little difference for the individual's eventual destiny.

Such differential patterns of childrearing do affect more than the worker's personality and aspiration level. They also determine his or her *style of self-presentation:* patterns of class loyalties and modes of speech, dress, and interpersonal behavior. Although such traits are by no means fixed into adulthood, their stability over the life cycle appears to account for at least part of the observed degree of intergenerational status transmission.

iv Evaluation A great deal of evidence points to the conclusion that the nature of work affects an individual's social life via his or her early socialization. The nature of work and the class structure that derives from the capitalist hierarchy have a strong influence on the structure of family life and education, which in turn perpetuates class divisions from generation to generation. Whereas those who have been critical of the alienating, unequal, and technically irrational character of the hierarchical division of labor have traditionally examined only the *direct* effects of work experience, it may be that the more important effects operate *prior* to entry into the labor force. Parents transmit the essentials of their own work experience to their children, and schools are organized as miniature reproductions of factories and offices.

There are of course a number of other ways in which class-based economic factors affect the kinds of jobs individuals eventually obtain. A young person growing up in a low-income area has little information on jobs, and severe financial pressures may curtail the number of years he can attend school. Guidance counselors, if there are any in his school, are less likely to encourage him to attend college. In any case, he is not likely to have many peers who do attend college. Family job contacts are likely to be limited to blue-collar jobs, and such contacts are likely to be the source of his first actual job. Circumstances as well as socialization help to determine the economic options for the individual, and circumstances vary perceptibly from class to class.

3 Overview

In theory, America is a democracy, the land of opportunity. In practice, the economic system makes some people far more equal than others: the highest-paid fifth of our population receives over 40 percent of the total wages earned, whereas the lowest fifth earns a mere 5.5 percent. That same privileged fifth also occupy the most desirable jobs in terms of working conditions, variety of responsibilities, self-direction, fringe benefits, prestige, and related emotional rewards. The lowest-paid 20 percent occupy those jobs that are most alienating, routine, fragmented, boss-directed, and limited. (Often the worker is simply an appendage to a machine). Those at the top of the hierarchy have a stake in the perpetuation of this system and tend to resist innovations that restructure work patterns at the lower levels. Such changes might increase worker participation and hence worker control.

The system might be more equitably adjusted through political participation. But studies show that those who fail to profit from the system also avoid political participation in it, whereas those who benefit from it tend to be more politically assertive. Work attitudes

and experiences are also reflected in different styles of family life and childrearing and those differences are reinforced in school and themselves further reinforce class divisions: middle-class children are prepared through socialization for middle-class occupations, whereas working-class children are prepared for working-class occupations. Circumstances associated with class (range of job contacts, years of schooling possible, available counseling, and the like) also combine to transmit social class and status from parent to child; hence intelligence—which is genetically transmitted to a considerable extent—tends to become socially stratified as well. This situation again contributes to inequality of incomes: those who score highest on tests of cognitive skills ultimately earn about twice as much as the lowest-scoring group does.

All things being equal, differences in cognitive skills do not in themselves account for the degree of disparity of incomes recorded in the United States. (Among the industrial nations, the United States is one of the most unequal.) Therefore, the traditional argument that education can be the great equalizer through its influence on the development of cognitive skills breaks down. One highly controversial study *Inequality: A Reassessment of the Effect of Family and Schooling* (1972) by Christopher Jencks, Herbert Gintis, Mary Jo Bane, and others, suggests that family background and quality of schooling and years of schooling and cognitive skills do not actually account for more than 25 percent of the observed inequalities in income among white nonfarm male individuals in the United States. Even if all those complex variables were equalized, *inequality would still be created anew within each successive generation.* Inequality, they argue, is due to so many factors—personality, weather (if you depend on crops), who you know, what the job market is like in your occupation, how much effort you are willing to expend, whether your store is in a high burglary district, whether the job interviewer thinks you look like her cousin and so on—that the list is almost endless. Jencks and his colleagues maintain that because sex, race, age, region, circumstances, luck, personality, effort, and a host of other variables (as well as years of schooling, cognitive skills, and family background) all affect how much an individual earns, then the only way equality among individual incomes can ever be dependably achieved is by adjusting the range of incomes directly. In essence all jobs should be made more equal in pay (though a slight difference would still be preserved to provide incentives for highly trained occupations).

Social reformers today operate under two very different philosophies. Some believe that we should work toward *equality of opportunity:* if everyone starts with the same advantages, those who have both the ability and desire to succeed will do so, and individual mobility will be assured because there will be no rigid socioeconomic barriers. Others, including Jencks and his associates, believe that we should work toward *equality of income,* because even if everyone does start with the same advantages, the end results will still be highly unequal.

D LOOKING AHEAD

1 Interview:
Kenneth E. Boulding

Kenneth E. Boulding is professor of economics and a program director at the Institute of Behavioral Science at the University of Colorado at Boulder. He was codirector of the Center for Research on Conflict Resolution for several years. His major works include *The Organizational Revolution, Conflict and Defense, Economic Analysis,* and *A Primer on Social Dynamics.* His current research deals with grants economics, zero and negative growth, and general social evolution.

DPG *As an economist, do you think that social problems are inherent in the nature of technology or in the social institutions that control and utilize technology? Will technology produce problems we won't be able to solve?*
BOULDING That's a slightly silly question. Technology is an integral part of the social system. After all, technology is something that's produced and utilized by people and by institutions. It doesn't come down from heaven. All societies have technology, although it ranges from bows and arrows to nuclear power stations. The real question is whether technological processes have a dynamic independent of the rest of the system, and I don't think they do. Technology is simply part of the social evolutionary process. Technology is the evolution of artifact and that goes along with the evolution of organization. You can't imagine an automobile without an automobile factory or without an automobile firm—without some large-scale organization. You couldn't have had the automobile in the Middle Ages.

DPG *Doesn't technology produce types of work situations that are alienating situations in which human beings suffer?*
BOULDING I think that's radical cant, but that doesn't mean there isn't a real problem. People have been alienated in their own societies for a very long time. If you're a Hopi in a Hopi society, you're not alienated, unless you don't like being a Hopi. Any society will produce misfits and rightly so, because it is only the failures of socialization that

produce change and evolution. On the other hand, in all evolutionary processes most mutations are adverse. Most social change is for the bad. The idealization of change as such is nonsense.

I would say that the Detroit factory worker, for instance, although he may not be entirely satisfied with his life, is not very alienated. He's much less alienated than, say, some radical economists are. They're alienated because it is fashionable to be alienated in their circles. But the victims of technology they bleed over are not so very alienated. They are Legionnaires, they're hard hats. They're very patriotic, which is the opposite of alienated. On the whole, the United States is one of the less alienated societies in human history.

DPG *Is the Western pattern of industrial and economic development with its pitfalls and socially undesirable concomitants inevitable for developing Third World countries?*
BOULDING Inequality has to be much greater in the poor countries than the richer, developed ones. If there are only a tenth as many automobiles as people, 10 percent will have automobiles and the other 90 percent won't. The distribution policy is more a function of the level of reproductive technology than it is of social institutions. The Eastern bloc and Russia have a pattern of development that is highly similar to that of the West. They haven't avoided any of these problems at all.

DPG *How about the Communist Chinese experiment?*

BOULDING Ask me in a hundred years. My hunch is that their method legitimates stagnation rather than produces development. It isn't just that the poor countries are not going to develop along Western lines, they're not going to develop at all. There just isn't enough of anything. The awful truth is that 4 billion people cannot all have developed standards of life. In the West development has avoided severe inequality; it has strengthened a sense of community; it has diminished alienation and unrewarded labor; it has improved the environment; it has encouraged arts, crafts, and spiritual activities. But all this is precarious, because it rests on the exploitation of irreplaceable resources and may contain a death sentence. Development may just hasten the day when everything will be gone. Of course, this evil day has been postponed very successfully for the last 100 years, because we've been increasing known resources much faster than we've been using them up. But how long can that go on? The earth's resource base is ultimately limited. Of course, if we go to a nuclear fusion and liquid hydrogen economy, or harness solar energy and stress recycling, the evil day can be postponed a long time. But it's clear that with the existing level of knowledge and technology, the rest of the world will find it extremely hard to develop beyond a certain point. Even Japan will have to slow down quite a bit. Maoism is how to be poor and like it. In 100 years the Western countries also may be dealing with the problem of maximizing the quality of life with limited resources and low consumption levels.

DPG *What effect would full economic equality have on women and their roles in the family and elsewhere?*

BOULDING The existing institutions result in a shocking waste of the resources of half the human race, and I think sexism has far more disastrous consequences than racism. On the whole, women have been subjugated because this subjugation had survival value in primitive cultures. Having kids is a drag, so you weight the dice so women will have to specialize in the production of children. No culture can survive unless the birth rate is equal to the death rate. Today there's a massive decline in fertility all over the Western world. The United States is now below a replacement reproductive rate—if this situation goes on, we'll die out. I think the emancipation of women is one of the major values

that may be achieved in the modern world. On the other hand, nothing is costless. Emancipation can easily create a new set of problems.

DPG *What kind of problems might it create?*

BOULDING Emancipation has costs in terms of childrearing. It also produces problems concerning the nature of the family. The nuclear family is terribly tough, mainly because this type of intimate and complex relationship is something that is very difficult to have with more than a very few people. This fact is the fundamental fallacy of communes. The communal relationship has very sharp diseconomies of scale. If you have to love 200 people, you don't have much time to do anything else. On the other hand, the nuclear family may be too small. You need a kind of onion pattern, with the extremely intimate community of the nuclear family and a series of progressively larger, less intimate communities reaching out to the world community.

The emancipation of women doesn't have to destroy the nuclear family, but it changes it. I think that the role of the sexes will be less differentiated in the future. But emancipation doesn't solve problems, it just raises more interesting problems. If we view it as a solution, we're in very great trouble indeed.

DPG *Do you think that work and the socialization of people for work has an immediate impact on leisure, family, and culture?*

BOULDING Obviously work has a profound effect on people's identity. Your identity is what you reply when I say, "What are you?" If you say, "I'm an automobile worker," or "I'm a professor," you have a work identity. Now it's important to have as satisfactory a work identity as possible, but after all, work is something you wouldn't do if you weren't paid to do it. Work is what you do for other people, in a sense. Work has an ethic of its own, and it's very valuable. I quarrel with the radical economists who are always touting labor but not the work ethic. Wage work has a high moral value. It creates identity in the sense that if I have a job it means that society is saying to me, "You are doing something for us that we think is valuable, and we pay you for it." The wage is the symbol of the value that society puts on your activity. Wage labor is *disalienating* in the sense that it gives a person a place and a status in the society, although obviously some jobs give more privilege and status than others. The old AFL motto, "Don't ask me what I do in my spare time," is a good value too. If you feel you're doing an honest day's work, making a contribution to the society, and getting wages in return, you should stop fussing about it.

DPG *So people should stop all this "sensitive plant" stuff?*

BOULDING That's right. The corporation should stop trying to be a church. You go to church on Sunday. There are important identities outside the work identity. If your work identity isn't totally satisfactory—and it isn't to a lot of people—you can be the Lord Grand Muckymuck of The Lodge or something.

DPG *Sociologists in the 1950s spoke of the end of ideology, but we now find ourselves with more questions than we have answers for. Do you think that there is any economic basis for the rise of the countercultural and radical student movements?*

BOULDING The economic base of the counterculture is simply affluence. It derives from what I have called the aristocratization of the middle class. Some elements of it are quite desirable; others are not. Human liberation doesn't depend on bell-bottom trousers, because cultural fashions come and go. On the other hand, I think part of the radical *Angst* rises out of the feeling that social democracy has been a bit of a fraud. I'd almost define social democracy as how you subsidize the rich in the name of subsidizing the poor. Poverty has diminished very substantially in this country, but it's only because we have all gotten richer. There hasn't been any real redistribution of wealth. The radicals have been raising some very good questions about the relations of the power structure of society to the political process of redistribution. But on the whole I think the countercultural and radical student movement has simply missed the most significant questions, the questions about the future of the developmental process itself. The major crisis of our age is what I've called the crisis of closure. People are beginning to sense that the earth is a closed system. Previously we've had the feeling of expanding on an infinite plain. Some of the anguish of young people today is a reflection of the fact that now there's nowhere to go. The space enterprise has made it extremely clear that the Earth is the only decent bit of real estate for a very long way.

DPG *Wouldn't you say it's more than just worries about the Earth's limited resources? Aren't the young more concerned with immediate assumption of pleasurable life styles, the distribution of wealth, and that kind of thing?*

BOULDING Yes, but the young are naturally more worried about the future than the old. On the other hand, I must say I've been disappointed in the radicals because they try to give nineteenth-century answers to twentieth-century questions. Marxism and neo-Marxism are essentially a reaction to the age of development. They have very little weight in the age of equilibrium, if that's what we have in front of us.

DPG *What are the main areas that sociology and the social sciences in general should be probing in the next 10 years or so?*

BOULDING One of the high priorities is the international system. It's probably the most pathological part of the troubled social system, as well as the most expensive and the most dangerous. Another priority is this problem of the limits of growth, population control, and so on. One of the things that may put great strain on the world in the next 100 years or so is differential population growth. It always has, as a matter of fact. The possible energy shortage could also have an enormous impact on the international system. I also still think there is need for an intellectual synthesis of the controversy about socialism.

In a sense the socialist solution is a feasible one. On the other hand it's also very disappointing in terms of the liberation of the human spirit. You see the socialist countries are, quite frankly, dreary. The capitalist countries are vulgar, but very exciting. The question of ideal social organization is still very much unresolved. This resolution involves social invention, and you certainly cannot predict that, I think.

DPG *The social sciences have been criticized sometimes because they fail to predict various developments, for example, the civil-rights movement or the countercultural movement. Do you think the social sciences can be useful in predicting new directions or developments?*

BOULDING I don't think they can predict very much, any more than the biological sciences can, because the subject matter of both is evolutionary systems, which have an inherent unpredictability because they essentially involve information and knowledge structures. You can't predict what we're going to know in the year 2000, or we'd know it now. Things are not wholly unpredictable, of course. It makes sense to make projections. It also makes a great deal of sense not to believe them.

Contempora

Part IV

Social Issues

Unit 22
Deviance

1 Definition
Deviance is conduct that is seen as involving a personally discreditable departure from a group's standards and that evokes reactions of a punitive nature toward the individuals involved in such behavior.

2 World Context
Behavior that deviates from group standards is almost as widespread as behavior that conforms to such standards. In some societies, however, deviance is not stigmatized.

3 American Context
In our society the deviant label imputes inferiority to the individual and tends to obscure his other social characteristics.

1 Questions
The basic issues concerning deviance pivot around the following questions: (1) How does society attempt to cope with deviant forms of behavior? (2) How does society itself, especially the state, contribute to deviance? (3) How do individuals and groups become deviant?

2 Evidence
a The "Burning Issue" Question
The conception of deviance as abnormal behavior whose root causes must be uncovered and "cured" was first expressed by early sociologists who wrote of "social pathology" and was further developed in the writings of the "Chicago" and functionalist schools. This correctional orientation has been criticized by recent theorists who view deviance as the result of societal labeling.
b The "Classical" Question
Sociologists have traditionally assumed that habitually acquired group standards of behavior are essential to the social order and have not considered that the state itself may be involved in the production of deviance. The labeling perspective recognizes conformity as the problem and examines the power relationships that contribute to deviance.
c The "Research" Question
Conventional explanations of deviance tend to stress poverty and other social circumstances without examining the dehumanizing social processes at work within those circumstances. The phenomenological perspective provides more subjective understanding but is supported by little empirical data.

3 Overview
The study of deviance is rapidly becoming one of the most creative areas of social thought, liberating society from unnecessary or outmoded restrictions on conduct.

DEVIANCE — A SOCIAL CONSTRUCT

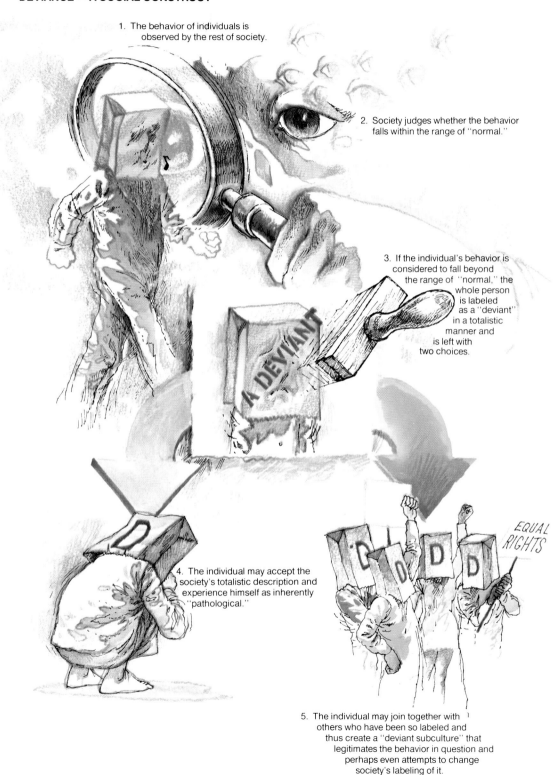

1. The behavior of individuals is observed by the rest of society.

2. Society judges whether the behavior falls within the range of "normal."

3. If the individual's behavior is considered to fall beyond the range of "normal," the whole person is labeled as a "deviant" in a totalistic manner and is left with two choices.

4. The individual may accept the society's totalistic description and experience himself as inherently "pathological."

5. The individual may join together with others who have been so labeled and thus create a "deviant subculture" that legitimates the behavior in question and perhaps even attempts to change society's labeling of it.

Type of Behavior and Person Punished	Number of Societies Measured	Percentage Punishing
Incest	54	100
Abduction of married woman	82	100
Rape of married woman	84	99
Rape of unmarried woman	55	95
Sexual relations during post-partum period	43	95
Bestiality by adult	15	93
Sexual relations during menstruation	73	92
Adultery		
(paramour punished)	88	89
(wife punished)	93	87
Sexual relations during lactation period	22	86
Infidelity of fiancee	57	86
Seduction of another man's fiancee	52	85
Illegitimate impregnation		
(woman punished)	74	85
(man punished)	62	84
Seduction of prenubile girl (man punished)	30	77
Male homosexuality	44	68
Sexual relations during pregnancy	49	67
Masturbation	16	44
Premarital relations		
(woman punished)	97	44
(man punished)	93	41
Female homosexuality	12	33
Sexual relations with own betrothed	67	10

B   DEFINITION AND CONTEXT

1   Definition

Recent conflicts among various segments of American society have called attention to the question of why men violate the rules and have obscured the corollary: Why do most men, most of the time, conform?

Sociologists who study deviance focus on social phenomena described in everyday language as alcoholism, addiction, crime, delinquency, dishonesty, perversion, prostitution, and so on—behaviors that are viewed in our society as departures from right conduct. Even though the term "deviance" is seldom used in everyday speech, labels such as "queer," "insane," "nut," "slut," and "pervert" may be applied by other people to the individuals involved in such behaviors. Thus deviance does not necessarily have a strictly scientific meaning, but is a ubiquitous and natural phenomenon of everyday life. It is also a relative term; that is, behavior that is regarded as deviant in one society is not necessarily regarded as deviant in another.

Deviance is conduct that is seen as involving a personally discreditable departure from a group's rules or standards and that evokes reactions of a punitive nature toward the individuals involved in such behavior. Criminality as a subdivision of deviance is dealt with in detail in Unit 23.

2   World Context

All known societies, past and present, are characterized by elaborate arrangements of rules and precepts within their definitions of social order. And even though most of the people most of the time conform to such strictures, *rule-violating behavior* or straying from group standards is almost as widespread as *conforming behavior.* Therefore deviance can be said to exist in all human societies.

Emile Durkheim emphasized the pervasive and persistent occurrence of deviance in the social order, even if that order be a "society of saints, a perfect cloister of exemplary individuals. . . . Crimes, properly so-called, will there be unknown; but faults . . . will create there the same scandal that the ordinary offense does." (*The Rules of the Sociological Method*, 1895) Durkheim reflected upon the universality of deviance, although he never used the term itself, and hypothesized that it serves a *social function.*

Most knowledge about deviance is based on studies conducted in American society. However, a few sociologists and cultural anthropologists have given us data regarding the existence of deviance in other cultures. Table 1 illustrates the cultural variability regarding 19 aspects of sexual behavior.

Dieter H. Seibel found in "Social Deviance in Comparative Perspective" (1972), a summary of studies of African societies, that social sanction or punishment was complementary to deviance and deduced three main characteristics of the *sanctioning process* in African societies:

1.   It is directed toward reintegration rather than alienation.

2. It does not attach moral labels to the deviant act.
3. It does not attach moral labels to the deviant person or group.

Thus in these African societies, in contrast to American society, the deviant is not *stigmatized* and the problem of *secondary deviance,* a person's emphasizing, elaborating, and extending his deviance because of the attention paid it, is avoided. Studies such as Seibel's underscore the *cultural relativism* inherent in the nature of deviance. Deviation is an inevitable feature of any society, the *incidence* and/or *content* of which varies, as does conformity, depending on time and place and on the definitions of right and wrong provided by the social order.

3   American Context

The way Americans—or members of any culture—view deviant behavior is mirrored in their attitude toward politics, war, foreign relations, and the like; there is a tendency to declare those groups and individuals who share "our" beliefs and manners of conduct as "good" and to condemn as "bad" those whose outlook or behavior is otherwise.

Most people regard *anomalies in behavior,* unless they are minor, as essentially *antisocial phenomena:* such instances of social deviance as crime, delinquency, addiction, alcoholism, sexual aberrations, and mental illness are seen as blights on the social structure that can be attributed to *individual pathologies* and "cured" either by treating or by punishing the erring individual.

This tendency to view deviance in absolute terms should not obscure other factors in American society that also influence our world view and reveal that agreement on what constitutes deviance is more apparent than real. One such factor is the heterogeneous composition of our society, with its attendant *cultural diversity.* The impact of this ethnic pluralism on the American *belief system* has occasioned numerous debates over the nature of values, and Kai T. Erikson has provided us with a case study of one of the great value conflicts of our history in *The Wayward Puritans* (1966).

Erikson's historical data showed how the process of defining certain beliefs and behaviors as heresy could serve to redefine and identify for the Puritans what was deviant and what was right conduct under changing conditions. Perhaps more significantly, his study emphasized the abstract and situational problems involved in such definition, for there is *dissensus* as well as *consensus* about the definition of deviance in a society. He also found that the tendency toward a *moral absolutism* still exists today—at least to the extent that the deviant is seen as a "miserable creature," outside the pale of conventional life. As Erikson aptly argues in an earlier work:

> Deviance is not a property inherent in certain kinds of behavior; it is a property conferred upon these forms by the audiences which directly, or indirectly, witness them. The critical variable, then . . . is the social audience, rather than the individual actor. . . . When a community acts to control the behavior of one of its members, it is engaged in

John Sinclair. The case of John Sinclair illustrates several issues of great interest in the study of deviance and crime. In 1969 penalties for marijuana use in Michigan ranged from zero time (suspended sentence or probation) to ten years in jail, and there was a mandatory minimum 20-year sentence for sale of the drug. That year Sinclair was sentenced in Detroit to 9.5–10 years in prison for possession of marijuana. He had also been charged with selling the drug, because he had given two marijuana cigarettes to police undercover agents disguised as "hippies." The charge of selling was dismissed because of the police entrapment process involved in the case. Sinclair's highly visible radical politics and advocacy of the counterculture—he was founder of the White Panther Party and the political rock group MC-5—may have influenced police activities toward him and the severe sentence given him more than did his gift of marijuana. What were the agents of social control really reacting to when they punished him with the upper limit of the possible sentence rather than with some lesser term? Sinclair was released in 1971 after the Michigan legislature established a maximum penalty of one year's imprisonment for possession of marijuana and four years' imprisonment for sale. What happened between 1969 and 1971 to make marijuana possession and sale seem more acceptable to the authorities of the state—or stiff penalties less acceptable?

(Facing page) **Table 1. Number of Societies Punishing Specific Types of Sexual Behavior.** In considering a table such as this one, it should be borne in mind that definitions of what constitutes specific types of behavior (for example, incest) may vary from society to society. (Source: Brown, "A Comparative Study of Deviations From Sexual Mores")

a very intricate process of selection. ("Notes on the Sociology of Deviance," 1962)

Expanding this argument, Robert A. Scott points out that in
American society the attribute of deviance may be conferred as the
result of merely inappropriate behavior or appearance or even
hereditary factors ("A Proposed Framework for Analyzing Deviance
as a Property of Social Order," 1972). Studies of the manner in
which handicaps and physical deformities lead to persons being labeled as deviant by "normals" suggest that those—for example,
sightless individuals or individuals lacking a limb—who do not fit
into our society's definition of normal appearance frequently find it
necessary to accommodate to society's stereotype of the "unfit."
The sightless or limbless person, for instance, may find his social interaction disrupted by the fact that other people stare at or away
from him or may act more helpless than he really is simply because
people expect him to be helpless. (See Unit 19.)

Nevertheless, deviant status is most frequently assigned as a
consequence of behavior so inappropriate as to evoke a reaction
from society or its *control agents*. Law violaters, the mentally ill, or
even political or religious dissenters may evoke this kind of reaction.

Nineteenth-century humanitarian reformers were aware of the
stigmatizing impact of law enforcement on adolescent law violators.
A youngster charged with one offense was frequently considered
"no good" ever after. In order to lessen these effects, the
humanitarians directed their efforts toward reforming the judicial
procedures. The result was the establishment of the juvenile courts,
which set up special procedures for processing delinquent, dependent, and neglected children.

Ironically, these reformers, characterized by Anthony Platt as
"the child savers," were also influential in setting up new *social
categories* for classifying and controlling "wayward" adolescents.
Thus they not only created new categories of deviance—youthful activities that previously had either been ignored or informally dealt
with—but also promoted their own traditional middle class values.

Deviance, then, is a broader category than one simply encompassing criminals or misfits, and Robert A. Scott suggests that
the concept of deviance in our society exhibits two distinctive characteristics. The term imputes *moral inferiority*—that is, criminals and
other dissidents are viewed as offenders against society's sense of
what is morally appropriate, although the mentally ill and physically
handicapped are not judged as harshly. And, the stigma of deviance becomes a *master status*. The thief is not seen as someone
who may have another normal status, as a husband and father, for
example, but essentially as a "thief." Similarly, the blind person is
given a special label; if he is a writer he is referred to as a "blind
writer."

It is apparent that deviance is not something apart from everyday social processes and beliefs, but rather is related to the
structure of our beliefs and behavior system. It is intertwined with
our definitions of right and wrong and intertwined with our definitions
of appropriate and inappropriate behavior. It is an outgrowth of, and
the corollary to, the definition of order that shows itself in day-to-day
social behavior.

Alcoholics on "Skid Row." In their complete "retreatism," such men
and women are perhaps even more extreme "drop-outs" than the
youth who more commonly receive the label.

C   QUESTIONS AND EVIDENCE

1   Questions

In a field of study as dynamic as that concerning deviance, it is not surprising to find a variety of emphases in social inquiry. The basic issues pivot around the following questions: (1) How does society attempt to cope with deviant forms of behavior? (2) How does society itself, especially the state, contribute to deviance? (3) How do individuals and groups become deviant?

2   Evidence

a   The "Burning Issue" Question

i   Context   When deviant behavior is readily observable rather than covert, it is frequently viewed as inimical to society's values and interests. Consequently the society, or its agents, is charged with the task of identifying the cause of the behavior in order to control or eliminate it. Sometimes these efforts take the form of suppression of information about the behavior, as well as the activity itself, so that the idea will not spread and contaminate the "innocent." The blacking-out in 1972 of two episodes of the CBS-TV situation comedy *Maude* in several cities because the show dealt with the topics of abortion and vasectomy illustrates this desire to censor even discussions of behaviors defined as deviant. The local station managers had a sound legal ground for their action, because state law forbade not only abortion but even its advocacy. And at least half of the phone calls and letters to the stations supported the managements' action. This example underlines the heterogeneity of our belief system and provides insights into society's largely futile attempts to suppress deviance. However, society employs many other tactics to isolate or eradicate deviance, and sociologists ask: *What sanctions and pressures does society exert against deviant forms of behavior?*

ii   Theory   Although blacking out *Maude* may seem an extreme example, conventional sociological attempts to deal with deviant behavior, though more subtle, may reflect the same attitudes. Daniel Glaser, in *Social Deviance* (1971), has suggested that the seventeenth-century Puritan colonists saw a greater range of behavior as seriously deviant than do contemporary Americans, and at first one might agree with this assertion. A closer look at American society, however, should incline the thoughtful observer to agree with Jack Douglas' contention that "the more democratic societies have become, the more rigid and autocratic . . . the foundation of the administration has become" (*American Social Order*, 1971). And even a small amount of social awareness permits one to recognize that those in the lower strata of society run greater risk of being identified and stigmatized by the formal bureaucracies of control (police, courts, and so on) than do those in the dominant upper or middle strata.

Society's stress on causes of unconventional or deviant behavior has been termed the *correctional orientation* by David Matza (*Becoming Deviant,* 1969). Much has been written about the various ways of treating the "miscreant," and it is an American sociological tradition to look upon deviance and deviators as "*pathological*." C. Wright Mills referred to early sociologists as "social pathologists," and the social surveys conducted by these reformers focused on the seamy side of urban life. The social pathologists were followed by the "Chicago school," who wrote and talked of *social disorganization* (an idea that frequently was translated to mean social pathology). We have also discussed the Chicago school in Units 6 and 17.

After World War II the concept of social disorganization was replaced by the emphasis of *functionalist* sociologists on scientific analysis. In their emphasis on the *causal explanations* (or *etiology*) of deviance, the functionalists sought systematically to analyze variations in rates of deviant behavior. They sometimes wrote more about the unintended or *latent* functions than about the intended or *manifest* functions of deviance and were inclined to see society as a system capable of correcting by appropriate policy any deviance that might occur within it. An example of these approaches is contained in Daniel Bell's essay on "Crime as an American Way of Life" (1953). Bell discusses how Arnold Rothstein and other gangsters of immigrant background moved into certain New York industries to gain wealth and power by shady means. As time went on:

> Rothstein's chief successors, Lepke Buchalter and Gurrah Shapiro, were able, in the early thirties to dominate sections of the men's and women's clothing industries, of painting, fur dressing, flour trucking, and other fields. In a highly chaotic and cut-throat industry such as clothing, the racketeer, paradoxically, played a stabilizing role by regulating competition and fixing prices. . . . When the NRA [National Recovery Administration] came in and assumed this [stabilizing] function, the businessmen found that what had once been a quasi-economic service was now pure extortion, and he began to demand police action.

With the introduction of government economic regulation, the context of the situation that made racketeering functional in the cutthroat industries changed. The irony of gangsters establishing orderly business practices ended. They became simply extortioners once again.

More recently, the "neo-Chicagoan" or "labeling" sociologists have renounced the correctional impulse, rejecting the assumption that deviance can be defined in absolute terms. They see deviance as the result of *social definitions* imposed on individuals and groups by others, rather than as the result of defects of character or social institutions. This orientation has focused on ideas such as *societal reaction* and *stigma*. More recently it has been elaborated by new theories stressing the *sociopsychological process* of becoming deviant.

iii Research The impulse of a society or group to correct deviant behavior seems reasonable and natural, given the need of such collectivities to maintain the social order. Sociological literature abounds with research studies that seek to explain deviant behavior in order to solve the social problem it creates. Most of these early studies were conducted from the standpoint of community morality, and this perspective is quite evident in the sociological surveys of

Burying a Hun. The casket of this former leader of the Boston Huns motorcycle gang was showered with beer and liquor during his burial and the empty containers thrown into his grave. Although this particular burial ceremony violated the customs of the wider society, it was considered appropriate behavior by the club members; it made use of highly valued commodities, beer and liquor, to pay last respects to an honored member of the group. At least seven gangs sent delegates to the funeral of the leader, who had been shot to death outside his club's headquarters.

Pittsburgh and New York City sponsored by the Russell Sage Foundation prior to World War I. These surveys described deviant behavior in terms of the social pathology of these communities, stressing the pathological nature of such diverse activities as various sports, gangs, crime, prostitution, and machine politics.

Research conducted by the Chicago sociologists focused on the idea that the social disorganization of the poor resulted in social dislocation and breakdown of ordinary social controls; this community disorganization released deviant impulses. One of the important works that proposed this social disorganization theory of deviance was Fredric Thrasher's study (*The Gang*, 1927) of 1,313 juvenile and adult gangs. This approach received further support through the work of Robert Faris and H. Warren Dunham, who studied the distribution of mental illness in Chicago. They discovered that most types of mental illness were most prevalent in areas of social disorganization at the center of the city and decreased progressively with movement away from the center (*Mental Disorders in Urban Areas*, 1939).

Robert K. Merton's "Social Structure and Anomie" (1938), which has been described as the most-quoted single paper in modern sociology, marked the high point of the functionalist theory of deviance. In this essay Merton used the concept of *anomie* (or anomy)—originally developed by Emile Durkheim in *The Division of Labor in Society* (1893) and *Suicide* (1897), two of his great contributions to sociology—to show how a "cardinal American virtue, ambition" could be translated into a "cardinal American vice, deviant behavior." In *Suicide* Durkheim discussed the condition of "deregulation" or "normlessness" that occurs in society in times of economic disaster or abrupt growth of wealth and power.

> . . . as the conditions of life are changed, the standard according to which needs were regulated can no longer remain the same; for it varies with social resources, since it largely determines the share of each class of producers. The scale is upset; but a new scale cannot be immediately improvised. Time is required for the public conscience to reclassify men and things. So long as the social forces thus freed have not regained equilibrium, their respective values are unknown and so all regulation is lacking for a time. The limits are unknown between the possible and the impossible, what is just and what is unjust, legitimate claims and hopes and those which are immoderate. Consequently, there is no restraint upon aspirations. If the disturbance is profound, it affects even the principles controlling the distribution of men among various occupations. Since the relations between various parts of society are necessarily modified, the ideas expressing these relations must change. Some particular class especially favored by the crisis is no longer resigned to its former lot, and, on the other hand, the example of its greater good fortune arouses all sorts of jealousy below and about it. Appetites, not being controlled by a public opinion become disoriented, no longer recognize the limits proper to them. Besides, they are at the same time seized by a sort of natural

Gang war in Philadelphia. Two rival street gangs armed with sticks, pipes, stones, bottles, nails and zip guns conduct a battle over territory. Assaultive behavior is one intragroup status ladder that is open even to those who occupy the lowest rung on the socioeconomic ladder of our society.

[agitation] simply by the greater intensity of public life. With increased prosperity desires increase. At the very moment when traditional rules have lost their authority, the richer prize offered these appetites stimulates them and makes them more exigent and impatient of control. The state of de-regulation or anomy is thus further heightened by passions being less disciplined, precisely when they need more disciplining.

Merton's theory assumed that aspirations were uniformly high in American society, that Americans of all classes pursue an identical set of ends or goals—especially those involving success as measured by money. As Americans learn that the means to achieve these goals are unequal, they are forced to *innovate*—to create new methods of attainment that may be regarded as deviant by those for whom traditional forms of behavior have proven adequate.

. . . other aspects of the social structure, besides the extreme emphasis on pecuniary success, must be considered if we are to understand the social sources of deviant behavior. A high frequency of deviant behavior is not generated merely by lack of opportunity or by this exaggerated pecuniary emphasis. A comparatively rigidified class structure, a feudalistic caste order, may limit opportunities far beyond the point which obtains in American society today. It is when a system of cultural values extols, virtually above all else, certain *common* success-goals *for the population at large* while the social structure rigorously restricts or completely closes access to approved modes of reaching these goals *for a considerable part of the same population*, that deviant behavior ensues on a large scale. ("Social Structure and Anomie," 1938)

A number of investigations followed Merton's analysis, and Delbert S. Elliot summarizes these findings and augments Merton's logic when he states that "the intense frustration of lower class boys in schools motivates them toward delinquent patterns of behavior in an attempt to recoup their loss of self esteem." ("Delinquency, School Attendance, and Dropout," 1966)

These studies made a number of assumptions germane to society's "common-sense" approach to deviant behavior. They assumed that the moral rules of our society are generally shared and that the basic problem in explaining deviance is to explain why specific individuals and groups do not follow these generally shared rules. They focused on the idea that because deviant behavior is found in disorganized communities, then there must be a relationship between these social dislocations and deviance.

Merton and the functionalists assumed a "moral road" to success. For them deviance arose where there is a lack of legitimate means adequate to the attainment of culturally acceptable goals and the individual is driven to take an illegitimate, innovative means to this end. Because disorganization and anomie occur mainly among the lower strata, these investigators believed that social policies of prevention and correction should focus on these deviance-prone groups.

iv Evaluation The popular conception that deviance was abnormal and must be explained in such a way as to uncover and "cure" the root causes of the evil was shared by early sociologists dealing with the phenomenon. This orientation of "seeking the cause in order to find the cure" suffered from several specific limitations, however. First, in seeing deviance as the product of disorganized communities, these sociologists overlooked the underlying order that existed within these communities. Niles Anderson's study *The Hobo* (1923) was an exception to the usual view among the Chicago school, as William F. Whyte's *Street Corner Society* (1955) was to the work of the functionalists. Both showed the existence of a distinct behavior system among the groups studied. Second, in focusing on the anomie of the lower classes, American sociologists stressed the *subcultural* aspects of deviance in a manner that depicted the lower-class individual as *constrained to deviance*. They emphasized the diversity within society in terms of the class system, but they overlooked the variety and diversity within the lower classes themselves. The third limitation is related to this problem. In assigning the cause of deviance to behaviors generated by subcultures that had developed in opposition to middle-class morality, sociologists tended toward an "oversocialized" conception of conventional behavior—people learn all that they do—and thus concluded that the deviant was "undersocialized"—had not learned the proper patterns. Viewing deviance as the result of a *deficiency in the socialization process* is related to the assumption that society (that is, the dominant or "straight" segments of society) is highly integrated rather than morally pluralistic. The idea that deviance might actually arise from a conflict over "moral" meanings and social definitions imposed on certain individuals and groups by the dominant power groups in society is a much more recent perspective, the *labeling perspective*.

b The "Classical" Question

i Context Thomas Hobbes, the English social philosopher, writing in the turbulent seventeenth century, was concerned with how society could establish and maintain social order. We have touched upon Hobbes in Units 5 and 11. The *Hobbesian question*, as this issue of social order came to be called, takes on a vastly different dimension in contemporary society. Hobbes and the social thinkers who followed him were reacting to the problem of general disorder; the present task is to develop a personal theory, an increased social consciousness regarding the problem of conformity within the social order. It is in defense of conformity that our leaders talk of "maintaining the national moral fiber" and dissidents are abused as unpatriotic bums. To see conformity as the key problem of the social order today is to acknowledge the presence of conflicting "moral meanings" in a society of ethnic and moral pluralism. It is also to acknowledge that man's capacity for freedom and for autonomous social action is to a considerable extent limited by that social order. And viewing conformity as the issue enables us to perceive the connection between the authority of the state and its involvement in the definition of what is conventional or "right" behavior. Therefore, many sociologists now ask: *How do individuals learn to observe rules and constraints habitually?*

ii   Theory Early man had to develop means whereby he could not only control nature but also regulate human relationships as increasing numbers of individuals gathered together. Ralph Linton, in *Tree of Culture* (1955), argues that the development of *culture* as a system whereby man could communicate and adapt to others was as crucial to his development as the discovery of the uses of fire.

Sigmund Freud, in one of his more sociological essays, *Civilization and its Discontents* (1930), deals with a tragic paradox, "the antagonism between the demands of instinct" and the "organic repression" of those instincts that paved the way for the development of complex civilization by harnessing basic human energy to the service of socially acceptable goals. Apropos of Hobbes, Freud argued that as a consequence of the "primary mutual hostility of human beings, civilized society is perpetually threatened with disintegration," and civilization must therefore "set limits to man's aggressive instincts." That Freud viewed the social order developed by civilization with considerable misgiving is apparent by a concluding statement to *Civilization and its Discontents:* "Men have gained control over the forces of nature to such an extent that . . . they would have no difficulty in exterminating one another. . . ."

Freud suggested no means whereby we could disentangle ourselves from the web of repressive civilization. The point is that he did not see the established social order as equivalent to the "good." With the exception of Karl Marx, who also dealt with the alienating effects of modern society, Freud was unique among clas-

Conformity—a social problem? Although all societies need conformity to perpetuate their existence, when does conformity itself become a social problem? Cannot blind conformity stand in the way of needed social change? From a perspective critical of conformity it is possible to see certain deviant behavior as socially productive in that arbitrary cultural barriers will occasionally be broken, thus allowing society to change in revitalizing directions.

Sit-in. Deviant actions by certain individuals can make others aware of the fact that some laws and customs are bad or contradict other more important rules—such as the proclaimed equality of citizens. The nonviolent sit-ins of the early 1960s, for which many blacks and some whites were arrested, pointed out the unfair and unconstitutional nature of laws requiring racial segregation, and these laws were repealed by legislative bodies or struck down by the courts.

sical thinkers in that he viewed the imposition of the social order with ambivalence. Most theorists, from Plato onward, had assumed the existence of a beneficent ultimate order in the affairs of mankind. Alvin Gouldner points out that the notion of social order as oppressive and tentative at best is very different from the functionalists' reliance on the concept of anomie, which led them to see deviance as the problem rather than the social order itself.

> [The functionalist] approach to deviant behavior is fundamentally different . . . from the Freudian or the Marxian, in which tensions are not necessarily seen as due to the lack of something, but may indeed derive from conformity with certain moral values or may be due to a conflict between opposing forces . . . simultaneously present. (*The Coming Crisis of Western Sociology,* 1970)

To view conformity as the problem in developing a perspective on deviance is to recognize, as Richard Quinney has so aptly pointed out in "From Repression to Liberation" (1972) that concepts such as alienation, authority, community, and the sacred must have different meanings in the contemporary world—which some have called "postindustrial"—than they had for the classical theorists: "They tended to support order for its own sake, we reject any order that oppresses us. Liberation is our goal—in theory and in action."

iii Research (Survey) In the social world we habitually act according to a variety of rules. These rules more often than not represent patterns of conduct that predate the time in which we live. In a very real sense, then, we live in a normative world we never made. Some of these rules are formalized into legal statutes, others are informal. Nevertheless, both serve to delineate a frame of reference, a *symbolic universe* shared—with great variations—by members of society. Sociologists have been more inclined to focus on the informal rules and agents of social control than on the formal. However, in serving the correctional viewpoint that social deviance can be "cured," sociologists frequently used official statistics in an uncritical manner—without careful consideration of the way statistics reflect the bias of the officials who create them and who designate "culprits." Durkheim's classic *Suicide* is frequently cited by introductory textbooks as a model of the scientific study of deviance. Yet as Jack Douglas has shown in his critique of that work (*Social Meanings of Suicide,* 1967), Durkheim uncritically used official statistics on suicide rates and official categorizations of individuals, and he deduced his typologies of suicide from these relationships.

Studies of mental illness (such as that by Faris and Dunham) have shown that people with schizophrenic disorders are concentrated in urban areas heavily populated by underemployed and unemployed (that is, the lower classes), and a number of studies of juvenile delinquency (including the classic *Delinquency Areas* by Clifford Shaw and Henry McKay, 1929) have emphasized the transmission of delinquent patterns through the lower-class culture. As numerous writers have pointed out, however, most people who are raised in poverty situations do not succumb to these various forms of deviance. Nevertheless, *poverty* has replaced *heredity* as the favored explanation of deviance today.

Although these studies did not discuss law-violating behaviors

A suicide. Suicide is not a "meaningless act." The "meaning" of a particular suicide is a complex function of the emotional and physical state of the individual involved, his social history, the social situation he finds himself in, and the cultural values of the wider society.

A male homosexual. Why does society insist on defining certain acts as "criminal" even when there are no victims (or the victim is the perpetrator himself or herself)? By criminalizing behaviors such as homosexuality and marijuana use, society itself makes the behavior into a "social problem." Prohibition showed how socially costly such a process can be. By attempting to outlaw the sale of liquor, it created the conditions for the forging of the domain of organized crime on a national and international scale as gangsters took over the liquor traffic and its big "profits."

exclusively, all were based on officially gathered statistics. Increasingly, as Jack Douglas points out in *American Social Order* (1971), "Sociologists who are committed to the statistical approach to the study of deviance rely almost wholly on official statistics since they are the most readily available." Thus not only does the state provide the definitions of deviance, but it also has "expanded its controls over the conditions whereby social information can be used." Nevertheless, one area where contemporary sociologists have made the public aware of the power of the state in defining what moral conduct must be is that of "*crimes without victims.*" In his study of abortion, homosexuality, and drug addiction, Edwin Schur suggests that "crimes without victims may be limited to those situations where one person obtains from another, in a fairly direct exchange, a commodity or personal service which is socially disapproved and legally proscribed." (*Crimes Without Victims,* 1965)

In the studies in *Outsiders* (1963) Howard S. Becker very effectively focused on the way the state labels behavior as deviant and also on the "conflict and disagreement" over the rules—that is, the political process through which deviance becomes defined. Becker introduced a simple typology to show the relationship between two dimensions of deviance: Whether or not acts are seen by "others" as really deviant and whether or not an act conforms to a particular rule. Table 2 illustrates the problematic interrelationship between *types of deviant behavior* and the *reaction system.* The case of *secret deviance* is singularly important because very little is known about deviant individuals who are not known to officials or therapists. In her investigation of a homosexual community, Evelyn Hooker found that homosexuals who were not under treatment or observation of social control agents did not share the problems fre-

quently associated with those in the clinical population ("The Adjustment of the Male Homosexual," 1965).

The social order represents an attempt by society and its agents to control individual and group behavior that seems to threaten definitions of order. Altogether, considerable effort is expended in American society in defining and processing of behavior thought to be contrary to the well-being of society.

iv Evaluation Classical social theorists were concerned with the problem of conformity to the extent that they saw man's unruly nature as a threat to the (assumed) moral order. Failure of social control would mean a state of "deregulation" or anomie. Conformity was to be rewarded and deviance eliminated in order to maintain the stability of society. The heritage of this emphasis on the need for conformity has perpetuated the myth of an all-pervasive social order in American society. Even though in most American communities the person in the street is daily confronted with evidence of ethnic, religious, and moral pluralism, Americans need to remind themselves —especially when formulating public policy—of the problematic meaning of morality and the hazards of demanding too much conformity. Conventional sociologists have not generally taken these factors into account in their studies of deviance. The individual or group seen as deviant has been studied as a "thing" apart from society or as a consequence of an aberration in the social structure. Studies of deviance have focused on the frequency of deviance in certain segments of society, and, of course, correctional or therapeutic programs have been proposed, but theories of deviance have not, until recently, considered the state itself as involved in the very production of deviance.

If our social consciousness can be heightened so that we see conformity as a problem and can recognize our overemphasis on it as a simplified way of maintaining the social order given the heterogeneous makeup of society, then we will see deviance as the consequence of power relationships in society and as a property conferred by social control agents. To the extent that we can develop this degree of awareness, the deviators will be seen as they are, for example, in Japan: fellow men who have been labeled deviant by the state but who are not "less than human" or outside of the collectivity. And we will have recognized a basic fact: those who confer the deviant label today represent the authority of the state. Furthermore, we will be informed about the nature of the deviators: they will generally be the poor and the powerless. Deviance can thus be seen as a political and social category rather than as a moral category.

Conventional sociology has failed to address the problem of order and conformity in relation to the process of creating deviance. The labeling perspective has not fully illuminated the nature of deviance either, although it has put it in perspective as a property conferred on an individual by others. It has not dealt, however, with the *power equation*—that is, how some members of society can violate rules without being labeled deviant. Furthermore, labeling focuses on the exterior complexity of deviance, but does not explain nor sensitize us to the subjective process whereby various individuals and groups develop deviant rather than conventionally accepted forms of behavior.

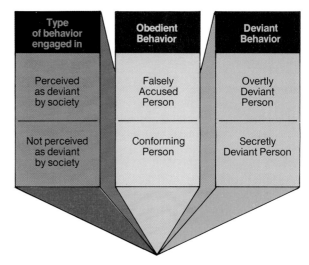

Type of behavior engaged in	Obedient Behavior	Deviant Behavior
Perceived as deviant by society	Falsely Accused Person	Overtly Deviant Person
Not perceived as deviant by society	Conforming Person	Secretly Deviant Person

Table 2. Types of Deviant Behavior. How should the presence of falsely accused persons and "secret deviants" affect our understanding of deviance-conformity as a whole? (Source: Adapted from Becker, *Outsiders*)

Gay liberation movement demonstration in New York City. This movement is encouraging homosexuals to acknowledge their sexual orientation publicly and thus rid themselves of socially induced feelings of guilt and inadequacy. Homosexuals now appear on television, write articles for national publications, publish their own magazines, lobby with politicians (promising political support in return for political action to repeal laws discriminating against them), and demonstrate publicly to protest harassment by police and other agents of social control.

c The "Research" Question

i Context The question most frequently asked by those concerned with deviant behavior—laymen and officials as well as social scientists—is: Why do they do it? David Matza has attributed this stress on causal explanations to society's desire to correct or rehabilitate the individual and to rid the social order of the phenomenon he represents. The question, given society's concern, is a legitimate one. Sociologists ask: *What is the process whereby the individual becomes deviant? To what extent are society and its agents involved in this process and what are the meanings and consequences of the process for the individual?*

ii Theory Traditional attempts to explain deviation have been influenced both by the *positivist school* of criminology of Cesare Lombroso (see Unit 23) and by the functionalists. Such explanations tend to emphasize the deterministic impact of such variables as biological factors, weak (or nonexistent) parental supervision, poverty, peer-group associations, and unequal access to opportunity. This deterministic orientation has been reflected in the treatment apparatus of our juvenile courts and has been built into our penal system in the name of rehabilitation. The reliance of these approaches on oversimplified causal connections was satirized by a street gang in the *West Side Story* song: "Gee, Officer Krupke . . . I'm depraved on accounta I'm deprived."

More recent pronouncements by political leaders on the need to get "tough" with criminals represent an equally simplistic backlash against the excesses of the deterministic approach to criminal deviance. As President Nixon stated in 1973, "Americans . . . were often told that the criminal was not responsible . . . but that society was responsible. I totally disagree with this permissive philosophy." Actually, the president's reduction of deterministic perspectives to the notion that the criminal is "not responsible" is clearly fallacious: certainly none of the proponents of the deterministic view deny that the individual is the direct and deliberate agent of his crime. Furthermore, to focus solely on the "culprit" is to obscure the role of society, because deviance is an enterprise that involves both the individual's behavior and society's response to that behavior.

In his excellent summary of the labeling perspective, *Labeling Deviant Behavior* (1971), Edwin Schur suggests that both individual involvement in deviant situations and whole deviant "careers" should be viewed as the result of basic response processes at various levels of *social interaction* between the deviating *social actor* and other members of society. "Deviant acts alone," then, "do not make a deviant; mechanisms of social labeling must also come into play." These *labeling mechanisms* themselves give rise to situations that provoke further forms of deviance, or secondary deviance. (An example would be a "hippie" harassed by police for his "radical" appearance who eventually becomes an "off the pigs" revolutionary.) The labeling orientation has by now become conventional wisdom in the study of deviance. More recently, *phenomenology* (a philosophic approach that seeks to describe and clarify without the distortions of any presuppositions, values, or intellectual principles, emphasizing instead immediate intuition of the whole experiential process or phenomenon) has been applied by David Matza to the study of deviance. This approach has much in common with the la-

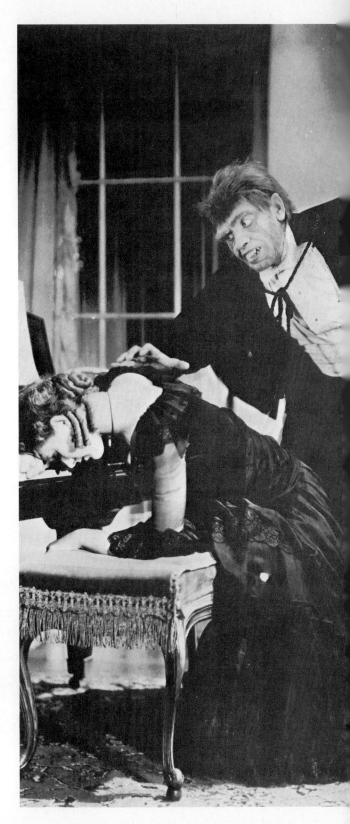

beling perspective. To summarize the salient details of the many theories that have sought to explain the process of becoming deviant, Matza, in his book *Becoming Deviant* (1969), explicates three "basic ideas or master conceptions": (1) *affinity* (circumstances contributing to an individual's competitive disadvantage, for example, poverty, low intelligence, racial discrimination); (2) *affiliation* (association with a deviant group or subculture); and (3) *signification* (the stigmatizing or labeling action of those in authority). He argues that separately each of these concepts is too abstract and simplistic to show the process of becoming deviant in its natural human context, and the human meaning of each can only be discovered in the context of the others. Any genuine attempt to understand deviance, Matza asserts, must also involve the following elements: (1) an attempt to appreciate the process from the subjective view of the individual involved; (2) a recognition that deviance is a complex system of socially constructed and shared meanings; (3) recognition of the intentionality and responsibility of the deviator throughout the process; (4) and a focus on societal reactions, especially agents and authorities of the state.

iii Research (Methodology) The idea of affinity has been a principal notion in explanations of becoming deviant—circumstances such as physical makeup, race, intelligence, family life, and socioeconomic status have been seen as causes of deviance, and sociologists' "favorite affinity" has been the relationship between poverty and pathology. Matza attacks this particular affinity in a critique of Robert Merton's "Social Structure and Anomie," which Matza describes as asserting that the lower class was "bombarded by the propaganda of success, yet prevented by class barriers from realizing that aim. . . . [Thus] the poor are more apt to stray from conventional avenues of achievement." Merton also came under attack by Matza for his reliance upon officially compiled statistics as the basis of his study. But the affinity of poverty and pathology cannot be dismissed merely because of this type of deficiency. Bernard Rosenberg's and Harry Silverstein's study of delinquency (*The Varieties of Delinquent Experience,* 1969) raises more questions about Merton's hypothesis, however, and supports Matza's skepticism about the use of affinity as a primary explanation of deviance.

Rosenberg and Silverstein explored the relationship between opportunity, aspirations, and delinquency by conducting in-depth interviews with delinquents and nondelinquents in high-delinquency areas of New York City and Chicago. To control the variable of *ethnicity* they selected a black community, a Puerto Rican community, and a Southern white community. They found that most of the youths in their study were uninterested in high levels of educational or occupational achievement. Most of those studied ranked low in aspirations with little commitment to success, as defined by the dominant culture. Rosenberg and Silverstein could not establish a link between high aspirations and success, but they did find a correlation between low aspirations and lack of success. Their general conclusion was that anomie is not limited to those in lower socioeconomic categories.

Rosenberg and Silverstein declared that if anomie exists it is endemic to the entire society and is really "moral anomie." "Moral anomie" refers not only to strain tending to deviance by those in

Frederic March as Mr. Hyde in film version of *Dr. Jekyll and Mr. Hyde* (1932). How much time does actual deviant behavior take up in the life of a person who is engaged in it? There is considerable range in such time spans, but no matter how frequently or how seldom a person engages in deviant behavior, once such behavior is known, the person is labeled a "deviant" in a totalistic manner.

low socioeconomic circumstances but also to a society-wide condition in which people refer to a group situation rather than to their own individual consciences in deciding what is right or wrong; this convergence of circumstances and exercise of the will to decide represents a more appropriate and logical conceptual relationship between affinity ("circumstance") and affiliation ("group") than earlier emphases.

Sociologist Erich Goode served as a consultant for the National Commission on Marihuana and Drug Abuse in 1971 and 1972, and he conducted research on whether marijuana use led to the use of more dangerous drugs. His findings fit rather well into Matza's concept of affiliation, for he discovered "that a given user's likelihood of experimenting with more dangerous drugs was closely related to his involvement with . . . a drug using subculture." He argues that "two factors account for the greater use of dangerous drugs among marijuana users in comparison with nonusers: (1) a process of selective recruitment, and (2) a process of selective interaction and socialization."

Matza's third master concept employed to conjoin major ideas in studying the process of becoming deviant is significant, the signifying or stigmatizing action of those in authority. The power of the state "dwarfs" the individual's power over the process; the individual is "banned"—that is, collectively represented as an outsider who is morally depraved—which forces him to affiliate with those who provide illegal services, which further *criminalizes* him.

Goode's study also provides an excellent demonstration of how signification works:

> The subterranean status of marijuana makes its use more than simply a question of selective recruitment into a specific activity by a certain "deviant" segment of society. The very criminal status of marijuana gives its use, possession, and sale an added . . . subcultural power not evidenced by the possession and use of the legal drugs. (*Drugs and American Society*, 1972)

He notes that the correlation between marijuana use and use of dangerous drugs would not disappear if marijuana were legalized, for the correlation also exists between use of marijuana and use of legal drugs. However, after legalization, the correlation would be no different from the current correlations between legal and illegal drugs. In light of the above findings, it is legitimate to ask, as John Kaplan has, in *Marijuana: the New Prohibition* (1970), "whether or not the criminalization of marijuana is part of the problem, rather than the solution." (See Units 10 and 24.)

iv   Evaluation   Conventional explanations of deviance tend to stress poverty and force of circumstances, including deviant subcultures as a compelling force, without viewing the dehumanizing social processes at work within those circumstances. There can be "no deprivation without deprivers." Even given such circumstances, the individual's "intentionality" mediates the process of becoming deviate. We should not turn into objects those we study by removing from them the responsibility of choice.

Matza's *phenomenological perspective* seeks to provide the subjective meaning of deviant behavior by stressing the need for in-

A Southern sheriff displays what he describes as the "tools of my trade." Who defines what constitutes "crime" and "deviance"? What is the role of the state in the production of "deviance"? Who controls the "controllers of deviance"?

Antiwar demonstrators jailed in Washington, D.C. 13,500 persons were arrested in the nation's capital in May 1971 during four days of protests against the war in Indochina. The charges against the demonstrators were later dismissed by the courts because during the mass arrests police violated provisions requiring due process of law. Generally in incidents such as this one, the wider society resists defining the police as criminal, even when they violate the law, and instead focuses on the "criminal behavior" of the persons the police arrest. Why is this so?

tuitive insights into deviance and the whole process of social control and by emphasizing the actual rather than assumed setting that surrounds specific human behavior. However, the new spirit that phenomenology brings to the study of deviance and control has yet to develop, as Edwin Schur points out, a sophisticated approach that will effectively bridge the gap between ''hard'' empirical data and subjective intuition (*Labeling Deviant Behavior,* 1971).

3   Overview

The sociological study of deviance has traditionally expended more effort on explaining aberrant behavior in order to correct it than it has on developing an understanding of deviance as a phenomenon that occurs naturally within the social order. Some sociologists have romanticized those who are stigmatized, but the error has far more often been in the direction of exclusively correlational emphasis. Consequently, pathology has been stressed rather than diversity, and explanations have ignored or obscured the complexity of the overlap between behaviors seen as ''bad'' and those perceived as ''good.''

      The ethnic and ethical pluralism of America has become more apparent as a result of the conflicts of the past decade, conflicts that have grown out of injustice and social policies that have been harsh and restrictive to many Americans. A clearer understanding of the problem of conformity and dissent is required if we are to effectively cope with these basic problems in the social order.

      The sociology of deviance is thus rapidly becoming one of the most creative areas of social thought. As we become more knowledgeable about the dynamics of social conduct, certain rules and expectations that characterize current roles and relationships will be replaced by others that may be more productive (that is, they may more accurately reflect human reality) and be less restrictive or repressive. This liberation of society from unnecessary or outdated prohibitions on conduct and from a narrowly circumscribed range of behaviors deemed ''normal'' or ''desirable'' should equally result in the liberation of diverse individuals from the stigma of being regarded—and treated—as deviants. In turn, this new climate may help to reintegrate such individuals into the social order and thereby enable them to have a responsible role in maintaining it.

1   Interview:
David Matza

David Matza is professor of sociology at the University of California at Berkeley and has been affiliated with the Center for the Study of Law and Society. His interests have focused on the study of deviance, and he is the author of the highly regarded books *Delinquency and Drift* and *Becoming Deviant*. He is currently doing research for a book on postwar American domestic politics.

DPG *From society's point of view, is there such a thing as a victimless crime?*
MATZA If by victim you mean what I mean—and that's also the legal meaning of victim—someone who is intentionally hurt by an act, then there are lots of victimless crimes. Gambling, prostitution, many forms of drug use, homosexuality—all would qualify. However, any argument that begins with society's point of view, or any group's point of view, or even the family's point of view runs into trouble, because equivocation takes place. The question then becomes: "Is anyone else harmed, either intentionally or unintentionally, as a consequence of the act?" By that kind of false reasoning, any act can have very harmful consequences.

DPG *Do we understand the nature of deviance sufficiently to develop policies to deal with it effectively?*
MATZA I don't think we have to have a full knowledge, or even scientific knowledge, to guide policy. The appropriate policies are pointed to by every kind of social or psychological research. Even common sense is adequate to develop policy.

DPG *What policies are appropriate in dealing with deviance?*
MATZA First, public policy should place priority on improving the law-enforcement system. Victimless crimes should be excised from the criminal code. That would give more legitimacy to the law. Many sections of the legal code no longer have legitimacy, and that leads to general disrespect. In addition, law enforcement must proceed again in a more legitimate manner, in a manner that is accepted by the population. That may mean more police, but, more than that, po-

lice who are respected in the areas in which they work. The second major thrust of public policy should be general economic and social reform in the usual sense of redistribution of income, a much lower unemployment rate than the United States has had for the last six or seven years, and much better opportunities for advancement in the educational system.

DPG *The present laws and statutes concerning victimless crimes like prostitution and gambling seem to be the expression of certain social attitudes. Don't we have to undergo a certain social enlightenment in order to effect changes?*
MATZA No, I think the American population, like most populations, follows the leader

on matters of that sort, although certain changes—like legalization of heroin—would be extremely difficult to impose from the top. However, laws could be passed legalizing gambling, prostitution, or minor drugs like marijuana. An element of the public would object, but the public as a whole would probably go along.

DPG *Do definitions of deviance vary in society over time and place?*
MATZA Obviously they do, but not as much as we tend to think. Laws vary tremendously with regard to victimless crimes. With regard to crimes like burglary, larceny, and assault, they vary only in detail. Although in many societies there is no private property in

the Marxian sense, there's *personal* property in all societies. And once you have personal property and a conception of an individual and his or her dignity, there are some restrictions put upon violations of the person and violations of personal property.

DPG   *We have various historical social attitudes that have petrified into numerous laws and statutes that would take a considerable effort to change. What developments might take place in our social attitudes to bring about the changes you mentioned?*

MATZA   I would say that the two basic facts in American history that account for most of the kind of social attitudes and legal codes we have are capitalism and puritanism. American puritanism has obviously been shaken, and it's hardly possible to speak of it any longer. The decline of puritanism might lead to some slight motion toward the elimination of victimless crimes, but I really doubt it. For example, in the state of California a referendum for legalized marijuana lost by two to one. And America is still very much capitalist. Capitalism is a more essential feature of our society than puritanism. The capitalist bias inherent in American law is illustrated best by the treatment of illegal immigration in the Southwest, the so-called wetback phenomenon. It is a crime to be an illegal immigrant, but it is no crime to hire one.

DPG   *Are there organizations in society that, in effect, process individuals toward deviance? If so, what role do the meanings that the individual brings to the situation have to affect the process?*

MATZA   I think that organizations like the police, the courts, and the prisons process people toward deviance, but I don't believe that an individual necessarily accepts any label that is put on him. I think the meanings the person attaches to those labels is crucial. But if a person is objectively processed by an institution, that can be much more consequential than any label. It seems to me that putting a person in prison has a very great impact, whatever meaning the individual attaches to it.

DPG   *What alternatives would you suggest to our established penal systems?*

MATZA   I don't think that much can be done within the framework of our moral and political economy—within the framework of capitalism. All I'd really suggest is that probation be used much more often, because it

has been shown to be just about as effective as imprisonment. I don't think merely letting everyone out of prison is a solution because there are all kinds of people who have been victimized by criminals. The simplest solution, perhaps the only solution, is to give us a more humane system. Under my conception of socialism—with public ownership of property, redistribution of wealth, and a more democratic system in which more people participate in decision making—there could doubtless be a more humane treatment of criminals. But it wouldn't follow automatically. A new consciousness would have to be developed.

DPG   *Would you say that most deviants want to "come in from the cold"—to escape from the social environments that label them deviant?*

MATZA   Yes, and there are numerous social environments that produce delinquency and crime. There's the poverty environment that forces a person to steal to feed his family. There are the middle-class kids who are ignored and rejected by their parents and the corporation executives who work in the kind of setting that systematically persuades them to do things that are criminal.

DPG   *So straightforward punishment is not going to achieve very much? It's almost as if people have to be socialized to a system that can involve their identity and allegiance.*

MATZA   Probably most psychological theories of enforcement and reinforcement would tend to support that contention. The whole B. F. Skinner tradition (given its limitations) more or less shows that positive reinforcement tends to work better than negative reinforcement. I don't think punishment per se is bad, though. Negative measures, even though they are not as effective as positive measures, are necessary to fulfill some social functions. Sometimes moral vindication is quite important. Simone de Beauvoir argued after the war that morally it would be unconscionable to countenance a society that did not execute Nazi war criminals. And I would largely agree with her.

DPG   *Does the rate of deviance in society vary by socioeconomic strata?*

MATZA   That's a very difficult question because you get different answers depending on the methods that are used. If you use official statistics, the answer is a clear yes. If you use self-reported delinquencies, the answer is a very ambiguous no. But there's

much question about the self-report method. Self-report evidence indicates that for some crimes, working-class and lower-class kids have higher rates, and for some crimes, middle-class kids have higher rates. My own gut feeling is that for a lot of serious delinquencies and crimes like burglary, assault, and robbery, there's a moderate correlation between class and serious violations. The lower class has the somewhat higher rate, I think.

DPG   *Do you see any current forms of deviance as representing the vanguard of broad social change in the future?*

MATZA   God, no! I think that most forms of deviance reflect the prevailing social system. I think ordinary crimes tend to be reflections and distortions of an almost precapitalist behavior. They're not even petit bourgeois, they're just petty exploitation. I haven't resolved for myself whether victimless crimes like homosexuality and drug use represent liberation or decadence. I mean decadence in the traditional sense of being an indication of a social system in decay. In other words, I think that a moral and political economy with a great deal of prostitution (which is the quintessential form of male chauvinism) and with a great deal of drug use is having some trouble. I think certainly we ought to accept things like drug use and prostitution—we are all somewhat different—but they are probably not vanguards. But homosexuality is probably neither liberation nor decadence. It's just homosexuality.

DPG   *What would you say were the most important areas that the sociological theorist of deviance should be attending to over the next 10 or 20 years?*

MATZA   I think the sociologist must look much more carefully at two streams of research that have had only a limited tradition in the past. One is the relationship between delinquency, crime, and unemployment. There's a lot of research on the relationship between social mobility and crime, but that's a somewhat different matter. Secondly, I think more research should be done into the connection between war and delinquency and crime. I think those two areas really need research, because, as a socialist, as well as a sociologist, I feel that war and unemployment are the major factors that underlie delinquency and crime.

Unit 23
Criminology

SCHEMATIC OUTLINE

A Introductory Graphics: The Criminalization Process

B Definition and Context

1 Definition
Criminality is a form of social conduct that is negatively evaluated and that is likely to elicit a politically organized punitive response from society. Criminologists study the causes, development, and effects of such behavior.

2 World Context
Definitions of crime and the punitive responses to it vary from society to society. The definition of crime through an institutionalized legal system is a relatively modern development.

3 American Context
Crime in the United States is partially shaped and supported by the social and economic systems. It is also a persistent political problem.

C Questions and Evidence

1 Questions
Three questions are basic to modern criminology: (1) Does punishment actually control crime? (2) What causes crime—nature or nurture? (3) What is the relationship between social class and crime?

2 Evidence
a The "Burning Issue" Question
Recent empirical research testing the long-established belief that punishment deters crime has not proved conclusive. It is clear, however, that the deterrence theory, by focusing only on controls over human behavior, tends to overlook the complex forces that impel men to act, the differences between expressive and instrumental crimes, and other factors.
b The "Classical" Question
The controversy about whether the basis of crime is to be found in man's innate constitution or in his environment has not been resolved. Most of the arguments on either side have been overly deterministic.
c The "Research" Question
Opportunity (or anomie) theories interpret crime among the lower classes as a response to inconsistencies in the social structure. The more recent theories of societal reaction (or labeling) assert that social stigmatizing increases the commitment of the criminal to deviance. Research provides little support for the opportunity perspective, slightly more for the labeling model. The latter tends to be overdeterministic, however, and cannot explain all crime.

3 Overview
Criminology is a relatively young science that still faces problems of definition, methodology, theory, and application. Broader perspectives are being developed.

D Looking Ahead

1 Interview: Gresham M. Sykes

SUPPORTING UNITS

  3 Biology and Society
  5 Socialization and Moral Development
  9 Social Stratification
17 Urban Society
21 Sociology of Economics
22 Deviance
24 Drugs and Drug Subcultures

ENCYCLOPEDIA ENTRIES

anomie
anonymity
capital punishment
chromosomal aberration
class
crime
criminology
delinquency
deviance
differential association theory
drugs and drug abuse
Lombroso, Cesare (1836–1909)
modes of individual adaptation
organized crime
police
prisons
professional crime
psychology and the law
social conflict
sociopathic personality
somatotypes
urbanism

THE CRIMINALIZATION PROCESS

1. **Patterning of Behavior.** A pattern of behavior develops and/or is recognized within a particular social group (such as the jobless in a certain area).

2. **Collective Perception of Threat and Influence Attempts.** The behavior is perceived as negatively affecting the interests or needs of other groups within the society (such as shopkeepers), and the affected groups try to influence the development of punitive controls.

3. **Establishing Formal Controls and Applying the Rule.** If they are successful, formal controls will be established to control the behavior, and at some point the prohibited behavior will be identified and violators apprehended.

4. **Punishment.** If the rules are successfully applied, the violator will be punished.

Country	Latest Year	Accident Rate	Suicide Rate	Homicide Rate
United States	1967	1.46	5.33	4.21
Australia	1967	0.65	3.02	0.56
Belgium	1967	0.15	0.80	0.20
Canada	1967	0.76	3.00	0.66
Denmark	1968	0.14	1.42	0.16
England and Wales	1967	0.13	0.40	0.10
France	1967	0.50	2.00	0.24
West Germany	1967	0.12	1.07	0.18
Ireland	1967	0.38	0.21	0.03
Italy	1967	0.29	0.70	0.50
Japan	1967	0.08	0.07	0.03
The Netherlands	1968	0.02	0.10	0.07
New Zealand	1967	0.92	1.61	0.11
Scotland	1968	0.19	0.35	0.04
Sweden	1968	0.16	2.25	0.08
Switzerland	1967	0.47	3.60	NA

Table 1. Deaths From Firearms in Various Countries (Rates per 100,000 Persons). Of these countries the United States ranks highest in all three categories: accidents with firearms, the crime of homicide with firearms, and the "deviant behavior" of suicide with firearms. An absence of gun-control legislation may be a major contributing factor to these conditions.

B DEFINITION AND CONTEXT

1 Definition

Just as deviance is a social concept (see Unit 22) encompassing all the forms of behavior that a particular society at a particular time deems threatening, harmful, or offensive, criminality is also a socially dependent and culturally relative concept. There is a difference, however: *criminality* is a special subdivision of *deviance* that is expressly punishable through formal sanctions applied by political authorities. The authorities evaluate and punish rule-breaking behavior of this sort—and thereby confer criminal status on the individual—by means of the *criminalization* process (itself a subdivision of the broader *stigmatization* process that attends deviant behavior). A homosexual may be stigmatized by society, but he can be legally constrained and accorded criminal status only in those communities where the authorities are empowered to intervene in, and apply, sanctions against homosexual acts.

Even though criminality is often viewed as antisocial behavior, it remains social in a very important sense. In violating social rules, criminal conduct is frequently oriented toward expectations of how other people will react (the victim, the authorities, one's peers, relatives, neighbors—or society at large), and it takes into account, through its attempts to evade, change, or flaunt the rules prohibiting it, central aspects of the social order. The perpetrator usually does not stumble into criminal activity inadvertently (although "ignorance of the law is no defense"), but carries it out with varying degrees of awareness that the activity is prohibited by rule, and that it entails a number of social consequences. Consequently, criminologists are concerned with investigating criminality as a form of social conduct that may be studied in terms of its causes, development, and effects.

Depending on their interests, criminologists have explored the nature of crime from two main perspectives: one focuses on crimi-

Country	Murder Rate
Sri Lanka	14.0
Kuwait	8.1
United States	7.2
Luxembourg	6.8
Singapore	5.2
Libyan Arab Republic	4.9
The Netherlands	3.9
West Germany	3.3
Ivory Coast	3.2
Fiji	3.0
Israel	2.6
Austria	2.5
Japan	2.2
Scotland	1.9
Malawi	1.9
Australia	1.8
Hong Kong	1.7
Korea (South)	1.5
Finland	1.2
Cyprus	1.2
Portugal	1.1
Sweden	0.6
Malaysia	0.5
England and Wales	0.4
Norway	0.2

Table 2. International Murder Rates (Based on 1969 Data).
Comparisons of the murder rates of various countries must be approached cautiously. The rates presented in this table show the number of persons per 100,000 inhabitants identified by the police as having committed or attempted willful murder, except for the United States, where the figure represents the number of actual killings per 100,000 inhabitants; in the United States attempts to kill are classified as aggravated assaults, not as murder. (This fact is also relevant to Table 3.) These rates reflect only detected offenders and crimes. The actual number of murders may remain undisclosed because of unreported offenses, which may vary greatly depending on a country's political situation and its national law enforcement levels. (Source: Interpol; Federal Bureau of Investigation, *Uniform Crime Reports*)

nality as a type of social *conduct,* and the other examines criminality as a social *status.* Both orientations can be incorporated into a broad definition: *Criminality is a form of social conduct that is negatively evaluated and that is likely to elicit a politically organized punitive response.* In other words, criminality involves behavior that is "officially actionable." But the way in which the behavior is defined, evaluated, and reacted to will of course depend on the prevailing conditions in a particular society.

2   World Context

It is clear that the actions defined or interpreted as crime show few if any *absolute characteristics.* The kinds of behavior considered criminal differ according to the structure of values and interests within different societies. The differences can be examined in terms of temporary as well as more basic aspects of social organization. For example, in a society where resources are so scarce that daily survival is problematic, infanticide may be accepted as necessary or desirable behavior. However, when survival is no longer in question and population expansion becomes desirable, infanticide and abortion may be forbidden. Similarly, if a society is organized around the protection of private property rights, it is likely to punish theft severely, wheras a society based on a single set of orthodox beliefs will probably focus its *control efforts* on acts that are defined as heresy, sedition, or subversion. By studying the acts that a society defines as criminal, the sociologist is able to construct a "mirror image" that helps him describe the essential values of the society as well as the priorities of powerful interest groups.

The definition of crime through an institutionalized legal system is a relatively modern phenomenon, closely connected with the growth, centralization, and specialization of governments. In fact, the evidence suggests that as societies become more complex, they move through several distinct stages of legal development. The simplest societies possess no legal system as we know it. This fact, of course, does not mean that they exercise no social control, merely that controls remain primarily informal. The first level of legal evolution occurs in societies that employ *mediation,* which involves the use of specialized non-kin arbitrators in the settlement of disputes and parallels the development of money and substantial property. The development of *police* (a special armed force available for norm enforcement), which represents the next stage in legal evolution, usually begins when societies establish a relatively specialized division of labor and provide for full-time government officials. The final step in the developmental sequence is the systematic use of specialized *counsel* (lawyers) in the settlement of disputes. Such use is characteristic of societies that possess a uniform system of judicial administration and a written legal code.

The *punitive responses* to criminal behavior also vary among societies. Incarceration in penal institutions is a relatively recent and by no means universal form of societal reaction. Capital and corporal punishment, mutilation, branding, fines, banishment, galley slavery have all been used instead of or along with imprisonment. Forms of punishment, like definitions and evaluations of crime, re-

Year	Total Crime Index	Violent Crime	Property Crime	Murder and Manslaughter	Forcible Rape	Robbery	Aggravated Assault	Burglary	Larceny $50+
1960	1,126.2	159.5	966.7	5.0	5.0	59.9	85.1	502.1	282.9
1961	1,141.0	156.8	984.2	4.7	9.3	58.0	84.7	512.3	289.5
1962	1,194.2	160.9	1,033.3	4.6	9.4	59.4	87.6	525.2	309.1
1963	1,295.2	166.7	1,128.6	4.5	9.3	61.5	91.4	568.8	344.7
1964	1,443.4	188.7	1,254.7	4.9	11.1	67.8	104.9	625.9	383.4
1965	1,515.5	198.1	1,317.4	5.1	12.0	71.2	109.8	653.2	409.7
1966	1,670.7	217.7	1,452.9	5.6	13.1	80.3	118.8	710.7	457.7
1967	1,926.2	250.5	1,675.7	6.1	13.8	102.1	128.5	814.2	530.3
1968	2,240.2	295.3	1,944.9	6.8	15.7	130.9	141.8	918.1	637.3
1969	2,482.7	325.1	2,157.6	7.3	18.2	147.3	152.3	968.9	756.6
1970	2,746.9	360.7	2,386.1	7.8	18.5	171.4	163.0	1,071.2	861.2
1971	2,906.7	392.7	2,514.0	8.5	20.3	187.1	176.8	1,148.3	909.2

flect the nature of social organization and the interests of those ap-plying social controls. They tend to vary according to social class: the rich are fined, the poor flogged.

Among the most important influences on the nature of puni-tive responses are definitions and redefinitions of the criminal. For example, a change in the image of the criminal was basic to the ef-forts of nineteenth-century reformers to offer correction to rather than punishment of the juvenile delinquent. Specific political condi-tions tend to alter the level and character of punishment—as shown most dramatically during the Stalinist purges of 1936–1938—and economic conditions also affect reactions to crime—the introduction of galley slavery as a punishment for crime in order to provide cheap labor for the economic expansion of European powers during the seventeenth century is an example.

3   American Context

Differences in values, cultural traditions, and social status are cen-tral to American society, and the fact that certain types of criminality are found more frequently among members of one sex than the other, or among members of particular cultural, ethnic, racial, and geographic groupings, suggests that important social forces are at work. But the criminologist cannot ignore the concerns, perspec-tives, and assumptions that are shared by the American people. Certain *characteristic values,* such as competition, material success, and individualism, may be central to the relationship between culture and crime. Of particular interest is the fact that those very values that support and help define *conformity* within our society, may also promote the emergence and growth of crime.

The American political-legal system differs substantially from its counterpart in continental Europe in that it is decentralized. Crimes are usually violations of state and local rather than federal laws, and the agencies for evaluating and punishing criminality (po-lice, courts, prisons) are organized, for the most part, on a regional rather than a national basis. The *localization* of legal controls makes it difficult to generalize about crime in national terms; the perception, evaluation, and response to crime is likely to vary greatly across the country.

Table 3. United States Index of Crime, 1960–1971 (Rates per 100,000 Persons). The Federal Bureau of Investigation crime index is based on the number of crimes of certain types reported in a year. These crimes fall into the two categories of violent crime and property crime. The index can be adjusted to show the crime rate per any given number of persons. The index shows a steady and substantial increase in major crimes reported throughout the 1960s. Why did this increase take place? (Source: Federal Bureau of Inves-tigation)

Crime Rate Ranking	City	Crime Index
1	Miami, Fla.	5,726
2	San Francisco, Cal.	5,512
3	Los Angeles, Cal.	5,443
4	New York, N.Y.	5,307
5	Detroit, Mich.	5,271
6	Denver, Colo.	4,899
7	Sacramento, Cal.	4,756
8	Jacksonville, Fla.	4,680
9	New Orleans, La.	4,439
10	Phoenix, Ariz.	4,403
11	Portland, Ore.	4,295
12	Baltimore, Md.	4,177
13	Washington, D.C.	3,973
14	Seattle, Wash.	3,956
15	Nashville, Tenn.	3,938

Table 4. Crime Index of Selected United States Cities, 1971 (Rates per 100,000 Persons). The table lists the top 30 standard metropolitan statistical areas with populations of more than 250,000 ranked according to Federal Bureau of Investigation crime-index fig-ures per 100,000 persons. The total number of crimes reported in the index categories in 1971 for Miami, a city of about 1.3 million population, was 75,080. (Source: Federal Bureau of Investigation, *Uniform Crime Reports,* 1972)

Crime is one of America's most persistent political issues, partly because it raises important questions of freedom and restraint. The most obvious dilemma is created by the conflict between social order and individual rights. In a *police state* the rights of the individual are sacrificed in the name of collective or national interests. In a democracy, however, individual rights must be balanced off against the need for social control. Harshly repressive punitive controls might be effective in reducing the level of crime, but those who support "due process" and individual freedoms might find the price too high. The political catchphrase "law and order" has become a rallying cry of the dominant culture in America. Attempting to further repress or remove those "elements" in society that it regards as most deviant (especially blacks and members of other disfavored minorities), it blames the "permissive philosophy" and the "soft-headed judges" of today for the rise in street crimes (mugging, rape, burglary, car theft, and so on), particularly in large cities. President Nixon has repeatedly advocated harsher criminal penalties—including a return to capital punishment—and has said, "Society is guilty of crime only when we fail to bring the criminal to justice. When we fail to make the criminal pay for his crime, we encourage him to think that crime will pay."

Legal controls in the United States often focus on the enforcement of *morality*. This tendency, which has a long history in America, reflects the belief that areas of private moral conduct are the just concern of the community. Sociologists are particularly interested in "*crimes without victims,*" such as homosexuality, drug addiction, prostitution, and abortion, because they raise questions about the limits of state authority and the extent of *public consensus* necessary to preserve or change a particular law. Americans have regularly tried to legislate social problems out of existence. (Prohibition is an example). This practice has two consequences. First, it produces an abundance of laws that cannot be completely enforced. There is selective rather than universal enforcement of the law, and the decision to arrest must often be made on grounds other than the behavior of the violator; that is, the police will arrest those they want to arrest and overlook violations by those whom they don't. Second, this practice leads to much unnecessary police activity and court cases and diverts the resources of enforcement agents to stigmatizing the unfortunate instead of the dangerous. It has been estimated, for example, that one out of three arrests in the United States is for public drunkenness. The use of legal rather than other more therapeutic means in handling this type of problem reflects what criminologists have referred to as the "overreach of the criminal law."

Finally, the American economic system shapes the *context of crime* in the United States. That system is a form of advanced monopoly capitalism. (It is capitalistic in that it is based on private ownership of the means of production, and it is monopolistic in that the control of most capital rests in the hands of a relatively few interrelated corporations.) This system has several implications for criminality. In one sense, crime can be the result of "business as usual." White-collar crimes, such as price-fixing, stock swindling, and consumer fraud, are by-products of the economic structure and the incentives for exploitative profit making that it provides. Similarly,

Pimp and prostitutes. Prostitution may be defined as participation in sexual relations for financial reward. If we were to take this definition literally, many men and women who have "married for money" would fall under the heading of "prostitutes." Clearly, the application of many social labels depends as much on the socioeconomic position as on the overt behavior of the individuals being judged.

organized crime may be interpreted as an extension of existing economic priorities. Perhaps most popular is the view that organized crime is a form of corporate enterprise offering consumer services that are in great demand (gambling, prostitution, drugs, and so on). Furthermore, the unequal distribution of wealth that is characteristic of capitalist societies may be important in the explanation of crime. For example, how do those who live in shabby, overcrowded tenements, with no dependable source of heat, with rats and faulty plumbing, react to the constantly televised image of the supposedly ''average'' American family's wall-to-wall carpeted $50,000 house in the suburbs?

C   QUESTIONS AND EVIDENCE

1   Questions

Three questions are basic to modern criminology: (1) Does punishment really control crime? (2) What causes crime—nature or nurture? (3) What is the relationship between social class and crime?

2   Evidence

a   The ''Burning Issue'' Question

i   Context   Throughout most of history man has assumed that *punishment* is the normal and appropriate response to crime. Only in recent years have social scientists attempted to investigate the relationship between punishment and crime carefully. Part of their interest is based on questions about the inevitability of punishment in society. Some have argued that punishment helps to preserve the basis of social order by defining the boundaries of acceptable behavior and providing a vehicle for collective revenge. Traditionally, however, punishment has been justified by reference to its deterrent effects. But opponents of punishment have raised important questions about its effectiveness as a deterrent and have argued that its social and personal costs may outweigh its positive effects.

Punishment in Public. The placement of offenders in the stocks in seventeenth-century New England illustrates a literal application of the ''deterrence theory.'' (''The Witch No. 2,'' lithograph by Walker, after Balser, 1892)

(Facing page) White-collar crime in the White House? *(Left to right)* H. R. Haldeman, White House Chief of Staff; James W. McCord, Security Coordinator for the Committee to Re-elect the President and the Republican National Committee; John Ehrlichmann, Special Assistant to the President for Domestic Affairs; John Mitchell, Attorney General of the United States; John Wesley Dean, Counsel to the President; and G. Gordon Liddy, Counsel to the Finance Committee to Re-elect the President. These men, onetime high-level appointees of the Nixon administration and/or re-election campaign, were some of the key figures in the Watergate scandal of 1972 and 1973. Accusations leveled at these and other political figures included their alleged involvement in various of the following offenses: breaking and entering in the nighttime, bribery, burglary, concealing evidence, conspiracy, "espionage" and "sabotage" against political opponents, extortion, false swearing, falsification of government documents, forgery, fraud, illegal electronic surveillance, invasion of privacy, misappropriation of funds, obstruction of justice, perjury, subornation of theft, violation of election campaign laws, violation of the charters of the Federal Bureau of Investigation and the Central Intelligence Agency, and violation of civil rights.

An excellent example of this debate is the controversy surrounding the use of *capital punishment* in the United States. Until the Supreme Court decision in Furman vs. Georgia (1972), no national guidelines for the application of the death penalty existed. That decision, which has, in effect, abolished capital punishment for the time being, was reached (in part) on the basis of studies by social scientists of the use and consequences of the death penalty. Nevertheless, the debate still rages, and sociologists continue to ask: *Does punishment really act as a deterrent to criminal behavior?*

ii Theory The oldest and most widely accepted views on the efficacy of punishment are found in the writings of Cesare Beccaria (*An Essay on Crimes and Punishments,* 1767) and Jeremy Bentham (*An Introduction to the Principles of Moral Legislation,* 1823) who represent the "classical" school of criminology. They provided the first formulation of what is now known as *deterrence theory,* which insists that there are good reasons to expect that punishment will prevent as well as control crime. The assumptions and predictions of this theory are relatively straightforward: man is portrayed as a rational creature who governs his actions by assessing the positive and negative consequences that are likely to follow from his acts; because he is interested in maximizing his rewards at all times, he will avoid behavior that is likely to have negative consequences (punishment). When the argument is stated in these terms, it is easy to understand why criminal penalties are expected to work. Because he realizes that conformity will be rewarded and criminality punished, the rational person will choose the former and resist the temptation of the latter. In order to ensure that crimes differing in *reward value* will be equally deterred, the *scale of punishments* should be adjusted to fit the crime; an offender who steals $1,000 should be more severely punished than a thief of $5—not because greater social harm is involved, but because the motivating forces are stronger with regard to the greater sum of money and need to be balanced accordingly.

Within this model two types of deterrence can be identified. *Specific deterrence* operates to control the behavior of the offender himself. When a criminal act is followed by punishment, the rational man is expected to learn that these acts are against his own best interest. If the punishment actually serves as a specific deterrent, the offender should refrain from committing the same or similar acts in the future. *General deterrence,* on the other hand, works through the example provided to the community by the punishment of the offender. By witnessing the consequences of criminal actions for others, the *conformer* decides against similar misconduct and is thereby prevented from following the example of the *deviant.*

According to this theory, the effect of punishment should depend on the exact nature and form that the punishment takes. Among the elements considered relevant to the effectiveness of punishment are its *certainty* and *severity*. Although it is unclear from the theory which of these characteristics is more important, deterrence should be maximized when punishments are both certain and severe. When punishment appears to be ineffective in controlling crime, supporters of deterrence theory will argue that the severity of punishment is not great enough (in which case pleas are made for increased penalties) or that the penalties that do exist have been applied inconsistently (in which case pleas are made for more rigorous enforcement and application of punitive controls). Rarely, if ever, are the assumptions and rationale for the theory seriously questioned by those who use it to support their decisions in the area of crime control.

iii   Research   Unlike the politician, who is willing to accept deterrence theory on the basis of its logical appeal, the criminologist must study its validity and applicability to social policy. The first systematic studies of deterrence theory were concerned with the effectiveness of capital punishment in preventing crime. Karl Schuessler (''The Deterrent Influence of the Death Penalty,'' 1952) attempted to

The electric chair in operation. This picture appeared on the front page of the *The New York Daily News* in 1928 with the following caption: ''Ruth Snyder's Death Pictured!—This is perhaps the most remarkable exclusive picture in the history of criminology. It shows the actual scene in Sing Sing death house as the lethal current surged through Ruth Snyder's body at 11:06 last night. Her helmeted head is stiffened in death, her face masked and an electrode strapped to her bare right leg. The autopsy table on which her body was removed is beside her. Judd Gray, mumbling a prayer, followed her down the narrow corridor at 11:11. 'Father forgive them, for they don't know what they are doing?' were Ruth's last words. The picture is the first Sing Sing execution picture and the first of a woman's electrocution.''

No executions have been performed in the United States since 1967, but currently public opinion is moving back toward a belief in the efficacy of the death penalty as a deterrent of crime. State legislatures are passing various laws maintaining the death penalty for certain categories of crime, despite Supreme Court rulings restricting capital punishment as it had been applied in most states. The fact is, however, that until we have a system where citizens perceive a direct relationship between the commission of a crime and a judicial process leading to conviction and punishment, it is very difficult, if not impossible, to assess the deterrent power of any punishment, including death in the electric chair.

determine whether fewer murders occur in places where murder is punishable by death than in places where it is not. By comparing the statistics for 15 contiguous states that had either retained or abolished the death penalty, he was able to correlate rates of homicide with differences in the use of capital punishment. No differences in murder rates were found, and Schuessler concluded that the death penalty had no special deterrent value. Several years later Leonard Savitz (''A Study of Capital Punishment,'' 1958) studied homicide rates before and after well-publicized executions in order to assess the impact (general deterrence value) of capital punishment and also found that the differences were insignificant. In 1967 Thorsten Sellin published a study ("Homicide in Retentionist and Abolitionist States") that demonstrated that homicide rates remained insensitive to the temporary abolition and eventual reinstitution of the death penalty in eleven states.

Although these studies did much to discredit deterrence theory, they left a great many questions unanswered. Does the deterrent value of punishment vary with the type of offense or group of potential offenders that are involved? Do variations in the level of punishment (certainty and severity) condition the effectiveness of punitive controls? How important are perceptions of punishment, as opposed to its actual application, in explaining deterrent effects?

In order to provide a more thorough test of the deterrence theory, a number of researchers have examined the relationship between the certainty and severity of punishment and levels of criminality. In "The Deterrent Influence of Punishment" (1966), for example, William J. Chambliss examined changes in the extent of illegal parking on a Midwestern university campus before and after the imposition of more certain and severe fines. His findings suggested that, in general, an increase in the certainty and severity of punishment did reduce the level of parking violations. However, because of the special nature of the behavior involved, Chambliss was cautious in his interpretation and urged further study of "those circumstances under which particular types of punishment do in fact act as a deterrent and those circumstances under which particular types of punishment have little or no effect."

In a later study, "Crime Rates and Legal Sanctions" (1969), Charles R. Tittle tested the impact of severity and certainty in terms of seven major offense categories—homicide, assault, sex offenses, robbery, larceny, burglary, and auto theft. As a measure of severity Tittle used the mean length of time served by felony prisoners released from state prisons in 1960, and he measured certainty by the ratio of the number of state prison admissions for "X" offense in 1960 and 1963 to the number of "X" crimes known to the police in 1959 and 1962. He found a strong positive relationship between greater certainty of punishment and lower crime rates, but similar association between greater severity of punishment and lower crime rates only for homicide. Although Tittle's study has been criticized for several methodological problems, it provided data that support rather than dispute the deterrence model.

The latest, and perhaps the most comprehensive, deterrence study is "Perceived Penal Sanctions and Self-Reported Criminality" (1972) by Gordon P. Waldo and Theodore G. Chiricos. In contrast to earlier researchers, these authors interviewed 321 students to determine the relationship between different types of reported criminality and individual perceptions of severity and certainty of punishment. Two types of crime were considered in the study: (1) marijuana use, a type of behavior where the law was not supported by the norms of the student community, and (2) theft, a crime where the law supported the moral codes of the group. No relationship was found between perceptions of severe punishment and admitted criminality for either type of offense. However, marijuana use was more likely than theft to be reduced by perceptions of the certainty of punishment. This finding seems to suggest that punishment operates as a deterrent only when laws are unsupported by the mores of the group. If *internalized norms* govern behavior, then the certainty of punishment (an external measure) becomes largely irrelevant to control of crime.

iv   Evaluation   Like any general view of behavior, deterrence theory offers an explanation that is both comprehensive and restrictive. It attempts to describe all aspects of the relationship between punishment and crime, but it provides a one-sided characterization of that relationship. This limitation results from the fact that the deterrence model is concerned only with controls over human behavior. It defines away the varied and complex forces that impel people to act or translates them into the rational language of rewards and costs. Having assumed absolute free will, the theorists are forced to abandon any consideration of causes beyond the basic calculation of positive and negative consequences.

An effective antidote to this bias is an orientation that focuses attention on the special features of the *social actor* and his act. For example, in *Crime and Legal Process* (1969) William J. Chambliss suggested that punishment will have a very different effect if a given act is *instrumental* than it will if that act is *expressive*. In most cases murder is an act expressive of an emotional state and therefore unlikely to be influenced by threats of punitive response. Such acts as embezzlement and illegal parking, on the other hand, are likely to be a rational or, at least, calculated means to a specific end. Such instrumental crimes are susceptible to control through the threat or

Street scene. One could almost believe that traffic-congested streets represent a successful conspiracy to create criminal behavior, such as parking violations. Here the owner of a car towed away by police during a crackdown on illegal parking in New York City in 1972 argues with officers. During this particular crackdown, policemen were supposed to hand out an average of 100 traffic tickets a day. One of the areas most crowded with illegally parked cars was that around the police station. However, few tickets appeared on cars in that area.

actual application of punishment.

Deterrence theory may also be complemented by assessments of the extent to which the offender is committed to crime as a way of life. Punishment is more likely to deter those who have a low commitment to their criminal activity than those who conceive of themselves as criminals and pattern their life around criminal behavior. In this regard, Frank Zimring and Gordon Hawkins ("Deterrence and Marginal Groups," 1968) have pointed out the value of what they call *marginal group analysis* for deterrence research. A class of persons that can be identified as "objectively on the margin of a particular form of criminal behavior" is especially important because "the utility of severe threats designed to prevent specific serious crimes depends on the effect of the threat on that limited marginal group." Here it is clear that a typology of "potential offenders" may substantially improve the predictive power of the deterrence model.

The research on deterrence, like much investigation in criminology, is suggestive rather than conclusive. The uneven quality of many of the studies can be attributed to the problems involved in isolating and measuring important factors. A number of open questions remain. Future research should address: (1) the relationship between certainty and severity of punishment; (2) the relationship between general and specific deterrence; (3) the process through which information about punishment becomes known, and how accurate (as opposed to inaccurate) knowledge of punishment affects behavior; (4) how perceptions of risk and the willingness to engage in risk taking affect the deterrence process; (5) the effects of drastic change, as might occur during wars or revolutions, in the structure of punishment; and (6) the extent to which punishment operates as a stimulus rather than a deterrent to crime. When more comprehensive studies of these and other matters are undertaken, criminologists will be able to describe the complicated relationship between punishment and crime in society more accurately.

b   The "Classical" Question

i   Context   From its birth criminology has been divided over the "true" causes of crime. Drawing their first perspectives from biology on the one hand and geographic studies on the other, nineteenth-century criminologists set the stage for one of the most enduring debates in the field. The biologically trained group, including Cesare Lombroso and his followers in Italy, believed that the basis of crime was to be found in man's nature, his innate constitution, whereas the "cartographers" (primarily Adolphe Quetelet and André Guerry) insisted that crime was an expression of environmental conditions. This conflict is part of the larger issue about whether human nature is genetically determined or environmentally conditioned, which has been outlined in detail in Unit 3.

A theory of crime that emphasizes biological causes is consistent with the identification and control of "criminal types." However, when the causes are located in the basic conditions of society, the elimination of crime depends upon the willingness of society to institute fundamental social change. The first perspective, which will be referred to as *typological,* supports, at least indirectly, the existing social order and its values. The second perspective, the *environmental,* is consistent with a "progressive" outlook on crime and its relation to society. Sociologists seek to determine: *What is the relationship between biological and environmental factors in the production of criminal behaviors?*

ii   Theory   In many cases it may be difficult for the criminologist to say that a particular theory stresses either nature or nurture; few theories that assert one position totally dismiss the other. Typological theories underscore the importance of inborn factors or of influences that take effect very early in social development. Because they hold that the causes of crime are internal, these theories often assume that the criminal is driven by powerful forces within his personality. Accordingly, efforts at correction must focus on the individual, and success remains problematic—if it is possible at all. In this view the causes of crime are indistinguishable from the basic nature of the criminal.

In contrast to the typological approach, environmental theories usually stress later personality development or influences outside the individual. These theories are optimistic insofar as they view man as malleable and see his crime as a product of changeable external forces. The criminal is different *only* by virtue of his experiences and situation, not because of any intrinsic quality that sets him apart.

Both of these theories are basically *deterministic*. Unlike deterrence theory, they reject the assumption of rationality and free will. Instead, they concentrate on the *causal process* through which an offender is compelled to commit his criminal act, irrespective of the punishments supplied.

Typological theories fall into two categories: those focusing on physical typologies and those concerned with mental types. Theories that focus on physical differences generally attribute tendencies toward antisocial conduct to the *constitutional inferiority* of the offenders. The earliest physiological explanations in the nineteenth century asserted that the criminal was a type of primitive "throwback" to an earlier stage of *human evolution*. Later biologically based theories emphasized the significance of *body structure* and *genetic makeup* in the production of criminal dispositions. Theories that describe the criminal in terms of mental types either support a view of inherited mental problems or see mental disturbances as growing out of the initial experiences of the child. In either case the emphasis is placed on basic mental characteristics that separate the criminal from the normal citizen. Such concepts as moral insanity and psychopathy have been introduced to explain how mental imbalance or deficiency is tied to criminal behavior.

Environmental theories in American criminology have taken two predominant forms: they argue either that crime is a natural consequence of learning a certain set of values or that it is the result of being in a particular position in the social structure. *Cultural theories* interpret criminality as the product of a process through which the offender incorporates a set of values that predispose him toward criminal conduct, and they emphasize the similarities between learning to behave criminally and other types of learning experiences. *Social class explanations* argue that the deprivations or advantages associated with social status, especially differences in the allocation of resources and prestige, will determine the form and incidence of criminal behavior. These inequities are seen at the core of the frustrations and tensions that produce criminal conduct.

iii Research (Survey) The systematic study of crime through scientific methods began most emphatically with the work of Lombroso, who was originally trained in medicine. On the basis of a careful examination of 338 Italian prisoners, he contended that measurable physical differences existed between criminals and normal men and women. These physical differences, which he called *stigmata,* were assumed to reflect a more primitive state of evolutionary development that carried with it a disposition toward criminal behavior. Lombroso explored such physical characteristics as shape and size of the head, asymmetry of the face, unusual types of hair and bone structure, and in *The Criminal Man* (1889) he reported what he felt were a significantly larger number of abnormalities among the prisoners than a comparison sample of Italian soldiers. He concluded that criminality was profoundly influenced by constitutional factors. The first scientific answer to the nature-nurture question was thus resolved in favor of the former position.

But the debate had just begun. Charles Goring's *The English Convict* (1913), which was based on precise comparisons of the physical attributes of 3,000 prisoners and a large number of nonprisoners, cast serious doubt on Lombroso's work. Utilizing more sophisticated methods, this study found no significant differences between the two groups in the number or types of physical abnormalities. Although Goring did not intend to question the assumptions of the typological approach (he proposed his own theory of *mental* inferiority), his findings seriously challenged physiological interpretations of criminal behavior. The discrediting of the "constitutional" approach, coupled with the distinctive nature of American social problems during the early twentieth century, paved the way for the development of an environmental approach to criminality. The recognition that crime was concentrated in large urban areas and the disorganizing effects of the Depression lent credence to the view that crime could be socially induced. The *ecological school* of criminology whose major proponents were Clifford Shaw and Henry McKay at the University of Chicago, studied the geographic distribution of crime during the late 1920s and 1930s. Such surveys revealed that crime was disproportionately concentrated in specific urban areas, which were termed "transitional zones." Most striking was the fact that, no matter what group inhabited these areas, the proportion of criminality in them remained consistently high. On the basis of these data the advocates of the ecological view concluded that "criminalistic subcultures" thrived in these areas and promoted participation in criminal activity. (See Units 17 and 22.)

But the constitutional approach was far from obsolete. During the 1930s a Harvard anthropologist, Ernest Hooton, resurrecting the ideas that Goring had challenged, asserted that the criminal did in fact represent a physically inferior type. His comparison of 13,873 prisoners with 3,203 nonprisoners led Hooton to conclude that physical and mental deficiencies occurred more frequently among the criminal sample (*The American Criminal,* 1939). Moreover, he was able to relate specific physical characteristics to particular types of criminal activity. Despite what appeared to be rather impressive evidence, Hooton's work was severely criticized and rejected by sociologists.

In 1949 William Sheldon's *Varieties of Delinquent Youth* reintroduced the concept of a criminal physical type. Drawing on the work of Ernst Kretschmer, Sheldon identified three genetically determined body types (*endomorph, mesomorph,* and *ectomorph*) and argued that they were related to variations in temperament and conduct. In a sample of 200 incarcerated delinquents Sheldon found a preponderance of mesomorphs and reasoned that this specific body type (musuclar) creates a disposition toward criminal conduct. Like Hooton, Sheldon was criticized for theoretical and methodological weaknesses. As a result, his work has had little influence on contemporary criminological thought.

During the 1940s and early 1950s another variant of the typological approach arose with the growing influence of psychiatric and psychological interpretations. Criminal behavior was ascribed to basic personality traits by such psychologically oriented researchers as Sheldon and Eleanor Glueck, who utilized the Rorschach Ink Blot Test and psychiatric interviews to identify psychological characteristics of delinquents. Other researchers used standardized tests, such as the Minnesota Multiphasic Personality Inventory, to study the differences in personality structure between criminals and noncriminals. In ''Personality Characteristics of Criminals'' (1950) Karl Schuessler and Donald P. Cressey surveyed the results of objective personality tests over the preceding 25 years and concluded that ''the doubtful validity of many of the obtained differences as well as the lack of consistency in the combined results, makes it impossible to conclude from these data that criminality and personality elements are associated.''

In the 1960s, however, a number of studies appeared to reconfirm the startling discovery made in 1961 that a significantly high proportion of men in mental institutions and prisons who were considered especially violent or aggressive had an extra chromosome (47 rather than the normal number of 46). This extra Y chromosome, in addition to being correlated with violent behavior, is associated with a spectrum of other characteristics: unusual sexual preferences, below-average intelligence, tall height, and acne. A fuller discussion of this anomaly, which is known as the *XYY syndrome* (Y is the male sex-determining chromosome and normal men are XY, normal women XX), appears in Unit 3.

This finding did not halt environmentally oriented research, which predominates today. Challenged by such urban problems as gang delinquency and stimulated by various sociological theories, criminologists began to analyze criminality as a product of unequal opportunity. Using official statistics, field research techniques, interviews, and questionnaires, sociologists tried to determine if delinquency was concentrated among the lower classes and if it could be explained as the result of frustrated aspirations. Although these studies were consistent with well-developed theories, they could not definitively demonstrate the environmental basis of crime. Moreover, as sociologists began to experiment with *unofficial* measures of criminal behavior a great many questions were raised about the exclusively lower-class basis of crime. It has recently been shown that, in certain categories, the number of crimes actually committed is far higher than reported—twice as high with respect to rapes and robberies, five times as high with respect to aggravated assault. Moreover, white-collar crimes such as embezzlement, which sometimes involve staggering sums of money, are often not officially recorded. Finally, prosperous or middle-class citizens who are involved with criminal infractions are rarely pursued by enforcement agents with the vigor applied to members of the lower class.

iv Evaluation After nearly a century of contradictory approaches, conflicting interpretations, and inconclusive findings, criminologists have failed to resolve the nature-nurture controversy. Rather than offering objective answers, their efforts seem to reflect the political climate of the time, the influence exerted by particular professional groups (biologists, psychologists, psychiatrists and sociologists), and the prevailing attitudes toward "pressing" social problems. This pattern may be partly due to the relatively young age of criminology as a discipline, but the practical nature of its subject matter is perhaps more significant. Much more than some behavorial sciences, criminology is judged in terms of its direct applications to specific problems. Criminologists are not encouraged to develop a general theory of human behavior that may have some distant and uncertain relation to the practical control of criminal behavior. They are asked to provide immediate and practical answers. Thus they have sought simple deterministic explanations of crime in terms of the individual or his environment. And their search for the causes of crime has been susceptible to fads in solving social problems and variations in political priorities.

To avoid rigid causal analysis, David Matza has suggested a type of "soft determinism." In *Delinquency and Drift* (1964) he argues that the attempt to find inexorable causes of crime is inevitably misleading and that the theorist must make some provision for voluntary action and individual choice. Rather then being defined as a victim of either nature or nurture, the criminal can be defined as existing in the state of "drift," which he resolves by choosing criminality or conformity. Dispositions toward criminal acts may be created by any number of factors, but the ultimate outcome will depend on an individual's decision to adopt one or another form of behavior. Thus, in this view, the individual is ultimately responsible for his own behavior.

Another solution posed by current criminology involves a fundamental rejection of earlier types of causal analysis. In an approach that has become extremely popular in the past few years, such sociologists as Howard S. Becker, Austin Turk, and Richard Quinney have sought to explain how individuals are *criminalized*, not why they commit criminal acts. This perspective avoids the problem of choosing between nature and nurture by directing attention away from the criminal actor and refocusing it on the process of societal reaction to the crime. In this perspective criminal status takes the place of criminal conduct as the concern of the criminologist.

c The "Research" Question

i Context Within any socially organized group certain differences develop that exert important influences on behavior and social life. As societies develop, those differences are invested with such specific meanings that people come to view themselves and one another as good or bad, depending on whether or not they possess certain qualities or occupy particular positions. It is not surprising,

Crime and conditioning: stills from *A Clockwork Orange* (1972). In this critical and popular success director Stanley Kubrick satirized the frequent attempts of social scientists to reduce human motivation to simplistic statements of cause and effect. The main character, Alex, an "ultra-violent" young man, was subjected to conditioning —ultimately unsuccessful—aimed at making him averse to sex, violence, and Beethoven.

therefore, that social position often defines worth by granting moral superiority to those who stand at the top of the social hierarchy and by considering those at the bottom of that ranking morally corrupt. Accordingly, in societies where economic achievement determines social status, poverty represents more than economic failure; it carries with it an implicit evaluation of the moral qualities of the poor.

This perspective influenced the writings of many early social thinkers. It was not uncommon in the nineteenth century to read about the "poor and criminal classes" as if they were one and the same. Although the association between poverty and crime remained a favorite topic for twentieth-century sociologists, the style of their analysis changed. Rather than assuming an identity of class and crime, they set out systematically to study the interrelationship in all its complexities. Expressing the most important focus of contemporary criminological theory and research, sociologists ask: *What is the relationship between social class and the causes and consequences of crime?*

ii Theory The most recent explanations of this relationship can be categorized broadly as opportunity (or anomie) theories and societal reaction (or labeling) theories. Although both approaches argue that class differences and social power are important in understanding the causes and consequences of crime, they differ in the assumptions that they make about the nature and basis of social order as well as the aspect of criminality that they seek to explain. Opportunity theories focus on criminal conduct, whereas societal reaction theories are concerned with the imposition of criminal status.

Opportunity theory is based on the writings of Robert Merton, particularly "Social Structure and Anomie" (1938), who reasoned, as we saw in Unit 22, that deviance can be explained by pressures relating to social structure in society. Merton termed those pressures the *strain toward anomie* and argued that they are created when the goals that a society instills in its members cannot be attained. The different allocation of opportunities permits certain segments of the population to reach important cultural goals (material success in our society) but prevents others, notably the lower classes, from doing the same. Socially disadvantaged groups experience the greatest gap between means and goals and, therefore, feel the greatest compulsion to reduce or overcome this gap.

In describing five types of cultural adaptation (conformity, innovation, ritualism, retreatism, rebellion), Merton presents three types of responses to anomie that are relevant to the understanding of crime—innovation, rebellion, and retreatism. *Innovation* occurs when an individual resolves the gap between means and ends by adopting illegitimate means. The innovator maintains his commitment to cultural goals but circumvents the ordinary means. When an individual engages in *rebellion,* he is rejecting both the means and the goals provided by the society and substituting his own; it is his way of repudiating a system within which he feels he cannot succeed. *Retreatism* involves an abandonment of conventional means and goals and an attempt to escape social demands. The retreatist, unlike the innovator and rebel, finds his solace in withdrawing from, rather than confronting and challenging, the frustrations that he feels.

Merton's theory of deviance was applied to the explanation of ·

532

Two populations. Which looks more criminal? Why?

criminal behavior by Albert Cohen in *Delinquent Boys* (1955). Utilizing the concept of anomie to explain the prevalence of violent delinquent gangs in lower-class areas, Cohen contended that the antisocial and hostile behavior of these groups grew out of their rebellion against middle-class standards that are imposed through such institutions as the public schools. These standards create a gap between the goals proclaimed by the institution and the very limited means the lower-class child has for achieving those goals. The lower-class youth faces a *problem of adjustment*, and the delinquent gang represents a *group solution*. As an alternative, albeit deviant, source of status and self-respect, the gang emphasizes *aggression*, which enables the individual to flaunt the conventional goals he finds so difficult to attain. Thus, in Cohen's words "the same value system, impinging upon children differently equipped to meet it, is instrumental in generating both delinquency and respectability."

Another extension of anomie theory is found in *Delinquency and Opportunity* (1960) by Richard A. Cloward and Lloyd E. Ohlin, who suggested that previous formulations such as Cohen's had been onesided in their exclusive concern with *legitimate* opportunities. Equally relevant, they argued, are the nature and extent of *illegitimate* opportunities available to youth. Considering the impact of both types of *opportunity structures*, Cloward and Ohlin identify three types of delinquent gangs. The *criminal gang* specializes in predatory crime and is found in areas where legitimate opportunities are absent but illegitimate opportunities prevail. *Conflict gangs*, similar to the type described by Cohen, are found in socially disorganized areas where even illegitimate opportunities are lacking, but violence may be used to enhance social status. The *retreatist gang*, which is organized around the search for kicks and escape, is made up of youth who have been unsuccessful in both legitimate pursuits and conflict activities; they are "double failures." This typology, which parallels Merton's original analysis (innovation, rebellion, retreatism), specifies the significance of different types of opportunity for the genesis and expression of criminal behavior.

Societal reaction theories examine the consequences of stigmatizing the criminal and assert that social labeling increases the commitment of the criminal to his deviance. In contrast to deterrence theory, the labeling model predicts that punishment will reinforce commitment to crime insofar as it supports a definition of self as criminal. A number of steps are crucial to the labeling process: (1) the commission of the original criminal act, (2) a negative official response, (3) a negative response from significant others, (4) internalization of the deviant label as an accurate description of self, and (5) initiation of subsequent behaviors that are consistent with the new definition of self. These behaviors complete the "vicious cycle" as the criminal begins to reflect those qualities that the label originally imputed to him. The criminality that occurs in the final stage is defined as a form of *secondary deviance* and is attributed directly to the initial labeling itself.

Labeling theory suggests that lower-class status increases the probability that stigmatizing will occur and decreases the chances of nullifying the label and its consequences. The higher level of criminality in the lower class is thus explained by the operation of the societal reaction system rather than by any special forces that precede

Cleveland motorcycle gang. Unfortunately—or fortunately—reality is never as clearcut as theory. A motorcycle gang, for example, can have elements of all three types of gangs—criminal, conflict, and retreatist. Badge reads: "Please be kind to me or I'll kill you."

the criminal act. Instead of claiming that members of the lower class are more likely to commit criminal acts and then be labeled, the theory suggests that they are more likely to be labeled and—as a consequence—to commit criminal acts. From this point of view, criminality depends upon the successful imputing of criminal status by the more powerful group to the less powerful group.

iii Research (Methodology)   Studies based on opportunity theory have focused almost exclusively on male delinquent behavior. The concern with the early development of criminal patterns as well as the prevalence of gang delinquency stimulated research on delinquent rather than adult criminal conduct. Three major propositions consistent with the concept of anomie directed this research: (1) the lower the social class, the higher the rate of delinquency; (2) delinquency is organized around specific types of criminal conduct; and (3) delinquent subcultures are formed in reaction or opposition to the predominant values of our society.

If the first proposition is true, delinquency should be concentrated in the lower classes. Unfortunately, *official statistics* tend to be unreliable measures of delinquency because official intervention is more frequent in cases of lower-class delinquency than in middle-class or upper-class delinquency. As an alternative approach, sociologists have begun to use *self-reports* to explore the relative distribution of delinquency among different social classes. Although the results varied in a number of ways, several researchers concluded that the relationship between social class and delinquency was con-

Prison. If one were carefully to design a social mechanism to ensure the occurrence of recidivism and "secondary deviance," one could hardly design one better than our prisons. They strip inmates of personal identity, label them formally, provide reinforcement of this new definition through peer groups and formal authorities, segregate them from "normal" society, deprive them sexually, and provide an environment for the learning and perfecting of "deviant" skills and the reinforcement of "deviant" attitudes.

siderably weaker than most of the anomie theorists had assumed. Maynard L. Erickson and LaMar T. Empey ("Class Position, Peers, and Delinquency," 1965), for instance, reported that lower-class and middle-class groups had similar patterns of delinquent involvement but both differed significantly from upper-class groups. Similar investigations also revealed that the greatest differences in distribution of delinquency occur in large urban areas rather than rural and small urban areas.

The second proposition suggests that delinquent groups should be specialized in terms of particular activities. In the most extensive study on this question, James F. Short, Jr., and Fred Strodtbeck used field techniques to search out and investigate delinquent gangs in Chicago. In *Group Process and Gang Delinquency* (1965) they reported that they were unable to locate a significant number of criminal or retreatist gangs but did find many conflict-oriented groups. Even in the conflict gangs, however, the majority of time was *not* spent in any type of assaultive or violent behavior. A more recent study by Michael J. Hindelang ("Age, Sex and the Versatility of Delinquent Involvement," 1971) also failed to locate delinquent groups organized around criminal, conflict, and retreatist

535

A "tough" self-image. The clear projection of a "tough" self-image involves the issuing of a challenge—especially toward the agents of social control. It is hardly surprising that police may overreact to individuals projecting truculent and hostile self-definitions.

behavior. These findings cast serious doubt on the assumptions that patterns of delinquency neatly correspond to types of available opportunities and that delinquent groups are organized in terms of obvious dimensions of antisocial behavior.

Finally, a number of studies have dealt with the basis of delinquent subcultures. Two studies—"The Conflict of Values in Delinquency Areas" (1951) by Solomon Korben and "Values and Gang Delinquency" (1963) by Robert A. Gordon, James F. Short, Desmond F. Cartwright, and Fred Strodtbeck—seriously questioned the oppositional nature of delinquent groups. These investigators found that delinquents were not alienated from the goals of middle-class society and that in many ways seemed to embrace rather than reject important aspects of conventional behavior. Instead of characterizing delinquents as negativistic and antisocial, these findings suggest that delinquents may be more committed to conformity than we ordinarily assume.

In sum, research fails to provide substantial support for predictions based on opportunity theory. Some critics have proposed that greater attention be given to group process, and others have stressed the importance of studying the reaction system.

To support the labeling approach, higher rates of lower-class crime should be shown to be a function of the prejudical application of criminal labels. Similarly, lower-class status should reduce the ability of offenders to defend themselves against these labels. A number of studies have addressed themselves to this issue, but the findings are far from consistent.

A relatively early study, *The Differential Selection of Juvenile Offenders for Court Appearance* (1963) by Nathan Goldman, utilized statistical comparisons and interviews with police in a number of communities and found that race significantly affected the referral of juvenile arrests to court. If arrested, black children were more likely to be referred to court than whites. Considering the relationship between race and social class, this finding seems to support the labeling model. It is necessary to add, however, that differential handling was more pronounced with regard to minor than major offenses.

A different type of study, "Police Encounters with Juveniles" (1964), by Irving Piliavin and Scott Briar, was based on observations of juvenile offenders in a single department. The researchers found that police tended to respond more severely to blacks and "tough-looking" youths. On the whole, the decision of police to arrest gave more weight to a juvenile's social characteristics than his behavior.

In contrast, Robert Terry's "The Screening of Juvenile Offenders" (1967), proved incompatible with the expectations of the labeling approach. Terry compared the relative weight of behavior and social attributes on the decisions made by police, probation officers, and a juvenile court judge in a Midwestern city. He found that the severity of societal reaction was more directly related to the amount of deviance engaged in than the social status or power of the offender or to the difference in social class between the offender and agents of social control.

More recently, Theodore G. Chiricos, Phillip D. Jackson, and Gordon P. Waldo studied judicial discretion in relation to social characteristics. The court system that they observed made provisions for withholding adjudication of guilt (that is, the imposition of a criminal label). In "Inequality in the Imposition of a Criminal Label" (1972), they reported that poorly educated and black offenders were less likely to be handled leniently, but that other class-related factors, such as occupational status and skill, did not influence decisions in the same way.

Another study tested the labeling model with respect to the treatment of drunken drivers. In "Human Deviance and the Labeling Approach" (1972) Harvey Marshall and Ross Purday compared convicted and never-convicted drinking drivers in terms of socioeconomic status, race, sex, and age. Social class was found to have a direct effect on the probability of conviction, though, as in the Goldman study, this effect was most significant for the least serious offenses.

Finally, the consequences of labeling for different class groups were investigated by Richard D. Schwartz and Jerome H. Skolnick. They examined the effects of a criminal court record on the employment opportunities of unskilled workers and the effects of medical malpractice suits on practicing physicians. In "Two Studies of Legal Stigma" (1962) they reported that unskilled offenders were discriminated against in applications for employment and, in contrast, that a protective environment helped doctors maintain or improve their practice after being sued for malpractice. (Also see Unit 19.) These findings indicate that social position colors the process of social evaluation with respect to informal as well as formal controls.

Research of this sort provides partial support for the labeling theory—especially with regard to discrimination by race. It has been observed that such *social characteristics* as social class do have some impact on the handling of offenders, particularly when their crimes are the least serious.

iv Evaluation New theories of criminality, like explanations of other social phenomena, have developed in response to earlier approaches that have become discredited. Opportunity theory, it has been argued, avoids the interactional process through which criminal behavior evolves, interprets criminal status as something one achieves rather than as a label that society imposes, assumes that the incidence and prevalence of criminal behavior is significantly higher in the lower class, and ignores the causes of secondary deviance. Each of these criticisms has helped define the substance and scope of the new labeling approach.

But the labeling model presents several problems of its own. The theory explains *how* labeling takes place, but not always why it occurs. The fact that lower-class, powerless persons are more likely to be labeled, and therefore to become committed to criminality, implies that the powerful create laws to protect themselves from the powerless. But this is only a partial answer to the question. The labeling approach has not yet been able to deal with "secret criminality," which does not involve labeling. If large groups of persons do in fact become criminal without any explicit societal reaction, then labeling may only be relevant to a limited number of cases. If that is so, the causes of *primary deviance* once again become important issues that can no longer be ignored.

Finally, the problem of "overdeterminism'" again arises. The

Revolt at Attica State Prison. An uprising by inmates protesting conditions at Attica State Prison in upstate New York in 1971 was crushed when 1,650 correction officers, local police, sheriffs' deputies, state troopers, and National Guardsmen stormed the facility. Thirty-five prisoners and 11 prison employees died in the uprising —all but four (three prisoners, one guard) of the 46 at the hands of the attacking law-enforcement officials, none of whom were indicted for their excessively violent behavior, which subsequent inquiry showed to be unnecessary for dealing with the situation at the prison. The photo at the bottom of the opposite page shows civil liberties attorney William Kunstler with a negotiating team of inmates. The other two pictures depict inmates in the yard of the prison, some masked to conceal their identities, before the police attack.

notion that people become what others say they are suggests that man is a passive agent who can be easily manipulated by informational cues or by the opinions and judgments of others. Theories of *socialization* and *interaction* (see Unit 5 and Unit 12)—especially those concerned with role-playing—seem to support the labeling theory in this regard, however.

3 Overview

Although sociology has made some progress toward the development of an integrated approach to crime, it has left a number of problems partially unresolved. Criminologists have usually relied upon legal categories (such as murder, rape, or robbery) in their analysis of criminal behavior, but those categories have been seriously criticized as overly restrictive. If the criminologist tends to overlook behaviors that are forms of "social injury" but not recognized as such by the government, he will ignore the relative nature of crime in society. A broader definition of crime is gaining more acceptance as criminologists begin to appreciate the complexity of relationships between law and social behavior.

A methodological problem stems directly from this definitional problem. The criminologist who employs legal definitions must assume that the only criminals are the "official criminals." He will use prisoners as the subjects for study, and, more subtly, will be preoccupied with "dramatic and predatory" crimes. This view is likely to ignore crimes that are committed by those who have the greatest ability to avoid criminalization—the economically and politically powerful. Conspicuously underrepresented in the research literature are studies of crime committed by powerful groups or individuals. If criminology is to become truly sophisticated in its methodology, it

must devote as much attention to the crimes of the privileged as to those of the deprived.

Criminology must formulate a theory that can explain criminality as both a status and a behavior. It is obvious that neither theories that emphasize the *antecedents* of criminal behavior nor those that direct attention toward the *consequences* of official handling can stand alone. Behaviors that come to be classified as crime have causes, but the process through which society defines and reacts to them is also significant. A comprehensive theory must incorporate both of these perspectives.

In practical terms, criminology is closely related to social policy. The pressure to supply information that will help solve the "crime problem" places the criminologist at the service of the crime controllers and makes it difficult, if not impossible, for him to study the nature of criminality objectively. In order to free himself from this constraint, the criminologist must define his clients as the *entire* society, not simply those who seek immediate and simple answers to what they consider to be crime.

The criminological perspective has already begun to broaden as researchers have applied insights developed in political sociology, sociology of law, and the sociology of deviant behavior. Political sociology provides some understanding of the process through which power is distributed and interests are reflected in legal controls; the sociology of law examines the foundations and development of legal controls; and perspectives in social deviance reveal the dynamics of social evaluation, stigmatization, and social control.

D   LOOKING AHEAD

1   Interview: Gresham M. Sykes

Gresham M. Sykes is chairman of the sociology department at the University of Houston. He is the author of *Society of Captives, Crime and Society, Law and the Lawless,* and *Social Problems in America.* He served as director of the administration of justice program of the board of advisers of the New Jersey prison system for several years and was criminology editor of the *Journal of Criminal Law, Criminology and Police Science.* His areas of current research are rehabilitation, labeling theory, and social problems.

DPG   *What are the challenges of crime in the decades ahead?*

SYKES   There is no question that crime has emerged as a very important social problem in America in a way that has not been true in the past. Furthermore, the study of crime—criminology—has emerged as an important part of sociology in a way that has not been true in the past. Criminology today deals with some of the issues that are most vital to sociology. The same social and intellectual forces that changed sociology have changed criminology as well. One of the most important of these is the question of the status of sociology as a science: Is it truly objective or do value judgments inevitably color research? And of course that question is important to criminology because criminologists study the application of the moral ideas embedded in the law. How objectively can we study that process?

As far as crime is concerned, there are several changes going on. The first is that the system of corrections is simply being overwhelmed. As the population grows and the crime rate remains the same (or possibly increases), the number of convicted criminals that have to be handled by the society begins to go up while the system for handling them does not grow at the same rate. Furthermore, the sheer cost of imprisonment, in terms of dollars and cents, is beginning to concern a great many people. And people have become thoroughly disillusioned with what the prison system can do. They no longer have the same kind of confidence in social intervention, or whatever you want to call it, that they used to.

Now all of these things are coming together. The public is being asked to pay more for the treatment of the offender precisely at a time when they've lost faith in the standard ways of treating offenders. I think what you're going to see, and are seeing, is a real withdrawal of public support for rather conventional and traditional ideas of rehabilitation, reform, and so on.

DPG   *Is criminology going to step into that void?*

SYKES   No. Criminology is going to study the problem, but I don't think that there are any very clear answers about what to do about it at the present time—from criminologists or anybody else. Many penologists would say that what we really need is a kind

of social reintegration that cannot be accomplished within a penal institution. It is has to be accomplished within the community. The problem is that nobody knows very much about what should be done in the community either.

Another problem is that there is tremendous pressure to get criminal law free of what a lot of people regard as irrelevancies—problems such as public drunkenness. It's been said that almost 40 percent of all police arrests involve drunkenness and that the police are simply being overwhelmed by handling cases they shouldn't be bothering with at all. This is, in part, an economic argument dealing with how we use our resources. The other argument is a moral one, saying that the police have no business handling this area anyway, no matter what the question of cost might be. Along with that is the idea that efforts to control such areas of human behavior, particularly drugs, are alienating large sections of the population and turning them against the legal system as well as against many of our concepts of authority.

DPG   *What do you think about that argument?*

SYKES   I think it's probably true to some extent. The attempts to enforce laws on marijuana have turned off an awful lot of young people and have really radically changed their ideas about law and order, the police, and so on. That's not necessarily a convincing argument that nothing should be done, but it has to be taken very seriously.

Another thing that is going on is that it seems quite possible that new crimes are coming into existence—or at least that the motivation for some criminal behavior is not the same as it used to be. A great deal of our theory about the causes of criminal behavior in the past really fell into two major camps. One was that criminals were psychologically disturbed and that was why they broke the law. The other was that people who committed crimes wanted what everybody else wanted but were frustrated in getting what they wanted and therefore turned to crime. What seems to be happening now is that some crimes are committed not because people are out after what everybody else wants, but because they're out after some rather new things. One example is the notion of excitement, a real search for "kicks" that has become a trait of the society in a very important way. What I have in mind here is really a kind of a notion of crime as sport, crime as a search for excitement.

DPG *Do you think we're beginning to see more of that?*

SYKES Yes. The problem of shoplifting certainly is tremendously on the increase, and it's not simply poor people who are shoplifting. It's middle-class people, and very often not from any driving economic need. That seems to me to be a new kind of crime, and it's going to be very hard to deal with.

Another kind of crime stems from the alienation of a portion of the population. This is something that has been treated in American criminology in the past, but the alienation here is a little bit different. This alienation doesn't come from people who have been frustrated by the social order and who therefore reject the goals of the society in a kind of a reaction formation. Rather, people who are perfectly capable of achieving the goals of the society have turned away from them. They really have turned off. Out of that alienation comes a highly symbolic form of deviant or criminal behavior that I think again is different from some of the behavior we've seen before. And, again, this alienation is not simply from the lower classes; you find it up and down the class ladder.

Some of the older forms of criminal behavior, then, are becoming infused with a new spirit. In a sense, at least, the motives behind them have a different meaning for the actors involved. Insofar as that is true, and we have some notion of trying to prevent crimes by dealing with the people who commit them, then all our ideas of rehabilitation, of reform, are going to be altered. If you were dealing with a kid who engaged in a crime because he couldn't make it in the conventional world, you could say to him, "Look, I'll give you vocational training, and I'll upgrade your educational levels," and so on and so on, and you might have some chance of doing something with him. You take a middle-class kid who has had complete access to all kinds of worldly goods, he'd probably laugh in your face if you talked about vocational training.

Another thing that's happening is that

large classes of behavior are simply slipping out from under normative controls. We used to talk about individuals who were no longer guided by norms, or who were not guided by conscience or internalized values, or whatever we wanted to call it. But I'm talking about a sociological phenomenon in which large areas of behavior have become divested of any ethical or normative imperatives for large masses of people over a long period of time. To cite a noncriminal example, over the years the stigma that used to be attached to divorce has lessened greatly. And just as the concept of fault in the legal sense is disappearing from the area of divorce as we change our divorce laws, I think the concept of wrongfulness of divorce is being eroded in the general public conscience.

I'm arguing here that there are a number of areas of criminal behavior—for example adultery, occasional use of drugs, and so on—for which this same sort of slipping out from moral sanctions may be occurring for a significant number of people. They no longer think such behavior is really *wrong;* they think it's just too bad if people do that sort of thing. Again, this situation becomes a very, very serious problem. But I think we may be seeing a shift in the whole philosophy of how we deal with crime—a turning away from trying to solve the problem by dealing with the criminal and directing more of our attention toward trying to deal directly with crime itself. Once at the University of California I saw a driveway, and there was a sign that said: "Do not drive down this driveway—Do not enter." And there was a set of steel teeth coming up from the drive at the point where a car would enter. Nobody drove down that driveway. There was no attempt here to catch the offender, to lecture him on good driving, to give him vocational training, or anything else. The punishment was right there, so nobody did it. I'm suggesting that this is one aspect of the way we're beginning to think about crime—that we make the commission of the crime much more difficult. We put better locks on our cars and deal directly with the delinquent kid who is out for a joy ride.

I think we will be pushed in the direction of putting better lighting in our streets rather than working with juvenile gangs. The whole move to buy up heroin near the source rather than to cure the addict represents the same kind of approach. The TV scanning screens that are being mounted on towers above business areas and storage facilities are part of this.

DPG *Crime prevention without increasing the punishment?*

SYKES What I would call an anticipatory prevention approach.

DPG *Do you think that's a fruitful direction for criminology?*

SYKES Well, there are some terrible problems. You could say that this is the ultimate police state that's bearing down on us. On the other hand, it may be a very rational, enlightened way of dealing with the crime problem.

In the past when we tried to protect the rights of the individual against the power of the state, we looked largely at procedural rules that would protect those rights after the suspected offender was detected and apprehended. Now, however, with efforts to forestall or prevent crime before it ever gets going, a lot of attention will shift to the protection of individual rights before detection. Our notions of privacy are going to come to the fore and are going to loom very much larger as a subject of social concern. As a criminologist, I'm convinced that that's something we should be working on and thinking about.

DPG *Do you see criminology as taking an active role in determining these matters?*

SYKES My feeling is that the voice of the criminologist very seldom seems to carry beyond the groves of academe. People have never paid much attention to it in the past, and I don't think they're going to pay too much more attention in the future. These are not matters that are settled by academic criminologists. It works more indirectly than that. I think you do have some influence by writing and talking to students, who in turn go out and become voting citizens. I myself feel that a number of government commissions have been far more useful than some of their critics thought they were. You don't see the payoff immediately; the commission doesn't submit a report that is implemented the next month. But sometimes these reports begin to stir up public attention, public concern, and something gets done maybe 10 years later. It's a very slow process. So if you ask me whether criminology can have an immediate impact, I would be very doubtful. Does it have some long-range impact? Almost certainly.

Unit 24
Drugs and Drug Subcultures

B Definition and Context

1 Definition

In medical terms, drug abuse occurs whenever a psychoactive drug is taken to such an extent that there is a possibility of mental or physical disorder; in legal terms, abuse occurs whenever such drugs are used for nonmedical purposes. A drug subculture is a group that does not accept the prohibitions, beliefs, and values of the predominant culture concerning psychoactive drugs.

2 World Context

Although drug taking is considered normal in nearly all societies, the drugs that are specifically endorsed by custom, religion, or law vary a good deal across cultures.

3 American Context

Most Americans are users of prescribed or unprescribed psychoactive drugs, but there is no consistent medically based attitude toward drugs in the United States. An ideological gap separates those using only legal drugs from those using the illegal ones, especially marijuana.

C Questions and Evidence

1 Questions

Among the questions sociologists ask about drugs are: (1) Why is marijuana illegal when other more harmful drugs are freely available? (2) Why do people start taking drugs? (3) What strategies can be used to handle heroin addiction?

2 Evidence

a The "Burning Issue" Question

Marijuana use in the United States is associated with a wide range of anti-establishment social and political attitudes. Public responses to it reflect the prevailing beliefs about the "ideological" aspects of the drug, and prohibitions should be reexamined to determine whether the penalties are too severe.

b The "Classical" Question

Various psychological and, more importantly, sociocultural factors account for the emergence of a drug subculture. Explanations in terms of physical disease, deviance, or psychopathology are less satisfactory than the sociocultural model.

c The "Research" Question

The British system of treating heroin addicts as sick individuals is, at least in the short run, more effective than the American system of legal prosecution coupled with haphazard rehabilitation programs. But cultural attitudes must change before the legal system can be reformed.

3 Overview

The solution to drug abuse must lie in providing valid and attractive alternatives to those who currently turn to psychoactive chemicals.

D Looking Ahead

1 Interview: Dana L. Farnsworth

CULTURAL ATTITUDES TOWARD DRUGS

1. In parts of North Africa marijuana is socially approved, but alcohol is unacceptable.

2. In the United States alcohol is socially approved, but marijuana is unacceptable.

3. Tobacco is smoked by over 57 million Americans and is legal.

4. Marijuana is smoked by over 13 million Americans and is illegal.

5. The dominant culture may perceive a subculture and its drugs as threatening the dominant values.

6. A subculture may perceive its drugs as an integral part of its own values and as a rejection of the dominant values.

Different cultures approve different drugs. A culture may approve some drugs, but a subculture within it may approve illicit drugs. The values of the dominant culture may strongly contrast with those of the subculture.

Yanomamo Indians in Brazil. These drug-using Indians employ a pipe to blow *ebene,* a hallucinogen, into each other's nostrils.

B DEFINITION AND CONTEXT

1 Definition

Although the United States has a long history of the use and abuse of a variety of drugs, current modes of drug usage have attracted national attention as one of the main problems facing American society. The issue has become controversial because of the emergence of an entire subculture that is regarded by the rest of society as deviant, threatening, and self-destructive.

The *psychoactive drugs*—chemical substances that are capable of modifying mental performance and individual behavior through their effects on emotions, feelings, consciousness, sensibility, and thinking—are potentially harmful to the individual. The degree to which they are harmful depends on the amount, frequency, and duration of use. In medical terms, *drug abuse* occurs whenever a psychoactive drug is taken to such an extent that there is a possibility of mental or physical disorder. In the legal terms defined by the mores of the dominant culture, abuse occurs whenever a psychoactive drug is used for nonmedical purposes.

A drug subculture is a group within a culture that does not accept a number of significant prohibitions and beliefs of the dominant culture; specifically, this variant subculture is characterized by a value system centered on the nonmedical use of psychoactive drugs. In the United States the principal drug subculture comprises a substantial section of the youth who are experimenting with a variety of drugs for the sole purpose of altering their state of consciousness. Generally this usage revolves around the *hallucinogenic* drugs (marijuana, LSD, psilocybin, mescaline, and allied compounds), but some elements within the subculture habitually use *nonhallucinogenic* drugs (amphetamines, barbiturates, or narcotics).

A subculture has several distinctive components that parallel the institutions and social system of the *dominant culture.* The drug subculture has organization (albeit loose); it has a common framework of values; it possesses ethical codes; it has a market and pricing system; it has a communications network and a special vocabulary; it has the elements of a stratification system. In addition, the subculture tends to advocate and reinforce certain patterns of behavior—passivity rather than hard work, present pleasure rather than deferred gratification, lack of ambition rather than subordination of enjoyment to future goals. Thus this subculture is characterized not only by its overt *behavior,* but also by its implicit *values,* which are at odds with those of the dominant culture.

2 World Context

Drug taking is considered normal in nearly all societies; most of the few exceptions are religious groups, such as the Mormons. The fully temperate individual is statistically deviant, for in nearly all cultures the demand for psychoactive substances is an accepted part of social life rather than the preoccupation of the abnormal few. Throughout the world men in search of bliss or oblivion seek experience in another dimension or in some altered state of consciousness through the use of psychoactive chemicals.

But although drug taking is considered normal in most cultures, the specific drugs permitted are usually strictly controlled by custom, religion, or law. In the United States alcohol is permissible but marijuana is not; in several parts of the Middle East marijuana is permissible but alcohol is not. In addition, all cultures make certain demands on drug users and disapprove of specific types of drug-induced behavior, such as violent aggression, loss of psychomotor control, and social incapacity stemming from mental or physical disorders.

The drugs that are specifically endorsed vary a great deal across cultures. According to a 1951 United Nations survey, there were then 200 million marijuana users in the world, principally in North Africa, India, and Mexico. In East Asia opium is the traditionally favored drug. In the Andes use of cocaine is normal. For the Indians of the American Southwest hallucinogens such as peyote have always been used, particularly in religious contexts. In the industrial societies of the world the normal drugs are alcohol, tobacco, and caffeine.

Attitudes toward drugs vary not only across cultures, but also within a particular culture over a period of time. When Sir Walter Raleigh first brought tobacco to England, its effects were much debated. During the plagues that swept Europe in the seventeenth century, rumor had it that those who smoked tobacco were spared from the ravages of the disease. King James I of England, on the other hand, anticipated modern research findings by declaring that smoking was "a custom loathesome to the eye, hateful to the nose, harmful to the brain, dangerous to the lungs." Yet in modern Britain the population spends as much on tobacco each year as it does on cars, furniture, TV sets, and refrigerators combined.

The sociologist is interested not only in which particular drugs are considered acceptable to specific societies, but also in why one drug rather than another is deemed acceptable, why certain people choose to take drugs at all, and why they choose to take the drugs they do. Analysis of the motives that people have for taking a particular drug may tell us a great deal about the meaning of drug taking in their society—and so may the *societal reaction* to that drug taking. The nature of the social response to a particular drug subculture is of significance in that it may serve to structure and define the status of the drug taken.

3   American Context

Americans have always been of a mixed mind about the nonmedical use of drugs; the use of psychoactive substances has almost invariably been countered with strong opposition. When the Pilgrims set sail for the New World in 1620, they took with them 14 tons of water—plus 42 tons of beer and 10,000 gallons of wine. But 20 years after they landed, Governor William Bradford was complaining in his diaries about excessive drunkenness in Plymouth.

A wide array of drugs was freely available in the United States from colonial times until the turn of this century. Some authorities suspect that the Civil War left a considerable number of narcotics addicts because casualties were administered morphine, a recently discovered opium alkaloid. In the last half of the nineteenth

Nineteenth-century advertisement for patent medicine. Mrs. Winslow's Soothing Syrup contained a grain of morphine per ounce. Widespread use of this and similar "curealls" brought on considerable addiction to morphine and other opium derivatives in the nineteenth century.

(Pages 546–547) **Table 2. Psychoactive Drugs and Their Effects.**

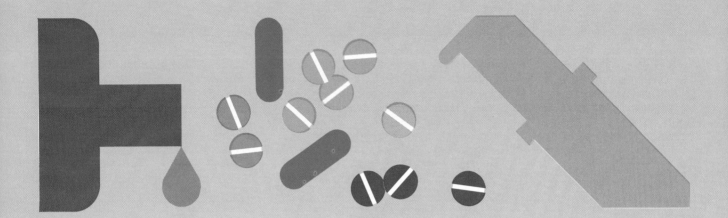

Morphine is injected into a vein, a muscle, or under the skin. Its potential for psychological dependency is great, as is its biological addiction potential. It has a calming, tranquilizing, sleep-inducing effect, but is of short duration and thus must be taken several times a day. It may reduce sexual desire. When taken without prescription, it renders the user a criminal. (Often individuals resort to criminal behavior to support their habit.)

Heroin is injected like morphine and has the same psychological and biological addiction potential. Both morphine and heroin do not, however, directly cause bodily deterioration, although users often neglect their physical needs and suffer from various deficiencies. Heroin use may cause menstrual irregularities; for female addicts, it reduces fertility. If a pregnant mother is addicted, she can pass this addiction on to her newborn baby, who will have possibly fatal withdrawal symptoms if this transmission of addiction is not known. The pupils are generally constricted by the drug, which impairs vision. Constipation and delayed ejaculation during sexual intercourse are also reported. Like morphine, heroin renders the user a criminal.

Methadone is taken orally, often with orange juice. It is usually taken to break a heroin addiction, but is itself addictive. Both biologically and psychologically, the addiction potential is great, but, interestingly, when the user comes off methadone, his psychological craving is for heroin. Weight gain and constipation are frequent side effects, as are increased fluid intake, delayed ejaculation, and possible numbness in hands and feet. Addiction can be passed on to the newborn by a pregnant mother. Unlike heroin and morphine, methadone does not block pain — though it does, if used regularly, block craving for heroin. When obtained through legitimate drug programs, the methadone user is not a criminal — and it is inexpensive enough not to cause him or her to resort to criminal behavior to support the habit.

Alcohol is taken orally; 10 to 12 percent of users are psychologically addicted and have a biological dependency (immediate withdrawal can cause convulsions, etc.). The body suffers through chronic use, with especial damage to the liver. Its use may also lead to serious malnutrition (as with barbiturates and tranquilizers). In moderate use motor control and sensory input processing are impaired. Psychologically, it leads to mood changes with possible impairment of emotional control and mental functioning ability. Socially, it may cause a person to be arrested on misdemeanor charges (unless serious additional charges like drunken driving, etc. are added). Excessive use is seen more or less as a social nuisance.

Long-acting barbiturates (phenobarbital) are taken orally and are moderately addictive psychologically and biologically. They induce sleep and act over a period of about eight hours. Side effects on mind and body are equivalent to alcohol, including hangover. If used without a prescription, barbiturate use renders the user a criminal.

Short-acting barbiturates (pentobarbital, secobarbital: brand names Nembutal and Seconal respectively) are taken orally, and start and end more quickly in their effects than do the long-acting. They also are more addicting than the long-acting. They, too, induce sleep, but may lead to impairment of emotional control and mental ability. They have the same side effects as alcohol, including hangover and loss of motor function. They are subject to the same criminal conditions as long-acting barbiturates.

Tranquilizers are taken orally. The most well-known are Miltown and Equanil (meprobamate), Librium (chlordiazepoxide), and Valium (diazam). They are moderately addicting, both psychologically and biologically; they have many of the same effects as barbiturates, except that a dosage large enough to calm a person down will not necessarily make him sleepy. Side effects include vision impairment, sex drive reduction, constipation (and a general drying of the mucous membranes), nausea, vertigo, and depression. Tranquilizers must be used with prescription, otherwise their use renders a person a criminal.

Sedatives-Hypnotics (non-barbiturate) are taken orally and are biologically and psychologically addictive to a significant degree. They are primarily taken to combat sleeplessness, and their possible side effects include lowering of the blood pressure, nausea, blurred vision, dizziness, facial numbness, and allergic reactions (hives). They relax the user and induce sleep, but must be used with a prescription.

Cocaine is derived from cocoa leaves and is sniffed through the nose, taken orally, or injected. It is often used in combination with morphine or heroin to reduce excess agitation and because the user also experiences the "rush" of the opiate. This combination of effects is called a "speedball." Although the psychological dependency potential is not very high, the biological addiction potential is great. The drug stimulates the central nervous system and produces the sought-after delusions of grandeur and euphoria in this manner. It also functions

as a local anaesthetic, reduces hunger, and dissipates fatigue, as well as causing indifference to pain. High doses may result in psychotic states. Cocaine use is criminal.

Amphetamines ("speed") best known are dextroamphetamine (Dexedrine), methamphetamine (Methadrine, Desoxine), and amphetamine (Benzedrine). They are taken orally and injected into the muscles, sometimes "mainlined" with heroin or other barbiturates. There is significant possibility that they are biologically addictive, and it is certainly the case that people become emotionally dependent on them. They are used to combat fatigue and stimulate the central nervous system. They increase work capacity and creativity and elevate the mood. Physical competence is increased (e.g., in athletics), and the self-image can be elevated. Side effects include hyperactivity and may lead to violent behavior, especially when used with barbiturates. Also, after their effectiveness wears off, the mood is often depressed, with fatigue and mental depression causing distress. High doses may result in paranoia and psychotic states. Use of amphetamines without prescription renders the user a criminal.

Solvents most commonly used are gasoline and glues. The vapors are inhaled. In glues the active agent is Toluene. The biological and psychological addiction potential has not been determined. Neurological effects include ataxia, itching, neuritis, paralysis of peripheral and cranial nerves. Psychologically, solvents elevate the mood, then produce drowsiness, hallucinations, and confusion. Usually solvents can be obtained legally; however, some municipalities have laws regarding the sale of hobby glues.

Caffeine is most commonly used in the form of coffee, tea, cocoa, and "cola" drinks — all of which are taken orally. These are all psychologically and biologically addictive to a significant degree. Caffeine stimulates the central nervous system, giving energy, allaying drowsiness, and allowing more rapid and clearer train of thought. Although generally motor skills improve under drug effect, newly-acquired motor skills may be impaired. Use of this drug is legal (including its purchase in tablet form, e.g. as Nodoz).

Nicotine appears in cigarettes, cigars, pipes, etc. The drug is inhaled (even from "non-inhaled" items). Both biological addiction and psychological dependency potentials are great. Psychologically the drug acts in a calming manner, as does the ritualized act of using it. Side effects include bronchitis, emphysema, cancer, coronary artery disease, shortened life expectancy; if a pregnant mother smokes, the body weight of her newborn will be reduced and rates of occurrence of premature births and aborted fetuses are doubled. Nicotine use is legal.

Cannabis appears in two available forms: *marijuana* and *hashish*. The former consists of dried leaves of the plant (also flowering tips), the latter of dried resin of the plant. (It is about five times stronger.) Both are smoked and ingested orally. There exists some possibility that cannabis may be both biologically and psychologically addictive to some degree. Its use results in relaxation, intensification of sensory stimulation, increase in self-confidence and feelings of creativity (though not necessarily actual creative behavior), and the experience of psychological insights into interactive social processes. The effects of the drug are

certainly influenced by the user's mood, expectations, and emotional environment. Heavy dosage can lead to loss of motor control and (rarely) to psychotic episodes. (It is easier to overdose on hashish than on marijuana.) Use is illegal, though there is tremendous variety in the nature of state laws and their enforcement.

Hallucinogens. The three varieties most commonly used are mescaline (peyote mushrooms or synthetic), psilocybin, and LSD. All are taken orally. There is no evidence of either psychological dependency or biological addiction potential. Effects vary enormously with psychological state of the user and his or her expectations. Most commonly, hallucinations of various kinds are experienced, as is an intensification of sensory stimulation. There are no recorded negative biological side effects, though there is some evidence of possible damage to genes and possibly an increase in the spontaneous abortion rate. Bad psychological reactions abound, especially when hallucinogens are taken in conjunction with alcohol. These reactions include paranoia and loss of ego control, i.e., psychotic states. Another unpleasant possibility for the user is the "flash" — the sudden and unexpected re-experience of portions of trips during "normal" states. The use of peyote, it should be noted, is often accompanied by nausea. Use of these drugs is illegal, and thus they are acquired through the black market. This situation introduces other dangers (besides criminal status for users): synthetic versions of the drugs may have large amounts of impurities — including dangerous dosages of strychnine (which is used as a catalyst in the chemical process of producing LSD).

century, narcotics addiction reached (in percentage terms) its highest level in American history, with at least 250,000 people (some 1 percent of the population) addicted. This addiction arose from the widespread and careless use of patent medicines containing opium and its derivatives in an alcohol base.

Throughout this period there were outcries against the use of drugs, particularly alcohol and tobacco. Various physical and psychological defects were attributed to tobacco chewing (it was not commonly smoked in the United States until 1870), including delirium tremens, perverted sexuality, insanity, and impotence. It was also widely argued that tobacco was a ''stepping stone'' to alcohol. The antitobacconists achieved a considerable measure of success; between 1895 and 1921 the sale of cigarettes was banned in 14 states. From the 1850s on temperance advocates achieved several political triumphs in their campaign against alcohol, and by 1913 about half the population lived under prohibition as the result of state laws. In 1919 the Eighteenth Amendment to the Constitution was ratified. Prohibition lasted until 1933, and state laws against the sale of cigarettes persisted until 1927.

The use of cannabis (marijuana and hashish) has a long history in the United States. In the 1850s a hashish club in New York City was attended by writers and artists. For decades marijuana was used mainly by underprivileged socioeconomic groups in cities and by certain insulated groups on the bohemian fringes of the wider society, but Americans as a whole were unconcerned. Early in this century, however, marijuana was made illegal in some states, mostly in the South and Southwest, when its use became associated with blacks and Mexican-Americans. In 1937 the federal government, under pressure from Harry Anslinger, commissioner of the Federal Bureau of Narcotics, legislated against marijuana. Anslinger's interest, as sociologist Donald Dickson has suggested (''Bureaucracy and Morality,'' 1968), may have derived from the fact that his bureau's budget had been cut by almost 26 percent in four years. The bureau responded by finding an issue that would permit it to widen its scope of operations and thus warrant additional funds. Anslinger started a concerted campaign against marijuana as the ''worst evil of all.'' In particular, an article coauthored by him and entitled ''Marijuana—Assassin of Youth'' (1937) was very widely circulated. Newspapers began to publish accounts of ''marijuana atrocities,'' and a stereotype emerged of the marijuana user as physically aggressive, mentally ill, and criminally inclined—the ''dope fiend.''

Although no comprehensive study was ever made of marijuana and its effects, the 1937 Marihuana Tax Act made use of the drug illegal. Laws on marijuana use were subsequently tightened in the 1950s. On this occasion Anslinger used the *stepping-stone theory* to justify further legislation. ''The danger is this: Over 50 percent of these young addicts started on marijuana. They started there and graduated to heroin; they took the needle when the thrill of marijuana was gone.'' Thus, until recently, marijuana use has been thought to be associated with a variety of social and individual ills, including crime and insanity.

What is the contemporary pattern of drug use in the United States? Almost every American is a user of prescribed or unpre-

Crusaders against drugs. The United States has been swept periodically by crusades against various drugs. The campaigns against tobacco and alcohol became major political forces in the nineteenth century. *(Opposite page)* Bible-brandishing temperance leader Carrie Nation (1846–1911) became famous for chopping up saloons with her ax. *(Above)* 1873 Currier & Ives lithograph depicts "Woman's Holy War" against beer, whiskey, gin, rum, brandy, wine, and liquors. (Left) Antiprohibition poster of 1888 suggests marriage as "a cure for prohibitionists." In 1919 the prohibitionists achieved their goal. The Eighteenth Amendment to the Constitution was passed, making prohibition the law of the land until 1933, when it was repealed. Laws regarding the use of psychoactive drugs change through time. Is it possible that the use of marijuana may soon be legalized?

scribed psychoactive drugs such as aspirin, sleeping pills, tranquilizers, stimulants, alcohol, and tobacco. Advertising has accustomed Americans to the idea that these substances provide solutions to a wide variety of problems. Some 225 million prescriptions for psychoactive drugs were written by doctors in 1971. About 70 percent of all prescriptions written in the United States are for these compounds, and they are used habitually by about 35 million Americans. "Warning," declares every cigarette pack or tobacco advertisement, "The Surgeon-General has determined that cigarette smoking is dangerous to your health." Cigarette smoking is a major factor of lung cancer in men and a significant cause in women; studies also indicate that smoking is a significant factor in coronary heart disease. There is evidence that women who smoke have a higher mortality rate for their infants than nonsmokers. Yet more than 57 million Americans continue to smoke tobacco; over 225,000

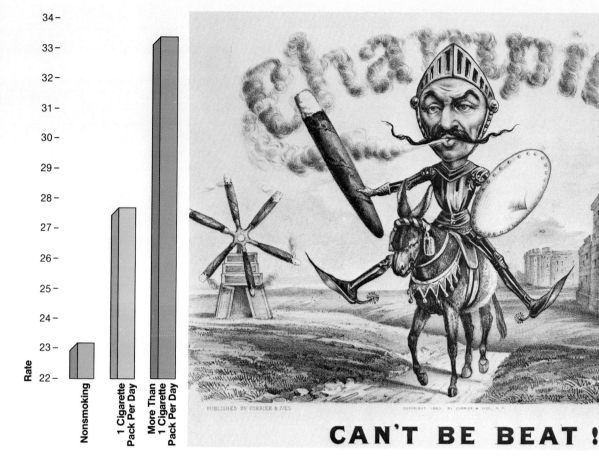

Rate

34 –
33 –
32 –
31 –
30 –
29 –
28 –
27 –
26 –
25 –
24 –
23 –
22 –

Nonsmoking

1 Cigarette Pack Per Day

More Than 1 Cigarette Pack Per Day

PUBLISHED BY CURRIER & IVES   COPYRIGHT 1880, BY CURRIER & IVES, N.Y.   115 NASSAU ST. NEW YORK.

CAN'T BE BEAT !

(Above left) **Figure 1. Mortality Rate per 1,000 Total Births, by Cigarette Smoking Category of Mother Around Time of Birth.** These data indicate that the more a prospective mother smokes, the more likely her baby is to be born dead. (Source: *New York Times,* Jan. 18, 1973; from Ontario Dept. of Health)

(Above right) 1880 Currier & Ives lithograph advertising Champion cigars.

of them can be expected to die during the course of a year as a result of factors connected with their smoking. Of any 20 adult Americans, about 17 drink moderately, two are problem drinkers, and one is a desperate alcoholic. Alcoholism directly afflicts more than 9 million Americans, and indirectly affects countless others who share in the consequences of the alcoholic's problem. According to the National Institute on Alcohol Abuse and Alcoholism, alcohol is a factor in half the highway fatalities each year. About half of the 5 million annual arrests in the United States are related to the misuse of alcohol, and the economic cost to the nation of alcohol abuse is an estimated $15 billion a year. About half the homicides and a quarter of the suicides are alcohol-related.

In addition to the use of legal drugs there is considerable use of illegal drugs. In 1972, 26 million Americans were estimated to have smoked marijuana at some time, with some 13 million currently using it; approximately 7.6 million were estimated to have taken a psychedelic drug, such as LSD or mescaline. There are at least 600,000 narcotics addicts in the United States.

There is no consistent medically based attitude toward drugs in the United States. The major problem is to determine which drugs are socially acceptable and which are not. The issue is further complicated by the fact that an ideological gap separates those using only the legal drugs from those using the illegal ones. The former tend to be older, more conservative, and more numerous; the latter are younger, more radical, fewer in number. Marijuana has become a common form of recreation for middle-class youth, and its use is spreading very rapidly into every ethnic, class, and geographical group among the younger generation. In fact, marijuana usage has now become so common in the United States that it is arguable that it is no longer marginal behavior, but a norm for the children of mainstream America. Marijuana has no known permanent effects and few transitory side-effects, yet the penalties for its use, sale, cultivation and possession are sometimes severe. Although America as a whole is a drug-using culture, those who take drugs that are not accepted by the wider society are considered deviant and criminal. (See Units 22 and 23 for a discussion of deviance and crime.)

C   QUESTIONS AND EVIDENCE

1   Questions

Drug use and the existence of a drug subculture have a number of social implications. Among the questions sociologists ask are these: (1) Why is marijuana illegal when other more harmful drugs are freely available? Can the prohibition of marijuana tell us anything about the relationship between drugs and society? (2) Why do people start to take drugs? What is the role of drug subcultures in initiating people into drug use? (3) What strategies exist for handling the problem of heroin addiction in America? Does sociological research suggest any directions that might be taken concerning this problem?

2   Evidence

a   The "Burning Issue" Question

i   Context   The issue of whether or not marijuana should be legalized is one that all Western industrialized countries are being forced to confront. A large portion of the youth in each of these countries is using marijuana, but governments and the general public remain strongly opposed to a more permissive attitude toward the drug. Nevertheless, several government commissions—in the United States, Britain, Canada, and Scandinavia—have recommended much lighter penalties or outright legalization of private use of marijuana. Most informed opinion accepts that in moderate use the drug is less harmful than tobacco or alcohol. The landmark first report of the National Commission on Marihuana and Drug Abuse (*Marihuana: A Signal of Misunderstanding,* 1972) found that:

> Looking only at the effects on the individual, there is little proven danger of physical or psychological harm from the experimental or intermittent use of the natural preparations of cannabis, including the resinous mixtures commonly used in this country. . . . The experimenter and the intermittent users develop little or no psychological dependence on the drug. No organ injury is demonstrable.

The generally conservative panel surprised many, including President Nixon who had appointed it, by recommending repeal of all criminal penalties for smoking marijuana. But the controversy over the continued prohibition of marijuana affects a large section of the American population, particularly its youth. According to the results of a national survey contained in the commission's second report (*Drug Use in America,* 1973), 8 percent of junior high students, 24 percent of senior high students, and 67 percent of college students reported having had some experience with marijuana. But 82 percent of the junior high students and 38 percent of the high school and college students with such experience reported that they no longer used the drug. Less than 2 percent of the students were heavy users—that is, used the drug more than once a day.

Given that marijuana is acknowledged to be one of the less harmful drugs and that it is already widely used in society, why does its use continue to be subject to criminal penalties? And why is marijuana usage perceived as a major social problem? Inconsistencies between the law and private behavior are not inevitably regarded as serious social problems; statutes on gambling, prostitution, adultery, or cigarette smoking by juveniles are frequently violated without much public or police attention. Sociologists ask: *What social factors can account for the proscription of specific psychoactive drugs in modern society?*

ii Theory   Several sociologists have postulated that the social reaction to particular drugs is directed not toward the pharmacological properties of the drugs concerned, but rather toward the people who use them. The real source of social concern, in this view, is the particular subculture that is associated with the drug and behavior patterns of that group. From this perspective the opposition of mainstream America to marijuana essentially stems from disapproval of the life style and attitudes of the young people who use it.

This opposition is further reinforced by the belief that marijuana usage is antecedent to and causally linked with the adoption of a "countercultural" life style. In *The Drugtakers* (1971) sociologist Jock Young suggests that the association of "hippie" values with drug taking is the real source of opposition to psychedelic drugs of all kinds; this opposition would otherwise be inexplicable when expressed in a culture that tolerates alcohol and tobacco:

> The hippies are a ready target for moral indignation: fascinating because they act out in an uninhibited fashion the subterranean goals which the rest of the population desires, immediately condemnable because they do not deserve any of the rewards. They are a new leisured class; they exist in a limbo which is outside the workaday world of the mass of the people. . . . It is not psychotropic drugs *per se* that evoke condemnation, but their use for unreservedly hedonistic and expressive ends. Society reacts, then, not to the use of drugs but to the type of people who use drugs; it reacts against the subterranean values of hippies and the use of drugs to attain these goals.

A similar approach was adopted by the National Commission on Marihuana and Drug Abuse in its 1972 report. The commission laid great stress on the "symbolic" role of marijuana. Marijuana is

Drug	Youth		Adults	
	%	Number	%	Number
Alcoholic beverages	24	5,977,200	53	74,080,220
Tobacco, cigarettes	17	4,233,850	38	53,114,120
Proprietary sedatives, tranquilizers, stimulants	6	1,494,300	7	9,784,180
Ethical sedatives	3	747,150	4	5,590,960
Ethical tranquilizers	3	747,150	6	8,386,440
Ethical stimulants	4	996,200	5	6,988,700
Marijuana	14	3,486,700	16	22,363,840
LSD, other hallucinogens	4.8	1,195,440	4.6	6,429,604
Glue, other inhalants	6.4	1,593,920	2.1	2,935,254
Cocaine	1.5	373,575	3.2	4,472,768
Heroin	0.6	149,430	1.3	1,817,062

perceived as more than a drug; its use is symbolic of the rejection of cherished values, and the public views it as inextricably linked with idleness, "dropping out," hedonism, sexual promiscuity, and lack of motivation. The commission argued:

> Use of marijuana was, and still is, age-specific. It was youth-related at a time in American history when the adult society was alarmed by the implications of the youth "movement": defiance of the established order, the adoption of new life styles, the emergence of "street people," campus unrest, drug use, communal living, protest politics, and even political radicalism. In an age characterized by the so-called generation gap, marijuana symbolizes the cultural divide.

iii Research It is clear that social attitudes toward drug use depend to some extent on the context in which they are used. For example, amphetamines are considered acceptable for the middle-class housewife who is feeling depressed, but unacceptable for the teenager at a Saturday night party. At the turn of the century nearly a quarter of a million people, predominantly white, middle-class and female, were addicted to narcotics as a result of opiated medications, but very few states regulated such patent medicines in any way. Yet in the first decade of this century, when narcotics use by ethnic minorities in the lower socioeconomic levels of urban centers began to attract public attention, every state rapidly enacted antinarcotics legislation, and the federal government passed the 1914 Narcotics Act (Harrison Act). Similarly, the specific use of marijuana by Mexican-Americans and by blacks was stressed several times in U.S. Bureau of Narcotics evidence to congressional hearings before passage of the Marihuana Tax Act in 1937.

Is marijuana smoking associated with a different value system from that of the dominant culture? In the late 1960s Edward A. Suchman tested the hypothesis that marijuana use was correlated with other expressions of the "hang-loose" ethic as defined by Jerry Simmons and Barry Winograd:

> One of the fundamental characteristics of the hang-loose ethic is that it is irreverent. It repudiates, or at least questions, such cornerstones of conventional society as Christianity, "my country right or wrong," the sanctity of marriage and premarital chastity . . . the accumulation of wealth, the right and even competence of parents, the schools and the government to head and make decisions for everyone—in sum, the establishment. (*It's Happening,* 1966)

In Suchman's study the dependent variable was the frequency of drug use by his student respondents, and the independent variable was the degree of adherence to the hang-loose ethic as determined by questions on values, attitudes, and behavioral patterns. In "The Hang-Loose Ethic and the Spirit of Drug Use" (1968) he reported that drug usage correlated highly with a wide range of social and political attitudes indicative of a rejection of the established order.

Table 1. Reported Experience with Drug Use for Recreational and Nonmedical Purposes by American Youth and Adults. The data are based on a 1972 survey by the National Commission on Marihuana and Drug Abuse. (Figures for alcohol and cigarette use refer only to use within the last seven days before the survey. Figures for proprietary and ethical drugs refer only to nonmedical use. The term "ethical drugs" means drugs restricted to sale only on a physician's prescription.) (Source: *New York Times,* March 23, 1973; from National Commission on Marihuana and Drug Abuse)

The more the student was rebellious, anti-establishment, and hedonistic, the more likely he was to smoke marijuana; the more conformist and moral in traditional terms the student was, the less likely he was to smoke the drug. Attitudes toward marijuana usage and adherence to the hang-loose ethic were highly correlated, and they reinforced each other.

Other studies have shown that subtle social, psychological, and behavioral changes may take place in long-term users of marijuana and the psychedelics: such people tend to orient only to the present. Some researchers believe the change in attitude is caused by prolonged use of the drug; others believe that the changes are the result of adoption of behavior patterns only coincidentally associated with drug usage.

Evidence on public attitudes toward marijuana tends to confirm the view that adults are at least as concerned with the "ideological" aspects of marijuana usage as with the pharmacological characteristics of the drug. A national opinion survey conducted for the first report of the National Commission on Marihuana and Drug Abuse found that 57 percent of the adult population believed that "if marijuana were legal, it would lead to teenagers becoming irresponsible and wild." Some 56 percent of the adult public also believed that "many crimes are committed by persons who are under the influence of marijuana." Some 70 percent of the adult population believed that "marijuana makes people want to try stronger drugs like heroin." (In fact, however, only 4 percent of marijuana smokers had tried heroin.) Of the population over 50 only 9 percent agreed with the statement, "Most people who use marijuana lead a normal life," but this statement was accepted by half of the young adults between 18 and 25. Furthermore, no less that 48 percent of adults believed that some people have died from marijuana abuse—although there is no record of a single fatality directly attributable to ingestion of marijuana. (The overdose amount necessary to cause death is so enormous that it is virtually unachievable.) The study also found that adults have a strong reaction to the "amotivational syndrome" they perceive in marijuana users: drugs are seen to threaten not just the health and sanity of the individual, but the morals of the society as a whole.

iv Evaluation The evidence seems to suggest that the more a drug problem threatens the values of the dominant culture, the more likely it is to be perceived as a legal rather than a medical matter. Although indigent—but not affluent—alcoholics are persecuted by the police to some extent, their addiction seems to involve no ideological program of social rebellion or protest, and the entire phenomenon of alcoholism is increasingly viewed as a sickness that threatens public health rather than public morality. But the implications of marijuana and other hallucinogens run much deeper; they touch on social issues such as radical protest, permissive morals, youthful rebellion.

If public attitudes toward marijuana are clouded by prejudice, the case for reexamination of the existing statutes is strengthened. Several writers have contended that even if marijuana use is in some way detrimental, any benefits derived from the laws are far outweighed by their damage to American society. In *Marijuana, the New Prohibition* (1971) John Kaplan asserts that prosecution of

Users of marijuana and psychedelics. If they retain their present orientation, will these young people be able to step into positions where they can shoulder the burden of planning for a more humane society?

marijuana users ties up police and courts, turns half a generation into prospective criminals, encourages disrespect between parents and children, spreads disbelief about the dangers of the genuinely hard drugs, and forces marijuana users into contact with drug peddlers.

Even if this social damage is considered acceptable, it may be that society will have to look anew at existing penalties to establish whether the punishments fit the crime—for penalties in many states are based on outdated conceptions of marijuana. The indications are, however, that public opinion is slowly moving in the direction suggested by Suchman when he completed his study of marijuana smokers:

To crack down on these youth with all the powerful forces of law and order and to justify such a restriction of freedom in the name of preventing crime or disease seems more an uncontrolled expression of adult moral indignation and righteousness than of human concern or social justice— and, sadly, an ineffective and destructive expression at that.

b The "Classical" Question

i Context   The fact that so many American citizens have chosen to experiment with psychoactive substances in a culture that prizes rationality and self-discipline rather than transcendence or hedonistic indulgence requires explanation. Despite widespread propaganda against the drugs, ranging from the threat of addiction to the danger of chromosome damage, millions of Americans have become involved in the drug subculture and its values. Sociologists ask: *What social factors account for the emergence of a drug subculture and encourage recruitment to it?*

ii Theory   Several perspectives have been applied to the question of why people take drugs and what role the drug subculture plays in the process. Four main models have been proposed, although some of them overlap and complement each other.

The first model, most frequently employed by law enforcement agencies and political figures, may be termed the *epidemic theory.* This model views the spread of a drug subculture as analogous to the progress of a disease. Just as a disease is spread by germs and their carriers, so drug taking is spread by the habituation potential of the drugs and by the peddlers why purvey them. Because of their pharmacological properties, the drugs are regarded as in some way "contagious"; that is, they infect the individuals with whom they come into contact, resulting in progression to further drug use. In this model the subculture is seen as a malignant growth that society must eradicate; its disappearance will virtually automatically eliminate drug abuse.

According to a second model, the *deviance theory,* the individual becomes involved in socially deviant behavior through a process much the same as that for other forms of deviance (such as criminality or sexual "perversion"). He takes part, in an exploratory way, in a deviant act; his act is observed and labeled as deviant by people whose opinion is significant to him; and finally he defines himself as a member of the deviant subculture and joins the group that will give continuing support to his deviant behavior. Such labeling tends to operate as a self-fulfilling prophecy: once the individual has been "typed" into a particular category, his subsequent experiences tend to reinforce behaviors associated with that category. Like the criminal or the mentally ill, the drug user is apt to find himself treated in terms of his past behavior even when he attempts a return to his earlier, "normal" life style.

A third model, the *psychopathological theory,* views the drug taker as an abnormal personality. Drug usage is regarded as an indication of psychological maladjustment. The use of a relatively innocuous drug such as marijuana indicates less serious disturbance, but the use of an addictive drug such as heroin indicates the presence of grave personal problems. The drug user thus tends to be contrasted with psychologically "normal" people who do not experience the need for flight from reality.

A fourth model is the *sociocultural theory.* This view accepts that psychological factors may predispose individuals to participate in drug taking, but emphasizes instead the social context in which the drug usage occurs. Particular social contexts may present problems for which drug taking provides a solution, or at least seems an appropriate response. The drug subculture itself is also stressed as

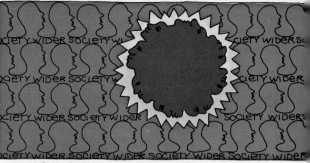

I. EPIDEMIC THEORY

DRUG SUBCULTURE AS A PRIME CARRIER AND SOURCE OF "DISEASE"

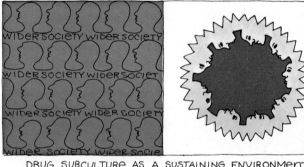

II. DEVIANCE THEORY

DRUG SUBCULTURE AS A SUSTAINING ENVIRONMENT FOR "DEVIANT" BEHAVIOR

III. PSYCHOPATHOLOGICAL THEORY

DRUG SUBCULTURE AS A CONTEXT IN WHICH "EMOTIONALLY DISTURBED" AND "WEAK" PEOPLE FIND "BAD" SOLUTIONS TO LIFE'S PROBLEMS.

IV. SOCIOCULTURAL THEORY

DRUG SUBCULTURE AS PART OF THE SOCIETY WITH BOTH SUBCULTURE AND SOCIETY IN DYNAMIC INTERACTION WITH EACH OTHER

a socializing context in which the use of drugs may be quite normal. The sociocultural model tends to reject the other three approaches as being too simplistic.

ii Research (Survey)   The epidemic model—that drug taking is contingent on the contagious influence of a subculture—is not generally accepted by social scientists. It's inadequacy, they believe, lies in its failure to consider either the wider social context in which drug taking occurs or the motivational factors in the individual. Jock Young's critique in *The Drugtakers* exemplifies the social-science response to this theory:

> The usual assumption implicit in theories of drug control is that subcultures connected with drug use must be eliminated in order to limit the spread of the "epidemic." My contention here is that . . . people accept socialization into drug cultures because they find the cultures attractive in terms of solving the problems they face; they do not "catch" drug addiction, they *embrace* it.

The deviance model has also been criticized by many sociologists. The contrast between a body of so-called normal people and a few deviants on the edge of society tends to equate normality with the middle-class life style and to view variation from that pattern as deviant or even pathological. As Young points out: "What is forgotten . . . is that hedonism, thrill-seeking, lack of employment, unstable formal marriages are often the *norms* of the groups from which drug users emanate." Those who reject the deviance model analyze the differences between the dominant culture and the drug subculture in terms of two sets of competing norms, one of which happens to be associated with a minority group (characterized by its "hang-loose" ethic). Other sociologists are reluctant, however, to abandon the deviance model. As Young suggests, to view the deviant in a new light would necessarily require the middle-class sociologist to reexamine his own unquestioned normality from the perspective of a subculture that prizes hedonism and transcendence.

The psychological model stresses motivational factors in the individual drug taker; these factors may impel a person to "escape reality" through the use of psychoactive chemicals. An example of this approach is that of D. P. Ausubel: "Differential susceptibility to drug addiction is primarily a reflection of the relative adjustment value which narcotics possess for different individuals." ("Causes and Types of Drug Addiction," 1961) This approach has been criticized by sociologists on several grounds. Although acknowledging the significance of individual motivational factors, sociologists are reluctant to see drug use purely as a manifestation of psychopathology. They contend that contextual factors may be at least as important as imagined differences between users and nonusers, and such factors may account for the initial emergence of a subculture or predispose individuals to join that subculture. Furthermore, several social scientists have queried the notion that there is necessarily something psychologically amiss with drug users. Kenneth Keniston, discussing a type of drug-using students whom he terms "seekers," asserts their basic stability:

Such students are less seekers after grades or professional expertise than seekers after truth. They are extremely open to the contradictory cross-currents in American society . . . continually struggling to experience the world more intensely, to make themselves capable of greater intimacy and love, to find some "rock bottom" from which they can sally forth to social and interpersonal commitments. . . .

Marijuana and the more powerful hallucinogens fit very neatly with the search for experience by such students. On the one hand, they promise a new kind of experience to a young man or woman who is highly experimental. On the other hand, they promise intensity, heightened sentience, intensified artistic perceptiveness, and perhaps even self-understanding. ("Heads and Seekers," 1968–1969)

The sociocultural approach focuses both on the wider society and on the subcultural context in which drug taking occurs. In this view the fact that different societies show differing incidences of the use of illegal drugs cannot be explained solely by reference to the psychological motivations of the participating individuals; drug taking instead must be seen as a response to features of the cultural context. Furthermore, the social group in which initiation into drug usage takes place is not seen merely as a passive environment; it plays a distinctive role in structuring the meaning of the drug experience.

Some theorists have stressed the role of the subculture as a *socializing peer group* that offers the opportunity for achieving status by demonstrating one's autonomy and independence. Initiation into the subculture may involve—as does entry to other forms of *youth culture*—a violation of various norms of decorum endorsed by the dominant culture. By taking drugs, the individual gains entry to the group, and his subsequent behavior is structured by his shared experiences. He becomes more involved in the group, views himself as a member of the subculture, and begins to sever contacts with conventional individuals and the conventional life style. In "Becoming a Marihuana User" (1953), Howard S. Becker stresses how the novice learns to respond to marijuana in terms of meanings defined by those who initiate him. After his first marijuana-smoking experience, the novice may feel that nothing much has happened to him; it is only when more sophisticated users in his new social setting assure him that he is being affected that he learns to recognize and approve his experience. In Becker's view membership in a drug subculture involves (often as a deliberate act of choice) making and sustaining social interactions and relationships that then influence further behavior. Becker suggests that in order to become a user, one has to be partly *resocialized,* discarding certain original definitions and prohibitions and adopting new ones espoused by the group. (For discussions of socialization and youth culture, see Units 5 and 25.)

iv Evaluation   Social scientists find the psychological and sociocultural approaches most useful in analyzing the problem of drugs in society. The perspectives are often combined, for the differences between them are largely differences of focus.

One conceptual problem that arises in accounting for drug subcultures and their continuous supply of recruits stems from the tendency to group all illegal psychoactive drugs together. In fact, some studies suggest that the marijuana user and the heroin user have different personality characteristics. According to these studies, the great majority of marijuana smokers are fundamentally indistinguishable from their "straight" peers except that they use the drug. In their case the evidence is strong that the actual use of the drug and willingness to experiment with it are the product of *contextual factors*—availability of the drug and an environment that allows redefinitions of what is appropriate behavior. Unit 10 discusses this point.

The psychological approach is of limited value in analyzing issues related to soft drugs because the use of the hallucinogens is found predominantly in relatively stable, middle-class environments. For heroin users, on the other hand, psychological factors may be much more important. Even here, however, different contextual factors are significant: heroin use, unlike that of marijuana and the psychedelics, is strongly correlated with poverty, deprivation, and general social disorganization. Because these social features decidedly influence personality development, even in this case the social and psychological perspectives are best combined.

Several aspects of social environment appear to predispose individuals to drug taking. For example, parental life syle is significant: marijuana users are more likely than nonusers to have parents who drink, smoke, and take prescribed psychoactive drugs. Use of tobacco or alcohol is also correlated with illicit drug use. In a high school study recorded in the 1972 report of the National Commission on Marihuana and Drug Abuse, 3 percent of the nonsmokers but 50 percent of the smokers had tried marijuana; 2 percent of the nondrinkers but 27 percent of the drinkers had used the drug.

Persons who are liable to use marijuana may be predicted statistically on the basis of familial, social, and cultural factors. For example, males, college students, and residents of urban areas in the Northeast and on the West Coast are overrepresented in relation to the national population. Similarly, a radical political stance, separate residence from parents, and a permissive attitude toward sexual behavior also correlate with the use of soft drugs. Again, the psychological factors are difficult to disentangle from those that are culturally determined.

Each of the four analytic perspectives adopts a somewhat different approach not only to the individual user but also to the drug subculture. In the epidemic model the drug subculture is the *prime carrier and source* of drug use. In the deviance model it provides the *sustaining environment* for the maintenance of deviance. In the psychopathological model it is merely the *context* in which the individual attempts to find a solution to his personal problems. In the sociocultural model drug use is related to the *total society;* it is seen as a product of a variety of social forces, and the subculture is viewed as a socializing agent that structures the experience of the individual. Indeed, some sociologists have even argued that if illicit drug taking is occurring in a society, the subculture serves a socially useful function. It is through the subculture that the individual learns how to administer the drug; if there were no norms surround-

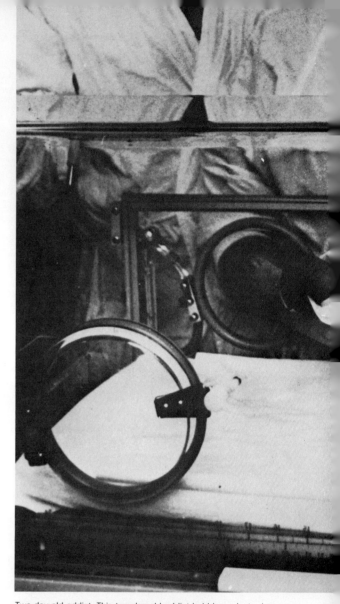

Two-day-old addict. This two-day-old addict held by a doctor in a Philadelphia hospital is a heroin addict suffering withdrawal symptoms from his mother's narcotics habit.

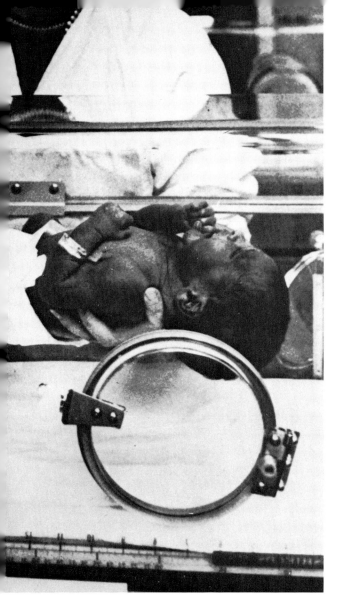

ing its use there would be a far greater danger of overdose, psychosis, and physical harm to the user.

c The "Research" Question

i Context President Nixon has described hard-drug addiction as America's "public enemy number one." Estimates of addiction rates vary widely, but the federal government accepts a figure of between 600,000 and 700,000 narcotics addicts in the United States. The sharp increase in the rate of addiction is another source of concern. The current estimate is double the figure for 1969, when the last official estimate was made, and it is about 13 times the estimated figure for 1960.

Heroin addiction was largely ignored by the larger society as long as it was regarded as almost exclusively a problem of the black ghetto. But whereas in 1960 over 90 percent of all known addicts were black, a quarter of them today are white—and many are middle-class suburban teenagers. In New York City one high school student out of every 20 is using heroin, and the drug has become the largest single cause of death for New Yorkers between the ages of 15 and 35. About one child in 40 in New York is born a heroin addict as a result of maternal addiction.

The 10,000-percent markup in price between the poppy fields of Asia and the junkie in "Needle Park" has attracted organized crime, and the heroin business is one of the major commercial enterprises in the United States today. Narcotics addiction is generally considered to be the principal source of street muggings and a major factor in a variety of other crimes, particularly burglary and fraud. In New York City alone heroin addicts steal goods worth a reputed $3 billion each year to support their habits. In terms of America's social, economic, health, and public order interests, the containment of heroin addiction is a problem of crisis proportions. Sociologists ask: *Does research suggest possible directions for public policy on heroin addiction?*

ii Theory Federal and local authorities in the United States view heroin users and addicts as criminals and pressure and prosecute them with the full force of the law. This approach is grounded in the belief that the heroin addict can be induced to give up his use of the drug in the face of legal penalties. It is assumed that with adequate funding of police and narcotics control efforts, heroin use can be reduced to manageable proportions.

In Britain the addict is treated as sick and, like any other sick person, is entitled to full treatment, including appropriate medication, at a nominal cost under the national health service. Just as the diabetes patient needs his insulin, the heroin patient needs his drug—so the British give it to him. The addict pays a standard rate applicable to all prescriptions, whatever their content—about 50 cents—and if he cannot afford even that, he gets his heroin free. An effort is made to persuade the addict to participate in a rehabilitation program. If possible, he is switched from heroin to the allied drug methadone, which, though also highly addictive, does not have many of the unpleasant effects associated with heroin and allows its user to lead a normal life. The British continue to prosecute heroin users who are not officially registered addicts. Only those who can satisfy a specially appointed doctor of their addiction are entitled to heroin or a heroin substitute, and the strength of the dosage is carefully calculated so that it is just sufficient to keep the patient functioning normally without getting "high." The addict may be prosecuted if he is found with heroin from any other source.

These contrasting approaches are reflected in public policy. In the United States the control of heroin takes three major lines of attack. First, the resources of the law are directed against all those involved in the heroin subculture—not only the pushers, but the addicts as well. Second, the resources of the narcotics squad and the U.S. Customs Service are directed at preventing heroin from actually entering the United States. Third, the United States is attempting to dry up heroin at its source: under the terms of an arrangement with the Turkish government, for example, the United States has in effect paid the Turkish poppy growers to stop growing their crop.

Critics of this three-pronged approach doubt its effectiveness. They point out that the size of the addict population in the United States suggests that policing is not a feasible deterrent. They also underscore the fact that many thousand dollars worth of heroin can be concealed in a single envelope, making the difficulties involved in maintaining a customs embargo on the drug almost insurmountable. And the belief that payment of $35 million to Turkish poppy growers will dry up the supply of heroin in the United States is considered naïve. Indeed, extensive poppy crops are being cultivated in Iran, Afghanistan, and other countries. And the "Golden Triangle" area of Southeast Asia has also been a source of drugs for Americans, particularly servicemen in Vietnam.

Critics of the British approach contend that legalized heroin would simply find its way onto the streets and thus would merely add to the dimensions of the problem. They argue that the British system solves nothing—the addict is still an addict. And they question whether it is sound social policy to distribute cheap or free narcotics to young addicts, who might otherwise have been forced to abandon their habits. This policy has also been criticized as a potentially racist approach to addiction in the United States, where 75 percent of the addicts are nonwhites.

iii   Research (Methodology)   Comparative research suggests the consequences of these alternative conceptual approaches. The most striking difference between the British and the American heroin problems lies in the relative size of the heroin subculture in each society. The British have contrived not only to keep their addiction levels at comparatively manageable proportions, but also to reduce the rate of addiction. The British have only one addict for every 21,000 persons; in the United States about one person in every 300 is a heroin user. A 1970 British figure puts the number of addicts at less than 2,700, which represents a decrease of over 200 from the previous year. There are, of course, several distinctive features of American society that encourage the growth of a heroin subculture, but the differential in rate of increase between Britain and the United States requires explanation.

Analysis of the British approach shows that their medical definition of the heroin problem has several social consequences. First, the black market in heroin has been considerably curtailed. When the addict can obtain a supply for a few dollars a week or even for nothing, there is little incentive for individuals or for organized crime

(Below and facing page) "DOA" from "OD": Dead on arrival from an overdose of heroin. The American street scene for heroin users is a never-ending rat race of constant criminal activities to raise money to pay for a constantly rising habit cost. The likelihood of spending time in prison or dying of an overdose of heroin or from impurities in the drug is an ever-present reality.

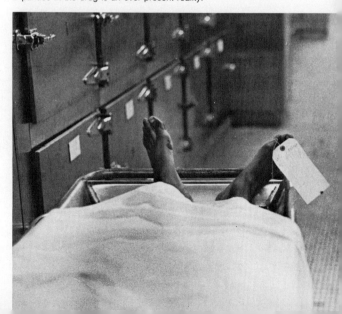

to risk the penalties involved in importing and peddling the drug. In the United States a vicious circle operates: the more successful narcotics agencies are in reducing the inflow of heroin, the higher the price rises, providing still greater encouragement for illegal importers of the drug.

Second, the British are able to maintain a comprehensive and up-to-date register of addicts. Because an unregistered addict finds his drug difficult to obtain, there is strong incentive for him to register for legal prescriptions. The British estimate that there are less than 200 unregistered addicts in the entire country, although certain observers put the figure somewhat higher. In the United States, however, no one really knows who the addicts are, or how many there are. The persecution of addicts as criminal offenders renders it extremely difficult to obtain an accurate picture of the problem or to encourage narcotics abusers to come forward for treatment (except in localities where methadone-maintenance programs have been instituted—programs currently sustaining well over 85,000 addicts).

Third, the British hard-drug user is able to remain economically active; over 40 percent of British addicts have full-time jobs. The American addict, by contrast, tends to spend his time hustling for the money for his next fix; his uncertain and risky routine makes a conventional way of life almost impossible.

Fourth, the British have kept the incidence of narcotics-related death to a negligible level. Narcotics deaths frequently result either from *overdosage* (when the victim uses unexpectedly concentrated heroin) or from *impurities* in the dosage (when the victim injects anything from soap to rat poison). Because British clinic heroin comes in a standard concentration and the addict knows how much is being administered, his only peril comes from illegally obtained street heroin—and deaths from this source have been alarmingly high. Analyses of samples of street heroin in the United States (where it is the *only* source of supply for five-sixths of the addict population) reveal that it may contain anywhere between 0 and 77 percent heroin. In New York City alone there were over 1,258 narcotics deaths in 1971, and the incidence in all American cities has risen very rapidly since the late 1960s.

Fifth, crime related to hard-drug addiction is virtually unknown in Britain. But in America a massive crime rate is an inevitable concomitant of the high price of illegal narcotics. The British are able to concentrate resources on the addict himself, while the contrasting United States approach may actually create crime by keeping the price of heroin at a high level and virtually forcing hundreds of thousands of addicts to resort to illegal activities to support the habits they are unable to abandon.

iv Evaluation In terms of the incidence of narcotics addiction, it is difficult to avoid the conclusion that the American approach has not worked, and it is unlikely that the problem will disappear in the face of continuing repression or haphazard rehabilitation programs. The implication for the foreseeable future is that American society will contain hundreds of thousands of addicts, all automatically defined as criminals, most of them obliged to resort to criminal acts to support their expensive habits. The likelihood is that this group of outlaws will pose a very substantial burden on law-enforcement offi-

In the United States today there are basically three ways addicts are being dealt with: (1) Most are treated as criminals and jailed. Jails solve few drug problems; they are overcrowded, and recidivism is very high. (2) Some are put into special programs in which they take methadone. Many addicts in such programs hold down jobs and are accepted by the wider society. As of 1969 the "failure" rate of such programs, according to one estimate, was 12 percent. (3) Some addicts are admitted into residential drug-treatment communities such as Synanon, Daytop, Odyssey House, and Horizon House (shown here). Only addicts with high motivation to quit drug use are admitted, and the "success" rate is therefore high. These communities function in terms of the psychopathology model. They assume that addicts need to remake their psyches, improving on their ego strengths and learning to communicate feelings to other people. It is believed that this process will enable ex-addicts to overcome the feelings of inadequacy and isolation that first propelled them into drug use.

cials, welfare agencies, ordinary citizens, and the very quality of life itself in America.

But does a study of the British system suggest that its adoption would offer any better solution? The British system is not a panacea; legalized heroin is simply a holding action. But it may be preferable to runaway addiction. The British argue pragmatically that although most addicts will stay addicts, addicts legally registered at clinics and leading relatively productive lives are better than desperate people hooked on dangerous, expensive, and illegal habits. British experience does suggest, however, that the problems associated with a black market in drugs will continue to persist to a certain degree and also that drug addiction cannot be solely attributed to (or controlled by) local factors.

Nevertheless, the arguments in favor of at least an experimental adoption of the British approach are strong. Why, then, is there continued resistance even to trial programs? One hypothesis is that the answer must be sought in attitudes toward drug use and drug users on the part of the predominant culture: without even considering the evidence, Americans recoil at the prospect of cheap, legalized dope. It may be that this tendency to reject out of hand, without even considering the evidence, ideas that cut against the grain of traditional American values is the major barrier to constructive new modes of thinking about ways of resolving America's drug problem.

3   Overview

Drug use is a product of reaction to social forces. And the social response to drug taking is colored by the perceptions that the dominant culture has of the people and values associated with the drugs in question. In each of the issues examined in this unit, social attitudes have been profoundly influential—on the continued prohibition of marijuana, on the way people perceive drug subcultures, on the approach to the problem of heroin addiction.

American attitudes toward drugs are often contradictory. Our culture endorses such potentially lethal drugs as alcohol and tobacco but forbids marijuana. Our culture endorses such dangerous activities as boxing, mountain climbing, and automobile racing because the experiential value of these activities is recognized, but the use of psychedelics for adventures of a different kind is not tolerated. Our culture prizes independence of thought and experimentation ("Make up your own mind," "Judge for yourself"), but not when these involve drugs ("Do your own thing").

If drug abuse is to be prevented, the answer must lie not in repression, but in finding valid and attractive alternatives for those who at present would rather seek meaning in the effects of psychoactive chemicals. As Kenneth Keniston comments in relation to student drug users: "Drug use is indeed a commentary of American society, but it is above all an indirect criticism of our society's inability to offer the young exciting, honorable and effective ways of using their intelligence and idealism to reform our society."

The issue is not whether or not to use drugs; it is *which* drugs a society approves of. Both Henry Kissinger, adviser to the President of the United States, and Chou En-lai, Premier of the People's Republic of China, apparently approve of this drug in liquid form, with which they are honoring each other on a state occasion.

D LOOKING AHEAD

1 Interview:
Dana L. Farnsworth

Dana L. Farnsworth is vice-chairman of the National Commission on Marihuana and Drug Abuse. A physician, he has held teaching and administrative positions with a number of hospitals and schools, including the Massachusetts Institute of Technology and Harvard University. He has been officer of many professional associations and editor of several journals. His works include *Mental Health in College and University; Living* (with Hein and Richardson); *Textbook of Psychiatry* (with Ewalt); *Psychiatry, Education, and the Young Adult; Dimensions in Health* (with others). He edited *College Health Administration; Psychiatry, the Clergy, and Pastoral Counseling* (with Braceland); and *Counseling and the College Student* (with Blaine).

DPG *Can we anticipate the eventual legalization of marijuana in the United States?*

FARNSWORTH Not in the foreseeable future. According to a comprehensive survey sponsored by the National Commission on Marihuana and Drug Abuse in 1972, only 14 percent of youth (12–17 years) and 16 percent of adults (18 years and over) had ever used marijuana and 7 percent of youth and 8 percent of adults were still using it. A sharp drop in usage was noted after the age of 25. Furthermore, only 8 percent of nonusing youth and 3 percent of nonusing adults indicated that they would try it if it became legalized. This lack of pressure toward legalization together with its strong disapproval by the great majority of citizens does not support a prediction that marijuana will become legalized until or unless strong unforeseen changes in attitudes come about. The analogy of prohibition of alcohol and its repeal during the early part of this century is not a good indication because a much higher percentage of the people at that time were in favor of the social use of alcohol than are now in favor of the social use of marijuana. Furthermore, the motivations toward the use of marijuana are not widely shared by the vast majority of people.

DPG *How would you compare marijuana to alcohol in terms of physical effect?*

FARNSWORTH Alcohol is much more harmful. Marijuana, at least in the concentration available in the United States, has a relatively innocuous physical effect. But people who use it excessively—those who are stoned to some extent practically every day—just aren't able to use their abilities effectively. To put it another way, alcohol tends to promote disorder and release violence, whereas marijuana is apt to have a more subduing influence. I know of no substantial evidence that marijuana leads to violence, although it may encourage relatively passive types of activity that are not in general favor. People who use amphetamines or cocaine, on the other hand, develop paranoid psychoses and violent behavior with considerable frequency.

DPG *Could you suggest a rational approach to marijuana, given scientific evidence on the subject, that might overcome social prejudices against it at this time?*

FARNSWORTH I believe that we should not move in that direction, because no country can survive and be effective if it has too many purely pleasure-producing drugs easily available. There are 9 million chronic alcoholics in this country already, and there is little that we can do about it, so I would strongly oppose official encouragement of any other pleasure-producing drug. Anyone who finds chemical solutions to problems without solving the basic issues that formed them—whether the drug involved is heroin, marijuana, alcohol, or cough medicine—is in a vulnerable situation.

DPG *In your work on the National Commission on Marihuana and Drug Abuse, did you come to any conclusions as to what measures, if any, should be used to determine what substances private individuals should be prevented from taking in America?*

FARNSWORTH Several drugs, including cocaine and heroin, should not be made available at all. Any of the narcotics or stimulants or sedatives that do not have adequate substitutes should be made as difficult to get as possible. Barbiturates and the other hypnosedatives present a special problem. They are very valuable drugs in medicine when used under supervision. Physicians, patients, pharmacists, and everyone else who is involved in the distribution process should be pressured to keep distribution within medically indicated channels.

DPG *Determining which drugs are legally permissible and which are not seems to be a sociopolitical decision, and as such it is derived from a certain set of value structures. Your formula seems to indicate an absolute value placed on the work ethic, getting the job done, subordinating present pleasure to the prospect of future rewards. Of course, another value orientation is subscribed to by people who choose immediate pleasures and who are not prepared to sacrifice them for the hardships of the work-ethic syndrome. Denying them pleasure-producing drugs surely amounts to the imposition of the values of one culture upon another. Do we have here a problem for democracy or freedom?*

FARNSWORTH The United States isn't a free country in the sense that it has free choice in all matters. It is a highly technological society. Throwing out the work ethic would mean a return to an agrarian, nontechnological society, and many people would be somewhat disappointed with the results. On the other hand, you can't say no one should be allowed to be irresponsible. Americans wouldn't stand for that either. You can have a relatively small percentage of people who are unable to postpone present pleasure for greater satisfaction later on as long as you have a reasonable percentage who do produce the goods. In a society like ours we have room for both. We just have to be sensible in distributing the advantages of both cultures. Justice Learned Hand once observed that any society that sets about obtaining complete freedom for everyone at all times ends up with freedom only for the savage few.

DPG   *So one can really say that freedom in America is essentially subject to economic priorities. Is large-scale use of hallucinogenics compatible with the economic priorities of our society, given that the former usually implies transcendence and hedonism, the latter the Protestant ethic?*
FARNSWORTH   Someone has to produce the goods. We have sufficient difficulty in keeping our minds under control as it is. Anything that tends to diminish that control is not very helpful to the individual. It may be all right for a person to become intoxicated when he's in a sheltered or protected situation. But to live in that state most of the time reacts against the individual and against his family and the community—they are deprived of his services. I don't believe we're in a position to encourage the use of hallucinogenic drugs.

DPG   *What would you say are the implications for the future when today's youth become the older generation themselves?*
FARNSWORTH   I think they'll be as conservative as their parents were about behavior that impairs their children's futures. I think the youngsters 10 to 16 are not going to buy some of the ideas their older brothers and sisters have been so ardently advocating. The evidence suggests that sophomores and freshmen in college and some of the high school students are becoming more conservative in all their attitudes. I'm not equating conservatism with being old-fashioned, but rather with an attitude encouraging the maximum degree of freedom for everyone by the use of wise restraints.

DPG   *Do you think that situation results from youngsters' more sophisticated knowledge of what drugs are and what they can do? In the 1970s many spokesmen for the youth culture—rock musicians and so on— are warning against dangerous use of drugs. Do you think the youth culture has learned to discriminate?*
FARNSWORTH   I'd like to be able to say that, but I'm not convinced that it's true. I'm afraid the trend toward greater conservatism is a cyclical affair motivated by influences I cannot be certain of now. It would be helpful if the youth culture were working in the direction of caution. Peer group influence is the major factor that motivates young people to take drugs.

DPG   *Many people use drugs as an "automatic problem-solver," but the problems return after the chemically induced sense of euphoria has disappeared. It's almost a theological discussion. What lies beyond drugs?*
FARNSWORTH   As a physician who has been involved in drug cultures as a nonparticipant observer, I find it incredible that anyone would choose drugs over the many other opportunities that may be available. The person who is badly handicapped, say by living in dire poverty and belonging to a minority group, may take drugs because it temporarily releases him from unbearable tensions. On the other hand, a college student may take drugs because he is angry at the social system and wants to show how alienated he is. There's quite an inconsistency here. One person takes drugs because he can't do anything else, and one takes drugs because he can do everything else.

DPG   *So people really take drugs for different reasons. If one's going to get at the root cause, one has to take each set of people or each individual according to his own thinking?*
FARNSWORTH   We should try to develop satisfying alternatives: equal opportunities, equal justice, a chance for each individual to do what he wants to do and is capable of

doing. This should be the major thrust of any program seeking to deal with large-scale drug use among the disadvantaged. It's a political problem as well as a social, economic, and ethical problem.

DPG   *How does one deal with the drug problem of the upper-middle-class kid who already has all the pleasures that go with wealth?*
FARNSWORTH   In this case the problem is more psychological. One way to a solution is to do everything we can to strengthen the nuclear family. Youngsters who have good relations with their parents and who have a feeling that schools mean something to them don't worry you if they get involved in drugs. They'll get themselves out. Another approach is to help those who are dissatisfied with many current conditions in our society (with more than ample justification) to find an activity or profession that will enable them to work directly toward the needed improvements in society. Many students are doing just that, but many other young people do not know what they can do. What is needed is not more drug education but better education for everyone, together with equal opportunity and equal justice.

DPG   *Can you identify emerging patterns of drug use, new drugs, or new contexts for old ones?*
FARNSWORTH   I see no useful emerging patterns of drug use for social or recreational purposes. There will be hundreds of new drugs developed in the near future that will have a capacity for harming the individuals using them much more seriously than those we already have. Legal controls will not be adequate. Only widespread attitudes of responsibility and awareness of what drugs can do to help us and how they may destroy us will enable this country and others to solve the problem. Legal controls are necessary. Social discrimination of a high order is necessary, but the truly effective controls are those exercised by informed persons who know what the limits of responsible use are. The drug problem is not confined to young people but involves all age groups. Our efforts to develop responsible drug use must center on alcohol—which is our number one problem—on the barbiturates, and the misuse of all legitimate drugs, as well as on such substances as heroin, cocaine, the hallucinogens, and marijuana.

Unit 25
Youth Culture

SCHEMATIC OUTLINE

A Introductory Graphics: The Development of Youth Culture

B Definition and Context

1 Definition
A youth culture is a distinctive subculture consisting of young persons whose norms, values, and roles differ sharply from those of the surrounding society.

2 World Context
Cultures around the world vary greatly in their attitudes toward the young. The concepts of childhood, adolescence, and youth are relatively new even in Western societies. The young have become demographically, and sometimes politically, significant in the modern world.

3 American Context
A distinctive youth culture has recently emerged as one of the most obvious and controversial features of American society. Its primary manifestations are political activism and the counterculture.

C Questions and Evidence

1 Questions
Three questions about youth are of particular interest: (1) What are the forms of youth culture in the United States, and how do they differ from the established culture? (2) How can we explain the rise of the counterculture among the youth? (3) Which students take part in protest and political activity?

2 Evidence
a The "Burning Issue" Question
Kenneth Keniston and other observers have developed several concepts to describe the attitudes and values of modern youth, stressing the function of youth cultures as a mode of accommodation to the tensions that arise through the discrepancies young people perceive between earler experience and later obligations.
b The "Classical" Question
Kenneth Keniston, Charles Reich, Robert Jay Lifton and others have described the difficult situation of the affluent young in contemporary America. They are able to choose whether or not they will "grow up" during a period of great technological change and social instability. Thus the counterculture is a reaction that is less political than earlier anti-establishment movements.
c The "Research" Question
Studies by Kenneth Keniston, Richard Flacks, and others have shown that radicalism is primarily associated with a small number of elite students. Their rejection of society is consistent with the values they learned as children and does not stem from the traditional sources of opposition.

3 Overview
Although youth culture is not homogeneous, there is a distinctive and historically unprecedented youth culture in the United States. Its ultimate significance has not yet been determined.

D Looking Ahead

Interview: Thomas J. Cottle

SUPPORTING UNITS

ENCYCLOPEDIA ENTRIES

adolescence
communes
counterculture
delinquency
drug culture
drugs and behavior
Erikson, Erik (b. 1902)
Flacks, Richard (b. 1938)
Goodman, Paul (1911–1972)
hippies
identity
Jesus freaks
Keniston, Kenneth (b. 1930)
Mead, Margaret (b. 1901)
population
Reich, Charles (b. 1928)
rites of passage
Slater, Philip (b. 1927)
social group
Sturm und Drang
youth culture

THE DEVELOPMENT OF YOUTH CULTURE

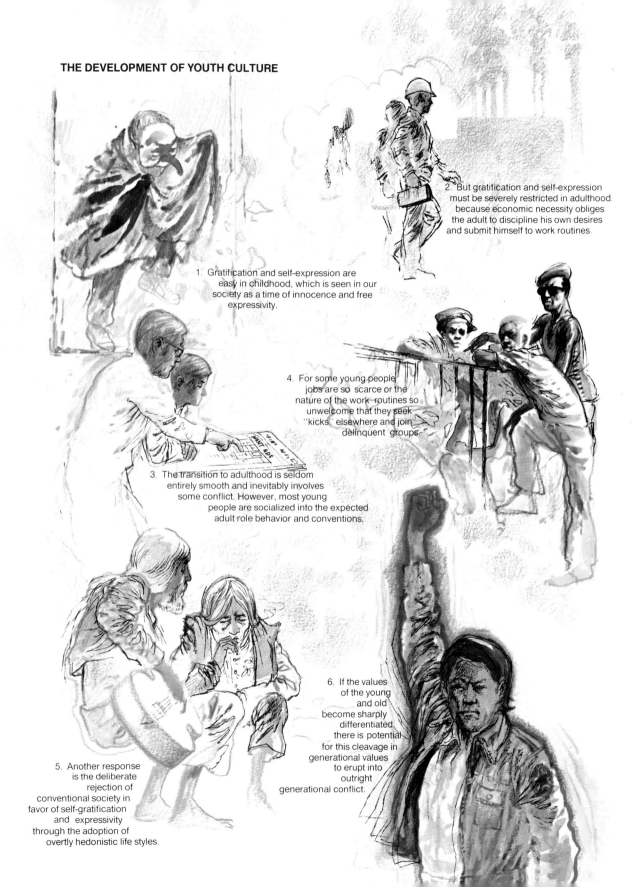

1. Gratification and self-expression are easy in childhood, which is seen in our society as a time of innocence and free expressivity.

2. But gratification and self-expression must be severely restricted in adulthood, because economic necessity obliges the adult to discipline his own desires and submit himself to work routines.

3. The transition to adulthood is seldom entirely smooth and inevitably involves some conflict. However, most young people are socialized into the expected adult role behavior and conventions.

4. For some young people jobs are so scarce or the nature of the work routines so unwelcome that they seek "kicks" elsewhere and join delinquent groups.

5. Another response is the deliberate rejection of conventional society in favor of self-gratification and expressivity through the adoption of overtly hedonistic life styles.

6. If the values of the young and old become sharply differentiated, there is potential for this cleavage in generational values to erupt into outright generational conflict.

B   DEFINITION AND CONTEXT

1   Definition

The category "youth" is as much a product of *social definition* as of *biological development*. Although all individuals pass through a roughly similar process of *maturation*, cultural definitions of youth are highly variable. The characteristics of various points in the life cycle are not physiologically predetermined, and many cultures scarcely recognize the period of youth at all. Even where this particular stage of life is recognized, its content and duration differ widely from society to society. In short, youth is a concept that must be seen not simply in chronological and biological terms, but in social and cultural terms as well.

In every society where the period of youth is perceived as a clearly marked-off stage in the maturation process, a youth culture has tended to develop. *A youth culture is a distinctive subculture consisting of young persons whose norms, values, and roles differ significantly from those of the surrounding society.* Many factors influence both the degree to which such cultures become differentiated from the surrounding society and also the specific content of the youth cultures themselves.

A youth culture is likely to develop in any society where there is an age-based *division of labor*. The complexity of modern mass industrial societies makes the emergence of such cultures almost inevitable. When young people are excluded from adult responsibilities for an extended period and are concentrated in specified locations, the schools, their *peers* became a *primary reference group*.

Social change can be measured by the degree of discontinuity between the culture of the old and the culture of the young. In a totally static society the *content of the culture* of young and old would be identical. No such society exists, of course, although in many small-scale traditional societies very little change takes place from one generation to the next. But wherever the young embrace cultural forms that are radically different from those of the established society, in times of rapid political, economic, or technological change, the implications are likely to be profound.

2   World Context

Societies around the world display great variation in their attitudes toward the young. Although most emphasize some transitions from childhood to adult status, the physiological facts of puberty and adolescence are always subject to a specific cultural interpretation. There may be variations in the age upon which attention is focused. *Initiation ceremonies*, for example, do not necessarily occur at puberty; they may take place much later and constitute social recognition of entry to *adulthood* rather than simply the reaching of a particular stage of maturation. The transition from childhood to adulthood may be marked by a brief formal ceremony, or it may be an extended process reaching into the early twenties, as in modern industrial states. In the latter instance the extended process is often divided into two recognizable phases: *adolescence*, in which the individual has passed puberty but remains legally dependent and ex-

Bar mitzvah, a ritual of transition in which a Jewish boy is initiated into manhood. Unlike the Australian Aborigine initiation ritual depicted on the opposite page, the *bar mitzvah* has lost most of its original emotional saliency for both initiates and the wider social group, which is not actually willing to grant the social rights and duties of an adult to a 13-year-old boy, even though he has gone through the public ritual. In Western industrial society transition into adulthood comes piecemeal and involves transitional states in which conflicting demands are placed on young people.

cluded from the labor force, and *youth*, in which the individual is physiologically adult and is legally able to be economically independent but is not a fulltime member of the labor force and is not responsible for the maintenance of an entire household.

The transition to adulthood can be painless, and its primary purpose may be to permit a *moratorium*, a period of pause, for the establishment of adult identities. Or it may be fierce, involving an *ordeal*—such as circumcision—inflicted on the novitiates by older members of society. Because men usually have a more dominant role in society than women, emphasis tends to be placed on the initiation of boys rather than girls. Entry to female adolescence is more likely to be viewed in terms of the requirements of a male-dominated society. For example in central Africa, where obesity is equated with beauty, the young girls are segregated in "fatting houses" and fed fatty foods until they are plump enough to be considered marriageable, whereupon they are produced before the tribe for the edification of the males. Modern Western societies still retain traces of earlier initiation rites—the "coming out" party of the debutante, the high school graduation ceremony, the bar mitzvah.

Australian Aborigine initiation rite—circumcision. In this ritual the boy is placed on a sponsor's body. He bites on a bundle of cotton yarn to give him strength and courage as the operation is performed. For the initiates and the wider social group, this ritual is highly charged emotionally and denotes a major shift in the social rights and obligations of the person being initiated. The great social significance of this ritual is attested to by the initiates' willingness to undergo the very painful subincision of the penis.

The willingness of youth in many cultures to undergo these initiation ceremonies and to accept with eagerness their adult roles points to one characteristic of youth that is highly variable. Nowadays the years between 13 and 21 are thought of as a time of turmoil and confusion, of rebellion and the defiance of parental authority. But, in fact, the rebellion of young people seems to be the historical exception rather than the rule. This fact is nowhere more apparent than in their general submission to ordeals for the prize of entry to adult culture.

Not only are the forms of adolescent and postadolescent behavior largely determined by their social context; the very notions of childhood, adolescence, and youth are culturally dependent creations. As such, they are relatively new to the Western world. In fact, they are European inventions of the past 400 years. Paintings before the Renaissance depict children as little adults, with the same clothing and facial features as their elders. As J. H. Plumb points out in an essay in *In the Light of History* (1972), the world of childhood, with its special books, boys, and clothing, did not exist at this time. Children were regarded as infants until about the age of seven, and thereafter they began to assume an apprenticeship to adult pursuits. Only in the seventeenth century did the child come to be segregated from the rest of the family as a special type of human being with a distinctive nature and distinctive needs.

The notion of adolescence is of even more recent origin. After 1880 increasing industrialization created a demand for personnel with certain skills and attitudes (see Unit 21), so that prolonged education became an economic necessity. The working family of parents and children together began to disappear, and greater affluence permitted the young to remain outside the labor force. Adolescence emerged during the early part of this century as a new period in the life cycle between childhood and adulthood. Today, as Kenneth Keniston comments in *Youth and Dissent* (1971), "A stage of life that barely existed a century ago is now universally accepted as an inherent part of the human condition."

The young have become demographically, and sometimes politically, significant in the modern world. The *age distribution* of the global population shows a steady increase in the proportion of children and adolescents—largely because of the rapid population increases in Asia, Africa, and Latin America. The question of age distribution was taken up in Unit 6. Young people have frequently been viewed as a radical force in countries all over the world. In recent decades this tendency has been particularly noticeable in the industrial countries of the West. But the ferment of the young is observable only at particular historical points; generally, the responses of the young seem as varied as those of their elders. Hitler's first electoral success in 1930 was achieved largely through the allegiance of some 4 million new voters. In South Africa young voters have consistently proved more reactionary than their parents since the vote was extended to them in the 1960s. There are indications that youth in the countries of Eastern Europe are bored by talk of revolution and socialism and are more interested in the "freer" life of the materialistic West. Surveys have shown, for example, that most young Poles seek marriage, security, children, college diplomas, professional advancement, prosperity, and well-furnished homes as their personal objectives in life.

Both Talcott Parsons, in "Age and Sex in the Social Structure of the United States" (1949), and Shmuel Eisenstadt, in *From Generation to Generation* (1956), have attempted to specify the particular conditions necessary for the development of a youth culture. They have called special attention to the gap that may exist between the *value climate* of "traditional" family life and the value climate of the "modern" occupational system in societies with a complex division of labor. In this view youth cultures tend to be *functional*, creating a period of adjustment between the old and the new. On this basis one would expect youth cultures to arise most pronouncedly in societies where the contrast between the old and the new is sharpest—that is, in "emerging" or developing countries. There is also a good deal of evidence to suggest that youth movements occur in only those contexts where political opposition is not identical with class opposition; in those countries where the opposition is largely class-determined, alienated youth can merge with existing adult forms of opposition, and thus no distinctive age divisions appear.

Yet it is probably true that the young throughout the Western world today have more in common with each other—in terms of shared tastes in dress and music and attitudes toward the older generation—than at any previous time in history. There is an identifiable and growing youth culture that cuts across national boundaries. Its inspiration and values are largely American in origin.

3 American Context

A distinctive youth culture has recently emerged as one of the most obvious and controversial features of American society. Yet in colonial times the social role of youth was insignificant. The principle that "the parent knows best" was enshrined in early colonial legislation: in 1646 the Massachusetts Bay Colony statutes decreed that if a man had a "stubborn or rebellious son" of at least 16 years of age, he could bring him to the magistrate's court, where "such a son shall be done to death." Although the social status of the young has changed since that time, parental rule until relatively late in life remains the American norm. The schools also exercise exceptional (and possibly unconstitutional) powers over their pupils—as evidenced by arbitrary searches of personal clothing and lockers, censorship of student publications, and punishment without due process or right of appeal. Even the exercise of personal choice in the matter of hair length has had to be won piecemeal in court cases across the country (only about half the cases have succeeded). Yet the social attitude to youth remains ambiguous. The contemporary United States is a very child-oriented society. Childhood is perceived as a time of spontaneity and innocence; the period is romantically contrasted with the grimmer realities of adulthood and old age. Americans do not grow old gracefully; the return to youth or the appearance of youth is a perennial search backed by a multi-billion dollar cosmetic industry.

The young in America receive more years of education than any other people in history. Since 1900 the amount of education received by the average American has increased by more than six

Induction into the armed forces—another ritual of transition. One of the features of mass, industrialized society is a shifting of the locus of rituals of transition out of the network of family and kinship relationships and into the context of complex, formally organized institutions, such as the United States Army.

years. In 1900 only 6.4 percent of Americans completed high school. Today some 80 percent do, and more than half of the high school graduates go on to some form of higher education—compared with only 26 percent after World War II. One consequence of this increase has been the emergence of a numerically significant youthful population that is (1) excluded from the labor force, (2) segregated from other age groups, and (3) concentrated together in large batches under conditions of high and intimate interaction. Education has become a major element in social change, and educational institutions have become the locus of unrest. It has been suggested that this phenomenon stems from the ambiguous, marginal position youth occupy in our society. Their major experience—education—emphasizes the ideal, but their lack of adult responsibilities frees them from those institutional ties and restraints that might otherwise induce caution and pragmatism.

Student activism is relatively new, however. The college generation of the 1950s was criticized for its careerism, apathy, and conservatism. It must be noted that during that decade, for the first time in America, the students who were attending colleges did not come predominantly from a small upper-class elite, but from newly achieved middle class backgrounds that placed a high premium on

(Below and facing page) College life, U.S.A. The United States has the largest percentage of young people going to college of any of the countries of the world. Thus college performs an unusual social function in America. It is a kind of four-year sanctuary for vast numbers of young people who would otherwise be entering the ranks of full social acceptance as adults but who still retain some of their nonadult status through living in a socially subordinate and financially dependent situation.

(Below) At a rock concert—the youth culture getting it together. Are they prophets or are they simply dropping out, abandoning a society they see as intrinsically not worth the effort to save? Theorists disagree, but the future may ride on the answer.

financial and professional achievement. Real affluence—the kind that Hollywood still tends to glamorize—suddenly seemed within reach of all graduating seniors who were willing to play the game according to clearly defined rules (a gray flannel suit, a ''sincere'' tie, a winning smile, and a heart devoted to the company image). Clark Kerr, president of the University of California, commented at the time, ''The employers will love this generation. They are not going to press many grievances. They are going to be easy to handle. There aren't going to be any riots.''

Yet within a matter of years the ''silent generation'' had disappeared. Such pastimes as cramming telephone booths gave way to protests and sit-ins for civil rights and peace. What had been only a small pocket of anti-establishment ''bohemians'' became a major and conspicuous force for political change.

Allied to but by no means identical with the youthful protest movement has been another phenomenon—the rise of a counterculture. This response has been cultural rather than political: it seems that the young find the cultural content of mainstream America so repellent that they have engaged in an ''anticipatory rejection'' of the roles their society will demand of them. In *The Making of a Counter Culture* (1969) Theodore Roszak describes ''a culture so radically disaffiliated from the mainstream assumptions of our society that it scarcely looks to many as a culture at all, but takes on the appearance of a barbaric invasion.'' The new culture questions the moral, economic, and social basis on which contemporary American society is founded.

The ''hippie'' ethic has spread, although in diluted form, through a substantial proportion of the youth of America. The new *life style* challenges the old ethic, which sees virtue in hard work, a ''conventional'' life style, deferral of physical and sexual gratification, competition, acquisitiveness, and the rational-scientific world view. Instead, the counterculture refuses to be bound by tradition or convention, disdains a settled and secure mode of living, and is willing to experiment in forbidden areas. It is marked by a deep distrust of machines and technology, which are seen as mastering rather than serving men.

The rise of this counterculture has attracted a great deal of attention from sociologists who perceive the movement as a social phenomenon of great importance. As Keniston remarked of the 1960s:

> No event in this decade was more significant than the rise of a youthful opposition—a dissenting order of the young, a counter-culture of the educated, privileged children of the American dream, who found the society they were to inherit failing and flawed. (*Youth and Dissent*, 1971)

C   QUESTIONS AND EVIDENCE

1   Questions

Three questions about youth are of particular interest: (1) What are the forms of youth culture in the United States, and in what ways are they different from the established culture? (2) How can we explain the rise of the counterculture among the youth? (3) Which students take part in protest and radical political activity?

2   Evidence

a   The "Burning Issue" Question

i Context   There has always been considerable cultural diversity in America. In the past, however, the society has usually stressed racial, religious, or ethnic distinctions—as in the cases, for example, of the Indians, the blacks, the Mormons, or the Italian and Irish minorities. The general tendency throughout American history has been for the dominant white Anglo-Saxon Protestant culture to absorb the others; the notion of the United States as a "melting pot" in which these distinctions have been all but eliminated is a myth. But the clash of generations, with the concomitant emergence of distinctive *subcultures* of youth that often depart radically from the mainstream middle-class culture, is relatively new.

What are the forms of youth culture in the United States today? Are they embraced by a minority or by the greater part of the youth? Is youth almost universally opposed to the "establishment," and does this response take a uniform character? What is the basis of the cleavage between youth and adult culture? In essence, sociologists ask: *What are the forms and distinguishing features of youth culture in the United States?*

ii Theory   One model that may throw light on the differences between youth culture and the established culture in America is that proposed by David Matza and Gresham Sykes in "Juvenile Delinquency and Subterranean Values" (1961). Their model was largely designed to interpret a particular form of youth culture that was attracting attention at that time—juvenile delinquency—but it still re-

Formal Values	Subterranean Values
Deferred gratification	Short-term hedonism
Planning future action	Spontaneity
Conformity to bureaucratic rules	Ego-expressivity
Fatalism, high control over detail, little control over direction	Autonomy, control of behavior in detail and direction
Routine, predictability	New experience, excitement
Instrumental attitudes to work	Activities performed as an end-in-themselves
Hard productive work seen as a virtue	Disdain for work

Table 1. Formal Values and Subterranean Values Contrasted.
This figure shows the two sets of values delineated by Matza and Sykes. (Source: Young, *The Drugtakers*)

veals certain characteristic features and values of contemporary youth that constitute the basis for their cultural divergence from conventional society.

According to Matza and Sykes, society is not only divided into horizontal *strata* based on class or status. There is also a fundamental vertical distinction based on the *value systems* of the individuals within society, regardless of their social location. Thus two competing value systems exist—the overt, official, or *formal* values of the society and its covert, unofficial, or *subterranean* values. In the formal system are found such values as security, stability, and predictability. In the subterranean system, on the other hand, are such values as excitement, experience, enjoyment.

Within conventional society subterranean values are unacceptable except in limited and institutionalized forms—for example, during vacations and at sporting events or festivals. These occasions are clearly marked off from the ordinary working life of the individual and are seen in some sense as a "reward" for labors conducted in deference to the formal values. As Jock Young suggests in *The Drugtakers* (1971), people have great difficulty in ordering their lives according to the formal values:

> There are cracks and strains. . . . People doubt the sanity
> of alienated work and the validity of their leisure. For they
> cannot compartmentalize their life in a satisfactory manner:
> their socialization for work inhibits their leisure, and their
> utopias of leisure belittle their work.

Some groups, however, are unwilling even to attempt this compartmentalization of existence. They are prepared to submit to the formal values, retaining only a part-time experience of the subterranean values; instead, these groups accentuate the subterranean values until the pursuit of them becomes the distinguishing feature of their own life style. The young are particularly likely to experience the tension between the two value systems, because most of their experience has emphasized the subterranean rather than the formal values.

Peter Pan and Wendy. Peter Pan's resistance to growing up is an expression of the ambivalent feelings many persons experience about taking on the burdens of adult responsibilities. (Still from 1924 film.)

Kenneth Keniston has pointed to the effect of conflicting images of youth and adulthood as they present themselves to the maturing adolescent. Society asks him to abandon his carefree life style in return for a new existence that offers little appeal—only a rigid separation of work and leisure, a reserved mode of conduct, an emphasis on the deferral of gratification, a concern for propriety, and the other restrictive patterns that seem to be the defining characteristics of mature adulthood in our society. It is not surprising that the young refuse to surrender the life style they have and enjoy for one that offers few compensating attractions.

Similarly, Herbert Marcuse in *Eros and Civilization* (1956) argued that the *socialization* of the child is aimed at bringing about a transition from, in Freudian terms, the "pleasure principle" to the "reality principle," from a world of free expression and enjoyment to one of labor and deferred gratification. Each individual, having experienced the paradise of play in childhood, possesses the implicit memory of a utopia where economic necessity does not stifle his desires. The tension is particularly felt by the young as they stand on the threshold of adult responsibility.

iii Research   Youth culture may be divided into four groups on the basis of social and economic background—"straight" middle class, "intellectual-bohemian" middle class, white working class, and black working class. The degree of involvement with subterranean values that each of these subgroups has thus depends on how strongly they feel their goals to be frustrated by the dominant culture: the black working class would obviously be the most alienated. But such a schematic division raises a number of questions. For example, how would we categorize "straight" middle-class juvenile delinquents? or "intellectual-bohemian" middle-class whites who identify with black militants?

Another way of analyzing youth culture in America is on the basis of three main forms of behavior—conventional, delinquent, and countercultural. Indications are that, despite the problematic nature of youth as a stage of life in the contemporary United States, the great majority of young people are *conventional*. They adopt the roles that are expected of them by the wider society, attending diligently to their work and their responsibilities; they focus their enjoyment on those activities that are socially acceptable. They tend, on the whole, to be as politically apathetic and as unquestioning of basic *social norms* as their parents are. In "What Generation Gap?" (1970), Joseph Adelson reported that an "overwhelming majority" of the young—as many as 80 percent—hold traditional values, with the same religious and political preferences as their parents.

Other studies have suggested that student dissent reached a peak in the late 1960s and that students are less activist today than a few years ago. Most young people retain an *instrumental approach* to the world and experience feelings of guilt if they deviate too far from the formal values of their society. Of course, even the conventional young can be considered a subculture: they have their own heroes, jargon, and leisure activities, which are not shared by the adult society. But these differences seem to represent little more than the slight discontinuity between the generations that might be expected in times of social change. The formal values of society are scarcely challenged by conventional youth.

The *delinquent* youth culture, on the other hand, may be seen as a deliberate attempt to pursue subterranean values in a hostile society. Delinquency among working-class youth is often a response to the feeling that the cards are stacked against them—that their school curriculum is irrelevant, that their future occupations are likely to be pointless and dull, that they will always be excluded from access to those things that are so highly prized in their materialistic society. Accordingly, interest is focused instead on the here and now, on leisure activities and the search for "kicks." The search for the fulfillment of the subterranean values may take the form of overtly illegal acts—partly because the financial means for the legally approved pursuit of hedonistic ends is lacking, partly because there is little fear of jeopardizing careers or peer group approval through "antisocial" acts.

Membership in a delinquent group can often be a useful element in the formation of personality. It may counteract feelings of insecurity, hopelessness, or boredom, and it may give the individual opportunities to "prove himself" by challenging the established order. Although the delinquent youth culture has tended to be neglected in recent sociology, it remains a widespread and recurrent feature of the industrial societies of the Western world.

The most recent and most controversial form of youth culture is the *counterculture*. Unlike the delinquent response, which arises principally among those of the young who do not have access to the material rewards of society, the countercultural response occurs almost exclusively among those who are able to enjoy the benefits of the middle-class life style. Bohemian life styles, in America as elsewhere in the world, are restricted to those affluent enough to reject the rewards that the less affluent continue to strive for. The countercultural young see the middle-class life style and its comforts as somehow inadequate, even offensive; in a deliberate act of choice, they reject those benefits in favor of a life-style in which experience, expressivity, and self-gratification become the main values. The key to this attitude is *alienation*—a feeling of being foreign to one's own environment, of separation from the values of one's culture, and a sense of the ultimate meaninglessness of one's destined role. In response, *personal autonomy* is asserted in matters of appearance, taste, values, and behavior; materialism and the rationalist, scientific approach that characterizes all industrial societies are rejected; and there is an interest in *altered states of consciousness* —via drugs, religion, or meditation.

One further element associated with the counterculture is rock music, which has been seriously neglected by sociologists. Recordings and performances provide a medium of communication, a source of role models, and a force for social cohesion among the countercultural young. In this regard it must also be noted that black youth have been more innovative and influential in the style of music, heroes, symbols, jargon, and fashions adopted by the youth culture today than has any other subgroup within it.

iv Evaluation The young in most countries tend to be socialized into adult roles that are not markedly different from those of their parents. In America, however, the socialization process is not as uniform or as successful as in most other societies. (We have discussed this socialization process in Unit 5.) The social extension of

Apart from the wider society. For some youths the value system of society is so lacking in meaning that they simply act as if it no longer existed—thus infuriating many of their elders.

579

childhood, with the interposed period of adolescence, has allowed the creation of various forms of youth culture with special sets of roles, feelings, and values. Such cultures are a *mode of accommodation* to the tensions that arise through the discrepancies that young people perceive between earlier experience and later obligations. Youth cultures, stranded in a society that exalts the formal values of self-discipline and hard work, attempt to provide outlets for the continuing desire of their members to indulge the subterranean values.

The tendency to view youth as a homogeneous mass is fundamentally misconceived. The National Guardsmen at Kent State University were of much the same age as the students they shot down in 1970. Young people do not come in neat, convenient categories. Certainly their political attitudes do not necessarily follow the formal-subterranean distinction: an ardent leftist can be otherwise conventional in his adherence to formal cultural norms, and some young people who have no political interests whatsoever may still reject every significant value of their society. Distinguishing between the activist and the alienated responses, Keniston points out that the usual grouping of the young into a general category of long-haired, scruffy, radical drug-users is quite inadequate. Instead, he argues, there must be a minimal distinction between those who are out to change society through commitment and action and those who avoid protest and prefer to withdraw into an intensified subjectivity. In reality, however, the lines here are blurred as well.

Although youth in the Western world are in an unprecedented state of ferment, the majority remain socially stabilized within the context of the established society. Yet there are times when youth may perceive a common interest and interdependence that overrides their individual differences. One striking recent example was the political protest against the Vietnam war: opposition among the young was broader, deeper, more intense and quicker to emerge than among adults.

b   The "Classical" Question

i Context   As Keniston observed, nothing in the social or political theory of the 1950s predicted the youth revolt of the 1960s and the early 1970s; social scientists were as unprepared for the phenomenon as the rest of the society. In the 1950s the silence of youth was taken as an indication that they had been effectively socialized into a conformist mass society. Theorists in the social sciences spoke of them in terms of incremental change, systems of control, social equilibrium, and the like. Indeed, the "end of ideology" was predicted, not only in the international sphere, but within America itself. *Consensus* rather than *conflict* was to be the pattern of the future. A few sociologists rejected this view—but their inspiration was usually Marxist, and the opposition they predicted was supposed to stem from the underprivileged working class.

The youth revolt, and especially the emergence of a hippie-influenced counterculture, cannot be explained in these terms. Yet some explanation is necessary, for the youth movement has had undoubted significance. Some writers have even postulated that *class struggle* itself is now outdated. Activist Tom Hayden has suggested "The struggle is no longer between wage earners and their bosses

(Above) The protest against the war in Indochina served as a cohesive force in the youth movement. Poster "And Babies" refers to massacre of unarmed Vietnamese civilians at Mylai by United States troops.

(Above right) Adolescence. In our society we expect adolescence to be a time of stress, an emotionally difficult period of adjustment to a changing metabolism and to new social expectations. Adolescence is, in fact, a miserable stage for many young people in *our* society, but cross-cultural research suggests that this situation is not inevitably the case elsewhere. For example, children raised in the *kibbutzim,* collectively-organized agricultural communities in Israel, exhibit few of the adolescent miseries Americans have come to expect as normal.

but between capitalists and their sons who don't want to tend the store.'' The emergence of a youthful counterculture, which rejects many of the most basic values of society, is of great social importance. Sociologists ask: *How can we explain the emergence of a mass counterculture among the youth of the contemporary United States?*

ii   Theory   The earliest and most extensive theoretical analysis of the counterculture is that of Kenneth Keniston. His "psychohistorical" approach elaborates on earlier studies by Erik Erikson on the stages in the life cycle.

At the turn of the century the natural stages of human development in America were considered to be the infant, the child, the young adult, and the mature adult. It was the psychologist G. Stanley Hall who created the term "adolescent" in 1904. Hall's massive *Adolescence: Its Psychology and its Relations to Physiology, Anthropology, Sociology, Sex, Crime, Religion, and Education* became a popular work, and "adolescence" soon became a household word. Hall's delineation of this stage of life was particularly relevant in a society where, for the first time, a cohesive but problematic age group was emerging—those who had attained puberty but were still denied adult responsibilities. Hall's classic description of the *Sturm und Drang* (a German phrase meaning literally "storm and stress") of adolescence has become an accepted component of the adolescent stereotype in our culture.

Erik Erikson believes that adolescence, in the particular historical context of the modern state, has become a time for the trial of *emergent identities:*

The adolescent mind is essentially a mind of the *moratorium*, a psychosocial stage between childhood and adulthood, and between the morality learned by the child, and the ethics to be developed by the adult. It is an ideological mind—and, indeed, it is the ideological outlook of a society that speaks most clearly to the adolescent who is eager to be reaffirmed by his peers, and is ready to be confirmed by rituals, creeds, and programs. . . . (*Childhood and Society*, 1950)

Keniston argues that in America today yet another category has emerged in the life cycle, a phase between adolescence and adulthood. He calls this period *youth* and regards it as an emergent stage: it is still optional, and its members still comprise only a minority of the relevant age group, 18–30. There are many young people in this age range, says Keniston, who refuse to settle down, to act as adults:

Millions of young people are in a stage of life that lacks even a name. Unprecedented prolongation of education has opened up opportunities for a new extension of psychological development, creating a "new" stage of life. We are creating on a mass scale a new breed of people whose development inclines them to be critics of our society, and architects of a better one. (*Youth and Dissent*, 1971)

Keniston stresses the particular *historical context* in which the psychological period of youth has appeared: a group of people, post-adolescent yet preadult, is emerging on a mass scale in a historical situation that presents them with new problems and challenges. Those experiencing the period of youth, then, are particularly susceptible to the appeal of a culture whose roles, beliefs, and norms seem more flexible than those of the surrounding society.

iii   Research (Survey)   A number of social scientists have turned their attention to the theoretical problems raised by the emergence of the youthful counterculture in America. One of the earliest was Theodore Roszak, whose *The Making of a Counter Culture* appeared in 1969. Roszak sees *technocracy* (see Units 16 and 20) as the focus of the rift between the generations, and he interprets the attitudes of the counterculture as a refusal to surrender spontaneity to artificiality, an insistence on the essential humanity of man in the face of an unnatural and ultimately dehumanizing technological society. The youthful rebellion, in Roszak's view, is a reassertion of life, individuality, and festival in the face of a society increasingly dominated by impersonal organization, remote experts, and stifling routines.

In *The Greening of America* (1970) Charles Reich argued that the counterculture emerged as a result of a perception by the young of the gap between the *stated ideals* of their parents' generation and their *actual practices*—the gap, for example, between the rhetoric of the president and the civics text books, on the one hand, and the facts of poverty, prejudice, exploitation, and racial inequality in America, on the other. The Vietnam war in particular, argued Reich, destroyed the faith the young had in their country as the internationally admired defender of truth, justice, and free institutions. Many of the young perceive the American dream as a sham and seek instead a new culture in which the finest ideals—of brotherhood, of love of nature, of spontaneity and joy—can be realized.

Anthropologist Margaret Mead in *Culture and Commitment* (1970) attributes the emergence of the counterculture to the sheer pace of technological change. In a traditional society, she points out, the young have merely to be socialized into an acceptance of the culture of their elders; when culture is virtually static, the old, with their greater experience, know more than the young. But the current pace of technological change is such that the entire social environment may change several times in a person's lifetime. The young are growing up in a world of which their parents have little knowledge; for the first time in history, it is the young who have more to teach the old than vice versa. The youth can no longer see their parents as relevant models for the world they are moving into, and commitment to the older values seems pointless. In a very real sense, suggests Mead, the pace of change is such that the parents of today do not have children and the children of today do not have parents. The young must make their way as best they can, continually exploring new *options* and seeking new *commitments*.

The exploration of options as the basis for an entire life style is emphasized in Robert Jay Lifton's notion of the "Protean Man." (The Greek god Proteus could change his form at will—but could never retain the same form for very long.) Lifton describes the Protean self-process as characterized by an endless series of experiments, some shallow, some profound, extending to all areas of human experience—political, sexual, ideological—in fact, to the whole pattern of existence. Like Keniston, Lifton stresses certain particular problems:

> The first is the world-wide . . . break in the sense of connection which men have long felt with the vital and nourishing symbols of their cultural tradition—symbols revolving around family, idea systems, religions, and the life-cycle in general . . . as irrelevant, burdensome, or inactivating. . . . The second large historical tendency is the flooding of imagery produced by the extraordinary flow of postmodern cultural influences over mass communications networks. These . . . permit each individual to be touched by everything, but at the same time cause him to be overwhelmed by superficial messages and undigested cultural elements, by headlines and by endless partial alternatives in every sphere of life. (*History and Human Survival*, 1970)

iv Evaluation For reasons connected with industrialization and consequent education and affluence, a stage of life implying the possible extension of the preadult existence has emerged in America. In a sense, the young now have a certain choice about whether or not they will "grow up." Moreover, they confront this choice in the midst of a historical situation marked by technological change, social instability, and loss of faith in established cultural tradition and anticipated social direction. The existing society lives in the shadow of nuclear holocaust or ecological disaster and offers only material comfort—not personal fulfillment.

The work of Keniston and other theorists sensitizes us to the difficult status of youth in modern industrial society. Taken in the context of the lure of subterranean values, these theories throw new light on the counterculture as a *charismatic* cultural reaction unlike other antiestablishment movements in the past. (See Units 8 and 20.) Earlier movements were more overtly political, comprising those who found themselves economically oppressed and who sought a radical transformation of society in which the wealth of the affluent would be justly redistributed. But the counterculture is largely a reaction by the economically privileged, and Harold M. Hodges, Jr., suggests that it is a reaction not against the present so much as against the grim and mechanized future the young see immediately ahead (*Conflict and Consensus*, 1971). Whether this cultural reaction will bring about basic changes in the social order remains to be seen. But Marxist theorists who looked for a mainly working-class radicalism are still looking; and liberal theorists who never anticipated that the prime beneficiaries of capitalism would, in part, reject the system are being obliged to reassess their approach.

c The "Research" Question

i Context Opinion polls in the 1950s showed students to be status-oriented, complacent, and uncommitted; their concerns were with their future careers and the comfortable life style they anticipated. But at the end of the decade students from Northern colleges began to take an active part in the burgeoning civil rights movement in the South. By the early 1960s students had extended the range of their political action, and more and more of them were involved in protest against the administration of the universities, the war in Southeast Asia, the exploitation of the environment, and the lack of responsibility of large corporations. Students became, after the blacks, the most critical and militant segment of American society. Often their militancy erupted into direct action or violence that attracted national attention.

The *women's liberation movement*—especially its radical and outspoken vanguard— was born in this period of energetic and angry protest: in the midst of all the fiery and idealistic demonstrations led by Students for a Democratic Society (SDS) and other such organizations, young women activists suddenly realized that all the interesting and policy-making leadership positions within the rebellious student ranks were automatically given to men; women were allowed to make the coffee, roll the "joints," wash the dishes, and run the mimeograph machine. In the good old days of Marxist class warfare, the "capitalist" was the "pig;" during the student upheavals of the 1960s, the policeman was the "pig;" in the days since women activists have recognized and rebelled against their secondary status, the term has been expanded to include every "male chauvinist pig."

By the end of the decade the word "student" seemed almost synonymous with "protester" in the public mind. A 1970 Gallup Poll showed that Americans deemed "campus unrest" to be the nation's main problem. At the same time, a majority of American students accepted the statement that "America is a sick society;" only 19 percent believed that their society was "on the right track," while three-quarters believed that "basic changes" were necessary.

New symbols for old. We are gradually changing the complex of symbols that help motivate our behavior and give meaning to our existence. What behavioral forms will emerge as an expression of this shift?

Although the high point of student protest seems now to have passed, the campus seems likely to provide a reservoir for activism and social concern. Who are the students who actually protest? Sociologists ask: *In what respects may student activists be distinguished from their student peers?*

ii Theory   Student activism has posed a particular theoretical problem: Why are the protesters drawn from the elite of society, rather than from the less privileged? As a result of his extensive interviews with "alienated" students, Kenneth Keniston contended that:

> The dissenters are drawn from among those who have benefited most from American society; they are usually the products of its most favored families; they have been the best educated; and they are, by traditional standards, those most likely to assume the national leadership in the future. Opposition among today's young, far from springing from deprivation, poverty, or discrimination, springs from affluence, wealth, and privilege. Never before have so many who had so much been so deeply disenchanted with their inheritance. (*Youth and Dissent*, 1971)

Similarly, in "The Liberated Generation" (1967), Richard Flacks argued that certain youths are attracted to radicalism not because they experience economic deprivation or because their opportunities are blocked. Instead, these highly privileged young people are indifferent to or even repelled by the opportunities they have for high status and income.

The new student left, then, is not a mere outgrowth of earlier radical trends in American society. It is not founded on the same economic discontent, and it lacks the Marxist or populist ideological inspiration of earlier radicalism as well as the programmatic approach to the new society that characterizes the older movements of the left. Any theoretical consideration of its nature must involve careful examination, using the tools of sociology and social psychology, of the *social context* and *personal biographies* of the student protesters themselves.

iii Research (Methodology)   In an extensive series of lengthy, in-depth interviews with student radicals, Kenneth Keniston found that most of them recalled early family atmospheres characterized by idealism and a warm, friendly relationship with their parents. In fact, the *core values* of the parents were in accord with the values expressed by their children. But although the parents—especially the fathers—were seen as idealistic and principled, they were also regarded as ineffectual. In the eyes of the students, the parents had principles but had failed to act on them. According to Keniston, the perception of his parents as dominated by powers beyond their control defines the basic tension in the young radical: he has principles and feels he must act on them.

Sociologist Richard Flacks, himself a former SDS leader, reached similar conclusions. His extensive surveys showed that the activists' conduct was entirely consistent with the parental attitudes. He argued that student protest, if anything, was a *result*, not a *revolt*. Flacks found that the typical family of the activist was middle or upper middle-class. Both mother and father were highly educated, and the father was usually a professional. Many of the parents tended to be political liberals. They saw themselves as permissive and democratic, and their activist children concurred in this judgment.

Both the student activists and their parents were characterized by humanistic values, whereas a control group of nonactivist students and their parents held to the values of the dominant culture. The activist parents were concerned with individual development and self-expression, with a spontaneous response to the world. Creativity was prized and encouraged, as were aesthetic and intellectual capacities. There was also a marked presence of what Flacks called *ethical humanism*—a sincere concern for the social condition of others—in parents as well as children. The values of activist and nonactivist families were very different, Flacks found. The parents of the nonactivist students were less permissive and less concerned with self-expression and ethical humanism; this attitude was shared by their offspring.

Unlike the activist students, the nonactivists did not experience a *significant tension* between the real and the ideal when they entered college or the work situation. But the activist students soon discovered that society at large expects them to be centrally motivated around goals and values they cannot accept. The pursuit of such goals implied to these students a hypocritical sacrifice of integrity. The result was an *activist response*—a turning to protest that is based on the values shared with parents.

Of course, Flacks does not see family background as the *sole* source of student activism. The specific impetus may vary from time to time and place to place. But he argues that parental values are an identifiable and significant factor in the making of a student radical.

Other investigators have found further variables that correlate with student activism. For example, Roger M. Kahn and William J. Bowers, in "The Social Context of the Rank and File Student Activist" (1970), reported that the academic department in which the student was enrolled was associated with his political values: social scientists, for example, were more likely to be activists than engineers. The likelihood of activism is also greater at the high-prestige universities than at those with lesser academic reputations because of a number of factors: (1) the more prestigious universities cost more and therefore have a higher percentage of students from affluent backgrounds; (2) the more prestigious universities are able to set tougher entrance requirements than most other schools and therefore have a higher concentration of "intellectual" students; (3) most prestigious universities are located in urban areas and, as such, are surrounded by a more potentially politically explosive atmosphere than schools in rural or small-town settings. (Princeton University, for example, which *is* in a pleasant suburb in New Jersey, is also notably conservative compared to other leading universities.)

iv Evaluation   Student radicalism seems to be associated primarily with a small number of elite students—mostly at the more prestigious colleges—who reject their anticipated roles as privileged members of their society. Their opposition is consistent with the values they have learned as children, and it does not stem from the traditional sources of opposition, poverty and misery. Their protest is a reaction to their *powerlessness*—not the powerlessness of the economically deprived, but the impotence of the idealistic young in the face of what they perceive as a rationalized, impersonal, competitive, bureaucratic society that betrays its own values and seems to destroy all spontaneity and expressivity. (Also see Units 8 and 16.)

Yet the militants' minority status should not be taken as an indication of their ultimate insignificance in American society. Such a view would ignore the historical role small, committed groups have played in the social transformation of many countries. Furthermore, there is evidence that since 1970, radical ideals have received such wide attention and exposure that the majority of students often tacitly or overtly support the objectives or the methods of the militants, particularly when the response of the establishment appears inappropriate or excessive—as when college administrators summon the

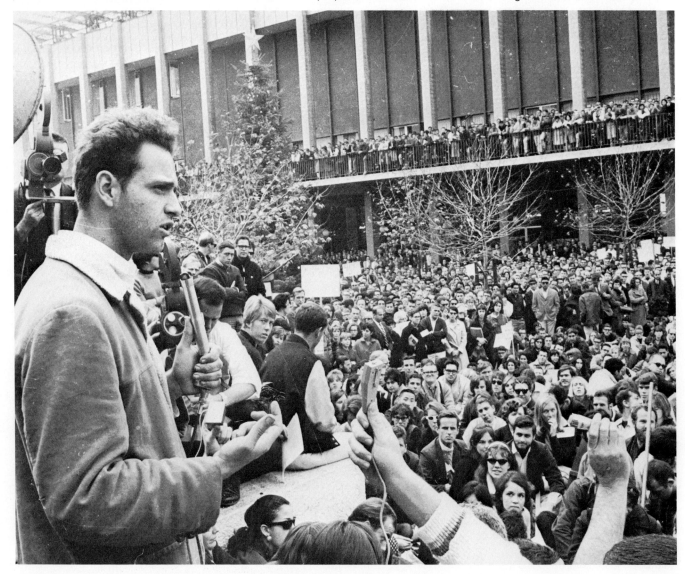

Where it all began. Mario Savio, one of the leaders of the Free Speech Movement at the University of California at Berkeley, tells rally that his group would continue efforts to expand political freedom on campus. The Berkeley protest about suppression of tables of civil rights literature and punishment for off-campus civil rights activity in 1964 was the start of several years of widespread student protests over war, racism, educational conditions, and other issues.

police to handle sit-ins and protests. Radicals call this *politicizing* the public—that is, making nonradicals sympathize, through dramatic confrontations and media publicity, with radicals' complaints and points of view.

3   Overview

Youth culture is not homogeneous. It takes many forms in the United States and around the world. In Europe and America many of the young assert that they are rebelling against the materialism of their society; they deplore the rationalist world-view and seek a more gentle and mystic alternative. In Asia and Africa, in contrast, many of the young see the problems of their countries as stemming precisely from the passivity and mysticism of their elders; they see a dynamic program of industrialization and *modernization* as the only means to end poverty and injustice in their societies.

Yet there is a distinctive and historically unprecedented youth culture in the United States, and its ultimate significance has not yet been determined. In his 1970 book *The New Reformation* Paul Goodman suggested that the youth culture may represent "a turning point of history." Goodman's view is shared by many sociologists, who feel that a generational *cleavage* as radical as that which exists in America and other Western societies today has the potential to work sweeping changes in the shape of our civilization. Other observers are more doubtful and consider that society is witnessing simply an aggravated example of generational *discontinuity;* the young may yet become only marginally different from their parents. Even if the youthful counterculture holds true to the original ideals exemplified at the famous Woodstock rock festival and elsewhere, the lack of a programmatic outlook may prove to be a failing. As C. H. Anderson observes, in *Toward A New Sociology* (1971), "Cultural boycotts and critiques without viable alternative life styles are useless and can easily degenerate into drugged oblivion, thus playing into the hands of the status quo." Kenneth Keniston, however, expresses an attitude of anxious optimism:

> A small band of a few million youths have not been able to persuade a nation of 200 million people that their world views and life styles constitute an inadequate basis for national policy. The youthful opposition is immensely vulnerable—not only to co-optation and repression, but equally to its own despair and its own potential for self-righteousness. It is indeed asking a lot today to ask the dissenting young to remain true as they grow older to their own principles of love, peace, justice and the celebration of human life. But we must ask it, both of ourselves and them. I am not confident that we can respond to the youthful opposition with understanding and change, or that it can respond with humanity and peace. But if together we fail, we may have lost what could have turned out to be the last bright chance to transform—and by renewing to preserve—our civilization. (*Youth and Dissent*, 1971)

Rally for Robert Kennedy, 1968. Even though many facets of youth culture are openly hostile to the culture of their parents' generation, it is a gross exaggeration to claim that there are no ties, that there is no continuity. Seeking social change by working for certain candidates through the electoral process is one clear example of the paths of the generations crossing.

D   LOOKING AHEAD

1   Interview:
Thomas J. Cottle

Thomas J. Cottle has been affiliated with the Education Research Center and the Medical Department of the Massachusetts Institute of Technology. He is now associated with the Children's Defense Fund of the Washington Research Project. He is author of *Time's Children, The Protest of Youth, Out of Discontent* (with Eisendrath and Fink), *The Abandoners, The Voices of School, The Present of Things Future* (with Klineberg), and *Black Children, White Dreams.* He is now working on studies of families living in poverty.

DPG   *In effect, then, the student movement has taken different forms?*

COTTLE   Yes, because important social changes have taken place. Jobs got tight, and the students got scared. Mr. Nixon had something to do with it. Students are afraid, and rightly so, that their scholarships will be taken away. Then, too, the ending of the war has eliminated the personal need of many students to be activists. In addition, some of the bolder students found that college activism had jeopardized their careers. The law schools and the medical schools were suddenly closed to them. Also, many students claim that admissions boards have changed their policies very drastically to screen out the potential activist—although admissions

McGovern campaign and the role of students there. But students are finding other modes of political action. Activism relates to the unearthly quiet in the country as a whole. The level of corruption is so high and so up front—the machinations of ITT, the Watergate scandals—if you're 18 or 19, you might well feel like quitting.

DPG   *Most of the discussion about youth culture centers on the culture of young people in college. What about working-class youth? What about black and Chicano youth? Are they part of the youth culture, or*

DPG   *Is student activism declining?*

COTTLE   I gather that it's changing. The visible part of it—the physical action we saw in the late 1960s—is declining. The shootings at Southern University in Louisiana in late 1972 caused absolutely no stir on the majority of the campuses. Today, students are involved in making certain political points by adopting different life styles. They're still working very hard on political concerns, though, and they're still actively hunting for programs that make academic and cognitive sense to them. But the media tend to cover the more dramatic events. They are not going to give these sorts of things a lot of play.

boards deny it, of course.

Phenomena like student activism are affected by what students do, but they're also affected by those who watch them. The media, and I fear the social scientists too, usually watch the large prestigious universities. They watch Harvard; they watch Berkeley; they watch the University of Chicago. They are not looking at the academic reform movements and local political concerns at the less well-known colleges. John Jay College in New York, for example, is changing its academic program and thereby altering the relationship between the students and the community. Students are currently initiating and carrying through strong, well-disciplined political movements, but the media are looking elsewhere now. I don't think student activism is dropping off. Look at the

do they largely assume the values of their elders?

COTTLE   I wouldn't look at it that way. When people of poverty backgrounds or people from discriminated-against minorities get into college, the scene is potentially different from anything their elders have experienced. I say "potentially" because there is racism and discrimination on just about every college campus. Some Chicanos and blacks are part of youth movements sponsored by white students, but they have terrific constraints placed on them. There is a great deal of distrust and self-consciousness. My impression is that the so-called youth movement tends to exclude the same people who have been excluded all along.

DPG *The rise of the counterculture has been compared to movements like ancient Christianity. Do you think it offers that kind of scope?*

COTTLE I think likening the youth movement to early Christianity is a rather grandiose notion. The counterculture, like early Christianity, does have a belief system that the main culture looks at with ambivalence. But there are so many differences. Christianity has a series of principles to which generations can adhere. Although there can be a dogmatism associated with certain aspects of the youth movement, it is a much more pluralistic enterprise. Furthermore, early Christianity was more of a separatist movement. It did not have the sociological dependence on the main culture that the youth movement presently does. Another dif-

elements of the youth culture have been quite successful in maintaining these ethics, and people live in harmony. But some of it is fraudulent. I also don't believe that the so-called youth culture is pure in the sense that the young people involved are totally happy when the movement excludes people younger or older than themselves. I don't think they're totally happy with homogeneous situations.

As far as the relationship between the larger culture and the youth culture goes, I think that part of the larger culture supports any kind of so-called deviation and then comes back to co-opt it or internalize it or in-

merely experiment with, affect these groups. If you go into the poorest neighborhoods of the black community in Boston, for example, you hear women talking about women's rights. Ten years ago these ideas were never articulated in exactly this way. But there are problems. The working class and the poor have a good bit of ambivalence toward the youth movement. Let's take a black urban area. The people watch, to a certain extent, to see what the students are doing, what effect the students' actions have. They also are in very close touch when students join hands with them in some kinds of programs—rent strikes, food boycotts, whatever. That's practical help, and it breaks a lot of stereotypes. The tensions are produced

ference is the inherently unstable membership of the youth movement. People enter it at a certain age and leave it when they get too old. The larger culture makes it very difficult for a person 28 or 35 to maintain certain practices that go along with being part of the youth movement.

DPG *Do you think the counterculture is being co-opted by the established culture?*

COTTLE We had better examine the terms more closely here. I don't like the phrase "counterculture" at all. "Counter" in that sense means *against* the main culture, and I don't think that is necessarily the primary motivation of this movement. The youth culture has a more positive base. There is an ethic of love. There is an ethic of attempting to break out of the invidious kind of competitiveness that pervades our society. Some

corporate it later on. Sometimes, naturally, the process is creative for the organization or institution that is doing the co-opting. But the youth movement is often co-opted in a way that neutralizes its creative aspects, and that's very tragic.

DPG *Do you feel that the counterculture is injecting a new consciousness into mainstream America?*

COTTLE Let me speak more about the experiences of young people who are not in the mainstream of the culture—working-class people, poor people. There can be no doubt that the movements of college students and the politics they invoke, even those they

when these very same students then try to seek jobs during the summer or even during the year and take away employment opportunities from poor people. Often young people want to have the experience of what it is to be poor or working class, but in the process they may cause serious problems inadvertently.

Unit 26
Social Change

CHANGE IN SOCIETY AND CULTURE

1. **Target Population.** Every social entity is a potential target for innovation and change through the adoption of technological inventions.

2. **Social Reorganization.** Often the adoption of new ideas or inventions necessitates the reorganization of social relationships.

3. **Cultural Change.** Shared assumptions and values must consequently be changed or rearranged.

4. **Target Population.** Every social entity is a potential target for innovation and change through the adoption of new ideas.

B   DEFINITION AND CONTEXT

1   Definition

In the language of sociology the term "social change" is not applied to just any change that involves people in society. If a single family moves from the country to the city and faces a new order of social relationships, work experiences, values, and life styles, the family might consider this move to be a social change, but the sociologist would not. If, however, a significantly greater than average number of families undertakes this shift in locale and life style within a given period of time, the sociologist may be interested in the phenomenon as a case of social change, simply defined as the appearance of new social patterns that are experienced by large or growing numbers of people. *Social change is an alteration of stable patterns of social organization and interaction, preceded or followed by changes in related values and norms. Social change is thus a persisting alteration in organization (social structure) and meaning (culture) within a given sphere of social life.*

2   World Context

An ancient Chinese curse said, "May your children live in interesting times." Since the beginning of human society most people in most societies have lived through "interesting times." The discoveries that fire could be harnessed, that minerals could be extracted from the earth and forged into tools, that crops could be planted and harvested in a single locale had profound implications for the nature of work and economic organization in early societies. Similarly, the Industrial Revolution and the rise of science have had a complex and crucial impact on world history; each major technological advance has carried with it new capabilities and social patterns and has rendered others obsolete. Changes in climate, physical environment, and population growth have also ranked close to discovery and invention as *sources* of social change.

The meeting of diverse cultures has also played an important role in stimulating change. In the modern age few societies have escaped the reverberations of this kind of influence. Nevertheless, there are still occasional reports of the discovery of an isolated tribe that has been totally devoid of any contact with the "outside" world. One such tribe, the Tasaday, was discovered recently in the forests of the Philippines. Within weeks, the members of the tribe were exposed to such wonders as canned food, radios, movie cameras, potent medicines in shiny capsules, and even a helicopter, and roads are being built into their jungle sanctuary. (See Unit 4.)

This sort of dramatic and sudden exposure to a more technologically sophisticated culture usually brings about radical and disruptive changes in a society. For example, the intervention of colonial powers in many Third World countries has produced drastic changes in their politics, societies, economies, and cultures, and those countries that have won their struggle for independence have rising aspirations for prosperity and modernization. However, problems linked to the colonial experience make the process of change a painful one: diverse indigenous cultures incorporated within arbitrary colonial boundaries clash with each other, economic systems

are weak, and the political systems are poorly equipped to handle the distribution of resources and resolve internal conflicts. The process of change in developing countries is closely watched by the major world powers, each of which offers aid and models for attaining social, political, and economic stability. Many sociologists have become interested in the developing nations as laboratories for studying social change, and some have even become involved in government efforts to monitor and influence the course of change in modernizing countries.

3 American Context

Americans seem to be living in an age of such perpetual change that the experiences of one generation take place in an entirely different context from the experiences of the next. Alvin Toffler's popular book *Future Shock* (1970) vividly describes the disorientation caused by the fact that technology is advancing faster than Americans can psychologically adapt to it. Labor-saving devices have altered home and work behaviors to the extent that the pursuit of leisure activities now appears to be replacing traditional American orientations of thrift and the Protestant work ethic. Within this century the extended family has been replaced by the nuclear family, and the nuclear family is currently undergoing changes as a result of an increasing divorce rate, a decreasing birth rate, new patterns of extramarital relations, and the emerging rights and independence of women in the society. (See Units 6, 7, 13.) Since the early 1960s there has been a significant incidence of protest and public pressure for social, economic, and political reorganization.

Although ours may seem an era of singularly broad or rapid change in the American experience, every generation since the birth of the nation has lived through a major epoch of change—and survived the consequences. The consequences of the American Revolution included the establishment of a new political system and a social order inspired by new ideals. Westward expansion and the

Social change among the Manus, an island people in the Pacific. Pokanau, a village elder, shown in 1929 and 1953. One man has not just simply changed his clothing; a whole society has become linked to the expanding industrial world. The story of Pokanau was told by Margaret Mead in *New Lives for Old* (1956).

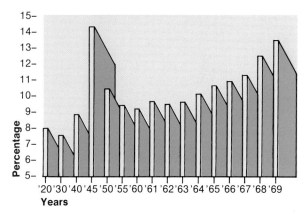

Figure 1. American Divorce Rate per Year, 1929–1969, per 1,000 Married Women 15 Years or More of Age. (Source: Public Health Service)

(Facing page) Detail of a painting by Bonito Romero of Taos, New Mexico. Traditional Indian themes and aspects of the wider American society are combined by this Pueblo Indian artist.

Table 1. American Family Characteristics, 1971. (Source: Bureau of the Census)

Characteristics	Number	Percentage
Total: All American families	**51,948,000**	**100.0**
White families	46,535,000	89.6
Black and other minority group families	5,413,000	10.4
Family size		
2	18,282,000	35.2
3	10,724,000	20.6
4	9,899,000	19.1
5	6,528,000	12.6
6	3,381,000	6.5
7	3,133,000	6.0
Children under 18 yrs. old		
0	23,161,000	44.6
1	9,163,000	18.5
2	8,915,000	17.2
3	5,380,000	10.4
4	4,878,000	9.4
Marital status of family head		
Married	45,222,000	87.1
Separated	1,263,000	2.4
Widowed	2,757,000	5.3
Divorced	1,584,000	3.0
Single	1,119,000	2.2
Age of family head		
25–34	10,649,000	20.5
35–44	10,840,000	20.9
45–54	11,065,000	21.3
55–64	8,473,000	16.3
65 or older	7,175,000	13.8

Policeman with rifle in black ghetto of Detroit after 1967 riots. *(Opposite page)* Detail of Hovenden's *The Last Moments of John Brown* (1883). Sometimes change can be accomplished in a relatively peaceful manner. However, if the institutions of a society tend to operate so as to ensure the chronic poverty of selected groups of people (for example, the blacks in America), then only when violence is a threat or a reality will the dominant groups of the society allow basic, structural change to take place. In 1859 John Brown and a small band of blacks and whites attempted to seize the federal arsenal at Harpers Ferry, Virginia, in order to touch off an uprising that would end slavery in America. Brown was captured by U.S. troops commanded—ironically—by Captain Robert E. Lee and hanged for treason shortly afterwards. At the time Brown's raid was condemned virtually unanimously in the North as well as the South. But the strains in American society over the slavery issue were such that two years later hundreds of thousands of U.S. troops were marching into battle—against forces commanded by Robert E. Lee—singing "John Brown's Body Lies A-Mouldering in the Grave, but His Soul Goes Marching On." Almost six years to the day after Brown was hanged, a constitutional amendment abolished slavery in America. But a hundred years after the Civil War, the unfulfilled promises of emancipation led to black uprisings in hundreds of cities, uprisings suppressed by local police and U.S. troops. What changes in American society have been brought about by these uprisings?

growth of railroads and communications bridging a largely untamed and unclaimed expanse of territory rich in resources broadened the spectrum of American activities and aspirations. Severe political, social, and economic cleavages led to the Civil War, a conflict that produced widespread repercussions throughout the American scene. And the latter part of the nineteenth century witnessed the crucial effects of the Industrial Revolution, Reconstruction, and the growth of urban centers. Since then Americans have experienced major immigrations, two world wars, a massive depression and a number of recessions, the spread of suburbs, the decay of cities, and so-called revolutions in technology, education, and civil rights.

Historical analysis allows sociologists to determine whether a given phenomenon reflects a significant alteration in social structure and culture or merely represents old practices in new guises. It may also provide useful information about the directions, patterns, and rates of particular changes. For example, the historical roots of the "liberation" of women since the mid-1960s may be traced back to the Industrial Revolution, when women were used in the factories as a source of cheap manual labor. This innovation was an initial step in drawing women out of traditional domestic roles and into new social and economic positions. Other sources of the changing role of women can be found in some rather unlikely places. It has been hypothesized, for example, that the replacement of the crank starter with an automatic starter in automobiles made women less dependent on men for transportation away from the household. Labor-saving appliances certainly decrease a woman's bondage to the home, and decreasing family size has made the role of mother less physically demanding and time-consuming. Other important factors in this *role change* include the woman's sharing of child-socialization duties with other agencies, her increasing longevity, her extended education, and the simple economic fact that one family breadwinner cannot provide the benefits that two often can (college educations for the children, a second car, a bigger home, and so on). The values and orientations of the culture lagged behind the rapid changes in the roles of women, however. During the 1940s and 1950s, for example, "ideologies" of motherhood developed and were reinforced. Prominent authors such as Dr. Benjamin Spock aggrandized the traditional role of "mother" at a time when the role was undergoing significant changes.

In the increasing tension that resulted between the *lag in cultural orientation* and *actual social practices*, alternative values and perspectives arose. These *new values* stimulated further *structural changes*. For example, the new values associated with individual expression and achievement among women not only filled the gap left by the change in the mother role, but in the United States also led to such structural changes as more career-oriented women working in higher-status jobs for more pay. These changes provide a clear-cut example of how elements of social structure and culture *interact* in the process of social change.

Although technology obviously has played a role in social changes pertaining to the role of women, it has even more fundamentally altered the framework in which all Americans live. It has been suggested that America is the first nation to have entered the "postmodern" or *technetronic age*—that we are, in a sense, already

living in the future, that we have overtaken the realm of science fiction, that our actual capabilities have outstripped any fantasies we might project. To what extent does our entire culture lag behind our current practices and knowledge, and to what extent has our culture been influenced by our rapidly expanding technology? Are there any theories that explain the nature of change in society as a whole?

C   QUESTIONS AND EVIDENCE

1   Questions

In explaining social change, sociologists ask a number of questions, ranging from specific research issues to broad theoretical concerns. For example: (1) Has the use of television in political campaigns significantly influenced voting behavior in presidential elections? (2) Is there a general pattern of social change, or is change too variable to conceptualize in a general theory? (3) What can explain the pattern of recent suburban growth in America?

2   Evidence

a   The "Burning Issue" Question
i   Context   Marshall McLuhan's *Understanding Media* (1964) has provided many insights into the influence of television on behavior.

Women's liberation movement. Women received the vote in 1920, but their struggle to find a politically significant basis for their self-identities in a society dominated by males emerged again intensely in the 1960s and 1970s. The women's movement focuses on the power to make the decisions regarding their own bodies (for example, the right to have an abortion) and their own life styles (for example, the right to remain unmarried without being subjected to formal and informal negative social sanctions) and on the right to advance in the job market without discrimination against them in pay or the types of jobs made available. Congressional representative Bella Abzug *(above left)* is a noted activist in the struggle for women's equality and has astutely used the media in her reform campaigns.

McLuhan tells us that television is a very special kind of medium. Unlike *"hot" media*, such as newspapers and radio, whose high-intensity images and detailed information provide a clear perspective for the perceiver, TV is a *"cool" medium* that involves more senses with incomplete, low-intensity images that invite sensory participation because the perceiver must complete the image in his own mind. TV has changed many features of our lives, from the way we spend leisure time to the way we receive and respond to information, images, and events. Increasingly, it has become the medium of politics. Considerable controversy has arisen as to whether this new medium has produced fundamental changes in American political orientations and practices. For example, media experts argue that the candidate's carefully packaged and projected TV image is now a central factor in political choice. Sociologists ask: *What role, if any, does television play in altering the electoral process?*

ii   Theory   To isolate television's role as a potential agent of change, one should first determine whether TV differs significantly from other media in regard to its treatment of political stimuli. Does TV have a higher political content than other media? Are televised political messages more memorable and/or persuasive than similar messages transmitted by other sources, such as radio? A related question is the degree to which, politically speaking, for TV "the medium is the message," in McLuhan's phrase. For example, does the introduction of a visual image of the candidate influence or alter the meaning of the political message? Consideration of these factors alone might lead a sociologist to formulate some strong hypotheses about TV and voting behavior, but the *target population* and its relationship to television must also be considered before a valid theoretical perspective can be developed.

In anticipating the effect of television on the target population, one must ascertain whether or not, prior to television, there was a major sector of the electorate that was not exposed to politics through other media. Another condition that might lead to television influence on voting behavior would be the existence of a target population with a previously unsatisfied need for political communication. Finally, one should consider whether TV treatments of politics present any significant challenge to the traditional bases on which voting decisions are made.

It is important to look at the *interaction between source and target* in developing any *model of change.* In this case one cannot focus solely on the characteristics of television itself, because it can be shown that TV does differ in important ways from other media in the realm of politics. Television sends 10 times the number of messages—and more memorable messages at that—into homes during the get-out-the-vote campaigns than does the nearest competing media source, radio. Also, the image projected by a candidate does seem to be significantly influenced by the television medium. If a sociologist considered these factors alone, he might be willing to make such predictions as ''TV leads to increased voting turnout'' or ''TV changes the basis of political choice.'' Study of the *target variables,* however, will encourage him to be a bit more cautious. It is a fact, for example, that television did not uncover any large sector of the electorate that was not exposed to politics through other media. During the late 1940s, when TV sets were first purchased in any number, 90 percent of the American adult population reported that they listened regularly to radio, and 80 percent reported that they read newspapers. And there appears to have been no great unsatisfied demand for political information before television arrived on the political scene. In fact, one of the major findings of media research is that those who seek information from new sources are generally well informed by other media. Finally, updated studies indicate that the major factor in voting choices is *party identification,* followed by *issue perception,* and that television appears not to have made any inroads into influencing either.

By referring to both the source of change and the nature of the target population, it is possible to outline the conditions under which significant television influence on voting behavior can be expected to occur. Two simple hypotheses can be constructed: (1) In general, television has no significant effect on voting turnout, the basic patterns of choice and voting trends over elections, and changes in vote decisions late in the campaign or on election day. (2) Television will have an effect in those occasional elections where traditional bases for making choices become blurred or where there exist marked personality and style differences between candidates.

iii Research   In ''Television and Voting Turnout'' (1965) William Glasser found that, as the first hypothesis predicts, television does not seem to have a significant impact on voting turnout. Even though a greater number of memorable voting reminders reach people by television, those who are urged to vote through TV appeals do not vote with greater frequency than those reminded by other media. However, Glasser did find a correlation between voting and ability to recall a reminder from *any* media source. In this sense TV is neither more nor less effective than any other medium. Glasser's data for this point were from just the 1960 presidential election, however. Has there been a trend toward higher voting over all the national elections since the advent of TV? Angus Campbell's analysis of turnout data for national elections over a thirty-year period demonstrated that no such trend exists ("Has Television Reshaped Politics?" 1962). Campbell's survey also found that there is no apparent relationship between increased television coverage of elections and the interest of the public in elections.

What about the importance of the candidate's *image* as a basis for electoral choice since the advent of television? According to the second hypothesis, image should play an important role in cases where normal bases for choice are blurred and/or sharp personal styles differentiate the candidates. The best example of such an election was the 1960 presidential contest between John Kennedy and Richard Nixon. Nixon espoused many of the issues and positions of the Democrats, and the issue of Kennedy's Catholicism may have subjected many Democrats to cross-pressures. The undeniable differences in personal styles were accentuated by the candidates' extensive television exposure during the debates. McLuhan feels that Nixon was too sharp and aggressive; he resembled the railway lawyer "who signs leases that are not in the interests of the folks in the little town." Campbell's surveys bear out the importance of candidate television image in that election. He relates an illustrative anecdote about an elderly lady who couldn't vote for Mr. Nixon because she didn't like the look in his eyes, "especially the left one."

In the elections of 1964, 1968, and 1972, charges were made (usually by losing candidates) that the "instant vote analysis" policy of the networks, which makes available information about the outcome of the election in the East before some people have voted in the West, is inequitable. This information may bias the decisions of the Western voter or even influence large numbers of people to stay home because they believe the election has already been decided. This hypothesis is plausible only if a sizable target population of late voters (1) are exposed to the early returns, (2) have not firmly decided for whom to vote, and (3) are not strongly committed to voting in the first place. A recent study by Kurt and Gladys Lang ("The Late Vote," 1971) shows that such conditions do not exist. The Langs believe the "law of minimal consequences" operates. They conclude that only an insignificant number of people remain after the target population of late Western voters is diminished by subtracting those who did not hear the early returns or had clearly made their voting choice and were committed to voting.

In short, it appears that television has not significantly affected voting patterns or turnout. The major change attributable to TV is the importance of visual image in making vote decisions in close or blurred elections.

iv Evaluation The hypothetical model indicates that television would cause significant voting changes if it constituted a distinctive medium for vote-related political stimuli and if a sizable target population was vulnerable to these distinctive effects of ''videopolitics.'' Research indicated that the second condition of the model was not met, and empirical evidence supports the expectation that no significant television-related changes have occurred in voting behavior in presidential elections.

The model does not imply that television has had no effect on politics. In fact, it has had several important *secondary effects*. For example, television has had considerable influence on the nature of political campaigns, and the high cost of purchasing TV time has made them far more costly. The result has been differential access to the public for the two major parties because of significant differences in party finances. If the cost of television campaigning continues to rise, the American party and election system may face a major crisis. This example points up the importance of looking for secondary effects that may be associated with any potential cause of change.

More research is needed on the effects of television upon politics. For example, sociologists would like to know how TV influences political orientations other than voting. Does videopolitics lead people to feel ''closer'' to government or more ''integrated'' into the political process? Will there be a shift in the future in the relationship between TV and politics? Different sources of data should also be utilized: too many ambiguities exist in a study such as Glasser's, where people were asked to recall if they were reminded to vote by any media. Finally, it may be interesting to look at *generational effects* of television on politics, because the 1970s mark the entry of the first ''television generation'' into the political arena.

b The "Classical" Question

i Context   Sociological theory has made considerable progress in identifying sources and mechanisms of change. However, sociologists have had little success in constructing a general or universal model of change that encompasses *historical trends, social dynamics,* and *structural alterations* and can stand up under empirical scrutiny. Each proposed model of change has attracted its adherents, and each illuminates some feature of social change. The integration of these different theoretical positions is a necessary step on the way to building a general model of change. Despite progress in the past decade, sociologists are still unable to answer the elusive question: *What is the basic set of historical trends, social dynamics, and structural configurations associated with social change?*

ii Theory   Sociology has struggled with two major controversies over the conceptualization of social change, both of which date back to the nineteenth century. The first controversy, which concerns whether or not social change is a deterministic process, has been largely resolved. The second, whether the natural state of societies tends toward equilibrium or conflict, is still the center of intense theoretical debate. We deal further with that debate in Units 4 and 27.

The *deterministic perspective* emphasizes the force of history in shaping human events. Determinist models propose that an inevitable pattern of change will occur in societies as a result of a universal *dynamic,* or principle of change, that pushes all societies in the same direction. Some determinist theories see the pattern as *linear;* this view is exemplified by the notion of universal progress from simple origins to complex civilizations. Others see the pattern as *cyclical:* societies progress to complex civilizations and then decay to their original simple roots, only to begin the process over again. Other theories interpret the dynamic in terms of the inevitable conflict between opposing groups in the social structure. Still others see the dynamic as simply the inevitable march of human progress. Whatever the specific principle, the basic assumption is that once an *institutional order* is established, all successive generations will be responsive to the social "laws" that inexorably control the course of human events.

Contemporary thinking and research have cast considerable doubt on the determinist position. It is now commonly assumed that the course of history is open to human influence. *Nondeterminist* conceptions of social change point to such sources of variability in the "paths" of societies as the intervention of one culture in the life of another and the rise of competing norms and values in institutional contexts. This new perspective has turned sociological attention toward finding *alternative patterns* of social change, rather than isolating a single, *universal form* of change.

The freedom to contemplate multiple patterns of change in a nondeterminist framework has been a major step in social-change theory. However, any theory of social change still faces two significant problems. First, there is the problem of discovering what social dynamics or principles lead to varying patterns of change. Second, a theory of change must come to grips with how patterns of change are reflected in the relationships among the basic units of society. In other words, a conception of the ways societies are put together is essential to an understanding of how change affects social structure.

If society is viewed as an organic whole in which all social units (roles, institutions, and so on) are interdependent, like the tissues and organs of the body, then change in one social sector might be visualized as ultimately leading to changes in all other sectors. If, on the other hand, social units are viewed as more fragmented and less interdependent, changes in one sector might be imagined to have relatively little effect on other sectors. If social units tend to accommodate each other so as to eliminate conflict and reduce tensions in society, there are few internal dynamics for change. If, on the other hand, relationships among people and institutions are potential sources of competing values and norms, this internal conflict might be the dynamic for change.

The view of society as a stable organism with systematically interdependent parts may be called an *equilibrium model* of society. The alternative perspective of a less interdependent, value-competitive social order can be termed a *conflict model* of society. Disagreement exists within the sociological community as to which model best reflects the actual nature of society. Is change largely a result of external pressures, as an equilibrium perspective might suggest? Or is change stimulated primarily by the potential value conflicts that arise within the social order, as a conflict perspective would maintain? There is disagreement also as to how change travels through and affects the social structure. Does an alteration in one area "vibrate" throughout the interlocking (or functionally interdependent) web of all social units, as an equilibrium perspective would contend? Alternately, is it possible that a change in one sector would not be felt in other isolated units of society, as a conflict model might argue?

A general theory of change must deal with such questions before alternative patterns of change can be meaningfully related to particular social contexts. The following sections explore some critical thinking in the area.

iii Research (Survey) The roots of contemporary conflict and equilibrium perspectives on change may be traced to several early or classical sociologists. Karl Marx viewed change as a historical process leading to the ultimate formation of a classless society. As

Pancho Villa and Fidel Castro. Called a "bandit" by some, Pancho Villa (1878–1923) was a cornerstone of the Mexican Revolution of 1910–1917, which brought major economic and social reorganization to that country. He was pursued (unsuccessfully) into Mexico by U.S. troops in 1916 and died by an assassin's hand in 1923. *(Opposite page)* Also called a "bandit," Fidel Castro gave up a law practice in Havana to lead a revolution that eventually eliminated the desperate and widespread poverty of Cuba and brought sweeping advances in education and health care for masses of people.

discussed in earlier units, in his theory the dynamic for change was the inevitable conflict between subordinate and ruling classes in the social order. Each subordinate class was destined to overthrow the ruling class and establish itself in the dominant position, and this series of *dialectical conflicts* was to end inevitably with the revolution of the proletariat and the construction of a stable, classless society. This theory was deterministic in the sense that it relied on the concept of *historical predictability*, which means that in any society, *patterns of class relationships* would develop around the *means of production*, and inevitable class conflicts and revolutions would result. Certain events and class actions might delay a particular phase of conflict, but nothing could alter the course of such change.

One of the early equilibrium theorists was Ferdinand Toennies. He theorized that the direction of change was linear progress toward societies of more and more complexity. Societies proceeded from traditional, simple, folk communities *(Gemeinschaft)* to complex, urban centers *(Gesellschaft)* in which roles were specialized (differentiated) and functionally interdependent. The change from *Gemeinschaft* to *Gesellschaft* was seen by Toennies as an irreversible result of the important social dynamics of population growth and industrialization. (See Units 6 and 17.)

Each of these theories has made important contributions to modern thought. Like most classical theories, however, they contain determinist assumptions. Max Weber made an important contribution in liberating theories of social change from determinist trappings. He argued (and demonstrated empirically) that although society's institutional network determines social relations and progress, certain key occurrences can change the basic institutional structure and alter the pattern and direction of social change. As we saw in Units 8 and 20, he pointed to the rise of *charismatic leaders and interventions of one culture in the affairs of another* (war, colonization, religious appeals, and so on) as important instances of potential nondetermined change in ongoing social processes.

Weber also emphasized that both social and cultural factors should be considered in the process of change. His stress on multiple factors and variability in change paved the way for such thinkers as Pitirim Sorokin to explore the possibilities of many patterns of change. Sorokin proposed that the major patterns of change included several types of linear trends, cyclical patterns, and variable or cyclical patterns with gradual trends. But the important work of Weber, Sorokin, and other thinkers did not resolve the equilibrium-versus-conflict dilemma.

FIDEL CASTRO
FIEL

Talcott Parsons stands as the towering figure among modern equilibrium theorists. His early work conceived of society as fixed in terms of its ultimate value structure and its mechanisms of interrelationship among social units. Within this model change consists of the differentiation of functions in the social system and the accompanying specialization of roles *(structural differentiation)* to accommodate this diffusion of functions. For example, the function of socialization is no longer the unique task of the family, but has become shared by a number of differentiated units—schools, occupations, voluntary associations, and the like. Systems of *norms* and *bridging institutions*, such as the courts, reduce conflict in the new structure and reintegrate all units in society. In this theory, often called *structural-functionalism*, a change in one sector results in change throughout society through a network of readjustments that reintegrate the system after the introduction of new structures.

In his early work Parsons had difficulty in explaining the dynamics of change and in visualizing change that might produce profound alterations in the basic framework of social values and interrelationships among units. During the past 15 years Parsons and others have made some headway in solving these dilemmas. For example, changes in personality as a result of conflicts between needs and social demands are viewed as one internal dynamic for change. Also, the process of reintegration may indeed require the formation of new values and mechanisms of interrelationships if equilibrium is to be reestablished. Thus, Parsons' recent thinking is that societies still tend toward equilibrium but that change (differentiation) may produce *new structural patterns and value systems* (a new framework for equilibrium) as a result of *reintegration.*

Despite these efforts to develop a theory of change within the equilibrium model, its critics are still dissatisfied. Contemporary conflict theorists, such as Ralf Dahrendorf, argue that although structural-functional theories account for the cement that holds societies together (the forces of integration) they do not adequately explain forces of disruption and change. The modern conflict perspective contends that *mechanisms of integration* do not fully function in society and that change-producing conflicts potentially exist within all social positions. This idea implies, much like Marxist theory, that in all social organization there exist roles that carry authority and relationships that involve domination and subordination. The pressures generated among unequal social groups lead to conflict over preserving or changing the status quo.

The conflict theorists argue that any adequate theory of social change must deal with both the integrative and the disruptive qualities of social relationships. Equilibrium theorists respond that they do account for disruptions, but that integrative mechanisms constantly operate to pull social units together. This impasse has not yet been resolved—and thus no theory of social change presents a clear picture of the relationships among social units and the social dynamics that lead to change.

iv   Evaluation   What are the prospects for resolving this dilemma? As theorist Wilbert E. Moore points out, "The mention of 'theory of social change' will make most social scientists appear defensive, furtive, guilt-ridden, or frightened." No simple solution has appeared for the disagreement between conflict and equilibrium (or structural-functional) models. Neither approach seems fully adequate to handle social change. Perhaps some compromise or integration of the two models could be made, but the fundamental opposition of their basic views on how social units relate to and influence one another would have to be overcome first.

There are, however, new trends in sociological thinking that regard change itself as a topic that is parallel in scope and complexity to social theory as a whole. In this sense change is seen as an integral and complementary aspect of all social process. Thus, rather than seeking a single global theory, sociologists have begun to generate narrower, middle-range theories of change that apply to the various subdisciplines and topical interests of sociology. This new orientation may eventually lead to separate general theories of political change, organizational change, demographic change, and so on. These perspectives may yield greater insights than the more elusive universal model of change that so intrigued earlier social scientists.

c   The "Research" Question

i   Context   A major shift in the population structure of the United States began after World War II, and we have discussed many aspects of it in Units 6 and 17. This shift, often called the "suburban boom," was characterized by a mass exodus from the cities to outlying, formerly rural, areas. The growth rate of these new population centers increased sharply, whereas population growth in the cities began to stabilize and, in some cases, decline. The very fact of such a rapid and marked population shift was enough to interest sociologists in it as a new case of social change, and we discuss their analysis in that regard in this unit. Its implications in terms of the life styles of many Americans, the conditions of the cities, and patterns of social integration have shown what an important role this population shift has played in the drama of contemporary America. Sociologists ask: *What factors account for the population shift to the suburbs, and how can we explain the pattern and direction of this change?*

ii   Theory   A change such as the suburban shift involves, at a minimum, four factors: (1) *facilitating conditions* make movement to areas outside of urban centers possible or feasible; (2) *motivating conditions* or events stimulate or trigger the shift; (3) a *target population* is affected by both the facilitating and the motivating conditions; and (4) certain *mechanisms of perpetuation* assure that successive generations of target populations will exist and be drawn to the suburbs even if original motivating conditions change or disappear.

The population structure of America had also shifted substantially around the turn of the century, when people left rural areas to come to the cities in search of new industry-related jobs. Cities not only provided jobs, but offered opportunities for living in the midst of transportation, consumer, and communication networks that supported both the domestic and economic needs of the population. In order for suburban growth to be possible, links had to be established between cities and their rural peripheries. Examples of such facilitating links were the advances in transportation and communications technology that allowed people to live outside of cities and still maintain economic and social contact inside urban boundaries. The building of commuter bus systems and railways, the spread of telephone service, the decentralization of consumer outlets, and, more importantly, the mass ownership of the automobile all facilitated the decentalization of population from urban centers to surrounding areas. None of these factors, however, directly accounts for the timing and the magnitude of the shift that occurred. Precipitating factors or motivating conditions were also necessary.

One such factor has been the pressure on urban centers associated with industrialization and rapid population growth. In ecological terms, the *carrying capacity* (the number of organisms comfortably handled by a given environment with limited resources) of the cities began to be reached during the 1940s and 1950s. In short, the cities began to be uncomfortable places in which to live. A more dramatic event occurred with the end of World War II itself. As millions of GIs returned home in search of jobs and housing, there was an increase in marriages and the birth rate, and the government began financing "overnight" housing developments outside of cities to accommodate the new demand. A related factor that attracted the population to the extraurban life style was the rising productivity of the economy (following more than 15 years of depression and war), which gave people the financial means to buy cars and houses and to free themselves from the necessity of living in the city.

The target population for these facilitating and precipitating conditions was large and growing. It consisted of young to middle-aged white, married persons, primarily of white-collar backgrounds. These people wanted to take their families out of the cities and had the economic resources to do so.

The "suburban revolution" did not stop here, however, for mechanisms of perpetuation developed to expand the suburban growth rate and appeal to other target populations. Industries began to decentralize their operations and follow their workers to the suburbs. Land, facilities, and taxes were often cheaper beyond the cities' borders, and the growth and diversification of manufacturing made it desirable to develop branch plants of parent companies. Industrial decentralization drew many blue-collar or working-class families out of the cities. A new working class, consisting of employees of service industries that provided domestic support functions for the new suburbs, developed.

An equally important perpetuation mechanism was the migration during the 1950s and 1960s of poor white and black families from rural Southern areas to the cities in search of better opportunities. The *population voids* in the cities began to be filled by ghettos of minorities and the poor, prompting many of the remaining urban whites to flee to the racially restricted sanctuaries of the suburbs.

If this simple model of surburban growth is accurate, it should be possible to generate some empirically valid hypotheses about the pattern and direction of suburban growth. (1) A simple proposition, given the particular mechanisms of perpetuation just identified, is that the suburban growth rate is still increasing at the present time. (2) Another hypothesis (which derives from identifying motivating conditions that appeal to diverse but largely white target populations) is that suburban social patterns incorporate a variety of economic and social characteristics but are racially homogeneous. (3) A final hypothesis is that, given the decentralization of industrial and consumer institutions and the consequent relocation of economic centers, the suburbs of today are becoming the cities of tomorrow. Research findings can be used to test the accuracy of each of these simple hypotheses.

iii Research (Methodology)   There are two basic types of research on suburban change. The most common is based on the *analysis of aggregate data*, such as census information. Such research provides a picture of the general trends in suburban growth and an estimate of the demographic composition of different suburban areas. The second major type of research is the *case study*, in which investigators select one community (or several) and interview residents to gather specific information about the life style of a community. Each type of research is suited to answering certain questions, and each can complement the other in building a general picture of suburbia. In many studies, however, only one method is used, and researchers draw inferences that would be more appropriate to the other approach.

To test the first hypothesis (that suburban growth is still going on), it is necessary to find the growth trend for all suburbs across America. Obviously the case-study approach will not provide this information. The best aggregate data source for our purposes is the U.S. Census. Such data present a comparative picture of urban, suburban, and rural populations over the past 60 years and show that not only has the population continued to grow, but that suburban dwellers are now the *modal population group* in the United States.

Figure 2. Percentage Distribution of United States Population by Place of Residence, 1910–1970. In this figure urban areas are defined as the central cities, and suburbs are defined as those parts of the standard metropolitan statistical areas that are not central cities. The percentage of the population living in rural areas declined drastically during the period shown. The percentage in urban areas rose steadily until 1950, except for a slight decline during the Depression of the 1930s. The percentage in suburban areas grew throughout this period, and particularly so after 1940. Since 1940 suburban living has gained so steadily at the expense of both urban and rural living that by 1970 there were more suburbanities than either of the other two groups. (Source: Adapted from Wattenberg and Scammon, "The Suburban Boom")

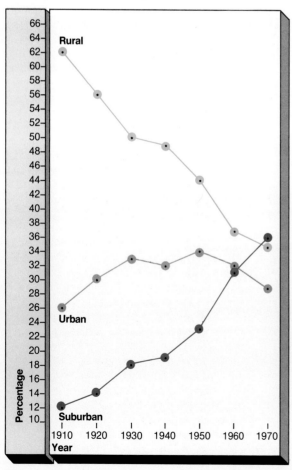

Perhaps the most frequent abuse of the case-study method occurs when it is used to deal with an issue such as suburban social patterns. Although racially homogeneous, suburban populations are diverse in social class and economic terms. Many case studies of the 1950s and 1960s (for example, the J. R. Seeley, R. A. Sim, and E. W. Loosley *Crestwood Heights* study of 1956, or William H. Whyte's *The Organization Man* of the same year) are in-depth, largely observational analyses of one or a small number of middle-class and upper-middle-class suburbs. Although disclaimers were usually made as to the generality of the profile, the proliferation of such case studies left a generation of students with the impression that all suburban dwellers were middle-class or upper-middle-class persons who regularly attended PTA meetings and mowed the lawns around their tract houses every Saturday. In recent years the case-study method has been used with greater sensitivity. There is now a tendency to utilize multiple cases and supplement the findings with aggregate data. For example, S. D. Clark employed this dual approach in a study of no fewer than 20 Toronto suburban areas (*The Suburban Society*, 1966). He found that suburban growth has involved diverse target populations of varying occupational, educational, and social backgrounds. Similar studies also tend to debunk the myth of the middle-class suburb. Although such studies do not show that the modal suburban dweller is not white-collar, middle-class, and white, they direct attention to the diversity that characterizes the contemporary pattern of suburban growth. It must be noted, however, that although great differentiation can be found among suburbs, each individual suburban neighborhood tends to be quite homogeneous—characterized either by a common religious or ethnic culture, by a common income level, by family size and stage, or by a particular style of living.

The third hypothesis proposes that suburban growth is directed toward the development of new urban centers. Early observers such as William Dobriner argued that urban patterns were transplanted to the suburbs along with city people and their occupations. According to this view, suburbs contain the "seeds" of new urban growth. More recent observers, however, have modified this view. S. D. Clark, for example, argues that people obviously abandon certain patterns when they enter the new social structure of suburbia. Although suburbs sometimes become new urban centers, the process and pattern of such growth are quite different from that of older metropolitan areas. The difference is one of the major reasons why there is such interest in the phenomenon of suburbanism. Clark argues that "there is a pattern of development of suburban society just as there is a pattern of development of any society. It is the recognition of such a pattern which distinguishes comparative sociological from historical analysis."

iv Evaluation   The study of suburban change is critical to an understanding of life in contemporary America. More people live in the suburbs than live in either urban or rural areas, and the life styles of suburbia differ significantly from the other two major residence patterns. Furthermore, the study of suburbia today may also shed light on the changing structure of metropolitan areas and the shape of tomorrow's cities. Equally important, the study of suburban change may help to explain the present crisis in the "old" cities. Such a search for secondary effects is a central part of any comprehensive study of social change. By understanding why people and industries are selectively leaving urban centers, sociologists may discover ways of altering this flow in an effort to save our established cities from economic instability and a population consisting largely of disenchanted racial and ethnic minorities and the poor.

3   Overview

In a very important sense, sociology as an academic discipline began with the attempt of thinkers such as Auguste Comte, Karl Marx, Ferdinand Toennies, Emile Durkheim, and Max Weber to understand the fundamental changes they perceived taking place in European society during and following the Industrial Revolution. The challenge of change to sociology continues today.

Thus far no thinker, classical or contemporary, has developed a general theory of social change that permits the accurate prediction of future events. Karl Marx, more than almost anyone else, believed that he had discovered such a theory. Nevertheless, despite his great insights into the nature of modern industrial society, most sociologists feel that his predictions of inevitable class warfare are too rigid and narrow. Sociologists have learned that human social life is not deterministic, that changes are caused by a number of factors that interact in complex ways, and that the human capacity to react to events creates new, unexpected possibilities for social life.

Although sociologists have ultimately failed to evolve a unified theory of change as a general process, they have had more success in handling discrete cases of change. Through the careful use of methodology and concepts, a given instance of change may reveal its main element and even its direction and pattern to sociological scrutiny. The recent trend toward abandoning the search for a single model of change permits some optimism about the development of new and flexible theories that will be open to empirical validation, revision, and refinement, and thus will have *predictive capabilities* as well.

D   LOOKING AHEAD

1   Interview:
Amitai Etzioni

Amitai Etzioni is professor of sociology at Columbia University and director of the Center for Policy Research. His books include *Comparative Analysis of Complex Organizations, Social Change* (with Eva Etzioni), *Modern Organizations, Political Unification, Studies in Social Change, The Active Society,* and *Demonstration Democracy.* He has consulted for and conducted studies for the Department of Labor, the National Science Foundation, the President's Commission on the Causes and Prevention of Violence, and other government agencies.

DPG   *Professor Etzioni, since the publication of your important book,* The Active Society, *and the more recent abridgement of the book by Warren Breed* (The Self-Guiding Society), *you have become well known for your theory of directed social change, which you call societal guidance. How fully developed is this theory?*

ETZIONI   Progress in social science over the recent years allows us now to develop a Keynesian theory of *societal* processes, that is, a theory of the factors which determine our capacity to manage society and of the conditions which allow us to improve our guiding capacity. Of course, even once we possess such a theory, however valid, this will only be the first step toward its effective use. At least a generation lapsed after Keynes published his seminal book before it became the basis for economic steerage. Hopefully, application of the theory will not be so long in coming this time around.

DPG   *What is the nature of this theory?*
ETZIONI   Its nature can be indicated by drawing upon an *analogue* from cybernetics. Cybernetics is still most developed in reference to guidance of mechanical and electrical systems. It assumes (a) one or more centers (command posts) that issue signals to the units which carry out the work; (b) communication lines which lead from the center or centers to the working units, carrying the instructions for what is to be done, and "feedback" lines which carry information and responses from the subject units to the center (in short, two-way communication links). (c) While many cybernetic models omit the conception of power, we see it as a main factor: if the steering units cannot back

up their signals with rewards or sanctions, they will be frequently disregarded (that is, the command post must be stronger than those who carry out its instructions). (d) A further subtlety is to distinguish, within the command centers, between subunits which absorb and analyze the incoming information and those which make decisions (that is, between knowledge-makers and policy-makers). When all these elements are available and function effectively, that is, communication lines are well linked and not overloaded, information and decision-making units have unimpeded access to each other, and so on, we have an effective control system.

DPG   *How can the cybernetics model be applied to social systems?*
ETZIONI   Some engineers and managers think that a social system, be it of a corporation or of a society, can be managed directly in this way. The government is viewed as the cybernetorial overlayer of society. The White House, Congress, state capitols, and city halls provide the command positions; universities, research institutes, government experts, and ''think-tanks''—the knowledge makers; the civil service and the media—the two way communication lines. I don't agree. As I see it, when a cybernetic model is applied to a social system, one must take into account, for both ethical and practical reasons, that the citizens cannot be coerced to follow ''signals'' unless those signals, at least to a significant extent, are responsive to their basic values and interests.

DPG   *What is the matter with the use of force—can't force be a very effective tool for the management of society and for the solution of some of the very difficult social problems that face us today?*

ETZIONI   If force is used, the system both violates rights and generates increasing levels of resistance, which become a major reason why the society is unable to manage its affairs effectively, whether the goals be collectivization of the farms or abolishing alcoholism. Effective societal cybernetics requires that the downward flow of control signals (from the government to the people) be accompanied by effective upward (from the people to the government) and lateral (among citizens) flows of signals which express the citizens' values and needs.

DPG   *You have written of active societies and compared them with passive societies. What's the difference?*
ETZIONI   The active society is capable of handling its problems through the process of societal guidance. The passive society is unable to handle its problems in this way. For a country like the United States to successfully adapt to the changes in the next decades and to provide a more meaningful and satisfying life for its people, it needs to become an active society.

DPG   *How can a country become an active society?*
ETZIONI   Very briefly, there are four elements in the process. The first factor is the amount and quality of *knowledge* an acting social unit possesses. All too often we have little knowledge about the underlying factors behind such problems as poverty, riots and urban problems and make policy on the wrong assumptions. The active society needs more research directed at social problems and a way of reducing the gap between the experts and the decision makers.

Secondly, we need to take advantage of the new tools of societal guidance such as the technology of communication, knowledge storage and retrieval, computation and research which have been developing rapidly since about 1955 to develop a better type of *decision making*. This new type of decision making needs to be deeper and more extensive than democratic decision making, but also much more humane than totalitarian decision making.

Third, the *distribution of power* in a society significantly affects its capacity to treat its problems and to change its structure and policies. I believe that the only way to assure that a society will be responsive to the membership-at-large is to give all members comparable amounts of control over its guidance mechanisms. This means that not just the right to vote, but the socioeconomic and educational prerequisites for its effective use, must be extended to all citizens before a democracy can be fully effective.

2 Interview:
Suzanne Keller

Suzanne Keller is professor of sociology at Princeton University. She is the author of *Beyond the Ruling Class* and *The Urban Neighborhood*. Her areas of current research include new towns, the family, and community.

DPG *Do you think that with increased communication capabilities all human societies will tend to become increasingly alike?*
KELLER My immediate answer would be no. Communication capabilities operate within a cultural system—of meanings, habits, and memories. The kind of communications revolution we have facing us is going to increase diversity—among individuals and among cultures.

DPG *With that increased communication, how can ordinary people cope with the growing flood of information?*
KELLER First of all, do they have to cope with it? People make use of selective devices. They tend to notice what interests them or what they need. Some people have the TV on all day, but it's just background until something happens to catch their attention.

DPG *But doesn't that kind of situation present a problem for the traditional notion of the informed citizen being the basis of a democracy?*
KELLER I think that we'll probably learn how to scan information better than we do, and we'll probably move toward increased centralization on the world level and increased decentralization on the local level, far greater decentralization because electronic communication can be much more representative of many views and interests. I don't know if you can satisfy those interests better, but future systems can certainly get at public opinions and hear people's responses better.

DPG *So you think that more sensitive mechanisms for tapping public opinion are perhaps the way to maintain at least the facade of democracy?*
KELLER Yes. And maybe more than a facade. The fundamental question today is: How, on what basis, do you make decisions, especially large-scale, collective decisions? Today we still try to operate under the notion

The final element involves *consensus building*. A program's chances to be successful are greater, assuming a given level of power backing, the more it is in accord with the values of the majority of the citizens. One of the great unanswered questions of our political life is what new or improved mechanisms for consensus building we will evolve. Elections are too infrequent and indirect to satisfy this need.

DPG *Assuming that a society becomes active in the sense that you have put forth, what values would it promote and what kind of a society would it be?*
ETZIONI I don't think that a social scientist can speak for man, identify his values and needs and proclaim them in the form of an ordered platform. The values a society effectively manages will have to be those *its citizens* will seek to advance.

DPG *What then is the role of social science in societal guidance?*
ETZIONI Social science's answer ought to be sheerly ''procedural;'' we should point to ways man may be more in command of societal process and less subject to his blind fluctuations, rather than spell out where precisely he should guide the processes.

that consensus is desirable and possible—that is, some single consensus, not shifting coalitions of views. But in the future people will argue very decidedly about the outcomes, as they do now about the means to given ends. I think the ends will be much more debated.

DPG *Could you give an example of the kinds of differing ends?*
KELLER We see it in community planning all the time. Will you teach a vocational curriculum at the school, or will you teach a math/science curriculum? People have to fight that out at local, community levels. Middle-class spokesmen may have more resources to draw on and may thus win more often than not. But the working class has numbers. There is no certainty what the outcome will be. This is just one of the unknowns that one learns to live with and deal with on a local, day-by-day level.

DPG *What about the problem of elitism?*
KELLER Elitism has always been here. I don't think the world will require a more centralized elite, but more diversified elites. Contrary to many of my colleagues and friends, I see both an increasing specialization of decision making and increased diversification, so that no single elite can dominate all others.

DPG *So the age of the generalized decision maker is coming to an end?*
KELLER Yes, the Renaissance prince is long dead. A single voice, caste, or point of view cannot speak for and organize the growing complexities of social systems any longer. It will be less and less possible for very small minorities to impose their wills on others by force. Increasingly, we will see more coordination and collaboration among policy-making groups, more give and take among diverse interests. Force and collusion will not automatically disappear, of course, but they will meet with greater resistance. All in all, I see a loosening up of the system.

DPG *What individual effects will the accelerating rate of change and the pressure to change have on ordinary people?*
KELLER This is a very intriguing question. My immediate gut feeling is that change is something that you can incorporate very easily if you start early enough. For children born under systems of accelerating change, it will just be the way things are. They won't be shocked at novelty—unlike their parents, born under a slower system, who may find change unsettling. The parents have been trained and are geared to a slower tempo.

DPG *Would you think, for instance, that children born today are going to be capable of changing in a way that their parents weren't?*
KELLER Absolutely. And *their* children will be even more so. The rate of change one perceives as too much is the rate that probably exceeds one's anticipation. Everything in human life has to do with expectations—mental images of how things *should be* in contrast to how they *are* in reality. The more one takes change for granted, the more one manages to incorporate it in one's view of the world.

People who travel a lot, for example, are much less locked in to one particular pattern. When in Rome they're capable of doing as the Romans do, yet not losing their bearings.

They still may call only one place home, and certain deep affections and loyalties abide, but they move with the tide, managing to juggle a different vocabulary, language, currency, and morals without great difficulty. They might be surprised, they might ask lots of questions, they might ponder about a great many things, but they're not notably disoriented. But when people who have been in one setting all their lives are put into another, they undergo tremendous disorientation. Not having prepared for it, they do not know how to deal with it.

Nothing I have read in psychology or in other fields leads me to believe that there is a maximum level of change beyond which people cannot adapt. I suspect that our tolerance level is probably much higher than anything we've experienced yet—especially since we attend to the world about us very selectively. So it will be not the overall rate of change that will matter to individuals but the rates of change in the areas closest to them.

When people are on a plane for the first time—and in a sense they have not lived in the twentieth century until that moment—they suffer all the apprehensions of the uninitiated. But most of them adjust very quickly and without ill effects.

In contrast to many other people, I therefore do not foresee only negative consequences of prospective changes. The impact of change will be selective, as are people's responses to the new. I also believe that the young are more able to accept change in several areas that threaten their elders—in family life, sexual relations, and morality.

DPG *What label do you prefer for the next era in mankind's life on earth?*
KELLER I would reject all the "post" terms—"postindustrial," "postcivilized," and "postmodern"—because I think these put the emphasis on the wrong aspect, on the past. I would prefer one that stresses the future and its possibilities and novelties. I think that the chief new phenomenon on the technical level is electronic connectedness, so "electronic society" is the term I would probably choose right now. However, this term

doesn't satisfy me either. It certainly isn't the term we will use in the future, I'm sure, because it's still one-sided. It doesn't give you a flavor of that new world.

DPG *How do you feel about the electronic society? Is it going to be worth living in?*
KELLER This is really a question of temperament, and my temperament happens to be optimistic and curious. My immediate response is that it will be an extremely interesting society to live in. It will tax more of our individual capacities; that is, more people will be able and will also be asked to work on the problems of society and to contribute their imaginations to the solutions. Today this is true for no more than a fraction of the population.

There will also be less monotony and drudgery than we've known in the past. I think Michael Harrington has proposed that we should act now to eliminate the dirty work of the society—the really dirty jobs—and to have machines do them. And that, I think, will be a great boon in human history. I believe it will raise the whole base of respect and participation for everyone.

It will be a difficult society for those who are used to the old system, of course. The transitional generations may find it very trying indeed. And, as always, some will benefit more from the new system than others. But I think that that sort of system has more capacity to use human capital and human resources. And that is my main wish and hope for the future.

Unit 27
Social Conflict and Peace

SCHEMATIC OUTLINE

A   Introductory Graphics: Conflict and Social Equilibrium

B   Definition and Context

1   Definition
Social conflict is a struggle over values and claims to status, power, and scarce resources in which the aims of the conflicting parties are not only to gain the desired ends, but also to neutralize, injure, or eliminate their rivals. Conflict and violence are distinct concepts, and sociologists also distinguish between negative peace—the absence of organized violence among human groups—and positive peace—a pattern of cooperation among human groups.

2   World Context
Conflict, both violent and nonviolent, has arisen between and within nations throughout man's history. In the next decade or so poverty will probably become a growing basis of such conflict.

3   American Context
Conflict has always characterized American society, though it has varied in amount and type. As a pluralist society, the United States is able to tolerate a fair amount of conflict.

C   Questions and Evidence

1   Questions
Three questions cover a variety of social contexts: (1) Why did some ghetto residents and not others participate in the riots in American cities in the 1960s? (2) What is the role of conflict in human societies? (3) Is it possible to solve international conflicts by means of social science diplomacy?

2   Evidence
a   The "Burning Issue" Question
Empirical studies generally do not support the standard sociological theory that participation in urban riots results from the frustrations of economic and social deprivation. Other, more direct approaches to the question must be tested.
b   The "Classical" Question
There is some evidence that conflict plays a fundamental role in social life. This insight—which has roots in the theories of Thomas Hobbes, Karl Marx, and Georg Simmel and has recently been restated by C. Wright Mills, Lewis Coser, Ralf Dahrendorf, and others—should probably be combined with the stress on consensus in the functionalist model of society.
c   The "Research" Question
Sociological interest in peace has become most active in John Burton's experimental diplomacy. To date, however, Burton's techniques have not been tested adequately.

3   Overview
Social conflict is an extremely complex matter, and our understanding of it is far from complete at any level.

D   Looking Ahead

1   Interview: Lewis A Coser
2   Interview: Johan Galtung
3   Interview: John Burton

SUPPORTING UNITS

3   Biology and Society
11   Small Groups
15   Race and Ethnic Relations
17   Urban Society
21   Sociology of Economics
22   Deviance
23   Criminology

ENCYCLOPEDIA ENTRIES

anarchy
automation
conflict theory
deprivation-frustration-aggression theory
dual society
evolutionary change
imperialism
interest group
migration
nationalism
poverty, culture of
rising expectations
role conflict
social change
social conflict
status
Third World

CONFLICT AND SOCIAL EQUILIBRIUM

There are many possible dimensions along which societies can experience internal conflict.
Religious divisions and political divisions are two major ones.

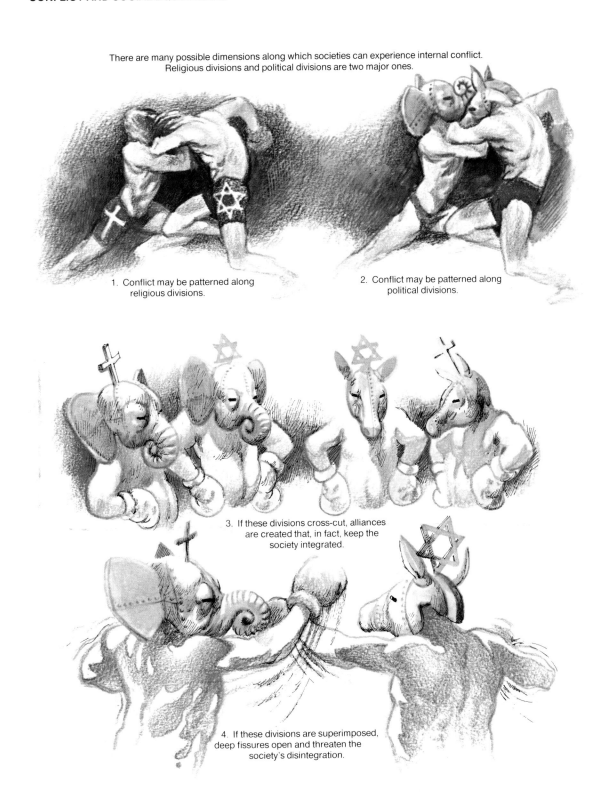

1. Conflict may be patterned along
   religious divisions.

2. Conflict may be patterned along
   political divisions.

3. If these divisions cross-cut, alliances
   are created that, in fact, keep the
   society integrated.

4. If these divisions are superimposed,
   deep fissures open and threaten the
   society's disintegration.

B   DEFINITION AND CONTEXT

1   Definition

There are two important reasons why the study of social conflict is of considerable importance. First, however undesirable social conflict may be, and however much men have attempted to design societies (called *utopias*) that would be conflict-free, it has remained ubiquitous in human life. Second, in order to attain peaceful relationships between people and nations, some understanding of the nature of conflict is essential.

"Conflict" and "peace" are everyday words that have special meanings in sociology. For example, conflict is sometimes confused with related concepts of violence or competition. In the *International Encyclopedia of the Social Sciences* Lewis Coser provides this definition: *Social conflict is "a struggle over values or claims to status, power, and scarce resources in which the aims of the conflicting parties are not only to gain the desired values, but also to neutralize, injure or eliminate their rivals."* Consider a foot race: as

Figure 1. Relationship Among the Concepts of Violence, Conflict, and Peace.

Spy Vs. Spy.

long as the runners compete for the prize without attempting to sabotage or push their rivals, it is an example of *competition* and not of conflict. Conflict and violence are also distinct concepts.

It is true that the most dramatic instances of conflict, such as riots and wars, involve violence, but it is also true that much of the conflict that characterizes human societies does not. Two rival lovers may use various stratagems to neutralize each other in their quest for the affections of a particular woman, but only rarely does their conflict involve violence. Labor conflict in the United States these days usually involves the ''neutralization'' of business firms by strikes without attacks on the firms' property or the persons of other workers. And, of course, violence as extreme as murder may be an act totally unrelated to ''a struggle over values,'' ''status,'' or ''scarce resources.''

The word ''peace'' is slightly more difficult to define because it is so emotionally charged. Every politician feels bound to stress his dedication to peace, however ruthless his policies may prove to be. Johan Galtung, a Norwegian peace researcher, has made a useful distinction in the *International Encyclopedia*. He defines *negative peace* as *''the absence of organized violence between . . . human groups''* and *positive peace* as *''a pattern of cooperation and integration between major human groups.''* Although ''peace'' is customarily used to refer to peaceful relationships between nations, it can characterize human relationships at every level, and it will be used in that broad sense in this unit.

Sociologists are increasingly coming to realize that conflict has been and probably will be a continuing factor in human social life, and that it is not necessarily destructive to society. The plain fact is that the interests of individuals and groups simply do not coincide much of the time. However, *violent* conflict need not be a constant factor in future human social life, despite the experiences of the past. Much of the effort of those sociologists engaged in peace research (or, as it is sometimes called, *conflict resolution* research) is directed toward understanding the conditions under which conflict may be kept from becoming violent. Nor does the level of conflict in a society like ours have to remain the same. These same sociologists are seeking to identify those conditions which lead to the absence of conflict—that is, peace.

2   World Context

During the twentieth century, as throughout man's history, there have been distressingly many violent conflict-relationships and all too few peaceful ones, especially of the positive kind. Leaving aside the relatively recent wars and hostilities that have been most in the public eye (Vietnam, the Arab-Israeli hostilities, and the Soviet invasions of Czechoslovakia and Hungary), over 150 armed clashes large enough to draw concerned international attention have occurred between nations since the end of World War II. In this same period, violent conflicts within nations have taken place in most parts of the world. Some of these have been wars of liberation from colonial oppression; others—for example, the violent situation in Northern Ireland between Catholics and Protestants—have resulted from religious conflict superimposed on competing nationalisms; and

still others—such as the Nigerian civil war (''Biafran War'') and the conflict preceding the Indian invasion of East Pakistan, which led to the creation of the new nation of Bangladesh—have been rooted in ethnic conflict. The conflict in industrial and industrializing nations between workers and owners has generally been resolved without violence, but the May 1968 French students' rebellion, which raised the barricades in Paris for several weeks, gained the mass support of French workers for a time and illustrates the potential for economic conflict to escalate into violence. It is likely that in the next decade or so poverty will become a growing basis of conflict both between nations and between the deprived and the elite within various nations.

Although violent conflict tends to dominate the headlines, conflict without violence is widespread and prevalent in the world today. One well-known form of nonviolent conflict is the Cold War between the ''free world'' and the Communist-governed nations. Billions of dollars for the military are spent by the major world powers each year to maintain a balance of power. Rivalry in international trade often appears to be more a form of conflict than of competi-

Biafran war *(above)* and French student-worker revolt *(right)*: two recent significant examples of violent situations taking place within the borders of the particular country involved. In 1966 the Ibo people attempted to split away from Nigeria, whose government was then controlled by the Hausa people, and form the new state of Biafra. The resulting civil war lasted three years and ended in defeat and mass starvation for hundreds of thousands of Ibos. In France in May 1968 a protest by students at the University of Nanterre about conditions there rapidly escalated within one month to a nationwide general strike by students and workers in an alliance that paralyzed the economy, brought the DeGaulle government to the brink of collapse, and for the first time in many years raised the possibility of revolution within a Western industrial country. The photo here depicts students at the Sorbonne in Paris with pictures of Mao Tsetung and other Marxist leaders. Surprisingly, only five persons died during the weeks of mass upheaval in France.

Striking auto workers at Ford River Rouge plant hurl bricks at non-strikers trying to get into plant. This 1941 strike led to the unionization of the Ford Motor Company, after decades of bitter—sometimes violent—opposition to unions by the large corporation.

tion—especially in recent years, when the value of the dollar has been under intense pressure. Conflict over the world's resources is increasing year by year. For example, fisheries in waters claimed by many nations to be international are being dangerously depleted by competing fishing fleets, and oil reserves are being exhausted by the industrial nations far more rapidly than new oil fields are being found or new sources of power are being developed.

Efforts to create peaceful relationships within and between nations have also characterized the period since World War II. In Western Europe, for example, the gradually expanding European Common Market is felt by its members to be both a guarantee against violence among the member nations and also a vehicle for mutual enrichment and support. The United Nations, which was created as an institutional mechanism to help bring about peace, has, at the very least, been able to foster negative peace. An ever-growing number of world multinational organizations, such as the International Monetary Fund and the United Nations Conference on the Environment, provide a context for reducing conflict in various areas to the level of competition.

3   American Context

Conflict has characterized our society since the first settlers dealt with the native Americans, the Indians, and, by violent and nonviolent means, ultimately deprived them of their land and the means to continue their way of life. The birth of the United States was the result of a colonial rebellion, and the establishment of the American social order involved continual conflict between groups with various economic, religious, ethnic, and ideological interests. Frequently this conflict became violent, as in the Civil War and in the decades of labor violence that preceded the acceptance of labor unions.

The amount and type of conflict in America have varied considerably over its history. To use labor conflict as an example, the number of strikes as well as the number of workers involved in the

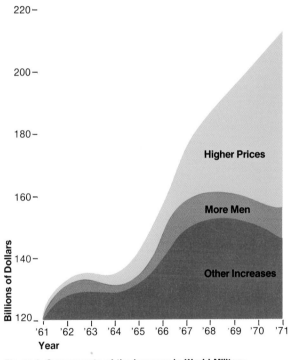

Figure 2. Components of the Increase in World Military Expenditures 1961–1971. On a worldwide basis prices increased an estimated 4 percent per year between 1961 and 1971. This increase accounts for the cost of actual expenditure (top line) above increases in spending for men (4 million added to world military forces) and technology. Most of the "real cost" increase has been due to investments in new technology and the accumulation of more sophisticated armaments. (Source: U.S. Arms Control and Disarmament Agency, *World Military Expenditures, 1971*)

strikes has risen and fallen over the years according to economic conditions and the pattern of contract negotiations. There has been a distinct shift in the type of labor conflict in the United States over the past century, however. Throughout the nineteenth and early twentieth centuries, management rejected the right of unions to strike, and violent conflict was often part of labor-management disputes. The general trend has been toward the reduction of violence as the right to form labor unions and to strike has become a legally recognized form of conflict. Today, in fact, even the long-fought-for right to strike is being voluntarily rescinded by some unions in favor of compulsory arbitration between labor and management.

Race relations in the United States show a different pattern and illustrate some important characteristics of conflict and peaceful relations. In many respects the mass of black people were not involved in overt challenges to discrimination in American life until the civil rights movement began in the 1950s. Of course, there had always been some protest by individuals and groups, but it was undertaken in difficult circumstances and against extreme odds. Especially in the South the lack of overt rebellion and protest on the part of the Southern blacks was due to the acute and pervasive white repression of them, as dramatically demonstrated by the many lynchings in the years following Reconstruction. Obviously blacks were not satisfied with the status quo and when the opportunity to overcome white power arose, this covert conflict broke into the open and, in contrast to labor-management conflict, has become more rather than less violent in recent decades. (See Units 9, 15, 20.)

This development pointedly raises a value question about conflict itself. Some Americans criticized the Rev. Dr. Martin Luther King, Jr., and other black leaders for "creating trouble and provoking violence." Many other observers have argued that American blacks could attain justice through direct conflict and have praised King's strategy for emphasizing *nonviolent techniques.* Other American leaders of movements of the oppressed, such as George Washington, have resorted to violence as the only form of conflict that would result in justice. These protesters (blacks, American revolutionaries) could not get what they considered to be their rightful power and share of scarce resources because their antagonists (whites, the British) sought to "neutralize, injure or eliminate" them when they tried. The sociological point here is that *conflict is not necessarily undesirable; nor is peace, in situations of injustice, necessarily desirable.*

Yet, even though American society is characterized by conflict relations between many individuals and subgroups, it does not tear itself apart. The many separate conflicts have not become one large conflict. In fact, large complex societies such as the United States are often characterized by *cross-cutting cleavages.* Catholic and Protestant may work side by side and even be members of the same ethnic group. Such *multiple affiliations* may sometimes lead people to oppose others in certain circumstances whom they regard as allies in other circumstances. *Pluralist societies,* which are characterized by a number of different ethnic, economic, and social groups, tend to be able to tolerate a fair amount of conflict without major upheaval. On the other hand, when *bases of conflict* become

(Facing page) Martin Luther King, Jr., was a charismatic leader who achieved significant social change while leading a nonviolent political movement for civil rights for blacks. It is possible, however, that the changes he wrought were at least partially the result of the threat of violence by more radical black activists; it was in the interest of the dominant white society to meet some of King's demands so as to "cool off" the more radical wing of the black movement. King himself died a victim of violence. He was assassinated by a white man in Memphis, Tennessee in 1968, while assisting a strike of sanitation workers.

I have a dream

Dr. King stares through the rain-spattered window of a police car after his arrest in Birmingham.

superimposed, a *fundamental division* of society as a result of conflict becomes much more possible.

Much of the strength of American society comes from its plural character. In addition, certain institutions, such as Congress and the Supreme Court, balance interests and tend to prevent possible types of conflict from building up and reinforcing each other to the point where the United States might be split into two or more warring camps. Among the other factors that have in the past facilitated the ability of American society to handle conflict and to promote peace, at least of the negative kind, are the capacity of the society to adapt to new conditions (such as the Depression) through political, legislative, and economic changes (such as the New Deal) and the widespread public acceptance of the legitimacy of the power of the police as well as respect for the "rule of law."

C   QUESTIONS AND EVIDENCE

1   Questions

Three questions cover a variety of social contexts: (1) Why did some ghetto residents and not others participate in the riots in American cities in the 1960s? (2) What is the role of conflict in human societies? (3) Is it possible to solve international conflicts by social-science diplomacy?

2   Evidence

a   The "Burning Issue" Question

i   Context   Several hundred lives were lost and millions of dollars worth of urban property was destroyed in the series of riots by blacks that occurred in many major American cities in the 1960s. After the disturbances in Los Angeles' Watts district in 1965, black residents in city after city were provoked into rage by incidents that sparked community reactions. Rampaging through the ghettos, they overturned cars, burned buildings, and looted stores. Such relatively short-lived movements—including religious revivals, programs for political reform, and revolutions as well as riots—are called *collective behavior* by sociologists.

The Kerner Commission, which was set up by President Lyndon Johnson to investigate the riots of the 1960s, reported that white racism and the conditions imposed on blacks were the fundamental causes. But this exploration does not deal with a much more specific issue. Sociologists are eager to comprehend the conditions and motives that lead people to take part in such a form of protest. By gaining some understanding of the process of social protest, they can learn something about collective behavior and violent conflict in general. They ask: *What special set of social factors produces the sudden emergence of riot behavior?*

ii   Theory   Ted Robert Gurr, a political scientist who has written much on violent conflict both in developing nations and in the American cities, argues that the sociological and popular cliché that frustration or discontent or despair are the causes of riots is fundamentally true. Relative rather than absolute deprivation characterizes

"Hard hats" march in New York City. The war in Vietnam spawned violence within the United States also. In May 1970 construction workers brutally assaulted antiwar demonstrators in New York City and engaged in several of what they called "pro-American" demonstrations. The police refused to intervene in the beatings until after the fact. Ironically, many of the "hard hats" stated that they were demonstrating because of their opposition to violence, which they identified with antiwar and campus demonstrations. These clashes led some observers to feel for a time that American society was on the brink of irreparable internal strife between blue-collar workers and middle-class youth.

the kind of discontent that triggers violent conflict according to the theoretical perspective Gurr develops in "Urban Disorder" (1968). *Absolute deprivation* describes the state of those who are poorest; *relative deprivation* refers to people who feel deprived in terms of what other people have.

Those who are relatively well-off may actually *feel* more deprived than those who are on the bottom. Gurr describes the process by which this deprivation leads to violent conflict:

> Underlying this relative deprivation approach to civil strife is a frustration-aggression mechanism, apparently a fundamental part of our psychological make-up. When we feel thwarted in an attempt to get something we want, we are likely to get angry, and when we get angry the most satisfying inherent response is to strike out at the source of frustration.

This *deprivation-frustration-aggression theory* can be applied directly to the situation in black ghettos. Ghetto blacks have been deprived economically, culturally, educationally, and in terms of their opportunities for a decent home and a safe environment. They realize the extent of their deprivation when they compare their situation with that of the middle-class white people shown to them in newspapers, magazines, and especially television ads and programs. Hence a high level of *relative* discontent may be characteristic of them.

Frustration was further promoted in the 1960s as black leaders directly highlighted inequities and criticized the white power structure, which failed to respond with improvements in the status of blacks or any decrease in the observed inequities. The particular riots, according to this theory, were triggered by specific blatant incidents of oppression or discrimination (such as police brutality) that occurred in public and led to confrontation.

iii Research   Several studies of city characteristics (such as average income in black census districts) have predicted that the worse the objective situation of blacks in the city, the greater the likelihood of a riot. The assumption here is that absolute deprivation measured in overall terms will indicate situations where blacks will be more frustrated and thus more prone to riot. In "The Causes of Racial Disturbances" (1970), Seymour Spilerman reviewed these studies and concluded that when the cities' black population size was taken into account, the deprivation theory did not work. As he put it, for the cities studied "differences in disorder-proneness cannot be explained in terms of variations in the objective situation of the Negro."

Spilerman made the logical suggestion that the best way to test the deprivation-frustration-aggression theory is to analyze the *behavior of individuals* instead of *city characteristics* to see if individuals participating in riots were more deprived and more frustrated than those who did not. Despite the difficulties of this kind of research, a number of careful studies of individual rioters have in fact been conducted. Ten of them examined individual participation in five different riots—Los Angeles (Watts area), 1965; Omaha, 1966; Detroit, 1967; Milwaukee, 1967; and Newark, 1967—and used a number of different sampling and interviewing techniques to

(Above right) Chronic poverty and relative deprivation. Chronic poverty is the womb of social conflict in the richest nation in the world. What is the experience of being *in* a wealthy society but not *of* it?

The riot in the Watts area of Los Angeles in 1965 is a clear example of some important aspects of collective behavior. The weather at the time was very hot, and thus an unusually large number of people were on the street and witnessed a routine arrest for drunken driving. The driver's mother arrived on the scene and became belligerent as the police began to take her son away. Gradually, the situation became more charged with emotion; the size of the crowd increased, and it focused its attention fully on the struggle between the police and the driver and his mother. All that was needed for an eruption was for one person to commit an overt act of violence. Someone did, and the crowd followed his example. Although many residents of Watts took part in the rioting and looting that followed, many others stood by and watched in bewilderment. Why did some riot and others not?

ask a wide variety of questions. All 10 studies depended on the deprivation-frustration-aggression theory as part of their explanatory framework, but, unfortunately, few of them asked about deprivation and frustration in the same way. Clark McPhail subsequently examined the 10 different reports in detail and concluded that on the whole their data did not support the deprivation-frustration-aggression theory ("Civil Disorder Participation," 1971). For example, five of the 13 strong relationships reported between deprivation and riot participation involved attitudes toward the police that were influenced by the fact that people were interviewed after they had been arrested.

iv Evaluation There is surprisingly little empirical support for the deprivation-frustration-aggression theory as an explanation for participation in these riots. Further testing will be required to determine whether the theory is still applicable to other areas of human conflict.

The deprivation-frustration-aggression theory is but one of several theoretical approaches to the explanation of riot behavior. Some sociologists have sought to explain riots by an examination of structural factors that differentiate riot cities from comparable nonriot cities. These variables include unemployment level, percentage of black store owners, and black policemen per thousand blacks. Another approach explains participation in violent conflict of this particular type in terms of the availability of certain kinds of people to take part in the riot. Rioters characteristically have been male and black and younger in age and lower in education than comparable nonrioters. McPhail points out that these are the characteristics of people who are more likely to be out of work and "hanging around" and thus available to take part in the riot when it suddenly starts. And, of course, in a sense they have the least to lose by participation. At the present time none of these alternative approaches has been demonstrated to be an unequivocally satisfactory explanation.

b The "Classical" Question

i Context Unit 26 discussed the question of whether the *conflict* or the *functionalist* approach was better able to account for social change. Taking this issue further, one can ask: What is the role of conflict in human societies—is it an aberration, or is it a fundamental, inescapable aspect of social life? In short: *Is conflict a necessary variable in human interaction?*

ii Theory Basically the conflict model or theory involves a set of assumptions about the role of conflict. These can be summarized as follows:

1. Conflict is very common in societies—so common that it is not the presence of conflict, but its absence which is surprising and abnormal.
2. As a result of the ubiquity of conflict, societies are at every moment subject to change.
3. Conflict is so ubiquitous that every element in society contributes to its change.
4. The social order rests on the constraint of some individuals and groups by others.

Clearly in this image of society tension and strife, but not necessarily violence, are part of the normal state of affairs. When groups and individuals have various interests, some of them contradictory, that lead them to oppose each other, change is simply a natural outcome of the push and pull of life. Power relationships always underlie the apparent harmony of the society and must be taken into account in sociological analysis.

The conflict model is not new to social thought, as we know from earlier units. Thomas Hobbes' "war of all against all" involved conflict assumptions, as did Karl Marx's postulation of the centrality and universality of *class conflict* in societies. Sixty-five years ago the German sociologist Georg Simmel wrote in his important essay "Conflict," "There probably exists no social unit in which convergent and divergent currents among its members are not inseparable, interwoven," and went on to analyze the role of conflict with considerable subtlety and depth.

After 1930 the conflict model was largely disregarded as sociologists and anthropologists pursued the implications of a new and exciting theoretical breakthrough, functionalist theory. Functionalists such as Kingsley Davis, Robert Merton, and especially Talcott Parsons dominated the relatively small number of sociological theorists. We have dealt with important aspects of functionalism in Units 4, 9, 20, 21, 22, and 26.

Very briefly, the dominant functionalist approach (of the consensus type) may be said to involve the following assumptions:

1. Every society is a system of interdependent parts. The elements of society are interconnected so that an event in one part of society has repercussions in many other parts of the society.

	Magnitude of Association						
	n.s.	0.00 0.09	0.10 0.19	0.20 0.29	0.30 0.39	0.40 +	Total
Deprivation							
Total	19	2	20	7	1	1	50
Percentage	38%	4%	40%	14%	2%	2%	100%
Frustration							
Total	19	3	34	18	9	1	84
Percentage	23%	4%	40%	21%	11%	1%	100%
Deprivation and Frustration							
Total	17		13	8		1	39
Percentage	43%		33%	20%		3%	100%
Total	55	5	67	33	10	3	173
Percentage	32%	3%	39%	19%	6%	1%	100%

Table 1. Magnitude of Association of Aggression-Deprivation-Frustration With Riot Participation. This table reports McPhail's statistical associations bearing on the deprivation-frustration-aggression (DFA) theory. Of the 173 (total in right-hand corner) associations, 50 are between various measures of deprivation and riot participation; 84 are between various measures of frustrations and riot participation; and 39 are between combined measures of deprivation and frustration and riot participation. Deprivation measures included such items as education, income, and personal experience of police malpractice. Most of the frustration measures dealt with the attitudes and expectations of the respondents (for example, regarding whites). The combined measures dealt with both experience of and opinion about such things as police malpractice. Of the 50 tests of the association of deprivation and riot participation, only two (4 percent) were of moderate magnitude of significance (a magnitude association of 0.30 or more). Of the 84 tests of the association of frustration with riot participation, only 10 (12 percent) were of moderate magnitude. Of the 39 tests of the association of deprivation and frustration with riot participation, only one (3 percent) was of moderate magnitude. Finally, of the total 173 associations bearing on the DFA theory, 32 percent were not significant. 61 percent of the associations were of a low magnitude (0.01 to 0.29), and 7 percent were of moderate magnitude. Thus, statistical support for the DFA theory is not very strong, because most of the associations were of a low magnitude of significance. (Source: McPhail, "Civil Disorder Participation")

For example, the introduction of the automobile has had enormous ramifications for the economic, social, and political life of the United States.

2. Each of these parts contributes to the functioning of society. Therefore, social analysis tries to answer the question: What function does this or that part of society have for the overall maintenance of the society? The function of presidential inaugurations, for instance, may be said to reinforce the legitimacy of the office of the presidency after an election.

3. Social systems have a strong tendency to maintain an equilibrium. A disturbance in society may result in a temporary change, but the system will generally return to its original equilibrium.

4. There is general agreement among actors in a social system on a certain set of social assumptions and values. This consensus on such matters as justice, equality, and the importance of religion is an important glue holding society together.

In the 1950s, however, Georg Simmel's work was "rediscovered" with Kurt Wolff's translation of *Conflict* in 1955 and Lewis Coser's systematization of many of Simmel's insights in his *The Functions of Social Conflict* (1956). At the same time there was a reaction against the functionalist assumptions, which seemed to support and justify the existing social order uncritically. C. Wright Mills' *The Sociological Imagination* (1959) and Ralf Dahrendorf's *Class and Class Conflict in Industrial Society* (1957) were very influential works of this type; they both looked to Karl Marx for inspiration but did not hesitate to criticize those aspects of Marx's thought that they deemed inapplicable to present social conditions. Finally, peace researchers and others, such as the sociologist of education and adolescence James S. Coleman, who wrote a short monograph, *Community Conflict* (1957), found social conflict an indispensable concept for their sociological analysis.

Clearly the functionalist assumptions about the role of conflict in society are the opposite of the conflict assumptions. To the pure functionalist, conflict is not a normal social characteristic, and society tends toward eliminating and reducing it whenever it occurs. Conflict is essentially unhealthy for society.

In contrast, to the conflict theorist conflict is by no means necessarily disruptive. It may create cohesion among the members of a society in the face of a common enemy. It may also promote the long-term health of society by forcing the direct consideration of problems that require solution. If ignored, such problems may erupt later in a much more severe and disruptive form.

The pure functionalist assumption of *shared common values* is sharply opposed by theorists such as Ralf Dahrendorf, who argues in "Out of Utopia" (1967) that only an ideal state enjoys such *cultural homogeneity*. The reality of social life is the inevitably clashing sets of individual and group interests. The ultimate glue holding society together for the conflict theorists is *coercion by force*.

iii   Research (Survey)   In one of the few attempts to test the relative merit of the functionalist and conflict approaches with empirical data, sociologist Randall Collins developed competing explanations

Talcott Parsons (b. 1902), functionalist theorist. Parsons is generally considered the "dean" of the American "sociological establishment," which portrays society as an equilibrium-seeking system. Critics charge that this perspective does not enable scholars to account adequately for the continuing presence of social conflict.

for the ever-rising educational requirements for job employment in the United States. A functionalist, arguing from the assumption that the needs of society determine the behavior and rewards of the individuals in society, would conclude that rapid technological change raises the skill requirements of jobs and therefore that people need progressively more education to fill these jobs successfully. (See Units 9, 13, 15, 18, 21.) A conflict theorist, arguing that status groups (such as Catholics or blacks) tend to occupy different occupational positions and that the occupants of the positions struggle over power, would conclude the educational demands of any occupational position are not fixed but vary according to the "bargaining" between persons who fill the positions and those who attempt to control them.

Collins examined such findings as: (1) 60 to 70 percent of the American business elite come from upper and upper-middle-class families; (2) these proportions held fairly constant from the 1800s to the 1950s; (3) sexual stereotyping of jobs is very widespread; (4) the educational level of the United States labor force has changed *in excess* of that which is necessary to keep up with skill requirements of jobs; and (5) better-educated employees are not generally more productive. He concluded that education requirements for employment primarily reflect employers' concerns for acquiring respectable and well-socialized employees; only secondarily do they ensure the provision of needed technical skills. ("Functional and Conflict Theories of Educational Stratification," 1971)

iv Evaluation Collins' study suggests that employers "neutralize" prospective employees of status groups different from their own by imposing arbitrarily high educational standards that ensure (1) that members of the dominant WASP (white Anglo-Saxon Protestant) group who have greater access to the best schools and the highest levels of education have the best chance for employment, and (2) that those members of other groups who do meet the educational requirements are socialized through the schools they attend into the dominant WASP way of life. Conflict plays a central role in society, therefore, even in an area where the functionalist model appeared to provide a satisfactory explanation.

Unfortunately, there are so few empirical studies comparable to Collins' that we cannot at this time define the degree to which conflict is fundamental to the life of society in any precise sense. It is clear that jobs do in part present technical requirements that require a certain level of education, so the power arrangements of status groups do not provide the whole explanation. This suggests that, although social conflict plays an *important* role in society, it cannot account for *all* of social life.

Dahrendorf endorses this perspective. He explicitly states that he does not claim for the conflict model "comprehensive and exclusive applicability":

> As far as I can see, we need for the explanation of sociological problems both the equilibrium and the conflict models of society; and it may well be that, in a philosophical sense, society has two faces of equal reality: one of stability, harmony, and consensus and one of change, conflict and restraint. ("Out of Utopia," 1967)

629

Indeed, Dahrendorf's work, and that of many conflict theorists, may be seen as an attempt to redress the imbalance created by the recent functionalist dominance of sociological theory.

c   The "Research" Question

i   Context   Following World War II a small group of social scientists from a number of countries sought a way to mitigate the Cold War and promote international understanding through the study of the causes of international conflict. In the ensuing decades various approaches to the study of peace gradually developed. They included: the *arms race approach,* a concept based on correlational analysis of data on national arms expenditures and international hostilities, developed by L. F. Richardson, British meteorologist, in *Arms and Insecurity;* the application of *game theory* to international conflict by Anatol Rapoport, mathematical biologist, in *Fights, Games and Debates,* among other works; and the application of *general systems theory* to international conflict by economist Kenneth Boulding in *Conflict and Defense.*

A relatively new approach, which might be termed *social-science diplomacy,* perhaps comes closest to linking academic theory with positive peace action and relating the public to the private sectors of society. Perhaps the best-known proponent of this approach is John Burton, Director of the Center for Analysis of Conflict at the University of London. Previously a high official of the Australian Ministry of External Affairs, Burton became disillusioned with conventional diplomacy as a means of resolving conflict and maintaining peace. He and a number of important sociologists have directed attention to the question: *Can violence be totally eliminated from conflict among nations?*

ii   Theory   Burton's basic hypothesis is that conflict behavior of individuals or groups, including nations, comprises *alterable components,* such as perception of external circumstances, the attitudes of opponents, goals, values, and the cost of the conflict. He further hypothesizes that conflict is largely *subjective* and therefore that understanding and direct experience can alter subjective perceptions and thereby change relationships.

According to this theory, the basic problem is *communication.* Burton believes that if the parties to a dispute are exposed to relevant information as well as to each other, they will see their own attitudes and behavior as illustrations of conflict theory, appreciate their own subjectivity, and thus change toward each other. The "relevant information" includes ideas about conflict resolution developed by social scientists connected with the peace research. For example, persons involved in violent conflict tend to believe that no other groups have ever been so oppressed and maltreated, have ever had such treacherous and bloodthirsty opponents; if the opposing parties can come to see that the unique features of their case are in fact universal, they may make a first short step in the direction of objectivity and accurate perception.

Emphasis on the fact that some conflicts have been resolved adds a further element of hope. In much international negotiation peace moves are doomed before they are even initiated because each side is so locked into suspicions of the other that any proposal, however sincere and sensible, is rejected out of hand as

North Vietnam
No figures available

Cambodia
1970 (from April). . . .
　　　　　1,000,000
1971 600,000
1972 400,000
　　　(through Oct.)

Laos
1964 130,000
1965 129,000
1966 128,000
1967 118,000
1968 137,000
1969 240,000
1970 270,000
1971 234,200
1972 268,400

South Vietnam
1964–66 .2,400,000
1967 463,000
1968 2,144,000
1969 590,000
1970 410,000
1971 136,000
1972 1,288,800
In camps as 1973 began 641,000

Figure 3. Refugees From the Indochina War. The figures depict just one aspect of suffering of just one war. There have been many wars in the twentieth century, and each war has had many aspects of suffering. (Source: *New York Times,* Jan. 31, 1973; from U.S. Agency for International Development and Cambodian government.)

Antiwar poster stamps of the 1930s. When will it ever end?

a trick. But some dawning comprehension of how groups behave and feel in conflict situations helps them to see that their own problems may not be insoluble. For example, they become aware of the *mirror image effect,* in which each side says of itself, "We are honorable and peaceloving people," and of the other, "They are savages solely bent on our destruction."

Burton's proposed technique for resolving international violent conflict is to remove discussion from the realm of political diplomacy into that of social science. Representatives of conflicting nations or groups are to be brought together in a completely neutral atmosphere for a seminar, with the nominal purpose of helping a group of social scientists learn more about the fundamental nature of conflict. The social scientists need not be particularly well informed about the specific issues, but they must be well versed in conflict theory and prepared with specific questions they wish to put to a group of people actually engaged in the conflict.

iii   Research (Methodology)   Thus far, only twice has Burton managed to bring contestants in violent struggles into his neutral setting where social scientists could make interpretations and comments. In one instance the struggle was international, in the other it was racial and religious, with international implications.

Given the fact that conflict situations are so tense and complex that even the most delicate and well-planned approaches can easily be disrupted by extraneous factors, it is not surprising that the results of his two experiments were mixed. On one occasion his theory was confirmed, to the extent that the conflict was resolved in a fashion that suggested that the meetings had been helpful. The other case was not so successful, and the conflict was not resolved.

iv   Evaluation   Many more cases are needed before the Burton approach can be adequately tested, of course. But social research in such "real world" situations is extremely difficult to carry out. Parties in desperate situations develop an almost paranoid aversion to contact with their enemies, and any sort of meeting seems to them to be dangerous. For this reason, dozens of invitations to take part in Burton's experiments have been turned down.

Burton has observed that if people were as interested in research on peace as in research on war, and if his work had been lavishly financed by foundations so that he could have provided luxurious facilities in an elegant and affluent setting, his invitations would have been taken more seriously. He continues, nevertheless, to work in this field, convinced that he has developed an original and pragmatic approach to conflict resolution.

3   Overview

Important though social conflict is to our understanding of society, our understanding of it is far from precise. The major achievements have been the reincorporation of the conflict perspective into the mainstream of sociological thought and the questioning of some of the weaker and less tenable assumptions of functionalism. There is, however, still no conflict theory in the sense of interrelated, testable propositions at a reasonable level of abstraction. Nor has any new synthesis of the functionalist and conflict perspectives gained wide acceptance.

The situation is no better at the middle-range level. The deprivation-frustration-aggression theory has gained rather wide currency as a way of understanding violent conflict behavior, but empirical research suggests that either it must be revised or another theory will have to be developed to explain riot behavior more adequately.

Finally, at the level of practice, the major achievement in recent years is simply the fact that such researchers as Burton are attempting to test ideas about the resolution of international conflict through scientific research. It is far too early to expect definitive results from such experiments, however.

An extremely wide range of behavior is subsumed under the concept of social conflict. Moreover, much conflict behavior, especially of the violent kind, erupts suddenly and runs its course swiftly. Finally, social conflict is a highly sensitive area of social life. Thus it is extremely difficult for the social scientist to study this topic with reasonable precision and objectivity.

D   LOOKING AHEAD

1   Interview:
Lewis A. Coser

Lewis A. Coser is Distinguished Professor of Sociology at the State University of New York at Stony Brook. His numerous works include *The Functions of Social Conflict, Sociological Theory* (with Rosenberg), *The American Communist Party* (with Howe), *Sociology Through Literature* (ed.), *Political Sociology* (ed.), *Continuities in the Study of Social Conflict,* and *Masters of Sociological Thought.* He is currently researching the sociology of publishing.

DPG   *Is there really a theory of social conflict, or just a theoretical perspective?*
COSER   Above all it's a theoretical perspective—a way of looking at the world. It sensitizes one to the fact that most social systems (even though there are common norms, consensual validations, and the like) also contain clashing and contending interests. We have made some progress toward one, but I don't think there is *a* theory of social conflict.

DPG   *Has conflict theory ever been helpful in understanding conflict in the early stages or in predicting its future course?*
COSER   It would have been easy to conceptualize what was going to happen on the racial and ethnic front 15 years ago if sociologists had translated the Marxist categories of worker versus management into racial upper class versus racial lower class. But Marxism was in bad repute until recently. People relied exclusively on the goody-goody theory that these conflicts could all be solved by better understanding. If sociologists had seen that these were real interests and power differentials at play, accurate predictions might have been made.

DPG   *In the last decade there's been a great deal of conflict on campuses. Were sociologists able to predict it?*
COSER   I would love to say that they were able to, but they didn't. I wrote my first book

on conflict, *The Functions of Social Conflict,* in 1954, and it was published in 1956. At that time, it was viewed as a totally maverick work. Nobody took conflict theory very seriously because the dominant idea was consensus theory. My general approach was that conflict was not necessarily a destructive phenomenon—that conflict was an engine of social change. Furthermore, I contended that one simply couldn't understand any society without realizing, even though there were common norms, common values, and so on, that interest groups or professional groups must necessarily clash with others in pursuit of their particular interests. But I wouldn't say that in the book I predicted the emergence of either the racial conflict or the student conflict.

DPG   *Would you say that conflict is very often a prerequisite for real harmony?*
COSER   Without conflict I think we would still be living in caves. The rise of all new salvation religions, scientific or philosophical systems, led to enormous conflict. The natural scientists talk about earthquakes as a natural phenomenon that readjusts the balance of the earth. Without these quakes the whole thing would blow up. I feel that conflict plays a somewhat similar role in social systems.

DPG   *What are the basic conflicts, in your view, in American society today? What conflicts might emerge in the next decade as we advance into what some have called the "postindustrial" society?*
COSER   We'll still be stuck with some of the old conflicts, of course. Race will still represent a major cleavage. Ethnic tensions play a considerably greater role than had been assumed until recently, so there will probably be contentions along those lines. To some extent, there'll be religious conflict. But I think that two newer ones will certainly mark the next 20 or 30 years—the conflict between the young and the old (or the middle-aged) and the conflict between men and women. I think the sex-role conflict, the redefinition of female roles, will probably be most decisive. It means the restructuring of the family, which is the basic nuclear institution of the society. I can even think of easier solutions to the racial conflict (not that they're really easy) than of solutions to the male-female thing.

DPG *Have Americans made any improvements in our approach to reducing conflict or managing conflict in the last 50 years?*

COSER From my point of view improvement does not mean doing away with conflict, but carrying on the conflict in relatively civilized, nonviolent forms. On that level we have made progress in the labor-management area. Labor-management contentions around the turn of the century were disorganized and exceedingly bloody; the police or the Pinkertons intervened on the side of management. Today management, by and large, has accepted the existence of unions, and it normally does not try to repress working-class movements in any drastic way. Conflict is carried on in a somewhat more civilized form. With regard to racial conflicts, progress is slower, but if you think of race relations in Alabama 15 years ago, the situation today represents a change for the better.

DPG *Have social science findings been absorbed and utilized by the establishment institutions in power in society?*

COSER That's a very complicated question. Social-science ideas certainly don't feed into the system as quickly as discoveries in the natural sciences, for example. Policymakers in Washington don't take out sociology textbooks and learn from them. Social science probably has the greatest impact indirectly through popularized accounts by people like Vance Packard. In that way ideas seep into both the general class of readers and elite groups. I think the input of social science into law, for example, has been quite significant. Several key Supreme Court decisions, for example, the school desegregation decision, were clearly based on social-science findings by scholars such as Kenneth Clark. On the other hand, a policymaker will often ask social scientists to work out a model program of doing something about poverty or community development. Then the project is executed. A nice report is delivered to the decision-maker. And nothing happens. It's largely a political decision, but it's also related to the fear of upsetting bureaucratic routines. On the other hand, many sociologists present their findings on such a high level of abstraction that the policy-maker simply doesn't know how to apply them.

DPG *Do you think it's utopian to expect that it's possible for human beings to develop social patterns that do not involve exploitation and conflict?*

COSER I would draw a distinction between exploitation and conflict. I can imagine a nonexploitative society (not that we are very near it), but I cannot imagine a society without conflict. I would love to see a society, and it's within the realm of the possible, where people don't have to engage in conflict about their daily bread, about the ordinary requirements for a decent living. These low-level conflicts won't appear, so people will have a chance to fight about the real issues: philosophy, morality, ethics, aesthetics, and so on. There are also issues that involve a time dimension. Do you want to have many good things right now or do you forgo some of your immediate satisfactions in favor of a later generation? That issue comes up in all planned economies. You deny the citizens a lot of good consumer products now, while you build steel factories that presumably will yield a dividend 30 years later. That kind of issue, I think, will still divide people after the conflicts over obtaining ordinary subsistence are solved.

DPG *What is the possible role of social scientists in conflict resolution?*

COSER An applied social scientist might very well serve as an arbiter or moderator or he might seek to eliminate the nonrealistic, emotional aspect of the conflict situation. He might say, "Look, there's real contention between the two parties, but that doesn't mean that you have to see the other as a devil." In other words, you can eliminate much of what the communications people call "noise," so that the channel is clear for a rational discussion of the real issues. But these real issues ultimately will have to be fought out between the parties, although hopefully not with machine guns or bombs. If you look at the evolution of mankind, many things that were once fought over in battles or in duels are now fought over in court. It's a somewhat more civilized way of handling it. More institutions of arbitration might be developed that could fulfill functions similar or complementary to the court. My basic idea, however, is that none of this does away with the conflict. It may channel it. It may civilize it. It may reduce its nonrational aspects. But it doesn't eliminate it.

DPG   *Do you think it is legitimate to use violence to resolve a conflict situation?*

COSER   It makes a great difference to me what kind of society you talk about. In a relatively open society like ours, I think the use of violence in most cases is not only morally repugnant but counterproductive. But if you talk about a totalitarian society where all the legitimate channels for conducting conflict are blocked, then either morally or practically I couldn't say violent conflict is a bad thing. If you have a military dictatorship somewhere in a Latin American republic or, say, South Africa, and people see no other way of doing away with it, that's it.

DPG   *What would you say was at the source of human conflict?*

COSER   I certainly don't go along with Robert Ardrey and other "territorial imperative" people who talk about basic human or animal instincts. One cannot rule out instinctual factors, but they have been modified so largely in the course of human cultural evolution that I think it's very difficult to impute anything very sensible from the behavior of baboons to the behavior of human beings in American culture. Let's simply say that egotistical drives on the part of both individuals and groups of individuals seem to be part of the human makeup. Groups may be even more prone to these drives—people normally fight much harder and often much dirtier when they think that they stand for the group, whether it's a nation or a religious group or an ethnic group, than they do to protect their purely private interests. When medieval knights fought each other, everything was governed by the rules of chivalry, and it was all very beautiful. When they fought the infidels on the Crusades, however, they were absolutely merciless because they fought in the name of the Christian God. And I'm told John Foster Dulles was privately a very moral and nice guy, but when it came to political affairs he represented the nation and was perfectly willing to play dirty pool in Guatemala.

DPG   *Do you think that in the foreseeable future mankind might set up some mechanism of conflict resolution and of peacemaking that could be permanently institutionalized so that we can avoid large-scale violence on the international scene?*

COSER   In some ways the invention of the hydrogen bomb means that large-scale human conflict is no longer possible. The benefits received can never be as high as the suffering inflicted. Of course, the major powers may still "hire" smaller powers to fight their wars by proxy. To a large extent the Vietnamese conflict represented that kind of activity. The Soviet Union and the United States and Communist China knew that they couldn't directly fight over the issue, and none of their policy-makers suggested it. The best they could do was to feed armaments to the poor bastards in Vietnam, and they fought it out for us.

I don't think in our lifetime we will see a world without wars. I don't believe in the lovely idea of world government at all. World government could become a world tyranny, to begin with. And I don't think that a world government would be free from tensions or conflict between the governors.

2 Interview:
Johan Galtung

Johan Galtung holds doctorates in mathematics and sociology and is professor of conflict and peace research and director-general of the International Peace Research Institute at the University of Oslo, Norway. Dr. Galtung is considered one of the world's pioneers in peace research, conflict theory, and the philosophy of science. His major works include *Essays in Peace Research, Volumes I–V; Methodology and Ideology; Theory and Methods of Social Research;* and *The European Community.*

DPG *Is the nation-state an outdated unit whose continued existence necessarily leads to war?*

GALTUNG Historical experience certainly seems to speak against the nation-state on this question. The transition to large-scale aggressive warfare seems to have accompanied the formation of the nation-state and vice versa. Territoriality seems to be the basic factor. The nomadic tribes generally did not engage in aggressive political and economic warfare because, for one thing, they had a much higher level of territorial flexibility than the nation-state does. Another reason is that settlement in the territorial nation-state was accompanied by bureaucratic social organization, social stratification, centralization, and so on. The structure of the nation-state is so similar to the structure of an army that it is not strange that the two go hand in hand.·

DPG *Is there any reason why the similarity in structures should necessarily lead to violence and hostilities?*

GALTUNG Not necessarily. Most of the states in the world are not at war at any given time. There are two possible reasons for this fact. One is the sheer distance between states. That's a negative reason and a rather depressing one, because the simple absence of any kind of contact couldn't be viewed as peace. Furthermore, better means of transportation and communication are gradually making this reason irrelevant. The other reason is that contiguous nation-states can exist in a symbiotic and very equitable relationship, as the Scandinavian countries do.

DPG *Is the relationship between Canada and the United States another example?*

GALTUNG No. I don't see the forty-ninth parallel as a parallel of peace except in the highly special sense that there are no actual direct wars going on. When you note that American investors control 70 to 80 percent of the Canadian economy, the relationship cannot be defined as equitable. An example of a rather equitable relationship would be that of the member countries of the European Common Market. If it hadn't been for the Common Market, I think that Germany would probably have exploited Italy more than it has.

DPG *You have stated that nation-states are structured like armies. Is there something inherent in the nature of hierarchical structure that leads to war and aggression between the hierarchies?*

GALTUNG If the hierarchies are exploitative—in the sense that those who are at the top get much more out of it than those at the bottom—I think that is in itself unpeace. And that's the kind of thing that has to be transformed if society is to be more peaceful. On the other hand, guerrilla warfare shows that it is quite possible to fight wars in nonhierarchical fashion. If all states somehow had a more horizontal organization, they would still be perfectly capable of fighting each other. However, if states had a more horizontal organization and also had good symbiotic relations among themselves, there would be considerably less chance of war.

DPG *What are the fundamentals of symbiotic relationships that would lead to a more peaceful relationship between states?*

GALTUNG In a symbiotic relationship two beings need each other so much that if one of them hits the other, he hits himself. When two countries have such a high level of trade between them that both of them depend on it, for example, they have a symbiotic relationship. Now this kind of relationship is not very easy to achieve in today's world because some nations are very big and some are very small. For example, when Cuba got out of its vertical relationship with the United States, it meant very little to the United States, but it meant a tremendous amount to Cuba. I do not think that we can easily get a more peaceful world unless nation-states become slightly more similar in size, which would mean cutting down the bigger states like the United States and the Soviet Union if possible.

DPG *Must society be fundamentally transformed if peace is to be preserved?*

GALTUNG I think that in many states today the structure depends on preparation for wars in order to survive. The capitalist version depends on the idea of the arms race as some kind of basic tonic that allows the economic system to function. In the state-capitalist version, which applies to the Soviet Union, the Red army and the arms race are used as a social mobilizing instrument (although of a somewhat sluggish variety). China uses to some extent the same technique. They need an outside threat to mobilize people.

DPG *Is there an essential connection between peace and justice?*

GALTUNG I would say that those two terms stand for two things so basically similar that the essential connection between them is logical. I define peace as the absence of violence, and violence is anything that impedes a human being's possibility of self-realization. Injustice is one of the basic ways of impeding people's possibilities of self-realization. For instance, when women are kept much more illiterate than men, there is unpeace at work. When blacks in certain parts of the United States have 10 years lower life expectancy than whites, that is unpeace. When Indians have an average life expectancy of 44 years in the United States, that is unpeace. The terminology is important. These conditions are *not* threats to peace in the sense that blacks and Indians *may* mobilize and start shooting, although that may also happen. The conditions are *in themselves* unpeace, which is a much broader category than conventional war.

DPG *Would you say the use of violence to eliminate conditions of oppression and exploitation is compatible with the pursuit of peace?*

GALTUNG Yes, in extreme cases, cases in which the difference between the living conditions of the high and the low in an exploitative relationship are so extreme that you can actually calculate the very high number of human lives lost through it. Let us say that you have a society where the 10 percent at the top have twice as high life expectancy as the 50 percent at the bottom. South Africa today represents such an extreme case, as did Cuba in 1958, before the revolution. Now if you calculate the number of lives lost through this kind of structural violence, it would be very hard to say that in all such cases direct violence is absolutely incompatible with the pursuit of peace. But, of course, our task is to try to bring about such changes nonviolently.

DPG *Would you say that the differential figures between the white upper 10 percent or whatever versus the black minority in America would constitute a case for justifiable violence?*

GALTUNG To answer that you also have to consider other channels available for achieving the same end. In South Africa, for example, all other channels seem to be entirely blocked. They may be clogged in the United States, but perhaps less deliberately than in South Africa. These channels have to be tried. But then the question arises, of course, of how many generations, perhaps how many centuries the oppressed will have to wait for those channels to be sufficiently open. For instance, how many years does it take before the white majority in the United States will decide by a vote to do something about the situation of the blacks? Let me summarize. I stand very firmly on the idea that a basic task of peace research is to explore nonviolent revolutionary methods—absolutely revolutionary, but also nonviolent. However, I think that in today's world exploitation is so extreme in *some* cases that one cannot exclude resort to direct violence.

DPG *What is the possible role of the social sciences in conflict resolution?*

GALTUNG It depends on what type of conflict you have. If you have a *horizontal* conflict, between equals, then the social scientist might act as a third party to some extent. He might point out possibilities of cooperation or act as a mediator or arbitrator. He might try to reduce violence and attempt to get a productive conflict resolution. In the case of vertical conflict between oppressor and oppressed, I see the social scientist's role as being unequivocally on the side of the oppressed. That means contributing to their level of consciousness and to their understanding of the situation; helping them in finding possibilities; and even participating with them in the battle. If there is a conflict between the Mafia in Sicily and the oppressed peasants, the task of the researcher is not to bring about a compromise between those two. His task is to help the oppressed peasant.

DPG *You seem to be implying a value-oriented social science.*

GALTUNG I think all social science is value-oriented. The social scientist who says that in a case between oppressor and oppressed he should be neutral and objective is in reality on the side of the oppressor. The distinction is not between value-oriented and neutral social science but between honesty and dishonesty. I try to stand for honesty.

3 Interview:
John Burton

John Burton is a former official of the Ministry of Foreign Affairs of Australia who is
now working on the theory and practice of
conflict resolution at the Center for Analysis
of Conflict at the University of London. He
is the author of *Conflict and Communication; Peace Theory; International Relations;
Systems, States, Diplomacy, and Rules;* and
World Society.

DPG *What are your present research interests?*
BURTON My particular interest is conflict,
particularly the inter-state level. But we have
been finding that conflict has to be looked at
at all levels. Consequently, I'm as likely to
become involved in industrial conflict situations or some particular aspects of socially
deviant behavior. All seem to be about the
same kind of relationships that exist at the
inter-state level. My focus of attention now is
the analysis and handling of conflict at all different social levels.

DPG *Is there a common approach or theory that you use in respect to this range of
conflicts?*
BURTON Yes, I think so. The traditional
approach to conflict has been to treat it as a
win-lose situation. This view is very deeply
ingrained—namely, that conflict is an undesirable struggle over scarce resources. If
you make this fundamental assumption that
conflict is win or lose, then you are led almost inevitably to a second assumption—
namely, that the only way you can handle
any conflict situation is by a third party intervening and employing some coercive
means. In other words, you either have a
win-or-lose fight, or you have judicial arbitration or conciliation. What I and my colleagues have been doing—not only in relation to inter-state conflict but also in industrial
conflict and conflict between individuals in
society—is challenging these two basic assumptions.
    When you look at the nature of conflict,
when you analyze it, it becomes clear that it
is not an objective thing but a highly subjective thing. It is a perceptual relationship, and
it involves a whole hierarchy of values. And
the order in which you put these values is of
course a subjective thing. So if conflict is
subjective in these terms, it is likely that relationships can be altered in such a way that a

positive outcome is possible. Take the Middle East conflict, for example. It looks as though territory held by one party can't be held by another. But when you analyze it, it is a conflict about security, and if you redefine security not in territorial terms but in terms of experienced security, then you are not interested in which heights are held by whom, but you are interested in the maximum amount of security that both sides can find. You end up by finding that an increase in security by one side leads to an increase in security on the part of the other.

So we have been looking at this question of conflict very closely to see if these fundamental assumptions are justified. If this is so, you move away from coercive deterrents and enforced settlements and explore quite a different range of settlements.

DPG   *Can you describe some of these non-coercive techniques?*
BURTON   You move away from a negotiating and bargaining framework into a problem-solving one. You bring the parties in dispute around a table with a panel of social scientists. The role of the third-party panel is not to adjudicate or arbitrate, but to see that the two parties are effectively communicating. Most important of all, it is their task to inject information about relationships so that the situation can be analyzed in such a way that the disputing parties can see that their situation is not unique and has many common factors with other conflict situations. This approach to conflict resolution is becoming more common.

DPG   *Is the nation-state outmoded? Its continued existence seems to lead to war.*
BURTON   The problem with that question is the use of the term "nation-state." In fact there are very few states that comprise only one nation, a homogeneous population group, and one of the problems of the contemporary world is that most states have two or three nations in them. Take Nigeria, for example, with the Ibo, Yoruba, and Hausa peoples within it, or even the United Kingdom of Great Britain and Northern Ireland. Most of the international conflicts we have had since 1945 have been spillovers of conflicts within states.

Furthermore, nation-states are a recent invention. Two or three hundred years is as far as we can go back and say that there existed an inter-state system. If nation-states as we know them today were to be broken up into smaller units based on homogeneous population groups, then I don't see that the nation-state would be considered outdated or leading to war. On the contrary, if there were a number of small political units of this character within a wider international economic framework, then I don't think it could be argued at all that the state contributed to war.

DPG   *What about ethnic identification?*
BURTON   One of the aspirations or values that people have is identifying with similar people with similar outlooks and values. Ethnic identification is a very primitive basic value. It involves the drive for security. For example, you have the child identifying with the family and the extended family and so on. Whenever you get some political situation such as that in Northern Ireland, environmental circumstances force people back into their own ethnic groups. Nigeria too is a case in point. The Ibos before the civil war had mixed fairly freely with other tribes but identified with their own ethnic group when the situation changed. The same is true of Canada. It seems to me we have to accept this fact. Most aware, educated, and sophisticated students, for example, don't necessarily hold these group values, but the vast majority of human beings do, especially when their security is threatened.

DPG   *Is there an essential connection between peace and justice?*
BURTON   I think we have to substitute the word "values" for "justice." There are certain human and social values attached to ethnic identification, to political participation, and so on. If one were to use the term "justice" to include the social and psychological values that are important to people, then I think this would give the term some meaning. And if you do that, there is a clear connection between peace and justice.

DPG   *Do you think it is possible to eliminate conflict of the type that leads to global war? Do you think it is possible to preserve a non-war situation for the foreseeable future?*
BURTON   If the aim is to preserve a non-war situation, then of course we do this by

deterrents, by threats, by defense, by alliances and so on. These measures do not solve the real problem at all. They are not unlike other devices, such as the balance of power that we have had in the past. In the short term preserving a non-war situation by these means is possible. In the long term I am sure that it is self-defeating.

What we are seeking are means of *peaceful* change rather than means of stopping change. My hunch is that the answers to these questions are already there in the literature if we can only coordinate the work that is being done at various levels. But of course the elimination of violent conflict means confronting many institutions. It means confronting social norms and role behavior. It means eliminating oppressive privilege. And it means some pretty fundamental changes and social reconstruction. And of course there are a lot of people who wouldn't want these to occur.

I think we have the answers in academic terms—in the sense that we might know what to do—but we don't have the answers in political terms. People in positions of privilege and political power would not be prepared to see the changes that would be required.

Selected Bibliography

Unit 1

Berger, Peter L. *Invitation to Sociology: A Humanistic Perspective.* Garden City, N.Y.: Anchor Books, 1963.

Bruner, Jerome S. *The Process of Education.* Cambridge: Harvard University Press, 1960.

Durkheim, Emile. *Suicide: A Study in Sociology.* George Simpson (ed.). J. A. Spaulding and George Simpson (trs.). New York: Free Press, 1968; first published in French, 1897.

Hammond, Philip E. (ed.). *Sociologists at Work: Essays on the Craft of Social Research.* New York: Basic Books, 1964.

Homans, George C. *The Nature of Social Science.* New York: Harbinger Books, 1967.

Horowitz, Irving Louis. *Professing Sociology: Studies in the Life Cycle of Social Science.* Chicago: Aldine, 1968.

Inkeles, Alex. *What Is Sociology? An Introduction to the Discipline and Profession.* Fundamentals of Modern Sociology Series. Englewood Cliffs, N.J.: Prentice-Hall, 1964.

Kaplan, Abraham. *The Conduct of Inquiry: Methodology for Behavioral Science.* San Francisco: Chandler, 1964.

Kuhn, Thomas S. *The Structure of Scientific Revolutions.* 2nd. ed. Chicago: University of Chicago Press, 1970.

LaCapra, Dominick. *Emile Durkheim: Sociologist and Philosopher.* Ithaca, N.Y.: Cornell University Press, 1972.

Loomis, Charles. "In Praise of Conflict and its Resolution," *American Sociological Review,* 32, 6: 875–890 (December 1967).

Lukes, Stephen. *Emile Durkheim: His Life and Work. A Historical and Critical Study.* Baltimore: Penguin, 1973.

Lynd, Robert S. *Knowledge For What? The Place of Social Science in American Culture.* Princeton, N.J.: Princeton University Press, 1969; first published, 1939.

Merton, Robert K. *Social Theory and Social Structure.* 3rd ed. New York: Free Press, 1960; rev. and enl. ed., 1957; first printing, 1949.

Mills, C. Wright. *The Sociological Imagination.* New York: Oxford University Press, 1959.

Parsons, Talcott. "Some Problems Confronting Sociology as a Profession," *American Sociological Review,* 24, 4: 547–559 (August 1959).

Sjoberg, Gideon and Roger Nett. *A Methodology for Social Research.* New York: Harper and Row, 1968.

Zeitlin, Irving. *Ideology and the Development of Sociological Theory.* Foundations of Modern Sociology Series. Englewood Cliffs, N.J.: Prentice-Hall, 1968.

Unit 2

Bernstein, Basil B. *Class, Codes and Control.* London: Routledge and Kegan Paul, 1971. Vol. 1.

——. "Social Class and Linguistic Development: A Theory of Social Learning," in A. H. Halsey, J. Floud, and C. A. Anderson (eds.), *Education, Economics and Society: A Reader in the Sociology of Education.* New York: Free Press, 1961.

Carroll, John B., and Joseph B. Casagrande. "The Functions of Language Classifications in Behaviour," in Eleanor Maccoby, Theodore Newcomb, and Eugene Hartley (eds.), *Readings in Social Psychology.* 3rd ed. Society for the Psychological Study of Social Issues. New York: Holt, Rinehart and Winston, 1958.

Hagstrom, Warren O. *The Scientific Community.* New York: Basic Books, 1965.

Kuhn, Thomas S. *The Structure of Scientific Revolutions.* 2nd ed. Chicago: University of Chicago Press, 1970; first printing, 1962.

Lawton, Denis. *Social Class, Language and Education.* New York: Schocken Books, 1968.

Mannheim, Karl. *Ideology and Utopia: An Introduction to the Sociology of Knowledge.* Louis Wirth and Edward Shils (trs.). New York: Harvest Books, n.d.; first published in German, 1929.

Marx, Karl. *Selected Writings in Sociology and Social Philosophy.* T. B. Bottomore and Maximilien Rubel (eds. and trs.). New York: McGraw-Hill, 1964.

Merton, Robert K. *Social Theory and Social Structure.* 3rd ed. New York: Free Press, 1968; rev. and enl. ed., 1957; first printing, 1949.

Mulkay, Michael J. *The Social Process of Innovation: A Study in the Sociology of Science.* Studies in Sociology. New York: Macmillan, 1972.

Sapir, Edward. *Language: An Introduction to the Study of Speech.* New York: Harvest Books, n.d.; first published, 1921.

Velikovsky, Immanuel. *Worlds in Collision.* New York: Delta Books, 1965; first published, 1950.

Weber, Max. *Economy and Society: An Outline of Interpretive Sociology.* 3 vols. Guenther Roth and Claus Wittich (eds.). Ephraim Fischoff, *et al.* (trs.). New York: Bedminster Press, 1968; first published in 4 vols. in German, 1922.

——. *From Max Weber: Essays in Sociology.* Hans Gerth and C. Wright Mills (eds. and trs.). New York: Oxford University Press, 1946.

——. *The Theory of Social and Economic Organization.* Talcott Parsons (ed.). A. M. Henderson and Talcott Parsons (trs.). Glencoe, Ill.: Free Press, 1957.

Whorf, Benjamin Lee. *Language, Thought and Reality: Selected Writings of Benjamin Lee Whorf.* John B. Carroll (ed.). Cambridge: Technology Press of the Massachusetts Institute of Technology, 1956.

Unit 3

Ardrey, Robert. *African Genesis.* New York: Dell, 1961.

Bodmer, W. F., and L. L. Cavalli-Sforza. "Intelligence and Race," in *Contemporary Psychology: Readings from Scientific American.* San Francisco: W. H. Freeman, 1971.

Bressler, Marvin. "Biology, Sociology, and Ideology," in David C. Glass (ed.), *Genetics: Proceedings of a Conference Under the Auspices of the Russell Sage Research Foundation, the Social Science Research Council, and The Rockefeller University.* New York: Rockefeller University Press and Russell Sage Foundation, 1961.

Carter, Cedric O. *Human Heredity.* Baltimore: Penguin, 1962.

Davis, Kingsley. *Human Society.* New York: Macmillan, 1949.

——. "The World's Population Crisis," in Robert K. Merton and Robert Nisbet (eds.), *Contemporary Social Problems.* 3rd ed. New York: Harcourt Brace Jovanovich, 1971.

Deutsch, Martin. "Happenings on the Way Back to the Forum: Social Science, IQ and Race Differences Revisited," *Harvard Educational Review,* 39, 3: 523–527 (Summer 1969).

Deutsch, Morton, and Robert M. Krauss. *Theories in Social Psychology.* New York: Basic Books, 1965.

Dicker, Martin, and Lois Dicker. "A Re-Examination of Sahlins' 'Origin of Society.' " Paper presented at the 70th Annual Meeting of the American Anthropological Association. New York, 1971.

Dobzhansky, Theodosius. *Mankind Evolving: The Evolution of the Human Species.* New Haven: Yale University Press, 1962.

——. *The Biology of Ultimate Concern.* Cleveland: World Publishing, 1967.

Etzioni, Amitai. "Violence," in Robert K. Merton and Robert A. Nisbet (eds.), *Contemporary Social Problems.* 3rd ed. New York: Harcourt Brace Jovanovich, 1971.

Ford, Amasa. "Casualties of Our Time," *Science,* 167, 3916: 256–263 (January 1970).

Gilula, Marshall F. and David N. Daniels, "Violence and Man's Struggle to Adapt," *Science,* 164, 3878: 396–405 (April 1969).

Gorer, Geoffrey. "Man Has No 'Killer' Instinct," in Ashley Montagu (ed.), *Man and Aggression.* New York: Oxford University Press, 1968.

Harlow, Harry F. and Margaret Kuenne Harlow. "Social Deprivation in Monkeys," *Scientific American,* 207, 5: 137–146 (November 1962).

Herrnstein, Richard. *"I.Q.,"* Atlantic (September 1971).

Hunt, J. McVicker. "Black Genes—White Environment," *Trans-action* (June 1969). Reprinted in Annual Editions *Readings in Human Development '73/74.* Guilford, Conn.: Dushkin Publishing Group, 1973.

Jensen, Arthur R. "How Much Can We Boost IQ and Scholastic Achievement?," *Harvard Educational Review,* 39, 1: 1–123 (Winter 1969).

Jolly, Alison. *The Evolution of Primate Behavior.* The Macmillan Series in Physical Anthropology. New York: Macmillan, 1972.

Kummer, Hans. *Primate Societies: Group Techniques of Ecological Adaptation.* Chicago: Aldine-Atherton, 1971.

Lorenz, Konrad. *On Aggression.* Marjorie Kerr Wilson (tr.). New York: Bantam Books, 1967; first published in German, 1963.

Matthews, John D., Robert Glasse, and Shirley Lindenbaum. "Kuru and Cannibalism," *The Lancet,* ii, 449–452 (August 24, 1968).

Mead, Margaret. "Warfare Is Only an Invention—Not a Biological Necessity," in Leon Bramson and George Goethals (eds.), *War.* Rev. ed. New York: Basic Books, 1968.

Montagu, Ashley. "The New Litany of 'Innate Depravity,' or Original Sin Revisited," in Ashley Montagu (ed.), *Man and Aggression.* New York: Oxford University Press, 1968.

Morris, Desmond. *The Naked Ape: A Zoologist's Study of the Human Animal.* New York: McGraw-Hill, 1967.

Pettigrew, Thomas F. "Race, Mental Illness and Intelligence: A Social Psychological View," in Richard H. Osborne (ed.), *The Biological and Social Meaning of Race.* San Francisco: W. H. Freeman, 1971.

Portmann, Adolf. *Animals as Social Beings.* Oliver Coburn (tr.). The Science Library. New York: Harper Torchbooks, 1964; first published in German, 1959.

Schaller, G. B. *The Mountain Gorilla: Ecology and Behavior.* Chicago: University of Chicago Press, 1963.

Skinner, B. F. *Beyond Freedom and Dignity.* New York: Knopf, 1971.

——. *Walden Two.* New York: Macmillan, 1972; first printing, 1948.

Stern, Curt. *Principles of Human Genetics.* 2nd ed. San Francisco: W. H. Freeman, 1960.

Stern, George C. "The Real Crisis in Education" (unpublished paper, Department of Psychology, Syracuse University, 1970).

Stinchcombe, Arthur L. "Environment: The Cumulation of Effects is Yet to be Understood," *Harvard Educational Review,* 39, 3: 511–522 (Summer 1969).

Stock, Robert W. "The XYY and the Criminal," *The New York Times Magazine,* October 20, 1968.

Tiger, Lionel. *Men in Groups.* New York: Vintage Books, 1970.

Tinbergen, Niko. "On War and Peace in Animals and Man," *Science,* 160, 3835: 1411–1418 (June 1968).

van Lawick-Goodall, Jane. *My Friends the Wild Chimpanzees.* Washington, D.C.: The National Geographic Society, 1967.

Washburn, Sherwood L., and David A. Hamburg. "Aggressive Behavior in Old World Monkeys and Apes," in Phyllis Dolhinow (ed.), *Primate Patterns.* New York: Holt, Rinehart and Winston, 1972.

Whitten, Phillip, and Jerome Kagan. "Jensen's Dangerous Half-truth," *Psychology Today* (August 1969).

Wilson, Edward O. "The Prospects for a Unified Sociobiology," *American Scientist,* 59, 4: 400–403 (July-August 1971).

Unit 4

Barthes, Roland. "Science versus Literature," in Michael Lane (ed.), *Introduction to Structuralism.* New York: Basic Books, 1971.

Chomsky, Noam. *Language and Mind.* New York: Harcourt Brace Jovanovich, 1968.

Cole, Robert. "Structural-Functional Theory, the Dialectic and Social Change," *Sociological Quarterly,* 7, 1: 39–58 (Winter 1966).

Dahrendorf, Ralf. *Class and Class Conflict in Industrial Society.* Rev. and tr. by the author. Stanford: Stanford University Press, 1959; first published in German, 1957.

——. *Essays in the Theory of Society.* Stanford: Stanford University Press, 1968.

Goodenough, Ward H. "Cultural Anthropology and Linguistics," in Paul Garvin (ed.), *Report of the Seventh Annual Round Table Meeting on Linguistics and Language Study.* Georgetown Monograph Series, 9. Washington, D.C.: Georgetown University Press, 1957.

Gouldner, Alvin W., and Richard A. Peterson. *Notes on Technology and the Moral Order.* Indianapolis: Bobbs-Merrill, 1962.

Jakobson, Roman. *Selected Writings.* 4 vols. The Hague: Mouton, 1962–1971.

——, and Morris Halle. *Fundamentals of Language.* 2nd rev. ed. The Hague: Mouton, 1956.

Leach, Edmund. *Claude Lévi-Strauss.* Modern Masters Series. New York: Viking, 1970.

Lenski, Gerhard. *Power and Privilege: A Theory of Social Stratification.* New York: McGraw-Hill, 1966.

Lévi-Strauss, Claude. *The Savage Mind.* The Nature of Human Society Series. Chicago: University of Chicago Press, 1966; first published in French, 1962.

Lévy-Bruhl, Lucien. *Primitive Mentality.* Lilian A. Clare (tr.).

Boston: Beacon Press, 1966; first published in French, 1922.

Marx, Karl. *Selected Writings in Sociology and Social Philosophy*. T. B. Bottomore and Maximilien Rubel (eds. and trs.) New York: McGraw-Hill, 1964.

Mead, Margaret. *Culture and Commitment*. Garden City, N.Y.: Natural History Press, 1970.

Parsons, Talcott. *Societies: Evolutionary and Comparative Perspectives*. Foundations of Modern Sociology Series. Englewood Cliffs, N.J.: Prentice-Hall, 1966.

Parsons, Talcott, *et al.* (eds.), *Theories of Society*. New York: Free Press, 1961. Vol. 1.

Piaget, Jean. *Structuralism*. Chaninah Maschler (tr.). New York: Basic Books, 1970; first published in French, 1968.

Reich, Charles. *The Greening of America: The Coming of a New Consciousness and the Rebirth of a Future*. New York: Bantam Books, 1971; first printing, 1970.

Sahlins, Marshall D., and Elman R. Service. *Evolution and Culture*. Ann Arbor: University of Michigan Press, 1960.

Sartre, Jean-Paul. *Search for a Method*. Hazel E. Barnes (tr.). New York: Knopf, 1963; first published in French, 1960.

Service, Elman R. *Primitive Social Organization*. New York: Random House, 1962.

Slater, Philip E. *The Pursuit of Loneliness*. Boston: Beacon Press, 1970.

Smelser, Neil J. *Essays in Sociological Explanation*. Englewood Cliffs, N.J.: Prentice-Hall, 1968.

———. *Theory of Collective Behavior*. New York: Free Press, 1962.

Tylor, Sir Edward Burnett. *Primitive Culture*. New York: Harper Torchbooks, 1958; first published, 1871.

van den Berghe, Pierre. "Dialectic and Functionalism: Toward a Theoretical Synthesis," *American Sociological Review*, 28, 5: 695–705 (October 1963).

Werner, Oswald. "Ethnoscience 1972," in Bernard J. Siegel, *et al.* (eds.), *Annual Review of Anthropology*. Palo Alto, Calif.: Annual Reviews, 1972. Vol. 1.

Unit 5

Berger, Peter L., and Thomas Luckmann. *The Social Construction of Reality: A Treatise in the Sociology of Knowledge*. Garden City, N.Y.: Doubleday, 1966.

Cooley, Charles H. *Human Nature and the Social Order*. New York: Schocken Books, 1964; first published, 1902.

———. *Social Organization*. New York: Schocken Books, 1962; first published, 1909.

Davis, Kingsley. *Human Society*. New York: Macmillan, 1949.

Elkind, David. "Erik Erikson's Eight Ages of Man," *The New York Times Magazine*, April 5, 1970. Reprinted in Annual Editions *Readings in Sociology '73/'74*. Guilford, Conn.: Dushkin Publishing Group, 1973.

Erikson, Erik. *Childhood and Society*. Rev. ed. New York: Norton, 1964; first printing, 1950.

Freud, Sigmund. *Civilization and Its Discontents*. James Strachey (tr.). New York: Norton, 1962; first published in German, 1930.

Goffman, Erving. *Asylums: Essays on the Social Situation of Mental Patients and Other Inmates*. Garden City, N.Y.: Anchor Books, 1961.

Goldfarb, William. "Psychological Privation in Infancy and Subsequent Adjustment," *American Journal of Orthopsychiatry*, 15, 2: 247–255 (April 1945).

Haan, Norma, M. Brewster Smith, and Jeanne Block. "The Moral Reasoning of Young Adults: Political-Social Behavior, Family Background and Personality Correlates," *Journal of Personality and Social Psychology*, 10, 3: 183–202 (November 1968).

Hampden-Turner, Charles, and Phillip Whitten. "Morals Left and Right," *Psychology Today* (April 1971).

Harlow, Harry F., and Margaret Kuenne Harlow. "Social Deprivation in Monkeys," *Scientific American*, 207, 5: 137–146 (November 1962).

Hartshorne, Hugh, and Mark A. May. "Studies in Deceit," in Hugh Hartshorne, *et al.* (eds.), *The Nature of Character*. The Character Education Inquiry, Teachers College, Columbia University. New York: Macmillan, 1928. Vol. 1.

Kohlberg, Lawrence. "Stage and Sequence: The Cognitive-Developmental Approach to Socialization," in David A. Goslin (ed.), *Handbook of Socialization Theory and Research*. Sociology Series. Chicago: Rand McNally, 1969.

Malinowski, Bronislaw. *Sex and Repression in Savage Society*. Cleveland: World Publishing, 1955; first published, 1927.

Mead, George Herbert. *Mind, Self and Society*. Chicago: University of Chicago Press, 1967; first published, 1934.

Piaget, Jean. *The Moral Judgment of the Child*. Marjorie Gabain (tr.). New York: Free Press, 1965; first published in French, 1932.

Rest, James, Elliot Turiel, and Lawrence Kohlberg. "Level of Moral Development as a Determinant of Preference and Comprehension of Moral Judgments Made by Others," *Journal of Personality*, 37, 2: 225–252 (June 1969).

Spitz, René A. "Hospitalism: An Enquiry into the Genesis of Psychiatric Conditions in Early Childhood," in *Psychoanalytic Study of the Child, 1*. New York: International Universities Press, 1945.

Turiel, Elliot. "An Experimental Test of the Sequentiality of Developmental Stages in the Child's Moral Judgments," *Journal of Personality and Social Psychology*, 3, 5: 661–668 (October 1966).

Unit 6

Berelson, Bernard. "KAP Studies on Fertility," in Bernard Berelson, *et al.* (eds.), *Family Planning and Population Programs*. Proceedings of the International Conference on Family Planning Programs, Geneva, 1965. Chicago: University of Chicago Press, 1966.

Chandrasekhar, Sripati. *Population and Planned Parenthood in India*. London: Allen and Unwin, 1961.

Davis, Kingsley. "Population Policy: Will Current Programs Succeed?," *Science*, 158, 3802: 730–739 (November 1967).

Ehrlich, Paul R., and Anne H. Ehrlich. *Population, Resources, Environment: Issues in Human Ecology*. Biology Books. San Francisco: W. H. Freeman, 1970.

Hartley, Shirley Foster. *Population: Quality versus Quantity: A Sociological Examination of the Causes and Consequences of the Population Explosion*. Sociology Series. Englewood Cliffs, N.J.: Prentice-Hall, 1972.

Lelyveld, Joseph. "Birth Curb Drive Slowing in India," *The New York Times*, April 20, 1969.

Loomis, Charles. "In Praise of Conflict and its Resolution," *American Sociological Review*, 32, 6: 875–890 (December 1967).

Malthus, Thomas Robert. *An Essay on the Principle of Population*. Anthony Flew (ed.). Baltimore: Penguin, 1971; first published, 1798.

Park, Robert E., Ernest W. Burgess, and Roderick D. McKenzie. *The City*. Heritage of Sociology Series. Chicago: University of Chicago Press, 1967; first published, 1925.

Poffenberger, Thomas, and Shirley Poffenberger. *Husband-Wife Communication and Motivational Aspects of Population Growth in an Indian Village*. New Delhi: Central Family Planning Institute, 1969.

Sorokin, Pitirim A., Carle C. Zimmerman, and Charles J. Galpin (eds.) *A Systematic Sourcebook in Rural Sociology*. 3 vols. New York: Russell and Russell, 1965; first published, 1930–1932.

Thomlinson, Ralph. *Population Dynamics*. New York: Random House, 1965.

Toennies, Ferdinand. *Community and Society (Gemeinschaft und Gesellschaft)*. Charles P. Loomis (ed. and tr.). East Lansing: Michigan State University Press, 1957; first published in German, 1887.

U.S. Bureau of the Census. *1970 Census of Population: General Social and Economic Characteristics*. Washington, D.C.: Government Printing Office, June 1972.

———. *Projections of Population of the U.S., by Age and Sex, 1970 to 2020*. Washington, D.C.: Government Printing Office, November 1971.

———. *Statistical Abstract of the United States: 1972*. 93rd ed. Washington, D.C.: Government Printing Office, 1972.

U.S. Presidential Commission on Population Growth and the American Future. *Population and the American Future*. Washington, D.C.: Government Printing Office, 1972.

Unit 7

Axelrod, Morris. "Urban Structure and Social Participation," *American Sociological Review*, 21, 1: 13–18 (February 1956).

Bell, Wendell, and Marion D. Boat. "Urban Neighborhood and Informal Social Relations," *American Journal of Sociology*, 62, 1: 391–398 (January 1957).

Billingsley, Andrew. "Family Functioning in the Low Income Black Community," *Social Casework*, 50, 563–572 (December 1969).

Bott, Elizabeth. *Family and Social Network: Roles, Norms, and External Relationships in Ordinary Urban Families*. Rev. ed. New York: Free Press, 1971; first printing, 1968.

Duvall, Evelyn. *Family Development*. 4th ed. Philadelphia: Lippincott, 1971.

Engels, Friedrich. *The Origin of the Family, Private Property, and the State*. Eleanor Burke Hancock (tr.). New York: International Publishers, 1972; first published in German, 1884.

Furstenberg, Frank F., Jr. "Industrialization and the American Family: A Look Backward," *American Sociological Review*, 31, 3: 326–337 (June 1966).

Gans, Herbert J. "Culture and Class in the Study of Poverty: An Approach to Anti-Poverty Research," in Daniel P. Moynihan (ed.), *On Understanding Poverty*. New York: Basic Books, 1969.

———. "The Negro Family: Reflections on the Moynihan Report," in Lee Rainwater and William B. Yancey (eds.), *The Moynihan Report and the Politics of Controversy*. Cambridge: Massachusetts Institute of Technology Press, 1967.

———. *Urban Villagers*. New York: Free Press, 1962.

Goode, William. *The Family*. Englewood Cliffs, N.J.: Prentice-Hall, 1964.

———. *World Revolution and Family Patterns*. New York: Free Press, 1963.

Gordon, Michael (ed.). *The Nuclear Family in Crisis: The Search for an Alternative*. New York: Harper and Row, 1972.

Greenfield, Sydney M. "Industrialization and the Family in Sociological Theory," *American Journal of Sociology*, 67, 3: 312–322 (November 1961).

Komarovsky, Mirra. *Blue Collar Marriage*. New York: Random House, 1964.

Lévi-Strauss, Claude. "The Family," in Harry L. Shapiro (ed.), *Man, Culture, and Society*. New York: Oxford University Press, 1956. Also in Arlene S. Skolnick and Jerome H. Skolnick (eds.), *Family in Transition: Rethinking Marriage, Sexuality, Child Rearing and Family Organization*. Boston: Little, Brown, 1971.

Lewis, Oscar. *La Vida: A Puerto Rican Family in the Culture of Poverty—San Juan and New York*. New York: Vintage Books, 1966.

Liebow, Elliot. *Tally's Corner: A Study of Negro Streetcorner Men*. Boston: Little, Brown, 1967.

Litwak, Eugene. "Geographic Mobility and Extended Family Cohesion," *American Sociological Review*, 25, 3: 385–394 (June 1960).

———. "Occupational Mobility and Extended Family Cohesion," *American Sociological Review*, 25, 1: 9–22 (February 1960).

———. "The Use of Extended Family Groups in the Achievement of Social Goals," *Social Problems*, 7, 3: 177–188 (Winter 1959–1960).

Mogey, John. "Family and Community in Urban-Industrial Societies," in Harold T. Christensen (ed.), *Handbook of Marriage and the Family*. Chicago: Rand McNally, 1964.

Murdock, George P. "World Ethnographic Sample," *American Anthropologist*, 59, 4: 664–687 (August 1957).

Parsons, Talcott. "The American Family: Its Relations to Personality and to Social Structure," in Talcott Parsons, *et al.* (eds.), *Family, Socialization and Interaction Process*. New York: Free Press, 1955.

———. "The Kinship System of the Contemporary United States," *American Anthropologist*, 45, 1: 22–38 (January-March 1943).

Rainwater, Lee. "Crucible of Identity," *Daedalus*, 95, 1: 172–216 (Winter 1966).

———, and William B. Yancey (eds.) *The Moynihan Report and the Politics of Controversy*. Cambridge: Massachusetts Institute of Technology Press, 1967.

Rodman, Hyman. "The Lower-Class Value Stretch," *Social Forces*, 42, 2: 205–215 (December 1963).

———. "On Understanding Lower-Class Behavior," in Marvin B. Sussman (ed.), *Sourcebook in Marriage and the Family*. 3rd ed. Boston: Houghton Mifflin, 1968.

Stephens, William H. *The Family in Cross-Cultural Perspective*. New York: Holt, Rinehart and Winston, 1963.

Sussman, Marvin B. "The Help Pattern in the Middle Class Family," *American Sociological Review*, 18, 1: 22–28 (February 1953).

———. "The Isolated Nuclear Family: Fact or Fiction?," *Social Problems*, 6, 4: 330–340 (Spring 1959).

———. "Relationships of Adult Children with their Parents in the United States," in Ethel Shanas and Gordon F.

Streib (eds.), *Social Structure and the Family: Generational Relations.* Englewood Cliffs, N.J.: Prentice-Hall, 1965.

———, and Lee Burchinal. "Kin-Family Network: Unheralded Structure in Current Conceptualizations of Family Functioning," *Marriage and Family Living,* 24, 3: 231–240 (August 1962).

U.S. Department of Labor. Office of Planning and Research. *The Negro Family: The Case for National Action.* ("The Moynihan Report") Washington, D.C.: Government Printing Office, 1965.

Valentine, Charles. *Culture and Poverty: Critique and Counter Proposals.* Chicago: University of Chicago Press, 1968.

Williams, Robin M. *American Society: A Sociological Interpretation.* 3rd ed. New York: Knopf, 1970.

Winch, Robert F., and Rae Lesser Blumberg. "Societal Complexity and Familial Organization," in Robert F. Winch and Louis W. Goodman (eds.), *Selected Studies in Marriage and the Family.* 3rd ed. New York: Holt, Rinehart and Winston, 1968.

Wirth, Louis. "Urbanism as a Way of Life," *American Journal of Sociology,* 62, 1: 391–398 (July 1938). Also in Albert J. Reiss, Jr. (ed.), *Louis Wirth on Cities and Social Life.* Chicago: University of Chicago Press, 1964.

Young, Michael, and Peter Willmott. *Family and Kinship in East London.* Baltimore: Penguin, 1957.

Unit 8

Adams, Robert L., and Robert J. Fox. "Mainlining Jesus: The New Trip" *Society* (February 1972). Reprinted in Annual Editions *Readings in Sociology '73/'74.* Guilford, Conn.: Dushkin Publishing Group, 1973.

Bellah, Robert N. "Reflections on the Protestant Ethic Analogy in Asia," *Journal of Social Issues,* 19, 1: 52–60 (January 1963).

Berger, Peter. *A Rumor of Angels: Modern Society and the Rediscovery of the Supernatural.* Garden City, N.Y.: Doubleday, 1969.

———. *The Sacred Canopy: Elements of a Sociological Theory of Religion.* Garden City, N.Y.: Doubleday, 1967.

Durkheim, Emile. *The Elementary Forms of Religious Life.* Joseph Wald Swain (tr.). New York: Free Press, 1965; first published in French, 1915.

Gallup, George, "Western World Sees Decline in Morality," *The New York Times,* September 1968.

Herberg, Will. *Protestant, Catholic, Jew: An Essay in American Religious Sociology.* Rev. ed. Garden City, N.Y.: Anchor Books, 1966. First published, 1956.

———. "Religion in a Secularized Society: The New Shape of Religion in America," in Richard D. Knudten (ed.), *The Sociology of Religion: An Anthology.* New York: Appleton-Century-Crofts, 1967.

Lenski, Gerhard. *The Religious Factor: A Sociological Study of Religion's Impact on Politics, Economics and Family Life.* Rev. ed. Garden City, N.Y.: Anchor Books, 1963.

Luckmann, Thomas. *The Invisible Religion: The Problem of Religion in Modern Society.* New York: Macmillan, 1967.

Martin, David. *A Sociology of English Religion.* New York: Basic Books, 1967.

Marx, Karl. "A Critique of Hegel's 'Philosophy of Right,' " in Lloyd D. Easton and Kurt Guddat (eds. and trs.), *Writings of the Young Marx on Philosophy and Society.* Garden City, N.Y.: Anchor Books, 1967; first written in German, 1843.

———. *Selected Writings in Sociology and Social Philosophy.* T. B. Bottomore and Maximilien Rubel (eds. and trs.). New York: McGraw-Hill, 1964.

"Poll Finds Church Attendance Is Down, but U.S. Holds Lead," *The New York Times,* December 22, 1968.

"Religious Views Assayed in Poll," *The New York Times,* December 26, 1968.

Stark, Rodney, and Charles Y. Glock. *American Piety: The Nature of Religious Commitment.* Research Program in Religion and Society of the Survey Research Center. Berkeley: University of California Press, 1968.

Swanson, Guy. *Religion and Regime: A Sociological Account of the Reformation.* Ann Arbor: University of Michigan Press, 1967.

Tocqueville, Alexis de. *Democracy in America.* Phillips Bradley (ed.). Henry Reeve (tr.). 2 vols. New York: Vintage Books; first published in two vols. in French, 1835, 1840.

Weber, Max. *Economy and Society: An Outline of Interpretive Sociology.* 3 vols. Guenther Roth and Claus Wittich (eds.) Ephraim Fischoff, *et al.* (trs.). New York: Bedminster Press, 1968; first published in 4 vols. in German, 1922.

———. *The Protestant Ethic and the Spirit of Capitalism.* Talcott Parsons (tr.). New York: Scribner, 1958; first published in German, 1904–1905.

———. *The Religion of China: Confucianism and Taoism.* Hans Gerth (ed. and tr.). New York: Free Press, 1968; first published in German, 1915.

———. *The Religion of India: The Sociology of Hinduism and Buddhism.* Hans Gerth and Don Martindale (eds. and trs.). New York: Free Press, 1967; first published in German, 1916.

———. *The Sociology of Religion.* Ephraim Fischoff (tr.). Boston: Beacon Press, 1968; first published in German, 1922.

Yinger, J. Milton. *Religion in the Struggle for Power.* Sociology Series. Durham, N.C.: Duke University Press, 1946.

Unit 9

Berger, Peter L., and Brigitte Berger. "The Blueing of America," *The New Republic,* April 3, 1971.

Bottomore, T. B. *Classes in Modern Society.* New York: Pantheon, 1966.

Dahl, Robert. *Who Governs? Democracy and Power in an American City.* New Haven: Yale University Press, 1961.

Dahrendorf, Ralf. *Class and Class Conflict in Industrial Society.* Rev. and tr. by the author. Stanford: Stanford University Press, 1959; first published in German, 1957.

Davis, Kingsley, and Wilbert E. Moore. "Some Principles of Stratification," *American Sociological Review,* 10, 2: 242–249 (April 1945).

Djilas, Milovan. *The New Class: An Analysis of the Communist System.* New York: Praeger, 1957.

Domhoff, G. William. *Fat Cats and Democrats: The Role of the Big Rich in the Party of the Common Man.* Englewood Cliffs, N.J.: Prentice-Hall, 1972.

———. *The Higher Circles: The Governing Class in America.* New York: Random House, 1970.

———. *Who Rules America?* Englewood Cliffs, N.J.: Spectrum Books, 1967.

Hodge, Robert W., Paul M. Seigel, and Peter H. Rossi. "Occupational Prestige in the United States, 1925–63," *American Journal of Sociology,* 70, 3: 286–302 (November 1964).

Hollingshead, August B. *Elmtown's Youth: The Impact of Social Classes on Adolescents.* New York: Wiley, 1949.

Hunter, Floyd. *Community Power Structure: A Study of Decision Makers.* Chapel Hill: University of North Carolina Press, 1953.

Lenin, Vladimir I. "Imperialism, the Highest Stage of Capitalism," in Henry M. Christman (ed.), *Essential Works of Lenin.* New York: Bantam Books, 1966; first published in Russian, 1916.

Lenski, Gerhard. *Power and Privilege: A Theory of Social Stratification.* New York: McGraw-Hill, 1966.

Lipset, Seymour Martin, and Reinhard Bendix. *Social Mobility in Industrial Society.* Berkeley: University of California Press, 1959.

Lynd, Robert S., and Helen M. Lynd. *Middletown, a Study in American Culture.* New York: Harvest Books, 1956; first published, 1929.

———. *Middletown in Transition: A Study in Cultural Conflicts.* New York: Harcourt Brace, 1937.

Marx, Karl. *Capital, a Critique of Political Economy.* 3 vols. Friedrich Engels (ed.). Samuel Moore and Edward Aveling (trs.). New York: International Publishers, 1967; first published in German, 1867–1894.

———. "A Critique of Hegel's 'Philosophy of Right,' " in Lloyd D. Easton and Kurt Guddat (eds. and trs.), *Writings of the Young Marx on Philosophy and Society.* Garden City, N.Y.: Anchor Books, 1967; first written in German, 1843.

Mills, C. Wright. *The Power Elite.* New York: Oxford University Press, 1956.

———. *White Collar: The American Middle Classes.* New York: Oxford University Press, 1951.

Mosca, Gaetano. *The Ruling Class.* Arthur Livingston (ed.). Hannah D. Kahn (tr.). New York: McGraw-Hill, 1960; first published in Italian, 1896.

Murdock, George P. *Social Structure.* New York: Macmillan, 1949.

Ossowski, Stanislaw. *Class Structure in the Social Consciousness.* Sheila Patterson (tr.). New York: Free Press, 1963; first published in Polish, 1957.

Parsons, Talcott. *The Social System.* Glencoe, Ill.: Free Press, 1951.

Perlman, Selig. *A History of Trade Unionism in the United States.* New York: Macmillan, 1922.

Rose, Arnold. *The Power Structure: Political Processes in American Society.* New York: Oxford University Press, 1967.

Warner, W. Lloyd, and Paul S. Hunt. *The Social Life of a Modern Community.* Yankee City Series, 1. New Haven: Yale University Press, 1941.

Weber, Max. "Class, Status and Party," in Hans Gerth and C. Wright Mills (eds. and trs.), *From Max Weber: Essays in Sociology.* New York: Oxford University Press, 1946.

———. *Economy and Society: An Outline of Interpretive Sociology.* Guenther Roth and Claus Wittich (eds.). Ephraim Fischoff, *et al.* (trs.). New York: Bedminster Press, 1968; first published in 4 vols. in German, 1922.

———. *The Theory of Social and Economic Organization.* Talcott Parsons (ed.). A. M. Henderson and Talcott Parsons (trs.). Glencoe, Ill.: Free Press, 1957; first printing, 1947.

Unit 10

Bendix, Reinhard. "Compliant Behavior and Individual Personality," in Neil J. Smelser and William T. Smelser (eds.), *Personality and Social Systems.* New York: Wiley, 1970.

Benedict, Ruth. *The Chrysanthemum and the Sword: Patterns of Japanese Culture.* Cleveland: Meridian Books, 1967; first published, 1946.

Cooley, Charles H. *Human Nature and the Social Order.* New York: Schocken Books, 1964; first published, 1902.

Durkheim, Emile. *The Division of Labor in Society.* George Simpson (tr.). New York: Free Press, 1964; first published in French, 1893.

———. *Suicide: A Study in Sociology.* George Simpson (ed.). J. A. Spaulding and George Simpson (trs.). New York: Free Press, 1968; first published in French, 1897.

Goode, Erich. "Multiple Drug Use Among Marijuana Smokers," *Social Problems,* 17, 1: 170–178 (Summer 1969).

Heider, Fritz. *The Psychology of Interpersonal Relations.* New York: Wiley, 1958.

Hoebel, E. Adamson. "Anthropological Perspectives on National Character," *Annals of the American Academy of Political and Social Science,* 370: 1–7 (March 1967).

Inkeles, Alex, Eugenia Hanfmann, and Helen Beir. "Modal Personality and Adjustment to the Soviet Socio-Political System," in Bert Kaplan (ed.), *Studying Personality Cross-Culturally.* Evanston, Ill.: Row-Peterson, 1961.

Lazar, Joseph. "Judicial Perspectives on National Character," *Annals,* 370: 16–22 (March 1967).

Levinson, Daniel J. "Role, Personality and Social Structure in the Organizational Setting," in Neil J. Smelser and William T. Smelser (eds.), *Personality and Social Systems.* New York: Wiley, 1970.

McAree, C. P., R. A. Steffenhagen, and L. S. Zheutlin. "Personality Factors in College Drug Users," *International Journal of Social Psychiatry,* 15, 2: 102–106 (March 1969).

Maccoby, Michael. "On Mexican National Character," *Annals of the American Academy of Social and Political Science,* 370: 71–72 (March 1967).

Mead, George Herbert. *Mind, Self and Society.* Chicago: University of Chicago Press, 1934.

Mead, Margaret. "National Character," in A. L. Kroeber (ed.), *Anthropology Today: An Encyclopedic Inventory.* Chicago: University of Chicago Press, 1953.

Merton, Robert K. *Social Theory and Social Structure.* 3rd ed. New York: Free Press, 1968; rev. and enl. ed., 1957; first printing, 1949.

Parsons, Talcott. *Social Structure and Personality.* New York: Free Press, 1964.

———, and Edward Shils. "Personality as a System of Action," in Parsons and Shils (eds.), *Toward a General Theory of Action.* New York: Harper and Row, 1951.

Preston, James D., and Patricia A. Fry. "Marijuana Use Among Houston High School Students," *Social Science Quarterly,* 52, 1: 170–178 (June 1971).

Smart, Reginald, and Dianne Fejer. "Illicit LSD Users: Their Social Backgrounds, Drug Use and Psychopathology," *Journal of Health and Social Behavior,* 10, 4: 297–307 (December 1969).

Smirnov, Georgii. "On the Concept of the Socialist Type of Man," *Voprosy Filosofii,* 25, 1: 26–35 (January 1971).

Strauss, Anselm. "Sociological Views and Contributions," in Edward Norbeck, *et al.* (eds.), *The Study of Personality: An Interdisciplinary Approach.* New York: Holt, Rinehart and Winston, 1968.

Tec, Nechama. "Family and Differential Involvement with Marijuana: A Study of Suburban Teenagers," *Journal of Marriage and the Family*, 32, 4: 656–664 (November 1970).

Unit 11

Argyris, Chris. "The Incompleteness of Social-Psychological Theory: Examples from Small Group, Cognitive Consistency, and Attribution Research," *American Psychologist*, 24, 10: 893–908 (October 1969).

Back, Kurt W. *Beyond Words: The Story of Sensitivity Training and the Encounter Group Movement*. New York: Russell Sage, 1972.

Bales, Robert F. *Interaction Process Analysis: A Method for the Study of Small Groups*. Reading, Mass.: Addison-Wesley, 1950.

———. *Personality and Interpersonal Behavior*. New York: Holt, Rinehart and Winston, 1970

———, and Fred L. Strodtbeck. "Phases in Group Problem Solving," *Journal of Abnormal and Social Psychology*, 46, 4: 485–495 (April 1951).

Bennis, Warren G. "Defenses against 'Depressive Anxiety' in Groups: The Case of the Absent Leader," *Merrill-Palmer Quarterly*, 7, 1: 3–30 (December 1961).

———, and Herbert A. Shepard. "A Theory of Group Development," *Human Relations*, 9, 4: 415–437 (November 1956).

Bion, Wilfred R. *Experiments in Groups, and Other Papers*. New York: Basic Books, 1959.

Dunphy, Dexter C. "Social Change in Self-Analytic Groups," in Philip J. Stone, *et al.* (eds.), *The General Inquirer: A Computer Approach to Content Analysis*. Cambridge: Massachusetts Institute of Technology Press, 1966.

Freud, Sigmund. *Group Psychology and the Analysis of the Ego*. James Strachey (tr.) New York: Liveright, 1967; first published in German, 1921.

———. *Totem and Taboo*. James Strachey (tr.). New York: Norton, 1950; first published in German, 1913.

Gibb, Jack R., and Lorraine M. Gibb. "Emergence Therapy: The TORI Process in an Emergent Group," in George M. Gazda (ed.), *Innovations to Group Psychotherapy*. Springfield, Ill: Charles C. Thomas, 1968.

Golding, William. *Lord of the Flies*. New York: Capricorn Books, 1955.

Hughes, Thomas. *Tom Brown's School Days*. Baltimore: Penguin, 1973; first published, 1857.

Koch, Sigmund. "The Image of Man Implicit in Encounter Groups," *Journal of Humanistic Psychology*, 11, 2: 109 (Fall 1971).

LeBon, Gustave. *The Crowd: A Study of the Popular Mind*. New York: Ballantine, 1969; first published in French, 1895–1896.

Lenneberg, Eric H. "A Biological Perspective of Language," in Eric H. Lenneberg (ed.), *New Directions in the Study of Language*. Cambridge: Massachusetts Institute of Technology Press, 1964.

Lewin, Kurt, Ronald Lippitt, and Ralph K. White. "Patterns of Aggressive Behavior in Experimentally Created 'Social Climates,' " *Journal of Social Psychology*, 10, 2: 271–299 (May 1939).

Mann, Richard D., *et al. Interpersonal Styles and Group Development: An Analysis of the Member-Leadership Relationship*. New York: Wiley, 1967.

Meador, Betty D. "Individual Process in a Basic Encounter Group," *Journal of Counseling Psychology*, 18, 1:70–76 (January 1971).

Mills, Theodore M. *Group Transformation: An Analysis of a Learning Group*. Englewood Cliffs, N.J.: Prentice-Hall, 1964.

———. *The Sociology of Small Groups*. Foundations of Modern Sociology Series. Englewood Cliffs, N.J.: Prentice-Hall, 1970.

Moreno, Jacob L. *Who Shall Survive? Foundations of Sociometry, Group Psychotherapy and Sociodrama*. Rev. ed. New York: Beacon House, 1953.

Parsons, Talcott, and Robert F. Bales. *Family, Socialization and Interaction Process*. Glencoe, Ill.: Free Press, 1955.

Rogers, Carl. *Carl Rogers on Encounter Groups*. New York: Harper and Row, 1970.

———. "The Group Comes of Age," *Psychology Today* (March 1969).

Schein, Edgar H. *Process Consultation: Its Role in Organization Development*. Reading, Mass.: Addison-Wesley, 1969.

Shaw, Marvin E. *Group Dynamics: The Psychology of Small Group Behavior*. New York: McGraw-Hill, 1971.

Slater, Philip E. *Microcosm: Structural, Psychological and Religious Evolution in Groups*. New York: Wiley, 1966.

Whyte, William H., Jr. *The Organization Man*. New York: Clarion Books, 1956.

Wolman, C., and H. Frank. "The Solo Woman in a Professional Peer Group," Working Paper No. 133, Department of Management, The Wharton School of Finance and Commerce, University of Pennsylvania, 1972.

Yalom, Irwin D. *The Theory and Practice of Group Psychotherapy*. New York: Basic Books, 1970.

———, and M. A. Lieberman. "A Study of Encounter Group Casualties," *Archives of General Psychiatry*, 25, 1: 16–30 (January 1971).

Zimbardo, Philip G. "The Human Choice: Individuation, Reason and Order versus Deindividuation, Impulse and Chaos," in William J. Arnold and David Levine (eds.), *Nebraska Symposium on Motivation, 1969*. Current Theory and Research in Motivation Series, 17. Lincoln: University of Nebraska Press, 1969.

Unit 12

Argyle, Michael. *Social Interaction*. Chicago: Aldine, 1969; first printing, 1959.

Backman, Carl W., and Paul F. Secord. "The Self and Role Selection," in Chad Gordon and Kenneth J. Gergen (eds.), *The Self in Social Interaction*. New York: Wiley, 1968.

Biddle, Bruce J., and Edwin J. Thomas. *Role Theory: Concepts and Research*. New York: Wiley, 1966.

Birdwhistell, Roy L. *Introduction to Kinesics*. Foreign Service Institute. Louisville, Ky.: University of Louisville Press, 1951.

Bixenstine, V. Edwin, Herbert M. Potash, and Kellogg V. Herbert. "Effects of Level of Cooperative Choice by the Other Player on Choices in a Prisoner's Dilemma Game. Part I," *Journal of Abnormal and Social Psychology*, 66, 4: 308–313 (April 1963).

Blau, Peter M. *The Dynamics of Bureaucracy: A Study of Interpersonal Relationships in Two Government Agencies*. 2nd ed. Chicago: University of Chicago Press, 1963; first printing, 1955.

Blumer, Herbert. *Symbolic Interactionism: Perspective and Method*. Englewood Cliffs, N.J.: Prentice-Hall, 1969.

Burns, Tom. "Non-Verbal Communication," *Discovery* (October 1964).

Chomsky, Noam. *Syntactic Structures*. New York: Humanities Press, 1957.

Deutsch, Morton. "The Effect of Motivational Orientation upon Trust and Suspicion," *Human Relations*, 13, 2: 122–139 (July 1960).

Ekman, Paul, and Wallace V. Friesen. "Constraint Across Cultures in the Face and Emotion," *Journal of Personality and Social Psychology*, 17, 2: 124–129 (February 1971).

Fast, Julius. *Body Language*. New York: Pocket Books, 1971.

Freedman, Jonathan L. "The Crowd—Maybe Not So Madding After All," *Psychology Today* (September 1971).

Friesen, Wallace V., and Paul Ekman. "Non-Verbal Behavior in Psychotherapy Research," in John M. Shlien (ed.), *Research in Psychotherapy*. Washington, D.C.: American Psychological Association, 1968. Vol. 3.

Gergen, Kenneth J. "Interaction Goals and Personalistic Feedback as Factors Affecting the Presentation of the Self" (unpublished dissertation, Duke University, 1962).

———. "Multiple Identity," *Psychology Today* (May 1972).

———. *The Psychology of Behavior Exchange*. Charles A. Kiesler (ed.) Topics in Social Psychology. Reading, Mass.: Addison-Wesley, 1969.

———, and Barbara Wishnov. "Others' Self-Evaluations and Interaction Anticipation as Determinants of Self-Preservation," *Journal of Personality and Social Psychology*, 2, 3: 348–358 (September 1965).

Goffman, Erving. *Interaction Ritual: Essays on Face-to-Face Behavior*. Garden City, N.Y.: Anchor Books, 1967.

———. *The Presentation of Self in Everyday Life*. Garden City, N.Y.: Anchor Books, 1959.

Hall, Edward T. *The Silent Language*. New York: Fawcett Books, 1969; first printing, 1959.

Homans, George C. *Social Behavior: The Elementary Forms*. New York: Harcourt Brace Jovanovich, 1961.

Jones, Edward E. *Ingratiation, a Social Psychological Analysis*. New York: Appleton-Century-Crofts, 1964.

———, Kenneth J. Gergen, and K. E. Davis. "Some Determinants of Reactions to Being Approved or Disapproved as a Person," *Psychological Monographs*, 76, 521 (1962).

Kelley, Harold H., John W. Thibaut, Roland Radloff, and

Donald Mundy. "The Development of Cooperation in the 'Minimal Social Situation,' " *Psychological Monographs*, 76, 19 (1962).

Kinzel, Augustus F. "The Body-Buffer Zone in Violent Prisoners," *American Journal of Psychiatry*, 127, 1: 59–64 (July 1970).

LaBarre, Weston. "The Language of Emotions and Gestures," in Warren G. Bennis (ed.), *Interpersonal Dynamics, Essays and Readings on Human Interaction*. Rev. ed. Homewood, Ill.: Dorsey Press,1968.

Lenneberg, Eric H. (ed.) *New Directions in the Study of Language*. Cambridge: Massachusetts Institute of Technology Press, 1964.

Linton, Ralph. "Concepts of Role and Status," in Theodore M. Newcomb and Eugene L. Hartley (eds.), *Readings in Social Psychology*. Society for the Psychological Study of Social Issues. New York: Holt, Rinehart and Winston, 1947.

Luce, Robert D., and Howard Raiffa. *Games and Decisions; Introduction and Critical Survey*. A Study of the Behavioral Models Project, Bureau of Applied Social Research, Columbia University. New York: Wiley, 1957.

McCall, George, and J. L. Simmons. *Identities and Interaction*. New York: Free Press, 1966.

Maslow, Abraham H., *et al.* "Some Parallels between Sexual and Dominance Behavior of Infra-Human Primates and the Fantasies of Patients in Psychotherapy," in Warren G. Bennis (ed.), *Interpersonal Dynamics, Essays and Readings on Human Interaction*. Rev. ed. Homewood, Ill.: Dorsey Press, 1968.

Mead, George Herbert. *Mind, Self and Society*. Chicago: University of Chicago Press, 1934.

Messinger, Sheldon L., Harold Sampson, and Robert D. Towne. "Life as Theater: Some Notes on the Dramaturgic Approach to Social Reality," *Sociometry*, 25, 1: 98–110 (January 1962).

Minas, J. Sayer, Alvin S. Scodel, David M. Marlowe, and Harve Rawson. "Some Descriptive Aspects of Two-Person Non-Zero-Sum Games," *Journal of Conflict Resolution*, 4, 2: 193–197 (June 1960).

Miyamoto, Frank S., and Sanford Dornbusch. "A Test of Interactionist Hypotheses of Self-Conception," *American Journal of Sociology*, 61, 4: 399–403 (January 1956).

Morris, Desmond. *The Naked Ape: A Zoologist's Study of the Human Animal*. New York: McGraw-Hill, 1968.

Park, Robert Ezra. *Race and Culture*. Glencoe, Ill.: Free Press, 1950.

Scheflen, Albert E. "Human Communication," *Behavioral Science*, 13, 1: 44–53 (January 1968).

———. "Quasi-Courtship Behavior in Psychotherapy," in Warren G. Bennis (ed.), *Interpersonal Dynamics, Essays and Readings on Human Interaction*. Rev. ed. Homewood, Ill.: Dorsey Press, 1968.

———, and Alice Scheflen. *Body Language and the Social Order: Communication as Behavioral Control*. Englewood Cliffs, N.J.: Prentice-Hall, 1972.

Sidowski, Joseph B. "Reward and Punishment in a Minimal Social Situation," *Journal of Experimental Psychology*, 54, 5: 318–326 (October 1957).

Sommer, Robert. *Personal Space: The Behavioral Basis of Design*. Englewood Cliffs, N.J.: Spectrum Books, 1969.

Thibaut, John W., and Harold H. Kelley. *The Social Psychology of Groups*. New York: Wiley, 1959.

Triandis, Harry C. "Cultural Influences upon Cognitive Processes," *Advances in Experimental Social Psychology*, 1: 2–48 (1964).

Watson, O. Michael, and Theodore D. Graves. "Quantitative Research in Proxemic Behavior," *American Anthropologist*, 68, 4: 971–985 (August 1966).

Weber, Max. *Economy and Society: An Outline of Interpretive Sociology*. Guenther Roth and Claus Wittich (eds.). Ephraim Fischoff, *et al.* (trs.). New York: Bedminster Press, 1968; first published in 4 vols. in German, 1922.

———. *The Theory of Social and Economic Organization*. Talcott Parsons (ed.). A. M. Henderson and Talcott Parsons (trs.). Glencoe, Ill.: Free Press, 1957; first printing, 1947.

Unit 13

Barry, Herbert, Margaret K. Bacon, and Irvin Child. "A Cross-Cultural Survey of Some Sex Differences in Socialization," *Journal of Abnormal and Social Psychology*, 55, 3: 327–332 (May 1957).

Beach, Frank A. "Retrospect and Prospect," in Frank A. Beach (ed.), *Sex and Behavior*. New York: Wiley, 1965.

D'Andrade, Roy G. "Sex Differences and Cultural Institutions," in Eleanor E. Maccoby (ed.), *The Development of Sex Differences*. Stanford Studies in Psychology, 5. Stanford: Stanford University Press, 1966.

Duverger, Maurice. *The Political Role of Women*. Paris: UNESCO, 1955.

Ford, Clellan S., and Frank A. Beach. *Patterns of Sexual Behavior*. New York: Harper and Row, 1951.

Gesell, Arnold. *The First Five Years of Life: A Guide to the Study of the Pre-School Child*. New York: Harper and Row, 1940.

Goode, William J. *The Family*. Foundations of Modern Sociology Series. Englewood Cliffs, N.J.: Prentice-Hall, 1964.

Kagan, Jerome. *Personality Development*. New York: Harcourt Brace Jovanovich, 1971.

Katcher, Allan. "The Discrimination of Sex Differences by Young Children," *Journal of Genetic Psychology*, 87, 1: 131–143 (September 1955).

Kinsey, Alfred C., Wardell B. Pomeroy, and Clyde E. Martin. *Sexual Behavior in the Human Female*. Philadelphia: W. B. Saunders, 1953.

———. *Sexual Behavior in the Human Male*. Philadelphia: W. B. Saunders, 1948.

Kohlberg, Lawrence. "A Cognitive Developmental Analysis of Children's Sex-Role Concepts and Attitudes," in Eleanor E. Maccoby (ed.), *The Development of Sex Differences*. Stanford Studies in Psychology, 5. Stanford: Stanford University Press, 1966.

Maccoby, Eleanor E. "Sex Differences in Intellectual Functioning," in Eleanor E. Maccoby (ed.), *The Development of Sex Differences*. Stanford Studies in Psychology, 5. Stanford: Stanford University Press, 1966.

Millett, Kate. *Sexual Politics*. Garden City, N.Y.: Doubleday, 1970.

Money, John, Joan Hampson, and John Hampson. "Imprinting and the Establishment of Gender Role," *Archives of Neurology and Psychiatry*, 77: 333–336 (1967).

Murdock, George P. "World Ethnographic Sample," *American Anthropologist*, 54, 4: 664–687 (August 1957).

Sorensen, Robert. *Adolescent Sexuality in Modern America: Personal Values and Sexual Behavior, Ages 13 to 19*. Cleveland: World Publishing, 1972.

Stephens, William N. *The Family in Cross-Cultural Perspective*. New York: Holt, Rinehart and Winston, 1963.

Unit 14

Blauner, Robert. "Death and the Social Structure," *Psychiatry*, 29, 4: 378–394 (November 1966).

Bowman, Leroy. *The American Funeral: A Study in Guilt, Extravagance and Sublimity*. Washington, D.C.: Public Affairs Press, 1959.

Brim, Orville G., *et al.* (eds.). *The Dying Patient*. New York: Russell Sage, 1970.

Chasin, Barbara H. "Value-Orientation and Attitudes towards Death" (unpublished dissertation, University of Iowa, 1968).

Choron, Jacques. *Death and Western Thought*. New York: Collier Books, 1963.

———. *Modern Man and Mortality*. New York: Macmillan, 1964.

Cohen, Sidney. "LSD and the Anguish of Dying," *Harper's* (September 1965).

Crane, Diana. "Dying and Its Dilemmas as a Field of Research," in Orville G. Brim, *et al.* (eds.), *The Dying Patient*.

Duff, Raymond, and August Hollingshead. *Sickness and Society*. New York: Harper and Row, 1968.

Erikson, Erik. "Identity and the Life Cycle: Selected Papers," *Psychological Issues*, 1, 1: 1–171 (1959).

Feifel, Herman (ed.) *The Meaning of Death*. New York: McGraw-Hill, 1959.

Freud, Sigmund. *Collected Papers*. 5 vols. Joan Riviere, Alix Strachey, and James Strachey (trs.). New York. Basic Books, 1959; first published in German, 1888–1938.

Fulton, Robert (ed.). *Death and Identity*. New York: Wiley, 1965.

Glaser, Barney G., and Anselm L. Strauss. "Awareness Contexts and Social Interaction," *American Sociological Review*, 29, 5: 669–678 (October 1964).

———. *Awareness of Dying*. Chicago: Aldine, 1965.

———. "Patterns of Dying," in Orville G. Brim, *et al.* (eds.), *The Dying Patient*.

———. "Temporal Aspects of Dying as a Non-Scheduled Status Passage," *American Journal of Sociology*, 71, 1: 48–60 (July 1965).

———. *Time for Dying*. Chicago: Aldine, 1968.

Gouldner, Alvin W. *The Coming Crisis of Western Sociology*. New York: Basic Books, 1970.

Hall, G. Stanley. *Senescence, the Last Half of Life*. New York: D. Appleton, 1922.

———. "Thanatophobia and Immortality," *American Journal of Psychology*, 26, 4: 550–563 (October 1915).

Harmer, Ruth M. *The High Cost of Dying*. New York: Collier Books, 1963.

Hillery, George A., *et al.* "Causes of Death in the Demographic Transition," paper presented at the Annual Meeting of the Population Association of America, Boston, April, 1968.

Hospice. "Philosophy Statement" (unpublished, New Haven, Conn., April 7, 1971).

Howard, Alan and Robert A. Scott. "Cultural Values and Attitudes Toward Death," *Journal of Existentialism*, 6, 22: 161–174 (Winter 1965).

Kalish, Richard A. "The Practising Physician and Death Research," *Medical Times*, 97: 211–220 (January 1969).

Kastenbaum, Richard A. "The Mental Life of Dying Geriatric Patients," *Gerontologist*, 7, 2: 97–100 (March 1967).

———, and Ruth B. Aisenberg. *The Psychology of Death*. New York: Springer, 1972.

Kaufmann, Walter. "Existentialism and Death," in Hermann Feifel (ed.), *The Meaning of Death*.

Kübler-Ross, Elisabeth. *Death and Dying*. New York: Macmillan, 1969.

Lasagna, Louis. "Physicians' Behavior Toward the Dying Patient," in Orville G. Brim, *et al.* (eds.), *The Dying Patient*. New York: Russell Sage, 1970.

Lifton, Robert K. *History and Human Survival: Essays on the Young and Old, Survivors and the Dead, Peace and War, and on Contemporary Psychohistory*. John Simon (ed.). New York: Random House, 1969.

Mitford, Jessica. *The American Way of Death*. New York: Simon and Schuster, 1963.

Morgenthau, Hans J. "Death in the Nuclear Age," *Commentary* (September 1961).

Parsons, Talcott. "Death in American Society—A Brief Working Paper," *American Behavioral Scientist*, 6, 9: 61–65 (May 1963).

Pattison, Mansell. "The Experience of Dying," *American Journal of Psychotherapy*, 21, 1: 32–44 (January 1967).

Quint, Jeanne. *The Nurse and the Dying Patient*. New York: Macmillan, 1967.

Rieff, Phillip. *Freud: The Mind of the Moralist*. Garden City, N.Y.: Anchor Books, 1961.

Saunders, Cicely. "The Last Stages of Life," *American Journal of Nursing*, 65, 3: 70–76 (March 1965).

Sudnow, David. *Passing On: The Social Organization of Dying*. Englewood Cliffs, N.J.: Prentice-Hall, 1967.

van Gennep, Arthur. *Rites of Passage*. Monika Vizedom and Gabrielle Caffee (trs.). Chicago: University of Chicago Press, 1960; first published in Dutch, 1908.

Weisman, Avery D. *On Dying and Denying: A Psychiatric Study of Terminality*. New York: Behavioral Publications, 1972.

Wolff, Kurt. "Helping Elderly Patients Face the Fear of Death," *Hospital and Community Psychiatry*, 18, 5: 142–144 (May 1967).

Unit 15

Adorno, Theodor W., *et al.* *The Authoritarian Personality*. New York: Norton, 1969; first printing, 1950.

Allport, Gordon W. *The Nature of Prejudice*. Studies in Prejudice. Garden City, N.Y.: Anchor Books, 1958; first printing, 1948.

Cox, Oliver C. *Caste, Class and Race*. New York: Monthly Review Press, 1970; first printing, 1948.

Jahoda, N. M. "X-Ray of the Racist Mind," *UNESCO Courier* (October 1960).

Marx, Karl. *Capital, a Critique of Political Economy*. 3 vols. Friedrich Engels (ed.). Samuel Moore and Edward Aveling (trs.). New York: International Publishers, 1967; first published in German, 1867–1894.

Merton, Robert K. "Discrimination and the American Creed," in Robert M. MacIver (ed.), *Discrimination and National Welfare*. The Institute for Religious and Social Studies, Jewish Theological Seminary. New York: Harper and Row, 1948.

———. *Social Theory and Social Structure*. 3rd ed. New York: Free Press, 1968; rev. and enl. ed. 1957; first printing, 1949.

Myrdal, Gunnar. *An American Dilemma: The Negro Problem and Modern Democracy*. 2 vols. 20th Anniversary Ed. New York: Harper and Row, 1962; first printing, 1944.

Nash, Manning. "Race and the Ideology of Race," *Current Anthropology*, 3, 3: 285–288 (June 1962).

Novak, Michael. *The Rise of the Unmeltable Ethnics: Politics and Culture in the Seventies*. New York: Macmillan, 1972.

Rex, John. *Race Relations and Sociological Theory*. New York: Schocken Books, 1971.

Simpson, George E., and J. Milton Yinger. *Racial and Cultural Minorities: An Analysis of Prejudice and Discrimination*. Social Science Series. New York: Harper and Row, 1965; first printing, 1958.

van den Berghe, Pierre. "The Dynamics of Racial Prejudice: An Ideal-Type Dichotomy," *Social Forces*. 37, 2: 138–141 (December 1958).

Whitten, Phillip, and Ian Robertson. "Racialism in Black Africa," *The Progressive* (April 1973).

Unit 16

Aron, Raymond. *Eighteen Lectures on Industrial Society*. T. B. Bottomore (tr.). London: Weidenfeld and Nicolson, 1967; first published in French, 1965.

———. *La lutte des classes: Nouvelles leçons sur les sociétés industrielles*. Paris: Editions Gallimard, 1964.

Blau, Peter M. *The Dynamics of Bureaucracy: A Study of Interpersonal Relationships in Two Government Agencies*. 2nd ed. Chicago: University of Chicago Press, 1963; first printing, 1955.

Durkheim, Emile. *The Division of Labor in Society*. George Simpson (tr.). New York: Free Press, 1964; first published in French, 1893.

MacIver, Robert M. *The Web of Government*. Rev. ed. New York: Free Press, 1965; first printing, 1947.

Marx, Karl. "A Critique of Hegel's 'Philosophy of Right,' " in Lloyd D. Easton and Kurt Guddat (eds. and trs.), *Writings of the Young Marx on Philosophy and Society*. Garden City, N.Y.: Anchor Books, 1967; first written in German, 1843.

———. *Selected Writings in Sociology and Social Philosophy*. T. B. Bottomore and Maximilien Rubel (eds. and trs.). New York: McGraw-Hill, 1964.

Merton, Robert K. *Social Theory and Social Structure*. 3rd ed. New York: Free Press, 1968; rev. and enl. ed., 1957; first printing, 1949.

Michels, Robert. *Political Parties: A Sociological Study of the Oligarchical Tendencies of Modern Democracy*. Eden and Cedar Paul (trs.). New York: Free Press, 1962; first published in German, 1911.

Ossowski, Stanislaw. *Class Structure in the Social Consciousness*. Sheila Patterson (tr.). New York: Free Press, 1963; first published in Polish, 1957.

Roethlisberger, F. J., and William J. Dickson. *Management and the Worker*. Cambridge: Harvard University Press, 1961; first printing, 1939.

Roszak, Theodore. *The Making of a Counter Culture: Reflections on the Technocratic Society and its Youthful Opposition*. Garden City, N.Y.: Anchor Books, 1969.

Schumpeter, Joseph A. *Capitalism, Socialism and Democracy*. 3rd ed. New York: Harper Torchbooks, 1950; first published, 1942.

Thompson, Victor. *Modern Organization*. New York: Knopf, 1961.

Weber, Max. *Economy and Society: An Outline of Interpretive Sociology*. Guenther Roth and Claus Wittich (eds.). Ephraim Fischoff *et al.* (trs.). New York: Bedminster Press, 1968; first printing in 4 vols. in German, 1922.

———. *The Theory of Social and Economic Organization*. Talcott Parsons (ed.). A. M. Henderson and Talcott Parsons (trs.). Glencoe, Ill.: Free Press, 1957; first printing, 1947.

Unit 17

Angell, Robert C. "The Social Integration of American Cities of More than 100,000 Population," *American Sociological Review*, 12, 3: 335–342 (June 1947).

Butler, Edgar W., Ronald J. McAllister, and Edward J. Kaiser. "Air Pollution and Metropolitan Population Redistribution," *Journal of the American Institute of Planners*, 37, 5 (September 1971).

Carstairs, George M. "Overcrowding and Human Aggression," in H. D. Graham and Ted R. Gurr (eds.), *The History of Violence in America: Historical and Comparative Perspectives*. Report of the National Commission on the Causes and Prevention of Violence. New York: Praeger, 1969.

Clinard, Marshall B. "Crime and the City," in Albert N. Cousins and Hans Nagpaul (eds.), *Urban Man and Society*. New York: Random House, 1970.

Drottboom, Theodore, Jr., Ronald J. McAllister, Edward J. Kaiser, and Edgar W. Butler. "Urban Violence and Residential Mobility," *Journal of the American Institute of Planners*, 37, 5 (September 1971).

Duncan, Otis Dudley, and Beverly Duncan. "Residential Distribution and Occupational Stratification," *American Journal of Sociology*, 40, 5: 493–503 (March 1955).

Freedman, Jonathan L. "A Positive View of Population Density," *Psychology Today* (September 1971).

Gans, Herbert J. (ed.) *People and Plans: Essays on Urban Problems and Solutions*. New York: Basic Books, 1968.

———. *The Urban Villagers*. New York: Free Press, 1962.

———. "Urbanism and Suburbanism," in T. Lynn Smith and C. A. McMahan (eds.), *The Sociology of Urban Life*. New York: Dryden Press, 1951.

Glazer, Nathan, and Daniel P. Moynihan. *Beyond the Melting Pot: The Negroes, Puerto Ricans, Jews, Italians and Irish of New York City*. 2nd ed. Cambridge: Massachusetts Institute of Technology Press, 1970; first printing, 1963.

Hall, Edward T. *The Hidden Dimension*. Garden City, N.Y.: Anchor Books, 1969; first printing, 1966.

Harris, Chauncy D. and Edward L. Ullman. "The Nature of Cities," *Annals of the American Academy of Political and Social Science*, 242: 7–17 (November 1945).

Hatt, Paul. "Spatial Patterns in a Polytechnic Area," *American Sociological Review*, 10, 3: 352–356 (June 1945).

Hoover, Edgar M., and Raymond Vernon. *Anatomy of a Metropolis: The Changing Distribution of People and Jobs within the New York Metropolitan Region*. New York Metropolitan Region Studies, 1. Cambridge: Harvard University Press, 1959.

Hoyt, Homer. *The Structure and Growth of Residential Neighborhoods in American Cities*. Federal Housing Authority. Washington, D.C.: Government Printing Office, 1939.

———. "The Structure of American Cities in the Post-War Era," *American Journal of Sociology*, 48, 4: 475–492 (January 1943).

Lynd, Robert S., and Helen M. Lynd. *Middletown, a Study in American Culture*. New York: Harvest Books, 1956; first printing, 1929.

McIntire, Davis. *Residence and Race: The Final and Comprehensive Report to the Commission on Race and Housing*. Berkeley: University of California Press, 1960.

McMahan, C. A. "Personality in the Urban Environment," in T. Lynn Smith and C. A. McMahan (eds.), *The Sociology of Urban Life*.

Mailer, Norman. "Why Are We in New York?" in Nathan Glazer (ed.), *Cities in Trouble*. The New York Times Series on Contemporary Affairs. New York: Quadrangle Books, 1970.

Moynihan, Daniel P. (ed.) *Toward a National Urban Policy*. New York: Basic Books, 1970.

New York City Planning Commission. *Plan for New York City 1969; a Proposal*. Peter S. Richards (ed.). Cambridge: Massachusetts Institute of Technology Press, 1969.

Pettigrew, Thomas F. "Racial Segregation and Negro Education," in Daniel P. Moynihan (ed.), *Toward a National Urban Policy*.

Riesman, David. *The Lonely Crowd: A Study of the Changing American Character*. New Haven: Yale University Press, 1950.

Sennett, Richard. *The Uses of Disorder: Personal Identity and City Life*. New York: Knopf, 1970.

Stouffer, Samuel. *Communism, Conformity and Civil Liberties: A Cross-Section of the Nation Speaks its Mind*. Garden City, N.Y.: Doubleday, 1955.

Suttles, Gerald D. *The Social Order of the Slum: Ethnicity and Territoriality in the Inner City*. Studies of Urban Sociology Series. Chicago: University of Chicago Press, 1970; first printing, 1968.

Taeuber, Karl E., and Alma F. Taeuber. *Negroes in Cities: Residential Segregation and Neighborhood Change*. Population Research and Training Center Monographs, University of Chicago. Chicago: Aldine, 1965.

Vernon, Raymond. *The Myth and Reality of our Urban Problems*. Joint Center for Urban Studies. Cambridge: Harvard University Press, 1966.

Wirth, Louis. "Urbanism as a Way of Life," in Albert J. Reiss, Jr. (ed.), *Louis Wirth on Cities and Social Life, Selected Papers*. Chicago: University of Chicago Press, 1964.

Unit 18

Armor, David. "Armor Answers Back on Busing," *Psychology Today* (April 1973).

———. "The Evidence on Busing," *Public Interest* (Summer 1972).

Boardman, Richard P. "A Comparison of the Academic Performances of 5th and 6th Grade Pupils in a Program of Public Transfer" (unpublished dissertation, Teachers College, Columbia University, New York, 1968).

Coleman, James S., *et al. Equality of Educational Opportunity*. 2 vols. Washington, D.C.: Government Printing Office, 1966.

Cremin, Lawrence A. *American Education: The Colonial Experience, 1607–1783*. New York: Harper and Row, 1970.

Davis, Allison. *Social Class Influences Upon Learning*. Cambridge: Harvard University Press, 1948.

Dentler, Robert A., Bernard Mackler, and Ellen Warshauer (eds.) *The Urban R's: Race Relations as the Problem in Urban Education*. New York: Praeger, 1967.

Deutsch, Martin P. "Minority Group and Class Status as Related to Social and Personality Factors in Scholastic Achievement," *Society for Applied Anthropology Monograph*.

Durkheim, Emile. *Education and Sociology*. S. D. Fox (tr.). Glencoe, Ill.: Free Press, 1956; first published in French, 1922.

Festinger, Leon. "Wish, Expectation and Group Standards as Factors Influencing Level of Aspiration," *Journal of Abnormal and Social Psychology*, 37, 2: 184–200 (April 1942).

Fox, David J., *et al. More Effective Schools*. New York: Center for Urban Education, 1968.

Gebhard, Mildred. "The Effect of Success and Failure Upon the Attractiveness of Activities as a Function of Experience, Expectation, and Need," *Journal of Experimental Psychology*, 38, 4: 371–388 (August 1948).

Goff, Regina M. "Some Educational Implications of the Influence of Rejection on Aspiration Levels of Minority Group Children," *Journal of Experimental Education*, 23, 2: 179–183 (December 1954).

Gordon, C. Wayne. *The Social System of the High School*. New York: Free Press, 1957.

Grant, David A., Harold W. Hake, and John P. Hornseth. "Acquisition and Extinction of a Verbal Conditioned Response with Differing Percentages of Reinforcement," *Journal of Experimental Psychology*, 42, 1: 1–5 (July 1951).

Guthrie, James W., *et al. Schools and Inequality*. Cambridge: Massachusetts Institute of Technology Press, 1971.

Hamblin, Robert L., *et al. The Humanization Processes*. New York: Wiley, 1971.

Hamilton, Charles. "Race and Education: A Search for Legitimacy," *Harvard Educational Review*, 38, 4: 669–684. (Fall 1968).

Hollingshead, August B. *Elmtown's Youth: The Impact of Social Classes on Adolescents*. New York: Wiley, 1949.

Hyman, Herbert H., *et al. Applications of Methods of Evaluation*. Berkeley: University of California Press, 1962.

Jencks, Christopher, *et al. Inequality: A Reassessment of Family and Schooling in America*. New York: Basic Books, 1972.

Katz, Irwin, Judith Goldston, and Lawrence Benjamin. "Behavior Productivity in Bi-Racial Work Groups," *Human Relations*, 11, 2: 123–141 (May 1958).

Kosloff, Martin. *Reaching the Autistic Child*. Champaign, Ill.: Research Press, 1973.

Mackler, Bernard. "The Little Black Schoolhouse," mimeographed paper. Center for Urban Education, New York, 1969.

Moore, Omar Khayam. *Autotelic Response Environments and Exceptional Children*. Hamden, Conn.: Responsive Environments Foundation, 1963.

Rosenthal, Robert and Lenore Jacobson. *Pygmalion in the Classroom*. New York: Holt, Rinehart and Winston, 1968.

Sexton, Patricia Cayo. *Education and Income*. New York: Viking, 1961.

U.S. Commission on Civil Rights. *Racial Isolation in the Public Schools*. 2 vols. Washington, D.C.: Government Printing Office, 1967.

Waller, Willard. *The Sociology of Teaching*. New York: Wiley, 1967; first printing, 1932.

Warner, William Lloyd, *et al. Who Shall Be Educated?* New York: Harper and Row, 1944.

Weinberg, Meyer. *Desegregation Research: An Appraisal*. 2nd ed. Bloomington, Ind.: Phi Delta Kappa, 1970.

Unit 19

Caplan, Gerald. *Principles of Preventive Psychiatry*. New York: Basic Books, 1964.

———. "Some Comments on 'Community Psychiatry and Social Power,'" *Social Problems*, 14, 1: 21–25 (Summer 1966).

Commission on Chronic Illness. *Chronic Illness in a Large City: The Baltimore Study*. Chronic Illness in the United States, 4. Cambridge: Harvard University Press, 1957.

Coser, Rose Laub. "A Home Away from Home," *Social Problems*, 4, 1: 3–17 (Summer 1956).

Davis, Fred. "Uncertainty in Medical Prognosis, Clinical and Functional," *American Journal of Sociology*, 66, 1: 41–47 (July 1960).

Dinitz, Simon, and Nancy Beran. "Community Mental Health as a Boundaryless and Boundary-Busting System," *Journal of Health and Social Behavior*, 12, 2: 99–108 (Summer 1971).

Freidson, Eliot. "Client Control and Medical Practise," *American Journal of Sociology*, 65, 4: 374–382 (January 1960).

———. *The Profession of Medicine: A Study of the Sociology of Applied Knowledge*. New York: Dodd, Mead, 1970.

Glaser, William A. "'Socialized Medicine' in Practise," *The Public Interest*, 1, 3: 90–106 (Spring 1966).

Goffman, Erving. *Asylums*. Garden City, N.Y.: Anchor Books, 1961.

Gove, Walter A. "Societal Reaction as an Explanation of Mental Illness," *American Sociological Review*, 35, 5: 873–884 (October 1970).

Hollingshead, August B., and Frederick C. Redlich. *Social Class and Mental Illness*. New York: Wiley, 1958.

Kasl, Stanislav V., and Sidney Cobb. "Health Behavior, Illness Behavior, and Sick-Role Behavior; I. Health and Illness Behavior," *Archives of Environmental Health*, 12, 2: 246–266 (February 1966).

———. "Health Behavior, Illness Behavior, and Sick-Role Behavior; II. Sick-Role Behavior," *Archives of Environmental Health*, 12, 4: 531–541 (April 1966).

Leifer, Ronald. "Community Psychiatry and Social Power," *Social Problems*, 14, 1: 16–25 (Summer 1966).

———. *In the Name of Mental Health: The Social Functions of Psychiatry*. New York: Science House, 1969.

Mechanic, David. *Medical Sociology: A Selective View*. New York: Free Press, 1968.

———. *Mental Health and Social Policy*. Englewood-Cliffs, N.J.: Prentice-Hall, 1969.

———. *Myths and Realities in Health Care: Essays on the Changing Organization of Health Services*. New York: Wiley-Interscience, 1972.

Parsons, Talcott. *The Social System*. Glencoe, Ill.: Free Press, 1951.

Peterson, Osler, *et al. An Analytic Study of North Carolina Medical Practise, 1953–1954*. Evanston, Ill.: Association of American Medical Colleges, 1956.

Phillips, Derek L. "Rejection: A Possible Consequence of Seeking Help for Mental Disorders," *American Sociological Review*, 28, 6: 963–972 (December 1963).

Quint, Jeanne C. "Institutionalized Practises of Information Control," *Psychiatry*, 28, 2: 119–132 (May 1965).

Rosenhan, David L. "On Being Sane in Insane Places," *Science*, 179, 4070: 250–258 (January 1973).

Roth, Julius. "Information and the Control of Treatment in Tuberculosis Hospitals," in Eliot Freidson (ed.), *The Hospital in Modern Society*. New York: Free Press, 1963.

Scheff, Thomas. *Being Mentally Ill: A Sociological Theory*. Chicago: Aldine, 1966.

Shiloh, Ailon. "Equalitarian and Hierarchical Patients: An Investigation among Hadassah Hospital Patients," *Medical Care*, 3, 2: 87–95 (April-June, 1965).

Srole, Leo. *Mental Health in the Metropolis: The Midtown Manhattan Study*. New York: Harper Torchbooks, 1970; first printing, 1962.

Suchman, Edward A. "Stages of Illness and Medical Care," *Journal of Health and Human Behavior*, 6, 3: 114–128 (Fall 1965).

Szasz, Thomas. *The Myth of Mental Illness*. New York: Harper and Row, 1961.

Zborowski, Mark. *People in Pain*. Behavioral Science Series. San Francisco: Jossey-Bass, 1966.

Zola, Irving K. "Culture and Symptoms—an Analysis of Patients Presenting Complaints," *American Sociological Review*, 31, 5: 615–630 (October 1966).

Unit 20

Berger, Peter L., and Brigitte Berger. *Sociology*. New York: Basic Books, 1972.

Binzen, Peter. *White Town, U.S.A.* New York: Vintage Books, 1970.

Burns, James MacGregor, and Jack Walter Peltason. *Government by the People: The Dynamics of American National Government*. Englewood Cliffs, N.J.: Prentice-Hall, 1969.

Dahl, Robert, and Charles E. Lindblom. *Politics, Economics, and Welfare: Planning and Politico-Economic Systems Resolved into Basic Social Processes*. New York: Harper Torchbooks, 1953.

Doob, Christopher B. "Dynamic Stagnation: Radicalism and Reform in an American Organization," unpublished paper, 1973.

Douglas, William O. *Points of Rebellion*. New York: Vintage Books, 1970.

Durkheim, Emile. *The Division of Labor in Society*. George Simpson (tr.). New York: Free Press, 1964; first published in French, 1893.

Eliade, Mircea. *The Sacred and the Profane: The Nature of Religion*. Willard B. Trask (tr.). New York: Harper Torchbooks, 1968; first printing, 1959; first published in German, 1957.

Ellis, William W. *White Ethics and Black Power: The Emergence of the West Side Organization*. Chicago: Aldine, 1969.

Engels, Friedrich. "On Historical Materialism," in Lewis S. Feuer (ed. and tr.), *Marx and Engels, Basic Writings on Politics and Philosophy*. New York: Anchor Books, 1959.

Hinton, William. *Hundred Day War: The Cultural Revolution at Tsinghua University*. New York: Monthly Review Press, 1972.

Horowitz, Irving L., and William Friedland. *The Knowledge Factory*. Observations Series. Chicago: Aldine, 1970.

Janis, Irving. *Victims of Groupthink: a Psychological Study of Foreign Policy Decisions and Fiascoes*. Boston: Houghton Mifflin, 1972.

Keniston, Kenneth. *Young Radicals: Notes on Committed Youth*. New York: Harvest Books, 1968.

————. *Youth and Dissent: The Rise of a New Opposition*. New York: Harcourt Brace Jovanovich, 1971.

Lundberg, Ferdinand. *America's Sixty Families*. New York: Vanguard Press, 1937.

Marx, Karl. *Selected Writings in Sociology and Social Philosophy*. T. B. Bottomore and Maximilien Rubel (eds. and trs.). New York: McGraw-Hill, 1964.

Mills, C. Wright. *The Power Elite*. New York: Oxford University Press, 1956.

————. *The Sociological Imagination*. New York: Oxford University Press, 1959.

Morgenthau, Hans J. *Politics Among Nations*. 4th ed. New York: Knopf, 1967.

Mott, Paul E. "Power, Authority and Influence," in Michael Aiken and Paul E. Mott (eds.), *The Structure of Community Power*. New York: Random House, 1970.

Pareto, Vilfredo. *The Mind and Society: A Treatise on General Sociology*. 4 vols. Arthur Livingston (ed.) Andrew Bongiorno and Arthur Livingston (trs.). New York: Dover, 1963; first printing, 1935; first published in Italian, 1916.

Parsons, Talcott. "The Distribution of Power in American Society," *World Politics*, 10, 1: 123–141 (October 1957).

Reich, Charles. *The Greening of America: The Coming of a New Consciousness and the Rebirth of a Future*. New York: Vintage Books, 1971; first printing, 1970.

Tocqueville, Alexis de. *Democracy in America*. Henry Steele Commager (ed.). Henry Reeve (tr.). New York: Oxford University Press, 1959; first published in French in two vols. 1835, 1840.

Turner, Jonathan. *American Society: Problems of Structure*. New York: Harper and Row, 1972.

Weber, Max. *Economy and Society: An Outline of Interpretive Sociology*. Guenther Roth and Claus Wittich (eds.). Ephraim Fischoff, *et al.* (trs.). New York: Bedminster Press, 1968; first published in 4 vols. in German, 1922.

————. *From Max Weber: Essays in Sociology*. Hans Gerth and C. Wright Mills (eds. and trs.). New York: Oxford University Press, 1946.

————. *The Protestant Ethic and the Spirit of Capitalism*. Talcott Parsons (tr.). New York: Scribner, 1958; first published in German, 1904–1905.

Unit 21

Clarke, Alfred. "Leisure and Occupational Prestige," in Eric Larrabee and Rolf Meyerson (eds.), *Mass Leisure*. New York: Free Press, 1958.

Coleman, James S. "Equality of Opportunity and Equality of Result," *Harvard Educational Review*, 43, 1: 129–137 (February 1973).

De Grazia, Sebastian. *Of Time, Work and Leisure*. Garden City, N.Y.: Anchor Books, 1962.

Featherstone, Joseph. *Schools Where Children Learn*. New York: Avon Books, 1973; first printing, 1971.

Graubard, Allen. *Free the Children: Radical Reform and the Free School Movement*. New York: Pantheon, 1972.

Jencks, Christopher. "Inequality in Retrospect," *Harvard Educational Review*, 43, 1: 138–164 (February 1973).

Kohn, Melvin. *Class and Conformity: A Study of Values*. Homewood, Ill.: Dorsey Press, 1969.

Kornhauser, Arthur. *The Mental Health of the Industrial Worker: A Detroit Study*. New York: Wiley, 1965.

Marx, Karl. *Contribution to the Critique of Political Economy*. N. I. Stone (tr.). New York: New World Books, 1970.

Meek, Ronald. *Economics and Ideology, and Other Essays*. New York: Barnes and Noble, 1967.

Montgomery County Student Alliance. "Wanted: A Human Education," in Ronald Gross and Paul Osterman (eds.), *High School*. New York: Clarion Books, 1971.

Palmore, Erdman. "Predicting Longevity: A Follow-Up Controlling for Age," *Gerontologist*, 8, 3: 259–263 (Winter 1969).

Polanyi, Karl. "Our Obsolete Market Mentality," in George Dalton (ed.), *Primitive, Archaic, and Modern Economics*. Boston: Beacon Press, 1968.

Postman, Neil, and Charles Weingartner. *Teaching as a Subversive Activity*. New York: Delacorte Press, 1969.

Project Talent Office. "Progress in Education: A Sample Survey," University of Pittsburgh, 1971.

Roszak, Theodore. "Education Contra Naturam," in Ronald Gross and Paul Osterman (eds.), *High School*. New York: Clarion Books, 1971.

Schlatter, Richard. *Private Property: The History of an Idea*. New York: Russell and Russell, 1973.

Special Task Force to the Secretary of Health, Education and Welfare. *Work in America*. Cambridge: Massachusetts Institute of Technology Press, 1973.

Torbert, William R. *Being for the Most Part Puppets*. Cambridge: Schenkman Books, 1973.

Verba, Sydney, and Norman Nie. *Participation in America: Political Democracy and Social Equality*. New York: Harper and Row, 1972.

Vroom, Victor H. "Industrial Social Psychology," in Gardner Lindzey and Elliott Aronsen (eds.), *Handbook of Social Psychology*. 2nd ed. Reading, Mass.: Addison-Wesley, 1969. Vol. 5.

Weber, Max. *Economy and Society: An Outline of Interpretive Sociology*. Guenther Roth and Claus Wittich (eds.). Ephraim Fischoff, *et al.* (trs.). New York: Bedminster Press, 1968; first published in 4 vols. in German, 1922.

————. "On Bureaucracy" and "The Meaning of Discipline," in Hans Gerth and C. Wright Mills (eds. and trs.), *From Max Weber: Essays in Sociology*. New York: Oxford University Press, 1946.

Whyte, William F. *Money and Motivation, an Analysis of Incentives in Industry*. New York: Harper Torchbooks, 1970; first printing, 1955.

Yankelovich, Daniel, *et al. Changing Values on Campus; Political and Personal Attitudes of Today's College Students*. New York: Washington Square Press, 1972.

Yinger, J. Milton. *Religion in the Struggle for Power*. Sociology Series. Durham, N.C.: Duke University Press, 1946.

Unit 22

Anderson, Niles. *The Hobo*. Chicago: University of Chicago Press, 1923.

Becker, Howard S. *Outsiders: Studies in the Sociology of Deviance*. New York: Free Press, 1963.

Bell, Daniel. *The End of Ideology: On the Exhaustion of Political Ideas in the Fifties*. New York: Collier Books, 1961; first printing, 1960.

Bell, Robert. *Social Deviance: A Substantive Analysis*. Homewood, Ill.: Dorsey Press, 1971.

Blum, Alan F. "Sociology, Wrongdoing, and Akrasia: An Attempt to Think Greek about the Problem of Theory and Practise," in Robert A. Scott and Jack Douglas (eds.), *Theoretical Perspectives on Deviance*. New York: Basic Books, 1972.

Clinard, Marshall B. *The Sociology of Deviance*. 3rd ed. New York: Holt, Rinehart and Winston, 1968.

Cloward, Richard A. and Lloyd E. Ohlin. *Delinquency and Opportunity: A Theory of Delinquent Gangs*. New York: Free Press, 1960.

Cohen, Albert K. *Deviance and Control*. Foundations of Modern Sociology Series. Englewood Cliffs, N.J.: Prentice-Hall, 1966.

Davis, Fred. "Deviance Disavowal: The Management of Strained Interaction by the Visibly Handicapped," in Howard S. Becker (ed.), *The Other Side*. New York: Free Press, 1964.

Douglas, Jack D. *American Social Order: Social Rules in a Pluralistic Society*. New York: Free Press, 1971.

Durkheim, Emile. *The Rules of the Sociological Method*. George E. G. Catlin (ed.) Sarah A. Solovay and John H. Mueller (trs.). New York: Free Press, 1958; first published in French, 1895.

————. *Suicide: A Sociological Study*. George Simpson (ed.). J. A. Spaulding and George Simpson (trs.). New York: Free Press, 1968; first published in French, 1897.

Elliott, Delbert S. "Delinquency, School Attendance, and Dropout," *Social Problems*, 13, 3: 307–314 (Winter 1966).

Erikson, Kai T. "Notes on the Sociology of Deviance," *Social Problems*, 9, 4: 308–314 (Spring 1962). Also in Howard S. Becker (ed.), *The Other Side*.

————. *Wayward Puritans: A Study in the Sociology of Deviance*. New York: Wiley, 1966.

Faris, Robert and Warren Dunham. *Mental Disorders in Urban Areas; an Ecological Study of Schizophrenia and Other Psychoses*. New York: Hafner, 1960; first printing, 1939.

Freud, Sigmund. *Civilization and its Discontents*. James Strachey (tr.) New York: Norton, 1961; first published in German, 1930.

Glaser, Daniel. *Social Deviance: Studies in Process and Change in American Society*. Chicago: Markham, 1971.

Goode, Erich. *Drugs in American Society*. New York: Knopf, 1972.

————. "Multiple Drug Use Among Marijuana Smokers," *Social Problems*, 17, 1: 48–64 (Summer 1969).

Gouldner, Alvin W. *The Coming Crisis of Western Sociology*. New York: Basic Books, 1970.

Hobbes, Thomas. *Leviathan*. C. B. MacPherson (ed.) Baltimore: Penguin, 1969; first published, 1651.

Hooker, Evelyn. "The Adjustment of the Male Homosexual," in Hendrik M. Ruitenbeek (ed.), *The Problem of Homosexuality in Modern Society*. New York: Dutton, 1963.

Kitsuse, John I. "Societal Reaction to Deviant Behavior: Problems of Theory and Methods," in Howard S. Becker (ed.), *The Other Side*. New York: Free Press, 1964.

Lehman, Timothy, and T. R. Young. "From Conflict Theory to Conflict Methodology," paper presented at the 67th Annual Meeting of the American Sociological Association, 1972.

Lemert, Edwin. *Social Pathology: A Systematic Approach to the Theory of Sociopathic Behavior*. Sociology and Anthropology Series. New York: McGraw-Hill, 1951.

Marris, Peter and Martin Rein. *Dilemmas of Social Reform: Poverty and Community Action in the United States*. Chicago: Aldine, 1967.

Matza, David. *Becoming Deviant*. Englewood Cliffs, N.J.: Prentice-Hall, 1969.

Merton, Robert K. "Social Structure and Anomie," *American Sociological Review*, 3, 5: 672–682 (October 1938).

————. *Social Theory and Social Structure*. 3rd ed. New York: Free Press, 1968; rev. and enl. ed., 1957; first printing, 1949.

Mills, C. Wright. "The Professional Ideology of Social Pathologists," *American Journal of Sociology*, 49, 2: 165–180 (September 1943).

Nicholas, David. "The Night They Pulled the Switch in Peoria," *T.V. Guide*, March 3, 1973.

Piven, Frances Fox, and Richard A. Cloward. *Regulating the Poor: The Functions of Public Welfare*. New York: Pantheon Books, 1971.

Quinney, Richard. "From Repression to Liberation: Social Theory in a Radical Age," in Robert A. Scott and Jack D. Douglas (eds.), *Theoretical Perspectives on Deviance*. New York: Basic Books, 1972.

Rosenberg, Bernard and Harry Silverstein. *The Varieties of Delinquent Experience*. Waltham, Mass.: Blaisdell, 1969.

Sagarin, Edward. *Odd Man In: Societies of Deviants in America*. Chicago: Quadrangle Books, 1969.

Schur, Edwin. *Crimes Without Victims: Deviant Behavior and Public Policy: Abortion, Homosexuality and Drug Addiction.* Englewood Cliffs, N.J.: Spectrum Books, 1965.

———. *Labeling Deviant Behavior: Its Sociological Implications.* Monograph Series in Sociology. New York: Harper and Row, 1971.

———. *Narcotic Addiction in Britain and America: The Impact of Public Policy.* Bloomington: University of Indiana Press, 1962.

Scott, Robert A. "A Proposed Framework for Analyzing Deviance as a Property of Social Order," in Robert A. Scott and Jack D. Douglas (eds.), *Theoretical Perspectives on Deviance.* New York: Basic Books, 1972.

———, and Jack D. Douglas. *Theoretical Perspectives on Deviance.* New York: Basic Books, 1972.

Seibel, H. Dieter. "Social Deviance in Comparative Perspective," in Robert A. Scott and Jack D. Douglas (eds.), *Theoretical Perspectives on Deviance.* New York: Basic Books, 1972.

Shaw, Clifford, Henry McKay, *et al. Delinquency Areas.* Chicago: University of Chicago Press, 1929.

———, and Henry McKay. *Juvenile Delinquency and Urban Areas.* Rev. ed. Chicago: University of Chicago Press, 1969; first printing, 1942.

Sutherland, Edwin H. *White Collar Crime.* New York: Holt, Rinehart and Winston, 1961; first printing, 1949.

Thrasher, Fredric. *The Gang: A Study of 1313 Gangs in Chicago.* Studies in Urban Sociology. Chicago: University of Chicago Press, 1927.

U.S. President's Commission on Law Enforcement and the Administration of Justice. *The Challenge of Crime in a Free Society, a Report.* Washington, D.C.: Government Printing Office, 1967.

Wallerstein, J. S., and C. J. Wyle. "Our Law Abiding Law Breakers," *Probation,* 35 (Spring 1947).

Whyte, William F. *Street Corner Society: The Social Structure of an Italian Slum.* 2nd ed. Chicago: University of Chicago Press, 1969; first printing, 1955.

Winslow, Robert W. *Society in Transition: A Social Approach to Deviancy.* New York: Free Press, 1970.

Wrong, D. H. "The Oversocialized Conception of Man in Modern Sociology," *American Sociological Review,* 26, 2: 183–193 (April 1961).

Unit 23

Beccaria, Cesare. *An Essay on Crimes and Punishments.* Henry Paolucci (tr.). Indianapolis: Bobbs-Merrill, 1963; first published in Italian, 1764.

Becker, Howard S. *Outsiders: Studies in the Sociology of Deviance.* New York: Free Press, 1963.

Bentham, Jeremy. "An Introduction to the Principles of Moral Legislation," in *The Utilitarians.* Garden City, N.Y.: Anchor Books, 1972; first published, 1823.

Chambliss, William J. *Crime and the Legal Process.* New York: McGraw-Hill, 1969.

———. "The Deterrent Influence of Punishment," *Journal of Research in Crime and Delinquency,* 3, 1: 70–75 (January 1966).

Chiricos, Theodore G., Phillip D. Jackson, and Gordon P. Waldo. "Inequality in the Imposition of a Criminal Label," *Social Problems,* 19, 4: 553–571 (Spring 1972).

———, and Gordon P. Waldo. "Punishment and Crime: An Examination of Some Empirical Evidence," *Social Problems,* 18, 2: 200–217 (Fall 1970).

Clark, John P., and Eugene P. Wenniger. "Socio-Economic Class and Area as Correlates of Illegal Behavior among Juveniles," *American Sociological Review,* 27, 6: 826–834 (December 1962).

Cloward, Richard A., and Lloyd E. Ohlin. *Delinquency and Opportunity: A Theory of Delinquent Gangs.* New York: Free Press, 1960.

Cohen, Albert K. *Delinquent Boys.* Glencoe, Ill.: Free Press, 1955.

Dentler, Robert, and Lawrence J. Monroe. "Early Adolescent Theft," *American Sociological Review,* 26, 5: 733–743 (April 1965).

Erickson, Maynard L., and Lamar T. Empey. "Class Position, Peers, and Delinquency," *Sociology and Social Research,* 49, 3: 268–282 (April 1965).

Glueck, Sheldon, and Eleanor T. Glueck. *Unraveling Juvenile Delinquency.* Commonwealth Fund Publications Series. Cambridge: Harvard University Press, 1950.

Gold, Martin. "Undetected Delinquent Behavior," *Journal of Research in Crime and Delinquency,* 3, 1: 27–46 (January 1966).

Goldman, Nathan. *The Differential Selection of Juvenile Offenders for Court Appearance.* New York: National Council on Crime and Delinquency, 1963.

Gordon, Robert A., James F. Short, Jr., Desmond S. Cartwright, and Fred L. Strodtbeck. "Values and Gang Delinquency: A Study of Street Corner Gangs," *American Journal of Sociology,* 69, 2: 109–128 (September 1963).

Goring, Charles. *The English Convict: A Statistical Study.* Reprint Series in Criminology, Law Enforcement and Social Problems, No. 137. Montclair, N.J.: Patterson Smith, 1972; first published, 1912.

Hindelang, Michael J. "Age, Sex, and the Versatility of Delinquent Involvements," *Social Problems,* 18, 4: 522–534 (Spring 1971).

Hooton, Ernest A. *The American Criminal: An Anthropological Study.* Cambridge: Harvard University Press, 1939.

Kobrin, Solomon. "The Conflict of Values in Delinquency Areas," *American Sociological Review,* 16, 4: 653–661 (October 1951).

Lemert, Edwin. *Social Pathology: A Systematic Approach to the Theory of Sociopathic Behavior.* Sociology and Anthropology Series. New York: McGraw-Hill, 1951.

Lombroso-Ferrara, Gina. *The Criminal Man, according to the Classification of Cesare Lombroso.* Reprint Series in Criminology, Law Enforcement and Social Problems, No. 14. Montclair, N.J.: Patterson Smith, 1968; first published in Italian, 1911.

Marshall, Harvey, and Ross Purday. "Hidden Deviance and the Labeling Approach: The Case for Drinking and Driving," *Social Problems,* 19, 4: 541–552 (Spring 1972).

Matza, David. *Delinquency and Drift.* New York: Wiley, 1964.

Merton, Robert K. *Social Theory and Social Structure.* 3rd ed. New York: Free Press, 1968; rev. and enl. ed., 1957; first printing, 1949.

Morris, Norval, and Gordon Hawkins. *The Honest Politician's Guide to Crime Control.* Chicago: University of Chicago Press, 1970.

Nye, F. Ivan, James F. Short, Jr., and Virgil J. Olsen. "Socioeconomic Status and Delinquent Behavior," *American Journal of Sociology,* 63, 4: 381–389 (January 1958).

Piliavin, Irving, and Scott Briar. "Police Encounters with Juveniles," *American Journal of Sociology,* 70, 2: 206–214 (September 1964).

Platt, Anthony M. *The Child Savers: The Invention of Delinquency.* Chicago: University of Chicago Press, 1969.

Savitz, Leonard D. "A Study of Capital Punishment," *Journal of Criminal Law, Criminology and Police Science,* 49, 4: 338–341 (November-December, 1958).

Schuessler, Karl. "The Deterrent Influence of the Death Penalty," *Annals of the American Academy of Political and Social Science,* 284: 54–62 (November 1952).

———, and Donald R. Cressey. "Personality Characteristics of Criminals," *American Journal of Sociology,* 55, 5: 476–484 (March 1950).

Schwartz, Richard D., and James S. Miller. "Legal Evolution and Societal Complexity," *American Journal of Sociology,* 70, 2: 159–169 (September 1964).

———, and Jerome H. Skolnick. "Two Studies of Legal Stigma," *Social Problems,* 10, 2: 133–142 (Fall 1962).

Shaw, Clifford R., and Henry D. McKay. *Juvenile Delinquency and Urban Areas.* Rev. ed. Chicago: University of Chicago Press, 1969; first printing, 1942.

Sheldon, William H. *Varieties of Delinquent Youth.* 2 vols. Human Constitution Series, 3. New York: Hafner, 1970; first printing, 1949.

Short, James F., Jr., Ramon Rivera, and Ray A. Tennyson. "Perceived Opportunities, Gang Membership and Delinquency," *American Sociological Review,* 30, 1: 56–67 (February 1965).

———, and Fred L. Strodtbeck. *Group Process and Gang Delinquency.* Chicago: University of Chicago Press, 1965.

Tannenbaum, Frank. *Crime and the Community.* New York: Columbia University Press, 1938.

Terry, Robert M. "The Screening of Juvenile Offenders," *Journal of Criminal Law, Criminology and Police Science,* 58, 3: 173–181 (June 1967).

Tittle, Charles R. "Crime Rates and Legal Sanctions," *Social Problems,* 16, 4: 409–423 (Spring 1969).

Tobias, John Jacob. *Crime and Industrial Society in the Nineteenth Century.* New York: Schocken Books, 1967.

Turk, Austin T. "Conflict and Criminality," *American Sociological Review,* 31, 3: 338–351 (June 1966).

Waldo, Gordon P., and Theodore G. Chiricos. "Perceived Penal Sanctions and Self-Reported Criminality: A Neglected Approach to Deterrence Research," *Social Problems,* 19, 4: 522–550 (Spring 1972).

Weber, Max. *Economy and Society: An Outline of Interpretive Sociology.* 3 vols. Guenther Roth and Claus Wittich (eds.). Ephraim Fischoff, *et al.* (trs.). New York: Bedminster Press, 1968; first published in 4 vols. in German, 1922.

———. *Law in Economy and Society.* Max Rheinstein (ed. and tr.). New York: Simon and Schuster, 1967.

Zimring, Frank, and Gordon Hawkins. "Deterrence and Marginal Groups," *Journal of Research in Crime and Delinquency,* 5, 2: 100–114 (July 1968).

Unit 24

Arnow, L. Earle. *Health in a Bottle: Searching for the Drugs that Help.* Philadelphia: Lippincott, 1970.

Ausubel, David P. "Causes and Types of Narcotics Addiction: A Psychosocial View," *Psychiatric Quarterly,* 35, 3: 523–531 (Fall 1961).

Barber, Bernard. *Drugs and Society.* New York: Russell Sage, 1967.

Becker, Howard S. *Outsiders: Studies in the Sociology of Deviance.* New York: Free Press, 1963.

Brecher, Edward M. and the Editors of *Consumer Reports. Licit and Illicit Drugs: The Consumers Union Report on Narcotics, Stimulants, Depressants, Inhalants, Hallucinogens and Marijuana.* Boston: Little, Brown, 1972.

Brenner, Joseph H., Robert Coles, and Dermot Meagher. *Drugs and Youth: Medical, Psychiatric and Legal Facts.* New York: Liveright, 1970.

Claridge, Gordon S. *Drugs and Human Behavior.* New York: Praeger, 1970.

Clarke, James W., and E. Lester Levine. "Marijuana Use, Social Discontent, and Political Alienation: A Study of High School Youth," *American Political Science Review,* 65, 1: 120–130 (March 1971).

Coles, Robert. *The Grass Pipe.* Boston: Little, Brown, 1969.

Dickson, Don T. "Bureaucracy and Morality: An Organizational Perspective on a Moral Crusade," *Social Problems,* 16, 2: 146–156 (Fall 1968).

Farnsworth, Dana L. "The Drug Problem Among Young People," *West Virginia Medical Journal,* 63, 12: 433–437 (December 1967).

Ginsberg, Allen. "The Great Marijuana Hoax," *Atlantic,* (November 1966).

Goode, Erich. *Drugs in American Society.* New York: Knopf, 1972.

———. "Multiple Drug Use Among Marijuana Smokers," *Social Problems,* 17, 1: 48–64 (Summer 1969).

Great Britain. Home Office. Advisory Committee on Drug Dependence. *Cannabis.* London: Her Majesty's Stationery Office, 1968.

Grinspoon, Lester. "Marihuana," *Scientific American,* 221, 6: 19–25 (December 1969).

———. *Marihuana Reconsidered.* Cambridge: Harvard University Press, 1971.

Huxley, Aldous. *The Doors of Perception.* New York: Harper and Row, 1954.

Kaplan, John. *Marijuana: The New Prohibition.* New York: World, 1972.

Keniston, Kenneth. "Heads and Seekers," *American Scholar,* 38, 1: 97–112 (Winter 1968–1969).

Leary, Timothy. "Interview with Timothy Leary," *Playboy* (September 1966).

———. *The Politics of Ecstasy.* New York: Putnam, 1968.

Lennard, Henry, *et al. Mystification and Drug Misuse: Hazards in Using Psychoactive Drugs.* San Francisco: Jossey–Bass, 1971.

Lindesmith, Alfred R. *The Addict and the Law.* New York: Vintage Books, 1965.

McGlothlin, William H. "Hallucinogenic Drugs: A Perspective, with Special Reference to Peyote and Cannabis," *Psychedelic Review,* 6: 16–57 (1965).

Melody, Roland. *Narco Priest.* New York: World, 1971.

Miller, Henry. "On Hanging-Loose and Loving: The Dilemma of Present Youth," *Journal of Social Issues,* 27, 3: 35–46 (1971).

Mitchell, A. R. K. "Misuse of Drugs in Modern Society," *Contemporary Review* (February 1972).

Orcutt, James D. "Toward a Sociological Theory of Drug Effects: A Comparison of Marijuana and Alcohol," *Sociology and Social Research*, 56, 2: 242–253 (January 1972).

Schur, Edwin M. *Narcotic Addiction in Britain and America: The Impact of Public Policy.* Bloomington: University of Indiana Press, 1962.

Simmons, Jerry and Barry Winograd. *It's Happening.* North Hollywood, Cal.: Brandon House, 1967.

Smith, David E. "The Characteristics of Dependence in High-Dose Methamphetamine Abuse," *International Journal of the Addictions,* 4, 3: 453–459 (September 1969).

——. "LSD and the Psychedelic Syndrome," *Clinical Toxicology,* 2, 1: 69–73 (March 1969).

——, (ed.) *The New Social Drug: Cultural, Medical and Legal Perspectives on Marijuana.* Englewood Cliffs, N.J.: Prentice-Hall, 1970.

——, and George R. Gay (eds.) *"It's So Good, Don't Even Try it Once": Heroin in Perspective.* Englewood Cliffs, N.J.: Prentice-Hall, 1972.

Solomon, David (ed.). *The Marihuana Papers.* Indianapolis: Bobbs-Merrill, 1966.

Suchman, Edward A. "The 'Hang-Loose' Ethic and the Spirit of Drug Use," *Journal of Health and Social Behavior,* 9, 2: 146–155 (June 1968).

Tec, Nechama. "Family and Differential Involvement with Marijuana: A Study of Suburban Teenagers," *Journal of Marriage and the Family,* 32, 4: 656–664 (November 1970).

U.S. National Commission on Marihuana and Drug Abuse. *Drug Use in America.* (2nd Report). Washington, D.C.: Government Printing Office, March 1973.

——. *Marihuana: A Signal of Misunderstanding.* (1st Report). 3 vols. Washington, D.C.: Government Printing Office, March 1972.

Weil, Andrew, Norman E. Zinberg, and Judith M. Nelsen. "Clinical and Psychological Effects of Marihuana in Man," *Science,* 162, 3859: 1234–1242 (December 1968).

Whitten, Phillip, and Ian Robertson. "A Way to Control Heroin Addiction," *Boston Globe Magazine,* May 21, 1972. Reprinted in Annual Editions *Readings in Social Problems '73/'74.* Guilford, Conn.: Dushkin Publishing Group, 1973.

Wittenborn, John R. (ed.) *Drugs and Youth.* Rutgers University Symposium on Drug Abuse. Springfield, Ill.: Thomas, 1969.

Young, Jock. *The Drugtakers: The Social Meaning of Drug Use.* London: MacGibbon and Kee, 1971.

Zinberg, Norman E. *Drugs and the Public.* New York: Simon and Schuster, 1972.

——, and Andrew Weil. "Cannabis: The First Controlled Experiment," *New Society* (January 1969).

Unit 25

Adelson, Joseph. "What Generation Gap?" *The New York Times Magazine,* January 18, 1970.

Anderson, Charles H. *Toward a New Sociology: A Critical View.* Homewood, Ill.: Dorsey Press, 1971.

Berger, Bennett M. "The New Stage of American Man, Almost Endless Adolescence," *The New York Times Magazine,* November 2, 1969.

Erikson, Erik. *Childhood and Society.* 2nd rev. ed. New York: Norton, 1963; first printing, 1950.

——, *Youth, Identity, and Crisis.* New York: Norton, 1968.

Flacks, Richard. "The Liberated Generation: An Exploration of the Roots of Student Protest," *Journal of Social Issues,* 23, 3: 52–75 (July 1967).

Goodman, Paul. *The New Reformation: Notes of a Neolithic Conservative.* New York: Random House, 1970.

Hall, G. Stanley. *Adolescence: Its Psychology and its Relations to Physiology, Anthropology, Sociology, Sex, Crime, Religion, and Education.* New York: D. Appleton, 1904.

Hodges, Harold M., Jr. *Conflict and Consensus: An Introduction to Sociology.* New York: Harper and Row, 1971.

Kahn, Roger M., and William J. Bowers. "The Social Context of the Rank and File Student Activist—a Test of Four Hypotheses," *Sociology of Education,* 43, 1: 38–55 (January 1970).

Keniston, Kenneth. *Youth and Dissent: The Rise of a New Opposition.* New York: Harcourt Brace Jovanovich, 1971.

Lifton, Robert Jay. *History and Human Survival: Essays on the Young and Old, Survivors the Dead, Peace and War, and on Contemporary Psychohistory.* John Simon (ed.) New York: Random House, 1969.

Marcuse, Herbert. *Eros and Civilization: A Philosophical Inquiry into Freud.* Boston: Beacon Press, 1956.

Matza, David, and Gresham A. Sykes. "Juvenile Delinquency

and Subterranean Values," *American Sociological Review,* 26, 5: 712–719 (October 1961).

Mead, Margaret. *Culture and Commitment.* Garden City, N.Y.: Natural History Press, 1970.

Parsons, Talcott. "Age and Sex in the Social Structure of the United States," in Samuel N. Eisenstadt (ed.), *From Generation to Generation.* Glencoe, Ill.: Free Press, 1956.

Plumb, J. H. *In the Light of History.* Baltimore: Penguin, 1972. See also "The Great Change in Children," *Horizon* (Winter 1971); reprinted in Annual Editions *Readings in Education '73/'74* and Annual Editions *Readings in Human Development '73/'74* (Guilford, Conn.: Dushkin Publishing Group, 1973.)

Reich, Charles. *The Greening of America: The Coming of a New Consciousness and the Rebirth of a Future.* New York: Vintage Books, 1971; first printing, 1970.

Roszak, Theodore. *The Making of a Counter Culture: Reflections on the Technocratic Society and its Youthful Opposition.* Garden City, N.Y.: Anchor Books, 1969.

Young, Jock. *The Drugtakers: The Social Meaning of Drug Use.* Observation Series. London: MacGibbon and Kee, 1971.

Unit 26

Bliss, Wesley L. "In the Wake of the Wheel," in Edward H. Spicer (ed.), *Human Problems in Technological Change.* New York: Wiley, 1952.

Campbell, Angus. "Has Television Reshaped Politics?" in Joyce Gelb and Marian Lief Palley (eds.), *The Politics of Social Change: A Reader for the Seventies.* New York: Holt, Rinehart and Winston, 1971.

——, *et al. The American Voter.* University of Michigan Research Center. New York: Wiley, 1960.

Clark, Samuel D. "The Process of Suburban Development," in John Kramer (ed.), *North American Suburbs: Politics, Diversity and Change.* Berkeley, Cal.: Glendessary Press, 1972.

——. *The Suburban Society.* Toronto: University of Toronto Press, 1966.

Dobriner, William M. *Class in Suburbia.* Englewood Cliffs, N.J.: Prentice-Hall, 1963.

Glasser, William A. "Television and Voting Turnout," in Joyce Gelb and Marian Lief Palley (eds.), *The Politics of Social Change: A Reader for the Seventies.* New York: Holt, Rinehart and Winston, 1971.

Horowitz, Irving L. "The Life and Death of Project Camelot," in Elizabeth T. Crawford and Albert D. Biderman (eds.), *Social Scientists and International Affairs.* New York: Wiley, 1968.

Lang, Kurt, and Gladys E. Lang. "The Late Vote: A Summary of Findings," in Joyce Gelb and Marian Lief Palley (eds.), *The Politics of Social Change: A Reader for the Seventies.* New York: Holt, Rinehart and Winston, 1971.

McLuhan, Marshall. *Understanding Media: The Extensions of Man.* New York: Signet Books, 1964.

Moore, Wilbert E. "A Reconsideration of Theories of Change," in Milton L. Barron (ed.), *Contemporary Sociology: An Introductory Textbook of Readings.* New York: Dodd, Mead, 1966.

Rossi, Alice S. "Equality Between the Sexes," in William J. Goode (ed.), *The Dynamics of Modern Society.* Chicago: Aldine, 1966.

Seeley, John R., R. Alexander Sim, and Elizabeth W. Loosley. *Crestwood Heights: A North American Suburb.* Toronto: University of Toronto Press, 1956.

Toffler, Alvin. *Future Shock.* New York: Random House, 1970.

Uliassi, Pio D. "The Prince's Counselors: Notes on Government Sponsored Research on International and Foreign Affairs," in Irving L. Horowitz (ed.), *The Use and Abuse of Social Science: Behavioral Science and National Policy Making.* New York: Transaction Books, 1971.

Wattenberg, Ben J., and Richard M. Scammon. "The Suburban Boom," in John Kramer (ed.), *North American Suburbs: Politics, Diversity and Change.* Berkeley, Cal.: Glendessary Press, 1972.

Whyte, William H. *The Organization Man.* Garden City, N.Y.: Anchor Books; first printing, 1956.

Unit 27

Burton, John W. *Conflict and Communication.* London: Macmillan, 1969.

Curle, Adam. *Making Peace.* London: Tavistock, 1971.

Doob, Leonard (ed.). *Resolving Conflict in Africa: The Fermeda Workshop.* New Haven: Yale University Press, 1970.

Freire, Paulo. *Pedagogy of the Oppressed.* Myra Bergman Ramos (tr.). New York: Herder and Herder, 1970.

Galtung, Johan. "Peace, Peace Theory, and an International Peace Academy," mimeographed paper, International Peace Research Institute, Oslo, February, 1969.

Gouldner, Alvin W. *The Coming Crisis of Western Sociology.* New York: Basic Books, 1970.

Gurr, Ted R. "Sources of Rebellion in Western Society: Some Quantitative Evidence," *Annals of the American Academy of Political and Social Science,* 391: 128–144 (September 1970).

——. "Urban Disorder: Perspectives from the Comparative Study of Civil Strife," *American Behavioral Scientist,* 11, 4: 50–55 (March-April 1968).

Horowitz, David (ed.). *Radical Sociology: An Introduction.* San Francisco: Canfield Press, 1971.

Kelman, Herbert. *International Behavior: A Social-Psychological Analysis.* New York: Holt, Rinehart and Winston, 1965.

Lakey, George. "Strategy for Non-Violent Revolution," *Peace News,* December 12, 1969.

McPhail, Clark. "Civil Disorder Participation," *American Sociological Review,* 36, 6: 1058–1073 (December 1971).

Nicolaus, Martin. "Text of a Speech Delivered at the American Sociological Association Convention, August 26, 1968," in Larry T. and Janice M. Reynolds (eds.), *The Sociology of Sociology: Analysis and Criticism of the Thought, Research and Ethical Folkways of Sociology and its Practitioners.* New York: McKay, 1970.

Roberts, Adam (ed.) *Civilian Resistance as a National Defence.* Baltimore: Pelican Books, 1969; first printing, 1967.

Sharp, Gene. *The Politics of Non-Violent Action.* Boston: Porter Sargeant, 1973.

Spilerman, Seymour. "The Causes of Racial Disturbances: A Comparison of Alternative Explanations," *American Sociological Review,* 35, 4: 627–649 (August 1970).

Index

Credits

1959) by Edward E. Jones and Harold B. Gerard in Figure 13.2 (page 567) of *Foundations of Social Psychology* (New York: Wiley, 1967); p. 287, (right top) Omnigraphics; p. 287, (bottom) Source: Adapted from Figure 14.4 (page 563) of Edward E. Jones and Harold B. Gerard, *Foundations of Social Psychology* (New York: Wiley, 1967).

Unit 13

p. 293, Joseph A. Smith from Craven and Evans; p. 294, (top) The Bettman Archive, (bottom) Howard Sochurek/Woodfin Camp and Associates; pp. 295–296, Source: From George P. Murdock, "Comparative Data on the Division of Labor by Sex," *Social Forces* 15 (May 1937): 551–553, cited in and adapted with permission of the publisher from Roy G. D'Andrade, "Sex Differences and Cultural Institutions," in Eleanor E. Maccoby (ed.), *The Development of Sex Differences,* Stanford Studies in Psychology 5 (Stanford: Stanford University Press, 1966), Tables 1 and 2, pages 177 and 178; p. 297, The Bettman Archive; p. 298, (top) Robert Malloch/MAGNUM, (bottom) © 1972 G. B. Trudeau. Distributed by Universal Press Syndicate; p. 299, Library of Congress; p. 300, Source: Mrs. Elizabeth Duncan Koontz, Deputy Assistant Secretary of Labor and Director of the Women's Bureau of the United States Department of Labor, adapted from "Myth and Reality in the Employment of Women," paper delivered at the 139th meeting (Washington, D.C., December 1972) of the American Association for the Advancement of Science; p. 301, Source: Adapted from "Woman's Work," *Newsweek,* February 12, 1973. Fenga & Freyer—*Newsweek,* February 12, 1973; p. 302, Library of Congress; p. 304, (top) Howard Petrick/Nancy Palmer Agency, (bottom) Leonard Freed/MAGNUM; p. 309, Source: Adapted from John Money, "Nativism Versus Culturalism in Gender Identity Differentiation," Figure 1, page 3, paper delivered at the 139th Meeting (Washington, D.C., December 1972) of the American Association for the Advancement of Science. Published by permission of the author, John Money, Ph.D.; p. 312, Karl Nicholason; pp. 314, 315, Wide World Photos; p. 317, UPI

Unit 14

p. 319, Joseph A. Smith from Craven and Evans; p. 320, (top) The Bettman Archive, (bottom) Claudia Andujar/Rapho Guillumette; p. 321, Courtesy Marvel Comics, Inc.; p. 322, Erik Hansen; p. 323, Omnigraphics; pp. 324–325, Norris McNamara/Nancy Palmer Agency; p. 326, (top left and right) Ken Heyman, (bottom) John Launois/Black Star; p. 327, (left) Donald Greenhaus, (right) Bruce Davidson/MAGNUM; p. 328, B. D. Vidibor; p. 329, (top) The Metropolitan Museum of Art, Harris Brisbane Dick Fund, 1943, (bottom) Museum of Modern Art Film Stills Archive; p. 330, (top) Culver Pictures, Inc.; pp. 330–331, Chester Higgins/Rapho Guillumette; p. 334, Cary Wolinsky/STOCK, Boston; p. 335, (top) Fred Ward/Black Star, (bottom) from *The New York Times Magazine,* December 26, 1971. © 1971 by the New York Times Company. Reprinted by permission; pp. 336, 337, William Goldschein

Unit 15

p. 339, Joseph A. Smith from Craven and Evans; p. 340, Owen Franken/STOCK, Boston; p. 341, UPI; p. 342, Source: Adapted from Stanley Garn, *Human Races,* 2nd edition (Springfield: Charles C. Thomas, 1965), pages 129–149. Courtesy of Charles C. Thomas, Publisher, Springfield, Illinois; p. 344,

Sygma; p. 345, (bottom) The Bettman Archive, (top) Wide World Photos; p. 347, Brian Cody; pp. 350–351, The Walters Art Gallery; p. 352, Wide World Photos; p. 353, The Bettman Archive; p. 354, Omnigraphics; p. 355, (top) Wide World Photos, (bottom) Sygma; p. 356, (top) Charles Gatewood, (bottom) Ian Berry/MAGNUM; pp. 357, 358, 359, Art Greenspon

Unit 16

p. 363, Joseph A. Smith from Craven and Evans; p. 364, Charles Harbutt/MAGNUM; p. 365, Burk Uzzle/MAGNUM; pp. 366–367, J. P. Laffont/Sygma; p. 368, (top) Wide World Photos, (bottom) Photo Researchers, Inc.; p. 369, UPI; p. 371, Omnigraphics; p. 372, Georg Gerster/Rapho Guillumette; p. 373, Karl Nicholason; p. 375, (left top to bottom) Wide World Photos, (right top to bottom) UPI, Wide World Photos, Wide World Photos; p. 376, Peter Menzel/STOCK, Boston; p. 377, (top) courtesy Pontiac Motor Division, GM Corp., (bottom) courtesy SAAB USA, Inc.; pp. 378, 379, Art Greenspon; p. 380, courtesy of Robert Townsend

Unit 17

p. 383, Joseph A. Smith from Craven and Evans; p. 384, Gunn Assoc.; p. 385, (left) Bruce Davidson/MAGNUM, (right) Elliot Erwitt/MAGNUM; p. 386, Sources: Statistical Office of the United Nations Department of Economic and Social Affairs, *World Social Situation,* 1957, page 114; *United Nations Demographic Yearbook, 1966;* p. 387, Sources: United States Department of Commerce, Bureau of the Census, *Statistical Abstract of the United States, 1960* (Washington: U.S. Government Printing Office, 1960), page 21; *Statistical Abstract of the United States, 1971* (Washington: U.S. Government Printing Office, 1971), page 16; pp. 388–389, Burk Uzzle/MAGNUM; p. 389, (top) United Nations Photo; p. 390, 391, (top) Leonard Freed/MAGNUM; p. 391, (bottom) Jeffrey Fox/Woodfin Camp and Associates; p. 394, (top) Source: Adapted from Chauncy Harris and Edward L. Ullman, "The Nature of Cities," *The Annals of the American Academy of Political and Social Science* 242 (November 1945), page 13, (bottom) Source: Adapted from Edward C. Burks, "Affluence Eludes Blacks, Puerto Ricans," *The New York Times,* August 17, 1972, p. 41. © 1972 by the New York Times Company. Reprinted by permission; p. 395, Wide World Photos; pp. 396–397, Ken Heyman; p. 397, (top) J. P. Laffont/Sygma; p. 398, (left) Elliott Erwitt/MAGNUM, (right) George Gardner; pp. 400–401, Courtesy ARCHIGRAM GROUP; p. 401, (bottom) SCALA/Florence-New York; p. 402, Erik Hansen; p. 404, Art Greenspon

Unit 18

p. 407, Joseph A. Smith from Craven and Evans; p. 408, (top) Marcia Keegan, (bottom) Alwyn Scott Turner/Rapho Guillumette; p. 409, (top) Stephen Potter/STOCK, Boston, (bottom) Courtesy Australian Department of External Territories; p. 411, (top) Constantine Manos/MAGNUM, (bottom) Mark Kane; pp. 412–413, © The Los Angeles Times Syndicate; p. 418, Source: Evans Jenkins, "School Funding Viewed as Chaotic and Unjust," *The New York Times,* March 11, 1973, page 52 (data from President's Commission on School Finance, *Review of Existing State School Finance Programs,* Vol. II, 1972). © 1973 by the New York Times Company. Reproduced by permission; p. 419, Source: Bureau of the Census, cited in *The Official Associated Press Almanac, 1973* (New York: Almanac Publishing, 1972), page 375. Reproduced by permission; pp.

420–421, Carol Ann Bales; pp. 422–423, Leo Stashin/STOCK, Boston; pp. 425, 426, 427, Erik Kansen

Unit 19

p. 429, Joseph A. Smith from Craven and Evans; p. 430, NYPL, Picture Collection; p. 431, Cary Wolinski; p. 434, Gunn Assoc.; p. 435, Ken Heyman; p. 437, Marcia Keegan; p. 440, Bruce Davidson/MAGNUM; p. 442, Ken Heyman; pp. 443, 444, 445, 446, 447, Art Greenspon

Unit 20

p. 449, Joseph A. Smith from Craven and Evans; p. 450, The Bettman Archive; p. 451, (top) The Metropolitan Museum of Art, gift of Joseph Verner Reed, 1964, (bottom) Library of Congress, Hine photo 1908/1910; p. 452, The Bettman Archive; p. 453, Sovphoto; p. 454, Omnigraphics; p. 455, Wide World Photos; p. 457, Erik Eibel; p. 458, (top left to right) Wide World Photos, Wide World Photos, Sygma, Wide World Photos, (bottom left to right) Wide World Photos, Sygma, © 1968 Los Angeles *Times* photo by Boris Yaro, Wide World Photos, Owen Franken/STOCK, Boston; p. 459, courtesy of the Italian Cultural Institute; p. 463, Wide World Photos; pp. 464, 466, Art Greenspon

Unit 21

p. 469, Joseph A. Smith from Craven and Evans; p. 470, (left) Burk Uzzle/MAGNUM, (right) Elliott Erwitt/MAGNUM; p. 471, courtesy Consulate General of Japan; p. 472, (left) John Running, (right) Erich Hartmann/MAGNUM; p. 473, Ewing Galloway; p. 474, Source: Peter Henle, "Exploring the Distribution of Earned Income" (*Monthly Labor Review,* 95 [December 1972]), page 22 (Washington: United States Department of Labor, Bureau of Labor Statistics); p. 475, Adapted from *Work in America: Report of the Special Task Force to the Secretary of Health, Education, and Welfare* (Washington: U.S. Government Printing Office, 1973), Table I, page 16; pp. 478–479, Burk Uzzle/MAGNUM; p. 480, courtesy General Motors Corporation; p. 481, courtesy Metropolitan Life Insurance Company; pp. 482–483, © The Frick Collection, New York; pp. 486–487, Norman Hurst/STOCK, Boston; pp. 488–489, (top) Ken Heyman; p. 490, courtesy Bank Street College of Education, "A Teacher Talks About Her Classroom," photos by Ellen Galinsky, funded by the Ford Foundation; pp. 491, 492, 493, Art Greenspon

Unit 22

p. 497, Joseph A. Smith from Craven and Evans; p. 498, Source: Julia S. Brown, "A Comparative Study of Deviation from Sexual Mores," *American Sociological Review* 17 (April 1952): 138; p. 499, Rainbow Energies photo by Richard Lee; pp. 502–503, Wide World Photos; p. 504, Philadelphia *Inquirer* photo by Richard Titley; p. 506, Charles Gatewood; p. 507, Wide World Photos; p. 508, (left) N.Y. Daily News Photo, (right) Arthur Tress/MAGNUM; p. 509, (top) Source: Adapted from Howard S. Becker, *Outsiders: Studies in the Sociology of Deviance* (New York: Free Press, 1963), page 20. Copyright © 1963 by The Free Press of Glencoe, A Division of the Macmillan Company, (bottom) Howard Petrick/Nancy Palmer Agency; p. 510, Lyrics to "Gee, Officer Krupke." Lyrics by Stephen Sondheim. © Copyright 1956, 1958 by Arthur Laurents, Leonard Bernstein, Stephen Sondheim, and Jerome Robbins. Lyrics © copyright 1957 by Leonard Bernstein and Stephen Sondheim. Used by permission of G. Schirmer, Inc., and Chapell & Company, Inc.; p. 510, photo, Museum of Modern Art Film Stills Archive; p. 512, Bob Adelman; p. 513, Ken Regan/Camera 5; p. 514, William Goldschein

Unit 23
p. 517, Joseph A. Smith from Craven and Evans; p. 518, Source: World Health Organization, cited in *The Official Associated Press Almanac, 1973* (New York: Almanac Publishing, 1972), page 147. Reproduced by permission; p. 519, Source: Interpol and the Federal Bureau of Investigation's *Uniform Crime Reports,* cited in *The Official Associated Press Almanac, 1973* (New York: Almanac Publishing, 1972), page 147; p. 520, (top) Source: Federal Bureau of Investigation, cited in *The Official Associated Press Almanac, 1973* (New York: Almanac Publishing, 1972), page 147. Reproduced by permission, (bottom) Source: Federal Bureau of Investigation, cited in *The Official Associated Press Almanac, 1973* (New York: Almanac Publishing, 1972). Reproduced by permission; p. 521, Burt Glinn/MAGNUM; p. 522, (left to right) Wide World Photos; pp. 522–523, Library of Congress; p. 524, N.Y. *Daily News* photo, © 1928 by Pacific and Atlantic Photos; p. 526, New York Times photo by Burton Silverman; p. 531, courtesy of Warner Brothers, Inc.; p. 532, (top) Arthur Tress/MAGNUM, (bottom) John Goodwin; p. 533, Michael Evans/Nancy Palmer Agency; p. 534, Danny Lyon/MAGNUM; pp. 534–535, Lee Romero; pp. 535, 536, Danny Lyon/MAGNUM; pp. 538–539, (top) Bill Whiting/Camera 5; p. 539, (bottom) UPI; p. 540, Art Greenspon

Unit 24
p. 543, Joseph A. Smith from Craven and Evans; p. 544, Claudia Andujar/Rapho Guillumette; p. 545, The Bettman Archive; pp. 546–547, Omnigraphics; p. 548, The Bettman Archive; p. 549, (left) The Bettman Archive, (right) Library of Congress; p. 550, (left) Source: Harold M. Schmeck, Jr., "Women Smokers Warned of Fetal and Infant Risks," *The New York Times,* January 18, 1973 (data from Ontario Department of Health), page 6. © 1973 by the New York Times Company. Reproduced by permission, (right) Library of Congress; p. 552, Source: "U.S. Drug Study Stresses Treatment, Not Penalties," *The New York Times,* March 23, 1973 (data from National Commission on Marihuana and Drug Abuse), page 37. © 1973 by the New York Times Company. Reproduced by permission; pp. 554–555, MAGNUM; p. 555, (top) Michael Hanulak/MAGNUM; pp. 556–557, Arlene Dubanevich; pp. 560–561, Wide World Photos; p. 562, Michael Hanulak/MAGNUM; p. 563, Leonard Freed/MAGNUM; p. 564, Wide World Photos; p. 565, Wide World Photos; p. 566, Erik Hansen

Unit 25
p. 569, Joseph A. Smith from Craven and Evans; p. 570, Richard Graber; p. 571, Axel Poignant; p. 573, Burk Uzzle/MAGNUM; p. 574, Ron Sherman/Nancy Palmer Agency; p. 575, (left) Hugh Rogers/Monkmeyer Press Photo, (right) Ken Regan/Camera 5; p. 577, Source: Jock Young, *The Drugtakers: The Social Meaning of Drug Use* (London: MacGibbon & Kee, 1971), Table 6, page 126. Reproduced by permission; p. 578, The Bettman Archive; p. 579, Owen Franken/STOCK, Boston; pp. 580–581, Steve Eagle/Nancy Palmer Agency; p. 581, Arthur Tress/MAGNUM; p. 584, Karl Nicholason; p. 588, UPI; p. 589, Ken Regan/Camera 5; pp. 590, 591, Erik Hansen

Unit 26
p. 593, Joseph A. Smith from Craven and Evans; p. 594, John Running; p. 595, (top) courtesy Dr. Margaret Mead from *New Lives for Old: Cultural Transformation—Manus, 1928–1953* (1956), Apollo, (bottom) Source: Bureau of the Census, cited in *The Official Associated Press Almanac, 1973* (New York: Almanac Publishing, 1972), page 438; p. 596, (left) Source: Bureau of the Census, cited in *The Official Associated Press Almanac, 1973* (New York: Almanac Publishing, 1972), page 438, (right) Tony Spina/Nancy Palmer Agency; p. 597, Thomas Hovenden, *The Last Moments of John Brown* (1883). Metropolitan Museum of Art, gift of Mr. and Mrs. Carl Stoeckel, 1897; p. 598, Sahm Doherty/Camera 5; p. 599, Santi Visalli/Photo Researchers; p. 604, Library of Congress; p. 605, Lillian Tonnaire/Nancy Palmer Agency; p. 608, Source: Ben J. Wattenberg with Richard M. Scammon, "The Suburban Boom," Table 1, page 73, in John Kramer (ed.), *North American Suburbs: Politics, Diversity, and Change* (Berkeley: The Glendessary Press, 1972). "The Suburban Boom" is adapted from *This U.S.A.* by Ben Wattenberg and Richard J. Scammon, Doubleday & Company, 1965. Reprinted by permission; pp. 611, 612, 613, Art Greenspon

Unit 27
p. 617, Joseph A. Smith from Craven and Evans; p. 618, (left) Gunn Assoc., (right) Reprinted from Mad Magazine with express permission. © 1973 E. C. Publications, Inc.; p. 620, (left) Bruno Barbey/MAGNUM, (right) Sygma; p. 621, (top) Courtesy AFL-CIO, (bottom) Source: United States Department of State, Arms Control and Disarmament Agency, *World Military Expenditures, 1971* (Washington: U.S. Government Printing Office), Chart I, page 2; p. 623, Corita Kent; pp. 624–625, Charles Gatewood; p. 626, (left) Los Angeles *Times* photo, (right) Bruce Davidson/MAGNUM; p. 627, Source: Clark McPhail, "Civil Disorder Participation: Critical Evaluation of Recent Research," *American Sociological Review* 36 (December 1971): 1064; p. 628, Courtesy Harvard University; p. 630, Source: Charles Mohr, "What War Has Meant to Saigon," *The New York Times,* January 31, 1973, page 16 (data from United States Agency for International Development and Cambodian Government). © 1968 by the New York Times Company. Reproduced by permission. Photo from Wide World Photos; p. 631, from the Papers of the National Library of Students' Peace Posters, Swarthmore College Peace Collection; pp. 633, 634, 635, Art Greenspon; p. 638, William MacDonald

Graphics by Gunn Associates appear on pages 52, 84, 108, 122, 136–138, 172, 173, 178, 179, 212, 295–296, 301, 309, 342, 386, 387, 394, 418, 474, 475, 498, 509, 518, 520, 550, 552, 577, 595, 596, 608, 621, 627, and 630.

Graphics by Omnigraphics appear on pages 262, 264–265, 287, and 300.

The Study of Society Staff

Phillip Whitten | Publisher
Peter J. O'Connell | Editor
Ron Zollshan | Designer
David Hunter | Graphics Consultant
Priscilla Fitzhugh | Photo Researcher
Carol Dudley | Production Supervisor
Glenn Cowley | Interviewer/Assistant to Publisher
Alix Nelson | Associate Editor
Cindy Pauk | Administrative Assistant

This book was set in Videocomp Helvetica by Kingsport Press, Inc., Kingsport, Tennessee.

Transparencies were processed and assembled by Robert Crandall Associates, New York, New York.

Color separations were processed by Electronic Color/Lehigh, Morton Grove, Illinois.

The text was printed in web offset lithography and bound by Kingsport Press, Inc., Kingsport, Tennessee.

Text paper is Warren Bookman Matte, furnished by Hobart McIntosh Paper Company, Boston, Massachusetts.

The cover material is Corvon 120, furnished by Wyomissing Corporation, Paper Division, Reading, Pennsylvania.

The cover was printed in offset lithography by Lehigh Lithographers, Pennsauken, New Jersey.